W9-APH-901

FAMILIES IN *Global and Multicultural* PERSPECTIVE

SECOND EDITION

This book is dedicated to our parents for teaching us to love and see the world in a different way—Daphine and Norman Ingoldsby and Waneta Wood Smith and Dalton Smith; and to our siblings for letting us be firstborns and still appreciating us—Tim Smith and Tom Smith; and Kirk Ingoldsby, Pamela Kimball, and Todd Ingoldsby. We also lovingly remember Patrick McKenry (1949–2004), a caring friend and accomplished colleague.

FAMILIES IN *Global and Multicultural* PERSPECTIVE

SECOND EDITION

EDITED BY

BRON B. INGOLDSBY
BRIGHAM YOUNG UNIVERSITY

SUZANNA D. SMITH
UNIVERSITY OF FLORIDA

SAGE Publications
Thousand Oaks ▪ London ▪ New Delhi

For information:

Sage Publications, Inc.
2455 Teller Road
Thousand Oaks, California 91320
E-mail: order@sagepub.com

Sage Publications Ltd.
1 Oliver's Yard
55 City Road
London EC1Y 1SP
United Kingdom

Sage Publications India Pvt. Ltd.
B-42, Panchsheel Enclave
Post Box 4109
New Delhi 110 017 India

Printed in the United States of America on acid-free paper

Library of Congress Cataloging-in-Publication Data

Families in global and multicultural perspective / editors Bron B. Ingoldsby, Suzanna D. Smith.— 2nd ed.
p. cm.
Rev. ed. of: Families in multicultural perspective. 1995.
Includes bibliographical references and index.
ISBN 0-7619-2819-7 (cloth)
1. Family—Cross-cultural studies. 2. Kinship—Cross-cultural studies. 3. Marriage customs and rites—Cross-cultural studies. 4. Sex role—Cross-cultural studies. 5. Home economics—Cross-cultural studies. 6. Multiculturalism. I. Ingoldsby, Bron B. II. Smith, Suzanna D. III. Families in multicultural perspective.
GN480.F35 2006
306.85—dc22

2005008578

05 06 07 08 09 10 9 8 7 6 5 4 3 2 1

Acquiring Editor: Jim Brace-Thompson
Editorial Assistant: Karen Ehrmann
Production Editor: Sanford Robinson
Copy Editor: Rachel Hile Bassett
Typesetter: C&M Digitals (P) Ltd.
Indexer: Julie Grayson
Cover Designer: Janet Foulger

Contents

Preface

Since the publication of the first edition of this volume, the globalization of the world economy has steadily proceeded to penetrate and absorb very diverse regions into a larger economic structure. In addition, far-reaching communication systems and new technologies have drawn together the far corners of the globe into a dynamic network of information exchange. Other events in various parts of the world—terrorist acts, armed conflicts, disease outbreaks, and natural disasters—have drawn attention to the interconnectedness of world cultures and political systems. In this context, the diversity and similarities of family life around the world also become more apparent. Yet, there is very little exchange of scholarly information about the world's families and communities to help us examine family life in a global perspective.

Families in Global and Multicultural Perspective travels across geographic, cultural, and historical boundaries to explore the diversity of the world's families. The key word is *diversity:* in family structure, processes, history, and social and environmental contexts.

In writing this text, we had three major goals, discussed in more detail in the following sections:

- To increase students' recognition of and respect for cultural diversity as it influences family life
- To meet educators' needs for a comparative family text
- To contribute to the development of new ways of thinking about families by examining cultural and family diversity within families

FAMILIES AND CULTURAL DIVERSITY

We live in an age of continuous change and ever-increasing interdependence as nations become integrated into a global political and economic system. However, U.S. citizens are often accused of being ignorant of and insensitive to the customs and lifestyles of other cultures. Most of us rarely speak foreign languages, although doing so would open up new relationships and cultural experiences. When we visit foreign countries, we seldom seek out nationals to better understand their society. Even in our own country, one of the most diverse in the world, we surround ourselves with those like us and often know little about others.

This is indicative of the ethnocentrism that is firmly rooted in our consciousness and behavior. We tend to see the world only through our own eyes, evaluating other cultures based on our beliefs and ways of doing things, judging their behaviors and beliefs as strange or inferior instead of different and valuable.

The internationalization of economies, governments, and cultures creates new opportunities for examining the diversity of social structures, including family life. As the reader will discover, throughout history and across the planet, there have been many approaches for managing the business of families, such as finding a mate, producing offspring, relating to family members, and earning a living. We find that families are central to life in every society; no matter what their structure, families adapt to a multitude of environmental, economic, and political pressures and survive.

Increasingly, the importance of families is being recognized, nationally and internationally. For instance, 1994 marked the celebration of the United Nations International Year of the Family (IYF), and the decade anniversary of this important event was celebrated in 2004. The overarching goal of the IYF was to stimulate local, national, and international actions in a sustained effort to promote awareness of family diversity, family needs, and gender-based inequality within families. In addition, the IYF encouraged the development of "family-sensitive" policies and services. Although individuals may disagree with any of the IYF's specific principles, we applaud the efforts of the international community to recognize the importance of families in all their various forms and to promote awareness of family diversity.

A COMPARATIVE FAMILY TEXT

Before the publication of the first edition (Ingoldsby & Smith, 1995), we surveyed a group of college and university professors to determine their needs in a comparative family life text. We asked this sample to choose, from a fairly comprehensive list, those topics they considered most important. The chapters included in this book were based on the priority areas these educators identified (Smith & Ingoldsby, 1992). Findings revealed that educators highly valued the traditional approaches to comparative family studies. Those who responded to the survey said it was important for a text to address the foundations of comparative family studies. These are family origin and universality, family functions, marital structure, kinship rules, and comparative research methods. We discuss these topics in two sections of this text, "Foundations of Comparative Family Studies" and "Family Structure."

Educators participating in the survey also placed a priority on topics pertaining to family development, particularly mate selection, marriage adjustment, parenting, divorce, and aging. These topics form the third section of this volume, "Family Development."

In addition, we found that educators were looking for a text that offered a closer look at contemporary concerns and particular cultural groups. Educators believed that students needed to be informed about family life in certain contemporary societies. In the text, examples from various regions are integrated into the chapters, as well as highlighted in individual chapters.

The final section, "Social Inequality in the Contemporary World," includes topics rarely included in comparative family texts but that are increasingly salient to comparative family studies: social inequality, as manifested in gender stratification; oppression of certain ethnic and cultural groups; and poverty. In fact, in our earlier survey, 96% of respondents viewed the topic of gender roles as very important.

We have attempted to be as comprehensive as possible in addressing each of the historical periods, world geographical regions, and major viewpoints that have shaped human families while still representing educators' main interest areas. Regarding historical periods, Chapters 3, 4, and 8 have drawn on material from ancient and pre-Renaissance history, but the text as a whole is strongest in detailing events from AD 1500 to the present day. As for world regions, our coverage of the Americas, Europe, Africa, and Asia is extensive, not only in individual chapters but throughout the text. In addition, in the second edition we have added chapters on the Middle East and Pacific regions, which were noticeable gaps in the first edition. Finally, the Judaic and Christian influences on families are well represented here, and other traditions, such as Islam and Confucianism, are also discussed.

One of the ways we have sought to increase student awareness and appreciation of diversity is with the inclusion of student exercises in each section, which will:

- Develop students' awareness of their own perspectives and biases regarding the major topics included in the text
- Help students to better understand the major concepts presented
- Give students an opportunity to apply these concepts

In the second edition, we have provided updated information about families around the world by expanding the contents to incorporate recent trends in family life and addressing information gaps that appeared in the earlier volume. Here we build on traditions established in the early scholarship of comparative family studies and also incorporate new material on changes in the world's families that have occurred in the decade since the first volume was published.

NEW WAYS OF THINKING ABOUT FAMILIES

The third goal for this text was to contribute to new ways of thinking about families. This is very natural for a text about family diversity, but it moves to areas of theory and research not traditionally addressed in comparative family studies.

A theory is a way of seeing things that allows us to organize and understand family life. Good theories provide explanations for our observations and allow us to predict what we should be able to find, given our theory's constructs and assumptions. Just as there is diversity in families, there are various theoretical frameworks for understanding family structure and interaction, each one providing certain insights and obscuring others.

Much of the landmark work in comparative family studies was rooted in theories that emphasized family structure and function. These frameworks presented what some have come to consider a narrow view of the world, based on Western family life, but they also provided important, basic concepts and the impetus for considerable research. Newer approaches that emerged in the 1960s, 1970s, and 1980s emphasized the impacts of social factors on families and introduced the language of family diversity and multiculturalism to our vocabularies. These frameworks created different ways of looking at and studying families and are also captured in this volume. In addition, the reader will notice more recent approaches that include the language of postmodernism, transitional economies, the Two-Thirds World, social inequalities, and gender; these reflect a continued interest in structural factors that have a profound effect on family and community life.

As we review the early ethnographic work in Part II, we see the family from the perspective of *structural-functional theory*. This approach, which focused on marital and kinship structures and family members' functional roles, has been used extensively by social scientists to organize and to explain research study results.

Later, family sociologists relied on *developmental theory*, which postulates that families can best be understood by knowing their stage of development in the "family life cycle." We follow such a perspective in Part III.

More recently, *feminist theory* has focused attention on the construction of family lives through socialized gender roles, gender differences in communication, and the systematic oppression of women in cross-gender interactions. This approach has coincided with the development of oppression-sensitive and structural models centered around the social construction of racial, ethnic, and class-based inequalities and their impacts on families.

These perspectives provide the theoretical grounding for Parts IV and V.

In closing, this book was written as a celebration of the diversity of family processes and experiences throughout the world. We approach this topic from the perspective that understanding differences in cultures, societies, and families helps to broaden and deepen our knowledge and appreciation of all families and can also help us to learn more about our own societies. We hope that readers will join us in this celebration.

Suzanna D. Smith
Bron B. Ingoldsby

REFERENCES

Ingoldsby, B. B., & Smith, S. (1995). *Families in multicultural perspective.* New York: Guilford Press.

Smith, S., & Ingoldsby, B. (1992). Multicultural family studies: Educating students for diversity. *Family Relations, 41,* 25–30.

Acknowledgments

We organized and edited this text with the assistance and support of a number of people. We particularly want to thank the scholars who contributed chapters in their areas of expertise. Most of them have already published extensively on the topics they cover here, and we felt that the reader would benefit greatly from their knowledge. Working with each of them made this project all the more enjoyable, and we very much appreciate their participation.

We also want to thank the wonderful staff at Sage Publications, including Jim Brace-Thompson, senior editor in charge of this project, for his thoughtful guidance and encouragement from the book's inception; Karen Ehrmann, editorial assistant, for her help and patience in preparing the manuscript for press; Rachel Hile Bassett, for her insightful copyediting; and Sanford Robinson, project editor, for his support and help in guiding the book to press. Thanks also to Tarrant Figlio, staff assistant at the University of Florida, who worked with us behind the scenes to attend to the many details of finalizing the project.

Part I

FOUNDATIONS OF COMPARATIVE FAMILY STUDIES

A Brazilian couple and the children at their wedding anniversary.

Introduction to Part I

Part I of this text provides the foundations necessary for the study of families from a comparative perspective. This includes an overview of families around the world, a summary of the methods used to conduct research on families in different societies, and a historical perspective on families in the West.

In Chapter 1, "Global Families," Smith provides an overview of major trends in family life worldwide such as the growth in female-headed households and aging families. She identifies some urgent problems families face, drawing out those that are particularly pressing for families in developing countries. Smith asks readers to think globally about families and identities, as well as to find ways the field can move forward toward a better understanding of families worldwide.

In Chapter 2, "Comparative Research Methodology," Lee and Greenwood provide an overview of the research methodologies that guide comparisons about human behavior across cultures. They review the major types of comparative family research—cross-cultural, cross-societal, and cross-national. They emphasize the methodological issues in comparative research that make it difficult for scholars to draw conclusions about similarities and differences between cultures. Lee and Greenwood also underscore the important interplay between theory and research.

In Chapter 3, "The History of the Euro-Western Family," Ingoldsby examines the historical roots of many U.S. families from ancient times through the colonial period and up to the present. He pays particular attention to the role of ideology regarding gender and power in shaping the marital and parent-child relationships of white families. Throughout the chapter, the reader traces the continued subordination of women and children to men within the family structure of the period.

CHAPTER 1

Global Families

Suzanna D. Smith

There are two constants—change and families.

—Perdita Huston

Families are important everywhere, regardless of family living arrangements and differences in who might be considered "family." Families all over the globe are facing many similar changes and difficulties as they attempt to adjust to the forces of modern life. This chapter introduces readers to these topics and also challenges students of the family to think globally about families in theory, research, policy, and practice.

DIVERSITY AND CONTINUITY

There is considerable diversity in families around the world in marital arrangements, in family formation, and in family composition, depending on cultural and religious practices and beliefs, economic conditions, and government policies and interventions. For example, in many countries, women are married at early ages and have their children young, often before they are out of their teenage years (Jensen & Thornton, 2003). In addition, children can be brought into a family not only by birth, but also through informal adoption when their biological parents die or are temporarily or permanently unable to care for them. Other family members are what anthropologists call "fictive kin." This is the "brother" or "sister" or "aunt" or "uncle" who is joined to a family group through feelings of affection and responsibility, and perhaps through distant biological ties as well (Leeder, 2004). Polygyny, the marital arrangement where husbands have more than one wife at one time, is common in areas of Africa, the Middle East, and Asia (Leeder; Chapter 6, this volume). Other research shows that there may be a fluid exchange of household members from rural to urban residences (Datta & McIlwaine, 2000), so that family includes those living in both areas; or that families may be clustered in neighborhood-based kinship networks that provide child care and housing (Chant, 1997a).

In many areas, poverty, war, natural disasters, and other calamities have torn families apart (Huston, 2001). For instance, women farmers scratch out meager livings from their family farms while their husbands are away for months or even years at a time in grueling and dangerous jobs in mines or on plantations. Or, desperately poor mothers leave their children in the care of other relatives and illegally cross one or two dangerous borders to find jobs in cities as maids and nannies. Families may send children to cities to work in private homes as domestics, in factories, or in the streets. Some children are simply abandoned because their families cannot care for them. Grandparents, whose own health and productivity may be limited, assume responsibility for families and even entire communities when children lose their parents to HIV/AIDS.

THE IMPORTANCE OF FAMILY

Although there is considerable diversity, there is also continuity—certain core values and practices remain constant. Most cultures emphasize the importance of extended family, the kin group beyond the nuclear family. In many parts of the world, the "traditional family" includes parents, children, and *grandparents,* whereas in the United States, the traditional family is typically defined as the mother, father, and their biological offspring (Huston, 2001). In fact, most of the world places a priority on these larger kin-group networks, rather than the conjugal couple and smaller nuclear family (Obaid, 2003; Sastry, 1999). In these systems, families come first in decisions, and the needs of the individual are considered later, if at all. In fact, individuals are often noticed only when they bring shame to the family, such as a premarital pregnancy.

Family members often depend on each other for survival and work cooperatively to ensure that the group's needs are met. In agricultural societies, families must team up together to produce sufficient crops for household consumption and market sales. In nomadic societies, families pool their resources to care for livestock and barter for market goods. Traditional practices and religious beliefs emphasize family responsibilities, rather than individual worth. The word of elders, particularly older men, is paramount. Elders are honored for their wisdom and respected for their decision-making authority, particularly in matters that affect the family, such as whom a son or daughter should marry. In contrast, in the industrialized world, there is a high value placed on individual freedom. Family members are encouraged to operate autonomously, even to establish lives apart from their families of origin to pursue their education or employment. In this context, elders have no more wisdom or value than younger family members and may even be considered a burden.

However, even within industrialized nations, extended kin groups have always been a part of U.S. families, although the nuclear family has been idealized (Coontz, 1997). Racial and ethnic minority groups have long emphasized extended family and community ties, in part to develop the collective strength to survive the devastating blows of slavery, racial discrimination, and the immigrant experience. There is little question that family is important, no matter where people live or what form their family takes.

Family Diversity

Family scholars know that there is enormous diversity in living arrangements including multigenerational, single-parent, adoptive, and foster family groups (Erera, 2003; Kaslow, 2001). In many parts of the developing world, households are fluid in membership, and "families" include both kin and pseudo-kin. In addition, women are frequently *de jure* household heads, where there is no man present on a regular basis because of divorce, separation, or widowhood, or *de facto* heads, where no male partner resides, yet a man contributes to household maintenance (Datta & McIlwaine, 2000).

When examining global families, using the biological nuclear family as a basis to judge the rest of the world would be an arrogant imposition of U.S. values (Huston, 2001). On a practical level, international interest in strengthening (nuclear) families diverts needed resources from those most in need of help (Chant, 1997a). Instead of searching for an elusive and even unattainable norm, our efforts would be better spent understanding the rich diversity of family life around the globe.

It is precisely this issue of family change in which we are interested, across the life cycle and in response to societal conditions. For example, family scholars have long studied how families are formed through mate selection, cohabitation, consensual unions, and marriages, as well as how they are dissolved through separation, divorce, or abandonment. With changes in aging and labor force participation, researchers are asking new questions about changes in the tradition of filial piety and how working families will continue to care for their parents and other relatives in later life. Some scholars argue that the term *household* has advantages in capturing structure and functioning at a point in time (Chant, 1997a). However, *family* incorporates many expected changes over the course of the life cycle that are shared with a primary social group.

Changing Families Worldwide

Family living arrangements are changing throughout the world (Kaslow, 2001; United Nations, 2000). Spouses or partners may live separately, couples divorce or separate, offspring live away from their families, and elderly people live alone. This section highlights several striking changes in family life around the globe: the rise in female-headed families, the growing importance of cohabitation in the marital life cycle, the increase in life expectancy and the corresponding need for caregiving of the elderly, the growth in women's labor force participation, and the emergence of same-sex families as another family form in some countries. Other changes in family life are also very important, particularly the rise in divorce and the diffusion of poverty, but because these are discussed in detail in other chapters, they are only briefly summarized here.

Throughout this chapter, the terms *developed, industrialized, North,* and *Western* are used interchangeably; *transitional economies* refers to areas of eastern Europe that recently entered the world market. The terms *developing, Third World,* and *South* are also used interchangeably. The literature on families around the world shows no distinctive pattern in choice of terminology.

Female-Headed Households

In many parts of the world women are increasingly likely to be heading households, for several reasons. Widowhood continues to be a major explanation for female headship; as populations and life expectancy have increased, more women are living longer and have a greater chance of being widowed. In addition, the divorce rate around the globe has been rising and has reached over 50% of once-married couples in some parts of the world (Huston, 2001). Legal custody is typically awarded to women, or women automatically assume responsibility for children. In addition, nonmarital childbearing has increased, because of greater social acceptance of out-of-wedlock sexual activity, even in countries where religious mandates have historically kept nonmarital birth rates low. Furthermore, when men migrate for employment, they often leave behind households headed by women.

Another factor in the increase in female-headed households is that in many countries, women are economically prepared to care for their children on their own. As a result of increased education and labor force participation, women are more likely to have access to and control over an income that enables them to support a family on their own if they choose. In many cases, women no longer have to endure unhappy marriages and domestic violence because of economic dependency on their husbands. As Perdita Huston (2001) notes, young women who are "generally better educated and more self-confident" are less willing to accept parental pressures to endure a marriage with an abusive or exploitative partner (p. 5).

The United States has the highest rate of lone-parent families among industrialized nations, with one third of families headed by a single parent. This is compared to highs of 20%–22% in most other developed nations and a low of 5% in Japan. In Canada, 22% of families were lone parents with children in 1996, up from 19% in 1991. Women head 80%–90% of lone-parent families (United Nations, 2000). Data are also available on women-headed households. These are not always the same as single-parent families, in that some woman-headed households may have an adult male present, and some may not have children in the home. However, these data do provide a good indication of how many women are responsible for supporting their households. As shown in Table 1.1, rates of female headship range from 9%–24% of households across regions, with an average of about 20% worldwide, based on data gathered between 1971 and 1985 (Chant, 1997a). The rates are highest in southern Africa, with 42% of households (and more in some countries) headed by women, and in the Caribbean, with 36% headed by women (United Nations, 2000).

Table 1.1 Women-Headed Households

Region	*Percentage*
Africa	
Northern Africa	12
Southern Africa	42
Rest of sub-Saharan Africa	21
Latin America and Caribbean	
Caribbean	36
Central America	22
South America	22
Asia	
Eastern Asia	22
Southeastern Asia	19
Southern Asia	9
Central Asia	24
Western Asia	10
Oceania	15
Developed regions	
Eastern Europe	27
Western Europe	29
Other developed regions	29

SOURCE: United Nations. (2000). The world's women 2000. New York: Author, p. 42.

In Africa, major reasons for female-headed households include high rates of male migration for work, the frequency of consensual or visiting unions and polygyny, and the preference among some kinship groups for matrilineal family structure rather than conjugal ties (United Nations, 2000). There seems to be an upward trend in women-headed households in some sub-Saharan African countries, because 8 of 12 countries surveyed by the United Nations reported an increase. In Latin America, the percentage of female-headed households increased in 5 of the 6 countries with data available. Reasons include later age at marriage in some countries, social acceptance of consensual unions, rape during armed conflict, and unwillingness of women to continue abusive relationships.

In the developed regions there is considerable variation in rates of female-headed households, with highs of about 40% in Scandinavian countries, 20% in Greece and

Portugal, and 17% in Japan. In developed countries the high rates are usually due to large numbers of older widows and young unmarried women living alone.

Many women who are heading families do so in extreme poverty. Uneducated and alone, they have few resources available to them. Extended family support, even if culturally mandated, may not be offered when those families are also poor and struggling (Huston, 2001). Or, women may live in multigenerational households where their own mothers are also impoverished (Akinsola & Popovich, 2002). In parts of Europe and the United States, children growing up in single-mother families tend to be at a financial and educational disadvantage relative to two-parent families (United Nations, 2000). Particularly devastating is a prevalent view that women-headed households are undesirable, that the women who head them are "immoral and unable to care for their children" (Datta & McIlwaine, 2000, p. 43). In large part, this may be because it is assumed that children without a father present will be somehow deviant—will do poorly in school, get in trouble with the law, and so on. The stigma and censure attached to women who head households disregard the circumstances under which they were formed, such as rape by boyfriends, male relatives, or strangers; separation after extramarital affairs and physical and sexual abuse; widowhood; and male outmigration and desertion (Datta & McIlwaine). In many cultures women must retain their married status or lose everything, even if their spouses are irresponsible, violent, or adulterous (Huston, 2001). In societies with extreme social disapproval of marital dissolution, such as the Philippines, female-headed households are less common (Chant, 1997a).

This bleak image of the situation for women-headed households does not hold true in all contexts: Women-headed households are not always poor and marginalized. Chant's (1997a) work in the Philippines confirmed that, although women may not have entered into household headship voluntarily, once in these units their lives were calmer and less stressful, because they had escaped the conflicts and burdens associated with their marriages. These women also claimed they may have become better mothers and tended to dedicate considerable time and resources to their children so that they could have good educations and have their needs met. Indeed, when women hold the purse strings, children are better fed and better educated, and female children receive the same opportunities as their male siblings (Chant, 1997b).

Cohabitation and Consensual Unions

Cohabitation refers to a heterosexual couple living in the same household without being legally married. The couple may plan to marry or may be testing out their compatibility prior to marriage, or the couple may be living together as an alternative to marriage. In any case, there is a presumption of both sexual and emotional intimacy and the potential for long-term commitment within or outside of legal marriage.

In Western developed nations, cohabitation rates have increased dramatically in the past few decades while marriage rates have declined (Katz, 2001). This phenomenon is widely viewed as one of the most important changes in family life in the past 40 years, dramatically altering the marital life course by offering a prelude to or replacement for marriage (Casper & Bianchi, 2002; Dharmalingam, 2002; Villeneuve-Gokalp, 1991). United Nations data on cohabitation for Europe show that 20% or more of women ages 20–24 years live in consensual unions in Switzerland, Austria, New Zealand, Norway, France, Netherlands, Finland, and Sweden. Although cohabitation is typically viewed as a recent Western phenomenon, consensual unions have long been common in other parts of the world (Castro Martin, 2002). A *consensual union* is defined as "a union in which couples share a household without being formally married," whereas a formal marriage has legal or religious sanction (Glaser, 1999, p. 57). Consensual unions are most popular in the Scandinavian countries: In Sweden, 44% of young women were living in consensual unions at the time of the survey; in Norway and Finland, 33% of young women were living with their intimate partners (Dharmalingam). In the United States, most young couples today live together prior to marriage; over half of U.S. unions started in the early 1990s began with cohabitation (Teachman, 2003). In Western industrialized countries, some unions are quickly followed by a wedding, whereas others never reach the altar because the couple rejects marriage entirely.

Studies show that it is increasingly common for children to be present in a cohabiting relationship. These may be children who were born to a previous marriage and then live with a custodial parent who lives with her or his new partner. Or, as is more and more common, they are conceived within the cohabiting relationship (Dharmalingam, 2002; Villeneuve-Gokalp, 1991).

Historically, there has been a high incidence of consensual unions in Latin America, particularly in the Caribbean and Central American subregion, and this form of relationship has been a basic part of the Latin American family system (Castro Martin; Glaser). Basically surrogate marriages, these relationships are not sanctioned through a government license or religious ceremony but are socially accepted as a desirable alternative to marriage for men and for women (Glaser). In some countries, such as Haiti, Panama, Costa Rica, Guatemala, El Salvador, Nicaragua, and the Dominican Republic, consensual unions outnumber formal marriages, making up more than 50% of all partnerships (Castro Martin; De Vos, 1999; Glaser). High levels, from one fourth to one half of unions, are found in Cuba, Guatemala, Colombia, Ecuador, Paraguay, Peru, and Venezuela. In other countries, such as Chile and Uruguay, consensual partnerships comprise less than 25% of unions (Castro Martin). Even within countries there are differences, with some regions having higher rates of consensual unions, as occurs in Brazil and Costa Rica, for example (De Vos; Glaser).

Census data collected over the past 30 years indicate that in Latin America in general, the already high proportion of consensual unions has remained stable or has moderately increased. Only one country, Guatemala, has seen declines in consensual unions (Castro Martin, 2002). Such partnerships are most prevalent among the young (15–24 years of age), but they are still very common at later stages of the life cycle (Castro Martin).

These relationships have advantages for both men and women. Couples choose a consensual union so they can get to know each other and assess the relationship before making a long-term commitment to marriage and so they can end the relationship more easily than a marriage (Glaser, 1999). Some traditional cultures practice bride robbing, where the bride is "stolen" from her parents by her prospective husband and the couple lives together for some days or months before the wedding. If the couple doesn't like the living arrangement, they may decide to break off the relationship (Cardoso, 2002).

Particularly important in determining whether a couple will marry or not is their financial situation. Poor economic circumstances may also serve as a barrier to formal marriage. Lower-income couples may choose consensual unions because they lack the financial resources to pay for a marriage license, wedding ceremony, or customary exchange of goods between families. However, a legal marriage, particularly a church wedding, is generally preferred, because it offers more security to the women and children, is perceived to be enduring, and is more clearly defined in terms of the status of the spouse and in-laws (Castro Martin, 2002).

Recent censuses indicate that consensual unions are more common in rural areas and among the socially and economically disadvantaged (Castro Martin, 2002; Glaser, 1999). Women in consensual unions are less educated and have less educated partners than married women. Higher educational achievement may give a woman greater bargaining power to attain the kind of relationship she wants, and it may also be a proxy for socioeconomic status. More educated (and wealthier) women are more likely to have property and to see a need to formalize their relationship (Castro Martin, 2002).

Men with few economic opportunities may feel unable to make a commitment to support a family (Glaser, 1999). In addition, if the relationship ends, men who separate from their partner will have fewer financial obligations to children, and these are more difficult to enforce than in the case of legal marriage. Although some legal protections have been established in some countries such as Costa Rica, usually when the consensual union is dissolved, separated women have almost no rights to goods or property acquired during the relationship. Furthermore, despite some laws requiring fathers to support children after separation, men often leave women to provide for children on their own (Glaser).

With regard to reproductive behavior and attitudes, for the most part, women who are married and in consensual unions are similar: Women in consensual unions seem to have fewer children over their lifetimes than married women, although the differences are very small. Regardless of union type, women want to have about the same number of children.

These facts indicate that throughout Latin America, consensual unions really are a parallel form of marriage where childbearing is common. Two socially respected forms of intimate partnerships exist side by side that are similar in their reproductive behavior (Castro Martin, 2002). However, these unions are a less binding legal, financial, and emotional commitment than marriage and do not last as long as legal marriages (Castro Martin; De Vos, 1999; Glaser, 1999). Consensual unions are more likely than formal marriages to be dissolved, either because the couple marries or because they end the relationship. Nevertheless, a large proportion of these unions (30%–45%, compared with 50%–65% of marriages) last 10 or more years in the consensual status (Castro Martin). Unfortunately, there is little information available about how many of these unions end in marriage or separation.

In short, there are a variety of intimate relationship structures around the world that are not adequately captured in neat dichotomies such as "married" and "not married." To this mix, we can now add another form of intimate relationship outside of marriage, "living apart together." These relationships are very much like cohabiting relationships except that the couple maintains separate households, with or without the intention to share a residence in the future (Dharmalingam, 2002; Leridon & Villeneuve-Gokalp, 1989; Trost, 2003). Such relationships are reported to have increased in France, Quebec, Sweden, and New Zealand, but few systematic studies have been done. It is increasingly likely that young couples will live with their parents rather than in their own residences while having an intimate relationship with a partner. The structure of these relationships is like the sexually intimate dating relationships of past decades, but there seems to be greater social and parental acceptance of the intimate union (Dharmalingam; Leridon & Villeneuve-Gokalp).

In summary, in the past few decades a variety of forms of intimate relationships have become more prevalent in the developed world. These have been driven by a number of factors, including greater social acceptance of sexual intimacy outside of marriage and the availability of modern contraception, delayed marriage, the rising divorce rate, children's personal experience with parental divorce, and women's economic independence (Casper & Bianchi, 2002; Raymo, 1998; Villeneuve-Gokalp, 1991). In addition, economic factors play a role in the decision to live together rather than marry. Men who do not have steady employment or are employed in unskilled jobs are more likely to cohabit because they cannot support their families (Villeneuve-Gokalp). Cohabitation or consensual unions have long existed as a common form of intimate relationship in the developing world, particularly in Latin America and the Caribbean. Social acceptance of these unions and poor economic conditions combined make consensual unions an attractive alternative to marriage.

What we have seen here is the amazing flexibility and fluidity of intimate unions outside of marriage. Even cohabiting and consensual unions do not follow a homogeneous pattern (Castro Martin, 2002; De Vos, 1999; Villeneuve-Gokalp, 1991). Some of these unions may be customary, based on tradition and recognized as binding under custom but not civil law. Or, they may be common-law unions, that is, long-lasting relationships that in some states are considered marriages. Others may be trial marriages, where the couple plans to marry after a period of time (De Vos). De Vos suggested that there may be as many as six types of intimate unions: civil marriage, customary marriage, religious marriage, common-law marriage, consensual union, and others (such as visiting unions, where a male partner stays in a woman's household for a short period of time and may produce children, or couples that do not live together but share children). Although an increasing number of couples choose not to marry, they do form conjugal relationships that may or may not result in marriage.

Aging and Elder Care

The United Nations calls the aging of the world's population unprecedented, without a parallel in human history (United Nations, 2002). At the beginning of the 21st century there were 600 million older persons worldwide, three times the number reported 50 years earlier. With a 2% growth rate per year, there will be more older than younger people throughout the world by the year 2050 (United Nations, 2002).

This steady increase in the aging population, particularly relative to the younger working-age population, has major implications for virtually every aspect of life. Aging will affect family composition and functioning; housing; health care; systems of financial support, such as pensions and Social Security benefits; as well as overall economic growth and consumer spending. The rapid increase in life expectancy and the explosion of the aging population may leave governments unprepared to address their problems and needs (Darkwa, 2000).

Worldwide, in 2000 there were nine people in the working ages to support each person aged 65 or older, down from 12 to 1 in 1950. By 2050, there will be four working-age persons for each person 65 and older. Thriving economic and political powers, such as Japan and Europe, are likely to face fiscal crises as their populations age (Hewitt, 2004).

Although aging is a worldwide phenomenon, there are huge differences between regions in the number and proportion of older persons. In the developed regions, almost one fifth of the population was 60 and older in 2000, and by midcentury one third of the population will be older adults.

In the less developed regions, only 8% of the population was over 60, but by 2050, this figure will shoot up to almost 20% (United Nations, 2002).

Furthermore, the median age will increase more rapidly in the less developed regions. In the United States the median age will rise by only about 3 years to midcentury but will increase more in other countries. For Mexico the median age will increase by 20 years, and it will be an "older" country than the United States, as will other Latin American countries. The Asian countries of Korea, China, Thailand, and Vietnam will also be "older" in median age than the United States by 2035. Japan is already the "oldest" country, with a median age of 41, due to low birthrate, lack of immigration, and high life expectancy. Other countries, including Italy, Germany, Bulgaria, Russia, and the rest of eastern Europe, face rapid aging (Hewitt, 2004).

In the more developed regions, men and women are less likely to be economically active at older ages than in the less developed areas. In the more developed areas, 21% of older men and 10% of older women were economically active, compared with 50% of older men and 19% of older women in the less developed regions (United Nations, 2002). In large part this is because men and women in less developed regions have more limited, if any, retirement coverage and lower earnings. Also, these older adults tend to work in the agricultural and informal sectors as farmers, artisans, and traders, where incomes are typically lower and less stable than in the formal sector, particularly for older women. Rarely are they covered by social insurance programs and pensions (Darkwa, 2000).

The fastest-growing age group is those 80 and older. Although this group currently represents one tenth of the total number of older persons, it is growing at a rate of 3.8% per year; by 2050 one fifth of older persons will be 80 and older. Most of these older persons are women, because women's life expectancy is higher than men's. At the oldest ages there are two to five times more women than men. In fact, 65% of those 80 and older are women (United Nations, 2002).

No matter what part of the world they are from, as people age, they turn to family members for help in carrying out the activities of their daily life (Rosenthal, 1997). Frail elders may need help with personal care such as dressing, grooming, and bathing, as well as preparing food and taking care of health needs. Caregivers of older adults may also provide emotional support by listening and helping with problems. In the industrialized world, there has been a trend for older adults to live with their spouse or, if widowed or divorced, to live alone (Rosenthal). Often this is out of choice, but in some cases a lack of understanding of the elderly, combined with a fast-paced work environment, may have discouraged the younger generation from taking good care of older relatives (Hui, 2000). In Hong Kong, the government has stepped in with comprehensive services to the elderly including income supports, special housing schemes, residential care services to enable the elderly to live independently or with a family member, ongoing health care, and social services (Hui, 2000).

Little is known about long-term care of the elderly in developing countries, although it is estimated that by 2025 72% of the world's elderly will live in the developing world (Shaibu & Wallhagen, 2002). For the most part, families take care of their elderly, usually at home (Shaibu & Wallhagen). In a study of elderly Ghanaians, Darkwa (2000) found that 99% lived in the community, frequently sharing a multigenerational home with other family members. In Botswana, caregiving took place in the elder's own home as long as possible and included simply visiting the elderly family member; making financial contributions; keeping up the elder's home; and providing assistance with intimate tasks in culturally accepted ways, such as bathing, dressing, toileting, and doing laundry. The poverty of caregiving families forced them to make serious choices between providing the resources their aging family member needed and putting food on their own tables (Shaibu & Wallhagen).

Although the research on family caregiving in developing countries is limited, it does appear that urbanization and rural-urban migration and other modern forces have weakened the capacity of the family to provide care and support to the elderly (Darkwa, 2000). In some areas, the family is facing a crisis of caring with the enormous growth in the older population and changes in traditional family life (Shaibu & Wallhagen, 2002).

A striking change in the family life of older adults has been their responsibility for taking care of their adult children and grandchildren. In recent years, grandparents have taken over when adult children are no longer able to care for their children because of drug and alcohol abuse, financial problems, or physical or mental illness (Pebley & Rudkin, 1999).

In the developing world, a primary reason for grandparents becoming caregivers has been the spread of HIV/AIDS, which has infected thousands of parents and an estimated 16 million children under the age of 15. These children may be orphaned or in the care of only one parent, who may also be ill. This figure could rise to 40 million children in the next decade (HelpAge International, 2003). When both parents die, the old and the young are left to support each other without the assistance and productivity of the middle generation.

Grandparents have often cared for the young, but seldom has their care been so urgently needed or extensive. The World Bank estimates that in 20 of 28 African and Latin American countries, more than one fifth of orphaned children were living with their grandparents. In South Africa and Uganda, which have been particularly hard-hit by HIV/AIDS, 40% of orphaned children are cared for by grandparents; in Zimbabwe, this rate is over half. In Zambia, Uganda, and Tanzania, grandparents are the largest single category of caregivers (HelpAge International, 2003). This dependence is often a burden for grandparents. It drains their limited economic resources, strains their physical capacity, and compromises their own health (Nyambedha, Wandibba, & Aagaard-Hansen, 2003). Although institutionalization of orphans is an option, children do better in a family environment and in the future can offer emotional and financial support to older adults. Thus, institutionalization may have negative effects on both generations (HelpAge International, 2003).

In any case, there is a need to explore other alternatives to family caregiving and long-term health care needs of older adults and their families (Darkwa, 2000). As Rosenthal (1997) suggests, the fundamental question is, "Who should have responsibility for the care of the elderly?" (p. 28). In the developed world, although the situation is far from easy, there is a growing interest in providing assistance to family caregivers through government programs and employer benefits so that older adults can remain in their own home or their family's home. In the developing world the answers to this question are complicated by demographic and social forces such as male out-migration, the rise in female-headed households, the HIV/AIDS pandemic, and the lack of government policies and business supports for the elderly.

Women's Labor Force Participation

Women make up an increasing share of the global labor force in almost all regions of the world, at least one third in almost all regions (except northern Africa and western Asia) and around half in some areas. The largest increase in the last 20 years has been in Latin America, where the proportion of women in the labor force grew from one fourth in Central and South America to one third in Central America and two fifths in South America (United Nations, 2000, p. 109). Women's labor force participation also increased in western Europe and other developed regions, so that at least half of women are working outside the home. Even in developed eastern Europe, where there has not been an increase, about half of women are in the labor force. Rates in sub-Saharan and southern Africa have remained at around 40%. In addition, even in western Asia and northern Africa, where women's employment has historically been low, rates have increased to over 20%.

There are several reasons for this change. One is that women have more control over their fertility, so they are freer to delay or limit childbearing while they pursue schooling and employment. Another reason has to do with increased opportunities. As the service sector has expanded, so have chances for women to find employment—in child care, restaurants, hotel and motel establishments, sales, health care, and so on. Women work primarily in the service sector in all regions. The exceptions are in Africa and southern Asia, where women workers are predominantly in agriculture, and central Asia, where they are split between agriculture and services. Unfortunately the service industry consistently pays less, offers fewer if any benefits, and is less stable compared with other economic sectors. Consequently, women, particularly low-income women, become trapped in low-wage jobs (United Nations, 2000).

In Africa, many women are pursuing self-employment in the growing informal sector by starting their own small-scale businesses where they are the employers as well as the labor, or they occasionally employ family or other workers (International Labor Organization, 2000). For example, women make prepared foods for the market and "employ" their children to sell the goods, or they brew beer and sell it to passersby on the street. This enables them to balance work and household responsibilities, much as women in developed countries do by reducing work hours or choosing self-employment.

Although women may be earning money for their families, they may still be unable to provide for their basic needs. In Zimbabwe, changes in economic policies have worsened poverty. Out of economic necessity, 80% of families working in the informal sector changed their eating habits and reduced their food intake. Over half of urban dwellers eliminated lunch and consumed less milk, meat, and bread (Rukuni, 2000).

Home-based work is an important and expanding type of employment, especially for women. Women may work for an enterprise to supply goods and services but carry out their work at home. Examples include piecework, where workers sew segments of garments at home for later assembly and sale, and indigenous crafts for market sale or export.

Women's increased labor force participation is closely tied to family life in important ways. A few decades ago, most women would enter the labor force in their early 20s and drop out during the child-bearing years, then go back to work after their children entered school or left home. By the end of the 20th century, women were remaining in the labor force throughout their child-bearing and child-rearing years. This shift to uninterrupted employment has been most common in Europe and North America. The same pattern is true for Latin America and the Caribbean, although activity rates are lower. However, in Africa, women's participation has always been high, and little has changed.

As women's labor force participation has become more acceptable and there are larger numbers of women in the labor force, governments and employers are offering more supports for working parents. For example, governments have established legislation supporting parental leave and child care. However, often policies require only unpaid leave, as in Australia, New Zealand, and the United States, although the Nordic countries do offer generous packages and a high level of compensation for earnings. In some Western countries, particularly in industries with a large number of professional female workers, such as banking, employers have begun to offer an array of family benefits. This includes part-time work, job sharing, and flexible leave as well as parental leave for mothers and fathers and child care and elder care benefits (United Nations, 2000). Indeed, the increase in women's labor force participation has important implications for older adults, as women juggle the demands of jobs with the needs of aging family members. The result is increased absenteeism for a large percentage of workers (Rosenthal, 1997). In the United States, the Family and Medical Leave Act mandates that employers in larger firms provide unpaid leave time for families caring for dependents, including the elderly. In addition, in the United States in 2002, 25% of employers provided help for employees to care for aging family members, compared with 11% in 1992 (Bond, Thompson, Galinksky & Prottas, 2002). Canada does not have a national policy to support employed caregivers, and, as in the United States, employer supports vary greatly depending on company size, corporate culture, and collective agreements (Rosenthal). In developing countries, such government and business policies would benefit family members, but these are rarely available (Darkwa, 2000).

Thus, societal changes are occurring at all levels as women have entered the workforce, and these have significant effects on family life. Women's labor force participation and family life are discussed in more detail in other chapters in this volume.

Same-Sex Families

The gay-rights movement in the United States, Canada, and Europe has given greater visibility to gay and lesbian families. The fact that same-sex families exist has recently been well documented by the Urban Institute in *Gay and Lesbian Families in the Census: Couples With Children* (Gates, 2003). Using data from the 2000 U.S. census, the study authors found that at least 1.2 million homosexuals reported living together as "unmarried partners" in census terms. Although gay and lesbian couples are concentrated in U.S. cities, they are "found virtually everywhere: in 99 percent of U.S. counties" (*Primary Sources,* 2004).

Like heterosexual couples, gay and lesbian couples desire lifelong commitments to a loving partner and, in many cases, want to have children (Benkov, 2003). They show a strong sense of personal responsibility to the relationship, despite the lack of formal, institutional supports, and are able to maintain these relationships over time (Kurdek, 1998). Cohabiting same-sex couples (who have committed relationships but are unable to legally marry) and married opposite-sex couples are remarkably similar in their satisfaction with their relationships (Kurdek; Means-Christensen, Snyder, & Negy, 2003).

In addition, many gay and lesbian couples have children. The census data show that more than one quarter of same-sex couples are rearing children. Like heterosexual parents, same-sex families have an average of two children (*Primary Sources,* 2004). In some cases, the child is the biological offspring of a previous heterosexual relationship; in other cases the child is brought into the relationship through adoption, surrogacy (a woman conceiving and carrying the fetus), donor insemination, or joint parenting (shared responsibility for a child with the biological parent or parents) (Benkov, 2003).

Even though homosexual families are establishing marriage-like relationships and having children, in most parts of the world they are not entitled to marry and do not have the same legal protections as married couples. Although there are a few historical examples of same-sex marriages since medieval times (Partners Task Force for Gay and Lesbian Couples, 2004), for the most part these families have struggled to gain social acceptance and legal rights.

However, in recent years, several nations and states have passed legislation that gives gay and lesbian couples the legal right to join in marital unions. In Europe, Scandinavia, and Canada, there is a trend toward liberalizing laws (Sterling, 2004). In April 2001, the Netherlands became the first country in the world to offer full, legal marriage to same-sex couples. Belgium followed in January 2003. Between 2003 and 2004, three Canadian provinces offered legal marriage to same-sex couples: Ontario in June 2003, British Columbia in July 2003, and Quebec in March 2004. Massachusetts was the first (and so far, only) state in the United States to offer legal marriage that is fully equivalent to an opposite-sex marriage license (Partners Task Force for Gay and Lesbian Couples, 2004). Sweden and Spain are also moving toward legalized same-sex marriage (Ford, 2004).

Various forms of civil unions establish an alternative legal status to marriage and some legal protections and benefits. A registered partnership allows couples to claim a status and benefits similar, but not equal, to those afforded married couples. This is possible in Denmark (and has been since 1989), Finland, Germany, Greenland, Iceland, Netherlands, Norway, Sweden, and the U.S. state of Vermont (Ford, 2004; Partners Task Force for Gay and Lesbian Couples, 2004). France has a civil solidarity pact for both gay and straight couples that offers some legal rights of marriage but is easier to dissolve. Parts of Australia have established similar measures, and Britain is also moving toward recognizing this kind of partnership (Ford; Partners Task Force for Gay and Lesbian Couples). Buenos Aires, Argentina, became the first city in Latin America to recognize civil unions in 2003 (Partners Task Force for Gay and Lesbian Couples). Although partnerships and civil unions appear to be gaining broader support, in some countries, this has occurred after years of legal, political, and religious battles (e.g., France; see Ford, 2004). Similar controversies have raged in the states that have attempted to pass legislation for gay marriages or civil unions.

Acceptance of gay and lesbian marriages is predicated on changing social attitudes in support of greater equality between gay and straight people. In most of the developing world, homosexuality is still considered a mental illness and is punishable by imprisonment and even death (Sengupta, 2003): Gay marriage is "unthinkable" (Sterling, 2004). Violence, blackmail, and harassment of gays are widespread (Sengupta). For example, in Saudi Arabia, nine men who confessed to "deviant sexual behavior," which involved dressing in women's clothing and having sex with each other, were sentenced to more than 2,000 lashes and 5 years in prison (Hays, 2000). In Somalia, two young women accused of having a lesbian relationship were sentenced to death ("Somalia: Lesbians," 2001).

In many countries, public discussion of sexuality in general is taboo (Ould, 2003). International human rights organizations have consistently tried to bring attention to the persecution of gays, but conservative North American organizations, the Vatican, and Islamic groups have derailed international discussions and resolutions (Sengupta, 2003). In this climate of hatred and fear, it is not surprising that there has been so little research on same-sex relationships in the developing world. Even development scholars have ignored same-sex sexuality in conversations about women's rights in the development process, giving the impression that no poor lesbians exist in the developing South (Swarr & Nagar, 2003).

Pertinent to this discussion is research showing that the particular social and economic context is a major determinant of how sexuality is articulated. Through comparative case studies in India and South Africa, Swarr and Nagar (2003) illustrated that lesbians were particularly vulnerable to attacks from former husbands and extended family, employers and colleagues, and strangers on the street. Homophobia was rampant and threatened the very lives of women who did not conform to the traditional expectations of the Indian or African woman. These women struggled to support their families while they also dreamed of an economically and emotionally stable future—one in which they could provide for their children, live without violence, and establish loving marriages with their lesbian partners.

Cardoso (2002) articulated a view of homosexuality that is quite different from the gay/straight dichotomy prevalent in industrialized nations. Some men in the Brazilian fishing village he studied were openly gay, and others were exclusively heterosexual. However, there was also a more ambiguous sexual practice of what would appear to readers from the North to be straight men having sex with gay men. In these cases, straight men were still considered "masculine," and they were not considered gay as long as they followed certain sexual practices and social roles. On the other hand, gay men were not viewed as equal to straight men, but neither were they marginalized in the local culture. Marriage did not really alter men's social relationships and behavior. Cardoso argued that numerous forms of male sexuality appear in the world's cultures and that the masculinity passed down from Northern Europe to the present-day industrialized nations is "practically unheard of elsewhere," where more fluid male sexual practices are accepted (p. 68).

In summary, gays and lesbians throughout the world struggle to find a life where they are accepted and respected and where they can establish a family life with a committed partner. As the gay-rights movement has opened up discussions about intimate partnerships and family relationships, we are learning more about how gay and lesbian couples create and define *family*. The limited research on gays and lesbians in developing countries suggests that sexuality is embedded in a particular economic and cultural context. The challenges of being gay are complicated by the need for resources in impoverished communities.

PRESSING ISSUES FOR THE WORLD'S FAMILIES

In addition to meeting the challenges of changes in family structure, gender roles, and the life cycle, families around the world are also facing pressing issues that profoundly affect their ability to rear their children, care for the elderly, and maintain healthy intimate partnerships. Some of those that appear to be particularly salient at this time include war and armed conflicts, poverty, and migration.

War and Armed Conflicts

As this chapter is written, flashpoints exist all over the world—Iraq, Israel, the West Bank and Gaza Strip, Indonesia, Pakistan, Sri Lanka, Sudan. In some countries, armed conflict has gone on for decades. War and armed conflicts have devastating consequences for families.

Although widowhood, divorce and separation, nonmarital childbearing, and male outmigration top the list of reasons for female household headship, many women are left to rear families alone while their husbands fight in wars and armed conflicts. For example, in areas of Sri Lanka embroiled in Tamil-Muslim ethnic violence, the proportion of female-headed households exceeded the national rates. One survey found that three fourths of area female-headed households came about as a result of the conflict (Centre for Women's Research, 2004). Women thrust into the role of household head because of conflict situations shouldered heavy economic and emotional burdens due to economic deprivation and family reliance on women as the sole breadwinner. As Muslim women, however, they had traditionally been confined to the home and lacked education, skills, and opportunities to generate an income. It was exceedingly difficult to change a lifetime of habits, to cope with the perceived vulnerability from being without male protection, and to interact in the public sphere (Centre for Women's Research). They had a pressing need for housing, property, and shelter, because families lost their assets and material possessions in the conflict or later resettlement (Centre for Women's Research). In some cases, women slipped into serious mental illness and desperately wished to end their lives. All women experienced psychological and emotional traumas from family members being killed, disabled, or mysteriously "disappeared." Without the body as evidence, women were unable to accept that their husbands were dead. Furthermore, a "good" widow would not remarry, even though this could restore confidence, improve financial conditions, and better their children's well-being (Shanmugum, 1999).

Similarly, in Guatemala, armed conflicts had devastating effects on families. Rape was used deliberately and frequently as a weapon of war, contributing to the formation of thousands of female-headed households. In today's postconflict period these mothers "live in a very traumatized state" and often have not returned to their villages or married (Datta & McIlwaine, 2000, p. 43).

In addition, children who have witnessed armed conflict have been deeply affected. Not only might they view a killing or disappearance, which is traumatic in itself, but anxious and grieving mothers may be unable to provide the nurturance and support that children need. Children find it very difficult to cope with their own grief and confusion and may experience their own psychological and physical problems as a result (Shanmugum, 1999). It is imperative that crisis counselors and disaster relief organizations address the unique needs of women and children suffering from armed conflict and its disturbing aftermath (Centre for Women's Research, 2004; Kaslow, 2001).

Poverty

Poverty negatively affects every aspect of family daily life and functioning. It is associated with higher infant and maternal mortality rates; malnutrition, disease, and overall poor health; reduced access to health care and other important services; substandard housing and contaminated water supply; family violence; brutal child labor; and child and adult prostitution (Huston, 2001; Narayan & Petesch, 2002; Weissman, 1997).

The United Nations (2003) reports that 1.2 billion of the world's population is absolutely poor, defined as living on less than a dollar a day. Over 900 million, or 70% of the poor, are women. Even though women's labor force participation is increasing, women still earn only one third of the world's total waged employment, and their share of national income is about a third. Women's wages are only three fourths of men's wages in the nonagricultural sector of 56 countries (Wee, 2000).

Women are hindered not only by low literacy and limited job skills, but by lack of full economic and legal rights. They work on land that is not theirs and that they will not inherit. They often do not control their income and cannot purchase household necessities such as food, clothing, and medicine. They may not even control their own labor. Their children may belong to their husband's family, and women may not have parental rights. These conditions are the result of traditional gender inequalities embedded in many religious, marriage, and kinship systems (Wee, 2000). Many countries are going through economic transitions that improve conditions for women such as increased education, labor force participation, and earnings. However, these are not always favorable, because they tend to transfer resources away from small-scale agriculture, where women work, to corporate farming or the large-scale urban sector (Wee). And, even though families are also transitioning to greater equality between men and women, women are still "caught between old and new ways of life" (Wee; see Huston, 2001, for a detailed summary of these transitions).

Another related issue is the growth of slums and shantytowns because of poverty, failed government policies, and explosive urban population growth (Azenga, 2001). An estimated 20%–50% of slum households are headed by women, whose low education levels and lack of job skills lead only to low and demeaning employment such as prostitution (Azenga).

For these women, finding clean water is a major task. They must travel long distances to water points that are privately owned and expensive. Consequently, they reuse water, endangering their families' health. Without drainage and sanitation, there is no place to pour used water and no toilet and bathroom facilities. The constant prevalence of stagnant water puts women and children at risk of malaria and typhoid outbreaks (Azenga, 2001). These conditions are found in many societies such as South Africa, Mexico, Egypt, and Vietnam (Azenga; Kaslow, 2001).

Basic living conditions can be improved if opinion leaders are committed to funding programs and services. Literacy skills would help women understand health practices that would reduce infant mortality and the spread of disease and, with some initial investments from outside sources, would enable women to start their own small-scale businesses, such as tailoring and crafts. Government support for newer and cheaper housing as well as for basic facilities can help women dramatically improve their families' lives (Azenga, 2001; Ndinda, 2003).

Migration

Migration is one way that men and women try to escape poverty. They may leave rural farms and villages for urban areas, or they may enter the international migration stream to other countries (Wee, 2000). In some cases, in parts of Jamaica, for example, migrants have found jobs that have allowed them to accumulate substantial earnings to return to their families, particularly if they initially were from higher-income families (Neufville, 2001). However, many migrants become deeply indebted to labor recruiters and are trapped in dangerous jobs or oppressive working conditions. In Asia, women migrants left their families for a more promising life in the garment industry and not only ended up earning low wages but were constantly vulnerable to job layoffs and, with economic crises, plant closures that eliminated jobs entirely. Many unemployed women and their children have been driven to prostitution and sex trafficking (Wee). In Lesotho, men have left their farms to work in South African mines, as well as factories, kitchens, and farms, and an estimated 40% of Lesotho's men ages 20–39 years are away in South Africa at any one time (Modo, 2001). A century of migration to South Africa has deeply affected family life, resulting in declining farm production, the abandonment of many wives and children, an increase in female-headed households without adequate resources to care for their families, and children living and working on the streets.

Typically, as able-bodied men have migrated from rural areas, women have been left to head farm households. In Zimbabwe, for example, half of rural households do not have the resources to meet basic food needs, and men migrate in search of jobs. In some areas of Africa, women head 50% of households and perform the agricultural labor and social roles of absent husbands while also taking care of their domestic responsibilities (Rukuni, 2000). In addition, youth migrate from rural to urban areas in search of a better life, leaving behind not only their parents but their grandparents and other older adults who need care (Darkwa, 2000). Peil (1989) reported that elderly family members left in rural Nigeria were not receiving adequate physical and social support as a result of migration.

Interestingly, in some situations there may be a close relationship between urban and rural households rather than an either-or residence. Responding to surveys in Botswana, urban women household heads asserted that they belong to larger families in rural villages. Ties between families located in rural villages and cities were maintained through cash remittances and also through exchanges of family members between rural and urban residences. Urban female heads often left their children with family members in their home communities and also took family members from rural areas into their city dwellings so that they could find employment or pursue education (Datta & McIlwaine, 2000). Whatever form migration takes, it clearly has significant impacts on family life.

Family Survival

How can families survive under these conditions? How can they ever reach a healthy level of functioning? Even under the most extreme conditions, women and their families have been survivors (Centre for Women's Research, 2004). Recent research on the health-promoting family may illuminate how, even under the most onerous circumstances, some families not only survive but sustain and develop their health and well-being (Christensen, 2004). Families can be empowered to build a livelihood for themselves, and this will come not only from developing skills that enable them to earn a living, but also from changing institutional policies so that they can receive basic resources through government or non-governmental services (Ndinda, 2003; Wee, 2000). In addition, at the same time that the United States has been expanding funding for "faith-based" organizations to meet the needs of vulnerable populations in local communities, some scholars in developing countries have also been calling on religious organizations to address family needs, for example, by providing adult day care for the elderly (Darkwa, 2000). Probably only through a combination of government policies, employer support, and grassroots efforts will families be able to overcome these enormous obstacles.

IMPLICATIONS OF CHANGES FOR FAMILY SCHOLARS

In recent years it has become quite clear that even distant areas of the world are interconnected into a globalized society, through international trade, rapid means of communication such as the Internet, supersonic travel, and even through the spread of disease (Myers-Walls, 2001; Waters, 2001). The people of the world are intertwined in numerous ways that are evident in daily life. And yet there is little discussion of global families—the ways families are changing around the world, the impacts of globalization on family life, or the challenges the world's families face (Waters).

The gathering of information about the world's families is hampered by the lack of suitable family theories to guide research, as well as the difficulties of conducting cross-cultural research. Regarding theory, Smith (1995) examined the major theories pertaining to the family and concluded that these traditional mainstream frameworks had limited power for helping us to understand families cross-culturally. The most promising were theories that were specifically geared to explaining families' situations in relation to their larger environments, such as human ecology, feminism, and multicultural frameworks.

In one sense, we may already know many "truths" about families around the world (Walters, Warzywoda-Kruszynska, & Gurko, 2002, p. 448). Research tells us that family relationships tend to be hierarchical, financial support for a family is shared by the adult couple, and women remain primarily responsible for housework and child care. These facts appear to be fairly universal. However, finely tuned cross-cultural studies reveal differences not only between, but also *within*, countries and cultures that would be overlooked if studies were conducted only at the large-scale country level.

Theoretical as well as empirical efforts could be directed toward helping us understand the causes of these differences. A number of chapters in this volume show that variation in socioeconomic class, which rests on education and income levels, is critical. So are race and ethnicity, urban or rural residence, gender, and age. These factors position an individual and family in the society and *structure* their opportunities and constraints. Studies of race, class, and gender within and across cultures would prove fruitful in helping us to understand variations in family life.

Another important concern for students of the family is the difficulty in gaining access to research on families beyond the borders of North America and Europe. Taken as a whole, the extensive literature on families in the industrialized nations reveals in-depth information about virtually every aspect of family life, such as marital and parent-child communication, the impacts of child care arrangements on attachment and child behavior, gender-based household division of labor, caregiving of older adults, longevity of cohabiting relationships, resilience of same-sex families, dynamics of family violence, and so on. In contrast, we know very little about the lives of families in the transitional economies and developing world, particularly in hard-to-reach rural areas. Although some international agencies have conducted useful large-scale surveys, rarely in the literature are the voices of families in the developing world heard speaking about their lives. (The extensive World Bank reports that focus on the lives of the poor provide a notable exception; see Narayan & Petesch, 2002.) Certainly the lack of resources and institutional support for research on families hamper the development of a true and complete understanding of the world's families.

As indicated in this chapter and throughout this volume, many problems are undermining the health and well-being of children and families, but child and family policies and programs could alleviate some of these concerns. At the millennium, interest in family-related policies appears to be growing in the United States (Bogenschneider, 2004). Canada and Europe, particularly the Scandinavian countries, have several decades of experience offering family-supportive policies and programs. In the developing world, formal policies mandating assistance with services such as housing, transportation, long-term care, and child care are rare, and few formal social welfare programs exist (Darkwa, 2000). Information about the West is readily available in the research literature, but information about family policies in the transitional economies or Two-Thirds World is much less accessible.

Increased contact and collaboration between family scholars and international aid agencies could provide more information about policy and practice pertaining to families worldwide. These agencies are on the leading edge of new knowledge about what is happening to families and households worldwide and how best to intervene, such as offering maternal education programs to reduce infant mortality and health and developing small-scale cottage industries to ameliorate poverty.

However, it is also important to recognize that social change occurs not only through large-scale government policies, but also through smaller, grassroots efforts that empower individuals and communities. For example, when poor single mothers in an area of South Africa were evicted from their squatter settlements, they mobilized not only to fight the expulsion, but also to obtain basic services. Through demonstrations and meetings with local authorities, they obtained water and sewage pipes and secured land tenure. Subsequently, they formed a committee that worked with local government and international donors to further upgrade the homes through "sweat equity," where most women participated in every aspect of building their own homes. They literally developed the power (skills, confidence, and organization) to transform their families' lives (Ndinda, 2003).

In conclusion, in our increasingly connected world, students are being challenged to think globally—to understand the international economy, to comprehend government systems and diplomacy, to use international technologies and, closer to home, to work and study side by side with immigrants from an array of far-flung cultures. This volume attempts to help students begin to think globally about family life. This means understanding family life in different cultures, near and far. It means developing an awareness of the context in which families live—the environmental and economic resources they have, or don't have, and how these affect their daily lives. It means being sensitive to varying cultural practices and traditions. Thinking globally and cross-culturally means valuing the lives of families and their members, no matter how different they might seem, no matter the problems they face. Families around the world are richly varied, responding to rapid social and demographic changes and both maintaining and adapting traditional ways of life to present-day circumstances and demands.

REFERENCES

Akinsola, H. A., & Popovich, J. M. (2002). The quality of life of families of female-headed households in Botswana: A secondary analysis of case studies. *Health Care for Women International, 23,* 761–772.

Azenga, B. (2001). Improving the conditions of African women living in slums. *Femnet News, 10*(1), 4.

Benkov, L. (2003). Reinventing the family. In A. S. Skolnick & J. H. Skolnick (Eds.), *Family in transition* (12th ed., pp. 415–436). Boston: Allyn & Bacon.

Bogenschneider, K. (2004). Building enduring family policies in the 21st century: The past as prologue? In M. Coleman & L. H. Ganong (Eds.), *Handbook of contemporary families* (pp. 451–468). Thousand Oaks, CA: Sage.

Bond, J., Thompson, C., Galinksky E., & Prottas, D. (2002). *Highlights of the national study of the changing workforce: Executive summary.* New York: Families and Work Institute. Retrieved January 31, 2005, from http://www.familiesandwork.org/summary/nscw2002.pdf

Cardoso, F. L. (2002). "Fishermen": Masculinity and sexuality in a Brazilian fishing community. *Sexuality & Culture, 6*(4), 45–72.

Casper, L. M., & Bianchi, S. M. (2002). *Continuity and change in the American family.* Thousand Oaks, CA: Sage.

Castro Martin, T. (2002). Consensual unions in Latin America: Persistence of a dual nuptiality system. *Journal of Comparative Family Studies, 33*(1), 35–55.

Centre for Women's Research. (2004). *Women surviving in situations of armed conflict.* Colombo, Sri Lanka: Author.

Chant, S. (1997a). Marginal (m)others: Lone parents and female household headship in the Philippines. *European Journal of Development Research, 9,* 1–34.

Chant, S. (1997b). *Women-headed households: Diversity and dynamics in the developing world.* Basingstoke, UK: Macmillan.

Christensen, P. (2004). The health promoting family: A conceptual framework for future research. *Social Science & Medicine, 59,* 377–387.

Coontz, S. (1997). *The way we really are: Coming to terms with America's changing families.* New York: Basic Books.

Darkwa, O. K. (2000). Toward a comprehensive understanding of the needs of elderly Ghanaians. *Ageing International, 25*(4), 65–79.

Datta, K., & McIlwaine, C. (2000). "Empowered leaders"? Perspectives on women heading households in Latin America and Southern Africa. *Gender and Development, 8*(3), 40–49.

De Vos, S. (1999). Comment on coding marital status in Latin America. *Journal of Comparative Family Studies, 30*(1), 79–93.

Dharmalingam, A. (2002). Marriage, cohabitation and marital dissolution in New Zealand. *Journal of Population Research, 19*(1), 121–136.

Erera, P. (2002). *Family diversity.* Thousand Oaks, CA: Sage.

Ford, P. (2004, May 27). France joins gay marriage debate. *Christian Science Monitor.* Retrieved June 11, 2004, from http:///www.csmonitor.com

Gates, G. (2003). *Gay and lesbian families in the census: Couples with children.* The Urban Institute. Retrieved June 11, 2004, from http://www.urban.org/urlprint.cfm?ID=8417

Glaser, K. (1999). Consensual unions in two Costa Rican communities: An analysis using focus group methodology. *Journal of Comparative Familiy Studies, 30*(1), 57–77.

Hays, M. (2000, May 23). The world: Saudi Arabia. *Advocate,* (812), 16.

HelpAge International. (2003). *Forgotten families: Older people as carers of orphans and vulnerable children.* Brighton, UK: International HIV/AIDS Alliance.

Hewitt, P. (2004). World in the balance. [Television series episode]. In *NOVA.* New York: Public Broadcasting Service. Interview text retrieved July 2, 2004, from http://www.pbs.org/wgbh/nova/worldbalance/voic-hewi.html

Hui, Y. F. (2000). The case in Hong Kong. *Ageing International, 25*(4), 47.

Huston, P. (2001). *Families as we are: Conversations around the world.* New York: The Feminist Press at the City University of New York.

International Labour Organization. (2000). *Skills development for the informal economy.* Retrieved January 21, 2005, from http://www.ilo.org/public/english/employment/skills/informal/who.htm

Jensen, R., & Thornton, R. (2003). Early female marriage in the developing world. *Gender and Development, 11*(2), 9–19.

Kaslow, F. W. (2001). Families and family psychology at the millennium. *American Psychologist, 56,* 37–46.

Katz, R. (2001). Effects of migration, ethnicity, and religiosity on cohabitation. *Journal of Comparative Family Studies, 32,* 587–608.

Kurdek, L. A. (1998). Relationship outcomes and their predictors: Longitudinal evidence from heterosexual married, gay cohabiting, and lesbian cohabiting couples. *Journal of Marriage and the Family, 60,* 553–568.

Leeder, E. (2004). *The family in global perspective: A gendered journey.* Thousand Oaks, CA: Sage.

Leridon, H., & Villeneuve-Gokalp, C. (1989). The new couples: Number, characteristics and attitudes. *Population: An English Selection, 44,* 203–235.

Means-Christensen, S. J., Snyder, D. K., & Negy, C. (2003). Assessing nontraditional couples: Validity of the marital satisfaction inventory-revised with gay, lesbian, and cohabiting heterosexual couples. *Journal of Marital and Family Therapy, 29*(1), 69–85.

Modo, I. V. O. (2001). Migrant culture and changing face of family structure in Lesotho. *Journal of Comparative Family Studies, 32,* 443–452.

Myers-Walls, J. (2001). How families teach their children about the world. In J. A. Myers-Walls, P. Somlai, & R. N. Rapoport (Eds.), *Families as educators for global citizenship* (pp. 3–12). Ashgate, UK: Aldershot.

Narayan, D., & Petesch, P. (2002). *Voices of the poor: From many lands.* New York: Oxford University Press and World Bank.

Ndinda, C. (2003). Housing delivery in Nthutukoville, South Africa: Successes and problems for women. *Journal of International Women's Studies, 5*(1), 29–41.

Neufville, Z. (2001, June 15). Development-Jamaica: Women bear unequal burdens of poverty. *Interpress Service.* Retrieved September 17, 2001, from http://archives.foodsafetynetwork.ca/agnet/2001/9-2001/agnet_september_17.htm#DEVELOPMENT

Nyambedha, E. O., Wandibba, S., & Aagaard-Hansen, J. (2003). "Retirement lost"—The new role of the elderly as caretakers for orphans in western Kenya. *Journal of Cross-Cultural Gerontology, 18,* 33–52.

Obaid, T. A. (2003, May). *Families: A cross-cultural perspective—New harmonies—Families holding relationships, work and the generations in balance.* Keynote address at the 50th conference of the International Commission on Couple and Family Relations, Leuven, Belgium. Retrieved February 6, 2005, from http://www.unfpa.org/news/news.cfm?ID=340

Ould, P. J. (2003). Passing in India. *Gay and Lesbian Review, 10*(3), 27–28.

Partners Task Force for Gay and Lesbian Couples. (2004). *Legal marriage report: Global status of legal marriage.* Retrieved June 11, 2004, from http://www.buddybuddy.com/mar-repo.html

Pebley, A. R., & Rudkin, L. L. (1999). Grandparents caring for grandchildren: What do we know? *Journal of Family Issues, 20,* 218–242.

Peil, M. (1989). Health and physical support for the elderly in Nigeria. *Journal of Cross-Cultural Gerontology, 4,* 89–106.

Primary sources: Ozzie and Harriet. (2004, May). *Atlantic Online, 293*(4), 44–46. Retrieved May 24, 2004, from http://www.theatlantic.com/issues/2004/05/primarysources.htm

Raymo, J. M. (1998). Later marriages or fewer? Changes in the marital behavior of Japanese women. *Journal of Marriage and the Family, 60,* 1023–1034.

Rosenthal, C. J. (1997). The changing contexts of family care in Canada. *Ageing International, 24*(1), 13–31.

Rukuni, M. (2000). Poverty amongst women. *WomanPlus, 5*(1), 7+. Retrieved May 12, 2005, from RDS Business Reference Suite, http://rdsweb1.rdsinc.com/texis/rds/suite?Session=4284f84d0l&isCached=n&ipCnt=1

Sastry, J. (1999). Household structure, satisfaction and distress in India and the United States: A comparative cultural examination. *Journal of Comparative Family Studies, 30*(1), 135–152.

Sengupta, J. (2003). How the U.N. can advance gay rights. *Gay and Lesbian Review, 10*(6), 32–34.

Shaibu, S., & Wallhagen, M. I. (2002). Family caregiving of the elderly in Botswana: Boundaries of culturally acceptable options and resources. *Journal of Cross-Cultural Gerontology, 17,* 139–154.

Shanmugum, G. (1999). Trauma in female headed households in Amparai: An empathetic analysis. *Nevedini: A Sri Lankan Feminist Journal, 7*(2), 5–17.

Smith, S. (1995). Family theory and multicultural family studies. In B. Ingoldsby & S. Smith (Eds.), *Families in multicultural perspective* (pp. 5–35). New York: Guilford.

Somalia: Lesbians sentenced to die. (2001, March). *Off Our Backs,* 3.

Sterling, T. (2004, March 5). Gay marriages common in the Netherlands. *Contra Costa Times.* Retrieved June 11, 2004, from http://www.contracostatimes.com/

Swarr, A. L., & Nagar, R. (2003). Dismantling assumptions: Interrogating "lesbian" struggles for identity and survival in India and South Africa. *Signs: Journal of Women in Culture and Society, 29,* 491–516.

Teachman, J. (2003). Childhood living arrangements and the formation of coresidential unions. *Journal of Marriage and the Family, 65,* 507–524.

Trost, J. (2003, November). *Cohabitation and marriage in Western countries.* Plenary presentation at the annual meeting of the National Council on Family Relations, Vancouver, British Columbia, Canada.

United Nations. (2000). *The world's women 2000: Trends and statistics.* New York: Author.

United Nations. (2002). *World Population Ageing: 1950–2050.* New York: United Nations Department of Economic and Social Affairs.

United Nations. (2003). World poverty and hunger fact sheet. *Bulletin on the Eradication of Poverty, 10,* 3. Retrieved February 6, 2005, from http://www.un.org/esa/socdev/poverty/documents/boep_10_2003_EN.pdf

Villeneuve-Gokalp, C. (1991). From marriage to informal union: Recent changes in the behaviour of French couples. *Population: An English Selection, 3,* 81–111.

Walters, L. H., Warzywoda-Kruszynska, W., & Gurko, T. (2002). Cross-cultural studies of families: Hidden differences. *Journal of Comparative Family Studies, 33,* 433–449.

Waters, W. F. (2001). Globalization, socioeconomic restructuring, and community health. *Journal of Community Health, 26,* 79–91.

Wee, V. (2000). Livelihood strategies of women in Asia. *Gender Studies News and Views,* 16+. Retrieved May 12, 2005, from http://rdsweb1.rdsinc.com/texis/rds/suite

Weissman, R. (1997). Stolen youth: Brutalized children, globalization, and the campaign to end child labor. *Multinational Monitor, 18*(1–2), 10–16.

CHAPTER 2

Comparative Research Methodology

GARY R. LEE AND NANCY A. GREENWOOD

INTRODUCTION

Research on human behavior, like most other types of scientific research, is based on the logic of correlation. This means that we examine the ways in which things go together in patterns. The things we study—traits, characteristics, or behaviors of individuals or other units of analysis, such as organizations or societies—are called *variables* because they take different values in different cases. In other words, they vary. Most variables vary from low to high values; in other words, they differ in quantity. *Correlation,* in its generic usage, is another term for *covariation,* which means the way variables vary together. We know, for example, that people with more education typically have higher incomes than those with less education (a **positive** correlation, meaning that the two variables tend to have similar values in most cases). We also know that the faster one drives, the lower one's gas mileage (a **negative** correlation, meaning that the variables tend to have opposite values).

The objective of behavioral science is not simply to observe and catalog correlations among variables involving human behavior, but rather to *explain* why we observe the patterns or correlations we do rather than some other patterns or correlations. The body of knowledge developed to predict and explain patterns of relations among variables is termed *theory.* The body of knowledge that guides us in the process of observing behavior and processing the information we obtain from those observations is termed *research methodology.* Although the latter is the focus of this chapter, theory and methods are intimately connected.

This chapter is explicitly about *comparative* research methods. In a literal sense, all social research is comparative (Lee, 1982). When we say, "Church attendance is negatively correlated with the probability of divorce," for example, we are saying that we have compared married persons who go to church frequently with those who go less frequently, and the latter were observed to divorce more often. This is a comparative statement. In practice, however, comparative research has come to mean research in which two or more *societies* are compared in some way.

Comparing societies is the only way of observing variation in the characteristics of societies and ascertaining how these characteristics affect the behavior of their members. Through comparative research, we are able to observe multiple societies with varying characteristics and to look for the ways in which these characteristics "hang together" in patterns and covary with the behavior of individuals. We cannot do this without comparing societies, because, within any single society, all characteristics of that society are "constants"—that is, they do not vary. We therefore cannot observe patterns of covariation among these characteristics or between these characteristics and the behavior of individuals. Studies conducted exclusively in the United States, for example, cannot tell us whether the behavior of Americans is caused by some characteristic(s) of the United States as a society, because there is no other society with differing characteristics with which the United States is being compared.

For example, we have evidence to the effect that in the United States (Lee & Ishii-Kuntz, 1987) and Israel (Litwin, 2001), the psychological well-being of older persons is positively related to the frequency with which they interact with their friends but unrelated to frequency of interaction with their adult children or other kin. Would this pattern also appear in societies such as Japan or Korea, where the culture places a much stronger emphasis on the value of intergenerational relations and a correspondingly lower emphasis on the value of independence from kin? Without comparative research, we do not know whether this pattern is specific to the United States or societies like the United States or is a general feature of human societies. More important, if these correlations do appear in some societies but not others, without comparison we do not know what particular features of societies might produce these patterns. Comparative research could provide evidence that would allow us to explain why these relations are observed in the United States and Israel by identifying the distinctive features of the societies in which these correlations appear.

Although comparative research is valuable, it is also difficult to do, and particularly difficult to do well. We will discuss some of the problems encountered in the conduct of comparative research and some of the ways researchers have attempted to resolve these problems. First, however, we will describe the various types of comparative research. (The names are arbitrary and are not necessarily shared by all comparative researchers, but we find them convenient.)

One type, *cross-cultural,* begins with descriptions of small, homogeneous societies by "ethnographers." A second type, *cross-societal,* uses descriptive statistics on societies' populations, such as census data, as its raw material. The third, *cross-national,* involves the conduct of separate but related surveys, experiments, or other studies in two or more societies, with the objective of comparing the results. Although all three types have in common a focus on comparing the characteristics of societies, they are quite different in terms of what they can do and how they attempt to do it. (The following section is based heavily on several previous publications on comparative methodology. See Lee [1982] for a general treatment of the issues, Lee [1984b] for a detailed discussion of cross-cultural research, and Lee and Haas [1993] for an analysis of cross-societal and cross-national methods. Also compare our division of comparative research into types with Ragin's [1987] distinction between "case-oriented strategies" and "variable-oriented strategies.")

TYPES OF COMPARATIVE RESEARCH

Cross-Cultural Research

One of the most common research methods used to gather information about other societies is the ethnographic method. Ethnography is concerned with the systematic, detailed description of the way of life (culture) of a group of people (society). The ethnographer accomplishes this primarily by direct observation, which involves living with the people under study, examining their customs and behaviors, interviewing key informants, and other strategies designed to allow the ethnographer to describe what it is like to be a member of this society.

One reason ethnographies are useful is that researchers are able to provide rich, complex descriptions of single societies or of communities within societies. Middleton (1965) lived among and studied the Lugbara of Uganda and wrote an ethnography describing their stratification system, religion, familial and kinship systems, and political structure; such contents are typical of ethnographies. Morris (1998) gave a rich account of the social life and customs of the Malawi of Africa; Peace (2002) did the same for an Irish village. Jacobs (1974) applied the ethnographic method to the study of an American retirement community. Each of these studies gives the reader a coherent picture of what life is like in the societies and communities described and what it might be like to be a member of the society or community.

However, according to our definition, research done in a single society (whether by ethnographic or other means) is not *comparative,* because it cannot examine variation in the properties of societies. But ethnographic research, although not inherently comparative, may be employed for comparative purposes if multiple ethnographies are compared. This type of research has been termed *cross-cultural* (Lee, 1982).

Ethnographies are written descriptions of the way of life of a group of people. To compare ethnographies systematically, one must code and quantify the information they contain. In other words, the written descriptions—words—must be turned into values of variables—numbers—which are then recorded in a form suitable for analysis. Because the ethnography has been a cornerstone of anthropological research for many decades, extending well back into the 19th century, thousands of ethnographies exist. Comparisons of all these written descriptions of societies would be impossible without quantification.

Fortunately, several data sets have been constructed, with codes assigned to a great many variables described in the texts of existing ethnographies (see C. R. Ember & M. Ember, 2001, Chapter 6). This makes it possible to compare literally hundreds of human societies in terms of the typical behaviors of their members and their characteristics as societies. Virtually all of these data sets exist as a result of the work of the anthropologist George Peter Murdock. Data sets include the Ethnographic Atlas (Murdock, 1967) with over 1,200 cases; the Standard Cross-Cultural Sample ($N = 186$; Barry & Schlegel, 1980; Murdock & White, 1969); and the Atlas of World Cultures ($N = 563$; Murdock, 1981). Many precoded data sets, including the latest additions to the Standard Cross-Cultural Sample, are available through the electronic journal *World Cultures.* In addition to the precoded data sets, the Human Relations Area Files (HRAF), based at Yale University, consist of categorized text from ethnographic studies of nearly 400 cultures that can be used to code variables that are not included in other data banks (see C. R. Ember & M. Ember, 2001).

It is possible to combine data from the precoded data banks with original codes from the HRAF. Ellis and Petersen (1992), for example, used a subset of the Standard Cross-Cultural Sample, in combination with original codes from 122 societies contained in the HRAF, to discover that, in societies where parents tend to value conformity in children, they are more likely to use physical punishment, lecturing, and other control techniques as disciplinary strategies than are parents in societies where self-reliance is highly valued in children.

Other recent studies have used cross-cultural data sets to examine issues such as the effects of cultural complexity and women's contributions to subsistence on women's status (Korotayev & Cardinale, 2003); the factors that influence women's role in agricultural production (Barry & Yoder, 2002); and the relationships between women's power and the frequency of divorce (Hendrix & Pearson, 1995). In each of these studies, the unit of analysis is the society or culture, not the individual. For example, Hendrix and Pearson found that divorce is more common in societies where women have more decision-making authority and marital roles are more segregated. With cross-cultural data, researchers cannot compare individuals or married couples, but they can compare societies among which the characteristics of marriages and marital roles differ. When we do this for a large number of societies, we are treating each society as a case in a cross-cultural survey, much as we treat individuals as cases in surveys within our own society. By the cross-cultural method, we can learn about the correlations among the characteristics of societies, but not about how these characteristics are related to the behavior of individuals within those societies.

The societies contained in cross-cultural data sets are small and relatively homogeneous. Many of them no longer exist, at least in the forms in which they were described in the ethnographies. No modern, industrial societies are contained in these cross-cultural data sets. This is because the ethnographic method isn't appropriate for the study of such societies, because the goal of ethnographic research is to describe the complete society. The United States and similarly complex societies are simply too large and diverse to be described in their entirety by observational methods.

One can, of course, conduct ethnographic research *within* large, complex societies such as the United States, but one cannot describe the entire society by doing so. For example, as noted earlier, Jacobs (1974) did an ethnographic study of a retirement community in the United States. Salamon (1992) studied farmers in the American Midwest and their connections to family and community ethnographically, supplemented by some survey and other data. She provides a thorough description and analysis of the way of life of the people she studied, but of course her study pertains only to the community of farm families she observed rather than to the entirety of American society. Wolf (1992) did a similar study of women employed in factories in Java, showing how industrialization in rural areas of a Third World country affects individual and family lives.

As valuable as these studies are, they do not describe the United States or Java as *societies,* but only the specific communities and types of people within these societies that were actually observed. However, this is not a criticism; these studies were never intended to describe entire societies. Ethnographic studies of entire societies and ethnographic studies of small communities within large societies should not be compared, because the units of analysis are different (Lee, 1982; Zelditch, 1971).

The purpose of cross-cultural research is not to describe the contemporary world, because many of the societies contained in the cross-cultural data banks no longer exist, or exist in a very different form. Instead, cross-cultural data may be very valuable for testing theories about the relations among characteristics or properties of societies. We will return to this issue later.

Cross-Societal Research

As noted earlier, cross-cultural research is useful for smaller, relatively homogeneous societies, because their populations may be observed directly and behavior is fairly uniform within the group. But large, complex societies cannot be described in full by the ethnographic method, and thus they are not included in cross-cultural data banks. Because these societies have very diverse populations, statistical descriptions are more accurate and useful than ethnographic descriptions based on observation.

There are many compilations of statistics on the populations of contemporary societies that provide information on the aggregate behaviors of members of these societies (e.g., average ages at marriage, divorce rates, or gross domestic product). These may be considered to be statistical counterparts of the ethnographic observations used in cross-cultural research. For convenience, we have labeled comparative research based on aggregate statistical descriptions of multiple societies *cross-societal* (Lee, 1982).

Again, cross-societal research does not allow the study of individuals within societies. The behavior of populations as aggregates is the focus of this type of research. We may discover through cross-societal research that divorce rates are higher in societies with higher rates of labor force participation by adult women (Trent & South, 1989). However, we cannot determine whether women who are employed are more or less likely to divorce than women who are not employed. Other recent cross-societal studies include investigations of the relations between systems of taxation and transfer payments and poverty rates (Moller, Bradley, Huber, Nielsen, & Stephens, 2003); effects of societal modernization on the environment and the sustainability of ecosystems (York, Rosa, & Dietz, 2003); and the interrelations between the accumulation of social capital and measures of democracy (Paxton, 2002).

Statistical data on contemporary societies are available through a great variety of sources. One of the richest is the United Nations' *Demographic Yearbook,* which publishes data on many social and demographic characteristics of societies each year. This is only one example, however; there are dozens of possible sources of data on the world's societies. Consequently, a major component of the cross-societal researcher's task is to assemble data from various appropriate sources that are relevant to the objectives of the research. Unlike cross-cultural research, there are few preexisting data sets (such as the Ethnographic Atlas) available in ready-to-analyze form. However, transcribing statistical data from published sources is not nearly as difficult or time consuming a task as is content-analyzing and coding written ethnographic descriptions of cultures.

Cross-societal research has been employed to study a great variety of family phenomena. For example, Trent and South (1989) were interested in the effects of certain structural properties of societies on the divorce rate. They obtained estimates of the crude divorce rates (number of divorces per thousand population) from the United Nations' *Demographic Yearbook* for 66 societies from around the world and constructed measures of several potential predictors of the divorce rate from a variety of sources. The predictors included societal modernization, the rate of labor force participation among adult women, and the sex ratio (number of males per 100 females). Their theory led them to expect that the more modern societies, those with higher rates of female labor force participation, and those with lower sex ratios (fewer men than women) would have higher divorce rates, and this is basically what they found. Their analysis shows that divorce covaries strongly with several dimensions of social structure and population composition.

Both cross-cultural and cross-societal research analyze data *on* societies, but not data *in* societies. That is, each provides one observation per variable per society, regardless of the number of individuals in each society who were observed in the collection of the original data. "Cross-national research," to which we now turn, involves the analysis of data collected *within* multiple societies.

Cross-National Research

Research conducted *within* two or more societies, either simultaneously or sequentially, may be termed *cross-national.* The objective is to obtain comparable data on some set of issues from samples of individuals or other units of analysis (e.g., organizations, political subunits) in all societies included in the research. Analyses are then conducted within each society in the study, and results are compared to determine whether relations among relevant variables are similar or different across the various societies in the sample.

Cross-national research is, in most respects, the most powerful of the various forms of comparative research, because it involves analyses on both the individual and societal levels (Kohn, 1987, 1989). It is the clearest way of ascertaining whether the characteristics of the societies in which they live affect the behaviors of individuals. However, it is also the most difficult and expensive form of comparative research because it requires the collection of original data in multiple societies; one rarely has banks of cross-national data to rely upon. Because of this, and because of the complexity of comparisons at multiple levels of analysis (individual as well as societal), it is virtually always the case that cross-national studies involve very small numbers of societies. Although cross-cultural studies can deal with over a thousand cultures simultaneously (the Ethnographic Atlas contains over 1,200 cases, for example), and cross-societal studies often involve a hundred or more societies, cross-national studies are generally restricted to no more than five or six countries at maximum, and most involve only two. However, in recent years collaboration between research organizations in different nations has produced data sets including 20 or more nations. For example, Batalova and Cohen (2002) used data from 22 nations to show that married couples who cohabited before marriage had more egalitarian divisions of domestic labor than couples who did not cohabit. (However, divisions of labor were more equal in countries with higher rates of cohabitation even among couples who had not cohabited themselves.) Stack and Eshleman (1998) found, with data from comparable surveys in 17 nations, that married persons report higher personal happiness than never-married persons in all but one nation (Northern Ireland), and that marriage has a considerably stronger positive effect on happiness than does cohabitation. These results are consistent with those found in most studies conducted in the United States (e.g., Lamb, Lee, & DeMaris, 2003), so we have some confidence that marriage has this effect in the great majority of contemporary societies.

We should note here that it is possible to compare multiple societies, in some cases, without collecting original data from each one. One may conduct a study in one society to replicate a study previously done in another. It is also possible to compare two or more studies done in multiple societies "after the fact," even if the studies weren't originally intended for this purpose, although one must be constantly aware of problems of comparability, which we will discuss shortly. But the best cross-national studies are generally those that are explicitly planned to be cross-national, because problems of comparability can be addressed at the design stage, and methods can be adapted to the explanatory objectives of the research project.

True cross-national studies are rare because of their difficulty and expense. They are, however, very valuable, for the reasons discussed earlier. But each type of comparative research has its own value, and each encounters its own versions of problems common to scientific researchers in all fields. We will briefly discuss a few of the major issues in the conduct of comparative research in the next section.

ISSUES IN COMPARATIVE RESEARCH METHODOLOGY

In any scientific investigation into human behavior, there are many issues that must be managed successfully in order to produce useful evidence and come to defensible conclusions. Most of these issues fall under three headings. First, *sampling* involves the selection of observations to be made from among the universe of all possible observations. Second, *measurement* is the process of assigning values to variables for each case. Third, *explanation* has to do with the interpretation of the evidence and the development of theory. Each of these issues is critical in any type of research, and the principles that guide the researcher to successful solutions to the problems each issue poses are identical regardless of whether research is comparative or noncomparative (Lee, 1982). However, comparative research presents some unique problems, and the ways in which the principles of good research are applied to these problems are somewhat different. We will briefly discuss each of these issues.

Sampling

The objective of behavioral science is to study the behavior of all human beings, or at least all members of a defined human population. However, no single study can possibly do this, and in any event it isn't necessary. Instead, studies are conducted on "samples" of relevant populations. The sample is the set of observations we actually make, which is a subset of all observations we could possibly make (the population). Provided that our samples possess certain properties, it is possible to "generalize" the results obtained from samples to populations with a high degree of confidence that we are correct.

Good samples possess two properties. The first is size. Although there is no handy rule that covers all cases, larger samples are better than smaller samples. This stands to reason, because the possibility that unusual events could occur in a high proportion of cases is greater in a smaller sample. The larger a sample, the more likely it reflects the characteristics of the population from which it was drawn.

However, this also depends upon another property of good samples: representativeness. A sample is representative to the extent that it possesses the same elements as the population, in the same proportions. In other words, if a population contains half males and half females, a sample should, too. Because it is impossible to know all the relevant characteristics of a population in advance of a study, or to intentionally choose observations that would collectively reflect these characteristics, behavioral scientists rely on *random* sampling methods to produce representative samples. *Random* simply means that we select the observations (cases) that comprise our samples by chance: Every member of the population has an equal chance of appearing in the sample, and the actual selection of cases is done by chance. If a random procedure is followed, and if the sample is large enough, the laws of probability ensure that the sample is highly likely to reflect or mirror the characteristics of the population. Then we can have some confidence that what we find to be true of the sample is also true of the population.

This, in brief, is the theory behind sampling. The same principles of sampling apply to all forms of behavioral research. Unfortunately, in the case of comparative research, it is essentially impossible to apply these principles to produce large, representative samples of the world's societies. The reasons for this differ according to the type of comparative research under consideration.

In cross-cultural research, as we noted earlier, it is possible to work with fairly large samples of cultures—over 1,200 in the case of the Ethnographic Atlas, and over 100 even in samples researchers construct independently (see, e.g., Ellis & Petersen, 1992). However, it is not possible to obtain representative samples of the world's cultures because we have data on only some of them and can't get data on many of the others. Many societies that have existed over the course of human history no longer exist, or they exist in a form highly altered from earlier forms as a result of contact with other societies. Those for which we have ethnographic data are surely different from those for which we do not (Lee, 1982, 1984b). Even if we were to use all of the ethnographic data available, we would have a biased (nonrepresentative) sample of the world's cultures, making generalizations from our sample to the population hazardous indeed.

We have a similar problem with cross-societal research even though the societies at issue are contemporary. There is a great deal of variation across societies in the amount and types of data that are collected from their populations and made available to the scholarly community. Trent and South (1989), in their cross-societal study of divorce, were able to come up with data on the divorce rate and other relevant variables for 66 societies around the world. Because there are fewer than 200 contemporary nations, this is a very high sampling fraction. But, as they demonstrated, the societies for which they had the necessary data were different from those for which they did not. The societies in their sample had higher gross national products, higher life expectancies, and lower fertility rates and were different from those not in the sample in several other ways as well. Generally, it is the more technologically advanced societies that are best able to collect population data and that are most likely to make it publicly available. This means that cross-societal samples also can't be fully representative of the world's societies; if the necessary data simply don't exist for certain societies, we can't create them.

The problem in cross-national research is somewhat different. Theoretically, we could choose any societies in the world to study and could therefore employ random methods of selection. But this usually isn't possible for political and logistic reasons, and furthermore the laws of probability don't apply to small numbers—remember, cross-national studies can include only a few societies. Although samples of individuals within societies may be large and representative, samples of societies themselves are inherently small and nonrepresentative.

The bottom line is that, for varying reasons, the principles of good sampling cannot be applied to the selection of societies for comparative research. Does this mean that good comparative research cannot be done? No. But it does mean that the objectives of this type of research must be adapted to the realm of the possible. Also, generalizing from samples to populations, which is a primary objective of survey research in contemporary societies, simply cannot be done. In other words, there is no type of comparative research that allows us to describe the population of societies in the world.

The objective of comparative research, however, is explanatory, not descriptive. We do this sort of research to test our ideas about *why* things go together as they do (C. R. Ember & M. Ember, 2001). What we need for this are samples of societies that allow our ideas to be tested fairly. We may, for example, have a theory that suggests a variety of reasons why arranged marriages should be more likely to occur in societies with extended family systems than in those with nuclear families (Lee & Stone, 1980). Although the ideal would certainly be a representative sample of all societies in the world, we can get by with a sample that includes a number of societies with extended family systems and a number with nuclear family systems. If, after comparing them according to type of mate selection system, we observe the difference we predict, then our reasoning (theory) gains credibility. If we do not observe this difference, then something about our reasoning is faulty and needs correcting, or perhaps our theory needs to be traded in for a completely different model.

In cross-cultural and cross-societal research, the general strategy is to employ all possible data—that is, if data are available for a society, use them. (There are certain important exceptions to this, as when a subset of cultures is selected according to some geographic criterion to test for the effects of cultural borrowing or "diffusion" [see C. R. Ember & M. Ember, 2001; Lee, 1982, 1984b; Lee & Haas, 1993; and Murdock & White, 1969]. These issues are beyond the scope of this discussion, however.) In cross-national research, it is vitally important to select societies that are appropriate for the comparison one wishes to make. If one has a hypothesis one believes to be universally applicable—that is, true in all human societies—one is well advised to test it in societies that differ as dramatically as possible, under the assumption that if it works at the extremes of a continuum it is likely to work in the middle. If, on the other hand, one has an hypothesis that a specific characteristic of a society has a specific effect on behavior, one should select societies that are as similar to one another as possible except on the characteristic in question. In this way, if the predicted differences are observed, one has narrowed the list of possible factors that might explain them, because a difference cannot be explained by a similarity.

In a study by Davis and Robinson (1991), education was shown to be positively related to consciousness of gender inequality among American women but negatively related to women's support for government efforts to combat inequality; this pattern did not hold in Austria, West Germany, or Great Britain. The authors argue that the United States may be different because of a tradition of emphasizing individualism and the primacy of the individual's role in solving problems. They suggest that "well-educated U.S. women adopt more individualistic solutions to women's disadvantaged position because of the U.S. educational system, which may emphasize personal effort and achievement more than systems in Britain and other European countries" (Davis & Robinson, p. 82). Although there is no means of verifying this speculation available in the authors' data, their suggestion is reasonable, because the four societies they studied are similar in so many other respects. (For more on the subject of selecting societies for cross-national research, see Kohn, 1987, 1989; Lee & Haas, 1993; and Przeworski & Teune, 1970.)

The point here is that comparative research is much more useful if it begins with a good theory. The theory predicts what will be discovered if certain observations are made. By making those observations and checking their outcomes against the predictions, one can learn something about the validity of the reasoning that produced the predictions. Without theory, one can only describe, and comparative research is very limited for descriptive purposes because of the impossibility of obtaining representative samples of the world's societies. If one doesn't have a theory that should be tested comparatively and that clearly stipulates what kinds of comparisons should be made to provide a constructive test, the value of the research probably will not justify its difficulty and expense (Kohn, 1987).

Measurement

Measurement is the process of assigning values to variables. Once observations are selected for inclusion in the sample, one must determine what value each observation takes. This may be as simple as ascertaining whether a respondent is male or female, or as complex as determining how "modern" a society is on a multidimensional index. In all research, each observation must be assigned a score for each variable.

In cross-cultural and cross-societal research, the values of variables are provided to the researcher in many cases. For example, in the Ethnographic Atlas, the type of family system that characterizes a society is precoded, in such a way that both family type (nuclear vs. extended) and marital type (monogamy, polygyny, polyandry) may be determined. The values for the variables, of course, refer to the "typical" or normative practice in the society, not to any specific family or set of families. In other cases, variables must be coded from original ethnographic reports or from compilations of the texts of these reports such as the HRAF. Problems may arise in each case (see C. R. Ember & M. Ember, 2001).

In precoded data sets, variables are not necessarily provided to the researcher in the form he or she finds most useful. Decisions must be made according to the objectives of the research, and codes for variables must often be recombined and reordered to suit those purposes. For example, Blumberg and Winch (1972) developed a theory of the relationship between "societal complexity" and family structure, which argued that the most complex families (i.e., extended family systems) are most likely to be found in the intermediate ranges of societal complexity. They decided that, in addition to consanguineally extended family systems, they would count societies as having complex families if they practiced frequent polygyny—the marriage of one husband to two or more wives. Their test of the theory was highly supportive. However, the theory was about family structure, not marital structure, but marital structure was an important component of their measure. It turns out that, if marital and family structure are separated, their theory predicts marital structure quite well but predicts family structure rather poorly (Lee, 1996). This is problematic for the theory, because it didn't address the topic of marital structure.

Problems are also encountered, usually much more obviously, when variables are coded directly from ethnographic reports. Balkwell and Balswick (1981) studied the status of the elderly and tested a theory that older persons have higher status in agricultural than hunting-and-gathering societies. To do this test, they had to code "status of the elderly" from ethnographic reports. They decided that any mention that older persons were ritually abandoned or killed would indicate low status for the elderly, regardless of other indicators. This seems eminently reasonable, particularly to contemporary scholars, who can't imagine abandoning or killing people simply because they have become too old. Their test was supportive: Older persons were shown to have higher status in agricultural societies.

However, Balkwell and Balswick (1981) overlooked the fact that older persons are killed or abandoned primarily in nomadic societies. It occurs when they become too weak or sick to keep up with the group in its travels. Because many groups must move in pursuit of food, slowing or stopping for older persons threatens the survival of the entire group. They are therefore faced with difficult choices between keeping their elders alive a little while longer or pursuing the food they need to keep the adults and children alive; if they stop, everyone may die.

The problem for Balkwell and Balswick (1981) was that these nomadic societies are almost exclusively hunting-and-gathering types. The members of agricultural societies don't move, because they must stay with the land on which their food is grown, so abandoning or killing old people who can't keep up simply isn't an issue. Of course, when the researchers coded the status of the elderly the way they did, hunting-and-gathering societies received much lower scores on this variable than did agricultural societies. When the variable is coded without regard to the practice in question, the direction of the relation remains the same, but it is much weaker (Lee, 1984a; Ishii-Kuntz & Lee, 1987). Balkwell and Balswick overestimated the strength of this relationship because they coded one variable in such a way that it was automatically and necessarily correlated with another variable, for a reason that had nothing to do with their theory.

Trent and South (1989), in their cross-societal study of divorce mentioned previously, showed that divorce rates are higher in more modern, complex, "developed" societies such as the United States than in those that are less technologically developed. The divorce rate they used, however, was the "crude" divorce rate, which is simply the number of divorces in a given year per 1,000 total population of the society in that year. With this measure, it is possible for a society to have a low divorce rate either because few marriages end in divorce, or because few people are married and thus are not exposed to the risk of divorce. Less "developed" societies typically have higher birth rates, lower life expectancies, and consequently high proportions of children in their populations; this means high proportions of unmarried persons. Thus, Trent and South's findings may mean, in part at least, that "less developed" societies have few divorces for the innocuous reason that relatively fewer people are married. A better indicator for their purposes would have been the "refined" divorce rate, which is the number of divorces per 1,000 married women in the population. Unfortunately, this was not available to them, so they did the best they could with what they had and warned their readers that there are problems with the use of the crude divorce rate.

Measurement in cross-national research can be very difficult. In addition to all of the usual problems of constructing good measures that are faced in noncomparative research (and there are many), the cross-national researcher is faced with the additional problems of comparability across societies and, frequently, comparability across languages. Having comparable measures is essential to comparative research because, if measures mean different things in different societies, then observed differences between those societies may be artifacts of the measures rather than true differences. The same measure (i.e., the same set of items or questions) may measure different things in different cultures, even if perfectly translated (Kohn, 1987; Lee, 1982; Lee & Haas, 1993; Przeworski & Teune, 1970; Walters, Warzywoda-Kruszynska, & Gurko, 2002).

Haas (1986) studied attitudes toward the breadwinning (provider) role among women in Sweden and the United States. To measure her dependent variable, she used two slightly different items in the two countries. In the United States, she asked respondents to agree or disagree with the statement that "The husband should be the main breadwinner in the family." In Sweden the comparable statement was, "The man should be the primary breadwinner in the family." The difference between the two statements is subtle but important, because the frequency of cohabitation is much higher in Sweden than in the

United States, and many of Haas's Swedish respondents were cohabiting and technically didn't have husbands. It is entirely possible to measure the same phenomenon in two or more societies by asking substantially different questions (Miller, Slomczynski, and Schoenberg, 1981; Przeworski & Teune, 1970; Walters et al., 2002).

Fortunately, a great deal of work has been done on how to create comparable measures and how to ascertain whether measures are in fact comparable (Kohn, Slomszynski, & Schoenbach, 1986; Kuechler, 1987; Miller et al., 1981; Przeworski & Teune, 1970). Unfortunately, space prohibits a careful treatment of these efforts here. Comparable measurement is difficult to achieve in cross-national research, and in all likelihood measures are never perfectly comparable, but it is possible to come close. It is, nonetheless, very important to be aware of the fact that noncomparability of measures may produce artifactual differences between nations in cross-national research. As Kohn (1987, 1989) points out, findings of cross-national similarity are unlikely to be due to noncomparable methods, but findings of differences between nations may be. One must always consider measurement error as a possible explanation for cross-national differences.

Although it takes somewhat different forms, measurement error is also a paramount concern in "qualitative" studies such as ethnographic reports. Here, the researcher observes the behaviors and customs of a group of people and interprets these observations in the context of the culture of the people as he or she understands it. A primary danger here is the unintentional application of the researcher's own cultural background to the interpretive process—in other words, ethnocentrism. Ethnographers are highly trained in methods designed to minimize the possibility of ethnocentric interpretations (Barnard & Good, 1984). It is important, for example, for the ethnographer to live with the people he or she is studying for some time, to learn the language, and to interview key informants extensively not only about customary behaviors, but also about the motivations and meanings underlying the behaviors. Interpreting the behavior of members of one society according to the culture of another society constitutes a serious form of measurement error.

Another form of measurement error in cross-cultural research arises in the process of coding ethnographic data. Coders may come to incorrect decisions about the values of variables based on misreading the ethnographic report, because of their own preconceived biases or knowledge of the theory to be tested, or because the ethnographic data are incomplete (C. R. Ember & M. Ember, 2001). Coders must be thoroughly trained, and it is always important to have variables coded by at least two different individuals so their codes can be compared and their consistency (reliability) determined.

Explanation

In the terminology employed here, *theory* is synonymous with *explanation. Theory* is the body of concepts, premises, assumptions, and knowledge that makes our empirical observations understandable; it is the attempt to answer the *why* question. There is no particular type or form of theory that is unique to comparative family scholarship, because comparative researchers tailor their explanatory strategies to the objects of their particular research efforts. There are, however, certain common problems that arise in the course of constructing comparative explanations. We can deal with only a few of these problems here.

One generic explanatory problem common to both cross-cultural and cross-societal research is often referred to as the "ecological fallacy." This is the assumption that what is true of aggregates is also true of individuals.

This assumption is often false. As an example, let us return to the study of divorce rates by Trent and South (1989). They discovered that, across most of their sample, divorce rates and rates of female labor force participation are positively related; that is, societies in which higher proportions of women are in the labor force have higher divorce rates than other societies. This does not mean, however, that employed women are more likely to divorce than nonemployed women. This may or may not be true (White & Rogers, 2000). It is possible that nonemployed women are more likely to divorce in populations where most women are employed. The discovery that two properties or characteristics of aggregate populations go together does not automatically imply that these same characteristics go together on the individual level; this must be determined separately.

A second major explanatory issue in comparative research is termed *overidentification*. Technically this refers to situations in which there are more ways to explain a difference among cases than there are cases in the analysis. This problem occurs most frequently and obviously in cross-national research, because it is a problem inherent in all small-sample research, and cross-national studies can deal with only a few societies. The problem arises when we attempt to explain a cross-national difference, either in the value of some criterion variable or in a pattern of relations among variables. The difference in question must be attributable to some other difference between the societies (because a difference cannot be caused by a similarity), but any two societies have an infinite number of differences between them, even if they were selected to be as similar as possible. Which difference accounts for the difference we are trying to explain?

Ono (2003) discovered that, in Japan, unmarried women's income seems to be a disincentive to marriage; that is, higher-income women are less likely to marry in a given time span than are lower-income women. But in the United States and Sweden, women's income predicts marriage positively: Higher-income women are *more* likely to marry than lower-income women. Ono theorizes that this is due to differences in gender role expectations. In Japan, men and women are expected to behave quite differently (for example, many fewer married Japanese women are employed than is the case in the United States or Sweden), and consequently each gender specializes in a certain type of activity (labor market for men, domestic market for women) and "trades" this activity to a member of the opposite sex in marriage. Higher-income women are less motivated to marry because they need a husband's income less. But in the United States and Sweden, men's and women's role expectations have become more similar, so both sexes are expected to participate in the labor force and are more desirable as marriage partners if their incomes are higher (see also Sweeney, 2002).

This reasoning certainly makes sense. But we do not know for certain that it is the correct explanation, because there are many other differences between Japan, on the one hand, and Sweden and the United States on the other, that could statistically "explain" this difference equally well. Rates of cohabitation are much lower in Japan than the other two countries. The populations of both the United States and Sweden are predominantly Christian; Japan's is not. Both cohabitation and religion distinguish Japan from the United States and Sweden in the same way that gender role differentiation does. So how do we know that Ono's (2003) explanation is the correct one?

In a purely objective sense, we don't and we can't. Because we have so few cases for analysis, an infinite number of variables will distinguish them in the same way, and there is no statistical means of choosing among the potential explanations. But Ono's (2003) theory has the great advantage of making sense. He derived hypotheses from this theory, tested them fairly, and found them to be supported. The theory therefore becomes more credible. This does not deny the possibility of alternative theories that might be equally consistent with the data, but at least we can say that Ono's theory was supported.

The best defense against overidentification is a good theory (Kohn, 1987; Lee & Haas, 1993). This is one more reason why comparative research should not be done without a theory, which provides the rationale for the comparison one is making as well as a credible explanation for the observed differences.

CONCLUSION

Good comparative research does not result from simply following a predesigned set of rules and procedures (Kohn, 1987; Zelditch, 1971). Instead, it involves creativity in assembling appropriate observations and employing these observations in a constructive manner. We have touched only briefly on some of the major issues in the method of comparative social inquiry here, and the reader is certainly not prepared by this abbreviated treatment to go out and do useful comparisons. But at least we have highlighted some of the issues.

Comparative research remains the only means of ascertaining how the characteristics of societies in which people live affect their behavior. It is, in fact, the only means of observing variation in the characteristics of societies, thereby rendering them amenable to scientific analysis. There are no easy solutions to the methodological problems posed by comparative inquiry, but our methods have become a great deal more sophisticated in recent years, and we are at least aware of the many pitfalls and obstacles to comparability.

Perhaps the best way to conclude this treatise is to echo Kohn's (1987) observation that, unless one has a compelling reason for doing comparative research, one is well advised not to do it. It can be a powerful means of analyzing the effects of society on behavior, which is what sociology is all about, but it is difficult to do well and is hard on resources. Although there are many specific compelling reasons to do comparative research, they can all be summarized by one generic term: theory. We compare societies in order to shed light on our thinking, to determine whether our ideas about the way the world works have merit. If we don't have ideas that need to be tested in this manner, there is little point in comparison. But if we do have ideas about how the characteristics of societies affect the behavior of their members, comparative research is the only way to generate empirical tests of these ideas.

REFERENCES

Balkwell, C., & Balswick, J. (1981). Subsistence economy, family structure, and the status of the elderly. *Journal of Marriage and the Family, 43*, 423–429.

Barnard, A., & Good, A. (1984). *Research practices in the study of kinship*. New York: Academic Press.

Barry, H., III, & Schlegel, A. (1980). *Cross-cultural samples and codes*. Pittsburgh, PA: University of Pittsburgh Press.

Barry, H., III, & Yoder, B. L. (2002). Multiple predictors of contribution by women to agriculture. *Cross-Cultural Research, 36*, 286–297.

Batalova, J. A., & Cohen, P. N. (2002). Premarital cohabitation and housework: Couples in cross-national perspective. *Journal of Marriage and Family, 64*, 743–755.

Blumberg, R. L., & Winch, R. F. (1972). Societal complexity and familial complexity: Evidence for the curvilinear hypothesis. *American Journal of Sociology, 77*, 898–920.

Davis, N. J., & Robinson, R. V. (1991). Men's and women's consciousness of gender inequality: Austria, West Germany, Great Britain, and the United States. *American Sociological Review, 56*, 72–84.

Ellis, G. J., & Petersen, L. R. (1992). Socialization values and parental control techniques: A cross-cultural analysis of child-rearing. *Journal of Comparative Family Studies, 23*, 39–54.

Ember, C. R., & Ember, M. (2001). *Cross-cultural research methods.* Walnut Creek, CA: AltaMira Press.

Haas, L. (1986). Wives' orientation toward breadwinning: Sweden and the United States. *Journal of Family Issues, 7*, 358–381.

Hendrix, L., & Pearson, W., Jr. (1995). Spousal interdependence, female power, and divorce: A cross-cultural view. *Journal of Comparative Family Studies, 26*, 217–232.

Ishii-Kuntz, M., & Lee, G. R. (1987). Status of the elderly: An extension of the theory. *Journal of Marriage and the Family, 49*, 413–420.

Jacobs, J. (1974). *Fun City: An ethnographic study of a retirement community.* New York: Holt, Rinehart & Winston.

Kohn, M. L. (1987). Cross-national research as an analytic strategy. *American Sociological Review, 52*, 713–731.

Kohn, M. L. (Ed.). (1989). *Cross-national research in sociology.* Newbury Park, CA: Sage.

Kohn, M. L., Slomczynski, K. M., & Schoenbach, C. (1986). Social stratification and the transmission of values in the family: A cross-national assessment. *Sociological Forum, 1*, 73–102.

Korotayev, A. V., & Cardinale, J. (2003). Status of women, female contribution to subsistence, and monopolization of information: Further cross-cultural comparisons. *Cross-Cultural Research, 37*, 87–104.

Kuechler, M. (1987). The utility of surveys for cross-national research. *Social Science Research, 16*, 229–244.

Lamb, K. A., Lee, G. R., & DeMaris, A. (2003). Union formation and depression: Selection and relationship effects. *Journal of Marriage and Family, 65*, 953–962.

Lee, G. R. (1982). *Family structure and interaction: A comparative analysis* (2nd ed.). Minneapolis: University of Minnesota Press.

Lee, G. R. (1984a). Status of the elderly: Economic and familial antecedents. *Journal of Marriage and the Family, 46*, 267–275.

Lee, G. R. (1984b). The utility of cross-cultural data: Potentials and limitations for family sociology. *Journal of Family Issues, 5*, 519–541.

Lee, G. R. (1996). Economies and families: A further investigation of the curvilinear hypothesis. *Journal of Comparative Family Studies, 27*, 353–372.

Lee, G. R., & Haas, L. (1993). Comparative methods in family research. In P. G. Boss, W. J. Doherty, R. LaRossa, W. R. Schumm, & S. K. Steinmetz (Eds.), *Sourcebook of family theories and methods: A contextual approach* (pp. 117–131). New York: Plenum.

Lee, G. R., & Ishii-Kuntz, M. (1987). Social interaction, loneliness, and emotional well-being among the elderly. *Research on Aging, 9,* 459–482.

Lee, G. R., & Stone, L. H. (1980). Mate-selection systems and criteria: Variation according to family structure. *Journal of Marriage and the Family, 42,* 319–326.

Litwin, H. (2001). Social network type and morale in old age. *The Gerontologist, 41,* 516–524.

Middleton, J. (1965). *The Lugbara of Uganda.* New York: Holt, Rinehart & Winston.

Miller, J., Slomczynski, K. M., & Schoenberg, R. J. (1981). Assessing comparability of measurement in cross-national research: Authoritarian-conservatism in different sociocultural settings. *Social Psychology Quarterly, 44,* 178–191.

Moller, S., Bradley, D., Huber, E., Nielsen, F., & Stephens, J. D. (2003). Determinants of relative poverty in advanced capitalist democracies. *American Sociological Review, 68,* 22–51.

Morris, B. (1998). *The power of animals: An ethnography.* New York: Berg.

Murdock, G. P. (1967). Ethnographic atlas: A summary. *Ethnology, 6,* 189–236.

Murdock, G. P. (1981). *Atlas of world cultures.* Pittsburgh, PA: University of Pittsburgh Press.

Murdock, G. P., & White, D. R. (1969). Standard cross-cultural sample. *Ethnology, 8,* 329–369.

Ono, H. (2003). Women's economic standing, marriage timing, and cross-national contexts of gender. *Journal of Marriage and Family, 65,* 275–286.

Paxton, P. (2002). Social capital and democracy: An interdependent relationship. *American Sociological Review, 67,* 254–277.

Peace, A. J. (2002). *A world of fine difference: The social architecture of a modern Irish village.* Dublin, Ireland: University College Dublin Press.

Przeworski, A., & Teune, H. (1970). *The logic of comparative social inquiry.* New York: Wiley-Interscience.

Ragin, C. C. (1987). *The comparative method: Beyond qualitative and quantitative strategies.* Berkeley: University of California Press.

Salamon, S. (1992). *Prairie patrimony: Family, farming, and community in the midwest.* Chapel Hill: University of North Carolina Press.

Stack, S., & Eshleman, J. R. (1998). Marital status and happiness: A 17-nation study. *Journal of Marriage and the Family, 60,* 527–536.

Sweeney, M. M. (2002). Two decades of family change: The shifting economic foundations of marriage. *American Sociological Review, 67,* 132–147.

Trent, K., & South, S. J. (1989). Structural determinants of the divorce rate: A cross-societal analysis. *Journal of Marriage and the Family, 51,* 391–401.

Walters, L. H., Warzywoda-Kruszynska, W., & Gurko, T. (2002). Cross-cultural studies of families: Hidden differences. *Journal of Comparative Family Studies, 33,* 433–449.

White, L. K., & Rogers, S. J. (2000). Economic circumstances and family outcomes: A review of the 1990s. *Journal of Marriage and the Family, 62,* 1035–1051.

Wolf, D. L. (1992). *Factory daughters: Gender, household dynamics, and rural industrialization in Java.* Berkeley: University of California Press.

York, R., Rosa, E. A., & Dietz, T. (2003). Footprints on the earth: The environmental consequences of modernity. *American Sociological Review, 68,* 279–300.

Zelditch, M., Jr. (1971). Intelligible comparisons. In I. Vallier (Ed.), *Comparative methods in sociology* (pp. 267–307). Berkeley: University of California Press.

CHAPTER 3

The History of the Euro-Western Family

Bron B. Ingoldsby

This chapter gives the reader an understanding of how the modern North American family with European roots came to be what it is. I trace certain aspects of family interaction from the time of the ancient Hebrews and through their European and colonial evolutions. This perspective helps one to understand how things came to be as they are today, both in their generalities and diversity. Because culture changes across time, this will supply part of the historical perspective within which we can understand family practices in the modern world.

However, this is only *part* of the perspective, because many millions of peoples do not share the white Christian heritage. It is simply not possible to give even an overview of the historical antecedents for the family of all the races and cultures of the world. Historians have thus far given us much more information on European family life because of the political dominance of the West in recent centuries. So, with some reluctance, but in order to provide a coherent picture, I am forced to narrow the focus to this particular group, as most family historians before me have done. We are able to provide some historical background for certain minority groups in other chapters of this text.

I also ignore certain aspects of family life that are explained in historical perspective in other chapters, such as mate selection and marital structure. Instead, my focus is on two often interrelated topics: sexuality and power. Much of Western history has been characterized by husbands' dominance over wives and parental dominance over children, and sex has been much of the rationale for that dominance.

The historical record provides us with much more information on what people were taught as to proper family behavior than it does on what people actually did. It also gives us more information about the wealthy and powerful than it does about the common people. The problem of norms versus actual behavior can be a thorny one, but one can assume that there is some correlation between what is written and what is practiced (Brady, 1991). In each case, I try to clarify when I am talking about proscriptions regarding behavior versus empirical behavior itself.

Finally, much of the historical literature about gender and family relations is religious in nature. It is precisely because so many Western norms have religious sanction that institutions such as patriarchy have been so impervious to change until very recent times. With these limitations in mind, I divide our look at the family into nine historical periods. Each builds on and alters its predecessor in various ways, leading eventually to today's family.

THE HEBREWS

The Hebrew nomads began to take possession of Canaan around the middle of the 12th century BC. Tribal life evolved into a nation, with a capital and temple in Jerusalem. In the sixth century BC, the kingdom of Judah was overthrown by the Babylonians, and the Jews remained under the control of various foreign powers until AD 70, when they were scattered as a people by the Romans. Their great legislator, Moses, was reared in Egypt, and much of their code seems to be borrowed from that civilization (Bardis, 1966).

The society of the Old Testament Israelites was clearly patriarchal. Wives were expected to be submissive to their husbands, and they were often viewed as little more than property. For instance, in the Ten Commandments of Exodus 20, they are listed with other domestic property as things not to be coveted when belonging to one's neighbor.

Marriages were simple affairs, arranged between families. A girl belonged to her father until she was sold (by means of the "bride-price") to her husband. Typically, betrothals were arranged at about the time of puberty (Kephart & Jedlicka, 1991). Although there is evidence of loving husband-wife relationships, love was not the key purpose of marriage. It was a responsibility expected of everyone in order to ensure the continuation of family lines through childbearing. The commandment to multiply and replenish the earth was taken seriously, and large families were seen as a sign of God's blessing. There was strong endogamous pressure in order to preserve their cultural identity (Queen, Habenstein, and Quadagno, 1985).

One piece of evidence for beliefs about female inferiority is in the area of reproduction. The Hebrews shared the almost universal tendency of primitive societies to label women as unclean, because of menstruation and childbirth, and to require purification (Fielding, 1942). Banishment was the penalty for a couple having intercourse during the woman's menstrual period (Leviticus 20:18 [King James Version for all biblical citations]), and menstruating women were to separate themselves from the rest of the community. When giving birth to a boy, the mother was considered unclean for 7 days and experienced a purification period lasting an additional 33 days. If she had a girl, then the time period was doubled (Leviticus 12:1–5).

However, the differential in gender status was nowhere more apparent than in the area of sexuality. The "double standard," where sexual activity is condemned for women but acceptable for men, seems to come from the Hebrews and other Middle Eastern groups. Although it may have been rarely enforced, women could be put to death for adultery and could suffer other serious penalties for fornication. Men were not to have intercourse with another man's wife, not because of the effect on the marital relationship, but because to do so would be a violation of the other man's property rights and would lead to a confusion of bloodlines. The importance of genealogy is seen in Deuteronomy 23:2, where illegitimate children and their offspring could not be part of the congregation for 10 generations.

Men were allowed to have as many wives and concubines (secondary wives, whose children did not have the same inheritance status) as they could support. Sex ratio constraints would have limited this practice to the wealthy; therefore, it was experienced by only a small minority. And although penalties existed for men who engaged in nonmarital sex, they were often minor. For instance, intercourse with a slave girl betrothed to another resulted in her being scourged, but the man was forgiven if he brought a ram as an offering to the priest (Leviticus 19:20–22).

Leviticus 18 focuses on forbidden marital or sexual relationships, and it is the basis for subsequent Western law on incest and related prohibitions. Intercourse with one's parents, siblings, and children is forbidden, as well as intercourse with aunts, uncles, and various in-law relations. Chapter 20 prescribes the death penalty for certain sexual relations, including adultery, some forms of incest, homosexuality, and bestiality. If a wife were accused of adultery, an ordeal was designed (Numbers 5) to test her claim of innocence. She would drink holy water, and if guilty, her belly would swell and her thigh would rot.

Today's high divorce rate concerns many, and it is often believed that divorce is a relatively new phenomenon invented by a decadent society. In fact, the termination of marriages has always been allowed under certain circumstances, even in societies that highly value marital stability. Hebrew men could divorce their wives for practically any reason, though the Hebrew women had no such recourse. Adultery and incompatibility were considered plausible grounds, but infertility (presumed to be the woman's fault) was the most common reason. Husbands, however, were subject to severe social disapproval if they divorced their wives for frivolous reasons, and under certain conditions they were not allowed to ever divorce. These conditions included when the husband and wife had had premarital intercourse, if she were taken into captivity, or if she was insane (Bardis, 1963a).

Children are always highly valued in agricultural societies as workers, and Old Testament stories give the impression of considerable love and devotion between parent and child. This does not mean that they were treated with the kindness and dignity expected today, however. Children were expected to be obedient, and severe punishment followed wrongdoing. Solomon stated, "He that spareth his rod hateth his son: but he that loveth him chasteneth him betimes" (Proverbs 13:24).

Beatings met with social approval, and it was possible (though apparently rare) to go further to curb disobedience. The Law of Moses permitted parents to kill any child who struck or cursed them (Exodus 21:15–17). Parental authority was virtually absolute. The practice of primogeniture, in which the eldest son inherits most of the family property, often resulted in sibling rivalry, especially if primogeniture was disregarded. The stories of Joseph and his brothers and of Jacob and Esau are prime examples. Daughters were seldom considered important enough to even be mentioned.

We have inherited a number of notions and practices from the Judaic codes. They include male dominance in marital and family relationships, the sexual double standard, and the justification of the mistreatment of children. Family life was private, and its members were the property of the husband, who could do basically as he saw fit.

THE GREEKS

Although there is some evidence of a matriarchal system in prehistoric Greece, by the time of the "golden age of civilization" it was very much a man's world. Female subservience in Hebrew culture seems benign when compared to the Greeks. Marriage was for social reasons, chiefly seen as necessary for securing an heir. As this quote from Demosthenes demonstrates, men went elsewhere for companionship: "We marry women to have legitimate children and to have faithful guardians of our homes. We maintain concubines for our daily service and comfort, and courtesans for the enjoyment of love" (quoted in Fielding, 1942, p. 204).

Now-famous Greek thinkers did not hesitate to speculate on proper family life. Plato, for instance, felt that common possession of wives, for the upper classes at least, would be better than monogamy, and that weak children should be allowed to die by exposure (Adams & Steinmetz, 1993).

Greek men were interested in intellectual qualities and did not see women as rational. In Athens, a wife's position was quite menial: She was not educated and could not leave the house without her husband's permission. If she did leave, she had to be veiled (so as not to arouse the desires of other men) and chaperoned (Fielding, 1942). She typically stayed in her own quarters and joined her husband only at mealtimes. Even this, however, was not permitted if there were dinner guests. The Greeks invented the chastity belt, because they felt that any man could talk any women into having sex with him, because of the woman's low reasoning skills.

There is considerable evidence that men considered women to be very inferior to them. Pericles held that the best reputation a woman could have was not to be spoken of among men for good or evil, and Aristotle regarded slavish obedience as the highest virtue for an uneducated wife. Spartan husbands could even arrange extramarital affairs for their wives in the interest of eugenics, so obsessed was this military society with producing physically superior children. The laws of Lycurgus permitted a "man of character" who had a passion for a modest and beautiful woman to ask her husband if he might mate with her in order to produce more excellent children. The husband could permit this, but Greek law also permitted a husband to kill an adulterer. In general, however, Spartan women had much more freedom than did their counterparts in the city-state of Athens (Bardis, 1964a).

Many of the beliefs still held by some about gender differences seem to come straight out of the literature of the Greeks. In Xenophon's *Oeconomicus,* the following quotes come from a discussion with Socrates:

> God from the beginning made the woman's nature for the indoor and the man's for the outdoor tasks and cares . . . knowing that to the woman's nature he gave and assigned the rearing of infants, he gave to her more affection for babies than to the man . . . he gave him a larger share of courage . . . So it is better for the woman to stay at home than to abide in the fields, but it is more disgraceful for the man to stay at home. (quoted in Bardis, 1964a, pp. 164–165)

In Homer's *Odyssey,* we see further evidence of male dominance: "But go now to the home, and attend to thy household affairs; to the spinning wheel and the loom, and bid thy maids be assiduous at the tasks that to them were allotted. To speak is the privilege of men" (quoted in Fielding, 1942, p. 202). Prostitution was also developed as a public service by the famous Athenian lawmaker Solon. According to Fielding, Solon's contemporaries commended him, exclaiming, "Solon, be praised! For thou didst purchase public women for the welfare of the city, to preserve the morals of the city that is full of strong, young men, who, without thy wise institution, would indulge in the annoying pursuit of better-class women" (quoted in Fielding, p. 204).

The better-class women referred to may have been the *hetairae,* a special class of mistresses trained to be women of beauty, charm, and intellect. These temple prostitutes had a life much freer than that of wives and often obtained considerable power and wealth. Men sought them out for sexual and intellectual companionship, and they enjoyed the highest status for women in Greek society (Bardis, 1964a).

In relation to the treatment of children, adoption was common when a couple had no sons. Only sons inherited, with the bulk of the family estate going to the eldest. The wife could not inherit her husband's property, and if a man had only daughters, one of them might be forced to marry a close relative, who would then be the recipient (Bardis, 1964a).

The double standard was quite exaggerated under the Greeks. For men, the social ideal seemed to be the full expression of sensuality with a minimum of restraints, whereas for women adultery was a criminal act, grounds for divorce, and justification for being put to death. A woman could sue her husband for divorce, but only with his consent or if she could prove cruelty (Bardis, 1964a).

Finally, the opinion of Greek women was so low that it formed part of the cultural approval of homosexuality. The actual incidence is unknown, but household illustrations portrayed homosexual relations, and Greek writers were open on the subject. Men turned to each other for intellectual and emotional support, and this frequent interaction and dependence is believed by some (see Kephart & Jedlicka, 1991) to be responsible. Actually, homosexuality does not appear to have been seen as abnormal by either the ancient Greeks or Romans. Passive or "feminine" behavior or positions were criticized in males, but as long as a man assumed the active role, the object of his passion did not seem to be important (Veyne, 1985).

Ancient Greece, then, represents the nadir for female status in family and general relations. Their subjugation was complete, with courtesans more valued than wives, and all men more valued than any woman.

THE ROMANS

Like the ancient Hebrew and Greek families, the Romans were patriarchal. In contrast, however, they were monogamous and did not approve of polygyny or concubinage. The early Romans were very much male centered, being patrilocal and patrilineal as well as patriarchal.

The Roman *familia,* or household, included everyone under the authority of the male head of the family, or *paterfamilias.* This typically included the man's wife, unmarried daughters, sons, and their spouses and children. Everyone in the male line was under the control of the *paterfamilias* until that person died, at which time each adult married male could start his own household.

In upper-class families, the girl's family provided a dowry, which became the property of the husband or of his *paterfamilias.* Lower-class weddings were often without ceremony or official witnesses, and their cohabitation was recognized as a common-law marriage. This validation of the private decision of the couple continues in many parts of the world today. Upper-class ceremonies included a contract and a procession (Bardis, 1963b).

As with the Hebrews, children, especially boys, were desired. The father had the right to reject children and would occasionally leave them to die or sell them. This was more likely to occur with deformed or female children. Most children were accepted into the household and received their educations by observing and working with their same-sex parent.

Men could divorce their wives for practically any reason, but they were restricted by social expectation to the causes of adultery, making poison, drinking wine, and counterfeiting house keys. The power of the *paterfamilias* was so great that he could not only divorce his own wife but could force a son to divorce, if he wanted him to, as well. When they married, daughters became members of their husband's family (Bardis, 1963b).

In the second century BC, Rome and Carthage were engaged in a long series of wars with each other. Major wars often serve as a turning point for societal customs, and the Punic Wars may be the best historical example of how wars can enhance the status of women. Because the men were away from home, on occasion for years at a time, their wives of necessity took over many of the household responsibilities.

They were already better off than their Greek counterparts in that they were not confined to family quarters, and they controlled child rearing to a certain degree. After the war, they became more independent. In many marriages, for instance, wives remained under their fathers' authority, instead of being transferred to the *manus* (control) of their husband. Because the father rarely exercised power over these adult daughters, they were able to gain some freedom and wealth (Bardis, 1963b).

According to Queen et al. (1985), divorce became easier to obtain and therefore more frequent. Women were able to secure divorces, and some upper-class Romans remarried frequently. Enough women became independently wealthy through inheritances from their fathers or husbands that laws were passed to discourage it. In essence, the status of the sexes became more egalitarian.

Many historians have also noted a change in sexual mores after Rome became an empire. People began to live sexually freer lives, with such activities as adultery and abortion becoming more common. Serious legal penalties were designed for adulterers—such as loss of property and even death, but enforcement was not regular. Prostitution became more acceptable, and statesmen decried the decaying moral values of the time (Bardis, 1963b).

To summarize, until the Punic Wars, the Roman household was the religious, educational, economic, and legal center of society. The father exercised considerable control over the lives of all family members. This power was gradually reduced, especially after the wars with Carthage. Many young people ceased to regard marriage as an obligation and assumed more personal control over the process. The legal and social status of both women and children improved. Men tended to view these trends with alarm and attributed moral degeneracy to these changes.

EARLY CHRISTIANITY

In the first century after the life of Jesus, domestic mores were not distinctly Christian, but were, rather, a mix of Jewish, Greek, and Roman customs. Gradually, however, a fairly homogeneous doctrine developed for marriage, sex, and family life. Although partially based on New Testament ideas, they also reflected repulsion from the lifestyle of upper-class Romans and an acceptance of the Persian notion of duality, which sees the body and spirit as opposed to each other (see Queen et al., 1985).

Although Rome was sacked in AD 410, its era had ended almost a century earlier when the Emperor Constantine allied the government with the Christian church. A persecuted cult became the state religion and eventually became the legal as well as social and moral successor to the empire in Europe (Tannahill, 1980). Indeed, no force has had greater influence than Christianity in shaping Western thought concerning the relation between the sexes.

In addition to the history of Jesus and the writings of Paul, our major source of information is the writings of influential early church fathers, such as St. Jerome, St. Augustine, and Tertullian. In a time of general illiteracy, reading and writing belonged to the monasteries, and they saved only information that supported the Church positions. As a result, the conclusions of these men were not seriously debated or modified and ended up having tremendous long-term impact (Tannahill, 1980).

It appears that Jesus taught that it was intended for adult men and women to leave their parents and marry and that the only acceptable reason for divorce was adultery. He also loved children and consistently treated women with dignity and respect. However, loyalty to his gospel was more important than family relationships (see Matthew 19).

St. Paul expands on these concepts and provides the basis for the ultimate devaluation of marriage and of women that developed in the early Christian church. In his first letter to the Corinthians (Chapter 7), he explains that although marriage is acceptable, it distracts disciples from their religious devotion (7:33–38), and therefore it is better to remain single if one can resist sexual temptation (7:8–9). However, there is nothing dishonorable about marital sex (see Hebrews 13:4).

Paul repeatedly makes it clear that women are to be subject to men. They are not to speak in church but should learn from their husbands instead (1 Corinthians 14:34–35). In his first letter to Timothy (2:9–14), he explains that women are to be modest and subject to men because Eve was the one who transgressed in the Garden of Eden. A cruel patriarchy was not condoned, however. Even though wives were to submit themselves to their husbands, and children were to obey their parents, husbands were commanded to love their wives and not abuse their children (Colossians 3:18–21). Although some argue that Paul was reacting to the "excesses" of Rome when he wished for the good old days of a clear hierarchy, he nevertheless provided justification for the subordination of women.

In the first few centuries AD, one notes considerable ambivalence on the part of church leaders toward such subjects as marriage, women, and sexuality. The Christian standards of monogamy, nonmarital chastity, and marital fidelity strengthened the nuclear family and attacked the double standard. However, according to Queen et al. (1985), even as the Roman emperors were penalizing citizens who refused to marry, the church fathers were praising them and according higher status to virgins and widows than to married couples.

Women were valued members of the church and were often idealized as charitable reflections of Mary. On the other hand, like Eve, they presumably tempted men into sin and away from devotion. And although sex was necessary for procreation (the making of more Christians and virgins), it was also the original sin that had to be overcome in subjecting the body to the spirit (Tannahill, 1980).

In the end, the church adopted a negative view on each of these issues. It came down to a rejection of physical pleasure and therefore a rejection of those things connected with it (from the male view, women and marriage).

A few quotes from early church leaders convey the inferior status of women. Tertullian said: "You are the devil's gateway: You are the unsealer of that forbidden tree: You are the first deserter of the divine law: You are she who persuaded him whom the devil was not valiant enough to attack." And Chrysostom declared that women are "a necessary evil, a natural temptation, a desirable calamity, a domestic peril, a deadly fascination and a painted ill" (quoted in Queen et al., 1985, p. 203). In 585, the Council of Macon seriously debated whether or not women had souls. The bishops decided that they do, but only by a one-vote majority (Bardis, 1964b).

That women were not to go to any effort to enhance their beauty was made clear in a letter from St. Jerome to a wealthy woman in 403. It contained advice on how to rear her daughter and included the following:

> Her very dress and outward appearance should remind her of Him to whom she is promised. Do not pierce her ears, or paint with white lead and rouge the cheeks that

> are consecrated to Christ. Do not load her neck with pearls and gold, do not weigh down her head with jewels, do not dye her hair red and thereby presage her for the fires of hell. . . . I know some people have laid down the rule that a Christian virgin should not bathe along with eunuchs or with married women, inasmuch as eunuchs are still men at heart, and women big with child are a revolting sight. For myself I disapprove altogether of baths in the case of a full-grown virgin. She ought to blush at herself and be unable to look at her own nakedness. (quoted in Queen et al., 1985, p. 209)

The condemnation of sexual pleasure itself was just as strong. The sole purpose of coitus was for procreation; anything else was lustful and therefore sinful. Any form of contraception was condemned, as were all "unnatural" acts such as anal and oral intercourse, homosexuality, and bestiality. Such crimes could result in a penance of fasting from all but bread and water for years; even a nocturnal emission demanded a few days of fasting or the reciting of psalms (Tannahill, 1980).

Probably no other culture has had such a stern code: All suggestive books, songs, and dances were forbidden as well. The Christian custom of kissing each other as a greeting became suspect, and second kisses were considered sinful. At least one church father, Origen, castrated himself in order to escape sexual desire. In 398 the Council of Carthage declared that, out of respect for the sacred nature of the wedding benediction, newlyweds should not have intercourse on their wedding night. This rule was later extended to three nights, but it could be avoided by paying a fee to the church (Queen et al., 1985).

Some saints tried to prove their superiority to the temptations of the flesh by marrying, but staying celibate. But such repression of natural urges can lead to obsessing on them. Jerome, who shunned even eating and washing as invitations to lust, was plagued with visions of dancing girls and was inflamed with lust as he fasted in the desert. Other monks and nuns complained of the devil tempting them to indecent acts in their dreams, and they believed in succubi, or erotic demons (Bardis, 1964b).

Over time, the church established control over marriage itself. In 305, the Council of Elvira forbade women to marry non-Christians. Couples were encouraged to have the approval of the bishop, and by the sixth century, relatives within the seventh degree (including affinal relations and godparents) were forbidden to marry. This meant that no one more closely related than third cousins could marry. To make sure that no one violated these restrictions, banns announcing a couple's intent to marry had to be posted in the church before the wedding so that anyone who thought they were too closely related could object to the marriage. These restrictions posed quite a burden in small towns, where almost everyone was related to some degree. After some ambivalence, marriages were declared indissoluble in 407, and remarriages could result in excommunication even if the spouse had been guilty of adultery (Queen et al., 1985).

Celibacy for church officials was encouraged from 398 on and was made mandatory in the 11th century. For the layman, however, interacting with women remained a dangerous necessity. To summarize, the status of women and of marriage declined during the early Christian era. In fact, women and sexuality were associated with evil. However, monogamous marriage and fidelity were strengthened. Not a lot was written about children, but there is some evidence that their status improved, because abortion, infanticide, and child selling were all condemned. These practices continued at various levels, however.

THE MIDDLE AGES

The time period in Europe from about AD 500 to AD 1500 is referred to as the Medieval Period or the Dark Ages, as well as the Middle Ages. It is generally seen as a time of slowed progression and loss of knowledge coming between the classic and Renaissance periods of history. We will say little of the first half millennium here, because it overlaps with early Christianity.

By the year 1000, the church had gained considerable control over marriage and family life. Even the nobility had conformed to the rules of indissoluble monogamy and kinship restrictions. Admonitions against adultery and fornication had had less effect. The larger kinship group, or clan, still had influence, but it was beginning to wane. Individual households took over marriage arrangements, with parents in control (F. Gies & J. Gies, 1987).

Important changes occurred in the 11th century. Here we find the first appearance of the surname, passed down the father's line. Also, the rule of primogeniture, in which the eldest son inherits the bulk of the family estate, became common. Both of these diminished the status of women and made things more difficult for noninheriting children. They could either leave home empty-handed or enter the church. Peasant girls did not have the option of the convent, so pressure to marry was great.

The focus of marriage shifted from family arrangement to the couple in the late 1100s when church leaders established that mutual consent with affection was the heart of a valid marriage. Minimum ages of 14 for the groom and 12 for the bride were set, except for the child marriages arranged by nobility, which became valid once consummated. Marriage was delayed for noninheriting sons, and it was socially acceptable for a single male (including á priest) to have a mistress (F. Gies & J. Gies, 1987).

Marriage became one of the seven sacraments in 1164, and marriages took place in the church and under the direction of clergy. In the middle 1500s, the Council of Trent distinguished between separation and annulment. The former could be granted for adultery, apostasy, or cruelty, but remarriage (never recommended anyway) was not allowed. An annulment declared that the marriage had not been valid from the beginning (usually for violating the incest restrictions, which had been relaxed to the fourth degree of kinship in 1215), in which case one could marry another person (Bardis, 1964b).

The Black Death, or bubonic plague, had tremendous impact on family life and society in general. The first outbreak was in Italy in 1347, and it returned in waves about every 10 years thereafter for the rest of the century. It afflicted the young at a higher rate than it did adults, but the mortality rates were very high for all groups. In some British districts as many as 65% of the inhabitants died, and in various cases entire villages were deserted (F. Gies & J. Gies, 1987). It is still the ultimate metaphor for calamity and remains with us even in children's games: "Ring around the rosie / Pockets full of posies / Ashes, ashes, we all fall down."

Its source is uncertain, but it is thought to have been carried by fleas on rats brought on boats from Turkey. Practice of sanitation was poor during these centuries (people rarely bathed, and they threw their trash into the streets), and people did not understand how diseases were transmitted. Education was limited and was often diverted into such philosophical puzzles as

"What language does a deaf-mute hear in his heart?" (Hebrew) and "What is the worst sin one can commit?" (sodomy). Moreover, although people understood such celestial events as rain and eclipses, other subjects closer to home were less clear. Many believed the fabulous tales about faraway lands: cyclopes, Amazons with tears of silver, snakes with jewels for eyes, and the Garden of Eden protected by a high wall. Fireflies were the souls of unbaptized dead infants, and alchemy was the most popular applied science (Tuchman, 1978).

Even though the plague was devastating at a personal level, it had positive consequences on society as a whole. It came at a time when overpopulation was resulting in a negative economic picture. Survivors were able to move onto vacated land, and improved agricultural techniques were developed. Laterborn children were able to have land, and the average size of holdings doubled.

Because of the surplus of land and shortage of workers, peasants were able to command higher wages and improve their living conditions.

Access to income allowed people to marry earlier. In Prato, Italy, the average age for marriage was 24 for men and 16 for women in 1371, whereas it had been 40 and 25 before the plague. The lowered age of marriage resulted in higher birthrates, which peaked in connection with each outbreak of the disease (F. Gies & J. Gies, 1987).

Information about the relationships of ordinary people indicates that young single men often resorted to prostitutes or rape for sexual experience. In courtship, a good deal of petting behavior was culturally acceptable, until about 1700. After that time, we see a dramatic drop in the rate of prenuptial pregnancy, indicating that Church teachings were having an effect (Flandrin, 1977). Legally and socially, women were considered inferior to men, but spouses tended to work together pretty much as equals, and love and affection often grew between them.

A great deal of literature has survived concerning the love and sex lives of the aristocracy, and it centers around the related concepts of chivalry and courtly love. Chivalry was a code of honor and behavior for knights, which grew out of the Crusades and was designed to combine warfare with religiosity. Men were expected to have great physical strength, which they showed off at tournaments when real battles were not available. It included treating women with respect, even though women were still seen as wicked. For instance, there was believed to be a special place in hell for women who plucked their eyebrows, and of the seven deadly sins, that of Ire was depicted as a woman (Tuchman, 1978).

Brought back from the Crusades were the veneration of Mary, from the Eastern Church, and the exotic harem, from the Muslims. Traveling entertainers, the troubadours, combined these into a powerfully attractive concept for the upper classes. The poems told of great ladies who symbolized purity and knights who were inspired to feats of heroism out of love for them. Such a lady would eventually return the feelings, but the relationship was never to be consummated, as she was always already married to a nobleman. Such songs were appealing to lonely women who were running the family castle while their husbands were off fighting somewhere and to traveling knights looking to go beyond the story line (Tannahill, 1980).

Courtly love, then, means the kind of love that went on at court. Essentially, the feeling was that only adulterous love could be true love, because marriages tended to be arranged for political or wealth purposes. The stories of King Arthur's court, which centered on this theme, became popular at this time. That romantic love could occur only outside of marriage was directly opposed to Church teachings and resulted in tension between culture and religion.

Whereas this would seem to do damage to the institution of marriage and encourage the sexual exploitation of women, it also encouraged men to treat women with greater gentleness and politeness. In fact, "courtesy" is based on the word *court* and refers to the way women were treated in royal courts. This glorification of seduction brought men and women together for more than just economic reasons and therefore set the stage for eventual psychological intimacy between the sexes in marriage.

Finally, theories that children were seen as miniature adults who did not receive much affection from parents have been undermined by more recent research. Law and custom gave them special protections as minors. Descriptions of children's play are very similar to what one would read today, and careful instructions for infant care are found. Some of this advice was not good, such as recommendations for swaddling and pressing an infant's ears and limbs into desired shapes, but the concern was there. The infant death rate was high, and parents mourned their loss, often consoling themselves with the belief that the child's soul would be reincarnated in later children born to the family.

Peasant women nursed their own babies, but the wealthy tended to hire wet nurses, who not only fed but also reared the children for them. A principal concern was the moral character of the wet nurse, because it was believed that bad traits could be passed to the baby via the breast milk. Infanticide persisted, but at lower rates; one study found only 2 likely infanticides out of 4,000 recorded deaths. Neglect was often fatal, because it was common to leave babies alone in the house near the fire while everyone else worked outside. Some children were apprenticed out at early ages, but many stayed at home and did chores assigned to them by their parents. Discipline was harsh by today's standards, but some church leaders spoke out against corporal punishment and in favor of love and affection (F. Gies & J. Gies, 1987).

During this time period, the view of women improved from negative to ambivalent, because they came to represent purity as well as inferiority. The courtly love complex encouraged men to treat them with more respect, and romance was introduced into sexual relationships. Childhood was recognized and protected to a greater degree than it had been in times past.

THE RENAISSANCE

The next two centuries is a short, but important, time period. The French term for rebirth refers to dramatic progress after centuries of stagnation. Some of this was brought about by the discovery of the New World, and part of it was a function of the Protestant Reformation. Luther, Calvin, and others spoke against the consanguinity rules that restricted mate choice, liberalized grounds for divorce (adultery, desertion, and cruelty), and declared that marriage and family life were superior to chastity. Some theologians concluded that the woman's pleasure was important for conception and advised husbands on how to bring their wives to orgasm (F. Gies & J. Gies, 1987).

Family structure shifted from large family lineages to the nuclear family, as outside agencies took over many of the traditional family functions. At first, loyalty was shifted from the clan to the patriarch. The wife was considered to be, along with the children, the property of the husband, who was the only legal entity in the group (in Queen et al., 1985).

A key aspect of the Renaissance was the creation of a middle class. With the rise of cities and commerce, other options besides agriculture became available. Nonnobles discovered that they could not only survive but also become rich as middlemen, engaged in the buying, transport, and selling of goods. The new economic situation led to what Laslett (1977) has called the uniquely "Western" family: nuclear family form, a small age gap between spouses, relatively late childbearing, and the presence of servants in households. Extended families did not function well within a commerce-based economy and gradually gave way to the smaller, more private and efficient nuclear structure.

This business class was influenced by the ideas of romantic love that had filtered down from the aristocracy. As a result they developed the art of "courtship." Employing the vocabulary and behaviors of courtly love, middle-class men began to use them on the women to whom they had been betrothed through parental matchmaking. During the time before their marriage, young men "courted" their future brides with adoring talk, gifts, and romantic poetry.

This kind of interaction led some to fall in love with each other, which called into question the idea that love and marriage could not coexist. This gradually led to rebellion against parental mate choice, as young people discovered that it was more gratifying to marry for love and that they, rather than any others, were the most qualified to make the selection based on that criterion. The behaviors of adulterous courtly love actually reversed the concept and brought love and marriage together, eventually leading to the replacement of arranged with free-choice marriages. This shift occurred slowly and did not find its culmination until the modern era.

COLONIAL AMERICA

This time period stretches from the early 1600s, with the Puritan settling of New England, to the mid-1800s and the industrial revolution. The Puritans came to America with the Protestant values of Europe. They believed strongly in marriage, strict childhood discipline, and paternal dominance. They felt that wives should be domestic and submissive, and in fact a woman could not engage in business without her husband's consent, and he owned all that she had.

However, life in the rugged New World modified patriarchy to some extent and shaped marriage in many ways. This was chiefly due to the shortage of women, which made them a scarce and valuable resource. Women served many economic functions and could choose their mates from a number of suitors. In addition to the making of clothes, food, and other household products, many women carried on income-producing activities outside of the home, such as teaching, retailing, and newspaper publishing (Queen et al., 1985). This does not mean that they were liberated in the modern sense. Wives could work at anything as long as it was acceptable to their husbands and could be understood as something that helped the family as a whole (Caffrey, 1991).

Europeans discovered that Native American families also had a sexual division of labor, but it was sometimes the reverse of what they were used to. Native American women were often the farmers. The Europeans tried to encourage them to make cloth while the men farmed, so as to fit their own sex role stereotypes. They also disapproved of Native American sexual practices, which were more permissive of premarital relations, polygamy, and homosexuality. White settlers often rationalized such perceived differences as justification for rape against not only Native American women, but also African slaves and lower social class European indentured servants as well (D'Emilio and Freedman, 1988). Slaves came from African cultures that were built around extended families. Marriage remained important to African Americans, and free choice was generally permitted, but the masters could interfere (Caffrey, 1991).

Because marriage was important for a comfortable life, and the Puritans were strongly opposed to nonmarital sex, singlehood was viewed with suspicion, and courtship was often brief. Remarriage was common for those widowed; in fact, the first marriage at Plymouth was between Edward Winslow and Susanna White, whose spouses had died only 7 and 12 weeks previously, respectively. In Connecticut, single males could not live alone without permission, and Hartford laid a tax on single men (Queen et al., 1985).

Typically, a young man had to receive the permission of the woman's father in order to begin courtship, and she could veto her parents' choice for her. Dowries seemed to be more important than love, but there were cases of young couples marrying in spite of parental objections. Marriage was a civil contract, but banns had to be posted for 2 weeks before the ceremony. Love was not expected before marriage, but it was hoped that it would develop as time went on.

Most important was chastity, because the Puritans opposed all sexual activity outside of marriage. Public confession was part of the repentance process for fornication, and records indicate that up to one third of couples engaged in premarital relations (Caffrey, 1991) in spite of the penalties attached, which included being fined, whipped, and forced to marry each other. Adultery could actually merit the death penalty, or at least the "scarlet letter," an *A* pinned to one's clothes or burned onto the face. The letter *I* was used for incest. To protect couples from themselves, young people were prohibited from riding off together with sinful intent, and "gynecandrical dancing" was condemned by church leaders (Queen et al., 1985).

Such views render the custom of "bundling" most interesting. Bundling was a courtship practice found to be common in the mid- to late 1700s. It meant that the courting couple would be in bed together, but with their clothes on. With fuel at a premium, it was often difficult to keep a house warm in the evenings, which was when a man would be visiting his betrothed at her home. In order to keep warm, they would bundle in her bed together. A board might be placed in the middle to keep them separate, or the girl could be put in a bundling or duffel-like chastity bag. At any rate, the girl's parents were usually in the room as well (Ingoldsby, 2003).

The word *puritanical* is often used to mean antisexual, but this is not an accurate understanding of this time period. Drawing much of their philosophy from the Old Testament Hebrews, the Puritans did not worship virginity; they felt that sex was good and meant to be enjoyed, but that it should be confined to marriage. In Morgan's (1942) classic study, he quotes from a sermon by John Cotton: "Women are creatures without which there is no comfortable living for man . . . They are a sort of Blasphemers then who despise and decry them, and call them a necessary Evil, for they are a necessary Good" (p. 592). Public displays of affection were not permitted, however, as evidenced by the case of a sea captain who was put in the stocks for 2 hours because he kissed his wife on their doorstep on a Sunday, and this was upon his return from a 3-year sea voyage!

The situation was somewhat different in the Southern colonies, which were more rural and included slavery. There was a chivalry much like that of the Middle Ages, in which upper-class white women were put on a pedestal. These women were treated with graciousness and respect, and their sexual purity was closely guarded. They were expected to turn a blind eye, however, to their husbands' infidelities, which often included the exploitation of female slaves. Penalties for sex crimes were limited to fines (and to women), and common-law marriages were recognized, in part because of a lack of clergy to perform the ceremony (D'Emilio & Freedman, 1988). In both the New England and Southern colonies, first marriages usually occurred when the man could afford to marry, generally in his late 20s.

So we see some general overall progress in the treatment of women from previous time periods. The same was true with respect to the treatment of children. The Puritans regarded having children as a commandment from God, and they seemed to spend more time with their children and to be more emotionally attached to them than had been their European ancestors. There was a significant decline in such practices as swaddling, wet nursing, and sending children out at young ages as apprentices.

However, the Puritans did accept the Calvinistic idea that children are born sinful and must be forced to be good. The goal of discipline was to the break the will of the child. Although this certainly included physical punishment, the focus was on internalized restraints. Children were taught that they were born evil and that their slim chance for salvation lay in obedience to and respect for their parents and other adults. These concepts were drilled into them in school, where they memorized such couplets as: "In Adams Fall / We sinned all" and "The Idle Fool / Is Whipt at school."

By the 1800s, this tradition of inherently sinful children was challenged as the values of society for children shifted from obedience to self-reliance, and the influence of philosophers such as John Locke and Jean-Jacques Rousseau increased. Locke said that children were born neither good nor bad, but as "blank slates" to be written on by experience, and Rousseau took the opposite stand of the Puritans in claiming that children were born good.

VICTORIAN AMERICA

The industrialization and urbanization of the 19th century brought with it important changes in the Western family. Before the time of factories and mass production, family members tended to spend their days together on their farms or in other commercial endeavors. Father, mother, and children worked with their animals, crops, and household chores, which included preserving food and making clothes. What education the children received they got from their parents.

With the advent of factory work, husbands, wives, and children went to work in the mills for wages. Eventually, child labor laws sent the younger children back home and into the public schools. The mothers stayed at home to care for the young children, and what many refer to as the "traditional" family was created. The literature of this time (see Queen et al., 1985) speaks of a sense of family disruption that resulted in an idealizing of the home as a refuge from the cruel outside world, and of women as its domestic center.

It became unacceptable for middle-class women to work for money outside of the home after marriage. As America struggled to adapt to democratic rather than hierarchical ways of thinking, the notion of separate spheres developed. Women were assigned the domestic sphere, where they were supposed to have authority. In reality, men were still the chief decision makers. Over time, both parental and male authority was undermined as the family wage economy of the colonial household was replaced by separate wages for individual workers (Caffrey, 1991).

According to Kephart and Jedlicka (1991), as young people moved to the cities for work, they became less influenced by their parents for mate selection. They did not have to worry about inheriting family land, and they were now interacting with prospective mates whom their parents had never even met. Love replaced parental permission, and the use of dowries disappeared. This resulted in a change from a controlled courtship to the freer dating that we are familiar with today.

From about the mid-1800s until World War I was a time typically referred to as the "Victorian Era," named after the queen who ruled England during much of this period.

Once again, the roles for women were restricted, similar to the chivalry of the Middle Ages and the Southern colonies. American and European society also experienced its most repressive attitude toward sexuality since the time of the early Christians.

Welter (1966) discusses the "cult of true womanhood" that emerged in the 1800s. There were four qualities a good woman was expected to have, the first being piety. Men were cautioned to look for a mate who was religious, probably because religion did not tempt women away from their "proper sphere," which was the home. The second trait was purity, which I discuss in greater detail later. Essentially, women were to avoid arousing sexual feelings in men. This advice is included in the book *The Young Ladies Friend:* "Sit not with another in a place that is too narrow; read not out of the same book; let not your eagerness to see anything induce you to place your head close to another person's" (quoted in Welter, pp. 159–160).

The third virtue of true womanhood was submission. Women were taught that they were weak and needed a husband as a protector. Being inferior to men (one physician said that "Woman has a head almost too small for intellect but just big enough for love"—see Welter, 1966, p. 162), wives were admonished to obey their husbands and to give advice only when it was asked for. The final and perhaps most important trait was domesticity. A woman's role in life was to maintain a cheerful home for her husband and sons. Housework and related tasks were extolled, and a truly patriotic woman was one who stayed at home, rather than wanting to vote or do other "male" things.

The Victorians were very antisexual and considered any intercourse except for the purpose of procreation to be excessive and degrading. Even in marriage it was embarrassing, and experts recommended limiting it to no more than once a month. Some foods common today were developed for the express purpose of lowering sexual desire in males. Such foods include corn flakes and Dr. Sylvester Graham's crackers.

In reference to the quality of purity, female clothing was heavy and designed to hide a woman's natural form, so as to reduce the sexual appetite of men. Even the legs of pianos and other furniture were covered so that one's mind would not be drawn to inappropriate thoughts. The sexes were often separated for certain dangerous activities, such as swimming and looking at classical art. Ladies were always expected to act in a dignified and discreet manner, and never to smoke, drink, or swear (Kephart & Jedlicka, 1991).

Medical experts supported the notions that sex could be unhealthy and that women were pure. This following example summarizes the popular view:

> There are many females who never feel any sexual excitement whatever. . . . The best mothers, wives and managers of households know little or nothing of the sexual pleasure. Love of home, children and domestic duties are the only passions they feel. As a rule, the modest woman submits to her husband, but only to please him; and, but for the desire of maternity, would far rather be relieved from his attentions. (Truitt, 1916, p. 162)

Too much sex could also be hard on the health of males. It was believed that the loss of semen sapped a man's strength and that intercourse should therefore be infrequent. Many books noted how it debilitated a man and could ruin his marriage as well (see, for example, Macfadden, 1904).

It is small wonder that Freud found sexual trauma and guilt to be at the base of most neurotic disorders. Denied intimate relations with their husbands, a woman's closest male-female relationships were often with her sons, which could partially explain such Oedipal-sounding songs as "I want a girl just like the girl who married dear old dad." There is considerable evidence that the typical Victorian family was far from the fancied ideal and that incest rates may have been fairly high, especially for the poor living in overcrowded conditions (Wohl, 1978). Men were considered to be weaker, so prostitution flourished as husbands spared their wives from their animal nature.

The Victorian era was a time of transition and paradox. The private, middle-class family had been developing since the time of the Renaissance, and movement for equality within that unit conflicted with patriarchal tradition. For instance, women were in charge at home, but under their husband's control; more permissive laws concerning such issues as abortion, divorce, and custody shifted power from husbands to male legislators and judges; intimacy and romance were valued, but the morally superior woman was to restrain her husband's lustful nature while meeting his needs; marriages were to be both passionate and sexless; fathers were to be the head of the home, but children were reared almost exclusively by the mother; a woman was to rear sons to function in the outside world, but she was to know nothing about it herself (Brady, 1991). Such contradictions certainly resulted in much confusion as husbands, wives, and children sought to know and interact with each other.

THE MODERN NORTH AMERICAN FAMILY

By the 1920s, Americans were emerging from this romantic but conflicted sexuality and into today's commercial and erotic sexual culture, in which sexual relations are expected to provide happiness and are not tied to reproduction. Since that time, sexuality for both males and females has come to be seen as a legitimate source of personal meaning and a necessary part of people's lives. With the acceptance of the erotic, the commercialization of sex has increased dramatically in recent decades. Since the 1960s and the decline of the baby boom, the demographics of the American family have changed along with the new sexual standard. The typical U.S. couple now marries later, has fewer children, and is more likely to divorce than was the case before the shift toward sexual equality in the 1920s (D'Emilio & Freedman, 1988).

Meanwhile, after millennia of stagnation, women were finally making dramatic progress in the area of political rights. One watershed event was the women's rights convention held in Seneca Falls, New York, in 1848. The three declared goals were all achieved in later decades in the United States: to gain legal and property rights for women, to allow women into higher education, and to procure full political rights.

Women were admitted into Oberlin College in 1883, and other colleges followed. Today, slightly more women than men enroll in U.S. colleges and universities. The Nineteenth Amendment to the Constitution gave women the right to vote in 1920, and other steps toward greater equality have followed. Some issues still remain, but for the first time in history men do not have absolute social and legal power over women. As with previous wars, the Civil War and the two world wars pushed women into the economic sphere and resulted in greater rights for women (Kephart & Jedlicka, 1991). Children also now have legal protections from the arbitrary use of power, such as laws prohibiting abuse, neglect, and sexual exploitation and nationwide reporting hotlines. In addition, child maltreatment has received increased media attention, which has further expanded public awareness and outcry about this issue.

Many look to the 1950s as a time of well-ordered, ideal family life. The age of marriage and parenthood declined, fertility increased, and the divorce rate dropped more than it had in 100 years. Much of the modern nostalgia for this period may be misplaced, however, because poverty rates exceeded those of subsequent decades, the push for gender equality was slowed, and many family dysfunctions were ignored.

As we enter the 21st century, marriage is still highly valued, but the median age for marriage continues to rise. Divorce rates increased throughout the 1960s, peaked in 1979, and have leveled off since that time. Modern Americans have many options in terms of their sexuality, family structure, and experience (Coontz, Ofstedal, & Ponzetti, 2003). High rates of nonmarital sexuality have been moderated by fears of sexually transmitted infections. Family life continues to react with resilience to the economic and cultural forces that affect it. We can expect change to be the constant.

CONCLUSION

Power and sexuality have always been linked in Western history. The "status quo" from which we start is the Hebrew culture, which provided a religious rationale for patriarchy over women and children. As inferior beings, they were to be benevolently controlled by their husband and fathers, and men were allowed more sexual expression than were women. The Greeks, who added a "scientific" rationale for the inferiority of women, intensified this.

Roman times saw the beginning of a system for bringing about gradual change, which is disruption and reaction. The Punic Wars disrupted the economic system, which enhanced the status of women by forcing men to allow them into the world of work. Early Christianity reacted to the perceived dangers of female equality by reemphasizing their inferiority by way of religious dogma. Women and sexuality became associated with evil. Church teachings, however, denounced the previously acceptable practices of killing or selling unwanted children.

The Middle Ages was a time of paradox, because the now-standard view of women as inferior and dangerous coexisted with a view that they were morally superior to males and should be treated with romance and respect. Whereas much of this was simply a seduction technique, it did raise the view of women in the eyes of many men and opened the door to true intimacy.

The economic changes of the Renaissance became an important turning point. As commerce led to the private, nuclear, middle-class family, couple relations became more intimate and therefore egalitarian. That is, as couples worked together, disconnected from the extended family, they came to like and respect each other more. As they recognized the pleasures of sexual and psychological intimacy, it became harder for one to treat the other as property.

Colonial America still held onto the importance of marriage as an economic union but recognized the value of women in this endeavor. In addition, sexual pleasure was seen as good for both sexes, but only if tied to family reproduction. Sex outside of marriage was seen as a threat to the social order. This shift toward greater equality, brought about by democratic political ideals and sex ratio and economic conditions, led to a conflicted sexuality in the Victorian period as couples valued intimacy and equality, but men still wanted to be in charge.

Physicians replaced ministers in the attempt to hold onto traditional ways of thinking. Doctors argued that menstruation diverted blood from the brain and made women irrational, indicating that they could not function in the public sphere. Scientists found that females had smaller brains than males (not taking into account differences in body size and weight) and argued that they were naturally inferior as a result (Caffrey, 1991).

Such efforts were insufficient to stem the tide in the direction of free mate choice based on love and the equality that such intimacy implied. World Wars I and II provided further disruptions to the economic and social order, resulting in more women in the workforce. This led to more equality in marriage and a greater acceptance of sexuality for men and women, both in and out of marriage.

However, there are those today who argue that society has become too permissive and that the rise in divorce rates, dual-career families, and single-parent families, which have resulted in part from greater gender equality, has harmed the quality of child rearing (Popenoe, 1993). Others maintain that the greater variety can be good for most participants.

Although it is clear that dramatic strides away from patriarchy and toward gender equality have occurred in the last 150 years, attitudes toward sexuality continue to shift. North American society is at present relatively permissive after a long tradition of either the double standard or sexual repression, but it is unclear what the future holds.

REFERENCES

Adams, B., & Steinmetz, S. (1993). Family theory and methods in the classics. In P. G. Boss, W. J. Doherty, R. LaRossa, W. R. Schumm, & S. K. Steinmetz (Eds.), *Sourcebook of family theories and methods: A contextual approach* (pp. 71–94). New York: Plenum Press.

Bardis, P. (1963a). Main features of the ancient Hebrew family. *Social Science, 38,* 168–183.

Bardis, P. (1963b). Main features of the ancient Roman family. *Social Science, 38,* 225–240.

Bardis, P. (1964a). The ancient Greek family. *Social Science, 39,* 156–175.

Bardis, P. (1964b). Early Christianity and the family. *Sociological Bulletin, 13,* 1–23.

Bardis, P. (1966). Marriage and family customs in ancient Egypt: An interdisciplinary study. *Social Science, 41,* 229–245.

Brady, M. D. (1991). The new model middle-class family (1815–1930). In J. M. Hawes & E. I. Nybakken (Eds.), *American families: A research guide and historical handbook* (pp. 83–125). New York: Greenwood Press.

Caffrey, M. (1991). Women and the American family. In J. M. Hawes & E. I. Nybakken (Eds.), *American families: A research guide and historical handbook* (pp. 223–257). New York: Greenwood Press.

Coontz, S., Ofstedal, M., & Ponzetti, J. (2003). United States. In J. Ponzetti (Ed.), *The international encyclopedia of marriage and family* (2nd ed., Vol. 4, pp. 1682–1688). New York: Macmillan Reference USA.

D'Emilio, D., & Freedman, E. (1988). *Intimate matters: A history of sexuality in America.* New York: Harper & Row.

Fielding, W. (1942). *Strange customs of courtship and marriage.* New York: New Home Library.

Flandrin, J. L. (1977). Repression and change in the sexual life of young people in medieval and early modern times. *Journal of Family History, 2,* 196–210.

Gies, F., & Gies, J. (1987). *Marriage and the family in the Middle Ages.* New York: Harper & Row.

Ingoldsby, B. (2003). Bundling. In J. Ponzetti (Ed.), *The international encyclopedia of marriage and family* (2nd ed., Vol. 1, pp. 181–182). New York: Macmillan Reference USA.

Kephart, W., & Jedlicka, D. (1991). *The family, society, and the individual.* New York: HarperCollins.

Laslett, P. (1977). Characteristics of the Western family considered over time. *Journal of Family History, 2,* 89–115.

Macfadden, B. (1904). *Superb virility of manhood.* New York: Physical Culture Publishing Co.

Morgan, E. (1942). The Puritans and sex. *New England Quarterly, 15,* 591–607.

Popenoe, D. (1993). American family decline, 1960–1990: A review and appraisal. *Journal of Marriage and the Family, 55,* 527–542.

Queen, S., Habenstein, R., & Quadagno, J. (1985). *The family in various cultures.* New York: Harper & Row.

Tannahill, R. (1980). *Sex in history.* New York: Stein and Day.

Truitt, W. (1916). *Eugenics.* Marietta, OH: S. A. Mullikin.

Tuchman, B. (1978). *A distant mirror.* New York: Alfred A. Knopf.

Veyne, P. (1985). Homosexuality in ancient Rome. In P. Ariès & A. Béjin (Eds.), *Western sexuality: Practice and precept in past and present times* (pp. 26–35). Oxford, UK: Basil Blackwell.

Welter, B. (1966). The cult of true womanhood: 1820–1860. *American Quarterly, 18,* 151–174.

Wohl, A. (1978). *The Victorian family.* New York: St. Martin's Press.

Part I Exercise: Comparative Family Research Study

Select a theoretical framework and conduct a comparative research study of:

1. intergenerational relationships, or
2. gender roles.

To conduct your study, follow the steps listed below:

1. Read the descriptions below of the two topics and the research questions. Select your topic.
2. Follow your instructor's directions for completing the research project

TOPIC 1: INTERGENERATIONAL RELATIONSHIPS

The world's elderly population is expanding rapidly because of extended life expectancy. As longevity has increased, so has the number of living generations in families. For the first time in history, it is not uncommon for three, four, and five generations of a family to be living. For many families throughout the world, grandparents, especially grandmothers, provide help with child care and household finances when needed.

Recent research has called attention to possible ethnic, racial, or cultural differences in grandparents' roles. For example, in African American families in the United States, elderly adults occupy a highly respected and significant position and often interact regularly with grandchildren. They are more likely than European Americans to live in three-generational households and to provide considerable emotional and instrumental aid to adult children and grandchildren (Taylor, Chatters, & Jackson, 1993; Tucker, Subramanian, & James, 2004).

In many cultures, the elderly traditionally hold a place of prestige and authority. However, in countries undergoing rapid urbanization and industrialization, there may be tension between younger and older generations as "traditional" and "modern" value systems come into conflict (Huston, 2001). Similarly, for some immigrant young people who want to assimilate to U.S. culture, grandparents may be a source of embarrassment for their "old-fashioned" (i.e., traditional) beliefs and practices (Halgunseth, 1994).

Research Questions

The purpose of this project is to compare intergenerational relationships in different cultures. You may choose one of two options:

1. Select two countries in the world for a library research project.
2. Conduct a case study of a minority or immigrant family in the United States (e.g., Asian/Asian American, Native American, African American, or Hispanic/Latino).

Option 1: Library Research on Two Countries. Use library materials to review the literature on grandparents' roles in two countries. One country should have a growing elderly population (e.g., Japan) or a history of reverence for older adults (e.g., China). Answer the following questions:

1. What are the traditional roles of grandparents in both cultures? What are the differences between grandmothers' and grandfathers' roles and degree of involvement with grandchildren?
2. How has the grandparent role changed in both countries in the past 10–20 years? Why have these changes occurred (e.g., high mobility of younger generations or changing value systems)?
3. How have the changes you identified affected intergenerational relationships between older and middle, as well as older and younger generations?

Option 2: Case Study of an Immigrant Family in the United States. This option gives you hands-on research experience. Before you begin your study, familiarize yourself with the research literature on immigrant families.

Conduct a case study of intergenerational relationships in one immigrant family in the United States. Interview family members from the older, middle, and younger generations. Find the answers to the following questions:

1. What is the traditional role of grandparents in the family's country of origin? What are the differences between grandmothers' and grandfathers' roles and degree of involvement with the grandchildren?
2. How is the grandparent role in the United States similar to or different from the role of the grandparents in the family's country of origin?
3. What are the sources of tension? What would each generation change about its relationships between older and younger generations if they could?

TOPIC 2: GENDER ROLES

Women worldwide have certain things in common. They are almost always responsible for the fundamental aspects of family life including child care, family health, and household care and management (see Chapters 1, 18, and 19, this volume).

Women differ in their degree of participation in labor force activities. This depends on a number of opportunities and constraints, such as available employment; women's level of education and training; their family income; societal, family, and personal attitudes toward women's employment and family roles; religious doctrines and cultural traditions; and child care or elder care responsibilities. Decision making within families also varies. In some cultures or classes, men are the primary decision makers, whereas in others husbands and wives share some decisions.

In many families in industrialized as well as developing nations, traditional gender roles are changing. This often creates tension in families as men and women struggle to negotiate and to redefine their family responsibilities while meeting their individual needs and aspirations.

Research Questions

The purpose of this exercise is to compare women's and men's work and family responsibilities in different cultures. You may choose one of two options:

1. Conduct a case study of one family not of U.S. origin.

2. Design a research study of gender roles in two countries in two different world regions.

Option 1: Case Study of a Family. This option gives you hands-on research experience. Before you begin, familiarize yourself with the research literature on gender roles in the country or countries and world region you plan to study. Identify one family not of U.S. origin and interview both the husband and the wife.

Option 2: Research Project. This option allows you to plan a research project to learn more about gender roles in a country or countries. This will involve identifying a study sample, collecting data, and overcoming problems you might encounter as you attempt to answer the questions below. Work with your instructor to plan this project.

For either option, answer the questions that follow.

1. What are the family responsibilities of husbands and wives from the country or countries you selected for study? What are the religious, economic, and social roots of gender roles in family and employment? (Note that in some countries, there may be differences among ethnic groups, and these should be identified.)
2. How are these men and women involved in income-generating activities within or outside the home?
3. Who (husband, wife, or both) is responsible for decisions about household tasks? Household expenditures? Children's health or activities? Women's income-generating activities and men's income-generating activities?
4. Are husbands' and wives' traditional responsibilities and attitudes toward men's and women's roles changing?

REFERENCES

Halgunseth, L. C. (2004). Continuing research on Latino families. In M. Coleman & L. H. Ganong (Eds.), *Handbook of contemporary families* (pp. 333–346). Thousand Oaks, CA: Sage.

Huston, P. (2001). *Families as we are: Conversations around the world.* New York: Feminist Press at the City University of New York.

Taylor, R., Chatters, L., & Jackson, J. (1993). A profile of family relations among three generations of black families. *Family Relations, 42,* 323–332.

Tucker, M. B., Subramanian, S. K., & James, A. D. (2004). Diversity in African American families. In M. Coleman & L. H. Ganong (Eds.), *Handbook of contemporary families* (pp. 353–363). Thousand Oaks, CA: Sage.

Part II

FAMILY STRUCTURE

African families are large, extended, and complex, representing several generations and including biological as well as adopted kin.

Introduction to Part II

Part II is grounded in the early scholarly literature that examined families from a cross-cultural perspective. This section presents key concepts for comparing families around the world. During the time in which most of this work was conducted, researchers were guided by the theory of structural functionalism. They were interested in the positions that were filled by various members of the family group and the functions the family system performed for society as a whole. These chapters provide an important starting point for understanding families in different cultures. Newer perspectives that offer different insights will be discussed in other sections.

In Chapter 4, "Family Origin and Universality," Ingoldsby focuses on the importance of the family as an institution to human societies worldwide. He begins by addressing the question "When and how did the family as we understand it begin?" He then turns to central questions in the debate about the universality of the family. Are there certain tasks important to any civilization that the family performs better than any other institution can? If so, does this mean that family organization is essential for the survival of any society and that it is therefore universal? This chapter explores important thinking on the meaning of the term *family*.

In Chapter 5, "Patterns of Kinship and Residence," Stanton broadens the scope of our investigation. He goes beyond the immediate family to consider the larger kin group, that is, all the others that a culture may include as relatives. Some surprising variety emerges. Differing needs and conditions lead societies to make various kinds of decisions in defining kin and in assuming the obligations that go with those connections. The chapter introduces readers to the terminology for describing kinship patterns and the rules that societies use to govern relations, including who can marry, where they can live, and who has authority in the household.

Chapter 6, "Marital Structure," addresses the fascinating complexity of the organization of marriage itself. Monogamy, or one husband to one wife, is only one of a number of ways societies manage interconnected issues of love, intimacy, sex, reproduction, economics, and power. Having multiple husbands or wives serves to meet the needs of many cultures, and Ingoldsby discusses how some of these arrangements function.

Chapter 7, "Religious Utopias and Family Structure," analyzes marital and family structure once again, but this time from a religious, rather than economic, perspective. Four modern Western Christian groups are discussed. Each is or was millennial, and members sought to redefine marriage and family to fit what they believed to be God's will for the last days. As Ingoldsby explains, the Shakers believed in celibacy, or no marriage at all, whereas at the other extreme, the Oneidans practiced group marriage for a generation. Members of the Latter-day Saints religion, that is, the Mormons, practiced polygyny until forced by the government to abandon it in favor of conventional monogamy. Finally, the Hutterian Brethren are monogamous but elevate the community over the family.

CHAPTER 4

Family Origin and Universality

Bron B. Ingoldsby

How did "family" as an organization in human society begin? What features make it attractive to so many of us, and is it universal? That is, what does the family "do," and is it found in all cultures? In this chapter, we will grapple with these difficult questions.

Looking at the family from the structural-functional framework that has guided this line of inquiry, I examine the research dealing with the following questions: How is the family defined? What are its functions in a society? What is its origin? And is it universal? We will then conclude with a new look at defining the family based on recent thinking about the meaning of family.

FAMILY DEFINITIONS

Before one can study the family, we have to know what a family is, and therefore it must be defined. However, in order to define it, it must be found in nature first—which is difficult to do without the definition to guide us! The first modern professional to attempt this was George Murdock (1949). In his landmark work, Murdock approached the chicken and egg simultaneously: He had a definition in mind, and he searched the world's cultures to see if it held true.

Anthropologists have been doing fieldwork for centuries, writing accounts of societies they visited and studied from their Western perspective. Murdock surveyed 250 of these ethnographic reports (collected today in most university libraries as the Human Relations Area Files or Ethnographic Atlas) focusing on "family" descriptions. His work resulted in this definition: "The family is a social group characterized by common residence, economic cooperation, and reproduction. It includes adults of both sexes, at least two of whom maintain a socially approved sexual relationship, and one or more children, own or adopted, of the sexually cohabitating adults" (Murdock, 1949, p. 1).

Murdock went on to use the term *nuclear family* for what he considered to be the most basic societal structure: "a married man and woman with their offspring" (Murdock, 1949, p. 1). He considered this to be a minimal structure, which was the norm in about a fourth of the societies he evaluated. In another fourth the dominant mode was *polygamous*, meaning two or more nuclear families united by the plural marriages of a spouse. The remaining half Murdock characterized as *extended*, where the nuclear family of a married adult resides with that of his or her parents.

Murdock concluded that "the nuclear family is a universal human social grouping" (Murdock, 1949, p. 2) that either stands on its own or serves as the basis for the more complex forms. For Murdock, this nuclear family fulfills so many essential functions that he declared it inevitable and therefore universal, at least in his impressive sample. Since that time, his claim has been tested, as will be reviewed later in this chapter.

In 1963, William Stephens's classic cross-cultural family text was published. He began with Murdock's (1949) definition, which he personally liked, but went on to discuss some problems with it. First of all, the ethnographic data, upon which we must all depend for this kind of work, often has an incomplete description of family customs. Second, some evidence had since surfaced that appeared to contradict Murdock's claims about family structure, function, and universality.

Stephens (1963) developed this definition of *marriage*: "Marriage is a socially legitimate sexual union, begun with a public announcement and undertaken with some idea of permanence; it is assumed with a more or less explicit marriage contract which spells out reciprocal rights and obligations between spouses, and between the spouses and their future children" (p. 5).

He added to this a definition for *family*: "a social arrangement based on marriage and the marriage contract, including recognition of the rights and duties of parenthood, common residence for husband, wife, and children, and reciprocal economic obligations between husband and wife" (Stephens, 1963, p. 8).

Stephens (1963) then went on to explain each of his key points, indicating that although they were generally true, there did appear to be exceptions to each point somewhere. In the end, he concluded that all societies have some kind of family kinship system but that he was unable to precisely define it.

FAMILY FUNCTIONS

Before examining further the issue of what the family *is* and how it is structured, we need to examine what the family *does*. Social institutions exist because they perform certain valuable functions for their members and for the society of which they are a part. The family is such an enduring institution among humans because of the critical societal functions that it handles.

Some of these functions, which the family used to perform, have been taken over by other institutions in the modern world. One of these is formal education. Public and private schools now teach the academic skills at a generally superior level to that which parents used to pass on to their children.

In many ancient cultures religion was family based. The father served as priest and directed the rituals of the local belief system. Today most people attend the services of an organized denomination if they desire religious instruction.

A complex medical practice has replaced home health care, and people tend to turn to movie theaters and other enterprises for entertainment, rather than the home. No doubt the reader can think of other examples in which other institutions have taken over a traditional family function because they can meet that need better than the family. As this occurs, the family adapts and focuses on what it does best.

And what does it do best? Once again we go to Murdock (1949), who postulated that the family fulfills four essential functions for society. Murdock claimed that the family must be universal because no other societal institution could take these over.

The first function is *sexual.* Murdock (1949) points out that sexuality must be controlled, and is controlled, in all societies:

> As a powerful impulse, often pressing individuals to behavior disruptive of the cooperative relationships upon which human social life rests, sex cannot safely be left without restraints. All known societies, consequently, have sought to bring its expression under control by surrounding it with restrictions of various kinds" (p. 4).

However, if sex is overregulated, personality maladjustments and insufficient population may result. All cultures have resolved this issue of needing to allow sexual expression, but not so much as to be socially destructive, through the institution of marriage. Sexual gratification is always a part of marriage, and that privilege serves to solidify the relationship.

This is not to say, of course, that sex occurs only in marriage. Nonmarital sex occurs in all cultures, with varying degrees of acceptance. But it may be safe to say that the majority of adult sexual expression occurs in marriage, and that it is the one context where sexual behavior is always socially acceptable.

Even within marriage, however, there are times when many societies frown on intercourse, such as during pregnancy, menstruation, and in connection with certain religious observances. In fact, Stephens (1963) speculates that for the average primitive society, sexual intercourse between husband and wife is legitimate only about half the time!

The key point here is that marriage (which is part of the nuclear family) is the *primary* sexual relationship in all societies. This leads to the second function, which is *reproduction.* It follows that if husbands and wives are having intercourse, then they will be the ones having children as well. We all know that many children are born out of wedlock, but the majority of children are born, according to society's preference, into a legal family. Any society must have children born into it in order to perpetuate it, and in every case they turn to the nuclear family (which is what a marriage becomes once children are introduced) for that critical element.

The third function of the family is *socialization*:

> It is also necessary for a society to do more than simply produce children; they must be cared for in a physical sense and they must be trained to perform the adult roles deemed appropriate for them in their culture. This involves more than the teaching of occupational skills; it revolves around the basic processes of language development and the transmission of culture. (Lee, 1982, p. 58)

In other words, society depends on the parents to love and nurture their children, to toilet train them and teach them to speak and otherwise act in what would be considered a civilized manner.

The final basic function of the nuclear family, according to Murdock (1949), is *economic.* By this, he was referring to the division of labor by sex. Chiefly because of the greater physical strength of men and the fact that women are the ones who bear the children, marital pairs have found it logical to divide responsibilities according to their capacities in order to enhance the survival of the group. To quote Murdock, "By virtue of their primary sex differences, a man and a woman make an exceptionally efficient cooperating unit. . . . All known human societies developed specialization and cooperation between the sexes roughly along this biologically determined line" (p. 7).

Although in the modern world there is little reason for a complete separation between the provider and domestic roles, few would argue against the notion that a man and a woman can provide for the needs of a family more easily than a single parent generally can. Nevertheless, the implication that women should be limited to expressive roles is a frequent criticism of structural functionalism. There is no reason to assume that *either* gender is capable of only one role.

Murdock (1949) claimed that society would cease to exist without the sexual and reproductive functions, that life would cease without the economic, and that culture would end without socialization:

> No society, in short, has succeeded in finding an adequate substitute for the nuclear family, to which it might transfer these functions. It is highly doubtful whether any society ever will succeed in such an attempt, utopian proposals for the abolition of the family to the contrary notwithstanding. (p. 11)

It can be claimed that there may be other functions in addition to these four that are central to the family. William Ogburn (1929) was one of a number of sociologists who took the position that urbanization and industrialization had stripped the modern family of many of its traditional functions. With other agencies taking over much of the economic, educational, protective, recreational, and religious functions, providing companionship and emotional support became the primary function of the family. Being relieved of some of the external social roles has allowed the family to better fulfill the remaining functions.

And in fact, being the chief source of love and affection may well be what the modern family does best. Many would argue that this is what gives the family its strength in our ever-changing and fast-paced world. In looking at the cultures throughout the world, it would have been difficult until very recently to make a convincing case that this is a universal family function not adequately provided for in other nonfamily ways. However, there is now evidence that love and psychological intimacy have become the cornerstones of modern family life.

Buss and his colleagues (1990) surveyed mate preferences in 37 cultures in all parts of the world. Almost 9,500 subjects responded to a list of 18 characteristics found in past research to be important to mate selection. Overall, love is considered to be the most important criterion for both sexes. It is more likely to hold the preeminent position in Western cultures, but it is sufficiently widespread to declare *love* as the fifth universal family function.

FAMILY ORIGIN

Many cultures have creation myths, and often they focus on what we call *family relations*. More than an actual recounting of the origin of the family, they can be seen as guidelines for how the family in that culture ought to be organized. Drawing from the Book of Genesis in the Old Testament of the Bible, we can draw the following conclusions concerning Judeo-Christian societies:

1. It is expected that men and women will form sexual relationships (Genesis 4:1 [King James Version for all biblical citations]).
2. Children are expected to result from this union (1:28).
3. The husband-wife bond (conjugal) is more important than are other relationships, such as the parent-child (consanguineal) bond (2:24).
4. There is a division of labor by sex, with females responsible for child rearing and males responsible for providing food (3:16-19).
5. Husbands have legitimate power over their wives (3:16).

This well-known story of Adam and Eve posits a family structure and function very similar to the one described in the previous section and makes the claim that the family began when humans did. The implication is that the husband-wife-child unit is a natural group that enhances survival and happiness.

It is presently considered to be beyond the reach of science to determine how and when the family originated. As a result, writings on the subject are necessarily speculative. A number of 19th-century social scientists, referred to as Social Darwinists, tried to place the family in an evolutionary sequence.

Building on the idea of progressive development from savagery to barbarism to civilization made popular by the work of Charles Darwin, the Social Darwinists proposed a similar process for the family. They did not all agree on the particulars, but basically the idea was that the family had progressed from some form of matriarchal group marriage, to patriarchy, to present-day monogamy. Not only is such a view ethnocentric and value based, but also there is no valid reason to assume that all cultures would follow the same family structure track. Historical research cannot tell us how the family originated, but we do learn from it that there are many different patterns of family life in addition to one's own (Queen, Habenstein, & Quadagno, 1985).

Karl Marx and Friedrich Engels adapted this evolutionary thesis to their own ideas about the role of economics in human civilization. They also presumed an original matriarchal group marriage system, which was replaced by the patriarchal oppression of monogamy when men gained control of the means of production (Hutter, 1988). Some feminist scholars today, who would also like to see a more fluid and equal family life replace an overly rigid and unfair structure, hold a version of this view.

In contrast, Westermarck (1903) was closer to the religious texts of the West in postulating that monogamy was the original form of marriage. He concluded that the nuclear family is based in biological instinct, and he referred to the monogamous habits of some lower animals for support of his theory.

More recent work on the origin of the family has focused on sex roles. One perspective is that whatever form the family takes, it always includes adults of both sexes and the pattern of interdependence between the sexes (Lee, 1982). The most illustrative example of this perspective is the work of Kathleen Gough (1971).

Gough (1971) postulated that during the Miocene period of prehistory the climate became drier, resulting in open grasslands replacing many subtropical forests. This caused some of the tree-dwelling primates to adapt to terrestrial life. These ground dwellers had to become active hunters, rather than simple foragers. Success was maximized by working in groups, which led to the development of language and eventually resulted in greater brain complexity.

The key to this theory is that not only were our new humans smarter, but living on the ground caused them to develop an upright stance, which resulted in a smaller pelvis size for the female. This meant that they could no longer carry a fetus for as long as before and still survive the birth process. Human babies began to be delivered sooner in their development.

As a result, these babies were born more helpless and therefore required more complete care than did other animals. This necessitated a mother-child closeness in which the mother had to spend much of her time and energy ensuring the child's survival. It then became efficient for her to obtain the help of others in carrying out the other life tasks of providing food, shelter, and so forth. The obvious solution was to bond with males, who were not encumbered with child care and who had the natural strength and fleetness for the other tasks.

As Lee (1982) expressed it:

> According to this logic, then, the family originated among human beings because a certain division of labor between the sexes was found to be convenient or efficient and maximized the probability of survival for individuals and groups. . . . The logic here implies that the origin of sex roles, or the differentiation between the sexes in terms of socially defined behavioral expectations, coincided with the origin of the family. If the argument is correct, then men have been assigned protective and productive tasks, and women have assumed domestic and child-care responsibilities, since the earliest periods of the existence of mankind. (p. 54)

Social and technological changes have significantly reduced this traditional division of labor, but it is not illogical to suppose that economic efficiency, as well as sexual attraction, is what has always brought men and women together. So we find that scientists like Murdock and Gough came to the same conclusion as the religious texts like the one referred to earlier. That is, adult men and women come together in a sexual union and share in the life skills necessary for their own survival and the rearing of their children.

Most modern scholars have abandoned the investigation of the details of the origin of the family. However, based on the sex role theory, those factors resulting in the origin of the family would be the same for all humans everywhere, because our biology and responses to the environment are similar. From this, many social scientists conclude that the family as we have described it must be universal.

FAMILY UNIVERSALITY

Is the family universal, and what does it mean if it is? We are not asking if everyone lives in a family. What we want to determine is whether or not the family exists everywhere as a social institution. If so, then it can be concluded that the family *may* be necessary, that is, that human society cannot survive without it. However, if just one society can be found that does not have the family as we define it, then we would have to conclude that, although common, alternatives to the family could be devised.

Murdock (1949) threw down the gauntlet, so to speak, when he declared that his study found the nuclear family to be universal. This can be tested empirically by sifting through the available data on the world's cultures, much as Murdock himself did. If just one society can be found that does not have the family, then we can conclude that either (a) the family is not universal; or (b) it may be, but not as previously defined.

There are two aspects to Murdock's definition. The first has to do with *structure*, meaning that the family will consist of at least a married man and woman and their dependent (natural, adopted, or both) children. The second part is *function*, or what the family does for society. In this case there are four functions: sex, reproduction, socialization, and economics. Therefore, one can reject Murdock's thesis by finding just one society in which the positions of husband, wife, and offspring do not go together or, even if they do, one or more of the four functions are not fulfilled by the family institution (Lee, 1982).

Over the years, researchers have accumulated data on some cultures that appear to contradict Murdock's conclusions. Some are fairly weak, but there are three from which a strong case can be made. They are: (a) lower-class black unions in Jamaica, (b) the Israeli kibbutz, and (c) the Nayar of southern India.

Jamaica

In her detailed study of three communities, Edith Clarke (1957/1999) concluded that marriage among the Jamaican poor was rare. A proper church wedding, with the accompanying feast and other costs, was too expensive. Those who could not afford it settled for illegal common-law unions, which Clarke referred to as *concubinage*. In some such unions, the father stayed with his family, but in other cases the woman would have a succession of lovers, with her children often "fatherless." Although families without someone in the "husband-father" position are common throughout the world because of death, divorce, or desertion, the claim that the mother-child dyad is a viable alternative to the nuclear family is better made if a society can be found where that form is in the majority. It has been reported that about two thirds of all children born to lower-class black Jamaicans are born to common-law unions. The claim is therefore made that Jamaican families are not nuclear, and fathers do not participate in the socialization and economic functions.

However, other scholars do not agree that these are fatherless families. Rodman (1966) points out that although couples tend not to marry until they are past the child-bearing stage (when they can afford it), most do eventually marry. In addition, children do grow up with their mother and the man she is living with, so they may be living in a stable and permanent family relationship, even if not with their biological father. So we find that legal marriage and the nuclear family are the cultural preference, and that although cohabitation may not be strictly legal, it is culturally acceptable.

The Kibbutz

Both Stephens (1963) and Lee (1982) discuss the Israeli kibbutz, which provides a stronger case against Murdock's (1949) assertions than does Jamaica. Kibbutzim are self-contained communities based on communistic ideals brought to Palestine in the 1920s by European Jews. Throughout history, there have been many communal social movements, and many of them have tried to replace the family as we know it. In general, few survive more than a few years. However, the kibbutz may be the most successful of them all.

In 1954, Spiro reported extensively on this movement. In the kibbutz, when a couple wishes to be together they simply have the manager move them into a two-person apartment. There is no marriage ceremony, but they are considered to be a "couple" until they decide to end the relationship. Children live not with their parents, but in a special area of the community where they are reared and educated by the adults assigned to that responsibility. All adults work somewhere in the community, and couples do not depend on each other economically. All domestic service is done at the community, rather than household, level, and all members are provided for.

At first glance, then, many aspects of Murdock's definition are not met. Parents and children live separately, violating the nuclear structure. And although sex and reproduction are family functions, socialization and economy are not. Closer inspection since the time of Spiro's original work, however, indicates that the kibbutz may be more family-like after all.

First of all, the couple relationships appear to be as stable and permanent as in the greater culture. The couple and their children know each other and spend as much time together as one might find in many modern busy dual-career families. During these evening and weekend visits much of the traditional socialization occurs, and although they may not live in the same room they are quite close by geographically. The strongest point is the economic one, where interdependence is at the group, rather than couple, level. However, there is evidence that members usually end up with traditional tasks. That is, the men are more likely to be assigned agricultural work, whereas the women find themselves in the kitchen or the nursery.

When they started in the early 1900s, kibbutzim were antifamilistic utopian experiments. But by the third generation, families had gained autonomy and collective dining rooms, and children's houses had faded away. Today parents have assumed responsibility for their children, and the community has much less control over their socialization (Smith, 1999).

The Nayar

Possibly the most interesting of our example is the Nayar. According to Lee (1982), "they have been used as a counterexample to just about every empirical generalization regarding cross-cultural family uniformity ever offered" (p. 101). Murdock recognized them as a society in his original work, but he rejected the conclusions about them, saying that the little work done on them could not be substantiated.

After extensive work by Gough in the 1950s supported the original contentions, Murdock tried to claim that they were not really a society after all. Although Gough's (1959) work is accepted as reliable, it is important to note that her ethnographic account is after the fact. That is, because of outside pressures, the culture that I am about to describe no longer exists in this form. Gough has reconstructed it from available documents and the memories of informants.

The Nayar were a warrior Hindu caste living principally in the Kerala province of South Malabar in India. Although part of the larger society, the Nayar were basically self-sustaining and could have continued their practices indefinitely if they had avoided outside interference. As warriors, the men traveled and were away from home a great deal, and their marital practices were an apparent adaptation to that situation.

Girls began adulthood at puberty with a ceremony, lasting about 4 days, in which they were united with a "ritual husband." This was called the *tali-tying* marriage, and it had no real significance in the girl's life after the ceremony. After this rite of passage, girls could then enter into *sambandham* relationships with other men, who were called "visiting husbands."

All adult females could marry as many visiting husbands as they liked. These relationships were formed and ended as the participants desired, resulting in a kind of fluid group marriage. These were basically sexual relationships, because there were very few economic responsibilities. The males gave small gifts on certain occasions, but they had no obligation to provide for the livelihood of the woman or their children. This was not considered to be promiscuity, however, but legally sanctioned and culturally approved marriages of the Nayar.

The legitimacy of children was important in the sense that a child should not be fathered by someone from a lower caste. In each case, one of the visiting husbands was asked to be designated as the father, which he accepted by paying for the midwife. At this point, his responsibility for and involvement in the child's life ended.

All spouses continued to live in their family of orientation, which was matrilineal. That is, a woman lived with her children, siblings, and mother and was provided for by her brothers (her children's uncles). Likewise, a man lived with his sisters and provided for their children but often spent the night with one of his wives. As mentioned before, this had worked well for men who traveled too much to develop a conjugal family life. The children who mattered to them were those of their sisters, rather than those of their wives.

Here we find that most of Murdock's conditions are not met. The family is not nuclear, because spouses did not live together. Sex and reproduction were couple functions, but socialization did not involve the father, and he had no economic responsibility for his wives and children. If we accept the Nayar as a once-viable society, then they are clear evidence that the nuclear family is not universal (Lee, 1982).

Summary

In 1975, Hendrix carefully analyzed Murdock's work with a review of 213 cases from the Human Relations Area Files. He found four cases where husband and wife remained in their mothers' homes throughout their lives, like the Nayar. Four other cases were like the kibbutz, where parents and children have separate residences, and there were a few others where the educational or economic functions were not performed by the nuclear family.

The Na of China are another female-centric society where male lovers are simply visitors, no one moves away from his or her childhood family, and children are reared by their mothers and uncles (Hua, 2001). On the other hand, at least one group, the Bari of Venezuela, believe that a child can have more than one father. The semen of additional lovers during pregnancy is believed to make for a healthier child. These secondary fathers are obligated to contribute to the food supply of the family during the pregnancy (Small, 2003).

In summary, then, we must conclude that although the nuclear family with its four functions is an extremely common and efficient way to organize family life, some alternatives are possible. Rather than rejecting the notion that the family is universal, it may be the definition that needs some adjustment.

THE FAMILY REDEFINED

Ira Reiss (1965) proposed an alternative to Murdock's definition for the family. The one function that he found to be universal was the socialization of the young; but this referred only to a certain kind, which he referred to as "nurturant socialization." Although it may not be the parents who provide for the physical care and education of their children, there are always relatives of some kind who give the love and emotional support necessary for healthy development.

Reiss (1965) concluded that the one common element in all societies is the nurturance of infants by a small primary group of kin: "The family institution is a small kinship structured group with the key function of nurturant socialization of the newborn" (p. 449). Commonly, that group is the parents in a conjugal relationship (the nuclear family), but occasionally it is the mother or relatives of the mother.

This accounts for groups like the Nayar and some Native American Indian tribes (see Driver, 1961) where residence is matrilocal and the father has minimal interaction with, or financial responsibility for, his wife and children. However, Reiss's definition, although unchallenged, is less specific and ambitious than is Murdock's. By that, we mean that although it is more technically correct, it is less satisfying because it tells us less about family life and relationships.

For most practical purposes, Murdock's definition is useful and more informative, with the other cases being exceptions to the general rule. One problem with Reiss's definition is that although it correctly captures the notion of family, it does not address marriage, which has always been a subpart of the definition. However, it may be the tendency to make family flow from marriage that has given much of the trouble to Murdock, Stephens, and others.

Without exception, marriage is a sexual adult relationship (and usually an economic and loving one as well) from which children may result. Family life focuses on the care of those children, but in rare cases the father plays no role in it. In those cases, people remain forever in their *family of orientation* and do not establish a new and separate *family of procreation*. So, although marriage and family generally go together, they do not always.

To help deal with this circumstance, the following definitions of *marriage* and *family* are offered. They are detailed enough to be useful but broad enough to qualify as universal.

Marriage: a culturally approved sexual relationship, which typically also contains economic and psychological expectations

Family: a kinship group providing the nurturant socialization of its children (natural or adopted)

CONCLUSION

There is a tendency to use the terms *marriage* and *family* somewhat broadly in our society today, where any long-term adult relationship is referred to as a marriage, and any group of people who love each other call themselves a family. However, the use of these terms needs to be restricted if they are to have a useful cultural and scientific meaning. In my view, even though there are many kinds of human relationships, the technical use of *marriage* and *family* should include the concepts of reproduction and child care.

Some suggest that part of the push to extend the definition of *family* is so that more individuals can benefit from government programs and benefits, which depend on the public definition of the term. Although understandable, this view also implies that families are the only legitimate groupings for long-term emotional and social support (Coontz, 1988). Perhaps new terms need to be developed for these other kinds of relationships. One proposal for these second-level intimacy groups is to combine the words *friend* and *family* into *friemily*.

Same-sex marriages, for instance, are at this writing a hot political topic in the United States. The courts and many state legislatures are battling over the definition of marriage as applied to same-sex unions. At present, there is more cultural approval for some kind of civil union category that would allow same-sex couples many of the legal privileges of marriage, but without the title, probably because of the religious meaning it has for many Americans. This could change in the future, however. Although a gay or lesbian couple cannot conceive their own offspring, they can, however, adopt, use artificial insemination, or bring in children from previous heterosexual relationships to become a family. The definition of *marriage* above is general enough to include these unions.

In addition, psychological intimacy is becoming a universal function of marriage and family. The direction of modern society points to a continuing deemphasis of economic interdependence in marriage, and to the increasing importance of the family as the critical source of love and affection in a fast-paced world.

To summarize, marriage and family are universal cultural institutions that perform critical functions for the preservation of human society. As Stephens (1963) has pointed out, even though there are logical alternatives, such as freely cohabiting bands, they have not been adopted. And although there are some mother-child dyad cultures, they are rare, leading to the conclusion that social fathers are sufficiently important to maintain the preeminence of the nuclear structure.

This does not mean that the debate is over, however. Although many serious scholars (see Popenoe, 1993) still maintain that the intact nuclear family is critical for proper childhood socialization, there are others (Stacey, 1993) who point out that this structure is more functional for men than it is for women. The role and importance of fathers in families continue to be debated (Marsiglio, Amato, Day, & Lamb, 2000). "Covenant marriage" appeals to traditional couples as a way of dealing with the high divorce rate (Hawkins, Nock, Wilson, Sanchez, & Wright

2002; Rosier & Feld, 2000). Current work points toward more personal, rather than societal, definitions of family (Gubrium & Holstein, 1990).

In the end, there are various ways to look at family, depending on what it is that one wants to understand. Until recently, most studies have focused on macrosocial issues, asking what it is that the family does for the larger community. Present research is beginning to turn that approach on its head and ask what the family does for its respective members.

REFERENCES

Buss, D., Abbot, M., Angleitner, A., Asherian, A., Biaggio, A., Blancovillasenor, A., et al. (1990). International preferences in selecting mates: A study of 37 cultures. *Journal of Cross-Cultural Psychology, 21,* 5–47.

Clarke, E. (1999). *My mother who fathered me: A study of the family in three selected communities in Jamaica.* Kingston, Jamaica: Press University of the West Indies. (Original work published 1957)

Coontz, S. (1988). *The social origins of private life: A history of American families 1600–1900.* New York: Verso.

Driver, H. (1961). *Indians of North America.* Chicago: University of Chicago Press.

Gough, K. (1959). The Nayars and the definition of marriage. *Journal of the Royal Anthropological Institute, 89*(1), 23–34.

Gough, K. (1971). The origin of the family. *Journal of Marriage and the Family, 33,* 760–771.

Gubrium, J., & Holstein, J. (1990). *What is family?* Mountain View, CA: Mayfield.

Hawkins, A., Nock, S., Wilson, J., Sanchez, L., & Wright, J. (2002). Attitudes about covenant marriage and divorce: Policy implications from a three-state comparison. *Family Relations, 52,* 166–175.

Hendrix, L. (1975). Nuclear family universals: Fact and faith in the acceptance of an idea. *Journal of Comparative Family Studies, 6,* 125–138.

Hua, C. (2001). *A society without fathers or husbands: The Na of China.* New York: Zone Books.

Hutter, M. (1988). *The changing family: Comparative perspectives* (2nd ed.). New York: Macmillan.

Lee, G. (1982). *Family structure and interaction: A comparative analysis.* Minneapolis: University of Minnesota Press.

Marsiglio, W., Amato, P., Day, R., & Lamb, M. (2000). Scholarship on fatherhood in the 1990s and beyond. *Journal of Marriage and the Family, 62,* 1173–1191.

Murdock, G. (1949). *Social structure.* New York: Free Press.

Ogburn, W. (1929). The changing family. *Publications of the American Sociological Society, 23,* 124–133.

Popenoe, D. (1993). American family decline, 1960–1990: A review and appraisal. *Journal of Marriage and the Family, 55,* 527–541.

Queen, S., Habenstein, R., & Quadagno, J. (1985). *The family in various cultures.* New York: Harper & Row.

Reiss, I. (1965). The universality of the family: A conceptual analysis. *Journal of Marriage and the Family, 27,* 443–453.

Rodman, H. (1966). Illegitimacy in the Caribbean social structure: A reconsideration. *American Sociological Review, 31,* 673–683.

Rosier, K., & Feld, S. (2000). Covenant marriage: A new alternative for traditional families. *Journal of Comparative Family Studies, 31,* 385–394.

Small, M. (2003, April). How many fathers are best for a child? *Discover,* 54–61.

Smith, W. (1999). *Families and communes.* Thousand Oaks, CA: Sage.

Spiro, M. (1954). Is the family universal? *American Anthropologist, 56,* 839–846.

Stacey, J. (1993). Good riddance to "the family": A response to David Popenoe. *Journal of Marriage and the Family, 55,* 545–547.

Stephens, W. (1963). *The family in cross-cultural perspective.* New York: Holt, Rinehart & Winston.

Westermarck, E. (1903). *The history of human marriage.* London: Macmillan.

CHAPTER 5

Patterns of Kinship and Residence

MAX E. STANTON

Virtually all human beings have a deep need to affiliate with others. This affiliation may be in the form of political alliances, friendship bonds, religious congregations, work gangs, and any number of other types of assemblages (Joyce & Gillespie, 2000). Membership in some of these groups creates strong, lifelong bonds and will be, for the most part, quite satisfying and rewarding for the individuals involved. Other types of affiliation may be short-lived but, nonetheless, often quite important—such as a party of workers who have banded together to fight a forest fire that might be threatening their homes and property.

Of all types of human affiliation, kinship is, with a few rare exceptions, the most permanent and has the greatest long-term impact on the life, behavior, and social identity of an individual (Cassell, 1993). There is no question that some other associations may have deep and significant impact on a person's identity and loyalties (e.g., the traditional military societies of the North American Great Plains peoples, the "clans" of the pre-1745 Scottish Highlands, or the age-sets of East Africa), but even these types of affiliation, and others that command so much social effort on the part of those who belong, do not replace the basic kinship units of their respective societies as the single most important locus of social obligations and identities (R. Fox, 1967; R. G. Fox, 1976).

Stack and Burton (1993) have noted that the lives of individuals are strongly affected by kinship network, even in modern Western society. Patterns of family interaction are "scripted" by kin in the areas of work, time, and roles. That is, the larger family often assigns such important activities as reproduction, care of dependent children or the elderly, and economic survival to individuals. Pressure to assume certain responsibilities for the good of the family can be both subtle and significant.

Because kinship is so central and "natural" in the life of the average person, most people do not give too much thought to the ways and manners in which various other societies reckon their terminology. If we hear terms such as *family, mother,* or *relatives,* we usually tend to think of them and other such terms in the context of our own personal experience, with little regard to the fact that there are a great number of ways throughout the world that people in various societies relate (or have related in the recent past) to these same terms. The tendency to think that our own type of kinship organization is normal and "correct" is especially strong if we have little or no contact with people from other societies.

The rural-to-urban migration trends of the latter half of the 20th century have brought millions of people from different cultures together in numbers unprecedented in history. Contemporary travel by air and over hard-surface, long-distance highways has also brought people of diverse heritages together. The current corpus of anthropological literature and related sciences is filled with this ongoing mass movement of people, families, and groups worldwide. Just a brief survey of my own academic bookshelves reveals a number of excellent works relating to the circumstances and consequences of the impact of rural-to-urban migration on the families, kinship systems, and residential patterns among the Native Americans and Pacific Islanders, the two groups warranting my specific academic focus (Barker, 1994; Benedek, 1992, 1995; DeMalie, 1998; Gershon, 2001; Jacobs, 1995; Lockwood, 1993; Macpherson, 2002; Metge, 1964, 1995; Modell, 2002; Nuttall, 2000; O'Meara, 1990; Rosenblatt, 2002; Shepardson, 1995; Small, 1997; Stanton, 1993; Strathern et al., 2002; Tapesell, 2002; Thomas, 1997).

International tourism is rapidly becoming the world's largest industry. Mass communication puts us in instantaneous contact with others in virtually all parts of the world. An increasingly large number of corporations and agencies are now multinational in scope, requiring both administrators and rank-and-file workers to travel and be transferred across international borders. It is important, therefore, to be aware of the significance of the differences existing between people and groups. In this chapter, I focus on kinship and residence patterns, two closely related aspects of these "significant differences." Kinship is one of the basic "building blocks" of any society. It is also one aspect of social interaction that can cause confusion between people of different cultural heritages. Residence, especially in traditionally oriented societies, also reflects long-term and deeply held cultural and moral group values (Crandall, 2000).

Members of ethnic minorities within a given society are usually acutely aware of the differences between their own patterns of kinship terminology and affiliation and those of the majority group (Kraybill, 2001; Maltz & Archambault, 1995; Pickering, 2000; Thomas, 1997). This reality first came to my attention when, in the mid-1960s, I visited the Hopi Indian Reservation in northeastern Arizona in the company of some fellow anthropology students. We were eager to see whether some of the things we had learned in the classroom would actually prove to be the case in the reality of the field. We had learned enough about Hopi kinship terminology to know that a person would refer to his or her mother's sister as "mother" and that the mother's sister's children would be referred to as "brothers" and "sisters." We spoke to a shy but cooperative girl of 8 or 9 years of age and asked her whether her mother had any sisters. She said "Yes," so we asked the girl what she called her. She replied, "Aunt Martha." We were somewhat disappointed, but we persisted, asking the girl whether there was a Hopi word she used. She said, "Ya, I call her my mother." We asked the girl whether her Aunt Martha had any children, and the girl replied that she did. We then asked what the girl called them. She replied, "Jimmy," "Annie," and so on. We asked her whether there was any word she used when she did not refer to them by name, and she said, "I call them my cousins." One of the students in our group then patiently asked whether she did not refer to them as her brothers and sisters. Her reply was classic and has had a profound impact on my understanding of the worldview of ethnic minorities: "Yes, I do call them my brothers and sisters—but I didn't know you white guys knew about that!" She was fully aware that we "white guys" as a general group knew very little about Hopi life and gave us the most appropriate answer for the specific context in which she found herself at the time.

Because there are still many Native American groups that continue to follow their traditional kinship rules; because there are so many people entering the United States from all parts of the world, many from places in which dramatically different types of kinship patterns are still practiced; and because ours is an ever-shrinking world wherein all inhabitants have become part of a "global community," it is essential for us as well-informed people to understand and appreciate the many varieties of kinship systems that persist throughout the world (Klein, 1995; Metge, 1995; Morton, 1996; O'Meara, 1990; Shepardson, 1995; Shimony, 1994). It is also essential not to think of differences as signaling inferiority to our own system. There are many people to whom these various forms of terminology make good sense and are preferred. In this chapter I discuss the various societal norms that have to do with lineage and family affiliations, rules and terminologies.

BASIC KINSHIP AFFILIATION

The most intimate group of kin for the majority of us comprises those in our immediate family. Whether they are our relatives by birth or adoption, they form the core of the world of our relatives. Beyond this first tier of relatives, there are other people to whom we are related, either through a genealogical link or through marriage. Those individuals to whom we are related through a direct genealogical link are our *consanguine* kin, meaning "by blood" (Parkin, 1997). (Anthropologists continue to use this term as a popular convention, even though it is now well known that our blood does not directly transmit our hereditary traits.)

There are two types of consanguine kin. Those people who are related to one another in a direct genealogical line are *lineal* kin (such as parent to child). In some cases, there is a distinction made between lineal kin who are descended from the direct line of a male and those who are descended from a direct line of a female. Kin who reckon their descent line through a common male ancestor are *cognatic* kin; those who trace their line through a common female ancestor are *agnatic* (sometimes also referred to as *uterine*) kin. Those relatives who are not in a direct parent-to-child line but who have a common more distant genealogical tie (such as siblings or first cousins) are *collateral* kin.

There are also those relatives to whom one is related by legal, nongenealogical ties. This would include all those individuals who have some sort of kinship affiliation through marriage (such as a spouse, brother-in-law, or what most Americans would refer to as an aunt- or uncle-by-marriage). These people are our *affinal* relatives. In most societies, affinal relatives are considered to be close and important members of the kinship network and are most often treated as important, vital parts of one's immediate kinship group. Another nongenetic tie is the *adoptive* relationship. In this situation, the expectation is that a person who is adopted into a kinship network assumes the social role equal to that of a person born into the same position, having all of the social rights, privileges, duties, and obligations as if he or she had inherited that position through birth (Keesing, 1975; Lowie, n.d./1968; Parkin, 1997; Scheffler, 2001).

Research by A. S. Rossi and P. H. Rossi (1990) provides us with an excellent understanding of the structure of kinship norms in the United States. Responses to vignettes that tapped the sense of obligation to help various relatives in times of crisis and celebration allowed the researchers to uncover basic principles underlying the U.S. kinship system. Briefly, their results were as follows:

1. In accordance with sociobiological theory, our sense of obligation to another person is a function of how closely related we are. That is, we show the highest levels of obligation to our own parents and children, followed by siblings, grandparents and grandchildren, aunts and uncles, nieces and nephews, and finally cousins.
2. Reflecting the emphasis on conjugal relations in our society, the position a person occupies is important, even when the person is not blood related. That is, in-laws, stepparents, and stepchildren are accorded the same level of obligation as are siblings, grandparents, and grandchildren, respectively.
3. More distant kin (aunts/uncles, nieces/nephews, and cousins) have about the same salience in our lives as do those nonrelatives with whom we frequently interact: our friends and neighbors.
4. Because of especially close bonds between mothers and daughters, there is a maternal tilt in the U.S. kinship system. Generally, women evoke more obligation than do men, especially if they are unmarried. There is also a tendency to be closer to the wife's relatives than to the husband's.

Other recent research on American families also strongly supports these research conclusions of A. S. Rossi and P. H. Rossi (Ehrlich, 2001; Galvin, 2001; Stone, 2000).

TYPES OF FAMILIES

The most common type of family is the *nuclear family*. It consists of at least one responsible adult male and female pair living commonly in a marriage arrangement with their children. The nuclear family may be part of a greater collection of families that are ultimately grouped together into an *extended family,* which has as its head a responsible adult (or, in some cases, a group or council of responsible adults). The extended family is a corporate economic and political unit as well as a kinship-based group. Members of this type of family work for the mutual benefit and welfare of all individuals and (nuclear) families that are recognized to be part of the unit. The extended family is an ongoing body with a geographical base, and it transcends the lifetimes of its members. The composition of the extended family with its nuclear families and independent single adults changes constantly, but the extended family itself continues on, with new leaders and new members as individuals depart or as the generations pass away.

The *joint family* has many of the elements of the extended family in that it is made up of any number of separate nuclear families and is an economic, geographical, and political entity as well as a kinship-based group. Also, one person or a small coalition of leaders ultimately heads it. The distinction between the two types is that the joint family is not an ongoing, long-term unit. It is made up of close relatives, usually brothers, who are affiliated together under the rule of their father. When the father dies or becomes unable to lead the family because of physical or mental problems. it becomes the task of the older brother to work to help his younger brothers within the joint family to set up their own independent family units separate from his own family. As he does this, his own children mature and remain within the joint family until he, the older brother himself, dies or is unable to continue on as its head. In the meantime, the brothers of the original joint family have gone on to establish separate joint family arrangements with their own children.

Historical research on the family has found a variety of family types in addition to those already mentioned. They often have a complex relationship to the larger society, principally the economic structure but to other aspects as well (see Farber, Mogey, & Smith, 1986; R. Fox, 1967).

In many parts of the world, there are social trends such as widespread divorce or the bearing (or adopting) of children by a single person. Families with one adult as a permanent member of the household are known as single-parent families. Divorce in particular can complicate multigenerational family relationships, as grandparents struggle to stay in contact with their grandchildren and perhaps their ex–children-in-law as well (Jacobson, Liem, & Weiss, 2001; Johnson, 1988; Skolnik, 1991).

It is also becoming recognized that some families are headed by homosexuals, who function as would a husband-wife pair. This type of family is known as a "same-sex union." Single-parent families are given the same legal status as those headed by a husband and wife. Same-sex families, as a socially acknowledged phenomenon, have yet to receive legal standing in most places where they are found (with Denmark, the Netherlands, and Canada serving as notable exceptions), and therefore, they lack the legitimacy enjoyed by the other forms of family units (Weston, 1992).

RULES OF DESCENT AND AUTHORITY

Because kinship typically implies special obligations and rights between its members that would not be expected between neighbors or strangers, it is too important to be left just to biology or chance. All cultures, then, have rules for defining who our important relatives are. This does not mean that cultures are ignorant of the other biological connections but simply that for the purposes of inheritance, marriage, and other aspects of life, certain lines matter, and others do not (Parkin, 1997; Peletz, 1995).

In many societies, an individual is affiliated to his or her family group exclusively through either the father's or the mother's family line: *unilineal* descent. If the inheritance passes through the father's side of the family, the arrangement is *patrilineal.* This means that primacy is given to ties from father to son to grandson, and so on through the male relatives. Taking one's surname from the father or husband is a *patrilineal* concept.

If the kinship affiliation is recognized through the mother's side, it is *matrilineal.* In this case, descent is traced through the mother and all the women in the line. Here, we would find that societal expectations about mutual aid or inheritance would focus on the mother's side of the family and would not apply to the father's. The Jewish people are an example of matrilineal religious descent. In order to be a Jew, your mother must be one, and the religion or ethnic identity of the father does not matter. Therefore, if a child's father is Jewish but the mother is not, that child is not a Jew.

There are also some societies that practice *double descent.* In these groups, a person (who is the referent, or center of discussion, and whom I shall call "ego") has distinctive rights and privileges that relate to both the line of inheritance from the father and other, distinct, rights that stem from the mother. The rules of double descent differ widely from group to group, but basically, one may inherit political or social rights from the father's group and land and other property from the mother—or another set of rights and privileges, depending on the specific rules of the particular group in question. The significant fact to remember in double descent is that whatever is inherited from the mother is not also inherited from the father.

Finally, there is the *bilateral* type of inheritance, in which ego has full and equal rights of inheritance to all property, social status, and privileges from both the father and the mother. This is the type of system common in the United States and most other modern Western societies. Like double descent, it is a nonunilineal descent system. Simply by following the rules of biology, bilateral descent cultures are indicating that kinship obligations are relatively minor and therefore can be shared with many people.

In 1949, the anthropologist George Peter Murdock made an in-depth survey cross-sampling of 250 societies throughout the world (a somewhat small, but carefully selected, representative sample of the more than 5,000 known social groups) and came up with the following statistics for the prevalence of the four types of descent rules: patrilineal, 42%; matrilineal, 20%; bilateral, 30%; and double descent, 7% (Murdock, 1949). The remaining 1% refers to a small number of societies that determine kinship in ways even more complicated than those just listed. In some, odd-numbered children are affiliated with the *mother's* family, and even-numbered offspring go with the *father's*. In a few other societies, kin group varies by the sex of the child.

In societies that recognize a known human ancestor as the common progenitor of either the patrilineal or the matrilineal group, the term *lineage* is used to designate a group of relatives. In those societies in which closely related people trace their common ancestry to a mythical being or natural force (often an animal, plant, natural object, or fictitious character), the term *clan* is used to designate the patrilineal or matrilineal group. It must be noted that there will not be both matrilineages and patrilineages in the same society. They are mutually exclusive groups. Also, there will not be a mixture of lineages and clans within a given society.

The terms *patrilineal* and *matrilineal* must not be confused with *patriarchal* and *matriarchal*. They are kinship designations and do not imply rule by men or by women. An analysis of Stephens's (1963) data indicates that about two thirds of all known societies are patriarchal. This means that the husband/father is given (by societal agreement and not by force) power over the members of his family and access to the best resources and privileges.

Matriarchies—societies in which women rule men within the home—are extremely rare. Stephens found perhaps 5 in a sample of 96 cultures. However, in most of these, the idea of Amazon women is more legend than real. Typically, women appear to have higher status than do men because transmission of property is matrilineal, but actual authority resides in male members of the female line. The people of the Five Nations of the Iroquois in Ontario and upper New York State are frequently cited as being matriarchal. For example, the senior women of a clan selected a person (or persons) to assume the position of *sachem* (chief) in one of the 50 leadership sets in the Iroquois council. However, the *sachem* was always a senior male of the clan to which the women who made the selection belonged (Bilharz, 1995; Fenton, 1978; Tooker, 1978).

There is a trend toward the egalitarian type of authority structure within the context of the independent nuclear families of the urbanized areas of the world. This is a recent trend and is most likely related to the facts that many of the traditional kinship supports for the family no longer function effectively within the reality of the mass culture of the urban setting and that, by necessity, the husband and wife must see each other as equals in an isolated team. Also, women are now able to honorably support themselves and their children in the absence of a husband/father in the household, which has surely made them far more independent than in previous generations.

In the Stephens (1963) sample, 12% of the cultures had a general egalitarian pattern, where the husband and wife made decisions jointly, and 15% divided authority into separate spheres. In the latter case, they were roughly equal in overall decision making, but each controlled his or her own domain. In a typical blue-collar marriage in the United States, for instance, the wife may be in charge of household decisions and child rearing, whereas the husband makes the "outside" decision about lawn, cars, and occupations.

TYPES OF POSTMARITAL RESIDENCE

In most urban, industrialized nations a newly married couple will choose a residence wherever social and economic conditions dictate. They may live in the near proximity of the relatives of either the bride or the groom, or they may move to a new location hundreds of miles away from any close relatives. This type of residence pattern is known as *neolocal* residence.

In the majority of societies, the conventional practice is for the husband to remain in close association with his close male relatives (father, paternal uncles, brothers, etc.). This pattern, *patrilocal* residence, is quite common in groups that have patrilineal lineages or clans. Patrilocal residence increases the authority of the groom's family, because he remains in his childhood home, but the bridge is removed from hers.

In societies that have matrilineal lineages or clans, it is quite common for the wife to reside with her husband and children in close proximity to her female relatives. This type of residence pattern is *matrilocal* (or *uxorilocal*). In some cases, the newly married couple resides with the family of the bride for a given period after the onset of the marriage (usually until the birth of the first child or shortly thereafter) and then moves to the vicinity of the groom's family to dwell for the remainder of their marriage. This pattern is *matri-patrilocal.*

In some cases, the family has the choice of dwelling either in close proximity to the relatives of the husband or in near proximity to the relatives of the wife. This type of residence pattern, *bilocal*, is quite common where extended families are found. Young married college students in neolocal societies occasionally resort to this pattern temporarily as part of their effort to become financially independent.

Finally, there are a few societies in which a young man, on reaching adolescence, leaves his parental household and goes to live with his maternal uncle (mother's brother). This pattern, *avunculocal*, is found only in societies that have matrilineal clans. The young man inherits his clan affiliation through his mother (she and her brother, having commonly inherited their clan membership from their mother, will therefore assume the son's social rights and responsibilities through his mother's clan). The mother's brother will pass on his social statuses and positions to his sister's son and not to his own son (who is a member of his wife's clan). A woman in a clan-type society will have a wide range of male relatives (her own siblings as well as her male parallel cousins) whom she will count as her brothers. There will, therefore, always be someone with whom the young man may go to spend his adolescence and young adult years (Goodenough, 1955/1968).

In the 1949 survey conducted by George Murdock, the following percentages for residence patterns were found: patrilocal, 58%; matrilocal, 15%; matri-patrilocal, 9%; bilocal, 8%; neolocal, 7%; and avunculocal, 3%. Murdock also determined from the survey that there was some correlation between residence patterns and kinship types. Of the groups represented, he found that 92% of those that practiced the patrilineal kinship arrangement were also patrilocal (or eventually became patrilocal by practicing the matri-patrilocal system). Of the matrilineal groups, 63% also practiced either matrilocal or avunculocal residence patterns.

Lee (1982) provides us with an excellent summary of the explanations for this pattern. Briefly stated, economic subsistence patterns determine the rules of residence, which in turn affect the rules of descent. The most primitive societies are based on hunting, which is almost exclusively a male activity. Because knowledge of the territory can be crucial for success, it is important that as adults, men stay in the same area in which they learned to hunt as children. This mandates patrilocal residence and then patrilineal descent, so that males will control the land.

Agricultural societies tend to be matrilocal and matrilineal when the major activities are crop and animal tending and harvesting. Women typically are assigned to these activities, so the land is passed on through their lines. If the sexual division of labor is such that working the land is mostly done by men (plow-based or pastoralist economies), then the males control the land. This results first in patrilocal residence, so that the male workers can stay together, and then in patrilineal descent in order to pass on this same condition to their sons.

Industrialized nations have economies based on wages rather than land, and it is not in the best interests of individuals to cooperate with large kinship groups. As a result, nuclear families predominate, residence is neolocal, and descent is bilateral.

Returning to the issue of postmarital residence by itself, surprisingly, only 7% of the societies in Murdock's (1949) sample were neolocal in their residence patterns. Keep in mind, however, that the groups chosen by Murdock were not all the same size. The large, urban industrialized societies of Europe, East Asia, and North America were given no more significance and weight than were the smaller, often more isolated groups of the Pacific, the Amazon basin, or sub-Saharan Africa. Nor were many of the groups as involved in the same degree of technological complexity and urbanization as they might be today. Also, in 1949, when Murdock published his findings, many of the trends toward urban migration and rapid technological change were not yet under way in many of the groups found in the sample, or these trends had just begun and had not yet appreciably affected the nature and structure of the societies represented.

Ethnographic data are only as current as the publication of the field data of the most recent researcher to emerge from the field, and Murdock's (1949) data were, in many cases, representative of the social reality that was reported in groups that had not been studied by anthropologists or other trained social scientists since before the worldwide economic depression of the 1930s and World War II. The great mass movement of people from isolated, rural, tradition-oriented societies to the rapidly expanding urban areas of the world did not get under way until the 1950s. Also, with the changes in traditional habitats brought on by such phenomena as deforestation, mineral exploitation, urban expansion, political strife, rapid population growth, and desertification, many groups have had to restructure their social organizations in such a way as to meet the demands of a cash economy, mass education, national politics, resource depletion, and other factors incompatible with the maintenance of a traditional way of life. It is highly probable that if the same 250 societies Murdock surveyed in 1949 were to be reentered into the statistics using the current social and economic realities, far more than 7% would be recognized as practicing de facto neolocal residence patterns because of the dramatically changed circumstances of recent years. We need only to look at ever-increasing rates of international migration and the rapid growth of the urban areas of Africa, Asia, Latin America, and elsewhere in the Pacific basin to know that significant social changes must be taking place that will have profound effects on the nature and expression of kinship relationships (Peletz, 1995; Sinclair, 2001; Strathern et al., 2002; Tapesell, 2002; White & Lindstrom, 1997).

To illustrate this dramatic change, consider the people of central Polynesia over the past four decades. In 1950, only a few Polynesians had left their traditional home villages and districts. The capital cities and port towns of these Polynesian islands were, for the most part, small colonial outposts. Virtually all Polynesians of central Polynesia still spoke their traditional languages, and most practiced their traditional extended family form of kinship. The cash economy made an impact only in the realm of plantation labor, which for the most part was manned by young adult males, who would leave their families for a few years to earn enough to return to their homes to finance the construction of a home and to provide themselves with some incidental goods and supplies (Doumengae, 1966; Lockwood, 1993; Metge, 1964; Oliver, 1961, 2002).

Today, just a generation later, more than half of the Cook Islanders now live in New Zealand, especially in the urban areas of Auckland and Wellington. Of the 4,000,000 Samoans in the world, more than 80,000 live in New Zealand, also principally in the urban areas. Well over 100,000 Samoans are found in the following metropolitan areas of the United States: Honolulu, Los Angeles, Seattle, and Salt Lake City. Another combined total of 25,000 Samoans reside in the two largest metropolitan areas of Australia: Sydney and Melbourne (Strathern et al., 2002).

Approximately half of all Tongans in the world now live in the urban areas of Auckland, Sydney, Honolulu, Los Angeles, San Francisco, and Salt Lake City (Small, 1997). Sizable concentrations of Polynesians are also found in and near San Diego, Phoenix, Washington, D.C., Kansas City, Seattle, Wellington, Noumea (New Caledonia), Melbourne, and Vancouver (Strathern et al., 2002).

French is now the language of preference for the adolescents of Tahiti over the native Tahitian language of their parents. Approximately three fourths of the 275,000 people of French Polynesia live in or near the capital of Pape'ete, now the bustling largest urban center of eastern Polynesia. All of the capital cities of the Polynesian island groups serve as magnets, drawing large numbers of the rural villagers into rapidly growing urban centers. It is difficult to find any remaining families in the outlying areas that have not been severely disrupted by this flow to the cities (Barker, 1994; Donner, 2002; Feinberg, 2002; Lockwood, 1993; Stanton, 1993).

A typical example is a Samoan classmate of mine, who was reared in Samoa with his four brothers and sisters. They all lived in a small village on the island of Savai'i in the Independent State of Samoa (former Western Samoa). He is the oldest of the five siblings in his family and was the first to leave his home village for the "outside" world. He left his home and family in 1963 to study in the United States. After his graduation, he stayed in the United States to fulfill a career in the Navy, living in the San Diego area until his 20-year retirement. One sister, married to an officer in the U.S. Army, has lived in Germany and in other parts of the world for the past 15 years. Another sister lives in Hawaii. His third sister lives in Auckland, New Zealand, and his brother lives in Virginia. My friend and his four siblings are all married to Samoans, but not one of the couples reared their children in the context of the traditional Samoan extended family of their youth. By the necessity of their circumstances, each of the brothers and sisters had their children in a neolocal family arrangement and in the midst of an urbanized, non-Samoan society. The experience of this friend and his siblings is not unusual; it is repeated many times throughout Polynesia (see also Gershon, 2001; Macpherson, 2002; Rosenblatt, 2002).

COUSIN RELATIONSHIPS

Anthropologists have developed a means of kinship reckoning whereby kinship ties are calculated in terms of one's cousins. This may seem to be a somewhat unusual way to look at kinship, but it helps us to get a much better look at the nature and function of kinship alliances within a society than if we were to consider only close consanguine or affinal relatives. In many societies, there is no differentiation between one's cousins (e.g., the Anglo American system). In this context, the term *cousin* does not convey any sense of relationship as to whether one's cousin is related through the mother's side of the family or that of the father. It does not indicate the gender of the cousin or imply whether the person is the offspring of one's mother's sister or brother or one's father's sister or brother. A cousin is a cousin, and that is all that is important.

Many Anglo Americans have close and affectionate ties with their cousins that are often lifelong in nature and, in some cases, as intense and valuable as the relationship with one's own siblings. However, the society that has a broad, general classification for one's cousins rarely imposes any important duties and responsibilities that bind such cousins into strong legal and political ties with each other.

In North American society, there is considerable confusion regarding the terminology used to classify cousins. This is especially true with regard to second cousins and first cousins once removed. Most North Americans know that their first cousin is the child of a sibling of their mother or father. For example, if your mother or father has a brother or sister, the child of this person is your first cousin. The child of your first cousin is your first cousin once removed, and you are the first cousin once removed to that same child. Your child and the child of your first cousin are second cousins to each other, but the child of your first cousin will not be a first or second cousin to you. That person is your first cousin once removed. This is where the confusion lies.

In popular discussion, most North Americans merge the term for their first cousins once removed and their second cousins into the same terminological classification of second cousin. We rarely use the terms *third cousin,* or *second cousin once removed, second cousin twice removed,* and so forth. It is just best to remember the generational distance you are from a given set of grandparents. If you are both two generations removed from your grandparents (your parents being the first generation away), you are first cousins. If you are both three generations removed, you are second cousins. If you are two generations removed from the specific set of grandparents and your cousin is three generations removed, you are one generation apart from one another, making you first cousins once removed.

In cases in which the only distinction between cousins is gender, this relationship is generally no more significant than that discussed above. This is especially the case in those societies that have gendered nouns and would have a term for a male and female cousin that is determined by a definite article (such as *el primo* or *la prima* in Spanish). There are, however, many cases in which a cousin might transfer his or her family loyalties and affiliations at marriage, which would effectively terminate the kinship ties that existed before marriage. In such cases, the use of gender to differentiate male and female cousins would imply that those cousins who are referred to by one specific term are guaranteed to be one's lifelong relations and those who are given another term will no longer count as close relatives after they are married.

There are many cases in which the gender of the siblings of one's parents determines the type of terminology one would use in reference to cousins. We shall see later that societies that have strong clans, or in which either the male lineage or the female lineage is the exclusive means by which one inherits his or her social identity, usually make a clear distinction between specific groupings of cousins. In such cases, it is vital to distinguish between those cousins who are members of one's clan or lineage and those who are not. This is accomplished by having a set of terms for "in-family" and "out-of-family" cousins. In such systems, the cousins who are the children of an aunt or uncle who are of the same sex as the parent in question (mother's sister or father's brother) would be "parallel cousins." Those cousins who are the offspring of an aunt or uncle who are the opposite sex of the parent in question would be "cross-cousins."

Those societies that make a distinction between parallel cousins and cross-cousins regard parallel cousins as close consanguine relatives and expect their members to behave toward these parallel cousins as they would toward their own siblings. It is common for a person of the opposite sex to treat such cousins with close respect. Persons of the opposite sex would show their respect for parallel cousins by practicing "avoidance relationships" during and after puberty. Such avoidance relationships also exist between brothers and sisters in these societies and would include such things as refusing to be alone in the same room with a sibling or parallel cousin of the opposite sex, refusing to dance with such a person, averting direct eyesight in public, refraining from profanity or coarse jokes, and so on. In these same societies, cross-cousins are not regarded as close relatives. In fact, there often exists a strong "joking relationship" between cross-cousins, especially between persons of the opposite sex. Such relationships might include extensive teasing, telling ribald jokes, flirting, and even sexual experimentation. Often, the relationship between cross-cousins of the opposite sex is so important to the people in these types of societies that they become *preferred* marriage partners and are encouraged to marry one another (Stone, 2000).

The practice of cross-cousin marriage is commonly found in societies that have clan systems. We might ask whether this type of close genetic inbreeding causes physical or mental problems in the groups in which the practice is found. The answer is, "Apparently not." It stands to reason that if there were noticeable genetic defects resulting from first-cousin marriages of cross-cousins, the practice would prove to be dysfunctional and would not be continued as frequently as it is. Because there are so many individuals who would qualify socially as cross-cousins, there is probably no noticeable increase in genetic defects, because although the marriage partner is closely related genetically, the pool of potential partners is so large that there is little chance of repeating the genetic pattern generation after generation. In cases in which close inbreeding has been known to cause problems, we find that not only was the genetic relationship close but the group had a rather limited number of members to begin with and was located in a geographically or socially isolated situation.

An interesting exception to the parallel-cousin avoidance practice of marriage exists in traditional Islamic societies. In Muslim Arab societies (and non-Arab Muslim societies that have adopted the Arab social model), the children of two brothers (parallel cousins through male siblings) are considered to be preferred marriage partners to the extent that a woman must receive the express permission of the son of her father's brother if she desires to marry another person. However, the children of two sisters (parallel cousins through female siblings) are considered to be as close in their relationship to one another as would be siblings, and any intimate relationship between them would be looked on as a type of incest.

The marriage of the children of brothers in Islamic societies has roots in the Old Testament and the Koran and follows a pattern that was once widespread throughout the region of Southwest Asia and North Africa. The avoidance of marriage between the children of sisters has less obvious roots. In Arab tradition, it is assumed that sisters maintain close relationships into adulthood (frequently becoming the wives of the same man in cases in which the husband chooses to follow the allowed practice of plural marriage). Because of this close affiliation between sisters, it is assumed that there will be times when both sisters are nursing their respective infants and will, occasionally, offer to nurse the child of the other sister if, for example, the mother is ill, tired, or busy with some other task and does not want to be interrupted. According to Arab tradition, children who have nursed from the same woman are considered to be siblings. Because of the potential for two women to marry the same man, the children of two sisters could well be the offspring of a common father, and it would make good sense to disallow any marital unions of this type.

KINSHIP TERMINOLOGY: THE SIX BASIC TYPES

As should already be apparent, there are many ways for the thousands of societies throughout the world to reckon their kinship affiliation. Fortunately, it is not necessary to learn the intricacies of each system in order to be conversant on the subject of kinship. As discussed earlier, most anthropologists have recognized the importance of the classification of cousins in unraveling the web of kinship (Parkin, 1997). Approximately 90% of all the world's societies can be grouped into one of six basic kinship types, which can be identified by the names used to refer to cousins and siblings. (Not all societies fall within one of these six kinship categories. Notable exceptions are the Navajo-Apache people of the American Southwest, the Ainu of Japan, the Fijians, and virtually all the aboriginal people of Australia.) Each of these kinship types is named after a society that uses (or recently used) the terminology characteristic of the classification. Because two groups happen to use the same type of kinship terminology does not imply in any way that there are any historical or cultural affiliations between them (Hocart, 1937/1968).

Some kinship types tend to merge a large number of people into a single term such as *brother* or *mother*. This tendency to "lump" a large number of relatives into one category is known as a classificatory system (Kroeber, 1909/1968). In other kinship types, a different set of terms is used for people who are the same genealogical distance from the referent (the person in reference to whom the relationships are being described, known as "ego" in a kinship chart). This may mean that the mother's brother is referred to by a different term than the father's brother, or that parallel cousins are given different designations from cross-cousins. Such a "splitting" of relationships is said to be a *descriptive* system (Evans-Pritchard, 1950). Of course, it is not possible to be totally classificatory (e.g., siblings—brother and sister—and parents—father and mother—are distinguished in all societies by their sex). Also, a strictly descriptive system does not include all the kinship combinations that are possible to describe (e.g., it would be somewhat cumbersome to have a specific term for the third-born son of your mother's oldest sister). The differences between classificatory and descriptive systems are a measure of degree of the number of separate kinship terms used. The six common kinship systems are described here in order of complexity of terminology from the most classificatory (the "lumpers") to the most descriptive (the "splitters").

The Hawaiian system employs the least number of specific kinship terms. All the adults in ego's parental generation are grouped together under the term *mother* or *father*. A person is fully aware of his or her specific biological parents, but all adults in the kin group are referred to as one's parents, and each person within this level of the kinship grouping will be treated as a parent by ego; in return, each person to whom ego refers as his or her parent will treat that person as his or her own biological child. All the members of the family in ego's own generation would be referred to as brother and sister, and all the members of the generation of ego's children would be called son or daughter (Oliver, 1989). This type of kinship terminology is most commonly found in the context of extended families (although not all groups that employ the Hawaiian kinship terminology have extended families as their basic kinship unit, and not all groups that have extended families employ the Hawaiian system in their terminology).

In the Eskimo (or Inuit) kinship system, the relations in ego's direct genealogical lineage are referred to as either mother or father in the parental generation, brother or sister in one's own generation, and son or daughter in the generation of one's children. The siblings of ego's parents are grouped together according to their sex as either uncle or aunt, and their children are collectively referred to as cousins. Although in some Eskimo-type systems there is a distinction made as to whether the cousins are males or females, no distinction is made as to whether a kinship linkage is from the mother's side of the family or the father's side. The Eskimo system is most often used where neolocal residence is practiced and when the independence of the nuclear family as a socioeconomic unit is necessary (Bohannan & Middleton, 1968). As most of us will recognize, the Eskimo type is the one that is predominantly used in Anglo American and Western European societies.

The next three kinship types are found in societies that depend on clans as their basic family organization. When most North Americans hear the term *clan,* they tend to think of the so-called Scottish clans. Actually, the clans of Scotland were based on obligations and loyalties as much (or more) to the geographical landlord as to someone who was close kin. In the anthropological sense, therefore, the Scottish clans did not operate as clans in the precise technical definition but much more as feudal fiefdoms (R. G. Fox, 1976).

Before proceeding, it will be helpful to discuss four basic characteristics of clan affiliation. These four characteristics should aid in gaining a better understanding of how clan systems operate. The four characteristics are as follows:

1. Clan membership is for life (one never changes clans, even in marriage).
2. All siblings belong to the same clan.
3. Clans are strictly exogamous units.
4. The ultimate leadership of a clan will always rest on a senior male (or coalition of males) who is a member of the clan.

In the Iroquois clan type of arrangement, ego merges the term for his or her parents with the parents' siblings of the same sex (thus, the father's brother will also be referred to as father, and the mother's sister becomes mother). A separate term will be used for the mother's brother and the father's sister. In some cases, societies that have masculine and feminine markers for a person's gender will add the feminine marker to the term used for father to refer to the father's sister (which in English would roughly be equivalent to "fatherette"), or the masculine marker would be added to the term for mother in reference to the mother's brother (roughly equivalent to "male mother"). In the Iroquois system, parallel cousins would belong to one's own clan (or to a closely affiliated clan) and would be referred to as brothers or sisters. It would not be possible for cross-cousins to be closely related through clan membership, and a term roughly equivalent to *cousin* would be employed. In many Iroquois-type systems cross-cousins become preferred marriage partners (Fenton, 1978; Shimony, 1994; Tooker, 1978).

The Iroquois system is found in both patrilineal- and matrilineal-type societies. It works out that regardless of which type is used, parallel cousins will always belong to ego's own clan (or to a very closely affiliated clan), and cross-cousins will never belong to a closely related clan (Lowie, n.d./1968).

The next two clan-type kinship systems are quite similar to the Iroquois system in many ways. The major difference is that in the Omaha system, which is only patrilineal, parallel cousins are treated in the same manner as in the Iroquois system, but cross-cousins are all lumped together with the term for either father or father's sister (on the father's side of the family), regardless of the generation of the person. In this system, therefore, not only is ego's mother's brother (maternal uncle) given a designation roughly equivalent to "uncle," but so is his son called uncle, and so would all the male descendants of that line be called by this same term (Taylor, 1969). Because the Omaha system is patrilineal, using the same term to refer to the mother's brother and all his male descendants is equivalent to saying "he who is a male in my mother's clan." The females in ego's matriline would all be referred to as mother, regardless of the generation. Thus, *mother* becomes a term used for any female who belongs to the mother's clan, including (of course) ego's mother herself. This practice of "lumping" all relatives of the mother's clan into a general category based on their sex is "cross-generational equivalence" (Keesing, 1975).

The matrilineal Crow kinship can be referred to as a sort of "mirror image" of the Omaha type. It follows the Iroquois system for the naming of ego's parallel cousins and all other relatives in the mother's clan (the clan to which ego also belongs). It employs cross-generational equivalence for the members of the father's clan. Ego uses the same term for cross-cousins on the father's side as he or she would use for the father or the father's sister (Taylor, 1969). The Crow system does get more complex when dealing with the members of ego's children's generation, but it is not necessary to discuss the intricacies of this system here.

The important key to understanding any of the clan-related kinship systems (the Iroquois, Omaha, or Crow type) is that each one allows the speaker (ego) to clearly differentiate between those relatives who are members of his or her clan and those who belong to the clan of the parent who is not of ego's own clan. Often, a person who is not a fellow clansperson but who is related through a genealogical tie will recognize a special social bond to ego and thus be of some help in times of need or grief.

In the three clan-based systems described here, clans are usually grouped together into alliances of closely affiliated clans. The most common such arrangement is one in which the whole society is divided into two basically equal units. Each of these two units would be referred to as a *moiety* (meaning "half"). There are other societies in which the clans are divided into three or more allied groups. Each of these alliances of closely related clans would be referred to as a *phratry* (Parkin, 1997). Technically, a moiety is a phratry, but it is such a common phenomenon in clan-like societies that such alliances are specifically referred to as moieties to set them apart from other types of phratries. People who belong to the same moiety or phratry treat one another in much the same manner as they would members of their own clan.

The final and most descriptive of the six kinship types is the Sudanese type (named after a region in eastern Africa and not a specific group). Ego employs a special term for each set of relatives in the parental generation. There is a specific and separate term for father, father's brother, and father's sister and for mother, mother's sister, and mother's brother. Also, each set of cousins has a separate term. Therefore, in ego's generation there would be a term for one's siblings and one each for the children of the father's sister, father's brother, mother's sister, and mother's brother. The Sudanese system is found most commonly in societies that have segmentary lineages. Ego would be able to trace his or her ancestry back to a known ancestor along with a large number of relatives. As long as the common relationship is not too distant in the past, all the members of ego's lineage would consider themselves to be close relatives. However, as the generations produce new children and these children grow to adulthood, the lineage becomes too large to be an effective kinship unit, so it is eventually necessary to divide the group into two or more new segments. When this division takes place, it becomes necessary for ego to be able to quickly distinguish those individuals who will remain in his or her lineage from those who are now part of another lineage. By having specific terms for a large number of relatives, ego will know who is a kinsperson and who is no longer a kinsperson by the terms that have been used all of his or her life (Evans-Pritchard, 1950).

As mentioned at the beginning of this section, those societies that do not fall conveniently into the six kinship types listed here are generally named after a society that uses (or recently used) the terminology characteristic of the classification. Some are closely related to the more common systems; for example, the Navajo observe a clan-based system but give more priority to all four of one's immediate parental lines (the two parental clans of the mother and the two parental clans of the father), thus placing them outside of the conventional clan system (Stone, 2000; Witherspoon, 1975). Others, such as the Fijian system, lie in an intermediate place between the Hawaiian system (regarding the generational classification of kin) and the Iroquois system, having generally five clan lines, *mataqali*, in a larger family group, *yavusa* (Nayacakalou, 1978; Roth, 1973; Thomas, 1997). Some, especially those found in Australia, are so completely unique as to place them in a category unrelated to any other forms understood by anthropologists (Hiatt, 1996; Oliver, 1989; Pelusey, 2000). Other groups, often referred to as utopian or intentional groups, have attempted to "rewrite the script" and invent or organize their own unique and distinct kinship and residential patterns. Most of these attempts have been ephemeral and have long since passed into oblivion. Some, however, have managed to survive, and in some cases succeed, becoming a recognizable long-term established social pattern. Among these successful "intentional" societies have been the Israeli kibbutz and moshav, the Old Order Amish, the Hutterian Brethren (Hutterites), and polygamous (polygynous) communities that have broken off from the Church of Jesus Christ of Latter-day Saints (Mormons).

In some cases these groups have undergone some degree of adjustment and redefinition of kinship and residential patterns, but they have nonetheless been able to sustain themselves on a long-term, multigenerational basis (Blasi, 1986; Bradley, 1993; Gavron, 2000; Hostetler & Huntington, 1992; Huntington, 1981; Jankowiak, 2001; Kraybill, 2001; Kraybill & Bowman, 2001; Spiro, 1975; Stanton, 1989; Weintraub, Lissak, & Azmon, 1969). Each of these groups and others (the list is certainly not exhaustive) may be thought to represent the successful redefinition of an alternative to traditional kinship and residential patterns that are worthy of further serious study and consideration. The nature of the focus of this chapter has led me to select only those groups that represent multiple communities within their movement located in geographically dispersed settlements. It is certain that there are a number of smaller, singular communities that have succeeded in surviving for a considerable span of time, but they might also be reasonably classified as a special type of an extended family rather than representing the successful emergence of an alternative social system.

CONCLUSION

Systems of kinship, marriage, and residence make sense to those who use them. Moreover, they are the first exposure a person has to his or her society. What we learn as young children tends to remain normal and comfortable throughout our lives. As many who work in cross-cultural settings know, insights into the family system of a group of people lead to a fuller understanding of their whole way of life.

An experience related by one of my professors illustrates this understanding. This professor began his anthropological field research among the Iroquois of the Six Nations Reserve near Brantford, Ontario, Canada. Each Sunday he attended a church service with his family in the non-Indian city of Brantford. One Sunday, a member of the congregation who was a successful businessman approached the young anthropologist and asked him whether he had been "out on the reserve" long enough to get to know something about what went on "out there." When my professor acknowledged that he had some basic idea of what was happening, the businessman then asked whether he could get an idea of the Iroquois concept of honesty. The businessman explained that he had a very hard-working employee who was an Iroquois. The Iroquois was one of his best workers, but it seemed he had a serious character flaw.

When the Iroquois man had come to work for him a few years before, he had not been employed for more than 3 or 4 months when he asked whether he could have a week off to go to his home reserve to participate in his mother's funeral in the traditional Native American manner. He offered to make up the lost time by deducting it from his vacation, but the owner of the business saw no need for that and excused him with his blessings and condolences. A few months later this same employee, now wanting to attend his father's funeral, again approached the owner. This time the owner decided that maybe it would be necessary to make up for the extra week by deducting it from the Iroquois's vacation time. Not too much later, the Iroquois worker asked for time off to attend his sister's funeral, and not much later on it was a brother, and then another sister. Finally, the businessman felt that he had had enough when he was approached so that the man could attend his mother's funeral. A man might have quite a large number of brothers and sisters, but it stood to reason to the businessman that once a person's mother had died, it would not happen again.

The business owner told his Iroquois employee that he now was convinced that he was using funerals as an excuse to skip work and that if he wanted to spend so much time back home with his people, he should just stay there. That had happened just a few days before, and the businessman was now asking the anthropologist whether he, as a Christian, had done the right and decent thing by terminating the employment of the Iroquois worker. At this point, my professor told the businessman that it might be beneficial for him to understand that every Iroquois probably refers to as many as 15 or 20 people as mother and an equal number as father, and perhaps as many as 100 persons would be considered brothers and sisters. After learning about their kinship system, the businessman had a better appreciation of the Iroquois customs. He apologized to the man he had fired, rehired him, and made arrangements for all of his Native American workers to use their vacation time to leave work for important traditional events such as funerals.

Because kinship is so central to the lives of us all, and because we all live in a complex world occupied by so many people from so many different cultures and groups, it would be wise to become more aware of and sensitive to the points of view of those around us.

REFERENCES

Barker, J. C. (1994). Home alone: The effects of out-migration on Niuean elders' living arrangements and social supports. *Pacific Studies, 17*(3), 41–81.

Benedek, E. (1992). *The wind won't know me: A history of the Navajo-Hopi land dispute.* New York: Vintage Books.

Benedek, E. (1995). *Beyond the four corners of the world. A Navajo woman's journey.* Norman: University of Oklahoma Press.

Bilharz, J. (1995). First among equals? The changing status of Seneca women. In L. F. Klein & L. A. Ackerman (Eds.), *Women and power in Native North America* (pp. 101–112). Norman: University of Oklahoma Press.

Blasi, J. (1986). *The communal experience of the kibbutz.* New Brunswick, NJ: Transaction Books.

Bohannan, P., & Middleton, J. (Eds.). (1968). *American museum sourcebooks in anthropology: Vol. Q9. Marriage, family, and residence.* Garden City, NY: Natural History Press.

Bradley, M. S. (1993). *Kidnapped from that land: The government raids on the Short Creek polygamists.* Salt Lake City: University of Utah Press.

Cassell, P. (Ed.). (1993). *The Giddens reader.* Stanford, CA: Stanford University Press.

Crandall, D. P. (2000). *The place of the stunted ironwood trees: A year in the lives of the cattle-herding Himba of Namibia.* New York: Continuum International.

DeMalie, R. J. (1998). Kinship: The foundation for Native American society. In R. Thornton (Ed.), *Studying Native America: Problems and prospects* (pp. 306–356). Madison: University of Wisconsin Press.

Donner, W. W. (2002). Rice and tea, fish and taro: Sikiana migration to Honiara. *Pacific Studies, 25*(1/2), 23–44.

Doumengae, F. (1966). *L'homme dans le Pacifique sud* (Publications de la Société des Océanistes No. 19). Paris: Musée de l'Homme.

Ehrlich, A. S. (2001). Power, control, and the mother-in-law problem: Face-offs in the American nuclear family. In L. Stone (Ed.), *New directions in anthropological kinship* (pp. 156–174). Lanham, MD: Rowman and Littlefield.

Evans-Pritchard, E. E. (1950). Kinship and the local community among the Nuer. In A. R. Radcliffe-Brown & D. Forde (Eds.), *African systems of kinship and marriage* (pp. 360–391). London: Oxford University Press.

Farber, B., Mogey, J., & Smith, K. (1986). Kinship and development [special issue]. *Journal of Comparative Family Studies, 17.*

Feinberg, R. (2002). Anutans in Honiara: A Polynesian people's struggle to maintain community in the Solomon Islands. *Pacific Studies, 25*(1/2), 45–70.

Fenton, W. N. (1978). Northern Iroquoian culture patterns. In W. C. Sturtevant (Ed.), *Handbook of North American Indians: Vol. 15. Northeast* (pp. 296–321). Washington, DC: Smithsonian Institution.

Fox, R. (1967). *Kinship and marriage: An anthropological perspective.* London: Penguin Books.

Fox, R. G. (1976). Lineage cells and regional definition in complex societies: The case of Highland Scotland. In C. A. Smith (Ed.), *Regional analysis: Vol. II. Social systems* (Studies in Anthropology, pp. 95–121). New York: Academic Press.

Galvin, K. (2001). Schneider revisited: Sharing and ratification in the construction of kinship. In L. Stone (Ed.), *New directions in anthropological kinship* (pp. 109–124). Lanham, MD: Rowman and Littlefield.

Gavron, D. (2000). *The kibbutz: Awakening from Utopia.* Lanham, MD: Rowman and Littlefield.

Gershon, I. (2001). Going nuclear: New Zealand bureaucratic fantasies of Samoan extended families. In L. Stone (Ed.), *New directions in anthropological kinship* (pp. 303–321). Lanham, MD: Rowman and Littlefield.

Goodenough, W. (1968). Residence rules. In P. Bohannan & J. Middleton (Eds.), *American museum sourcebooks in anthropology: Vol. Q10. Kinship and social organization* (pp. 297–316). Garden City, NY: Natural History Press. (Reprinted from *Southwestern Journal of Anthropology, 12,* 22–37, 1955)

Hiatt, L. R. (1996). *Arguments about aborigines: Australia and the evolution of social anthropology.* Cambridge, UK: Cambridge University Press.

Hocart, A. M. (1937). Kinship systems. In P. Bohannan & J. Middleton (Eds.), *American museum sourcebooks in anthropology: Vol. Q10. Kinship and social organization* (pp. 29–38). Garden City, NY: Natural History Press. (Reprinted from *Anthropos, 32,* 345–351, 1937)

Hostetler, J. A., & Huntington, G. E. (1992). *Amish children: Education in the family, school, and community* (2nd ed.). Orlando, FL: Holt, Rinehart & Winston.

Huntington, G. E. (1981). Children of the Hutterites. *Natural History, 90*(2), 34–47.

Jacobs, S. (1995). Continuity and change in gender roles at San Juan pueblo. In L. F. Klein & L. A. Ackerman (Eds.), *Women and power in Native North America* (pp. 177–213). Norman: University of Oklahoma Press.

Jacobson, D., Liem, J. H., & Weiss, R. S. (2001). Parenting from separate households: A cultural perspective. In L. Stone (Ed.), *New directions in anthropological kinship* (pp. 229–245). Lanham, MD: Rowman and Littlefield.

Jankowiak, W. (2001). In the name of the father: Theology, kinship and charisma in the American polygynous community. In L. Stone (Ed.), *New directions in anthropological kinship* (pp. 264–284). Lanham, MD: Rowman and Littlefield.

Johnson, C. L. (1988). *Ex familia.* New Brunswick, NJ: Rutgers University Press.

Joyce, R. A., & Gillespie, S. D. (2000). *Beyond kinship: Social and material reproduction in house societies.* Philadelphia: University of Pennsylvania Press.

Keesing, R. M. (1975). *Kin groups and social structure.* New York: Holt, Rinehart & Winston.

Klein, L. F. (1995). Mother as clanswoman: Rank and gender in Tlingit society. In L. F. Klein & L. A. Ackerman (Eds.), *Women and power in Native North America* (pp. 28–45). Norman: University of Oklahoma Press.

Kraybill, D. B. (2001). *The riddle of Amish culture* (Rev. ed.). Baltimore: Johns Hopkins University Press.

Kraybill, D., & Bowman, C. F. (2001). *On the backroad to Heaven: Old Order Hutterites, Mennonites, Amish, and Brethren.* Baltimore: Johns Hopkins University Press.

Kroeber, A. L. (1968). Classificatory systems of relationship. In P. Bohannan & J. Middleton (Eds.), *American museum sourcebooks in anthropology: Vol. Q10. Kinship and social organization* (pp. 19–27). Garden City, NY: Natural History Press. (Reprinted from *Journal of the Anthropological Institute, 39,* 77–84, 1909)

Lee, G. R. (1982). *Family structure and interaction: A comparative analysis* (2nd ed.). Minneapolis: University of Minnesota Press.

Lockwood, V. (1993). *Tahitian transformations: Gender and capitalist development in a rural society*. Boulder, CO: Lynne Rienner.

Lowie, R. H. (1968). Relationship terms. In P. Bohannan & J. Middleton (Eds.), *American museum sourcebooks in anthropology: Vol. Q10. Kinship and social organization* (pp. 39–59). Garden City, NY: Natural History Press. (Reprinted from *Encyclopedia Britannica,* 14th ed., n.d.)

Macpherson, C. (2002). From moral community to moral communities: The foundations of migrant social solidarity among Samoans in urban Aotearoa/New Zealand. *Pacific Studies, 25*(1/2), 71–93.

Maltz, D., & Archambault, J. (1995). Gender and power in Native America: Concluding remarks. In L. F. Klein & L. A. Ackerman (Eds.), *Women and power in Native North America* (pp. 230–249). Norman: University of Oklahoma Press.

Metge, J. (1964). *A new Maori migration: Rural and urban relations in northern New Zealand.* London: Athlone Press.

Metge, J. (1995). *New growth from old: The whānau in the modern world.* Wellington, New Zealand: Victoria University Press.

Modell, J. S. (Ed.). (2002). Constructing moral communities: Pacific Islander strategies for settling new places [Special issue]. *Pacific Studies, 25*(1/2).

Morton, H. (1996). *Becomimg Tongan: An ethnography of childhood.* Honolulu: University of Hawaii Press.

Murdock, G. P. (1949). *Social structure.* New York: Macmillan.

Nayacakalou, R. R. (1978). *Tradition and change in the Fijian village.* Suva, Fiji: University of the South Pacific Press.

Nuttall, M. (2000). Choosing kin: Sharing and subsistence in a Greenlandic hunting community. In P. Schweitzer (Ed.), *Dividends of kinship: Meanings and uses of social relatedness* (pp. 33–60). New York: Routledge.

Oliver, D. (1961). *The Pacific islands* (Rev. ed.). (Natural History Library). New York: Anchor Books.

Oliver, D. (1989). *Oceania: The native cultures of Australia and the Pacific islands: Vol. 2.* Honolulu: University of Hawaii Press.

Oliver, D. (2002). *Polynesia in early historic times.* Honolulu, HI: Bess Press.

O'Meara, T. (1990). *Samoan planters: Tradition and economic development in Polynesia.* Orlando, FL: Holt, Rinehart & Winston.

Parkin, R. (1997). *Kinship: An introduction to basic concepts.* Malden, MA: Blackwell.

Peletz, M. (1995). Kinship studies in late twentieth-century anthropology. *Annual Review of Anthropology, 24,* 343–372.

Pelusey, M. (2000, July-September). Skin stories. *Australian Geographic, 59,* 102–111.

Pickering, K. A. (2000). *Lakota culture, world economy.* Lincoln: University of Nebraska Press.

Rosenblatt, D. (2002). *Titirangi* is the mountain: Representing Maori community in Auckland. *Pacific Studies, 25*(1/2), 117–140.

Rossi, A. S., & Rossi, P. H. (1990). *Of human bonding: Parent-child relations across the life course.* New York: Aldine de Gruyter.

Roth, G. K. (1973). *The Fijian way of life* (2nd ed.). Melbourne: Oxford University Press of Australia.

Scheffler, H. (2001). *Filiation and affiliation.* Boulder, CO: Westview Press.

Shepardson, M. (1995). The gender status of Navajo women. In L. F. Klein & L. A. Ackerman (Eds.), *Women and power in Native North America* (pp. 159–176). Norman: University of Oklahoma Press.

Shimony, A. A. (1994). *Conservatism among the Iroquois at the Six Nations reserve.* Syracuse, NY: Syracuse University Press.

Sinclair, K. (2001). Mischief on the margins: Gender and primogeniture, and cognatic descent among the Maori. In L. Stone (Ed.), *New directions in anthropological kinship* (pp. 156–174). Lanham, MD: Rowman and Littlefield.

Skolnik, A. (1991). *Embattled paradise: The American family in an age of uncertainty.* New York: Basic Books.

Small, C. A. (1997). *Voyages: From Tongan villages to American suburbs.* Ithaca, NY: Cornell University Press.

Spiro, M. E. (1975). *Children of the kibbutz.* Cambridge, MA: Harvard University Press.

Stack, C. B., & Burton, L. M. (1993). Kinscripts. *Journal of Comparative Family Studies, 24,* 157–170.

Stanton, M. (1989). The maintenance of the Hutterite way: The family and childhood life-cycle in the communal context. *Family Science Review, 2,* 373–388.

Stanton, M. (1993). A gathering of saints: The role of the Church of Jesus Christ of Latter-day Saints in Pacific Islander migration. In B. McCall & J. Connell (Eds.), *A world perspective on Pacific Islander migration: Australia, New Zealand and the USA* (Center for South Pacific Studies, Pacific Studies Monograph No. 6, pp. 23–37). Sydney, Australia: University of New South Wales.

Stephens, W. N. (1963). *The family in cross-cultural perspective.* New York: Holt, Rinehart & Winston.

Stone, L. (2000). *Kinship and gender: An introduction* (2nd ed.). Boulder, CO: Westview Press.

Strathern, A., Stewart, P. J., Carucci, L., Poyer, L., Feinberg, R., & Macpherson, C. (2002). *Oceania: An introduction to the cultures and identities of Pacific Islanders.* Durham, NC: Carolina Academic Press.

Tapesell, P. (2002). *Marae* and tribal identity in urban Aotearoa/New Zealand. *Pacific Studies, 25*(1/2), 141–171.

Taylor, R. B. (1969). *Cultural ways: A compact introduction to cultural anthropology.* Boston: Allyn & Bacon.

Thomas, N. (1997). *In Oceania: Visions, artifacts, histories.* Durham, NC: Duke University Press.

Tooker, E. (1978). The league of the Iroquois: Its history, politics, and ritual. In W. C. Sturtevant (Ed.), *Handbook of North American Indians: Vol. 15. Northeast* (pp. 418–441). Washington, DC: Smithsonian Institution.

Weintraub, D., Lissak, M., & Azmon, Y. (1969). *Moshava, Kibbutz, and Moshav: Patterns of Jewish rural settlement and development in Palestine.* Ithaca, NY: Cornell University Press.

Weston, K. (1992). *The families we choose: Lesbians, gays, kinship.* New York: Columbia University Press.

White, G. M., & Lindstrom, L. (Eds.). (1997). *Chiefs today: Traditional Pacific leadership and the postcolonial states.* Stanford, CA: Stanford University Press.

Witherspoon, G. (1975). *Navajo kinship and marriage.* Chicago: University of Chicago Press.

CHAPTER 6

Marital Structure

Bron B. Ingoldsby

This chapter looks at marriage rather than the more complex issue of family. The number of social positions that make up a family determines family structure. With marriage, however, there are only two positions: husband and wife. Cohabiting couples would be considered as if they were legally married for this type of analysis. Therefore, marital structure refers simply to the number of *individuals* who occupy each of those two positions or roles within a given marriage.

Homosexual unions cannot be considered here for a couple of reasons. First, we have little global data on same-sex domestic relationships. In the United States, for instance, census statistics only recently have begun to tell us about opposite-sex cohabitation. And second, if we take away one of the two positions, this type of analysis does not work. As a result, an investigation of same-sex marital structure is beyond the scope of this chapter.

There are, then, four possible types of marriage structure, depending on the number of persons of each sex who occupy each position within a given marriage (Lee, 1982). The type most familiar to those from modern Western societies is *monogamy,* or one husband and one wife. Because it is often the only legal option, it is so common that many people make the mistake of considering monogamy the only natural or legitimate marital form.

The other three possibilities are all forms of plural marriage, or *polygamy.* In each case, the structure is determined by the number of husbands or wives simultaneously married to their opposite-sex counterparts:

Table 6.1 Types of Marital Structure

Marital Type	*Husbands*	*Wives*
Monogamy	One	One
Polygyny	One	Two or more
Polyandry	Two or more	One
Cenogamy	Two or more	Two or more

Drawing on medical terms for the sexes, *polygyny* means "many females," whereas *polyandry* refers to many males. *Cenogamy* is the term for "group marriage," as *cen* is the root for "hundred." More recently, the term *polygynandry* (Sangree & Levine, 1980) has also been applied to the situation of a marriage consisting of plural husbands and wives.

It has been tempting for some to consider the plural marriage forms to be at least exotic, if not unnatural. Book titles such as *Strange Customs of Courtship and Marriage* (Fielding, 1942) reveal the Eurocentric bias of some writers who have helped shape public opinion.

Monogamy is certainly the most common of the marital types; the generally equal sex ratio throughout the world sees to that. It works well with our modern economic structure and probably provides for greater interpersonal intimacy, but this does not make it more "natural." As we shall see, polygyny in particular has been a common adaptation to the complexities of the human condition.

In the most extensive examination of the Ethnographic Atlas, Murdock (1967) analyzed marital structure in 1,157 societies. As with all studies in which societies rather than individual marriages are counted, polygyny emerges as the preferred marital structure in the world.

Monogamy was the only permitted form of marriage in 14.5% of the cultures; polyandry was the norm in only seven, or 0.6%; cenogamy doesn't appear as the preferred marital style in any of the cases surveyed; and polygyny is practiced in 84.8% of the world's cultures. In 42% of the polygynous societies, it was practiced only occasionally, which means in fewer than 20% of all marriages.

It must be remembered that modern industrialized societies are not included in the data banks of the Ethnographic Atlas, but the results are nonetheless impressive. It should also be kept in mind that even in polygynous societies, the majority of marriages might be monogamous because of sex ratio constraints. However, polygyny is the ideal for which the citizens strive.

Modern societies, heavily influenced by European colonialism, are overwhelmingly monogamous, but many citizens end up practicing what is now called "serial monogamy." They marry, divorce, and remarry, sometimes more than once. In this way, one has more than one spouse, but only one at a time. Those who enter into cohabitation relationships increase their total number of partners even more.

POLYGYNY

The Baganda are one of the larger Bantu tribes living in present-day Uganda in east-central Africa. They are an agricultural people who enjoy a mild climate. Before British domination brought Western social changes, polygyny was the dominant marital form. The king may have had literally hundreds of wives, chiefs dozens, and commoners two or three. Queen, Habenstein, and Quadagno (1985) provide an excellent summary of this well-known example of polygyny.

Girls usually married at about age 14, and boys shortly thereafter, as soon as they could acquire property. A wife could be inherited or captured in war, but she was usually purchased from her parents. The bride-price (what the groom pays the bride's family in order to marry her; see Chapter 8, this volume, for a complete explanation), typically involving goats, cattle, and cowry shells, could often take up to a year to accumulate. Once agreed upon, the wedding would take place as soon as the bride-price was paid. The bride would be fed well to make her plump and would be veiled in bark cloth.

Wives were valued for two things. The first was their economic productivity. The wife's primary responsibility was to cultivate a family garden plot, and whenever she would wear out her hoe, her husband would reward her with a goat (and probably a new hoe) for her diligence.

Wives were also valued for producing children. The Bagandans had a number of beliefs concerning children and especially legitimacy. A woman would give birth in her garden, hanging on to a plantain tree and supported by a female assistant. The medicine man was called only in difficult cases, but he was generally not wanted because of his primitive obstetrics and because needing him indicated to the Bagandans that the child had been conceived in adultery.

If the firstborn to a chief were male, he would be killed, because it was considered to be bad luck for the father. Breech births were also killed (it was believed that they would grow up to be murderers), but twins were cause for rejoicing. A child's umbilical cord was saved and brought to a special clan ceremony. It would be dropped into a container of beer, water, and milk, and if the cord sank, then the child was considered to be the product of adultery and was disowned.

The next day the child was named. The paternal grandfather would recite the names of clan ancestors, and when the child laughed it was believed that the soul of that ancestor had entered the child's body, and that was the name given. Children generally lived with a brother of the father after weaning. Grandparents could also ask for a child to live with them at any time.

Explanations for Polygyny

Western scholars first supposed that the sex drive was at the root of the practice of having plural wives. Men were presumed to have a greater desire for sexual variety than do women, and because they typically control the authority structure, it was thought that they simply imposed their will upon the women to gratify themselves. But as Lee (1982) demonstrates, this explanation has a number of flaws to it. First of all, there is no evidence that the male sex drive is innately stronger than it is for females. Second, women also favor the polygynous system. There are a number of economic advantages to living in a polygynous household (e.g., greater wealth for all), and it is often a senior wife who encourages her husband to marry again.

Third, the fact of the roughly equal sex ratio means that only some men can enter plural marriage. As a valuable resource, there is usually an expensive bride-price to pay for each wife, so it is only the older men, who have had the time to gain wealth, who can afford additional wives. It is the younger men who are believed to have the more intense sexual urges, but they may not yet have even a first wife.

Finally, even though there may be some theoretical evidence that males value sexual variety, it does not necessarily follow that they would try to acquire multiple wives. Instead, they would seek multiple sexual partners, which is not the same thing. Men in most societies are able to obtain sex without marriage, even though marriage always includes sexual privilege. Because sex is available elsewhere, marriage would be a high price to pay for that aspect alone.

Other arguments have been offered as well. Whiting (1964) claims that polygyny is more likely to be acceptable in cultures that have postpartum sex taboos until the infant is weaned. This enables the couple to space children so that the mother can properly feed each one. Polygyny therefore provides a regular sexual outlet for the husband. Ember (1974) reports that polygyny fills the need for all women to marry in societies where there are fewer men because of high warfare mortality rates.

Marriage and Economy

The explanation that has shown the most promise and received the most attention among scholars (see Lee, 1982) has been the link between marital type and economic subsistence patterns. It has been widely reported that in polygynous societies, the wealthiest families are most likely to be polygynous.

The implication is that the more women and their children can contribute to the production of wealth, the more likely polygyny is to be practiced. We find this in light agriculture and animal husbandry economies, where the more wives a man has, the more fields can be tended and the more animals cared for. The wealth generated exceeds the expenses of any additional consumer, because virtually everyone can be a worker.

As a result, women are attracted to the economic advantages of being a multiple wife. Sociobiologists (Devore, 1979) have reported similar strategies in the animal kingdom as well. Male blackbirds that control the richest wetland will have many females attach to them, whereas the less fortunate males on the rocky edges may be lucky to entice even a single mate.

A good example of this argument that having plural wives is for economic reasons, rather than to have an exotic harem, is the Siwai:

> It is by no mere accident that polygynous households average more pigs than monogamous ones. Informants stated explicitly that some men married second and third wives in order to enlarge their herds. They laughed at the writer's suggestion that a man might become polygynous in order to increase his sexual enjoyment. ("Why pay bride price when for a handful of tobacco you can copulate with other women as often as you like!") (Oliver, 1955, p. 352)

With the family as the unit of production, it follows that the economy might influence family size. In primitive hunting-and-gathering societies, children will consume much more than they produce, and the same is true for modern industrialized societies. These societies tend to be monogamous, whereas the agricultural societies that have a high female contribution to subsistence tend to be polygynous.

Other Possibilities

However, the economic explanation doesn't fit the facts as perfectly as originally thought. Goody (1973) points out that although polygyny is practically universal among native African societies, it is more frequent in West Africa, even though women contribute more to production in East Africa. Also, about 90% of preagricultural societies practice polygyny, even though women make relatively low contributions to subsistence in those hunting, fishing, and herding cultures.

In these cases it may be women's reproductive value that leads to the taking of plural wives. That is, more wives means more sons being born, who will be the workers in a male-oriented economy. Some research (Lee & Whitbeck, 1990; Verdon, 1983) has indicated that the reasons for polygyny are many and complex: economy, social status, tradition, biosocial, for political connections and lineage advantages, and others, even possibly including the before-discredited idea of sexual access. In light of the fact that most societies permit the practice of at least occasional polygyny, it may be that scholars have pursued the explanation from the wrong vantage point. Goody (1976) argues that it is monogamy that requires an explanation, and that we should be looking for the constraints that push a society away from polygyny and toward monogamy.

There are also a number of groups that have attempted, with varying degrees of success, to intentionally restructure marriage for religious reasons. Some of these, which have had an impact on modern Western culture, will be examined in some detail in Chapter 7 of this volume.

Drawbacks to Polygyny

In polygynous societies wives are scarce, and therefore valuable, resources. As a result, they are expensive to obtain, and we find that the custom of paying the girl's family a bride-price is more common in polygynous cultures. This custom helps to deal with the problem of the sex ratio, because men need time to generate the wealth necessary to afford additional wives. Women often marry shortly after puberty and are therefore much younger than their husbands. This means that there are always more women in the marriage pool than there are men, making polygyny possible.

Stephens (1963) recounts problems with jealousy in some polygynous households, and indeed many Westerners today consider it to be only natural that a woman would resent sharing her husband with others. However, the idea of sexual exclusivity is learned rather than innate, and therefore jealousy would be less common in cultures that do not espouse that value (Lee, 1982).

In short, there may be nothing intrinsically anxiety producing about plural marriages. In Ware's (1979) study of polygyny in Nigeria, she found that the majority of women were pleased to have their husband take an additional wife, mainly because it gave them help in their domestic tasks. It must be remembered that even though it is expensive to establish a polygynous arrangement, in the long run it usually creates more wealth for all members than it costs.

Stephens (1963) mentions that in the political system of the Trobriand Islands, a husband receives an annual large food gift from the kinsmen of each wife. This makes it economically profitable to have as many wives as possible. In other cases, plural wives are a status symbol for prominent families. In general, polygyny has not been associated with low status for women, so they tend not to oppose it.

However, Stephens (1963) also quotes the following Indian Hindu proverb: "A thousand moustaches can live together, but not four breasts" (p. 56). So how is the possibility of jealousy dealt with? Essentially there are two approaches: (a) If the cowives are sisters or other close relatives, then they tend to share the same residence; and (b) if they are not related they are usually given separate households. This first approach, *sororal polygyny,* is very common in polygynous societies. It is apparently assumed that sisters can handle sexual jealousy and close quarters better than others would (Lee, 1982).

Nonrelative plural marriage is called *hut polygyny,* where each wife has her own home, or "hut," and the common husband visits each in rotation. This reduces interaction between the wives and their children and also results in periods of father absence.

In summary, polygyny has flourished everywhere except in Christian Europe and North America, and it brings advantages to the wives as well as the husband. This is particularly true for the senior wife, who often has authority over the others. It remains popular in places even when it is not economically advantageous, and it has mechanisms for dealing with family conflict.

POLYANDRY AND POLYGYNANDRY

Murdock (1957) originally identified four societies as being characterized by polyandry: the Toda, the Tibetans, the Nayar, and the Marquesans. In 1967, he found three more, and since that time a few others have been identified. Although certainly rare compared to monogamy and polygyny, entire cultures have found it suitable for their particular circumstances, and it would be inaccurate to call polyandry unnatural, as early ethnographers sometimes did.

In addition to permitting women to marry multiple husbands, many of the polyandrous societies allow the husbands to marry additional wives under various circumstances, resulting in group marriage. As the two often go together, I will discuss them together as well.

For the sake of clarity, we need to distinguish between two types of group marriage. Typically, people think of group marriage as being a situation where a group of men are all married to the same group of women and vice versa. They all know each other and may share the same residence. I restrict the term *cenogamy* for this type of group marriage. Another type, *polygynandry,* is also likely to occur in polyandrous cultures. In this case, both men and women may have plural spouses, but the spouses are not the same people. The woman visits her various husbands and the man visits his wives, but each may not know the spouses of their partners.

Because there are not many recognized polyandrous societies, I will describe some of them and then attempt to explain the predisposing conditions for this particular marital structure.

The Toda

The Toda were a pastoral tribe living in small villages in South India. Western anthropologists began studying them in the late 1800s. They had a complex kinship system and cared for herds of sacred buffalo. Polyandry existed for centuries as the dominant marital type.

When a Toda woman married a man, she was automatically married to all of his brothers, even those who may not have been born yet. This is called *fraternal polyandry*, and like its counterpart sororal polygyny, there is very little evidence of jealousy. There was no concern about who the biological father was, but a social or legal father was chosen for each child. One brother, usually beginning with the eldest, would make a ceremonial bow and arrow and "give the bow" to his pregnant wife to achieve that status.

Female infanticide was practiced, as is true for many nonliterate societies. In the Toda case, of course, it reduced the number of potential wives so that polyandry could (or had to) occur. Unlike with the Baganda, twins were considered bad luck, and one was killed even if both were boys. Todas preferred to marry cross-cousins. In fact, if a Toda died unmarried, then he or she was ritually married to a cross-cousin so that there would be no singles in the Toda afterlife.

Todas maximized heterosexual outlets for males in various ways. Because Todas were often married as children, there were typically very few mature women available for marriage. An older man, perhaps widowed, who didn't have the time for a child bride to grow up could negotiate for an already married woman from her husbands. This wife transfer was effected by giving some buffalo, which increased the wealth of the original husbands. This in turn enhanced their competitiveness for a new and younger wife.

Another marital type was a system we might call *consort-mistress*. The Todas were divided into two endogamous groups, or moieties. One married within his or her own moiety but could enter into a legitimate sexual relationship with someone from the other group. Typically a man obtained permission, through payment, from the desired woman's husbands. A ceremony was held and visits were scheduled.

Although betrothals were often arranged during the infancy of those involved, a girl did not move into her husband's home until after puberty. Shortly before puberty, it is reported that a young man from any clan except the girl's clan would deflower the girl. Not to do so was considered disgraceful.

The Toda household revolved around care of the buffalo and dairying activities. Women had relatively little to do, because they were not allowed to engage in anything having to do with the sacred buffalo, including preparing food that included milk products. Wives could be divorced for being incompetent or lazy, but adultery was considered normal and not grounds for censure. If a wife were barren, then the husband would try to take on an additional wife.

Inheritance was patrilineal, with only males inheriting. Women owned very little—only a few personal possessions and their dowry. Although males were dominant in many ways, few societies give as much freedom and leisure to women as the Toda did (Queen et al., 1985).

Tibetans

Before the Chinese conquest of Tibet, anthropologists (Prince Peter, 1965) reported its inhabitants to be practicing a classical polyandry. The economy was agricultural, but land was scarce because of the high altitude. In addition, all the land was owned either by the church, the government, or the landed aristocracy. The peasants had to rent the land at a cost that often exceeded half of their income. There was little incentive to try to increase one's holdings, because surplus production usually went to rent and taxes.

Like the Todas, the Tibetans practiced fraternal polyandry and female infanticide. Still, there was often an excess of females because many men joined monastic groups. An unmarried female had the option of also joining a religious order, becoming a prostitute, or living in her brother's household. The Todas differ from the Tibetans in that the predisposing condition seems to be a lack of productive activities for women, such that each man doesn't need a spouse of his own. For the Tibetans, it is more a strategy to keep the birthrate down in a poor environment. The land cannot support many people, and if each generation of sons were to subdivide their inheritance, then the plots would become too small (Lee, 1982).

Other South Asian Groups

Other polyandrous groups for which we have data include the Nyinba of Nepal (Levine, 1980). As with their neighbors, polyandry is fraternal, though all other marital structure possibilities are present among the Nyinba. Polyandry once again appears to be a successful adaptation to a harsh environment and scarce resources, and a way to avoid subdividing land holdings. In case of infertility, men prefer to marry an additional wife who is a sister of the first.

Another Himalayan culture is the Pahari. They justify polyandry with a Hindu tradition of five deified brothers who shared a common wife. Once again, there is a narrow survival margin for population versus land. Monogamy and polygyny are also acceptable, depending on each family's financial condition (Berreman, 1980).

Sri Lanka is home to the ancient Kandyan culture (Kemper, 1980). Their Buddhist traditions deemphasize the ritual importance of marriage, so there is very little ceremony. This is especially true for cross-cousins, who are considered married from birth. Monogamy is the norm and has been the only legal option since 1859; however, cases of polyandry have been found even later than the 1950s. As with most of the cultures permitting polyandry, sexuality is rarely restricted and is not considered to be a defining characteristic of marriage.

When a man allows other husbands into his marriage, it is generally for economic reasons and is positively associated with sacrifice and solidarity. Polygyny, on the other hand, is far less respectable. Kandyans say that polyandry is to unify the family, meaning to concentrate male earning power. Women define their polyandrous marriages not in terms of shared sexuality, but of shared food. A husband is someone she cooks rice for, and although a man's extramarital affairs are tolerated, society would not accept his eating in public with a mistress. So it is economy rather than sexuality that defines marriage.

Finally, there are the Nayar, who were described in Chapter 4 of this volume. Even though Murdock (1967) saw them as an example of polyandry, they are clearly a case of polygynandrous group marriage and do not meet the general characteristics that are found in most polyandrous societies.

Rationale

What are those characteristics? First of all, polyandry as we have discussed it so far is generally fraternal. That is, brothers stay together on the family farm, and one wife moves in with them. Second, polyandry is a response to economic poverty, which demands that land not be divided and that the birthrate remain low. Third, female infanticide is often practiced. Fourth, the economy tends to be male oriented, with few productive tasks assigned to women, making them less necessary. Fifth, sexuality has few restraints and does not generate the jealousy found in romantic cultures. Finally, in most cases additional wives are also permitted, resulting in cenogamy. However, group marriage is not the goal, just an acceptable by-product of certain conditions, such as infertility or unexpected wealth.

Polyandrous groups in other parts of the world support many of these predisposing conditions to various degrees. The Marquesans (southern Polynesia) practiced fraternal polyandry and female infanticide, and well-to-do households might marry additional wives and become cenogamous. Jealousy was considered inappropriate, and family heads might arrange for additional husbands for an already married daughter because each male worker would add to the family wealth (Stephens, 1963).

The Kaingang were wandering hunters in the jungles of Brazil; in this culture about 14% of all marriages were polyandrous (Lee, 1982). Women were encouraged to attract additional lovers and husbands, because each man could help hunt and protect the group.

The Yanomama Shirishana people have been extensively studied by Peters (1982). In the 1950s polyandry was the dominant marital type for this small Amazonian tribe. Fraternal polyandry was common, but "associated polyandry," where the husbands are not brothers (as with the Kandyans) also occurred. Female infanticide was practiced but did not appear to be related to food shortages.

Marriages began monogamously, with a young adult male paying bride-price for an infant girl and consummating the marriage after puberty. After the couple had had a few children, another male would join the group, usually because he could find no mate of his own. He would be welcomed as another meat provider for the group.

Later, if the younger husband could obtain a wife of his own through capture in a raid, then he would leave the polyandrous arrangement. It was also common for a man to leave his wife when she reached menopause and move in with a younger bride. The first wife would then be cared for by her sons or sons-in-law. In the case of the Yanomama, economic considerations do not seem to have played a part. Instead, polyandry was a short-term adjustment to a sex ratio imbalance.

Nigerian Polygynandry

Many conclude (see Cassidy & Lee, 1989) that polyandry has been adequately understood. Essentially, it is a response to (a) extreme societal poverty, mandating a low birthrate; and (b) limited productive economic roles for women. However, more recently investigated cases in the Jos Plateau of Northern Nigeria point to greater complexity. One major contrast is that in South Asian cases the wife has a fixed residence, which she shares with her husbands, who tend to be close relatives. The polyandrous Nigerian tribes, however, have a system in which each husband (husbands tend not to be related) has his own separate residence, and the wife shifts from one to another (Sangree & Levine, 1980).

The Abisi

The Abisi number around 3,300 (Chalifoux, 1980) and are divided into six clans. A woman cannot have more than one husband per clan. Typically a young woman is married to three men on the same day, but she will live with them separately in a certain order. She begins with the "first marriage," which was arranged by her clan. After this betrothal, the girl is free to select her second husband, and this is called the "love marriage." She chooses from her various suitors, and this marriage is popular with the young people, but it doesn't have the same social status as the first marriage.

The third groom is selected by the parents, usually from the remaining suitors, and this is called the "home marriage," referring to the home of the girl whose family arranged it. (Parents also select the first marriage, but on a more formalized basis of clan exchanges.) Most men also enter into each of these three types of marriages, so marriage is polygynous for them while it is polyandrous for the women, resulting in polygynandry for the culture.

A woman usually stays with her first husband for a year (to leave earlier means a smaller dowry for her) at which time she must move in with her love marriage husband. At the end of the next year the third husband may claim his wife, but more than half of Abisi women refuse to go to their home husband. All of these men, even the rejected suitors, have paid a bride-price to the girl's family. This free labor is the economic incentive for parents to promote polyandry for their daughters.

Women may move back and forth between husbands as they desire, and they may also enter into a fourth marriage, called the "grass marriage." Typically, while gathering wood in the bush, the woman is enticed by an older man who is better established financially than her younger husbands and can therefore offer more economic security. Parents are informed of the liaison later, and the union is validated by payment of a goat and two hoes.

The Abisi system is one of polygynandrous group marriages, in that the plural marriages of each sex are separate. The focus is on polyandry for the women, with polygyny as a natural by-product. Although there are economic considerations, first marriages have important lineage and political significance. The system also seems to be designed for dealing with the legitimization of sexual attraction to more than one person and could be seen as healthier than the monogamy-with-adultery pattern common in modern Western society. It also avoids the psychological tension one might expect to find at a higher level in cenogamous households, where all of the marital participants share the same residence.

The Irigwe

Another Nigerian society is the Irigwe (Sangree, 1980), for whom divorce did not even exist until 1968. Parents arrange first marriages while the individuals are still small children. The prospective groom's family performs substantial farm labor for several years before the marriage is consummated. Parents will do this in spite of the fact that in most "primary marriages," couples rarely stay together for more than a few weeks. The main incentive for the boy's family is that the work shows the community that this family's sons and daughters are good candidates for "secondary marriages."

Secondary marriages are initiated by the couple themselves and involve a much smaller bride-price. A daughter is encouraged by her parents to enter into several secondary marriages during the teen years. She is obligated to spend only a few nights with each husband, and the parents benefit from the flow of bride gifts.

A woman remains married to all of her husbands throughout her life, but there is a culturally determined system for residence. Once she becomes pregnant for the first time, she will stay with that husband, who is designated the legal father. Subsequent shifts from one husband to another are determined by health crises with the children. A diviner often ascertains that the particular illness is rooted in the child's poor "soul state," which can be improved only by a change of residence.

Competition for secondary wives fosters hostility between tribal sections, but it also controls the hostility. That is, Irigwe men are suspicious of men from other sections who might want to take their wives in secondary marriage, which can lead to fights among the competing males. However, once a man's wife has cohabited with another man, that man must be treated with caution and respect because of the Irigwe belief that a cohusband can cause the first husband's death, if he is ill or injured, merely by the new husband's presence. As a result, men sharing the same wife tend to be polite to each other and to avoid one another when possible.

The Irigwe, then, have a system different in approach but similar in result to that of the Abisi. Both societies are polygynandrous, with men paying for wives who will control the living arrangements. The traditional exchange of economic security for sex and children seems evident, with variety substituted for stability.

The Birom

The Birom (Smedley, 1980) have a practice called *cicisbeism,* which is not quite polyandry, because the multiple unions do not result in legal status. This term refers to a situation in which a married woman is permitted socially approved sexual relations with men not defined as a legal husband. A woman retains her full status with her "real" husband throughout her life. Prior to colonialism, this custom was widespread and overt and was considered a necessary part of the social system.

The key aspects of this system are as follows. The right of sexual access to another man's wife is obtained by the payment of a fee, usually a goat, to the woman's husband. A woman chooses her own cicisbeo, or lover, and is expected to have some. The woman does not leave her husband but receives her lovers in her own home. Any children she may have from these men belong to her husband, the one person to have paid a bride-price for her.

The advantages for Birom women include expanded economic support and sexual variety, but what benefits do the men derive? For one thing, of course, they are the cicisbeos to other men's wives, thereby maximizing sexual variety for everyone in a legitimate context, and minimizing (by sharing with others) economic and other marital obligations. More important, however, is that the practice provides an alliance system for men called *njem.* To become a leader in the community, a man needs a group of followers, and these are the lovers of a man's wife and the husbands of his own mistresses. Men gain wealth and power through cicisbeism, but it is the women who determine who the leaders will actually be, because they are the ones who choose the njem partners.

Also, the women receive material support for themselves and their children every year from their cicisbeos, which they do not have to share with their husbands. This annual support provides them with economic security. The men gain politically, but they have been more willing in recent years to do away with the njem than have the women.

Summary

The previously mentioned and other polyandrous African societies exhibit complicated systems of spouse circulation (Muller, 1980), which is very different from "classic" south Asian polyandry. For multiple-husband cultures in Asia, the explanation is chiefly economic: a poverty and land scarcity that force brothers to share a wife. It serves to intensify affinal relationships. The Nigerian version, in contrast, serves to increase the extent and variety of affinal ties (Levine & Sangree, 1980). Husbands are not brothers, and coresidence does not occur. The land is not as poor, so economics is an issue of lesser importance. Polygyny always occurs along with the polyandry, and the status of women seems to be higher. As with the Asians, sex is "looser" than in monogamous societies, but it is more central to the meaning of marriage.

Prince Peter (1980) disagrees that polyandry, or any marital structure, can be purely the result of economic, kinship, social necessity, or other rational cultural factors:

> But do human creatures act rationally in response to so deep an emotion as the passionate, sexual instinct of reproduction? Are they sufficiently aware of their unconscious urges and drives, not to speak of complexes carried over from childhood and securely entrenched by infantile amnesia, to be able to do so? Is there not a predominant psychodynamic correlate of polyandry, which is being neglected here, as an intermediary between ecological and sociological reasons for the custom and its actual institution? Personally, I think so, and feel that this factor is sadly left out by those investigating polyandry. (p. 374)

Prince Peter goes on to suggest homosexual tendencies and the Oedipus complex as the psychodynamic correlate, in spite of researchers' inability to empirically connect these Freudian concepts with family structure. However, his general point is well taken, in that there probably is more to marriage than just culture and economy. The relevance of sexual and psychological intimacy and other microsocial and clinical concepts in the understanding of marital structure seems warranted.

CENOGAMY

The fourth and final type of marital structure is cenogamy. This is group marriage where the husbands and wives share the same spouses. Although we find the practice of group marriage in polyandrous societies, Murdock (1967) found no cases of a society that had group marriage as its dominant or preferred structure.

Stephens (1963) mentions two groups that he considered marginal. The Siriono of Bolivia are technically monogamous, but spouses are permitted to engage in sexual intercourse with the wife's sisters or the husband's brothers, real and classificatory. Unlike the Birom, however, there appears to be no economic or political component to this system.

The other case that looks like cenogamy but that most writers have concluded is another example of sexual hospitality, are the Reindeer Chukchee. Stephens (1963) quotes the ethnographer Bogoras, who wrote about them in 1909:

> The Chukchee group marriage includes sometimes up to ten married couples. The men belonging to such a marriage-union are called companions in wives. . . . Each companion has a right to all the wives of his companions, but takes advantage of his right comparatively seldom, namely, when he visits for some reason the camp of one of the companions. Then the host cedes him his place in the sleeping-room. . . . The union, in group marriages, is mostly formed between persons who are well acquainted

> . . . especially between neighbors and relatives. Second and third cousins are almost invariably united by ties of group-marriage; brothers, however, do not enter into such unions. The inmates of one and the same camp are seldom willing to enter into a group-marriage, the reason obviously being that the reciprocal use of wives, which in group-marriage is practiced very seldom, is liable to degenerate into complete promiscuity if the members of the group live too close together. . . . Not to be connected with such a union, means to have no friends and good-wishers, and no protectors in case of need. (quoted in Stephens, pp. 47–49)

It may be that the purpose of Chukchee cenogamy is the same as it is for Nigerian polygynandry. That is, men trade their wives' sexuality for a male network that exists for their political or economic benefit. There is, however, one clear case of true cenogamy as the dominant marital structure in a society. Because it was based on religious ideology, the Oneidans will be discussed in Chapter 7 of this volume.

CONCLUSION

Stephens (1963) suggests that monogamy as a cultural preference gained preeminence in modern societies because the early Catholic fathers outlawed polygyny. Their general repugnance for sexual pleasure resulted in an ideologically based marital structure now considered normal. Monogamy's foundation is stronger than that, of course. One spouse at a time best fits the even sex ratio and the economic structure of the non–family-based, consumer-oriented society in which most of us presently live. It also provides for the deeper psychological intimacy now widely valued in marriage and implies greater equality between the sexes than do some of the plural marriage forms.

Polygamy in its various forms, however, has been a successful strategy in many societies for dealing with the complexities of human civilization and intimacy. Each culture must find a balance in handling the issues of economy, status, sexual exclusivity and variety, chastity, parental power, paternity, kin networks, politics, jealousy, religion, and related concerns. Depending on the relative importance of these considerations, men and women have been very creative in dealing with marital structure. The Abisi, for instance, settled on four different marriages for each person, so as to meet the needs of kin organization (first marriage), romance (love marriage), parental authority (home marriage), and economic security (grass marriage). In contrast, modern Western culture generally ignores the first and third considerations and tries to combine the fourth (economics) with the highly valued second (romance).

Marital structure continues to make adjustments to modern realities. In South Africa, a large percentage of the black males are separated from their families to work in the mines. The women and children manage the family farms at a subsistence level. These realities have led to later ages of marriage and more premarital sexual involvement. There are high rates of spouses living with other companions while separated or preferring cohabitation over marriage (Modo, 2001). Fewer than half of black families in the United States consist of married couples. Much of this is due to a shortage of black males in the marriage market because of incarceration and poor income-earning opportunities. Miller and Browning (2000) conclude that many adult women are willing to "share a man" rather than have no husband figure at all. If so, then this would be an informal polygyny.

In marital structure, then, we find a fascinating variety. The various approaches reflect our attempts to deal with the complexities of human intimacy, with all its beauty and pain, joy and confusion.

REFERENCES

Berreman, G. (1980). Polyandry: Exotic custom vs. analytical concept. *Journal of Comparative Family Studies, 11,* 377–384.

Cassidy, M., & Lee, G. (1989). The study of polyandry: A critique and synthesis. *Journal of Comparative Family Studies, 20,* 1–12.

Chalifoux, J. (1980). Secondary marriage and levels of seniority among the Abisi (piti), Nigeria. *Journal of Comparative Family Studies, 11,* 325–344.

Devore, I. (1979, November). *Sociobiology.* Paper presented at the National Council on Family Relations, Boston, MA.

Ember, M. (1974). Warfare, sex ratio, and polygyny. *Ethnology, 13,* 197–206.

Fielding, W. (1942). *Strange customs of courtship and marriage.* New York: Garden City Pub.

Goody, J. (1973). Polygyny, economy and the role of women. In J. Goody (Ed.), *The character of kinship* (pp. 175–190). London: Cambridge University Press.

Goody, J. (1976). *Production and reproduction: A comparative study of the domestic domain.* London: Cambridge University Press.

Kemper, S. (1980). Polygamy and monogamy in Kandyan Sri Lanka. *Journal of Comparative Family Studies, 11,* 299–324.

Lee, G. (1982). *Family structure and interaction: A comparative analysis.* Minneapolis: University of Minnesota Press.

Lee, G., & Whitbeck, L. (1990). Economic systems and rates of polygyny. *Journal of Comparative Family Studies, 21,* 13–24.

Levine, N. (1980). Nyinba polyandry and the allocation of paternity. *Journal of Comparative Family Studies, 11,* 283–298.

Levine, N., & Sangree, W. (1980). Conclusion: Asian and African systems of polyandry. *Journal of Comparative Family Studies, 11,* 385–410.

Miller, R., & Browning, S. (2000). Sharing a man: Insights from research. *Journal of Comparative Family Studies, 31,* 339–346.

Modo, I. (2001). Migrant culture and changing face of family structure in Lesotho. *Journal of Comparative Family Studies, 32,* 443–452.

Muller, J. (1980). On the relevance of having two husbands: Contribution to the study of polygynous/polyandrous marital forms of the Jos plateau. *Journal of Comparative Family Studies, 11,* 359–370.

Murdock, G. (1957). World ethnographic sample. *American Anthropologist, 59,* 664–687.

Murdock, G. (1967). Ethnographic atlas: A summary. *Ethology, 6,* 109–236.

Oliver, D. (1955). *A Solomon island society.* Cambridge, MA: Harvard University Press.

Peter, Prince of Greece and Denmark. (1965). The Tibetan family system. In M. Nimkoff (Ed.), *Comparative family systems* (pp. 192–208). Boston: Houghton Mifflin.

Peter, Prince of Greece and Denmark. (1980). Comments on the social and cultural implications of variant systems of polyandrous alliances. *Journal of Comparative Family Studies, 11,* 371–376.

Peters, J. (1982). Polyandry among the Yanomama Shirishana revisited. *Journal of Comparative Family Studies, 13,* 89–96.

Queen, S., Habenstein, R., & Quadagno, J. (1985). *The family in various cultures.* New York: Harper & Row.

Sangree, W. (1980). The persistence of polyandry in Irigwe, Nigeria. *Journal of Comparative Family Studies, 11,* 335–344.

Sangree, W., & Levine, N. (1980). Introduction. *Journal of Comparative Family Studies, 11*(3), i–iv.

Smedley, A. (1980). The implications of Birom cicisbeism. *Journal of Comparative Family Studies, 11,* 345–358.

Stephens, W. (1963). *The family in cross-cultural perspective.* New York: Holt, Rinehart & Winston.

Verdon, M. (1983). Polygyny, descent, and local fission: A comparative hypothesis. *Journal of Comparative Family Studies, 14,* 1–22.

Ware, H. (1979). Polygyny: Women's views in a transitional society, Nigeria 1975. *Journal of Marriage and the Family, 41,* 185–195.

Whiting, J. (1964). Effects of climate on certain cultural practices. In W. Goodenough (Ed.), *Psychological anthropology* (pp. 511–544). Homewood, IL: Dorsey Press.

CHAPTER 7

Religious Utopias and Family Structure

BRON B. INGOLDSBY

In general, social scientists attribute variation in marriage and family structure to economic conditions and pressures. Although there is little doubt that family life has had its focus around survival, there are other forces at work as well. In this chapter I examine the influence of religious belief and practice on the family. We will focus on four Christian groups that came to or had their origin in the United States. Each group practiced communalism and was led by a young, charismatic leader.

We learn that faith can have a major impact on lifestyle, even when it is strongly opposed by the majority in society. We also see the difficulty in creating a long-term alternative to the traditional family. The Shakers, with their opposition to marriage and reproduction, and the Oneidans, who favored group marriage, lasted only a few generations. The Mormons have continued to flourish, but only after giving up polygyny. The Hutterites are monogamous but consider the community to be more important than the family. They have endured with little change until very recently.

SHAKER CELIBACY

Ann Lee was born in Manchester, England, in 1736. She grew up poor and uneducated. At the age of 22 she joined a small religious group led by James and Jane Wardley. The Wardleys had left the Society of Friends and promoted un–Quaker-like religious services that included considerable singing, shaking, and other noisy behaviors. They became known as the "Shaking Quakers" and eventually just as Shakers (unless otherwise indicated, information for this section comes from Foster, 1991, and Kephart, 1982).

Ann married Abraham Stanley in 1762, and over the course of time endured four very difficult pregnancies. All four of their children died in infancy. Ann came to see childbirth as a godly punishment for giving in to sexual desire. Her fear of the pains related to fertility led her to regard her own marriage bed "as if it had been made of embers."

Ann began to preach against all carnal behaviors, and townspeople reacted with claims of blasphemy and mob attacks against her and the small group that she was beginning to influence. In 1770, she was imprisoned for disturbing the peace, in connection with the Pentecostal services of the Shakers. During her 2 weeks there, she experienced an "open vision" in which she saw Adam and Eve engaging in intercourse. She became certain that this was the transgression that resulted in the Fall from the Garden of Eden. Shortly thereafter, Jesus Christ himself appeared to her and confirmed that it was her mission to share this message with the world.

The Wardleys believed that Christ's second coming was imminent, as did many Christian sects, but they believed that he would come in the form of a woman. Ann's experiences convinced the Wardleys that she was that woman, and she quickly became the spiritual leader of the group. Shortly after her prison experience, Mother Ann Lee (as she became known by her followers) felt directed to take her group to America, where it would be more successful. The official name of the religion was the United Society of Believers in Christ's Second Appearing, and they referred to themselves simply as "Believers."

In 1774, Ann Lee and eight followers, which included her husband but not the Wardleys, sailed to New York. In the first 5 years they gained only one convert, but that number was cancelled out because Ann's husband gave up after years of celibacy and left the group. However, their patience paid off with the conversion of Joseph Meachem, an influential Baptist minister, who would take over the leadership of the group when Ann Lee died in 1784 at the age of 48. Following his death in 1796, Lucy Wright, whom he had selected as the female leader, continued to guide the Shakers for another 25 years.

Membership increased to an all-time high of about 17,000 (though it may have been considerably higher than that) at about the time of the Civil War. Shakers lived in 19 societies scattered over eight states. The head community was in New Lebanon, New York. Each community had a membership that varied from about 100 to 4,000. Within each community, the members were divided into "families" of about 100 persons. Each family was headed by two elders and two elderesses, who were accountable only to their counterparts in New Lebanon.

Living in a Shaker society meant obeying strict rules concerning confession of sins, rejection of marriage in favor of celibacy, manual labor (Ann Lee said to "put your hands to work, and your hearts to God"), and communal living instead of private property. Those who were attracted to this lifestyle included some who were unhappy in their marriages, older individuals, women (twice the number of men), and those whose personality types made them comfortable with the emphasis on humility and obedience. Economically, it was ideal for those who were not comfortable with the rigors of capitalism, and it was a haven for the widowed and others who were disadvantaged. The security of group living with like-minded people in an orderly (except for the frenzied dancing of the Sunday services) society would be attractive to many.

Everyone worked and learned a trade, and the Shakers became known for their straightforward, high-quality products. Their furniture is still appreciated as a distinctive art form, even though the religion itself has had very little impact on the greater society. Members were never paid for their work, and inventions were shared rather than patented. Inventions credited to the Believers include the circular saw, brimstone match, clothespin, flat broom, and many machines for household and other work.

Recognizing that "the joys of celibacy" were sometimes difficult, the sexes were separated in Shaker societies. Men and women slept and worked in different rooms, and hallways were made wide enough so that one person could pass another without touching. All work was considered equal, but this separation mandated a division of labor that was very traditional. Each man was assigned a woman to look after his clothing and related needs in exchange for performing some heavy menial tasks, but sisters had to be careful so that "mending or setting buttons on the brethren's clothes while they have them on" did not occur.

Men, women, and children were all served separately in the dining halls, with pork forbidden and other meats eaten sparingly. Perhaps in reversion to one Quaker custom, conversation was forbidden during mealtimes. Women wore formless attire so as not to arouse physical feelings in the men, and pets were not allowed, because they might engender maternal feelings in girls. Members interacted with the outside world only during trips to other Shaker communities.

The Shakers had a saying: "There is not dirt in heaven." Cleanliness and order were important values. They indulged in very little ornamentation. They also abstained from involvement in public life by not voting or serving in the military. In their religious services they acted out "gathering in the good" and "shaking out the evil." They were also spiritualists, in the sense of believing they could communicate with the dead. Mother Ann and American Indians were the most common manifestations.

No children were ever born into Shaker communities, so they expanded by adult conversions and by adopting orphans. The large majority of these youth, however, left the church when they reached adulthood. It is one thing to choose this lifestyle, but most individuals found a life without love, sex, or intellectual pursuits undesirable. Children with natural family ties (whose parents joined the movement) were more likely to continue as Shakers as adults than were those children who had been adopted by the society (Cosgel, 2000). Eventually, the Shakers gave up on bringing in children, and this spelled the eventual end for the movement. Because they believed that the millennium was at hand, it was not a concern that the human population would die out if everyone were to follow their celibate example.

Membership began to decline after the Civil War. The Shaker handicraft economy could not compete with the factory assembly lines of the industrial revolution, and avoiding the greater society became more difficult with the advent of the railroad. Increased government involvement in welfare programs and a healthier national attitude about sexuality after the Victorian era also undermined key components of Shaker society. By 1925, most of the Shaker villages were gone, and only a few Believers were left. Nevertheless, except for the Hutterites, it was the largest and longest-lasting communal experiment that we have seen in America.

ONEIDAN CENOGAMY

John Humphrey Noyes, born in 1811, was an apprentice lawyer turned minister by a religious revival that occurred in Vermont in 1831. Two years later, he graduated from Yale Theological Seminary, but he soon developed radical ideas that took him out of the Protestant mainstream. He proposed a "Perfectionist" doctrine, which stated that Christ had already returned to earth in AD 70 and that redemption from sin was therefore an already accomplished fact. By 1839, Noyes was the leader of a small Bible study group, and in 1846 he founded what was called the Putney (after his hometown, where they had gathered) Community. The group's discussions focused on spiritual, economic, and sexual equality. Noyes's radical ideas and practices outraged many in the area, so in 1848, Noyes moved his flock (which would eventually reach about 300 members) to former Indian lands along Oneida Creek in central New York State (unless otherwise indicated, the material for this section comes from Foster, 1991, and Kephart, 1982).

What became known as the Oneida Community grew and in many ways flourished over the next few decades. In 1862, the Oneidans completed the Mansion House, a spacious brick building that still stands, in which most of the members lived (another branch of Perfectionists lived in Connecticut). Each adult had his or her own bedroom, but all other living spaces were designed to promote togetherness and group interaction. The Oneidans practiced economic communism in that there was no private ownership of property. Holding "all things in common" was designed to help the members overcome selfishness.

To avoid problems of discrimination, community jobs were rotated every year. The community functioned much like an Israeli kibbutz and was quite successful. Their economic base was originally the sale of excellent steel traps developed by a member, but in 1877 the Oneidans began manufacturing silverware—an enterprise that continued after the demise of the religious group.

A second pillar of the society was what came to be called *mutual criticism.* Even though the goal was perfection, it was recognized that individual behavior problems could occur. Major infractions were rare, and there were no law enforcement officers. Instead, whenever someone deviated from the group norms or manifested a significant personality weakness, a committee of trusted peers was called in. The subject sat quietly while each member of the group voiced his or her criticisms!

Apparently, the Oneidans had considerable trust in and affection for each other, because the method was generally successful, such that the recipients of mutual criticism indicated gratitude and felt uplifted by the experience. Many would in fact request a criticism when they felt they needed it. The practice was even extended into the sphere of physical illnesses (called in this context *krinopathy*), where it was considered effective in energizing one's immune system to throw off a disease.

The most dramatic aspect of the society, however, was its practice of cenogamy, or group marriage. Noyes considered monogamy to be selfish love and developed the idea of *complex marriage,* which the Oneidans all apparently practiced. He felt that it was natural for all men to love all women and vice versa, and therefore each adult in the community was considered married to all the adults of the opposite sex.

After nearly a decade of contemplation, Noyes put the idea into practice in Putney. A driving force may have been his attraction to Mary Cragin, who along with her husband George was one of the 40 or so faithful original members of the group. Noyes was very distraught when she died in 1851 in a boating accident, and he often presented her as the personification of spirituality.

The community was managed by committees, and the feelings of women were considered in the practice of complex marriage. If a man desired sexual relations with a particular woman, he would submit a request to the Central Committee. A female go-between would deliver the message so that a woman could without embarrassment turn down a proposal that did not appeal to her. Noyes did not believe that sex was the duty of women for the pleasure of men; in fact, women had considerably more responsibility, freedom, and respect than were found in the larger culture at the time.

Noyes had two programs related to children that were important to the Perfectionist doctrine. First, he felt that scientific principles used in the breeding of superior animals could also be successful with humans. Second, for the first 20 years of the community, he had the Oneidans refrain from bearing children so that they could become economically stabilized. An additional benefit was that it allowed the sexes to be amative without having to worry about pregnancy. Noyes had originally instituted a ban on fertility in Putney in order to spare his legal wife, Harriet, who had experienced five difficult childbirths in the first 6 years of their marriage, and four of the children had died. Birth control would spare her such future agonies.

For birth control, Noyes advocated *coitus reservatus,* which is sexual intercourse without male ejaculation. Common medical opinion of the time indicated that frequent ejaculation was not good for men, but developing such control is difficult. Older women in the community benefited, because Noyes mandated that until a man could learn this coital control, sexual relations had to be limited to women past menopause. The method's success is manifested by the fact that only 12 unplanned births occurred during this time period.

In support of the practicality of this approach, Noyes compared the learning of self-control to boating on a river (Noyes, 1872):

> The situation may be compared to a stream in the three conditions of a fall, a course of rapids above the fall, and still water above the rapids. The skillful boatman may choose whether he will remain in the still water, or venture more or less down the rapids, or run his boat over the fall. But there is a point on the verge of the fall where he has no control over his course; and just above that there is a point where he will have to struggle with the current in a way which will give his nerves a severe trial, even though he may escape the fall. If he is willing to learn, experience will teach him the wisdom of confining his excursions to the region of easy rowing, unless he has an object in view that is worth the cost of going over the falls. (p. 8)

In 1869, the group began a eugenics (called "stirpiculture" by Noyes) program. Couples wanting to become parents had to make a formal application to the appropriate committee, which decided if the couple had the superior physical and mental traits desired. The program was in effect for the last decade of the group's existence, and 58 children were born during that time. Reports indicate that as a group, these children were very healthy and well adjusted.

Outside pressure against this radical reformulation of family life and structure led to public campaigns against what was labeled "free love" and "animal breeding." Probably to escape charges of statutory rape (Noyes had fathered about a dozen children, some apparently with women who were legal minors), Noyes fled to Canada in 1879, and the community disbanded shortly thereafter (Kephart & Jedlicka, 1991). There was also internal dissension, because many in the younger generation had not experienced the beginnings and resented some of the sexual and other rules, which were designed to benefit the aging leadership.

A fascinating account of life in the Oneida Community is found in the diary of Tirzah Miller (Fogarty, 2000). Tirzah was a niece and longtime lover of Noyes, and she also revered him as her spiritual leader. Her entries detail the problems of "special love" with one man and the demands to treat everyone in the community equally. In the end, she has children with more than one man, and when the group disbands, she follows Noyes to Niagara Falls rather than marrying her beloved Edward. Through her eyes, we see the aging Noyes as he increases his micromanagement of the lives of the members and contemplates ever more radical sexual practices, such as having a child with his own sister or daughter.

As is true with most modern communal groups, the Oneidans did not survive the loss of their charismatic leader. They wisely chose to disband on their own terms, rather than be forced to by internal and external pressures. Nevertheless, a truly cenogamous culture did thrive for an entire generation. This indicates that group marriage is possible. Moreover, once again, the causes have little to do with economics or other traditional explanations, and everything to do with religious belief.

MORMON POLYGYNY

One reason for polygyny that has received little attention is religion. Modern Christianity has been strongly promonogamy and has ignored the institutionalization of polygyny among the Old Testament Hebrews. One exception has been the Church of Jesus Christ of Latter-day Saints (LDS), commonly known as the Mormons. The LDS church is one of the largest and fastest-growing denominations in the United States today, and its members practiced polygyny on a fairly large scale during its early history. It has received little attention from family sociologists, however, and much of what has been reported in the past has been biased.

Mormon prophet Joseph Smith founded the LDS church in New York State in 1830. He later stated that he had received a revelation from God indicating that as part of the restoration of ancient Christian practices, the Saints (as church members call themselves) should return to the practice of plural marriage. This was part of a wider vision of "celestial marriage," which is the name for the LDS belief that marriage can be eternal, that is, that it continues in the afterlife (Church of Jesus Christ of Latter-day Saints, 1981, section 132).

Wyatt (1989) makes it clear that this practice did not begin for the traditional sexual or economic reasons. First, early Mormons came from puritan New England and found polygyny personally distasteful; second, they correctly predicted the persecution that would come to them because of it; and finally, it was older men who had the plural wives, just as in other cultures, and not the younger ones at their sexual peak.

In addition, there is no evidence that there was an excess of Mormon women who needed husbands, or that there were any economic benefits to plural marriage. Most plural wives had to support themselves and lived at a subsistence level. In short, Mormons practiced polygyny for the ideological reason that they believed God required it of them. The Prophet Joseph, as he was generally referred to by his followers, was a powerful religious leader, and a large number of the individuals who believed in him claimed to have had their own confirming spiritual experiences convincing them that the practice of polygyny was from God (Newell & Avery, 1984).

Smith carefully introduced the practice to trusted associates in the early 1840s, after the church had moved its headquarters to Nauvoo, Illinois. There was much secrecy involved, because polygyny was illegal and attracted much persecution from nonmembers. Moreover, many of the church members themselves had difficulty accepting the doctrine. Smith married about 33 women in the last few years of his life, which caused considerable stress in his relationship with his first wife, Emma Hale. It resulted in the defection of a number of key church leaders and played a major role in the dynamics that led to the arrest and mob killing of the Mormon prophet (Newell & Avery, 1984).

After Smith's murder by an anti-Mormon mob in 1844, the church was led to the Salt Lake valley in present-day Utah by their new prophet, Brigham Young. Emma, who had remained faithful to her husband/prophet and his religion until his death, stayed behind in Nauvoo and eventually supported their son, Joseph Smith III, in leading a reorganized version of the church, which was founded on monogamy. In 1852, the Utah church publicly admitted to the practice of polygyny and in the following decades suffered ever-greater federal prosecution and persecution. Finally, in order to avoid imprisonment, disenfranchisement, and the seizure of property and other financial assets, Church President Wilford Woodruff declared an end to the practice of plural marriage in 1890. Some church members were unwilling to give up the practice, which resulted in splinter groups that still exist today (Van Wagoner, 1989).

Although Wyatt (1989) claims that it was the lack of an economic basis that doomed Mormon polygyny in the long run, he offers no evidence for this. However, economics did play a role in the dynamics of plural marriage. Plural wives tended to be young women who were economically disadvantaged, often immigrants arriving in Utah from Europe. The men who married them were wealthier than the average frontiersman and thus could afford to take on a larger family (Daynes, 2001). When the practice of "the principle," as the Mormons called it, was given up, it was because the church president declared that it was now God's will for them to submit to secular authority.

In the American case, polygyny was purely ideological. It was embedded in an antipolygamy culture and lacked an economic rationale. In spite of this, polygyny persisted for more than 50 years, and there are still some splinter groups from the LDS church that practice plural marriage in the American West.

Early Mormons believed that having many wives and children were signs of God's favor and a requirement for His blessings. Having large families is still an expectation for devout Mormons, and it is clear that the key philosophical reason for Mormon polygyny was to bring children into the true religion. Although the husband was, of course, older with each plural wife he married, the average age for each wife was always 19, and a man tended to remarry when his current wife passed the child-bearing years. First wives averaged eight children, whereas subsequent wives averaged six. However, about 60% of the men who participated in polygyny married only one plural wife (Embry, 1987).

Life "in the principle" was difficult. Husbands were often absent, on church missions or avoiding federal marshals, and the wives worked at home or on their farm with their children. The divorce rate was higher for polygynous marriages than it was for the monogamous ones, and from a generation or so after the formal ending of polygyny, church members were content to be in the cultural mainstream in U.S. society with monogamous marriages. In fact, today, the church is noted for its conservative family values. Its marriage and fertility rates are higher than the national average, and traditional sex role behaviors are promoted within the context of heterosexual monogamous marriage (Ingoldsby, 1989).

HUTTERITE MONOGAMY

The Hutterites are an Anabaptist group, along with the Amish and the Mennonites, which was founded by Jacob Hutter in central Europe in the middle 1500s. The official name of the religion is the Hutterian Brethren. Today, they total about 45,000 members living in over 400 colonies. They are the oldest family communal group in the Western world, but the community is considered to be more important than the family. They believe that salvation is found in total submission to the group, which is more important than the individual. One of their original basic tenets was that believing Hutterites must separate from nonbelieving spouses (Huntington, 1997).

Continually persecuted, many moved to Russia in 1770, where they were promised toleration for their beliefs and practices. This lasted about 100 years before the czars forced them into the national schools and the military. Between 1874 and 1877, all 800 surviving Hutterites immigrated to the

United States. About half were not practicing communal living and eventually joined the Mennonites. The others settled in South Dakota into three colonies, each with a different leader. Even to the present day, each of these groups, or *Leut,* maintains its own council of elders, has minor custom differences, and seldom intermarries, even though relations are friendly across groups. From most to least conservative in their practices, they are called the *Lehrerleut,* the *Dariusleut,* and the *Schmiedeleut.*

World War I brought persecution from the U.S. government, because the Hutterites refused military service, so as a group they made arrangements with the Canadian government, which granted them immunity from the draft. As a result, almost all of them moved to western Canada. Since that time, many have moved back to the United States, and there are colonies along the northern tier states from Washington to Minnesota.

Originally craftsmen, they turned to agriculture when the industrial revolution made their skills obsolete (Peter, 1971). The Hutterites live together in communities and speak a German dialect as well as English. Unlike the Amish, they do accept and use modern devices such as automotive equipment and electricity. Each community, or *Bruderhof* (which is a colony within a Leut), is administered by a council of six men, usually elected for life. The spiritual leader is the preacher. There is also a business manager, a farm boss, and a German teacher (Kephart, 1982).

Kinship Structure

All Hutterites are descended from 18 families. Four names have since died out, so there are only 14 Hutterite surnames. Society is patriarchal and kinship is patrilineal and patrilocal, so men have lifelong association in the same community, whereas women usually leave their colony of birth at marriage. They have maintained the extended family, with three or four generations in the same community but not necessarily under the same roof.

They believe in a hierarchy of relationships that is ordained by God. Men have higher status than women, and the elderly deserve the respect of the young. The sex and age ranking is seen in all settings, be it church, school, work, or meals. Males sit on one side of the room and females on the other, with the oldest in the back. After church services, for instance, the males file out first, with the oldest woman following the youngest boy (Hofer, 1991, 1998).

Because of the high intermarriage that occurs, a colony might have only one or two family names but consist of 8 to 14 extended families all related to each other to some degree. Other colonies may have as many as seven family names. The three Leut have been endogamous since 1879. However, within these groups an incest taboo is maintained that includes up to first cousins on both sides (Peter, 1971).

The House Child

The sequence and details of child care were originally described by Hutterite leader Peter Riedemann in 1545, and these ideas are still basically followed. As a result, much of their childrearing practice has not been altered as it has in the greater society by Freudian and other ideas that have come along since the 1600s (Huntington, 1997). However, since about 1980, some modernizing influences have been noted. Parents now toilet train their children at about age 2 rather than at 3 months; and nursing may go all the way to the second birthday, but solid foods are introduced somewhere between 6 and 12 months (Ingoldsby, 2001), whereas it used to be as early as 1 month after birth (Hostetler, 1974).

When the child is an infant, it is common for the mother's female relatives to visit her and care for the demanding needs of both the new mother and the infant. The mother is allowed time off from her regular duties to attend to the needs of her newborn infant and to recover from the pregnancy.

The late infancy stage is a time for the house child to venture beyond the mother to a greater range of peers and associations within the colony. When the child gets a little older, the mother is reassigned back to her original job, so the rest of the community helps to raise the child. In effect, the colony becomes a large extended family tending to the needs and welfare of the young Hutterite (Stanton, 1989).

In the early years of the group, the Hutterites believed that "as soon as the mother hath weaned the child she giveth it to the school." Today the nuclear family is not so limited in its functions, but the schools do play a large part in the lives of Hutterite youth (Hostetler, 1974).

Kindergarten

Children stay with their families until they are 3, at which time they go to the community kindergarten, which usually lasts from 7 or 8 in the morning to 4 in the afternoon. Throughout their six-day-a-week program, the children are separated from the rest of the colony, including parents and siblings, from early in the morning to mid- or late afternoon. The children sing together, memorize together, eat together, and even take their midmorning and midafternoon naps together.

Young children are considered to be willful, and strict punishment, including strapping, is used. They are expected to learn to obey, pray, share, and sit properly. In the area of toys, one can see the differences between the Leuts. For the most conservative Lehrerleut, none are permitted. The Dariusleut will tolerate small toys brought from home, and the Schmiedeleut provide them in the school (Hostetler, 1974).

However, many Dariusleut colonies have stopped running kindergartens. Although it has been a cornerstone of putting the community over the family in child rearing throughout most of Hutterite history, they are just not getting around to organizing them now. This means, of course, that small children are now spending those years with their families (Ingoldsby, 2001).

Just as there is a wide variety of parenting styles in the greater society, so is there among the Hutterites. Most are loving parents, and the use of corporal punishment has declined in the last generation. Feeling that the colony is a safe place, many families supervise their young children less than many outsiders consider safe (Ingoldsby & Smith, 2005).

School

Next there is a 10-year period, from ages 6 to 16, which is a time of intensive preparation for the young Hutterite to prepare to fully embrace the Hutterian way of living. A large part of this period is spent in the big school. The local school board instructor teaches from the normal provincial curriculum, and the German teacher provides the moral and religious instruction. The instruction takes place in a one-room classroom with children from the 1st to the 10th grades in attendance.

The English school is staffed by a teacher provided by the government who teaches at the colony. Before and after those classes, the Hutterites run their own classes, which teach German and the Hutterian way of life. This way government demands are met and the children get a minimal education for interacting in the larger world, but they are not corrupted from their way of life (Kephart, 1982).

The schooling system successfully separates Hutterite children from the outside world. Having close, primary, intimate, concrete relations with the colony and only a secondary, generalized relationship with the outside world, Hutterites find it hard to interact with and relate to the outside world, so defection is rare (Peter, 1971). The public school teachers are discouraged by Hutterite leaders from using very much modern technology in the classroom or from dealing with sensitive topics such as sex and evolution. Because critical thinking is limited, so may be the intellectual development of many Hutterite youth (Smith & Ingoldsby, 2005).

Adolescence

Adolescence is from 15 to baptism (which is around age 20); during adolescence, adult work is learned and begun. Corporal punishment stops here. Termed "the foolish years," minor deviations are expected, such as smoking and having a radio. Serious problems such as suicide, drug addiction, arson, or sexual immorality are virtually nonexistent (Kephart, 1982). At this point, the adolescents begin to eat with the adults in the dining hall.

The young adult occupies an apprentice position. The boys in this group do most of the colony's hard labor and enjoy the opportunity to demonstrate their strength and stamina. Almost all the boys in this age group find ways to generate cash of their own. A boy may share this cash with his sister in exchange for her sewing him clothes that depart from the accepted pattern in some small way. This is, however, against the expectations of the good basic communal commitments of the Hutterites. Adolescents are still considered to be immature emotionally and in need of more religious instruction, but moodiness or poor work performance is not tolerated (Hostetler, 1974).

Most opportunities for meeting and becoming involved with members of the opposite sex come by visiting other colonies, for weddings, funerals, or other activities. In general, young people are given considerable privacy by adults for get-togethers (Smith & Ingoldsby, 2005).

Hutterite preachers condemn dating as a carnal or romantic activity, but it occurs anyway. Parents will usually veto a child's choice that they do not like, or colony leaders will intervene if the partner is considered inappropriate (such as a first cousin). Hostetler (1974) gives us this quote from a 16-year-old girl on relationships:

> When boys or girls from other colonies come and visit we all go together in the evening. If the visitors have never been here before, one of our group does the introducing (so the boys know what the girl's name is when he wants her for a date). Then we sit and talk or play. If a boy wants a date, he goes out with one of our guys and tells him; then he calls out the girl he wants. If she wants, she goes along with him. If not, she says no. Sometimes the boys don't like it if we refuse, but you can't tell a girl to go along if she doesn't want to. It's only in leap year that the girls call the boy for a date. Otherwise the boy has to do the calling. In wintertime we really get a lot of visitors because there's not much work to do. In all the colonies each boy gets a two-week vacation. Then they can go and visit whenever they please. (p. 223)

A more recent description of Hutterite dating (Hofer, 1998) is more physical:

> A date could be as simple as going for a walk or sitting in a dark corner holding hands, talking, and kissing. On a typical date however, a couple meets in a private room, preferably with a cot or bed on which to sit or lie on (most Hutterites don't have sofas in their homes). Sometimes several dating couples will use the room simultaneously, each minding their own business, on separate cots. And so, usually with the lights off, the couple "dates" often in horizontal position. I was told that this is not universally practiced among the Schmiedeleit, but I do know it is among the Lehrerleit.

> I suspect that most young people of all three leit date this way. (p. 51)

Hutterite leaders are uncomfortable with the dating style, and it is kept hidden from outsiders, which is not surprising given the strong religious stance they have of confining sexual relations to marriage. Therefore, Hutterite dating, although still conservative, has become romantic. Love and sexual attraction may be as important as orthodoxy in mate selection.

Marriage

The Hutterites invented a matching procedure where once or twice a year the marriageable youth were assembled, and the preacher gave each male a choice of three females from which to select a wife. The young man would have to wait for the next time if he didn't want to marry any of the three. This changed to personal choice in 1830 following the uproar caused when a young girl refused to marry an older man (Peter, 1971). However, one must marry a Hutterite, and interfaith marriages never occur in the Hutterite church (Hofer, 1998). Most colonies are like a large extended family where everyone is either a relative or feels like one, so one usually goes outside the colony to find a spouse. Because one can't marry until after baptism, and because visiting across colonies is relatively infrequent (for weddings, funerals, etc.), courtships of 3 or 4 years are not uncommon (Kephart, 1982).

After it is informally known that a couple wishes to marry and any objections with the families or the colony are worked out, the formal procedure begins the Sunday before the actual wedding:

1. The boy asks the preacher's help, which is granted.
2. The elders consider his request and lecture him on proper behavior, and he is encouraged to confess his sins.
3. The next day father and son travel to the girl's colony to get her parents' permission.
4. The day after, they are put together in the girl's church.
5. They celebrate for 2 days in the girl's colony and for the rest of the week in the boy's.
6. They are married on Sunday, including a lecture on the submissive role of the wife and the kind, protective role of the husband.
7. There is no honeymoon but an immediate return to the normal routine. Marriages are durable because of the strong community relations, and divorce is unknown (Kephart, 1982).

Weddings do not take place right before Christmas or Easter, and they rarely occur during the planting or harvest seasons. Half of all Schmiedeleut marriages occur in November or December (Hostetler, 1974). The bride typically wears a blue brocade wedding dress, along with her usual kerchief head covering instead of a veil. The groom wears a black suit (made for him by his fiancée) with a white shirt and black tie. Wedding cakes seem to be getting fancier, and pictures are now usually taken. It is a happy time, with lots to eat and drink (Hofer, 1998).

There is pressure to marry, in that men cannot grow beards until they are married, and a beardless male is visibly set apart and not allowed to move into the upper authority levels. The marriage bond is relatively weak in that the couple is generally together only at night, and in some colonies their bedroom is next to that of the husband's parents during the first year. Overt affection is discouraged, but romantic love is being infiltrated from Canadian society. Wives have a sense of loyalty and devotion to their husbands, but the men are more concerned with other men, because they are the ones who vote on advances in the occupational hierarchy (Peter, 1971). Once again, since about 1980, an increase in love and affection in marriage has been noted, with a resulting focus on family over work structure (Ingoldsby, 2001).

In 1950, the median age at marriage was 22.0 years for women and 23.5 years for men. Only 1.9% of the men and 5.4% of the women over the age of 30 had never been married, and only one divorce and four desertions had been reported since 1875 (Hostetler, 1974). In recent years, the age of marriage has increased, and marital problems have become more common (Smith & Ingoldsby, 2005).

Fertility

In 1954, Eaton and Meyer published their landmark study on Hutterite fertility. They documented that from 1880 to 1950 the Hutterites grew from 443 to 8,542 persons. This represents an annual increase of 4.12%, which appears to be the world's fastest natural growth rate. Eaton and Meyer established the Hutterites, with their average family size of slightly over 10 children, as the demographic standard, and they estimated that maximum fertility for humans is 12 to 14 children.

Because Hutterites don't marry at the beginning of a woman's fertility and because there is virtually no premarital sex, the actual number of children is lower than the theoretical maximum. Birth control is considered to be murder, and Eaton and Meyer (1954) noted that it was often not used even when medically recommended. Natural methods, such as coitus interruptus, are considered to be sinful. These sexual beliefs and practices have been substantiated in other research (Lee & Brattrud, 1967).

Since the time of Eaton and Meyer's research, a 33% drop in their birthrate has been confirmed. Peter (1966, 1980) attributed the decline to later age of marriage and speculated that the purpose was to delay colony divisions or in order to save money and to avoid having idle workers. Although it is true (Laing, 1980) that age of marriage is increasing and colony size decreasing, others (Boldt & Roberts, 1980) believed that some forms of birth control must be practiced, which could represent a weakening of church authority and a change in core values.

In 1985, access was given to the medical records of all Hutterites treated at a clinic in a small southern Alberta town. There are six colonies (three Lehrerleut and three Dariusleut) that patronize that clinic for treatment. The clinic had medical records on 48 married Hutterite women. It was found that 12.5% of the women have used oral contraceptives, IUDs, or both. An additional 25% have had a tubal ligation or hysterectomy, meaning that over one third of the sample has made use of some form of birth control. This was confirmed by other medical doctors and Hutterite leaders (Ingoldsby & Stanton, 1988).

Later Life

The Hutterites believe that the aged are to be respected and deserve rest. Women are usually relieved of regular colony jobs in their late 40s. Most will continue with food preparation, because that is preferred to being alone in their apartments. Men will move to council positions. Having a large family is seen as insurance against loneliness in old age, and a grandchild may be assigned to run errands for someone with health problems.

In terms of personality type, Hutterites are generally considered to be extraverted rather than introverted, sensing rather than intuitive, feeling rather than thinking, and judgmental rather than perceptive. The time of death is seen to be controlled by God, and children who die young are envied for having avoided life's temptations and struggles. Most colonies have cemeteries, but funerals are low-key (Hostetler, 1974).

Conclusion

Superficially, Hutterite society may appear unchanging. Many colonies hold firmly to the traditional rules concerning dress, food, recreation, and so on, even as important shifts have been occurring in family size and relations. Although still very communal by outside standards, there is evidence that individualism is on the rise with the Hutterites (Huntington, 1997).

In visiting a Dariusleut colony, one gets the feeling of an extended family sharing an inherited farm. It is not so much communalism as it is togetherness. Rather than the apartment row, every nuclear family has its own home. This includes mobile homes brought onto the property. Families do their own laundry, and furniture stays in a family from one generation to the next, rather than going back to the community.

Although there is a community dining hall, each house has a kitchen with a microwave and refrigerator, and people can eat at home if they choose to. There are many store-bought goods in addition to those the colony produces. Each adult is given a personal monthly allowance, and everyone has personal knickknacks. They are comfortable with picture taking. One sees children's books, pop cans, and toys in the rooms. Unlike the Lehrerleut, their furniture is soft and comfortable.

Gender relations are still quite conservative by modern standards. There is a clear division of labor by sex, and boys expect to be waited on by the girls. A public school teacher commented that her efforts to have boys and girls take turns sweeping the classroom floor were met with resistance by the boys, who viewed this as women's work and pointed out that their mothers and sisters cleaned up after them (Ingoldsby & Smith, 2005).

Most important is the family interaction, which reminds one of the idealized American families of the 1950s, that is, still technically patriarchal, with occasional blustering on the part of the father, but with the mother doing pretty much what she wants. There is a real affection that leads to greater gender equality in decision making. Without the TV, families engage in easy, happy conversations. Word games and jokes are common, with extended kin dropping in and out throughout the evening.

The center of life now seems to be the family, with the colony as a shared business extended family. They remain faithful to key tenets and are not threatened by societal incursion in minor areas. They are still conservative enough to be set apart and are less individualistic than are members of the greater society. But the family is now psychologically over the community, which has become a support rather than the center (Ingoldsby, 2001).

RELIGION AND FAMILY

In this chapter, we have examined four Christian millennial groups that have attempted to alter marital and family structure to fit their beliefs. As can be seen, it is very difficult for modern Western groups to successfully get away from the monogamous nuclear family. The attempts by the Shakers and Oneidans to practice celibacy and group marriage resulted in the demise of their religious organizations, and the Mormons survived only by giving up polygyny for traditional monogamy. Finally, the monogamous Hutterites are evolving from a communal to a family-centric society as they adapt for their own survival and growth.

REFERENCES

Boldt, E., & Roberts, L. (1980). The decline of Hutterite population growth: Causes and consequences—A comment. *Canadian Ethnic Studies, 12*(3), 111–117.

Church of Jesus Christ of Latter-day Saints. (1981). *Doctrine and covenants.* Salt Lake City, UT: Author.

Cosgel, M. (2000). The family in utopia: Celibacy, communal child rearing, and continuity in a religious commune. *Journal of Family History, 25,* 491–503.

Daynes, K. (2001). *More wives than one: Transformation of the Mormon marriage system 1840–1910.* Chicago: University of Illinois Press.

Eaton, J. W., & Meyer, A. (1954). *Man's capacity to reproduce: A demography of a unique population.* Glencoe, IL: Free Press.

Embry, J. (1987). *Mormon polygamous families: Life in the principle.* Salt Lake City: University of Utah Press.

Fogarty, R. (2000). *Desire and duty at Oneida.* Bloomington: Indiana University Press.

Foster, L. (1991). *Women, family and utopia.* Syracuse, NY: Syracuse University Press.

Hofer, S. (1991). *Born Hutterite.* Winnipeg, Manitoba, Canada: Hofer.

Hofer, S. (1998). *The Hutterites: Lives and images of a communal people.* Winnipeg, Manitoba, Canada: Hofer.

Hostetler, J. (1974). *Hutterite society.* Baltimore: Johns Hopkins University Press.

Huntington, G. (1997). Living in the ark: Four centuries of Hutterite faith and community. In D. Pitzer (Ed.), *America's communal utopias* (pp. 319–351). Chapel Hill: University of North Carolina Press.

Ingoldsby, B. (1989). Mormon marriage: A review of family life and social change. *Family Science Review, 2,* 389–396.

Ingoldsby, B. (2001). The Hutterite family in transition. *Journal of Comparative Family Studies, 32,* 87–97.

Ingoldsby, B., & Smith, S. (2005). Public school teachers' perspectives on the contemporary Hutterite family. *Journal of Comparative Family Studies, 36,* 249–266.

Ingoldsby, B., & Stanton, M. (1988). The Hutterites and fertility control. *Journal of Comparative Family Studies, 19,* 137–142.

Kephart, W. (1982). *Extraordinary groups: The sociology of unconventional life styles.* New York: St. Martin's Press.

Kephart, W., & Jedlicka, D. (1991). *The family, society, and the individual.* New York: HarperCollins.

Laing, L. M. (1980). Declining fertility in a religious isolate: The Hutterite population of Alberta, Canada, 1955–71. *Human Biology, 52,* 288–310.

Lee, S. C., & Brattrud, A. (1967). Marriage under a monastic mode of life: A preliminary report on the Hutterite family in South Dakota. *Journal of Marriage and the Family, 29,* 512–520.

Newell, L., & Avery, V. (1984). *Mormon enigma: Emma Hale Smith.* Garden City, NY: Doubleday.

Noyes, J. (1872). *Male continence.* Oneida, NY: Office of Oneida Circular.

Peter, K. (1966). Toward a demographic theory of Hutterite population growth. *Variables, 5*(Spring), 28–37.

Peter, K. (1971). The Hutterite family. In K. Ishwaran (Ed.), *The Canadian family* (pp. 289–303). Toronto, Ontario, Canada: Holt, Rinehart & Winston.

Peter, K. (1980). The decline of Hutterite population growth. *Canadian Ethnic Studies, 12*(3), 97–109.

Smith, S., & Ingoldsby, B. (2005). Dating and educational behaviors of Hutterian youth. *Communal Societies, 25.*

Stanton, M. (1989). The maintenance of the Hutterite way: The family and childhood life-cycle in the communal context. *Family Science Review, 2,* 373–388.

Van Wagoner, R. (1989). *Mormon polygamy: A history* (2nd ed.). Salt Lake City, UT: Signature Books.

Wyatt, G. (1989). Mormon polygyny in the nineteenth century: A theoretical analysis. *Journal of Comparative Family Studies, 20,* 13–20.

Part II Exercise: The Ethnic Genogram

Can you trace your family to its country or countries of origin? In this exercise, you will attempt to do so. Here are the procedures to follow:

1. Draw a genogram of your family, starting with yourself at the bottom. Trace only upward through parents, parents of parents, and so on. Do not show siblings in any generation. Use gender symbols for all family members, including yourself (triangles for males and circles for females).
2. Include the branches upward (backward through the generations) until you reach a person who emigrated from another country. If different branches emigrated during different generations, there will be different "heights" at spots. Or, if all eight of your great-grandparents came to the United States during their lifetimes, the top of your tree will have eight branches, and the top will be flat.
3. For each person at the top of your genogram, indicate above his or her gender symbol the country from which the person came. If you are not absolutely sure, put a question mark at the top. You may know the region (e.g., Caribbean) or continent but not the specific country. Include this information if it applies, but be as specific as you can.
4. If you have no idea which generation came to the United States, use dotted lines at the top of the applicable branches and try to estimate how many additional generations are involved before reaching an immigrant.
5. Some people may have moved twice or more between different countries during their lifetimes. Ignore this and show only the last country before coming to the United States. You can make an exception if residence in the intermediate country did not last long.
6. In some cases, branches may terminate at the top with "Native American." Of course, if these could be traced back further, they might show that an ancestor came across the Bering Strait thousands of years ago. Ignore this, but do indicate the tribal affiliation of the Native American ancestor if you know it.
7. Some of you will have complicated genograms if a person was raised for a significant period of time by a stepparent or was adopted. Include whatever information you have about "blood" relations and other kinds of relationships.
8. Work out your genogram in a preliminary version until you complete it. Then, redraw it neatly and turn in only the edited final version, making sure it is easy to read.
9. Include historical circumstances related to immigration if known. These might include religious or ethnic persecution, famine,

EDITORS' NOTE: Thanks to David Klein, Department of Sociology, Notre Dame University, for sharing his original version of this exercise.

war, following family and friends, slavery, forced relocation or resettlement, criminal incarceration/deportation, and so on.

10. You should indicate if a person was a racial minority group member in his or her country of origin. For example, a Hmong person (a Vietnamese ethnic group) might have come from Laos or Thailand. The point is, countries by themselves may not tell the whole story of your ethnic heritage, so you may need to clarify this.

Part III

FAMILY DEVELOPMENT

A multiethnic marriage in Hawaii.

Introduction to Part III

Part III takes a developmental approach to major stages in family life—mate selection and marriage, parenting, divorce, and later life. Just as an individual changes through time, so does a family. How these family changes are experienced depends in large part on the culture in which one lives, as these chapters illustrate.

In Chapter 8, "Mate Selection and Marriage," Ingoldsby looks at the beginning stages of the family life cycle. Historical and cross-cultural evidence points to a variety of practices concerning the process or rules of mate selection and around the customs of the wedding itself. Adjustment issues within the marriage also vary in importance by culture. The original meanings behind some of the marriage customs in Western societies are explained in this chapter as well.

In Chapter 9, "Parenting Practices Worldwide," Myers-Walls, Myers-Bowman, and Posada provide a multidimensional view of the cultural context of parenting. Based on the National Extension Parent Education Model, their chapter analyzes the similarities and differences in parenting cross-culturally from important dimensions of guidance and motivation, nurturance, understanding, care of self, and advocacy.

Chapter 10, "International Divorce," by McKenry and Price, provides a sweeping look at what has become the most common form of family dissolution. They examine the major reasons for rising divorce rates in every region of the world as well as the social forces that work against divorce. McKenry and Price urge readers to understand divorce from a global perspective that is closely tied to changes in economic, political, and religious systems.

This section concludes with Chapter 11, "Diversity in International Aging Families," in which Miller and Meredith discuss the unprecedented growth in the world's aging population and its dramatic impacts on families. After providing an overview of this demographic transition, they conclude with an in-depth analysis of the changing treatment of the elderly in China.

CHAPTER 8

Mate Selection and Marriage

BRON B. INGOLDSBY

The institution of marriage is very popular throughout the world. The large majority of adults desire and participate in this union. The average age for first marriage in the United States is about 25 for women and 27 for men (Whitehead & Popenoe, 2001). There are many others who choose not to formalize their stable sexual relationship and cohabit instead. In the United States in the year 2000, there were 4.9 million households with unmarried different-sex partners (Simmons & O'Connell, 2003).

Marriage, as normative as it is, is approached in many different ways. Even though it is common for most North Americans to marry in their 20s, it can occur much earlier in some other cultures. It has been common for girls especially to marry at puberty, and infant betrothals are not unknown. How mates are chosen also varies considerably from one culture to another. As we will see in this chapter, the free mate choice based on love, which is common in the modern West, has not been the way people in most other societies have selected their companions. The rituals connected with the wedding ceremony have been many and varied as well. What one expects from a spouse and how spouses get along is also an area that is heavily affected by culture.

We will examine three general topics: (a) mate-selection procedures, (b) wedding customs, and (c) marital adjustment. Few, if any, areas of human activity have been invested with as much specified activity and meaning as has marriage.

MATE-SELECTION PROCEDURES

Historically, there have been three general approaches to choosing one's mate. They are: marriage by capture, marriage by arrangement, and free-choice mate selection. I examine each of them in turn.

Marriage by Capture

Although it has probably never been the usual method of obtaining a wife, men have taken women by force in many times and places. This typically occurred in patriarchal societies, in which women were often considered as property. Often women were seized as part of the spoils of war, and other times a specific woman was forced into marriage because the man wanted her and could not afford the bride-price or obtain the permission of her parents. The capture and marriage of a woman was legal in England until the reign of Henry VII, who made it a crime to abduct an heiress (Fielding, 1942).

The ancient Hebrews would seize wives under certain circumstances. A dramatic example is recounted in the Old Testament (Judges 21 [King James Version for all biblical citations]), where it was arranged for young women to be kidnapped from other areas to serve as wives so that the tribe of Benjamin would not die out after a war that they had lost.

There was also a formal procedure for dealing with wives captured in warfare:

> When thou goest forth to war against thine enemies, and the Lord thy God hath delivered them into thine hands, and thou hast taken them captive, And seest among the captives a beautiful woman, and hast a desire unto her, that thou wouldest have her to thy wife; Then thou shalt bring her home to thine house; and she shall shave her head, and pare her nails; And she shall put the raiment of her captivity from off her, and shall remain in thine house, and bewail her father and her mother a full month: and after that thou shalt go in unto her, and be her husband, and she shall be thy wife. And it shall be, if thou have no delight in her, then thou shalt let her go whither she will; but thou shalt not sell her at all for money, thou shalt not make merchandise of her, because thou hast humbled her. (Deuteronomy 21:10–14)

At least she was given time to get used to the idea and was never sold into slavery! Fielding (1942) cites a number of different cultures, including the Australian aborigines, who frequently resorted to marriage by capture in the recent past. The Yanomama of the Amazon are reported (Peters, 1987) to use capture as one of their mate-selection options. One village is often raided by another for the specific purpose of finding wives. If a man captures a young, attractive female, he must be careful, because other men from his own village may try to steal her from him.

In the popular musical *Seven Brides for Seven Brothers,* the concept of marriage by capture is acted out, and one of the songs is based on the historical incident of the "rape of the Sabine women." There are many cultures that still have remnants of the old practice of marriage by capture in their wedding ceremonies. In each of them the match is prearranged, but the husband pretends to take his bride by force, and she feigns resistance.

One example is the Roro of New Guinea. On the wedding day, the groom's party surrounds the bride's home and acts out an assault on it. The bride attempts to run away but is caught. Then a sham battle ensues, with the bride's mother leading the way and crying at the loss of her daughter when the daughter is taken off to the groom (Fielding, 1942).

Marriage by Arrangement

It appears that the most common method of mate selection has been by arrangement. Typically, the parents, often with the aid of certain relatives or professional matchmakers, have chosen the spouse for their child. This form of mate choice is more common where extended kin groups are strong and important. Essentially, marriage is seen as being of group, rather than individual, importance, and economics is often the driving force, rather than love between the principals.

Arranged marriages have been considered especially important for the rulers of kingdoms and other nobility. Care had to be taken to preserve bloodlines, enhance wealth, and resolve political issues. It is believed, for instance, that the majority of King Solomon's 700 wives and 300 concubines were acquired for the purpose of political alliances.

Stephens (1963) identifies four major considerations that determine mate choice in societies where marriages are arranged. The first is *price.* The groom's family may need to pay for the bride, with either money or labor. In some cultures the situation is reversed, with the bride's family paying a dowry to the husband. In other cases, there is a direct exchange, where both families make payments to each other or simply trade women for each other's sons.

The second consideration is *social status.* That is, the reputation of the family from which the spouse for one's child will come is very important. A third determinant is any *continuous marriage arrangement.* This refers to a set pattern for mate selection, which is carried on from generation to generation. For instance, cousin marriages are preferred in many societies.

The final criteria for mate choice are *sororate and levirate* arrangements, which refer to second marriages and tend to be based on bride-price obligations. These terms are explained more fully later in the chapter. Stephens also notes 19 societies (including some large ones, such as China and Renaissance Europe) that have practiced child betrothals or child marriages. This means that the marriage is arranged before puberty and can even be worked out before the child is born.

One example of variety within arranged marriages are the Yanomama of Venezuela, already mentioned as practicing marriage by capture as well. The ideal match is between cross-cousins, and the majority of unions fall into this category. Most betrothals are made before the girl is 3 years of age. A man will initiate these arrangements at about the time he becomes a hunter, which is shortly after turning 15 years old. Another acceptable form of mate selection is sister exchange, in which two unrelated single males wish to acquire wives and have sisters who are not promised to anyone, so they simply trade sisters (Peters, 1987).

Some societies have provided an "out" for couples who have strong personal preferences that go against the arrangement of their families. This is to permit elopement. Stephens (1963) gives this account of the Iban of Borneo:

> When a young woman is in love with a man who is not acceptable to her parents, there is an old custom called *nunghop bui,* which permits him to carry her off to his own village. She will meet him by arrangement at the waterside, and step into his boat with a paddle in her hand, and both will pull away as fast as they can. If pursued he will stop every now and then to deposit some article of value on the bank, such as a gun, a jar, or a favor for the acceptance of her family, and when he has exhausted his resources he will leave his own sword. When the pursuers observe this they cease to follow, knowing he is cleared out. As soon as he reaches his own village he tidies up the house and spreads the mats, and when his pursuers arrive he gives them food to eat and toddy to drink, and sends them home satisfied. In the meanwhile he is left in possession of his wife. (p. 200)

Following is a detailed look at some of the specific mechanisms of arranged marriages.

Bride-Price

Throughout much of human history, marriage has been seen as chiefly an economic transaction. As an old German saying goes, "It is not man that marries maid, but field marries field, vineyard marries vineyard, cattle marry cattle" (Tober, 1984). The purpose of a bride-price is to compensate the family of the bride for the loss of her services. It is extremely common and is indicative of the value of women in those societies. Stephens (1963) reports that Murdock's World Ethnographic Sample yields the following breakdown on marriage payments:

Marriage Payment	*Number of Societies*
Bride-price	260
Bride service	75
Dowry	24
Gift or woman exchange	31
No marriage payment	152

This means that in 62% of the world's societies a man must pay in order to marry a woman. The price is usually paid in animals, shell money, or other valuable commodities, and often exceeds one's annual income. Some cultures prefer payment in service, often many years of labor to the bride's parents, or at least permit it for suitors who cannot afford to pay in goods. One famous example from the Old Testament is that of Jacob, who labored seven years for each of Laban's two daughters, Leah and Rachel (Genesis 29).

Dowry

The dowry appears to be an inducement for a man to marry a particular woman and therefore relieve her family of the financial burden of caring for her. Although relatively rare, it is a sign of a culture that places a low value on women. Actually, the key purpose of a dowry is probably to stabilize a marriage, because the dowry is not given to the husband but is something that the bride brings with her into the marriage. For example, in Cyprus before the time of British influence, the expected dowry was often a house. If the husband divorced his wife, or if he mistreated her and she left him, then the dowry went with her. Like modern-day wedding gifts or the bride's trousseau, it was an investment in the marriage and was intended to reduce the chances of a breakup (J. Balswick, personal communication, 1978).

The dowry has been around for a long time. The Babylonian code of Hammurabi (1955 BC) clearly stated that the wife's property stayed with her if her husband divorced her and passed on to her children when she died. Ancient Greece and Rome also considered the dowry to be essential in any honorable marriage (Fielding, 1942).

Recent research in the southern Indian state of Kerala (Billig, 1992) differentiates between the traditional dowry and an actual groom-price. Groom-price is money paid by the bride's family directly to the husband to use as he sees fit. In the 1950s and 1960s rapid population growth resulted in more young women looking for husbands a few (average of 7) years older than themselves.

This surplus of potential brides increased the value of husbands. Popular revulsion for the groom-price has resulted in a decrease in the age difference (now 5 years), women lowering their social status expectations for their husband or increasing their own education, and a government outlawing of the practice.

Sororate and Levirate

These terms refer to marriage practices designed to control remarriages after the death of the first spouse. In cultures that practice the sororate, a sister replaces a deceased wife. Assume that a man has paid a good bride-price for his wife, but sometime later she becomes ill and dies. He has lost his wife and the bride-price. Therefore, to make good on the original bargain, the parents who received the bride-price provide the man with a new wife. This new wife is an unmarried sister or other close relative of the first wife. Here we see how marriage is often more of an economic transaction than a personal relationship.

Much more widely practiced has been the levirate. Under this system, it is the husband who dies, and his wife must be married to a brother of the deceased man. There are various reasons for this practice. One is that the wife belonged to her husband as part of his property, and as such would be inherited along with the other possessions by a near relative. Another is that it is presumed that women need someone to take care of them, and brothers-in-law (which is the meaning of the Latin word *levir*) should assume that responsibility. It has been reported that the levirate has been practiced by the New

Caledonians, the Mongols, the Afghans, the Abyssinians, the Hebrews, and the Hindus, as well as certain American Indian and African tribes (Fielding, 1942).

The chief reason for the Hindus and Hebrews was religious and had to do with the importance of having a son in the family. Hindu men needed a son to perform certain sacrifices, so if a man died before having a son, then a boy born to his former wife and brother would carry out those ceremonies in his name (Fielding, 1942).

For the Hebrews, it was also important that every man have a son, so that his name would not die out. There was a ritualized penalty for a man who refused to marry his brother's widow and rear a son in his name:

> And if the man like not to take his brother's wife, then let his brother's wife go up to the gate unto the elders, and say, My husband's brother refuseth to raise up unto his brother a name in Israel, he will not perform the duty of my husband's brother. Then the elders of his city shall call him, and speak unto him: and if he stand to it, and say, I like not to take her; Then shall his brother's wife come in to him in the presence of the elders, and loose his shoe from off his foot, and spit in his face, and shall answer and say, So shall it be done unto that man that will not build up his brother's house. (Deuteronomy 25:7–9)

In earlier times, the punishment for refusing to practice the levirate was more severe than the ritual just described. In Genesis 38 we read of Judah's son Onan and how he was killed by the Lord for refusing to impregnate his dead older brother's wife! The book of Ruth in the Old Testament is also an excellent example of how the levirate worked. It is an account of how Naomi has no more sons for her daughter-in-law Ruth to marry, so she arranges for another male relative, Boaz, to take on the responsibility.

Matchmaking

There are various ways in which two young people can be brought together. Typically, the parents of both families will work out the details among themselves and then announce the match to their children. The initial go-between in Turkey has been the boy's mother, who would inspect potential choices at the public baths and then give reports to her son (Tober, 1984). The popular musical *Fiddler on the Roof* is about father-arranged marriages. Often, hired go-betweens, or matchmakers, assist in making the arrangement. They might act as intermediaries between the families or suggest potential spouses. Checking for astrological or other religious signs and requirements could also be part of their job.

In the 1800s, bachelor pioneers in the American West would sometimes find a wife by ordering one from a mail-order catalog. Even today, many Asian families will publish matrimonial want ads in search of a respectable spouse for their child (Tober, 1984). The following, found in the classified section of a Philippine newspaper, is a common method of spouse hunting today.

> FOREIGNERS: video match a decent friendship marriage consultant office introducing a beautiful single educated Filipina view friendship to marriage.

> LADIES: Australian European businessmen newly arrive in town sincerely willing to meet decent Filipina view friendship to marriage. Ambassador Hotel suite 216.

Internet dating and marriage services in the United States, Japan, Russia, and elsewhere manifest the continued utility of professional matchmaking, even in societies where the individuals involved make the final decisions themselves. There are also magazines designed for singles that include matrimonial or relationship want ads.

There are immigrants to Western societies who are not comfortable with love-based unions and prefer to have their marriages arranged by their parents or through a mediator. It is estimated, for instance, that up to 90% of the marriages in the East Indian community in Edmonton, Alberta, Canada, are to some degree arranged (Jimenez, 1992). Some ethnic Indians return to the Indian subcontinent to find a spouse, whereas others allow their parents to find a match locally for them. Some place ads in newspapers such as *India Today* or *India Abroad,* which focus on desired background characteristics such as education, religion, and age. In deference to Western customs, the young people can veto any match that does not appeal to them, and a dowry is rarely accepted.

Free-Choice Mate Selection

As noted in Chapter 3, love gradually became the principal criterion for marriage in the Western world after the Renaissance. The shift from kinship and economic motives to personal ones in mate selection led to the conclusion that the individuals themselves, rather than their parents or others, were best qualified to make the decision. In societies where the basic family unit is nuclear, both romantic love and free mate choice are more common. This is because extended kin groups are not important enough to see marriage as needing to be group controlled. The people of most cultures throughout the world today marry for love over any other consideration (Buss et al., 1990).

Even though free choice is the mate-selection method of the modern United States, one should not conclude that it is the most common approach in the world. In a survey of 40 societies, Stephens (1963) found only 5 in which completely free mate choice is permitted. An additional 6 allowed the young people to choose their spouse, but subject to parental approval. Twelve other cultures had a mix of arranged marriages and free-choice (usually subject to approval) unions, and the final 16 allowed only arranged marriages.

And even free choice does not mean that you can marry anyone. All societies have marital regulations. First is the rule of *exogamy.* This means that you must marry outside of your group. Typically, this refers to certain relatives who are unavailable as marriage partners. Exogamous rules are generally the same as the incest taboos of the society, which prohibit sexual intercourse between close blood relatives. Other societies go beyond that, however. In classical China, two people with the same surname could not marry, even if there was no kinship relation (Hutter, 1981).

The second rule is called *endogamy*, which means that a person must marry within his or her group. This refers to social pressure to marry someone who is similar to oneself in various important ways including religion, race or ethnic group, social class, and age. These factors have been found to be related to marital compatibility and are precisely the kinds of things considered by parents in arranged marriages. One reason why the divorce rate seems to be higher in free-choice societies may be that many couples ignore endogamy issues and allow romantic love to be practically the sole consideration in mate selection. There is a tendency for marriages to be fairly homogamous, however, even in free mate choice societies.

A final factor is *propinquity* (geographical nearness). It is of course impossible to marry someone who lives so far away from you that you never meet. At another level, however, this principle refers to a human tendency to be friends with people with whom it is convenient to interact. Let us say that you leave your hometown to attend college elsewhere. You left a boyfriend or girlfriend back at home, and you also meet someone new at college. All other things being equal, which one will you marry? Generally, it will be the one at school with you, simply because it is easier.

Some Examples

Free mate choice is on the rise in China today. However, it is very different from the courtship pattern in North America. Young people will gather information about each other first and check for mutual suitability before going public with their relationship. In fact, dating will follow, rather than precede, the decision to marry. Typically the couple knows each other for well over 2 years before marrying. This cautious approach is paying off, because the quality of these marriages seems to be higher than that of arranged unions (Liao & Heaton, 1992).

The Igbo are a people living in present-day Nigeria (Okonjo, 1992). About 55% of the Igbo had their marriages arranged, whereas the remaining 45% are in free-choice unions. Most of the latter are younger, indicating a move from arranged to free-choice marriages, a shift we see occurring throughout much of the world today. Regardless of mate-selection method, premarital chastity is very highly valued among the Igbo.

As the Igbo move to free mate choice based on love, their various arranged practices are falling into disfavor. Customs that are quickly disappearing include the following. One is *woman-to-woman* marriage. In this situation, an older childless woman pays the bride-price to marry a younger female, usually a cousin. A male mate is chosen for the "wife" to have children with, but they belong to the older female spouse, who has the legal role of "husband."

Another way of securing an heir is *father-to-daughter* marriage. If a man has no sons, he may prohibit a daughter from marrying. She has children from a male mate (not the father), but her sons are considered to be her father's. Women whose husbands turn out to be impotent are allowed to have a lover from whom to have children, who are considered to be the legal husband's. Other arranged customs seldom practiced anymore are the levirate and child marriages.

Courtship and Sex

One final area that we will explore in this section on mate selection is the issue of premarital sexuality in courtship. There is considerable variation across cultures concerning the acceptability of premarital sexual relations. Most are fairly permissive, however. Of 863 societies in Murdock's Ethnographic Atlas, 67% impose little restriction on premarital sex (Murdock, 1967). The largest proportion of permissive societies are found in Pacific regions, and the most restrictive are the Arab and Muslim nations (Tseng & Hsu, 1991).

In the Marshall Islands, sexual activity begins around puberty. It is common to have many different partners, to cohabit with a few, and to eventually marry a more permanent mate. There is no stigma to being an illegitimate child or an unwed mother, and having children does not seem to reduce a woman's chances of finding a future mate (Tseng & Hsu, 1991). In this culture, sexuality is just seen as part of life, with no special taboos or significance attached to it.

The Hopi also included sexuality as part of their courtship procedure. A girl was allowed to receive suitors in her late adolescence. The boys would sneak into her house at night and sleep with her, and the parents would pretend not to notice if the boys were considered good marriage prospects. Eventually, she would become pregnant, and then select her favorite lover as her husband. The families involved would then arrange the marriage. As a result, a Hopi boy would never have intercourse with a girl he was not willing to marry (Queen, Habenstein, & Quadagno, 1985).

Estimates vary, but certainly well over half of all Americans experience intercourse before marriage. The "sexual revolution" of the 1960s and 1970s had a major impact on premarital behavior: In the 1930s only 15% of American women had experienced premarital coitus. In spite of fairly high rates of sexual experience, there is still widespread disapproval of premarital coitus in American society. In comparison, other Western countries appear to be more relaxed about it. Much of today's caution has to do with the dangers associated with sexually transmitted diseases and unwanted pregnancies.

WEDDING CUSTOMS

There are many rituals and practices that occur in connection with the act of getting married. Contemporary couples typically participate in many of these without giving much thought to what they might mean and why they are being done. My purpose here is to provide some insight into the depth and richness of marriage by recounting some of the principal Western wedding customs along with their history and meaning. Unless otherwise noted, the following information comes from Chesser (1980) or Tober (1984).

The Ring

This may be the oldest and most universal symbol of marriage. Some ancient peoples used to break a coin in half, with each partner taking one piece. The idea of this love match is still found in today's necklace jewelry. This practice may have evolved into using rings, which we know were used by ancient Egyptians, Greeks, and Romans.

The right hand is considered to be dominant over the left, and originally men wore the engagement ring as a symbol of their control of the relationship. When women began wearing engagement and wedding rings, the rings were moved to the left hand as a sign of submission. Another possible theory is that the ring should be worn on the fourth finger of the left hand because there is a vein in that finger that runs straight to the heart. The *vena amoris* doesn't exist, but that finger is still a logical place for jewelry, because it is probably the least used in daily activity (Fielding, 1942).

The ring's circular shape is indicative of never-ending love, and in the 17th century, social pressure led to the preference for gold as the material because it does not tarnish. The ring gains even greater symbolism with the inclusion of a precious stone. The clarity and durability of the diamond make it the most popular, as does the idea that it represents innocence. Other stones have been assigned special meaning as well. For instance, the emerald promises domestic bliss, and the ruby is a sign of love. Its red color is also supposed to have the power to ward off evil spirits. A more dangerous one is the aquamarine, believed to give its wearer the power to read another's thoughts.

Setting the Date

One important decision that a couple must make is when to marry. Today convenience seems to be the determining factor. However, many cultures and religions have had beliefs about good- and bad-luck times of the year for marrying, and much effort was often expended to set the date at a time when the gods, or stars, would smile on the new couple.

Here are a few guidelines: January is a good-luck month because the Greeks dedicated it to Hera, a goddess of fertility. February and March are bad for Catholic and Orthodox adherents because one should give up good things during Lent. The folklore says, "Marry in Lent, live to repent." April is considered to be a good month because springtime is illustrative of the reproduction wished upon the new couple. May is not so good because Catholics dedicate the month to the Virgin Mary, the patron saint of chastity. July and August are inconvenient times for farmers, who need to be getting the harvest in. The Irish believed that "they that wive between sickle and scythe shall never thrive."

The autumn months are considered to be good times to marry because of the connection between harvest and fertility and because of good astrological signs. December, finally, is a bad-luck month because of the British belief that "you always repent of marriage before the year is out." The following rhyme also indicates that certain days of the week are better than others:

Monday for wealth,
Tuesday for health,
Wednesday is the best day of all.
Thursday for losses,
Friday for crosses,
And Saturday, no luck at all.

Candles

Candles are another symbol of love. Apparently an evolution from the Roman torches used to light the way of the wedding procession, one popular ritual today is to have a large candle representing God's love used to light two other candles, which represent the couple getting married.

The Bridal Veil

Many cultures believe in the "evil eye," where one can be made ill by the covetous stares of powerful individuals. The veil, then, is designed to protect the bride from the evil spirits that might attend all the looking-at she is certain to get. The Romans preferred that the veil be red, because that is the most effective color for warding off evil.

The Wedding Gown

Most people are aware that a white gown is intended to represent the bride's virginity, a guarantee that grooms expected from her family. This rhyme tells us of some attitudes toward bridal gown colors:

Married in red, wish yourself dead;
Married in black, wish yourself back;
Married in blue, you'll always be true;
Married in green, ashamed to be seen;
Married in grey, go far away;
Married in brown, live out of town;
Married in white, chosen all right.

Children

The purpose of including children in the wedding party (today's flower girl and ring bearer) is to serve as a visible encouragement for the age-old purpose of marriage: fertility.

The Kiss

Although not a legal requirement, the kiss historically sealed the wedding vow. Although wedding participants prefer to do their own kissing today, the priest used to give the groom the "kiss of peace," and then he would kiss his bride. The priest's assistants would then kiss all of the wedding guests.

The Wedding Cake

There are many superstitions surrounding this important centerpiece of most receptions. Often multitiered and decorated with hearts, lovebirds, and flowers, small figures of the bride and groom often adorn the top. It is considered bad luck for a bride to bake her own cake or to taste it before it is formally cut. If a section is saved, however, it will perpetuate the couple's love.

The cake is actually another symbol of fertility, and in times past it was broken over the bride's head. It was believed that cutting the cake would magically facilitate the breaking of the bride's hymen or maidenhead, and thereby aid in the birth of the first child. We have since developed the less messy custom of throwing rice (also representative of fruitfulness) or other materials on the couple.

Attendants

The bridesmaids and groom's attendants appear to be remnants of the marriage by capture sometimes practiced. The bride had women trying to protect her from capture, whereas the groom had his friends to assist him in the assault (Fielding, 1942).

Flowers

In the Middle Ages, the wealthy adorned themselves with their finest jewelry. Peasant brides could not afford such things, so they imitated the practice by using flowers. They have since assumed a place of prominence in wedding plans, with a bouquet for the bride, corsages for others, and floral arrangements throughout the room. Modern selections are based on personal preference, but originally some had special significance. One favorite, the orange blossom, meant fruitfulness.

Talismans

There are various good-luck articles that superstition dictates a bride should work into her wedding clothes. A penny in your shoe is supposed to guarantee a lifetime of good fortune. Something old: a family heirloom to give a sense of continuity from one generation to the next. Something new: as most of the bride's clothes will be, to put things on an optimistic note. Something borrowed: usually from a happily married friend and based on the idea that happiness rubs off. Something blue: a symbol of fidelity.

Throwing the Garter and Bouquet

The person who catches these objects is to be the next to marry. Custom dictates that when throwing her bouquet, the bride must not face her girlfriends, so that she cannot direct it into the hands of a favorite. Throwing the garter comes from an old British custom called "flinging the stocking." Guests would invade the bridal chamber, and the women would take the groom's stockings while the men grabbed the bride's. They would take turns throwing them, and whoever tossed the one that landed on the bride or groom's nose was the next to marry! By the 1500s, the bride's garter was so highly prized that guests would rush her at the altar trying to get it. In self-preservation, she began to take it off, and her husband would throw it out to the unmarried males.

Evil Spirits

It has been a common religious belief that malicious spirits are attracted to weddings, because of their sacred nature. As a result, many diversions are used to throw them off of the bride's trail. She enters through one church door, but exits from another. Car decorating, noise making, and following the couple as they leave for their honeymoon are all to frighten the devil away from the newlywed couple. Carrying the bride over the threshold is to shake off demons that have been following along the soles of her feet. Finally, sprinkling holy water on the marriage bed is intended to drive off spirits that are attracted to the sexual act.

The Honeymoon

Honey refers to mead, an alcoholic drink made from fermented honey, and moon refers to the lunar month. Essentially, it indicates a time in which the new couple should be free from the cares of the world and allowed to get to know each other. Its central purpose has been the consummation of the marriage.

In many European and Mediterranean cultures it has been very important that the bride be found to be a virgin. Proof of this would be that she would bleed from first intercourse, and the stained bedsheet might be hung from a window the following morning as evidence to all of her purity and the proper consummation of the new union.

MARITAL ADJUSTMENT

The last topic for investigation in this chapter is the quality of the marriage relationship itself. I shift from a structural-functionalist approach to a developmental focus for this section. This will allow us to see how marital concerns can change and be influenced by the stages in the life cycle through which the couple progresses. This information on cross-cultural variation comes from Wen-Shing Tseng and Jing Hsu (1991).

Intimacy

How one would assess the quality of one's marriage depends on what is expected in a marriage relationship. In the United States and Canada today, the emphasis is on psychological intimacy and emotional sharing, in addition to task performance. That is, one's satisfaction is influenced by whether or not the spouse acts in hoped-for ways in the areas of child care, housekeeping, economic support, and sexual activity. Certain negative behaviors, such as gambling, abuse, drug use, and infidelity, can present major threats to marital stability and happiness.

However, what many Westerners want the most, especially women, is a deep and close friendship. Most young Americans today desire to marry a "soul mate" with whom they can share their deepest feelings (Whitehead & Popenoe, 2001). The traditional marriage of times past in which each spouse simply performed the expected tasks would be considered hollow by today's standards. The happiest marriages appear to be those couples that know each other well and enjoy doing things together.

Expected closeness varies by culture, however. For instance, the Japanese family tends to have a very clear sexual division of labor. The husband has his work and associates with his colleagues there. He does not participate in child care or housework and is fairly unaware of how his wife and children spend their time. She also knows little about his life. It is not considered wise to overload a single relationship with too many concerns, so adults have various friends and relatives in whom they confide.

In the United States and Germany, research indicates that husbands and wives are significantly more involved in each other's lives. Husbands are home more often and interact more in each other's social lives. Confiding in others about the marital relationship is likely to be considered a betrayal rather than a wise action.

Toleration of extramarital affairs varies greatly among different societies. Conservative cultures consider it unforgivable and a principal rationale for divorce. In other cultures, there is a double standard. In the Philippines, for instance, extramarital sex is not tolerated in the wife, but it is acceptable, *macho* behavior for husbands to have many lovers. The Toda, discussed in Chapter 6, consider affairs for either sex to be natural and not a cause for concern. In Micronesia, there is a long postpartum sex taboo, and extramarital behavior on the husband's part is considered to be frequent.

Stress

There are many events that are stressful to family functioning. Some are unexpected, such as certain disasters, illnesses, or work-related conflicts. Others are more normative, including the life-cycle stresses expected from parenthood, children leaving home, retirement, and widowhood.

Certain types of stresses are more important in some cultures than they are in others, however. For example, Nigerian families consider procreation to be very important in marriage. Fertility is a blessing, and "barrenness" is a curse. Infertility can be a major source of conflict and unhappiness for many Nigerian couples as a result.

In Korea, it is still considered to be very important that married women be housewives and not work outside the home. Many young women are well educated, but fewer than 15% have jobs. Modernization has made housework easier and more monotonous, and as a result many Korean housewives are developing neurotic symptoms in response to their unfulfilling lifestyle. It is common enough that psychiatrists have labeled this phenomenon the "housewife syndrome."

Finally, household structure can have an impact on how stress is experienced. In extended families, there are other family members to provide a buffer when there is conflict in a couple's relationship. These other members can give psychological as well as economic support. However, extended families have interpersonal conflicts that are less likely to occur when households are nuclear. Problems are most likely to erupt between the wives of brothers and between mother-in-law and daughter-in-law over issues of household duties and power structure. Most young couples would prefer to establish their own nuclear family if they could.

Life-Cycle Issues

Each phase of the marital life cycle has its own unique challenges, which may be viewed differently from one society to the next. In the *marriage establishment phase,* the couple must replace fantasy with reality and make the adjustments necessary for living with another person. Each spouse has his or her own ideas about how family life should be, and these adjustments are even more complicated when one enters a large or extended family system. Many cultures are patrilocal, requiring the bride to move in with and be subject to her in-laws. There are many stories of the hardships endured by these young wives when they lose the support of their family of origin.

There are various interactive patterns a couple might develop. The dominant-submissive pattern is common. One spouse controlling the other is considered dysfunctional in many societies, but a dominant husband and submissive wife would be seen as not only normal but even ideal in a patriarchal culture. Another pattern is the "obsessional husband and the hysterical wife." In this pattern, the husband is intellectual and emotionally distant, and the wife complains about his being cold and uninvolved. Whereas Western clinicians would consider this to be a mismatch, a couple in Japan would not be likely to be labeled dysfunctional.

In the *child-bearing and -rearing phases,* couples deal with fertility and child socialization. In some cultures, having large families or having children of a certain sex is more important than it is in others. Asian cultures are most likely to value having sons over daughters. Not meeting those societal expectations can result in anxiety and conflict for the couple.

It is not uncommon for husbands and wives to disagree on how children should be reared and disciplined. Cultures also differ on whether the focus of childhood should be enjoyment or learning through hardship. These differences will be even more difficult if the husband and wife come from different cultures and bring with them the conflicting approaches of their society. For instance, a husband of Hawaiian heritage may feel that children should be quiet at mealtime and that physical punishment is the best approach for discipline. A wife from the mainland United States is likely to feel that dinnertime should include discussions between parents and children and that striking children is abusive.

In the *empty-nest phase,* the couple must get used to having their children leave home and being alone again. The impact of this would be much less in extended families, where there are always others around, and to which many married children return. In nuclear families, as children leave and workers retire, the couple may need to reestablish their relationship. This could be especially difficult for those couples that had separate life activities. In Japanese families, for instance, the retired husband has lost his social network and has no involvement in his wife's activities. Some couples will consider divorce once the children are gone and they see that they have little to keep them together.

Widowhood is the final phase. Generally, women are most likely to outlive their husbands, and how that loss is dealt with depends to some degree on culture. Traditional Hindu society is very hard on widows. No matter how young she may be, a widow is expected never to remarry and to live a life of seclusion, interacting only with close family members.

The matrilineal Trobriand Islanders have highly structured mourning rituals, followed by seclusion for the widow for a time between 6 months and 2 years. After that, she puts on a gaily decorated outfit and, after some ceremonial dancing, is allowed to remarry. Evidence indicates that societies that see death as natural and that provide grieving ceremonies and family support—such as the Samoans—find widowhood less painful than do those that are uncomfortable with death and ignore the subject as much as possible (e.g., in the United States).

CONCLUSION

This chapter has examined mate-selection practices that have been common in many times and places throughout the world. Although largely an economic or political transaction beyond the control of the couple themselves, it is becoming in modern times a free-choice situation based on affection.

One's wedding day is often considered to be the most important day in a person's life. There are many customs and rituals associated with getting married, many with deep meaning unknown to today's couples. I have analyzed some of the principal ones here. Finally, some of the major influences on marital adjustment and how these can differ by culture have been discussed.

REFERENCES

Billig, M. (1992). The marriage squeeze and the rise of groom price in India's Kerala state. *Journal of Comparative Family Studies, 23,* 197–216.

Buss, D., Abbot, M., Angleitner, A., Asherian, A., Biaggio, A., Blancovillasenor, A., et al. (1990). International preferences in selecting mates: A study of 37 cultures. *Journal of Cross-Cultural Psychology, 21*(1), 5–47.

Chesser, B. (1980). Analysis of wedding rituals: An attempt to make weddings more meaningful. *Family Relations, 29,* 204–209.

Fielding, W. (1942). *Strange customs of courtship and marriage.* New York: New Home Library.

Hutter, M. (1981). *The changing family: Comparative perspectives.* New York: John Wiley & Sons.

Jimenez, M. (1992, July 26). Many Indo-Canadians follow age-old custom. *Edmonton Journal,* p. B3.

Liao, C., & Heaton, T. (1992). Divorce trends and differentials in China. *Journal of Comparative Family Studies, 23,* 413–429.

Murdock, G. (1967). Ethnographic atlas: A summary. *Ethology, 6,* 109–236.

Okonjo, K. (1992). Aspects of continuity and change in mate-selection among the Igbo west of the river Niger. *Journal of Comparative Family Studies, 23,* 339–360.

Peters, J. (1987). Yanomama mate selection and marriage. *Journal of Comparative Family Studies, 18,* 79–98.

Queen, S., Habenstein, R., & Quadagno, J. (1985). *The family in various cultures.* New York: Harper & Row.

Simmons, T., & O'Connell, M. (2003). Married-couple and unmarried partner households: 2000. Washington, DC: U.S. Census Bureau. Retrieved May 14, 2005, from http://www.census.gov/prod/2003pubs/censr-5.pdf

Stephens, W. (1963). *The family in cross-cultural perspective.* New York: Holt, Rinehart & Winston.

Tober, B. (1984). *The bride: A celebration.* New York: Harry N. Abrams.

Tseng, W. -S., & Hsu, J. (1991). *Culture and family: Problems and therapy.* New York: Haworth Press.

Whitehead, B., & Popenoe, D. (2001). *The state of our unions: The social health of marriage in America.* New Brunsusick, NJ: Rutgers University, National Marriage Project.

CHAPTER 9

Parenting Practices Worldwide

JUDITH A. MYERS-WALLS,
KAREN S. MYERS-BOWMAN, AND GERMÁN POSADA

INTRODUCTION

Parenting has been identified as "the most challenging and complex of all the tasks of adulthood" (Zigler, 1995, p. xi). Parenting also is central to the transmission and expression of cultures (Harkness & Super, 1995). Parents are embedded in cultural settings, so parenting styles and practices differ from one culture to the next. Parents also transmit and alter the culture through the ways that they care for and teach their children. As Flanagan (2001) put it, "In the values we emphasize with our children, we are creating the personalities and principles that will shape the global environment of the next millennium. The choices we make in child rearing will fundamentally affect the kind of world they will create" (p. 34). Therefore, when discussing families and cultures it is critical to include parents, parenting practices, and parent-child relationships as part of the conversation. In this chapter, we will explore some ways that cultural context is evident in parenting and how understanding culture will help in understanding parenting. We will do this by examining basic parenting skills and practices in six categories, looking at research that has demonstrated how those practices vary (or not) by cultural setting, and providing the reader with exploratory questions to ask when considering parents in any cultural setting in order to understand them more completely and adapt programming or interventions appropriately.

DEFINING PARENTING

It is tempting to assume that everyone knows what a parent is and that there is therefore no reason to define the term. However, the study of families across cultures provides a strong reminder that such an assumption is not wise, because there is a significant amount of variability in the structures and activities of parenting. Despite this diversity, there is a core that comprises the commonalities of parents and parenthood. We will look at some of these core parenting concepts within this section.

Clearly one definition of *parent* refers to a person who contributes to biological reproduction that results in the birth of a child. There are limits to this definition, however. For example, Smith (1999) has said that this term refers to one static event that occurred in the past. He recommends use of the word *parenting,* which is action oriented and emphasizes what a parent *does.* He defines *parenting* as "assuming responsibility for the emotional, social, and physical growth and development of a child" (p. ix). In a similar way, Brooks (2004) describes parenting as a process that involves "a series of actions and interactions on the part of parents to promote the development of children" (p. 5). Parenting is what a parent *does* and therefore includes a wide variety of forms and actions. The parenting job also can be done by a variety of people, including mothers, fathers, grandparents, siblings, and other caregivers with formal or informal ties with and responsibility for a child. The constellation of people who perform the parenting job takes many forms in different cultures. When we use the word *parent,* we are referring to anyone who is acting in a parenting role by nourishing, protecting, and guiding a child. We will specify if the research we are using was limited to a particular subgroup of parents or caregivers, but when such a designation is not made, the assumption should be that we are referring to anyone in a culture who assumes some level of parenting responsibility.

Some authors have differentiated between parenting behaviors or practices and parenting style (Darling & Steinberg, 1993; Stevenson-Hinde, 1998). Parenting behaviors or practices have been described as "behaviors defined by specific content and socialization goals" (Darling & Steinberg, p. 492). On the other hand, *parenting style* has been defined as "a constellation of attitudes toward the child that are communicated to the child and that, taken together, create an emotional climate in which the parent's behaviors are expressed" (Darling & Steinberg, p. 488). Stevenson-Hinde indicated that the difference between practices and style may be difficult to identify but suggested that it is a distinction to keep in mind. Because much of the literature on parenting and culture does not make the distinction between practices and style, our review will not always be able to differentiate between the two, but we will mention the issue where it is relevant.

DEFINING *CULTURE*

The other major concept in this chapter also deserves a clear definition: *culture.* Discussions of culture often include a presentation of a set of characteristics, behaviors, rituals, and beliefs that are used to describe a group of people who: (a) live within (or originated from) a specific country or geographical region, (b) share a religious affiliation, (c) claim common ancestry or heritage, or (d) are grouped together for other reasons. This descriptive approach implies that culture is a static, unchanging entity that exists outside of and has a unidirectional impact upon individuals and families—*all* individuals and families in a specific area or group. This suggests that people are products of their cultures. That is, it assumes that the culture is the powerful force that helps shape the people according to a culturally determined image. Although sets of descriptors can be helpful in depicting and understanding some variations in human values, behaviors, and goals in different groups, this method also can be narrowing and may limit one's recognition of the dynamic and continuously changing nature of cultural identity and experience (Laird, 2000; Strauss & Quinn, 1997). Therefore, it is important to move beyond "the idea that culture is a *thing*" (D'Andrade, 1995, p. 250) and examine the dynamic *process* of culture.

Instead of a stereotyped and unchanging conceptualization, we use the term *culture* to refer to recurring, common objects and events of a group of people and the shared meanings they create about such objects and events (Strauss & Quinn, 1997). This broadens the concept to include a wide variety of cultural contexts rather than implying that culture is limited to ethnic or national groups that have clear boundaries or are easily separable from each other. Thus, cultures include many shifting and overlapping identities. How can this be applied to parents—the focus of this chapter? Parents can share experiences and create meaning with people with whom they share some characteristics and expectations and with whom they identify—such as people who read the same books (e.g., Dr. Spock, James Dobson, murder mysteries, or the Book of Mormon) or watch the same television shows they do (e.g., *Oprah,* the History Channel, or professional wrestling); people whose children attend the same classes or are in the same activities as their children (e.g., "soccer moms," "stage mothers," or parents of children in Montessori schools); and people who have had similar education or training to theirs (e.g., transcendental meditation, business management, or midwifery), even if they live in different parts of the world (Strauss & Quinn). This highlights the concept that people can be members of multiple cultural groups.

Also, because culture is composed of shared meanings, it is constantly in motion, changing in meanings and definitions. It is constantly evolving and can be understood only in the context of examining the past, present, and projected future according to the individuals and families involved in the culture. Although they may not be conscious of this time context, parents appear to apply it in their parenting behaviors; studies have shown that parents try to prepare their children to live in the future world they anticipate more than preparing them for the present (Flanagan, 2001).

When professionals talk about becoming culturally sensitive or culturally competent, they often are referring to the process of learning about or knowing how to work with "the other," or those different from oneself (Laird, 2000). The approach rarely includes reflection on one's own cultural characteristics or background. This reflects the belief that cultural characteristics focus on difference and contrast (e.g., male-female, black-white, rich-poor)—in other words, me-you or us-them. Although this can be very helpful, there are also potential pitfalls in this approach. One problem with this perspective is that, when taken by the dominant culture, "different from" often means or implies "less than" (Laird). This perspective encourages the professional to rely on stereotypes or to overgeneralize assumptions to an entire group of people. It can create a kind of competition or judgment that we would like to avoid in this chapter. Instead, we will provide you with a tool to help you take the perspective that has been described as "informed not-knowing" (Shapiro, as cited in Laird, p. 102). This means that we encourage you to become as informed as possible about both yourself and those you perceive as different from you in order to be culturally aware and responsible in your professional interactions with others while recognizing the limitations of being an outsider. We believe this is especially important for white people in the United States, some of whom think that culture is something that other people have. "An open-minded appreciation of cultural differences concerning ethical values is essential in evaluating the child-rearing practices of a subculture that is not one's own" (Baumrind, 1994, p. 362). What strategies can students and professionals in the family field use to achieve this?

Falicov (1995) outlined four positions that can be taken when examining cultural issues: universalist, particularist, ethnic focused, and multidimensional. The *universalist* perspective asserts that families share important similarities—that they are more alike than different. For example, all children need love and discipline, and all parents provide some combination of nurturance and control. Taken to an extreme level, this position implies that all families could be viewed and treated the same way. Although the universalist position discourages professionals from overemphasizing differences and group membership, it also may lead professionals to ignore real differences that exist among groups and may discourage adapting practices to fit the needs of those groups. An extreme universalist approach presents the opportunity for inaccurately focusing on what one person asserts as universal or normal when that person's assertion may be merely "'local' knowledge or beliefs based on the cultural forms developed or 'invented' by specific subgroups" (Falicov, p. 374). It also leads to the danger that some types of families—the presumably "universal" families—may become the standard of comparison by which other families are judged (Allen, 1978; Scanzoni, Polonko, Teachman, & Thompson, 1989; Wilson, 1986). This can develop "a default norm . . . representing the majority group or the group in power" (Myers-Walls, 2000, p. 363).

In direct contrast to the universalist position is the *particularist* perspective. This view maintains that families are more different from each other than they are alike. From this extreme position, it is not possible to make generalizations, because each family is considered to be unique. A person using this perspective may refer to the culture of a family, but that culture would not be shared with anyone else outside that specific family. One is required to uncover the intricacies of each family while making no assumptions or presumptions based on group membership or characteristics.

The *ethnic-focused* perception stresses how families differ by ethnicity. "This position focuses on regularities of thoughts, behavior, feelings, customs, and rituals that stem from belonging to a particular group" (Falicov, 1995, p. 374). Again, there are some helpful aspects to this approach, but at its extreme it can lead to what has been called a "tourist approach" to learning about culture, in which the traits and customs are presented for cultures as though one is visiting each culture as an outsider. To become culturally competent under this approach requires separate, focused training sessions about each cultural group with which one may come in contact. Several limitations of this approach include: (a) the tendency to stereotype members of particular groups based on overgeneralizations (e.g., assuming that every Hispanic parent accepts male dominance in the family or that every African American parent believes in and uses physical punishment); (b) holding the false assumption that all members of a group are more similar to each other than they are different, so that a professional can talk with two or three parents in one group and thereby find out what all parents in that group think or need; and (c) assuming an outsider who is learning about a culture is completely objective and can learn about the culture without his or her own background or assumptions affecting any conclusions he or she draws about that culture. It also can give the impression that training about families that is not focused on an ethnic group is neutral or culture free (Falicov).

The *multidimensional* position provides a much broader perspective for learning about and dealing with culture. This viewpoint refers to culture as

> those sets of shared world views, meanings and adaptive behaviors derived from simultaneous membership and participation in a multiplicity of contexts, such as rural, urban or suburban setting; language, age, gender, cohort, family configuration, race, ethnicity, religion, nationality, socioeconomic status, employment, education, occupation, sexual orientation, political ideology; migration and stage of acculturation. (Falicov, 1995, p. 375)

This means that understanding the cultural context of a female teacher in Greece with two biological children who lives in a small city and is Greek Orthodox requires more than just knowledge about national Greek traditions and practices when one is using the multidimensional perspective. This perspective requires that we know enough to ask good questions and to notice many dimensions of culture when they are right in front of us (Laird, 2000). We have adopted this fourth approach to examining parenting across cultures. Therefore, throughout the chapter we propose questions that will help the reader accomplish this goal.

PARENTING AND CULTURE

As described above, in this chapter we are taking a multidimensional approach to understanding the cultural context of parenting. We will do this by focusing on how parents differ from each other in ways related to the multiplicity of their group memberships and contexts. At the same time that we look at differences, we believe that there are some key tasks and perspectives that all parents share. Several authors have assumed that parents in all settings want common outcomes for their children. For example, LeVine (1974, 1988) described three universal goals of parents: (a) the physical survival and health of the child, (b) the preparation of the child for economic and practical self-maintenance, and (c) the development of the child's ability to maintain cultural practices and values. Taking a more detailed approach to shared parenting tasks, Smith, Cudaback, Goddard, and Myers-Walls (1994) developed a model of critical parenting behaviors that appear to "facilitate the development of caring, competent, and healthy children" (p. 15). They listed 29 practices that arose from research findings associating those practices with positive outcomes in children (admittedly using primarily U.S. samples) and placed them into six categories. They called their list the National Extension Parent Education Model (NEPEM). Their attempt was to create a model that was as broadly applicable as possible. As they put it, "We believe that the more abstract practices we identified are critical for U.S. children regardless of the culture that nurtures their growth" (p. 17). A national survey of the model was conducted with administrators, university-based specialists, and local parenting educators employed by or collaborating with the Cooperative Extension Service. Respondents indicated overwhelmingly (90%) that they felt the words and phrases identified in the model were free of cultural, racial, and sexual bias (Smith et al.). The six categories of the model are: Guide, Nurture, Understand, Motivate, Advocate, and Care for Self (see Table 9.1).

Because of the support it has received; because the model has been used in several other countries, by Early Head Start, and by the U.S. Congress as a framework; and because it is the only comprehensive model of parenting behaviors found by these authors, we will use the parenting practices identified in NEPEM as an organizing structure for examining parenting in international or multicultural settings. Each following section provides a brief description of the relevant NEPEM category (or categories) and a brief summary of research literature highlighting some similarities and differences in the parenting practices across cultures. A list of questions related to the parenting practices is provided in Table 9.2. These questions are an expansion of an effort by Myers-Walls, Myers-Bowman, and Dunn (2003) and are designed to assist anyone studying or working with parents from diverse cultures.

Guide and Motivate

One category of the NEPEM model refers to a commonly identified and important function of parenting: guiding children. According to Smith and his colleagues (1994), parental guidance includes "the development of personal strength in children and the benevolent expression of authority

Table 9.1 The National Extension Parent Education Model

Icon & Category		*Priority practice*
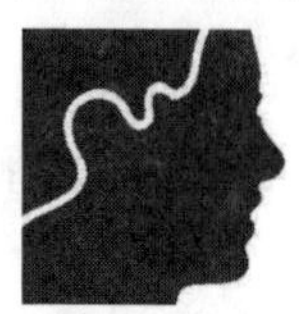	CARE FOR SELF	• Manage personal stress. • Manage family resources. • Offer support to other parents. • Ask for and accept support from others when needed. • Recognize one's own personal and parenting strengths. • Have a sense of purpose in setting child-rearing goals. • Cooperate with one's child-rearing partners.
	UNDERSTAND	• Observe and understand one's children and their development. • Recognize how children influence and respond to what happens around them.
	GUIDE	• Model appropriate desired behavior. • Establish and maintain reasonable limits. • Provide children with developmentally appropriate opportunities to learn responsibility. • Convey fundamental values underlying basic human decency. • Teach problem-solving skills. • Monitor children's activities and facilitate their contact with peers and adults.
	NURTURE	• Express affection and compassion. • Foster children's self-respect and hope. • Listen and attend to children's feelings and ideas. • Teach kindness. • Provide for the nutrition, shelter, clothing, health, and safety needs of one's children. • Celebrate life with one's children. • Help children feel connected to family history and cultural heritage.
	MOTIVATE	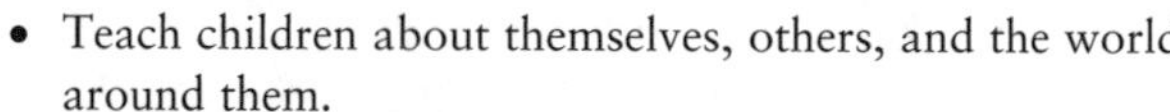 • Teach children about themselves, others, and the world around them. • Stimulate curiosity, imagination, and the search for knowledge. • Create beneficial learning conditions. • Help children process and manage information.
	ADVOCATE	• Find, use, and create community resources when needed to benefit one's children and the community of children. • Stimulate social change to create supportive environments for children and families. • Build relationships with family, neighborhood, and community groups.

Developed by Charles A. Smith, Dorothea Cudaback, H. Wallace Goddard, and Judith A. Myers-Walls in collaboration with extension professionals throughout the United States. This project was supported by the Extension Service, U.S. Department of Agriculture, and the Cooperative Extension Service, Kansas State University, under special project number 92-EXCA-2-0182.

Table 9.2 Questions to Guide Exploration of the Cultural Context of Parenting

Questions related to the National Extension Parent Education Model (NEPEM) categories of Guide and Motivate

- How do parents teach (e.g., model, verbally instruct, physically guide) appropriate behavior and attitudes?
- How do parents establish limits for their children, how are limits enforced, and what forms of discipline do parents use with their children?
- How do parents monitor their children's activities?
- How do parents stimulate curiosity and the search for knowledge?
- How is interpersonal conflict resolved within the culture, and how does this affect the ways in which parents model and teach problem-solving skills?
- How do parents provide children with opportunities to learn and acquire responsibility and other fundamental values within their social context?

Questions related to the NEPEM category of Nurture

- How do parents and children interact (e.g., explore issues of proximity and distance, physical contact, carrying, cosleeping, verbal expressions, provision of material goods), and how is affection expressed? Does it vary by the sex or age of the child and the caregiver?
- How do parents focus on connecting with children or establishing independence? Is one emphasized over the other? Does it vary by time in the life course?
- Who is primarily responsible for caring for children at different ages (e.g., parents, grandparents, siblings, day-care providers, teachers, all adults)? Is this responsibility connected to women more than men—or vice versa?
- How do the socioeconomic status of the community and the availability of community services affect the ability of parents to meet their children's basic needs?
- Whose needs in the culture are dominant (parents, children, elderly, certain social groups), and what is the role of the children? Are they seen as mostly a blessing or a burden?

Questions related to the NEPEM category of Understand

- What are the expectations for children's behavior and abilities at different ages and stages?
- What do parents believe their children can achieve at different ages, and how do they try to facilitate children's development?
- Who are considered to be parenting experts—older family members, younger family members, scholars, people with specific training, community leaders?
- How do parents become competent or successful in learning about children and their development?
- How do parents determine their parenting goals?
- Do parents feel that parenting is easy and comes naturally, or do they feel it requires training, expert advice, or hard work?
- What do parents believe are the causes of children's development and behavior?

Questions related to the NEPEM categories of Care for Self and Advocate

- What economic and employment resources are available to families, and how do families manage the resources that are available to them?
- How do parents represent their children's needs to community agencies and organizations?
- Whose needs are dominant—children's or adults'?
- What is a "good" parent?
- What are parental preferences regarding child behavior?
- How do people define common values, which values are emphasized by parents and the larger society, and how are the values communicated or reflected in parenting practices?

by parents" (p. 28). Parents need to identify, introduce, and enforce reasonable limits while also gradually giving freedom to children and encouraging them to be appropriately responsible for themselves. Parents also must communicate values, nurture self-control, and respond to their children's misbehavior. Issues in this category are closely related to the NEPEM category of Motivate, which outlines the parenting practices that support child learning, curiosity, and the search for learning. Because the major goal of discipline is teaching children proper behavior, we will discuss the two categories together.

In his cross-cultural research with parents, LeVine (1988) found that different cultural groups meet these parenting goals in a variety of ways. Therefore, we need to understand how the parents' disciplinary and education-related behaviors are related to the broader cultural models and expectations about parental and child behavior. Parenting styles are closely related to how parents guide their children, because, as mentioned earlier, parenting styles reflect a combination of parental attitudes and behaviors regarding children. Therefore, the guidance parents provide for their children occurs within the emotional environment created by the parents' styles.

Baumrind (1966, 1971) developed four categories of parenting styles based on combining the dimensions of warmth or responsiveness—"the parent's emotional expression of love" (Baumrind, 1996, p. 410) and control or demandingness—"parents' attempts to integrate the child into the family and society by demanding behavioral compliance" (Darling & Steinberg, 1993, p. 489)—exhibited by parents toward their children. The four styles are (a) authoritative/democratic (high warmth and high control), (b) authoritarian (low warmth and high control), (c) permissive (high warmth and low control), and (d) neglectful (low warmth and low control).

Research conducted in the United States with primarily white, middle-class families based on these parenting styles has consistently shown that they are closely related to children's behavior and outcomes (Darling & Steinberg, 1993). Authoritative parenting appears as the optimal parenting style for this cultural group, because it seems to result in a multitude of positive child outcomes (e.g., competence, internalization of parental values, etc.). However, "in other cultural contexts, authoritarian parenting is more likely to be the norm and [is] less likely to be associated with negative child outcomes" (Rudy & Grusec, 2001, p. 202). For example, African American mothers who live in high-risk areas have been found to use authoritarian parenting techniques without this resulting in negative consequences for the children (Kelley, Power, & Wimbush, as cited in Rudy & Grusec). This has been attributed to the necessity of keeping the children safe in an unsafe environment by demanding the children's obedience. The same point can be seen when looking at another cultural group. Chinese parents consistently score higher on scales of authoritarian parenting and are more restrictive than American mothers, but, once again, the children do not show negative effects from this parenting style (Chao, as cited in Rudy & Grusec; Dornbusch, Ritter, Leiderman, Roberts, & Fraleigh, 1987; Ho & Kangh, 1984).

Why does one parenting style work well in a certain culture, but not in another? One possible explanation is that authoritative parenting fits well with the dominant values in Western cultures that emphasize individualism and achieving success through upward mobility (Rudy & Grusec, 2001, p. 203). At the same time, non-Western cultures emphasize cooperation and collectivism and may face situations in which the parents must be vigilant about a child's safety (e.g., high poverty, high crime, war). In the latter settings, children must learn to follow the instructions of their parents and to cooperate with others in order to survive and succeed. "Socialization practices that are normative for a culture are generally well accepted by children" (Baumrind, 1996, p. 409). Therefore, it is important to examine cultural context to understand how and why parenting styles are related to the socialization of children. It is also important to keep in mind that parents may demonstrate several parenting styles. For example, although parents in a particular cultural group may exhibit tendencies toward a specific style in certain situations and contexts, they could exhibit a different style in a different set of contexts or situations, and individual parents may vary from the cultural norm.

When learning about or working with parents of different cultural groups, then, it is important to examine the following specific aspects related to parenting style: how warmth and emotional support are provided by parents, what different patterns and communication strategies are used, the prevailing social standards regarding social and behavioral control, and goals and expectations for children. It also is important to examine the rationale parents have for their own behavior as well as their ideas about what kinds of outcomes they want to encourage for their children.

As mentioned above, the goals of guidance and discipline overlap with the NEPEM category of Motivate, which addresses the encouragement and support of children's learning. Parents teach their children appropriate behavior, attitudes, values, and other information both deliberately and unintentionally. Therefore, in considering how parents guide their children, we need to take into account the diversity of methods they use to convey to children what they need to learn. Cross-cultural studies on parental behavior, preferences, and beliefs find both similarities and differences in specific aspects of this task among cultures (e.g., Fisher, Wang, Kennedy, & Cheng, 1998; Harwood, Miller, & Irizarry, 1995; LeVine, 1988; Posada et al., 2002; Zavalkink & Riksen-Walraven, 2001).

One variation among cultural groups is the basic premise of whether parents acknowledge their modeling role and whether they feel it is important. Wright (1998) studied parenting practices in France, Japan, and the United States. He found that French parents perceive child development as progressing independently of parenting; therefore, they are likely to believe there is no need to monitor their own behavior. Parents in Japan, however, focus heavily on traditions and carrying on cultural practices, so they have high expectations that children will repeat what parents do. Wright also looked at U.S. parents and found that they place emphasis on individual abilities and using the "right" information. This may lead some U.S. parents to assume that children are making their own independent decisions, such that parental behavior does not matter. At the same time, it may lead other parents to focus on their own independent choice to be responsible parents, and they may rely on information sources that stress modeling and that encourage parents to be very conscious of the impact of their own behavior.

Parents establish limits and teach appropriate behaviors in the context of parent-child relationships. These relationships create an atmosphere that can either facilitate or make more difficult the parents' role of guiding their children's socialization and motivating them to learn (Ainsworth, Bell, & Stayton, 1974; Darling & Steinberg, 1993; Waters, Kondo-Ikemura, Posada, & Richters, 1991). Relationships set the stage for and influence the guidance parents provide in different aspects of a child's life (such as relationships with peers, academic achievement, norms of good behavior, etc.). For example, secure child-parent attachment relationships early in life help children to be more open and receptive to their parents (Waters et al.). Close relationships between parents and children also make the modeling of positive behaviors more powerful. Waters and colleagues proposed that children are committed to their families' values and norms of behavior when the parents: (a) respond promptly and appropriately, (b) help the child recover when upset and then help the child to reengage in the environment, (c) facilitate the child's explorations and effective transactions with the surroundings, (d) monitor the child's activities, and (e) cooperate with ongoing child behavior. Generally, the children's commitment to the parents' values is unspoken and occurs long before the family norms and rules of good behavior are either explained or enforced. This process is assumed to take place in all cultures, but it is very important to explore how it takes place specifically within the cultural context of interest. Some of the cultural variations in other aspects of the parent-child relationship will be addressed in more detail in the Nurture section below.

In summary, research has confirmed that the categories of Guide and Motivate are critical to parenting in any culture, but the ways that those functions are accomplished vary by culture. See Table 9.2 for important questions to ask when examining the guidance and motivational roles of parents in any cultural group.

Nurture

The Nurture category in NEPEM (Smith et al., 1994) deals with the parenting skills that are required to meet the physical and emotional needs of the child. These include securing children's health, safety, nourishment, and shelter along with expressing affection, building self-respect, and helping children understand and feel connected to their family history and cultural heritage. Parental care and nurturance are expressed in diverse ways across different cultures, as indicated by the cross-cultural literature on parenting behaviors and practices (e.g., Fisher et al., 1998; Sharma & LeVine, 1998; Super & Harkness, 1986; Wu et al., 2002). However, this literature also provides evidence in support of some cross-cultural commonalities of some aspects of caring for and nurturing children (e.g., Fisher et al.; LeVine, 1988; Posada et al., 1995). That research cues us in to the importance of attending to both the functions of parenting and the specific ways those functions may be fulfilled in different contexts (Bowlby, 1982; Daly & Wilson, 1983; LeVine, 1982).

Because parent-child relationships are essential for providing nurturance, we present information on cross-cultural research conducted on this topic, focusing primarily on attachment. *Attachment* refers to "an enduring affectional tie that unites one person to another, over time and across space" (Thompson, as cited in Brooks, 2004, p. 46). All human infants have the inclination and basic ability to develop an attachment relationship with one or a few primary caregivers (Bowlby, 1982), and attachment continues to be a theme in family relationships throughout the life cycle. Securely attached infants and children balance exploration with seeking proximity to attachment figures. Although this balance between wandering away and checking in with the "home base" varies by child and by specific setting, the function of this behavior pattern is to protect the infant (and later the child or adolescent) while he or she takes advantage of opportunities for learning within the environment.

Some aspects of attachment relationships seem to be fairly universal. Ainsworth and her colleagues (Ainsworth, Blehar, Waters, & Walls, 1978) suggested that parents who (a) are aware of their children's signals and interpret them correctly, (b) respond to the children promptly and appropriately, (c) cooperate with their children's behavior, and

(d) are accepting and accessible have children who are confident in their caregivers' availability and response. In other words, sensitive parents have children who are secure in their attachment relationships (see a meta-analysis of 65 studies by de Wolff & van IJzendoorn, 1997).

Despite the number and overall consistency of studies that give the impression that attachment issues are universal, most research has used middle-class samples in industrialized societies such as Canada, Germany, and the United States (Belsky, 1999; de Wolff & van IJzendoorn, 1997). In a relatively recent review of child-mother relationships from non-Western cultures (i.e., in Africa, China, Japan, and Israel), van IJzendoorn and Sagi (1999) concluded that current cross-cultural research is rare and that more studies are required to determine if the attachment issues are similar across cultures. Addressing this shortcoming, a few studies have been conducted in South America. They have supported the general conclusions of attachment theory in samples from both low and middle socioeconomic status groups from Chile and Colombia (Posada et al., 1999; Posada et al., 2002; Valenzuela, 1990, 1997).

Therefore, research findings, although scant, seem to support the hypothesis that, across many different cultures, children become attached to their caregivers, and the quality of care provided by parents is associated with children's attachment security. However, research also has shown that the ways parents demonstrate caregiving behavior and establish attachment relationships vary by culture (Posada et al., 1999; Posada et al., 2002). Thus, although quality of care seems to be universally related to security in attachment, the definition of quality and the expression of attachment relationships appear to vary according to the context in which the relationship takes place. (It also is important to note that most studies of attachment have focused on infants and that investigations looking at older children and adolescents with their parents may yield a different picture.)

When trying to understand nurturance in different cultural contexts, it is important to examine parent-child interactions. Although it seems critical that all children establish firm attachments with their parents, we also need to examine *how* those attachments are constructed in different cultures. How do parents regard a child's perspective? How are parents' responses adapted to cultural socialization goals overall? Answers to these questions can be derived from observations of actual parenting behavior as the parent becomes attuned with her or his child and of how the timing and appropriateness of parental responses to the child's signals are managed.

The broader context also is important to consider when determining the quality of care children receive. Beyond the parent-child relationship, the primary premise of this chapter is that parents nurture their children within a system broader than that of the dyad. From the start, children are members of a family and a cultural group. Thus, some of the questions regarding the Nurture category are concerned with the physical and social settings of the family in which the child's needs are perceived and met. For example, some studies have illustrated that the quality of maternal care is influenced by difficult living conditions, such as stressors and marital conflict (Howes & Markman, 1989; Owen & Cox, 1997; Vaughn, Egeland, Sroufe, & Waters, 1979). Therefore, parents living in cultures experiencing political violence, serious environmental disasters, and distressed economic conditions may struggle to nurture their children in an optimal way (see Scheper-Hughes, 1985). We need to examine the living conditions of families, the objects and toys children are provided, space for the child at home, and safety issues.

To further understand the context of nurturing children in various cultural settings, other issues should be addressed concerning typical parental behavioral strategies to deal with children at particular ages—for example, physical contact, family activities, feeding routines, games and other play activities, household tasks, and hygienic practices. Finally, several issues related to this category also overlap with other areas of the NEPEM model (e.g., Guide, Motivate, Care for Self, and Advocate), such as the caretakers' preferences about child behavior; their socialization goals and educational expectations regarding their child; the resources available to achieve those goals; and issues about stress, social support, and depression.

Clearly, nurturance is an important aspect of parenting and takes place in every culture. See Table 9.2 for important questions to ask when examining the variability in parental nurturing behaviors across cultures.

Understand

The category Understand in NEPEM is concerned with the parenting task of understanding children's development and the processes associated with it. Parents must determine the basic needs of their children and recognize how the needs change as children grow and mature and how parents and children influence each other in different ways throughout the life course, in order to evaluate the reasonableness of their expectations for their children's behavior in choosing their parenting strategies. A number of cross-cultural studies have addressed issues related to this category. Much of the research has reviewed parents' expectations regarding the timing of various milestones and transitions. Other studies have explored parents' perceptions of their children and their parenting knowledge level and attitudes toward parenting training.

What parents think about children's development will affect what they do as parents. Keller, Yovsi, and Voelker (2002) studied mothers in Cameroon and Germany to investigate the apparent early development of motor skills in African infants. They found that mothers in Cameroon expected their infants to be capable of and to need significant physical activity at an earlier age than did German mothers. Therefore, mothers in Cameroon provided a high amount of physical stimulation. In contrast, German mothers provided prompt verbal response and verbal stimulation rather than physical stimulation. In a separate study, Suizzo (2002) found that Dutch parents tried to minimize stimulation of any kind and scheduled only very few activities for their children. They believed that overstimulating children was a major danger. The parents in each of these countries tended to judge their approaches as "right." In fact, Keller and colleagues (2002) found that mothers from Cameroon and Germany both judged the mothers in the other country as interacting inappropriately with their babies. Mothers in Cameroon also tended to show more concern for their children's health and safety than did German mothers, a concern that is likely related to the higher infant mortality rates in Cameroon. The cultural differences measured by these studies are examples of how developmental expectations can lead to parenting behaviors. This understanding both leads to and stems from differences in outcomes for children, in that parents who expect behaviors from children are likely to create situations that make those behaviors more likely, and observing those behaviors continues to support the expectation.

Some authors have questioned whether developmental differences that have been measured among countries are attributable to differences in parental perceptions or to measurable differences in ages and stages of development. Russell, Hart, Robinson, and Olsen (2003) asked Australian and U.S. mothers to describe their 4-year-old children's behavior. On the surface, these countries are very similar,

but the results of the study showed that U.S. mothers rated their children as being more active, aggressive, and emotional; higher on sociability; and lower on shyness than the Australian mothers rated their children. It cannot be determined from these data whether the reported differences between children in the two countries are actual behavioral differences or whether the parent (and, in this study, also teacher) ratings are affected by their culturally influenced definitions of positive behavior. As Russell and colleagues reported, "Actual difference could arise from cultural differences in expectations for children's behavior, as well as contrasts in parenting practices. . . . [C]ulture variables may influence both children's behavior and [the parents'] perceptions of behavior" (p. 82). When working with parents in different cultural contexts, then, it is important to assess parent expectations as well as to examine children's developmental accomplishments using standardized norms.

Consistent with some of the discussion in the Care for Self section below, it is important to note that, even when some central parenting values are shared, varying cultures may define the value differently or may try to achieve it using very different strategies. This can affect parents' attempts to facilitate their children's development. For example, a number of countries value independence and encourage it in their children. German parents attempt to nurture independence by leaving children at home alone to care for themselves, whereas French parents avoid holding their babies too much and do not cosleep (Suizzo, 2002). Some authors have said that U.S. parents assume that children are born dependent biological organisms, so they systematically work to help children become independent (Caudill & Weinstein, 1962). U.S. parents do this by giving children their own bedrooms and celebrating what they can do for themselves. So, although German, French, and U.S. parents all value independence, they use very different methods to encourage their children to become independent and also may define independence and its value differently. As Suizzo concluded, "in order to understand variation in how parents rear children and how children develop, we must examine not only what is observable, such as children's physical environments and parents' caregiving behaviors, but what is less apparent—the contents of parents' minds" (p. 297).

Parents' understanding of children's development also plays a role in parents' perceived need of assistance in developing child-rearing skills. For example, some researchers have found that parents in Italy see development as natural and inevitable, and they expect that family members will envelope the child and participate in child care (New, 1988). Because of these factors, Italian parents have little or no interest in parenting education. In Japan, on the other hand, studies have shown that parents tend to feel primarily responsible for outcomes with their children (Stevenson, Azuma, & Hakuta, 1986; Stevenson & Lee, 1990), and parenting success is thought to be due primarily to parental effort but not ability. With their emphasis on parental hard work, it can be assumed that knowledge or ability may take a secondary role, so Japanese parents also do not emphasize parent education. Bornstein and colleagues (1998) discovered, however, that both Italian and Japanese mothers reported low levels of perceived competence in parenting, and both groups reported willingness to invest time and energy in parenting. Japanese mothers, however, reported less satisfaction with their parenting and reported less success with balancing parenting with the rest of their lives. In contrast, French parents tend to depend on intuition in parenting and report that parenting is easy (Bornstein et al.; Suizzo, 2002). As a result, French parents reported that they were not likely to seek out parenting programs.

Again, the parenting-culture relationship is complex and involved. It is possible that parents in interdependent, communalist societies who share responsibility for parenting with others are likely to report lower levels of child development knowledge and are less likely to feel a need for parenting instruction or support because of the availability of child-rearing partners (Bornstein & Cote, 2003). One clear conclusion, however, is that any parenting intervention or educational effort should be based on an understanding of cultural attitudes regarding the parent's role in influencing child outcomes. See Table 9.2 for important questions to address when examining children's developmental progress and parents' understanding of this process.

Care for Self and Advocate

Care for Self is not always seen as a parenting skill, but Smith and his colleagues (1994) argued that it is a key foundational piece for accomplishing the other tasks of parenting. The Care for Self category includes the management of stress, time, and resources; connection with others; and identification of strengths, goals, and philosophical approaches related to children and parenting. The Advocate category of NEPEM also is not always incorporated in considerations of parenting, although it includes important parenting tasks. It consists of skills related to identifying community resources to help children and representing children's needs and values to resource providers.

Several studies related to these domains have looked at the impact of varying income levels of individual parents and of cultural groups. These provide insight into how resource levels affect parenting. For example, Kaufman and Rizzini (2002) reflected on the management of both resources and stress when they describe how parental unemployment leads both to family stress and changes in child care conditions. Durbrow, Peña, Masten, Sesma, and Williamson (2001) explored this relationship when they looked at mothers who were living in poverty in the Philippines, St. Vincent (a Caribbean island), and the United States. Although these are very different cultures, the researchers identified at least one theme that appeared to be consistent across all three limited-resource cultures: a focus on obedience in the children. In a similar way, Bornstein and colleagues (1998) reported that Argentine parents experienced a significant amount of insecurity in their lives and also demonstrated authoritarian parenting styles. These high levels of parental control are consistent with classic studies by B. B. Whiting and J. W. M. Whiting (1975), who found that socioeconomic status was related to parenting goals and styles. Their interpretation was that societies with limited resources stressed the qualities related to the expectations that members of that society must work together and maintain strict standards in order to ensure survival, and that all members of such societies need to share responsibilities. This is consistent with the earlier statements about authoritarian parenting in low-resource populations. On the other hand, societies with abundant resources and whose basic needs are met comfortably are able to encourage the development of entrepreneurship and creativity so that individuals can distinguish themselves from each other and get ahead. As Whiting and Whiting put it, "methods of socialization adopted by different cultures prepare the children for the adult roles that they must assume when they grow up" (p. 71). These socialization practices are heavily influenced by the availability of resources.

Economic conditions can have a ripple effect on several areas of parenting. Kaufman and Rizzini (2002) noted some consequences of unemployment in Brazil: "When fathers are unable to fulfill the role of provider they are less likely to be involved in other ways in their children's lives (and/or . . . mothers are less likely to facilitate or encourage this involvement)" (p. 143). They noted that these conditions often are accompanied by maternal employment, resulting in children frequently being left to care for themselves. Although increasing maternal employment appears to be a relatively universal trend, these authors contrast results for the middle class with those for families with limited resources. The relative availability of resources and safety of the community are critical concerns when evaluating these trends. "The tendency seems to be that the children of the poor continue to be expected to care for themselves—and even to contribute to the family income—while middle class children may be left alone within the relatively protected spaces of homes and gated apartment complexes" (Kaufman & Rizzini, p. 143). In another study, Posada and colleagues (1999) reported that quality of maternal care was associated with socioeconomic status. Mothers living in poverty were found to be less sensitive to and cooperative with their children's behavior than middle-class mothers. Overall, findings suggest that parenting approaches that vary across countries are affected at least in part by the economic and employment conditions in the country or among subgroups of the country. Some parents may have more in common with parents of similar social status in other countries than with parents in their own country who have a different income level.

Additional issues in the Care for Self category are knowing one's parenting strengths and having a sense of purpose and philosophy in parenting. In the Advocate category, one is expected to be able to use those values to choose or create services for children and to represent one's values to service providers. The importance of parenting strengths, values, and philosophy leads us to explore what parents consider to be important and what vision they hold for their children's futures. These issues have been addressed by a number of researchers who have examined parenting values and their relationship to parenting practices across cultures. For example, Watanabe (2001) reported findings from a study that asked parents in six countries—Japan, Republic of Korea, Thailand, Sweden, the United Kingdom, and the United States—what lifestyles they did *not* want for their children as they grew older. One conclusion is that some countries are more restrictive (e.g., Republic of Korea) than others (e.g., the United Kingdom) in that they listed, respectively, more or fewer lifestyles that they did not want for their children. A variety of other patterns could be identified. For example, parents in the three Eastern countries (Korea, Japan, and Thailand) reported more discomfort with the idea of their children raising children who were not biologically related, such as stepchildren or adopted children, whereas parents from countries in the West (United States, United Kingdom, and Sweden) reported more discomfort with the idea of their children living with their parents as adults. These reported attitudes are consistent with observed parenting behaviors in those countries; many Western families travel to Eastern countries such as China and Korea to adopt a child, and many Asian couples expect to live with one set of parents when they marry.

Inglehart, Basañez, and Moreno (1998) took a very straightforward and extensive approach to investigate values across 43 countries in which adults were asked (among other questions) how important it was to teach children certain values in the home. The results from this study provide a reminder of the complexity of analyzing parenting values in different countries. The body of research described earlier suggested that obedience was likely to be especially important to parents in countries with limited resources. When the adults in the study by Inglehart and colleagues were asked about the importance of teaching obedience in the home, however, the picture became complicated. The country reporting the highest importance of teaching obedience was Nigeria, one of the poorest countries in the study—as would be expected on the basis of the previous studies. However, the second highest importance level for obedience was reported by Iceland, one of the 10 richest countries included in the study. At the same time, Iceland provided the highest rating of the importance of responsibility, and Nigeria provided the lowest. The authors concluded that the constellation of questions included in their study allowed for the identification of several regions in the world that could be clustered together because of shared values. Using our multidimensional approach to culture, however, we reach a different conclusion—that the overlap of values and uniqueness of cultural identities make cultural clustering clumsy and unsatisfying. The valuing of obedience needs to be viewed in the context of the other values held simultaneously by the culture and in the context of the understanding of obedience by people in that setting. Another issue to consider is related to language. Although all of the surveys used translations from the same original questionnaire, the nuances of each language mean that individuals from different countries may have responded to a slightly different concept when rating each item in the survey. For example, one can imagine that the word used for "obedience" in China could refer to more rigid standards than the word used for the similar concept in Iceland, or vice versa.

In addition to clustering countries that seem to share many values, another approach is clustering values that seem to represent certain countries. For example, Jose, C. S. Huntsinger, P. R. Huntsinger, and Liaw (2000) and Wu and colleagues (2002) listed values that appear to characterize Chinese culture and parenting, including restraint of emotion, modesty, filial piety, protection, persistence, directiveness, shaming/love withdrawal, and maternal involvement. When Wu and colleagues measured behaviors representing those values in Chinese and U.S. mothers, however, they found that all of the values they investigated were present to some degree in both cultures. However, they felt that the emphasis, meaning, and effect of each value varied across countries, and that parenting behaviors that may look similar could be associated with different values or goals. (Consider the discussions of independence and safety earlier in this chapter.)

A consideration of these studies confirms that values are very difficult concepts to measure. The fact that various cultures place different meanings on values is part of the challenge to understanding the influence of values, and it is also important to recognize the many components of value concepts. For example, a focus on either independence or interdependence has been said to characterize countries, and these dimensions have been used as variables in studies comparing countries. As Keller and colleagues (2003) have pointed out, these concepts include at least two dimensions: relatedness-separateness (also described as interpersonal distance), and autonomy-heteronomy (also described as agency or the ability to make one's own decisions and take action). Studies that do not recognize and examine both dimensions when they investigate the independence/interdependence variable will be likely to report confusing and inconsistent results. As Keller and colleagues (2002) put it, "It is difficult to compare ethnotheoretical accounts across cultural contexts . . . because different discourse styles and different orientations to children may need different systems of assessment" (p. 410).

An interesting way to assess values in a cultural context is to examine the content of typical children's stories and fairy tales. As a Taiwanese colleague of ours noted, children's stories in Chinese-related cultures do not include princes and princesses (C.-Y. Tang, personal communication, September

28, 2004). Instead, the focus in China and Taiwan is on stories that show cooperation, self-sacrifice, and filial piety, whereas in Western societies the emphasis in classic children's stories is on royalty, magical intervention, and individual accomplishment. This observation leads us to suggest that an additional possible strategy to discover the developmental goals and values in a society is to examine children's stories.

In summary, some of the stress- and resource-management skills and orientation that parents bring to the tasks of parenting appear to vary in different parenting contexts and cultural groups, and those variations are associated with parenting styles and behaviors. It is possible that the values create the cultural practices, the practices influence the values, or the practices and values are thoroughly intertwined in an inseparable fashion. See Table 9.2 for questions to guide an examination of cross-cultural differences regarding the NEPEM categories of Care for Self and Advocate.

CONCLUSION

Parents around the world deal with the daily tasks, unexpected events, frustrations, and joys of parenting. Groups of parents share experiences and understandings of the world with others around them, creating a cultural context for their parenting. This chapter has used the National Extension Parent Education Model (see Table 9.1) and cross-cultural research literature to review parenting practices and how they may vary according to cultural context. We have presented several issues and tasks that appear to be universal, but we also have highlighted a wide array of differences among groups of parents in varying cultural contexts. Using a multidimensional perspective of culture, we have stressed the constantly evolving nature of parenting and suggested that parents and other individuals belong to many different cultural contexts at once.

Table 9.2 provides a list of questions one should ask when trying to understand parents' cultures. These questions can help students understand the relationship between cultural context and parenting practices. They also can assist professionals as they adapt programming and expectations to fit the needs and characteristics of the various parents whom they serve. This list is a revision and expansion of the Cultural Characteristics Questionnaire (Myers-Walls et al., 2003) that we (and our students) have used to explore similarities and differences in family issues across cultures. In the same way, we encourage you to consider the questions in Table 9.2 for any population or subgroup you study or with whom you work. We hope this will help make your learning and programming experiences successful and relevant.

REFERENCES

Ainsworth, M. D. S., Bell, S. M., & Stayton, D. F. (1974). Infant-mother attachment and social development: Socialization as a product of reciprocal responsiveness to signals. In M. P. M. Richards (Ed.), *The integration of a child into a social world* (pp. 99–135). New York: Cambridge University Press.

Ainsworth, M. D. S., Blehar, M. C., Waters, E., & Wall, S. (1978). *Patterns of attachment*. Hillsdale, NJ: Lawrence Erlbaum.

Allen, W. (1978). The search for applicable theories of black family life. *Journal of Marriage and the Family, 40*, 117–131.

Baumrind, D. (1966). Effects of authoritative control on child behavior. *Child Development, 37,* 887–907.

Baumrind, D. (1971). Current patterns of parental authority. *Developmental Psychology Monograph, 4*(1), 1–103.

Baumrind, D. (1994). The social context of child maltreatment. *Family Relations, 43,* 360–368.

Baumrind, D. (1996). The discipline controversy revisited. *Family Relations, 45,* 405–414.

Belsky, J. (1999). Interactional and contextual determinants of attachment security. In J. Cassidy & P. R. Shaver (Eds.), *Handbook of attachment* (pp. 249–264). New York: Guilford Press.

Bornstein, M. H., & Cote, L. R. (2003). Cultural and parenting cognitions in acculturating cultures: 2. Patterns of prediction and structural coherence. *Journal of Cross-Cultural Psychology, 34,* 350–373.

Bornstein, M. H., Haynes, O. M., Azuma, H., Galperin, C., Maital, S., Ogino, M., et al. (1998). A cross-national study of self-evaluations and attributions in parenting: Argentina, Belgium, France, Israel, Italy, Japan, and the United States. *Developmental Psychology, 34,* 662–676.

Bowlby, J. (1982). *Attachment and loss: Vol. 1. Attachment.* New York: Basic Books.

Brooks, J. (2004). *The process of parenting* (6th ed.). Boston: McGraw-Hill.

Caudill, W., & Weinstein, H. (1962). Maternal care and infant behavior in Japan and America. *Psychiatry, 32,* 12–43.

Daly, M., & Wilson, M. (1983). *Sex, evolution, and behavior* (2nd ed.). Belmont, CA: Wadsworth.

D'Andrade, R. G. (1995). *The development of cognitive anthropology.* New York: Cambridge University Press.

Darling, N., & Steinberg, L. (1993). Parenting style as context: An integrative model. *Psychological Bulletin, 113,* 487–496.

de Wolff, M. S., & van IJzendoorn, M. H. (1997). Sensitivity and attachment: A meta-analysis on parental antecedents of infant attachment. *Child Development, 68,* 571–591.

Dornbusch, S. M., Ritter, P. L., Leiderman, P. H., Roberts, D. F., & Fraleigh, M. J. (1987). The relation of parenting style to adolescent school performance. *Child Development, 58,* 1244–1257.

Durbrow, E. H., Peña, L. F., Masten, A., Sesma, A., & Williamson, I. (2001). Mothers' conceptions of child competence in contexts of poverty: The Philippines, St. Vincent, and the United States. *International Journal of Behavioral Development, 25,* 438–443.

Falicov, C. J. (1995). Training to think culturally: A multidimensional comparative framework. *Family Process, 34,* 373–388.

Fisher, K. W., Wang, L., Kennedy, B., & Cheng, C. -L. (1998). Culture and biology in emotional development. In D. Sharma & K. W. Fisher (Eds.), *New directions for child development: Vol. 81. Socioemotional development across cultures* (pp. 21–44). San Francisco: Jossey-Bass.

Flanagan, C. (2001). Families and globalization: A new social contract and agenda for research. In J. A. Myers-Walls & P. Somlai, with R. N. Rapoport (Eds.), *Families as educators for global citizenship* (pp. 23–40). Aldershot, UK: Ashgate.

Harkness, S., & Super, C. (1995). Culture and parenting. In M. H. Bornstein (Ed.), *Handbook of parenting* (Vol. 2, pp. 211–234). Mahwah, NJ: Lawrence Erlbaum.

Harwood, R. L., Miller, J. G., & Irizarry, L. N. (1995). *Culture and attachment: Perceptions of the child in context.* New York: Guilford.

Ho, D. Y. F., & Kangh, T. K. (1984). Intergenerational comparisons of child-rearing attitudes and practices in Hong Kong. *Developmental Psychology, 20,* 1004–1016.

Howes, P., & Markman, H. (1989). Marital quality and child functioning: A longitudinal investigation. *Child Development, 60,* 1044–1051.

Inglehart, R., Basañez, M., & Moreno, A. (1998). *Human values and beliefs.* Ann Arbor: University of Michigan Press.

Jose, P. E., Huntsinger, C. S., Huntsinger, P. R., & Liaw, F. -R. (2000). Parental values and practices relevant to young children's social development. *Journal of Cross-Cultural Psychology, 31,* 677–702.

Kaufman, N. H., & Rizzini, I. (2002). *Globalization and children: Exploring potentials for enhancing opportunities in the lives of children and youth.* New York: Kluwer Academic/Plenum.

Keller, H., Papligoura, Z., Kuensemueller, P., Voelker, S., Papaeliou, C., Lohaus, A., et al. (2003). Concepts of mother-infant interaction in Greece and Germany. *Journal of Cross-Cultural Psychology, 34,* 677–689.

Keller, H., Yovsi, R. D., & Voelker, S. (2002). The role of motor stimulation in parental ethnotheories: The case of Cameroonian Nso and German women. *Journal of Cross-Cultural Psychology, 33,* 398–414.

Laird, J. (2000). Theorizing culture: Narrative ideas and practice principles. *Journal of Feminist Family Therapy, 11*(4), 99–114.

LeVine, R. A. (1974). Parental goals: A cross-cultural view. *Teachers College Record, 76,* 226–239.

LeVine, R. A. (1982). *Culture, behavior, and personality: An introduction to the comparative study of psychosocial adaptation.* New York: Aldine.

LeVine, R. A. (1988). Human parental care: Universal goals, cultural strategies, individual behavior. In R. A. LeVine, P. M. Miller, & M. M. West (Eds.), *Parental behavior in diverse societies* (pp. 3–12). San Francisco: Jossey-Bass.

Myers-Walls, J. A. (2000). Family diversity and family life education. In D. H. Demo, K. R. Allen, & M. A. Fine (Eds.), *Handbook of family diversity* (pp. 359–379). Oxford, UK: Oxford University Press.

Myers-Walls, J. A., Myers-Bowman, K. S., & Dunn, J. (2003). Cultural characteristics questionnaire: What does your target population look like? In D. Bredehoft & M. Walcheski (Eds.), *Family life education: Integrating theory and practice* (pp. 186–188). Minneapolis, MN: National Council on Family Relations.

New, R. S. (1988). Parental goals and Italian infant care. In R. A. LeVine, P. M. Miller, & M. M. West (Eds.), *New directions for child development: Vol. 40. Parental behavior in diverse societies* (pp. 51–63). San Francisco: Jossey-Bass.

Owen, M. T., & Cox, M. (1997). Marital conflict and the development of infant-parent attachment relationships. *Journal of Family Psychology, 11,* 152–164.

Posada, G., Gao, Y., Fang, W., Posada, R., Tascon, M., Schöelmerich, A., et al. (1995). The secure-base phenomenon across cultures: Children's behavior, mothers' preferences, and experts' concepts. In E. Waters, B. Vaughn, G. Posada, & K. Kondo-Ikemura (Eds.), Care giving, cultural, and cognitive perspectives on secure-base behavior and working models: New growing points of attachment theory and research (pp. 27–48). *Monographs of the Society for Research in Child Development, 60*(2–3, Serial No. 244).

Posada, G., Jacobs, A., Carbonell, O. A., Alzate, G., Bustamante, M. R., & Arenas, A. (1999). Maternal care and attachment security in ordinary and emergency contexts. *Developmental Psychology, 35,* 1379–1388.

Posada, G., Jacobs, A., Richmond, M., Carbonell, O. A., Alzate, G., Bustamante, M. R., & Quiceno, J. (2002). Maternal caregiving and infant security in two cultures. *Developmental Psychology, 38,* 67–78.

Rudy, D., & Grusec, J. E. (2001). Correlates of authoritarian parenting in individualist and collectivist cultures and implications for understanding the transmission of values. *Journal of Cross-Cultural Psychology, 32,* 202–212.

Russell, A., Hart, C. H., Robinson, C. C., & Olsen, S. F. (2003). Children's sociable and aggressive behavior with peers: A comparison of the US and Australia, and contributions of temperament and parenting styles. *International Journal of Behavioral Development, 27,* 74–86.

Scanzoni, J., Polonko, K., Teachman, J., & Thompson, L. (1989). *The sexual bond.* Newbury Park, CA: Sage.

Scheper-Hughes, N. (1985). Culture, scarcity, and maternal thinking: Maternal detachment and infant survival in a Brazilian shantytown. *Ethos, 13,* 291–317.

Sharma, D., & LeVine, R. A. (1998). Child care in India: A comparative developmental view of infant social environments. In D. Sharma & K. W. Fisher (Eds.), *New directions for child development: Vol. 81. Socioemotional development across cultures* (pp. 45–64). San Francisco: Jossey-Bass.

Smith, C. A. (1999). Preface. In C. A. Smith (Ed.), *The encyclopedia of parenting theory and research* (pp. ix–x). Westport, CT: Greenwood Press.

Smith, C. A., Cudaback, D., Goddard, H. W., & Myers-Walls, J. A. (1994). *The National Extension Parent Education Model Final Report.* Manhattan: Kansas State Cooperative Extension Service.

Stevenson, H. W., Azuma, H., & Hakuta, K. (Eds.). (1986). *Child development and education in Japan.* New York: Freeman.

Stevenson, H., & Lee, S. (1990). Contexts of achievement: A study of American, Chinese, and Japanese children. *Monographs of the Society for Research in Child Development, 55*(1–2, Serial No. 221).

Stevenson-Hinde, J. (1998). Parenting in different cultures: Time to refocus. *Developmental Psychology, 34,* 698–700.

Strauss, C., & Quinn, N. (1997). *A cognitive theory of cultural meaning.* Cambridge, UK: Cambridge University Press.

Suizzo, M. A. (2002). French parents' cultural models and childrearing beliefs. *International Journal of Behavioural Development, 26,* 297–307.

Super, C. M., & Harkness, S. (1986). The developmental niche: A conceptualization at the interface of child and culture. *International Journal of Behavioral Development, 9,* 545–569.

Valenzuela, M. (1990). Attachment in chronically underweight young children. *Child Development, 61,* 1984–1996.

Valenzuela, M. (1997). Maternal sensitivity in a developing society: The context of urban poverty and infant chronic undernutrition. *Developmental Psychology, 33,* 845–855.

van IJzendoorn, M. H., & Sagi, A. (1999). Cross-cultural patterns of attachment. In J. Cassidy & P. R. Shaver (Eds.), *Handbook of attachment* (pp. 713–734). New York: Guilford Press.

Vaughn, B., Egeland, B., Sroufe, A., & Waters, E. (1979). Individual differences in infant-mother attachment at twelve and eighteen months: Stability and change in families under stress. *Child Development, 50,* 971–975.

Watanabe, H. (2001). Transformations of family norms: Parents' expectations of their children's family life style. In J. A. Myers-Walls & P. Somlai, with R. N. Rapoport (Eds.), *Families as educators for global citizenship* (pp. 81–90). Aldershot, UK: Ashgate.

Waters, E., Kondo-Ikemura, K., Posada, G., & Richters, J. E. (1991). Learning to love: Mechanisms and milestones. In M. R. Gunnar & L. A. Sroufe (Eds.), *Minnesota symposia on child psychology: Vol. 23. Self processes and development* (pp. 217–255). Hillsdale, NJ: Lawrence Erlbaum.

Whiting, B. B., & Whiting, J. W. M. (1975). *Children of six cultures: A psychocultural analysis.* Cambridge, MA: Harvard University Press.

Wilson, M. N. (1986). The black extended family: An analytical consideration. *Developmental Psychology, 22,* 246–256.

Wright, B. (1998). A cross-national study of self-evaluations and attributions in parenting: Argentina, Belgium, France, Israel, Italy, Japan, and the United States. *Developmental Psychology, 34,* 662–676.

Wu, P., Robinson, C. C., Yang, C. M., Hart, C. H., Olsen, S. F., Porter, C. L., et al. (2002). Similarities and differences in mothers' parenting of preschoolers in China and the United States. *International Journal of Behavioral Development, 26,* 481–491.

Zavalkink, J., & Riksen-Walraven, M. (2001). Parenting in Indonesia: Inter- and intracultural differences in mothers' interactions with their young children. *International Journal of Behavioral Development, 25,* 167–175.

Zigler, E. (1995). Foreword. In M. H. Bornstein (Ed.), *Handbook of parenting* (Vol. 2, pp. xi–xii). Mahwah, NJ: Lawrence Erlbaum.

CHAPTER 10

International Divorce

PATRICK C. MCKENRY AND SHARON J. PRICE

INTRODUCTION

Marital dissolution is universal. Every country and society has mechanisms for ending unhappy marriages (Yorburg, 2002). Data regarding marital dissolution, however, are not consistent from country to country, and in fact, some countries do not register divorces. In the United States, however, there is almost a preoccupation with divorce rates, which during the past decade have stabilized in this country. In contrast, a majority of countries have witnessed an increase, whereas a few have experienced a decrease in divorce rates.

Provisions for divorce are of ancient origin. The first written regulation was incorporated into the Babylonian legal code of Hammurabi around 2000 BC. This regulation provided that a husband could divorce his wife at will, with no stated reason required. Throughout much of Western history, divorce has been more a prerogative for husbands than for wives. Cherlin (1996) has divided access to divorce into three periods: (a) *era of restricted divorce:* prior to the mid-19th century, when divorce was rare and existed to protect the property of men; (b) *era of divorce tolerance:* from the mid-19th century until 1970, when divorce existed to improve a sense of individual well-being, especially among women, if certain grounds for divorce could be proved; and (c) *era of unrestricted divorce:* from 1970, when no-fault divorce first became available, eliminating most barriers to divorce in virtually every Western nation. Divorce, in fact, has increasingly come to be seen as a human rights issue—the right to divorce is seen as an important advance in the social status and position of women, because marital dissolutions are formalized with provisions made for alimony, division of property, child maintenance, and housing (Prendiville, 1988; Yorburg, 2002).

The universal existence of marital dissolution typically is viewed by social scientists as functional rather than reflecting personal, family, or societal failure. Divorce is usually viewed as an important element in family systems—an escape valve for the tension that inevitably rises from a dysfunctional relationship (Goode, 1963). However, almost no society places a positive value on divorce. Rather, most penalize parties to a divorce. For example, some groups impose fines, prohibit remarriage, or insist that the bride-price be returned. Industrialized societies often apply religious, economic, and legal pressures to encourage the continuation of marriage, and all societies have used equally effective informal controls such as censure, gossip, and condescension (Cherlin, 1992; Kephart & Jedlicka, 1988).

Legal grounds for contested divorces vary to some extent across societies. In societies where divorce is difficult to obtain, the grounds for divorce may not represent the real reason for the divorce; in such cases there is a tendency toward dishonest annulment, fabrication of legally accepted offences, and migratory divorce and separations (Price & McKenry, 1988). There are, however, some common grounds across many cultures: adultery, sterility, economic incapacity, thievery, impotence or frigidity, desertion, and cruelty (Kephart & Jedlicka, 1988).

Much scholarly attention has focused on societal reasons for the high divorce rates in recent years, especially in Western society. It is commonly believed that industrialization and the conjugal family system that accompanies it operate in such a way as to drastically increase the frequency of divorce over nonindustrial societies. In industrialized societies, families are no longer obligated to remain together as self-sufficient economic and productive units but instead are voluntarily held together for emotional gratification. Where marriage is based on personal choice and where marital happiness and the emotional tie between husband and wife are more highly valued, divorce rates are typically higher (Hendrix & Pearson, 1995; Lee, 1982). As voluntary unions without strong kin support, the mutual dependence of the husband and wife increases high expectations for companionship, intimacy, and emotional support. With the kin group less available, there is also less pressure on the married couple to remain together when there are marital problems.

Some researchers have focused on the change in female status that accompanies industrialization as a major factor in divorce (Hendrix & Pearson, 1995; Pearson & Hendrix, 1979). These authors have focused on measures of female status including participation in public ceremonies, property inheritance, and achieved position. These authors point to a direct relationship between the decline in patriarchy and the increase in divorce rates. Seccombe and Lee (1986) argue that it is not female status per se, but the independence of wives from husbands that occurs with industrialization that is the crucial variable. Regardless, such resources allow a woman to more easily leave an unsatisfactory marriage.

Goode (1993) and Yorburg (2002) note that one of the most striking reasons for higher divorce rates among industrialized nations is the declining stigma attachment to divorce. That is, there is little loss of respectability or individual rights after a divorce in most industrialized societies today.

Cross-cultural research on divorce is often limited, dated, and deficit oriented. Too often, the study of divorce has rested on the assumption of one normative family form—the Western, industrialized nuclear family—as the model for all families. However, increasingly, social scientists are accepting a multicultural perspective that is fundamental to understanding not only families, but also the societies in which they reside. Consequently, the focus of this chapter is on the historical and cultural context of divorce, societal factors affecting divorce rates, and societal responses to individuals and families after divorce in selected countries.

NORTH AMERICA

North America, including the United States and Canada, represents increasingly diverse populations. These countries are characterized by an increase in persons who have migrated from other countries, bringing with them significant cultural differences in family patterns and life, including divorce.

United States

Similar to most Western, industrialized societies, rates of marriage in the United States have decreased since the late 1940s, whereas the rates of divorce have increased. As previously mentioned, however, divorce rates in the past 20 years in the United States have stabilized and even experienced a minimal decrease, whereas most other Western, industrialized nations are experiencing a continuing increase in their divorce rates. Also, there has been a pronounced decline in remarriage among Americans, even though approximately 75% of divorced individuals remarry; this decline surpasses those of most other Western nations. Much of the change in marital behavior may be explained by changing economic circumstances and an accompanying uncertainty about an economic future for young men, whereas economic opportunities have increased for young women. Thus, it has been difficult for individuals to replicate the model of marriage lived by their parents and grandparents (Teachman, Tedrow, & Crowder, 2001). Such economic changes reflect a continuation of long-term shifts in production and family roles associated with the industrial revolution (Goode, 1963). Also, economic instability, poverty, and loss of economic opportunity for some groups in the United States have limited marriage and encouraged divorce. In recent years, this uncertainty has increased the focus on divorce and remarriage because of the downward economic mobility often experienced by these individuals and the increasing number of children involved. An increase in individualism and decrease in sense of community have also been related to recent changing marriage patterns in the United States (Coltrane & Collins, 2001).

The United States is often thought of as a "melting pot," wherein various subcultures are assimilated and largely indistinguishable in their family lives. In reality, however, significant cultural differences remain in family patterns and lifestyles. These cultural differences are clearly reflected in the patterns of divorce and remarriage among the three largest ethnic minority groups in the United States: African Americans, Latinos, and Asian Americans.

African Americans

During a period of relative stability in overall divorce rates among white Americans, the divorce rate for African Americans increased by 17% in the 1980s (Martin & Bumpass, 1989). By 1998, the divorce rate among blacks was twice that of whites (422 per 1,000 vs. 190 per 1,000), the highest of any American ethnic minority group (U.S. Bureau of the Census, 1998). Racial differences in divorce rates persist independently of such compositional variables as socioeconomic status, religiosity, region of residence, and parental marital stability (Teachman, 1986; Yorburg, 2002). Cultural factors related to divorce among African Americans include: racial discrimination and resulting economic stress, women's independence, different male-to-female earning ratios, hypogamy, teen births, and the disproportionate ratio of African American women to men (Cherlin, 1998; Staples & Johnson, 1993; Yorburg). In spite of higher divorce rates, there is some evidence that African Americans may adjust better than white Americans to divorce (Gove & Shin, 1989; Kitson, 1992; McKelvey & McKenry, 2000). The better adjustment of African Americans to divorce has been explained by (a) strong extended family ties and resources, (b) greater acceptance of alternative child-rearing structures, and (c) the more normative nature of separation and divorce in the African American community (Taylor, Tucker, Chatters, & Jayakody, 1997).

African Americans, particularly women, are also less likely to remarry following divorce (Taylor et al., 1997). Possible explanations include the following: (a) fewer black men are available, especially men of similar or higher social status; (b) strong support is given to single mothers by the African American community (Staples & Johnson, 1993); and (c) marriage may be less central to the well-being of African Americans than it is for whites (Ball & Robbins, 1986).

Latinos

In spite of the fact that Latinos share many characteristics with African Americans (e.g., lower socioeconomic status, lower education levels, and younger average age at marriage), the divorce rate among Latinos is about the same or slightly lower than that of whites when socioeconomic status is controlled. The most commonly cited reasons for greater marital stability are (a) the strong emphasis placed on family, and (b) prohibition against divorce by the Catholic Church (Faust & McKibben, 1999; Zinn & Eitzen, 1996).

It should be noted that the rate of divorce among Latinos varies considerably by subculture. For example, Cuban Americans have divorce rates much lower than the United States as a whole, and Puerto Rico has much higher rates. The Cubans who migrated in large numbers in the 1960s were disproportionately middle-class professionals who have maintained economic stability primarily in south Florida, where the majority reside. Puerto Rico's high divorce rates can be explained, in part, by the rapid social change since 1950, moving from an agricultural to an industrialized state. This has affected marital stability by changing the traditional role of women in terms of (a) a need for increased income because of decreases in household production and changes in consumption patterns; (b) an increase in employment opportunities for women outside the home; and (c) an increase in the educational level of women, which has also contributed to an increase in women's employment. Sociopsychological changes needed for adaptation to such change have been lacking in Puerto Rico, resulting in conflict between expected gender roles of traditional patriarchal society and the presence of women in the roles of breadwinner. Other related factors include the mass exodus of the population from rural to urban areas (including migration to the U.S. mainland) and the extensive and successful campaign by private groups and the government in promoting the use of contraceptives and sterilization (Canabal, 1990).

Asian Americans

The diversity of Asian Americans makes it extremely difficult to speak about any one pattern of divorce and remarriage. In spite of the lack of research, Asian American families are assumed to be strong, stable, cohesive, and conforming. They also place a strong emphasis on education and economic well-being—two factors highly related to marital stability ("Asian Families Stay Together," 2003). As a result, data do indicate that Asian Americans, in general, exceed white Americans in terms of marital stability as well as education and median income. Also, more than 80% of all Asian American children reside in two-parent families (Fong, 1998). Interestingly, the more assimilated Asian Americans, such as the Japanese Americans, have the highest divorce rates compared to other Asian American groups.

Asian Americans are generally more group and family oriented, not as individualistic as are other Americans. Asian Americans expect parents to stay together—a tradition that may come from the Buddhist religion and other traditions in which the children are taught to respect their parents and ancestors. Also, Asian Americans don't have many social alternatives outside the family; the family is central.

Canada

Canada has long held the distinction of having one of the lowest rates of divorce among industrialized nations. Prior to 1968, divorce was granted primarily on grounds of adultery. In 1968, divorce laws were changed to include various other grounds, including marital breakdown. No-fault divorce followed soon after (Kanwar & Swenson, 1997). Since the no-fault provision, the divorce rate in Canada has increased by 500% (Ambert, 1998). However, even in Canada today, a marriage still cannot be terminated because the relationship has stagnated or because one or both partners wish a change unless there is a 1-year separation with the idea that the marriage is over. The 1-year period can be reduced in cases of adultery or physical or mental cruelty that makes marriage intolerable. Current divorce legislation represents a compromise between the wholly restrictive law of the 19th century and a move toward unilateral divorce (Eichler, 1988). Canadian society, particularly the conservative influences of religion, government, and family, has sought to maintain the status quo despite attempts for change in access to divorce similar to that of other Western industrialized nations.

Canadian divorce laws still seek to encourage reconciliation. The 1985 act, the most recent change in Canadian divorce law, requires divorce attorneys to discuss the possibility of reconciliation and to inform clients of available counseling. Also, the act requires lawyers to promote negotiated settlements and mediation of support and custody disputes. This act, however, was followed by a sharp increase in the divorce rate (Kanwar & Swenson, 1997). In 1989, the crude divorce rate in Canada was 3.1 per 1,000, about the same as England and Wales. The 1998 crude divorce rate represented a slight decrease; it was 2.28 per 1,000 individuals, almost half the U.S. rate (4.19 per 1,000 individuals) (United Nations, 2000), and historically changes in divorce rates in Canada have paralleled those of the United States, even though the magnitude of the rates has been less (B. W. Robinson & McVey, 1985). Similarly, about 10% of Canadian families with children are single parents, compared with 25% in the United States. As in the United States, there is an east-west difference in divorce rates, with the western provinces generally having higher divorce rates because of younger populations, greater individualism, and less influence of the Catholic Church (Peters, 1983). Also, it should be noted that Canada is distinguished by its higher proportion of Catholics and immigrants from traditional societies, both of whom discourage divorce (Nett, 1993). Reasons cited for increasing divorce rates in Canada include better opportunities for women that allow them to be independent, decreasing stigma in divorce, and higher expectations for marriage. Simpler divorce laws and family reform laws that give divorced women a larger share of the family assets have also been cited as major factors (Eichler, 1988; Peters).

Remarriage has become significant in Canada. The majority of divorced individuals remarry, often within 3 years of the divorce. Remarriages account for over 25% of all marriages. However, as in the United States, the marriage and remarriage rates in general are declining in Canada because of economic uncertainties, changing values toward marriage, and changing roles of women.

EUROPE

Traditionally, divorce rates among the various European countries have varied, with the

Table 10.1 World Divorce Rates

Country	Divorce Rate Per 1,000 Individuals
Countries with the highest divorce rates in the world	
1. Maldives	10.97
2. Belarus	4.63
3. United States	4.34
4. Cuba	3.72
5. Estonia	3.65
6. Panama	3.61
7. Puerto Rico	3.61
8. Ukraine	3.56
9. Russia	3.42
10. Antigua and Barbuda	3.40
Divorce rates in selected countries	
United Kingdom	2.6
Sweden	2.4
Canada	2.28
Uruguay	2.01
France	2.0
Japan	1.92
Israel	1.56
Egypt	1.18
China	.79
Mexico	.48
Italy	.60

SOURCE: United Nations (2000, 2001); "Countries With the Highest Divorce Rates" (n.d.).

NOTE: It should be noted that many nations do not have publicized divorce rates.

more highly industrialized and urbanized northern Europe having more liberal divorce legislation than southern Europe. Between 1980 and 1998, however, there has been an ascending pattern and definite convergence of divorce rates across the 15 countries that constituted the European Union in 1998. Divorce is almost universally available to women in European Union countries, although it is exceptionally difficult and complex in the Republic of Ireland (Burley & Regan, 2002). In general, more women than men apply for divorces or legal separations.

Similar to the United States, a large part of the postwar divorce phenomenon can be seen as a function of economic and cultural modernity: (a) economic change has provided the means by which women might become more independent in marriage (through access to resources and job opportunities); and (b) cultural parameters determining the legal and financial availability of the divorce option have changed, resulting in more liberal laws and the availability of women's work (Castles, 1998). Increased divorce rates may also be the result of growing individualization and secularization and less emphasis on marriage and raising children (Cherlin & Furstenberg, 1988; Dronkers & Kalmijn, 2002). Like the United States, a recent and increasing phenomenon is the decline of remarriage rates of the divorced because of a decrease in economic incentives and in cultural pressures to marry. Remarriages are still frequent in some southern European countries such as Italy, Portugal, and Greece, where marriage is still highly institutionalized (Rothenbacher, 2003).

A wide variation in divorce rates exists among European nations, although there is increasing convergence among these nations (Cherlin & Furstenberg, 1988). The United Kingdom and Sweden lead, with Italy having the lowest rates (United Nations, 2000; see Table 10.1).

Italy

Historically, Italy has had a strong antidivorce tradition, with Italian families characterized by the stability of both their nuclear and their extended families. Italy, in fact, had no legal provision for divorce until 1970, whereas most other European nations have permitted divorce under some circumstances since the mid-1800s. Also, unlike other nations in Europe, the stability of the family lessened only moderately as a result of the introduction of divorce legislation (Sgritta, 1988).

There are still strong legal deterrents to divorce in Italy, including the following: a lengthy period of separation is required (3 years); the legal procedures are expensive, long, and drawn out; and child-support benefits are low. As a result, it is thought that there are a number of separations that do not end in divorce, and only about 1% of Italian households constitute single-parent families (Henneck, 2003).

Additional deterrents to divorce in Italy include the influence of the Catholic Church; low rates of women in the labor force; a chronic housing shortage; inadequate child care; lack of part-time work; and the significant social control exerted by kin and community, especially in the less urbanized areas (Henneck, 2003). Sgritta (1988) concludes that the legal costs of separation and divorce, along with the hardships and economic costs associated with searching for and renting an independent dwelling, are onerous for most Italians, especially in cases where the wife is not gainfully employed.

United Kingdom

The United Kingdom/Britain resembles the United States in its pattern of divorce and remarriage, largely because of the influence of the common English-speaking culture. The United Kingdom (led by England and Wales) has a rising divorce rate that is also the highest in western Europe (National Statistics, 2005). Likewise, Britain has the highest proportion of children living in one-parent families compared to other European nations; specifically, 24% of British children live in single-parent families compared with a European average of 14% (Gibb, 1999). More lenient legislation, greater secularization, and various economic and employment problems are thought to be major explanations for the continuing increase in divorce and single-parent families in the United Kingdom since 1970 (Gibb).

Similar to the United States, a frequent consequence, as well as cause, of single parenthood is poverty. Over half of all single-parent families live below their respective national poverty lines in both nations. Over half of the single-parent families in the United Kingdom must rely on government benefits as a result of adverse economic conditions, gender inequity in income, and limited availability of child care. The tendency of British social policy has been to assume that single mothers are parents first and workers second; thus, single mothers are guaranteed economic support for as long as their children are dependent (Kiernan, 1988). The remarriage rate in Britain is considered relatively low and declining. In the past, a major motivating factor in remarriage has been enhanced economic well-being for single mothers (Miller, 1984).

Sweden

The Swedish rate of divorce has been one of the highest in Europe since World War II, following the United Kingdom and Russia. This long-term trend has continued through the 1990s. Like many other European nations, Sweden has moved away from an adversarial approach to a variation of no-fault divorce. Divorce can be obtained immediately upon application if both spouses are in agreement. However, if children are involved or if one spouse resists the divorce action, a reconsideration period of 6 months is mandated (Andersson & Guiping, 2001).

The divorce rate in Sweden would be a more valid indicator of relationship or family stability in Sweden if the very high rates of cohabitation were included. The Swedish divorce rate is somewhat surprising because so many factors associated with divorce in the United States are mitigated in Sweden, including poverty, teen pregnancies, early marriage, interethnic and interfaith unions, and high residential mobility. Popenoe

(1988) suggests that much more research is needed to understand the reasons for the high rates of divorce and general relationship instability in Swedish society.

Similar to the United States, Sweden also has a high proportion of single-parent families. Yet there are two noticeable differences between the two nations regarding single parents: (a) in Sweden, almost all children are born to parents who live together; and (b) as a nation, Sweden is a strong welfare state focused on protecting children. Consequently, the economic situation of single-parent families in Sweden is not characterized by the high level of relative deprivation seen in the United States (B. Hoem & J. M. Hoem, 1988; Popenoe, 1988).

France

France, like Sweden, has experienced very high rates of cohabitation, out-of-wedlock births, and divorce in recent years. These divorce rates are surprising because they are inconsistent with other European nations outside the Nordic group; also, France is a predominantly Catholic nation (Roussel & Théry, 1988). However, France has gone so far as to recognize the family status and legal rights of cohabiting relationships (both heterosexual and homosexual) (Henneck, 2003). Other factors related to high divorce rates include smaller families, a large percentage of women in the labor force, quality child care, and child benefits.

All these changes are thought to reflect wider cultural change related to (a) a new image of women and their role in the family, and (b) value differences of the "baby boom" generation reflecting greater individualism (Roussel & Théry, 1988). Also, it should be noted that more lenient attitudes toward divorce have existed in France for many generations; for example, the French Revolution (1789–1799) secularized marriage and introduced very liberal divorce legislation, although it was repealed about 25 years later (French Embassy, 1981).

Historically, the French government has been concerned with changes from traditional family patterns, especially declining birthrates; thus, there has been strong state intervention on behalf of families with children. Divorced or otherwise single mothers traditionally have been viewed as victims by the state and have received special assistance. However, much debate has ensued over the continuation of such policies.

Russia

Russia, as part of the former Soviet Union, experienced an extraordinary increase in divorce prior to its demise as a republic in 1991; the divorce rate tripled between 1960 and 1980 and increased by almost 50% between 1990 and 2000. Statistical data in the 1980s placed the Soviet Union as second in divorce only to the United States among major industrial nations (Moskoff, 1983; "Russia, Eastern Europe," 2001). The divorce rate has remained high through the 1990s, but it is still second to the United States. Contrary to the United States, however, the rate of remarriage among Russians is increasing. Children are less an obstacle for either divorce or remarriage, and there is a desire to live independently from one's family of origin. The Russian population is increasingly abandoning a long-held tradition of maintaining large, extended families. As economic and other incentives to preserve extended families disappear, the process of family dissolution has intensified (Vishnevsky, 2003).

The irretrievable breakdown of marriage is still the only formal ground for divorce since the Family Code of 1995. The power of the state authorities to investigate the reasons for divorce has been significantly limited in noncontested cases. In essence, a divorce by mutual consent is much the same as no-fault divorce in other nations. The couple goes to court only if they have children or if one spouse does not agree to the divorce. All legal custody is joint, and child support, which represents a specified minimum based on prior earnings, must be arranged by the divorcing spouses. Alimony is still provided according to need and lack of labor capacity. Again, the spouses agree to a certain sum, and the court determines if it is a fair amount based on what the court would have given in a contested case.

The reasons for the high divorce rates in the USSR and now Russia have not been carefully studied. In addition to changing gender roles, such that the wife is less dependent on the husband, the following factors are often mentioned: decline in institutional restraints (e.g., extended family and divorce legislation); economic distress; the greater acceptance of cohabitation and singlehood; the greater educational level of the population, with commensurately greater expectations; and adoption of democratic, Western values regarding family (Antokolskaia, 2002; Vishnevsky, 2003).

LATIN AMERICA

Two major influences on divorce laws and practices in Latin America have minimized the divorce rates in Latin America: (a) the strong influence of the Catholic Church, which has failed to accept divorce as a marital option; and (b) the belief that men are superior to women, should provide for their family, maintain proper links with kin, maintain their honor, and expect honor from others—that is, *machismo*. Divorce laws, however, have gradually changed, frequently in the midst of strong protest. Uruguay enacted divorce legislation in the early 20th century, and "it was as socially revolutionary as when Italy did so" (Quale, 1988, p. 273). The revolutionary nature of these changes in the divorce law was also evident in Mexico when a governor was thrown out of office for attempting to pass divorce legislation in 1915 and 1923. However, when Mexico broke with the church during the revolution (1911–1917), divorce was made possible and in several places very easy to secure (Cubitt, 1988). Similarly, Juan Perón was thrown out of office in 1965 when Argentina liberalized divorce laws, passed legislation enabling women to vote, and mandated equal pay for equal work. Colombia legalized divorce for civil marriages in 1973, Brazil in 1977, and Argentina in 1987 (Quale, 1988). By 2004, all Latin American countries had legalized divorce.

In spite of divorce not being legal for many years, Latin American countries appear to have had provisions for ending unhappy marriages. Although annulments were usually available only under the rules of the Catholic Church, several countries approved the dissolution of marriages. For example, in Brazil, if a man unknowingly married a woman who was not a virgin, he could have the marriage adjudged "void." In addition, there was annulment of civil marriages, where witnesses would attest to facts, true or false, that there were some procedural error or errors in the civil marriage process. In countries such as Chile, all marriages were classified as civil, even if performed in the church (Lewis, 1994); therefore, this type of annulment was available to all couples.

In most Latin American countries, however, women were expected to stay with their husbands, regardless of circumstances including cruelty or unfaithfulness. In addition, women often viewed social and legal divorce as a threat to their positions and would therefore avoid divorce even when it was legally available (Quale, 1988). As a result, there is a serious lack of reliable divorce statistics for Latin American countries, which has been attributed to the prevalence of consensual unions, which are not systematically registered (Quale).

Several factors, however, have been reported to be related to significant changes in divorce rates in Latin American countries over the last few decades. For example, even though these data may be questionable, several sources report that after the revolution in Cuba, the divorce rate increased until at present approximately 75% of all marriages end in divorce. This increase has been attributed to couples having to live apart because of work assignments, the prevalence of common-law arrangements, women's increased education and labor force participation, and the availability of state assistance for children (Americans for Divorce Reform, n.d.; Shaikh, 2000).

Several authors have also attributed the increase in divorce in Brazil (about 25% of all marriages end in divorce) to the changing roles of women that have accompanied industrialization and modernity. Furthermore, in Brazil the Constitution of 1988 specified that there is no longer a male head of the family, that men and women have the same rights and duties, and that women's rights to work can no longer be questioned. Today, urban and middle-class Brazilian women are more likely to be economically secure enough to live without a husband; in 1990, 73% of requests for divorce were made by women (Westfried, 1997). Divorced women in Brazil may encounter some prejudice, but they can, in general, return with their children to their families of origin, where they will find the assistance and nurturance needed. In addition, divorced women may also secure the full support of their ex-husbands' kin in raising their children (Westfried).

Similarly, in Mexico, the younger cohorts of women are not as dependent on men as they were in the past. They often are earning their own money and therefore need no longer stay prisoners in an unhappy and perhaps abusive marriage. Although they may not be free to remarry in the Catholic Church, they may choose a new partner in a free union, thereby retaining their freedom (LeVine, 1993; Westfried, 1997).

ASIA

Similar to many other parts of the world, divorce laws and practices have been changing and continue to change in Asian countries. These changes are attributed to several factors including changes in religious beliefs and laws, political revolutions, urbanization, changing roles of women, industrialization, advances in technology, and, in some cases, Western influences.

Japan

Japan has experienced significant changes in divorce laws and trends. In 1883, it was believed that Japan had the highest divorce rate (3.4/1,000 population) in the world. However, the Civil Law Act of 1892 reduced the divorce rate by half (Yuzawa, 1990), and this low rate continued until after World War II, during which time, because of impoverishment, men and women stayed together in order to survive (Katsutoshi, 1986). At present, even though the divorce rate in Japan has almost doubled since 1990 ("State Targets Single Moms," 2002), it is still in the middle band of divorce rates at 2.27/1,000 population (Curtin, 2002). This increase is attributed to: (a) 1990s growth and subsequent slowdown in the Japanese economy accompanied by an increase in employment opportunities for women and economic pressures on families; (b) baby boomers reaching divorceable age; (c) ease of getting a divorce; (d) decrease in the influence of the extended family; and (e) women's desire to live more rewarding lives (Katsutoshi; Yuzawa).

Women's desire to live more rewarding lives may be reflected in the significant increase in middle-aged couples divorcing in Japan. Although the divorce rate in Japan still appears flat when compared with those of the United States and Europe, in the last few years, divorces among older people have been skyrocketing, reflecting profound changes in a traditionally conservative society (French, 2003, p. A3).

This trend is attributed to changes in women's expectations regarding marriage. In the past, women in Japan were often expected to suffer in silent dignity. This is becoming less so because of the influence of TV, availability of jobs, and a "trickle-up" women's liberation movement, in which grown daughters, often still living at home, prod their mothers to stop putting up with emotionally barren or abusive relationships with their husbands (French, 2003).

In the 1800s, only men were allowed to initiate divorce in Japan. Today, approximately three quarters of all petitions for divorce are initiated by women. Data indicate, however, that in 90% of the divorces in Japan, the husband and wife mutually agree. In fact, divorce has long been a simple matter in Japan, requiring little more than the agreement and signatures of both parties and a trip to city hall to file the papers.

Approximately 70% of all divorces in Japan involve children, a complete reversal from the 1960s. Prior to 1947, only fathers received custody of children; more recently, approximately 75% of the mothers receive custody of their children (Katsutoshi, 1986). Japan's laws, however, ignore the individual rights of parents to see their children after a divorce (Kakuchi, 2003). Unlike many countries, Japan has no specific laws pertaining to visitation, and consultations between judges and children are not common, making it difficult (if not impossible) for the parent who does not have custody to gain access to his or her children. In addition, Japan has no system for the collection of child-support payments from noncompliant fathers. Specifically, there is no tracking of noncompliant fathers, no requirement to conduct DNA tests in order to establish paternity, and no means for deducting money from the delinquent father's salary. This has resulted in very serious hardships for many Japanese mother-headed families. Historically, single mothers have been able to claim the child allowance granted by the state. Recently, however, there has been a move to reduce the child-rearing allowances for single mothers in a bid to reduce the divorce rate as well as the increased amounts paid out because of the increasing divorce rates in families with young children. In addition, although the government traditionally has paid child-rearing allowances until the child reaches 18, it proposes to stop paying the full child-rearing allowances when a child turns 5. This new law states that a divorced father has an obligation to contribute to the cost of raising his children, but no consequences for nonpayment are specified ("Government May Slash," 2002; "State Targets Single Moms," 2002).

India

India has a rich and diverse religious and cultural heritage. It is characterized as multiracial, multireligious, and multilinguistic and varies by geographical locale and a caste system based primarily on birth, occupation, and region. Historically, castes were extremely segmented and governed all areas of an individual and family's sociocultural and religious lives. Since independence, however, many caste rigidities have been reduced (Mullatti, 1995).

In India, religion provides a common base and is an all-encompassing way of life. Over 80% of the population is Hindu; the remainder belongs to religions such as Christianity, Islam, and Jainism. Christians and Muslims are generally converts from Hinduism and therefore follow most of the socioreligious beliefs and practices of that religion.

The Hindu family and marriages are steeped in age-old customs and traditions. Marriage is considered almost compulsory, that is, as essential for men and even more so for women (Mullatti, 1995; Pothen, 1989). For this reason, prior to 1970 there were very few divorces. However, there was a gradual increase between 1970 and 1976. In 1976, the 1955 Hindu Marriage and Divorce Law was amended to allow no-fault divorce by mutual consent (Sharma, 1989). Since then, the number of divorces has steadily increased, but at a much slower rate than in the United States (Amato, 1994). Available data regarding divorce, however, are probably an underestimate, because no one compiles this information. Furthermore, in rural areas marital dissolutions are granted by caste (*panchayat*) councils, and no records are kept of these. In addition, a large number of couples separate permanently but never file for divorce (Amato). Specifically, forward (or higher-status) castes constitute the single largest category that pursues legal divorce. In contrast, most of the illiterate or lower castes prefer seeking divorce through caste panchayats or private transactions (Rao & Sekhar, 2002). Research that has focused on divorce increased over the last decade, but there are still a very limited number of studies because of a lack of adequate data and negative attitudes associated with divorce in India. Researchers, therefore, are denied access to relevant information (Amato; Rao & Sekhar).

A combination of factors, similar to other countries, contributes to marriages ending in divorce in India. The most common reasons include cruelty (including physical and mental abuse and neglect), adultery (valid grounds for both sexes, but adulterous women are judged more harshly than men), desertion (disruption of cohabitation for at least 3 years or if a spouse has not been heard from for at least 7 years), impotency (inability to consummate the marriage or refusal by one spouse to do so), and chronic disease (mental and physical illness and sexually transmitted diseases) (Amato, 1994; Choudhary, 1988; Diwan, 1983; Fried, 1997; Kapoor & Crossman, 1996).

A primary reason for the increased divorce rate in India appears to be the changing roles of women; that is, women with college educations and women in the labor force are more likely to divorce in order to end marital incompatibility. In addition, an increasing number of women live in nuclear families prior to marriage and therefore often have difficulty adjusting to living in a joint or extended family after marriage (Rao & Sekhar, 2002).

In India, divorce is viewed as a personal tragedy for men and women, but it produces greater problems for women. In general, men do not experience increased economic hardship or much stigma associated with divorce, freeing men to remarry. Marital disruption, for women, often results in serious economic problems. These problems are even greater if women have custody of their children (about 80% of the divorces) (Amato, 1994). At least 50% of the fathers do not try to maintain contact with their children, and only about 19% provide any child support (Amato; Pothen, 1989). Divorcees in India may for a short time turn to their parents or siblings for a place to live and economic assistance. However, families often refuse or are hesitant to provide such support because they are ashamed that their daughter is separated or divorced from her husband; they are poor and unable to help or share already scarce resources; and they believe they have fulfilled their obligation to their daughter by arranging her marriage and providing a dowry (in most cases, dowries are not returned in case of divorce) or may view her as hurting her sister's chances of marriage (Amato; Pothen, 1989; Weiss, 1999). Therefore, even if at a bare subsistence level, these women strive to establish their own home, and remarriage is not a viable alternative for divorced women in India.

Pothen (1986, 1989) reported that some children in India were upset as a result of their parents' divorce, whereas others were reconciled to the situation and were viewed as being as happy and well adjusted as could be expected. Indian culture, however, may have the advantage of the support of a number of relatives other than parents, which could contribute to the transition of the parents' divorce.

China

Divorce has been possible in China for over 1,500 years. For example, a mutual consent divorce was theoretically possible in China in approximately AD 600 (Jeng & McKenry, 2000). In Ancient Law, three types of divorce were recognized: (a) mutual consent; (b) repudiation (seven grounds for men, three grounds for women); and (c) "intolerable acts against principles of conjugality." The 1931 Chinese Soviet Republic Laws, however, were based on the antifamily 1926 Soviet Family Code and permitted unrestrained divorce, including for the first time allowing women to initiate divorce (Naltao, 1987).

Divorce practices in China vary by regions of the country (Huang, 2001), and divorce statistics are often not considered reliable (Wang, 2001). Indications are, however, that divorce was on the increase prior to 1949 (United Nations, 1985, 1986) and soared with the passage of the marriage law of the People's Republic of China. Specifically, although China's divorce rate is lower than those of many European countries and the United States, the rate almost tripled between 1979 and 1998 (United Nations, 1985, 1986; Wang).

The 1981 Marriage Law of China was based on the premise that marriage is based on love, understanding, and mutual respect, which will result in loyalty and dedication to the nation (J. Robinson, 1989, p. 651). No precise grounds for divorce were included in this law, but divorce was granted in the event of complete and permanent breakdown of a marital relationship, that is, "breakdown of affection" (Platte, 1988). In traditional China, however, men initiated almost all divorces. Following the communist takeover it is estimated that as many as 70% of the divorces were initiated by women (Bullough & Ruan, 1994).

Recently, however, the 2001 Marriage Law of the People's Republic of China has been debated and passed into law (International Divorce Law Office, 2001; Pipi, 2001). This law presents clear grounds for divorce (domestic violence, abandonment, gambling and drug addiction, separation for 2 years). It also specifies procedures for securing a divorce, what is common property in dividing assets after a divorce, and parental responsibilities including child visitation rights.

Reasons for divorce in China are similar to those in other countries. They vary between rural and urban areas and include wife battering, bigamy, infidelity (Naltao, 1987; Pipi, 2001), disagreement over household duties, and mistreatment of women after the birth of a daughter (Platte, 1988). More global reasons for the rapid increase in China's divorce rate since 1979 include: (a) political and legislative changes (divorce laws changed several times, married couples were separated from one another for punishment or reeducation, government controlled availability and assignment of housing); (b) economic growth (China has experienced over two decades of significant economic expansion; therefore, many people could improve their skills, pursue higher education, change jobs, and increase income, resulting in incompatibility of spouses; also, housing conditions improved); (c) individualism and

Western influence (resulting from economic reform, exposure to democratic ideas, and changes in attitudes toward marriage and divorce); and (d) demographic changes (more people married—young and old—resulting in more people in the potential divorce pool; and increase in childlessness) (Wang, 2001). Several authors, however, contend the financial independence of women in the workforce is driving China's divorce rate (D'souza, 2002).

Under the new marriage law both parents are responsible for the upbringing of their children (International Divorce Law Office, 2001). Child custody, however, follows the "tender years doctrine," with mothers maintaining custody of their young children. Property owned individually before marriage is retained after marriage, and property acquired during marriage is divided equally unless received as a gift or inheritance. In rural China, however, many women forfeit claims of property, and in all cases, judges are given wide discretion in the distribution of marital property.

Israel

Israel, part of western Asia, is marked by cultural diversity; traditional families and modern lifestyles; influence of Western culture and Middle Eastern heritage, values, and practices (ranging from orthodox to secular religions); and an almost constant state of war, threat of terrorist attacks, and security risks (Lavee & Katz, 2003). This country has been built by immigration from Europe, Islamic countries (especially North Africa), Russia, Ethiopia, United States, United Kingdom, and Canada. In spite of this diversity, the dominant form of families in Israel is the traditional nuclear family composed of a mother, father, and their children.

In Israel, there has been a slow decline in marital stability, particularly since the mid-1980s (Katz & Peres, 1995). In 1995, the divorce/marriage ratio for Jewish couples was 30%; for Muslims it was 11%. The Jewish population is more likely to divorce than Arabs, and among Jewish couples, those of European or American origin divorce more than those of Asian or African origin (Lavee & Katz, 2003.

A unique feature of divorce in Israel is the religious legal system that regulates marital and family status. A myth of gender equality has accompanied the Zionist movement and the formation of the state of Israel (Lavee & Katz, 2003). For example, there is evidence in the law that makes divorce harder to obtain for women than men. Protest over this discrepancy resulted in a double system of courts being established: The Marital Status Law of 1953 determined that all matters of marriage and divorce are delegated to the various religious courts: Jewish rabbinic, Sharai Islamic, Christian, and Druse (Saltzman, 2003). All issues of property division and child custody may be determined by a civil court, but the divorce, per se, remains solely under the authority of the religious court (Saltzman).

In rabbinic courts, it is the father's absolute obligation, regardless of other issues, to support a child until the child achieves maturity. The amount of this obligation varies with the child's age, father's income, to a limited extent the mother's income, and special needs of the child (Saltzman, 2003). In cases where the father is delinquent in this obligation, the National Insurance Institute provides limited support (Eldar-Avidan & Haj-yahia, 2000). Spousal maintenance exists only as long as the marriage and is the responsibility only of the husband; there is no Jewish form of post-divorce alimony. In general, distribution is equitable with the exception of premarriage property, inheritance, and gifts (Saltzman).

Arab Countries

Arab countries cover a wide geographic area in eastern Asia and extend into parts of

Africa. However, although there are differences in interpretations, these countries share a basic belief in the Koran. This area of the world has also witnessed a multitude of wars, changes in governments, riches provided by oil, abject poverty, Western influences, technology, and some changes in attitudes and practices associated with family life—including divorce.

It is difficult to discuss divorce rates in Arab countries or of Arabs living in Israel. In many countries the data are not reliable for reasons, including divergent standards for record keeping. Also, scholars in the Arab countries have not been particularly concerned with divorce trends or the consequences of divorce (Aghajanian & Moghadas, 1998). This may be because "divorce was always taken for granted as a possible outcome of marriage in the Arab world" (Goode, 1993, p. 251).

In general, there are no strong trends in divorce rates; that is, some countries are experiencing a reduction in their divorce rate, whereas others may be experiencing a slight increase (Aghajanian & Moghadas, 1998; Goode, 1993). For example, in Iran the divorce rate has decreased since 1966. This trend has been attributed to the 1967 Family Protection Law (which made divorce a legal and secular action), the Islamic Revolution, and the Iran-Iraq war (Aghajanian & Moghadas). In contrast, the slight increase in the divorce rate in Saudi Arabia has been attributed to couples not being allowed to see each other before marriage, family interference, differences in behavior and attitudes (especially roles of husband and wives), impotence, sterility, age differences, and sickness (Al-Khateeb, 1998).

In most Arab countries a marriage occurs with the conclusion of a marriage contract. If a marriage has been contracted by two competent persons in the presence of two witnesses and been adequately publicized, it is complete and binding and requires no religious or other rites or ceremonies (International Divorce Law Office, 2003). Parents or other family members arrange marriages, in most countries, with the spouses meeting only when the details of the contract are completed. In other countries, such as Egypt and Saudi Arabia, marriages are often "semi-arranged" and therefore dependent on parents choosing; however, the couple is given the chance to know each other before the wedding (Al-Khateeb, 1998).

The Koran clearly discourages divorce, but it does not forbid it. Rather, divorce is allowed if circumstances warrant or necessitate it, or if there is hopeless failure of one or both parties to discharge their marital duties (Social Laws of Islam, 2003). Historically, and today, in some parts of the Arab world, only men were allowed to seek a divorce. Men could simply say "I divorce thee" three times in front of two witnesses to effect a divorce (i.e., *talaq*). Recently, however, several countries have changed the laws regarding divorce, often over the protest of fundamentalist clerics. For example, in Iran, as a result of the Islamic Revolution in 1979 and a return to more traditional religious practices, the Special Civil Court replaced the Family Protection Court with judges who were Islamic scholars. New laws were based on the Koran and the strong desire to protect the family from instability and divorce. Under Islamic law, the judge is advised to do his best to convince the husband and wife to reconcile (Aghajanian, 1986). However, couples that mutually consent to divorce may simply register their divorce with a notary public before two witnesses. (The necessity of women's consent, however, in such a strongly patriarchal society is questionable.)

In addition, in 2000 Egypt put in place one of the Arab's world most far-reaching reforms of family life by making divorce an equal opportunity to end an unhappy marriage (Tunisia has a similar law). Under this law, a woman may divorce her husband, with or without his assent. She must, however, return to him any money or property he paid when they married.

Fundamentalists, however, do not approve of changes to the laws that give the husband a right to divorce his wife unilaterally, that prevent men from marrying additional wives, or that allow women to get jobs outside the home. Therefore, any decrees or laws made in one year may be challenged or repealed in subsequent years (Goode, 1993). For example, in 1979, President Anwar el-Sadat of Egypt issued a decree allowing a woman to divorce her husband if she objected to his taking an additional wife; the decree was later declared unconstitutional.

It appears that the fundamentalists have tried to reaffirm the subordinate position of women (Goode, 1993). This is apparent in countries such as Saudi Arabia, which finds itself between the push of modernity and the conservative interpretation of Islam. Over the last few decades, women's participation in public life has become more restricted; the sexes are increasingly separated; and the legal equality granted to women is circumscribed by the courts, which give men more rights in marriage, divorce, child custody, maintenance, and inheritance (Al-Khateeb, 1998).

In most Arab countries, however, if it is part of the prenuptial contract, women may seek a divorce. In addition, many families have protected their daughters against unilateral divorce by men by including a prenuptial agreement decreeing that the husband must pay a specific sum of cash and jewelry (*Mahr*) to his wife at any time she requests. In case of divorce, the husband is required to pay the *Mahr* in full, and it is assumed the larger the *Mahr,* the more reluctant a man would be to initiate a divorce (Aghajanian & Moghadas, 1998; Goode, 1993).

Divorce for Arabic women living in Israel is often associated with psychosocial and economic problems including a marked reduction in their status (Al-Krenawi & Graham, 1998; Lavee & Katz, 2003). These women are often employed in low-paying positions or unemployed because of pressure to confine their activities to domestic roles, job hours that conflict with child care, and inability to move in search of employment. Remarriage is not viewed as a viable alternative; therefore, such women are dependent on parental or other family members or court-ordered support from the husband. In addition, Arab cultural norms maintain that divorced women should live with their parents or a close male relative. This arrangement often produces conflict, and because a divorced woman is seen as sexually seductive, she may seldom be allowed to leave the residence (Al-Krenawi & Graham).

Under Islamic law, when parents divorce, male children stay with their mother until age 7 and female children until age 9. Furthermore, there are no issues regarding alimony or child support; the divorced wife receives support until the end of *idda* (usually 3 months) to be certain she is not pregnant. Ideally, the husband supports his children in the house of their mother's father, but it is assumed in the case of his failure to do this that the mother and children are cared for by one or the other of the respective families (Goode, 1993).

In several countries (Tunisia, Syria, Egypt), husbands may have to pay longer. In Tunisia, if a man divorces his wife without good cause he must pay 1 year's support, and sometimes he may pay alimony for the rest of his former wife's life (Goode, 1993). In Egypt, if the wife does not want to be divorced, the husband may have to support her for 2 years (Goode, 1993). In addition, with the 2000 changes in Egyptian law, she may call on the Egyptian government to garnish her former husband's wages, and if he disappears or cannot pay a court-ordered living allowance, she may draw from a special state bank to support her family (Sachs, 2000).

Women remarry after divorce at a lower rate than men in the Arab world. However, most divorces take place early in marriage; therefore, divorced women are still young, generally resulting in a high rate of remarriage. Marriage is also viewed as the only acceptable status and as necessary for women (Aghajanian & Moghadas, 1998; Al-Khateeb, 1998; Goode, 1993). For example, in Saudi Arabia women are denied access to many services and offices; for example, if a woman wants to apply for a job or pay bills (among other things), she needs to have a man do this for her. A woman is made to feel she cannot live without a man, and marriage is an identity card for her to enjoy her rights as a human being (Al-Khateeb). The bride-price for divorcées, however, is lower than for first marriages. Her family also has a stake in her getting remarried because she would be a financial burden and would inherit part of the family property (half that of her brothers) if she remained unmarried.

CONCLUSIONS

A multicultural and international approach to divorce is a challenging and important endeavor. It is plagued with inconsistent data and, in many cases, a shortage or absence of scholarship. What literature is available (including the Internet and newspapers) generally focuses on limited and inconsistent demographic data, macrostructural factors, and historical trends. Research on the processes associated with divorce and postdivorce life is often negligible.

An international approach to divorce, however, is very important. We are increasingly part of the global village in contrast to the traditional, more limited view of our own culture, country, state, or neighborhood. It is imperative that scholars and students are knowledgeable about what is happening to families around the world. There is a lack of commonality in the laws and practices associated with divorce, and there does not appear to be any significant move to merge. Therefore, it is important that people who travel, work, and marry persons from other countries and cultures understand the implications of these differences. For example, it is not uncommon for people to marry and divorce in other countries with the erroneous assumption that laws and practices are like those in the United States.

It is clear, however, that all countries and cultures have developed mechanisms for the dissolution of marriages. Different societies have responded in a wide range of ways, ranging from punitive measures to supportive environments and programs. Therefore, the number of persons experiencing divorce differs based on location. It is expected, however, that because of increasing urbanization, industrialization, advances in technology, Western influence, and changes in the roles of women, the rate of divorce will increase in many countries. Some may view this trend as positive, because people no longer have to live in unhappy marriages. At the same time, this means that an increased number of people, especially women and children, are living in poverty because of lack of job skills and financial support. Therefore, divorce is becoming an issue of human rights and equity, with demands for the right of divorce and fair settlements. To address this challenge implies not only confronting the issue of divorce and dissolution, but the societal institutions related to the economy, politics, and religion. Incorporating a multicultural and global perspective when confronting these issues may provide insights that will help improve the lives of adults and children.

REFERENCES

Aghajanian, A. (1986). Some notes on divorce in Iran. *Journal of Marriage and the Family, 48,* 749–755.

Aghajanian, A., & Moghadas, W. (1998). Correlates and consequences of divorce in an Iranian city. *Journal of Divorce and Remarriage, 28,* 53–71.

Al-Khateeb, S. A. H. (1998). Women, family and the discovery of oil in Saudi Arabia. *Marriage and Family Review, 27,* 167–187.

Al-Krenawi, A., & Graham, J. R. (1998). Divorce among Arab women in Israel. *Journal of Divorce and Remarriage, 29,* 103–119.

Amato, P. R. (1994). The impact of divorce on men and women in India and United States. *Journal of Comparative Family Studies, 25,* 207–221.

Ambert, A.-M. (1998). *Divorce: Facts, figures, and consequences.* Child and Family Canada. Retrieved May 16, 2003, from http://www.cfc-efc.ca/docs/vanif/00005_en.htm

Americans for Divorce Reform. (n.d.). *Divorce statistics collection: Non-U.S. divorce rates.* Retrieved April 14, 2005, from http://www.divorcereform.org/nonus.html

Andersson, G., & Guiping, L. (2001). Demographic trends in Sweden: Childbearing developments in 1961–2000, marriage and divorce developments in 1971–1999. *Demographic Review, 5,* 1–13.

Antokolskaia, M. (2002). *Grounds for divorce and maintenance between former spouses.* Utrecht, The Netherlands: University of Utrecht, Molengraff Institute for Private Law.

Asian families stay together. (2003). Scripps Howard News Service. Retrieved April 15, 2005, from http://www.divorcereform.org/mel/rasian.html

Ball, R. E., & Robbins, L. (1986). Marital status and life satisfaction among black Americans. *Journal of Marriage and the Family, 48,* 389–394.

Bullough, V. L., & Ruan, F. F. (1994). Marriage, divorce, and sexual relations in contemporary China. *Journal of Comparative Family Studies, 25,* 383–393.

Burley, J., & Regan, F. (2002). Divorce in Ireland: The fear, the floodgates, and the reality. *International Journal of Law, Policy, and the Family, 15,* 202–222.

Canabal, M. E. (1990). An economic approach to marital dissolution in Puerto Rico. *Journal of Marriage and the Family, 52,* 515–530.

Castles, F. G. (1998). *Comparative public policy: Patterns of post-war transformation.* Cheltenham, UK: Edward Elgar.

Cherlin, A. (1992). *Divorce, marriage, and remarriage.* Cambridge, MA: Harvard University Press.

Cherlin, A. (1996). *Public and private families.* New York: McGraw-Hill.

Cherlin, A. J. (1998). Marriage and marital dissolution among black Americans. *Journal of Comparative Family Studies, 25,* 147–158.

Cherlin, A., & Furstenberg, F. F. (1988). The changing European family. *Journal of Family Issues, 9,* 291–297.

Choudhary, J. M. (1988). *Divorce in Indian society: A sociological study of marriage disruption and role adjustment.* Jaipur, India: Printwell.

Coltrane, S., & Collins, R. (2001). *Sociology of marriage and the family: Gender, love, and property.* Belmont, CA: Wadsworth.

Countries with the highest divorce rates in the world. (n.d.). Retrieved April 14, 2005, from http://www.aneki.com/divorce.html

Cubitt, T. (1988). *Latin American society.* New York: John Wiley & Sons.

Curtin, J. S. (2002). Japanese child support payments in 2002. *Glocom Platform from Japan.* Retrieved April 14, 2005, from http://www.glocom.org/special_topics/social_trends/20020909_trends_s6

Diwan, P. (1983). *Family law: Law of marriage and divorce in India.* New Delhi, India: Sterling.

Dronkers, J., & Kalmijn, M. (2002). Divorce and inequality. *Divorce in cross-national perspective: A European research network.* Retrieved April 15, 2005, from http://www.iue.it/Personal/Dronkers/DivorceandInequality.htm

D'souza, L. (2002). Is divorce China's new fad? *Hard News Care Archives.* Utah State University, Department of Journalism and Communications. Retrieved April 14, 2005, from http://www.hardnewscafe.USU.edu/archive/oct2002/1009_divorce.html

Eichler, M. (1988). *Families in Canada today: Recent changes and their policy consequences.* Toronto, Ontario, Canada: Gage.

Eldar-Avidan, D., & Haj-yahia, M. M. (2000). The experience of formerly battered women with divorce: A qualitative descriptive study. *Journal of Divorce and Remarriage, 32,* 19–40.

Faust, K. A., & McKibben, J. N. (1999). Marital dissolution: Divorce, separation, annulment, and widowhood. In M. B. Sussman, S. K. Steinmetz, & G. W. Peterson (Eds.), *Handbook of marriage and the family* (pp. 475–500). New York: Plenum.

Fong, T. P. (1998). *The contemporary Asian American experience: Beyond the model minority.* Upper Saddle River, NJ: Prentice Hall.

French, H. W. (2003, March 25). As Japan's women move up, many are moving out. *New York Times,* p. A3.

French Embassy. (1981). Women and divorce in France. *International Journal of Family Therapy, 3,* 62–82.

Fried, M. (1997). *Divorce in India.* Retrieved April 14, 2005, from http://www.emory.edu/English/Bahr/Divorce.html

Gibb, F. (1999, June 15). Divorce ends two out of four weddings. *London Times.* Retrieved from http://www.fact.on.ca/newpaper/ti990615.htm

Goode, W. (1963). *World revolution and family patterns.* London: Collier & Macmillan.

Goode, W. (1993). *World changes in divorce patterns.* New Haven, CT: Yale University Press.

Gove, W., & Shin H. (1989). The psychological well-being of divorced and widowed men and women: An empirical analysis. *Journal of Family Issues, 10,* 122–144.

Government may slash child-care allowances. (2002, February 8). *Japan Times Online.* Retrieved May 16, 2005, from http://www.japantimes.com

Hendrix, L., & Pearson, W. P. (1995). A spousal interdependence, female power, and divorce: A cross-cultural examination. *Journal of Comparative Family Studies, 26,* 217–232.

Henneck, R. (2003). *Family policy in the US, Japan, Germany, Italy, and France: Parental leave, child benefits/family allowances, childcare, marriage, cohabitation, and divorce.* Council on Contemporary Families. Retrieved April 15, 2005, from http://www.contemporaryfamilies.org/public/articles/Int%271%20Family%20Policy.htm

Hoem, B., & Hoem, J. M. (1988). The Swedish family: Aspects of contemporary developments. *Journal of Family Issues, 9,* 397–424.

Huang, P. C. C. (2001). Women's choice under the law. *Modern China, 21,* 3–58.

International Divorce Law Office. (2001). *China divorce law: Marriage law of the people's Republic of China* Retrieved April 15, 2005, from http://www.international-divorce.com/d-china.htm

International Divorce Law Office. (2003). *Islamic family law.* Retrieved April 15, 2005, from http://www.international-divorce.com/d-islamic.htm

Jeng, W. -S., & McKenry, P. C. (2000). A comparative study of divorce in three societies: Taiwan, Singapore, and Hong Kong. *Journal of Divorce, 34,* 143–161.

Kakuchi, S. (2003). Foreign spouses in Japan seek easier child custody laws. *International Divorce Law Office: Japanese divorce and custody law.* Retrieved April 15, 2005, from http://www.international-divorce.com/d-japan.htm

Kanwar, M., & Swenson, D. (1997). *Issues in Canadian sociology.* Dubuque, IA: Kendall/Hunt.

Kapoor, R., & Crossman, B. (1996). *Subversive sites: Feminists engagements with law in India.* New Delhi, India: Sage.

Katsutoshi, Y. (1986). Divorce, Japanese style. *Japanese Quarterly, 33,* 416–420.

Katz, R., & Peres, Y. (1995). Marital crisis and therapy in their social context. *Contemporary Family Therapy, 17,* 395–412.

Kephart, W. M., & Jedlicka, D. (1988). *The family, society, and the individual.* New York: Harper & Row.

Kiernan, K. E. (1988). The British family: Contemporary trends and issues. *Journal of Family Issues, 9,* 298–316.

Kitson, G. C. (with Holmes, W. M.). (1992). *Portrait of divorce: Adjustment to marital dissolution.* New York: Guilford Press.

Laish, A. (1975). *Women and Islam in a non-Moslem state.* New York: Wiley.

Lavee, Y., & Katz, R. (2003). The family in Israel: Between tradition and modernity. *Marriage and Family Review, 35,* 193–217.

Lee, G. R. (1982). *Family structure and interaction: A comparative analysis.* Minneapolis: University of Minnesota Press.

LeVine, S. (1993). *Women and social change in urban Mexico.* Madison: University of Wisconsin Press.

Lewis, J. J. (1994). Chile—Divorce. *Encyclopedia of women's history.* Retrieved April 15, 2005, from http://womenshistory.about.com/library/ency/blwh_chile_divorce.htm

Martin, T. C., & Bumpass, L. L. (1989). Recent trends in marital disruption. *Demography, 26,* 37–51.

McKelvey, M. W., & McKenry, P. C. (2000). The psychological well-being of black and white mothers following marital dissolution. *Psychology of Women's Quarterly, 24,* 4–14.

Miller, J. (1984). *Living standards of low-income, one-parent families: Movements out of poverty* (Discussion Paper 209). York, UK: University of York, Social Policy Research Unit.

Moskoff, W. (1983). Divorce in the USSR. *Journal of Marriage and the Family, 45,* 419–425.

Mullatti, L. (1995). Families in India: Beliefs and realities. *Journal of Comparative Family Studies, 26,* 11–25.

Naltao, W. (1987). Divorce: Traditional ideas receding. *Beijing Review, 11,* 23–25.

Nett, E. M. (1993). *Canadian families: Past and present.* Toronto, Ontario, Canada: Butterworths.

Pearson, W., & Hendrix, L. (1979). Divorce and the status of women. *Journal of Marriage and the Family, 41,* 375–385.

Peters, J. F. (1983). *Divorce: The disengaging, disengaged, and re-engaging process.* In K. Iswaran (Ed.), *The Canadian family* (pp. 225–248). Toronto, Ontario, Canada: Gage.

Pipi, L. (2001). New marriage law sparks concern. *Beijing Review, 44,* 14–16.

Platte, E. (1988). Divorce trends and patterns in China: Past and present. *Pacific Affairs, 61,* 428–445.

Popenoe, D. (1988). What is happening to the family in Sweden? In N. D. Glenn & M. T Coleman (Eds.), *Family relations* (pp. 92–99). Chicago: Dorsey.

Pothen, S. (1986). *Divorce: Its causes and consequences in Hindu society.* New Delhi, India: Shakti Books.

Pothen, S. (1989). Divorce in Hindu society. *Journal of Comparative Family Studies, 14,* 558–582.

Prendiville, P. (1988). Divorce in Ireland: An analysis of the referendum to amend the constitution. *Women's Studies International Forum, 4,* 355–363.

Price, S. J., & McKenry, P. C. (1988). *Divorce.* Newbury Park, CA: Sage.

Quale, G. R. (1988). *A history of marriage systems.* New York: Greenwood.

Rao, A. B. S. V. R., & Sekhar, K. (2002). Divorce: Process and correlates: A cross-cultural study. *Journal of Comparative Family Studies, 33,* 541–563.

Robinson, B. W., & McVey, W. W. (1985). The relative contributions of death and divorce to marital dissolution in Canada and the United States. *Journal of Comparative Family Studies, 16,* 93–109.

Robinson, J. (1989). Family policies, women, and the collective interest in contemporary China. *Policy Studies Review, 8,* 648–662.

Rothenbacher, F. (2003). European family indicators. *Eurodata Newsletter, 3,* 1–2.

Roussel, L., & Théry, I. (1988). France: Demographic change and family policy since World War II. *Journal of Family Issues, 9,* 336–353.

Russia, Northern, Eastern Europe. (2001). *Migration News, 8.* Retrieved April 15, 2005, from http://migration.ucdavis.edu/mn/more.php?id=3100_0_4_0

Sachs, S. (2000, March 1). Egypt's women win equal rights to divorce. *New York Times,* p. A5.

Saltzman, N. J. (2003). Domestic relations laws in Israel. *International Divorce Law Office: Israel family law.* Retrieved April 15, 2005, from http://www.international-divorce.com/d-israel.htm

Seccombe, K., & Lee, G. R. (1986). Female status, wives' autonomy, and divorce: A cross-cultural study. *Family Perspective, 10,* 241–249.

Sgritta, G. B. (1988). The Italian family: Tradition and change. *Journal of Family Issues, 9,* 372–396.

Shaikh, N. (2000). *Cuban women: Before and after the revolution.* Retrieved April 15, 2005, from http://www.saxakali.com/caribbean/nshaikh.htm

Sharma, B. K. (1989). *Divorce law in India.* New Delhi, India: Deep and Deep.

Social Laws of Islam. (2003). *Islamic laws regarding divorce.* Retrieved April 15, 2005, from http://www.jamaat.org/islam/divorce.html

Staples, R. S., & Johnson, L. B. (1993). *Black families at the crossroads: Challenges and prospects.* San Francisco: Jossey-Bass.

State targets single moms in bid to fight divorce rate. (2002, June 8). *Japan Times Online.* Retrieved May 16, 2005, from http://www.japantimes.com

Taylor, R. J., Tucker, M. B., Chatters, L. M., & Jayakody, R. (1997). Recent demographic trends in African American family structure. In R. J. Taylor, J. S. Jackson, & L. Chatters (Eds.), *Family life in Black America* (pp. 14–62). Thousand Oaks, CA: Sage.

Teachman, J. D. (1986). First and second marital dissolution: A decomposition exercise for whites and blacks. *Sociological Quarterly, 27,* 571–590.

Teachman, J. D., Tedrow, L. M., & Crowder, K. D. (2001). The changing demography of America's families. In R. M. Milardo (Ed.), *Understanding families into the new millennium: A decade in review* (pp. 453–465). Lawrence, KS: National Council on Family Relations.

United Nations. (1985). *Demographic yearbook.* New York: Author.

United Nations. (1986). *Demographic yearbook.* New York: Author.

United Nations. (2000). *The world's women: Trends and statistics.* New York: Author.

United Nations. (2001). *Demographic yearbook.* New York: Author.

U.S. Bureau of the Census. (1998). *Marital status and living arrangements.* Washington, DC: U.S. Government Printing Office.

Vishnevsky, A. G. (2003). *Family, fertility, and demographic dynamics in Russia: Analysis and forecast.* Retrieved April 15, 2005, from http://www.rand.org/publications/CF/CF124/CF124.chap1.html

Wang, Q. (2001). China's divorce trends in the transition toward a market economy. *Journal of Divorce and Remarriage, 35,* 173–189.

Weiss, L. (1999). Single women in Nepal: Familial support, familial neglect. *Journal of Comparative Family Studies, 30,* 243–256.

Westfried, A. H. (1997). The emergence of the democratic Brazilian middle-class family: A mosaic of contrasts with the American family (1960–1994). *Journal of Comparative Family Studies, 28,* 25–53.

Yorburg, B. (2002). *Family realities: A global view.* Upper Saddle River, NJ: Prentice Hall.

Yuzawa, Y. (1990). Recent trends of divorce and custody in Japan. *Journal of Divorce, 13,* 129–141.

Zinn, M. B., & Eitzen, D. S. (1996). *Diversity in families.* New York: Harper.

CHAPTER 11

Diversity in International Aging Families

RICHARD B. MILLER AND WILLIAM H. MEREDITH

GLOBAL AGING

The world's population is growing older. Whereas children historically have dominated populations, an increasing proportion of the global population consists of older persons. In 2000, an estimated 419 million people, or 6.9% of the world's population, were over the age of 65. The elderly population is currently increasing by 750,000 people each month, and within two decades, it is estimated that the older population will grow by 2 million on a monthly basis (National Research Council, 2001). The unprecedented growth of the global elderly population led the United Nations General Assembly to declare 1999 the International Year of Older Persons (Hayward & Zhang, 2001).

The trend toward global aging is due to a demographic transition in which populations shift from high mortality and high fertility to low mortality and low fertility (Serow, 2001). As fewer children are born and people survive into middle and late adulthood, the median age of the population becomes older. Moreover, the proportion of older people becomes larger. Consequently, as this demographic transition occurs, populations become "grayer."

The changing demographic structure of the population is having a dramatic impact on the composition of families, as well as relations between generations. Traditionally, the demographic characteristics of high fertility and short life expectancy created families with many children, but relatively few generations alive at the same time. However, as the fertility rate declines and life expectancy increases in aging societies, the family structure changes to what have been described as "beanpole families" (Bengtson, Rosenthal, & Burton, 1996). That is, families have fewer children, and more generations are alive at the same time, creating families that are "long and lean."

The increase in longevity is making it possible for family members to experience longer-lasting relationships with their kin (Bengtson, 2001). For example, using U.S. data, Uhlenberg (1996a) found that in 1900 a 40-year-old adult had a 62% probability of having at least one parent still alive. By 2000, the probability had increased to 95%. Likewise, in 1900 only 21% of adults at the age of 30 had at least one grandparent still alive, but in 2000 the percentage had more than tripled, to 76%. Uhlenberg (1996a) illustrates the dramatic impact that increased longevity has on family composition by reporting that "it is more likely that 20-year-olds alive now have a grandmother still living (91%) than that 20-year-olds alive in 1900 had a mother still living (83%)" (p. 685).

The changing family structure in aging societies affects family relationships. For example, because adults have fewer children and adults are living longer, a new stage of the life course, the "empty nest" stage, has developed (Uhlenberg, 1996b). One implication of this new stage is that the grandparent role is now more distinct from the parenting role, thus allowing middle-aged adults to enjoy their relationships with their grandchildren without the competing demands of simultaneously raising young children of their own (Uhlenberg & Kirby, 1998). Another implication of the "empty nest" stage is that couples are now spending many years together without children in the home, thus placing a greater emphasis on compatibility and emotional satisfaction in the couple relationship.

These demographic changes have also affected the need for middle-aged children to become caregivers. As the number of adults surviving into later life increases, more adult children will face the necessity of caring for their disabled parents (Bengtson, 2001). This issue of caregiving is compounded by decreasing fertility rates, which will lead to fewer siblings with whom middle-aged children can share the care of their parents (Kinsella, 2000; Uhlenberg, 1996b). For example, an unintended consequence of the one-child policy in China, implemented in 1979, has been to severely limit the number of potential caregivers for China's aging population in the future (Zhan, 2004).

Thus, these demographic changes of lower mortality and fertility rates are having a dramatic impact on the world population, leading to a general aging of the population. An important implication of global aging is that it is leading to changes in family composition, as well as changes in relationships and roles within families.

Diversity in Global Aging

Although the world population is generally getting older, there remains considerable diversity in the demographic transition among nations (Kinsella, 2000). For many decades, Europe has had the highest proportion of people over the age of 65, with 14.0% of the population being elderly in 2000. In contrast, the percentage of elderly in Asia was 5.9%, Latin America had 5.5%, and only 2.9% of the population in Africa was over the age of 65 (National Research Council, 2001). Among individual countries, Italy has the oldest population, with 18.1% being over the age of 65. In contrast, only 3.6% of the population in the Philippines is elderly, and people over the age of 65 comprise only 2.7% of the population in Kenya (Kinsella & Velkoff, 2001).

For illustrative purposes, the aging characteristics of four countries, Sweden, China, Brazil, and Egypt, will be examined. These four countries represent different continents of the world, as well as distinctive cultures. Sweden is representative of European countries, which have considerably older populations than less-developed countries. Even though China, Brazil, and Egypt are all less-developed countries, they represent different continents, as well as distinctive cultures. For example, most Chinese believe in various forms of Eastern religions, such as Buddhism and ancestor worship, whereas Brazilians are generally Christian, and Egyptians are mainly Muslim.

Figure 11.1 shows the Aging Index for the four countries, which is a common statistic

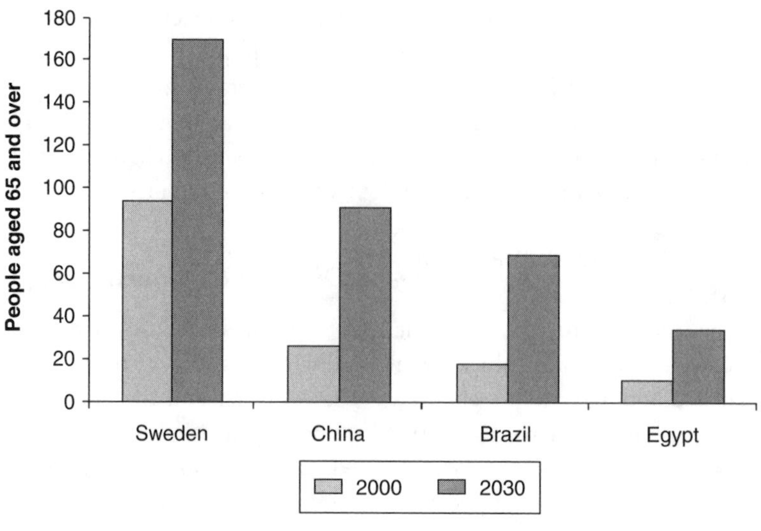

Figure 11.1 Aging Index: 2000 and 2030 (People aged 65 and over per 100 people aged 0–14)

SOURCE: Kinsella and Velkoff (2001), p. 14.

used to represent the age composition of a population. The Aging Index represents the number of people 65 years old and older per 100 children aged 0 to 14. As indicated in Figure 1, Sweden's Aging Index in 2000 (94) is nearly four times greater than that of China (27), five times more than that of Brazil (18), and nine times higher than that of Egypt (11). Although all four of the countries will experience dramatic growth in the aging population over the next 25 years, Sweden will continue to have a much larger proportion of elderly people compared to China, Brazil, and Egypt. In fact, demographers project that older persons in Sweden in 2030 will significantly outnumber children.

These variations in aging populations are due to differences in each country's demographic transition to an aging population, which is a gradual process that takes many years to fully complete. The beginning of the transition is indicated by declining mortality rates, which usually occurs first among children, as infectious diseases are controlled (National Research Council, 2001). This change actually creates a temporarily younger population because more children survive early childhood. The most important part of the transition, though, is the decrease in fertility rates (Kinsella, 2000; Serow, 2001). As the number of children declines, the proportion of the elderly in the overall population increases. This proportion increases as the fertility rate remains low and the high birthrate cohorts eventually move into old age (Stone & Myers, 2001).

All four countries have at least begun the demographic transition, because all of them have experienced a significant decrease in mortality rates. In 2000, Sweden had the highest life expectancy among women, at 82.4 years, but the other three countries also had average life expectancies among women that reached into later life, with averages of 73.3, 67.6, and 65.5 years for China, Brazil, and Egypt, respectively (Kinsella & Velkoff, 2001). However, the differences in fertility rates among the four countries help explain the differences in each country's proportion of elderly. Fertility rates in Sweden (1.5 children per adult woman), China (1.8), and Brazil (2.1) are at or below the replacement

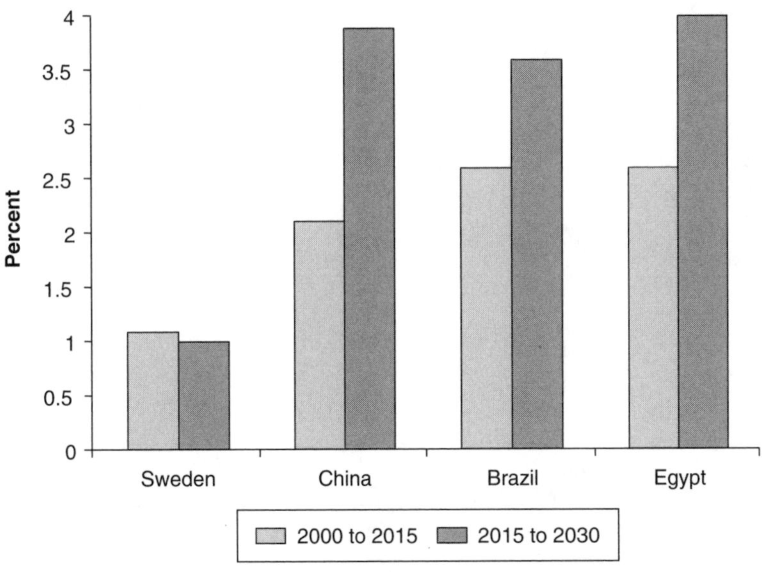

Figure 11.2 Average Annual Growth Rate for Older Age Groups: 2000 to 2015 and 2015 to 2030

SOURCE: Kinsella and Velkoff (2001), p. 130.

rate of 2.1 children per adult woman, whereas Egypt's fertility rate is 3.2 (Kinsella & Velkoff). Sweden has completed the demographic transition to an aging population, with China and Brazil in the middle phases of the transition. As the earlier high-fertility cohorts move into later life, the proportion of elderly in China and Brazil will rise dramatically. Egypt, on the other hand, is still in the early phase of the transition, with an increased life expectancy but an ongoing high fertility rate. For Egypt, the transition to an aging population will continue to progress when the fertility rate declines to a lower level.

Although Sweden has the highest proportion of elderly among the four countries being examined, its growth rate of elderly is not expected to increase significantly over the next few decades. On the other hand, as illustrated in Figure 11.2, the growth rate of the elderly in China, Brazil, and Egypt will increase dramatically (Kinsella & Velkoff, 2001; Shuman, 2001). For example, it took Sweden 85 years for the percentage of the population of people aged 65 and over to increase from 7% to 14%. However, it is projected that it will take China only 27 years to experience a similar increase in the proportion of elderly in the population (Kinsella & Velkoff). Thus, virtually all countries throughout the world, even those with currently young populations, will become proportionately aging societies, and the process will take a much shorter span of time.

As mentioned previously, the phenomenon of aging societies will have a significant impact on family composition and roles. One effect of declining fertility and mortality rates will be the increased responsibilities of adult children to care for their frail, elderly parents. Figure 11.3 illustrates the Elderly Support Ratios for Sweden, China, Brazil, and Egypt in 2000, 2015, and 2030. This ratio refers to the number of people over the age of 65 for every 100 people between the age of 20 and 64, suggesting the number of available adults in

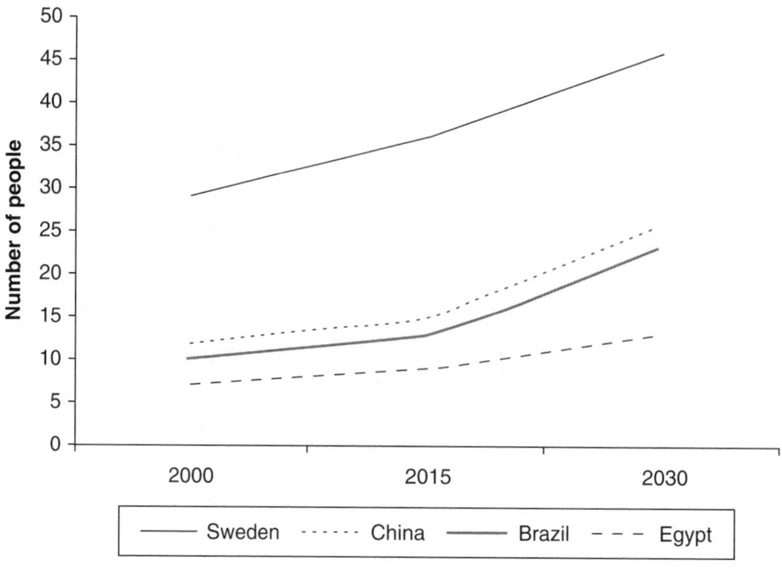

Figure 11.3 Elderly Support Ratios: 2000, 2015, and 2030

NOTE: Elderly support ratio is the number of people 65 years and over per 100 people 20 to 64 years.

SOURCE: Kinsella and Velkoff (2001), p. 154.

the workforce providing financial and caregiving support to the elderly. A high ratio creates the concern that there will not be enough adults to support the elderly population. Figure 11.3 shows that Sweden already has a high Elderly Support Ratio, indicating that there is a large concentration of elderly compared with nonelderly adults. Moreover, the ratio in Sweden will increase dramatically over the next 30 years. Conversely, China, Brazil, and Egypt currently have small Elderly Support Ratios; however, the ratios will increase substantially, especially in China and Brazil, over the next 30 years.

One similarity among these four countries is that widowhood among older women is common. Worldwide, women live longer than men (Hayward & Zhang, 2001). For example, a 65-year-old Swedish woman in 2000 could expect to live another 20.3 years, compared with only 16.4 years for men. Likewise, the gender discrepancies for Brazil, China, and Egypt were 3.8, 2.5, and 2.3 years, respectively (Kinsella & Velkoff, 2001). Because women live longer, they are more likely than men to spend the later years of their lives as widows. In fact, the majority of older women are widows (National Research Council, 2001).

Diversity in Cultural Norms

These demographic changes interface with societal norms, cultural values, and government policies to influence family interaction (Myers, 2000). That is, in addition to the diversity in the proportion of elderly in populations among countries affecting the composition of families, different norms, values, and policies among countries also affect the way that families interact with elderly family members.

For example, Denmark and Portugal, both western European countries, have very different rates of older people living alone. Fifty-two percent of older Danish women live alone, compared to 24% of Portuguese women. This difference reflects dissimilar social and economic policies between the two countries. Older women in Denmark have access to more "elder-friendly" housing and receive more financial support from the government, which allows them to live independently of their children (Kinsella & Velkoff, 2001, p. 67). Likewise, among less developed countries, 16% of Bolivian older women live alone, compared to only 7% of Taiwanese women. In general, older people in less developed countries are more likely to live with their adult children than older people living in developed countries, thereby leading to fewer older people living alone (Kinsella & Velkoff).

Culture also plays an important role in the proportion of elderly who live in institutions. Although 8.7% of the elderly in Sweden live in long-term care, only 3.9% of Italian elderly live in similar circumstances. Thus, in countries with a similar proportion of elderly, in the same region of the world, and both having developed economies, Sweden has a proportion of elderly in residential care that is double the proportion in Italy (Kinsella & Velkoff, 2001). These differences in norms and values are often represented in different government policies. The considerable differences among countries in public policy regarding the financing of long-term care provide a case in point. For example, the elderly and their families in Great Britain are required to pay for their own care until their assets, such as property and savings, are reduced to a specified level. On the other hand, the elderly in Canada, which is part of the British Commonwealth, pay for long-term care based on their income, rather than level of assets (Merlis, 2000).

The family has traditionally provided care for disabled, frail elderly family members, with the government having a minimal role (Meeks, Nickols, & Sweaney, 1999). This cultural norm is still dominant in most less developed countries (Shuman, 2001). For example, there is a strong cultural norm for Brazilian families to care for the elderly (Ramos, 1993), and "the family is still considered the most important institution for the care of the elderly" in Egypt (Fadel-Girgis, 1983, p. 589). In developed countries, however, the culture has changed so that the state has taken over much of the responsibility for caring for the elderly (Kim, Bengtson, Myers, & Eun, 2000). For example, nearly half (45%) of the disabled elderly in Sweden receive professional care (Shea et al., 2003), with a sizable portion of them receiving home-based services, such as bathing, grooming, house cleaning, and help with household chores (Kinsella & Velkoff, 2001).

In parts of Asia, the demographic transition that is leading to an aging society is clashing with traditional norms of families caring for the elderly (Kim et al., 2000). The traditional Asian culture that emphasizes the important role of the family and its duty to the elderly has placed the care of the elderly almost exclusively on the family. However, the drastically reduced fertility and mortality rates in some of the Asian countries, such as South Korea, have created a burden on too few children to care for too many surviving parents. Although many families are reluctant to share the responsibility of caring for their elderly family members with the state, the practical reality of the need for additional help is gradually forcing the state to offer formal services and the families to accept them.

A closer look at one country will provide an illustration of aging families from an international, cross-cultural perspective. China has an ancient culture with strong norms of family solidarity and filial piety, or respect for elders (Kim et al., 2000). In recent decades, the country has undergone substantial societal changes because of communist political rule. Within this cultural environment, the Chinese society is aging. More older people live in China than in any other country (Kinsella & Velkoff, 2001), and the population is aging rapidly (Fan, 2002; Riley, 2004; Yi & Vaupel, 2002). What does aging look like for families in China?

Chinese Families in Later Life

The Traditional Chinese Family and the Elderly

The beliefs that form the basis of the Chinese family can be traced directly to Confucius (551–479 BC), whose ideas became the basis of Chinese social and political life for more than 2,000 years. Confucian ideas penetrated to the core of the lives of ordinary Chinese people, effectively defining for them what it meant to be human and acting as the guiding principles of Chinese social life (Ikels, 1993; Smith, 1991).

There were many distinctive characteristics of the traditional family in China. First and foremost, the Chinese family was patriarchal. Roles were clearly defined, with males, particularly the father and eldest son, having the most dominant positions (Hsu, 1971a). Authority passed from the father to the eldest son, whose authority and decisions were absolute. Females, relegated to a subordinate position in the traditional Chinese family, were expected to please and obey their fathers, and if married, were subordinate to their husbands and their husbands' parents. The norm for women was compliance (Smith).

A second characteristic of the traditional Chinese family was that it was patrilocal; that is, the married couple lived with the husband's parents (Ikels, 1993). According to this custom, the grandparents, their unmarried children, and their married sons, together with their wives and children, all lived in one household. Because of patrilocal residence, daughters were considered less valuable than sons; parents felt that daughters were being reared at their expense for the benefit of another family or clan (Sung, 1967). In some cases, particularly if the family was extremely poor, infanticide of the female child was practiced. Because of its patrilocal residence pattern, the traditional family in China was also an extended family in which many generations and their offspring lived under one roof. Ideally, the more generations living under the same roof, the more status the family had. Besides the prestige factor, the extended family structure of the Chinese family provided another important function. In an agriculturally based economy, there was an urgent need for many workers to cultivate and till the land and harvest the crops. An isolated nuclear family would be at a disadvantage in this economy. The extended family system was a much more suitable arrangement, providing the family with additional laborers as well as providing the members of the extended family with some degree of economic security.

According to the Chinese system of patrilineal descent, the household property and land were to be divided equally among the sons, either at the father's death or at the marriage of the youngest son. However, in exchange for the property and land, the sons were expected to reciprocate by sharing equally in the responsibility for the care and support of their parents in their old age (Hsu, 1971b; Wong, 1988).

Ancestor worship was greatly emphasized in the traditional family in China. It was believed that a Chinese male could achieve some form of immortality only if his family line were continued through the birth of sons. One of the greatest sins that a man could commit was to die without having any sons to carry on the family line and perform the ancestor worship rituals; therefore, an intense desire to have sons existed among the Chinese.

Filial piety was a highly cherished value in the traditional Chinese family. Filial piety is a set of moral principles, taught at a very young age and reinforced throughout one's life, which emphasizes reverence toward the nation's leaders and one's elders. Duty, obligation, importance of family name, service, and self-sacrifice to the elders—all essential elements of filial piety—characterized Chinese family relations. The meaning of filial piety is threefold: to have gratitude for the care given by one's parents, to respect and love one's parents, and to be attentive to one's parents' desires (Hsu, 1971a; Li, 1985). Complete devotion to parents was expected. Such devotion was taught in childhood through emphasis on obedience, proper conduct, moral training, and the acceptance of social obligations (Ho, 1986). A familiar proverb states: "Of all the teachings of the classics, filial piety comes first" (Kong, 1989, p. 22).

Chinese families emphasized social order and the need to "do the right thing." In families, this required children, no matter how old, to remain deeply loyal to their parents and to value them. An old Chinese saying goes, "The elderly are a family's greatest treasure" (Yu, 1987, p. 211).

Marriage was a family concern, not a private matter between a couple in love. The major purpose of marriage was to carry on the family line (Wu, 1987). Love was not a prerequisite for marriage and was discouraged. Because the bride lived with the husband's parents, the parents felt that they should have an important voice in the decision about who would live with them. The arranged marriage, another characteristic of the traditional Chinese family, kept parents from leaving things to chance.

The Communist Revolution and the Elderly

The Confucian concern for social order and for obeying those in a higher position resulted in few changes occurring in the family system of China for more than 2,000 years. However, in 1949, the Communist Revolution shook the very foundations of the family system as it had been known. The Marriage Law of 1950 abolished arranged marriages; restricted payments for brides, as well as much of the ritual and ceremony associated with marriages; and provided greater access to divorce. In effect, the law not only put an end to the feudal marriage code but also encouraged marriages based on mutual affection. The Marriage Law basically set up a legal system to manage family legal issues, and it guaranteed the rights of women as part of the new system (Davis & Harrell, 1993). A new Marriage Law of 1981 retained the basic spirit of the earlier law while extending some of its provisions. Later marriages were to be officially encouraged, men and women were supposed to enjoy equal status in the home, both partners were to share the responsibility of caring for their parents and their children, and divorce was to be granted in cases of "complete alienation" even if only one party felt it was necessary (Smith, 1991).

Although the law "officially" changed, many aspects of traditional marriage and family remained, and the age-old concept of filial piety as it related to the care of the elderly parents was legitimized. The General Principles of the Marriage Law state that "the lawful rights and interests of the aged are protected" and that "within the family, maltreatment and desertion is prohibited." Article 15 of the Marriage Law further states, "Children have the duty to support and assist their parents. When children fail to perform the duty of supporting their parents, parents who have lost the ability to work or have difficulty providing for themselves have the right to demand that their children pay for their support." Article 22 stipulates: "Grandchildren or maternal grandchildren who have the capacity to bear the relevant costs have the duty to support and assist their grandparents whose children are deceased." Chapter 7 of the Criminal Law states:

> Whoever vilely mistreats an aged member of his family shall be sentenced to imprisonment for not more than two years, or to detention, or to public surveillance. Whoever, having responsibility for supporting an aged person, flagrantly refuses to support that person, shall be sentenced to imprisonment for not more than five years, to detention, or to public surveillance. (quoted in Tsai, 1987, pp. 572–573)

It should also be noted, too, that children, in turn, may depend on the support, both economic and emotional, of their parents (Li, 1985).

The Chinese government sees filial care as the best solution for the future to the problems of aging in China (Ikels, 1993). The parent-child reciprocal relationship is the backbone of Chinese culture (Tsai, 1987). Respect, love, and care for the elderly have always been traditional Chinese virtues. The proverb "We should respect our elders" dates back at least 2,000 years (Lin, 1984). Caring for the aged is regarded as an obligation in each household, and adult children have a duty to care for their parents according to the law.

It would appear that the obligations to the elderly are as protected under the legal codes of the Communist government as they were in the traditional past; nevertheless, the status of the elderly has declined. The elimination of ownership of private land that occurred with the Communist Revolution weakened the hold that elderly parents had on their children. If parents could not pass on land to their children, the children might have fewer feelings of obligation.

The official curb on ancestor worship further reduced the past prerogatives of the elderly, because without state sanction for these beliefs and rituals, parents cannot as effectively invoke the threat of supernatural punishment against those children who desert them or fail to support them (Davis-Friedmann, 1991; Gu & Liang, 2000).

The Elderly in the Chinese Family Today

Retirement. Whereas age 65 most often marks the onset of old age in the West, in China withdrawal from the full-time workforce usually comes well before age 65. In urban China, women workers may retire at age 50, women cadre (government- and state-sponsored employees) retire at 55, and men retire at age 60.

As the result of government pensions, urban retirees enjoy a high degree of flexibility in their leisure activities. Many retirees spend their years in various ways, such as gardening, taking care of their grandchildren, reading, doing arts and crafts, or visiting with friends. The elderly are often seen in parks visiting or doing morning exercises such as *tai-chi* or *qi-gong* (Li, 1985). Elderly men are often seen carrying pet birds in cages, a common hobby of older persons, or playing cards and chess. Urban elderly represent an elite group, relative to retirement, compared to their rural counterparts.

However, in recent years, the elderly have been taking different roles. The trend is for older persons, particularly men, to take new positions after retirement. Going back to work after retirement is displacing the traditional "baby-sitting the grandchildren at home" as a lifestyle for older people in China. Older persons may be self-employed, starting up part-time businesses, acting as advisers to their original work units, or counseling middle school students and helping them organize activities in their spare time. China's retirees are returning to work for reasons that include financial problems due to inflation, invitations from their original work units, or a strong commitment to their work. Because China has had a one-child-per-family policy,

Chinese extended families have become smaller. There are no longer many grandchildren for the urban elderly to care for, which gives them considerably more discretionary time.

In rural areas, where 80% of the population lives, retirement age for men is determined by their health status. They retire when they can no longer do the physical labor on the farm. Women retire when they achieve the status of a grandmother. Age, itself, is of less importance. Men gradually take on less strenuous jobs as their physical strength declines, or they work until family fortunes permit them to pass on primary financial responsibilities to their sons. When rural men stop working, they tend to socialize and relax with friends away from home. Women continue working in the home to assist family members with child care and household tasks as long as their health allows. Rural elderly remain very much a part of their families and are very dependent on them. Yi and Vaupel (2002) have found that the elderly in rural areas are more active in daily living than are urban elderly. This may be because facilities and services to assist the elderly in their lives are less available in rural areas, thereby forcing the rural elderly to perform daily activities by themselves. This frequent exercise may enable them to maintain their capacities for daily life longer than their urban counterparts. The rural elderly are likely to continue to perform garden work or even to do light labor in the fields, which may help them maintain their capacity for daily living.

Living Arrangements. In rural families, the model continues to be for an elderly parent to live with a married son (Johnson, 1993). For the urban elderly, living with adult children is more a response to economic necessity. In the urban family, the ideal is for married children and their parents to live separately until the time that the parents are too old to manage on their own. At that time of need, a married child will rejoin the parents, or an elderly parent will move to the home of a married child. Although urban residents are more dissatisfied with the necessity to live with elderly parents than are rural residents and actively search for alternatives, urban elderly maintain multigenerational homes as often as rural elderly do. However, housing shortages and the economic advantages of joint living make multigenerational households a practical choice.

Whereas the previously cited reasons encourage joint living, the economic benefits of large households make multigenerational living desirable. In both urban and rural areas, one household is usually a more efficient unit of consumption than are two smaller ones. Food costs are lower, as well as the cost of furniture and most other items. The need for child care is also an important consideration. In both urban and rural China, mothers work outside the home. In rural areas there is little day care, and even in urban areas, where day care is more common, there are still times that it is unavailable and the parents cannot be present. In both rural and urban areas, the typical solution is for the grandmother to stay at home with the grandchildren (generally only one grandchild in the cities), do the housework, and take care of other important tasks such as food shopping and cooking.

Even when young people live separately from their parents, which occurs more frequently than it did in the past, even in the rural areas (Fan, 2002), they all try to live close by in order to render mutual help (Jia, 1988). Coresidence, however, is still a viable and widely used option, and elderly persons in need of support still rely mainly on their immediate family members. In fact, it should be noted that 87% of the elderly in Wuhan live with their immediate family. It should be emphasized that residence in separate households does not necessarily mean functionally separate families. They may continue providing great assistance to each other (Gu & Liang, 2000).

Younger family members regard the role of the elderly in household work and child care as being important for the maintenance of the family's lifestyle. When the elderly parents can no longer care for themselves because of poor health, which places heavy burdens on their children, they will be viewed as having provided several decades of support to their children and grandchildren (Davis-Friedmann, 1991).

Although most families still live together, in the large cities an increasing number of elderly are living in retirement homes. Originally, such homes were shelters for childless widows and widowers unable to earn a living by themselves. Now, however, care centers for the elderly are available for paying residents who have children and a regular income. In the past, living in such residential centers would have been considered unthinkable for elderly persons who had living children. Even when elderly do not live with their children, the children generally remain in close contact with their parents.

Financial Arrangements. The majority of China's urban elderly derive their income from pensions or part-time employment, although many are also supported by their children. Although China's urban elderly are more reliant on the state, those who live in the rural areas are bound more closely to their families (Shi, 1993). However, change is evident in the rural areas as well.

Pensions and salaries account for the majority of the total income for the urban elderly (Ikels, 1993). The remainder comes from financial support from children and spouses. Although filial piety and the parent-child reciprocal relationship are the backbone of Chinese culture, there are also practical reasons in urban areas why children provide care for their elderly parents. The elderly person's pension may be larger than the child's salary, because pay is based on years worked. In a country of limited means, such economic support may be very welcome in a household, particularly when one considers the household and child care work assistance that the elderly are expected to provide in the household (Tsai, 1987). Therefore, the elderly provide both tangible and intangible returns for the family (Shi, 1993).

Because of the changing dynamics of the Chinese family, many couples that expected their children to care for them are fearful that their children may not be willing or able to support them after they retire. Consequently, in rural areas, and especially in developed rural areas, saving for retirement has also become a trend. Because the elderly in the rural areas do not receive pensions, the government is encouraging rural one-child families to purchase retirement insurance. Parents of only children who buy the insurance will receive monthly payments from the insurance company after reaching retirement. This represents a fundamental change in the approach to the care for the elderly. The traditional intergenerational approach is gradually being replaced by an investment approach. However, people in the less developed areas still rely on their sons for old-age support.

Another important trend is the increasing development of health insurance. The policies often take the form of a prepaid medical insurance plan. However, at present, the great majority of rural residents are without health insurance. In a study in Wuhan, 71% of urban residents had health coverage, compared to only 13% of rural residents (Henderson et al., 1995).

Another change in China is the movement of people from rural areas to urban areas, where many settle down when they find adequate employment. Although they may send money back to their parents to help support them, the function of caring for the elderly by the family is being weakened (Zhu & Xu, 1992).

Relationships Between Elderly Parents and Children. Few elderly, particularly in the countryside, can imagine a life isolated from their children's everyday lives. However, within the multigenerational family setting, the relationships between the generations often vary based on the child's gender. Mothers generally develop strong emotional ties with their children, as opposed to fathers, and in old age, mothers receive the benefits of their early attention in terms of particularly close ties with adult sons and daughters. Many parents, however, still place more emphasis on their sons than on their daughters, and ties with adult sons are especially strong. Because parents continue to be more likely to live with their sons, it is difficult for married daughters to sustain the same level of daily interactions as their brothers do (Davis-Friedmann, 1991).

Particularly in the urban areas, patterns of behavior are changing. Elderly parents are increasingly likely to divide their attention between sons and daughters. In fact, parents are often as intensely involved with their daughters as with their sons. In general, urban elderly are more likely to observe bilateral kinship as opposed to the patrilateral loyalties of the rural elderly (Davis-Friedmann, 1991). This is in part due to the government's conscious attempt to raise the status of women in society.

The preferred parent-child relationship remains one of mutual interdependence. When they live together, parents and children are in almost constant contact, share their meals, and pool their money in a common household budget. Contact with children who do not live together with their parents is more variable. They are more likely to visit their parents on their days off if they live in the same city or on holidays if they live farther away.

Because of the extreme concern about security in old age and the belief in continuance of the male lineage that exists among rural Chinese, parents of only daughters and those unable to have children face significant problems. Daughters often leave to become a part of another family and may live far from their parents. The traditional solution for the absence of male children, still used today, is to adopt a young boy or to adopt a son-in-law at the time of a daughter's marriage. In the latter case, the parents may require the son-in-law to take the surname of the father-in-law. The son-in-law might choose to do this in order to honor the father-in-law or for economic reasons such as inheritance. Generally, a young man would not take the surname of his father-in-law unless he had a brother to carry on his own father's name.

In the cities, in contrast to the rural areas, parents rarely form favored relationships with just one child if they have more than one child. Rather, they are more likely to move from child to child depending on family size and room available at any given household. Urban elderly maintain strong ties with all their children throughout old age. It is common for siblings to split the financial obligations for elderly parents (Davis-Friedmann, 1991).

In both urban and rural areas, children provide for elderly parents and parents turn for help to adult children without guilt, because both believe that the previous care of the children requires the children to reciprocate in their parents' old age (Zhan, 2004). However, most Chinese agree that there is one limitation on this responsibility. All generations believe that the needs of the elderly are less important than the immediate needs of the grandchildren. Both grandparents and parents give priority to the grandchildren, because they represent the future of the family.

CONCLUSION

Thus, the global population is aging, and the graying of the population is having a significant impact on family composition and interaction. Some family roles are being redefined as a result of these changes, and families, as well as the overall society, must make changes to adapt to more elderly people. However, although virtually every country is experiencing an increasingly older population, there is substantial diversity among countries in their stages in the aging process. Most developed countries, especially those in western Europe, have already reached the point where a substantial proportion of the population is elderly, whereas less developed countries have begun the demographic transition and anticipate dramatic changes as their population ages in the next few decades.

In addition to diversity in population composition, cultural norms and values also create substantial variety in the ways that societies interact with older family members. Household arrangements, utilization of professional care and long-term care facilities, caregiving practices, and government involvement all differ according to societal customs. In addition, as illustrated with the example of China, many of these traditional norms are changing in the face of political and social transformations.

Yet, despite this diversity, developed and less developed countries alike will be faced with the challenges of meeting the needs of their increasing older population. Social institutions and norms will need to continue to adapt to the many changes brought about by older populations. Families will be required to modify and transform family roles in order to adapt to the emerging "beanpole" structure of families. Moreover, governments will need to address the needs of the escalating older population. Health care, housing, and financial security are all issues that will require the attention of public policymakers. Particularly, with fewer adult children available to care for their elderly family members, traditional means of family caregiving will become inadequate in helping the elderly. Governments will need to develop public policies that will meet the needs of the population of elderly who can no longer care for themselves.

REFERENCES

Bengtson, V. L. (2001). Beyond the nuclear family: The increasing importance of multigenerational bonds. *Journal of Marriage and Family, 63,* 1–16.

Bengtson, V. L., Rosenthal, C. J., & Burton, L. M. (1996). Paradoxes of families and aging. In R. H. Binstock & L. K. George (Eds.), *Handbook of aging and the social sciences* (4th ed., pp. 253–282). San Diego, CA: Academic Press.

Davis, D., & Harrell, S. (1993). Introduction: The impact of post-Mao reforms on family life. In D. Davis & S. Harrell (Eds.), *Chinese families in the post-Mao era* (pp. 1–24). Berkeley: University of California Press.

Davis-Friedmann, D. (1991). *Long lives.* Stanford, CA: Stanford University Press.

Fadel-Girgis, M. (1983). Family support for the elderly in Egypt. *Gerontologist, 23,* 589–592.

Fan, C. C. (2002). Population change and regional development in China: Insights based on the 2000 census. *Eurasian Geography and Economics, 43,* 425–442.

Gu, S., & Liang, J. (2000). China: Population aging and old age support. In V. L. Bengtson, K. D. Kim, G. C. Myers, & K. S. Eun (Eds.), *Aging in East and West: Families, states, and the elderly* (pp. 59–93). New York: Springer.

Hayward, M. D., & Zhang, Z. (2001). Demography of aging: A century of global change, 1950–2050. In R. H. Binstock & L. K. George (Eds.), *Handbook of aging and the social sciences* (5th ed., pp. 69–85). New York: Academic Press.

Henderson, G., Jin, S., Akin, J., Li, Z., Wang, J., Ma, H., et al. (1995). Distribution of medical insurance in China. *Social Science and Medicine, 41,* 1119–1130.

Ho, D. V. F. (1986). Chinese patterns of socialization: A critical review. In M. H. Bond (Ed.), *The psychology of the Chinese people* (pp. 1–37). Hong Kong: Oxford University Press.

Hsu, F. L. K. (1971a). *The challenge of the American dream: The Chinese in the United States.* Belmont, CA: Wadsworth.

Hsu, F. L. K. (1971b). *Under the ancestor's shadow: Chinese culture and personality.* Stanford, CA: Stanford University Press.

Ikels, C. (1993). Chinese kinship and the state: Shaping of policy for the elderly. In G. Maddox & M. P. Lawton (Eds.), *Annual review of gerontology and geriatrics: Vol. 13. Kinship, aging, and social change* (pp. 123–166). New York: Springer.

Jia, A. (1988). New experiments with the elderly care in rural China. *Journal of Cross-Cultural Gerontology, 3,* 139–148.

Johnson, G. E. (1993). Family strategies and economic transformation in rural China: Some evidence from the Pearl River Delta. In D. Davis & S. Harrell (Eds.), *Chinese families in the post-Mao era* (pp. 103–138). Berkeley: University of California Press.

Kim, K. -D., Bengtson, V. L., Myers, G. C., & Eun, K. -S. (2000). Aging in East and West at the turn of the century. In V. L. Bengtson, K. -D. Kim, G. C. Myers, & K. -S. Eun (Eds.), *Aging in East and West: Families, states, and the elderly* (pp. 3–16). New York: Springer.

Kinsella, K. (2000). Demographic dimensions of global aging. *Journal of Family Issues, 21,* 541–558.

Kinsella, K., & Velkoff, V. A. (2001). *An aging world* (U.S. Census Bureau, Series, P95/01-1). Washington, DC: U.S. Government Printing Office.

Kong, S. L. (1989). *Chinese culture and lore.* Toronto, Ontario, Canada: Kensington Educational.

Li, X. (1985). The effect of family on the mental health of the Chinese family. In W. S. Tseng & D. Wu (Eds.), *Chinese culture and mental health* (pp. 85–93). Hong Kong: Academic Press.

Lin, X. (1984, September 4). Nationwide concern for elderly. *China Daily,* p. 4.

Meeks, C. B., Nickols, S. Y., & Sweaney, A. L. (1999). Demographic comparisons of aging in five selected countries. *Journal of Family and Economic Issues, 20,* 223–250.

Merlis, M. (2000). Caring for the frail elderly: An international review. *Health Affairs, 19,* 141–149.

Myers, G. C. (2000). Comparative ageing research: Demographic and social survey strategies. In V. L. Bengtson, K. -D. Kim, G. C. Myers, & K. -S. Eun (Eds.), *Aging in East and West: Families, states, and the elderly* (pp. 243–259). New York: Springer.

National Research Council. (2001). *Preparing for an aging world: The case for cross-national research.* Washington, DC: National Academy Press.

Ramos, L. R. (1993). Brazil. In E. B. Palmore (Ed.), *Developments and research on aging: An international handbook* (pp. 25–40). Westport, CT: Greenwood Press.

Riley, N. E. (2004). China's population: New trends and challenges. *Population Bulletin, 59,* 3–36.

Serow, W. J. (2001). Economic and social implications of demographic patterns. In R. H. Binstock & L. K. George (Eds.), *Handbook of aging and the social sciences* (5th ed., pp. 86–102). New York: Academic Press.

Shea, D., Davey, A., Femia, E. E., Zarit, S. H., Sundstrom, G., Berg, S., et al. (2003). Exploring assistance in Sweden and the United States. *Gerontologist, 43,* 712–721.

Shi, L. (1993). Family financial and household support exchange between generations: A survey of Chinese rural elderly. *Gerontologist, 33,* 468–480.

Shuman, T. (2001). Third world aging. In G. L. Maddox (Ed.), *The encyclopedia of aging* (3rd ed., pp. 1019–1022). New York: Springer.

Smith, C. J. (1991). *China: People and places in the land of one billion.* Boulder, CO: Westview Press.

Stone, L., & Myers, G. C. (2001). Demography. In G. L. Maddox (Ed.), *The encyclopedia of aging* (3rd ed., pp. 282–285). New York: Springer.

Sung, B. L. (1967). *Mountains of gold.* New York: Macmillan.

Tsai, W. (1987). Life after retirement: Elderly welfare in China. *Asian Survey, 27,* 567–576.

Uhlenberg, P. (1996a). Mortality decline in the twentieth century and supply of kin over the life course. *Gerontologist, 36,* 681–685.

Uhlenberg, P. (1996b). Mutual attraction: Demography and life-course analysis. *Gerontologist, 36,* 226–229.

Uhlenberg, P., & Kirby, J. B. (1998). Grandparenthood over time: Historical and demographic trends. In M. E. Szinovacz (Ed.), *Handbook on grandparenthood.* Westport, CT: Greenwood Press.

Wong, M. (1988). The Chinese American family. In G. H. Mindel, R. W. Huberstein, & R. Wright (Eds.), *Ethnic families in America* (pp. 230–258). New York: Elsevier.

Wu, B. (1987). The urban family in flux. In Women of China (Eds.), *New trends in Chinese marriage and the family.* Beijing, Republic of China: China Books and Periodicals.

Yi, Z., & Vaupel, J. W. (2002). Functional capacity and self-evaluation of health and life of oldest in China. *Journal of Social Issues, 58,* 733–748.

Yu, G. (1987). Spending the remaining years at ease. In Women of China (Eds.), *New trends in Chinese marriage and the family.* Beijing, Republic of China: China Books and Periodicals.

Zhan, H. J. (2004). Willingness and expectations: Intergenerational differences in attitudes toward filial responsibility in China. *Marriage and Family Review, 36,* 175–200.

Zhu, C., & Xu, Q. (1992). Family care of the elderly in China: Change and problems. In J. I. Kosberg (Ed.), *Family care of the elderly: Social and cultural changes* (pp. 67–138). Newbury Park, CA: Sage.

Part III Exercise: Mate Selection

The purpose of this exercise is to help you to see how your own marriage could be if you lived in another culture. Type a one-page response to each of the following scenarios.

1. If your parents were to select your spouse for you, what kind of person would they choose, and how would this choice match (or not match) your personal preferences? Consider such issues as race, religion, social class, compatibility, and physical attraction. Also, what kind of dowry or bride-price could your parents afford to pay, and how would this affect their selection of a spouse for you?
2. Assume that the sororate or levirate is practiced where you live. If you have a same-sex sibling or cousin who has been married or seriously involved with someone, imagine what it would be like if that person died and you had to marry his or her spouse. How well would the two of you get along?
3. Now assume that you live in a culture where it is mandated that you marry a cross-cousin. For males, that would be the daughters of the uncles on your mother's side of the family, and the daughters of the aunts on your father's side. For females, it would be your father's sister's and mother's brother's sons. List those people by name, and indicate how happily you think that you could live together.
4. Reflecting on your answers to the above questions, what did you learn about what is important to you? How are these preferences rooted in your own culture and mate-selection systems?

Part IV

INTERNATIONAL FAMILY VARIATION

African woman at the market.

Introduction to Part IV

Part IV covers contemporary family life in certain countries and cultural regions of the world. We begin with immigration to the United States from Latin America and Asia. This is followed by more in-depth analyses of the Islamic Middle East, Kenya, Latin America, and Japan.

In Chapter 12, "Asian and Latino Immigrant Families," Kawamoto and Viramontez Anguiano discuss the two major immigrant groups to the United States. They explain the family, gender, and intergenerational issues, as well as education, health, government policies, and family dynamics influencing these populations in similar and different ways.

In Chapter 13, "Families in the Islamic Middle East," Sherif-Trask places the Middle Eastern Muslim family within its historical, cultural, and religious contexts. She provides an overview of the research on these families and carefully explains the role of Islam in family life. Sherif-Trask also discusses the tensions between traditional and modern expectations of marriage, divorce, and parenting.

In Chapter 14, "Families in Sub-Saharan Africa," Wilson and Ngige provide a detailed description and analysis of traditional and contemporary African family life, with an emphasis on East Africa. Marriage, sexuality, parenting, gender relations, and other topics are presented within the context of modernization.

In Chapter 15, "Families in Latin America," Ingoldsby assesses key aspects of family life in the countries of Central and South America. He reviews the historical development of mate selection and cohabitation and provides an overview of family relations in selected countries where sufficient research exists. The topics of familism, machismo, abandoned street children, and domestic violence are also discussed.

In Chapter 16, "Families in Japan," Murray and Kimura begin with a historical overview of the Japanese family, based on the *ie* model, which focuses on the importance of the generational continuity of the household. The modern, post–World War II family, with its nuclear and Western influences, is presented across the life cycle, including mate selection, marriage, gender relations, parenting, and the elderly.

CHAPTER 12

Asian and Latino Immigrant Families

WALTER T. KAWAMOTO
AND RUBEN P. VIRAMONTEZ ANGUIANO

Now more than ever, the culturally diverse tapestry that constructs our country's reality is at the forefront. The United States has been characterized as a place where immigrants and their families could find a new beginning. Although there are many interesting trends among contemporary immigrants, such as Arab and Muslim (Cheng, 2003) and European immigrant families from the former Soviet Union, especially from Russia (Iskow, Kitanov, & Ferlazzo, 2002), this chapter will focus on families from the two groups that are consistently at the center of immigrant issues, Asian and Latino families.

We have chosen this focus for a variety of reasons. Demographically, these two groups represent the top two contemporary immigrant groups. Within these groups, Mexicans, Chinese, Vietnamese, Cambodians, and Koreans are the largest subgroups (Becerra, 1998; Fong, 2000; Lee, 1997), even though the populations for recent immigrants are generally regarded as undercounted (Fong, 2000). Politically, both groups are just now becoming more active in the national political arena and have often been known to work together toward a common goal (Saito, 2000). Academically, they have been featured together in major urban studies such as the Children of Immigrants Longitudinal Study (Rumbaut, 2000). But most of all, both these groups share the social stigma of the archetypal immigrant/foreigner (Takaki, 2001). We have chosen to explore these groups together to illustrate the depth of their connections and the complexity of their distinctiveness.

AN OVERVIEW OF LATINO AND ASIAN IMMIGRANT FAMILIES

Although Latinos and Asians have been a part of and have immigrated to the United States for over 150 years, the most recent waves have changed the cultural landscape of the United States (Becerra, 1998; Fong, 2000). Over the last few decades, the population of these groups has risen throughout the United States. The impact of mostly Mexican and Central American immigrant families has propelled the Latino population to 38 million (El Nasser, 2003), making them the largest ethnic minority in the United States. At the same time, a series of contemporary Asian immigrant waves, beginning with the Immigration Act of 1965 and led by Southeast Asian immigrants, has swelled the Asian American population to around 11 million (Yeh & Inose, 2002), making them one of the fastest-growing ethnic groups. The immigrant Latino population numbers 12.8 million, which is almost half of the foreign-born population in the United States (U.S. Bureau of the Census, 2001b). Since 1990, 86% of the growth in the Asian American population has been due to immigration (U.S. Bureau of the Census, 2003), and more than half of all Asian Americans are foreign born (Lee, 1997).

There are some interesting geographic characteristics of these two communities. Traditionally, the majority of Latino families would migrate to historically Latino-based states, such as the southwestern region (California, Texas, Arizona, and New Mexico) for Mexicans and Central Americans and Florida and New York for Cubans, Puerto Ricans, and other Caribbean-based groups. The recent wave has migrated and settled throughout the United States, including the Southeast, South, Midwest, and Northwest, in high numbers. For example, North Carolina reported a more than 300% increase of Latinos throughout the 1990s (Associated Press, 2001; U.S. Bureau of the Census, 2003). The Great Lakes region, which includes Minnesota, Illinois, Wisconsin, Michigan, and Ohio, reported a significant increase of Latinos in the last decade of the 20th century (Aponte & Siles, 1997). Most of the Southeast Asian immigrants ended up in coastal and urban states, such as California, Texas, Washington, New York, and Florida (Fong, 2000).

The Family

Immigrant Latino and Asian families are faced with an array of familial, cultural, and social risk factors including high poverty rates, physical and mental health factors, educational challenges, and fear of deportation (Gim, Atkinson, & Whiteley, 1990; Trueba, 2002). *Familism* within Latino families has been characterized as a collective flexible support network that provides social, emotional, and financial support within the family. The support network comprises nuclear, extended, and fictive kin members. The family serves as the cornerstone of the Latino and Asian immigrant communities and is key to the cultural socialization of children within the family and larger society (Tam & Detzner, 1998; Viramontez Anguiano, 2004). Moreover, Latino immigrant families have demonstrated their resiliency through their cultural capital. The collective nature of these families is grounded in their linguistic pride, their religiosity, and spirituality. Asian American immigrants enter this country with a similar set of ideals based upon harmony and specified roles of mutual obligation (Hsu, 1971; Tam & Detzner, 1998).

The complex nature of resiliency in Asian American immigrant families is seen several other ways. Sometimes it is about perception, such as when Lee (1997) concluded that positive identification with ethnicity and culture can better predict positive mental health than a high acculturation rate for many Asian immigrants. I. S. Kim's (1981) study of Korean Americans in New York revealed strong survival instincts and opportunity seeking. Other times, having a physical community resource such as a nearby ethnic neighborhood is important in facilitating resilience (Koranyi, 1981; Lee, 1997). Ethnicity-based churches, professional organizations, and recreational groups are key resources that also foster resiliency in the Korean American immigrant community (Min, 1988) and a principal element of resiliency in other ethnic groups (H. I. McCubbin, M. A. McCubbin, A. I. Thompson, & E. A. Thompson, 1998). Up to 70% of Korean American immigrants attend Korean-based Christian churches (S. C. Kim, 1997). Finally, it is important for therapists to approach families with respect for the strength and resiliency it took to make it to this country, often surviving life-threatening conditions (Boehnlein, Leung, & Kinzie, 1997).

Immigrant Latino and Asian families and individuals often experience a familial and cultural gap when they migrate to a foreign country such as the United States. This gap can be quite stressful for the immigrant family, which is faced with understanding and adapting to a mainstream culture that emphasizes individualism and emancipation from the family (Hetts & Sakuma, 1999; Wodarski, 1992). As a result, Latino and Asian immigrant families typically experience feelings of social and cultural isolation and struggle to function as family systems, especially when considering gender issues, intergenerational factors, and the process of acculturation and assimilation as related to family dynamics (Benokraitis, 2002; K. K. Dion & K. L. Dion, 2001; McAdoo, 1999; Portes & Hao, 2002; Taylor, 2002; Vega, 1995). Moreover, the immigrant families struggle within various ecological social systems outside the family system, including the educational, physical and mental health, economic, and political systems (Landau, 1982; J. F. Smart & D. W. Smart, 1995; Trueba, 2002; Zuniga, 2002).

Gender

Gender plays a pivotal role in Latino families, and consequently, understanding gender is critical to understanding Latino families and their adaptation to the United States. Recent migration research has hypothesized that gender should be conceptualized as a social system (K. K. Dion & K. L. Dion, 2001; Hondagneu-Sotelo, 1999). Immigration and feminist researchers have also hypothesized that traditional sex role theory has hindered the holistic understanding of gender by promoting gender as a static social construct. Traditional sex role theory neglects to examine important fluid systemic factors including inequalities, social change, historical factors, power relations, and political and economic issues (Thorne, 1993).

With this in mind, the fluidity of gender as a social system results in a process of renegotiation that transpires within Latino and Asian immigrant families, particularly about family work, including child care, household chores, and family relations. These domestic tasks were typically a female's responsibility in the home country and now are being renegotiated based on different social contexts in the host country, as mainstream women work outside the home, and more and more husbands and partners participate in household labor. Often Latino and Asian immigrant women have had to balance traditional expectations of family work and postmodern realities of the United States. The fact is that work is not an option for women in these families; it is a necessity. For example, K. C. Kim and S. Kim (1998) estimate that three fourths of Korean immigrant women are currently employed. The expectation is that women must sacrifice for the family. This sacrifice is expressed in unexpected ways, such as the anecdotal report of a Vietnamese immigrant woman who wants to live a separate life but stays in the house to be there for the children (Leung, Boehnlein, & Kinzie, 1997).

The renegotiation process also occurs outside the family system in other systems, especially in the workplace. For example, the opportunity to earn higher wages enables immigrant women to gain more familial power (K. K. Dion & K. L. Dion, 2001; Menjivar, 1999). This process also happens in immigrant Asian families, and the strain has resulted in well-documented negative outcomes, including higher levels of depression, poor overall mental health, and some physical problems and at-risk outcomes (S. C. Kim, 1997; Lee, 1997; Noh, Wu, Speechly, & Kaspar, 1992). For example, Korean immigrants have a divorce rate five to six times higher than Koreans in general (I. S. Kim, 1981), suggesting that many immigrant couples are not able to resolve problems with newfound gender roles. K. C. Kim and S. Kim (1998) report that part of the tension comes from the quality of the jobs encountered. Unfavorable jobs necessitate female employment and discourage positive attitudes about female employment. Typically, these unfavorable jobs do not get better for Korean immigrant women, and they are not likely to be able to move to better jobs (or have the family survive on one income), prolonging the heavy burden of their dual roles. K. C. Kim and S. Kim conclude that Korean immigrant women are also willing participants in creating this double burden, sacrificing themselves for the greater resiliency of their families. However, subsequent generations of Korean American women are less inclined to accept this role. This trend is also supported by evidence of increased demands for equality in the family by Vietnamese immigrant women (Leung et al., 1997).

Yee (1987) reports that Japanese and Vietnamese elderly women seem to be given more of a functional role in families, thus fostering an easier adaptation into elder status. This function was also evidenced by the work of Tam and Detzner (1998), who found that although both maternal and paternal Chinese immigrant grandparents were active as caregivers for their grandchildren, the grandmothers tended to be more active than the grandfathers.

Another aspect to consider when examining the interface between gender and Latino and Asian immigrant families is the familial socialization process of gender. Research has demonstrated that daughters and sons are often socialized in different manners that could lead to different outcomes (Das Gupta, 1997). Latino immigrant families are more restrictive with their daughters than their sons. This is based on traditional cultural values that are rooted in Catholic beliefs about women and their sexuality. Moreover, within this context parents encourage conservative Catholic gender values out of concern for a possible unwanted pregnancy. On a positive note, K. K. Dion and K. L. Dion (2001) found that often daughters demonstrated high levels of ethnic pride as a result of the traditional Catholic styles of socialization.

Intergenerational[1] Realities

A critical issue for Latino immigrant family systems is the intergenerational challenges that its members face. Unlike European immigrant families, who assimilated through the process of "straight-line" assimilation, Latino immigrant family assimilation is a segmented process. The process of straight-line assimilation was carried out by the first generation, who spoke their native language at home and learned English to function in the work system; a second generation, who learned fluent English but still communicated with their parents in their parents' language; and finally the third generation, which primarily spoke English and had very little or no knowledge of their European ancestors' language (McKeever & Klineberg, 1999).

The process of segmented assimilation is based on resource factors including financial, social, and human capital that the immigrant families brought with them. They brought these resources to the communities that they initially settled, or colonized in the case of Mexicans in the Southwest, and they were influenced by the circumstances under which they arrived. This cultural transition has also been governed by the cultural, social, political, and economic climate of the United States and its response to Latino immigrant families. The United States has changed dramatically over the last few decades.

Earlier waves of European immigrants had fewer economic and cultural barriers when compared to the current anti-immigrant environment toward Latinos and other immigrants (Fernandez-Kelly & Schauffler, 1994; Portes, 1995).

Latino immigrant families often live in impoverished communities, enroll their children in a struggling public school system, and frequently experience constant anti-immigrant sentiment (McKeever & Klineberg, 1999). These overarching factors often influence the 1.5 generation (*1.5 generation* can be defined as the children who were born in a foreign country but immigrated with their parents to the United States), the second generation, and subsequent generations of Latino children and youth. Constant struggle with acculturative stress can determine whether Latino children and youth will show positive or negative developmental outcomes. The search for positive Latino identity development within a turbulent U.S. mainstream can become a daunting task for Latino children and youth (Garcia Coll et al., 1996). Although developmental and family researchers have consistently found the psychological and social advantages associated with bilingualism to be a key component of positive Latino identity, the U.S. mainstream culture has continued to be structured by an environment based on English monolingualism, despite the negative developmental outcomes related to immigrant Latino and other immigrant multilingual groups (Cummins, 1976; Hakuta, 1986; Portes & Hao, 2002). Consequently, multigenerational Latino children and youth express feelings of being culturally isolated and stratified, which affect their educational and economic success (Ogbu, 1991).

Asian American immigrants experience similar feelings of isolation, along with other concerns. It begins with the complex elements of entry into the United States. Family reunification is traditionally the leading reason for the immigration of Korean women and elderly family members (S. C. Kim, 1997), but then family members are often forced to live in different parts of the country because of employment opportunities (Tam & Detzner, 1998). Furthermore, although reunification is welcome, the current procedures, which usually require individual family members to come at different times based on U.S. immigration preferences, are very disruptive to the family's stability (Kao & Lam, 1997). Most Asian American immigrant families are founded on ancient traditions of intergenerational obligation (Lee, 1997; H. I. McCubbin et al., 1998). These traditions are under significant pressure to change or to be lost altogether. Kao and Lam (1997) report that a specific tradition, respect and obedience given to elderly women by daughters-in-law, is an especially disturbing loss to the traditional family dynamic. The classic intergenerational dynamic is that of the parents and grandparents with traditions more in keeping with the country of origin finding themselves at odds with the younger, more Westernized members of the family. These elders expect obedience and work, whereas the youth emphasize independence and assertiveness (Lee, 1997). Intergenerational conflict may be connected to the disparity between the acculturation rates of elders and youth (Lee, 1997). This can lead to loosening of the tradition of filial piety and neglect for elderly parents (Kao & Lam, 1997). Evidence of this dynamic is especially apparent for Vietnamese American families (Leung et al., 1997).

Intergenerational conflicts are often influenced by the specifics of the ages of the children at migration. Migrate with younger children, and the family is vulnerable to parental reversal of hierarchies (McGoldrick, 1982). Dependence on bilingual children to translate for monolingual elders can cause resentment on either side (Lee, 1997). This is exacerbated when it comes to issues such as mental health, and it may be so bad that some cases have been reported where an adult child has exaggerated symptoms simply to have his or her elder removed from the home (Kao & Lam, 1997). With older children, there is a greater danger of a loss of connectedness (McGoldrick). Loss of this interconnectedness can lead to feelings of isolation and disengagement (Landau, 1982; Tam & Detzner, 1998). Many work to maintain a sense of connectedness through family associations and social clubs (Lee, 1997).

Asian American small businesses often incorporate the entire family working long hours together, sometimes resulting in heightened tension (Lee, 1997). Tam and Detzner (1998) note that this heightened use of family members, from a family resource management perspective, can also work out well for immigrant families. They focused on the idea that immigrant elders, despite stress from the move to the United States, often provide substantial help to the family in the form of caretaking for their grandchildren. The grandparents also provided child-rearing advice when they were not able to provide actual child care.

Serious issues persist for multigenerational[2] Asian American immigrant families. The unexpectedly high cost of caring for elderly in the United States can be a source of tension (Leung et al., 1997). Of the various Indochinese groups served by Oregon Health Sciences University, Vietnamese immigrants had the highest incidence of parent-child relationship problems (Leung et al.). A study by Ikels (1983) indicated that ultimately, many elders preferred the dangers of living in their home country to the frustrations of living in the United States.

ACCULTURATION AND FAMILY DYNAMICS

Coupled with gender and intergenerational dynamics is the process of acculturation and assimilation as it relates to immigrant Asian and Latino family systems. The issue of assimilation and acculturation of families of Asian and Latino background within and compared to a European American mainstream society has been well documented (Benokraitis, 2002; Fong, 2002; Marger, 2003; McAdoo, 1999; Taylor, 2002; Vega, 1995). A general overview of this process will be presented, specifically focusing on family dynamics, including spousal relationships and parent-child relationships. This general overview will center on immigrant Asian and Latino families and how their experiences compare to those of nonimmigrant Asian Americans, Latinos, and mainstream European Americans.

Acculturation

Central to the assimilation and acculturation discussion are the realities of the social space where Asian and Latino families have found themselves within the larger American cultural tapestry. This must be elaborated as a cultural-historical backdrop before centering on family dynamics. Moreover, when examining acculturation, it is important to understand that acculturation is a continuum that also may encompass assimilation. Specifically, a basic definition for *acculturation* is when various cultural threads of the ethnic and mainstream cultures become intermeshed (McAdoo, 1999), and *assimilation* is the gradual process that occurs over time in which one set of cultural traits is replaced and a new set acquired through participation with the mainstream (McAdoo).

Historically, the melting-pot philosophy focused on the primacy of all people assimilating into mainstream society such as ethnicity would not be significant. This type of thinking is consistent with straight-line assimilation described earlier. McAdoo (1999) eloquently illustrated this social space when she shed light on the melting pot and its limitations. She discusses the melting-pot fallacy as she describes families of color who did not melt or assimilate into mainstream America like their European American counterparts. She argues that the melting-pot philosophy had its shortcomings because it did not take into account the cultural roots and history of people of color, including Asians and Latinos, and the discrimination that they have experienced. She argues as well that this philosophy was more appropriate for those individuals who were predominantly of European origin. Asians, Latinos, and other ethnic minorities have been identified as "unmeltable ethnics." These ethnic groups, who actively intermesh their family culture and mainstream values and beliefs without significantly diluting them, often become part of a societal "salad bowl," "tossed salad," or "stir-fry." The intermeshing of traditional family culture and mainstream values has also been referred to as "acculturation" (McAdoo). Marger (2003) further provides a social and familial backdrop to this discussion by describing today's American ethnic hierarchy through three tiers. The top tier comprises European American Protestants of various national origins; here, ethnicity is of no real significance except to distinguish this tier from the other ethnic tiers. The second tier is made up of Catholics of various national origins except Latinos. This tier also includes Jews and some Asians (Japanese Americans and Korean Americans), whose acculturation is an intrinsic part of social and family life. The last tier is made up of African Americans, Latinos, Native Americans, and other Asians, whose family ethnicity has a major impact on daily social and family life. Other researchers, such as Taylor (2002), have also contributed to the paradigms of assimilation and acculturation literature that illustrate the cultural-historical backdrop of ethnic minority families in the United States. McAdoo goes on to describe how the study of ethnicity is experiencing a paradigm transformation where there is a shift away from assimilation to the mainstream and a pull toward valuing cultural diversity. However, she cautions that American society has not created an environment for cultural pluralism, that this shift is still in its infancy, and that there is considerable resistance to embracing pluralism. This backdrop will serve as a foundation for enhancing further understanding of family dynamics comparisons between immigrant Asian and Latino families and mainstream European American, nonimmigrant Asian American, and Latino families.

Spousal Relationships

Immigrant Asian and Latino couples are faced with the challenges of retaining traditions, adapting to mainstream European American values and beliefs, and maintaining their relationships. Immigrant Asian couples' traditional values usually are rooted in Buddhism, Confucianism, Hinduism, and Islam, which dictate roles for males and females within spousal relations and the family. Furthermore, immigrant Asian couples are accustomed to values grounded in collectivism, patriarchal lineage, and hierarchical relationships. Vertical relationships between husband and wife are the norm, compared to egalitarian values that are more common among mainstream European Americans (Fong, 2002; Hildebrand, Phenice, Gray, & Hines, 2000; Kitano & Daniels, 2001).

Immigrant Latino couples, similar to their Asian counterparts, struggle with adapting to their host country. Often spousal relationships are neither male dominated nor egalitarian but are on a continuum and are affected by other social factors, including gender, work, and other family values and beliefs (Baca Zinn, 1983; Baca Zinn & Wells, 2001). For example, whether a mother works outside the household is an important social factor to consider. Moreover, spousal relationships are centered on the collective nature of Latino families rooted in familism, which emphasizes interdependence (Baca Zinn & Wells, 2001; Vega, 1995), compared to mainstream European American family values, which stress independence and individuality (Lynch & Hanson, 1997).

Today, multigenerational Asian Americans, especially Japanese Americans, Chinese Americans, and Filipino Americans, are more likely to be acculturated into mainstream America. Specifically, Asian American women have the highest rate of intermarriage in the United States (Fong, 2002; Hildebrand et al., 2000; Kitano & Daniels, 2001; Takagi, 2002). Asian American women are striving to be more independent and less interdependent. Asian American men are also more accepting of egalitarian roles in their spousal relationships and their families (Hildebrand et al.,). Multigenerational Latinos, depending on the subgroups, also echo signs of the "salad bowl," "tossed salad," or "stir-fry" in spousal and family relations. Traditional Latino spousal relationships were often neither male dominated nor egalitarian, but today the egalitarian role is becoming more prevalent among Latino couples (Baca Zinn & Wells, 2001; Pessar, 2002; Vega, 1995). Latino couples mix traditional collective familism values with mainstream values such as independence and autonomy in their marital relationships and family life. However, although multigenerational Latinos are becoming more acculturated, they still resemble earlier Latino immigrants in mate selection, which tends to be endogamous (U.S. Bureau of the Census, 2000).

Parent-Child Relations

The generation gap and reciprocal nature of the parent-child relationship can be turbulent for any family. As illustrated by Belsky (1984), parenting can be influenced by many factors and determinants, and in the case of immigrant families the continuum of acculturation and assimilation plays a critical role in the parent-child relationship. As early as the 1940s Mexican Pachucos or "Zoot Suiters" drew a distinction from their immigrant parents and mainstream European Americans in the way that they dressed, spoke, and identified themselves as Americans (Acuna, 1972). Asian and Latino children and youth often struggle with ethnic identity and their role in their family, community, and the large mainstream U.S. society, as illustrated earlier in the intergenerational realities section. The differences between immigrant Asians and Latinos, multigenerational Asian Americans and Latinos, and mainstream European Americans are on a continuum rather than dichotomous. Research has demonstrated that often immigrant Asian and Latino parents fear that the more acculturated and possibly assimilated their children become, the less likely they are to value their traditional family and cultural values. Specifically, multigenerational Asian and Latino parents often engage in a variety of parenting styles and familial patterns that may range from collectivistic to more independent (Lin & Liu, 1999; Martinez, 1993). However, research has found that acculturated multigenerational Asians and Latinos are more likely to strike a balance between collectivism and independence when compared to their mainstream European American counterparts, thus placing them somewhere between the immigrants and mainstream European Americans (Baca Zinn & Wells, 2001; Fong, 2002; Hildebrand et al., 2000; Kitano & Daniels, 2001; Vega, 1995).

Another important aspect of the parent-child relationship is the value of being bilingual or multilingual, which can be very stressful on the family and the community. Although bilingualism and multilingualism are highly valued by immigrant families, parents often fear that their children will be discriminated against if they speak more than

one language (Cummins, 1976; Hakuta, 1986; Portes & Hao, 2002). This reality of being bilingual or multilingual has also echoed in multigenerational Latino and Asian households for generations, which has resulted in speaking patterns that are not exclusive depending on the region of the United States. These patterns among multigenerational Latinos include speaking only English, speaking mostly English but understanding Spanish, bilingual fluency varying by the individual, or speaking "Spanglish," a combination of Spanish and English. Similar results have been found among multigenerational Asian Americans, who present even more patterns of language use because they can be multilingual (Cummins; Hakuta; Portes & Hao, 2002). Because of the process of straight-line assimilation discussed earlier, most mainstream European Americans are monolingual English speaking, and thus the developmental, familial, and social issues associated with speaking more than one language are often not a reality in the parent-child relationship.

Immigrant parents also fear that through the acculturation process their relationship with their children will grow further apart and their children will adopt at-risk behaviors. This fear is supported by research that has demonstrated that the more acculturated and assimilated some Asian and Latino children and youth become, the more likely they are to engage in risk behavior including drug abuse, unprotected sex, and criminal behaviors (Fong, 2002; Hildebrand et al., 2000; Kitano & Daniels, 2001; McArthur, Viramontez Anguiano, & Nocetti, 2001; Vega, 1995; Viramontez Anguiano, 2004). This conclusion is affected by multiple factors, including peer relationships (especially during adolescence), socioeconomic status (SES), and education, as well as other SES and educational outcomes, health outcomes, and other social factors that are beyond the scope of this chapter. In short, the process of acculturation and assimilation as it relates to family dynamics, coupled with gender as a social system and generational realities, provide a foundation for understanding the differences and similarities that immigrant Asian and Latino families have with multigenerational Asian and Latino families and mainstream European Americans.

EDUCATION WITH BARRIERS

Historically, multigenerational Latino families in the Southwest and West have struggled to forge a positive relationship with educational systems despite cultural and language differences (Delgado-Gaitan, 1992). These differences have resulted in the misconception that Latinos do not value education. Understanding the value of education to Latino families is important when debunking these misconceptions. Galindo (1996) defined *educacion* (education) in a broader sense than the formal education that typically takes place in an academic setting. To be *educado/a* (educated) implies that an individual must be well mannered and respected by the family, within the Latino community, and across the larger society, in addition to having educational success through formal education. As a result of the lack of bridges between multigenerational Latino families and educational systems, Latino children continue to struggle at all levels of education (Brice, 2002; San Miguel & Valencia, 1998).

Asian American immigrants, on the other hand, suffer from the "positive" misconception that they are all highly motivated and disciplined at academics. Although this may be a relatively accurate characterization for some of the groups such as South Asian, Chinese, and Japanese Americans, many in the very recent immigrant groups, such as Cambodian and Vietnamese Americans, are struggling to succeed academically (Lee, 1997). This misconception is also restricting.

It tells Asian American immigrants that they are supposed to be good in certain fields (science and math) while steering them away from other disciplines.

An estimated 50 million students are in the K-12 grades in the United States; 6 million are of Latino descent, and 2 million of these speak Spanish as their primary language (Gonzalez-Ramos & Sanchez-Nestor, 2001). Many school districts have been overwhelmed in their efforts to serve immigrant Latino children and their families. Regions such as the Southeast and Northwest that traditionally have not been populated with high numbers of Latinos have recently been challenged with cultural and language differences. The educational hurdles that immigrant Latino children face are most prevalent in rural and urban inner-city school districts, which struggle to recruit and retain qualified bilingual and culturally sensitive educators and staff with the limited resources they have. These districts are faced with providing Latino children, especially those with limited English proficiency, with a "makeshift" education (Holman, 1997; McLaughlin, Liljestrom, Lim, & Meyers, 2002; Schnaiberg, 1994). This is visible throughout the United States in the lack of access to technology and equal opportunity to learn the uses of technology (R. Duran, J. Duran, Perry-Romero, & Sanchez, 2001; National Center for Education Statistics, 2000). It is also prevalent in preparing immigrant Latino children for the state standardized exams that children are required to take throughout their K-12 education (Viramontez Anguiano, 2004). Latino immigrant children are dealt an educational card that limits them from competing with other children in school.

With a few distinctions, Asian immigrant children face similar challenges. Watson (2001) details a Hmong community and its supportive school district that teamed up to help children and their families deal with language barriers to learning and participating more fully in society. Although they all also reported communication frustrations, Yeh and Inose (2002) discuss how different Asian groups responded differently to different educational barriers. One distinction of note was that the Korean immigrants tended to utilize religious support networks more often than Chinese and Japanese immigrant students.

Another important factor is the relationship between immigrant parents, their children, and schools. Previous research has documented that Latino family involvement contributes to the educational success of children (Chavkin & Gonzalez, 1995; Delgado-Gaitan, 1992). Also, Bankston and Zhou (2002) and Chao (2000) report that the interaction between culture, family, and academic success for Asian immigrants is a complex relationship between parental status, values, and self-concept.

And yet school systems throughout the United States have not been able to close the cultural and educational gap that exists with immigrant families. Research has found that immigrant Latino families and their children struggle with similar cultural and educational issues that American-born Latinos have struggled with for decades, in addition to their struggles as immigrants in the United States (Holman, 1997; Katz, 1999; Ramirez, 2003; Viramontez Anguiano, Johnson, & Davis, 2004; Viramontez Anguiano, Theis, & Chavez, in press). However, there are signs of hope: The Asian and Latino immigrant youths in a cross-cultural study of San Diego schools actually had lower dropout rates than the district norm (Rumbaut, 2000).

HEALTH AND MENTAL HEALTH

The Latino population, especially immigrant Latino families, is the ethnic group with the highest uninsured rate in the United States (Ku & Matani, 2001). Latino families are poorly positioned to access the health care system because of their low family income and a higher likelihood that their employers do not provide medical insurance (Brice, 2002; Ginzberg, 1991; Palinkas & Arciniega, 1999; Zambrana, 1995). Immigrant Latino families have been particularly affected by the passage of the Personal Responsibility and Work Opportunity Reconciliation Act (PRWORA) of 1996, which significantly limited eligibility for Medicaid and public benefits (Joyce, Bauer, Minkoff, & Kaestner, 2001). This legislation had a devastating impact on access to health care services for Latino immigrant families and their children. To compound the situation, Latino and Asian immigrants often do without medical care because of several factors, including fear of being deported, language and cultural barriers, and frustration with understanding medical applications and paperwork (Berk & Schur, 2001; Boehnlein, 1987; Joyce et al., 2001; Parangimalil, 2001; Strug & Mason, 2002). Other factors include the lack of literacy programs, skills training, and work programs that would give immigrants an opportunity to earn higher wages that would pay for medical care (Strug & Mason; Tumlin & Zimmermann, 2003). Many elderly Asian immigrants do not understand all of their options; for example, some believe that an admission of mental illness will prohibit their ability to bring other family members to the United States (Kao & Lam, 1997).

Coupled with a lack of health insurance and the PRWORA, immigrant Latino families are at risk for chronic health conditions such as diabetes, hypertension, cardiovascular disease, and obesity due to changing dietary patterns and hereditary factors (Darrigo & Keegan, 2000). Hepatitis and tuberculosis are among the health concerns Asian immigrants face (Coalition for Asian American Children and Families [CACF], 2001). Latino immigrant parents struggle with competing social systems, such as schools, media, and peer groups, that often encourage unhealthy dietary habits when compared to the immigrant families' traditional food habits (McArthur et al., 2001). This significant change in dietary habits has a strong relationship with chronic health conditions.

Immigrant Latino families also struggle to access quality mental health care. The Surgeon General of the United States reported that Latino immigrant families in urban and rural environments did not have access to quality mental health care (McCarthy, 2001). Additional research (Garrison, Roy, & Azar, 1999; Gonzalez-Ramos & Sanchez-Nestor, 2001; Vega & Lopez, 2001) has found that available mental health care is generally not culturally and linguistically sensitive and rarely has qualified bilingual therapists. Furthermore, there is a need to expand clinical practice guidelines and program standards for culturally competent mental health providers and services (Garrison et al.; Gonzalez-Ramos & Sanchez-Nestor; Vega & Lopez).

Although Latino immigrant families continue to struggle with physical and mental health systems, it is important to point out their resiliency. The lack of access to quality health and mental health care has resulted in Latino immigrant families having to depend on their nuclear and extended family and their community. It is not uncommon for Latinos to seek counseling from their local church or faith-based organization. Organizations such as Catholic Social Ministries, Lutheran Social Services, and other organizations provide mental health services to Latino immigrant families. Some of these organizations have also developed basic health clinics that serve Latino immigrant families (Viramontez Anguiano, Brumley, & Perry, 2002). There have also been efforts to develop health education–based programs within the Latino community that promote the culture and positive health, such as the Promotora program (S. Kim, Koniak-Griffin, Flaskerud, & Guarnero, 2004; I. N. Ramos, Marlynn, & K. S. Ramos, 2001; Zuvekas, Nolan, Tumaylle, & Griffin, 1999). This program is made up of Latinos who are promoting general health education.

Asian American immigrants share many of the same needs for culturally competent mental health care (CACF, 2001), and this need is especially acute given what we know about the mental health of Asian American immigrant families. Kinzie (1989) reports a high rate of disorders, and Sue and Zane (1987) support this with the finding that recent Asian immigrants report higher levels of anxiety than earlier Asian immigrants. Uba (1994) identifies a variety of disorders that Asian American immigrants are suffering from, including dissociative disorders, paranoia, and schizophrenia. Most of the disorders can be traced to the trauma that many of the refugees faced in the struggle to make it to the United States (Kinzie et al., 1990; Boehnlein et al., 1995; Kao & Lam, 1997). Multiple traumas are relatively high for Asian immigrants; for example, one man was forced to leave his wife in Vietnam, and one of his sons who did make it to the United States was killed in gang violence (Leung et al., 1997). Many Asian American elderly in San Francisco's Chinatown are more likely to report a physical concern (e.g., insomnia, poor concentration) that may be directly related to a mental health issue, because it is socially more acceptable to seek help for physical ailments than for psychological disorders. Finally, both Asian (Kao & Lam) and Latino (Avila & Parker, 2000) cultures have spiritual traditions around the treatments and sources of physical and mental pain that may be especially powerful for recent immigrants and immigrant elders. Although clinicians and others need not endorse or practice any of these customs, such traditions should at least be acknowledged and respected. Add to these frustrations the fears of being reported by hospital staff to government officials and of being deported, and seeking any health services becomes a major issue for families (Waller, 2003).

SOCIAL SERVICES

Immigrants often rely on their family and community before they seek out public social services, and they are unlikely to solicit social services for several reasons, including pride, distrust or fear of government institutions, and cultural beliefs (S. C. Kim, Lee, Chu, & Cho, 1989). Immigrant Latino families face an array of barriers when soliciting and utilizing social services, ranging from a lack of understanding the system to difficulty accessing services. Asian immigrant families often utilize the outreach efforts of religious organizations before they use public services (Lee, 1990). Families may perceive religious organizations as more culturally sensitive and responsive to their needs. Moreover, religious organizations have consistently played a major role in the social and spiritual welfare of immigrant Latino families in the United States. Thus, it is important for public social services to develop trusting relationships and helping environments with immigrant families in an effort to better serve families and their needs (Gupta & Pillai, 2002; Viramontez Anguiano & Kawamoto, 2003). Organizations should launch community-specific initiatives (Rama, 1997); otherwise, immigrant communities will be forced to bypass existing programs and create their own to be able to serve their families and communities (Zion, 2001).

IMMIGRATION POLICY

Immigrant families have always been profoundly affected by immigration policies, which affect their family structure as well as their work and family lives. Throughout the 20th century, immigration policies have been affected by the perceptions and views of the American government and the public in general toward various immigrant populations. Most recently, the anti-immigrant and anti-Latino/Asian sentiment in states such as California and others has created feelings of fear for some immigrant families (Ikeda, 2002; J. F. Smart & D. W. Smart, 1995). To compound the issue, the recent terrorist attacks in the United States have created a web of fear of foreigners among the American public (Phares, 2001).

Although the Immigration Reform and Control Act of 1986, also known as "Amnesty," allowed the opportunity for permanent citizenship, many immigrants did not take advantage of this opportunity and thus have retained their unnaturalized status. This state of the perpetual immigrant creates a harsh reality for immigrant families, knowing that a family member could be deported despite many years of hard work that they have contributed to this country. With the constant demand for laborers in the service, agricultural, construction, and tourist industries, it is common for immigrants to struggle with their place of employment because of their status (Martinez-Brawley & Zorita, 2001). Their struggle encompasses the reality that on any given day, they could be dismissed from their job because they are illegally working, or worse, as mentioned above, they could be deported and separated from their family.

On a positive note, across the nation, immigration issues are seen in a variety of political contexts, including bills such as Arizona Republican Jim Kolbe's (2003) Border Security and Immigrant Improvement Act. This bill seeks to simultaneously save the lives of immigrants who would otherwise die in the dangerous border crossing (Rotstein, 2003), which would benefit U.S. taxpayers from the challenge of caring for immigrants who do make it over, and would still make it possible for immigrants to work in the United States. Immigration policy has also been affected by another key political issue, lesbian and gay marriages. Presently, a U.S. citizen engaged or married to an immigrant is allowed to bring in his or her significant other, but lesbian and gay couples in similar circumstances are barred from having their partner immigrate. There is a move to make it possible for committed partners to be united with the Permanent Partners Immigration Act ("Immigration Law a Roadblock," 2003).

The White House recently reviewed its immigration policy in an ambitious attempt to have an "orderly, safe, and humane" policy toward our borders (Seper, 2003). This policy to make it easier for immigrants to legally obtain jobs was received as a small step in the right direction within a larger, complicated discussion on how to deal with immigrant issues (Westphal, 2004), although it remains the subject of debate and some controversy.

ECONOMIC DIVIDE

Immigrant Latino families struggle to provide for their children in a highly competitive economic atmosphere. These families have the lowest annual family median income ($12,111) of ethnic groups in the United States (U.S. Bureau of the Census, 2001a). The economic struggles of immigrant families are due to a combination of barriers to occupational and educational opportunities. Immigrants often have a low level of educational attainment and work in blue-collar jobs (Tumlin & Zimmerman, 2003). Mexicans and Central Americans are more likely to work in manufacturing and labor-intensive occupations in the farming, forestry, and fishing industries (Borjas, 1996; U.S. Bureau of the Census, 2001a). These types of occupations often have dangerous working conditions and do not provide benefits to their employees. This has created an underclass of individuals and their families who are filling these occupations that other individuals would not consider. As a result, immigrant Latino families, especially Mexicans and Central Americans, have the highest rates of poverty in the United States (U.S. Bureau of the Census, 2001a).

The situation for Asian immigrants is somewhat more complicated. The first waves of contemporary immigrants (post-1965 to the late 1970s) were relatively better educated and were from urban areas (Fong, 2000); these immigrants have often suffered from underemployment or "downward mobility" (Lee, 1997), where they have encountered a glass ceiling keeping them from the professional jobs for which they are qualified (S. C. Kim, 1997). Nevertheless, their remarkable economic and educational successes earned them the status of "model minority." In the last 20 years, Asian immigrants have tended to be less educated and have come from more rural backgrounds. These immigrants share many of the frustrations and barriers identified earlier for Mexican and Central American immigrants (Fong, 2000).

CONCLUSION

The process of coming to the United States has been contextually explored to the point where models of adaptation and migration have been developed, including straight-line assimilation and segmented assimilation (Fernandez-Kelly & Schauffler, 1994; McKeever & Klineberg, 1999; Portes, 1995). In this chapter we reviewed the challenges faced by immigrant families in their work and family lives in the United States. Adjusting to life in the United States is often difficult, particularly for first-generation immigrants, and may be felt for many generations to come. Many educational, economic, and policy barriers exist that make it difficult for immigrant families to fully participate in U.S. society.

Although we can see the wounds from the immigrant transition and the barriers to success of Asian and Latino immigrant families, we must not lose sight of the strengths of these families. Many Asian (Boehnlein et al., 1997; I. S. Kim, 1981) and Latino (Arriaza, 1997) immigrants have displayed remarkable survival skills in the face of numerous dangers to make it to this country and thrive. Some of these skills include their family and community resiliency, cultural resiliency, and collectivistic orientation. Moreover, often, the key to survival is the support of social networks, such as the local religious community (Lee, 1990).

Students of the family must work to assist or provide the supports that immigrant families need to become fully functioning members of U.S. society, including improving educational services to immigrant children and families, facilitating greater access to health care, and ensuring that social services are accepting and culturally appropriate. Often this requires working with local communities and grassroots social support systems. In addition, we can support the strong social networks that are in place working to get immigrants naturalized (Fong, 2000) and fostering civic participation. Without this important final step in their journey to the United States, Asian and Latino immigrant families will remain stalled in isolation, and anti-immigrant movements will only be encouraged (Ong & Nakanishi, 2000). If Asian and Latino immigrant families break out of their internally and externally imposed isolation, they will help the United States continue to mature and become a full member of the international community. Professionals in other countries are already multicultural and often multilingual, and immigrants are helping American society to reach its potential as a true multicultural community.

NOTES

1. The term *intergenerational* identifies the relationship between different generations.

2. *Multigenerational* in this chapter will not only refer to the relationship between generations but it may refer to two or more generations.

REFERENCES

Acuna, R. F. (1972). *Occupied America: The Chicano's struggle toward liberation.* San Francisco: Canfield Press.

Aponte, R., & Siles, M. E. (1997). *Winds of change: Latinos in the heartland and the nation* (Statistical Brief 5). East Lansing: Julian Samora Research Institute, Michigan State University.

Arriaza, G. (1997). Grace under pressure: Immigrant families and the nation-state. *Social Justice, 24,* 6–26.

Associated Press. (2001, April 1). Census shows North Carolina top in country in Hispanic growth. *Daily Reflector* (Greenville, NC), p. A1.

Avila, E., & Parker, J. (2000). *Woman who glows in the dark: A curandera reveals traditional Aztec secrets of physical and spiritual health.* New York: Penguin Putnam.

Baca Zinn, M. (1983). Familism among Chicanos: A theoretical review. *Humbolt Journal of Social Relations, 10,* 224–238.

Baca Zinn, M., & Wells, B. (2001). Diversity within Latino families: New lessons for family social science. In A. S. Skelnick & J. H. Skelnick (Eds.), *Family in transition* (11th ed., pp. 381–407). Boston: Allyn & Bacon.

Bankston, C. L., & Zhou, M. (2002). Being well vs. doing well: Self-esteem and school performance among immigrant and nonimmigrant racial and ethnic groups. *International Migration Review, 36,* 389–416.

Becerra, R. M. (1998). The Mexican-American family. In C. H. Mindel, R. W. Habenstein, & R. Wright (Eds.), *Ethnic families in America: Patterns and variations* (pp. 153–171). New York: Prentice Hall.

Belsky, J. (1984). The determinants of parenting: A process model. *Child Development, 55,* 83–96.

Benokraitis, N. V. (2002). The changing ethnic profile of U.S. families in the twenty-first century. In N. V. Benokraitis (Ed.), *Contemporary ethnic families in the United States: Characteristics, variations, and dynamics* (pp. 1–15). Upper Saddle River, NJ: Prentice Hall.

Berk, M. L., & Schur, C. L. (2001). The effect of fear on access to care among undocumented Latino immigrants. *Journal of Immigrant Health, 3,* 151–156.

Boehnlein, J. K. (1987). A review of mental health services for refugees between 1975 and 1985 and a proposal for future services. *Hospital and Community Psychiatry, 38,* 764–776.

Boehnlein, J. K., Leung, P. K., & Kinzie, J. D. (1997). Cambodian American families. In E. Lee (Ed.), *Working with Asian Americans: A guide for clinicians* (pp. 37–45). New York: Guilford Press.

Boehnlein, J. K., Tran, H. D., Riley, C., Tan, S., Vu, K. C., & Leung, P. K. (1995). A comparative study of family functioning among Vietnamese and Cambodian refugees. *Journal of Nervous and Mental Disease, 183,* 510–515.

Borjas, G. J. (1996). The earnings of Mexican immigrants in the United States. *Journal of Development Economics, 51,* 69–98.

Brice, A. E. (2002). *The Hispanic child: Speech, language, culture and education.* Boston: Allyn & Bacon.

Chao, R. K. (2000). Cultural explanations for the role of parenting in the school success of Asian-American children. In R. D. Taylor & M. C. Wang (Eds.), *Resilience across contexts: Family, work, culture, and community* (pp. 333–365). Mahwah, NJ: Lawrence Erlbaum.

Chavkin, N. F., & Gonzalez, D. L. (1995). *Forging partnerships between Mexican American parents and the schools* (Report No. RC020348). Washington, DC: Office of Educational Research and Improvement. (ERIC Documentation Reproduction Service No. ED388489)

Cheng, M. M. (2003, December 11). Call to liberate detained aliens. *Newsday.* Retrieved December 18, 2003, from http://www.newsday.com/mynews/ny-nyreg113579890dec11,0,803485

Coalition for Asian American Children and Families (CACF). (2001). *Child and family health of New York's Asian American community.* Retrieved January 4, 2004, from http://www.cacf.org/publications/index.html#factsheets/FS_ health.pdf

Cummins, J. (1976). The influence of bilingualism on cognitive growth: A synthesis of research findings and explanatory hypotheses. *Working Papers on Bilingualism, 9,* 1–43.

Darrigo, T., & Keegan, A. (2000). Diabetes and Latinos: A community at risk. *Diabetes Forecast, 53,* 42–46.

Das Gupta, M. (1997). "What is Indian about you?": A gendered, transnational approach to ethnicity. *Gender and Society, 11,* 572–595.

Delgado-Gaitan, C. (1992). School matters in the Mexican-American home: Socializing children to education. *American Educational Research Journal, 29,* 495–513.

Dion, K. K., & Dion, K. L. (2001). Gender and cultural adaptation in immigrant families. *Journal of Social Issues, 57,* 511–521.

Duran, R., Duran, J., Perry-Romero, D., & Sanchez, E. (2001). Latino immigrant parents and children learning and publishing together in an after-school setting. *Journal of Education for Students Placed at Risk, 6,* 95–113.

El Nasser, H. (2003, July 19). 39 million make Hispanics largest U.S. minority group. *USA Today,* p. A01.

Fernandez-Kelly, M. P., & Schauffler, R. (1994). Divided fates: Immigrant children in a restructured U.S. economy. *International Migration Review, 28,* 662–689.

Fong, T. P. (2000). The history of Asians in America. In T. P. Fong & L. H. Shinagawa (Eds.), *Asian Americans: Experiences and perspectives* (pp. 13–30). Upper Saddle River, NJ: Prentice Hall.

Fong, T. P. (2002). More than "family values": Asian American families and identities. In T. P. Fong (Ed.), *The contemporary Asian American experience: Beyond the model minority* (2nd ed., pp. 221–269). Upper Saddle River, NJ: Prentice Hall.

Galindo, R. (1996). Reframing the past in the present: Chicana teacher role identity as a bridging identity. *Education and Urban Society, 29,* 85–102.

Garcia Coll, C., Lamberty, G., Jenkins, R., McAdoo, H. P., Crnic, K., Wasik, B. H., et al. (1996). An integrative model for the study of developmental competencies in minority children. *Child Development, 67,* 1891–1914.

Garrison, E. G., Roy, I. S., & Azar, V. (1999). Responding to the mental health needs of Latino children and families through school based services. *Clinical Psychology Review, 19,* 199–219.

Gim, R., Atkinson, D., & Whiteley, S. (1990). Asian American acculturation, severity of concerns, and willingness to see a counselor. *Journal of Counseling Psychology, 37,* 281–285.

Ginzberg, E. (1991). Access to health care for Hispanics. *Journal of the American Medical Association, 265,* 238–241.

Gonzalez-Ramos, G., & Sanchez-Nestor, M. (2001). Responding to immigrant children's mental health needs in the schools: Project Mi Tierra/My Country. *Children & Schools, 23,* 49–62.

Gupta, R., & Pillai, V. K. (2002). Elder care giving in South Asian families: Implications for social service. *Journal of Comparative Family Studies, 33,* 565–581.

Hakuta, K. (1986). *Mirror of language: The debate on bilingualism.* New York: Basic Books.

Hetts, J. J., & Sakuma, M. (1999). Two roads to positive regard: Implicit and explicit self-evaluation and culture. *Journal of Experimental Social Psychology, 35,* 512–560.

Hildebrand, V., Phenice, L. A., Gray, M. M., & Hines, R. P. (2000). *Knowing and serving diverse families* (2nd ed.). Englewood Cliffs, NJ: Merrill & Prentice Hall.

Holman, L. J. (1997). Meeting the needs of Hispanic immigrants. *Educational Leadership, 54,* 37–38.

Hondagneu-Sotelo, P. (1999). Gender and contemporary U.S. immigration. *American Behavioral Scientist, 42,* 565–576.

Hsu, F. L. K. (1971). *Under the ancestor's shadow: Kinship, personality, and social mobility in China.* Stanford, CA: Stanford University Press.

Ikeda, S. D. (2002, June 19). "I'm Vincent Chin!": The hate crime that "created Asian America": Remembering June 19, 1982 as the defining moment for Asian American political identity. *Asian-American Village.* Retrieved January 5, 2004, from http://www.imdiversity.com/villages/asian/Article_Detail.asp?Article_ID=11491

Ikels, C. (1983). *Aging and adaptation: Chinese in Hong Kong and the United States.* Hamden, CT: Archon.

Immigration law a roadblock for gay couples. (2003, November 24). *Seattle Post-Intelligencer.* Retrieved December 11, 2003, from http://seattlepi.nwsource.com/national/149655_gay24.html

Iskow, R., Kitanov, S., & Ferlazzo, L. (2002). Overcoming historic fears: Slavic immigrants organize for change. *Social Policy, 33,* 43–47.

Joyce, T., Bauer, T., Minkoff, H., & Kaestner, R. (2001). Welfare reform and the perinatal health and health care use of Latino women in California, New York City, and Texas. *American Journal of Public Health, 91,* 1857–1864.

Kao, R. S., & Lam, M. L. (1997). Asian American elderly. In E. Lee (Ed.), *Working with Asian Americans: A guide for clinicians* (pp. 208–223). New York: Guilford Press.

Katz, S. R. (1999). Teaching in tensions: Latino immigrant youth, their teachers, and the structures of schooling. *Teachers College Record, 100,* 809–840.

Kim, I. S. (1981). *New urban immigrants: The Korean community in New York.* Princeton, NJ: Princeton University Press.

Kim, K. C., & Kim, S. (1998). Family and work roles of Korean immigrants in the United States. In H. I. McCubbin, E. A. Thompson, A. I. Thompson, & J. E. Fromer (Eds.), *Resiliency in Native American and immigrant families* (pp. 225–242). Thousand Oaks, CA: Sage.

Kim, S., Koniak-Griffin, D., Flaskerud, J. H., & Guarnero, P. A. (2004). The impact of lay health advisors on cardiovascular health promotion. *Journal of Cardiovascular Nursing, 19,* 192–199.

Kim, S. C. (1997). Korean American families. In E. Lee (Ed.), *Working with Asian Americans: A guide for clinicians* (pp. 125–135). New York: Guilford Press.

Kim, S. C., Lee, S. U., Chu, K. H., & Cho, K. J. (1989). Korean Americans and mental health: Clinical experiences of Korean American mental health services. *Asian American Psychological Journal, 13,* 18–27.

Kinzie, J. D. (1989). Therapeutic approaches to traumatized Cambodian refugees. *Journal of Traumatic Stress, 2,* 75–91.

Kinzie, J. D., Boehnlein, J. K., Leung, P. K., Moore, L. J., Riley, C., & Smith, D. (1990). The high prevalence of PTSD and its clinical significance among Southeast Asian refugees. *American Journal of Psychiatry, 147,* 813–917.

Kitano, H. L., & Daniels, R. (2001). The present status of Asians Americans. In H. L. Kitano & R. Daniels (Eds.), *Asian Americans: Emerging minorities* (3rd ed., pp. 181–204). Upper Saddle River, NJ: Prentice Hall.

Kolbe, J. (2003, October 30). Immigration reform bill a necessity. *Denver Post,* p. B-07.

Koranyi, E. (1981). Immigrants' adaptation in aged population. In L. Eitinger & D. Schwartz (Eds.), *Strangers in the worlds* (pp. 220–231). Bern, Switzerland: Hans Huber.

Ku, L., & Matani, S. (2001). Left out: Immigrants' access to health care and insurance. *Health Affairs, 20,* 247–256.

Landau, J. (1982). Therapy with families in cultural transition. In M. McGoldrick, J. K. Pearce, & J. Giordano (Eds.), *Ethnicity and family therapy* (pp. 552–572). New York: Guilford Press.

Lee, E. (1990). Family therapy with Southeast Asian refugees. In M. P. Mirkin (Ed.), *The social and political contexts of family therapy* (pp. 331–354). Needham Heights, MA: Allyn &Bacon.

Lee, E. (1997). Overview: The assessment and treatment of Asian American families. In E. Lee (Ed.), *Working with Asian Americans: A guide for clinicians* (pp. 3–36). New York: Guilford Press.

Leung, P. K., Boehnlein, J. K., & Kinzie, J. D. (1997). Vietnamese American families. In E. Lee (Ed.), *Working with Asian Americans: A guide for clinicians* (pp. 153–162). New York: Guilford Press.

Lin, C., & Liu, W. T. (1999). Intergenerational relationships among Chinese immigrant families from Taiwan. In H. P. McAdoo (Ed.), *Family ethnicity: Strengths in diversity* (2nd ed., pp. 235–252). Thousand Oaks, CA: Sage.

Lynch, E. W., & Hanson, M. J. (1997). *Developing cross-cultural competence: A guide for working with children and their families.* Baltimore: Paul H. Brookes.

Marger, M. N. (2003). Foundations of American ethnic hierarchy. In M. N. Marger (Ed.), *Race and ethnic relations: American and global perspectives* (pp. 140–172). Belmont, CA: Thomson/Wadsworth.

Martinez, E. A. (1993). Parenting young children in Mexican American/Chicano families. In H. P. McAdoo (Ed.), *Family ethnicity: Strengths in diversity* (pp. 184–199). Thousand Oaks, CA: Sage.

Martinez-Brawley, E. E., & Zorita, P. M. B. (2001). Immigrants, refugees and asylum seekers: The challenges of services in the Southwest. *Journal of Ethnic and Cultural Diversity in Social Work, 10,* 49–67.

McAdoo, H. P. (1999). Families of color: Strengths that come from diversity. In H. P. McAdoo (Ed.), *Family ethnicity: Strengths in diversity* (2nd ed., pp. 3–15). Thousand Oaks, CA: Sage.

McArthur, L. H., Viramontez Anguiano, R. P., & Nocetti, D. (2001). Maintenance and change in the diet of Hispanic immigrants in eastern North Carolina. *Family and Consumer Sciences Research Journal, 29,* 309–335.

McCarthy, M. (2001). U.S. mental-health system fails to serve minorities, says U. S. Surgeon General. *Lancet, 358,* 733.

McCubbin, H. I., McCubbin, M. A., Thompson, A. I., & Thompson, E. A. (1998). Resiliency in ethnic families: A conceptual model for predicting family adjustment and adaptation. In H. I. McCubbin, E. A. Thompson, A. I. Thompson, & J. E. Fromer (Eds.), *Resiliency in Native American and immigrant families* (pp. 3–48). Thousand Oaks, CA: Sage.

McGoldrick, M. (1982). Ethnicity and family therapy: An overview. In M. McGoldrick, J. K. Pearce, & J. Giordano (Eds.), *Ethnicity and family therapy* (pp. 3–21). New York: Guilford Press.

McKeever, M., & Klineberg, S. L. (1999). Generational differences in attitude and socioeconomic status among Hispanics in Houston. *Sociological Inquiry, 69,* 33–50.

McLaughlin, H. J., Liljestrom, A., Lim, J. H., & Meyers, D. (2002). LEARN: A community study about Latino immigrants and education. *Education and Urban Society, 34,* 212–232.

Menjivar, C. (1999). The intersection of work and gender: Central American immigrant women and employment in California. *American Behavioral Scientist, 42,* 601–627.

Min, P. G. (1998). The Korean American family. In C. H. Mindel, R. W. Habenstein, & R. Wright (Eds.), *Ethnic families in America: Patterns and variations* (pp. 223–253). New York: Prentice Hall.

National Center for Education Statistics. (2000). *Stats in brief: Internet access in U.S. public schools and classrooms: 1994–99.* Washington, DC: U.S. Department of Education.

Noh, S. H., Wu, Z., Speechly, M., & Kaspar, V. (1992). Depression in Korean immigrants in Canada: Correlates of gender, work, and marriage. *Journal of Nervous and Mental Disorders, 180,* 578–582.

Ogbu, J. U. (1991). Immigrant and involuntary minorities in comparative perspective. In M. A. Gibson & J. U. Ogbu (Eds.), *Minority status and schooling: A comparative study of immigrant and involuntary minorities* (pp. 3–33). New York: Garland.

Ong, P., & Nakanishi, D. (2000). Becoming citizens, becoming voters: The naturalization and political participation of Asian Pacific immigrants. In T. P. Fong & L. H. Shinagawa (Eds.), *Asian Americans: Experiences and perspectives* (pp. 369–387). Upper Saddle River, NJ: Prentice Hall.

Palinkas, L. A., & Arciniega, J. I. (1999). Immigrant reform and the health of Latino immigrants in California. *Journal of Immigrant Health, 1,* 19–30.

Parangimalil, G. J. (2001). Latino health in the new millennium: The need for a culture-centered approach. *Sociological Spectrum, 21,* 423–429.

Pessar, P. R. (2002). Grappling with changing gender roles in Dominican American families. In N. V. Benokraitis (Ed.), *Contemporary ethnic families in the United States: Characteristics, variations, and dynamics* (pp. 66–71). Upper Saddle River, NJ: Prentice Hall.

Phares, R. (2001). US/Mexico border: In the wake of the attacks border tightens, relationships chill. *Bimonthly Journal of the Religious Task Force on Central America and Mexico, 21*(4). Retrieved May 14, 2005, from http://www.rtfcam.org/report/volume_21/No_4/vol__21_no__4.htm

Portes, A. (1995). Children of immigrants: Segmented assimilation and its determinates. In A. Portes (Ed.), *The economic sociology of immigration: Essays on networks, ethnicity, and entrepreneurship* (pp. 248–280). New York: Russell Sage Foundation.

Portes, A., & Hao, L. (2002). The price of uniformity: Language, family and personality adjustment in the immigrant second generation. *Ethnic and Racial Studies, 25,* 889–912.

Rama, J. P. (1997). Ambitious mentors guide and encourage. *Hotel & Motel Management, 212,* 25.

Ramirez, A. Y. F. (2003). Dismay and disappointment: Parental involvement of Latino immigrant parents. *Urban Review, 35,* 93–110.

Ramos, I. N., Marlynn, M., & Ramos, K. S. (2001). Environmental health training of *promotoras* in *colonias* along the Texas-Mexico border. *American Journal of Public Health, 91,* 586–572.

Rotstein, A. H. (2003, December 11). Arizona ranch family is sued for rounding up immigrants. *San Diego Union Tribune.* Retrieved December 22, 2003, from http://www.signonsandiego.com/news/uniontrib/thu/news/news_1n11rancher.html

Rumbaut, R. G. (2000). Profiles in resilience: Educational achievement and ambition among children of immigrants in southern California. In R. D. Taylor & M. C. Wang (Eds.), *Resilience across contexts: Family, work, culture, and community* (pp. 257–294). Mahwah, NJ: Lawrence Erlbaum.

Saito, L. T. (2000). Asian Americans and Latinos in San Gabriel Valley, California: Ethnic political cooperation and redistricting 1990–1992. In T. P. Fong & L. H. Shinagawa (Eds.), *Asian Americans: Experiences and perspectives* (pp. 388–397). Upper Saddle River, NJ: Prentice Hall.

San Miguel, G., Jr., & Valencia, R. (1998). From the treaty of Guadalupe Hidalgo to Hopwood: The educational plight and struggle of Mexicans in the Southwest. *Harvard Educational Review, 68,* 891.

Schnaiberg, L. (1994, February 23). Immigration's final frontier. *Education Week, 13,* 22–26.

Seper, J. (2003, December 12). White House verifies immigration review. *Washington Times.* Retrieved December 21, 2003, from http://washingtontimes.com/national/20031211-114734-2215r.htm

Smart, J. F., & Smart, D. W. (1995). Acculturative stress of Hispanics: Loss and challenge. *Journal of Counseling and Development, 73,* 390–396.

Strug, D. L., & Mason, S. E. (2002). Social service needs of Hispanic immigrants: An exploratory study of the Washington Heights community. *Journal of Ethnic and Cultural Diversity in Social Work, 10,* 69–88.

Sue, S., & Zane, N. (1987). The role of culture and cultural techniques in psychotherapy: A critique and reformulation. *American Psychologist, 42,* 37–45.

Takagi, D. Y. (2002). Japanese American families. In R. L. Taylor (Ed.), *Minority families in the United States: A multicultural perspective* (3rd ed., pp. 164–181). Upper Saddle River, NJ: Prentice Hall.

Takaki, R. T. (2001). A different mirror. In M. L. Anderson & P. Hill Collins (Eds.), *Race, class, and gender: An anthology* (4th ed., pp. 52–65). Belmont, CA: Wadsworth/Thomson Learning.

Tam, V. C. W., & Detzner, D. F. (1998). Grandparents as a family resource in Chinese-American families: Perceptions of the middle generation. In H. I. McCubbin, E. A. Thompson, A. I. Thompson, & J. E. Fromer (Eds.), *Resiliency in Native American and immigrant families* (pp. 243–264). Thousand Oaks, CA: Sage.

Taylor, R. L. (2002). Minority families in America: An introduction. In R. L. Taylor (Ed.), *Minority families in the United States: A multicultural perspective* (3rd ed., pp. 1–17). Upper Saddle River, NJ: Prentice Hall.

Thorne, B. (1993) *Gender play: Girls and boys in school.* New Brunswick, NJ: Rutgers University Press.

Trueba, H. T. (2002). Multiple ethnic, racial, and cultural identities in action: From marginality to a new cultural capital in modern society. *Journal of Latinos in Education, 1,* 7–28.

Tumlin, K. C., & Zimmermann, W. (2003). *Immigrants and TANF: A look at immigrant welfare recipients in three cities.* Washington, DC: Urban Institute.

Uba, L. (1994). *Asian Americans: Personality patterns, identity, and mental health.* New York: Guilford Press.

U.S. Bureau of the Census. (2000). *Statistical abstract of the United States* (120th ed.). Washington, DC: Author.

U.S. Bureau of the Census. (2001a). *Hispanic or Latino origin for the United States, median incomes, educational attainment, poverty rates and labor participation for all regions.* Washington, DC: Author.

U.S. Bureau of the Census. (2001b). Profile of the foreign-born population in the United States: 2000. In *Current population reports: Special studies* (pp. 23–206). Washington, DC: Author.

U.S. Bureau of the Census. (2003) *The foreign born population: 2000* (Census 2000 brief CK2BR-34). Washington, DC: Author.

Vega, W. A. (1995). The study of Latino families: A point of departure. In R. E. Zambrana (Ed.), *Understanding Latino families: Scholarship, policy, and practices* (pp. 3–17). Thousand Oaks, CA: Sage.

Vega, W. A., & Lopez, S. R. (2001). Priority issues in Latino mental health services research. *Mental Health Services Research, 3,* 189–200.

Viramontez Anguiano, R. P. (2004). Families and schools: The effect of parental involvement on high school completion. *Journal of Family Issues, 25,* 61–86.

Viramontez Anguiano, R. P., Brumley, B. M., & Perry, S. P. (2002). *Latino families speak in eastern North Carolina: Strong families build strong communities.* Unpublished manuscript.

Viramontez Anguiano, R. P., Johnson, C., & Davis, T. E. (2004). The education of Latino children: Rural Latino families and schools in eastern North Carolina. *Journal of Early Education and Family Review, 11,* 33–49.

Viramontez Anguiano, R. P., & Kawamoto, W. T. (2003). Serving rural Asian American and Latino families and their communities: A call for a rural paradigm shift. *Journal of Extension, 41,* 1–3.

Viramontez Anguiano, R. P., Theis, J., & Chavez, M. (in press). The politics of educating Latino children: Latino family and educational systems. *Inquiry: Critical Thinking Across the Disciplines.*

Waller, D. (2003, December 8). Should hospitals snitch? *CNN/Time.* Retrieved December 21, 2003, from http://www.cnn.com/2003/ALLPOLITICS/12/08/ timep .hospitals.tm/index.html

Watson, D. C. (2001). Characteristics of Hmong immigrant students. *Childhood Education, 77,* 303.

Westphal, D. (2004, January 9). Analysis: Bush targets Latino voters. *The Sacramento Bee.* Retrieved January 10, 2004, from http://www.sacbee.com/content/politics/story/8067714p-9000369c.html

Wodarski, J. S. (1992). Social work with Hispanic Americans. In D. F. Harrison, J. S. Wodarski, & B. A. Thyer (Eds.), *Cultural diversity and social work practice* (pp. 71–105). Springfield, IL: Thomas.

Yee, B. (1987). Adaptation in old age: Japanese and Vietnamese elderly women. *Asian American Psychological Journal, 12,* 38–50.

Yeh, C., & Inose, M. (2002). Difficulties and coping strategies of Chinese, Japanese, and Korean immigrant students. *Adolescence, 37,* 69–83.

Zambrana, R. E. (1995). Family and child health: A neglected vision. In R. E. Zambrana (Ed.), *Understanding Latino families: Scholarship, policy, and practice* (pp. 157–176). Thousand Oaks: Sage.

Zion, L. (2001). The long road from Vietnam leads to European bakery. *San Diego Business Journal, 22,* 12.

Zuniga, M. E. (2002). Latino immigrants: Patterns of survival. *Journal of Human Behavior in the Social Environment, 5,* 137–155.

Zuvekas, A., Nolan, L., Tumaylle, C., & Griffin, L. (1999). Impact of community health workers on access, use of services, and patient knowledge and behavior. *Journal of Ambulatory Care Management, 22,* 33–44.

CHAPTER 13

Families in the Islamic Middle East

BAHIRA SHERIF-TRASK

Throughout the Middle East, family remains a central and significant institution in the lives of most individuals. Although we cannot speak of a "typical" Middle Eastern Muslim family, many families share, to varying degrees, characteristics related to historical, religious, and cultural influences. This is not to imply that these families have not changed over time, nor that they are not affected by global forces. Middle Eastern Muslim families, like families around the world, are influenced by socioeconomic and historical factors that affect different social classes and regions in a multitude of ways. Because of the current interest in the role of Islam in this part of the world, this chapter seeks to give readers an overview of some of the Muslim injunctions with respect to family life and how they play out differently depending on the social location of individuals. It also seeks to dispel several of the misconceptions that readers may have, especially with respect to the role of women.

The Middle East is characterized by a high degree of heterogeneity with respect to geography, economics, politics, and social practices. The geographic position of this region has made it a crossroads for many different peoples over thousands of years. Many of the divisions and boundaries that exist today have resulted from the impact of various occupations and colonialism, as well as constantly changing political and economic contexts. However, most inhabitants of North Africa and the Middle East share a common cultural and religious heritage: Jews, Christians, and Muslims all trace themselves back to the Old Testament and share the same holy places in the central Middle East, such as Jerusalem. A common cultural and religious heritage is reflected in similar practices with respect to family life. We find, for example, that throughout the Middle East, family continues to play a central role in social life, that many aspects of the marriage contract remain the same among Muslims and Jews, and that women share practices such as veiling even if they are not Muslim.

DEFINING THE MIDDLE EAST

The Middle East and North Africa are located in a region that includes an area that stretches from Morocco to Iran and covers a distance of approximately 3,400 miles. There are various definitions of the Middle East, some of which include North Africa (Morocco, Algeria, Libya, Tunisia, and Egypt), the central Middle East (Lebanon, Syria, Jordan, Israel, Occupied Territories, Saudi Arabian Peninsula, Iraq, and Iran), as well as Turkey, Pakistan, and Afghanistan (Eickelman, 1981). Most of the land in North Africa and the Middle East is desert or semiarid and characterized by the prevalence of urban areas, irrigation agriculture, and pastoral nomadism. However, the whole area is not clearly delineated by natural borders. Part of the region is cut off from sub-Saharan Africa and from the Indo-Pakistani subcontinent by mountains and deserts, but in the north the boundaries with some of the former Soviet Muslim republics are political borders, not geographic ones.

It is interesting to note that this region is not characterized by a common identity, even though people share some similar religious, historical, and linguistic experiences. This is an issue that is often glossed over in the West, because of lack of knowledge about the diversity of peoples, rural/urban differences, and the multiple interpretations of Islam and other religions that are practiced in the Middle East and North Africa. For example, over the last half century, Turkey has openly stressed its ties with Europe rather than with its Muslim neighbors. This has occurred despite the fact that the majority of Turks are Muslim and have had strong historical ties with the Arab world. Because of historical circumstances and geographic location, Pakistan and Afghanistan have a stronger South Asian identity and are often not included under the Middle Eastern umbrella.

In terms of language, most of the region is Arabic speaking; however, there are many dialects, which makes communication difficult. Although written Arabic is relatively standard, the many variations of spoken Arabic can make it virtually impossible, for example, for someone from Morocco to understand someone from Iraq. Also, in Israel people speak, read, and write Hebrew, and in Iran the dominant language is Persian. The Middle East is also the region with the world's primary reserves of oil. It is estimated that at least 70% of the world's known reserves of oil can be found in the central Middle East. The dominance of oil economies has had a significant impact on the societies and families in this region with respect to globalizing influences.

The impact of geography for individuals living in this part of the world cannot be overemphasized. Middle Eastern families live in oil-rich nations such as Saudi Arabia and the United Arab Emirates, as well as in countries with much poorer economies, such as Egypt and Lebanon. There are major variations in lifestyles within these societies as well, because some families live in urban areas, some live on agricultural lands, and others still are nomads. There are other differences as well: Families live under an array of political systems that include governments modeled on the French system as well as political dictatorships and monarchies. People in the Middle East also represent an array of races, including African, Caucasian, and Asian. The heterogeneous nature of this area makes it difficult to speak of a uniform experience for all the families in this region. It is possible, however, to delineate some common cultural and historical roots and shared impacts due to globalizing influences.

RESEARCH ON MIDDLE EASTERN FAMILIES

The study of Middle Eastern families is in its infancy and can be understood only in the context of the study of other non-Western families. Early social scientific writings on non-Western families (Asian, Indian, Islamic) in historically literate societies presented a singular view of families as characterized by traditional, patriarchal values and behaviors (Ortiz, 1998). This depiction was based on the assumption that male dominance and age-based authority were the primary features of these families. Moreover, descriptions of non-Western families relied on models that highlighted a complete segregation of gender roles, with husbands being the breadwinners and authority figures while women were assumed to be submissive, passive wives whose roles were primarily as full-time homemakers. Change within these families was predicted to occur through an acculturation or assimilation process whereby families moved from traditional patriarchal forms to the more idealized egalitarian nuclear models of Western families.

These traditional portrayals have been heavily criticized in recent years (see Ortiz, 1998, for example). Much of this criticism centers on the fact that traditional perspectives on *non-Western* families were based on the assumption that *Western* families were models of equality, ignoring the reality that Western families were themselves patriarchal and class based and commonly deviated from an egalitarian ideal. This perspective also ignored the considerable changes that have affected all societies differentially, including issues of globalization, urbanization, increasing numbers of women in the labor force, rising divorce rates, and technology. Further, although studies of Western families are theoretically driven and are increasingly incorporating postmodern concepts such as agency into their analyses (the idea that individual actors act and react to their conditions and thus effect change), non-Western families are still studied by using culture or, as in the case of Middle Eastern families, religion as the dominant paradigm.

Until very recently, studies of the family in Middle Eastern societies also have been hampered by the unproven assumption that the family, in all parts of the Muslim world, is an institution that can be termed interchangeably as either the *Arab* family, the *Islamic* family, or the *Oriental* family (as commonly cited from Barakat, 1985). This family has been described in opposition to its Western counterpart. It is assumed that the institution of the Muslim family has not undergone the significant structural transformations that are associated with the rise of capitalism in the West, nor has it been the object of "modernization," which promoted individualism at the expense of family control (Tucker, 1993a). Most ethnographic studies still emphasize rural or very poor families, and the findings from these studies are used to make assumptions about all other "Islamic" families, ranging from Morocco to Indonesia, as well as Muslim families residing in the West. For the most part, conclusions drawn from these data ignore the many regional, cultural, and class differences. Even so, ethnographic evidence from these studies indicates that, far from being an unvarying institution, Islamic families change in size, in composition, and according to historical and social circumstances.

A second, equally important problem with studies conducted on Islamic families pertains to the problem of gender. Until recently, primarily male researchers conducted fieldwork in the Islamic world. Because of gender segregation, these male field-workers had problems gaining access to households and therefore had to use their male informants' insights to draw conclusions about family life. Much of this observation emphasized the idea that men were all-powerful, the primary decision makers, and the economic providers. This aided in shaping a distorted Orientalist view of the Islamic family as a patriarchal family in which women are subjected, oppressed, and invisible (Singerman, 1995).

A rapidly growing interest in women's issues in the Islamic world has sought to answer this question by examining the relationship between women and Islam. Although I do not intend to review this expansive literature at this point, I would just like to mention that the proliferation of feminist studies that now exists (almost all of which are conducted by women) basically entertains two opposing views: (a) that women's status was raised with the advent of Islam by giving women certain rights; and (b) that Islam suppresses women by not giving them equal rights with men. Within this context, Western feminist scholarship on women has led to the recognition that gender is not a given but is historically and socially constructed according to particular local realities. Nevertheless, in the case of Muslim women, Western feminist scholars usually perceive Islam as the primary agent of their definition (Bernal, 1994).

This assumption, however, is problematic, because there is actually little agreement even on what the central texts of the religion have to say about gender. The Koran offers only very general guidance on the subject, and the hadiths, the sayings of the Prophet, allow for a wide variety of interpretations because of their number and variety. In contrast, the shari'a, Islamic law, does contain certain rules for governing gender relations, particularly within the family (Tucker, 1993b). Some of these are well known, such as polygyny, unilateral divorce for men, and child custody rights for the father. On the other hand, Muslim women, whether they are married or not, and unlike their Christian counterparts, are full legal personae with unabridgeable property rights (Tucker, 1993b). It is important to point out that these laws are enforced differentially between countries, and even across societal classes, and they are often evoked as ideals, rather than as practical measures.

A further impediment to objective research on the institution of the Islamic family is the fact that many Western feminists consider the family as the agent of women's suppression, and this assumption is carried over to the Islamic case. This has discouraged detailed investigations of women's actual roles, responsibilities, and relationships within Islamic families. Nonetheless, there is a slowly growing awareness that the application of theories that were derived to understand certain historical and economic Western phenomena provide a distorted lens when used to view the roles of women and men in Islamic societies. It is becoming increasingly clear that topics of Western feminist inquiry such as legal equality; reproductive freedom; and the opportunity to express and fulfill the individual self, whether through work, through art, or through sexuality, do not accurately portray Muslim women's lives (Tucker, 1993b).

In recent years, most of the research and interest in non-Western contemporary families, including Middle Eastern families, has centered almost exclusively on demographic and family-planning issues. Most of this research is based on census and survey data and has greatly increased our understanding of the relationship between population dynamics and the concerns of families in developing countries. For example, over the last 20 years solid empirical data and analysis have been accumulated through a series of World Fertility Surveys, which focus on family, fertility, and the changing position of women in the household. Nonetheless, in contrast to research on Western families, very little work has been done on the effects of colonization, migration, urbanization, integration into the global economy, and changing internal dynamics within households. This gap in the family literature is due to multiple factors: a lack of research tools that lend themselves well to cross-cultural investigation, linguistic issues, difficulty in gaining access to subjects, lack of area studies, and little if any international training of professionals in family studies. Furthermore, I would argue that underlying these issues is a continued reliance on the assumption that non-Western families in particular are governed primarily by unchanging cultural values, traditions, and laws—and thus are "understood." However, as I have pointed out, we actually have a very elementary understanding of Middle Eastern Muslim families. In order to gain a clearer picture of Middle Eastern Muslim families, it is necessary to examine the context in which they live, including the cultural, religious, legal, economic, and sociopolitical influences on their lives. This is not possible in a brief chapter such as this. It is, however, instructive to examine some of the basic Islamic religious concepts with respect to family life, because this tends to be the focus of so much of Western concern and interest—with the caveat that religious ideals provide only *one* source for individuals with respect to how they structure their lives.

THE ROLE OF ISLAM

Although there exists in North Africa and the Middle East much greater diversity with respect to religion, culture, and class than most people from other parts of the world realize, Islamic values influence, in various ways, the social life of many peoples in this region of the world (including those that are not Muslims). The word *Islam* is an Arabic word meaning "submission to the will of God." A Muslim is anyone who follows the religion of Islam. Although Islam is one of the youngest religions in the world (its inception dates to AD 622), it is the fastest-growing religion, with currently approximately 1.3 billion adherents—most of whom do not live in North Africa and the Middle East but instead in Pakistan, India, and Southeast Asia.

Islam is a monotheistic religion that is very similar to Judaism and Christianity. All Muslims believe that there is only one God, and they regard the Old and New Testaments as revelations that came from God (Allah). Much of the moral code with respect to human behavior is identical in Islam, Judaism, and Christianity. A primary difference, however, is that Islam does not accept the Christian concept of the Trinity nor Jesus as the Son of God. Instead, Jesus is regarded as a prophet who was then followed by Muhammad, the last prophet. This makes Muhammad the most important prophet to Muslims. Furthermore, there are two major strands of Islam, Sunni Islam and Shi'a Islam, with their distinction resulting from a crisis of succession after the death of Muhammad.

Islam is more than a set of beliefs and ritual practices. It constitutes a system of thought and includes rules of behavior that were transmitted to the Prophet Muhammad from God. These rules are understood to be a series of commands that assist individuals in every aspect of their lives. Thus, every pious Muslim has to fulfill the five "pillars of Islam." These include: the proclamation that there is no God but Allah, and Muhammad is his Prophet; five daily prayers performed in the direction of Mecca; the fast of Ramadan, during which Muslims may not eat or drink from sunrise to sunset for a whole month; charitable giving; and the hajj, the pilgrimage to the Holy City of Mecca that every Muslim is expected to perform once in his or her lifetime. Furthermore, every Muslim is expected to be moderate and not to drink alcohol, eat pork, or gamble.

The commands found in the Koran are thought to be divine; they were revealed once and hence may not be changed in any form. God's will is also expressed in the sunna, containing the traditions about and the sayings of the Prophet Muhammad. The canon law, or shari'a, is composed of the Koran as well as the sunna. It is the sunna that provides the basis for interpretations of the Koran and for an adaptation of its commands to present-day societies. A prominent piece of the shari'a are the laws dealing with family issues, and specifically the areas of marriage, divorce, and succession. Thus, family roles and responsibilities can be identified in the law. The link between the law, the religion, and God's will explains why in all North African and Middle Eastern countries changes to the personal status law raise such concern and outrage.

The Shari'a and Family Life

From a formal perspective, a major part of Islamic law, the shari'a, is preoccupied with family issues, specifically marriage, divorce, and succession. Thus, family roles and clearly delineated aspects of gender-based responsibilities can be readily identified in the law (Esposito, 1982). Most countries in the Arab world follow civil law but have retained the familial aspects of the shari'a. It has been argued persuasively that many Islamic countries have maintained Islamic family law because the law is sacred and peculiarly immutable (Beck & Keddie, 1978). Although this is largely the case, and Islamic law does provide the basis for much of family law, in this area, as in all others, there has been a process of some selection and revision. There are injunctions in the Koran that are not reexpressed in law and that have been totally ignored, and there are observed "Islamic" customs, such as circumcision, that are neither mentioned in the Koran nor written into law. Nevertheless, Islamic family law contains a number of elements that help to delineate distinct ideals of family and gender relations. It also provides the foundation for legal rights and procedures throughout the Middle East. In most of the Arab world, the shari'a is constantly reinterpreted by religious and legal authorities and then implemented in the courts. Family law is carefully detailed in the sacred and secular legal codes, but this does not guarantee that it is either applied or enforced with great consistency (Esposito). It is important to note that historically, the interpretation and transmission of the shari'a has always been in the domain of male lawyer-theologians. This has had major implications for women when it comes to legal rulings with respect to familial issues.

MARRIAGE AS THE BASIS OF FAMILY

Unlike in the West, all Muslim men and women are expected to marry, and marriage is governed by a complicated set of legal and social rules (Sherif, 1999b). Religiously and socially, the founding of a Muslim family is based on the concept of a contractual exchange, legally commencing with a marriage contract and, subsequently, its consummation. In all schools of Islamic law, marriage is seen as a contract whose main function is to legitimize sexual relations between a man and a woman. The fundamental requirements for a valid Muslim marriage are (a) consent of the wife; (b) consent of the legal guardian, *al wali;* (c) two legal witnesses; and (d) payment of dower, or *mahr*. Through the signing of the contract, women are to receive the *mahr,* a suitable home, maintenance (food, clothes, and gifts), and a partial inheritance from men (Sherif, 1999b). According to all schools of Islamic law, women are not required to share in the costs and expenditures of their spouse or their male relatives. Neither are women expected or required to work outside of the home. In return for their financial responsibility, the men acquire access to the sexual and reproductive abilities of women, as well as authority as the head of the family.

Beyond its legal components, marriage is also regarded as a religious obligation and is invested with many ethical injunctions. This can be attributed primarily to the fact that any sexual contact outside marriage is considered *zina,* fornication, and is subject to severe punishment. Furthermore, Islam condemns and discourages celibacy. In this manner, marriage acquires a religious dimension; it becomes the way of preserving morals and chastity through the satisfaction of sexual desires within the limits set by God. Muslim jurists have gone so far as to elevate marriage to the level of a religious duty (Sherif, 1999b). The Koran (Pickthall, Trans., 1976) supports this notion in the verse that states, "And marry such of you as are solitary and the pious of your slaves and maid servants" (24:32), which is commonly interpreted as advocating marriage in order to "complete the religion." A common hadith, still often quoted, particularly among men, states that "the prayer of a married man is equal to seventy prayers of a single man." Thus, all individuals are encouraged to marry, and societal provisions, such as the importance of family reputation, discourage being single. For both men and women, marriage is the only acceptable alternative to living at home. In this way, both natal and conjugal families play a crucial role in the lives of Muslims.

Marriage and Polygyny

Although Westerners often assume that polygynous families are the norm in the Middle East, and although polygyny is allowed by the Koran, in actuality it is very uncommon throughout the Middle East. The Koran permits men to have up to four wives but advocates that should a man choose this option, each wife needs to be treated equally. The Koran then warns that in reality this is impossible to practice. In contrast to the stereotypical Western image of Muslim men with multiple wives, ethnographic evidence indicates that men bemoan the difficulties of supporting one wife in today's economy, and strong social sanctions work against their even considering polygyny as a viable option (Sherif, 1996). There is some evidence that some men who are either very poor or very rich secretly have several wives (somewhat akin to the concept of a mistress in the West); however, this is not an acceptable lifestyle to most individuals throughout the Middle East.

The issue of polygyny can best be understood by examining a country case study, in this case Egypt. It is interesting to examine both male and female views in light of a 1979 ruling in Egypt, also known as "Jihan's law," so named after Sadat's modernist wife, who introduced a decree outlawing polygyny as an option for men. This law caused considerable debate in the media as well as among secular and religious elites concerning the Personal Status Laws and their relationship to the shari'a (Islamic law). The amendment was eventually partially changed on procedural grounds in 1985. However, in June of that year, a similar law (Law No. 100) amending the 1925 and 1929 laws was put into place, where it still remains (Karam, 1998). The new law stipulates that in the case of a polygynous union, the first wife retains the right to divorce her husband, but it is no longer her automatic right. Instead, she now has to prove that her husband's second marriage is detrimental to her either materially or mentally. Further, the first wife now has the right to sue for divorce only in the first year of the new polygynous marriage. Nonetheless, as mentioned previously, it is extremely uncommon to find polygynous marriage in Egypt or elsewhere in the Middle East.

DIVORCE AND ITS IMPLICATIONS FOR FAMILY

If marriage represents the legal union of two individuals and the social alliance of two families, a divorce represents the breakup of the same relationships. As Mir-Hosseini (1993) writes,

> Divorce is often a key to a deeper understanding of marriage. Legally, it is at the point of divorce that approved marital behavior is rewarded and spouses who violate the norms are punished. Socially, divorce represents the point at which the inducements to leave prevail over the social and cultural forces that have so far kept the couple together. Personally, divorce represents the failure of a human relationship; it happens when the parties are no longer willing to negotiate. (p. 54)

Divorce is perceived as an extremely serious process with social consequences that have long-term effects far beyond the unhappiness of the two people in the marriage. Because of these serious implications, prominent Islamic discourses advocate that divorce be avoided under all conditions.

Contrary to common misperceptions, divorce is treated as a serious matter in both the Koran and the hadith, as well as by Islamic law (see Beck & Keddie, 1978; Mernissi, 1987; Haeri, 1989, for further discussion). Several suras (2:225–232; 65:1–7) deal in detail with divorce, and an authenticated hadith (i.e., a statement by the Prophet Muhammad) states, "No permissible thing is more detested by Allah than divorce." Socially, divorce is perceived as an extremely undesirable event throughout the different societies in the Middle East. There are heavy social stigmas attached to divorce, and it is commonplace, therefore, for the families of two disputing parties to try to work toward a conciliation of a feuding couple (Sherif, 1996).

Divorce implicates men and women differently, in both the legal and social domains. According to Islamic law, a Muslim husband has the unilateral right to divorce his wife without having to justify his actions before any legal body or any witnesses. A wife, however, in order to initiate a divorce, must place her claim before a shari'a court and argue her case on the basis of certain legal precepts. In most countries in the Middle East, however, a number of social and often legal sanctions prevent men from exercising this unilateral right. Furthermore, a careful examination of Islamic law reveals that although it may make it relatively easy for a man to divorce his wife in some ways, it limits his actions in other ways (Esposito, 1982).

For most individuals, going to court in order to execute a divorce is often the last step in a long, arduous process. The same lengthy, intertwined processes that led to the actual marriage also work toward preventing its easy dissolution. Because, as we have seen, marriages involve many more people than just the conjugal couple, it is almost impossible for a couple to have marital problems without the knowledge of a large number of other people. Families of both the husband and the wife tend to intervene in a troubled marriage. Often, the injured wife asks her father or another male relative to speak to her husband on her behalf. In unusual cases, the wife will also ask her mother or her sister to speak with her husband's mother or even with her spouse. It is considered more appropriate and productive for men to speak to one another, without the interference of "women's talk" (Sherif, 1996).

Legally, the most concrete factor that prevents divorce is that portion of the *mahr* that becomes owed to the wife upon the dissolution of the marriage. Women who stipulate a *mahr* in their contracts will use it primarily as a bargaining tool, should their husband threaten to divorce them. Thus, the *mahr* acts as a deterrent to divorce, and it gives a wife some financial security and bargaining power. For example, Mir-Hosseini (1993), in her detailed study of divorce cases in both Iran and Morocco, reports that among recently divorced young couples, women have returned to the practice of asking for *mahrs* that are well beyond the means of the bridegroom (in the currency of gold coins, because of high inflation). Iranian women have adopted this strategy in order to protect themselves from men's rights to divorce and polygyny. Mir-Hosseini also found that with this renegotiated function of *mahr*, the marriages of Iranian women tend to be more secure than they were before the revolution.

Besides the *mahr*, the *'idda* also acts as a deterrent to divorce. According to Islamic law, a divorce cannot be finalized until the *'idda* requirement is completed. The *'idda* is the period between an actual separation and the final termination of marriage, and it carries with it, while it lasts, certain obligations and rights for both spouses. These include a temporary legal restraint from marrying, the mutual entitlement to inheritance, and the maintenance and lodging of the wife. By definition, the *'idda* is a waiting period and a period of sexual abstinence for a woman, starting immediately after a divorce or the husband's death. During this time a woman may not remarry and, in the case of divorce, must wait three menstrual cycles before the divorce is final (Koran 2:228). The *'idda* is thought to have been introduced as a major reform to the pre-Islamic practices of easy marriage and divorce (Watt, 1956). That the Koran is expressly concerned with the well-being and maintenance of the unborn child can be seen in the fact that it clearly states that if a woman is divorced before the consummation of her marriage, she is not required to perform the *'idda* (Koran 2:234). Other interpretations, which imply that the *'idda* was stressed in order to limit the rights of women, do not hold up against this argument.

Several references in the Koran imply that by introducing the *'idda,* Muhammad was trying to introduce clarity into the father-child relationship (2:228, 234; 65:4). By insisting that the woman reveal her pregnancy during a period of divorce or widowhood, the actual genitor was forced to take on the responsibility of fatherhood. This desire to solidify the father-child relationship can also be seen in the Islamic rejection of previous adoption practices (Koran 33:4, 5, 37).

The period of the *'idda* gives the husband the right to resume marital relations, including sexual intercourse, with his wife, even without her consent. During this period, the wife may not marry another man, and the husband may not take a fifth wife. In other words, this gives the man the right to change his mind about terminating the marriage and forces the couple to stay together for a period of time. The importance of the *'idda* indicates the value that Islam places on attempting to preserve the marital relationship, because it provides time for a reconciliation (Degand, 1988). Because the wife is obligated to stay with her husband under the same roof, the *'idda* provides the opportunity for continued interaction and a possible continuation of the marriage. This becomes even more likely in case of a pregnancy, in which the woman is entitled to a full year of financial support. The *'idda* strives to preserve her physical and psychological well-being during a period of potential great strain, whether she is pregnant or not. In the case of a pregnancy, the unborn child is guaranteed that its mother has access to adequate nutrition and shelter from the commencement of conception. This ensures as much as is possible the health of the child. In other words, the *'idda* is a form of financial and psychological insurance for a woman and her born and unborn children (Sherif, 1996).

PARENT-CHILD RELATIONSHIPS

Children, specifically, occupy a special place in Islamic thinking on family. The Koran encourages all men and women to marry and to consider the children who result from these unions as a blessing. Islam stresses the importance of the founding of the family through marriage and the reproduction of society through birth (24:32; 2:221). Because sexual activity outside of marriage is prohibited, reproduction can take place only within the framework of the family. The desire for children is a striking feature of Middle Eastern societies (Sherif, 1996). Many couples wish to have a child within the first year of marriage, and even though the Koran clearly forbids the one-sided favoring of sons over girls (Koran 42:49–50), the cultural value of boys remains high among both men and women and across all social classes. Women desire sons in order to gain prestige, and men hope for sons in order to pass on their name and family reputation. Religiously, socially, and legally, children occupy a central position in the social organization of Islamic societies. Children are seen as the vital generational link. These views on the important roles of children find their origins in classic Islamic literary and religious discourses (Degand, 1988).

The Koran and the sunna are extremely concerned with motherhood, fatherhood, and the protection of children from the moment of conception until the age of maturity. Islam stresses the rights and obligations that parents have to their children and, reciprocally, the rights and obligations children have to their parents. The legal aspects of Islam deal with the socioeconomic conditions of the children, both within the family and in case of divorce or the death of the parents (Schacht, 1964).

According to the law, the relationship between parents and children parallels the rights and obligations that are established through marriage, notwithstanding specific social content. The shari'a has developed specialized topics that reflect the highly protective attitude of the Koran toward minor children and aged parents. Specifically, the primary legal relationship between parents and children centers on the question of adequate maintenance of dependent children and needy parents. The economic and social welfare of children is a major responsibility of parents, and it is enforceable under Islamic law (Fluehr-Lobban, 1987). Conversely, it is the legal responsibility of children to take care of their aged parents both financially and socially. Ethnographic evidence indicates that, for most Middle Eastern families, the welfare of both children and old people centers around the capabilities of the extended family (Sherif, 2005).

According to Islamic law, every Muslim infant is entitled to *hadana,* which loosely translates into the fulfillment of the physical and emotional needs of a child (Degand, 1988). This includes, besides the care and protection of the child, his or her socialization and education. A child is entitled to *hadana* from the day of birth. Under the shari'a, custody is defined as the caring for the infant by women who have the lawful right to bring the child up during the period when the child cannot do without care (Nasir, 1990).

The *hadana* encompasses two phases. The first phase lasts, independent of the sex of the child, from birth until the time that the child has reached the stage of discernment. The second phase, which follows right after that point, differs in time span depending on the sex of the child. The *hadana* of a boy ends when he has reached sexual maturity and when he is considered to have attained a degree of social maturity that will allow him to live an independent life, that is, adulthood. The situation differs for girls, who remain in the *hadana* of their parents until they get married. One reason for this seems to lie primarily in the concern for the protection of women (Degand, 1988).

Hadana rules are organized around the various stages of development of a child and guarantee that adult interests do not stand in the way. In the initial phase of life, the child must be nursed either by its mother or by a wet nurse, in which case her fee becomes the responsibility of the father. According to the Koranic ruling, this period lasts approximately 2 years, depending on the individual circumstances. The development of a permanent emotional relationship to a caretaker becomes the next central component of the weaning phase. It is advised that the need of a child for care, love, and tenderness is usually satisfied by the mother. Should she, however, not feel able to take care of the child and be in charge of its upbringing, either for physical or psychological reasons, she may delegate this task to another female relative or to a hired nursemaid. However, whoever takes over the initial upbringing of the child must fulfill a series of physical and psychological criteria that will further the well-being of the child in this phase of life. Although there is a stress on the "natural" inclination of women to take care of young children, it is interesting to note that historically the classical jurists who wrote on these issues did not feel that gender roles could not be reversed, with the woman becoming the breadwinner and the man caring for his children (Degand, 1988). This points to a historical realization that gender roles can, at times, be determined by social factors and not always by biology.

As soon as the practical goals of the initial socialization—personal hygiene; learning to walk, eat, and dress—have been realized, and the child is at a point in his or her intellectual development to be discretionary, usually between the ages of 5 to 7 years, the child's upbringing and well-being begin to compete with the interests of the adults. The adults' interests lie primarily in preparing both boys and girls for their future gender roles. The preparation of the boy for his future role as provider and guardian lies in the hands of the father or a male relative. A girl is prepared for her tasks as wife, housewife, and mother by her mother or other female relatives. In this phase of socialization, most of the responsibility for the child's well-being still lies in the hands of the mother. Biological parents may be replaced, depending on the circumstances, by sociological parents, who may assist in raising a child but who are legally forbidden from adopting it (Sherif, 1996).

It is important to note that not only do the parents have obligations toward their child or children, but children are also responsible for their parents. This obligation is described both in the Koran and in the shari'a. Specifically, adult children, both sons and daughters, are responsible for financing their parents, if the parents' economic situation requires this (Sherif, 2005). Children are obligated to take care of their parents for two reasons: (a) the importance placed on familial ties, and (b) because respect toward one's parents (*birr al-walidain*) is among the most important values in Islamic societies. To a greater or lesser extent, these values continue to pervade contemporary Middle Eastern societies, with some form of family obligation remaining the norm contrary to predictions of the "Westernization" (i.e., increasing individualization) of individuals in this part of the world.

THE CONTINUING IMPORTANCE OF FAMILY

The Role of the Family of Origin

Throughout the Middle East, the importance of family for women and men in all arenas can hardly be overestimated. Even though women, upon marriage, become incorporated into the household of their husbands, they remain members of their natal families. They retain their fathers' family names after marriage and, in case of divorce or widowhood, are expected to move back to their natal home (Sherif, 1996, 2005). Men bear the financial responsibility of caring for all single women in their families, even if these women have been previously married. Thus, women are brought up with the expectation that their primary ties and ultimate sources of economic security will be in their relationships to their fathers, brothers, and sons. These relationships with both female and male members of the immediate family remain the strongest links in women's lives (Macleod, 1991).

The Role of Extended Families

Some version of the extended family still remains the ideal among the various Middle Eastern societies and classes. Most individuals consider living in the same building or neighborhood as fathers, brothers, sisters, mothers, or cousins as the best situation (Macleod, 1991). Extended families do not follow the traditional patterns in which genealogically related persons of two generations live together or in which married siblings form one household. Rather, extended families are based on the incorporation of unmarried relatives into a family. Widows, divorcees (especially those with no children), and bachelors do not live independently and would risk being stigmatized should they make this choice. Further, unmarried sons or daughters live with their parents until marriage, irrespective of age. After divorce or the death of a spouse, both men and women, especially if they do not have children, are expected to return to their parents if the parents are still alive; otherwise, they are supposed to live with a brother, sister, or other relative. Also popular is the "borrowing" of a child by a relative with no children of his or her own. Among lower-class people, one tends to find this phenomenon more often among grandparents who need the assistance of a child for housework. Among more well-to-do families, an uncle or aunt will offer to take care of a sibling's children for an extended time period, primarily for sentimental reasons or because the biological parents already have other pressing obligations, such as an extended leave abroad (Sherif, 1996).

Another common middle- and lower-class family pattern is the incorporation of nonrelatives, such as apprentices and work assistants, into a particular household. Such individuals have a special position, because even though not all of them sleep in the house of their employer, their food and laundry are part of that of the household. Upper-middle- and upper-class families are characterized by the presence of domestic servants, who may or may not live in the household. Often, domestic live-in servants will come from the family's natal village, even if the family has not lived there in several generations (Rugh, 1984).

Migrants, an often ignored group in the academic literature, exhibit an alternative family pattern: They do not usually bring their families when they first enter the city from the countryside. When they first arrive in the city, they tend to live in the same neighborhoods as others from their original natal village. Each will live with other relatives in the local neighborhood until he becomes established and acquires a house of his own (Rugh, 1984).

For most Middle Easterners, the continuing primacy of extended families can be explained by the sense of place, congenial setting, and social networks for financial and personal support that come through the association with families. People perceive life in the West, with its emphasis on individual desires and pursuits, as lonely and self-centered. Although the actual composition of households may vary widely within the community or even within a larger extended family, the structure and ideology of family remain crucial for most Muslims because of the network of resources and sense of identity it continues to provide (Macleod, 1991).

CONTEMPORARY CHALLENGES FOR FAMILIES

Families in the Middle East have not been immune to the challenges with respect to family life facing individuals all over the world. Westernization and globalization have differentially affected all families with respect to gender roles, child rearing, and maintenance of aging parents (Sherif, 1999a). In the contemporary Middle East, some of these challenges are compounded by an increasingly fervent religious fundamentalism that is affecting even highly secular individuals. Married couples, in particular, find themselves at the center of a debate that places them in a double bind. Dominant religious and often political discourses uphold and promote a stereotyped, male-centered vision of the husband as the economic provider. Simultaneously, intensifying Islamist movements around the region are calling for a "return" of women to their "traditional" place at the center of the family, as wives and mothers. For married women, especially ones who choose to or must work, these visions are particularly problematic. Such women are caught between ideologies that devalue their contributions to their families and to the larger society and social conditions that have necessitated or at times encouraged them to redefine their household roles (Sherif, 1999a).

Recent calls by fundamentalists to restore a "traditional" or "Islamic" order have centered much of their rhetoric around the "appropriate" place and roles for women. Women are eulogized in the press and in sermons as the repository of "traditional" values: The ideal woman is a wife and a mother; she is a woman who raises a new generation of Muslims, wears the veil, guards her modesty, obeys her husband, and expresses her views only through him. She takes care of her family, and because the family is at the heart of Muslim society, she performs the most fundamental task in society (Macleod, 1991; Sherif, 1999a). Within this description, there is no room for the economic pressures that force women to work outside the home; to interact with unrelated men; or to negotiate a new distribution of household roles in order to deal with the pressures of marriage, work, and children. As a result, working Muslim women are continually forced to redefine and renegotiate their positions against a backdrop of public expectations, balancing interpretations of holy texts against existing societal factors that influence their family's social position. This reconfiguration of religious practice and belief is connected to the larger-scale socioeconomic transformations taking place around the globe.

On the one hand, through education and working, women have been given new opportunities for education, mobility, and the capacity to contribute to the financial and economic progress of their families. On the other, they receive little acknowledgment for their increased workloads, and instead, they attract increased criticism for their inability to live up to the socioreligious ideal. In one sense, women are the point of convergence of opposing ideological currents, and their experience is created by this clash. It is primarily within the sphere of marriage that these conflicting understandings of male and female roles are symbolically and ideologically negotiated (Sherif, 1999a). For many Muslims, the border that divides the West from the East is drawn in a moral sphere where women represent the symbolic boundary between all that is good and evil and between all that is moral and corrupt. At issue is the debate over which aspects of individuals' lives are public and which are private. The former is popularly thought to be the realm of work and of men, whereas the latter is that of the family and of women. However, the line between these domains is unclear, and this ongoing debate is, therefore, an ever-growing source of conflict in Muslim societies.

Parallel to the situation in Western societies, the family has become the ideological battleground for contemporary disputes: Must the traditional family unit, with a provider father and a homemaker mother, be reaffirmed in order to reinforce a moral order? Do the conditions of modern economic life allow women to stay home taking care of the children? What are the appropriate gender roles within the household, and who should raise the children? The Muslim response to these questions parallels that of Christians and Jews—to promote those practices perceived as ideally strengthening the family unit and to denounce those perceived as weakening it. However, modern economic and social conditions do not create an environment that allows for "ideal" rules and roles to be instituted. Nor does the current world system allow for communities and societies to go back in time. With an increasing number of women working, old patterns of authority are increasingly giving way to new roles and expectations, even in highly conservative societies (Sherif, 2000). Ethnographic evidence indicates that both gender role definitions and family life are subject to societal pressures and economic constraints (Sherif, 1996). With this in mind, any examination of Islamic families must not only encompass an overview of religious ideals, but must also include attention to economic and social factors as well as regional, gender, and class variation.

CONCLUSION

Changing economic conditions and new perceptions of the relative value of education and of wage employment have promoted new configurations of family strategies among all types of communities in the Middle East. Today, even in the most patriarchal family contexts, decisions concerning education, employment, spending, and so on are, to a large extent, reached somewhat more collaboratively between husband and wife. In part, this stems from the fact that because of economic circumstances, many families are forced to depend on the earnings and contributions of women and children as well as adult males. Access to new opportunities has been distributed unequally, leading to relative economic disadvantages between families, communities, and countries. Nevertheless, not all families, even those within a single community or class, have experienced these shifts in identical ways. Social conditions dictate that families of different classes have differential access to knowledge, enforcement of their rights, and economic privileges. For middle- and upper-class individuals, their power is enhanced through social policies, informal and formal organizations, as well as opportunities for employment outside the home. For poor and rural families, survival is the priority. Even very recent studies (Amin & al-Bassusi, 2004) generalize about the situation of Middle Eastern or country-specific families. However, class, education, and socioeconomic access matter, and they affect families differentially. What is often ignored in studies of Middle Eastern families is that especially poor women and children are taken advantage of in both the public and private spheres of their lives. The lives of all individuals in the Middle East are not the same, and we cannot make universal assumptions about people's experiences. In order to assist families, contemporary social policies and religious forces must take into account the varied access to the structure of opportunities.

Family strategies reflect this range of experience. The marital bond remains primary, given that most women marry young and are bound to their spouses through social and economic ties. In turn, the husband has the right to demand obedience and submission from his wife as part of the legal definition of marriage. However, in contemporary Middle Eastern societies, the husband's power is modified by the woman's control over her dower and other capital, as well as by the relationships she has with other members of her family (Sherif, 1999a). Women are not universally oppressed and subjugated by religious values and their families. In fact, an examination of the formal, religiously based aspect of family relationships allows for the understanding that many provisions of Islam with respect to the domain of the family attempt to protect the individuals within it and do not just aim to subjugate women, as is commonly held to be the case. However, what has happened over time is that patriarchal *interpretations* of religious injunctions often disadvantage and even at times oppress women in their families. In the current climate of opposing forces of fundamentalism and globalization, women are often caught in the middle of the debate. Women's positions are particularly complicated vis-à-vis men, because they are perceived as representing the "honor" of their families. Their behavior is what is understood to be a symbolic marker of the reputation of the larger entity of the family. Still, in today's economic climate, women also act as social place markers and contribute with their labor to upholding the family's status within its social sphere. This opposes the societal model that places much emphasis on patrilineal ancestry and kinship ties among men. Through changes in women's contributions to the household, men's traditional authority is beginning to deteriorate within the family, with repercussions for all the members. What this discussion illustrates is that Middle Eastern Muslim families are not immune to the forces and challenges that are affecting families around the world. As in other regions, they are trying to find indigenous solutions to contemporary challenges. Some may try to turn to traditional religious precepts in this quest, but ultimately, every family has to find its own solution to its particular set of circumstances.

REFERENCES

Amin, S., & al-Bassusi, N. (2004). Education, wage work, and marriage: Perspectives of Egyptian working women. *Journal of Marriage and Family, 66,* 1287–1299.

Barakat, H. (1985). The Arab family and the challenge of social transformation. In E. W. Fernea (Ed.), *Women and the family in the Middle East: New voices of change* (pp. 27–48). Austin: University of Texas Press.

Beck, L., & Keddie, N. (1978). Introduction. In L. Beck & N. Keddie (Eds.), *Women in the Muslim world* (pp. 1–34). Cambridge, MA: Harvard University Press.

Bernal, V. (1994). Gender, culture, and capitalism: Women and the remaking of Islamic "tradition" in a Sudanese village. *Comparative Studies in Society and History, 36,* 36–67.

Degand, A. (1988). *Geschlechterrollen und Familiale Strukturen im Islam: Untersuchungen Anhand der Islamisch-Juristischen Literatur* [Gender roles and family structures in Islam: Research based on the Islamic judicial literature] (Europaeische Hochschulschriften). Frankfurt, Germany: Peter Lang.

Eickelman, D. (1981). *North Africa and the Middle East: An anthropological approach.* Englewood Cliffs, NJ: Prentice Hall.

Esposito, J. (1982). *Women in Muslim family law.* Syracuse, NY: Syracuse University Press.

Fluehr-Lobban, C. (1987). *Islamic law and society in the Sudan.* London: Frank Cass.

The glorious Koran: Text and explanatory translation (M. Pickthall, Trans.). (1976). Albany: State University of New York Press.

Haeri, S. (1989). *Law of desire: Temporary marriage in Iran.* London: I. B. Tauris.

Karam, A. (1998). *Women, Islamisms and the state: Contemporary feminism in Egypt.* New York: St. Martin's Press.

Macleod, A. (1991). *Accommodating protest: Working women, the new veiling and change in Cairo.* New York: Columbia University Press.

Mernissi, F. (1987). *Beyond the veil: Male-female dynamics in modern Muslim society* (Rev. ed.). Bloomington: Indiana University Press.

Mir-Hosseini, Z. (1993). *Marriage on trial: A study of Islamic family law: Iran and Morocco compared.* London: I. B. Tauris.

Nasir, J. (1990). *The status of women under Islamic law and under modern Islamic legislation.* London: Graham and Trotman.

Ortiz, V. (1998). The diversity of Latino families. *Understanding Latino families: Scholarship, policy and practice.* Thousand Oaks, CA: Sage.

Rugh, A. (1984). *Family in contemporary Egypt.* Syracuse, NY: Syracuse University Press.

Schacht, J. (1964). *An introduction to Islamic law.* Oxford, UK: Clarendon.

Sherif, B. (1996). *Unveiling the Islamic family: Concepts of family and gender among upper-middle class Muslim Egyptians.* Unpublished doctoral dissertation, University of Pennsylvania, Philadelphia.

Sherif, B. (1999a). Gender contradictions in families: Working wives among upper-middle class Muslim Egyptians. *Anthropology Today, 15*(4) 9–13.

Sherif, B. (1999b). The prayer of a married man is equivalent to seventy prayers of a single man: The significance of marriage to Muslim Egyptians. *Journal of Family Issues, 20,* 617–632.

Sherif, B. (2000). Understanding the rights of women: The Egyptian example. In L. Walters (Ed.), *Women's rights in an international perspective* (pp. 71–84). Westport, CT: Greenwood.

Sherif, B. (2005). Treat your elders with respect and kindness. In M. Aguilar (Ed.), *Rethinking aging in Africa: Colonial and post-colonial and contemporary representations* (pp. 273–291). Lawrenceville, NJ: Africa World Press.

Singerman, D. (1995). *Avenues of participation: Family, politics, and networks in urban quarters of Cairo.* Princeton, NJ: Princeton University Press.

Tucker, J. (1993a). The Arab family in history: "Otherness" and the study of the family. In J. Tucker (Ed.), *Arab women: Old boundaries, new frontiers* (pp. 195–207). Bloomington: Indiana University Press.

Tucker, J. (1993b). Introduction. In J. Tucker (Ed.), *Arab women: Old boundaries, new frontiers* (pp. vii–xviii). Bloomington: Indiana University Press.

Watt, W. (1956). *Muhammad at Medina.* Oxford, UK: Clarendon Press.

CHAPTER 14

Families in Sub-Saharan Africa

STEPHAN M. WILSON AND LUCY W. NGIGE

INTRODUCTION

This chapter examines families in sub-Saharan Africa generally with a particular emphasis on East African families In fact, the opening section on traditional perspectives and universal family features is applicable all over Africa, whereas the final sections on contemporary and emerging perspectives focus on East African family trends—past, present, and future. The traditional East African concept of family extends to a wider group compared to the nuclear family of husband, wife, and their children; thus, it is correctly referred to as the "extended family." Included in this definition are parents, grandchildren, grandparents, siblings, aunts, uncles, children, as well as other immediate relatives related by blood, marriage, or adoption. In many ways, this is a (family) system built upon mutual obligations that underlie the power and authority of an extended family ethos; however, the ethos goes beyond blood, marriage, and adoption.

East African families include everyone from the *sasa* (i.e., present and from this time forward), including living relatives, remembered dead relatives (i.e., who were known to people who are still alive), as well as the unborn family members who will become the continuation of the family lineage (Mbiti, 1969). The extended family system is an interdependent, multidimensional network of relationships that binds various relatives together for mutual support in a system of privileges, obligations, and shared identity. Although there is a distinction between marriage and family, these two organizations are intricately connected. Marriage is largely defined in terms of producing and nurturing children, as we shall argue in this chapter. It can also be regarded as an involuntary linkage, which is determined at birth and binds past, present, and future generations to each other in an ongoing family lineage.

Benefits of extended family social organization include provision of a network of relationships through which members assume mutual responsibilities toward one another; provision of a forum for individuals to contribute meaningfully toward the common good of the family institution, strengthening the cohesion and sense of belonging of members in the community; promotion of communal participation of members in family events and ceremonies such as naming, initiation, marriage, childbirth and child rearing, funerals, inheritance, and succession (i.e., positions of family leadership). Also, extended family systems create a support network by offering services to one another, particularly to the needy members such as widows; orphans; elderly; and those who are disabled, ailing, and dying (Bitrus, 2000; Unah, 2002).

In sub-Saharan African extended families, collectivism often takes precedence and overrides individual needs and interests (i.e., familism prevails over individualism). The family is a source of both collective identity and tension (Madhavan, 2001). However, it is best represented by an associative rather than a communal model, especially given the need to reconcile competing allegiances to natal and affinal kin. Madhavan (and others) cite the great variance "in the extent to which family members feel a genuine community of interests or, conversely, exploit the relationship for their own ends" (p. 505). The African family can also be conceptualized as

> a network of blood relationships and kinship ties extending beyond man [*sic*], wife or wives, and children to the clan and the entire community. This is so because since the human community is regarded as an aggregate of interacting and interpenetrating life-forces, what affects the individual or his immediate family affects the existential harmony of the whole group. (Unah, 2002, p. 268)

However, the family social structure organized around the extended family system is not without costs to the elementary (i.e., a mother and her children) family and the individual members in it. For instance, social organization around the extended family may support dependency, in that unproductive and less productive members can make demands on the more productive members for their support, and these can be carried on from one generation to another. It can be burdensome to some individuals because everyone is related, and there is often an expectation that every needy relative, whether justifiable or not, has a right to be supported by all other relatives. This is not simply a cultural imperative. It is exacerbated by the economic situation and especially the absence of well-developed public or private welfare systems with benefits. Support may range from provision of basic needs such as food, clothing, and shelter to more expensive needs such as education and health care. These perennial needs are often supported at the expense of one's individual and nuclear family needs and standard of living.

The extended family system broadens the scope for family conflict: Tension between two members may be transmitted to other (extended) relatives and even to an entire clan (i.e., a large group of relatives who recognize their shared ties to a common ancestor). Problems with in-laws in general, and in particular the relationships between mothers-in-law and their daughters-in-law, who live together in the same homestead, have the propensity to extend out to other parts of the larger family or even to the clan level. There is also the likelihood of misappropriation of private property in the name of extended family rights in matters of inheritance and succession. For example, in most traditional patriarchal systems (East African social systems continue as patriarchal, though many older patterns have changed), women and girls could not own or inherit property from either their family of origin or their family of procreation. If a man died, his sons inherited his wealth, and if he had no sons, his brothers inherited the deceased man's property without reference to the surviving wife and daughters—although contemporary law reflects changes in customary principles. Finally, culturally sanctioned practices such as initiation into adulthood and marriage are controlled by the family, and these practices can take precedence over individual rights and preferences. Child betrothal, female genital mutilation (FGM), girl-child marriage, parent-arranged marriages, polygyny, and widow inheritance, to mention but a few practices where culture and collectivism prevailed over individual rights and preferences, were some of the costs of the extended family system to its individual members. However, the principle of mutual reciprocity also provides for rewards of mutual responsibilities to individuals (i.e., the extended family is obligated to them).

Rapid cultural, socioeconomic, political, and technological changes affecting East African society have also affected the extended family system. For the past century, external contact and interaction with the non-African world have contributed to weakening rather than strengthening the extended family system (Bitrus, 2000). Some of the factors that favor individualistic over collectivistic family systemic organization include contact with Western culture, adoption of nonindigenous religions, values espoused by European colonialism, rural to urban migration, increasing commitment to higher education and paid employment, increased mobility and communication devices, the HIV/AIDS pandemic, and even increased use of national and international languages that enable intermarriage; these myriad factors influence the East African way of life.

TRADITIONAL AFRICAN FAMILY LIFE

In this section, we examine historic patterns and origins of African families from a traditional perspective, which includes some of the distinguishing features of traditional and family universality as well as diversity across varied ethnic backgrounds, in particular across East Africa. We also explore historic African marriage dynamics, from mate selection and premarital negotiations to the marital relationship and dissolution of marriage. Finally, we review fundamental aspects of family life that include parent-child relationships, legitimacy of children, socialization and child care support systems, the status of women and girls, division of labor, and care of the aged. Most of the language that follows is in past tense, though very many of the customs persist in some form and continue as vital, though sometimes transformed, components of family life in contemporary sub-Saharan Africa. The following section is a historic overview of East African family life from the time period just prior to independence (1963) and just after (i.e., roughly, the last 50 years).

Family Universality and Diversity

A universal characteristic of family systems in East Africa is the extended family. However, it must be pointed out that there is great diversity of customs surrounding family formation and structure across various ethnic communities. For instance, in Kenya, there are 42 distinct ethnic groups, each with its own distinctive indigenous language and culture. Ethnic identity is still a pervasive force in contemporary Africa. A person born into a particular ethnic community cannot change his or her ethnic membership, even though he or she may be "adopted" ritually into another ethnic group. According to Mbiti (1969), there were five main distinguishing features of different ethnic communities in Africa. First, each group had its own distinct language and not simply a dialect. Second, each ethnic group had its own geographic area, with varying sizes depending on whether they were nomadic pastoralists or non-nomadic agricultural peoples. Third, each group had a unique culture and shared a common history, customs, morals, ethics, and social behavior. Fourth, each group had its own distinct social and political organization in terms of family life, age groups, marriage customs, and traditional forms of government. Finally, each group had its own unique religious system. A person born into a particular society participated in the entire religious life of that society.

Of course, East African families are typified by a vast variety of ethnicities and customs; we can examine only the broad universal features that are salient across communities. These include the predominant patriarchal kinship system, the extended family system, the initiation of the young into adulthood, the collective and institutional nature of marriage, polygynous marriages, the payment of bride-wealth by the groom's family to the bride's family, (in many societies) widow inheritance, and a strong emphasis on childbearing and large families (Mair, 1969; Mbiti, 1969; Phillips, 1969; Watson, 2000; Wilson, Ngige, & Trollinger, 2003).

There are several distinguishing features of African families that have implications for the individual, the nuclear family, and the community at large. Among the most important are the following eight features.

Patriarchal Kinship System. A prevailing feature of traditional East African family life is a patriarchal kinship system. Kinship controls the social relationships among people in a given community; for example, kinship generally governs marriage customs and determines the behavior of an individual in relationship to others in his or her social world. Kinship governs the whole life of an individual. In each particular ethnic group, the kinship system connects everyone to others, including departed members and those yet to be born (Mbiti, 1969). Children are expected to learn the genealogies of their family heritage from family elders. Genealogies serve two purposes: social and organizational. The social aspect is concerned with establishing relationships between individuals, whereas the organizational deals with dividing the larger society into clans, households, and families. In some African cultures, clan members are not allowed to marry within their clans (exogamous clans), whereas in others, marriage is permitted within clans (endogamous clans). Furthermore, clans are divided into two types: patriarchal clans, where descent is traced through the father's lineage, and matriarchal clans, where descent is traced through the mother's lineage. The dominant kinship system in East Africa is the patriarchal type (Kenyatta, 1953; Sankan, 1971; Schafer, 1997; Snell, 1954; Watson, 2000).

Extended Family System. Throughout sub-Saharan culture, the extended family system is a universal feature. The nuclear family of husband, wife, and their children (i.e., family of procreation) was considered incomplete without the extended family. The polygynous family of a man, his multiple wives, and their children was the norm for most East African societies (Madhavan, 2001). Each wife and her biological children (which may be referred to as an elementary family) resided in their own house and were allocated their own property by the male head of the extended household. In patriarchal societies, each of these female-headed elementary family households lived in the same homestead and generally worked together under the authority of the common male head. The polygynous household remained cohesive until the death of the male head. Thereafter, each individual wife's household was allocated a portion of land as an inheritance. Among the Kikuyu, Embu, and Meru (all of these are ethnic groups in Kenya), when sons became of age and got married, they established their own homesteads on the portion of land allocated to them (Leaky, 1977).

Initiation of the Young Into Adulthood. Most ethnic communities in East Africa included initiation of boys and girls (including circumcision rites) into adulthood as a prerequisite to marriage, such as the Kikuyu (Cagnolo,

1933; Kenyatta, 1953), the Maasai (Sankan, 1971), the Nandi (Snell, 1954), and the Kamba (Wilson et al., 2003). The initiation ceremony was followed by instruction on sexual matters and marital duties. Among the ethnic communities that did not practice FGM as part of the initiation rites (e.g., the Luo), special initiation schools were set up to teach girls about sex and procreation and to prepare them for marriage (Ominde, 1987). Initiation schools existed also among the Chagga of Tanzania and Baganda of Uganda (Mair, 1969). Among the Maasai, tests of physical courage and endurance in young males were also performed as part of the initiation into adulthood. For instance, young Maasai men were expected to kill a lion as proof of bravery and readiness to protect their family and community in times of danger (Beckwith & Saitoti, 1980; Saitoti, 1986).

Collective and Institutional Nature of Marriage. Traditional East African marriages were and still are regarded as an alliance between two families and to a lineage rather than merely between two individuals (Madhavan, 2001; Phillips, 1969; Wilson et al., 2003). Traditionally, parent-arranged marriages were the norm, rather than the exception from young adult individual choice, in selecting a mate. Child betrothal and girl-child marriages were other forms of marriage where cultural and parental choice prevailed over individual rights and preferences. Divorce and separation were also highly discouraged because of the subsequent cost to the extended family of returning bride-wealth to the groom's family should a woman be found guilty of the grounds for divorce. At the extreme, but very rarely, there was total disregard of the individual woman's circumstances even where she was mistreated by her husband or by her in-laws (P. L. Kilbride & J. C. Kilbride, 1990).

This section deals with historical patterns. Today, one can speak with many older women who were married "traditionally" who will say that they suggested to their parents whom they wanted to marry or at least had some private say before their parents "arranged" the marriage for them. This may well reflect an intermediate stage between complete parent control and the practice of individual choice that has been emerging in recent years.

Polygynous Marriages. Polygynous marriages have been customary in sub-Saharan Africa. In most ethnic groups, marriages traditionally were potentially and predominantly polygynous. Polygyny exists today, though there is some question whether polygyny is a modern contradiction (P. L. Kilbride & J. C. Kilbride, 1990). Polygyny was regarded as a status symbol; it reflected male dominance and the fundamental inequality between men and women (Madhavan, 2001; Mair, 1969). A monogamous man was considered poor because he could not afford to marry multiple wives. Both sororal polygyny (i.e., marriage of sisters or close relatives to the same man) and polygyny of one man married to two or more nonrelatives were practiced throughout Africa.

Payment of Bride-Wealth. The payment of goods or services (sometimes called "dowry" in East Africa) by the groom's family is a salient feature of African customary marriage (Watson, 2000; Wilson et al., 2003). However, there is great diversity of traditions about the types, amounts, and duration of bride-wealth payment across communities. There are also diverse regulations governing the repayment of bride-wealth in the cases of divorce or death of the woman. The universal significance of bride-wealth includes compensation to the bride's family for the loss of the services provided by their daughter, a sign of marriage alliance between the two families, enhancement of marriage stability, and a symbol to mark the formalization of marriage.

Widow Inheritance. Widow inheritance resulted from the need to provide for widows and orphans (Snell, 1954). Because of the institutional nature of marriage as an alliance between two families and as an allegiance to a lineage, a widow was automatically inherited by a (lineage through the) surviving brother-in-law or deceased husband's close relatives. Children born of such a union were considered as the deceased man's children. Widow inheritance was considered as family insurance for widows and orphans and as providing for a continuation of family lineage for the deceased across many communities in Africa (Mair, 1969; Watson, 2000). Where a wife predeceased her husband, the man was expected to remarry a young wife. It should be noted that there was no cultural prescription for inheritance of widowers.

Childbearing. Importance was given to childbearing and large families. As in many collectivist societies, having children was the main goal of marriage, and every couple was expected to bear as many children as nature would allow. It was almost as though marriage was synonymous with having children in traditional marriages. Women were highly regarded and valued for their childbearing capabilities (Achatz, 1990; LeVine et al., 1994). Therefore, a childless woman was of little or no value to her husband, her family, or the community at large. So important was the proof of fertility that an impotent man would seek the assistance of a brother or close male relative to produce children for him "in secret." Likewise, a childless wife would seek the assistance of a sister or a close female relative to play the role of a cowife and bear children for her. Among the Kikuyu, Nandi, Kisii, and Kamba, a barren wife could also "marry another woman" (gynaegamy) to produce and raise children for her (Schafer, 1997; Wilson et al., 2003).

African Marriage Dynamics

As stated earlier, East African families' lives are characterized by much diversity among communities and across varied cultures. These cultural orientations permeate every aspect of an individual's life and experiences throughout the life course. Marriage as an institution has been subjected to traditional customs and practices in African society. It should be noted that, in general, culturally sanctioned (collectivist) practices related to mate selection and marriage took precedence over individual rights and preferences (Wilson et al., 2003). In this section, we attempt to examine the distinguishing features of African customary marriages across ethnic groups. These practices include the collective and institutional nature of the marriage transaction and relationship as portrayed in child betrothal, girl-child marriage, parent-arranged marriages, polygyny, bridewealth payment, marriage by service and by exchange, widow inheritance, and dissolution of marriage.

Mate Selection. Two types of mate selection existed in traditional East African communities: parental choice and restricted individual choice with parental approval. The predominant mate-selection method was parental choice of suitors for their children, because marriage was regarded as an alliance between two families rather than two individuals. This was demonstrated in child betrothal among the Maasai (Sharman, 1979), the giving of a daughter in marriage as compensation for a debt among the Kikuyu (H. Kibathi, personal communication, 2003), and the giving of a sister as a substitute for a barren wife among the Luo (Ochola, 2003). Parent-arranged marriages were also the preferred form of mate selection among families with similar socioeconomic status (Wilson et al., 2003). Cases of forced marriage existed among the Maasai, such as if a girl became pregnant before marriage and the lover was reluctant to marry her. In such circumstances, the girl's father could demand bride-wealth from the offending party's family, and the girl's family could press her lover's family to marry the girl to her lover in order to "cover the disgrace" (Beckwith & Saitoti, 1980; Hollis, 1979). The practice of girl-child marriage is another form of parent-arranged marriage where the girl's consent is taken for granted. Among the Maasai, even today, prepubertal girls are sometimes married off (i.e., not just promised but actually married) without their consent to older men who may be their father's or grandfather's age-mates.

Individual choice was limited, and when it occurred, parental approval was a necessary prerequisite to marriage. Among the Chagga of Tanzania, the Baganda of Uganda, and the Luhyia and Maasai of Kenya, a young man could choose his bride-to-be and secure her consent, but he had to secure parental approval (from her parents) before marriage negotiations could begin (Bleeker, 1963; Mair, 1969). If parents were dissatisfied with their children's choices, they had the prerogative of denying their children consent to marry. In such cases, children acquiesce to their parents' wishes without causing undue family conflicts. However, there were cases of elopement to escape from a parent-arranged marriage for which a couple had no inclination. In such cases, the lover arranged to formalize the marriage by paying bride-wealth and also to avoid paying fines to his father-in-law.

Prohibitions of marriage even with somewhat distantly related persons existed across many African communities, thereby restricting the choice of possible mates. Among the Kikuyu, Embu, Meru, and Kamba of Kenya, members of the same clan were prohibited from marrying (Leaky, 1977). In the choice of mate, emphasis was laid on personal character and family background and social status rather than mutual attraction and love. In fact, love as the basis for marriage initiation appears to be a contemporary notion to which the decision-making generation (i.e., the elders) among traditional East Africans did not give much attention (Wilson et al., 2003). In contemporary times, marriage based on emotional bonds appears to be increasing, though it has not eclipsed patterns of family input or choice in mate selection or investment in marital maintenance whether or not emotional bonds persist.

Premarital Sexual Relations. In most traditional communities, virginity at marriage was highly valued and regarded (Watson, 2000). Among the Baganda, Kikuyu, Nandi, Luhyia, and Luo communities, virginity was not only highly valued but also rewarded. A special gift was awarded to the mother of a virgin bride at the time of marriage (Kenyatta, 1953; Leaky, 1977; Mair, 1969; Snell, 1954).

A deflowered girl was considered a disgrace to the family and clan. Permissive premarital sexual indulgence was prohibited, and when it occurred, the culprits were severely punished (although the girl often paid a more severe penalty than the boy). For example, among the Meru, a girl who became pregnant before initiation into adulthood faced a death penalty together with her lover (Nyai, 1961). In contrast, among the Nandi, it was the newborn child who was killed, and the girl would be married off as a subsequent wife in a polygynous family (Snell, 1954). Among the Kikuyu, a girl who gave birth to a child before marriage was regarded as a reject, or *gicokio,* and could only be married to an old man as a cowife. Her lover was required to pay a fine in the form of cattle to the girl's family (Kenyatta, 1953). Such a girl also fetched a lower bride-wealth for her family than a virgin girl (Snell).

In a few communities, such as the Kamba, premarital sexual relations were permitted. A Kamba girl was expected to have had prior sexual experience as part of the preparation for consummation of marriage. Among the

Maasai, restricted premarital sexual relations were allowed, provided such experiences did not lead to pregnancy. In this case, young prepubertal girls would have sexual relations with young circumcised males known as *morans,* with or without intentions to marry (Hollis, 1979; Sharman, 1979). Among the Kikuyu, premarital sexual relations were restricted to love-play known as *ngweko,* where penetration was not permitted. These premarital unions did not necessarily lead to marriage, because the latter was predominantly a parent-arranged affair (Kenyatta, 1953).

Premarital Negotiations and Bride-Wealth. The transfer of bride-wealth (i.e., including money, goods, and material) from the groom's family to the bride's family is a tradition practiced throughout sub-Saharan Africa. The institution of bride-wealth payments has multiple meanings: It is a recognition of the wife's value and a token of appreciation by the groom's family to the bride's family; it formalizes and legalizes the marriage; it establishes the legitimacy of children; and it is a pledge for the maintenance of marriage and must be returned if the marriage is dissolved (Mair, 1969; Watson, 2000; Wilson et al., 2003). The type of bride-wealth system, the amounts, and duration of payment vary according to the different ethnic groups. Traditionally, cattle were the most common form of bride-wealth, and in modern days the monetary equivalent for cattle is often given in place of cattle. The amount of bride-wealth ranges from a fixed amount to a variable number, with a well-defined minimum among the Kikuyu (Kenyatta, 1953), the Nandi (Snell, 1954), the Maasai (Sankan, 1971), and the Kamba (Wilson et al.). The mandatory minimum requirement for bride-wealth payment was made before formalization of the marriage. However, the rest of the bride-wealth was paid in installments over a long period of time (Mair) and in many cases might not be paid fully for many years or ever (Wilson et al.). In such an arrangement, the unpaid bride-wealth was a symbol of the obligations and responsibility that the groom had to his bride's family across their lives. Even today, cases among Kamba, Meru, and Embu families might be found where a widowed husband who had not paid the full bride-wealth might have to complete a symbolic payment before his dead wife's family would release him to marry again (S. M. Wilson, personal communication, 2003).

Marriage Without Bride-Wealth. Several forms of marriage without bride-wealth transfer existed, but they were regarded as inferior to marriage with bride-wealth. These were elopement, cohabitation, and marriage by service. A marriage without bride-wealth did not give a husband all the rights that bride-wealth would secure. For example, a husband could not claim damages against an adulterer; children from such a union between him and his wife belonged to their mother's kin, and therefore he could not claim legitimacy of his children. If his wife died in childbirth, he was liable to pay a fine. Finally, he could not receive bride-wealth for his own daughters because he did not give it for his wife. Instead, the wife's brothers would receive bride-wealth for their nieces (Mair, 1969). In the Maasai community, if a woman eloped with a man, she was relegated one stage below a properly married wife. She would be referred to as *enkapiani* instead of the highly esteemed wife known as *esainoti.* Should the union break down because of disagreements, the woman was allowed to return to her parents' home with her children (Sankan, 1971). A marriage without bride-wealth could be formalized at a later stage to enable the man to acquire the rights of a recognized marriage by offering his father-in-law the customary required bride-wealth.

Cohabitation is a union recognized as a kind of marriage in which the husband moved in to the girl's hut and lived with her in her family's homestead. If the reverse had taken place, and the girl moved to the man's hut, it would have been considered an elopement. Among the Birwana of Tanzania, cohabitation was preceded by a formal agreement between the two parties in the presence of a witness other than the girl's parents (Mair, 1969). The girl's parents preferred cohabitation to elopement because their daughter remained under their protection and lived in close proximity. Cohabitation could also be formalized by paying the required bride-wealth as in customary marriage.

Marriage by service was practiced by the Nyakyusa of Tanzania. The son-in-law did not give cattle for bride-wealth but was required to cultivate and build a house for his father-in-law in exchange for a wife. However, this form of union denied him some rights, such as legitimacy of children, which were regarded as belonging to his father-in-law (Mair, 1969).

Marriage by exchange of girls was practiced among the Maasai. This usually occurred when two young men exchanged their sisters in marriage. For this kind of union to be recognized, the normal customary processes of bride-wealth transfer would be followed later (Sankan, 1971).

Traditionally, most girls were married at a young age, immediately after reaching puberty and after undergoing the rite of initiation into adulthood. The girls' ages ranged from 12 to 14 years. Men contracted marriage at a later age because of the requirement of the rite of passage (initiation) into adulthood and, perhaps more practically, accumulation of sufficient bride-wealth to facilitate marriage. Their ages at first marriage were between 20 and 25 years or older (Wilson et al., 2003).

Order of marriage was culturally defined and systematically followed. Traditionally, siblings married in order of age. This meant that an older brother had to get married before his younger brothers. If the first son delayed in contracting marriage, then all subsequent sons of marriageable age had to wait longer for their turn to marry. The same applied to daughters. Sisters got married according to their birth order. Other rules of marriage and birth order were defined. Among the Luo community, a firstborn son was not allowed to marry a firstborn daughter. Similarly, lastborn sons were not permitted to marry lastborn daughters. These regulations were put in place in order to avoid the negative consequences that were believed would befall such couples. In the case of firstborn children, many expectations were placed upon them to support their siblings and parents in old age. Therefore, when such a pair of firstborns married, their marriage would suffer double responsibility in terms of extended family obligations.

Marital Relationships. Newly wedded couples were trained about marital relations and the processes of conception, childbearing, and child rearing by their elders. Their seniors trained men and women separately. Mothers-in-law and older women often instructed women. Likewise, fathers and other male relatives taught men. Information on sexual taboos was also disseminated at this time. For example, postpartum sexual abstinence was the norm for as long as a child was breastfeeding (Kenyatta, 1953). Husband-wife relationships were expected to be cordial and respectful at all times. A husband's authority over his wife or wives was culturally sanctioned. The extended family played a mediating role in case of differences or tension between members of the couple.

Decision Making Within Marriage. Decision making within East African marriages is generally not egalitarian (Kihaule, 2002). Consistent with Resource Theory, the social position of husband is generally advantaged over that of wife (wives) because of his greater wealth, (often) education, power, job opportunities, and so forth. Although interpersonal relations between African wives and husbands are expected to be cordial and respectful, traditional and rural marriages usually involve unequal input into family decision making. However, in a study of 600 families randomly selected in Dar Es Salaam City, when wives were employed and educated and when they contributed comparable money to the household, it was found that they held more egalitarian influence and contributions to family decision making (Kihaule).

Sexual Activity in Marriage. Historically, East African traditional marriage was regarded, first and foremost, as an institution for childbearing and continuation of the family lineage (Mair, 1969). The central goal of sexual activity was procreation. Bearing and raising many children conferred status on the parents, particularly the mother, and showed the success of the marriage. A childless couple was viewed with suspicion, and culturally sanctioned arrangements were made for a "proxy" husband or wife to beget children who would be accounted as the legal issue of childless couples in many ethnic communities in Kenya, such as Kikuyu and Kamba. Among the Luo, a sister to the bride was the preferred cowife should the bride turn out to be barren ("sororate polygyny," or the marriage of one man to sisters or close female relatives). Widow inheritance, which was widely practiced among Luo, Luhyia, and Kikuyu, allowed the deceased man's brothers or close kin to remarry his widow and both raise children for him and further add to the deceased man's lineage. If a man died before he was married, a ghost marriage could be performed in which a proxy husband married a woman on behalf of the dead man to beget children to continue the lineage of the departed relative. In all these examples, the principal role of sexual activity for procreation and continuation of family lineage was evident.

Extramarital Relationships. Marital fidelity was expected of married couples, although under certain circumstances (which varied from one ethnic group to another), some form of extramarital relations were allowed. For example, a Maasai man could allow his friend who was an age-mate temporary sexual access to his wife without sanctions (D. Simotwo, personal communication, 2003). A Luo man could request his brother's assistance in discharging his marital duties if he was unable to do so (Ochola, 2003). Among the Kamba, an impotent man could likewise seek assistance from his brothers or close male kin in producing children for him while he was still alive (Mutiso, 2003). Children born of such unions legally belonged to the incapacitated husband. In general, there was strong conviction about the sanctity of marriage, though the cultural proscriptions and expressions of that sanctity varied across communities and from one familial circumstance to another.

Where there was no "justification" for extramarital affairs, such unions were outlawed as adultery and were sanctioned accordingly. Marital infidelity by either husbands or wives was punished, although a wife's infidelity was more severely punished than her husband's. The sanctions for a wife's adultery included wife beating; divine punishment in the form of difficult childbirth; and, in cases of serial adultery, separation and divorce (Mair, 1969). In addition, the husband had a right to claim compensation from the offending party. The wife's lover could be assaulted or charged a fine, or in extreme cases he could be killed. In most cases, an adulterous man was charged before a council of elders and was compelled to pay a fine or else he would be beaten by men in his own age-grade and be expelled from the council of elders (*kokwet*) (Snell, 1954).

Dissolution of Marriage. In all communities, marriage was regarded as a lifelong relationship and as the foundation and continuation of family life across generations. As such, every attempt was made to safeguard marriages from separation and divorce and to reconcile differences between spouses. After all, these were obligations to the two families and to the lineage, even beyond whatever responsibilities and feelings the two spouses had for each other. However, where marital conflict and incompatibilities occurred, separation or divorce was possible. A woman could separate from her husband if she was mistreated by him or her in-laws and return to her family of origin (i.e., parents). Among the Kikuyu, Kamba, and Maasai, the deserted man was expected to go to and to pacify his wife and retrieve her from her parents, pay some compensation for mistreating her, and make a pledge to be of good conduct henceforth (Kibathi, 2003; Mutiso, 2003; Sankan, 1971). If the woman was the offending party, her husband could send her back to her parents to be trained in her role as a wife and her marital duties and to return to her husband when she was ready. Such a separation was a disgrace to the woman's parents, and they did their best to train their daughter on how to overcome her shortcomings and reconcile with her husband. On those relatively rare occasions when it occurred, separation usually occurred immediately after marriage and during the first years of marital adjustment. After children were born, it was extremely difficult to separate such a couple. Serious matrimonial differences were settled by a council of elders (Snell, 1954).

Dissolution of marriage was a costly affair and required serious grounds for its sanction. Divorce was, therefore, rare and highly discouraged. The grounds for divorcing a man were different from those for divorcing a woman. Traditionally, a wife could divorce her husband if he was impotent among the Turkana (Atonia, 2003), the Luo (Ominde, 1952), and the Kisii (A. Akunga, personal communication, 2003). In contrast to this practice, a man was not permitted to divorce his wife if she was barren. Instead, he was encouraged to take a second wife while maintaining the first one. A wife could be divorced if she was guilty of serial adultery or witchcraft or if she threatened her husband's life (Mair, 1969; Schafer, 1997; Snell, 1954).

The consequences of divorce to both parties were far-reaching and costly. If a man was the guilty party, the council of elders could fine him, and he suffered the loss of the bride-wealth he had given the wife's family upon marriage. A man who had previously been divorced was stigmatized in the community and was unlikely to contract a marriage alliance with another family because of his history as a marriage failure. In some communities, he would lose all legitimacy rights over his children (Mugo, 1982). If the woman was the guilty party, she lost all matrimonial property she had acquired during the marriage. Child custody could be awarded to her husband, and her family most likely would be required to return the bride-wealth given for her at marriage. In such cases generally, she was despised and stigmatized because of the failure of the marriage, and she was most likely to be a subsequent wife in a polygynous marriage (Sankan, 1971; Snell, 1954; Watson, 2000).

CONTEMPORARY FAMILY LIFE

Family life in East African communities is characterized by more similarities than differences across groups. Extended families live in close proximity, and, when they occur in contemporary East Africa, polygynous households usually live in the same homestead (i.e., a house and adjoining land occupied by one family). The most prominent feature of family life continues to be the collective lifestyle, which emphasizes achieving common family goals. In a patriarchal system, the authority of the male household head is predominant. However, in the elementary family of a mother and her children, the mother is regarded as the head. Married adult men own property, and they make decisions about its generation and allocation (Ngige, 1993). In the following section, many patterns reflect a fidelity to historic patterns; where they have changed or are shifting, mention is made of these developments.

Legitimacy of Children

All children born to a woman whose husband had given a bride-wealth to her family are regarded as his legitimate children. Fathers expect to receive their daughters' bride-wealth at the time of marriage, and if he has sons, he likely will expect to provide bride-wealth for their wives. Sons were and still are expected to support their parents in old age. Historically, upon the death of their father, sons alone inherited his property. Because girls were given away in marriage, they were not considered as heirs in matters of inheritance and succession. Among the Luhyia and Meru communities, biological paternity is critical, in that a man takes responsibility for all the children that he begets, whether their mothers are married to him or not (W. Muchai, personal communication, 2003; S. Waudo, personal communication, 2003). In contrast, among the Kikuyu, an unmarried mother takes full responsibility for raising children born out of wedlock. Such children were regarded as illegitimate and could obtain support only from their maternal grandparents.

In communities that practice leviratic marriage (i.e., where a man dies and his widow is inherited by his male next of kin), such as the Luo, children born of the leviratic union were regarded as the legitimate children of the deceased man (Ochola, 2003). In communities such as the Kisii, Kikuyu, Nandi, and Kamba, where gynaegamy (woman-to-woman marriage) was practiced, a childless senior wife "took a young wife" to bear and raise children for her. The younger wife played the role of a surrogate mother, and children born of such unions legitimately belonged to the senior wife (Wilson et al., 2003). Finally, in those communities that practiced ghost marriage, if an unmarried man died, his brother or next of kin took a wife for his departed relative, and children from such unions were counted as the legitimate children of the dead kin (Mair, 1969). Although diminished, these patterns persist in contemporary families, particularly in rural areas.

Sex Preference

Historically, male children were preferred over female children because of the emphasis on continuity of the family lineage in patriarchal societies. However, girls were more valued because of their childbearing capabilities and their potential for wealth generation in the form of the bride-wealth that would come to their family of origin when they were married. Males diminish family resources, because their family is expected to pay bride-wealth for their wives. In giving and receiving bride-wealth, a fair balance was reached in resource distribution across clans.

Parent-Child Relationships

In general, African children are highly valued and regarded as the linkages in the lineage between the past and present as well as between the present and future generations (Mbiti, 1969). In a typical polygynous household, the mother-child relationship is of special importance. An early study of infancy in Uganda indicated that the growth of attachment of the infant to the mother in particular, and to other members of the household in general, played a key role in the social development of the child among Baganda children (Ainsworth, 1967), and this applies to Kenyan children as well (LeVine et al., 1994). As children grew older, boys identified with their fathers and were socialized for male gender roles, and similarly girls identified with their mothers and were trained in their culturally defined roles as future wives and mothers.

Girls are highly valued and protected by their fathers and brothers, first and foremost as female children who are vulnerable, and second, because of their role in wealth generation in the form of bride-wealth at the time of marriage, and because of their role as linkages in establishing family alliances with in-laws. Boys have a special relationship with their parents into old age, even today. Firstborn sons are responsible for taking care of their fathers in old age, and lastborn sons take care of their mothers in their advanced age. Among the Maasai, these are the only two sons who were special, and their inheritance was clearly defined and indisputable. The eldest son inherits all his father's property and debts. Thereafter, he distributes the property and debts among his brothers. The youngest son inherits his mother's property (Sankan, 1971).

Child Care Support

The child's own parents, particularly mothers, are responsible for care and upbringing of their children. Other members of the extended family such as stepmothers (i.e., cowives), grandparents, and other extended relatives also play a part. Traditionally, every older person is expected to play the role of a parent (i.e., child socializer/nurturer/supervisor) to every younger person. In every community, there were well-defined child care support systems for orphans. For example, if a father died, the biological mother took custody of children with the assistance of a paternal uncle until those children were launched and formed their own families. In case of a mother's death, the father had legal custody, but the responsibility of care and maintenance was placed under a stepmother, a paternal aunt, or paternal grandmother. In case both parents died, the responsibility of child care was placed under a senior sibling, preferably an adult brother, and if there were no such brothers, the duty fell upon the child's senior paternal uncle as a proxy father and an older sister, aunt, or grandmother who played the role of a proxy mother. Only in the rare event when there was no male relative on the paternal side would the child be placed under the care of the maternal relatives (Kenyatta, 1953; LeVine et al., 1994; Ominde, 1987; Snell, 1954). These patterns are being challenged by recent events related to HIV/AIDS.

Socialization of the Young

Parents are primarily responsible for nurturing and socialization of their children. However, in an extended family system there was also communal responsibility for socializing the young. Historically, all adults were responsible for the upbringing of all children, regardless of biological ties. Young boys and girls learned proper gender roles from older men and women, respectively. The discipline of children was a collective responsibility, where each senior person guided, counseled, and meted punishment to any errant child when justified. However, mothers had the primary duty of disciplining their children, in particular their daughters. Fathers took the chief responsibility for sons' discipline after their initiation rite into adulthood. During rites of passage from one developmental stage to another, children were prepared to undertake their normative developmental roles. During the initiation into adulthood stage, youth were prepared for marriage and family life in special initiation schools (LeVine et al., 1994).

The Status of Women and Girls

The notion that traditional African women were subjugated by men is a subject of debate. In our discussion on the place of girls in family life, we have found that daughters were highly valued and regarded with respect, particularly by their fathers, and highly protected by their brothers. It is our belief that their place in the family was not just in relation to the roles they played in wealth creation, establishing family alliances, and child-bearing function, but they were valued first and foremost as female children. At marriage, brides were highly regarded, and families went to great lengths to acquire wives who would be valued and respected by their sons and who would bring honor for their new families. Family wealth was transferred from a groom's family to a bride's family in exchange for a wife. At childbirth there were celebrations, and new mothers received special gifts from their husbands and in-laws. At every stage of the family life cycle, a woman's role was recognized and appreciated. We indicated earlier that virginity was highly regarded (Watson, 2000) and that the mother of a virgin bride received a special gift for raising her daughter well (Kenyatta, 1953; Leaky, 1977; Mair, 1969; Snell, 1954).

In her individual house composed of herself and her children, a mother was regarded as the head. She commanded respect from her children and made decisions pertaining to her children's welfare. She could negotiate with her husband on matters pertaining to her house. In a polygynous household, all cowives were equal, and a husband was expected to treat his wives equally regardless of his preference for any. The husband was expected to consult the first wife in matters that would affect the entire household, including taking a subsequent wife. Her opinion was important and could not be taken for granted. If a woman felt that her rights had been abused, or she was subjected to ill treatment by her husband, she sought redress. Two options were open to her. First, she could return to her parents for temporary protection until her differences with her husband were sorted out. Alternatively, if the offence was serious, she could sue her husband for divorce in an elders' court (Mugo, 1982).

There were traditional rites that could promote a woman to the highest social status, which enabled her to perform certain ritual roles (Kenyatta, 1953; Mair, 1969; Watson, 2000). The traditional birth attendant (female) was one of the most respected members of every community. Her social status was equivalent to that of a male traditional healer.

From the foregoing discussion, the general assumption that traditional African women were simply subservient to men is not supported. Although contemporary gender and family patterns are rapidly shifting and these modify gender relations and expectations, superficial characterizations have too often been made by those who fail to attend to the subtleties of traditional East African family life and culture.

Division of Labor

A division of labor based on gender role socialization from early childhood has long existed. It was the responsibility of the men to attend to the nondomestic sphere of family life, such as tending cattle, hunting wild game, and protecting the family from insecurity. In addition, older men trained and socialized younger men for their roles in society. Men had the sole right to acquire, distribute, or dispose of wealth when the need arose. Women's responsibilities were confined to the domestic sphere of household production. Their duties included but were not limited to child rearing, agricultural production, carrying *kuni* (i.e., fuel wood), fetching water, food preparation and preservation, and house care (Ngige, 1993; Schafer, 1997). In a polygynous household, each wife fed her own children. In addition, each wife prepared a meal for her husband daily. There is a Kikuyu saying, "a polygynous man would starve to death in his own hut alone" if he relied on rotational meals from his cowives—each wife assumed that it was another's duty to feed him. Some responsibilities were shared, such as house building, planting, and harvesting crops. Among the Kikuyu, men would erect the structure for a hut, and women completed the mud walls and thatching (Leaky, 1977). Among the Nandi, men constructed the foundation and roofing, and women completed the walls (Snell, 1954). Among the Maasai, house construction was the responsibility of women (Hollis, 1979). Again, these patterns persist in some form as at least a referent to which contemporary families compare themselves.

Care of the Aged

In earlier generations, the primary duty of caring for aged parents fell to one's own children. As stated earlier, firstborn sons were responsible for taking care of their fathers in old age, and lastborn sons took care of their mothers in their advanced age. The eldest son was the principal heir of his father's estate, and he would normally become the head of the household upon his parent's death. The responsibility of taking care of one's parents was rarely evaded because of natural ties of affection and also because of the potential sanctions (e.g., a possible curse on the children) should they fail in their obligations (Mugo, 1982). In recent times, the economic well-being of the elderly has begun to deteriorate because of a diminishing emphasis on the extended family network and the tradition of mutual obligations across generations (Watson, 2000). There has been an increase in the number of nursing homes and retirement homes and institutionalization of the care for the elderly, particularly in urban areas.

SUMMARY OF EMERGING TRENDS AND IMPACTS ON CONTEMPORARY FAMILIES

The 1999 Kenya population and housing census reported changes that reflect changing families in many ways, including population, fertility, and nuptiality as well as mortality, migration, and urbanization. Other trends are noted in education, labor, unemployment, housing, gender issues, and population projections. In the following section, results are summarized from the Central Bureau of Statistics 1999 population census report (Kenya, 2001).

Contemporary East African Family Life

In this section, we more specifically examine contemporary East African families in transition and several emerging perspectives that have implications for marriage and family dynamics. We note that rapid socioeconomic, political, public health, and technological changes affecting society have also affected the extended family system. For the past century, external contact and interaction with Western ideas and institutions, arguably, have weakened traditional East African extended family systems. Among these influences have been contact with Western culture; introduction of modern/imported religions such as Christianity, Islam, and Hinduism; and the emergence of formal education, secular codified law, colonialism, modern economies, a new political order, industrialization and urbanization, the rural-urban drift in search of education and employment opportunities, the HIV/AIDS pandemic, increased mobility of family members and absence from each other, and ethnic intermarriage, to name a few social and other contextual forces that have demanded adaptations in family patterns, lifestyles, and values. On the whole, in East Africa as in other parts of the world, the movement toward globalization has had a tremendous impact on contemporary families.

There are several contemporary shifts that, although not explicitly family changes, do powerfully shape family life. Among these are several societal shifts related to migration, economics, residence, and the social forces that shape family formation.

Among the major shifts have been those from rural to urban residence and livelihood and changes from little to increasingly higher levels of education and modernization. These shifts, in turn, have led to new challenges in daily living motivated by increasing distances from kin for child care, exchanges of services and support, and redefinition of what is family. The following are several of the major themes of emerging and ongoing family changes in contemporary East African family life.

Rural-Urban Migration. The population of people migrating from rural to urban areas has increased over time from 10% in the 1970s to 19% in 1999. This has several implications for families, such as decreased control by the extended kin, more freedom of choice in mate selection by the younger generation, smaller family sizes, and reduced prevalence of multigenerational families (Kenya, 2002).

Educational Attainment. The 1999 population census reported that 58% of the population had completed primary school, 17% had attained a secondary school education, and less than 1% had completed a tertiary or university level of education. Often, community and family continue to be emphasized over the individual, and traditions that interfere with the attainment of formal education continue to be widely practiced. Despite these facts, many consider the Kenyan educational system to be a shining example of successful mass education (Buchmann, 2000). School enrollment for boys and girls are comparable at the primary school level up to about age 14. From age 15 upward, the female dropout rate is higher than the male rate. It is more difficult to maintain girls in school. In general, the level of educational attainment has been associated with increased age at marriage for both men and women and with later ages at first birth for women. By extension, this reduces total fertility per woman (Kenya, 2002). The majority of young women report that they would prefer to marry in their mid- to late 20s and have fewer than five children (Achatz, 1990).

Labor Force. Unemployment problems have remained consistently high, from 7% in the 1970s to at least 20% by 1999. The female unemployment rate rose from 18% to 26%, reflecting a depressed female participation in the labor market. The 1999 census reported that 69% of the working population aged 15–64 years was self-employed in the rural areas. About 15% of employed persons were self-employed in family-related business in urban areas. Unemployment leads to poverty in families, inability to provide for basic needs, and a declining standard of living for families (Kenya, 2002).

Women and Gender Issues. In 1999, 37% of all households were female headed, compared to 35% in 1989. More females (62%) than males (38%) had not attended school. Out of the population working for pay in 1999, 71% were males and 29% were females. The implication is that wage employment is still dominated by males both in urban and rural areas. As far as economic activity is concerned, 58% of the women, compared to 42% of the men, were economically inactive in 1999. The general conclusion is that though there have been efforts to improve gender equity, women still continue to occupy a disadvantaged position socially, economically, and politically (Kenya, 2002).

Beyond the shifts that influence family life listed above, other major shifts have more direct and intimate influence on contemporary family life. The following generalizations have been made in terms of the transitions taking place that have an impact on the family. For instance, changes include the following: shifts from collectivism to individualism, from polygyny to monogamy, and from large to small families (as well as postponement of marriage to later ages); increases in the number and proportion of nonmarital families; decline in the fertility rate and the increased adoption of modern contraception; a shift from initiation to alternative rites of passage to adulthood; an increase in one-parent households and cohabitation of unmarried adults; a shift in child care arrangements; institutional care of HIV/AIDS orphans; and a decrease in the length of the East Africans' adult life span.

Ongoing and Emerging Changes

Historic patterns of East African family life that persist to current times compete with modifications to those patterns and with challenges that compel some changes or elimination of these historic patterns. There are shifts in patterns and external circumstances that motivate new patterns. These combine to shape current and as yet unseen futures for East Africans.

Shift from Collectivism to Individualism. One of the distinguishing features of contemporary East African families is the decline in centrality of the extended family system and the increasing emergence of centrality of the nuclear family system. There is a decreasing authority and dominance of the extended family over nuclear families and over individuals. For instance, marriage appears to be changing to more of an individual matter rather than being the traditional collective family concern. There is more freedom of choice in mate selection by the young and a shift from parental choice of suitor to self-choice. This corresponds to an emerging shift from parent-arranged marriages to individual companionship marriages. Girls have more freedom of choice in mate selection today than in the past. Bride-wealth payment has shifted from transfer of cattle and nonmoney goods and services to the transfer of money from the groom's to the bride's family. In most instances, the groom raises the bride-wealth by himself without assistance from relatives, especially among the urban and more educated. The traditional significance of bride-*wealth* has shifted from a positive token of appreciation and recognition of the value of a wife to a modern commercialized understanding of bride-*price*. The trend toward demanding a high payment of bride-wealth for daughters is becoming common in modern Kenya. In contemporary East Africa, the more highly educated the girl, the more the bride-price (i.e., in distinction to the traditional idea of bride-wealth) she is expected to fetch. Wedding ceremonies have undergone changes from a traditional, relatively inexpensive and prolonged marriage ritual to an expensive 1-day Western-type wedding ceremony. Modern couples have a choice of legally recognized marriage contracts from Christian, Islamic, Hindu, and civil marriage in addition to the legally recognized African customary marriage (Kayongo-Male & Onyango, 1984).

Shift From Polygynous to Monogamous Marriage. Several factors are associated with the shift from polygynous to monogamous marriages, such as religion, cost of maintaining an extended household, the location of residence, and level of education. Unlike the African customary and Islamic marriages, which are potentially polygamous, Christian, Hindu, and civil marriages are monogamous. People who profess Christianity account for 92.2% of the population, Muslims account for 5.1%, and the rest practice other religions (Kenya, 1999). The cost of maintaining a family and maintaining a high enough standard of living is a deterrent to polygynous marriages, which lead to large families. In addition, the shift from rural to urban residence and the increasing cost of housing do not support the traditional polygynous homestead. The rate of polygynous marriages in Kenya is declining. Available statistics in Kenya indicate that the practice of polygyny has declined from 30% in 1977 to 16% in 1998, with the highest proportions being among older women (Kenya, 1999).

Data from Tanzania indicated that 29% of married women were in a polygynous union (Tanzania, 1997), whereas in Uganda the figure for the same period was 30% (Uganda, 1996). Across East African countries, an inverse relationship was found between polygyny and the level of education among women. In Kenya, data showed that 29% of the women in a polygynous marriage had no formal education compared to 11% with secondary education (Kenya, 1999). In Tanzania, the corresponding figures were 39% and 22%, respectively (Tanzania, 1997), whereas in Uganda the figures were 32% and 27%, respectively (Uganda, 1996). Related demographic developments in Kenya indicated that older women (25%) were more likely to be in a polygynous union than younger women (10%). Polygyny was higher among rural women (17%) than their urban counterparts (11%). In Kenya, there were substantial geographical variations in the practice, with Central Province having the lowest (4%) and Nyanza the highest (24%) rate. Differentials in the age of women and urban-rural residence for Tanzania and Uganda parallel those observed for Kenya.

Marital Status. More women are choosing to remain single, thus reducing the level of fertility. However, this has resulted in an increased number of births outside marriage. An increase in age at first marriage has been reported, from the early teen years to the early 20s for women and mid-20s for men.

Increase in One-Parent Households. Whereas marriage was practically universal for women of reproductive age in traditional settings, the current trend shows that only 59% are currently married; 3% are living with a man; 8% are widowed, divorced, or separated; and 30% have never married (Kenya, 1999). More women are remaining single and choosing to have children outside of marriage. Likewise, whereas extended families were the norm in traditional families, contemporary families are characterized by a combination of nuclear families with two parents, single parents, and children living with neither parent, but there still exist extended family obligations and loyalties (e.g., providing support to immediate family members and more distant relatives). According to the 1998 Kenya Demographic and Health Survey (KDHS), 58% of children under 15 years of age were living with both their parents, 26% were living with their mother alone, 3% were living with their father alone, 10% were living with neither parent, and 3% did not indicate their living arrangements. As long as the numbers of premarital childbirths, separated couples, and divorced couples keep on increasing, the number and proportion of one-parent households may be expected to continue rising. Of the 29% of children currently living in households that are maintained by one parent, the majority live with their mother alone, which accounts for 26% of all households with children (Kenya, 1999).

Increase in Cohabitation. Whereas in traditional society, cohabitation was rare and was regarded with scorn until the couple formalized their marriage, in modern East African society, an increasing number of young people are postponing marriage and opting to live together informally as unmarried couples (Frederiksen, 2000). The 1998 KDHS survey reported that 3% of the women were living together with a man, compared to only 1% of men reporting they were cohabiting. In Tanzania, the figures are 6.7% and 4.1%, respectively, indicating a higher incidence of cohabitation than in Kenya (Tanzania, 1997). The figures in Uganda are 9.1% for women and 3.1% for men (Uganda, 1996). Given recent trends, the future proportion of young couples living together before marriage (or as an alternative to marriage) seems likely to increase. Another category of cohabiting couples are working adults who are not currently living with their spouses. Formal education and employment coupled with urbanization have resulted in prolonged separation between husbands and wives. In Kenya, more men than women are engaged in the labor market and live in urban areas. Out of the national population working for pay in 1999, 71% were males and 29% females (Kenya, 1999). Wage employment is still dominated by males in urban areas. Married men living in towns find it difficult to live with their wives and children because of the high cost of living compared to rural areas. This kind of spousal separation for long periods encourages cohabitation of married men with unmarried women and vice versa.

Housing. The changing profile of household structure (i.e., marriage structure, household composition, and household size) is related to housing, particularly to extant urban housing. Between 1989 and 1999, household size declined from 5.0 to 4.4 persons. In terms of home ownership, 71% were owners compared to 73% in 1989, and 29% were renters compared to 27% in 1989. Only 30.6% had access to piped water, compared to 31.9% in 1989. These statistics show deterioration in housing amenities even though household size had decreased.

Shift in Child Care Arrangements. Whereas in traditional society, relatives within the extended family system provided voluntary and free child care services, the shift to a nuclear family involves an increasing amount of distance and reduction of extended family obligation to assist with details of everyday family life, such as assistance with child care. Thus, in modern East African family life, parents in general and particularly mothers with young children must provide most care themselves or engage hired help. Where both parents work outside the home, domestic workers, referred to as maids or house-helps, are employed to provide child care services. Reports from employed Kenyan women with a child under 6 years of age indicated that 42% took care of their children while working, 17% had a relative to look after their children, 15% had their children under the care of a sibling, 10% engaged hired help, 2% had their children taken care of by husband or partner, and the rest (12%) had children cared for by neighbors or friends (Kenya, 1999).

Population Increase. Shifts in marriage structure (i.e., increasingly monogamous) notwithstanding, the population continues to increase. The total population of Kenya continued to rise from 21.4 million in 1989 to 28.6 million in 1999. Of this total 50.3% were females and 49.7% males. There were more persons (54.6%) in the younger age groups (0 to 19 years) than in the older age groups (20 to 80 and above), who accounted for 45.4% in both urban and rural areas. As the population increased over the 10-year period, population density also increased from 37 to 49 persons per square kilometer, thereby exerting increasing pressure on land and other resources (Kenya, 2001).

Fertility. Despite the complex changes in family life, including the decreasing numbers of polygynous marriages but increasing population, the overall rate of fertility is declining. The total fertility rate dropped from 8.1 in the 1970s, to 6.7 in the 1980s, and down to 4.7 in the 1990s. In 1999, the fertility rate for married mothers was almost double (6.1) that for single mothers (3.4). Rural-urban differences were noticeable, with rural women having more children (5.2) than urban women (3.1 children). Fertility differentials by women's education were remarkable: Women with no education had an average of 5.8 children compared with 3.5 for women with secondary education. Women's education is, therefore, associated with reduced fertility.

According to the KDHS, which was conducted on a nationally representative sample in 1998, fertility preferences continue to change from the desire for large to small family size, with 53% of women and 46% of men indicating that they did not want to have any more children. Another 25% of the women and 27% of the men reported a desire to delay having their next child for 2 years or longer. Thus, about three fourths of women and men wanted either to limit or to space their childbirths. According to the survey, if all unwanted births were avoided, the fertility rate would fall from 4.7 to 3.5 children per woman (Kenya, 1999).

Shift From Large to Small Family Size. Several factors are associated with the shift from large to small family size, among them the increasing postponement of marriage and the resulting rising age at first marriage, the declining fertility rate, and increased use of modern contraception to space or limit births. The average size of a Kenyan household has decreased from 5.0 persons in 1989 to 4.4 persons in 1998. Urban households were on average smaller, with 3.3 persons compared to rural households with 4.6 persons (Kenya, 2001). The move to smaller family size is also partially a reflection of alternative family forms (e.g., the variety of single-parent and nonmarital households), increasing use of family planning, and the postponement of the age at first marriage.

Postponement of Marriage. For most societies, marriage marks the point in a woman's life when childbearing becomes socially acceptable. Women who marry early have, on average, a longer duration and exposure to childbearing. Therefore, societies with an early age at first marriage tend to have higher fertility levels. The age at which East African women and men first marry has risen in recent years. Traditionally, a girl was betrothed at an early age, and by puberty (12 to 14 years) she was married to a young man quite a few years older. In recent years, the age gap between men and women at marriage has been declining, with women marrying at a later age. Kenyan women marry, on average, at 20 compared with age 25 for men, whereas in Uganda the ages are 17 and 23 years, and in Tanzania 19 and 24 years, respectively. On average, East African men first marry 5 years later than do East African women. Rural-urban differentials also exist, with urban men and women marrying at least 2 years later than their rural counterparts.

A similar pattern is observed for both males and females for education differentials; those with secondary education marry 5 years later than those with no formal education (Kenya, 1999; Tanzania, 1997; Uganda, 1996).

Use of Family Planning. Knowledge and use of modern family-planning methods have continued to rise over the years. By 1998, virtually all married women (98%) and men (99%) were knowledgeable about modern contraception. Use of contraception rose from 27% in 1993 to 39% in 1998, with noticeable differentials by education. Only 23% of women with no formal education compared to 57% of women with secondary education were using contraception to either space or limit births. From the foregoing discussion it is evident that the traditional emphasis on childbearing and large families has been challenged by contemporary ideas and demands on families through postponement of marriage, declining fertility rate, and use of contraceptives (Bankole & Ezah, 1999; Kenya, 1999; Kimuna & Adamchak, 2001). However, the increased use of family planning is associated with higher levels of education and improvements in spousal communication (Kimuna & Adamchak).

Shift From Initiation to Alternative Rites of Passage. The initiation of youth into adulthood was a prerequisite to marriage among many ethnic communities in East Africa. Since the introduction of formal education and Christianity, FGM as a form of initiation for girls has been proscribed. Instead, alternative rites of passage have been introduced in communities where FGM was almost universally accepted, such as the Maasai, the Meru, and Kisii communities. According to the 1998 KDHS report, the prevalence of FGM in Kenya has declined significantly over the past two decades, from 50% in the oldest age cohort to 25% in the youngest cohort. However, there exists a wide variation across ethnic groups, from virtually no FGM practice among the Luo and Luhyia to very widespread or universal practice among the Kisii and Maasai. In terms of future trends, three fourths of Kenyans reported that they would like to see the FGM practice stopped and alternative rites of passage introduced (Kenya, 1999). Criticism and widespread social disapproval of FGM has led to decreased practice. However, beyond the informal condemnation, in 2002 the Government of Kenya formally outlawed FGM following the enactment of the Children's Act of 2002, which criminalizes FGM. Thereafter, the communities that still practice FGM, such as the Maasai and Meru, have begun to introduce alternative rites of passage that are similar to the old schools of initiation but without the FGM practice. However, old customs die slowly. In Tanzania, 18% of the women are circumcised. Young girls and urban women are less likely to be circumcised (Tanzania, 1997).

Childhood Mortality. In Kenya, there was a consistent decrease in childhood mortality from 170 per 1,000 live births in the 1960s to 97 in the 1990s. However, this trend was reversed between 1989 and 1999, during which time the childhood mortality rate increased to 120. A high rate of childhood mortality is associated with three factors: young mothers, short preceding-birth interval, and low level of maternal education. Attainment of a completed primary education was associated with 25% reduction in childhood mortality compared to 48% reduction for mothers with a secondary level of education. Expectations for single parents and other emergent family forms and demands are facing increasing challenge with the rising tide of AIDS orphans; the demands for provision of social and financial support have in many cases exceeded the capacity of extended families to meet the challenge.

Adult Life Expectancy. There was a consistent increase in life expectancy from 49 years in the 1960s to 54 in the 1970s, and then to 59 in the 1980s. However a noticeable drop has been reported in the 1990s, to 57. The major factor contributing to the recent reversal in the trend toward an increasing life span for people in sub-Saharan Africa is HIV/AIDS.

HIV/AIDS. On the African continent, about 26.4 million people are currently infected with HIV/AIDS. In Kenya alone, 2.2 million are infected, and 1.5 million people have developed AIDS since the beginning of the epidemic in 1984. Of these, 75% of AIDS cases occur in adults between the ages of 20 and 45, with male and female cases being about equal. The peak ages for AIDS cases are 20–24 years for women and 30–34 years for men. Young women in the age groups 15–19 and 20–24 years are more than twice as likely to be infected as males in the same age groups. About 10% of reported AIDS cases occur in children under 5 years of age. Most of these cases are caused by mother-to-child transmission (National AIDS Control Council, 2001).

Institutional Care of HIV/AIDS Orphans. A study of HIV/AIDS orphans in Kenya found more than 900,000 such children in 2000, which is expected to increase to 1.5 million by 2005. With the advent of the HIV/AIDS pandemic and the increased number of AIDS orphans, child care has shifted from the extended family to include institutional care (child orphanages). A study by UNICEF in 14 Kenyan districts found over 80,000 children in institutional care in 1997. By 2001, the number had risen to 350,000 children enrolled in 228 institutions. As the burden of orphans continues to rise, institutional resources will not be available to sustain care at an acceptable standard. Because not all needy children can be enrolled in institutions, elderly grandmothers and older siblings as young as 10 to 12 years continue to provide care to the majority of orphans (UNICEF, 2001). The problem is further compounded because many families have multiple sets of HIV/AIDS orphans living with elderly grandparents who are already struggling to care for other relatives or their own deceased adult children's orphaned children and who are themselves unable to provide for their long-term interests. These elders are often living in communities where the number of families in similar circumstances outstrips the capacity of the community to support them.

CONCLUSION AND IMPLICATIONS FOR THE FAMILY OF THE FUTURE

Contemporary East African families are undergoing new and large challenges to the traditional patterns that have served them so well over recent times. It is clear that ideas about marriage, parent-child interactions, extended family relations, and mate selection are undergoing major alterations. Although many changes have occurred, there has not been a complete transformation to a Western or other style of family life, nor is that likely ever to transpire. East African culture is unique, draws from different resources and history, and is likely to create its own adaptations to contemporary demands. It is clear that the understanding, expectations, meaning, and family organization around both gender and generation are shifting in ways that change present-day family life and that these imply a myriad of changes for the future that are difficult to predict.

In this chapter, we have documented a variety of ways in which current East African families have less emphasis on and control by extended family than was true only a few years ago. This is related to the increasing demands on the younger generation for attaining higher levels of education, increased young adult choice and control in mate selection (i.e., decreasing amounts of control by elders and the extended family), a changing balance of privilege to obligation in relations with extended family, and changing perspectives about children's value to parents and role in families. Each of these themes reflects changes in how family life plays out and provides some insights about changes that may be imminent.

Increased choice in mate selection by adults reflects an emerging ideology of "romance" as a criterion for marriage. This ideology may be imported from other cultures but might not be well matched to (extended) families that have defined marriage as a structure supported and controlled by the extended kin (i.e., the larger family has a stake) and who expect fidelity and submission of the marriage to the larger entity. Shifts in the basis (i.e., to a "romantic" criterion) for marriage choice alter the power of choice versus obligation and transform relations across generations, alter the understanding of male-female relations (e.g., how and by whom roles are performed such as domestic, child socializer, breadwinner) in marriage, and potentially alter how parents think about their female and male children. Thus, marriage choice patterns have potentially far-reaching effects on family life.

The balance of privilege to obligation in relationship with extended family is both a precursor to and reflection of changes in family size and what it means (e.g., each additional child as an asset who produces labor vs. each additional child as an increased economic and material burden). Smaller families may also presage how parents "invest" in their children (e.g., with fewer children, there may be increases not just in economic investments but also in time, emotional connections, and companionship). Fewer children could portend increased attention and valuing of marital roles over parenting roles and a shift in understanding the nature of marriage and family from an extended family to nuclear family ideology.

Changing perspectives about the value of children both reflect and may foreshadow other changes in perspective. It is clear that for many families in contemporary East Africa, children occupy a different meaning than was true in a less complex and rural lifestyle. The large number of street and homeless children in urban areas, the increasing number of AIDS orphans, and the reported rise in child abuse all suggest either an incapacity of traditional family patterns or that the force of these contemporary realities overwhelms traditional patterns of family life.

The decrease in family size reflects an economic reality; not only is it more expensive to provide the child care, food, education, clothes, health care, and other amenities expected by modern parents, but the responsibility of caring for children has increasingly moved from being shared with extended family to the nuclear family. These changes have intensified the control and felt onus by modern parents (especially urban parents). This in conjunction with higher levels of education contributes to changing expectations and mandates of modern parents and children compared to previous generations (i.e., changes in the style and nature of parent-child relationships).

Modern East African families are increasingly more nuclear in their organization and functioning. Although there continue to be felt obligations to the extended family (e.g., for social and financial support), married couples have fewer obligations to (and rights from) extended families than was formerly true. There is more nuclear family and parental control of family matters, related particularly to marriage and children. It seems likely that these patterns will continue (i.e., increasing control over marriage and children by the nuclear family) to evolve with less and less support expected or given by extended family. This may be the price of modern family life for escaping disproportionate levels of control by extended family; with this, however, comes decreased resource contributions from extended family. Modern East African families are likely to have fewer supports based on internal resources and therefore will make ever-increasing demands for formal, external support. The next generation may give birth to the so-called modern welfare state.

The social and economic impact of HIV/AIDS on the family, community, and society at large is far reaching as people continue to be infected and die in enormous numbers. One of the worst impacts of AIDS deaths on families is the increasing number of AIDS orphans. These children lack proper care, provision of basic needs, and above all nurturing socialization by their immediate families. Although many East African contemporary families valiantly struggle to provide for HIV/AIDS victims, in the end, it may overwhelm both their capacity to give support and some of the system of felt obligations typical of East African extended family life. AIDS will also have a significant impact on population size; AIDS deaths reduce the number of people in the reproductive age group and produce subsequently fewer births. AIDS has affected the health sector by increasing the number of people seeking HIV/AIDS-related health services, thereby increasing the cost of health care to every country in sub-Saharan East Africa. Furthermore, AIDS impoverishes families by decreasing household labor and income and increasing medical and funeral expenses. The family loses its potential for future income when children drop out of school to care for their ailing parents and to supplement family incomes. It increases child labor when children as young as 10 become full-time caregivers or child laborers in place of their sick or dying parents ("AIDS awareness," 2001).

HIV/AIDS is fundamentally challenging traditional patterns of how families take care of their vulnerable members. In many cases, adults with AIDS feel stigmatized or fear for the fate of their children once they are dead, because adult family members are already troubled by a large number of other family AIDS orphans who collectively exceed their ability to adequately provide for them. AIDS is greatly increasing the population of children who will be cared for poorly or not at all. AIDS is changing the face of how families take care of severely ill or dying family members. It is confronting East African families with challenges that traditional family patterns do not accommodate.

Assuming that the observed decline in fertility is maintained, it is anticipated that fertility will fall to 3.6 births per woman by 2010 and 3.2 births per woman by 2020. Given the predetermined impact of HIV/AIDS and its future course, life expectancy at birth is anticipated to drop from 50 years to 46 years by 2005. Considering the vigorous efforts directed toward combating the HIV/AIDS pandemic, the prevalence rate is expected to attain a constant level of 13% within the next 10 years, and thereafter, the rate is expected to decrease to 8.0% by 2020. Taking into account the interplay of fertility, mortality, migration, and the effect of the HIV/AIDS pandemic, the total population of Kenya is still expected to increase, but more slowly than in the last two decades (Kenya, 2001).

Contemporary East African families are dynamic and characterized by both continuity and change. Some of the highly regarded traditions such as collectivism and the extended family system, polygyny, parent-arranged and early marriages, bride-wealth payment, high fertility rates, FGM, and widow inheritance continue to undergo an evolution (e.g., the impact of HIV/AIDS on widow inheritance is obvious). Some aspects of traditionally accepted customs have been largely discarded or even outlawed (e.g., FGM through the enactment of the Children's Act of 2002), although not all communities have complied with the law. Other customs, such as parent-arranged marriages, bride-wealth payment, and widow inheritance, have been modified by consent of the parties involved. Other practices have been retained, such as strong loyalty to the extended family system and, to a smaller extent, the practice of polygyny. Some new practices have been adopted, for instance modern contraception to space and limit births. Alternatives have been introduced to fill the gaps in discarded practices such as FGM, which include alternative rites of passage to adulthood. Other modern practices involve the institutional care of orphans and the elderly rather than the communal care structures that existed in traditional societies. Informal unions such as cohabitation, single adulthood, single-parent households, and independent and unattached widows are examples of the African family in transition. Nevertheless, the Western bias toward and ethos about nuclear families seem unlikely to simply replace the traditional beliefs and ethos about the extended family.

Diversity of family life is increasing in Kenya. It is also clear that among educated, modern East Africans, family life is ostensibly more Western. However, it would be a mistake to simply see them as becoming more Western. Even with the myriad changes discussed herein, it is clear that modern East African families have additional and persistent themes that are African, not mere replication or imitation of European or American family patterns. In particular, we note that nuclear families are expected (a norm) to include selected live-in dependent relatives. Further, in African family life, there is a continuing centrality and meaning/requirement of children to marriage and family life. Even with the greatly increased family diversity, there is, for example, suspicion, invalidation, and doubt about childless couples and homosexual marriages.

Some family diversity is recognized in contemporary statutory law. However, even the law is not consonant with social, cultural, religious, and other realities, and these are often inconsistent with African traditions; for example, the definition of marriage as monogamous in contrast to polygamous. Additionally, legitimacy of children based on parents' marital status is in conflict with the traditional definition of legitimacy based on the status of bride-wealth payment by the husband/father to the wife/mother of the child in question, and the law of inheritance and succession is in conflict with the existing customary practice. For instance, among the majority of Kenyan ethnic groups, female children, regardless of age and marital status, do not inherit property from their parents or their parents-in-law.

Modern East African families are at a crossroads—trying to mesh traditional and contemporary expectations. Some would argue that the myriad new and changing demands have been met by family adaptations and transitions (cf. Wilson et al., 2003), whereas others would argue that East African families are facing a crisis of social change (Weisner, Bradley, & Kilbride, 1997). In this effort, we find a cultural lag manifested in a set of dichotomies, including those between rural and urban families, between younger and older generations, between more educated and less educated, between the affluent and the poor, between Christians and non-Christians, and between ethnocentric and nonethnocentric communities. We also note that families have undergone a transition from strict adherence to traditional customary regulation of marriage and family life to a more flexible and individually focused choice of lifestyle. The gaps in knowledge for further investigation include understanding the impact of modernization on the quality of life of contemporary families in the face of rapid sociocultural, economic, political, technological, and global change.

REFERENCES

Achatz, M. (1990). *Orientation of female secondary school students to work, marriage, and family in Western Province, Kenya.* Unpublished doctoral dissertation, University of Michigan, Ann Arbor.

AIDS awareness. (2001). *Kenyaweb.* Retrieved June 13, 2003, from http://www.kenyaweb.com/health/aids/impact.html

Ainsworth, M. D. S. (1967). *Infancy in Uganda: Infant care and growth of love.* Baltimore: Johns Hopkins University Press.

Atonia, M. (2003). *Marriage and family life among the Turkana.* Unpublished manuscript, Kenyatta University, Nairobi, Kenya.

Bankole, A., & Ezah, A. (1999). Unmet need for couples: An analytical framework and evaluation with DHS data. *Population Research and Policy Review, 18,* 579–605.

Beckwith, C., & Saitoti, O. T. (1980). *Maasai.* New York: Abrams.

Bitrus, D. (2000). *The extended family: An African Christian perspective.* Nairobi, Kenya: Christian Learning Materials Centre.

Bleeker, S. (1963). *The Maasai: Herders of East Africa.* New York: William Morrow.

Buchmann, C. (2000). Family structure, parental perceptions, and child labor in Kenya: What factors determine who is enrolled in school? *Social Forces, 78,* 1349–1379.

Cagnolo, C. (1933). *The Akikuyu: Their customs, traditions and folklore.* Nyeri, Kenya: Mission Printing School.

Frederiksen, B. (2000). Popular culture, gender relations and the democratization of everyday life in Kenya. *Journal of Southern African Studies, 26,* 209–222.

Hollis, A. C. (1979). *The Maasai: Their language and folklore.* Westport, CT: Negro Universities Press.

Kayongo-Male, D., & Onyango, P. (1984). *The sociology of the African family.* Essex, UK: Longman.

Kenya. (1999). *Kenya demographic and health survey: 1998.* Calverton, MD: Macro International.

Kenya. (2001). *The Republic of Kenya: 1999 population and housing census.* Nairobi, Kenya: Central Bureau of Statistics.

Kenya. (2002). *The 1999 population and housing census popular report.* Nairobi, Kenya: Central Bureau of Statistics.

Kenyatta, J. (1953). *Facing Mount Kenya: The tribal life of the Gikuyu.* London: Secker & Warburg.

Kihaule, D. C. P. (2002). *The Tanzanian family: Participation of women in family decision-making process. A descriptive-empirical study in Dar Es Salaam.* Unpublished doctoral dissertation, Pontificia Universitas Gregoriana, Facultas Scientiarum Socialium, Rome.

Kilbride, P. L., & Kilbride, J. C. (1990). *Changing family life in East Africa: Women and children at risk.* University Park: Pennsylvania State University Press.

Kimuna, S., & Adamchak, D. (2001). Gender relations: Husband-wife fertility and family planning decisions in Kenya. *Journal of Biosocial Science, 33,* 13–23.

Leaky, L. S. B. (1977). *The Southern Kikuyu before 1903.* London: Academic Press.

LeVine, R. A., LeVine, S., Leiderman, P. H., Dixon, T. B., Richman, A., & Keefer, C. H. (1994). *Child care and culture: Lessons from Africa.* New York: Cambridge University Press.

Madhavan, S. (2001). Female relationships and demographic outcomes in sub-Saharan Africa. *Sociological Forum, 16,* 503–527.

Mair, L. (1969). *African marriage and social change.* London: Frank Cass.

Mbiti, J. S. (1969). *African religions and philosophy.* London: Heinemann.

Mugo, E. N. (1982). *Kikuyu people.* Nairobi, Kenya: Kenya Literature Bureau.

National AIDS Control Council. (2001). *AIDS in Kenya: Background, projections, impact, interventions and policy.* Nairobi, Kenya: Author.

Ngige, L. W. (1993). *Intra-household resource allocation, decision making and child nutritional status in rural Thika, Kenya.* Unpublished doctoral dissertation, Michigan State University, East Lansing.

Nyai, C. (1961). *The changing position of women among the Meru of Kenya.* Rome: International Institute of Social Studies.

Ominde, S. H. (1952). *The Luo girl: From infancy to marriage.* Nairobi, Kenya: Kenya Literature Bureau.

Ominde, S. H. (1987). *The Luo girl: From infancy to marriage.* Nairobi, Kenya: Kenya Literature Bureau.

Phillips, A. (1969). Introduction to African marriage and family life. In L. Mair (Ed.), *African marriage and social change* (pp. vii–xiv). London: Frank Cass.

Saitoti, O. T. (1986). *The worlds of a Maasai warrior: An autobiography.* New York: Random House.

Sankan, S. S. (1971). *The Maasai.* Nairobi, Kenya: Kenya Literature Bureau.

Schafer, R. (1997). Variations in traditional marriage and family forms: Responses to changing patterns of family based social security systems in Sierra Leone and Kenya. *History of the Family, 2,* 197–210.

Sharman, M. (1979). *Kenya's people: The people of the plains.* London: Evans Brothers.

Snell, G. S. (1954). *Nandi customary law.* Nairobi, Kenya: Kenya Literature Bureau.

Tanzania. (1997). *Tanzania demographic and health survey: 1996.* Calverton, MD: Macro International.

Uganda. (1996). *Uganda demographic and health survey: 1995.* Calverton, MD: Macro International.

Unah, J. (2002). African theory of forces and the extended family relations: A deconstruction. *Analecta Husserliana, 74,* 265–276.

UNICEF. (2001). *Situation of AIDS orphans and vulnerable children in Kenya.* Nairobi, Kenya: Author.

Watson, M. (2000). Rites of passage: Birthing, naming, coming of age, marriage, elderhood, widowhood and death. In M. Watson (Ed.), *Modern Kenya: Social issues and perspectives* (pp. 246–268). Lanham, MD: University Press of America.

Weisner, T. S., Bradley, C., & Kilbride, P. L. (1997). *African families and the crisis of social change.* Westport, CT: Bergin & Garvey.

Wilson, S. M., Ngige, L. W., & Trollinger, L. J. (2003). Connecting generations: Kamba and Maasai paths to marriage in Kenya. In R. R. Hamon & B. B. Ingoldsby (Eds.), *Mate selection across cultures* (pp. 95–118). Thousand Oaks, CA: Sage.

CHAPTER 15

Families in Latin America

BRON B. INGOLDSBY

INTRODUCTION

The Latin American region runs from the Northern to the Southern Hemisphere and includes Mexico, Central and South America, and the Caribbean. Dozens of languages and dialects are spoken; economies include small-scale family farming and huge corporate plantations, high-tech and cottage industries; in some areas the traditional ways of life of indigenous cultures are preserved, whereas in others, such as large cities, culture and family life are transformed. In this chapter, I attempt to provide some background on family life in the Hispanic world. Because this area is so large and diverse, by necessity the sweep will be broad. This chapter will focus particularly on patterns of mate selection, highlight family patterns in some countries, and discuss family concerns that have been analyzed at length in the historical as well as more contemporary literature. We begin with the recognition that two major undercurrents have a profound effect on family life—poverty and patriarchal norms.

Poverty is a pervasive part of Latin American life. An estimated 40% of families in Latin America have insufficient income for essential needs, and another 28% can be categorized as "working poor" (David, 1987). Economic challenges families face and the roles of women in providing for their families are prominent themes in the literature.

When the Spaniards came to the Americas, they worked hard to impose their family ideals on the indigenous populations. That ideal was a patriarchal, monogamous, nuclear family (Munoz, 1983). Before this pressure, there had been significant variety among local peoples, including polygyny, cousin marriages, extended clans, and the more familiar patriarchal power and strict separation of tasks by sex (Boremanse, 1983).

The interplay between poverty and patriarchy is evident in the case of male out-migration to the United States or other countries in search of work to support their families (Wiest, 1983). When they are successful in locating jobs, their income allows the family to live better, but their absence strains the relationship. These separations may last for years, and although men are permitted to live their lives away from their home countries without interference, a wife rarely has affairs in her partner's absence out of fear of violence or abandonment. Even though the mother is responsible for the children, the absent father is the final decision maker and thus retains a presence in the home. This pattern holds in Mexico and other countries, where in many families patriarchal notions establish controls that limit women's activities and make it difficult for women to support themselves (Chant, 1993).

In contrast, in some subcultures, such as the black Caribs of Guatemala (Gonzalez, 1983), women change companions fairly frequently in search of economic support. They have also discovered that they can provide for themselves as well as their migrating menfolk can, and as a result, they are less likely than they were in the past to look up to men as leaders.

Another example comes from the area of health practices in Mexico. Anesthesia is often avoided in childbirth, because many Mexicans believe that the mother must endure pain in order to be a "real mother." This has nothing to do with the pros and cons of natural childbirth but is related to the biblical idea of women bringing forth children in sorrow. Some attribute miscarriages and other problems to *susto,* which means a "terrible fright." Even when their health is in danger, some women will avoid birth control, because the cultural view is that their main purpose in life is to reproduce. It is often believed that having children is proof of the husband's virility, and that using birth control might tempt the wife to have affairs (Haffner, 1992), a view that is enforced by male elders and community norms.

Studies indicate an increase in health risk-taking behaviors, such as the use of alcohol, tobacco, and other drugs, by adolescents in Latin America. Urzua (1993) found that 70% of Chileans consume alcohol by the time they finish high school, and a third had tried various chemical substances. He attributes this in part to sociocultural changes that come with modernization, leading to a disconnect between education and training and job opportunities. Another cause is the destabilization of the family brought about by increasing rates of separation and divorce and reduced day-to-day family interaction and communication. He found a positive correlation between family separation or illness and the prevalence of teen risk behaviors.

MATE SELECTION

A few studies have addressed the particular traits that Latinos look for in a potential mate (Gibbons, Richter, Wiley, & Styles, 1996; Styles, Gibbons, & Schnellmann, 1990). Teens in Guatemala, Mexico, Iceland, and the United States were asked to rank in order of importance the top 10 qualities of the ideal person of the opposite sex. It was hypothesized that these rankings would reflect the collectivistic or individualistic values of each of these cultures, and study results confirmed this projection. The U.S. sample, for example, demonstrated individualistic traits by valuing qualities such as having lots of money, being fun and sexy, and being physically attractive. Guatemalan adolescents showed collectivistic values by ranking "liking children" as important and "being attractive" as less important. Finally, respondents from Iceland and Mexico demonstrated mixed results, with Mexican teens valuing intelligence, kindness, and honesty, but also appearance.

An exhaustive study of birth and marriage records in Venezuela revealed mate-selection patterns to be very similar to those found in the United States (Jaffe & Chacon-Puignau, 1995). Women preferred to marry men who had a similar educational attainment, occupational level, age, and nationality. Husbands were older than wives in 70% of the cases, with the average age of marriage being 20 for women and 22 for men. Among unmarried couples, there was less parental investment by men and greater focus on the physical characteristics of men by women, whereas with married couples, men and women both focused on social characteristics, such as education, rather than beauty.

Couple-formation research in Ecuador (Schvaneveldt & Ingoldsby, 2003) revealed basic similarities between the United States and other societies. Young people in Ecuador marry for love, and they prefer a partner who is attractive, better off financially, healthy, and emotionally stable. Traits that made a potential companion unattractive included sexual problems, health issues, obesity, and difficult personalities. Previous cohabitation was not an issue.

Recently, many persons in Latin America have migrated into larger urban centers. Feldman (1994) found that rural peasants in Peru and Mexico who move to larger cities still tend to marry someone from their village area. It appears that economic associations exist in urban areas in which membership is based on common origin. These organizations form the basis for social interaction and, ultimately, mate-selection practices.

As in North America, changes in gender roles have occurred in Latin America, and these transitions have affected couple-formation practices. Rosenberg (1983) studied the impact of female employment on couple formation in Bogotá, Colombia. Interviews with employed women and their housewife neighbors revealed that working women married on average 2 years later (22 instead of 20) and had fewer children across the life span. In a related study, Heaton and Forste (1998) examined survey data from large samples acquired in Colombia, Peru, and Bolivia for changes in marriage and fertility patterns. Results indicated that the greater the educational level of a woman, the later the age of marriage (two thirds of uneducated women are married by the age of 20), the higher the rates of contraceptive use, and the fewer the number of children. Evidence indicates that the practice of cohabitation throughout Latin America is widespread (De Vos, 1999). Goldman and Pebley (1986), using data from rural surveys in Colombia, Costa Rica, Mexico, and Peru, found that over a third of all unions in these countries are consensual. Women who were older, better educated, and practicing Catholics were most likely to legally marry rather than cohabit. Interestingly, pregnancy did not increase the likelihood of a couple's legalizing their union. Moreover, there was very little use of birth control in these samples; those who are worried about the legitimacy of their children probably chose to form legal unions instead of cohabiting.

Studies on cohabitation in the United States demonstrate an increased risk of divorce for those who live together prior to marriage. In Latin America, the relationship between cohabitation and subsequent divorce is less clear. Some research shows that cohabitation actually increases marital stability, with part of this phenomenon due to the fact that the women who marry after cohabiting are older, and later age of marriage is correlated with marital stability. Other research indicates that cohabitation results in higher rates of eventual divorce (De Vos, 1999). Although the relationship between premarital cohabitation and subsequent divorce is not clear in Latin America, consensual unions are common and have a lengthy history in the region.

Castro Martin (2002) found that consensual unions have been an integral part of the family system in Latin America for centuries. Many poorer couples delay formal marriage because of the high cost involved. In most of Central America, consensual unions outnumber legal marriages, and the rate ranges from 25% to 50% in northern South American countries. In Mexico, Brazil, and the southern cone, the rates tend to be under 25%. Cohabitation rates also tend to decrease with age, because there is a tendency to formalize relationships as time passes.

Price (1965) described "trial marriages" as an important first step toward marriage in Andean cultures since the days of the Incas. During pre-Columbian times, premarital sexual relations were common and received social approval in the highlands of Peru. References to the "diabolical" custom of trial marriage are found as early as 1539, which was only a few years after the arrival of Pizarro. According to Price, a trial marriage generally preceded a Catholic wedding for the modern-day Quecha. Courtship behaviors included considerable sexual freedom, playful fighting, and gift exchanges. Free mate choice existed, but mate selection was endogamous, with virtually all couples marrying someone who resided within 10 miles of the community. The period of patrilocal cohabitation is called *watanaki,* which means having a year together. The young man simply informed his parents that he wished to enter into *watanaki* with a particular girl. Subsequently, his parents gave their approval and then visited her parents, who usually feigned surprise and indignation before giving their consent. Only about 7% of modern marriages among the indigenous people are not preceded by this trial marriage.

In summary, the literature on Latin American couple-formation practices indicates that cohabitation before marriage is common and culturally accepted. Latin American couples tend to be more endogamous and marry at younger ages than U.S. couples. Women are about 2 years younger than are the men at marriage, which is similar to the pattern in North America. Better-educated women tend to marry later and have fewer children, also similar to U.S. patterns. In contrast to studies on U.S. samples, some Latin Americans rank inner qualities and personality traits as being more attractive than the physical or individualistic traits of a potential mate.

THE LATIN AMERICAN FAMILY

In this section, I summarize some of the existing research pertaining to selected countries in Latin America. Both regional differences and general trends can be seen. Of particular importance is a shift to smaller nuclear families and single-parent and stepfamily households. In addition, family size is dropping because of declining fertility rates in recent decades, from an average of 11 children to fewer than 5 in the last two generations. Women have entered the paid labor force in large numbers since the 1970s; in most urban areas of Latin America, over half of women aged 25–34 are economically active. In large part, women are working outside the home out of economic necessity, even though throughout Latin America, men generally earn about 20% more than women do in urban areas, and the percentage can be considerably higher in rural areas. Without women's contributions, however, the poverty index would increase by 10% to 20% in most countries (Economic Commission for Latin America and the Caribbean, 1995).

Argentina

One major transition experienced recently is a movement toward greater autonomy and individuality. Young men in particular are moving out of their childhood homes and living on their own before marriage (Jelin, 1994). This has been hindered to some degree by the economic crisis of the 1970s, which has made it more difficult for them to find work. Women have also questioned traditional roles, and those who are better educated have moved into the workforce, which has contributed to the rise in male unemployment (Wainerman & Geldstein, 1994).

The 20th century witnessed an overall declining birthrate but an increase in adolescent fertility. In 1997, two thirds of all families in Argentina were classified as nuclear, down slightly from the previous decade because of an increase in individual and extended-family households (Palmero, 2002). In the late 20th century, there has been in increase in common-law unions, age at first marriage, number of children born out of wedlock, and separations. Other family forms, such as couples without children, female-headed households, and stepfamilies have all increased.

The present Argentine family is less patriarchal, with the husband sharing the breadwinning role and greater equality for women. However, as marital unions become less formal, they also appear to be less stable, with an increase in female-headed households and poor families (Palmero, 2002; Wainerman & Geldstein, 1994).

Brazil

Brazil is the fifth-largest nation in the world, and unlike its Spanish-speaking neighboring countries, the predominant language is Portuguese. In early colonial times, the economy was agrarian, and families tended to be extended, including workers as well as relatives and centered in a strong patriarch. Upper-class marriages were often arranged, whereas consensual unions were the norm for others. The Europeans benefited from Native American and African slave labor. Slave families were often separated so as to undermine the cohesion of the African groups (Metcalf, 2005).

The Catholic Church promoted the ideal of the stable monogamous family, sending women from Europe to marry colonialists as replacements for their Native American concubines. As in North America, the late 1800s saw a shift from extended to nuclear families and a new idealization of women as wives and homemakers who focused on their children. Mate selection moved to free choice based on love (Nunes, 2000).

Families in the more urban areas, such as Sao Paolo, have tended to be smaller and nuclear in structure. Children leave their parents to marry and build an independent life. As women have become more educated, the emotional and sexual needs of spouses have received more consideration (Correa, 1982). In the latter third of the 20th century, there has been an increase in the number of dual-worker, single-parent, and remarried families (Goldani, 1994). A dramatic increase in families in poverty has shifted much of the responsibility for survival to the adult women in the family, and there is some evidence that this has led to role overload (Diniz, 2002).

Since the 1980s, Brazilian families have experienced a decrease in average family size, a decrease in the percentage of couples without children, and an increase in the percentage of single-parent families and female-headed households (Oliveira, 1996). The average age at first marriage is 25.8 for men and 22.7 for women, with 93% of the population marrying by the age of 45 (United Nations Development Programme, 2000).

The most dramatic changes have come since the industrialization and modernization of the 1950s and 1960s. The rights of women, children, and the elderly have been expanded, and divorce has been legalized. Much of this was formalized in the 1988 Constitution (Genofre, 1995). Informal marriages are more common among the poor, though they aspire to legal marriage, which is seen as superior and more stable. In 1991, 21% of marriages in Brazil ended in divorce or separation (Oliveira, 1996).

Although the ideal of the traditional patriarchal family remains, diversity is being recognized. Consensual unions and the legitimacy of resulting children have legal status equal to that of formal marriage, and gay marriages have been recognized. Groups of Native Americans and African groups are gradually gaining better legal recognition and treatment as well (Diniz, 2002).

Regarding parenting practices, parents are given wide latitude by society in the discipline of their children, including corporal punishment. The line between discipline and abuse is rarely defined, and public consciousness of domestic abuse is new. Poverty is a major stressor, forcing many children into the labor market. The two main reasons that children leave home are domestic abuse and poverty (Lozano, 1997).

Another aspect of family life and gender relations is sexuality. There is a "culture of ambivalence" in relation to female sensuality. On the one hand, it is celebrated in the media and fashion, but it is also still believed that men have stronger sexual needs that are harder to control, leading to a continued acceptance of the sexual double standard (Parker, 1991).

In summary, Brazilian families and culture are shifting in the direction of valuing individual over traditional rights. Many of the patterns discussed here mirror those in Western industrial nations. Some scholars attribute these family changes to a modernization process that can be seen as both a crisis and an achievement in that it obscures and denies the importance of traditional practices, but also affords new opportunities for expression and equality, particularly for women (Sarti, 1995).

Costa Rica

Costa Rica has been strongly affected by the entrance of women into the paid labor force. Only about half of the population fits the traditional family structure of a couple and their children born within the marriage. The following information comes from a large survey undertaken at the University of Costa Rica (Vega Robles, 2000).

This study revealed that, regarding family structure, 57% of Costa Rican families are conjugal nuclear; 18% are extended; 16% are mother-child; and about 7% are what are called "large families," meaning households with at least two couples and other relatives. Masculine authority is recognized, in that 68% of households list the husband/father as the head of the home. The wife/mother was considered to be the head in 20% of the cases, and another family member in the remaining 12%. Overall, about 27% of adult women indicated that they participate in the workplace, but this increased to 52% for women who headed households.

Patriarchal values and beliefs about women were dominant during the time of the coffee economy in the later 19th century. These beliefs were called into question in the 20th century because of economic and political changes and the influence of feminist ideas. At present, patriarchal values are still strong, and women are uncertain as to their ability to enjoy a happy married life as well as participate in paid employment. There are concerns that female-headed households contribute to the disintegration of the family. Another study (George-Bowden & Burgess, 2000) confirmed that there continues to be resistance to changes in women's roles in Costa Rica, and in Latin America in general. There are laws to safeguard women's rights, but they are not always enforced, and textbooks continue to portray women mostly in domestic roles. Costa Ricans tend to believe that discrimination due to race, wealth, or gender has been eliminated, but the evidence is that these problems still continue to some degree (George-Bowden & Burgess).

Mexico

In Mexico, the family is a central concept to the culture, transcending generations and individuals. The pre-Hispanic Aztecs were generally monogamous, except for the nobility, who were permitted to practice polygamy. Marriage was a family affair, where the parents, rather than the couple themselves, made decisions about the selection of a spouse—but with the aid of fortune-tellers.

When the Spanish came, they imposed their traditions of monogamy and the importance of the extended family. One's family position determined his or her status in society as well. The Catholic Church allowed young people to select their own spouses and did not permit divorce. The father was the head of the house, and children were expected to honor and obey their parents (Gonzalez Gamio, 1997).

The contemporary Mexican family contains characteristics of both its Native American and European heritage, with the indigenous people representing traditionally feminine norms and the Spanish promoting the masculine *macho* cultural expectations. In reality, there are many types or approaches to family life in the contemporary society (Sanchez-Aragon, 2002). About three fourths of today's families have the nuclear structure, and the rest live in extended families (Instituto Nacional de Estadistica Geografia e Informatica [INEGI], 2000).

Marriage is popular, with over 95% of Mexicans marrying by age 50. Although some cohabit, over 80% are formally married. The average age of marriage is 26 for men and 23 for women (INEGI, 2000).

Contemporary married couples report communication difficulties as well as disagreements over child rearing, domestic chores, and finances while they form more egalitarian and individually based unions (Espinosa Gomez, 2000), and men are not participating in child rearing and housework at the same rate that women are entering the workforce. Although in recent decades, women's legal rights and economic opportunities have improved, men continue to exert their authority, including through coercion and domestic violence (Jordon, 2002). This may be a time of transition, because the large majority of Mexicans surveyed still believe that a good family is headed by a strong father who is supported by a sacrificing mother, along with growing acceptance of more egalitarian roles (Sanchez-Aragon, 2002).

Peru

Half of Peru's population lives in poverty, and the rate is even higher in rural areas and with the indigenous population (Instituto Nacional de Estadistica e Informatica del Peru [INEI], 2002). The ideal family type is patriarchal, with the wife subordinate to her husband and responsible for the education of their children. The *macho* double standard of sexuality continues, with the view that it is more difficult for men to control their desires and that women are morally superior and should remain chaste (Fuller, 1993).

Men generally believe that having many children is an indication of faithfulness in a wife, and that birth control is related to infidelity. In addition, having many children enables men to keep wives at home and, for women, ensures the financial support of their husbands. They are also an economic investment for the parents, who will depend on them for support in their later years (Ruiz-Bravo, 1995). In spite of the traditional advantages of larger family size, the average number of children has fallen from seven in 1950 to three in 2002, due mainly to a sharp decrease in fertility for urban women (INEI, 2002).

About one fourth of families in Peru are female-headed households (Fuller, 2000). Usually this occurs when the father in a cohabiting relationship has abandoned his family. These families usually suffer from inferior housing and reduced access to public services. As a result, many attempt to migrate to other countries in order to better provide for their children (Carbajal Mendoza, 2002).

Venezuela

Here, family dynamics have historically been described as matrifocal, with the mother as the stable decision maker (Pollak-Eltz, 1975). The cultural pattern has been considered matrilineal, even though it may appear to outsiders as patrilineal. Grandmothers have been key figures in this system. In one study of poor families in Caracas, half of the nuclear family groups lived in the grandmother's household, and the other half were in her neighborhood.

In these families, the group is basically women and children, with the husband/father as a marginal figure, even with formal or legal marriages. Women gain their status in society through motherhood, and even more fully when they become grandmothers and assist in the rearing of their grandchildren. Women are identified with the home and men with the streets.

Formal marriage is a desired ideal, but cohabitation is also seen as respectable and is common, especially among the poor (Hurtado Salazar, 2002). Of course, not all Venezuelan families are characterized as having the mother or grandmother at the center, but family research in this country has focused on this type.

FAMILY IDEALS

So, what is the "typical" Latin American family like? Some earlier research (Ingoldsby, 1980) indicated that psychological intimacy is not as highly valued in Latin America as in the United States. Comparisons of couples from the United States and Colombia found that high-satisfaction marriages in the United States were characterized by a high level of emotional expressiveness between spouses. This was not true for the Colombian couples, however. Their satisfaction was associated with having a similar level of expressiveness, be it high, medium, or low. Also, Colombian women and men were equally likely to say what they feel, and their level of expressiveness was at the same level as that of U.S. males. U.S. females were significantly more expressive as a group than their male counterparts.

More recent research in Ecuador (Ingoldsby, Horlacher, Schvaneveldt, & Matthews, 2005) indicated that the amount of expression of emotion in Latin American marriages has not increased, and that in fact, the women may be even less expressive than in the past. However, emotional expressiveness is now more strongly correlated with marital satisfaction. Sharing positive feelings while suppressing anger, especially by the husband, contributes significantly to happier relationships. These findings suggest that in recent years married couples have been moving to valuing more companionate marriages.

Unfortunately, the literature on Hispanic families has not explored this issue in depth. Rather, it has focused on what might be called "ideal types." The first, called *familism*, is a prominent cultural ideal that describes a close, loving, and religious family. The second type is *machismo*. Here, I argue that although machismo has historically been socially accepted, at least by lower-income families, it is an abuse of patriarchy due in large part to poverty.

Familism

Familism refers to a type of social organization that places the family ahead of individual interests and development. It is part of a traditional view of society that highlights loyalty and cooperation within the family (Perez, 2001). It includes many responsibilities and obligations to immediate family members and other kin, including godparents. Extended family members often live in close proximity to each other, with many often sharing the same dwelling. It is common for adult children to supplement their parents' income. In many ways, the Hispanic family helps and supports its members to a degree far beyond that found in individualistically oriented Anglo families.

A feeling of duty is developed among the members for each other, and there is a strong belief in the importance of having children (Popenoe, 1988).

Kephart and Jedlicka (1991) claimed that a large majority of Mexican American young people comply with parental rules in the following areas: (a) dating and marriage within their ethnic and religious group, (b) having parental approval and some supervision of dating, and (c) complete abstinence from sexual intercourse before marriage. American-born Hispanics were less likely to insist on the tradition of chaperoning their daughters on their dates, and it seems unlikely that all teens adhered to the no-sex rule. Nevertheless, these authors have given us a very positive picture of Latin American family life that also includes lower mental illness and divorce rates, greater personal happiness, and a secure feeling about aging.

Machismo

Two principal characteristics appear in the study of machismo. The first is aggressiveness. Each *macho* must show that he is masculine, strong, and physically powerful. Serious differences of opinion, verbal or physical abuse, or taunts and challenges must be responded to with fists or other weapons. The true *macho* shouldn't be afraid of anything, and he should be capable of drinking great quantities of liquor without necessarily getting drunk (Giraldo, 1972).

The other major characteristic of machismo is hypersexuality. The impotent and the homosexual are scoffed at—the preferred goal is the conquest of many women. To take advantage of a young woman sexually is cause for pride and prestige, not blame, and some men will commit adultery just to prove to themselves that they can do it. Excepting the wife and a mistress, long-term affectionate relationships should not exist. Sexual conquests are to satisfy male vanity. Indeed, one's potency must be known by others, which leads to bragging and story-telling. A married man should have a mistress in addition to casual encounters. His relationship with his wife is that of an aloof lord-protector. The woman loves, but the man conquers; this lack of emotion is part of the superiority of the male (Giraldo, 1972).

In the *macho* world, women believe in male superiority and prefer for their men to be strong and to protect them. According to the cultural stereotype, a man must protect his female relatives from other men, because women should be virgins when they marry. Knowing that other men are like himself, the macho is very jealous and, as a result, allows his wife very few liberties.

It appears that machismo may result from feelings of inferiority, possibly induced in early childhood. This is accomplished by avoiding feminine traits and emphasizing strong masculine ones. Ingoldsby (1991a) found that Latin American fathers showed a lack of affection toward their sons. The emphasis in the father-son relationship was on respect—characterized by separation, distance, and fear of the father as the domestic legislator of severe punishments.

Giraldo (1972) developed a circular model to explain the continuation of machismo across generations. Father-son relations and child-rearing practices and education created inferiority feelings in the boy. These were compensated for by the psychological mechanism of acting superior toward women and children by way of the cultural institution of machismo. This compensation produced child-rearing practices that created an inferiority complex in a new generation, and so on. Machismo, then, is a cultural trait to satisfy the psychological need resulting from the inferiority complex in men. The culture provides the way to its satisfaction, looking for feelings of superiority and transmitting them through the generations.

Female Support of Machismo

Some authors suggest that the woman's role in Latin American society serves to support machismo. The machismo ideal that expects that women of all classes should be virtuous and secluded goes back to colonial times in Latin America (van Deusen, 1997). Women were expected to be submissive and dependent and even to endure physical punishment from men. They were expected to be sexually passive, presumably waiting to be conquered by their virile partners. The cult of virginity, that is, the norm for women to stay virgins and to be indifferent toward sex until marriage, gave men the job of protecting their own female relatives and also made them feel even more macho when they succeeded in seducing a female partner. This line of thinking proposes that all of these culturally valued female traits are idealized in support of machismo. Following this simple line of reasoning, it becomes impossible to be a *macho* without a virgin to seduce, an inferior to protect, a submissive to dominate, or sisters to protect (Giraldo, 1972).

In other early work, Stevens (1973) discussed the other side of machismo, which she called *marianismo*. This term referred to the concept that women, particularly mothers, are semidivine, spiritually and morally superior to men. Although girls learn that they must cater to their father's whims and that they are less important than their brothers, they also learn that their mother is venerated and respected by all male family members. For this sainthood, women had to have many children, which not only satisfied the *macho* need for producing offspring but provided homage for the mother. Nevertheless, women could, if they were subtle, engage in men's activities, ultimately giving women the satisfaction of participating in a variety of roles and more freedom from the constraints of gender than men had. Stevens's construct referred mainly to the mestizo middle class, where labor was divided based on certain ideal characteristics for the members of each sex. This system depended on being able to continue to exploit the poorer indigenous members of the society as domestic servants.

According to this theory, male dominance is a myth, in part perpetuated by the women themselves because it preserves their way of life, which has certain advantages for them. However, it seems likely that what appears to be a mutually agreed upon relationship may in fact be enforced by male violence. Many women may have stayed with and accepted machismo out of fear, economic dependency, and the desire for their children to have a father. In addition, as discussed elsewhere in this chapter, there is evidence that, buttressed by financial resources from labor force participation and higher education levels, many women are challenging men's authority and refusing to accept a submissive role.

In summary, two prevailing ideals of the Latin American family are familism and machismo. No doubt they have both been correct to some extent, defining different families in a diverse society. Familism has represented the traditional ideal, still adhered to by many families. Machismo has also been a common style. In reality, Latin American families are diverse and changing as egalitarian relationships, divorce and remarriage, and nonmarital births become more common, and as violence and patriarchy are called into question.

STREET CHILDREN

One of the most negative outcomes of the *macho* family is its treatment of unwanted children, an area that has received some public media attention in recent years. A widespread problem throughout Latin America is the proliferation of young children living on their own in the streets. UNICEF estimates that there are over 40 million children surviving on their own without parental supervision. Aptekar (1990) claimed that this is not as tragic and threatening as might be believed. His research suggested that the children were not so much abandoned as they were encouraged into early independence. This was virtually a necessity in poor, female-headed households. Most writers have seen it in a more negative light, however.

Who They Are

Paul Velasco (1992) interviewed 104 street boys in Guayaquil, Ecuador, and the following profile emerged. They ranged in age from 8 to 18, with 13 the most common age (31%, with 12- and 14-year-olds at about 15% each). The large majority, 62%, had been on the street for less than 2 years, and on average they had a third-grade education.

Over half of these boys had seen their parents within the last year. This is consistent with research that indicates that street boys are not lost in the sense of not knowing where their home and family are. In order to survive, each boy had one or two "jobs." Selling and begging are common, but shining shoes was the work they mentioned most often (38.5%). Another 19% identified themselves as "artists," with about half of them acting like clowns for money and the others being comics or singers. Few admitted to being thieves, though they were feared by the community, especially for violence and stealing car parts. They typically stayed within a certain part of town and slept on the sidewalks, or even in the sewers to avoid harassment by adults. They formed their own small communities, as exemplified by the fact that four fifths went by nicknames given to them by their comrades.

The Colombian term for runaway or abandoned children who live on their own and on the street is *gamine*. There are an estimated 5,000 *gamines* in Bogotá alone, and *gamines* in smaller cities and towns remain uncounted. They are mostly boys (there are girls as well, but they have received less attention by researchers and the media), and as in Ecuador, they live in small groups, controlling a territory where they sleep at night under cartons or sheets of plastic. They work hard each day to survive, by begging or stealing (Ingoldsby, 1991b).

Why They Leave Home

There are many suggested reasons why these boys leave their homes, including lack of love at home, child abuse, neglect of basic needs due to parental unemployment, too much unsupervised free time, and escaping overwork by parents for the freedom of the streets. Parental rejection appears to be the chief cause, as parents already burdened by unemployment, poverty, and financial stress find marriage and child rearing extremely difficult. To quote de Nicolo, a Catholic priest in Colombia who has established many orphanages for abandoned street children, "Due to poverty it is impossible to hold the family together" (J. de Nicolo, personal communication, 1987).

The predominant pattern resulting in a *gamine* appears to be as follows: A young man moves from the country to the city in search of a better life. He doesn't find it because unemployment is consistently and extremely high, creating widespread poverty. He does fall in love and marries. This young husband cannot find work, becomes depressed, and eventually leaves his wife and children.

Another man moves in with the children's mother. This "stepfather" (informally so, because divorce and remarriage are rare in Colombia) is not interested in the offspring of a previous union; he pushes the boys away, generally when they are 8–12 years old; rejected, they leave for the street. Almost half (47%) of all *gamines* have stepfathers. The mother, for fear of violence and retaliation by her new husband, doesn't try to bring her sons back (Ingoldsby, 1991b). Clearly, this sequence takes place in an environment characterized not only by poverty but by violence. In a climate of isolation and without adequate social supports and resources, families find it nearly impossible to break the cycle of unemployment and poverty, desertion and child abuse and neglect. Similar conditions can result in abandoned children in any culture of poverty, not just in Latin America.

FAMILY VIOLENCE

Child abuse and domestic violence (also called spouse abuse or intimate partner violence), now widely discussed in U.S. society, received very little attention in the United States before 1970. Even though violence does not fit our notion of what home life should be, it affects thousands of women and children each year. Leading researchers have concluded that family violence is more common in male-dominant marriages and in societies that condone violence in general. Another predictor is the privacy of the conjugal family, which could predispose Western societies toward violence.

However, family violence is widespread throughout the world (Straus, 1977). For example, studies in Oceania (Counts, 1990) attributed domestic violence to patrilocal residence and bride-price: Paying for a wife and controlling her environment increased cultural support for male dominance. According to one study, in 84.5% of 90 different societies, wife beating was found to occur at least occasionally (Levinson, 1989).

The serious problem and pervasiveness of intimate partner violence in the United States has received considerable attention in recent years. For instance, public polls have indicated that one fifth of all spouses approve of a man slapping his wife under certain circumstances. More assaults and murders are committed within the family than in any other context. In fact, one third of all women killed are victims of their husband or boyfriend, and a woman is more likely to kill her husband than to kill anyone else (Wells, 1991).

Wife abuse is consistently mentioned as commonplace in traditional Hispanic families. One study (Straus & Smith, 1989) found that almost one fourth of Latino couples experienced violence in their relationship, a rate over 50% higher than for Anglo couples. Elements of machismo may contribute to this situation. One factor is alcohol abuse. Estimates indicate that from 40% to 95% of all wife-beating situations are ones in which the husband has been drinking. Another is male dominance, or the man's right to force compliance to his wishes within his family. The last is low self-esteem, often related to financial problems. All of these predictors of spouse abuse are aspects of being a *macho* male (B. Ingoldsby & V. Ingoldsby, 1981).

Divorce is less acceptable and the family more hierarchical in Latino than in Anglo families. Many Latino men are reluctant to admit to using force to control women and instead claim that they are being protective. In addition, one study found that, compared to their Anglo counterparts, Latinas were more "tolerant" of physical and emotional abuse in their family life. They may be less likely to leave abusive relationships because of cultural traditions of sticking with their original marital commitments, and not wanting to get their family of origin involved in fights with their husband (Campbell, Masaki, & Torres, 1997).

CONCLUSION

Tragically, the poverty that permeates large segments of the Latin American population breaks down not only family structure but even the personal dignity necessary for traditional familism to function, and replaces it with the excesses of machismo such as desertion, intimate partner violence, and child abandonment. There is evidence, however, of movement toward what Western clinicians and scholars would describe as a more functional, healthy family.

A survey of 71 married women in Panama (Stinnett, Knaub, O'Neal, & Walters, 1983) revealed fairly egalitarian beliefs concerning marriage. Large majorities believed that (a) women should receive education equal in quality to that of men; (b) women should receive equal pay for equal work; (c) women are just as intelligent as men; (d) women are just as capable of making important decisions as are men; and (e) a wife should express her opinions even if her husband doesn't ask for it, and she should voice her disagreements with him.

On the other hand, most agreed that the husband is the head of the family, the wife must obey her husband, and the woman's place is in the home (even though 77% of the sample worked outside the home). This indicates a "separate but equal" attitude compatible with the familism construct.

Finally, some research has shown that Hispanic/Latino families that rate themselves as "strong" and that have a high level of marital satisfaction also value the rewards of companionate relationships. Casas, Stinnett, Williams, DeFrain, and Lee (1984) collected data from nine Latin American countries using Stinnett's Family Strengths Inventory. The most important factors for maintaining a happy family life were: (a) love and affection, (b) family togetherness, (c) understanding and acceptance, (d) mutual respect and appreciation, (e) communication and relationship skills, and (f) religion. Wives emphasized love and affection more than husbands did, and husbands were more likely than wives to mention the importance of religion.

A national survey of values in Mexico indicated positive attitudes toward gender equality. Men and women with higher socioeconomic status believed that husbands and wives should be equal and share in the work of household chores. This was also true for males with androgynous personalities (Beltran, Castanos, Flores, & Meyerberg, 1994). Dominican families who immigrated to the United States tend to become more egalitarian. After some initial resistance, husbands gave up many of their privileges, helped more with child care and domestic chores, and permitted their wives to work and participate in family decision making (Pessar, 1995).

There is evidence that a growing number of Latin American families value love and affection in the husband-wife and parent-child relationships more than they do the traditional authority/submissiveness approach. All of this bodes well for familism, which avoids not only the abuses of patriarchy, but the possible disengagement of Western individualism as well.

REFERENCES

Aptekar, L. (1990). How ethnic differences within a culture influence child rearing: The case of Colombian street children. *Journal of Comparative Family Studies, 21*, 67–79.

Beltran, U., Castanos, F., Flores, J., & Meyerberg, Y. (1994). *Los Mexicanos de los noventa: Una encuesta de actividades y valores: Parte I.* Unpublished manuscript.

Boremanse, D. (1983). A comparative study of the family lives of the northern and southern Lacandan Mayas of Chiapas (Mexico). *Journal of Comparative Family Studies, 14,* 183–202.

Campbell, D., Masaki, B., & Torres, S. (1997). Water on rock: Changing domestic violence perceptions in the African American, Asian American, and Latino communities. In E. E. Klein, J. Campbell, E. Soler, & M. Ghez (Eds.), *Ending domestic violence: Changing public perceptions/halting the epidemic* (pp. 64–87). Thousand Oaks, CA: Sage.

Carbajal Mendoza, M. (2002). Peru. In J. Ponzetti (Ed.), *The international encyclopedia of marriage and family* (pp. 1217–1223). New York: Macmillan.

Casas, C., Stinnett, N., Williams, R., DeFrain, J., & Lee, P. (1984). Identifying family strengths in Latin American families. *Family Perspective, 18*(1), 11–17.

Castro Martin, T. (2002). Consensual unions in Latin America: Persistence of a dual nuptiality system. *Journal of Comparative Family Studies, 33,* 35–55.

Chant, S. (1993). Family structure and female labor in Queretaro, Mexico. In L. Tepperman & S. Wilson (Eds.), *Next of kin* (pp. 205–210). Englewood Cliffs, NJ: Prentice Hall.

Correa, M. (1982). Repensando a familia patriarcal Brasileira. In M. Correa (Ed.), *Colcha de retalhos: Estudos sobre a familia no Brasil* (pp. 13–38). Sao Paolo, Brazil: Editora Brasilience.

Counts, D. A. (1990). Domestic violence in Oceania: Conclusion. *Pacific Studies, 13,* 225–254.

David, P. (1987). Children in despair: The Latin American experience. *Journal of Comparative Family Studies, 18,* 327–337.

De Vos, S. (1999). Comment on coding marital status in Latin America. *Journal of Comparative Family Studies, 30,* 79–93.

Diniz, G. (2002). Brazil. In J. Ponzetti (Ed.), *The international encyclopedia of marriage and family* (pp. 170–174). New York: Macmillan.

Economic Commission for Latin America and the Caribbean (ECLAC). (1995). *Social panorama of Latin America.* Santiago, Chile: United Nations Publications.

Espinosa Gomez, M. (2000). Exploración de los problemas familiares. *La psicología social en Mexico, 8,* 217–224.

Feldman, K. (1994). Socioeconomic structures and mate selection among urban populations in developing regions. *Journal of Comparative Family Studies, 25,* 329–343.

Fuller, N. (1993). *Dilemas de la femininedad. Mujeres de clase media en el Peru.* Lima, Peru: Fondo Editorial Pontificia Universidad Católica del Peru.

Fuller, N. (2000). *Significados de paternidad y reproducción entre varones urbanos del Peru.* Lima, Peru: Fondo Editorial Pontificia Universidad Católica del Peru.

Genofre, R. (1995). Family: A juridical approach. In M. do C. B. de Carvalho (Ed.), *The contemporary family in debate* (pp. 97–104). São Paolo, Brazil: Cortez.

George-Bowden, R., & Burgess, N. (2000). Forces that shape rural and urban life in Costa Rica. *Family Science Review, 13*(3–4), 119–132.

Gibbons, J., Richter, R., Wiley, D., & Styles, D. (1996). Adolescents' opposite-sex ideal in four countries. *Journal of Social Psychology, 136,* 531–537.

Giraldo, O. (1972). El machismo como fenómeno psicocultural. *Revista Latinoamericana de Psicologia, 4,* 295–309.

Goldani, A. (1994). As familias Brasileiras: Mundancas e perspectives. *Cadernos de Pesquisa, 91,* 7–22.

Goldman, N., & Pebley, A. (1986). Legalization of consensual unions in Latin America. *Social Biology, 28,* 49–61.

Gonzalez, N. (1983). Changing sex roles among the Garifuna (black Carib) and their implications for the family. *Journal of Comparative Family Studies, 14,* 203–213.

Gonzales Gamio, M. (1997). Aspectos históricos de la familia en la cuidad de Mexico. In L. Solis Panton (Ed.), *La familia en la ciudad de Mexico: Presente, pasado, y deviner* (pp. 33–47). San Angél, Mexico, D.F.: Pax Mexico.

Haffner, L. (1992). Translation is not enough: Interpreting in a medical setting. *Western Journal of Medicine, 157,* 255–259.

Heaton, T., & Forste, R. (1998). Education as policy: The impact of education on marriage, contraception, and fertility in Colombia, Peru, and Bolivia. *Social Biology, 45,* 194–213.

Hurtado Salazar, S. (2002). Venezuela. In J. Ponzetti (Ed.), *The international encyclopedia of marriage and family* (pp. 1693–1697). New York: Macmillan.

Ingoldsby, B. (1980). Emotional expressiveness and marital satisfaction: A cross-cultural analysis. *Journal of Comparative Family Studies, 11,* 501–515.

Ingoldsby, B. (1991a). The Latin American family: Familism vs. machismo. *Journal of Comparative Family Studies, 22,* 57–61.

Ingoldsby, B. (1991b). Street children and family life. *Family Science Review, 4,* 73–77.

Ingoldsby, B., Horlacher, G., Schvaneveldt, P., & Matthews, M. (2005). Emotional expressiveness and marital adjustment: A follow-up cross-cultural analysis. *Marriage and Family Review.*

Ingoldsby, B., & Ingoldsby, V. (1981). The macho male and wife beating. *Proceedings of the Ohio Council on Family Relations Annual Convention,* 48–51.

Instituto Nacional de Estadistica e Informatica del Peru (INEI). (2002). Retrieved May 19, 2005, from http://www.inei.gob.pe

Instituto Nacional de Estadistica, Geografia e Informatica (INEGI). (2000). *Censo nacional de población.* Retrieved April 22, 2005, from http://www.inegi.gob.mx

Jaffe, K., & Chacon-Puignau, G. (1995). Assortative mating: Sex differences in mate selection for married and unmarried couples. *Human Biology, 67,* 111–120.

Jelin, E. (1994). Familia: Crisis y despues. In C. H. Wainerman (Ed.), *Vivir en familia* (pp. 23–48). Buenos Aires, Argentina: Losada.

Jordon, M. (2002, June 30). In Mexico, an unpunished crime. *The Washington Post,* p. A01. Retrieved May 18, 2005, from http://www.pulitzer.org/year/2003/international-reporting/works/post4.html

Kephart, W., & Jedlicka, D. (1991). *The family, society, and the individual* (7th ed.). New York: HarperCollins.

Levinson, D. (1989). *Frontiers of anthropology: Vol. 1. Family violence in cross-cultural perspective.* Newbury Park, CA: Sage.

Lozano, A. (1997, May 29). Characteristics of the children who live and work in the streets of São Paolo. *Jornal Folha de São Paolo,* section 3, p. 7.

Metcalf, A. C. (2005). *Family and frontier in colonial Brazil.* Austin: University of Texas Press.

Munoz, J. (1983). Changes in the family structure of the Pokaman of Petapa, Guatemala in the first half of the 16th century. *Journal of Comparative Family Studies, 14,* 215–227.

Nunes, M. (2000). Women, family and Catholicism in Brazil: The issue of power. In S. Houseknecht & J. Pankhurst (Eds.), *Family, religion, and social change in diverse societies* (pp. 347–362). New York: Oxford University Press.

Oliveira, M. (1996). The Brazilian family near the year 2000. *Journal of Feminist Studies, 4*(1), 55–63.

Palmero, A. (2002). Argentina. In J. Ponzetti (Ed.), *The international encyclopedia of marriage and family* (pp. 78–82). New York: Macmillan.

Parker, R. (1991). *Bodies, pleasures and passions—Sexual culture in contemporary Brazil.* Sao Paolo, Brazil: Best Seller.

Perez, A. (2001). Familism. In J. Ponzetti (Ed.), *The international encyclopedia of marriage and family* (pp. 546–549). New York: Macmillan.

Pessar, P. (1995). *A visa for a dream: Dominicans in the United States.* Boston: Allyn & Bacon.

Pollak-Eltz, A. (1975). Household composition and mating patterns among lower-class Venezuelans. *International Journal of Sociology of the Family, 5,* 85–95.

Popenoe, D. (1988). *Disturbing the nest: Family change and decline in modern societies.* New York: Aldine de Gruyter.

Price, R. (1965). Trial marriage in the Andes. *Ethnology, 4,* 310–322.

Rosenberg, T. (1983). Employment and family formation among working-class women in Bogota, Colombia. *Journal of Comparative Family Studies, 14,* 333–345.

Ruiz-Bravo, P. (1995). Estudios, practices y representaciones de genero. Tensiones, desencuentros y esperanzas. In G. Portocarrero & M. Valcarcel (Eds.), *El Peru frente al siglo XXI* (pp. 441–468). Lima, Peru: Fondo Editorial Pontificia Universidad Católica del Peru.

Sanchez-Aragon, R. (2002). Mexico. In J. Ponzetti (Ed.), *The international encyclopedia of marriage and family* (pp. 1126–1130). New York: Macmillan.

Sarti, C. (1995). Family and individuality: A modern problem. In M. do C. B. Carvalho (Ed.), *The contemporary family in debate* (pp. 39–50). São Paolo, Brazil: Cortez.

Schvaneveldt, P., & Ingoldsby, B. (2003). An exchange theory perspective on couple formation preferences and practices in Ecuador. *Marriage and Family Review, 35,* 219–238.

Stevens, E. (1973). The prospects for a women's liberation movement in Latin America. *Journal of Marriage and the Family, 35,* 313–321.

Stinnett, N., Knaub, P., O'Neal, S., & Walters, J. (1983). Perceptions of Panamanian women concerning the roles of women. *Journal of Comparative Family Studies, 14,* 273–282.

Straus, M. (1977). Societal morphogenesis and intrafamily violence in cross-cultural perspective. *Annals of the New York Academy of Sciences, 285,* 719–730.

Straus, M., & Smith, C. (1989). Violence in Hispanic families in the United States: Incidence rates and structural interpretations. In M. Straus & R. Gelles (Eds.), *Physical violence in American families: Risk factors and adaptations to violence in 8,145 families* (pp. 341–368). New York: Transaction Books.

Styles, D., Gibbons, J., & Schnellmann, J. (1990). Opposite-sex ideal in the U.S.A. and Mexico as perceived by young adolescents. *Journal of Cross-Cultural Psychology, 21,* 180–199.

United Nations Development Programme. (2000). *World marriage patterns.* Retrieved May 15, 2005, from www.un.org/esa/population/publications/worldmarriage/worldmarriage.htm

Urzua, R. (1993). Risk factors and youth: The role of family and community. *Journal of Adolescent Health, 14,* 619–625.

van Deusen, N. (1997). Determining the boundaries of virtue: The discourses of *Recogimiento* among women in seventeenth-century Lima. *Journal of Family History, 22,* 373–389.

Vega Robles, I. (2000). Prospective analysis of the family process in Costa Rica. *Family Science Review, 13*(3–4), 1–9.

Velasco, P. (1992). [Study of street youth in Guayaquil, Ecuador]. Unpublished raw data.

Wainerman, C., & Geldstein, R. (1994). Viviendo en familia: Ayer y hoy. In C. H. Wainerman (Ed.), *Vivir en familia* (pp. 183–283). Buenos Aires, Brazil: Losada.

Wells, J. (1991). *Choices in marriage and family*. San Diego, CA: Collegiate Press.

Wiest, R. (1983). Male migration, machismo, and conjugal roles: Implications for fertility control in a Mexican municipio. *Journal of Comparative Family Studies, 14,* 167–181.

CHAPTER 16

Families in Japan

COLLEEN I. MURRAY AND NAOKO KIMURA

Fairy tales and folktales deal with motifs that reflect universal issues, and they also give us an insight into elements that are specific to the culture in which the story is told (Kawai, 1996a). European and American tales typically include a superior character (often a father) who sets down a taboo (e.g., a forbidden food, horrible room, or dangerous forest), and a character who is found guilty of breaking the taboo and is punished. The male hero, who sometimes is also the breaker of the taboo, has to fight against something (e.g., dragon, troll, or black knight) in order to get a treasure. That treasure is the beautiful maiden, and marriage is the valued final goal, so the couple lives happily ever after. Japanese tales also include a prohibitor/hero (often a woman) who sets down a taboo (e.g., forbidding a beautiful room or meadow), but when that taboo is broken, there is no direct punishment of the transgressor. It is the prohibitor who, seeing that the taboo was broken, is sad and disappears sorrowfully (e.g., turning into a bird), leaving the transgressor to feel the shame of having been seen. Japanese fairy-tale heroes are strong women, with strong wills and a sense of self and purpose; their personalities reflect simultaneous multiple layers and complexity. It is when men develop their capacity for "emptiness/nothingness" that blissful marriage to the feminine spiritual energy is possible. However, the masculine figures rarely rise to this goal, so in most cases when a couple marries, there is a tragic separation and no happy ending. In Western fairy tales breaking a taboo leads to a hero's adventure; in Japanese tales breaking of a taboo leads to the loss of everything.

Kawai (1996a) argues that from a Jungian perspective, the gender of characters has no physical meaning and is merely a reflection of the psyche, with feminine characters representing the ego and multiple layers of consciousness. However, it would appear that these tales can also tell us something about families within a culture. In addition to marital relationships, tales address parent-child relationships. In Japanese tales (developed before the process of conception was understood), the mother-daughter bond is strongest. Even when interrupted by a male (e.g., father or husband), the primordial unity between women eventually is revived and the male intrusion is eliminated, so the tales end with the mother-daughter relationship in a state as if nothing had ever happened. Father-daughter bonds in Japanese tales are also strong, but the strongest bond in Western tales is between father and son. Perhaps scholars have exaggerated the uniqueness of Japanese culture. However, if fairy tales do reflect cultural values and beliefs it would appear that there are, or at least were at some time, differences between family systems in Japan and those in Europe or the United States.

Japan's geographic location may contribute to the nature of its family system. It is a country composed of 4 main islands and approximately 3,900 smaller ones. Although it has experienced some diverse influences since early settlement, its island nature has afforded it limited occupation by outsiders until after World War II. Thus, Japan has developed indigenous family systems that, throughout history when confronted with outside influences, have found ways to integrate new philosophies with existing models. Although outside writers contrast the traditional Japanese family to modern Japanese families, the traditional family (sometimes referred to as a *stem family*) represents only a single stage in the family evolution process that has been going on for many centuries. Throughout Japan's history, outside philosophies and practices have been incorporated in family life, each time being adapted and grounded within the current and indigenous family system.

EARLY JAPANESE FAMILIES

The structures and roles related to family have undergone many changes during Japan's long recorded history. The earliest historical accounts suggest that prior to 100 CE, society was stratified, with ruling families that observed rituals to remember ancestors (Hendry, 2003). Families were polygamous; men and women were equal in relationships, with a husband visiting his wife and eventually living with her; and children were raised at the wife's home (Kaku, 1999). In the seventh century, Chinese influence brought to Japan Confucian practices, Buddhist theory, bureaucratic systems such as unified civil law, and the patriarchal family. An example of integration of old and new can be seen during the Heian era (794 to 1185 CE); in line with the Chinese patriarchal family concept, the husband became the head of family, although this existed within a matrilocal residence system, with husbands marrying into their wives' families (*muko-iri*) (Sougou joseishi kenkyuukai, 1992). Divorce and remarriage were common; marriage was a custom rather than legal status; marriage ceremonies were only for ruling families; and sexual behavior before marriage was the norm.

As unifying bureaucracies proved ineffective, there was a move away from Chinese approaches and toward a more regional feudal system (Hendry, 2003). Marriage became a ceremony among commoners. There was a movement toward monogamy (although there often were concubines or other wives), living in a house that the husband prepared, with wives marrying into their husbands' families.

During the 16th century, there was great regional strife, coinciding with the arrival of the first European explorers and missionaries. When the strife ended, Christianity was seen as a threat, nearly all Europeans were expelled, Japanese were prohibited from travel abroad, and a bureaucratic class system based on occupation was instated. New laws required families to register with a local Buddhist temple. Although during the Edo era (1603 to 1868 CE) Japan was isolated from the rest of the world, Confucian and Christian thought increasingly influenced Japanese family life. Eventually, a wife became expected to leave her family and live with her husband and his family; baby boys were more valued than girls, even if the boy's mother was a concubine; and women's affairs were prohibited by law. Although families arranged marriages among the samurai class, commoners often chose their own spouses.

THE *IE*

The policy of isolation ended with the Meiji era (1868 to 1912 CE), and various European systems of government were tried out. The concept of marriage based on free choice and love was reintroduced. Traditionalists feared that outside ideas would produce social ruin. A new series of laws was enacted, the Civil Code of 1898, which described a "family system" in a manner that reflected compromise between traditionalists (including indigenous, Taoist, and Confucian ideologies) and those wanting international influence (Hendry, 2003; Ishikawa, 2001). This family model was based on the indigenous Japanese system of samurai families from the 17th century to the 19th century, and it continues to be a legal and social force in Japan today (Maree, 2004), not only in families, but in corporations and organizations that were based on this model.

In the Civil Code of 1898, marriage became a legal structure, and families were required to register with local government, not a temple. Wives and husbands were to have the same family name, and marriage meant marrying into the husband's family (*yome-iri*) (Kaku, 1999; Kodama & Fukuda, 2000). Arranged marriages became common for all classes. During the early 1900s, men had to be at least 30 years old and women at least 25 to marry without parental permission. The indigenous term for the family system that became the legal structure in the Civil Code is *ie,* and it has some similarity to the European view of aristocratic families as a *house* (e.g., "the House of Windsor"), in which there is a continuing line that requires each generation to produce an heir (Hendry, 2003). A critical aspect of the *ie* system is its emphasis on continuity. Members include ancestors (those who died long ago and are now forgotten as individuals), those recently deceased who are still remembered in ceremonies, and descendants who are not yet born. Living members (who do not always reside in the particular house associated with the *ie*) are responsible for its continuity, through practices that remember ancestors and ones that ensure continuity of *ie* after their own deaths. In the original samurai family model, the *ie* itself was the unit that owned property. Under the Civil Code of 1898, property was registered with a specific individual who represented the *ie*, served as its head, managed its affairs (although delegation was possible), was legally responsible for its members, and could be removed by decision of its family council if the head was determined to be detrimental to continuity of the *ie*.

An *ie* was often associated with a particular occupation, and each member contributed to that occupation in whatever manner was possible, working toward continuity of the *ie*. Members were subordinate to the head, with a hierarchy based on age, gender, and expectation of future movement into the head position (Ishikawa, 2001). Confucian and Taoist principles of loyalty and benevolence influenced relationships; younger members were to be indebted to older members for their care, and, in turn, they were to take care of older members when needed. These relationship patterns were not based on a philosophy that valued individuals; more important, they were seen as contributing to the continuity of the *ie*.

Although the law stipulated inheritance through the oldest son, the rule of continuity was viewed as more important than the method of achieving that continuity. Blood ties were desirable, but not essential. Therefore, if no elder son was available (or competent), the heir could be a younger son, a son-in-law, a new spouse, a child of a concubine (who would be brought up by the wife), an adopted relative, and even an adopted nonrelative. It was expected that marriages would be arranged, because that would enhance continuity of the *ie*. If the eldest son's wife was barren or seen as unfit (even during middle age), this unsuitable wife (*yome*) could be returned to her family of origin.

POSTWAR JAPAN AND THE *IE*

Following the end of World War II, Allied forces (particularly the United States) provided the next influx of foreign influence. As a part of reconstruction efforts, many changes were introduced. A new constitution, based on democracy, was created. Land reform allowed families to buy their own land, polygamy was prohibited, women were given voting rights, fathers were identified as heads of households, nuclear families were registered at the time of marriage, extramarital relationships were seen as a social problem rather than a crime, and there were constitutional provisions aimed at virtually demolishing the family system of *ie* (Ishikawa, 2001; Shikata, 1999). For example, all children were supposed to inherit equally and share equal responsibility for the care of their parents. (However, in practice, the land or property was often so small that further division would not be realistic.) The *ie* was blamed for many of the evils of the war, because it was seen as a model that had governed all levels of institutions and systems, producing extreme nationalism. This family form was seen as a relic of the feudal era and as incompatible with the new era of democracy. However, just as in the past, families found ways to cope with discrepancies between these new laws and their own beliefs.

Thus, some principles and practices related to *ie* continue to exist within many nuclear families today (Hendry, 2003). Houses still contain a Buddhist altar (*butsudan*) (in addition to a Shinto god-shelf) where the memory of ancestors is preserved, ensuring the existence and continuity of *ie*. The postwar constitution actually encouraged continuity of *ie*, because it required that one member of a family be chosen to care for genealogical records and utensils used in religious rites. On the New Year's holiday or during the summer festival of Obon (a time for remembering ancestors), families make trips to visit their relatives and *butsudan* in order to pay respects to ancestors. In cases where a house has been passed down through several generations, the members still living in the home may conceptualize it as an *ie*. This is especially true if the family owns its land or if there is an *ie* occupation where the demands of work are still shared. Urban families may live near one another, with a retirement home (*inkyo-ya*) built close to the main house. Frequently, rural families live and work together in a variety of forms, but often with the inheritance structure of *ie* still in place (Tsutsumi, 2001). For many Japanese who live in urban areas, there is no physical *ie* dwelling passed down through generations. Thus, it may appear that no elements of *ie* exist. There is debate over the extent to which elements of *ie* continue to exist or have influence in modern Japan.

THE *IE*, SELF-CRITICISM, AND FAMILY STRENGTHS

Approaches to studying and understanding families reflect the culture in which the study takes place. Western cultural emphasis on the individual and factors such as self-esteem, praise, positive self-evaluation, happiness, and accomplishments are reflected in researchers' choices to study "family strengths." From a strengths perspective, identifying and focusing on shortcomings or deficits is viewed as detrimental to family well-being. In contrast, Japanese literature draws attention to potential drawbacks, problems, critical appraisals, and negative characteristics (Heine, Lehman, Markus, & Kitayama, 1999; Karasawa, 2001; Kitayama, Markus, Matsumoto, & Norasakkunkit, 1997.) Westerners may be surprised to find there does not seem to be a universal need for positive self-regard. A critical focus is more characteristic of the view of the individual and family in Japanese culture. There is a greater response to failure feedback (Heine, Kitayama, & Lehman, 2001) and stronger emphasis on the process of becoming better than there is on identifying existing strengths. Self-criticism and negative information are seen not as indicative of low self-esteem, but as serving to improve the social and psychological consequences for the future. From early in life, Japanese children are taught to attend to negative aspects of themselves, because this is an essential step to constructing an interdependent form of identity (Kitayama et al.). Improvement in a family would be highly valued because it could lead to eliminating features that are negative or undesirable; building on already existing positive characteristics would be seen as self-serving. Focusing on failings, and then perfecting actions, would affirm one's sense of belongingness to the family. Thus, although the information presented in this chapter may seem to focus on the negative, it is consistent with Japanese family literature because it would promote the relationality and embeddedness of the individual within the family, and the family within broader society. It is consistent with the views that self-criticism is a virtue and that lack of critical perspective (implying that one is already satisfied) would appear arrogant in the eyes of others. Thus, the concept of *ie* influences not only the family structure, but also the characteristics of families that are chosen for study in Japan.

FAMILY STRUCTURE AND DEMOGRAPHICS

Currently, the dominant family form in Japan is the nuclear family. Although nuclear families appear on the surface to function independently, the value of continuity for the larger family system still influences nuclear family decisions. In addition to the integration of the nuclear family and the continuing family life of the *ie*, Japanese families have undergone additional evolution, particularly since the late 1970s, when economic and social changes altered life circumstances for many. The period that followed, and that continues today, has been called the "age of nonmarriage" (*hikon jidai*) in response to a series of demographic trends (Hirota, 2004). With recent polls (Cabinet Office, 2004) showing that 60% to 70% of Japanese expect no change in their living circumstances or income, with an additional 25% to 35% expecting decline and worsening, it does not appear that family-related trends will reverse in the foreseeable future.

Marriage

During the latter half of the 20th century, nearly everyone in Japan married. It was viewed as an essential step toward mature, responsible adulthood (Goldman, 1993). However, attitudes are changing. A recent poll ("Marriage Is Not Everything," 2003) reported that approximately 54% of adults think it is better to marry, and 44.5% think that people do not need to marry if they choose not to do so. Yet, those numbers mask large age-related variation. Only 30% of those in their 20s think it is better to marry than not marry, whereas 80% of those who are age 70 or older think it is better to marry.

Although most Japanese marry, the rate of marriage has declined. In 1970 one in five women aged 25–29 had not yet married; in 2000 over half (54%) of women in this age group had not married (Raymo, 2003a). Average age of first marriage in 1950 was 23 years for women and 26 for men; in 2001, average age was approximately 27 for women and 29 for men. In 1970, nearly all women who married did so by their early 30s. It is not clear whether more of these unmarried young adult women will marry at later ages or will not marry at all, but it does appear that this trend is occurring for women with various educational attainment levels (Raymo, 2003a). Of those who do marry, the percentage of couples in which the wife is older has doubled in the past decade, accounting for more than 23% of marriages.

A variety of factors have been discussed in terms of their contribution to the decline in marriage rates. In addition to national economic problems and high unemployment among young adults, there has been an increase in women's economic independence (Ono, 2003). Independent, employed women also have high expectations for partners; these expectations contribute to a sense of *kekkon kanbatsu* ("marriage drought," or lack of available acceptable men). Many urban singles (including 80% of unmarried women) live with their parents and view marriage as a less desirable alternative; they enjoy the freedom and romance of the single lifestyle, without the responsibility of managing a household, with mothers to cook for them, and with encouragement from family members to continue living with their parents. Raymo (2003a) has pointed out that this trend away from marriage is important to watch because it exists in a nation where alternative family forms (e.g., cohabitation and nonmarital childbearing) are strongly discouraged; where women (even those with higher education) have limited career promotion opportunities; and where families have a critical role in meeting the needs of the elderly. Raymo (2003b) has also suggested that having access to parental resources may contribute to later marriage, not by keeping adult children at home as what some are calling "parasite singles" (*parasaito shinguru*) (Yamada, 2000), but by facilitating the child's independence for those who wish to remain single but cannot afford separate housing.

Divorce

Divorce in early Japan was more common than it has been recently. During the Edo era, rates were high for all except the high-class samurai families (Ishikawa, 2001). In 1883, at the beginning of the Meiji era, the divorce rate was 3.38%. Today, although the divorce rate in Japan (2.3%) is low compared with that in the United States (4.1%), the annual divorce rate in 2001 was comparable to that of Germany, France, and Sweden (Ministry of Health, Labor, and Welfare, 2002a). The number of divorces has nearly doubled in 20 years, with most divorces occurring during the first 5 years of marriage, but an increasing number of divorces now occur after the husband retires and the children leave home (Ishikawa). The law prohibits a woman from marrying within 6 months of her divorce. The majority of young adults think divorce is a life experience that is neither good nor bad. The major reason stated by men and women for divorce is "mismatched personalities." In general, reasons men give for divorce tend to be vague and involve some problems of not getting along with each other emotionally. Reasons given by women tend to be more concrete, such as a husband's physical abuse, relationships with other women, not bringing home income, and drinking too much.

Kateinai rikon (domestic divorce) is used to describe husbands and wives who have very little conversation, communication, and sexual relations, but who do not seek a legal divorce. Many adults (especially when one parent is not Japanese) remain in unhappy marriages, largely because Japanese laws ignore the rights of parents to see their children after a divorce and the rights of children to see both parents (Kakuchi, 2003). Although Japanese law recognizes divorce that is granted on mutual consent, unlike Western law, it does not acknowledge custody as a separate issue from the divorce. Children are seen as belonging to the family, and there are no specific laws about visitation rights or joint custody. As divorce rates rise and marriages between Japanese and foreign nationals increase, Japan will be faced with considering child custody laws. It would appear that custody situations are changing. In 1950, Japanese fathers were given custody of about 50% of children, and Japanese mothers were given custody 40% of the time, with 10% shared. In 1994, mothers were given custody nearly 80% of the time, with fathers receiving custody in less than 20% of cases (Ishikawa, 2001).

Although young adults do not view divorce as a serious stigma, divorced parents do face discrimination in terms of employment and have difficulty meeting child care and housekeeping demands. Women initiate most divorces but then often face serious economic problems. The employment system is set up with the major wage earner assumed to be the father. Thus, men receive wages and additional fringe benefits to support their families, and full-time positions and benefits are more difficult for women to obtain. The wage system encourages a woman to remain in a marriage. Wives' average earnings are 12.2% of their husbands' average income. If she earns no income or a small income, a wife is exempt from tax and pension funds, so the system favors full-time homemakers. Although this system recognizes the value of unpaid work at home, it also contributes to keeping women in part-time or underpaid work positions.

Households

The most common form of household (32.5%) continues to be that of a married couple with child(ren) (Ministry of Health, Labor, and Welfare, 2004). Other common and increasing compositions include one-person households (23%) and married couples without child(ren) (21.4%). Over 10% of households include three generations. Most single-parent households are composed of widowed mothers and their children. The size of workers' households has remained around 3.1 to 3.5 persons for the past 8 years. The postwar common definition of family is based on blood relationships; this definition has contributed to difficulties in recruiting foster families to care for children (Fukushima, 2001).

The family definition based on blood also poses challenges for other types of households. Since the mid-1970s Japan has gradually become more accepting of homosexuality (McLelland, 2000). In the past, gay men generally entered marriages of convenience, rather than living as openly gay. Now an increasing number of gay men live alone (Lunsing, 2001). Lesbians are more likely to live in households in coupled relationships, one of the most common forms of alternative household structures. The legal strength of the *ie* is visible when one considers rules that affect same-sex couples, such as the registration system in which each household is headed by the husband. Same-sex couples have difficulties with property and inheritance rights. If one dies without a spouse or children, property is divided among parents or siblings; and if one is hospitalized, only the immediate family is legally entitled to make decisions on behalf of another. To deal with these problems in same-sex couples, the older partner can adopt the younger (thus becoming "family" in the legal sense) or attempt to draw up legal agreements and register them with a local notary (a "joint living agreement," an option yet to be tested in court) (Maree, 2004).

Cohabiting couples are not a new form of household. They have existed throughout Japanese history. Under the Meiji Civil Code people became cautious about marriage and divorce. Therefore, in 1900 people often lived together prior to filing marriage paperwork in order to see if the relationship would work (Shikata, 1999). Currently, the only form of legally recognized relationship is a marriage between two opposite-sex members. However, there have been calls to acknowledge diversity in coupled relationships, including recognition of cohabiting couples and same-sex couples (Yoshizumi, 1994).

Birthrate and Life Expectancy

In this country of 128 million, the birthrate has been declining dramatically. The birthrate is about 1.35 children per woman. This is far below the 2.1-child birthrate needed to maintain a stable population. Following the recent birth to Japan's royal middle-aged couple, births to women over age 30 are losing their stigma. If women are delaying marriage, rather than choosing never to marry, and if the Japanese government is successful in creating an environment where children are more desirable, we can expect that the need for infertility services will increase, and more couples will experience stresses associated with infertility and its treatment.

In 2003, every age group under 35 years had far fewer members in 2003 than in 1997. In addition, Japan has the longest life expectancy in the world, calculated in 2001 as over 78 years for males and nearly 85 years for females (Ministry of Health, Labor, and Welfare, 2002b). It is estimated that by 2040 one third of the population will be over age 65, and only 11% will be under age 14 (Foreign Press Centre, 2002, p. 10). Families today do provide support and care for the elderly at levels higher than were expected when postwar Japan moved from the multigenerational *ie* structure to nuclear families. However, pressures related to declining birthrates and extended life span give reason for concern as to whether there will be sufficient working-age family members to meet the needs of elderly relatives in the future.

COUPLE FORMATION AND MARRIAGE

There have been many paths throughout Japanese history that led to family formation or marriage. Japan involves a combination of individualistic and collectivist beliefs and customs that coexist, and they are reflected in dating and marriage. Arranged marriages (*omiai* or *miai*), in which the family makes the marriage partner choice without input from the bride or groom, have existed at various times. Romantic love marriages *(ren'ai kekkon)* also existed before post–World War II Western influence. Today, approximately 90% of marriages are classified as *ren'ai*, not because Western influence has been so powerful, but because underlying values of individualization and self-expression existed at various times throughout Japanese civilization and are just being reinvigorated (Yamazaki, 1994). Similarly, unmarried couples during early periods in history were involved in sexual relationships, spouses lived separately, and couples experienced some level of gender equality. By the mid-1960s, the recent trend toward love marriages and dating was underway.

Dating

Japanese adults distinguish dating that is just for fun (*deto*) from dating that leads toward marriage (*otsukiai*). One can *deto* casually, picking partners who are fun and dating many people. Dating with the expectation of leading toward marriage is largely a process of getting to know one another in a serious way, assessing compatibility and the potential for financial security. Public displays of affection are becoming more common, and sexual abstinence before marriage does not pose major concerns.

Studies of college-aged and young adult women indicate they have high expectations of a future spouse, seeking a man who is taller than 5 feet 7 inches, with a high salary and high level of education, who will help with child care and housework, tolerate a wife's ambitions, and is not the eldest or only child (both are positions that can bring greater responsibilities for taking care of his aging parents or may require that she move in with his family) (Nicotera, 1997; Traphagan, 2003). Young men indicate they are seeking someone who is physically attractive, a good cook, kind, young, loving, and honest.

Unmarried Japanese women often speak of their rejection of spoiled Japanese men, unfair work environments based on traditional models (where educated women become "office ladies" doing menial jobs), and their idealization of the "liberated" West (Hirakawa, 2004). During the 1980s, there began an exodus of young women from Japan to the West, seeking what they perceived to be a liberating, more egalitarian environment where they could pursue education, employment, and possibly romance or marriage with Western men (Kelsky, 2001). Many of these Japanese women who attended university in other countries then returned to Japan, adding to the ranks of unmarried educated women. A qualitative study of women returning to Japan following education in the United States found that women were equally divided on whether Japanese men saw experiences abroad as making these women more or less desirable dating partners (Murray & Kimura, 2003; Murray, Kimura, & Peters, 2000). Half of the women had dated only Japanese men since their return, and one fourth had dated mostly non-Japanese men (typically Anglo Americans). All of the women felt some pressure from their families to marry (especially from mothers), but none felt pressured by fathers. All those over age 28 said they were currently looking for a marriage partner, and many indicated they were experiencing the "marriage drought" of acceptable eligible men.

When young adults are ready to marry, they quit casual dating. Some seek help in locating a partner, through coworkers, siblings, or friends. Others may use the services of a *nakodo,* a well-respected person with many connections who can identify a potential spouse and also serve as a source of advice. The first meeting of the couple begins with the possibility that this will lead to *otsukiai,* or serious dating.

Marriage

It is a misconception to dichotomize arranged marriages and romantic love marriages. Most marriages contain elements of both; families making arrangements generally consider the feelings and input from the couple; and love marriages are usually also based on practical reasons, compatibility, and liking one another. Love marriages might more accurately be called "free choice marriages," because romance is not always involved. In addition, what distinguishes relationships in Japan from those in the United States is not specifically romance, but the attempt in the United States to maintain romance over time and reliance on it as a major factor in maintaining family cohesion (Rothbaum, Pott, Azuma, Miyake, & Weisz, 2000). Couples in the United States appear to work harder at their relationships, but relationships in Japan appear more stable.

Couples date an average of 6 to 7 months before arranged marriages, and 2 years before love marriages. Only 1% of Japanese identify themselves as Christians; but in 2000, 67% of weddings were Western

Christian style (usually in church with a minister or priest), 20% were Shinto style (where only close family and *tamomare nakodo* attend), 10% were "marrying in front of people" (getting support of family, friends, and community), and less than 2% were Buddhist (Abe, 2001). One's personal religion and choice of religious ceremony do not need to be consistent. They are part of a pool of coexisting beliefs and practices.

At the wedding and reception, the bride's father often shows his sadness, and may even cry in public. When children are growing up, a father often spends more time with his daughter than son, in anticipation of her marrying and leaving the family. There is no symbol of marriage that is uniquely Japanese, although Western-style rings are often used today. A symbol of marital status is not seen as necessary because it is assumed that all relevant people will already know one's marital status. After the wedding some women may begin to dress more conservatively, which signals that they are not trying to impress other men. Men seem to have no comparable change in appearance.

An emerging issue deals with the legal requirement that new spouses must adopt one of their family names and register themselves as a married couple under that last name. Typically, the woman joins her husband's family, takes her husband's last name, and cares for his parents. At that time her name is removed in the government registry from her family of origin and moved to the roll of her husband's family, showing that her first line of obligation is to his family. In practice, she will probably continue to ask her own mother for help, remain emotionally attached to her family of origin, and give help to her parents.

Although in rural areas wives may provide the major support for their in-laws, in urban areas young couples are more likely to have their own small apartment. In some families, the parents' house is modified, with additional floors added or a separate entrance for the new couple. Because many families today have only one child, daughters are feeling more need to care for their own parents and continue their family name. The law requires that a couple choose a family name, but it does not specify that the name must be that of the husband (although in 1986 98.5% of couples chose the husband's family name) (Shikata, 1999). Some couples are reaching compromises in which the husband agrees to move in with the wife's family, care for her parents, and maintain her family's grave site, in exchange for the wife's agreeing to take his family name. This compromise is more likely when the husband has a brother to carry on duties with his own parents; however, it frequently results in competition between the two sets of parents. Thus, we see that although Confucian ideology has created some patriarchal aspects to Japanese society, there are also elements of gender equality that existed during early history (rekindled in recent times)—both of which attempt to coexist in family life.

ROLES AND RELATIONSHIPS IN FAMILIES

As in many countries, the main purposes of marriage in Japan have been to provide a structure in which to create and raise children; care for dependent individuals; and provide economic security, physical safety, and welfare. Shikata (1999) suggested that many of the functions of the family have been lost, because other institutions (fire departments, police, schools, religions) now meet those needs. Today's limited functions seem to include fulfilling sexual needs, child care and nurturance, continuing the human species, exchanging affection, and providing a place to relax. Although a main purpose of *ie* was to ensure continuity of the family, members of nuclear families today expect their relationships to meet a combination of traditional (e.g., economic security, procreation, continuity) and modern (e.g., love, fulfillment, companionship) needs.

Men's and Women's Roles

It may be a challenge for nuclear families to meet the range of expectations of those who marry. In the modern family, the husband's main role is to work and bring home money. One type of family often discussed is the "salaryman family," which appeared during the mid-1960s in urban areas and has seen some decline as the economy deteriorated. Although the majority of families were not of "salarymen," this form was considered desirable, because it ensured a family's future and because wives did not have to work in a family business. In the "salaryman family" (consisting of a wage-earning husband who works outside the home, his wife, and children), it is assumed that a man will rarely take a major role in the lives of his children or wife. Jobs often demand that he put in long days at work, with required work-related socialization in the evening. By the time he gets home the children are asleep, and there is little physical space that is his own, so he seems to be "in the way." Some Japanese men report a fear of going home, because they feel there is no place there for them. It is often assumed that the wife's role in these families is to take care of her husband, children, and older family members. She also plays a strong role in her children's education. In many cases she controls family finances and provides the husband with an allowance.

Contemporary women's expectations of a marriage are not well met by the salaryman model. More women are faced with balancing the demands of work and family, some are pursuing demanding careers, and some are deciding not to have children; therefore, women are seeking more cooperation from their husbands in housework and child care. Some men appear to be making efforts to comply (Ishii-Kuntz, 2003). This participation also may take place when, because of a poor economy, men may be unemployed or underemployed. However, husbands' time spent participating in housekeeping and child care is still much smaller than that of wives, even in dual-income families. A 2001 government survey on time use found that in dual-income families, Japanese husbands spent an average of 9 minutes a day in housekeeping and 5 minutes a day in care of preschool children; their wives spent 3 hours 31 minutes in housekeeping and 25 minutes in child care. In single-income households, men spent 7 minutes per day in housekeeping and 13 minutes in child care; their wives spent 4 hours 49 minutes in housekeeping and 1 hour 48 minutes in child care (Ministry of Public Management, Home Affairs, Posts, and Telecommunications, 2002). This division of labor may help explain why the number of married women who are employees grew by only 2% from 1983 to 2003, even though female employees overall grew by 15%. In fact, the percentage of the female labor force that is composed of married women actually dropped during that period, from 68% of all working women to 60% of all working women (Ministry of Public Management, Home Affairs, Posts, and Telecommunications, 2004).

Domestic violence has also been a social problem in Japan. About 23.5% of murders of adult women are committed by the husband (Fukushima, 2001). A 1998 survey in Tokyo found that 60% of the women who responded reported they had experienced some kind of violence or abuse from their husbands. Of these, 35% reported physical violence, 20% reported sexual violence, and the remainder reported psychological abuse. However, men typically report that they are not aware of their violence and abuse. A national survey conducted in 2000 reported that 1 in 20 women had experienced *life-threatening violence* by their husbands. The major reason for not reporting the violence was that the women thought that if they endured, things would get better. Japan lacks adequate shelters and counseling services for women who have experienced domestic violence; even women who locate a shelter then may have no home to return to except that of their husbands.

Other Adult Family Relationships

The elderly compose another group of family members who may have unmet expectations. Older family members, who had engaged in providing loyalty and care for their elders, had expected a reciprocal system in which they would receive such care and support during their own older years. These older generations would like *ie* to continue, for their ancestors, for the family occupation, and for their own personal needs. In the nuclear family structure, the strict hierarchical system has diminished, and older adults generally have less power and authority in the family than they did in prior generations. However, there still seems strong reciprocal concern for family members across the generations, regardless of housing arrangements.

When adults (ages 20 to 69) are asked about what they do as a family, most report spending time together during the New Year's holiday, including shared activities, decorating the house for the holiday, visiting shrines, and having a party. Most reported other shared times including birthday parties, celebrating Christmas and Mother's Day, and visiting graves during the Obon festival (a time of remembering dead ancestors) (AERA Mook, 1998).

PARENTING

In the *ie* family system, paternal principles were strong. Women were not the only ones raising children; young, able-bodied wives were often sent to work in the family occupation while their children were cared for by frail grandmothers or grandfathers. After World War II, when the *ie* system was abolished, maternal principles gained in power. Fathers spent long hours away at work, and without spousal companionship the mother-child bond became the strongest, closest relationship within the family (Kawai, 1996b). Japanese child rearing tends to strengthen the mother-infant bond (Doi, 1996). This intensification of the mother-child relationship is magnified by the lack of other family members (e.g., aunts, uncles, cousins, and grandparents) present to share in child care and emotional socialization.

Mothering

The mother-child relationship is seen as the core of the nuclear family, often with the father still on the sidelines. Mothers generally are responsible for the psychological foundation of the family, financial management, care of the elderly, structuring the environment for the child's educational success, and providing child care and emotional socialization. Doi (1973) has described the *amae* relationship that exists between mother and young child. This term characterizes the feelings and behaviors of the child as a state of dependency on benevolence or indulgence of the mother, which leads to a secure relationship. It can also be used to describe, in a reciprocal fashion, how the child's behavior affects the interaction (Holloway & Minami, 1996). Although Japanese and U.S. mothers do not differ in most categories of contact (e.g., kissing, hugging, picking up, comforting), Japanese mothers spend longer periods in close physical contact and have less eye contact with infants than U.S. mothers. Thus, in Japan, there is more equipment focused on promoting proximity to infants (e.g., Snugglis), whereas in the United States there is more equipment focused on promoting distance (e.g., walkers and swings) (Rothbaum et al., 2000).

Fathering

Because of fathers' long work hours, the small amount of time they spend with their children is generally on weekends in the companion role, such as playing or taking baths with their preschool children or going for drives and family picnics with older children. Fathers' involvement in child care or housework is generally seen as "helping" the wife, rather than assuming these tasks as part of the father role (Hara & Minagawa, 1996). There is indication that men are attempting to reinvent fatherhood (S. Steinberg, Kruckman, & S. Steinberg, 2000). Because they lack role models and are dissatisfied with their own childhood, fathers of newborns seem to use their own fathers as a point of reference for how to be different. Although many of today's fathers are trying to improve, they still perceive themselves as relatively inadequate caregivers and better at the tasks of financial providing. They also perceive themselves as sharing the physical workload at home, although the majority of wives claim to be totally responsible for child care and household duties, while adding that they saw their husbands as integrated into the family. Because Japan has one of the world's lowest birthrates, there has been discussion about how to make having children a more desirable situation for couples. One idea that has emerged in this discussion has been the introduction of paternity leave. The Equal Employment Opportunity Law of 1998 allows for parental leave for 1 year. Many mothers take parental leave to stay home for children, but fathers rarely take paternal leave. It is unclear whether the context of fathers' workplace environment (still often based on principles of *ie*) is amenable to this change.

Parenting Behaviors

It is inaccurate to assume that socialization of children in Japan is exclusively focused on creating dependence and situation-centeredness, whereas that in Western nations focuses on independence and is individual centered (Murray & Kimura, 2003; Rothbaum et al., 2000; Tobin, 2000). Japanese relationships have both public (*tatemae*) and private (*honne*) contexts (Doi, 1986), and child socialization is highly focused on learning *kejime,* that is, how to adjust one's behaviors, speech, and expectations based on the contextual demands of the immediate situation (Tobin). Unlike parents in the United States, a Japanese parent would be less likely to emphasize learning to be "true to your beliefs" or "completely honest."

In Japan, nonverbal, mutually empathic parent-child relationships have been encouraged more than the child's ability to assert the self. Mothers model empathy, and children are to learn subtle cues of gesture and tone (Holloway & Minami, 1996). When children are noncompliant, it is attributed to immaturity, not to intent. Japanese parents expect more compliance and emphasize *healthy dependence*; U.S. parents exert more direct control and emphasize *healthy conflict* (Rothbaum et al., 2000). Japanese parents are more likely to avoid confrontations and back down when children resist their requests. Rather than using direct control and specific rules, they model deference and restraint, using reasoning, anxiety induction, shaming, appeals to the child's interests, and appeals to the child's awareness of the consequences for others when they have been hurt (Rothbaum et al., p. 1130). Similar to children in the United States, stressful early life events and poor parenting practices appear to have more lasting effects on personality traits of sons than daughters (Kitamura & Fujihara, 2003).

Rather than punishment, Japanese mothers focus on helping children understand how their misbehavior will evoke negative reactions from outsiders, who may then ridicule or create danger for the child. This encourages the child's alliance with the mother, who is seen as able to help the child avoid these negative repercussions. Japanese children are also taught the difference between behavior expected at home from that expected outside the home. Indulgence of the child's behavior is more likely to happen within the home. Therefore, Japanese parents may threaten to banish the disobedient child from the home, in contrast to parents in the United States, who threaten to ground the child inside the home.

Parenting Adolescents

Parenting adolescents is becoming more of a challenge in Japan today. Japanese adolescents can be expected to have developed skill at attending to subtle cues and avoiding conflict, and they do not seem to have extensive interaction with their parents. Nearly 50% of adolescents say they have not talked with their father in the past week, and 15% say they have not talked to their mother. They retreat to their rooms to study, and parents who want their children to excel in educational endeavors do not intrude. In fact, a popular style of desk includes a button that, when pushed, rings a bell in the kitchen to summon mother with a snack or for help. Adolescents who are also exposed to Western values and stereotypes of adolescents through television, Internet, and music may seek to be fashionable by finding ways to integrate these Western behaviors and values into their lives. Another trend adolescents experience involves having a mother who is employed. Continuous maternal employment, especially if the mother uses supportive parenting behaviors, appears to have a positive effect on early adolescents' independence (Suemori, 2003). Thus, it appears that Japanese families are not simply socializing their adolescents for the collectivist lifestyle, as many outsiders mistakenly expect.

CHILDREN

Traditionally, the Japanese say that until the age of 7 children are "among the gods" or "children belonging to god" (*nanatsu mae kami no uchi*). This idea is often used by writers to explain customs such as the practice of burying a dead infant under the floor of the house, so the family stays closer to the infant, who can then serve as a guardian of the family (e.g., Hara & Minagawa, 1996). It also explains why infanticide and abortion were considered not as murder, but as returning children to the gods. During their early years, children are viewed as innately good, so parents are not likely to scold or strictly train them (Ishikawa, 2001). Ceremonies when children are born and when they turn 3, 5, and 7 years old are rites of passage to becoming part of the human world. Some scholars have suggested that what the Japanese really mean is that children under age 7 are "subhuman" but that it would be too harsh to use language of that nature (Chen, 1996). In either case, with decreased infant mortality, smaller family sizes, and lower abortion rates for all women except teenagers, the traditional view of children may no longer be a common image.

During times of social change and economic problems, children may be among the first to suffer. The first child abuse and neglect association was built in 1990. The Japanese Ministry of Health and Welfare recognized the problem of child abuse in large cities by starting to provide telephone counseling during the early 1990s. Analyses suggested that abuse was the result of nuclearization of the family, isolated mothers with an absence of relatives nearby who could advise and help with child rearing, and the limited experiences parents had in understanding children because of their own development within a small family where they may not have had any siblings (Chen, 1996). However, government and societal attitudes that "it can't happen," "it is better not to intervene in family problems," and "it is better for children to be with their families" delayed passage of any related legislation (Shikata, 1999). It was not until 2000 that the Child Abuse Prevention Act was passed. Currently, no official statistics are kept on child abuse cases (McCurry, 2004).

ELDERLY

Prior to World War II, the average life expectancy in Japan was less than 50 years. Today, it is among the longest of the industrialized nations. In 1978, only 8% of the population was 65 years or older. By 2000, older adults accounted for 17% of the population, and by 2010, it is expected to be 22%. Coupled with the very low fertility rate of Japan, this creates a situation where fewer older adults will have adult children available to assist in their care and share housing. The family support ratio (i.e., female population age 40–59 divided by population of both sexes ages 65–84) was 1.75 until 1960 (meaning there were 1.75 middle-aged women available for every 1 older adult). In 1995, that ratio was 1.09, and by 2025 it is projected to be 0.6 (approximately one potential female caregiver for every two elderly persons). Over 90% of in-home caregivers of the elderly are women, with the majority of those being spouses of the elderly (Traphagan, 2003). However, most societal concern is focused on the middle-aged daughters and daughters-in-law in the "sandwich" generation, who may be providing care for their children and their parents.

Barriers to women's labor force participation might be assumed to leave many women available to meet the caregiving obligations of their parents and in-laws. However, in the era of nuclear families, family obligatory caregiving and traditional living arrangements have been replaced by voluntary family caregiving and a variety of living arrangements. In 1971, 75% of adults over age 65 lived with one of their children and his or her family. By 1995, that proportion was under 40% (Hara & Minagawa, 1996). Coresidence, however, does not necessarily mean two or three generations living under one roof (Traphagan, 2003). It can include variations such as a small grandparent house in the same compound; a remodeled parental home with separate entrances; or prefabricated two-household homes (*nisetai jutaku*) designed for two related families, each with separate facilities.

The reality of multigenerational households may not live up to the expectations of older adults. Busy middle-aged working couples may spend less time with the elderly than if they lived apart and made intentional visits. Older adults may feel taken advantage of when they are continuously used as free child care providers who support their working daughters or daughters-in-law (Brown, 2003). Oldest sons and only sons may be handicapped in the marriage market, because potential spouses see the expectation of caregiving for their in-laws as a negative factor in choice of marrying that man. Daughters-in-law who had married a younger son may feel resentful at being thrust into the caregiver role when older sons of the elderly in-laws move away or refuse to provide elder care. Those same in-laws may see the expectation of care as a fair transaction, in exchange for the support they had provided other aging family members in earlier years. Caregiving in a multigenerational family structure is associated with both health risks and protective health behaviors (Takeda et al., 2004). Women providing care report more caregiving worries and more sedentary behaviors but fewer future health and financial worries and less smoking or drinking. Regardless of family structure, men most often report worries about financial security and work; however, those in multigenerational structures smoke more as a way to cope with the stress of multiple roles.

As the family system changes, traditional obligations are often reinvented. An increasing number of older adults are living alone (Raymo & Kaneda, 2003), including those who are widowed, unmarried, divorced, as well as those who had no children or lack harmonious relationships with their children. With fewer family members to care for traditional family grave sites, older adults may opt for *eitai kuyobo,* a grave eternally cared for by an organization or temple (Kawano, 2003). With more one-child families, a daughter may assume the care of her parents, rather than her in-laws; family succession by daughters (rather than sons) is increasing. This will require new models, because most caregiving plans and community expectations are based on the assumption that it is daughters-in-law who will provide care.

RITUALS AND FAMILIES

Families share in rituals across the life span. Japan has been influenced by many different religious traditions that now pervade the secular sphere. Many people say they are not religious but practice a variety of activities that seem religious, including both Shinto and Buddhist elements. Rituals during life tend to be celebrated out in the community as a whole (e.g., festivals) and often reflect the ideology of Shinto (the indigenous Japanese religion). Underlying these rituals are often principles of pollution and purification. Such rituals include those associated with birth and childhood, entry into adulthood, middle-age years of calamity (*yakudoshi*), retirement, and old age. Marriage ceremonies, even Christian/Western ones, often include both Shinto and Buddhist elements.

Memorials related to death and ancestors are more concerned with family continuity, are usually conducted at home, and are based primarily on Buddhist principles, except for families that are exclusively Shinto, the imperial family, and those in Okinawa (Hendry, 2003). Although there are regional variations, the following is representative of general death-related activities (Hammond, 2001). In Buddhist funerals today, the body is usually washed at the hospital (although the family used to do this, and occasionally still does). Many of the practices associated with death, funerals, and memorials use the symbolism of reversal, such as dressing the body in a white garment that is fastened in a manner opposite to the usual way; but the deceased may also be dressed in a man's suit or woman's kimono. Wreathes of blue, yellow, and green are hung outside the home. Usually, the eldest son makes arrangements together with the mortuary regarding the funeral. Altars are assembled at the funeral site (or at the home) by the mortuary staff, and usually flowers and fruits are placed on them. The body is placed on dry ice in the mortuary or by the altar, and the family stays close by until it is time to place the body in the casket, after which time the family dresses in black.

Guests come to pay their respects to the family and deceased either at home or the temple, bringing condolence money. Individuals ring bells and offer prayers and incense. Visitors offer their condolences to the family members, who are seated near the body. Visitors then go to another room for food and drinks. The Buddhist priest arrives and is offered green tea. During the wake, the priest lights incense and reads a sutra while family members (in hierarchical order) go to the incense urn and offer incense before returning to their seats. Visitors may then also repeat this ritual. The family stays up with the deceased for the night. The next day the funeral is held at the temple. A posthumous name is chosen, and it is inscribed by the priest on a wooden tablet that will later be placed at the family's *butsudan*. Each family member adds a pinch of incense to a fire in order to say farewell, and the priest finishes the readings. The casket is loaded into the hearse.

At the crematorium, the family watches as the casket is slid into the oven. At the appointed time, the family returns to the crematorium, and the body is slid back out. Each member is given a set of chopsticks to pick up the bone fragments and put them into the urn. Two family members pick up each bone fragment in unison and put it into the urn. This is the only time in Japan that two people hold the same thing with two sets of chopsticks. Sometimes two urns are filled—one for the temple and one for the family grave. Gravestones have a hollow space inside for placement of the urns of the family. Memorial services are held on each of the first 7 days, and at varying frequencies until the 49th day, usually with the priest present. Memorials for the individual also are held on the 100th day; the 1-year anniversary; and after 3, 5, 7, 13, 25, 33, and either 50 or 60 years. After that time, the individual loses an individual identity and becomes part of the larger nameless group of ancestors who are considered (and honored) as a group. Thus, through these activities, the emphasis on continuity associated with *ie* coexists with the living members and their nuclear families.

CONCLUSION

Since the end of World War II, the Japanese media have continuously discussed the family as being in crisis. Ochiai (2002) suggests that this may be because the idealized image of a nuclear family does not match the "real" family. She suggests viewing the family as continuously in transition and as part of a historical process, functioning within the broader societal context that exists. Given the many changes in society and family throughout Japan's long history, this process view of family life is warranted. From this perspective, the recent low marriage and fertility rates, coupled with an increasing proportion of the population who are elderly adults, would be results of past socioeconomic circumstances and government policies, as well as prompters of new ones. They are but a link in the long chain of what constitutes family in Japan.

How will these circumstances play out in an environment grappling with the coexistence of the nuclear family and *ie*? The ability to adapt foreign ideas and use them to create innovations within existing systems has been a strong feature throughout Japanese society. The combining of Western and Japanese family systems is in process. Its outcome is unclear, but we can be sure it will result in a family system model with its own special identity, rather than a replica of Western families. We can look forward to the continued reinvention of Japanese tradition, by the Japanese people.

REFERENCES

Abe, T. (2001). *Konyaku to kettsukonn no techou* [Notebook on engagement and marriage]. Tokyo: Shougattsukan.

AERA Mook. (1998). *How to look at family study* (Extra Report & Analysis Special No. 39). Tokyo: Asahi Shimbun.

Brown, N. (2003). Under one roof: The evolving story of three generation housing in Japan. In J. W. Traphagan & J. Knight (Eds.), *Demographic change and the family in Japan's aging society* (pp. 53–71). Albany: State University of New York Press.

Cabinet Office. (2004). *Feeling on living conditions*. Tokyo: Statistics Bureau, Ministry of Public Management, Home Affairs, Posts and Telecommunications. Retrieved from http://www.stat.go.jp/english

Chen, S. (1996). Are Japanese young children among the gods? In D. W. Shwalb & B. J. Shwalb (Eds.), *Japanese childrearing: Two generations of scholarship* (pp. 31–43). New York: Guilford Press.

Doi, T. (1973). *The anatomy of dependence*. New York: Kodansha International.

Doi, T. (1986). *The anatomy of self*. Tokyo: Kodansha International.

Doi, T. (1996). Foreword. In D. W. Shwalb & B. J. Shwalb (Eds.), *Japanese childrearing: Two generations of scholarship* (pp. xv–xvii). New York: Guilford Press.

Foreign Press Centre. (2002). *FFJ—Facts and figures of Japan*. Tokyo: Author.

Fukushima, M. (2001). *Aremo kazoku koremo kazoku* [This is a family, this is also a family]. Tokyo: Iwanami.

Goldman, N. (1993). Perils of single life in contemporary Japan. *Journal of Marriage and Family, 55*, 191–204.

Hammond, B. (2001). *Japanese Buddhist funeral customs*. AELS, Inc. (Tanu Tech). Retrieved April 22, 2005, from http://www.tanutech.com/japan/jfunerals.html

Hara, H., & Minagawa, M. (1996). From productive dependents to precious guests: Historical changes in Japanese children. In D. W. Shwalb & B. J. Shwalb (Eds.), *Japanese childrearing: Two generations of scholarship* (pp. 9–30). New York: Guilford.

Heine, S. J., Kitayama, S., & Lehman, D. R. (2001). Cultural differences in self-evaluation: Japanese readily accept negative self-relevant information. *Journal of Cross-Cultural Psychology, 32*, 434–443.

Heine, S. J., Lehman, D. R., Markus, H. R., & Kitayama, S. (1999). Is there a universal need for positive self-regard? *Psychological Review, 106*, 766–794.

Hendry, J. (2003). *Understanding Japanese society* (3rd ed.). London: Routledge Curzon.

Hirakawa, H. (2004). Give me one good reason to marry a Japanese man: Japanese women debating ideal lifestyles. *Women's Studies, 33*, 423–451.

Hirota, A. (2004). Kirishima Yoko and the age of non-marriage. *Women's Studies, 33*, 399–421.

Holloway, S. D., & Minami, M. (1996). Production and reproduction of culture: The dynamic role of mothers and children in early socialization. In D. W. Shwalb & B. J. Shwalb (Eds.), *Japanese childrearing: Two generations of scholarship* (pp. 164–176). New York: Guilford Press.

Ishii-Kuntz, M. (2003). Balancing fatherhood and work: Emergence of diverse masculinities in contemporary Japan. In J. E. Roberson & N. Suzuki (Eds.), *Men and masculinities in contemporary Japan: Dislocating the salaryman doxa* (pp. 198–216). London: Routledge.

Ishikawa, M. (2001). *Sociology of modern families*. Tokyo: Yuhikaku.

Kaku, K. (1999). *Otoko to onnano monogatari nohonshi* [Men and women's stories in Japanese history]. Tokyo: Kodansha.

Kakuchi, S. (2003). Foreign spouses in Japan seek easier child custody laws. *International Divorce Law Office: Japanese divorce and custody law*. Retrieved April 15, 2005, from http://www.international-divorce.com/d-japan.htm

Karasawa, M. (2001). A Japanese perception of self and others: Self-critical and other-enhancing biases. *Japanese Journal of Psychology, 72*, 195–203.

Kawai, H. (1996a). *The Japanese psyche: Major motifs in the fairy tales of Japan.* Woodstock, CT: Spring.

Kawai, H. (1996b). *Kazoku kankei wo kanngaeru* [Thinking about family relationships]. Tokyo: Kodansha.

Kawano, S. (2003). Finding common ground: Family, gender, and burial in contemporary Japan. In J. W. Traphagan & J. Knight (Eds.), *Demographic change and the family in Japan's aging society* (pp. 125–144). Albany: State University of New York Press.

Kelsky, K. (2001). Who sleeps with whom, or how (not) to want the West in Japan. *Qualitative Inquiry, 7,* 418–435.

Kitamura, T., & Fujihara, S. (2003). Understanding personality traits from early life experiences. *Psychiatry and Clinical Neurosciences, 57,* 323–331.

Kitayama, S., Markus, H. R., Matsumoto, H., & Norasakkunkit, V. (1997). Individual and collective processes in the construction of the self: Self-enhancement in the United States and self-criticism in Japan. *Journal of Personality and Social Psychology, 72,* 1245–1267.

Kodama, A., & Fukuda, T. (2000, June 25). *Jituwa atarashii fuufudousei* [In fact, a wife and husband having the same family name is a new phenomenon]. *Asahi Shimbun Weekly AERA,* pp. 112–114.

Lunsing, W. (2001). *Beyond common sense: Sexuality and gender in contemporary Japan.* London: Kegan Paul.

Maree, C. (2004). Same-sex partnerships in Japan: Bypasses and other alternatives. *Women's Studies, 33,* 541–549.

Marriage is not everything. (2003, September 19). *Yomiuri News.*

McCurry, J. (2004). Japan makes progress in facing up to post-traumatic stress. *Lancet, 363,* 1782.

McLelland, M. (2000). Is there a Japanese "gay identity"? *Culture, Health & Sexuality, 2,* 459–472.

Ministry of Health, Labor, and Welfare. (2002a). *International comparison of divorce rates.* Tokyo: Statistics and Information Department, Ministry of Health, Labor, and Welfare. Retrieved April 22, 2005, from http://web-jpn.org/stat/stats/02VIT33.html

Ministry of Health, Labor, and Welfare. (2002b). *International comparison of life expectancy at birth.* Tokyo: Statistics and Information Department, Ministry of Health, Labor, and Welfare. Retrieved April 22, 2005, from http://web-jpn.org/stat/stats/02VIT25.html

Ministry of Health, Labor, and Welfare. (2004). *Composition of households.* Tokyo: Statistics Bureau, Ministry of Public Management, Home Affairs, Posts, and Telecommunications. Retrieved April 22, 2005, from at http://www.stat.go.jp/english

Ministry of Public Management, Home Affairs, Posts, and Telecommunications. (2002). *Housework sharing (1986–2001).* Tokyo: Statistics Bureau & Statistics Center. Retrieved April 22, 2005, from http://web-jpn.org/stat/stats/ 18WME51.html

Ministry of Public Management, Home Affairs, Posts, and Telecommunications. (2004). *Female employees by marital status (1983–2004).* Tokyo: Statistics Bureau & Statistics Center. Retrieved April 22, 2005, from http://web-jpn.org/stat/stats/18WME31.html

Murray, C. I., & Kimura, N. (2003). Multiplicity of paths to couple formation in Japan. In R. R. Hamon & B. B. Ingoldsby (Eds.), *Mate selection across cultures* (pp. 247–268). Thousand Oaks, CA: Sage.

Murray, C. I., Kimura, N., & Peters, D. (2000, November). *Japanese women's experiences with dating and marriage desirability after higher education in the United States.* Paper presented at the annual meeting of the National Council on Family Relations, Minneapolis, MN.

Nicotera, A. M. (1997). Japan. In A. M. Nicotera (Ed.), *The mate relationship: Cross-cultural applications of a rules theory* (pp. 77–92). Albany: State University of New York Press.

Ochiai, E. (2002). *The Japanese family system in transition* (2nd ed.). Tokyo: Yuhikaku.

Ono, H. (2003). Women's economic standing, marriage timing, and cross-national contexts of gender. *Journal of Marriage and Family, 65,* 275–286.

Raymo, J. M. (2003a). Educational attainment and the transition to first marriage among Japanese women. *Demography, 40,* 83–103.

Raymo, J. M. (2003b). Premarital living arrangements and the transition to first marriage in Japan. *Journal of Marriage and Family, 65,* 302–315.

Raymo, J. M., & Kaneda, T. (2003). Changes in the living arrangements of Japanese elderly: The role of demographic factors. In J. W. Traphagan & J. Knight (Eds.), *Demographic change and the family in Japan's aging society* (pp. 27–52). Albany: State University of New York Press.

Rothbaum, F., Pott, M., Azuma, H., Miyake, K., & Weisz, J. (2000). The development of close relationships in Japan and the United States: Paths of symbiotic harmony and generative tension. *Child Development, 71,* 1121–1142.

Shikata, H. (1999). *Kazoku no houkai* [Disruption of families]. Tokyo: Minerva.

Sougou joseishi kenkyuukai [General Women's Studies Research Group]. (1992). *Nihon jossei no rekishi: Sei iai kazoku* [History of Japanese women: Sexuality, love, and family]. Tokyo: Tokyo University Press.

Steinberg, S., Kruckman, L., & Steinberg, S. (2000). Reinventing fatherhood in Japan and Canada. *Social Science & Medicine, 50,* 1257–1272.

Suemori, K. (2003, November). *Maternal employment and early adolescents' independence in Japan.* Paper presented at the annual meeting of the National Council on Family Relations, Vancouver, British Columbia, Canada.

Takeda, Y., Kawachi, I., Yamagata, Z., Hashimoto, S., Matsumura, Y., Oguri, S., & Okayama, A. (2004). Multigenerational family structure in Japanese society: Impacts on stress and health behaviors among women and men. *Social Science & Medicine, 59,* 69–81.

Tobin, J. (2000). Using "the Japanese problem" as a corrective to the ethnocentricity of western theory. *Child Development, 71,* 1155–1158.

Traphagan, J. W. (2003). Contesting coresidence: Women, in-laws, and health care in rural Japan. In J. W. Traphagan & J. Knight (Eds.), *Demographic change and the family in Japan's aging society* (pp. 203–226). Albany: State University of New York Press.

Tsutsumi, M. (2001). Succession of stem families in rural Japan: Cases in Yamanashi prefecture. *International Journal of Japanese Sociology, 10,* 69–79.

Yamada, M. (2000). Kekkon no genzaiteki imi [Current meaning of marriage]. In K. Yoshizumi (Ed.), *Kekkon to paatonaa kankei* [Marriage and partner relationships] (pp. 56–80). Kyoto, Japan: Mimreruvashhobou.

Yamazaki, M. (1994). *Individualism and the Japanese: An alternative approach to cultural comparison.* Tokyo: Japan Echo.

Yoshizumi, K. (1994). The presence of nonmarital couples. *Municipal Problems, 85*(8), 23–27.

Part IV Exercise: The Story of José and Lana

Before you begin this exercise, write a one-page paper summarizing your answers to these questions:

1. How do you usually react to people from other countries, particularly people from parts of the developing world? What stereotypes do you tend to have? How do your beliefs about cultural differences influence your reactions? Have you had any experiences that influenced your reactions? Say anything else you wish about your own response to cultural differences.
2. Are you satisfied with how you react to diversity? Is there anything you would like to change about your response?
3. Read the description below, and then answer the additional questions.

Imagine that you are José or Lana. Recently you have immigrated illegally to the United States from El Salvador with your mother, Doña Maria; your grandmother, Doña Margarita; and your four brothers and sisters.

You came to the United States because there was nothing left for your family in your country. Your father divorced your mother a few years ago and moved from the village to Salvador. He said he would send money, but he didn't. No one in the village has heard from him, and you fear he may be dead. Your family's farm has been ruined by war.

Your mother wanted you to have a chance at a better life. She took all her savings and paid them to a man you didn't know to help you make it to the Mexican border. You hated having to sneak across the border. You were frightened and worried about being caught. Your mother is constantly fearful about being discovered now, and you feel an underlying tension almost all the time at home. But what choice did you have, and what choice do you have now?

You mother wants you to go to school, but she depends on you to help her, so there is no time. Your mother has a limited education. She works as a maid, and because she can't make much money, she works two jobs. She doesn't get any help from the government because she is afraid of being caught. But she works so hard that a lot falls on you at home. You help your mother with the younger children. If you are Lana, you do almost all the housework; if José, you go from house to house asking people if they need yard work done, garbage hauled, or windows washed to try to make some extra money. You spend time listening to your grandmother—she is very sad and cries a lot.

You know a little English from listening to the radio. You sometimes go to the university library and try to read the newspapers. You like being around the college students and hope that someday you will also be able to get an education. Usually you go to the library late in the evening when your mother has come home and the younger children are fed, bathed, and in bed. This is the only time of day you really have to yourself, and sometimes you stay up late just to read and think. Tonight at the library, right before closing you notice that a student seems to have left some papers behind—no one is around and they are lying loose on the table next to you. You decide to read them to see what this student is learning and to see if you might want to try to return them to her or him.

Now answer the additional questions below. Discuss your responses with your peers.

1. Go back and read the paper you wrote about your reaction to diversity—but read it through the eyes of José or Lana. Write, from José or Lana's perspective, whether he or she would consider you to be a desirable candidate for a friendship, and why or why not.

2. Respond to José or Lana in your own words, telling José or Lana how you feel about the judgments you made. Are you changing as you read this book, and how?

Part V

SOCIAL INEQUALITY IN THE CONTEMPORARY WORLD

In Hutterite communities, all wealth is shared equally. Males have authourity over females in the formal decision-making structure.

Introduction to Part V

Part V examines dimensions of social inequality due to stratification brought about by gender, race, ethnicity, and class. Social stratification gives some groups greater access to resources such as income and political influence—and therefore greater power—than others have. Such inequality can have profound effects on family life.

In Chapter 17, "American Indian Families: Strength and Answers from Our Past" Cheshire discusses the strengths and challenges facing American Indian families today. After providing a historical background, she focuses on such issues as intermarriage, foster families, education, and elders. The poverty and oppression that American Indians have experienced is a good illustration of the concerns of this section of the text.

In Chapter 18, "Women in the Two-Thirds World," Russo and Smith focus on women in the major regions of Africa, Asia, Latin America, and the Caribbean. They include an overview of indicators of women's welfare, including their health, education, income, and workforce participation. Ideological and historical factors are identified, specifically gender stratification, colonialism, and capitalist expansion. The chapter also analyzes the ways in which women's lives in various regions are influenced by various cultural beliefs and societal norms about proper gender and family roles.

In Chapter 19, "Household Division of Labor in Industrial Societies," Haas turns our attention to gender and family relations in modern industrialized nations. She examines how families divide responsibility for household work and how this division of labor is related to the status of women and men in society. Haas traces the historical development of the gender-based division of labor that separates men's and women's activities and offers explanations for why this has occurred. She then compares various industrial societies on the degree to which they adhere to the "doctrine of separate spheres," by providing detailed cross-cultural examples of traditional, transitional, and egalitarian societies.

In Chapter 20, "Poverty and Family Policy in a Global Context," Rank and Yadama discuss how poverty affects families worldwide. The situations for both developed and developing nations are explained, as well as strategies for dealing with poverty. Policies that can build assets and provide safety nets for families are presented.

CHAPTER 17

American Indian Families: Strength and Answers From Our Past

Tamara Cheshire

We survive war and conquest; we survive colonialism, acculturation; assimilation; we survive beating, rape, starvation, mutilation, sterilization, abandonment, neglect, death of our children, our loved ones, destruction of our land, our homes, our past, and our future. We survive, and we do more than just survive. We bond, we care, we fight, we teach, we nurse, we bear, we feed, we earn, we laugh, we love, we hang in there no matter what.

—Paula Gunn Allen, 1992, p. 43

This chapter will examine the problems facing, as well as the resiliency of, American Indian families. The characteristics of American Indian families are extremely diverse. Available literature on normative American Indian families is limited because of the tendency of researchers to focus on problems in human behavior. The need to address normative families is essential in order to counteract stereotypical misconceptions. There is also a need to address the problems facing the Indian community so that positive changes can be made in the various areas that affect Indian families. This chapter will provide the reader with ideas on how to support American Indian families via their strengths.

Issues affecting American Indian families today include: high rates of intertribal and interethnic marriage, the distinctive needs of Indian children in foster care, the unmet opportunities in higher education, the persistence of poverty, the promise of access to quality health care, and the disease of substance abuse. Family strengths observed within the interactions of American Indian families—between elders, children, and other kin—can be utilized to help deal with the challenges affecting American Indian families today.

TERMINOLOGY

Whether to use *Native American, American Indian, Indian, Indigenous,* or some other term to identify a particular group is confusing to many scholars. Because anyone who is born in America is a native to this land, I have chosen to use the terms *American Indian* or *Indian* to identify indigenous families. To be most accurate is to identify families by their specific tribal affiliation and last name, but because this chapter will address American Indian families in general, it is not appropriate to use tribal affiliation in this instance.

Other terms that are of importance include *intertribal community, enrollment, blood quantum, Indian education, contact,* and *Indian Country. Intertribal community* means a group of American Indians from different tribes making up a community. Some of these community members may be intertribal themselves. Their heritage or bloodline may be from more than one tribe, making them as individuals intertribal.

Enrollment refers to being enrolled within a particular tribe. This term is very important because being enrolled with a particular tribe, especially one that is recognized by the federal government via treaty, means that rights and services will be provided for members of that tribe as specified by the treaty or agreement between the tribe and the federal government. This land deal between governments is one of the defining distinctions between American Indian communities and any other group in the United States.

Blood quantum is also a very important term that will come up in this chapter. Tribes maintain records of the genealogical makeup of each member, his or her blood quantum. To be enrolled in a tribe, there is often a blood quantum requirement for membership. Defining membership is one of the central elements of tribal sovereignty. If a person does not meet the blood quantum requirement, he or she cannot be enrolled, does not have services available to him or her, and is generally not recognized as being a member of that tribe. Although individuals who are no longer recognized can state that they are American Indian (many official records, including the census, are based on self-definition), they cannot be enrolled as an official member of a tribe, and they do not participate in the rights and responsibilities of that nation.

Indian education refers to federally funded programs that exist within many individual school districts to reinforce cultural traditions and teachings for American Indian children. These programs were created to reverse the damage done to three to five generations of American Indians who lost their cultural traditions because they were forced to attend boarding schools and abandon their Indian identity.

The term *contact* refers to the time of contact in history of the indigenous people of the Americas with Europeans and the devastation that ensued. The final term, *Indian Country,* refers to both reservation and urban Indian communities across North America.

HISTORICAL AND CULTURAL BACKGROUND

American Indian tribes thrived long before the invasion of the Americas. Complex civilizations formed with sophisticated architecture, agrarian systems, and medical knowledge. Each tribe had its own distinctive language, religious system, and history, which often reflected the natural environment. Contact with other tribes through trade led to the realization that most American Indians shared many common values, including respect for others and the environment.

The arrival of European immigrants negatively affected indigenous cultures across the Americas. Not only did the European invaders inflict their economic system and social and religious values on Indian people, but they also brought and spread disease in an attempt to annihilate the indigenous population. The introduction of disease had the most impact on elders and children, which in turn affected cultural transmission and retention by destroying sources of oral history (C. Colley, personal communication, 1992).

As Europeans established governments and took Indian lands, they institutionalized a series of barriers to prevent American Indians from continuing their traditions. By taking over tribal homelands and forcing the inhabitants to migrate to distant reservations, the U.S. government uprooted native peoples from one vital source of their cultural identity—their natural environment. In order to survive in the inhospitable surroundings of the newly formed reservations, tribes had to abandon some traditional ceremonies, rituals, and ways of life. Tribes adapted by developing new resources and cultural patterns in order to survive. Cultural cohesion was further subverted when the U.S. government terminated tribes and refused to recognize them as distinct, autonomous, self-governing entities, forcing them instead to adapt to the political and legal system of the European immigrant culture (Pevar, 1992). Governmental policies that focused on genocide placed enormous strain on the traditional ways of life of American Indians. Eventually, they were forced to submit to a paternalistic system that necessitated their reliance on the federal government for their physical survival.

Despite changes dictated by these drastic upheavals, American Indian culture has proven itself to be both dynamic and resilient. Tribal elders have worked to preserve their people's distinctive heritage by passing down language, traditions, stories, and oral histories from generation to generation. Today, American Indian men and women are taking political stances and are serving on tribal councils that make decisions regarding sovereignty, enrollment, and the availability of resources that will affect the next generations.

AMERICAN INDIANS TODAY

Currently there are 2.4 million American Indians in the United States, representing almost 1% of the total U.S. population (U.S. Bureau of the Census, 2000b). Of the 2.4 million American Indians, 1.4 million are children under the age of 18 (Willeto & Goodluck, 2003). Current census data also reveal an overall increase in the American Indian population from the previous census.

The American Indian population has a median age of 28 years (Willeto & Goodluck, 2003), which indicates younger families. Larger families are to be expected, because the majority of the overall population is children. The average family size for American Indian families is 3.6 people, compared to 3.1 people for the total U.S. population (Willeto & Goodluck).

American Indian families experience a higher rate of child poverty than the general population. Numbers reveal that between 27% and 31% of American Indian children experience poverty, compared to 9% of non-Hispanic white children. An estimated 40%–46% of American Indian female-headed households live in poverty, compared to 26% for non-Hispanic white female-headed households (Willeto & Goodluck, 2003). For American Indian families, the median family income ranges between \$33,000 and \$36,000 a year, whereas non-Hispanic white families earn between \$54,000 and \$55,000 a year (U.S. Bureau of the Census, 2000a). According to Willeto and Goodluck, American Indian families experience high rates of poverty because of lower median incomes and the need to support larger families. Because lower median incomes are associated with service sector jobs that don't require a secondary education, and because women who do not have a higher education have a higher number of births, one can clearly see how poverty is pervasive and perpetual.

Even though the high school dropout rate for American Indians is much higher than the U.S. national average (Willeto & Goodluck, 2003), the number of American Indians receiving a bachelor's degree has doubled from 1984 to 2000, "jumping from 4,246 in 1984 to 8,711" (Shirley, 2004, p. 88). Only 65.6% of all American Indians 25 years old and over have a high school diploma or higher, and only 9.4% have a bachelor's degree or higher (U.S. Census Bureau, 2000a). Specific statistical data are not available on the exact number of American Indians returning to their reservations or their urban communities after graduating from college.

Census numbers indicate a major shift away from reservations to urban areas. It is estimated that only 35%–40% of American Indians live on reservations today, with as many as 60%–65% living in urban areas (U.S. Bureau of the Census, 2000a; Willeto & Goodluck, 2003).

American Indians are the only ethnic group that has a specific legal relationship with the federal government via treaties. Treaties guarantee a nation-to-nation relationship between Indian tribes and the federal government. There are 558 federally recognized tribes in the United States today (Willeto & Goodluck, 2003), and more are petitioning for federal re-recognition each day.

THE AMERICAN INDIAN FAMILY

American Indian families are diverse. Individuals identify themselves not only as members of specific families, but as members of a tribe, which creates a larger kinship structure to draw upon, with many families interrelated. Family membership is the most important group membership a person can have besides tribal membership. "In many American Indian communities, belonging to or aligning with the right family determines community status, economic opportunity, or even political power" (Kawamoto & Cheshire, 1997, p. 18). In close-knit communities both on and off the reservation, extended-kin ties can take on significant importance.

American Indian families can be found in many different living arrangements, including large extended-kin households. Having an extended family living together in the same household provides many positive resources, such as assistance with child care, money, transportation, and emotional and moral support. However, living in the same household as one's adult children and grandchildren can also cause a certain amount of stress on individuals in the family. Elders in the home may criticize their own children about the way they parent, the job they have, or the lack of money they make, but these adult children find that the availability of child care and other resources often outweighs parental criticism.

American Indian families also live in nuclear-family households with two parents, divorced parents, and single-parent mothers or single-parent fathers, on and off the reservation. For American Indians who are separated from their families, fictive kin provide a much-needed support system in the place of extended family. The whole community may share in the raising of a child and assist with child care, food, or money while the parents (or parent) work or go to school. In intertribal communities with few elders, kinship roles are expanded, and elders serve as grandparents to all the children in the community. Nuclear family structure is still the norm, although typical family size varies from region to region.

From small nuclear families to large families with many extended kin living in the same home, all Indian households are affected by economics and by a lack of living space. Urban families gravitate to small living spaces, which cost less and do not accommodate large numbers of people. Regardless of these cramped quarters, many Indian families take in additional people, including neighbors, friends, and members of extended family. On reservations, federally supported housing once built small homes without running water and electricity. These homes were meant for nuclear families, not larger extended families. Tribally supported housing in some communities is currently being designed for the extended family, with larger kitchens and living room areas in addition to five, six, or seven rooms or more.

MARRIAGE/INTERMARRIAGE

Prior to and after the invasion of the Americas by Europeans, intermarriage occurred among tribes and between indigenous peoples and new immigrants in order to facilitate alliances, promote trade, and adhere to traditional incest taboos. Needless to say, high rates of intermarriage have occurred within the American Indian population (Sandefur & Liebler, 1996; Sandefur & McKinnell, 1986). Snipp (2002) would say that intermarriage levels have exceeded 50%. The major concern with intermarriage is that it was utilized alongside other strategies (boarding schools, relocation programs, termination) as a means of assimilating American Indians (Bieder, 1986).

There is a valid fear of the loss of culture as Indian families intermarry. There is also a concern about the loss of resources for family members with diminished genetic bloodlines, who are determined ineligible for services guaranteed to tribal members (Wagner, 1976). Some Indian families (on and off the reservation) are encouraging their children to "marry Indian" in order to maintain enrollment of future generations and keep the transmission of cultural traditions intact. According to Kawamoto (1995), many intermarried Indian families are active in preserving cultural traditions because they fear the dilution of American Indian culture. A number of Indian families maintain their cultural traditions by being very active in their communities, which facilitates a supported Indian identity, which in turn leads to further cultural transmission of traditions (Cheshire, 2001).

INDIAN CHILDREN

Because more than half of all Indian families are intermarried (Snipp, 2002), a large number of American Indian children have mixed heritage. Some American Indian children have as many as six tribes they can identify as part of their ancestry. Because each tribe determines its own enrollment criteria based upon its sovereign rights as an individual nation, an American Indian child may qualify to enroll in many of his or her tribes, but each person must choose only one to enroll in because of federal government restrictions. On the opposite end of the spectrum, there are many American Indian children in urban areas who are not eligible for enrollment in any tribe. Either their blood quantum is smaller than what is required by the tribe or they do not fit other criteria to be enrolled (e.g., being born on the reservation, having a living relative on the reservation who will sponsor them). These children are the ones who fall through the cracks because they do not qualify for any of the needed resources provided by urban Indian programs, tribes, or the federal government. These children are more likely to be placed in non-Indian foster and adoptive homes. This means that the child is even further separated from his or her Indian identity, which in turn can cause major problems when the child reaches adolescence and adulthood.

The cultural identity of a child is very important to that child's individual perception of self. This individual perception of self is significant, because it affects how a child deals with racism, peer pressure, drug and alcohol use, teen sexual activity, and depression.

American Indian youth living in non-Indian foster or adoptive homes are at a high risk of being isolated. In fact, these children are six times more likely than other youth in the United States to commit suicide (Johnson & Tomren, 1999). These youth are isolated not only from their family, but from their community and tribal support network. When they experience external stressors regarding acculturation from their foster or adoptive parents, in addition to their teachers, peer group, society in general, and the media, they have nowhere to turn for support. Among American Indian youth ages 15–19, suicide is the second leading cause of death (Johnson & Tomren), and their suicide rate is almost three times higher than the national average. Other than suicide, additional high-risk behaviors are likely, such as high dropout rates in school (Wood & Clay, 1996), gang involvement, and substance abuse (Herring, 1994). Thousands of American Indian children remain at risk in non-Indian homes (Berlin, 1987), despite attempts to place them with Indian families in response to the Indian Child Welfare Act.

Congress passed the Indian Child Welfare Act in 1978. This act was passed because of research done on Indian families revealing that a majority of Indian children were being forcibly taken from their homes and placed with white foster and adoptive families, where they were being assimilated into white society (Madrigal, 2001). In passing the Indian Child Welfare Act, Congress was attempting to undo early assimilation techniques that were focused on Indian children.

During the late 1800s, thousands of Indian children were forcibly removed from their homes and placed in boarding schools where they were taught to be white and serve whites. This created an entire generation of Indian people who had lost much of their culture. They had been beaten, raped, and starved in order to "kill the Indian, but save the man" (Pratt, 1892/1973, p. 46). Unfortunately, they had also lost the ability to parent their own children (Rogers, 2001), because they had been taken away from their own parents and were raised by missionaries who were more interested in converting them to Christianity than teaching them to be parents. So the boarding school experience essentially gave birth to an entire generation of American Indian parents who had limited skills in parenting (Rogers) other than the strict rule enforcement of the boarding school system that taught them violence and self-hatred.

Today, when a child is taken into custody by the state, the social worker must identify the racial/ethnic identity of the child. If that child is American Indian, the tribe is contacted. Once this happens, the tribe determines if the child is eligible for enrollment. The caseworker must do research into the lineage of the child. If the tribe chooses to enroll the child, then the child is placed in an American Indian foster home until the matter is resolved and the child is either returned to his or her parent(s) or placed in an American Indian adoptive home chosen by the tribe. American Indian adoptive families have become an important tool in the preservation of American Indian communities.

When a tribe supports the identity of a child by enrolling the child and providing him or her with resources such as health care, education, and specifically cultural knowledge, the tribe is making a world of difference in that child's life. This tribe becomes an extension of the family, a caretaker. In all matters, the tribe is concerned about the child, an extension of their nation, a member of their family, and they will protect the child at all costs because the child is their future.

AMERICAN INDIAN FOSTER FAMILIES

County, state, and private foster care agencies are finding it increasingly difficult to recruit and retain foster parents (Brown & Calder,

2000). The shortage of foster parents holds true and is even more apparent in Indian Country. Because American Indian children first and foremost must be placed in American Indian foster homes (according to the Indian Child Welfare Act), and with significant numbers of American Indian children in the foster care system (over 10,000 children estimated for 2001 by the U.S. Department of Health and Human Services, Administration for Children and Families [2001]), the Indian community is experiencing a crisis.

The scarcity of foster homes and the obstacles to recruiting and retaining foster parents has been blamed essentially on inadequate support (Brown & Calder, 2000; Walter, 1993). Support to foster parents occurs in different forms (Sellick, 1992), but it is found to correlate positively with increased retention (Chamberlain, Moreland, & Reid, 1992; Martin, Altemeier, Hickson, Davis, & Glascoe, 1992), quality of care (Steinhauer et al., 1988), and decreased placement breakdown (Tinney, 1985).

Because foster parents often encounter more complicating circumstances when it comes to raising other people's children, it is difficult to recruit and retain foster families. Foster parents are required to provide the child placed in their care with a safe, loving, and secure home, while being part of a team effort, often working with a number of different social workers, counselors, lawyers, judges, administrators, and the biological parents toward reunification. Foster parents experience high rates of burnout and emotional stress (Aldgate, Bradley, & Hawley, 1996). Many of their needs are not considered. Foster parents are expected to make certain social and economic sacrifices to their own detriment.

Foster parents cannot always rely on an extended network of available family and friends to take on some of the tasks of parenting, because they either don't have access to this type of support or they have utilized these resources beyond their extent. Heavy regulations on who can care for foster children also prevent many foster parents from being able to utilize the teenager down the street for impromptu child care. Some foster parents believe it is their duty alone to care for their charges and feel that they will be judged as unworthy parents and have their licenses taken away if they ask for help, even in the most difficult situations. The demands of parenting in difficult circumstances place foster families at a higher risk of breakdown.

Respite care on a regular basis can provide immediate relief from the normal stresses of being a parent, and it can build parents' self-esteem and confidence. When foster children or parents unexpectedly become ill, alternative plans must be implemented. A very limited number of programs watch ill children, and foster parents don't always have access to these types of programs or other resources that will help them with this matter. This one issue can cause a foster family to break down because of the hardship they will experience economically if they are forced to choose between caring for the ill child or keeping their jobs. Crisis respite care can provide relief to sick parents or to parents who have been taking care of an ill child for an extended amount of time. Respite care can also provide early diversion from potential physical abuse and allow foster parents to address their own problems (Aldgate et al., 1996). General and crisis respite care are necessary for foster parents to continue with the assistance they provide to children, the community, tribes, and the state.

It is extremely difficult to recruit, certify, and retain American Indian foster homes. Foster care maintenance rates of pay to provide for the child(ren) in care are not adequate to cover the costs to care for the child, let alone pay for respite care (Dougherty, Yu, Edgar, Day, & Wade, 2002). There are inherent barriers in the foster care delivery system, and this has made the recruitment of American Indian foster homes challenging, to say the least. Unfortunately, there are many American Indian children who are placed in non–American Indian homes because there is not a sufficient number of American Indian foster homes where children can be placed. Once homes are found, it is difficult to retain them because of the lack of resources and support for foster homes. Foster homes would benefit from community mental health services to address the unique stressors in a foster care environment. Given the resources and support, more American Indian foster homes will be retained and will serve as an encouragement for more American Indians to pursue becoming foster parents. Outside funding sources are necessary to provide respite care to this population. Tribes that have been able to establish economic stability and even prosperity can contribute to the needs of American Indian foster families by creating programs that provide much-needed, quality respite care and counseling services not only to the foster families themselves, but also to the biological parents of the children in foster care.

INDIAN EDUCATION

Indian education programs were created in the 1970s in response to boarding schools and relocation programs. In the late 1800s the federal government supported Richard Pratt, a captain in the U.S. Army who founded the Carlisle Indian Boarding School. His idea was to "civilize" and assimilate Indian children into white society (Baldridge, 2001; Christensen & Manson, 2001) by kidnapping them and placing them in boarding schools managed and partly funded by many diverse Christian churches. The concept here was to save the Indian from himself, to beat the culture and traditions out of him (Rogers, 2001) because the children would be better off dead than to live as "uncivilized heathens." Boarding schools were designed to take care of the "Indian problem" that the U.S. government was facing. The so-called Indian problem was essentially indigenous people holding the government accountable for the treaties it made, meaning that the federal government had to live up to its part of the agreement and provide Indian people with the resources they needed to survive, in exchange for the land that was forcibly taken in treaty agreements (Pevar, 1992). The federal government didn't want to honor those treaties, so they decided to create a strategy to assimilate all American Indians. Boarding schools, the termination of tribes, and relocation programs were all part of the onslaught, or final attack, against Indian people.

The termination of tribes essentially began in the early to mid-1900s. Congress found a loophole when it came to breaking treaties. They could terminate a tribe's status as a sovereign nation, thereby negating or voiding out the original treaty and any other agreements the tribe had made with the federal government (Pevar, 1992). This way, Congress did not have to fulfill the promises it had made to tribes regarding provisions for basic needs and survival, including food, housing, health care, land set aside as a reservation, education, and access to natural resources. During this period of termination, over 100 tribes were affected, and relocation programs encouraged Indian people to move from the reservation, or what was left of it, to urban areas where they were promised work and housing. These relocation programs were another way to force assimilation upon Indian people. What was not expected, but did happen, was that many people who moved to the urban areas (Portland, OR; San Francisco; Chicago; etc.) created their own programs and services within their communities that helped with housing and health care and, most of all, maintained cultural traditions. Indian education was a backlash against forced assimilation techniques of boarding schools and relocation programs. Successful Indian education programs value the critical role of family in the development of skills and Indian identity in children. Educational goals and self-esteem through Indian culture go hand in hand. Indian education programs are essential, because "Indian children critically need to have meaningful contact with successful role models who are also Indians and can accurately interpret and teach their mutual tribal heritage" (Farris, 1976, p. 387).

POVERTY, DOMESTIC VIOLENCE, DRUG AND ALCOHOL ADDICTION

Because American Indian families have higher rates of poverty, domestic violence, drug addiction, alcoholism, teen pregnancy, and fetal alcohol syndrome than other ethnic groups in the United States, we must look into the causes of these plagues upon Indian families. One question we must ask ourselves is, How can one population of people experience so many problems? Again, this relates back to family, community, society, and the federal government's impact on tribes. I realize that many of the above-mentioned issues can and do relate to individual decision making, but one must also look at external forces that influence these decisions. One's environment and the people who wield the power in that environment can place individuals into positions that afford them only limited choices, each with immense penalty. Essentially, American Indian families have faced the more powerful oppressor, the federal government, and have not fared well. American Indian families face extreme poverty on and off the reservation. One type of oppression, poverty, is compounded when alcohol and drugs are introduced to the community. Lack of resources or skills to deal with the effects of poverty is not conducive to "saying no" to drugs and alcohol. In fact, drugs and alcohol are used to cope with the effects of other forms of oppression, including racism and sexism. Unfortunately, many behaviors are learned, and this includes limited coping skills. Generation after generation unknowingly continues the cycle of addiction, domestic violence (Kawamoto, 2001), and teen pregnancy, which in turn feeds into poverty, self-hate, internalized oppression, and depression.

There are programs that are utilizing traditional ways to overcome these problems in the Indian community. The Sacramento Urban Indian Health Project Inc. (SUIHPI) has established drug and alcohol programs that infuse traditional ways to create a more effective approach to deal with addiction. SUIHPI has established informative workshops for American Indian teens regarding pregnancy and sexually transmitted diseases as well.

ELDERS

Besides issues with Indian youth, Indian elders are experiencing life-cycle transitions. Elders contribute to familial cohesiveness and stability (Kawamoto & Cheshire, 2003). They help to maintain cultural norms by serving as mentors and advisors who reinforce culturally specific roles and responsibilities (Baldridge, 2001). However, elders are becoming more and more dependent on health services for heart disease, diabetes, and cancer (Baldridge). These health services are not equipped to handle the large number of elders who need assistance, nor are they up to current standards (Baldridge). In addition, elders need trained professionals to visit their homes and check on their medical status. This is difficult when elders live on remote reservation land. Often, family members are not as available to help as they were before because they have moved to urban areas in response to the lack of jobs on the reservation. Many family members simply cannot assist with the needs of elders from such a distance. It is up to extended family and the community to help (Hennessy & John, 2002; John, 1988). Often, elders don't have transportation to doctor's appointments or to pick up prescriptions. They also don't have access to many nursing home facilities or adult day care programs. There is a great need for the development of such programs on reservations (Baldridge). The growing needs of elders put an additional strain on the family (Manson, 1989). American Indian families with these additional responsibilities find themselves unprepared, and elders experience neglect and abuse (Brown, 1989). Elders isolated from family who therefore rely on hired caretakers are also at risk. Without tribal support, there will continue to be a lack of available resources and programs that assist the elderly. The federal government and tribes need to take an active role in providing much-needed programs for the American Indian elderly.

FAMILY STRENGTHS AND CHALLENGES—CONCLUSION

Even though a majority of American Indians live in urban areas (Snipp, 2002), the Indian community is essentially split between urban areas and reservations. One would think that these two distinct communities would have different strengths and challenges, but they both depend on tradition, family, elders, and community for survival. Both urban and reservation American Indian families face many challenges including poverty, drug and alcohol addiction, high rates of teen pregnancy, inadequate health care, and many forms of oppression, supported and often sponsored by the federal government.

One must realize that when a group of people, even though diverse, have in common the same hardships, they often find ways to rise above and draw strength from their shared identity and traditions. In order to support Indian families, it makes sense to recognize the positive strategies Indian families have already created and gear programs to family needs.

Family strengths, including the roles of kin in providing economic and emotional support, are important to the cohesion of the American Indian family. Even though a majority of American Indians have been relocated to urban areas, kin ties remain in the larger scheme of what is considered to be "family." Instead of strict blood ties, we see intra- and multitribal relationships that provide family support. For example, a family that is Cherokee may find another Cherokee family (intratribal) or a Lakota family or an Apache family (multitribal) in an urban area to help provide support. Unfortunately, this custom of reaching out and incorporating other American Indian families as extended kin into a support network may make it difficult for these families to achieve economic stability, because they continue to help support other families.

Tribes are considered to be an extension of family, and in accordance with government regulations, they can legally advocate for American Indian families when families are in danger of collapse. With recent economic stability, tribes can fund programs that provide respite care for children and elders alike. By providing respite for these two age cohorts, efforts can be made to promote positive cultural transmission between the generations.

In addition, service providers can research and utilize techniques used by tribes and tribal colleges to recruit, teach, and retain American Indians who are facing obstacles obtaining higher education. American Indians who are experiencing domestic violence situations, teen pregnancy, drug and alcohol abuse, fetal alcohol syndrome, and poverty need support through the creation of counseling programs specifically designed with historical information in mind. Without the historical knowledge of why these problems persist within this group, there is no hope for successful programs. Service providers must not only do historical research, but they must apply the information obtained to fully serve their constituents.

Because Indian nations are sovereign entities, the federal government should limit its involvement with tribes to avoid power struggles and recognize the ability of tribal nations to determine their own needs. Once these needs are determined, the federal government should provide services because of the legal and ethical ramifications of treaty agreements.

To counter stereotypes and end oppression, we must educate first ourselves, and then others. The next step is to act by advocating for funding to create programs and provide services for American Indian families both on and off the reservation.

REFERENCES

Aldgate, J., Bradley, M., & Hawley, D. (1996). Respite accommodation: A case study of partnership under the Children Act. In M. Hill & J. Aldgate (Eds.), *Child welfare services—Developments in law, policy, practice and research* (pp. 160–169). London: Jessica Kingley.

Baldridge, D. (2001). Indian Elders: Family traditions in crisis. *American Behavioral Scientist, 44,* 1515–1527.

Berlin, I. N. (1987). Suicide among American Indian adolescents: An overview. *Suicide and Life-Threatening Behavior, 17,* 218–232.

Bieder, R. E. (1986). *Science encounters the Indian, 1820–1880.* Norman: University of Oklahoma Press.

Brown, A. (1989). A survey on elder abuse at one Native American tribe. *Journal of Elder Abuse and Neglect, 1,* 2.

Brown, J., & Calder, P. (2000). Concept mapping the needs of foster parents. *Child Welfare, 79,* 729–747.

Chamberlain, E., Moreland, S., & Reid, K. (1992). Enhanced services and stipends for foster parents: Effects on retention rates and outcomes for children. *Child Welfare, 71,* 387–401.

Cheshire, T. (2001). Cultural transmission in urban American Indian families. *American Behavioral Scientist, 44,* 1528–1535.

Christensen, M., & Manson, S. (2001). Adult attachment as a framework for understanding mental health and American Indian families: A study of three family cases. *American Behavioral Scientist, 44,* 1447–1465.

Dougherty, S., Yu, E., Edgar, M., Day, P., & Wade, C. (2002). *Planned and crisis respite for families with children: Results of a collaborative study.* Washington, DC: Child Welfare League of America, ARCH National Respite Network and Resource Center, and Casey Family Programs National Center for Resource Family Support.

Farris, C. (1976). Indian children: The struggle for survival. *Social Work, 21,* 386–389.

Gunn Allen, P. (1992). Angry women are building: Issues and struggles facing American Indian women today. In M. L. Andersen & P. Hill Collins (Eds.), *Race, class, and gender: An anthology* (pp. 42–46). Belmont, CA: Wadsworth.

Hennessy, C. H., & John, R. (2002). Elder care in Pueblo Indian families. In N. V. Benokraitis (Ed.), *Contemporary ethnic families in the United States* (pp. 368–377) Upper Saddle River, NJ: Pearson Education.

Herring, R. D. (1994). Substance use among Native American Indian youth: A selected review of causality. *Journal of Counseling & Development, 72,* 576.

John, R. (1988). The Native American family. In C. H. Mindel, R. Habenstein, & R. Wright (Eds.), *Ethnic families in America* (3rd ed., pp. 325–363). New York: Elsevier.

Johnson, T., & Tomren, H. (1999). Helplessness, hopelessness, and despair: Identifying the precursors to Indian youth suicide. *American Indian Culture and Research Journal, 23,* 287–301.

Kawamoto, W. (1995). *Stability and process issues in intermarriage: A study of marital satisfaction and problem solving in American Indian intermarried and European American endogamous families.* Unpublished doctoral dissertation, Oregon State University, Corvallis.

Kawamoto, W. (2001). Community mental health and family issues in sociohistorical context: The Confederated Tribes of Coos, Lower Umpqua, and Siuslaw Indians. *American Behavioral Scientist, 44,* 1482–1491.

Kawamoto, W., & Cheshire, T. (1997). American Indian families. In M. K. DeGenova (Ed.), *Families in cultural context: Strengths and challenges in diversity* (pp. 15–34). Mountainview, CA: Mayfield.

Kawamoto, W. T., & Cheshire, T. C. (2003). A "seven generation" approach to American Indian families. In M. Coleman & L. H. Ganong (Eds.), *Handbook of contemporary families: Considering the past, contemplating the future* (pp. 385–393). Thousand Oaks, CA: Sage.

Madrigal, L. (2001). Indian Child Welfare Act: Partnership for preservation. *American Behavioral Scientist, 44,* 1505–1511.

Manson, S. M. (1989). Long-term care in American Indian communities: Issues in planning and research. *Gerontologist, 29,* 38–44.

Martin, E. D., Altemeier, W. A., Hickson, G. B., Davis, A., & Glascoe, F. E. (1992). Improving resources for foster care. *Clinical Pediatrics, 31,* 400–404.

Pevar, S. (1992). *The rights of Indians and tribes: The basic ACLU guide to Indian and tribal rights.* Carbondale and Edwardsville: Southern Illinois University Press.

Pratt, R. (1973). Kill the Indian, save the man: Official report of the Nineteenth Annual Conference of Charities and Correction. In F. P. Prucha (Ed.), *Americanizing the American Indians: Writings by the "friends of the Indian" 1880–1900* (pp. 260–271). Cambridge, MA: Harvard University Press. (Original work published 1892)

Rogers, B. (2001, May). A path of healing and wellness for Native families. *American Behavioral Scientist, 44,* 1512–1514.

Sandefur, G. D., & Liebler, C. A. (1996). The demography of American Indian families. In G. D. Sandefur, R. R. Rindfuss, & B. Cohen (Eds.), *Changing numbers, changing needs: American Indian demography and public health* (pp. 196–217). Washington, DC: National Academy Press.

Sandefur, G. D., & McKinnell, T. (1986). American Indian intermarriage. *Social Science Research, 15,* 347–371.

Sellick, C. (1992). *Supporting short-term foster carers.* Aldershot, UK: Avebury.

Shirley, V. (2004, June 17). On the right path. *Black Issues in Higher Education,* 88–91.

Snipp, M. C. (2002). *American Indian and Alaska Native children in the 2000 census*. Baltimore: The Annie E. Casey Foundation; Washington, DC: The Population Reference Bureau.

Steinhauer, P. D., Johnson, M., Snowden, M., Santa-Barbara, J., Kane, B., Barker, P., et al. (1988). The foster care research project: Summary and analysis. *Canadian Journal of Psychiatry, 33,* 509–516.

Tinney, M. (1985). Role perceptions in foster parent associations in British Columbia. *Child Welfare, 64,* 73–79.

U.S. Bureau of the Census. (2000a). *Census Bureau facts for features: American Indian heritage month: November 2000*. Washington, DC: U.S. Census Bureau, Public Information Office. Retrieved November 20, 2004, from http://www.census.gov/Press-Release/www/2000/cb00ff13.html

U.S. Bureau of the Census. (2000b). *Statistical abstract of the United States: 2000 (population section)*. Washington, DC: U.S. Department of Commerce, Economics and Statistics Administration. Retrieved October 20, 2004, from http://www.census.gov/prod/2001pubs/statab/sec01.pdf

U.S. Department of Health and Human Services, Administration for Children and Families. (2001). *Child welfare outcomes 2001: Annual report to Congress executive summary*. Retrieved November 15, 2004, from http://www.acf.hhs.gov/programs/cb/publications/cwo01/chapters/executive.htm

Wagner, J. (1976). The role of intermarriage in the acculturation of selected urban American Indian women. *Anthropologica, 18,* 215–229.

Walter, B. (1993). In need of protection: Children and youth in Alberta. Edmonton, Alberta, Canada: Children's Advocate.

Wood, P. B., & Clay, W. C. (1996). Perceived structural barriers and academic performance among American Indian high school students. *Youth & Society, 28,* 40–60.

Willeto, A., & Goodluck, C. (2003). *American Indian children: State-level measures of child well-being from the 2000 census* (Kids Count Pocket Guide). Baltimore: The Annie E. Casey Foundation.

CHAPTER 18

Women in the Two-Thirds World

SANDRA L. RUSSO AND SUZANNA D. SMITH

INTRODUCTION

> *We are the ones who first plowed the earth when Modise [God] made it. We were the ones who made the food. We are the ones who look after the men when they are little boys, when they are young men, and when they are old and about to die. We are always there. But we are just women, and nobody sees us.*
>
> —Setswana poem

Around the world, women are simultaneously workers, mothers, partners, and consumers. According to the United Nations (UN), women perform at least two thirds of the world's paid and unpaid labor (United Nations, 1991b). Women's unpaid, unseen work including such tasks as housework and care of dependents supports entire economies, keeping countries, as well as families, functioning. Increasingly, around the world, women also participate as paid laborers in all manner of jobs, from factory workers to teachers, from sex-trade workers to physicians. Because three fourths of the world's population, as well as 75% of the world's women, live in the Third World (Brydon & Chant, 1989), it is essential that an understanding of women worldwide be based on knowledge of Third World women's experiences.

WHAT IS THE "THIRD WORLD"?

People from other countries often dislike terms such as *Third World, underdeveloped, developing,* and *the South* in reference to countries that are not part of the so-called West (i.e., the United States, Europe, or Japan). They view these phrases as paternalistic and condescending, because they suggest that one side is seen as "better" than the other side. For example, the oppositional phrase *North/South* positions the North as a group of affluent, privileged nations and communities. In comparison, then, the South must contain economically and politically marginalized nations and communities. These categories are also used for *Western/non-Western* (with Japan included

AUTHORS' NOTE: The authors would like to express their gratitude to Nitesh Tripathi, Alana Lynch, and Brianne McCarthy in the preparation of this document.

in the Western category). These are not neat geographic boundaries; they are categories that reflect the haves and have-nots of the world.

The phrase *Third World* came into use during the Cold War when the West (e.g., the United States and Europe) was seen as the First World, communist countries were the Second World, and the remaining nations comprised the Third World of nonaligned forces. Because these countries were also poor, mostly located in tropical regions, and not well developed economically, they were also called *underdeveloped* or *developing*. The Third World has come to be defined as nations or peoples who were once under Western rule, are relatively poor, and are largely nonwhite.

The term *Third World,* however, cannot possibly encompass the enormity of those geographical regions wherein the majority of the world's population lives. It may be more appropriate to use the terms *One-Third World* and *Two-Thirds World,* which describe the social minorities (of the developed countries) in contrast to the majorities (in the developing countries) (Esteva & Prakash, 1998). This terminology focuses on the quality of life led by peoples and communities in the North and South. The "One-Third World" has, overall, a higher standard of living and better quality of life by most indicators, such as education and health, than the "Two-Thirds World."

In this chapter, we use *One-Third World/Two-Thirds World* or *First World/Third World,* or *North/South* to indicate social minority/majority and levels of economic development for the various regions of the world. We also use *developed* and *developing,* again focusing on economic and social indicators of well-being. We concentrate on poor women because they make up such a large portion of the world's inhabitants. Of the 1.2 billion people who live on less than $1/day, over half are women (World Bank, 2000/2001). Women in upper-class households around the world are usually able, through access to resources and education, to avoid many of the social inequities faced by poor women. Being poor and a woman is to be at the bottom of the social hierarchy—vulnerable to malnutrition, illness, job exploitation, dangerous living and working conditions, discrimination, and violence (Agarwal, 1985).

CONSTRUCTION OF THE TWO-THIRDS WORLD

Colonization

Early European colonists, mostly men, imposed Western patriarchal notions of family and households onto colonial societies, with a certain ideology regarding women's proper place in society. This ideology dictated that women's appropriate place was in the home and that their concerns should revolve around child rearing and household duties. Women who accompanied male colonizers as wives, missionaries, or teachers reinforced these stereotypes about proper feminine behavior (Enloe, 1989) in their interactions with local women by focusing on motherhood and wifely duties while ignoring other significant roles and responsibilities undertaken by indigenous women.

These notions of gender roles became more firmly established during colonial rule of the South from the 1880s to the 1960s. European missionaries, authorities, and businessmen had little regard for traditional family and community relationships that characterized indigenous peoples of conquered lands. European colonists presumed that men had supreme authority in the family and community, depriving indigenous women of any property, rights, personal autonomy, and public authority they might have had prior to colonization. Women came to be regarded as primarily dependent on men (Manuh, 1998).

By the 19th century, the United States had joined the fight for territorial expansion and sought to become the major economic and geopolitical power in the Western Hemisphere. During the mid-20th century, most former colonies achieved independence through peaceful and nonpeaceful means. Where armed struggles for national liberation occurred, women often participated equally (e.g., Central America, Zimbabwe, Uganda). Yet, after new nations emerged, women usually found themselves discarded or disregarded in the new, formal political processes and institutions. Women were often reminded that they had the important role of mothers and were relegated back into the household sphere.

Globalization and Development

Former colonies continue to depend on a global economic system of production driven by the industrialized North. Joining these former colonies in their growing dependence upon the First World are the new *transition economies.* This term is applied to those nations that have emerged from socialist and communist regimes and are struggling to adjust to capitalism and globalization. Globalization is about making goods and services available worldwide. In the global economy, goods and services are equally exchanged and shared across countries and cultures through free-trade agreements. Jobs are created and move around the world according to wage rates and market demands. Corporations that conduct business across national boundaries are fostered. Government services are privatized, reducing the number of civil service employees. Globalization profoundly affects women and households in developing countries as government jobs evaporate, people migrate for work, and families are fractured.

It is important to note that globalization occurs not only because of the growth of capitalism and free trade, but also because of foreign aid offered by the North to the South. Wealthier countries provide assistance for more than one reason. Occasionally, this assistance is for humanitarian needs, but increasingly it is for economic and political gains. The latest development approach, called the Millennium Development Goals, stresses reducing poverty and improving lives so as to increase economic growth, create more jobs, and enhance people's productivity (United Nations Development Programme [UNDP], 2003). It appears that even development assistance serves the global economy with its focus on creating new jobs and markets virtually everywhere.

Poverty and Development

Anywhere in the world, people are able to identify who is poor and what constitutes poverty. Poverty can mean no food or clean water, or it can mean unstable livelihoods and lack of health insurance. The causes, situations, and vulnerability of people to poverty vary by country and region (Narayan & Petesch, 2002). Poor people identify different reasons for poverty: In Bosnia, it was the war; in Brazil and Jamaica, it is the lack of jobs; in Nigeria, poor governance; and in Bangladesh, it is the many risks (hunger, poor health, lack of assets, floods, crime, and lack of dowry) that often combine in waves to rock the poor (Narayan & Petesch). In most cases, poor people recognize the gender dimensions of their situation and the increased vulnerability of poor women.

The international donor community wants to reduce poverty by lowering the number of poor people while also addressing nonincome quality of life indicators that are so essential to well-being. These include basic needs, such as food and good nutrition, health care and the attributes of a healthy life, education, and housing, at minimum (UNDP, 2003).

An alternative approach to addressing basic needs has been pioneered by Amartya Sen, who focuses on the ability, or the *freedom,* a person has to live a full life and to realize his or her potential through individual choices (Sen, 1999). These capabilities are present in all of us, but many obstacles can block their fulfillment (Little, 2003). The limitations placed on a person by poverty are obvious; being female compounds these. Women and girls have less access to food in times of scarcity as well as during normal times. They have limited or no access to health care and education throughout their lives (United Nations, 2000). Women are also restricted in their abilities to assert their economic rights (e.g., land and property ownership). The cumulative effects of these limitations stunt the development of girls and women as fully capable human beings. Their freedoms are constrained—freedom to choose where to live, how to live, with whom to live; how to use their capabilities to pursue their life plans; and even what their life plans ought to include (Little).

A 50-year-old woman from the Kyrgyz Republic expresses confusion and dismay over changes in women's roles and responsibilities:

> A woman must obey her husband, as the man is head of the household, father of the children. Older people say, don't look upon your husband, don't threaten your husband, or else you will go to hell. Wherever men get together, women must go round. Girls were taught from their childhood to be obedient, never walk without head covering, wear long dresses. Now girls have opened up; they wear trousers. Women seek work in the cities. I can hardly understand what is going on. (quoted in Narayan & Petesch, 2002, p. 292)

GENDER ROLES IN THE HOUSEHOLD

What is meant by *gender roles,* and how are these changing? The term *gender,* which does not easily translate into other languages, has been used to distinguish biologically determined activities, norms, and roles (e.g., giving birth) from those that are socially determined (e.g., washing dishes). The shared expectations of appropriate gender behavior vary across cultures. For example, a study of 224 cultures found 5 in which men do all the cooking and 36 in which women do all of the house building (Williams, Seed, & Mwau, 1995). Gender norms and roles are idealized; the daily reality of people's lives can be considerably different.

Gender inequalities are prominent and often debilitating in the Two-Thirds World. There are substantial differences in the situations of men and women in many developing countries. In addition to the restrictions associated with poverty discussed above, women are often denied economic and political rights, such as the opportunity to work outside the home or to hold public office. They may not have any decision-making power within the household, either. They may be denied access to social necessities such as health care and education, or other measures of well-being. As we discuss later in this chapter, some traditional practices show a marked bias against women and girls, with sometimes mortal consequences. These patterns of gender discrimination raise issues of social justice and human welfare (Little, 2003). Feminists attribute women's subordinate position in society to *gender stratification,* also called *patriarchy* (Huber, 1988). As a result of patriarchy or gender stratification, women are excluded from fully participating in society and are denied access to opportunities, resources, and decision making.

Patriarchal traditions throughout the world place the father as the head of the household and the key authority figure. Most important, perhaps, is that placing primary emphasis on the role of the father effectively renders the mother invisible (Karmi, 1993). Family structures are often vertical, with no possibility of power sharing within the household. Customary and religious laws as well as the laws of the country often uphold this tradition. In many countries with strong customary laws, women's rights may still be at risk even when national laws are more equitable. Honor killings in Pakistan and other Islamic countries and loss of jointly acquired property upon a husband's death under traditional tribal laws in East Africa are two examples of traditional laws taking precedence over national laws.

In many societies, the stay-at-home wife represents the cultural ideal. She not only fulfills her maternal responsibilities, but she symbolizes her husband's wealth and status. Poor women working outside the home in order for their families to survive do not live up to this cultural ideal. Although poverty affects both men and women, it is the combination of poverty and *expectations* about gender that doubly marginalizes women.

Unpaid, Unseen Labor: Women at Home

For the majority of women in the Two-Thirds World, home is where they spend most of their time and energy. The value of women in societies is usually linked to their roles as mothers; other roles or activities are perceived as less important. Motherhood is often the primary source of identity; that is, it defines who the woman is as a person. Although women do work outside the home, paid employment is seen as allowing women to better fulfill their mothering roles and is not seen as a career giving them meaning in life (Tiano, 2001). Children provide both an identity to women (as mothers) and security, because children are expected to support parents as they age.

The "job" of being a mother, along with the tasks associated with maintaining the household, such as marketing, preparing food, and cleaning, seldom have any economic value in almost any society. These tasks can consume as much as 12–18 hours a day, especially when the household is in poverty. The *sexual division of labor,* that is, the division of tasks that are seen as either appropriate to men or appropriate to women, places an undue burden on women around the world. The double workday of women, aptly called the *accumulation of labor,* is noted even in the North and wherever women work both outside the home and inside the home (Sen, 2001). No study has surfaced to show that men take on household tasks equitably when the wife works outside the home. *Time poverty* is used to refer to the situation in which many women find themselves working double days.

Women work at home in a variety of tasks ranging from child care to agricultural production to small-scale enterprises. Whether this work is actually done in the home, near the home, or in the village depends on the culture. In some Islamic societies, from Nigeria to Pakistan, women are not allowed to leave the family compound after marriage unless accompanied by an adult male. This is known as *purdah*. In Nigeria, for example, Hausa women often live in purdah, and are seldom, if ever, seen, represented, or recognized. Still, these home-based women carry out all forms of subsistence production and income-earning labor from their homes. All women, from aristocrats to commoners, engage in multiple forms of labor at home, much of which is time-consuming, unending "women's work," and part of which is home-based income-earning work (Adamu, 1998; Pittin, 2002).

Marriage is the destiny of most girls in the Two-Thirds World. Their value to the family may be based solely on whom they marry, so there is great interest in marrying a girl to someone with wealth and status in the community. Arranged marriages are common in many cultures, and a young woman may have little or no choice in the decision. Marriage can also be a career strategy for young women who have no other options. Girls often do not have the opportunity to attend school. Marriage gives respectability to women and some modicum of authority from which to operate.

Aside from the work of child rearing and household maintenance, perhaps one of the least understood economic and political domestic tasks that women and households perform is *kin work* or *family status production.* This work, simply defined, consists of those tasks, such as writing letters, visiting, exchanging gifts, and attending ritual events, that maintain and expand social ties with kin, work colleagues, or other socially advantageous contacts. Although this work has no immediate tangible benefits, ultimately it is critical for the household's survival. Throughout Latin America and the Middle East, network building is a survival strategy women undertake to cope with often unstable and changing social and economic situations (Holmes-Eber, 2003). Having strong networks, often called *social* or *political capital,* reduces women's vulnerability. Evidence suggests that, for poor women in many areas of the world, new support networks are lessening the incidence of family violence and increasing women's participation in the public sphere (Narayan & Petesch, 2002).

Changing Gender Roles and Relations

Gender roles are not static but may change over time as the society changes and is reshaped by factors such as globalization, new technologies, environmental pressures, conflicts, health epidemics, and the rise of religious fundamentalism. Change can also come from deliberate efforts by governments and others to change social policies, often as a result of pressure by citizens and voters. Many governments have put in place laws and policies to raise the status of women in their countries. For example, as more women become lawyers, they inform other women of their rights, such as inheritance and property owning, which are written into secular laws.

The most noticeable change in social practice is the reduction of the father's traditional role as the sole source of economic survival (Karmi, 1993). For instance, when the state takes on some of the father's roles (e.g., free child care) or, in contrast, fails to provide support (e.g., collapse of pension schemes), women leave the home to earn wages for household needs. When economies go through recessions or, as in many parts of the world, nearly collapse, women often add or increase their paid employment outside the home. Poor women are typically supplementary earners, but as poverty deepens, they may become the primary earners. This does not necessarily change traditional gender roles and, in fact, can worsen the situation at home for women when they are still expected to fulfill their roles as mothers and wives. For example, in Bosnia-Herzegovina, Kosana's husband became an invalid and now she must support her husband and two children. She says,

> I started to work twice as much on the land so that I could manage to produce some to sell—I sell milk, cheese, cream, but it is all very little. The money leaves the house far more easily than it makes its way in. The children always need textbooks and sneakers. . . . I buy my husband medication every seven days as with every change in the weather he is struck down with pain. I am lucky he has not started to drink the way others do. (Narayan & Petesch, 2002, p. 224)

Women at Work

The relationship between production and reproduction is often described as paid versus unpaid labor; *productive* activities take place outside the home, whereas *reproductive* activities occur in the home. The latter include not only childbearing but also child rearing, dependent care, cooking, cleaning, and maintenance of the household, all activities that do not normally earn a wage. Some women have home-based work and businesses that allow them to earn an income without leaving their home environs. In addition, women who are the primary food producers are sometimes able to sell or trade the surplus for cash.

Most women work outside the home either in the *informal* sector (e.g., as domestic servants) or in the *formal* sector (paid jobs), often at wage rates lower than men's (Narayan & Petesch, 2002). The impact of globalization on employment opportunities within Southern countries and around the world has been profound. In the export industries, women account for about 80% of the 27 million workers worldwide in *export-processing zones*. This work carries both benefits and risks. Benefits include formal-sector work and standardized working conditions; however, salaries are often low and enforcement of health and safety standards lax. Specific risks include exposure to toxic substances and muscular skeletal problems (Asis, 2003).

Migration

Not every region or country can provide jobs for people who want them. Past patterns of migration are changing as increasing numbers of women, not men, are migrating away from their homes and even their countries in search of paid labor. One out of every 35 persons worldwide is an international migrant (International Organization for Migration [IOM], 2003). Estimates are that some 175 million persons (2.9% of the world population) are migrants, and 48% of these are women (IOM). Massive labor migration of women is a global phenomenon with a high social cost. Women workers are particularly vulnerable to discrimination and abuse (Forestieri, 1999).

Women migrate to a wide array of jobs including jobs as sex workers, domestic workers, and mail-order brides. Other types of migration include refugee migration, immigration "shopping" (to find a new home, especially to Canada and Australia which have less restrictive immigration laws), undocumented workers, skilled transients who only temporarily work in another country, and unskilled contract workers hired for short periods of time.

Trafficking

Human trafficking, especially of women and children, is becoming an increasingly serious problem. Trafficking in human beings is different from smuggling, which is the transportation of illegal goods or people across borders to new markets. Trafficking involves recruitment or force and exploitation for the broker's profit. An estimated 2.5 million people are trafficked each year for prostitution, the sex industry, domestic service, and forced labor, and this problem is worldwide (International Labor Organization, 2005). The problem of trafficking is seen in different ways. Is it a criminal, moral, migration, human rights, public order, or labor issue? A gender perspective raises questions about the impact of trafficking on women, their rights, opportunities, education and empowerment, health, traditional gender roles, poverty, and the gendered labor market (Foundation of Women's Forum, 1998).

CRITICAL ISSUES FOR WOMEN AND GIRLS IN DEVELOPING COUNTRIES

A decade ago, *The State of the World's Children 1992* used the term *the apartheid of gender* (Grant, 1992) to describe the disparity between males and females in education, employment, and health. Women in developing countries clearly had not advanced in the same ways that men had in the previous 40 years. Only in the industrialized countries of Sweden, Finland, and France did women approach men's success. Even in these countries, however, women and men were not equal on these indicators of well-being (Jacobson, 1993).

New data on the world's women (United Nations, 2000) show that women made major gains at the end of the 20th century. However, new forms of gender apartheid have emerged for women and girls as they bear the burdens of intimate violence, armed conflicts, and refugee conditions. In some cases, such as Afghanistan under the Taliban, national governments have blatantly sanctioned the elimination of basic rights of women and girls. However, gender apartheid exists in many countries in different forms, such as honor killings, arranged marriages, and sex-selective abortions. The following sections provide an overview of the critical issues for women and girls in the developing world.

Education

Major goals for the United Nations in the new millennium include universal primary education for both boys and girls by the year 2015 and the elimination of the gender gap in education, preferably by 2005 and no later than 2015. The gender gap in primary and secondary schooling is closing; in some countries, progress has been dramatic (United Nations, 2003a). The biggest improvements have been in regions where girls' enrollment was significantly lower than boys', including parts of Africa and Southern Asia (United Nations, 2003b). In many other countries, education is almost universal, and there are few if any differences between boys and girls, particularly at the primary levels. In several Latin American and southern African countries, there is even a female advantage (World Bank, 2005).

Within countries, children from wealthy families are much more likely to have completed higher levels of schooling than children from poorer families. Combining wealth and gender shows an enormous educational gap for women, with poor girls being much less likely to complete even primary school than wealthier girls and boys. For example, although 90% of wealthy Indian boys have completed fifth grade, less than 20% of poor girls have. Only 19% of poor women have completed Level 8, the highest level of basic education (World Bank, 2005). In some areas, such as Eastern Europe and Central and Eastern Asia, basic education has stagnated or declined because of war, economic transitions, and reduced government spending on education (United Nations, 2000).

Improved literacy is a major goal of international organizations and national governments. Worldwide, literacy improved at the end of the 20th century. *Illiteracy* is defined as the inability to read or write a simple sentence about one's daily life; illiteracy rates refer to the percentage of the population that is illiterate. Women comprise two thirds of the 876 million illiterates in the world. This figure is not expected to decline significantly in the next 20 years (United Nations, 2000). Young adults and older women who never had the opportunity to enroll in school have high rates of illiteracy (United Nations, 1991b, 2000). Rural women may be two or three times more likely to be illiterate than their counterparts in urban areas (United Nations, 2000); rural women have little time or energy to spare for literacy training (United Nations, 1991a). Future efforts to increase women's literacy must target rural communities.

In higher education, women and men have achieved nearly equal enrollment in most countries except those in sub-Saharan

Africa and Southern Asia. Women have also made rapid gains in advanced training in traditionally "male" fields of law, business, and science and engineering (United Nations, 2000). In some regions of the developing world, such as West Asia and the Caribbean, women's enrollment has surpassed that of men. In South America, women's enrollment equals men's. However, large gaps still exist, particularly in many countries in sub-Saharan Africa, where, in some cases, fewer than two women out of a thousand may be enrolled beyond the secondary level. This gender gap in education is heightened when, because of economic crises, governments and families have less money to spend on education (United Nations, 2000).

Improvements in women's access to education are linked to advancements in health and economic conditions for women as individuals and for the family as a whole. Women who are educated are more likely to find better-paying jobs, to control their fertility, to be in overall good health, and to have children who are more educated and in better health (United Nations, 2000). In contrast, women who lack education or training typically cannot get steady, well-paid work that could give them the resources to improve their lives. Women in Bihar State, India, note that 25 years ago,

> there was no education. Women could only count. Now a few in the village can sign their names. . . . In the past the responsibilities of the women were cooking, as well as planting seeds and other such agricultural [jobs]. Earthwork [construction work] was avoided and shopping was taboo. Now the women tend cattle, collect grass, go out to shop for the home, and accord priority to earning money. (quoted in Narayan & Petesch, 2002, p. 170)

Reproductive Health

Reproductive health refers to physical, mental, and social well-being in matters related to the reproductive system. Reproductive health includes the ability to have a safe sex life and to reproduce, and the freedom to decide when to have children and how many to have. Access to reproductive health care is considered a basic right by international agencies. This includes adequate prenatal care so that women can have healthy pregnancies and safe deliveries; family planning information and supplies; nutritional information and an adequate diet; and assistance from health care workers trained to identify health problems such as cervical cancer (Population Reference Bureau, 1994; United Nations High Commission for Refugees [UNHCR], 1999).

In most of the developing world, a woman's status depends on her ability to bear children. In some countries, 30% of women are pregnant or lactating at any given time. It should be noted that many women do not wish to become pregnant but are not using any method of family planning, because of lack of access to contraceptive information and supplies or because of family pressures to conceive (UNHCR, 1999). The "son wish" drives many pregnancies, because male children are valued and celebrated more than girls by their families. Female fetuses are more likely to be aborted than carried to full term if the mother has a choice (Population Reference Bureau, 1994).

For pregnant women in developing countries, there are a number of risks associated with reproduction. Many receive little or no help with pregnancy and delivery. Although the World Health Organization (WHO) recommends that women receive at least four prenatal visits, half of women in most South Asian countries and one third in many sub-Saharan countries do not receive any prenatal care. In addition, of the countries in these two regions, 60% of mothers do not have any trained personnel attending their deliveries, and even fewer of them give birth in health care facilities. In the developing world, there are few backup services for high risk-pregnancies (United Nations, 2000).

In parts of the developing world, women continue to marry early and bear children at young ages. Early childbearing takes a heavy toll (UNFPA, n.d.). For example, a young woman's underdeveloped pelvis can lead to complications during labor, and there may be repeated obstetrical problems throughout life. Often, young women die during pregnancy or delivery and become part of the 515 million annual maternal deaths worldwide (WHO, n.d.). According to the United Nations, "the risk of dying from complications related to pregnancy or childbirth is 25 times higher for girls under 15 and two times higher for 15 to 19 year olds, compared to women in their midtwenties" (UNFPA, n.d.). When maternal mortality occurs, the woman leaves behind the child and perhaps other children, resulting in further deprivation and suffering for the family. Unable to care for children, families are often torn apart (Population Reference Bureau, 1994).

Children in the developing world are also at greater risk of infant and child mortality. In an attempt to make up for these real or anticipated child losses, women often continue childbearing for as long as possible, especially when they have no choice regarding the spacing of children. This increases the stress on their bodies and traps women and children in a cycle of poor health and nutrition (United Nations, 1991a). This is reflected in fertility rates that are higher in countries with high infant and maternal mortality rates and high levels of poverty.

Cultural beliefs and practices result in a tendency for women and girls to consume smaller amounts and less nutritious food. In some countries, food taboos discourage pregnant women from eating fruits, vegetables, milk, rice, eggs, and other high-calorie foods. These nutritional deficiencies compromise women's health, physical development, and ability to bear children and increase their susceptibility to illness, pregnancy complications, and maternal death (United Nations, 1991a). Men in many Third World countries have higher status and as a result receive better and more food (Agarwal, 1985; Jacobson, 1993; United Nations, 1991b). In many societies, men are fed first, and women and children receive whatever is left to eat. Men and boys are the first to receive medical care, as well. This results in higher mortality rates for girls than boys (Jacobson; Sen, 2001; United Nations, 1991b).

HIV/AIDS

Over 42 million people are living with HIV/AIDS; 19.2 million of these are women. AIDS deaths in 2002 totaled 3.1 million, of which 1.2 million were women and 610,000 were children (UNAIDS, 2002). Sub-Saharan Africa leads the world in the numbers of people infected with the HIV/AIDS virus. In that region, 29 million adults and children are living with HIV/AIDS, and 3.5 million were newly infected in 2002. Unless there are greatly expanded prevention and treatment efforts, the African AIDS death toll is expected to continue to increase and then peak at the end of this decade. In some Southern African countries, infection rates are higher than had been thought possible, with over one third of the population living with the virus (Botswana, 38.8%; Lesotho, 31%; Swaziland, 33.4%; and Zimbabwe, 33.7%) (UNAIDS).

HIV/AIDS clearly affects women who pick up the disease from their male partners. Yet, many women believe they have no power to challenge their situation in life. The combination of "dependence and subordination can make it very difficult for girls and women to demand safer sex (even from their husbands) or to end relationships that carry the risk of infection" (UNAIDS, 2002, p. 2). The spread of AIDS in sub-Saharan African is also associated with high rates of male migration to urban areas as well as female migration within rural areas. Migrants are more likely than nonmigrants to engage in risky sexual behavior, such as having multiple recent sex partners and not using a condom with those partners (Brockerhoof & Biddlecom, 1998).

The disease has devastated African families, killing 2.4 million Africans in 2002. HIV/AIDS has created famines and food crises not linked to natural weather cycles and environmental conditions, which tend to destroy the very old and the very young. HIV/AIDS has shattered the core of the agricultural production system by killing the main producers—the young and productive husbands and wives who run family-based farms. Women and children are enlisted to care for the ill, thereby diverting their time and energy from farming and paid jobs (McPherson, 2003; UNAIDS, 2002). HIV/AIDS also disrupts the transmission of knowledge from one generation to another, because parents die before young people can acquire useful information about farm and household management (McPherson).

The infection rates for the rest of the world trail far behind those of Africa, but other regions of the developing world are also suffering. The Caribbean has the second highest prevalence rates in the world. Haiti is hardest hit, with a national adult HIV prevalence of over 6%, followed by the Bahamas, where the prevalence is 3.5%. Half of HIV/AIDS cases in the Caribbean are women. Over 1.5 million people in Latin America are living with HIV/AIDS, and nearly one third of them are women. Rapid increases in the spread of the virus are being observed in Eastern Europe and India (UNAIDS, 2002).

In Latin America, and probably in parts of Asia, the "feminization" of the epidemic is attributed to the high number of men who have sex with both men and women. There are high rates of unsafe sex among men across the entire region—low rates of condom use, high numbers of sexual partners, and low perceptions of risk. The HIV prevalence rate among male partners is high throughout the region, ranging from 8% to 28% in 10 Central and South American countries (UNAIDS, 2002).

In addition, HIV is spreading throughout the region through the sharing of injecting drug equipment. HIV also spreads because of the combination of high population mobility and inequities in social development. In Central America, the AIDS epidemic is concentrated among the poor and outcast (who are also more likely to use drugs), who are forced to migrate in search of employment. The economic problems striking several countries can encourage the spread of the epidemic (UNAIDS, 2002).

In 2002, an estimated 7.2 million people in Asia and the Pacific were living with the virus, a 10% increase since 2001. Nearly half a million South Asians died of AIDS in 2001. About 2.1 million young people ages 15–24 are affected. In China, the 1 million living with the disease could grow to 10 million by the end of the decade. In Indonesia, injecting drug use in on the rise, and so is the spread of HIV/AIDS (UNAIDS, 2002).

It is difficult to obtain detailed information about the Middle East and North Africa, but evidence indicates that about half a million people are living with the disease; 37,000 died from it in 2002. Outbreaks of infections have occurred among injecting drug users, many of whom have extramarital relations and do not use condoms. Men who have sex with men, as well as sex workers and their clients, are also at high risk. Without prevention and intervention programs, the disease could spread to other sectors of the population (UNAIDS, 2002). Still, traditional practices that isolate women have tended to keep prevalence rates low.

Despite the dire circumstances of many of the world's developing countries, there has been progress in reducing HIV/AIDS prevalence. For example, Cambodia has stabilized the highest rates of adult HIV in the world and has reduced high-risk behaviors. Prevalence among sex workers, a particularly vulnerable group, was cut by one third in 4 years as consistent condom use tripled during the same time period. Prevention programs targeted at injecting drug users, such as those in parts of Latin America, have also been successful. Yet programs targeting specific sectors, such as drug users and sex workers (where women predominate), are not enough to stop the epidemic. Education and prevention efforts must also be instituted among the general population. There are examples of declines in prevalence rates in some countries when sexually active adults adopt safe-sex practices such as using condoms, seeking antenatal care, and abstaining from sexual activity (UNAIDS, 2002).

Women, particularly poor and uneducated women, continue to be at high risk of infection and also to bear the cost of caring for infected partners. Awareness and knowledge levels remain lowest among women in rural areas, where women often cannot read and therefore are unable to obtain reliable information or to follow recommended practices provided in health care information.

Domestic Violence

According to a study released by the UNICEF, it is common for 20% to 50% of women and girls in most countries to have experienced physical violence at the hands of an intimate partner or family member (UNICEF, 2000a). More than 60 million women are missing from population statistics due to acts of violence or neglect. This is domestic violence, violence perpetrated by one intimate partner or family member against another, whether it occurs within or outside of the home. One of the most appalling and destructive issues for women is domestic violence, because it is carried out by the most trusted people in a woman's life—family members such as husbands, boyfriends, cohabiting partners, fathers, stepfathers, brothers, uncles, and other male relatives. Despite the severity of the problem worldwide, only 44 governments have created legislation to address domestic violence (UNICEF, 2000a).

Acts of domestic violence may be acts of commission, meaning overt violence such as beatings or marital rape, or they may be acts of omission, wherein a woman is deprived of something essential such as food or health care, or is repeatedly insulted and belittled. Although physical violence produces physical scars, just as damaging are neglect and psychological abuse. These acts include forced isolation, threats of violence, denial of economic support, and humiliation. These often hidden forms of violence are harder to report and leave a woman feeling uncertain and powerless. Indeed, all types of domestic violence are committed to intimidate and control a woman's identity and actions (UNICEF, 2000a). UNICEF reports a list of almost unspeakable types of domestic violence perpetrated against women throughout the life cycle by family members. Violence may begin before birth, in the sex selection and abortion of female fetuses and beating of the pregnant woman, and continue in infancy through female infanticide and physical and psychological abuse and neglect. In childhood, beatings and psychological abuse may continue, and other forms of violence may appear such as incest, child prostitution, and pornography. During adolescence and adulthood, the forms of violence expand even further to include workplace violence such as harassment and battering; dating and courtship violence, including date rape; marital rape and forced pregnancy; forced prostitution and pornography; and more. Even in old age, other forms of violence appear, such as forced suicide or homicide of widows. Many women suffer throughout their entire lives (UNICEF, 2000a).

Extensive media coverage has raised public awareness of child abuse, child homicide, and wife battering. Efforts to combat or prevent child maltreatment and intimate violence have become widespread, including mandated state reporting systems, networks of child protection agencies and domestic violence shelters, and laws and social policies tightening up prevention and intervention strategies. Many countries around the world are beginning to put laws and practices into place that will protect women and children from domestic violence. However, governments face continued resistance from traditional belief systems.

Violence is an issue that pervades women's lives and that will take efforts from many groups to change, partly because it is frequently justified on the basis of cultural beliefs and traditions. For example, *dowry violence* in India and Pakistan occurs when women are burned "accidentally" in kitchen fires by their husbands, who believe that their demands for a dowry have not been met. An estimated four women per day are burned to death in Pakistan as a result of domestic disagreements. *Acid attacks* are used to disfigure and even kill women and girls over a variety of disputes such as failure to meet dowry demands, rejection of marriage proposals, and other family disagreements. In Bangladesh, an estimated 200 such attacks take place every year. In some countries, women are killed in the name of their family's "honor." *Honor killings* are justified on almost any grounds, including alleged adultery, premarital relationships (but not necessarily sexual), rape, or falling in love with someone of whom the family does not approve (UNICEF, 2000b).

Early marriages are also considered a form of violence. In India and Bangladesh, for example, marriage when a girl is beyond puberty is considered an embarrassment to the family. In one area of Northern India, 56% of girls were married by the time they were 14 (Hunger Project, n.d.). Early marriages undermine a girl's health and development in many ways. They result in childhood or teenage pregnancy, which can cause problems for the health of the mother as well as her children, such as miscarriages and low birth weight. Early marriages lower the chances that girls will complete their education and be able to support themselves and their families, leading to poverty and the malnutrition of mother and children.

In transitional economies in Eastern Europe, violence is rooted not in culture and tradition but in current grim economic conditions that create acute, long-term stress in families. The disappearance of government-sponsored jobs and supports has put increasing economic pressure on families. Women have entered the labor market and now carry the double burden of caring for home and family as well as earning what may be the only household income through paid employment. Men have been unable to keep up with the socially expected provider role, leading to a profound sense of powerlessness and failure and many pernicious problems, such as serious physical ailments and depression. Gender roles are changing, leading to conflicts at home. Men may react violently, abusing wives and children, but also neglecting and abandoning their families. Suicide is increasing among men and youth in transition economies as unemployment and depression increase. Alcohol is often used to manage stress, but it puts a tremendous economic and emotional strain on family members and also results in violence. Similar patterns have emerged in countries all over the world where men are displaced or unemployed because of changing economic conditions (Rademacher, Schafft, Patel, Koch-Schulte, & Narayan, 2000).

The outcomes of domestic violence for women and girls are dramatic and insidious. Women sustain long-term injuries such as lacerations, fractures, and damage to internal organs. They suffer psychologically, experiencing serious problems that compromise their health and ability to function on a daily basis, such as depression, anxiety, eating disorders, and posttraumatic stress disorder. It is not uncommon for violence against women to result in death—through suicide, murder, maternal mortality, and HIV/AIDS.

Violence against women also harms their children. Children who have observed violence in their homes, as victims of child abuse or witnesses to domestic violence, are more likely to have problems themselves compared with children who have not experienced domestic violence. They have more health and behavior problems and more trouble eating and sleeping; they run away and even commit suicide. Studies in several developing countries confirm that the offspring of women who are beaten are less likely to survive infancy and childhood, probably because their mothers cannot bargain with their husbands to provide adequate care and resources for their children (UNICEF, 2000b).

No matter where in the world domestic violence occurs, its roots are deeply embedded in cultural expectations of what is appropriate behavior for women and girls. Social, economic, and legal systems support these expectations. For example, in many countries, women do not have equal status under the law; they may not inherit property after their husband's death, they may not hold political office, they may not be permitted to divorce. When men are considered in control of family life, religious laws uphold this arrangement, and police and judiciary systems do not take women or domestic violence seriously (UNICEF, 2000a).

International organizations advocate a comprehensive approach for addressing the problem of domestic violence. Education and intervention must include the family, as well as community system of elders and religious groups; legal reforms, such as legislation that would hold the perpetrator accountable; responsive health care providers; and other interventions, such as battered women's shelters.

Female Genital Cutting

One form of violence that has received considerable attention in recent years is female genital cutting (FGC) or female genital mutilation. This involves cutting or removing portions of a woman's external genitalia or other injury to the female genital organs for cultural or other nonmedical reasons (UNFPA, 2003). An estimated 130 million women and girls have experienced FGC; probably 2 million are affected each year.

FGC is carried out and perpetuated based on a number of different cultural beliefs. It is viewed as a way to control female sexuality, preserve virginity, and enhance men's sexual pleasure. It is a rite of passage that initiates young women into adulthood. In some societies it is viewed as an aesthetic or hygienic practice and may be considered a prerequisite to marriage. Sometimes, it is performed on girls as young as 5 to 8 years old (UNFPA, 2003).

The health impacts of FGC are serious and may be life threatening (UNFPA, 2003), including numerous gynecological, reproductive, and child-bearing problems as well as increased risk of HIV/AIDS. FGC may also have lasting psychological impacts. The practice is found throughout Africa, in some parts of Asia, and in several countries in the Arab peninsula, although it is outlawed in some countries where it is practiced. It also occurs among immigrant groups that have settled in Canada, Europe, and the United States (Brydon & Chant, 1989; Townsend & Momsen, 1987; UNFPA, 2003).

International health organizations and many governments in the developing as well as developed world view FGC as a form of violence against women that must be eliminated. A number of laws and proclamations have been ratified, providing legal and economic sanctions against the practice of FGC, and arrests have been made in several countries where FGC has been commonly practiced (UNFPA, 2003). International campaigns against FGC have in some cases resulted in changing attitudes toward the practice and declines in the procedure. For example, in Egypt in the 1990s, girls were 10% less likely to undergo the procedure than their mothers had been. Even many circumcised girls expressed ambivalence or thought the procedure was unnecessary (El-Gibaly, Ibrahim, Mensch, & Clark, 1999).

Missing Women

One hundred million women in the world have gone missing. The term *missing women* refers to distorted sex ratios, where there are much lower ratios of females to males than expected. We would expect that the ratio would be about one to one, or that there would be slightly more females than males because of higher male mortality at all ages. In regions where both girls and boys receive adequate food, clothing, and shelter, such as Europe, North America, and Japan, the female-to-male ratio is 103–105 women to 100 men. The lower female-to-male ratio is most obvious in South Asia, China, and parts of the Middle East. The ratios are 97:100 in Egypt and Iran, 95:100 in Bangladesh and Turkey, 94:100 in China, 93:100 in India and Pakistan, and 84:100 in Saudi Arabia. In India's Punjab state, notorious for higher female mortality, the ratio is 87 women for every 100 men (Sen, 2001). This overmortality of females is not due to natural causes.

The term was first used in the late 1980s by Nobel laureate economist Amartya Sen to refer to the many girls who are simply *not alive* because of unusually high mortality rates. These girls are never given a chance to reach maturity because of their families' consistent neglect and discrimination, as well as significant biases against women and girls in the delivery of health care (Hunger Project, n.d., section "Unwanted Before Birth"; Sen, 2001). In the past decade, millions of girls have been killed because of cultural biases against female children and changing economic conditions that make it difficult for families to fulfill their social contracts for female offspring. Amniocentesis is used to identify the sex of the fetus; parents or relatives can then choose to induce or force abortion. Female infanticide is also practiced. In early childhood, girls are deliberately malnourished and deprived of needed medical care, leading to higher female child mortality. Girl children in India are breastfed for a shorter period of time, are fed less, and receive poorer-quality food during childhood. Girls are much less likely to receive health care when they are ill (Hunger Project, n.d.; Sen, 2001).

Why does this occur? In South Asia, families assume from birth that a daughter will belong to her husband's family. This means that money spent to raise and care for a daughter is often considered "wasted" (Hunger Project, n.d., section "Unwanted . . . ").

Refugee and Emergency Situations

There were nearly 12 million refugees in 2001, and the largest groups were from Asia (48%) and Africa (27%). Refugees are those who are out of their country and cannot return because of fear of persecution based on race, religion, national origin, political beliefs, or membership in a particular social group; those who have fled their country because of armed conflict; and those who have been allowed to stay in a host country for humanitarian reasons (UNHCR, 2002, section on statistics). In most regions, women and girls make up about half of the refugee population (UNHCR, 2001); many of them are single mothers who head their households. Adult men in refugee situations are often disabled, aged, or with their households only temporarily (Byrne & Baden, 1995). Refugees typically live in camps, where women are discriminated against in the distribution of food, clothing, and shelter, just as they are in their home countries. They are frequently victims of violence, such as sexual abuse and rape, forced prostitution, and beatings perpetrated by spouses, family members, refugee workers, or gangs. They are five times as likely to be infected with HIV/AIDS as a male refugee (Byrne & Baden).

The dismal situation for refugees also applies to women and girls in other emergency situations. Emergencies vary by how fast they occur and how long they last and include: natural disasters, such as earthquakes and floods; sudden technological or communication, transportation, and information system problems; slow-onset emergencies, such as drought; permanent emergencies such as widespread poverty; mass population displacements due to other emergencies; and complex emergencies associated with armed conflict (Byrne & Baden, 1995).

The conditions and crises leading to emergency and refugee situations break down social norms and community support patterns. Because of the collapse of their normal lives and communities, women and men are left without the usual practices and rules that guide social interactions and support. Men may take their frustrations out on women, and, in the unfamiliar camp environment, violence against women may be tolerated. Women do not have the usual social networks they have at home for assistance and safety (Byrne & Baden, 1995; 24 Hour Exile, 2003).

Not everyone suffers equally, and some may benefit (Byrne & Baden, 1995). Men tend to have more ways to deal with emergencies, because they have access to and control of more resources, such as cash, large livestock, and ownership of property. Women may be forced to use survival strategies that hurt them in the long run. For example, they may eat last and least, or they may sell off small livestock under their control. If the family sells its possessions, women's property often goes first, leaving them particularly vulnerable if the family breaks up. Not only do poorer women have fewer resources, but their pleas for help from household members may be rejected. It is not uncommon for women, children, and the elderly to be abandoned in crisis situations. In some emergencies, women may gain some autonomy and leadership in camp communities, whereas in armed conflict situations, more conservative attitudes tend to prevail, and women's rights and mobility decrease (Byrne & Baden).

Relief programs often register only men, not their wives, rendering women invisible in the camps. Whether it involves food aid, tools and seeds, or training, these are directed to male heads of households, even though women may have primary responsibility at home for food production and distribution. There is an increasing push among humanitarian relief agencies to address what happens to women and children in emergency situations and in the camp environment. Special programs are designed to meet women's particular needs, such as the provision of reproductive health care by female medical personnel and protection against physical violence.

Coping With Crises

The issues discussed above are often crises, problems, or at the very least challenges for women and their families. How do families respond to these situations? How do they resolve them? Available coping strategies may be inadequate to deal with the many complex and often life-threatening situations we have discussed in this chapter. In fact, coping strategies may set off other problems.

For example, with regard to the HIV/AIDS crisis, families with infected members are depending more on the elder generation to care for the adults with AIDS and their offspring. Tragically, an estimated 10 million children are now "OVCs," or orphans and vulnerable children, because they have lost both parents to HIV/AIDS. Elders often provide care for the adults and children, but it is an enormous burden for them, because they also must do the laborious work necessary to sustain the household. Their increased *vulnerability* leads to greater impoverishment of the household and ever more serious health problems. Children themselves must work to earn an income and produce food and must also care for sick family members. In some instances, children head their own households or have no choice but to live on the streets (HelpAge International, 2003). In short, these families and others facing crises are particularly *vulnerable*. They are to some degree defenseless against external shocks and stress and find that they have limited capacity to recover without sustaining damaging losses such as physical illness, impoverishment, and psychological harm (Byrne & Baden, 1995).

Resources are essential for coping with crisis. These resources might take the form of money, material goods, social support, or personal characteristics of family members such as education. Families in developing countries typically lack the resources that would enable them to cope effectively with crisis situations. Modern crises such as wars and famines crumble social support and kin networks, shattering women's traditional sources of emotional and practical support and leaving them even more vulnerable. Two-Thirds World families often lack human capital resources that would help them deal with a situation. Women are doubly affected, because they are more likely than men to lack access to material and social resources (Byrne & Baden, 1995).

POLICY AND PRACTICE: EMPOWERING WOMEN

In this chapter, we discovered that gender stratification and patriarchal systems determine the relationships between men and women within households and in communities. We have taken the position that women have been marginalized in the process of colonialism and capitalist expansion into rural and urban systems of production and are even further marginalized by globalization.

In short, women have fewer economic and human capital resources than men and have more family and work responsibilities. Under worsening economic conditions, families are being split apart in efforts to make ends meet, whereas women are expected to hold them together. Given these dire circumstances, what is the future for Two-Thirds World women?

Many argue that empowerment of women is critical. At its most basic level, empowerment means that women have or gain greater control over their lives so that they achieve greater equity in society and their relationships. Empowerment refers to expanding choices and the freedom to shape their own lives (Everett, 1989; Sen, 2001).

In large part, empowerment may depend on women's ability to gain and control valuable social resources such as education and income (Coltrane, 1992). Empowerment is developed through education by improving women's literacy rate and enrollment in primary and secondary schools. Empowerment is promoted in the workplace with assurances of gainful employment, but also through recognition of the value of women's contributions to production with domestic work, child care, and subsistence agriculture. Social and health care services that assist women in supporting their families also empower women (Blumberg, 1989). A 40-year-old woman from Ghana says,

> I managed to save a little and feed my children at the same time. When I managed to save enough, I started selling cooked yam, and here I made more money and managed to save. I was lucky to meet a friend who gave me secondhand clothes on credit to sell. This I did very well and started building up my capital. Now I am trading with my own money. My first two children are in secondary school and my last child, who is 18 months old, is in a creche [day-care center]. I managed to get out of poverty because I was not ready to give up, and so I fought hard and with the help of a friend, I succeeded. I believe with hard work and luck one could get out of poverty and be self-sufficient. (quoted in Narayan & Petesch, 2002, p. 28)

Women's Associations

Women often are empowered through their relationship with women's associations. There are five general categories of women's groups: national, employment-based, voluntary, grassroots, and feminist (Ziyambi, 2002).

National associations, national machineries, and official women's associations are usually a reliable indicator of the official position on gender issues, because they are in most cases administered and led by government officials, or wives of government officials (Ziyambi, 2002). The government often subsidizes these groups, and their physical location is often in or near the president's office. These can be either weak or strong associations, depending on the national context. There have been major campaigns to increase the number of women in governance by electing women to public office or appointing them to political leadership positions. For example, in Brazil, the civilian government established the National Council on Women's Rights, which allowed women access to shaping the new constitution (Racioppi & O'Sullivan See, n.d.)

Employment-based groups are usually the women's sections of trade unions or professions with large numbers of women, such as teaching and nursing. These groups are often more autonomous than official associations, operating along clear, self-perpetuating guidelines or with constitutions, and they are often financed by member subscriptions as well as donor funds (Ziyambi, 2002). In industrialized nations, women have organized for women's rights and their full participation in the public sphere (Johnson-Odim, 1991). For instance, as women's labor force participation has increased, so have efforts to equalize women's and men's salaries for comparable work, to free women from sexual harassment in the workplace, and to establish national parental leave policies and other family-supportive acts that enable parents to be productive workers.

Women may find that either voluntary associations or grassroots groups help them address these needs. Some regimes and governments tolerate certain kinds of women's groups, assuming that they are not political. Examples include the Mothers of the Plaza de Mayo in Argentina, who organized as mothers to protest the disappearance of their children under the military dictationship of the 1970s, using their position as mothers to protect themselves from police repression during their political protests. Other regimes, for example, the former USSR, repressed all forms of social activism and association (Racioppi & O'Sullivan See, n.d.)

Voluntary associations provide services and engage in welfare activities by offering training in basic skills, shoring up support networks, and operating child care facilities. They can mobilize, network, and educate the wider population about their concerns and issues. These associations may have close ties with international women's associations or religious institutions from which they may receive funding or other assistance (Ziyambi, 2002).

Grassroots groups can be found in both rural and urban areas and are predominantly self-help groups that grow out of local conditions to meet specific needs of women and households. The local or national government, national or international nongovernmental organizations (NGOs), and international donors sometimes assist these groups. Examples from the Third World suggest that women's social actions are often motivated by their desire to improve the quality of their families' lives (Nash, 1990; Safa, 1990). Women want their rights as wives and mothers to be affirmed as a legitimate basis for incorporation as full participants in the public world and use their domestic role to give them strength and legitimacy in making demands of the state (Safa). Often, women have organized simply to survive (Enloe, 1989; Nash; Safa).

Feminist groups are made up of more educated women who are working toward basic changes in their society to support women's rights in one or more areas. They may tackle specific issues, such as reproductive rights, violence against women, access to education, and women's legal rights. They use both legal means and the media to publicize and advance their causes, advocating for women wherever they can. Often, they receive support from international donors. These groups are usually urban based, although not necessarily, and small in size. Examples include Women and Law in Southern Africa and the Federation of African Media Women Zimbabwe.

Feminism has long operated at the margins of policy and practice, seemingly because those espousing feminist causes (e.g., educated elite or middle-class women) had little power to make a difference. Since the advent of the UN Decade(s) for Women, starting in Mexico City in 1975 and occurring every 10 years since, women of all classes, races, and nationalities, working from local to international levels, have made serious inroads into policy and practice around the world. Key among these have been Third World feminists, women speaking, writing, and practicing in developing countries. These women frame the issues around feminism differently, in some cases, than do Western feminists.

By and large, the interests of Western feminists have been rights based, for example, the right to work and the right to vote. Third World feminists, whose voices finally began to be heard in the 1980s, conflate women's rights with class, race, and ethnicity issues and are more interested in resistance and hearing/knowing the oppressed. Race, ethnicity, and other markers shape women's multiple identities and map the discriminations and inequities they face on account of their identities as women (Crenshaw, 1991). Feminists in the South, who continue to struggle with social inequities in their countries, also have to address the multiple identities, experiences, and issues facing women in their quest for social justice. The simultaneity and intersection of their issues recognize that women have to construct their multiple identities in relation to others.

Role of Government and International Agencies

One of the most important actions taken by the international community with regard to women's rights is the Convention on the Elimination of All Forms of Discrimination Against Women (CEDAW). This agreement obligates those countries that have ratified or acceded to it to take all appropriate measures to ensure the full development and advancement of women in all spheres—political, educational, employment, health care, economic, social, legal, and marriage and family relations (United Nations, 2003a). It also calls for the modification of social and cultural patterns of conduct in order to eliminate prejudice, customs, and all other practices based on the idea of inferiority or superiority of either sex. The UN General Assembly passed CEDAW in 1981. As of April 2003, 173 nations are party to the convention, and an additional 3 have signed the treaty, binding them to do nothing in contravention of its terms. The United States is one of the last countries still holding out on ratification (United Nations, 2003a).

A number of international organizations work on behalf of women. These include intergovernmental agencies such as the various UN agencies (UNIFEM, UNICEF, INSTRAW). The number of international NGOs, associations, institutes, centers, and universities that focus on topics such as human and women's rights, labor rights, housing rights, work against trafficking, reproductive health, women in politics, and women and AIDS continues to grow annually. Although many of these are based in the North, a growing number are found in Southern countries.

CONCLUSION

In this chapter, we explored the similarity and diversity of women's lives in the major regions of the Two-Thirds World. We found that preference is given to men and boys in the distribution and control of three critical social and human resources—education, employment, and health. Women have lower educational achievement and receive relatively little encouragement to attend school. They are responsible for most of the work that gets done in the home and in factories, markets, and fields but are relegated to low-paying jobs or marginal work in the informal sector. Despite the importance of reproduction in developing countries, women and girls are deprived of an adequate, nutritious food supply, with measurable negative effects on their own health and the health and survival rates of their offspring. Finally, they suffer the tragic consequences of domestic violence, female genital cutting, and other practices that impair their physical and psychological health and that of their children.

We have found that women are becoming empowered, as social practices slowly change. Women are entering the workforce in greater numbers, they are receiving more education, and they are taking responsibility for their health and that of their children. Legal practices are also helping women to attain higher status in their countries. Not all stories of poor women are sad stories; many are encouraging. Awareness of the issues they face and why we should be concerned about poor women around the world is necessary for the continued empowerment and encouragement of these women. As a woman in Bihar, India, says, "[I wish] to have my children be educated and employed. They would then become good citizens and lead happy lives" (quoted in Narayan & Petesch, 2002, p. 173).

REFERENCES

Adamu, F. L. (1998). Gender myths about secluded women in Hausa Society of Northern Nigeria. In M. E. Kolawole, (Ed.), *Gender perceptions and development in Africa: A socio-cultural approach* (pp. 231–241). Lagos, Nigeria: Arrabon Academic Publishers.

Agarwal, B. (1985). Women and technological change in agriculture: The Asian and African experience. In I. Ahmed (Ed.), *Technology and rural women: Conceptual and empirical issues* (pp. 67–114). London: George Allen and Unwin.

Asis, M. M. B. (2003). Asian women migrants: Going the distance but not far enough. *Migration Information Source.* Retrieved May 17, 2005, from http://www.migrationinformation.org/Feature/display.cfm?ID=103

Blumberg, R. L. (1989). *Making the case for the gender variable: Women and the wealth and well-being of nations.* Washington, DC: U.S. Agency for Women in Development.

Brockerhoff, M., & Biddlecom, A. E. (1998). *Migration, sexual behavior and HIV diffusion in Kenya* (Policy Research Division Working Paper No. 111). New York: Population Council. Retrieved June 29, 2003, from http://www.popcouncil.org/publications/wp/prd/111.html

Brydon, L., & Chant, S. (1989). *Women in the Third World.* New Brunswick, NJ: Rutgers University Press.

Byrne, B., & Baden, S. (1995). *Gender, emergencies and humanitarian assistance: Bridge (development-gender)* (Rep. No. 33). Brighton, UK: Institute of Development Studies, University of Sussex.

Coltrane, S. (1992). The micropolitics of gender in nonindustrial societies. *Gender and Society, 6,* 86–107.

Crenshaw, K. (1991). Mapping the margins: Intersectionality, identity politics, and violence against women of color. *Stanford Law Review, 43,* 1241.

El-Gibaly, O., Ibrahim, B., Mensch, B. S., & Clark, W. H. (1999). *The decline of female circumcision in Egypt: Evidence and interpretation* (Policy Research Division Working Paper No. 132). New York: Population Council. Retrieved June 29, 2003, from http://www.popcouncil.org/publications/wp/prd/132.html

Enloe, C. (1989). *Bananas, beaches, and bases.* Berkeley: University of California Press.

Esteva, G., & Prakash, M. S. (1998). *Grassroots post-modernism: Remaking the soil of cultures.* London: Zed.

Everett, J. (1989). *The global empowerment of women.* Washington, DC: Association for Women in Development.

Forestieri, V. (1999). *Improvement of working conditions and environment in the informal sector through safety and health measures* (ILO Safe Work Papers). Geneva, Switzerland: International Labor Organization. Retrieved May 17, 2005, from http://www.ilo.org/public/english/protection/safework/sectors/informal/inform1.htm#summa

Foundation of Women's Forum. (1998). *Trafficking in women for the purpose of sexual exploitation.* Retrieved June 27, 2003, from http://www.qweb.kvinnoforum.se/papers/traffickingreport.html

Grant, J. (1992). *The state of the world's children 1992.* Oxford, UK: Oxford University Press.

HelpAge International. (2003). *Forgotten families: Older people as carers of orphans and vulnerable children.* Brighton, UK: International HIV/AIDS Alliance.

Holmes-Eber, P. (2003). *Daughters of Tunis: Women, family, and networks in a Muslim city.* Boulder, CO: Westview Press.

Huber, J. (1988). A theory of family, economy, and gender. *Journal of Family Issues, 9,* 9–26.

Hunger Project. (n.d.). The condition of women in South Asia. Retrieved April 22, 2005, from http://www.thp.org/sac/unit4/

International Labor Organization. (2005). A global alliance against forced labor. Geneva, Switzerland: Author. Retrieved May 17, 2005, from http://www.ilo.org/dyn/declaris/DECLARATIONWEB.DOWNLOAD_BLOB?Var_DocumentID=5059

International Organization for Migration. (2003). Facts and figures on international migration. *Migration Policy Issues, 2*. Retrieved June 27, 2003, from http://www.iom.int

Jacobson, J. (1993). Closing the gender gap in development. In L. R. Brown (Ed.), *The state of the world 1993* (pp. 61–79). New York: W.W. Norton.

Johnson-Odim, C. (1991). Common themes, different contexts: Third World women and feminism. In C. T. Mohanty, A. Russo, & L. Torres (Eds.), *Third World women and the politics of feminism* (pp. 314–327). Bloomington: Indiana University Press.

Karmi, G. (1993). The Saddam Hussein phenomenon and male-female relations in the Arab World. In H. Afshar (Ed.), *Women in the Middle East: Perceptions, realities and struggles for liberation* (pp. 146–157). New York: St. Martin's Press.

Little, D. (2003). *The paradox of wealth and poverty: Mapping the ethical dilemmas of global development*. Boulder, CO: Westview Press.

Manuh, T. (1998). *Women in Africa's development* (Africa Recovery Briefing Paper No. 11). Retrieved March 7, 2003, from http://www.un.org/ecosocdev/geninfo/afrec/bpaper/maineng.htm

McPherson, M. F. (2003, March). *Scaling up of HIV/AIDS activities: A critique*. Working paper presented for the U.S. Agency for International Development and Harvard University, Washington, DC.

Narayan, D., & Petesch, P. (2002). *Voices of the poor: From many lands*. Washington, DC: World Bank.

Nash, J. (1990). Latin American women in the world capitalist crisis. *Gender and Society, 4*, 338–353.

Pittin, R. I. (2002). *Women and work in Northern Nigeria: Transcending boundaries*. The Hague, The Netherlands: ISS.

Population Reference Bureau. (1994). *Conveying concerns: Women write about reproductive health*. Washington, DC: Population Reference Bureau.

Racioppi, L., & O'Sullivan See, K. (n.d.). *Engendering the democratic transition in Russia: Women, politics, and civil society*. Retrieved June 26, 2003, from http://www2.isp.msu.edu/cers/Racioppi%20See.htm

Rademacher, A., Schafft, K., Patel, R., Koch-Schulte, S., & Narayan, D. (2000). *Can anyone hear us?* New York: Oxford University Press for World Bank.

Safa, H. (1990). Women's social movements in Latin America. *Gender and Society, 4*, 338–353.

Sen, A. (1999). *Development as freedom*. New York: Alfred A. Knopf.

Sen, A. (2001, October 27). Many faces of gender inequality. *Frontline, 18*(22). Retrieved May 2, 2003, from http://www.hinduonnet.com/fline/fl1822/18220040.htm

Tiano, S. (2001). From victims to agents: A new generation of literature on women in Latin America. *Latin American Research Review, 36*, 183–203.

Townsend, J., & Momsen, J. H. (1987). Towards a geography of gender in developing market economies. In J. Momsen & J. Townsend (Eds.), *Geography of gender in the Third World* (pp. 27–81). London: Hutchinson.

24 Hour Exile. (2003). *Facts on women refugees.* Retrieved June 7, 2003, from http://www.mbcbl.org/exile2003/exile2003women.htm

UNAIDS. (2002). AIDS epidemic update. Geneva, Switzerland: Joint United Nations Programme on HIV/AIDS (UNAIDS) and World Health Organization (WHO). Retrieved June 3, 2003, from http://www.unaids.org/worldaids day/2002/press/update/epiupdate2002_en.doc

UNFPA. (2003). *What are the different types of FGC?* Retrieved May 20, 2003, from http://www.unfpa.org/gender/faq_fgc.htm#1

UNFPA. (n.d.). *Supporting adolescents and youth: Fast facts.* Retrieved July 3, 2003, from http://www.unfpa.org/adolescents/facts.htm

UNICEF. (2000a). Domestic violence against women and girls. *Innocenti Digest, 6,* 1–23. Retrieved June 4, 2003, from http://www.unicef.org/vaw/domestic.pdf

UNICEF. (2000b). *Violence against women and girls still a global epidemic.* Retrieved June 8, 2003, from http://www.unicef.org/newsline/00pr45.htm

United Nations. (1991a). *Women: Challenges to the year 2000.* New York: Author.

United Nations. (1991b). *The world's women 1970–1990.* New York: Author.

United Nations. (2000). *The world's women 2000.* New York: United Nations.

United Nations. (2003a). *Division for the Advancement of Women: Convention on the Elimination of All Forms of Discrimination Against Women: 29th Session.* Retrieved May 9, 2003, from http://www.un.org/womenwatch/daw/cedaw/

United Nations. (2003b). *World and regional trends: Data for years around 1990 and 2000.* Retrieved June 12, 2003, from http://unstats.un.org/unsd/mi/mi_worldregn.asp

United Nations Development Programme. (2003). *Millennium Development Goals.* Retrieved April 22, 2005, from http://www.undp.org/mdg/

United Nations High Commission on Refugees. (1999). *Reproductive health in refugee situations.* Geneva, Switzerland: Author.

United Nations High Commission on Refugees. (2001). *Women, children and older refugees.* Geneva, Switzerland: Author. Retrieved April 22, 2005, from http://www.unhcr.ch

United Nations High Commission on Refugees. (2002). Committee on the Elimination of Discrimination Against Women. Retrieved June 27, 2003, from http://www.unhchr.ch/html/menu2/6/cedw.htm

Williams, S., Seed, J., & Mwau, A. (1995). *The Oxfam gender training manual.* Oxford, UK: Oxfam Publishing.

World Bank. (2000/2001). *World development report 2000/2001.* Retrieved June 27, 2003, from http://www.worldbank.org/poverty/wdrpoverty/report/ch1.pdf

World Bank. (2005). *World development indicators 2005.* Retrieved May 17, 2005, from http://www.worldbank.org/data/wdi2005/wditext/Section1_1_3.htm

World Health Organization. (n.d.). *1995 maternal mortality estimates for U.N. regions.* Retrieved June 27, 2003, from http://www3.who.ch/whosis/mm/mm_region_1995

Ziyambi, N. M. (2002). *Historical overview of women's groups in Zimbabwe.* Retrieved May 9, 2003, from http://www.scholars.nus.edu.sg/landow/post/africa/ziyambi2.html

CHAPTER 19

Household Division of Labor in Industrial Societies

LINDA HAAS

This chapter describes how families in industrial societies divide responsibility for the work that must be done to support their families. Of particular interest is how this work is allocated on the basis of gender and how this gender-based division of labor is related to the status of women and men in society. The focus here is on three types of work prevalent in industrial societies: breadwinning, housework, and child care.

Unlike agricultural subsistence economies, in industrial societies most of the products and many of the services that families need must be purchased, including food, clothing, consumer goods, and leisure activities. *Breadwinning* involves responsibility for wage earning outside the household. This earned income is essential for family survival and comfort. Although individuals typically are employed because of the need for income, employment also has other benefits to individuals, including opportunities for self-fulfillment and social contacts. *Housework* is the work that must be done to keep family members fed, clean, and comfortable and to keep the home in good order. It includes cooking, dishwashing, shopping, housecleaning, laundry, and clothing care. This important and necessary work has been generally undervalued and invisible; even those who perform most of it tend to downplay its significance. In order for families to reproduce themselves, children must be born or adopted and cared for. The practical aspects of *child care* include feeding, washing, and arranging for substitute care. Children also need love, security, guidance, and instruction in order to develop self-respect and the skills necessary to get along in society. Play and parent-child interaction thus become important for nurturing the attributes desired in a given society.

This chapter focuses on these three types of activities because they take up most of family members' time and because they have received the most attention from researchers. Other types of work performed by families include house and lawn maintenance, care of sick family members, care of frail elders, maintenance of kin relations, financial management, and securing the family's position in the larger social community.

In industrial societies, the responsibilities of breadwinning, housework, and child care have traditionally been assigned to individuals on the basis of their assigned sex category. Men are regarded as more responsible for breadwinning, whereas women are considered more responsible for housework and child care. Either sex might cross over gender boundaries, but such behavior is often viewed as unusual because these responsibilities tend to be assigned to one sex (Coltrane, 1998; Potuchek, 1997; Williams, 2000). Women, especially wives and mothers, have entered the labor force in dramatic numbers in the past few decades. This development has the potential to dramatically change attitudes about gender roles in the family, as well as the actual division of labor for breadwinning, housework, and child care (Waite & Nielsen, 2001). This chapter shows, however, that the tendency for men and women to assume distinctive social roles within the family persists.

This chapter will discuss the following topics:

1. How the household division of labor in industrial societies became gender based
2. How the household division of labor is organized in various contemporary industrial societies
3. Why some societies have developed a more egalitarian approach to the division of labor
4. What future trends can be foreseen in the household division of labor in industrial societies

HOW THE HOUSEHOLD DIVISION OF LABOR BECAME GENDER BASED

Historical Perspectives

Anthropological evidence suggests that a gender-based division of labor in human societies has always existed (Kimmel, 2004). Yet before industrialization (i.e., the development of capitalism and market economies), there was no universal pattern for the division of labor that always assigned one task to women and one task to men, such as we might expect if the division of labor had some basis in biological sex differences. For example, in some societies women grew crops, whereas in others it was men. Before industrialization, men were not exclusively responsible for production of goods and services needed for the family's survival. Aronoff and Crano's (1975) study of 862 nonindustrial societies found that women contributed 44% of the food eaten by their families.

In preindustrial societies, women's work was not confined to the home. They gathered herbs, roots, fruits, and seeds; tended and harvested crops; fetched firewood and water; and raised small livestock (Stephens, 1963). They were often involved in economic exchanges outside the household when they sold or bartered surplus products of their labor to outsiders. The "housework" that women did was qualitatively and quantitatively different from that done by women in industrial countries today. Food preparation involved butchering, curing meats, and grinding grains, not just cooking. Clothing care involved tanning hides, spinning, weaving, and garment construction, not just laundry. Women were considered to be more responsible for housecleaning and child care, but these activities took up a small proportion of their time and were considered less important and less worthy of effort compared to women's other work (Crano & Aronoff, 1978). Dwellings were small and simply furnished, and high standards of cleanliness were not maintained. Children were regarded as little adults who did not require constant adult attention; the care of the youngest was often left to older siblings. Each parent was responsible for the moral upbringing and skills training of same-sex children (Faragher, 1990; Shorter, 1977).

Impact of Industrialization

Industrialization led to a dramatic redefinition of men's and women's household roles. As factories began manufacturing goods once produced in the home, family members were drawn into wage labor. Many of the first factory workers were women. Eventually, as factory work came to be seen less as a peripheral activity and more as the mainstay of the new economy, men entered the labor market and thereby gained control over this new source of cash income, power, and prestige (Jackson, 1992). A powerful set of beliefs—*the doctrine of separate spheres*—arose to justify men's monopolization of wage work (Padavic & Reskin, 2002). This doctrine maintained that men were naturally more suited for wage labor in the public sphere outside the home, whereas women were by nature more suited to perform housework and child care in the private sphere. Men would provide income for women and children so that goods and services previously produced in the home could be purchased; women would care for men's personal needs, the house, and children. Although labor was divided along gender lines, men's and women's activities were viewed as complementary in that they supported similar ends, the survival and economic advancement of the household unit. The resulting gender differences in power, economic resources, and social status were seldom discussed or challenged until the second wave of feminism began in the 1960s (Shorter, 1977).

The belief in natural differences and the desirability of complementary roles of women and men became entrenched first in the middle class, where families could survive on the pay of a single wage earner. Eventually, this ideology shaped the aspirations (if not the reality) of the working class as well. Trade union leaders, politicians, clergy, educators, writers, physicians, politicians, and even female social reformers promoted the doctrine of separate spheres. Some of these groups had vested interests in men having privileged access to cash income and women remaining subordinate to men; others believed devoutly in women and men having different biological capacities and divine missions (Padavic & Reskin, 2002).

In accordance with the idea that men were to be family breadwinners, men had greater access to jobs that would provide cash income essential to obtain the necessities of urban life. Women were supposed to concentrate on doing unpaid work within the home. The character of this work was substantially different from what it was like before industrialization. Many tasks women had spent so much time on before industrialization, such as food production, food processing, and clothes making, were less necessary because food and clothes could be purchased. Instead, women were expected to devote themselves to housework, which "as a distinctive form of labor emerges only with industrialization" (Ferree, 1991, p. 111). Dwellings, furnishings, and wardrobes became more elaborate, and women spent more time maintaining them. Standards for cleanliness escalated; domestic scientists warned women to eliminate germs to preserve family health. In time, new products and machines were invented for women to use to maintain their possessions and homes in even better condition (e.g., washing machines, vacuum cleaners). The amount of time women spent in housework increased dramatically (Oakley, 1974).

Standards for child care changed even more, which shaped women's new social identities in important ways. Childhood came to be viewed by clergy, psychologists, and physicians as the most crucial stage in the development of the individual. Children were seen as needing special protection, education, and nurturing in order to develop normally. Mothers were regarded as the ideal parents to do this, because religion and popular opinion maintained that they were more moral, spiritual, and tender than men were (Rotundo, 1985). The "cult of motherhood" was promoted from pulpits and in the mass media, and motherhood began to represent "the greatest achievement of a woman's life, the sole true means of self-realization" (Oakley, 1974, p. 186). Women's time spent with children increased significantly, and women's personal and social identities became tied up with being mothers. Children's need for full-time care by mothers was used to justify women's exclusion from the paid labor market.

It is important to note that the doctrine of separate spheres did not succeed in excluding women entirely from wage labor. For example, in 1900, one fourth of U.S. women worked for pay outside the home; in France, nearly one third did (J. Lewis, 1992). Many (but not all) women who worked for pay were single, poor, minority, or immigrant women whose families could not afford to conform to the dominant middle-class ideal promoting women as full-time housewives and mothers. Employers benefited from these women's need for work, using them as a low-paid labor force. Other women worked for pay at home—taking in boarders, sewing, and doing laundry—in a hidden labor market not counted in employment statistics (Bose, 1987).

Recent Developments

In nearly all industrial societies, women's entrance into the labor market has dramatically increased in the past three decades. In the United States, 60% of all women were in the labor force in 2000 (Padavic & Reskin, 2002). In the 15 nations of the European Union (EU), the average employment rate of females ages 15–64 was 54% in 2000 (Eurostat, 2000). More wives have been drawn into the labor market, from all social classes. Mothers of young children, who previously did not enter the labor force until their children went to school, have entered the labor market in record numbers. Women are now a highly visible part of the paid labor force in industrial societies, composing between one third and one half (Padavic & Reskin).

There are several reasons for this change. Smaller family sizes, reliable birth control technology, and higher educational attainment have made women more eligible for employment. Women's labor force participation is also affected by changes in the economy related to the development of the service sector. The availability of service jobs has attracted women into the labor market; these jobs are also often regarded as consistent with women's traditional responsibilities for nurturing and service (Padavic & Reskin, 2002; Waite & Nielsen, 2001).

In many industrial societies, a decline in real earnings since the 1970s has made two incomes crucial for the maintenance of families' standard of living. This decline is attributed to the elimination of many formerly well-paying manufacturing jobs and the development of a two-tier wage system that offers lower wages and slower pay increases to new entrants in the labor market. With women providing between 25% and 42% of family income in most industrial societies, their contribution to the household's economy is considerable (United Nations, 2002).

Women have also entered the labor market to enjoy the benefits of economic independence, including more control over family resources, more say in family decision making, and less vulnerability to economic misfortune after divorce. Like men, women take on paid work to serve their communities, develop skills and talents, and pursue personal interests. In many countries, a strong feminist movement has helped women realize the advantages of earning one's own income and the benefits of seeking self-fulfillment outside the home. The Organisation for Economic Cooperation and Development (OECD), which represents most industrialized societies, promotes mothers' participation in paid employment "to maintain their labour market skills, to ensure adequate resources for families . . . and to make further progress toward gender equity." The OECD maintains that "the skills of mothers will be increasingly needed in the labour market as the population of working age in most OECD countries begins to shrink" (OECD, 2001, p. 129).

Despite the increasing employment of wives and mothers, women's opportunities for highly paid work remain limited. Their wages in comparison to men's have not risen to any significant extent, although some improvements are noticeable in some countries. Women's low wage potential and segregation in the lower-status areas of the labor market keep women economically dependent on men, who remain, for the most part, their families' primary breadwinners. Being a good family breadwinner is the surest route for men to achieve recognition as good husbands, fathers, and citizens. Women are still evaluated more for their performance as housekeepers and mothers. (Television commercials provide a good example of this.) Women's unpaid family work lacks social recognition as work. It is seen as something women do because they love their families or as something they want to do in their leisure time. Women must arrange their participation in the paid labor market around family needs, whereas men are able to devote themselves to their jobs and careers without having to be concerned about their responsibility for child care or their spouses' occupational involvement (Gerson, 1985).

In summary, industrialization resulted in men being assigned the most visibly productive and highly valued responsibility in the family, namely breadwinning. Meanwhile, women were assigned the lower-status tasks of housework and child care, redefined to encompass more activities with a higher set of standards than had previously existed. Women's job opportunities were limited, because women were considered to be less suitable laborers than men and were held responsible for home and children. This same division of labor persists to a greater or lesser extent in all contemporary industrial societies. However, important differences exist not only in the way breadwinning, housework, and child care are assigned and performed as responsibilities but also in terms of the directions societies are taking in this regard.

CROSS-NATIONAL VARIATIONS IN THE HOUSEHOLD DIVISION OF LABOR

Industrial societies can be divided into different types based on the extent to which the society promotes gender equality in the family. For the purposes of this chapter, three types of societies are distinguished: *traditional*, *transitional*, and *egalitarian*. The specific criteria used to determine whether a society falls in one group or another are described below.

1. ***Shared breadwinning.*** This concerns the extent to which women, including mothers of young children, are income providers for their families. To be income providers, women must be employed outside the home for pay. Such employment needs to be supported through legislation that promotes equal opportunities at the workplace, so that women have access to a wide range of jobs at pay levels that are above poverty level

(defined internationally as earning less than 50% of the nation's median earned income). Companies and social policies need to provide support for working mothers (e.g., family leave policies, subsidized and regulated public child care). Otherwise, women's wages are reduced and their opportunities for feeling responsible for breadwinning are limited (Stier & Lewin-Epstein, 2001).

For breadwinning to be shared by men and women, women's wage work must be defined as contributing money for the family's basic needs, and women must be as obligated as men to be financial providers for their families (Haas, 1986). Three major types of breadwinning arrangements exist cross-culturally: "strong male breadwinner" nation-states, where the ideal is the husband and father bringing home wage income; "dual breadwinner" (or "weak male breadwinner") states, where the ideal is for both wives and husbands to bring home wage income; and "modified" breadwinner states, where men remain families' primary breadwinners and women engage in paid work mainly before and after periods of domestic responsibilities (J. Lewis, 1992).

2. ***Shared domestic work.*** This concerns the extent to which women and men share the work of caring for family members and their living quarters. The most common measure of sharing housework and child care is comparing how much time each spouse spends. Because spending time in household labor does not necessarily mean a person is involved in the planning and administration of it, it is also desirable to know to what extent men and women share equally in the overall responsibility for housework and child care.

3. ***Integration of public and private spheres.*** Integration of public and private spheres would exist when working parents of both sexes prioritize family and work roles to an equal degree, and when both sexes are assumed to share responsibility for housework and child care.

This is also known as "reconciliation of work and family life" and is widely regarded as an important prerequisite of gender equality at home and in public life. At the workplace, both sexes would have easy and affordable access to programs designed to help them combine breadwinning, housework, and child care responsibilities (e.g., parental leave, child care, time off for sick children, part-time work, flexible work scheduling). Working conditions and standards for career advancement would take into account that most workers have family responsibilities, and family work would become as socially valued as paid employment. For example, there would exist wage replacement programs for people who do unpaid family work (e.g., stay home to care for children), as well as assurances that such time would not hurt them later in terms of job security, advancement, seniority, and retirement benefits.

Using these criteria, societies are labeled *traditional* if available research evidence suggests that they meet almost none of the above criteria, *transitional* if they are beginning to meet some, and *egalitarian* if they meet nearly all three. It is in fact difficult to classify societies, because data on societies are incomplete; often, little research has been done or made available to an international audience. At other times, the information provided on different societies is not comparable. For example, international statistics about women's labor force participation involve different definitions of "participation," age ranges, and base years. Survey data on the household division of labor for individual couples is even more difficult to compare cross-nationally, because researchers employ different methods for gathering data.

To minimize potential bias in assigning countries to one group over another, it is helpful to look at research on gender role attitudes, because attitudes have a significant impact on the domestic division of labor (Crompton & Harris, 1999; Shelton & John, 1996). Government and workplace policies can also be analyzed as proxies for cultural definitions of men's and women's roles, because policies are often affected by cultural perspectives on gender. According to Pascall and Manning (2000), "Social policies reflect assumptions about gender relations within households and affect those relations" (p. 250). Such policies can support or help to erase boundaries between work and family and establish whether caring for family members is a public or a private responsibility. Research on EU member states has found that tax policies favoring women's employment, child care programs, and paid family leave help families' efforts at integrating work and family roles (OECD, 2001).

Below are descriptions of societies that fit each type—traditional, transitional, and egalitarian.

Traditional Societies

A rather strict gender-based division of household labor characterizes traditional industrial societies, with the man being responsible for breadwinning and the woman (even if employed for pay) having primary responsibility for home and children. Work life and social policy are structured to perpetuate this division. The following industrial societies appear to fit into this category: Austria, Belgium, Czech Republic, Germany, Greece, Ireland, Italy, Japan, the Netherlands, Poland, and Spain. In this chapter, Japan and Spain are featured.

Japan

Historically, Japan was a strongly patriarchal society, influenced by Confucian ethics. Men exercised direct control over the lives of wives and children and expected absolute obedience and respect. After World War II, however, more democratic ideals emerged. Laws granted women more authority in marriage and over children (Ishii-Kuntz, 1993). According to Siketo (2003), contemporary Japanese society remains sharply stratified by gender, where men are expected to be "principal earners" for their families and women are expected to be "accommodators," adjusting their participation in the labor market to family needs and remaining primarily responsible for housework and child care.

Legislation mandates equal employment opportunities for Japanese women, and research indicates that Japanese women experience less job segregation than do women in many other industrial nations, including the United States and the United Kingdom (Nakata & Takehiro, 2002). But women make up only 41% of the labor market (United Nations, 2000). Although over half (54%) of Japanese wives are in the labor force, only one third of mothers are employed (OECD, 2001). Japan remains a strong "male breadwinner" state. Women's tendency to quit work while children are young causes them to lose job opportunities when they return to a labor market that rewards continuous service (Ishii-Kuntz, 1993).

When women are in the labor market, they tend to hold jobs that have less security and status than men's, especially if they work for large corporations. Women's share of administrative and managerial jobs has stayed steadily low, at less than 10% (Wirth, 2001). Women's regular hourly pay in 1999 averaged only 61% of men's, which is a larger disparity than in most industrial societies (OECD, 2001). Siketo (2003) suggests that the gender wage gap is due to women's tendency to discontinue their employment to care for children and to their working part-time. Although government legislation technically prohibits paying part-timers less than full-timers or penalizing those who drop out of work to care for family members, this remains a common practice. Part-time workers' average hourly wage is only 70% that of full-time workers. The government encourages women's working part-time by exempting part-time work from taxation (Siketo).

Men's jobs typically require considerable overtime hours. Although some observers have concluded that men's devotion to work has contributed to Japan's financial success, there is now concern about fathers' absence from children's lives. One national survey found that fathers spent 3 minutes a day on weekdays and 19 minutes per day on weekends in child care activities. A cross-national study found that 37% of Japanese children never interacted with their residential fathers (even to eat meals together), compared with 15% of U.S. children and 20% of German children. Absence does not necessarily make fathers weak parents, however. Fathers remain psychologically present through mothers' "daily talk," which continually affirms that fathers are authority figures and breadwinners, and thus at the center of the family. A six-nation study showed that Japanese children respect their mothers much less than children in other societies, reflecting Japanese society's devaluation of women's unpaid family role (Ishii-Kuntz, 1993; 2003).

There are signs that Japanese women's orientation toward employment is changing. Thirty years ago, almost half of employed wives "retired" from paid employment after becoming mothers; by 1997, only 19% did so (Gottfried & O'Reilly, 2002). An increasing percentage of young Japanese women is remaining single, because they believe it would be difficult to be married and still fulfill their personal and professional aspirations (Sugihara & Katsurada, 2002).

Japanese women's attitudes have also become more egalitarian over time (Sugihara & Katsurada, 2002). In 1995, 75% of women ages 25–64 agreed that "Work life should be an important element of life for women just like men," and 64% disagreed that "Men should work outside the home and women should maintain the home." However, two thirds of women still agreed that "Women are more suited for household work and childrearing than men are" (Yamaguchi, 2000). Younger women and women with more education were more likely to express egalitarian gender roles attitudes; however, the impact of education on women's attitudes was far weaker in Japan than has been found for the United States (Yamaguchi, 2000).

Although wives' labor force participation has increased, the division of labor in Japanese households generally remains quite traditional. Japanese wives' duties focus primarily on housework, financial management, care of elderly relatives, and close attention to children, especially supervision of their schooling. In Batalova and Cohen's (2002) study of housework in 22 industrial countries (which included the United States, Sweden, the United Kingdom, and Russia, also discussed in this chapter), Japan scored the most traditional on a measure of "gender division of labor within couples," which measured the extent to which women did laundry, cared for sick family members, did shopping, and planned dinner. A 1996 time-use study found that wives with toddlers (ages 1–2) spent 4 hours and 46 minutes per day on housework, compared to 21 minutes per day for their husbands (Siketo, 2003).

In 1996, the Council for Gender Equality declared that men and women should equally share responsibility for work and family (Siketo, 2003). To reduce men's absorption in paid work, government policy now limits the total days and hours employees can work, and annual leaves must be taken (Siketo). Men's tendency to work overtime will be difficult to break, because work organizations are structured on the "long hours" model (Fujimoto, 1999). Research shows that men's increased time off work has been converted into more leisure time, rather than to more time spent in housework and child care (Siketo).

Government policy also encourages the private sector to expand services that workers can purchase, to reduce women's workload at home. But these efforts have resulted in "an overall decline in the wages and working conditions of care workers," reflecting a "low appreciation of women's work" (Peng, 2001, p. 195). Concern over a declining fertility rate and fathers' frequent absence have led to amendments in the Childcare Law, allowing fathers to take leave to care for a sick child (Araki, 1998), and to family leave legislation making leave available to fathers as well as mothers (Sato, 2000). However, such leave is compensated at only 40% of usual earnings, and those who take leave have been found to suffer wage penalties after they return to their jobs (Siketo, 2003). Women's low proportion of seats in Parliament (9%) has been offered as one explanation for why gender equality has been slow to evolve in Japan (Mikkelsen, 2000).

Spain

Like Japan, Spain has historically been a society dominated by men. A strong Catholic tradition has emphasized traditional gender roles in the family (Gonzalez-Lopez, 2001). Moreover, the 40-year-long dictatorship of Francisco Franco "abolished rights and liberties for the entire population and impeded Spanish women's efforts to gain the same social achievements as other European women" (Martinez-Hernandez, 2003, p. 601). Franco's death in 1975 paved the way for the development of a women's movement and a new government that was more positive about improving women's position. However, the end of the dictatorship was also associated with economic developments that slowed down women's integration into the labor market, including decreased international investment, an oil crisis, rising unemployment partly caused by the return of emigrants, and an economic recession (Carrasco & Rodriguez, 2000).

Although women now have full legal status and the constitution now grants equality of husband and wife, Spain is still considered to be one of the most traditional societies in Europe in regard to women's labor market status and the extent to which breadwinning, housework, and child care are shared by women and men. In most industrial societies, women take for granted that they can plan the timing, spacing, and number of children because of modern birth control technology and abortion rights. In Spain, on the other hand, contraceptive information and sale were outlawed until 1979. Contraceptives are still not available for free, and abortion rights are limited (Martinez-Hernandez, 2003).

The unemployment rate for Spanish women (counting only those looking for work) is double that of men (20% vs. 10%) (Martinez-Hernandez, 2003). Only 40% of women are employed for pay, which is the lowest female labor force participation in Europe (Martinez-Hernandez). Spain remains a strong "male breadwinner" state. Spanish women work in a narrow range of occupations considered appropriate for women, in the service sector and in civil service (where antidiscrimination laws are most effective). In 1998, women's hourly wages were only 61% of men's (OECD, 2001). However, women's share of administrative and managerial jobs is on a steady incline, tripling from 1985 to 1995 (from 4% to 12%) (Wirth, 2001).

In two-parent households with children, where husbands work full-time, only 36% of Spanish wives were employed for pay full-time, with an additional 8% being employed part-time in 2000 (EU, 2002). But attitudes toward maternal employment are changing.

In 1996, only 28% of Spanish women felt that the ideal way of life was for the woman to stay home when the children were young. Forty percent stated that ideally, women should combine a job with homemaking and caregiving throughout their lives (Duran, 2000). A 1998 study of couple families with at least one child under 6 found that 60% preferred that both mothers and fathers worked full-time, whereas 12% preferred that the man worked full-time while the woman worked part-time (OECD, 2001). In 2000, 42% of mothers with children under 6 were employed, compared to 30% 10 years earlier (OECD, 2001).

According to Carrasco and Rodriguez (2000), "Women do not relinquish responsibilities for the care of others when they become employed. They respect the value of emotional and social relationships that generate links of solidarity and create the complex fabric of human relations that make a market economy possible" (p. 49). To cope with work-family conflict, women elect to have fewer children. The total fertility rate has dropped over time, to 1.14 births per woman in 1998, from 2.78 in 1975 (Carrasco & Rodriguez, 2000).

Gonzalez-Lopez (2001) states that women's higher occupational aspirations have not been accompanied by changes in institutions that will help women integrate work and family responsibilities. Following changes in the treaty for the EU, which Spain joined in the 1980s, legislation now calls for the reconciliation of work and family life. In 1996, fathers and mothers were given the right to share 10 weeks of paid leave after childbirth (with the mother having exclusive right to an additional 6 weeks at the beginning). The government has also enacted job-guaranteed unpaid parental leave, for a maximum of 3 years. However, Comas (2001) found that work-family legislation so far has mainly benefited women. For example, less than 1% of workers who took parental leave in 2000 were men.

Critics of Spanish social policy say what is needed is a shorter working day for all, non-transferable parental leave for men, greater employment opportunities for women, and more government provision of child care (Comas, 2001). The Spanish president recently promised to develop a policy to provide day care for the children of working parents (Martinez-Hernandez, 2003). Currently, less than 2% of children ages 0 to 3 are cared for by publicly funded facilities (Carrasco & Rodriguez, 2000). Valiente (2003) reports that recent expansion of preschool programs in Spain has not increased the proportion of women in the paid workforce because programs have short hours and long holidays and are designed for children older than 3 years.

Although national legislation is beginning to develop supports for working parents, no concern is yet shown about men increasing their participation in housework or child care. A 1996 time-use study found that employed women spent 47.2 hours per week on household work, compared to 13.7 for men. Women's domestic hours, however, had declined since 1991, whereas men's had risen (Duran, 2000). Gonzalez-Lopez's (2001) research found that as women's employment increases, men's share of domestic work is likely to increase. Spanish men's attitudes toward participating in housework and child care became more positive during the 1990s (Martinez-Hernandez, 2003). Increased institutional support for sharing domestic roles may come about in the future, because women's share of positions in the Spanish legislature has increased dramatically, from 3% in 1980 to 23% in 2000 (Mikkelsen, 2000).

Transitional Societies

Some transitional societies (e.g., China, France, Israel, Russia, and former Soviet nations such as Estonia) have made substantial efforts to implement policies to encourage women to assume an active breadwinning role, including the development of programs to help working mothers, such as maternity leave and day care. These societies, however, fall short of being considered egalitarian, because they have not promoted men's greater participation in unpaid family work and because the motivations behind programs that improve women's employment opportunities have usually had little to do with the promotion of gender equality. This section features France and Russia, which have remained transitional societies over the past 10 years.

In other transitional societies (e.g., Australia, Canada, New Zealand, the United Kingdom, and the United States), there is little government policy that provides support to working mothers or promotes men's participation in unpaid family work, but there is strong acceptance of women's employment, women's status in the labor market is relatively high, men's participation in unpaid work is increasing, and individuals are finding ways to integrate work and family responsibilities. This chapter features the United Kingdom and the United States, which have moved from being traditional societies to becoming transitional societies in 10 years' time.

France

Like Spain, France has a formal tradition of traditional gender roles in the family, with the man as the primary breadwinner and the woman more responsible for home and child care. Until the 1960s, legislation made the husband the financial and moral head of the family and put him formally in charge of all major decisions about children (Laubier, 1990). Despite this, French women have a history of working in family-owned businesses and in agricultural labor, with 30% registered as doing so in 1966. Historically, French men have not felt that their masculinity is threatened by having a working wife, in contrast to British men (J. Lewis, 1992).

As in other industrial societies, French women increasingly entered the labor force in the 1960s. By 2000, in households with children where husbands worked full-time, 45% of French wives also worked full-time, with 16% working part-time (EU, 2002). French women are increasingly likely to have a continuous attachment to the workforce, independent of whether or not they have children (Crompton, Hantrais, & Walters, 1990). In 1999, 56% of mothers with children under 6 were employed, up slightly from 53% 10 years earlier (OECD, 2001).

In the 1970s, strong laws were established to discourage sex discrimination and sex segregation of workplaces. For a time, French women enjoyed relatively high wages compared to women in other societies, with "only" a 15% gender wage gap (Reed-Danahay, 2003). In 2001, however, government statistics discovered that the wage gap between men and women had increased to 22% (Meilland, 2002). The gender wage gap appears to be largely due to women's greater tendency to work part-time; male full-time and part-time workers make higher hourly wages than female part-time workers.

Maternity leaves grant French women 16 weeks off with 84% pay for the first child and longer periods for later children. Parents receive tax credits for child care expenses. The supply and quality of child care facilities has improved to a level now considered to be among the best in Europe (J. Lewis, 1992). In the 1990s, 35% of children aged 0–3 were in publicly funded day care facilities, along with 99% of those ages 3–6 (Morgan, 2002).

Maternity leave and child care policies, however, have not been based on the premise that women should be family breadwinners, in contrast to some other societies (e.g., Russia and Sweden). They have been justified in terms of how they benefit children and provide encouragement to French couples to have children (J. Lewis, 1992). Nevertheless, according to Fagnani (2002), the availability of excellent care for their children makes

"French women feel legitimized to be in employment" (p. 104).

Officially, women have been given the choice of whether or not to work. In reality, because of the way benefits and taxes are formulated, one-earner families are somewhat better off, and highly paid professional women are encouraged to work part-time (J. Lewis, 1992). Attitudes toward women's roles remained mixed. Almost half (45%) of women in 1996 stated that ideally, women should combine a job with homemaking and caregiving throughout their lives, whereas one third still believed that the ideal way of life is for women to stay home when children are young (Duran, 2000). A 1998 study of couple families with one child under 6 found that about half (52%) preferred that both parents worked full-time (OECD, 2001). France, along with the other societies in the "transitional" group, could be called a "modified male breadwinner" state.

Research shows that French fathers are increasing their participation in the daily care of young children and that men's attitudes toward sharing child care are becoming more positive over time (Laubier, 1990). No progress seems evident, however, when it comes to French men sharing housework. According to Reed-Danahay (2003), "women, despite their high levels of employment outside the home, do 80% of the domestic chores. In 60% of French households, men do no domestic labor at all" (p. 221). One study found that married men do less housework after they get married than they do when they are single. When they participate in domestic work, French men prefer cooking over cleaning or shopping (Laubier).

The future of French gender roles is uncertain. There is a tendency for the government to reduce benefits to working parents by denying these benefits to the more highly paid workers as a way to improve the conditions of low-income families and reduce social expenditures (J. Lewis, 1992). This discourages some women from being employed, especially during the child-rearing years. Changes in the labor market have reduced the supply of full-time jobs in women's traditional areas, although part-time working women in France still receive excellent benefits.

French women's share of political power has been somewhat lower than other areas of Europe (including Spain). By 2000, women held only 11% of seats in the legislature, up from 5% 20 years previous (Mikkelsen, 2000). This will soon change, because "the law of parity," passed in 2000, requires electoral ballots to list both female as well as male candidates (Reed-Danahay, 2003). Increased political representation may bring women's interests in employment rights and work-family integration to the forefront of social debate.

Russia

Russia is unique in the length of its official commitment to the concept of women's equality, one of the goals of the Bolshevik Revolution in 1917. Soviet policy was based on the premise that gender equality depended on women taking their place beside men in the paid labor market. Accordingly, Russian women gained legal rights unheard of in the rest of the world, including the right to work and to receive equal pay (Broschart, 1992). Policymakers promised to shift unpaid family work to the public sphere, through the establishment of child care facilities, public laundries, and communal dining halls (Goldman, 1991). Interest in women's participation in the paid labor market was not, however, based on an ideological commitment to women's equality alone. Russia badly needed women as labor power because of a strong push for economic expansion.

By 1940, millions of Russian women had joined the labor market, making up almost 40% of all industrial workers. World War II brought on an even greater demand for female labor power, as a way to compensate for heavy casualties among men (Lapidus, 1988). Yet the promised public services that would relieve women of unpaid family work (with the exception of some child care) never materialized on a wide scale (Goldman, 1991). Moreover, a decision was made to emphasize heavy industry and construction; this meant that the consumer products that would make unpaid family work easier were not produced (Lapidus). After first downplaying the importance of the family as an important institution in the new society, authorities concluded that strong family relationships were necessary for social stability, economic productivity, and population growth (Lapidus). New emphasis was placed on women's family roles to help bolster family stability. The women's section of the Communist Party was disbanded, and organizations to promote women's interests were outlawed, making it difficult for women to influence social policy development (Goldman).

The 1960s were characterized by continued labor shortages. To encourage more women to enter employment, more day care facilities were created, and women's wages and pension benefits were improved (Lapidus, 1988). Consumer shortages continued to be common, and women spent long hours waiting in lines to purchase food and other necessities. At home, they took care of domestic work without the help of refrigerators, washing machines, and hot water. Because of the poor quality of day care facilities (with overcrowding, poor sanitation, and inferior food), children often became sick, and women were forced to miss work (Goldman, 1991). To reduce their heavy domestic burdens, women had fewer children (Lapidus).

By 1985, women made up 51% of the Russian labor force, concentrated in jobs traditionally associated with women's roles (e.g., clerical work) but also in jobs nontraditional for women in the West (e.g., semiskilled agricultural work). Almost all (97%) women in the prime childbearing years of ages 25–44 were employed full-time for pay (Broschart, 1992). The original Bolshevik goal of women's full entrance into the labor market was finally reached, basically through forced employment. But women's dual responsibilities for employment and family work caused problems. Working women had poorer health, higher absenteeism, and lower productivity than did men. The birthrate remained very low and the divorce rate very high. It became clear that women were working much harder than men. Studies found that women did 18 to 21 more hours of household work per week than men in dual-earner households, and that men had 50% more leisure time (Goldman, 1991; Lapidus, 1988).

The backlash against communism in the early 1990s resulted in questioning of the idea that gender equality called for women's full participation in the labor force. A minister of labor at a 1993 press conference stated, "Why should we employ women when men are unemployed? It's better that men work and women take care of children" (Nechemias, 2003, p. 553). More moderate policymakers considered moving women into less difficult jobs to protect their health, increasing the supply of consumer goods and services to make their lives easier (refrigerators, mass transit, public laundries), and increasing the length of maternity leave. Making men more responsible for household and child care and granting women greater access to more highly paid jobs were not considered (Nechemias).

Gender segregation in the labor market in Russia persists today, and as in other industrial countries, it is associated with women earning less wages, despite legislation that calls for equal pay for equal work (Nechemias, 2003). Women make 70% of men's wages because they dominate the low-paying sectors of the economy (Mikkelsen, 2000). But sex segregation in the labor market is not the only reason why women earn less. Women's responsibility for housework and child care forces them to pick more convenient and less demanding jobs and leaves them less time for additional training and education (Broschart, 1992).

There has been a resurrection of traditional family values, associated with an increased interest in following the tenets of the Russian Orthodox Church, part of the effort "to counterbalance past collectivism" (Degtiar, 2002, p. 50). There are reports that "the ideological climate is pushing women into traditional relationships" (Pascall & Manning, 2000, p. 252). The doctrine of separate spheres appears to be reemerging in Russia. Most Russians assume that there are important personality and biological differences between the sexes that lead to women prioritizing family over work roles (Nechemias, 2003). Before the "second Russian Revolution," only 20% of Russian women said they would leave the labor force if their husbands earned much more, because they valued their economic independence and obtained personal satisfaction from work (Broschart, 1992). Today, over twice as many women (43%) say they work only out of financial necessity and would prefer to stay home if they could (Mikkelsen, 2000). Although most Russian men say that wives should have the right to work and that partners should equally share household and child care responsibilities, the average Russian man also insists "that there should be a cozy and orderly home and well-kept children waiting for him when he returns from work, as a necessary condition for this 'equality'" (Arutiunyan & Zdravomyslova, 1997, p. 167). Russian students are more likely than American students to disagree that work in the home should be shared by wives and husbands and more likely to agree that women ought to have more time off work in order to care for their families (Henderson-King & Zhermer, 2003). In Batalova and Cohen's (2002) study of housework in 22 industrial countries, Russia scored in the middle of nations in terms of how equally shared the division of labor was for laundry, caring for sick family members, shopping, and dinner planning (above Japan, but well below the United Kingdom, Sweden, and the United States).

The transition to a market economy has resulted in cuts in social services that once enabled women to work (e.g., day care, paid parental leave) (Pascall & Manning, 2000). Gender equality is not the most pressing issue for the Russian government, particularly because the issue of women's equality tends to be associated with now outmoded communist ideology. Women's opinions seem unlikely to have much influence on public policy, because Russian women have little power in society. They make up only 8% of parliamentary membership (Mikkelsen, 2000).

United Kingdom

The United Kingdom has a long history of restricting the employment rights of wives and mothers. Historically, men were defined as family breadwinners, and women were expected to be caregivers. Extreme emphasis was placed on the importance of full-time motherhood for children's healthy development, and the majority of men and women disapproved of mothers of small children working outside the home (Alwin, Brown, & Scott, 1992). Policymakers believed that government should not support women's work through day nurseries or paid maternity leave (Pascall, 2003).

In the 1970s, women gained some legal employment rights and access to benefits that would make it easier for them to be working mothers (e.g., 18 weeks of paid maternity leave, although not all women were eligible). But day care for children under 3 was still virtually nonexistent (Brannen, 1992; J. Lewis, 1992). Mothers of young children had the lowest labor force participation rate in Western Europe (Sorrentino, 1990). Women's limited job opportunities and the lack of support services for working parents perpetuated their segregation into the low-paid sector of the labor market, which meant that they remained dependent on men, who were families' main breadwinners (J. Lewis). At the beginning of the 1990s, high unemployment and economic recession made it very difficult for women to advance in the labor market. Women's rights to maternity leave were reduced, making Britain the only society where women were losing such privileges rather than gaining them (Brannen).

Brannen's (1992) study offers interesting insights on mothers who returned to full-time employment after childbirth in the 1980s, something few women in the United Kingdom dared to do at the time. Her sample included mainly professional women earning high incomes. The vast majority said that men and women should share equally in family work, but almost none practiced this arrangement. The women still defined their husbands as the family breadwinners, and husbands expressed greater interest and commitment to paid employment than wives. Wives were more concerned about maintaining emotional closeness in the marriage than they were in demanding that their husbands do an equal share of housework and child care. To compensate for not being home full-time, women spent as much time with children as possible and remained primarily responsible for child care, which relieved their feelings of guilt.

By the beginning of the 21st century, social arrangements appeared to be on a different trajectory. Equal employment legislation in the 1980s calling for women to receive equal treatment and equal pay in the labor market appears to have increased women's likelihood of being employed outside the home. Adherence to social directives associated with EU membership also forced the United Kingdom to pay more attention to equal employment opportunity for women and the reconciliation of work and family life. By 1999, 56% of mothers with children under age 6 were in the labor market, compared to 43% 10 years earlier (OECD, 2001).

Although married mothers are now more likely to remain employed, they do so on conditions different from fathers. By 2000, only 29% of married women with children with full-time employed husbands worked full-time, with an additional 40% working part-time (EU, 2002). According to Auer (2002), "part-time employment by mothers seems to be the major approach in dealing with the tensions between paid work and parenthood in the United Kingdom" (p. 211). Mothers' full-time employment is preferred by only 42% of couples with children under 6 (OECD, 2001). Highly educated professional women are more likely to retain a lifelong attachment to the labor market, whereas less educated women with fewer employment opportunities are likely to follow a more traditional path, working part-time after children are born (McCulloch & Dex, 2001). U.K. men have the longest average workweek of all EU member states, averaging 46 hours, with 29% working over 48 hours a week. Long working hours make it difficult for employed fathers to participate actively in household work and child care (Auer).

The majority of working mothers occupy jobs in the lowest-status occupations, with severely low wages and especially short hours (Pascall, 2003; Warren, 2000). This means that their wages cannot contribute as much to the family as men's can. This reduces their chances of sharing breadwinning as well as their ability to convince men to participate more in unpaid family work.

Overall, women's hourly wages were 65% of men's in 1999 (OECD, 2001). Women with higher education can become mothers and sustain their earnings at a high level without suffering an extreme wage penalty. Women with lesser education, however, incur a big income penalty if they try to leave and reenter the labor market (Pascall).

Almost half of women (45%) still agreed in 1996 that the "ideal way of life is for the woman to stay home when the children are young," whereas only 37% believed that it was ideal for women to combine a job with homemaking and caregiving throughout their lives (Duran, 2000). The division of household labor remains rather traditional, according to Batalova and Cohen's (2002) study of 22 nations (well above Russia and Japan, but below Sweden and the United States). Women are still more likely than men to do chores such as laundry, caring for sick family members, shopping, and dinner planning. Young women's attitudes, however, are becoming more nontraditional. According to the British Household Panel Survey, conducted in 1994 and again in 1997, girls are increasingly more likely than boys, their mothers, and their fathers to disagree that "a husband's job is to earn money, a wife's job is to look after the home and family" (Burt & Scott, 2002).

As in other industrial societies, British women's share of seats in the national legislature is increasing, from 3% in 1980 to 18% in 2000 (Mikkelsen, 2000), which may someday affect the level of public support for working parents. In 2000, the Labour government announced a "work-life balance campaign" to encourage employers to provide flexible working arrangements to employees, by providing information and advice, establishing an alliance of leading employers to promote good practice, and offering funds to encourage employers to explore development of new policies (Arrowsmith, 2001). The government appears to be emphasizing the "business case" for work-family arrangements, hoping to encourage employers to provide necessary supports for working parents (e.g., career breaks, flextime mainly directed at women), rather than providing them through public funds (S. Lewis, 1999). Auer (2002) describes the United Kingdom as a "neoliberal, flexible economy. . . . This model emphasizes a strong belief in market forces . . . which assumes that the marketplace will not only lead to high economic performance but also to fair and just social results" (p. 205). Research suggests, however, that this strategy is unlikely to be successful. Evans's (2002) study of policies and practices in existence in various countries found that when governmental policy for work-family integration is lacking, there is little evidence that companies step up to provide needed programs.

The United States

The last transitional society to be examined is the United States. U.S. women have entered the labor force in record numbers during the last three decades, making up 48% of the workforce by 2002. The most dramatic increases have been for mothers of small children. By 2001, 62% of married mothers with at least one child under 6 were in the labor market, compared to 30% in 1970. By 1999, 62% of mothers with one child under 6 were employed, compared to 54% 10 years earlier (OECD, 2001). In 2001, both parents were employed in 62% of families with children, up from 35% in 1975 (Padavic & Reskin, 2002; U.S. Bureau of the Census, 2002).

As in other societies discussed so far, U.S. women's employment opportunities remain inferior to men's. Women have less access to prestigious, well-paid jobs, and those traditionally available to women are low paid in comparison to men's jobs requiring similar skill levels. Although women's average pay levels have gradually risen in recent years, women still receive only 68% of men's hourly wages (OECD, 2001). The relatively disadvantaged status of women in the labor force reinforces the male-as-breadwinner ideal (Padavic & Reskin, 2002). The 2002 National Study of the Changing Workforce found that women's contribution to family earnings in dual-earner couples was 42% (Bond, 2003).

There has been a substantial shift in attitudes toward role specialization in U.S. families. In 1977, three fourths (74%) of men and half of women (52%) said they believed "men should earn the money and women should take care of the home and children." By 2002, these proportions had dropped to 42% for men and 37% for women (Bond, 2003, p. 4). By the 1990s, the vast majority of both men and women endorsed less segregation of male and female roles, and most viewed maternal employment in a positive light, although there is evidence that there is a "leveling off of the egalitarian trend" (Thornton & Young-DeMarco, 2001, p. 1014). The 2002 National Study of the Changing Workforce also found an increase in the proportion of employees who felt that "a working mother can have just as good a relationship with her child as a mother who does not work outside the home," from 49% of men and 70% of women thinking this in 1977 to 64% of men and 78% of women thinking this in 2002 (Bond, p. 5).

There appears to be a significant shift in the actual division of household labor as well. In Batalova and Cohen's (2002) study of housework in 22 industrial countries, the United States scored second as the most egalitarian society studied, on a measure of the "gender division of labor within couples" (behind Norway and just above Sweden). Men's relative share of domestic work has risen because working women spend less time doing domestic work and because men are willing to do more (Bianchi, Milkie, Sayer, & Robinson, 2000). Full-time employed women still do more housework, averaging 12.6 hours per week compared to 9.9 for men (Padavic & Reskin, 2002). Men's level of involvement in active child care has also increased over time. According to Pleck (1997), the amount of time fathers are actively engaged with children is 44% of the level of mothers. Contradictory evidence, however, is provided on men's sense of responsibility for domestic work by the 2002 National Study of the Changing Workforce, which found no change in men's self-reports of taking greater responsibility for house-cleaning or the routine care of children from the 1977 to 2002 time period (Bond, 2003).

When U.S. men are involved in unpaid family work, they do so on their own terms—they tend to take on tasks with more discretion (e.g., household repairs), clear boundaries (e.g., mowing), more leisure (e.g, playing with children), and less time commitment (e.g., putting away clean dishes) (N. Gunter & B. Gunter, 1990). As in many other societies, U.S. women tend not to express dissatisfaction with the unequal division of work in the home, although they are more likely than men to describe their own household division of labor as unfair (Kluwer, Heesink, & Van de Vliert, 2002). The more time they spend in traditionally female domestic chores, the lower American women's wages are over time (Noonan, 2001).

The U.S. government has made little effort to develop social policies to help working parents. When it comes to public subsidies for child care, maternity leave, and parental leave, the United States usually appears at the bottom of the list of industrial countries (Kamerman, 2000). The few leave policies that do exist at the national, state, and workplace level are gender neutral (e.g., family leave policies), but in practice only women are encouraged to take advantage of them (especially because they are usually unpaid) (Kamerman). Individuals (mostly mothers) are forced to develop their own strategies for balancing work and family roles, often by working part-time, which reduces family income and career opportunities. In 1998, 24% of women ages 20–39 worked part-time (Mikkelsen, 2000). It has been estimated that U.S. women suffer a "pay penalty" of 7% per child in terms of lifetime earned income (Padavic & Reskin, 2002). The idea that work should be restructured to allow both men and women opportunities to develop relationships with children has not been seriously considered.

Because employment and family commitments are so strong in the United States, it is not surprising that reports of conflict between work and family roles are high. Only 1 in 10 dual-earner couples with a preschooler report that they manage both roles successfully. Couples are more likely to report success when they have supportive supervisors, work an ordinary 40-hour week or less, and have job security (Moen & Yu, 1999). U.S. companies seem increasingly aware that it is in their economic interest to help workers combine employment and family roles. As indicated above, however, workplace supports are unlikely to be sufficient in the absence of national policy making promoting the integration of work and family life.

It seems likely that the United States will continue to experience redefinition of gender roles in the near future. Recent changes in the political climate in the United States favor women's concerns and support dual-earner lifestyles as well. The number of women elected to government office has risen, up from 4% in 1980 to 13% in 2000 (Mikkelsen, 2000), and many new female officeholders seem inclined to push for social policies to encourage gender equality.

Egalitarian Societies

Egalitarian societies, the last category to be considered, manifest equal sharing of breadwinning, housework, and child care by men and women. In these societies, the social importance of unpaid family work is recognized and the division between private and public spheres of social life is eliminated, in an effort to maximize the well-being of children and advance gender equality. There are no societies that fully fit in this category, but one country, Sweden, has made very serious efforts toward these goals, so it will be described here. Denmark, Finland, and Norway could also be discussed in this category, but they lag behind Sweden.

Sweden

Gender equality has been a goal of social policy in Sweden since the late 1960s. Gender equality is defined as women and men having "the same rights, obligations, and possibilities to have a job that gives them economic independence, to care for children and home, and to participate in political, union, and other activities in society" (Statistiska Centralbyrån, 1992, p. 5). This policy was outlined first in a publication prepared for the United Nations in 1968. It has continuously been included in the official programs of all trade unions, political parties, and government agencies (Haas, 1996).

The government's current plan for equality calls for workplaces to develop strategies to eliminate job segregation and pay differences, reorganize work life so that both sexes can combine parenthood and employment, and give women more access to power and responsibility in work life. There has been a long series of programs and laws that have been developed in Sweden to help bring about gender equality (Swedish Institute, 2003). A majority of these aim to improve women's employment opportunities so they can become family breadwinners on an equal level with men. Compared to women in other societies, Swedish women have had unusual access to educational opportunities and job training. Women have entered the labor market because of plentiful job opportunities (especially in the public and service sectors), high wages (the result of union efforts to lessen class differences by raising the wages of the lowest-paid workers), and by a tax system that taxes their incomes separately from those of their spouses (Haas, 2003b).

The Swedish government has also been active in providing a high level of support services and programs for working parents, which have helped women maintain a continuous attachment to the labor force and encouraged men to participate in early child care. One program involves the heavy subsidization of public child care of high quality. Three fourths of Swedish children ages 1–6 are in publicly provided child care, compared to less than 5% of children in Spain and the United Kingdom (Perrons, 2000). Other programs include paid family leave. Fathers get 10 days off with 90% pay at childbirth to take charge of the household while mothers recuperate from childbirth and to get to know their babies. Then each parent is entitled to 2 nontransferable months of paid parental leave (at 80% of regular pay), and each couple has an additional 9 months of paid parental leave that either can take, on a part- or full-time basis. Families are entitled to 50 days off with 80% pay to care for sick children and have the right to reduce the workday to 6 hours (with a reduction in pay) (Haas, 2003a).

Why has Sweden developed such a radical approach to gender relations, in comparison to other countries? Interest in equality is closely related to and influenced by deep-rooted social values and the nature of political culture in Sweden. One important Swedish value that relates to interest in gender equality is productivity. Policymakers' interest in women's labor force participation is related to their desire to boost society's productivity and to meet Sweden's need for labor power, which was particularly pressing in the 1970s and 1980s. This labor shortage led to recognition of the importance of women's labor power and the development of specific programs designed to enhance women's lifetime attachment. However, there is an ideological component as well. Working at a job is seen as good and important for an individual to do, apart from its economic benefits (Sandqvist, 1992).

Another important social value is children's welfare, a concern that has been strong since the 1930s Depression, when the Swedish birthrate dropped to below replacement levels. Swedish children are seen as benefiting from having two parents who enjoy economic independence and the opportunity to seek personal fulfillment outside the home, and from the economic security of being in a two-earner household. Having close relations with fathers who are involved in their daily care is also considered important for children's healthy development. Day care is seen as a positive way for children to learn intellectual, social, and emotional skills. It is considered appropriate that workplaces adjust to the needs of children by allowing parents time off to care for them (Haas, 1996). This is an interesting contrast to the situation in other societies, such as Japan or the United States, where children's welfare has been used as a rationale for discouraging women from employment and for encouraging their full-time absorption in child care.

A third important value in Sweden is social equality. Although the economy is based on the pursuit of profit, it is widely accepted that no family should live in impoverished conditions and that there should not be a huge gap between those who earn the least and those who earn the most. Social equality is the basic tenet of the Social Democratic Party, which has ruled alone or in coalition in the Swedish government since the 1930s. To some extent, Swedish concern for gender equality is a spin-off from the concern for social equality, making it possible for women and their children to live in comfortable circumstances, even without the support of a father (Haas, 2003b). According to Winkler (2002), "by the end of the twentieth century, Swedish solo mothers were much less likely to be poor than their sisters in the United States, and this difference was largely attributable to the sort of social policies for which Sweden is known" (p. 273).

Currently, 45% of the members of Parliament are women. No other society has such a high representation of women at the top level of government (Swedish Institute, 2003). This has played a big role in policy making designed to meet the dual agenda of productivity and gender equality.

How successful has Sweden been in eliminating the traditional division of labor for breadwinning, housework, and child care? The answer is "somewhat successful." When it comes to breadwinning, Swedish women are almost as likely as men to be in the labor force, having the highest labor force participation rate of women of all industrial societies. In 2002, 79% of women ages 20–64 were employed (compared to 84% of men) (Statistiska Centralbyrån, 2002). The "dual-breadwinner" family is the norm. Nearly all women and men (97%) agree that "it is just as important for a woman to have a job as it is for a man," a higher proportion than in France, Spain, and the United Kingdom (Plantenga & Hansen, 2001). Having young children has little effect on women's paid employment. Over three fourths (78%) of mothers with children under 6 were employed in 2000 (OECD, 2001). One study found that the vast majority of parents believed breadwinning responsibility should be shared equally by mothers and fathers, as early as the mid-1980s (Haas, 1993).

Swedish women earn 41% of family income (Haas, 2003b). Swedish women do not earn more money in comparison to men because 37% work part-time (Mikkelsen, 2000). A large number of jobs in the public and service sectors were established as part-time jobs to attract women into the labor force, and women have taken more advantage than men of legislation that allows parents to work part-time until their children reach school age. Unlike in Britain, where women also tend to work part-time, Swedish women tend to work longer hours (30 per week), receive prorated benefits, and have job security. A 1998 study of EU states found that two thirds of couples with a child under 6 preferred that both parents work full-time (OECD, 2001). Sweden has become a "dual-breadwinner" state.

Women's contribution to family income is also reduced because of wage differences between the sexes. Although Sweden ranks high internationally in terms of reducing the gender pay gap, a pay gap does still exist. In 2000, Swedish women's hourly wages averaged 85% of men's (Swedish Institute, 2003). Some of the pay gap is due to differences in the types of jobs men and women hold. Sweden has a highly sex-segregated labor market that is only slowly changing in response to government efforts to train more young people in nontraditional fields. In 1999, almost half of all employed women worked in child care, elder care, social work, health care, or education, compared to only 14% of men (Haas, 2003b). Some researchers have speculated that Swedish women are less motivated to seek nontraditional jobs because there are few wage differences between traditionally female and male jobs. Swedish women also seem to reject the notion that traditionally male jobs are more worthwhile to have (Sandqvist, 1992).

As early as 1981, the vast majority of Swedish men agreed that men's roles should be changed to make them equally responsible for home and children. In spite of the widespread acceptance of egalitarian ideology, Swedish men do not do 50% of the work (although they appear to come closer than men in other societies). In Batalova and Cohen's (2002) 22-nation study, Swedes scored slightly behind the United States in terms of sharing traditionally female chores like laundry, dinner planning, caring for sick family members, and shopping. Research shows that Swedish men have been doing more housework and child care over time (since 1957, when the first measurements were taken), both relative to women and in an absolute sense. A 2001 time-use study found that men's share of time spent in household work, shopping, child care, repair, care of others, and errands was 42% of all time spent by the couple, up from 34% in 1992 (Haas, 2003a). In 1998, the vast majority of fathers (85%) were actively involved in caring for their young children, up dramatically from 1% in 1960 (Fürst, 1999). When men's and women's labor market and household work hours are totaled, Swedish men and women work the same number of hours, whereas in other societies men have noticeably more leisure (Haas, 2003b).

Inequality is still evident. Recent research indicates that Swedish women are more likely than men to want to work fewer work hours because of family responsibilities, and women also report higher levels of psychological distress than do men (Nordenmark, 2002). Only 29% of a random sample of wives saw their relationship as equal, and 45% of women perceived the division of labor for housework as unfair (Nordenmark & Nyman, 2003). Swedish fathers take advantage of programs to assist working parents with child care, but not to the same degree as do mothers. They take a small proportion of the parental leave available (16%), with mothers taking the vast majority of days (Haas, 2003b).

Nevertheless, in 2001, 70% of all Swedish men took parental leave after childbirth to care for their child alone while the child's mother returned to work (up from 50% 10 years earlier). Nearly all fathers take the 10 days off immediately after childbirth, and fathers and mothers fairly equitably share time off to care for sick children. Only a few other countries (generally in the EU) grant paid parental leave to fathers, but none of them comes close to having as many fathers take leave as in Sweden (Haas, 2003a).

Swedish social policies help to break down the distinction between public and private spheres. Employers do not have complete control over the work lives of their employees, because legislation grants workers rights to stay home with children at frequent intervals. Many leave benefits are directly tied to employment, because compensation levels are determined by pay levels. Taxes on employers' payrolls help to pay for these programs. These practices give the impression that unpaid family work, particularly child care, is a valued social activity that should be fairly compensated. The time parents spend at home with children is also credited toward seniority and retirement benefits (Jonung & Persson, 1990).

Several developments in Sweden make progress toward gender equality likely. In the 1990s, a poor economy and a government deficit appeared to threaten support for programs designed to bring about an egalitarian division of labor in the home. In response to the conservative political climate, Swedish feminists became more active in pressing for the reduction of gender inequality. New feminist organizations were formed, including a women's political party, an alliance of women politicians organizing across party lines, and a league of trade union women organizing across union boundaries.

Feminists objected to government policy making that appeared to value productivity over reproduction and the public sphere over the private. They called for measures that would restructure work life to maximize family well-being and gender equality, for example, by instituting a 6-hour workday for all workers. The women's party folded, and the 6-hour day for all was never implemented, but women's share of positions of power throughout society continues to increase; more legislation to promote gender equality has been enacted; and it is expected that with more women in power, barriers to gender equality will be more discussed and challenged.

The reelection of the Social Democrats in 2002 promises a continuation of liberal social policies. Even during the 1990s recession, the Social Democratic government fulfilled a longtime campaign pledge of making day care available to all parents, and in 2002, the rates for day care were drastically reduced (Haas, 2003b). Support for working parents and for gender equality has been sustained, even when women's labor power has not been in high demand.

WHY SOME SOCIETIES ARE MORE EGALITARIAN THAN OTHERS

The descriptions of the seven societies above show that each society approaches the issue of the household division of labor somewhat differently, depending on social values, economic circumstances, and political priorities. Although each society is in its own way unique in how it comes to define men's and women's roles, the information provided can be used to develop hypotheses concerning why some societies are more egalitarian than others.

We have seen that all the industrial societies featured have experienced and been affected by the entrance of women into the labor force during the past few decades. Some societies, however, notice and appreciate this development more than others. Women's labor force participation will lead to a redefinition of who is responsible for breadwinning, as well as an increase in men's share of household work and public interest in support programs for working parents, when women's work involvement is defined as being essential for the society's economic growth and families' economic survival.

In most of the societies mentioned in this chapter, mothers are highly likely to work part-time. When the number of hours of part-time work is "short" (less than 20, which is common in the United Kingdom), women appear to remain more responsible for household work and child care, compared to societies where mothers work full-time or work "long" part-time (e.g., 30 hours a week, which is common in Sweden). Tijden's (2002) study of 15 EU member states found that women are more likely to be responsible for looking after the home and shopping if they work part-time, but the differences between part-time workers and full-time workers were not substantial—87% of part-time workers felt more responsible than their partners for this domestic work, whereas 80% of full-time workers did. Consequently, mothers' likelihood of working part-time does not seem to be a major factor influencing men's participation in domestic work.

The birthrate drops in all industrial societies with the advent of birth control and a lessened need for family laborers. Some industrial societies, however, seem to become more concerned about this development than others, usually in connection with productivity issues, and seek to develop social policies that would encourage people to have more children. Societies that both recognize the importance of women's labor power and are concerned about the birthrate are more likely to develop policies that support women in their dual roles as workers and parents. Evidence concerning OECD countries "shows that high levels of female employment rates need not be incompatible with relatively high fertility rates—paradoxically, there is currently a positive correlation between female employment rates and fertility rates across OECD countries" (OECD, 2001, p. 153). When women maintain a continued presence in the workforce, their earning potential increases, and it becomes less obvious that they should always be the ones to shoulder the burden of domestic chores. Men then become more likely to share family responsibilities, starting with child care.

Since industrialization, a cult of motherhood has existed, which portrays children as needing their mother's full-time attention and considers mothers as being fulfilled only through parenting activities. When societies develop policies to support working mothers (e.g., job protection and paid maternity leave, publicly supported child care), mothers choose to remain in the paid labor force (Gornick, Meyers, & Ross, 1998). Societies like Sweden's that aim for fathers to become more responsible for early child care also are helping to break down gender specialization in parenting and the distinction between the private (family) and public (work) spheres.

Industrialization also brought increased concern for the welfare of children. Research in Sweden suggests that concern for children can lead to societal support for mothers' working, by providing services like paid parental leave and high-quality, affordable day care, partly because policymakers believe economic security is the most important determinant of child well-being. These same societies also show more interest in fathers developing close relations with children.

Another important determinant of the domestic division of labor is women's power in society. Industrialization helped to consolidate men's power over women by giving them greater access to the more valued public sphere and opportunities to make money. Although all industrial societies have extended political rights to women over the years (starting with the vote), women are typically underrepresented in positions of formal power in government or at the workplace. As "gender empowerment" increases, we might expect a more egalitarian division of labor. "Gender empowerment" has been measured by an index based on women's share of parliamentary seats, women's share of administrative and managerial posts in companies, women's share of professional and technical occupations, and women's share of earned income. Apparala, Reifiman, and Munsch's (2003) cross-national study of 13 European nations found that citizens expressed more egalitarian attitudes toward household work and child care when they lived in countries with more "gender empowerment." Similarly, Batalova and Cohen's (2002) 22-nation study of the division of housework found that couples had a more egalitarian division of labor if they lived in countries with more "gender empowerment." As women gain access to power positions, or resources that translate into power, issues of gender equality appear more likely to be raised on the national level and appropriate social policies developed.

Finally, societies differ in the extent to which government policy is regarded as an appropriate instrument for bringing about social change. In some societies, the government has tried to stay out of the business of encouraging changes in gender roles, partly because government is not looked upon as trustworthy or wise. Cultures that accept the state as fundamentally benevolent seem more likely to establish new structures and expectations for family roles.

FUTURE TRENDS

Both as a fact and as an ideal, the division of labor that assigned wage labor to men and unpaid family work to women is dramatically changing in industrial societies. Women are in the labor force to stay, and they increasingly maintain an attachment to work even during their child-bearing and child-rearing years. But women are not yet able to share equally in the responsibility for providing family income because of the persistence of traditional attitudes, labor market discrimination, the structure of male-dominated work organizations, and husbands' lack of interest and participation in domestic work. We have on our hands what sociologist Arlie Hochschild (1989) calls "a stalled revolution." Some governments and workplaces reinforce this stalled revolution by developing policies that make it easier for women (but not men) to balance employment with primary responsibility for housework and child care. Not much progress has been made in recognizing that men's employment should also be responsive to family life. Only in Sweden is men's greater participation in family life becoming mandated and expected. The Swedish case suggests that it might be possible to construct new social norms about the domestic division of labor, based on an equal valuing of caring and productivity.

REFERENCES

Alwin, D., Brown, M., & Scott, J. (1992). The separation of work and family. *European Sociological Review, 8,* 13–36.

Apparala, M., Reifiman, A., & Munsch, J. (2003). Cross-national comparison of attitudes toward fathers and mothers' participation in household tasks and childcare. *Sex Roles, 15,* 189–204.

Araki, T. (1998, April 1). Recent legislative developments in equal employment and harmonization of work and family in Japan. *Japan Labour Bulletin,* 5–10.

Aronoff, J., & Crano, W. (1975). A re-examination of the cross-cultural principle of task segregation and sex-role differentiation in the family. *American Sociological Review, 40,* 12–20.

Arrowsmith, J. (2001). Government calls for better work-life balance. *European Industrial Observatory On-line.* Retrieved April 22, 2005, from http://www.eiro.eurofound.ie/2001/02/feature/uk0102115f.html

Arutiunyan, M., & Zdravomyslova, O. (1997). Russian parents. In U. Björnberg & J. Sass (Eds.), *Families with small children in eastern and western Europe* (pp. 159–173). Hants, UK: Ashgate.

Auer, M. (2002). The relationship between paid work and parenthood. *Community, Work & Family, 5,* 203–218.

Batalova, J., & Cohen, P. (2002). Premarital cohabitation and housework. *Journal of Marriage and Family, 64,* 743–755.

Bianchi, S., Milkie, M., Sayer, L., & Robinson, J. (2000). Is anyone doing the housework? *Social Forces, 79,* 191–237.

Bond, J. (2003). *Highlights of the national study of the changing workforce.* New York: Families and Work Institute.

Bose, C. (1987). Dual spheres. In B. Hess & M. Ferree (Eds.), *Analyzing gender* (pp. 267–285). Newbury Park, CA: Sage.

Brannen, J. (1992). Money, marriage and motherhood. In S. Arber & N. Gilbert (Eds.), *Women and working lives* (pp. 54–70). London, UK: Macmillan.

Broschart, K. (1992). Women under glasnost. In S. Arber & N. Gilbert (Eds.), *Women and working lives* (pp. 118–127). London, UK: Macmillan.

Burt, K., & Scott, J. (2002). Parent and adolescent gender role attitudes in 1990s Great Britain. *Sex Roles, 46,* 239–245.

Carrasco, C., & Rodriguez, A. (2000). Women, families and work in Spain. *Feminist Economics, 6,* 45–57.

Coltrane, S. (1998). *Gender and families.* Thousand Oaks, CA: Pine Forge Press.

Comas, C. (2001). Law on reconciliation of work and family life examined. *European Industrial Relations Observatory On-line.* Retrieved April 22, 2005, from http://www.eiro.eurofound.ie/2001/07/feature/es0107154f.html

Crano, W., & Aronoff, J. (1978). A cross-cultural study of expressive and instrumental role complementarity in the family. *American Sociological Review, 43,* 463–471.

Crompton, R., Hantrais, L., & Walters, P. (1990). Gender relations and employment. *British Journal of Sociology, 41,* 329–349.

Crompton, R., & Harris, F. (1999). Attitudes, women's employment, and the changing domestic division of labour. In R. Crompton (Ed.), *Restructuring gender relations and employment* (pp. 105–127). Oxford, UK: Oxford University Press.

Degtiar, L. (2002). The transformation process and the status of women. *Russian Social Science Review, 43,* 48–60.

Duran, M. (2000). The future of work in Europe. In European Commission (Ed.), *Gender use of time* (pp. 77–138). Luxembourg: Office for Official Publications of the European Communities.

European Union (EU). (2002). *Impact of children on women's employment.* Retrieved April 22, 2005, from http://europa.eu.int

Eurostat. (2000). *Community labour force survey 2000.* Retrieved April 22, 2005, from http://europa.eu.int

Evans, J. (2002). Work/family reconciliation, gender wage equity and occupational segregation: The role of firms and public policy. *Canadian Public Policy, 28,* S187–S216.

Fagnani, J. (2002). Why do French women have more children than German women? *Community, Work & Family, 5,* 103–119.

Faragher, J. (1990). The Midwestern farm family at mid-century. In N. Hewitt (Ed.), *Women, families and communities: Vol. 1* (pp. 181–196). New York: Pearson Education.

Ferree, M. (1991). Feminism and family research. In A. Booth (Ed.), *Contemporary families* (pp. 103–121). Minneapolis, MN: National Council on Family Relations.

Fujimoto, T. (1999, September). *The impact of sex composition and workplace climate on the provision of family responsive policies among Japanese employers.* Paper presented at the annual meetings of the American Sociological Association, Chicago.

Fürst, G. (1999). *Sweden—The equal way.* Stockholm, Sweden: Swedish Institute.

Gerson, K. (1985). *Hard choices.* Berkeley: University of California Press.

Goldman, W. (1991). A "non-antagonistic" contradiction? *Gender and History, 3,* 337–344.

Gonzalez-Lopez, M. (2001). Spouses' employment careers in Spain. In H. Blossfeld & S. Drobnic (Eds.), *Careers of couples in contemporary societies* (pp. 146–174). New York: Oxford University Press.

Gornick, J., Meyers, M., & Ross, K. (1998). Public policies and the employment of mothers. *Social Science Quarterly, 79,* 35–54.

Gottfried, H., & O'Reilly, J. (2002). Reregulating breadwinner models in conservative welfare systems. *Social Politics, 9,* 29–59.

Gunter, N., & Gunter, B. (1990). Domestic division of labor among working couples. *Psychology of Women Quarterly, 14,* 355–370.

Haas, L. (1986). Wives' orientations toward breadwinning in Sweden and the United States. *Journal of Family Issues, 7,* 358–381.

Haas, L. (1993). Nurturing fathers and working mothers. In J. Hood (Ed.), *Men, work and family* (pp. 238–261). Newbury Park, CA: Sage.

Haas, L. (1996). Family policy in Sweden. *Journal of Family and Economic Issues, 17,* 47–91.

Haas, L. (2003a). Parental leave and gender equality: Lessons from the European Union. *Review of Policy Research, 20,* 89–114.

Haas, L. (2003b). Sweden. In L. Walter (Ed.), *The Greenwood encyclopedia of women's issues worldwide: Europe* (pp. 621–652). Westport, CT: Greenwood Press.

Henderson-King, D., & Zhermer, N. (2003). Feminist consciousness among Russians and Americans. *Sex Roles, 48,* 143–155.

Hochschild, A. (1989). *The second shift.* New York: Viking.

Ishii-Kuntz, M. (1993). The Japanese father. In J. Hood (Ed.), *Men, work and family* (pp. 45–67). Newbury Park, CA: Sage.

Ishii-Kuntz, M. (2003). Balancing fatherhood and work. In J. Roberson & N. Suzuki (Eds.), *Men and masculinities in contemporary Japan* (pp. 198–216). New York: Routledge.

Jackson, S. (1992). Towards a historical sociology of housework. *Women's Studies International Forum, 15,* 153–172.

Jonung, C., & Persson, I. (1990). Hushållsproduktion, marknadsproduktion och jämställdhet [Household production, market production and equality]. In C. Jonung & I. Persson (Eds.), *Kvinnors roll i ekonomin* [Women's role in the economy] (pp. 9–85). Stockholm, Sweden: Finansdepartementet.

Kamerman, S. (2000). Parental leave policies. *Social Policy Report, 14,* 3–16.

Kimmel, M. (2004). *The gendered society.* New York: Oxford University Press.

Kluwer, E., Heesink, J., & Van de Vliert, E. (2002). The division of labor across the transition to parenthood. *Journal of Marriage and Family, 64,* 930–943.

Lapidus, G. (1988). The interaction of women's work and family roles in the U.S.S.R. *Women and Work, 2,* 87–121.

Laubier, C. (1990). *The condition of women in France.* London: Routledge.

Lewis, J. (1992). Gender and the development of welfare regimes. *Journal of European Social Policy, 2,* 139–173.

Lewis, S. (1999). Work-family arrangements in the UK. In L. den Dulk, A. van Doorne-Huiskes, & J. Schippers (Eds.), *Work-family arrangements in Europe* (pp. 41–56). Amsterdam, The Netherlands: Thela-Thesis.

Martinez-Hernandez, E. (2003). Spain. In L. Walter (Ed.), *Greenwood encyclopedia of women's issues worldwide—Europe* (pp. 601–620). Westport, CT: Greenwood Press.

McCulloch, A., & Dex, S. (2001). Married women's employment patterns in Britain. In H. Blossfeld & S. Drobnic (Eds.), *Careers of couples in contemporary societies* (pp. 175–200). New York: Oxford University Press.

Meilland, C. (2002). Gender pay disparities examined. *European Industrial Observatory On-line*_Retrieved April 22, 2005, from http://www.eiro.eurofound.ie/2001/09/feature/fr0109106f.html

Mikkelsen, L. (2000). *Women and men in Europe and North America.* New York: United Nations.

Moen, P., & Yu, Y. (1999). Having it all. *Research in the Sociology of Work, 7,* 109–139.

Morgan, K. (2002). Forging the frontiers between state, church and family. *Politics & Society, 30,* 113–148.

Nakata, Y., & Takehiro, R. (2002). Employment and wages of female Japanese workers. *Industrial Relations, 41,* 521–546.

Nechemias, C. (2003). Russia. In L. Walter (Ed.), *Greenwood encyclopedia of women's issues worldwide—Europe* (pp. 554–576). Westport, CT: Greenwood Press.

Noonan, M. (2001). The impact of domestic work on men's and women's wages. *Journal of Marriage and Family, 63,* 1134–1145.

Nordenmark, M. (2002). Multiple social roles. *Gender, Work and Organization, 9,* 125–145.

Nordenmark, M., & Nyman, C. (2003). Fair or unfair? *European Journal of Women's Studies, 10,* 181–209.

Oakley, A. (1974). *Woman's work.* New York: Vintage.

Organisation for Economic Cooperation and Development (OECD). (2001). *OECD employment outlook.* Paris: Author.

Padavic, I., & Reskin, B. (2002). *Women and men at work.* Thousand Oaks, CA: Pine Forge Press.

Pascall, G. (2003). United Kingdom. In L. Walter (Ed.), *Greenwood encyclopedia of women's issues worldwide—Europe* (pp. 719–742). Westport, CT: Greenwood Press.

Pascall, G., & Manning, N. (2000). Gender and social policy. *Journal of European Social Policy, 10,* 240–266.

Peng, I. (2001). Women in the middle. *Social Politics, 8,* 191–196.

Perrons, D. (2000). Flexible working and the reconciliation of work and family responsibilities. In European Communities (Ed.), *Gender use of time* (pp. 1–45). Luxembourg: Office for Official Publications of the European Communities.

Plantenga, J., & Hansen, J. (2001). Assessing equal opportunities in the European Union. In M. Loutfi (Ed.), *Women, gender and work* (pp. 273–304). Geneva, Switzerland: International Labour Office.

Pleck, J. (1997). Paternal involvement. In M. Lamb (Ed.), *The role of the father in child development* (pp. 66–103). New York: Wiley.

Potuchek, J. (1997). *Who supports the family?* Stanford, CA: Stanford University Press.

Reed-Danahay, D. (2003). France. In L. Walter (Ed.), *The Greenwood encyclopedia of women's issues worldwide—Europe* (pp. 205–222). Westport, CT: Greenwood Press.

Rotundo, E. A. (1985). American fatherhood. *American Behavioral Scientist, 29,* 7–25.

Sandqvist, K. (1992). Sweden's sex-role scheme and commitment to gender equality. In S. Lewis, D. Izraeli, & H. Hootman (Eds.), *Dual-earner families* (pp. 80–98). London: Sage.

Sato, H. (2000). The current situation of "family-friendly" policies in Japan. *Japan Labour Bulletin, 39*(2), 7–10.

Shelton, B., & John, D. (1996). The division of household labor. *Annual Review of Sociology, 22,* 299–322.

Shorter, E. (1977). *The making of the modern family.* New York: Basic Books.

Siketo, T. (2003, March). *Principal earner and accommodator in household.* Paper presented at the meeting of Research Committee 28, International Sociological Association, Tokyo.

Sorrentino, C. (1990, March). The changing family in international perspective. *Monthly Labor Review*, pp. 41–58.

Statistiska Centralbyrån. (1992). *Om kvinnor och män i Sverige och EG* [Women and men in Sweden and the European Community]. Stockholm, Sweden: Author.

Statistiska Centralbyrån. (2002). *På tal om kvinnor och män* [Talking about women and men]. Stockholm, Sweden: Author. Retrieved April 22, 2005, from http://www.scb.se

Stephens, W. (1963). *The family in cross-cultural perspective*. New York: Holt, Rinehart & Winston.

Stier, H., & Lewin-Epstein, N. (2001). Welfare regimes, family-supportive policies and women's employment along the life-course. *American Journal of Sociology, 106,* 1731–1760.

Sugihara, Y., & Katsurada, E. (2002). Gender role development in Japanese culture. *Sex Roles, 47,* 443–452.

Swedish Institute. (2003). Equality between women and men. *Fact Sheets on Sweden.* Retrieved April 22, 2005, from http://www.sweden.se/templates/cs/BasicFactsheet____4123.aspx

Thornton, A., & Young-DeMarco, L. (2001). Four decades of trends in attitudes toward family issues in the United States. *Journal of Marriage and Family, 63,* 1009–1037.

Tijden, K. (2002). Gender roles and labor use strategies. *Feminist Economics, 8,* 71–99.

United Nations. (2002). *The world's women*. New York: Author. Retrieved April 22, 2005, from http://unstats.un.org

U.S. Census Bureau. (2002). *Statistical abstract of the U.S. 2002*. Washington, DC: U.S. Government Printing Office. Retrieved April 22, 2005, from http://www.census.gov

Valiente, C. (2003). Central state childcare policies in postauthoritarian Spain. *Gender & Society, 17,* 287–292.

Waite, L., & Nielsen, M. (2001). The rise of the dual-earner family. In R. Hertz & N. Marshall (Eds.), *Working families* (pp. 23–41). Berkeley: University of California Press.

Warren, T. (2000). Diverse breadwinner models. *Journal of European Social Policy, 10,* 349–371.

Williams, J. (2000). *Unbending gender*. New York: Oxford University Press.

Winkler, C. (2002). *Single mothers and the state*. New York: Rowman & Littlefield.

Wirth, L. (2001). Women in management. In M. Loutfi (Ed.), *Women, gender and work* (pp. 239–249). Geneva, Switzerland: International Labour Office.

Yamaguchi, K. (2000). Married women's gender-role attitudes and social stratification. *International Journal of Sociology, 30,* 52–89.

CHAPTER 20

Poverty and Family Policy in a Global Context

MARK R. RANK AND GAUTAM N. YADAMA

When thinking about global family concerns, one particularly pressing issue is poverty. Poverty affects families in virtually all of the world's nations, although the precise nature and extent of poverty vary from country to country. The magnitude and reach of poverty upon the peoples of the world prompted the United Nations in 1995 to declare that the decade from 1997 to 2006 was to be the "First United Nations Decade for the Eradication of Poverty," with the general theme being that "eradicating poverty is an ethical, social, political and economic imperative of humankind."

The detrimental effects of poverty upon families and individuals have been well established and extensively documented. Poverty negatively affects the health, education, and life chances of individuals and family members. It places an undue burden and stress upon families and households. It also infringes upon family members' ability to fully partake in various opportunities, rights, and freedoms. As Amartya Sen (1992) has persuasively argued, one of the central meanings of impoverishment is "poverty as lack of freedom" (p. 152).

Given its detrimental nature, what can be done to reduce the extent and severity of poverty in the world today? Obviously, this is a monumental question and task, as the United Nations is fully aware. This chapter can only scratch the surface of such an important and huge question. There are, however, some generalizations that can be made. In particular, we would like to discuss several of the conditions and policies that would appear critical in alleviating poverty within families in both the developed and developing world, although the specifics themselves will obviously vary depending upon the national and cultural context.

THE EXTENT OF POVERTY ACROSS NATIONS

Before discussing various strategies for reducing poverty, it is important to provide a brief overview regarding the extent of poverty across nations and how it is measured. Over 200 years ago, in his treatise *Wealth of Nations* (1776), Adam Smith defined poverty as a lack of those necessities that "the custom of the country renders it indecent for creditable people, even of the lowest order, to be without." This type of definition is what is known as an absolute approach. One defines a minimum threshold for living conditions, and individuals who fall below that threshold are considered poor. An example of this approach is the manner in which the United States' official poverty line is calculated. The U.S. poverty line is established by estimating the income needed for different sizes of households to obtain what is considered a minimally adequate basket of goods and services for the year. In 2003, the poverty line for a family of four was drawn at $18,810 (U.S. Bureau of the Census, 2004).

Alternatively, one can measure poverty in a relative sense. For example, individuals who are in the bottom 20% of the income distribution might be considered poor. Alternatively, the poor could be defined as those whose incomes fall below 50% of the population's median income. This is often the type of measure employed in European countries.

A third type of measure seeks to encompass more than just low income by incorporating additional measures of deprivation such as levels of illiteracy, early mortality rates, and so on. The focus here is on the concept of social exclusion as well, or "the inability to participate in the activities of normal living" (Glennerster, 2002, p. 89). As the *Human Development Report* of 2003 notes,

> Poverty involves much more than the restrictions imposed by lack of income. It also entails lack of basic capabilities to lead full, creative lives—as when people suffer from poor health, are excluded from participating in the decisions that affect their communities or have no right to guide the course of their lives. Such deprivations distinguish human poverty from income poverty. (United Nations Development Programme, 2003, p. 27)

This type of measure has been used most notably by the United Nations in their construction of a human poverty index for both the developing and developed nations, and it will be used as well in our discussion and analysis of global poverty.

Developed Countries

Table 20.1 draws upon an analysis by Timothy Smeeding, Lee Rainwater, and Gary Burtless (2000) that uses the Luxembourg Income Study (LIS) to compare the rates of poverty across 18 developed nations. Begun in the 1980s, the LIS contains income and demographic information on households in more than 25 different nations from 1967 to the present. By standardizing variables across 70 data sets, it allows one to conduct cross-national analyses regarding poverty and income inequality.

In Table 20.1, a relative measure of poverty is employed in the first three columns—the percentage of persons living with incomes below half of the median income. In the case of the United States, this works out to approximately 125% of the official U.S. poverty line (which for a family of four in 2003 would be $23,513).

What is apparent in Table 20.1 is that poverty rates in the United States are substantially higher than those found in the other 17 nations. The overall U.S. rate using this measure stands at 17.8%. The next closest country is Italy, at 13.9%, followed by the United Kingdom, Canada, Spain, and Israel, with the Scandinavian and Benelux countries falling near the bottom. The average for all 18 nations is 8.6%.

Looking at the rates for children and the elderly, we can see the same patterns. The United States leads all nations in having the highest rates of child poverty at 22.3%, with the overall average standing at 9.9%. The Scandinavian and Benelux countries again

Table 20.1 Extent of Income Poverty Across 18 Developed Countries

	Percentage of Population Below 50% of Median Income		*Percentage of Population Below U.S. Poverty Line*	
Country (Year)	*Overall*	*Children*	*Elderly*	*Overall*
United States (1997)	17.8	22.3	20.7	13.6*
Italy (1995)	13.9	18.9	12.4	—
United Kingdom (1995)	13.2	20.1	13.9	15.7
Canada (1994)	11.4	15.3	4.7	7.4
Spain (1990)	10.4	12.8	11.4	—
Israel (1992)	10.2	11.6	17.2	—
Netherlands (1994)	7.9	7.9	6.2	7.1
Germany (1994)	7.5	10.6	7.0	7.3
France (1994)	7.4	6.7	10.2	9.9
Denmark (1992)	7.1	4.8	11.1	—
Norway (1995)	6.9	3.9	14.5	4.3
Switzerland (1992)	6.9	7.5	7.4	—
Australia (1994)	6.7	15.0	28.9	17.6
Austria (1992)	6.7	5.9	17.4	—
Sweden (1992)	6.5	2.6	2.6	6.3
Belgium (1992)	5.5	4.4	11.9	—
Finland (1995)	5.0	4.1	5.1	4.8
Luxembourg (1994)	3.9	4.4	6.7	0.3
Overall Average	8.6	9.9	11.6	8.6

*Data for the United States in this column are for 1994.

SOURCE: Smeeding, Rainwater, and Burtless (2000).

tend to have the lowest rates—the child poverty rates for these countries are 2.6% for Sweden, 3.9% for Norway, 4.1% for Finland, and 4.4% for Belgium and Luxembourg.

Only in the case of the elderly does the United States not lead the developed world. Here, the U.S. poverty rate of 20.7% is second from the top, falling behind only Australia's rate, with the overall average being 11.6%.

The final column of Table 20.1 estimates the overall poverty rates for a subset of these nations using an absolute measure. One critique that could be leveled at columns 1 to 3 is that although the United States has extremely high rates of relative poverty, the standard of living that poor Americans experience is potentially greater than that of the poor or near-poor in many of the comparison countries, because the overall levels of U.S. income are higher. Consequently, column 4 recalculates the rates of poverty by applying the official U.S. poverty line to 11 countries for which the data allow such comparisons.

Using this measure, Australia, the United Kingdom, and the United States have the highest levels of poverty at 17.6%, 15.7%, and 13.6%, respectively. France, Germany, Canada, and the Netherlands fall in the middle of the pack, whereas Norway, Sweden, Finland, and Luxembourg again display the lowest rates of poverty.

Further analyses also show that the purchasing power of U.S. households at the 10th percentile of the income distribution is far below that of comparable households in other Western countries. Among 12 major industrialized countries, only the poor in Australia and the United Kingdom had less purchasing power than their U.S. counterparts (Smeeding & Rainwater, 2001; see also Jencks, 2002). On the other hand, the purchasing power of wealthy Americans at the 90th percentile of the income distribution far surpassed their counterparts in all other countries. A similar story can be told with respect to children (Rainwater & Smeeding, 2003; Smeeding, 2002).

What makes the high absolute rate of U.S. poverty particularly glaring is that each country in Table 20.1, with the exception of Luxembourg, has a per capita income level well below that of the United States. These range from 67% of the U.S. level for the United Kingdom to 86% for Norway. Consequently, even though the United States is considerably wealthier than each of the comparison nations, it has a higher level of absolute poverty than nearly all the comparison countries.

Table 20.2 looks at a similar set of countries (Ireland and Japan are added, whereas Switzerland, Austria, and Israel are omitted) using the human poverty index developed by the United Nations. As discussed earlier, this approach attempts to measure the broader notion of deprivation. Components of the index include the percentage of the population at birth not surviving to age 60, the percentage of the population lacking functional literacy skills, the percentage of the population who have been unemployed for 12 months or more, and the percentage of the population whose income is below 50% of the median income (which was also used in the first three columns of Table 20.1).

Once again, we see that the United States leads the other nations in terms of the extent of poverty. According to the human poverty index, 15.8% of the U.S. population lives in poverty, followed by 15.3% of those in Ireland, 14.8% in the United Kingdom, and 12.9% in Australia. As in Table 20.1, those countries with the lowest rates of poverty tend to be the Scandinavian countries (Sweden, Norway, Finland, and Denmark) and Benelux countries such as the Netherlands and Luxembourg.

Looking at the individual components of the human poverty index, the United States is at the top in terms of mortality, illiteracy, and falling below 50% of the median income. Only in the case of long-term unemployment does the United States not lead the developed nations. Here we see that countries such as Italy, Spain, Germany, and France tend to have the highest rates.

In summary, among the developed countries examined in Tables 20.1 and 20.2, the United States has the highest rates of poverty, with Ireland, the United Kingdom, Australia, Italy, and Canada also having relatively high rates of poverty. Countries such as France and Germany fall in the middle of the pack, whereas the Scandinavian and Benelux countries such as Sweden, Norway, Finland, and Luxembourg tend to have relatively low rates of poverty.

Developing Countries

The severity and depth of poverty in the developing world is obviously much more extreme than that found in the developed world. As Layi Erinosho (2004) notes,

> More than two thirds of the poor in the world are in developing countries. There is more grinding poverty in the developing than in the developed countries. . . . It is therefore not surprising that the searchlight on poverty is often directed at third world countries. (p. 1)

Yet it is also true that the extent of poverty varies widely across the developing world. Countries in sub-Saharan Africa tend

Table 20.2 Extent of Poverty and Deprivation as Measured by Human Poverty Index Across 17 Developed Countries

	Components of Human Poverty Index				
Country	*Human Poverty Index*	*Not Surviving to Age 60*	*Lacking Functional Literacy*	*Long-Term Unemployment*	*Below 50% of Median Income*
United States	15.8	12.6	20.7	0.3	17.0
Ireland	15.3	9.3	22.6	3.2	12.3
United Kingdom	14.8	8.9	21.8	1.3	12.5
Australia	12.9	8.8	17.0	1.4	14.3
Belgium	12.4	9.4	18.4	3.2	8.0
Canada	12.2	8.7	16.6	0.7	12.8
Italy	12.2	8.6	—	6.1	14.2
Japan	11.1	8.7	—	1.4	11.8
Spain	11.0	8.8	—	4.6	10.1
France	10.8	10.0	—	3.3	8.0
Luxembourg	10.3	9.7	—	0.5	3.9
Germany	10.2	9.2	14.4	4.2	7.5
Denmark	9.1	11.0	9.6	0.9	9.2
Netherlands	8.4	8.7	10.5	1.6	8.1
Finland	8.4	10.2	10.4	2.4	5.4
Norway	7.2	8.3	8.5	0.2	6.9
Sweden	6.5	7.3	7.5	1.1	6.6

SOURCE: United Nations Development Programme (2003).

NOTE: Values are percentages.

to have the highest poverty rates, followed by those in South Asia, North Africa, the Middle East, East Asia and the Pacific, and finally the Latin American and Caribbean countries.

Table 20.3 includes a sampling of 20 developing countries from across the different world regions. The data are again taken from the *Human Development Report* prepared by the United Nations Development Programme (2003). As in the previous table, Table 20.3 uses a human poverty index (HPI) in order to gauge poverty; however, the specifics are somewhat different than those used for the developed countries. The HPI for developing countries includes

> deprivations in three dimensions: longevity, as measured by the probability at birth of not surviving to age 40; knowledge, as measured by the adult illiteracy rate; and overall economic provisioning, public and private, as measured by the percentage of people not using improved water sources and the percentage without sustainable access to an improved water source and the percentage of children under weight for age. (United Nations Development Programme, 2003, p. 61)

We can see that the sub-Saharan African countries in Table 20.3 tend to have the highest values in terms of poverty. Ethiopia has an estimated 56% of the population residing in poverty, followed by Mozambique, the Central African Republic, and Senegal. The South Asian countries of Bangladesh, Nepal, and Pakistan have around 40% of their populations living in poverty. The East Asian countries of Vietnam, Indonesia, the

Table 20.3 Extent of Poverty and Deprivation as Measured by Human Poverty Index Across 20 Developing Countries

	Components of Human Poverty Index					*Below Income Poverty Line*	
Country	*Human Poverty Index*	*Not Surviving to Age 40*	*Adult Illiteracy Rate*	*Lack of Access to Water Source*	*Children Under Weight*	*Less Than \$1 a Day*	*Less Than \$2 a Day*
Ethiopia	56.0	43.0	59.7	76	47	81.9	98.4
Mozambique	50.3	56.0	54.8	43	26	37.9	78.4
Central African Republic	47.8	55.3	51.8	30	24	66.6	84.0
Senegal	44.4	27.7	61.7	22	18	26.3	67.8
Bangladesh	42.6	17.3	59.4	3	48	36.0	82.8
Nepal	41.9	19.3	57.1	12	48	37.7	82.5
Pakistan	40.2	17.8	56.0	10	38	13.4	65.6
India	33.1	15.3	42.0	16	47	34.7	79.9
Egypt	30.5	8.6	43.9	3	4	3.1	43.9
Algeria	22.6	9.3	32.2	11	6	<2	15.1
Vietnam	19.9	10.7	7.3	23	33	17.7	63.7
Indonesia	17.9	10.8	12.7	22	26	7.2	55.4
Philippines	14.8	7.4	4.9	14	28	14.6	46.4
China	14.2	7.1	14.2	25	10	16.1	47.3
Thailand	12.9	10.2	4.3	16	19	<2	32.5
Ecuador	11.9	10.3	8.2	15	15	20.2	52.3
Brazil	11.4	11.5	12.7	13	6	9.9	23.7
Mexico	8.8	7.6	8.6	12	8	8.0	24.3
Trinidad and Tobago	7.7	9.1	1.6	10	7	12.4	39.0
Costa Rica	4.4	3.7	4.3	5	5	6.9	14.3

SOURCE: United Nations Development Programme (2003).

NOTE: Values are percentages.

Philippines, China, and Thailand have between 12% and 20% of their populations in poverty, whereas the Latin American countries have the lowest rates of poverty in terms of the HPI, between 4% and 12%.

Not every country from these regions, however, falls into these general patterns. For example, some countries in sub-Saharan Africa have much lower rates of poverty than those in Table 20.3—34% of Nigeria's population are in poverty, 32% in Congo, and 26.4% in Ghana. On the other hand, some Latin American and Caribbean countries have much higher rates of poverty than the countries shown in Table 20.3. The poverty rate for Haiti is 41.6%, and poverty in Nicaragua stands at 24.3%. What this points out is that although there are general patterns across broad regions of the developing world, there are also a number of exceptions to the rule. As we will discuss in the next section, the patterns in both the developing and developed nations can be largely understood in terms of the presence or absence of certain conditions and policies that help to reduce the extent and severity of poverty.

The two far-right-hand columns employ an absolute measure of poverty by estimating the percentages of the population in each of these countries living below $1 a day and $2 a day. As with the developed countries, it is somewhat difficult to make comparisons in terms of income poverty across different nations and regions of the world, in that the cost of living can and does vary. Nevertheless, as the *Human Development Report* states, "Behind this approach is the assumption—based on national poverty lines from a sample of developing countries—that, after adjusting for cost of living differences, $1 a day is the average minimum consumption required for subsistence in the developing world" (United Nations Development Programme, 2003, p. 42).

We see a somewhat similar pattern in terms of how these countries compare with respect to these two measures of poverty. Again, the sub-Saharan African countries tend to have the highest rates of poverty, whereas the Latin American and Caribbean countries tend to have the lowest. In some cases, a country's rate of poverty as measured by living below a dollar a day is much higher than its rate of poverty as measured by the HPI. For example, 81.9% of Ethiopians live on less than a dollar a day, whereas 56% are counted as poor by the HPI. On the other hand, 30.5% of Egyptians are considered poor in terms of the HPI, but less than 2% live on less than a dollar a day.

To summarize, poverty varies widely across both the developed and developing worlds. Among the developed nations, the United States has the highest levels of poverty, followed by the United Kingdom, Ireland, Australia, Canada, and Italy; those with the lowest rates of poverty are the Scandinavian and Benelux countries. Within the developing world, countries in sub-Saharan Africa and South Asia display the most severe levels of poverty, whereas the Latin American nations tend to have the lowest rates.

STRATEGIES FOR ADDRESSING POVERTY WITHIN DEVELOPED COUNTRIES

Having briefly discussed the extent of poverty within a global context, we now turn to those conditions and policies that can effectively reduce the severity of poverty within countries. Our discussion is divided into strategies pertaining to the developed and to the developing worlds.

With respect to the developed world, there are at least three broad conditions and policies that are essential to reducing poverty. These include ensuring the availability of jobs that will economically support a family, providing an effective social safety net that also incorporates key social and public goods, and building individual and community assets. Each is discussed below.

Ensuring the Availability of Decent-Paying Jobs

Essential to any overall strategy to reduce poverty are policies that will increase the availability of jobs that can support a family above the poverty line. As Bradley Schiller (2004) notes, "Jobs—in abundance and of good quality—are the most needed and most permanent solution to the poverty problem" (p. 272).

The problem of not enough jobs has played itself out somewhat differently within an American versus a European context. Within the United States, the economy over the past 25 years has done relatively well in terms of creating new jobs. The problem has been that many of these jobs are low paying or lacking in basic benefits, such as health care. The result has been that although unemployment rates have been relatively low in the United States (averaging between 4% and 6%), working full-time does not ensure that a family will be lifted out of poverty or near poverty. For example, Smeeding, Rainwater, and Burtless (2001) found that 25% of all American full-time workers could be classified as being in low-wage work (defined as earning less than 65% of the national median for full-time jobs). This was by far the highest percentage of the developed countries analyzed, with the overall average falling at 12%.

In contrast, the European economies have been much more sluggish in terms of creating new jobs over the past 25 years, resulting in unemployment rates much higher than in the United States. In addition, workers have remained out of work for longer periods of time (as seen in the long-term unemployment rates in Table 20.2). However, for those who are employed, workers are generally paid more than their American counterparts, resulting in substantially lower rates of poverty (Gallie, 2002).

What then can be done to address the related problems of jobs that do not pay enough to support a family, and not enough jobs in the first place? Two broad initiatives would appear essential. The first is transforming the existing job base so that wages will support a family (which is particularly relevant within an American context). The second is the creation of enough jobs to employ all who are in need of work (which is particularly relevant within a European context).

Within the context of the United States, one might begin with the following benchmark—individuals who are employed full-time throughout the year (defined as working 35 hours per week over a 52-week period, or 1,820 hours) should be able to generate earnings that will enable them to lift a family of three above the poverty threshold. Such a family might include a married couple with one child, a one-parent household with two children, or a three-generation household of mother, grandmother, and son. The 2003 poverty threshold for a family of three in the United States was set at $14,680. Consequently, in order to lift such a family above the poverty line, an individual needs to be earning no less than $8.07 an hour.

There are at least two specific ways of accomplishing this. One is to raise the minimum wage to a level that will support a family above the poverty line and then index the minimum wage to inflation so that it will continue to keep such a family over the poverty line in the future. A second approach is to provide a tax credit (such as the Earned Income Tax Credit) that supplements workers' wages so that their total income for the year lifts them above the poverty line.

The minimum wage in the United States went into effect in October 1938 at an initial level of $0.25 an hour. The basic concept was that no employee should fall below a certain wage floor. There was an underlying value that workers should receive a fair wage for a fair day's work. However, unlike Social Security, the minimum wage has never been indexed to inflation; changes in the minimum wage must come through congressional legislation. Years often go by before Congress acts to adjust the minimum wage upward, causing it to lag behind the rising cost of living. For example, the minimum wage remained at $3.35 an hour between 1981 and 1989, substantially eroding its purchasing power. The current minimum wage in the United States stands at $5.15 an hour, a rate that went into effect in September 1997. At this wage, an individual working full-time during the year (52 weeks at 35 hours per week) would earn a total of $9,373, far short of the $14,680 need to lift a family of three above the poverty line.

To lift such a family above the poverty line, an individual needs to be earning at least $8.07 per hour. Consequently, what is needed is to raise the minimum wage to approximately $8.00 per hour, and then index the minimum wage each year to the rate of inflation so that it will maintain its purchasing power. The phase-in period to raise the minimum wage might take place over several years in order to spread out the increase.

The positive impact of tying the minimum wage to the poverty level for a family of three and then indexing it to the rate of inflation would be substantial. First, it would establish a reasonable floor below which no full-time worker would fall. Second, it would allow such a worker to support a family of three above the official poverty line. Third, it would reinforce the value that Americans have consistently attached to work. Fourth, it would remove the political wrangling from the minimum wage debate. Fifth, it would address in a limited way the increasing inequities between CEOs who earn three or four hundred times what their average paid workers earn.

A second approach for supplementing and raising the earnings of low-income workers is through the tax structure, specifically through the use of tax credits. The primary example of such a credit in the United States is the Earned Income Tax Credit (EITC). The EITC was enacted in 1975 and underwent a significant expansion during the 1990s. In fact, it currently represents the largest cash antipoverty program in the United States and is frequently considered one of the more innovative American economic policy ideas (see Ventry, 2002, for a historical and political background of the EITC).

The program is designed to provide a refundable tax credit to low-income workers, with the vast majority going to households with children. In 2002, a family with one child could qualify for the EITC if its earned income was below $29,201 (or $30,201 for married couples), whereas a family with two or more children could qualify if its household income was under $33,178 (or $34,178 for married couples). The maximum credit for a one-child family was $2,506; the benefit rose to $4,140 for a family with two or more children. The credit is normally received in a lump-sum payment as part of an overall tax refund for the previous year. Because it is a refundable credit, families receive the payment even if they do not owe any taxes.

The goals of the EITC are to deliver economic relief at the low end of the earnings distribution and to furnish a strong work incentive. An individual cannot qualify for the EITC without earned income, and the impact is particularly strong at the lower levels. For example, for a head of household who was earning $7.50 an hour (and her total annual earnings were under $10,000), the EITC would effectively raise her wage by an additional $3.00, to $10.50 an hour. The program thus provides a significant supplement to low earners as well as an incentive to work. In 2002, it was estimated that 19 million Americans benefited from the EITC and that it pulled approximately 5 million individuals above the poverty line who otherwise would have fallen into poverty (Schiller, 2004). For families that remain in poverty, the EITC has helped to reduce the distance between their household income and the poverty line. It has also enabled families to purchase particular resources that can improve their economic and social mobility (e.g., school tuition, a car, or a new residence) or to meet daily expenses (Meyer & Holtz-Eakin, 2002).

In order to make the EITC even more effective, its benefits should be expanded so that they provide greater assistance to low-income workers without children. The vast majority of the EITC benefits go to families with children. Yet there is no compelling reason why such benefits should not also be provided for individuals without children. Further work also needs to be done in order to increase the feasibility of receiving the EITC throughout the year, rather than as a lump sum during the tax season (although many families do prefer this way of receiving the EITC). Third, some households that qualify for the EITC fail to claim and take advantage of the tax credit. Better education of tax filers about the benefits of the EITC appears warranted. Fourth, state EITC programs should be encouraged as an additional antipoverty component on top of the federal EITC benefits. Finally, consideration should also be given to modestly increasing the size of the credits currently given to families (although, as mentioned, considerable expansion occurred in the early 1990s, and the federal program may currently be close to its optimal size; e.g., see Liebman, 2002).

The policy of an expanded EITC, in conjunction with the raising and indexing of the minimum wage to the level of a living wage, would substantially help working men and women in the United States who, in spite of their efforts, are unable to get themselves and their families out of poverty or near-poverty. In addition, such policies begin to address (although in a very limited way) the increasing inequalities and perceived unfairness of the American income distribution and wage structure.

With respect to the problem of producing an adequate number of jobs (which affects the European Union to a greater extent than the United States), in many ways, this is a much more difficult task than supplementing and raising the wages of existing jobs. Nevertheless, it is essential that a sufficient number of jobs be available to meet the demands of the existing labor pool.

Various labor demand policies have the potential to generate a more robust rate of job growth. Several approaches can be taken. First, economic policy should seek in a broad way to stimulate job growth. This would include fiscal policies such as increasing government expenditures, enhancing tax incentives for investment, or enacting consumer tax cuts. Monetary policy can provide a stimulus by making access to credit easier and cheaper (Schiller, 2004).

A second approach is to provide targeted wage subsidies to employers in order to stimulate job creation. Although the details of such programs can vary considerably, the basic concept is that an employer receives a monetary subsidy for creating a position or hiring an individual (often from a targeted population) that the employer might not have hired without such an incentive. This approach could be aimed at businesses and industries that are potential employers of individuals from lower-income or lower-skill backgrounds.

A third strategy for creating jobs is through public service employment. As Ellwood and Welty (2000) note in their review of the effectiveness of public service employment programs, if done carefully and judiciously, they can help increase employment without displacing other workers, and they can produce genuinely valuable output. Such an approach appears particularly pertinent for those out of work for long periods of time.

Taken as a whole, an overall strategy for reducing poverty in the developed world must begin with a set of policies that will increase the availability of jobs that can economically support families above the poverty threshold. To a large extent, poverty in developed nations is the result of not having a job, or having a job that is not able to viably support a family. Policies must address these shortcomings within the developed free-market economies.

Providing an Effective Social Safety Net and Access to Key Social Goods

A second key strategy for reducing poverty within developed countries is ensuring the existence of an effective social safety net along with providing access to key social and public goods such as health care, a quality education, child care, and affordable housing.

No matter how strong economic growth may be, some individuals and families will invariably fall between the cracks. Whether through the loss of a job, a sudden disability, or some other unanticipated event, there are times and situations in people's lives when a social safety net is needed. In developed countries, this has taken the form of various programs and policies encompassed under the social welfare state, whereas in developing countries the role of the social safety net has more typically been fulfilled by the extended family.

Hyman Minsky (1986) points out that free-market economies are prone to periods of instability, such as periodic recessions and economic downturns. Safety net programs help to serve as automatic stabilizers for the economy during these periods. That is, they grow during times of need and diminish during more prosperous times. For example, as rates of unemployment rise, more individuals draw on unemployment insurance to weather the temporary economic problems caused by the lack of jobs. As economic conditions improve, more people are able to find jobs and so no longer need unemployment insurance. In this fashion, safety net programs help to automatically stabilize the instability inherent within Western economies. A social safety net is therefore important in assisting individuals and families during times of need and in alleviating the economic instability associated with recessionary periods.

One of the reasons for the high rates of poverty in the United States, compared to the low Scandinavian rates, is the result of differences in the extent and depth of their social safety nets. Compared to other Western industrialized countries, the United States devotes far fewer resources to programs aimed at assisting the economically vulnerable (Alesina & Glaeser, 2004; Organization for Economic Cooperation and Development, 1999). In fact, the United States allocates a smaller proportion of its gross domestic product (GDP) to social welfare programs than any other industrialized country except Japan (Gilens, 1999). As Charles Noble (1997) writes, "The U.S. welfare state is striking precisely because it is so limited in scope and ambition" (p. 3).

In contrast, most European countries provide a wide range of universal social and insurance programs that largely prevent families from falling into poverty. These include substantial family or children's allowances, which are designed to transfer cash assistance to families with children. Unemployment assistance is far more generous in these countries than in the United States, often providing support for more than a year following the loss of a job. Furthermore, health coverage is routinely provided, along with considerable support for child care.

The result of these social policy differences is that they substantially reduce the extent of poverty in Europe, whereas U.S. social policy has only a small impact upon poverty reduction. As Rebecca Blank (1997) notes,

> the national choice in the United States to provide relatively less generous transfers to low-income families has meant higher relative poverty rates in the country. While low-income families in the United States work more than in many other countries, they are not able to make up for lower governmental income support relative to their European counterparts. (pp. 141–142)

This effect can be clearly seen in Table 20.4. The data in this table are based upon an analysis of the Luxembourg Income Study conducted by Veli-Matti Ritakallio (2001). For a household, poverty is defined as having disposable income of less than half of the country's median annual income. Eight

Table 20.4 Comparative Analysis of Governmental Effectiveness in Reducing Poverty Across Selected Countries

Country (Year)	*Pretransfer Poverty Rates*	*Posttransfer Poverty Rates*	*Reduction Factor*
Canada (1994)	29	10	66
Finland (1995)	33	4	88
France (1994)	39	8	79
Germany (1994)	29	7	76
Netherlands (1994)	30	7	77
Norway (1995)	27	4	85
Sweden (1995)	36	3	92
United Kingdom (1995)	38	13	66
United States (1994)	29	18	38

SOURCE: Luxembourg Income Study, adapted from Veli-Matti Ritakallio's (2001) computations.

NOTE: Values are percentages.

European countries and Canada are compared to the United States in terms of their pretransfer and posttransfer rates of poverty. The pretransfer rates (column 1) indicate what the level of poverty would be in each country in the absence of any governmental income transfers such as welfare payments, unemployment compensation, or social security payments. The posttransfer rates (column 2) represent the level of poverty after governmental transfers are included (which is how poverty is officially measured in the United States and many other countries). Comparing these two levels of poverty (column 3) reveals how effective (or ineffective) governmental policy is in reducing the overall extent of poverty in a country.

Looking first at the rates of pretransfer poverty, we can see that the United States is on the low end of the scale. Norway's pretransfer poverty rate is 27%, followed by the United States, Canada, and Germany at 29%. The Netherlands' pretransfer rate is 30%; Finland stands at 33%, Sweden at 36%, and the United Kingdom at 38%. France possesses the highest level of pretransfer poverty at 39%.

When we examine the posttransfer rates of poverty, listed in column 2, we see a dramatic reversal in terms of where the United States stands vis-à-vis the comparison countries. The average posttransfer poverty rate for the eight comparison countries in Table 20.4 is 7%, whereas the United States' posttransfer poverty rate stands at 18%. As a result of their more active social policies, Canada and Europe are able to significantly cut their overall rates of poverty. For example, Sweden is able to reduce the number of people who would be poor in the absence of any governmental help by 92%. The overall average reduction factor for the eight countries is 79%. In contrast, the U.S. poverty reduction factor is only 38% (with much of this being the result of Social Security).

One of the reasons why the Scandinavian countries have such low rates of poverty found in Tables 20.1 and 20.2, and why the United States has such high levels of poverty, is a result of the nature and scope of their social safety nets. The Scandinavian countries are able to lift a significant percentage of their economically vulnerable above the threshold of poverty through governmental transfer and assistance policies. In contrast, the United States provides substantially less support through its social safety net, resulting in poverty rates that are currently among the highest in the industrialized world. In summarizing this research, Jurgen Kohl (1995) notes,

> If there is a common pattern behind the bewildering variety of rates and risk of poverty in the advanced Western countries, it is perhaps this: Differences in the extent and the relative risks of poverty reflect the differing capabilities and/or willingness of welfare states to cope with social risks and problems by means of social policy programmes. . . . Cross-national comparisons provide examples that adequate social programmes can contain the poverty risk of vulnerable groups and, thereby, the extent of poverty in society in general. (p. 272)

In addition to providing a social safety net, it is also critical that governments make available easy and affordable access to several key social and public goods. In particular, a quality education, health care, affordable housing, and child care are vital in building and maintaining healthy and productive citizens and families.

The European countries provide far greater access and coverage to health care, affordable housing, and child care than does the United States (although it is also true that the social welfare states in many of these countries have been under increasing retrenchment pressure; Korpi, 2003). All of them provide some form of national health care. In addition, many provide accessible, affordable, and good-quality child care and subsidized housing. In addition, European countries do not display the wide fluctuations in educational quality that American children are subjected to at the primary and secondary levels.

The result is that these policies have the effect of mitigating the harshness of poverty and economic vulnerability. In addition, there is a belief that there are certain social and public goods that all individuals have a right to, and that making such resources accessible results in more productive citizens and societies in both the short and the long run. As stated in the European Union Council's communication to the Nice European Council,

> the European social model, with its developed systems of social protection, must underpin the transformation to the knowledge economy. People are Europe's main asset and should be the focal point of the Union's policies. Investing in people and developing an active and dynamic welfare state will be crucial both to Europe's place in the knowledge economy and for ensuring that the emergence of this new economy does not compound the existing social problems of unemployment, social exclusion and poverty. (Esping-Andersen, 2002, p. 121)

Providing access to these vital social and public goods is essential to any overall strategy of alleviating poverty.

Building Assets

Social policies are frequently designed to alleviate the current conditions of poverty. Indeed, the strategies of creating work and providing a social safety net are both aimed at improving the current economic conditions of individuals and families. This is understandable, given that poverty affects children and adults in the here and now.

Yet approaches to poverty alleviation must also pay attention to longer-term processes and solutions. In particular, the accumulation of assets is crucial, both across the individual life course and within the communities in which families reside. The acquisition of such assets allows families to more effectively function and, for our purposes, to reduce their risk of poverty. These assets enable households to ride out periods of economic vulnerability. They also allow for the growth and strengthening of individual and family development. Assets build a stake in the future that income by itself often cannot provide. Unfortunately, the opportunities to acquire such assets have often been in short supply for lower-income families.

One innovative policy tool for building the assets of the poor has been the concept of Individual Development Accounts (or IDAs). This approach has been pioneered by Michael Sherraden (1991, 2001). Sherraden (1991) argues that government policy should provide incentives and resources that would allow low-income individuals and families to build their economic assets, much as it does for middle- and upper-class families. For example, the tax expenditure policy of allowing home mortgage deductions on federal income tax returns in the United States has allowed millions of Americans to lower the costs of owning a home and thus has enabled them to build equity in this major asset. His assertion is that "asset accumulation and investment, rather than income and consumption, are the keys to leaving poverty" (Sherraden, 1991, p. 294). Government policies should attempt to facilitate the building of individuals' and families' resources through asset accumulation.

To do this, Sherraden has formulated the concept of Individual Development Accounts, which allow poor individuals and families to participate in matched savings accounts, with the match being at least 1:1 and often much higher. Accumulated assets in these accounts can be used for a broad array of development purposes intended to strengthen a family's economic position, such as job training, education, starting a small business, or owning a home. The IDAs "can have multiple sources of matching deposits, including governments, corporations, foundations, community groups, and individual donors" (Sherraden, 2000, p. 161). IDAs are designed to provide a vehicle for lower-income families to save and a financial incentive for them to do so. The savings themselves are intended to be used at a later time to further build and strengthen a household's assets and human capital.

The 1996 federal welfare reform legislation in the United States included a provision allowing states to use part of their block grant money to establish and fund IDAs. Both Presidents Bill Clinton and George W. Bush have demonstrated strong support for the concept, and more than 40 states have some form of IDA policy. The concept is also gaining ground in countries such as Canada, Taiwan, and the United Kingdom. Evidence from a large demonstration project in the United States indicates that IDAs do indeed enable poor families to save and accumulate assets (Schreiner, Clancy, & Sherraden, 2002).

Additional asset-based development policies could be developed as well. One recent example is the idea of a children's trust fund. Beginning at the child's birth, a government would contribute monetary funds on a regular basis into an account for each child. It would be universal in that all children would be entitled to such a fund, yet it would also be progressive in that lower-income families would receive a proportionally greater amount of resources than middle- or upper-income children. At age 18, children would be allowed to use their trust funds for particular purposes such as furthering their education, receiving technical training, or perhaps investing in a home a bit later in life. As Sherraden (2002) notes, such a policy has the potential to "reduce class divisions, increase opportunity, spark individual engagement and initiative, and increase both economic growth and active citizenship" (p. 4). The idea of a children's trust fund has been adopted in the United Kingdom, and discussions are beginning to take place in the United States.

Singapore, with its Central Provident Fund (CPF), is an example of a developed country that has invested heavily in the concept of asset building. Introduced in 1955, the CPF is a mandatory pension fund that allows members to use their savings for housing, medical expenses, and education.

Just as individuals thrive with the acquisition and development of assets, so too do communities. Poor neighborhoods are often characterized by their lack of strong community assets, such as quality schools, decent housing, adequate infrastructure, economic opportunities, and available jobs. These, in turn, affect the life chances of residents in such communities.

Strengthening the major institutions found within lower-income communities is vital, because they have the power to improve the quality of life, foster the accumulation of human capital, and increase the overall opportunities for community residents. Among such institutions are schools, businesses and industries, lending establishments, community centers, and so on. A wide range of strategies can be used to strengthen these institutions to meet the needs of the community. Creating greater equity in funding across school districts, attracting businesses to lower-income communities, opening up the lending practices of banks and savings and loans to people in economically depressed areas—all would provide substantial benefits.

Some of the techniques and policies for arriving at such goals would include community development strategies, grassroots organizing techniques, neighborhood movements such as the rise of community development corporations, and tax incentive policies targeted at businesses that choose to locate in a specified impoverished area. Strengthening the resources and assets of economically vulnerable communities, in conjunction with individual and family asset building, is vital to an overall poverty reduction strategy for the developed world.

STRATEGIES FOR ADDRESSING POVERTY WITHIN DEVELOPING COUNTRIES

It is important to begin our discussion of developing countries with a brief description detailing the conditions of poverty found in the developing world. These conditions are clearly more extreme than those found in the developed world. We then turn to a discussion of three broad strategies for addressing such poverty.

A majority of the world's 1.2 billion poor who survive on less than $1 a day reside in 117 low- and lower-middle-income countries. Poverty in these countries tends to be widespread, severe, and chronic. Of the 1.2 billion living on less than $1 a day, 69% are concentrated in sub-Saharan Africa and South Asia, whereas another 24% are in the East Asia and Pacific region (United Nations Development Programme, 2003).

Aggregate numbers, however, mask the actual social and economic conditions that such poor families must endure, the livelihood strategies they deploy (many times undermining their chances of ever escaping poverty), and the inability of debt-burdened governments to intervene effectively. Poor families in developing countries are more vulnerable to food shortages, disease burden, children dropping out of school or not enrolling at all, and infant and child mortality. In addition, they are less likely to have access to productive assets, health services, clean water, and sanitation (United Nations Development Programme, 2003; World Bank, 2004).

Poverty initially predisposes individuals and households to these deficiencies, but a vulnerability to food shortages and a lack of productive assets and services deepen poverty, making it chronic and persistent (Mehta & Shah, 2003). In addition, weak governments that ignore the plight of the poor and political institutions that represent only the narrow interests of the elite have given rise to civil conflicts that further exacerbate poverty and limit the choices those in poverty have for mere survival.

Approximately 75% of the 1.2 billion poor in developing countries live in rural areas, and this figure is expected to be around 60% in the year 2025 (International Fund for Agriculture Development [IFAD], 2001). A significant portion of the rural poor are landless agricultural laborers. In Bangladesh, for example, 69% of the poor and 80% of the extreme poor are landless (IFAD, 2002, p. 20). Lack of productive assets in an agrarian economy not only restricts the labor market mobility of the poor, but also makes them vulnerable to economic and environmental shocks. They are the first to suffer in a stagnant economy, and they bear the greatest and immediate burden of crop failures due to poor rainfall or excessive monsoons. Under such conditions, it is the poor—rural and urban—who experience hunger; disease; and deprivation of food, safe drinking water, sanitation facilities, health, shelter, and access to emergency services (Townsend & Gordon, 2004).

Inaccessibility of land is both a cause and outcome of being poor. Even small amounts of productive land can enable poor families to be independent subsistence producers instead of being trapped in oppressive patron-client relationships. Secure land ownership gives the poor greater control to combine their labor, skills, and management, and it boosts household productivity and income. For example, a 10% increase in land ownership in El Salvador is associated with a 4% increase in per capita income (IFAD, 2001, p. 76). Distribution of land and other productive assets in South Asia and sub-Saharan Africa, however, is highly skewed and significantly contributes to persistent and chronic poverty.

Women in particular have very little access to land, but they make up a significant portion of the rural poor. For example, in sub-Saharan Africa, a high percentage of rural households are headed by women (Agarwal, 1998; World Bank, 2001b). Social and legal norms that exclude women from owning property have a devastating impact in perpetuating chronic poverty among female-headed households. Initial conditions that dispossess the poor (and particularly women) of productive assets result in widespread deprivation during times of shock, be it from contraction of the economy, civil war, or an HIV/AIDS epidemic.

Lack of access to land, civil war, and weak economies converge to erode the livelihoods and dignity of the poor. For example, the poor in Tajikistan in the early 1990s experienced such conditions. Elizabeth Gomart (2001) recounts the experience of a poor Tajik family,

> A family living in a small village in the Vose district of eastern Khatlon, near the city of Kuliab, has fallen into poverty as a result of the civil war. . . . The husband works at the collective farm but has not received a salary in years. . . . He and his wife cannot feed their seven children, who have not gone to school in two years. In the corner of the house is a heap of dying grass from which the mother says she will make bread. Her older child takes care of cattle for relatives in exchange for bread. A few days ago, when the mother went begging with a group of women from her village, she was bitten by a dog. The wound became infected, but the family cannot afford the medicines to treat it. Her arm is visibly infected and possibly gangrenous. . . . There is no tabib (traditional healer) in the village, and the family is faced with the decision of whether to sell their only cow to buy medicine or let the illness run its course. (pp. 60–61)

Girls and women often bear a disproportionate burden of poverty. Economic crises and conflicts further destabilize already vulnerable rural and urban livelihood strategies and substantially increase the burden on women and girls to engage in livelihoods that rob them of their dignity and undermine their physical, social, and mental well-being. In many cities of Central Asia, rapid economic transition has led to high rates of unemployment, forcing women into prostitution and greatly increasing their vulnerability to HIV/AIDS and more poverty (Kuehnast, 2003).

Rates of HIV infection among the poor provide yet another window into the complexity and intractability of poverty in developing countries. An estimated 38 million people worldwide are currently living with HIV (UNAIDS, 2004b). The worst affected areas are sub-Saharan Africa, South Asia (particularly India), and China. Sub-Saharan Africa has two thirds of all the people living with HIV (25 million), India has another 4.6 million, and it is estimated that China will have 10 million living with HIV by 2010 (UNAIDS, 2004b). The implications of these staggering numbers for poverty are many, ranging from their impact on slowing economic growth rates, to reducing stocks of human capital, to severely affecting agricultural productivity and thereby directly contributing to persistent food shortages. The AIDS epidemic will reduce the working-age populations in sub-Saharan Africa and Asia and likely lead to a contraction of many national economies (UNAIDS, 2004b).

Moreover, AIDS-affected households often suffer severe poverty due to financial burdens of the disease and loss of productive employment. Families saddled with the loss of a breadwinner and increased financial strain from the disease will experience an acute drop in income. Studies in South Africa and Zambia found that AIDS-affected households experienced a decline of 66% to 80% in their monthly income (UNAIDS, 2004b). With 70% of the workforce employed in agriculture, Africa's agricultural base is most affected, giving rise to food shortages, increase in hunger, and a decline in agricultural exports and much-needed foreign exchange (UNAIDS, 2004b). Recent data on the AIDS epidemic also indicate a disproportionate increase in HIV infection among women. Worldwide, women now constitute 50% of all people living with HIV; in sub-Saharan Africa, women make up 57% of all HIV-infected adults, and 75% of HIV-infected youth are women and girls (UNAIDS, 2004b).

The agricultural base is seriously threatened with the loss of adult agricultural workers to AIDS, contributing further to already widespread hunger, which is estimated to affect 183 million in sub-Saharan Africa and another 426 million in Asia and the Pacific (United Nations Development Programme, 2003). The impact of the AIDS epidemic is also likely to undermine the ability of countries to educate the next generation, vital for alleviating poverty and growing the economy. This could mainly unfold in the following way: Schools will be burdened by a shortage of teachers as they fall ill, combined with a growing number of orphans (11 million in sub-Saharan Africa, according to Population Action International, 2004), who without an education will likely join the ranks of the extreme poor. Another externality of the AIDS crisis is that "children, especially girls, from AIDS-affected families are often withdrawn from schools to compensate for loss of income through a parent's sickness and related expenses, to care for sick relatives and look after the home" (UNAIDS, 2004a, p. 9).

Given the complicated nature of poverty in developing countries, policy and program strategies to reduce poverty must address a complex array of factors, from the immediate and short-term needs of the poor to ensuring fundamental rights of the poor to engage and participate in the development process.

At the outset, poverty reduction strategies must ensure economic growth combined with investments in the social sector. Promoting economic growth and infrastructure development while addressing key social development concerns, such as disparities in access to food, health, education, productive assets, clean water, and sanitation, is essential for addressing poverty in developing countries. Generally, the architecture of poverty reduction in developing countries must rest on three pillars that are mutually reinforcing—pro-poor economic growth, social development, and good governance (Asian Development Bank, 2004).

Pro-poor Economic Growth

Pro-poor economic growth is "the type of growth that enables the poor to actively participate in economic activity and benefit proportionally more than the nonpoor from overall income increase" (Pernia, 2003, p. 2). High levels of public debt, however, undercut pro-poor growth. Ensuring that public debt is sustainable and debt burdens are reasonable is the first condition for pro-poor growth. High levels of external debt directly undermine a government's ability to engage in a range of growth-inducing strategies, such as attracting external foreign direct investment to generate growth, undertake capital expenditures on infrastructure development, and promote an investment climate for private-sector development. Moreover, fiscal burdens imposed by high debt force governments to either raise taxes or drastically reduce government spending. In most developing countries where the tax base is narrow and governments are unable to collect taxes, the outcome is reductions in government spending, which directly affect vital services to the poor. As the proportion of spending on debt servicing increases, there is a concomitant reduction in the ratio of social-sector spending in country budgets (United Nations Development Programme, 1999). Partially as a result, the World Bank and the International Monetary Fund in 1996 began a debt initiative to reduce unsustainable external debt of heavily indebted poor countries.

Debt aside, an important dimension of economic growth is to pursue policies that enhance growth in rural areas. Given that a large proportion of the poor in developing countries live in rural areas, and their livelihoods are dependent on agriculture, it is imperative that growth strategies focus on rural areas and on enhancing productivity in agriculture. Khan (2001) illustrates the importance of growth in the agricultural sector in his analysis of poverty in Nepal from 1977 to 1992:

> In Nepal the overall growth in GDP was high enough to prevent a rise in the incidence of poverty if not to bring about a fall in it. But the growth in GDP was largely concentrated in the growth of income in non-agricultural and non-rural activities. The growth of agricultural GDP declined sharply. This, along with a moderate rise in inequality in the rural economy and a sharp rise in inequality in the urban economy, resulted in a rise in the incidence of poverty. (pp. 141–143)

For growth to be pro-poor and to make substantial inroads in poverty, it should be broad based and should particularly affect those sectors of the economy in which the poor are concentrated (such as agriculture). Economic growth must connect with the livelihoods of the poor and be steered into those sectors of the economy where the vast proportion of the poor earn their livelihood. Sectoral composition of growth, therefore, is important; in particular, the distribution of growth between rural and urban areas is critical for poverty reduction (Alarcón, 2001; McKinley, 2001).

Yet another factor in economic growth and its impact on reducing poverty is an enabling environment. An enabling environment concerns investments and strategies that leverage the productivity of poor families. Beyond expanding employment for the poor, there is accumulating evidence for the importance of expanding access to productive assets by way of investments in rural roads, irrigation systems, access to credit, and technical support to raise agricultural productivity (Alarcón, 2001). A key productive asset in the context of developing countries is agricultural land. An increase in landlessness in rural areas significantly reduces the chances of poor families participating in the nonfarm growth in the economy (Ravallion & Datt, 2002). Land redistribution, therefore, is a critical initial condition for realizing pro-poor growth. Here, it is important to note that many developing countries have legislated land redistribution, but in practice, distribution remains skewed in favor of the rich.

Another facet of land as a productive asset is women's lack of inheritance rights to land in many developing countries. Even when there are rights to property stipulated in the law, women still find it difficult to own land because social norms prevail and work against their owning land, as do local governments and courts that are lax in enforcing the letter of the law (Royal Tropical Institute and Oxfam, 2001). Land distribution as a strategy for poverty reduction is a challenge for countries, because governments not only have to formulate policy for land redistribution, but also enforce such redistribution and ensure that women are equal beneficiaries to land in practice as well as in law.

The other types of infrastructure investments that have a salutary effect on reducing poverty are rural roads and irrigation systems. Economic growth, when combined with rural road construction and development of irrigation systems, has a strong poverty-reducing effect. Studies show that an increase in agricultural productivity due to investments in roads accounts for approximately 20% of poverty-reducing effects in India, and 30% in China (Yao, 2003). In Vietnam, households living in villages with paved roads have a 67% greater probability of getting out of poverty than those who live in villages without paved roads (Glewwe, Gragnolati, & Zaman, 2000). Investments in roads, irrigation, and electricity tend to positively influence agricultural and nonagricultural productivity as well as nonagricultural employment. Irrigation and electricity investments also have independent effects on increasing the incomes of poor households, but what is most interesting is that in India and Bangladesh, rural electrification boosts the use of irrigation, thereby significantly reducing poverty incidence (Songco, 2002, as cited in Ali & Pernia, 2003).

Social Development

A second overall strategy for poverty reduction in developing countries is an emphasis upon social development. Government investments in health, education, and sanitation have been shown to improve health outcomes in both the short and long run. Better health, in turn, contributes to increases in income by raising the productive capacities of poor households in the short run; in the long run, as longevity increases, so do savings rates of households, contributing to overall economic growth (Bloom, Canning, & Jamison, 2004). Moreover, complementarities between health and education reduce the poor's vulnerability to disease and, as a result, achieve reductions in poverty. The AIDS pandemic in sub-Saharan Africa, South Asia, and China, however, has severely affected prospects for sustained economic growth. Through strategic and targeted investments in health, education, and sanitation, developing nations can overcome the staggering impact of disease on the economy, and particularly on the poor. Social-sector investments must ensure that the elite does not capture these public services.

Even when investments in social development are pursued, the poor, for a variety of reasons, often fail to benefit from them. A recent *World Development Report* highlighted four ways in which services are failing poor people around the world: (a) Although governments are spending approximately a third of their budgets on health and education, much of that spending benefits the well-to-do rather than the poor. (b) Public spending in the social sector, even when deliberately targeted to the poor, is often not reaching the service providers in the trenches. (c) A disproportionate number of professionals—teachers and doctors—prefer to serve in urban areas, resulting in rural schools and clinics remaining understaffed; as a consequence, rural segments of the economy do not get a lift from public spending. (d) Poor people tend not to utilize primary health care clinics when their children are sick, and they fail to send their children to school, especially girl children (World Bank, 2004).

Three overarching principles should guide health programs aimed at poverty reduction. First, poor households' access to the programs must be improved as well as their knowledge of health services. Second, there is a need to focus on increasing the technical quality of the health services provided to the poor. And third, health interventions for the poor must be predicated on the health profile of the poor (World Bank, 2001c). If inaccessibility is an issue in a given country, then staffing and technical quality of the services provided is irrelevant until accessibility problems are solved. Similarly, the relevance of health services to the needs of the people is significant only when those services become accessible to the poor in their communities.

Investments in education complement health-promotion strategies in reducing poverty. Education, along with health, significantly contributes to increasing the productivity of the poor. However, more than 100 million children in the developing countries (especially girls) are not in school (World Bank, 2001a). Promoting primary education is fundamental for reducing poverty in developing countries. At the same time, adult literacy is also critical, because 880 million adults in the developing countries are illiterate, with significant implications for overall productivity of these economies (World Bank, 2001a). Increasing public spending on education and health to at least 20% of total government expenditure is the first step in achieving positive poverty reduction outcomes, whereas universal primary education can address gender disparities and adult literacy.

In tandem with an increase in aggregate public expenditures, primary health care and schools need greater input from communities. More than other public services, the success of health and educational programs is predicated on the active involvement of communities, especially the poor and women (primary targets of health and education programs). The opportunities for effective social development lie in forging partnerships between communities and local governments to supply and maintain essential public goods and resources. Thus, social development strategies must not only encompass planned investments and change undertaken by the state, but must also focus on affecting development through active participation of local communities, through strengthening civil society to represent the interests and preferences of people, and through leveraging social relationships and structures to affect economic outcomes (Serageldin & Grootaert, 1999). This leads to a final strategy for reducing poverty in developing nations.

Good Governance

Good governance represents a third important strategy for poverty reduction in developing countries. Economic development does not automatically transform into social goods unless those citizens most likely to benefit from such transformation have an influence over the development process. A significant way in which citizens influence this process is through political acts. Sustained social development is realistic in societies where there is a higher rate of civic and political engagement. Pursuit of social development merely as a technology is to overlook the full potential of a social development approach, and even more grave is to discount the ability of ordinary citizens to represent their own interests through civic and political means. Sustained social and economic development must focus on capacity building and on bringing citizens who were previously on the margins into the fold of civic and political representation. Underlying our focus on civic and political engagement is an emphasis on political efficacy, that is, "the self-confidence and sense of competence on the part of the citizenry that their political action may produce a change in policy or a redress of grievances" (Diamond, 1999, p. 171).

State-society synergy amounts to a reorientation of the state toward partnership with elements of civil society, and the enabling of governance to address critical social service needs and preferences of its people. State-community partnerships have the potential of contributing to the vibrancy of civil society and to the consolidation of democracy as the interests of the disadvantaged and disenfranchised become well represented in these partnerships (Haynes, 1997).

Two processes are crucial for good governance leading to effective social and economic development—active civic engagement and reorientation of the role of the state. Democratic and open systems seldom develop from the top down. They are more likely to emerge, deepen, and consolidate over time from the bottom up. Therefore, citizens in various aggregations of family, community, region, and nations must be partners with the state to determine the variety of policy and program strategies for contributing to their well-being.

For example, it has been shown that the poor benefit from better-quality public goods and services when citizens are active in making their needs known and organize to monitor the local government response to meeting those needs through public services. In effect, when the poor actively engage in local governing arrangements, there is a greater likelihood of better public services. In Bangalore, India, a citizen report card initiative that rated public services such as hospitals, roads, water supply, and trash pickup resulted in the Bangalore City Corporation and Development Authority, which responded in constructive ways to improve public goods and services throughout the city, affecting not only middle-income households but the poor as well (Paul, 1998).

The Education Guarantee Scheme in Madhya Pradesh, India, illustrates how citizen preferences for primary education and subsequent inclusion in the governance of newly established schools can produce universal access to education, significantly benefiting the poor. Under this project, the state government of Madhya Pradesh provided primary schools in rural areas lacking a school, as long as 25 learners in a community demanded such a school. These schools were to be locally governed by management committees with active citizen engagement. After 18 months under the program, the state of Madhya Pradesh, with large numbers of poor and low literacy rates, now claims universal access to primary education (Osmani, 2000).

The other component of good governance is that the state itself is important in framing the role of citizens, civil society actors, and the institutional arrangements that generate political and personal empowerment in citizens—precursors to civic and political engagement (Agrawal & Yadama, 1997; Degnbol-Martinussen, 2002; Lowndes &

Wison, 2001; Yadama & DeWeese-Boyd, 2001). As Sobhan (2002) notes, "To elevate the sovereignty of the citizens from fiction to reality demands an appreciation of the role of civil society in assembling citizens to assert their rights" (p. 154). Democratic institutions foster conditions for the formation of voluntary associations and generate confidence in state and nonstate institutions (Paxton, 2002). Under such conditions, citizens are empowered to act collectively on social and political fronts. Petro (2001), in explaining high rates of economic performance in the Novgorod region of Russia, firmly concludes that the state is a significant factor in fostering social trust, and an important exogenous factor is "stable state institutions that allow for predictable engagement among social actors, and a credible system of enforcing social norms" (p. 241). This necessitates conceptualizing the role of the state from one that is distant from people to one that is more responsive, transparent, and accountable to citizens.

A recent study from Indonesia examined the impact within districts as to the quality of governance (transparency, accountability, rule of law, and elimination of corruption) upon reductions in poverty. Results indicated that those districts with good governance practices (where there was greater transparency and accountability and lower corruption) had a 6.5% higher poverty reduction rate than those districts with poor governance practices (Sumarto, Suryahadi, & Arifianto, 2004).

In summary, reducing poverty in developing countries is dependent upon the governments of such countries actively engaging in three broad strategies—pro-poor economic growth policies, social development, and good governance. As is apparent from our discussion of these strategies, they are closely intertwined with each other. Pursuing one without the other two will likely not produce a significant reduction in the extent of poverty. For example, a growing economy and the creation of greater opportunities in the labor market are important. Yet even with an expanding economy, large numbers of poor families who suffer from ill health and illiteracy will be unable to take advantage of such growth. Therefore, investments in health, education, and other forms of social development are essential if the returns from a growing economy are to reach the poor. Likewise, economic growth without a responsive and accountable government that incorporates the needs of the poor will likely fail to reduce poverty appreciably. Consequently, sustained poverty reduction in developing countries is possible only when economic growth, social development, and good governance are pursued simultaneously.

CONCLUSION

Although we have discussed many different policies for addressing the issue of poverty within a global context, there are several broad commonalities that underlie such policies. The first is the obvious importance of economic opportunities. Although the specifics vary from country to country, the existence of viable economic opportunities is paramount if families are to avoid poverty. In the developed world, this translates into economies that are able to produce a sufficient number of jobs to adequately support a family. In developing nations, this means encouraging pro-poor growth and distributing land in an equitable fashion.

A second overarching theme from our discussion is the importance of governmental policies that provide access to key social goods. These goods are essential for families to develop and prosper. In the developed world, they include ensuring that citizens are able to secure health insurance, child care, affordable housing, quality education, and a viable social safety net. In the developing world, they translate into access to clean water and sanitation, health programs, and primary education.

Finally, it is important that such policies actively involve those who are most affected by poverty—that is, the poor themselves. Citizen participation is critical in the development and implementation of any overall strategy designed to reduce poverty among the world's households and families.

REFERENCES

Agarwal, B. (1998). *A field of one's own: Gender and land rights in South Asia.* New York: Cambridge University Press.

Agrawal, A., & Yadama, G. N. (1997). How do local institutions mediate market and population pressures on resources? Forest panchayats in Kumaon, India. *Development and Change, 28,* 435–465.

Alarcón, D. (2001). National poverty-reduction strategies of Chile, Costa Rica and Mexico: Summary of findings. In T. McKinley (Ed.), *Macroeconomic policy, growth, and poverty reduction* (pp. 185–200). New York: Palgrave.

Alesina, A., & Glaeser, E. L. (2004). *Fighting poverty in the US and Europe: A world of difference.* Oxford, UK: Oxford University Press.

Ali, I., & Pernia, E. M. (2003). *Infrastructure and poverty reduction—What is the connection?* (ERD Policy Brief Series No. 13). Manila, Philippines: Asian Development Bank.

Asian Development Bank. (2004). *Fighting poverty in Asia and the Pacific: The poverty reduction strategy.* Manila, Philippines: Asian Development Bank.

Blank, R. M. (1997). *It takes a nation: A new agenda for fighting poverty.* Princeton, NJ: Princeton University Press.

Bloom, D. E., Canning, D., & Jamison, D. T. (2004, March). Health, wealth, and welfare. *Finance and Development,* pp. 10–15.

Degnbol-Martinussen, J. (2002). Development goals, governance and capacity building: Aid as a catalyst. *Development and Change, 33,* 269–279.

Diamond, L. (1999). *Developing democracy: Toward consolidation.* Baltimore: Johns Hopkins University Press.

Ellwood, D. T., & Welty, E. D. (2000). Public service employment and mandatory work: A policy whose time has come and gone and come again? In D. E. Card & R. M. Blank (Eds.), *Finding jobs: Work and welfare reform* (pp. 299–372). New York: Russell Sage Foundation.

Erinosho, L. (2004). Key items for developing countries. *CROP Newsletter, 11,* 1–2.

Esping-Andersen, G. (2002). *Why we need a new welfare state.* Oxford, UK: Oxford University Press.

Gallie, D. (2002). The quality of working life in welfare strategy. In G. Esping-Andersen (Ed.), *Why we need a new welfare state* (pp. 96–129). Oxford, UK: Oxford University Press.

Gilens, M. (1999). *Why Americans hate welfare: Race, media, and the politics of antipoverty policy.* Chicago: University of Chicago Press.

Glennerster, H. (2002). United States poverty studies and poverty measurement: The past twenty-five years. *Social Service Review, 76,* 83–107.

Glewwe, P., Gragnolati, M., & Zaman, H. (2000). *Who gained from Vietnam's boom in the 1990s? An analysis of poverty and inequality trends* (World Bank Working Paper No. 2275). Washington, DC: World Bank.

Gomart, E. (2001). Between Civil War and land reform: Among the poorest of the poor in Tajikistan. In N. Dudwick, E. Gomart, & A. Marc, with K. Kuehnast (Eds.), *When things fall apart: Qualitative studies of poverty in the former Soviet Union* (pp. 57–93). Washington, DC: World Bank.

Haynes, J. (1997). *Democracy and civil society in the Third World: Politics and new political movements.* Cambridge, UK: Polity Press.

International Fund for Agriculture Development (IFAD). (2001). *Rural poverty report 2001: The challenge of ending rural poverty.* New York: Oxford University Press.

International Fund for Agriculture Development (IFAD). (2002). *Assessment of rural poverty: Asia and the Pacific.* Rome, Italy: Asia and the Pacific Division, IFAD.

Jencks, C. (2002). Does inequality matter? *Daedalus, 131,* 49–65.

Khan, A. R. (2001). Macroeconomic policies and poverty: An analysis of the experience in ten Asian countries. In T. McKinley (Ed.), *Macroeconomic policy, growth, and poverty reduction* (pp. 126–152). New York: Palgrave.

Kohl, J. (1995). The European community: Diverse images of poverty. In E. Oyen, S. M. Miller, & S. A. Samad (Eds.), *Poverty: A global review* (pp. 251–286). Oslo, Norway: Scandinavian University Press.

Korpi, W. (2003). Welfare-state regress in Western Europe: Politics, institutions, globalization, and Europeanization. *Annual Review of Sociology, 29,* 589–609.

Kuehnast, K. (2003). Poverty shock: The impact of rapid economic change on the women of the Kyrgyz Republic. In N. Dudwick, E. Gomart, A. Marc, & K. Kuehnast (Eds.), *When things fall apart* (pp. 33–55). Washington, DC: World Bank.

Liebman, J. B. (2002). The optimal design of the Earned Income Tax Credit. In B. D. Meyer & D. Holtz-Eakin (Eds.), *Making work pay: The Earned Income Tax Credit and its impact on American families* (pp. 196–234). New York: Russell Sage Foundation.

Lowndes, V., & Wison, D. (2001). Social capital and local governance: Exploring the institutional design variable. *Political Studies, 49,* 629–647.

McKinley, T. (2001). The macroeconomic implications of focusing on poverty reduction. In T. McKinley (Ed.), *Macroeconomic policy, growth, and poverty reduction* (pp. 201–226). New York: Palgrave.

Mehta, A. K., & Shah, A. (2003). Chronic poverty in India: Incidence, causes and policies. *World Development, 31,* 491–511.

Meyer, B. D., & Holtz-Eakin, D. (2002). *Making work pay: The Earned Income Tax Credit and its impact on America's families.* New York: Russell Sage Foundation.

Minsky, H. P. (1986). *Stabilizing an unstable economy.* New Haven, CT: Yale University Press.

Noble, C. (1997). *Welfare as we knew it: A political history of the American welfare state.* New York: Oxford University Press.

Organization for Economic Cooperation and Development. (1999). *Social expenditure database 1980–1996.* Paris: Author.

Osmani, S. R. (2000). Participatory governance and poverty reduction. In A. Grinspun (Ed.), *Choices for the poor: Lessons from national poverty strategies* (pp. 121–143). New York: United Nations Development Programme.

Paul, S. (1998). *Making voice work: The report card on Bangalore's public services.* Bangalore, India: Public Affairs Centre.

Paxton, P. (2002). Social capital and democracy: An interdependent relationship. *American Sociological Review, 67,* 254–277.

Pernia, E. M. (2003). *Pro-poor growth: What is it and how is it important?* (ERD Policy Brief Series No. 17). Manila, Philippines: Asian Development Bank.

Petro, N. N. (2001). Creating social capital in Russia: The Novgorod model. *World Development, 29,* 229–244.

Population Action International. (2004). *How the HIV/AIDS pandemic threatens global security* (Fact Sheet No. 26).Washington, DC: Author.

Rainwater, L., & Smeeding, T. M. (2003). *Poor kids in a rich country: America's children in comparative perspective.* New York: Russell Sage Foundation.

Ravallion, M., & Datt, G. (2002). Why has economic growth been more pro-poor in some states in India than others? *Journal of Development Economics, 68,* 381–400.

Ritakallio, V.-M. (2001). *Trends of poverty and income inequality in cross-national comparison* (Luxembourg Income Study Working Paper No. 272). New York: Maxwell School of Citizenship and Public Affairs, Syracuse University.

Royal Tropical Institute (KIT) and Oxfam. (2001). *Gender perspectives on property and inheritance: A global source book.* Amsterdam: KIT.

Schiller, B. R. (2004). *The economics of poverty and discrimination.* Upper Saddle River, NJ: Prentice Hall.

Schreiner, M., Clancy, M., & Sherraden, M. (2002). *Saving performance in the American Dream Demonstration: A national demonstration of individual development accounts.* St. Louis, MO: Center for Social Development, Washington University.

Sen, A. (1992). *Inequality reexamined.* New York: Russell Sage Foundation.

Serageldin, I., & Grootaert, C. (1999). Defining social capital: An integrating view. In P. Dasgupta & I. Serageldin (Eds.), *Social capital: A multifaceted perspective* (pp. 40–58). Washington DC: World Bank.

Sherraden, M. (1991). *Assets and the poor: A new American welfare policy.* Armonk, NY: M. E. Sharpe.

Sherraden, M. (2000). From research to policy: Lessons from individual development accounts. *Journal of Consumer Affairs, 34,* 159–181.

Sherraden, M. (2001). Asset-building policy and programs for the poor. In T. M. Shapiro & E. N. Wolff (Eds.), *Assets for the poor: The benefits of spreading asset ownership* (pp. 302–323). New York: Russell Sage Foundation.

Sherraden, M. (2002, September 19). *Asset-based policy and the Child Trust Fund.* Speech at a dinner hosted by Chancellor of the Exchequer Gordon Brown, 11 Downing, London. (Available from the Washington University Center for Social Development, St. Louis, MO)

Smeeding, T. M. (2002). *Real standards of living and public support for children: A cross-national comparison* (Luxembourg Income Study Working Paper Series No. 345). New York: Maxwell School of Citizenship and Public Affairs, Syracuse University.

Smeeding, T. M., & Rainwater, L. (2001, June). *Comparing living standards across countries: Real incomes at the top, the bottom, and the middle.* Paper presented at the conference "What Has Happened to the Quality of Life in America and Other Advanced Nations?" Levy Institute, Bard College, Annandale-on Hudson, New York.

Smeeding, T. M., Rainwater, L., & Burtless, G. (2000). *United States poverty in a cross-national context* (Luxembourg Income Study Working Paper Series No. 244). New York: Maxwell School of Citizenship and Public Affairs, Syracuse University.

Smeeding, T. M., Rainwater, L., & Burtless, G. (2001). U.S. poverty in a cross-national context. In S. H. Danziger & R. H. Haveman (Eds.), *Understanding poverty* (pp. 162–189). Cambridge, MA: Harvard University Press.

Sobhan, R. (2002). South Asia's crisis of governance: Avoiding false solutions. In K. Haq (Ed.), *The South Asian challenge* (pp. 148–181). New York: Oxford University Press.

Sumarto, S., Suryahadi, A., & Arifianto, A. (2004). *Governance and poverty reduction: Evidence for newly decentralized Indonesia.* Jakarta, Indonesia: SMERU Research Institute.

Townsend, P., & Gordon, D. (2004). *World poverty: New policies to defeat an old enemy.* Bristol, UK: Policy Press.

UNAIDS. (2004a). *Report on the global AIDS epidemic: Executive summary.* Geneva, Switzerland: Joint United Nations Programme on HIV/AIDS.

UNAIDS. (2004b). *Report on the global AIDS epidemic: Fourth global report.* Geneva, Switzerland: Joint United Nations Programme on HIV/AIDS.

United Nations Development Programme. (1999). *Debt and sustainable human development* (Technical Advisory No. 4). New York: Bureau for Development Policy, United Nations Development Programme.

United Nations Development Programme. (2003). *Human development report 2003.* New York: Oxford University Press.

U.S. Bureau of the Census. (2004). *Income, poverty, and health insurance coverage in the United States: 2003* (Current Population Reports, Series P60–226). Washington, DC: U.S. Government Printing Office.

Ventry, D. J. (2002). The collision of tax and welfare politics: The political history of the Earned Income Tax Credits. In B. D. Meyer & D. Holtz-Eakin (Eds.), *Making work pay: The Earned Income Tax Credit and its impact on American families* (pp. 15–66). New York: Russell Sage Foundation.

World Bank. (2001a). Education and poverty. In *Poverty reduction strategy paper source book.* Unpublished report, World Bank.

World Bank. (2001b). *Engendering development.* New York: Oxford University Press.

World Bank. (2001c). Health, nutrition, and population. In *Poverty reduction strategy paper source book.* Unpublished report, World Bank.

World Bank. (2004). *World development report 2004: Making services work for poor people.* New York: Oxford University Press.

Yadama, G. N., & DeWeese-Boyd, M. (2001). Co-management of forests in the tribal regions of Andhra Pradesh, India: A study in the making and unmaking of social capital. In B. Vira & R. Jeffery (Eds.), *Analytical issues in participatory natural resource management* (pp. 90–107). New York: Palgrave.

Yao, X. (2003). *Infrastructure and poverty reduction—Making markets work for the poor* (ERD Policy Brief Series No. 14). Manila, Philippines: Asian Development Bank.

Part V Exercise: The Arias Family

Eduardo and Ramona Arias live in a rural area of the Philippines. They are 43 and 39, respectively, and have been married for 21 years. They live in the same village in which they were born, and both of their extended families live nearby. The couple has four children: Christina, age 16; Maria, 14; Lilianna, 11; and Frederico, 9. After finishing primary school, Christina began working in a packing shed at a nearby pineapple plantation. There are few other jobs in the area, especially for women. She lives at home. The three youngest children are in school. Eduardo tends to favor Frederico and is exceedingly proud to have a son. He expects that some day Frederico will take over the family business.

The Arias family earns a living from agricultural production, primarily from sugar cane and pineapples. Almost all their products are destined for foreign markets, although they also raise food crops and livestock for their own consumption and domestic-market sales. Eduardo employs a few men who assist him in his fields year-round. During peak times in the production cycle, Eduardo hires a few day laborers looking for work.

Ramona does not work in the fields, but she does prepare food for the workers. She also handles all the household and child care duties. Although Eduardo spends time with his wife and children, this is limited to evening meals and church on Sunday. During the week, he frequents a cafe where he socializes with his men friends.

Ramona considers Eduardo a good husband because he provides for the family and spends time with them whenever he can. As far as she knows, he does not cheat on her. The family has been able to make a better living than their parents did, thanks to Eduardo's good business sense and frugality. Indeed, Eduardo often reminds Ramona of the need to conserve money and resources. A few times, he believed that she was spending money "frivolously"; he became angry, hit Ramona, and demanded that she be more careful with "his" money. At these times, Ramona turned to prayer, asking God's forgiveness for both Eduardo and herself.

Recently, the family has had a crisis to cope with, Christina's pregnancy. Although several of Christina's friends had become pregnant, Ramona and Eduardo did not expect this of their daughter. They have told no one—not their parents, friends, or priest—about this situation.

Eduardo did confront the young man's parents, telling them how irresponsible and disrespectful their son Ernesto is. They were apologetic but said, "After all, what can we do? What is done is done." Eduardo wondered bitterly what he could have expected from those people. Ernesto's father is a laborer on the plantation and spends his hard-earned money on beer. Eduardo knows little about the mother—he and Ramona rarely see her at church, where most of the area families attend and socialize. They have heard that she sometimes works as a domestic for the plantation managers. Eduardo never approved of Christina seeing Ernesto, and now his fears have been justified. He expected that she would have a traditional wedding and start her family nearby or even in the Arias compound.

Ernesto refuses to take any responsibility for the child. He plans to move to the city to look for work and a more exciting life than the one here in the village. Eduardo angrily confronted Ernesto, accusing him of taking advantage of Christina. Eduardo tried to force the young man to marry her, to no avail. Since then, Eduardo has not seen Ernesto near the house, or anywhere he, Ramona, and Christina normally spend time. After his initial anger, Eduardo has been somewhat distant from his daughter. Ramona urges her husband to control his temper and tries to soothe Christina's feelings of fear, hurt, and rejection. Ramona expects that when the baby comes, she will have responsibility for child care while Christina returns to her work at the plant. Ramona considers this her duty, as a mother and grandmother, as well as her destiny, like the women in the generations before and after her. However, Ramona vows to insist that the younger girls go on to high school or some other training so they can find other opportunities outside this village and its traditions. Even if they have to travel some distance or live with their aunt in the nearby town, she wants them to have other chances in life.

Answer the following questions about the Arias family, individually or in small groups.

1. How are this family and community linked to the larger global system? How might this connection affect the Arias family?
2. What evidence do you see of traditional gender roles in the Arias family? What signs are there that these gender arrangements might be changing, and what signs are there that they are similar to the past?
3. How does the social context, including the rural setting and the local labor force, affect the family, especially the women?
4. How do you see social class played out in this story? How do inequalities affect individual and family opportunities and the relationship between families?
5. How do the families cope with the changes in their lives? What resources do they have, and how might these influence their decisions?

Author Index

Subject Index

About the Editors

Bron B. Ingoldsby is Associate Professor in the School of Family Life at Brigham Young University. He received his PhD in child and family development from the University of Georgia. A leader in the area of cross-cultural family research, he is the author of numerous professional publications, including (with Raeann Hamon) *Mate Selection Across Cultures*. His current research focuses on family change among the Hutterian Brethren and marriage in Latin America. He is an accomplished teacher-scholar in the area of cross-cultural family studies. He was honored as the 2002 recipient of the Jan Trost Award for Outstanding Contributions to Comparative Family Studies by the National Council on Family Relations (NCFR).

Suzanna D. Smith is Associate Professor in the Department of Family, Youth and Community Sciences at the University of Florida. She has a PhD in child and family development and a master's degree in social work and is a Certified Family Life Educator (CFLE). In addition to teaching, she develops extension programs for families through the Florida Cooperative Extension Service. Her research has focused on difficult economic transitions and their impacts on women and their families, particularly in rural and natural resource–dependent communities. She also has experience in human services, offering resources and support to children, women, families, and the elderly in need. Her international work has included research and training programs in Cameroon, Burkina Faso, Haiti, and Korea, as well as coursework for international students and faculty.

About the Contributors

Tamara Cheshire received her master's degree from Oregon State University. She is an adjunct faculty member in the Department of Anthropology at Sacramento City College. Tamara teaches courses in Ethnic Studies (specifically Native American Studies) and Family Studies as well. She is Lakota, and her interests are American Indian education, American Indian families, and tribal sovereignty issues. She is a certified foster parent with the American Indian Child Resource Center of Oakland, California.

Nancy A. Greenwood is an Associate Professor of Sociology and Director of the Health and Aging Program at Indiana University—Kokomo, where she teaches family, gender, and aging courses. Her research interests include cross-cultural families, the well-being of the elderly, and the scholarship of teaching and learning. She is currently writing a book about students' first contact with sociology in the introductory course.

Linda Haas earned a PhD from the University of Wisconsin—Madison. She is Professor of Sociology at Indiana University in Indianapolis, teaching courses on gender, family policy, and families and work. Her research interests focus on the linkages between gender, family, and work in postindustrialized societies, with a focus on Sweden. She holds an honorary doctorate in social sciences from the largest university in Scandinavia, Gothenburg University. Publications include *Equal Parenthood and Social Policy* (SUNY Press, 1992) and *Organizational Change and Gender Equity* (with P. Hwang and G. Russell; Sage, 2000).

Walter T. Kawamoto, PhD, is an independent scholar whose graduate work was funded by the National Institute of Mental Health. He is a Sasakawa Fellow, whose most recent study sponsored by the Japanese Ministry of Education was the U.S. sample of an international study of people of Japanese descent. His first original class, at Syracuse University, focused solely on Latino families. He has recently taught or created classes focusing on American Indian, Asian American, and interethnic families at California State University, Sacramento.

Naoko Kimura is a doctoral candidate in counseling and educational psychology at the University of Nevada, Reno. She holds a master's degree in human development and family studies from that institution. Her interests include theory development in international studies, as well as the experiences of college-age and older adults. She has published in the *Journal of Selected Papers in Asian Studies* and presented her research at meetings of the National Council on Family Relations. She is currently working at a community-based social service center in Tokyo as a researcher on an international study.

Gary R. Lee (PhD, University of Minnesota, 1973) is Professor and Chair of the Department of Sociology at Bowling Green State University. He has done comparative research, using cross-cultural data banks such as the Ethnographic Atlas and the Human Relations Area Files, on issues ranging from marital and family structure to the status of the elderly. His current research involves the consequences of marital status: the economic and psychological implications of marrying, divorcing, and becoming widowed. He also has a funded research project on cohabitation among older people.

Patrick C. McKenry (deceased) was Professor of Human Development and Family Science and African-American and African Studies at The Ohio State University. He received his MS and PhD from the University of Tennessee in child and family studies and was a postdoctoral fellow at The University of Georgia in child and family development. He served as Visiting Professor in the Department of Maternal and Child Health, University of North Carolina at Chapel Hill, and in the School of Family Studies at the University of British Columbia. His work focused on family stress and coping, with particular interest in gender, cultural, and lifestyle variations. He published over 100 journal and book chapters, and coauthored or coedited five books with Sharon J. Price.

William H. Meredith is currently the Director of the School of Family Studies and Human Services at Kansas State University. Previously he was a department head, associate dean, and an interim dean at the University of Nebraska. He received a master's degree in family and child development from Kansas State University and a master's degree in social work and a PhD in human resources from the University of Nebraska. Much of Dr. Meredith's initial research focused on Indochinese refugee families. Over the last 15 years, his focus has been on Chinese families, and he has made seven research trips to China.

Richard B. Miller received his PhD in sociology from the University of Southern California. He is currently a Professor in the School of Family Life and the Director of the Gerontology Program at Brigham Young University (BYU). Prior to working at BYU, he taught at Kansas State University for 11 years. His research focuses on marital relationships over the life course, global aging, and marriage and health. He has published articles in numerous journals, including *Journal of Marriage and the Family, Family Relations,* and *International Journal of Aging and Human Development.*

Colleen I. Murray is Director of the Interdisciplinary PhD Program in Social Psychology and Associate Professor of Human Development and Family Studies at the University of Nevada, Reno. She received her PhD from The Ohio State University. Her research interests include cross-cultural examination of the social construction of meaning for adolescents and families, media reporting of mass tragedies and grief of family survivors, and development of methodology and theory in family studies. She has published in journals such as *Family Relations, Journal of Social and Personal Relationships, Journal of Selected Papers in Asian Studies,* and *Journal of Early Adolescence.*

Karen S. Myers-Bowman, PhD, CFLE, is an Associate Professor in Family Studies and Human Services at Kansas State University, where she teaches graduate and undergraduate courses in the areas of parenting education, families and diversity, family theory, delivery of human services, and family life education. Her research interests focus on how parents and children talk about war and peace issues. Her current projects involve a multinational project (along with Judith A. Myers-Walls) exploring this issue within cultures around the globe.

Judith A. Myers-Walls, PhD, CFLE, is an Associate Professor and Extension Specialist in Child Development and Family Studies at Purdue University. She has her master's and doctoral degrees in child development. She creates materials and provides educational experiences through the Cooperative Extension Service and teaches classes in working with parents and family life education. She has done research and published in the areas of parenting education, cultural context of families, the family's role in educating for global citizenship, and how parents and children discuss war and peace issues.

Lucy W. Ngige is a Senior Lecturer and Chair of the Department of Family and Consumer Sciences at Kenyatta University in Nairobi,

Kenya. She holds a PhD and an MA in Family and Child Ecology from Michigan State University and a BEd degree from the University of Nairobi, Kenya. She has published on the changing African marriage and family dynamics. Her research interests are on international families and cross-cultural perspectives. She is also a consultant for the African Union on a continental plan of action for the family in Africa.

Germán Posada, PhD, is an Assistant Professor in the Child Development and Family Studies Department at Purdue University. He has a doctoral degree in developmental psychology. His research interests are in the study of child-parent attachment relationships and parenting. He is specifically interested in investigating the development of the secure base phenomenon, its relation to the quality of caregiving and characteristics of the family, and children's behavioral outcomes. Important emphases of his work are the study of those issues from a cross-cultural perspective and the use of observational methodologies in naturalistic settings.

Sharon J. Price, Professor Emerita in the Departments of Child and Family Development and Sociology at The University of Georgia, retired in 2000. She published extensively in professional journals; coauthored or coedited five books with Patrick C. McKenry; and won several teaching awards, including the Osborne Award, presented by the National Council on Family Relations, and the highest honor for teaching at The University of Georgia, the Josiah Meigs Award. She was active in professional organizations and served in many capacities, including President of the National Council on Family Relations. She received her MS and PhD in sociology at Iowa State University

Mark R. Rank is the Herbert S. Hadley Professor of Social Welfare in the George Warren Brown School of Social Work at Washington University, St. Louis, Missouri. His areas of research interest have focused on the topics of poverty, inequality, social welfare, and the family.

Sandra L. Russo is Director of Program Development in the International Center and Associate Director of the Transnational and Global Studies Center at the University of Florida. She received a PhD in agronomy from the University of Florida. Her research currently focuses on human-environmental conflicts in the South African transboundary region, with a focus on gender issues. While primarily working in Africa, she has also worked in Latin America and the Middle East on environmental resource management, farming systems, and community involvement projects with an emphasis on gender and participation. She has worked with numerous international donor organizations.

Bahira Sherif-Trask, PhD, is an Associate Professor in the Department of Individual and Family Studies at the University of Delaware. She is by training a cultural anthropologist whose areas of interest include issues of cultural diversity; gender, work, and family; and intergenerational relationships. She has conducted research on these topics in the United States, Europe, and the Middle East.

Max E. Stanton is currently a Professor of Anthropology and Geography at Brigham Young University, Hawaii Campus. He earned his doctorate in anthropology from the University of Oregon and wrote his dissertation on the changing kinship and political institutions in a Samoan immigrant community in Hawaii. His current research interests include: a 20-year investigation of Hutterite communities in the upper Great Plains and the Columbia River Basin of Washington State of the United States and the prairie provinces of Canada; the economic and social impact of tourism in Easter Island; and interethnic relationships between the Indo-Fijians and ethnic Fijians of the island nation of Fiji.

Ruben P. Viramontez Anguiano is an Assistant Professor of Human Development and Family Studies at Bowling Green State University. He received his PhD in family and child ecology from Michigan State University. His research addresses ethnic families and their communities from an ecological perspective. Taking an inductive approach, he focuses on the interaction between Latino families and schools, Latino families and health, and Latino families and their communities in general. His teaching focuses on family and cultural diversity and family systems and other social systems courses.

Stephan M. Wilson is a Professor and Department Chair of Human Development and Family Studies at the University of Nevada, Reno. He holds an MS and PhD in family studies and human development from the University of Tennessee, Knoxville. His areas of scholarly interest include East African, Chinese, and Appalachian families. In particular, he is interested in adolescent social competence in these and other cultural settings. Other interests include family influences on lifestyle choices and transitions to young adulthood and family wellness. He has lived and worked in Kenya for 3 years as a U.S. Peace Corps volunteer in the 1970s and as a Fulbright Visiting Professor in 2000.

Gautam N. Yadama is an Associate Professor at the George Warren Brown School of Social Work at Washington University in St. Louis. His research has addressed issues related to poverty, the role of nongovernmental organizations in sustainable development, and governance of common pool resources. His particular interests are in understanding how impoverished communities in the least developed countries partner with the state to supply and manage critical public goods.

John W Severinghaus
Oct 27, 2006

see p271

HYPOXIA AND EXERCISE

ADVANCES IN EXPERIMENTAL MEDICINE AND BIOLOGY

Recent Volumes in this Series

Volume 580
THE ARTERIAL CHEMORECEPTORS
Edited by Yoshiaki Hayashida, Constancio Gonzalez, and Hisatake Condo

Volume 581
THE NIDOVIRUSES: THE CONTROL OF SARS AND OTHER NIDOVIRUS DISEASES
Edited by Stanley Perlman and Kathryn Holmes

Volume 582
HOT TOPICS IN INFECTION AND IMMUNITY IN CHILDREN III
Edited by Andrew J. Pollard and Adam Finn

Volume 583
TAURINE 6: UPDATE 2005
Edited by Simo S. Oja and Pirjo Saransaari

Volume 584
LYMPHOCYTE SIGNAL TRANSDUCTION
Edited by Constantine Tsoukas

Volume 585
TISSUE ENGINEERING
Edited by John P. Fisher

Volume 586
CURRENT TOPICS IN COMPLEMENT
Edited by John D. Lambris

Volume 587
NEW TRENDS IN CANCER FOR THE 21ST CENTURY 2006
Edited by López-Guerrero, J.A., Llombart-Bosch, A., Felipo, V. (Eds.),

Volume 588
HYPOXIA AND EXERCISE 2006
Roach, R., Wagner, P.D., Hackett, P. (Eds.),

HYPOXIA AND EXERCISE

Edited by

ROBERT C. ROACH
Colorado Center for Altitude Medicine and Physiology
University of Colorado at Denver Health Sciences Center
Denver, Colorado, USA

PETER D. WAGNER
Department of Medicine
University of California San Diego
La Jolla, California, USA

PETER H. HACKETT
Telluride Medical Clinic
Ridgway, Colorado, USA

Editors:

Robert C. Roach, Ph.D.
Research Director
Altitude Research Center
Mail Stop F524,
PO Box 6508
University of Colorado
Health Sciences Center
Aurora, Colorado
80045-0508
rroach@hypoxia.net

Peter D. Wagner
UCSD Dept Medicine
0623
9500 Gilman Avenue
La Jolla, CA 92093-0623
pdwagner@ucsd.edu

Peter H. Hackett
Telluride Medical Center
500 W. Pacific
Telluride, Colorado 81435
hackett@hypoxia.net

Library of Congress Control Number: 2006927789

Printed on acid-free paper.

ISBN-10: 0-387-34816-6
ISBN-13: 978-0387-34816-2
e-ISBN: 0-387-34817-4

Proceedings of the 14th International Hypoxia Symposium, held in Chateau Lake Louise, Lake Louis, Alberta, Canada, February 22-27, 2005.

Printed in the United States of America.

9 8 7 6 5 4 3 2 1

springer.com

The 14th International Hypoxia Symposium was dedicated to the memory of Dr. John T. "Jack" Reeves.

As most of you know, Dr. John T. "Jack" Reeves passed away in September, 2004 following a motor vehicle-bicycle accident. Jack was a former Professor of Medicine, Pediatrics and Surgery and Professor Emeritus at the University of Colorado Health Sciences Center, having joined the faculty in 1972. He made exceptional contributions in teaching/mentoring, research, administration and leadership. He was a scientist of international stature. He made major advances at the molecular, cellular, animal and human level with regard to the pulmonary circulation and adaptation to high altitude. For many years Jack was a senior member of the Cardiovascular Pulmonary Laboratory of the School of Medicine within the Department of Medicine and most recently played a significant role in the establishment of the Colorado Center for Altitude Medicine and Physiology (CCAMP). He was a key, active and memorably vocal member of the Hypoxia family. No one who ever met Jack at Hypoxia will forget him; his spirit lives on within the Hypoxia community.

In honor of Jack, we established The Reeves Prize for Presentation Excellence. This prize will be awarded at the biennial International Hypoxia Symposium to the speaker judged to present the most outstanding scientific talk, with special emphasis on clarity of presentation skills that were cherished, taught and practiced by Jack. The recipient will be named at the closing banquet by the organizers of the International Hypoxia Symposia with funds coming from the John Sutton Fund, McMaster University, the Colorado Center for Altitude Medicine and Physiology, University of Colorado at Denver and Health Sciences Center, and the International Hypoxia Symposia. The winner for 2005 was Dr. Randy Sprague. See his written contribution starting on page 207.

PREFACE AND ACKNOWLEDGEMENTS

The International Hypoxia Symposia convenes every other year to bring together international experts from many fields to explore the state of the art in normal and pathophysiological responses to hypoxia. Representatives from 18 countries joined together in February 2005 for four days of intense scientific discourse in the dramatic mountain setting of Lake Louise, Canada.

The 14th International Hypoxia Symposium was a rewarding experience due to the outstanding faculty and the lively participation of our largest-ever group of participants. At this, our fourth meeting as the organizers, we were especially pleased that the experience known as the Hypoxia Meetings can continue to prosper. We remain always thankful for the kind and wise guidance of Charlie Houston, the originator of the Hypoxia meetings.

As editors of the Proceedings of the International Hypoxia Symposia, we strive to maintain a 28 year tradition of presenting a stimulating blend of clinical and basic science papers focused on hypoxia. Topics covered in 2005 included a history of high altitude physiology, arterial hypoxemia in exercise, sleep and hypoxia, genetic components of adaptation to hypoxia, erythropoietin, cell stress pathways and hypoxia, the role of red blood cells, ATP release and hemoglobin in the control of vasoreactivity, exercise and altitude training, the eye at high altitude and pulmonary hypertension in high altitude residents. An update on methods to measure the hypoxic ventilatory response was also featured.

The abstracts from the 2005 meeting were published in High Altitude Medicine & Biology Dec 2004, Vol. 5, No. 4: 471-509. Late abstracts are presented staring on page 311, this volume.

We hope that this collection of papers especially prepared for this volume allows us to share with a broader audience some of the intellectual excitement that embodies the spirit of the Hypoxia meetings.

In 2005 we had the generous support of a number of organizations and individuals, including the U.S. Army Research and Development Command, The White Mountain Research Station, our International Advisory Committee. At the meeting we were greatly helped by Barbara Lommen, Paige Sheen, Mollie Pritcher, Gene and Rosann McCullough and Andy Subudhi who each made a tremendous effort to make every delegate feel at home, and to make the meeting go very smoothly.

Please join us by the light of the full moon in February 2007 at the Chateau Lake Louise, Lake Louise, Alberta, Canada for the 15th International Hypoxia Symposium.

Robert C. Roach, Peter D. Wagner, Peter H. Hackett, Editors, Fall 2005
(www.hypoxia.net)

CONTENTS

HYPOXIC VASOREGULATION: INTERACTIONS OF RED CELLS, ENDOTHELIUM AND SMOOTH MUSCLE

HYPOXIA: STATE OF THE ART

FUTURE DIRECTIONS IN HYPOXIA RESEARCH

AUTHORS FOR CORRESPONDENCE

Christophe Bonny
Unit of Molecular Genetics, CHUV
CH1011 Lausanne, Switzerland
Email:Christophe.Bonny@chuv.hospvd.ch
(Chapter 12)

Tiziana Borsello
BDCM, rue du Bugnon 9
CH1005 Switzerland
Email: borsello@marionegri.it
(Chapter 13)

Douglas Corfield
Keele University, School of Life Sciences
Keele, Staffordshire, United Kingdom,
ST5 5BG
Email: d.corfield@keele.ac.uk
(Chapter 7)

Steven Deem
University of Washington
Dept. of Anesthesiology, Box 359724
Harborview Medical Center
Seattle WA United States 98104
Email: sdeem@u.washington.edu
(Chapter 19)

Jerome A. Dempsey
Univ of Wisconsin, Med Sci Bldg
1300 University Ave Rm4245
Madison WI United States 53706
Email: jdempsey@wisc.edu
(Chapter 2)

Hérve Duplain
CHUV, Département de Médecine Interne
CH1011 Lausanne, Switzerland
Email: hduplain@hospvd.ch
(Chapter 14)

Martin Flück
Department of Anatomy- University of Bern
Baltzerstrasse 2
CH3000 Bern Switzerland
Email: flueck@ana.unibe.ch
(Chapter 16)

Max Gassmann
University of Zurich
Institute of Veterinary Physiology
Winterthurerstrasse 260
CH-8057 Zurich Switzerland
E-mail: maxg@access.unizh.ch
(Chapter 11)

Mark T. Gladwin
National Institutes of Health
NHLBI-CVB
10 Center Drive Bldg 10-CRC
Room 5-5142
Baltimore MD United States 20892-1454
Email: mgladwin@mail.nih.gov
(Chapter 17)

Susan R. Hopkins
University of California, San Diego
Division of Physiology
9500 Gilman Dr
La Jolla CA United States 92093-0623
Email: shopkins@ucsd.edu
(Chapter 3)

Benjamin D. Levine
Institute for Exercise and Environmental Medicine
7232 Greenville Ave, Suite 435
Dallas TX United States 75231
Email: benjaminlevine@texashealth.org
(Chapter 20)

Andrew T. Lovering
University of Wisconsin Medical School
RM 4245 MSC, 1300 University Ave.
Madison WI United States 53706-1532
Email: atlovering@wisc.edu
(Chapter 4)

James S. Milledge
Northwick Park Hospital
137 Highfield Way
London United Kingdom WD3 7PL
Email: jim@medex.org.uk
(Chapter 1)

Lorna G. Moore
Univ of Colorado at Denver & Health Sciences Center
4200 East Ninth Avenue, Box B133
Denver CO United States 80218
Email: Lorna.G.Moore@UCHSC.edu
(Chapter 10)

Mary J. Morrell
National Heart and Lung Institute
Sleep and Ventilation Unit
Royal Brompton Hospital, Sydney Street
London United Kingdom SW3 6NP
Email: m.morrell@imperial.ac.uk
(Chapter 8)

Daniel S. Morris
NHS, 27 Elsdon Road
Gosforth United Kingdom NE3 1HY
Email: danielsmorris@hotmail.com
(Chapter 21)

Frank Powell
University of California San Diego
UCSD Dept. of Medicine 0623A
9500 Gilman Dr
La Jolla CA United States 92093-0623
Email: fpowell@ucsd.edu
(Chapter 24)

Urs Scherrer
Department of Internal Medicine, BH 10.642
Centre Hospitalier Universitaire Vaudois
CH1011 Lausanne, Switzerland
Email: urs.scherrer@chuv.hospvd.ch
(Chapter 22)

Mark D. Shriver
Pennsylvania State University
409 Carpenter Bldg
University Park, PA, United States, 16802
Email: mds17@psu.edu
(Chapter 9)

M. Celeste Simon
University of Pennsylvania
456 BRB II/III, 421 Curie Boulevard
Philadelphia, PA United States 19104-6160
Email:celeste2@mail.med.upenn.edu
(Chapter 15)

Randy Sprague
Saint Louis University
1402 South Grand Blvd
St. Louis, MO, United States 63104
Email: spraguer@slu.edu
(Chapter 18)

Kenneth B. Storey
Institute of Biochemistry
Carleton University
Ottawa, Ontario, Canada K1S 5B6
Email: kbstorey@ccs.carleton.ca
(Chapter 23)

William Whitelaw
Department of Medicine
University of Calgary
Calgary, Alberta, Canada T2N 1N4
Email: wwhitela@ucalgary.ca
(Chapter 6)

John B. West
University of California San Diego
UCSD Dept. of Medicine 0623A
9500 Gilman Dr
La Jolla CA United States 92093-0623
Email: jwest@ucsd.edu
(Chapter 2)

Contact information for the Authors of the Late Abstracts see individual abstracts in the Late Abstracts section

Chapter 1

A TRIBUTE TO JOHN BURNARD WEST

James S. Milledge
President, International Society of Mountain Medicine, Harrow, Middlesex, UK.

Abstract: John West is well known to the "Hypoxia" community for his many contributions to the physiology and Pathophysiology of high altitude and for his leadership of the 1981 American Medical Research Expedition to Everest. He is known to the wider medical world for his researches into respiratory physiology especially gas exchange in the lung and perhaps even more for his numerous books on these topics. His publication list numbers over 400 original papers. His research career started in the UK but since 1969 he has been Professor of Medicine at UCSD, leading a very productive team at La Jolla. He has been honoured by numerous prizes and named lectureships, the latest honour being to be elected to the Institute of Medicine, National Academies (USA).

Hypoxia and Exercise, edited by R.C. Roach *et al.*
Springer, New York, 2006.

Key Words: biography, gas exchange, altitude physiology, altitude pathology, cardio-respiratory physiology, space medicine

INTRODUCTION

It is entirely fitting that this year when he has recently been honoured by being elected a Member of the Institute of Medicine, National Academies, the Symposium organisers should select John West to be the scientist who we are honouring. I am pleased to be asked to compose this tribute but if it is not as fulsome and laudatory in tone as some previous ones, I ask John's indulgence and plead the twin handicaps of the British love of understatement and an old friend's licence to tell it as he sees it!

I have known John West as a friend, expedition companion and scientific colleague for about 45 years. We first met in 1960 when preparing for the 1960-61 Himalayan Scientific and Mountaineering Expedition, popularly known as the Silver Hut Expedition. I was, even then, aware of his reputation as a bright young medical researcher at the Postgraduate Medical School, Hammersmith Hospital where he had done work on lung gas transfer, exploiting the unique opportunity afforded by the MRC cyclotron sited there.

Since then our paths have crossed and re-crossed. He invited me on his American Medical Research Expedition to Everest (AMREE) in 1981, and we were together on a trek in Sikkim in 2000. From 1985 to the present we have worked as joint authors, with Michael Ward, on the textbook "High Altitude Medicine and Physiology" as well as frequent meetings at conferences and social occasions.

John is a man of many parts, researcher, teacher, author, editor, and organiser/administrator. His interests also include music, ham radio, radio-controlled gliders, tennis, skiing, mountaineering and of course he is a family man.

In this short tribute I can only give the reader a flavour of the man and a few personal reminiscences. No doubt there will, in time, be a full biography of John B. West!

The Researcher

John West is probably best known to the Hypoxia community for his research work in the field of high altitude medicine and physiology. His interest in the effects of altitude hypoxia followed naturally from his early work on pulmonary gas exchange which started when he was a junior doctor at the Postgraduate Medical School. The MRC cyclotron could produce short-lived radio-isotopes of oxygen. The oxygen-15 could be inhaled or infused either as O_2 or CO_2 and the activity counted over the chest wall. This resulted in a number of important papers in 1960. The one I remember reading at the time I first met John was in the *BMJ*. There was also one in *J. Appl. Physiol.* in the same year. This was the time when I was working with Dr Griffith Pugh (honoured at Hypoxia 1993) preparing for the Silver Hut Expedition of which he was the Scientific Leader. John had also been invited to be a member and we met doing base line exercise experiments at Griff's MRC lab in Hampstead and again in Oxford for control of breathing studies, my particular responsibility (Figure 2).

The work John did on the Silver Hut was again on gas exchange. He measured the diffusing capacity of the lung for carbon monoxide and showed there to be no change with acclimatization, apart from the small effect of increased haemoglobin concentration. He was also involved, as we all were, in the exercise studies and with Mike Ward measured $\dot{V}O_2$ max on the Makalu Col (7440m), still, 44 years later, the highest altitude at which it has been measured! (Figure 3) The reduction in $\dot{V}O_2$ max with altitude, he showed, was largely due to diffusion limitation, again a matter of gas exchange.

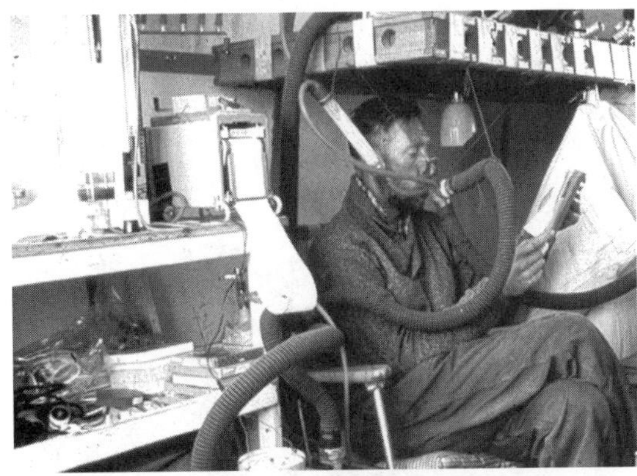

Figure 2. John West as subject of a control of breathing experiment inside the Silver Hut, 1961.

Figure 3. John West and Michael Ward setting up the bicycle ergometer on the Makalu Col, (7440m) to measure $\dot{V}O_2$max on themselves.

After the Silver Hut, he did a post-doc fellowship with Herman Rhan (an Honouree at Hypoxia 1991) in Buffalo and then became leader of a MRC Respiratory Physiology Group at the Hammersmith studying pulmonary gas exchange. He had a sabbatical year 1967-8 with NASA at the Ames Research Center. Here he has the opportunity to work on computer models of gas exchange. He put in his first research proposal to NASA on lung function in astronauts at the end of this year and since then has had a continuing connection with space research on the effect of micro-gravity on gas exchange.

In 1969 John joined the faculty of University of California, San Diego where he is still working as Professor of Medicine. On arrival, his NASA project was approved and a check for $100,000 started his career in La Jolla on the right foot! Work on computer modelling of gas exchange led, in collaboration with Peter Wagner, to the multiple inert gas method for measuring V/Q ratio inequalities in health and disease. His more recent research includes work on stress failure of the alveolar-capillary wall as part of the mechanism of high altitude pulmonary edema and the use of oxygen enrichment of room air in high altitude living quarters.

Publications

John's bibliography is impressive and can be found on the web at: http://medicine.ucsd.edu/faculty/west/.

He has published 424 papers, in 290 of which he is the first author (68.4%). The great majority of these have been in prestigious peer reviewed journals. By today's standards he was a late starter. His first paper, on ventilation-perfusion ratio inequality in the lung by single breath analysis, was in *Clinical Science* in 1957 when he was 28 and had been qualified for 6 years. However once John got started, he was soon churning out significant papers in respectable numbers as shown in Fig 4.

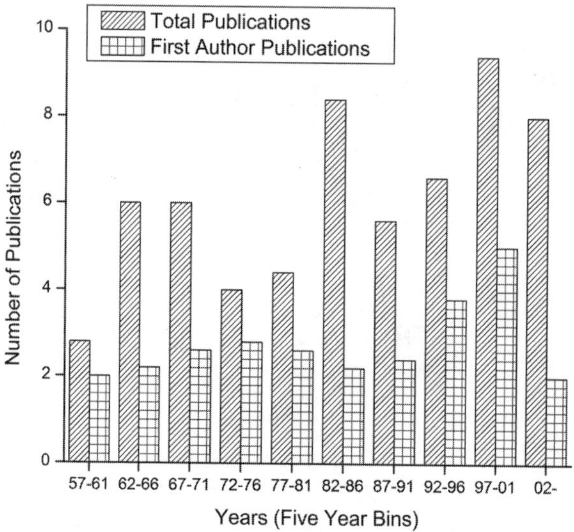

Figure 4. Papers published by John West, average number per year in 5 year bins, showing 1st author and totals.

As impressive as the numbers and quality of his papers, is the fact that with the passing years his output, far from diminishing, has actually increased! There is a significant linear increase in numbers of paper with each quinquennium of his career ($p=0.015$). If the trend continues, I can confidently predict, that on reaching his centenary, he will be publishing at the rate of 16.5 papers per year!

The Teacher

I cannot report on John's ability as a teacher in medical school though I am sure his courses are very well appreciated. As a lecturer I have heard him on numerous occasions and can vouch for his ability to give a clear and exciting account of even the most difficult of subjects such as *V/Q ratio inequalities*. His lecture on AMREE and Peter Hackett's solo summit climb is exciting in both scientific and mountaineering content and style. Evidence of the widespread appreciation of his abilities as a lecturer is the number of prestigious named lecturers he has been asked to give: 57 at the last count, mostly in the USA but also in UK, Canada, Australia and Russia.

However, I think that his most important role as a teacher is as author of numerous textbooks and monographs. These have made him well known to the wider medical world. John has 21 books on his publications list; in some, he is the editor of multi-author books or conference proceedings but in the majority he is sole author. The titles range from *Ventilation/Blood flow and Gas Exchange,* his first monograph, through *The Use of Radioactive Materials in the Study of Lung Function; Translations in Respiratory Physiology*, his first assay into the history of our subject, to *Gravity and the Lung: Lessons from Microgravity,* his latest book. For the Hypoxia community, John's excellent history of our subject, *High Life,* and our joint book *High Altitude Medicine and Physiology* are, no doubt the best known. However, John's most influential book is probably *Respiratory Physiology - The Essentials* followed by *Pulmonary Pathophysiology - The Essentials.* The former was originally written for Medical Students and both are required reading for many postgraduate courses. Both books have been translated into many languages and have gone into 7 and 6 editions in English, respectively. Mention John West's name to any young anaesthetic trainee and (s)he is likely to respond, "Not *The* John West of *Respiratory Physiology*!"

Also important in the wider teaching role of promoting scientific communication, is John's work in the thankless task of editorship. He showed early promise of this by starting a journal whilst still a school boy at Prince Alfred College in Adelaide. The PAC Science Journal is still being published 60 years later! John is on the editorial board of 17 learned journals and of course is the Editor-in-chief and founder of our own, very successful journal, *High Altitude Medicine and Biology.* We all hope his latest journal proves to be as long lived as his first!

The Man

He chose to head up quite a small division of physiology at La Jolla rather than build up a big empire but his organisational abilities are considerable. Anyone who can put together an Everest Expedition, especially one that carries through both scientific and mountaineering objectives as he did with AMREE has to have such skills in spades! He has received numerous honours including being elected President of the American Physiological Society and the International Society of Mountain Medicine. His most recent honour, last year, is to have been elected to the Institute of Medicine of the National Academy of Sciences (USA)!

I personally owe John a lot, in that he was one of three or four men who influenced me in becoming interested in academic medicine and specifically respiratory physiology. We had many long discussions whilst trekking on the Silver Hut Expedition or sharing a tent in the Western Cwm on AMREE. One of the earliest of these I remember was his unfolding to me the beauties of the Rhan/Otis O_2/CO_2 diagram! Happy days!

John never claimed to be a climber but he has a love of mountains and enjoys trekking and skiing. The pinnacle of his mountaineering was probably, at the end of the Silver Hut Expedition. He made a solo ascent to the Makalu Col and organised the rescue of the near dead climber, Pete Mulgrew, from the Col when other members of the team were exhausted and devoid of drive.

John has been fortunate in having a wonderfully supportive wife in Penny and two children to be proud of in Joanna and Robert.

SELECTED REFERENCES OF JOHN B. WEST

Books

1. West, J.B. Respiratory Physiology - The Essentials. 7th edition. Philadelphia: Lippincott Williams & Wilkins, 2005.
2. West, J.B. Everest - The Testing Place. New York: McGraw-Hill, 1985.
3. West, J.B. High Life: A History of High-Altitude Physiology and Medicine. New York: Oxford University Press, 1998.

Articles

1. West, J.B. and C.T. Dollery. Distribution of blood flow and ventilation-perfusion ratio in the lung, measured with radioactive CO2. *J. Appl. Physiol.* 15: 405-410, 1960.
2. West, J.B. Diffusing capacity of the lung for carbon monoxide at high altitude. *J. Appl. Physiol.* 17: 421-426, 1962.
3. Pugh, L.G.C.E., M.B. Gill, S. Lahiri, J.S. Milledge, M.P. Ward, and J.B. West. Muscular exercise at great altitudes. *J. Appl. Physiol.* 19: 431-440, 1964.
4. West, J.B., C.T. Dollery and A. Naimark. Distribution of blood flow in isolated lung; relation to vascular and alveolar pressures. *J. Appl. Physiol.* 19: 713-724, 1964.
5. West, J.B. Ventilation-perfusion inequality and overall gas exchange in computer models of the lung. *Resp. Physiol.* 7: 88-110, 1969.
6. Wagner, P.D., H.A. Saltzman and J.B. West. Measurement of continuous distributions of ventilation-perfusion ratios: theory. *J. Appl. Physiol.* 36: 588-599, 1974.
7. West, J.B. and P.D. Wagner. Predicted gas exchange on the summit of Mt. Everest. Resp. Physiol. 42: 1-16, 1980.
8. West, J.B., P.H. Hackett, K.H. Maret, J.S. Milledge, R.M. Peters, Jr., C.J. Pizzo and R.M. Winslow. Pulmonary gas exchange on the summit of Mt. Everest. *J. Appl. Physiol.*: Resp. Environ. Exercise Physiol. 55: 678-687, 1983.
9. West, J.B., S.J. Boyer, D.J. Graber, P.H. Hackett, K.H. Maret, J.S. Milledge, R.M. Peters, Jr., C.J. Pizzo, M. Samaja, F.H. Sarnquist, R.B. Schoene and R.M. Winslow. Maximal exercise at extreme altitudes on Mount Everest. *J. Appl. Physiol.*: Resp. Environ. Exercise Physiol. 55: 688-698, 1983.
10. Winslow, R.M., M. Samaja and J.B. West. Red cell function at extreme altitude on Mount Everest. *J. Appl. Physiol.*: Resp. Environ. Exercise Physiol. 56: 109-116, 1984.
11. West, J.B. Human physiology at extreme altitudes on Mount Everest. *Science* 223: 784-788, 1984.
12. West, J.B. Highest inhabitants in the world. *Nature* 324: 517, 1986.
13. West, J.B., K. Tsukimoto, O. Mathieu-Costello and R. Prediletto. Stress failure in pulmonary capillaries. *J. Appl. Physiol.* 70: 1731-1742, 1991.
14. Prisk, G.K., H.J.B. Guy, A.R. Elliott, R.A. Deutschman III and J.B. West. Pulmonary diffusing capacity, capillary blood volume and cardiac output during sustained microgravity. *J. Appl. Physiol.* 75: 15-26, 1993.
15. West, J.B., O. Mathieu-Costello, J.H. Jones, E.K. Birks, R.B. Logemann, J.R. Pascoe and W.S. Tyler. Stress failure of pulmonary capillaries in racehorses with exercise-induced pulmonary hemorrhage. J. Appl. Physiol. 75: 1097-1109, 1993.
16. West, J.B. Oxygen enrichment of room air to relieve the hypoxia of high altitude. *Resp. Physiol.* 99: 225-232, 1995.
17. West, J.B. Snorkel breathing in the elephant explains the unique anatomy of its pleura. *Resp. Physiol.* 126: 1-8, 2001.
18. West, J.B. Thoughts on the pulmonary blood-gas barrier. *Am. J. Physiol.*: Lung Cell. Mol. Physiol. 285: L501-L513, 2003.

Chapter 2

ADVENTURES IN HIGH-ALTITUDE PHYSIOLOGY

John B. West
Department of Medicine, University of California San Diego, La Jolla CA, USA.

Abstract: I have probably had more fun doing high-altitude physiology than most people. Some 45 years ago I applied to be a member of Sir Edmund Hillary's Silver Hut expedition and was accepted in spite of having no previous climbing experience. On this project a group of physiologists wintered at an altitude of 5800 m just south of Everest and carried out an extensive research program. Subsequently measurements were extended up to an altitude of 7440 m on Makalu. In fact the altitude of these field measurements of $\dot{V}O_{2max}$ has never been exceeded. This led to a long interest in high-altitude medicine and physiology which culminated in the 1981 American Medical Research Expedition to Everest during which 5 people reached the summit and the first physiological measurements on the summit were made. Among the extraordinary findings were an extremely low alveolar PCO_2 of 7-8 mmHg, an arterial pH (from the measured PCO_2 and blood base excess) of over 7.7, and a $\dot{V}O_{2max}$ of just over one liter/min. More recently a major interest has been the pathogenesis of high altitude pulmonary edema which we believe is caused by damage to pulmonary capillaries when the pressure inside some of them increases as a result of uneven hypoxic pulmonary vasoconstriction ("stress failure"). Another interest is improving the conditions of people who need to work at high altitude by oxygen enrichment of room air. This enhances well-being and productivity, and is now being used or planned for several high-altitude telescopes up to altitudes of 5600 m. Other recent high-altitude projects include establishing an international archive on high-altitude medicine and physiology at UCSD, several books in the area including the historical study *High Life*, and editing the journal *High Altitude Medicine & Biology*.

Key Words: Everest, stress failure, oxygen enrichment, gas exchange, history

INTRODUCTION

Naturally it is a great pleasure and honor to be recognized in this way by the 14th Hypoxia Symposium. I have attended essentially all of the symposia since the first at Banff

Hypoxia and Exercise, edited by R.C. Roach *et al.*
Springer, New York, 2006.

Springs Hotel in 1979 and on every occasion there has been a very special mixture of science and camaraderie. Long may the tradition continue.

I want to take the opportunity to relate some of the high points in a career in high-altitude physiology. This talk is directed at the young people in the audience who are starting their careers. The gray hairs in the front row know most of this but I hope will indulge me.

SILVER HUT EXPEDITION

There can be few introductions to a new area of science as dramatic as being invited to join Sir Edmund Hillary's 1960-1961 Himalayan Scientific and Mountaineering Expedition now universally known as "Silver Hut". In 1959 I had had several years of training in respiratory physiology, first at the Medical Research Council Pneumoconiosis Research Unit in South Wales, U.K. and then at the Postgraduate Medical School, Hammersmith Hospital, London. But I knew almost nothing about high-altitude physiology and, apart from some skiing, had never been on a mountain. It happened that I was sitting next to someone at a meeting of the (British) Physiological Society when she happened to remark that Griff Pugh was arranging a medical research expedition to the Himalayas. I knew something of Griff because he had been the physiologist on the first successful ascent of Everest some six years before. On a whim I decided to approach him and to my astonishment he invited me to join the expedition of which he was scientific leader. Of course Ed Hillary also wanted to interview everybody before taking them on. The story I tell is that I met him in London and he asked me to climb a flight of stairs whereupon he said "Please join us." This may be apocryphal. However the whole process was a remarkable piece of serendipity for a 30 year old.

The expedition was in three parts (1, 4). In September of 1960 a large group walked in to the Everest region carrying pieces of the Silver Hut which was then erected on a glacier at an altitude of 5800 m (19,000 ft) about 10 miles south of Everest (Figure 1). A group of about 7 physiologists then lived in the Silver Hut during the winter studying the effects of acclimatization at this very considerable altitude over several months. Happily two of these are here today including Jim Milledge and Sukamay Lahiri (Figure 2). In the spring the third phase of the expedition took place when we were rejoined by the climbers and the group moved across to Makalu, the fifth-highest mountain in the world at 8481 m. The plan was to try and climb this without supplementary oxygen but a severe illness in one of the climbers near the summit prevented this.

Interestingly some new information on the planning of the expedition has recently come to light. Pugh's daughter, Harriet Tuckey, is writing a biography of her father and she has been mining the Pugh archive at UCSD (see below). She came across some correspondence in 1958 between Pugh and Philip Hugh-Jones about a possible physiological expedition to Kamet (7756 m) in the Garhwal Himalayas about 300 km northeast of New Delhi. Kamet was one of the peaks that attracted the remarkable early British mountaineer/physiologist Alexander Kellas (1868-1921) and he carried out physiological studies on Kamet in 1920 (5, 7). However funding for a major physiological expedition would have been very difficult to come by at that time, and in the event Pugh found himself with Hillary on an expedition in Antarctica in 1959 where apparently the plan of the hybrid scientific and mountaineering expedition was hatched. Remarkably Hillary was successful in obtaining almost all of the funding for the expedition from the American publishers of *World Book Encyclopedia* (1).

There is no space here to do justice to the science of the Silver Hut expedition which has been the subject of at least two communications in previous Hypoxia Symposia (3, 8). In the Silver Hut itself there were extensive studies of exercise, pulmonary gas exchange including arterial oxygen saturation and the diffusing capacity of the lung, control of ventilation, blood studies, electrocardiogram, basal metabolism, weight loss, intestinal and psychomotor function. When the party moved to Makalu the physiological studies were extended up to Camp 5 on the Makalu Col at 7440 m where maximal exercise and electrocardiograms were studied, and alveolar gas samples were obtained as high as 7830 m. The Silver Hut expedition was the most ambitious and successful high-altitude field expedition of its time and a number of its conclusions are still cited.

Figure 1. Silver Hut at an altitude of 5800 m.

Figure 2. Four of the physiologists on the Silver Hut expedition. Left-to-right: Sukhamay Lahiri, West, Griffith Pugh, Jim Milledge. The photograph was taken in 1977.

1981 AMERICAN MEDICAL RESEARCH EXPEDITION TO EVEREST

Of all the projects in my academic career, none has given more satisfaction than the privilege of leading this expedition which obtained the first physiological measurements at the highest point in the world. Following the success of the Silver Hut expedition I often wondered whether it might be possible to make measurements high on Mt. Everest. The data point for maximal oxygen consumption that Mike Ward and I obtained on the Makalu Col (7440 m) (Figure 3) renewed the intriguing question originally posed by Kellas in 1921: can a human being reach the Everest summit without supplementary oxygen? The answer came in 1978 in dramatic fashion when Messner and Habeler made their memorable ascent, a feat that has now been repeated many times.

In many respects AMREE owed a lot to Silver Hut. For example the design of the Base Camp laboratory at 5400 m was a smaller version of the Silver Hut structure. However whereas the principal scientific question of the Silver Hut expedition was what physiological changes take place in lowlanders when they are exposed to an altitude of 5800 m for several months, the question we hoped to answer on AMREE was what physiological adaptations allow humans to reach the summit of Mt. Everest.

Again it is impossible to do justice to the science here. However the general plan of the expedition was to place laboratories at the Base Camp (5400 m), Camp 2 (6300 m) and if possible carry out some measurements at the highest Camp 5 (8050 m). Each of these sites had its own experimental projects. However in a sense they were all focused on the central aim of getting measurements at the highest possible altitude, hopefully the summit. In this the expedition was extremely lucky and a number of measurements were indeed made at an altitude of 8050 m and above, including the summit (Figure 4). Some of the most dramatic results are shown in Table 1 where it can be seen that on the summit the extreme hyperventilation reduced the alveolar PCO_2 to 7-8 mmHg with an extraordinary respiratory alkalosis and pH (based on the alveolar PCO_2 and measured base excess) of over 7.7 (11). The maximal oxygen consumption measured on extremely well-acclimatized climbers with an inspired PO_2 of 43 mmHg corresponding to the Everest summit was just over 1 liter.min^{-1} (10). It is a lucky person who can be involved an experiment like this once in a lifetime.

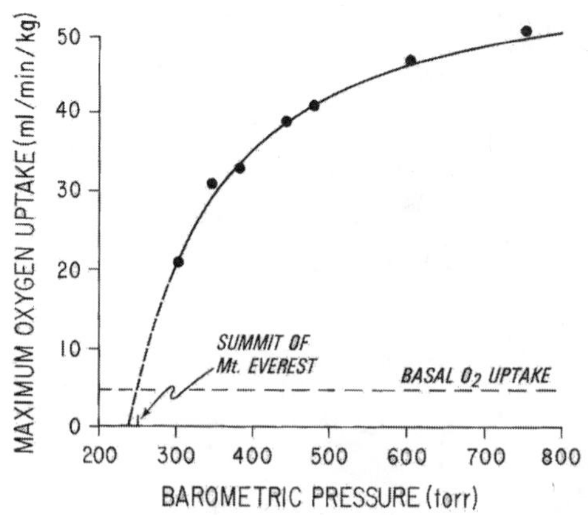

Figure 3. Maximal oxygen consumption plotted against barometric pressure at different altitudes. The lowest point was obtained on the Makalu Col (7440 m). Extrapolation of the line suggests that all the oxygen available on the Everest summit will be required for basal metabolism. These were the data available prior to AMREE.

Figure 4. Chris Pizzo, M.D. sitting on the summit of Mt. Everest collecting samples of alveolar gas.

Table 1. Alveolar gas and estimated arterial blood values on the summit of Mt. Everest.

ALTITUDE	BAROMETRIC PRESSURE	INSPIRED PO2	ALVEOLAR PO2	---ARTERIAL VALUES--- PO2	PO2	pH
m	mmHg	mmHg	mmHg	mmHg	mmHg	
8848 (summit)	253	43	35	28	7.5	>7.7
Sea level	760	149	100	95	40	7.40

PATHOGENESIS OF HIGH-ALTITUDE PULMONARY EDEMA

Of course the opportunities for field experiments such as Silver Hut and AMREE are rare and most of us spend most of our time in the more humdrum environment of the laboratory. But in some way this next project has given me as much satisfaction as any, particularly as it started with a seemingly simple question but has progressed to an intriguing biological problem.

In the late 1980s the pathogenesis of high-altitude pulmonary edema (HAPE) was a puzzle. There was a wealth of evidence that pulmonary hypertension played a vital role. For example catheterization studies showed high pulmonary artery pressures in patients with HAPE, susceptible individuals tended to have an unusually strong hypoxic pulmonary vasoconstriction response, pulmonary vasodilator drugs were useful both for treatment and prevention, and a restricted pulmonary vascular bed was a risk factor as was exercise. Then in 1986 Brownie Schoene and Peter Hackett boldly performed bronchoalveolar lavage on climbers with HAPE high on Denali and made the critical observation that the edema fluid was of the high-permeability type (6). This immediately suggested that the capillary wall was damaged and raised the question of whether the pulmonary hypertension could be the mechanism.

Nobody had previously exposed pulmonary capillaries to graded increases in hydrostatic pressure and examined them by electron microscopy for ultrastructural changes. When Odile Mathieu-Costello and I did this we were astonished to see obvious disruptions of the capillary endothelium and alveolar epithelium at pressures that we believed could occur in HAPE (Figure 5). Incidentally, it is perhaps surprising that no one has bothered to repeat these ultrastructural studies that were first published 14 years ago. We then recognized a feature of pulmonary capillaries that had apparently previously been overlooked, namely because of the excruciatingly thin blood-gas barrier required for gas exchange, the wall stresses become enormous at high capillary pressures. We therefore coined the term "stress failure" which was borrowed from engineering, and we stated in 1991 that this could explain the pathogenesis of HAPE (12). This explanation has stood the test of time.

But the project did not stop there. One day while we were doing experiments someone walked into the lab and asked us whether we knew that racehorses bled into their lungs. I had never heard of this before but indeed it transpires that every Thoroughbred in training breaks its pulmonary capillaries as evidenced by hemosiderin-laden macrophages in tracheal washings (13). The reasons for this extraordinary situation is that these animals have been inbred for hundreds of years for great speed and this requires an enormous cardiac output. The horses therefore have very high left ventricular filling pressures leading to high pulmonary venous and capillary pressures. Interestingly elite human athletes also apparently develop changes in the integrity of their blood-gas barrier during maximal exercise (2). A further example of edema caused by stress failure is high states of lung inflation caused for example by PEEP in the intensive care unit.

What ultimately turned out to be of greater biological interest were questions like what is responsible for the strength of this highly vulnerable blood-gas barrier. The answer apparently is the type IV collagen in the basement membranes. Another question was how special is the makeup of the mammalian blood-gas barrier, the answer being not special at all in that the three-ply design (alveolar epithelium, extracellular matrix, capillary endothelium) has been highly conserved since animals first ventured on to land, such as the ancestors of the present-day lungfishes some 400 million years ago. Finally how is it that the blood-gas barrier is able to remain so excruciatingly thin but just strong enough to withstand the maximal physiological stresses to which it is exposed. The answer presumably is that it is being continually regulated in response to the wall stress, a lively area of research at the present time. Thus this project has been exceptionally stimulating because what appeared to be a relatively simple question on pathogenesis of HAPE has led us into much more fundamental questions of lung biology.

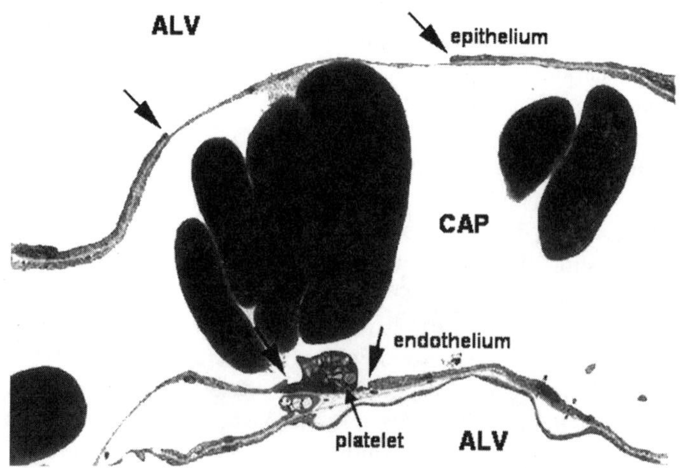

Figure 5. Ultrastructural changes in the wall of a pulmonary capillary when the capillary hydrostatic pressure was raised. The arrows at the top show a disruption in the alveolar epithelial layer; the arrows at the bottom show a break in the capillary endothelial layer with a platelet adhering to the exposed basement membrane. ALV, alveolus; CAP, capillary lumen. Modified from (12).

OXYGEN ENRICHMENT OF ROOM AIR AT HIGH ALTITUDE

In contrast to the last project, this subject has no broad biological significance. Indeed it might be argued initially that it is trivial from a scientific point of view. Yet it also has proved to be enormously satisfying because it is changing the way that people work at high altitude and, for example, makes it possible for astronomers to operate at altitudes that would be impossible without this advance.

The general principle could hardly be simpler. The detrimental effects of high altitude are caused by the low PO_2 in the air and so the obvious way to circumvent these is by raising the PO_2. Of course this can be done using portable oxygen equipment but this is cumbersome and awkward to use 24 hours a day. The solution is to add oxygen to the ventilation of the room thus raising its concentration (9). At a typical facility at an altitude of 5000 m, the oxygen concentration is raised from 21 to 27%, and this reduces the equivalent altitude (based on the inspired PO_2) to about 3200 m. Since most people working at these altitudes already have some acclimatization, an altitude of 3200 m is easily tolerated.

This procedure has some interesting technical problems. First it has only become economically feasible since the introduction of oxygen concentrators that produce oxygen from air. These are now used by the thousands in homes of people with chronic lung disease. The concentrators work by pumping air at high pressure through a tube of synthetic zeolite with the result that the nitrogen is preferentially adsorbed and the effluent gas has a high oxygen concentration. These concentrators are robust, self-contained and typically only require about 350 watts of electrical power to produce 5 $l \cdot min^{-1}$ of 90-95% oxygen. This is then fed into the ventilation duct of the room. A typical room containing 2 people at an altitude of 5000 m requires 4 concentrators. It is also possible to provide the oxygen from liquid oxygen tanks but the running costs are about ten times higher in a typical facility.

The amount of ventilation with fresh air is an important factor. Clearly the higher the ventilation, the more oxygen that has to be generated. We use the ASHRAE (American Society of Heating, Refrigeration, and Air Conditioning Engineers) 1975 standard which is 8.5 $m^3 \cdot h^{-1}$ per person. The CO_2 concentration in the room is monitored and kept at or below 0.3%. Much higher concentrations can be present without causing a health hazard or the occupants being aware of them, but the CO_2 level is a useful index of the adequacy of ventilation. Of course the oxygen concentration is also monitored.

Another important issue is the possible fire hazard. This has been carefully studied by the National Fire Protection Association and it is possible to choose a room oxygen concentration that provides substantial benefit to the occupants at high altitude but that is below the fire hazard level. It should be remembered that although the PO_2 of the air in the room at high altitude is raised by the addition of oxygen, the resulting PO_2 is always far below the sea level value.

The principal use of oxygen enrichment of room air to date has been in high-altitude telescope facilities. The longest experience has been in a radiotelescope operated by the California Institute of Technology at an altitude of 5050 m in north Chile (Figure 6). This has been in continuous operation for 5 years and the astronomers are adamant that the project could not have gone ahead without room oxygen enrichment. A number of other high-altitude telescopes are installing or planning oxygen enrichment of room air. The principle has also been used in the sleeping quarters of the Collahuasi mine which is situated at an altitude of about 4500 m though the dormitories are lower at 3800 m. Sleep is often impaired at high altitude and oxygen enrichment of room air has proved to be very valuable to some of the miners.

Rarely in my experience does a project progress from an idea to implementation in a few years. However in this case the Cal Tech astronomers were using it in their telescope less than 5 years after the initial description (9) and this certainly resulted in a warm fuzzy feeling.

Figure 6. Oxygen-enriched room at the Cal Tech radio-telescope (5050 m). The oxygen concentration in the room is 27% giving an inspired PO_2 equivalent to that of an altitude of 3200 m. Courtesy of the California Institute of Technology.

HISTORY OF HIGH-ALTITUDE PHYSIOLOGY AND A JOURNAL

The last adventure is something of a hodgepodge but no less satisfying for that. We are fortunate at UCSD to have an excellent archival library known as the Mandeville Special Collections Library. Some years ago I was talking to the librarian about depositing some material there and she suggested that we start an archive in high-altitude medicine and physiology. This was done and as far as we know is the only such archival collection in the world.

The primary purpose of an archival collection of this kind is to gather correspondence, documents, experimental protocols, laboratory notebooks, field journals and the like. Published material is of less interest because it is available elsewhere. The archive now contains a very extensive collection from Griffith Pugh which was referred to earlier. Another large collection is from Ulrich Luft, and there are various amounts of material from other workers in the field including Bruno Balke, Elsworth Buskirk, Erik Christensen, David Bruce Dill, Thomas Hornbein, Steven M. Horvath, Herbert Hultgren, Alberto Hurtado, James S. Milledge, Nello Pace, Edward J. Van Liere, Michael P. Ward, Oscar A.M. Wyss and myself. An archive like this increases in value as time passes and more material is added. The archive can be accessed on the web at <roger.ucsd.edu> and searching for the title High Altitude Medicine and Physiology Collection. Potential donors should contact the librarian in charge, Lynda Claassen <Lynda@library.ucsd.edu>.

Another historical interest has been researching some prominent figures in high-altitude medicine and physiology including: Robert Boyle, George Finch, Stephen Hales, Alexander Kellas, and Thomas Ravenhill. This interest has been stimulated by the enlightened policy of the editors of the *Journal of Applied Physiology* who have welcomed occasional historical articles. The most ambitious product of this research has been the book *High Life: A History of High-Altitude Physiology and Medicine* which I am glad I took the trouble to write because it is so useful for reference.

A final adventure in this list has been the journal *High Altitude Medicine & Biology*. Initially I was reluctant to take this on because I thought there were enough journals and I told the publisher so. However Mary Ann Liebert was very persuasive and she convinced me that there was a niche and indeed I now think she was right. There are a number of articles in the area that are important but do not fit easily into existing clinical, physiological or other biological journals. It was gratifying to see the Journal adopted by the International Society for Mountain Medicine, and its trajectory is definitely upward as befits its topic.

Hopefully other adventures in high-altitude physiology and medicine will come my way but even if they do not I have had more than my share and am grateful for this.

REFERENCES

1. Hillary E and Doig D. *High in the Thin Cold Air*. New York: Doubleday and Co., Inc., 1962.
2. Hopkins SR, Schoene RB, Martin TR, Henderson WR, Spragg RG, and West JB. Intense exercise impairs the integrity of the pulmonary blood-gas barrier in elite athletes. *Am J Resp Crit Care Med* 155: 1090-1094, 1997.
3. Milledge JS. The Silver Hut expedition. In: *Hypoxia: Man at Altitude*, edited by J.R.Sutton, N.L. Jones and CSH Houston. New York: Thieme-Stratton, 1982.
4. Pugh LGCE. Physiological and medical aspects of the Himalayan scientific and mountaineering expedition 19601961. *Br Med J* 2: 621-633, 1962.
5. Rodway GW. Prelude to Everest: Alexander M. Kellas and the 1920 high altitude scientific expedition to Kamet. *High Alt Med Biol* 5: 364-379, 2004.
6. Schoene RB, Swenson ER, Pizzo CJ, Hackett PH, Roach RC, Millis WJ, Jr., Henderson WR, Jr., and Martin TR. The lung at high altitude: bronchoalveolar lavage in acute mountain sickness and pulmonary edema. *J Appl Physiol* 64: 2605-2613, 1988.
7. West JB. Alexander M. Kellas and the physiological challenge of Mt. Everest. *J Appl Physiol* 63: 3-11, 1987.
8. West JB. The Silver Hut expedition, high-altitude field expeditions, and low-pressure chamber simulations. In: *Hypoxia and Molecular Medicine*, edited by Sutton JR, Houston CS, and Coates G. Burlington, VT: Queen City Printers, 1993.
9. West JB. Oxygen enrichment of room air to relieve the hypoxia of high altitude. *Respir Physiol* 99: 225-232, 1995.
10. West JB, Boyer SJ, Graber DJ, Hackett PH, Maret KH, Milledge JS, Peters RM, Jr., Pizzo CJ, Samaja M, Sarnquist FH, Schoene RB, and Winslow RM. Maximal exercise at extreme altitudes on Mount Everest. *J Appl Physiol* 55: 688-698, 1983.
11. West JB, Hackett PH, Maret KH, Milledge JS, Peters RM, Jr., Pizzo CJ, and Winslow RM. Pulmonary gas exchange on the summit of Mt. Everest. *J Appl Physiol* 55: 678-687, 1983.

12. West JB, Tsukimoto K, Mathieu-Costello O, and Prediletto R. Stress failure in pulmonary capillaries. *J Appl Physiol* 70: 1731-1742, 1991.
13. Whitwell KE and Greet TR. Collection and evaluation of tracheobronchial washes in the horse. *Equine Vet J* 16: 499-508, 1984.

Chapter 3

EXERCISE INDUCED ARTERIAL HYPOXEMIA: THE ROLE OF VENTILATION-PERFUSION INEQUALITY AND PULMONARY DIFFUSION LIMITATION

Susan R. Hopkins
Department of Medicine, University of California, San Diego, La Jolla, CA, USA.

Abstract: Many apparently healthy individuals experience pulmonary gas exchange limitations during exercise, and the term "exercise induced arterial hypoxemia" (EIAH) has been used to describe the increase in alveolar-arterial difference for oxygen ($AaDO_2$), which combined with a minimal alveolar hyperventilatory response, results in a reduction in arterial PO_2. Despite more than two decades of research, the mechanisms of pulmonary gas exchange limitations during exercise are still debated. Using data in 166 healthy normal subjects collated from several previously published studies it can be shown that ~20% of the variation in PaO_2 between individuals can be explained on the basis of variations in alveolar ventilation, whereas variations in $AaDO_2$ explain ~80%. Using multiple inert gas data the relative contributions of ventilation-perfusion ("$\dot{V}A/\dot{Q}$") inequality and diffusion limitation to the $AaDO_2$ can be assessed. During maximal exercise, both in individuals with minimal ($AaDO_2 < 20$ Torr, x = 13±5, means ± SD, n = 35) and moderate to severe ($AaDO_2$= 25-40 Torr, x = 33±6, n = 20) gas exchange limitations, $\dot{V}A/\dot{Q}$ inequality is an important contributor to the $AaDO_2$. However, in subjects with minimal gas exchange impairment, $\dot{V}A/\dot{Q}$ inequality accounts for virtually all of the $AaDO_2$ (12±6 Torr), whereas in subjects with moderate to severe gas exchange impairment it accounts for less than 50% of the $AaDO_2$ (15±6 Torr). Using this framework, the difficulties associated with unraveling the mechanisms of pulmonary gas exchange limitations during exercise are explored, and current data discussed.

Key Words: multiple inert gas elimination technique, pulmonary gas exchange, perfusion heterogeneity

Hypoxia and Exercise, edited by R.C. Roach *et al.*
Springer, New York, 2006.

INTRODUCTION

For many years researchers have been fascinated by the apparent paradox that some highly aerobically trained humans and animals experience pulmonary limitations to maximal exercise performance. These are of sufficient magnitude to cause a reduction in arterial partial pressure of oxygen (PaO_2) and saturation (5, 17, 42, 52). This condition, termed exercise induced arterial hypoxemia (EIAH), poses a potential limitation to maximal exercise performance. Evidence suggests that a consequence of EIAH is that even small amounts of EIAH have a significant detrimental effect on limiting O_2 transport and utilization during maximal exercise (16, 40). The reader is referred to an excellent review of the topic (8), which reviews the potential causes of EIAH in detail and provides the framework for classification of the severity of hypoxemia which is utilized here.

Definitions of EIAH

In the past EIAH was defined in terms of a decrement in PaO_2 from resting levels, but this definition does not allow hypoxemia related to inadequate ventilation, to be distinguished from that due to from inefficient gas exchange. For example, a subject could have a increased alveolar-arterial difference for oxygen ($AaDO_2$) to 40 Torr, but if they were able to reduce markedly hyperventilate, and reduce the partial pressure of carbon dioxide to 25 Torr, PaO_2 would be maintained near resting levels. Thus, the effect of inefficient gas exchange would be obscured by a brisk hyperventilatory response. The most appropriate classification of the severity of EIAH therefore, depends on the type of research question is being asked. Where one is concerned with issues related to systemic oxygen transport and delivery, then arterial oxygen saturation (SaO_2) is the best indicator of the consequences of EIAH. If the main research question is concerned with efficiency of gas exchange, then a classification based on the extent of the increase of the $AaDO_2$ with exercise is more appropriate. An $AaDO_2$ greater than 25 Torr is consistent with a mild gas exchange impairment, whereas $AaDO_2$ greater than 35-40 Torr consistent with a severe gas exchange impairment (7). Similarly, when the hyperventilatory response to exercise is considered, a $PaCO_2$ at maximal exercise in the 35-38 Torr range represents a borderline hyperventilatory response and $PaCO_2$ greater than 38 Torr, an absent hyperventilatory response (7). The use of these different criteria allow the identification of key components of EIAH, which individually may not result in a decrement in PaO_2 or SaO_2. It should be noted that EIAH is not confined to humans and is especially notable in the horse which develops a large $AaDO_2$ during maximal exercise, associated with a considerable decline in PaO_2 (to ~70 Torr) and SaO_2 (~88%) (8, 52).

Why don't we know more about EIAH?

Despite considerable research effort, the causes of EIAH are still debated. Once issue is that the amount of data collected in healthy normal exercising subjects is rather small compared to the clinical data collected in patients with disease. In research studies, because of the technical difficulties associated with data collection, many studies are conducted using 8-12 subjects and generalizations to populations are therefore limited. Also, many of the desirable measurements can only be made indirectly, such as the quantification of pulmonary diffusion limitation using the multiple inert gas elimination technique (49). Many investigators have chosen not to measure body temperature during exercise studies where arterial blood gas data is collected, since measuring temperature accurately often requires unpleasant and/or invasive monitoring. Since blood gases are measured at a standard electrode temperature of 37°C the true PaO_2 is underestimated, the $PaCO_2$ is overestimated. The use of pulse oximeters to estimate oxyhemoglobin saturation has induced a negative bias to the data such that the incidence of EIAH is greatly overestimated amongst populations of subjects (57). In the discussion that follows, temperature corrected arterial blood gas and inert gas data obtained in healthy normal subjects have been assembled from published sources (3, 5, 11, 13, 14, 22, 25, 28, 36, 39, 42, 51, 57), and used to discuss mechanisms of EIAH with special reference to ventilation-perfusion inequality and pulmonary diffusion limitation of oxygen transport.

Who gets EIAH?

Figure 1 shows the increase in the $AaDO_2$ and associated fall in PaO_2 from 198 exercise tests in healthy normal subjects exercising at 90-100% of $\dot{V}O_2$ max (data from 58 female, 123 male exercise tests, a total of 181 research subjects). The aerobic capacity of these subjects spans the physiologic range of $\dot{V}O_2$ from 30 to ~ 80 ml/kg/min. There is a negative relationship between $\dot{V}O_2$ max and PaO_2 at $\dot{V}O_2$ max, such that the subjects that have the highest $\dot{V}O_2$ max experience the greatest fall in PaO_2. However the PaO_2 during heavy and maximal exercise is highly variable even among populations of similar aerobic fitness. For example, at an oxygen consumption of 70 ml/kg/min the PaO_2 varies from 110 to 53 Torr. Even at more modest levels of $\dot{V}O_2$ max, there is a similar range of responses and although EIAH is often most pronounced at maximal exercise, there is a clear trend among some subjects towards developing a reduction in PaO_2 even during moderate exercise (17).

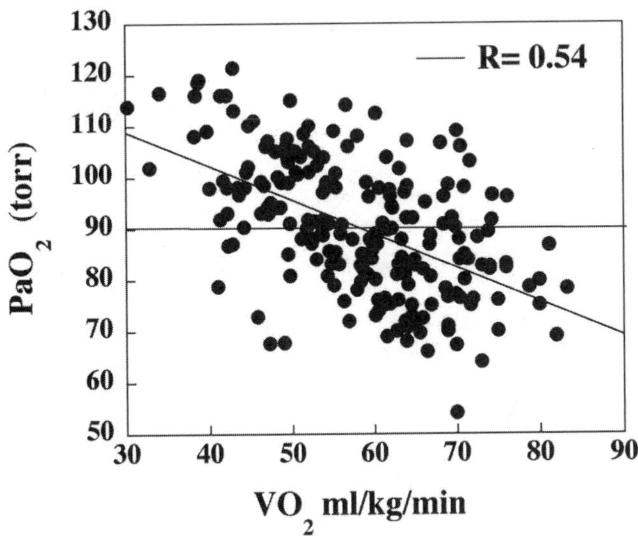

Figure 1. Arterial partial pressure of oxygen (PaO_2) obtained during cycling or treadmill running exercise at 90-100% of $\dot{V}O_2$max as a function of $\dot{V}O_2$. Data are from 181 exercise tests in 58 women and 123 men (some subjects were tested more than once). PaO_2 is reduced in subjects with higher $\dot{V}O_2$, although there is marked individual variability.

The gas exchange response to different exercise types varies even among the same subjects exercising at the same absolute and relative oxygen consumption (12, 23). For example, there is an approximately 10% lower PaO_2 during treadmill running than during cycling exercise (23). Although it might be tempting to attribute the reduction in PaO_2 with running exercise to differences in alveolar ventilation, (and indeed $PaCO_2$ is greater during running than cycling) the efficiency of gas exchange also differs between the two exercise types and the $AaDO_2$ is greater during running (23), for reasons that are obscure. Women have significantly smaller lung volumes and a lower resting diffusing capacity for carbon monoxide than males, even when corrected for body size and lower hemoglobin levels (35, 46, 48). How these differences in pulmonary structure may manifest themselves functionally as EIAH has been recently reviewed (26).

MECHANISM(S) OF EIAH

What is the role of inadequate hyperventilation?

Inadequate hyperventilation during high intensity exercise is implicated as a contributor to EIAH (5, 18, 32, 41). However the extent of hyperventilation is highly variable between individuals. Figure 2 shows the relationship between PaO_2 and $PaCO_2$ in the same subjects as Figure 1. Since, at a constant metabolic rate, alveolar ventilation is inversely proportional to alveolar partial pressure of CO_2, $PaCO_2$ is used as an indicator of alveolar ventilation. Of these subjects, only 12 (7%) exhibit an absent hyperventilatory response as previously defined, whereas 114 (~70%) of subjects have an adequate hyperventilatory response. Even in the subjects with an absent hyperventilatory response, the variation in PaO_2 is substantial, ranging from 71-106 Torr, and PaO_2 is only loosely associated with $PaCO_2$ ($R^2 = 0.2$). Perhaps this is not surprising, since if the $AaDO_2$ is not substantially increased, frank hypoventilation, with $PaCO_2$ is increased above normal resting values is rare, and thus PaO_2 will not be reduce by this mechanism. However, the effects of limited hyperventilation on PaO_2 are amplified when gas exchange efficiency is impaired and the $AaDO_2$ is increased.

A number of mechanisms for the failure of some subjects to lower $PaCO_2$ below 35 Torr during exercise are possible including: a decreased peripheral chemoreceptor function (18), respiratory muscle fatigue (37, 38) and mechanical constraints imposed on inspiratory and expiratory flow (31, 32). This last explanation is the most likely. In young fit subjects almost all of the maximal expiratory flow volume curve may be approached during exercise (31) and even when helium-oxygen mixtures are used to remove expiratory flow limitation EIAH is not completely abolished (32). In addition the metabolic demands of the respiratory muscles themselves, consuming up to 15% of the total oxygen consumption, may also contribute to EIAH (6). Also, although ventilatory muscle fatigue may not play a major role during short term maximal and very low intensity exercise, respiratory muscle fatigue has been demonstrated during high intensity exercise (30) where it may further contribute to relative hypoventilation.

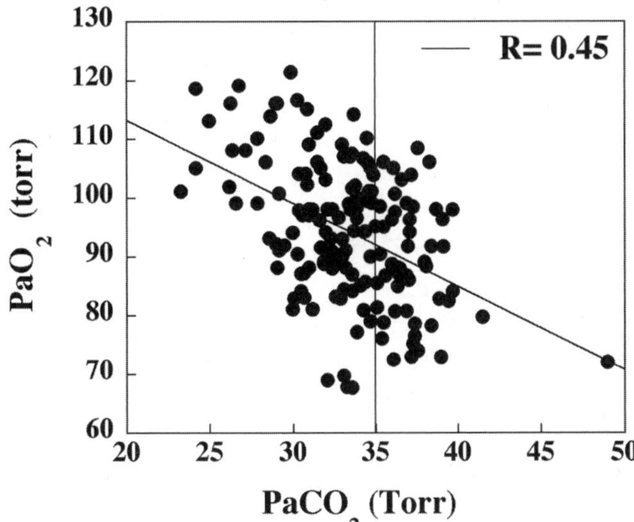

Figure 2. The relationship between PaO_2 and the partial pressure of carbon dioxide in arterial blood ($PaCO_2$, indicative of alveolar ventilation) from the same subjects and conditions as Figure 1. The majority of the subjects had an adequate hyperventilatory response as indicated by a $PaCO_2$ less than 35 torr, and frank hypoventilation is rare. There is a loose association between PaO_2 and $PaCO_2$, but marked inter-subject variability.

How important are differences in efficiency of gas exchange?

Figure 3 shows the $AaDO_2$ during near maximal or maximal exercise in 175 of the subjects from Figure 1. The variability in individual response is striking and the $AaDO_2$ varies almost 10 fold (~5-50 Torr) at any given level of $\dot{V}O_2$. While it can be appreciated that although most of the subjects who have an $AaDO_2$ greater than 25 Torr are exercising at a $\dot{V}O_2$ above 60 ml/kg min, there are still some who experience an $AaDO_2$ greater than 25 Torr at a $\dot{V}O_2$ of less than 50 ml/kg/min.

In determining any potential relationship between increased $AaDO_2$ and a decreased PaO_2 an interesting statistical problem arises. Regression analysis assumes that the X and Y variables are measured independently from one another. If the value of Y is used to calculate X, then these variables are said to be intertwined, and the regression analysis is invalid. Indeed, in these subjects, PaO_2 and $AaDO_2$ are highly related, and 85% of the variation in PaO_2 is explained on the basis of $AaDO_2$. Thus it is tempting to conclude that individual variation in gas exchange efficiency are important, however it is difficult to be sure because PaO_2 is used to calculate $AaDO_2$ and the variables are intertwined!

In Figure 4 subjects have been grouped according to the extent that the $AaDO_2$ is increased during maximal exercise, in order to compare subjects who experience a definite gas exchange limitation ($AaDO_2$ greater than 25 Torr, n = 69) to subjects that have minimal or no gas exchange limitation ($AaDO_2$ that is less than 20, n = 69). Figure 4A shows the $AaDO_2$ between the two groups. As expected, since they were grouped based on $AaDO_2$, the extent of gas exchange limitation is significantly greater in those subjects with an $AaDO_2$ greater than 25 and averages 33±6 Torr. That this difference in gas exchange efficiency has an effect on PaO_2 is not surprising and figure 4B shows the PaO_2 between the two groups. In the group with no gas exchange limitation, PaO_2 is maintained at normal resting levels, or is perhaps elevated slightly. However in the subjects with definite gas exchange limitations PaO_2 is reduced and averages 84 Torr.

Thus, it seems clear that gas exchange efficiency and an increased $AaDO_2$ is important in the development of EIAH. Potential mechanisms of reduced gas exchange efficiency with exercise and an increased $AaDO_2$ with exercise include intra-pulmonary or extra-pulmonary shunting, ventilation-perfusion $\dot{V}_A/\dot{Q}$ inequality, pulmonary diffusion limitation. A potential role of intrapulmonary shunts are discussed in Chapter 4.

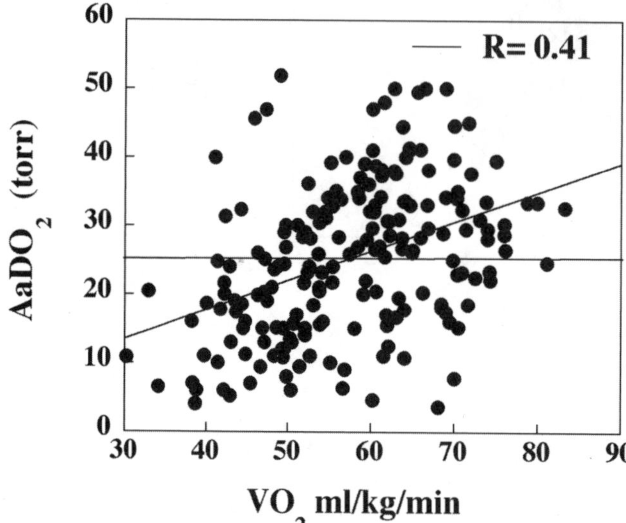

Figure 3. The relationship between alveolar arterial difference for oxygen ($AaDO_2$) and $\dot{V}O_2$ from the same subjects and conditions as Figure 1 and 2. Gas exchange is less efficient in subjects capable of higher oxygen consumptions, but at a $\dot{V}O_2$ of 70-80 ml/kg/min there is a 5-fold difference between the subjects with the greatest gas exchange limitations and the least.

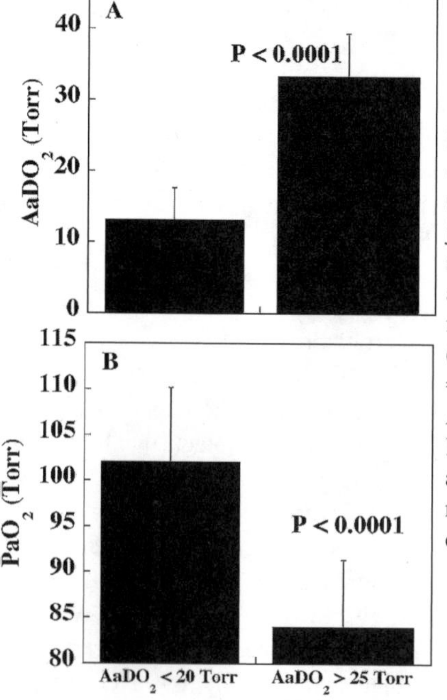

Figure 4. $AaDO_2$ data from a subset of the data presented in the preceding figures ($AaDO_2$ data were not available on all subjects). Subjects were grouped as having no significant gas exchange limitation ($AaDO_2$ at 90-100% of $\dot{V}O_2$ max <20 Torr, n = 69) or moderate to severe gas exchange limitation ($AaDO_2$ at 90-100% of $\dot{V}O_2$max > 25 Torr, n = 69). PaO_2 data from the same subjects as A. Subjects with no significant gas exchange limitation did not experience a fall in PaO2 at 90-100% of $\dot{V}O_2$max whereas subjects with moderate to severe gas exchange limitations experience a fall in PaO_2.

Multiple inert gas elimination technique

For decades, the multiple inert gas elimination technique has been used for measuring ventilation-perfusion ($\dot{V}A/\dot{Q}$) inequality (53, 54). Despite the reliability and versatility of the multiple inert gas elimination technique, there are some significant drawbacks. It is time consuming and somewhat technically difficult to perform, it requires sampling of arterial blood and mixed expired gases, and it requires an independent measure of cardiac output, if pulmonary mixed venous blood is not sampled. This has limited the technique to only a few research centers in the world, despite more than 30 years of use.

Using inert gas data, the relative contributions of $\dot{V}A/\dot{Q}$ inequality, diffusion limitation of oxygen transport, and intrapulmonary shunt to the $AaDO_2$ can be estimated (15). Trace amounts of six marker gases of differing solubility (sulfur hexafluorane (SF_6), cyclopropane, ethane, enflurane, ether, and acetone) that, unlike oxygen, have a linear relationship between solubility in blood and partial pressure are infused into a peripheral vein. Cardiac output and the concentration of the six gases in arterial blood and mixed expired gases are measured, and by using basic principals of mass balance, a distribution of pulmonary blood flow and ventilation relative to $\dot{V}A/\dot{Q}$ ratio of the lung can be obtained. This method considers the lung "as if" it were comprised of fifty individual gas exchange units with different $\dot{V}A/\dot{Q}$ ratios equally spaced on a logarithmic scale. Computer algorithms can be then be used to partition total ventilation and cardiac output between the fifty $\dot{V}A/\dot{Q}$ compartments to minimize error between data predicted from the modeled $\dot{V}A/\dot{Q}$ distributions and experimentally measured data (19). Using these distributions, a global index of $\dot{V}A/\dot{Q}$ inequality can be calculated. The LogSD$\dot{V}$ and LogSD$\dot{Q}$. (the standard deviation of the ventilation and perfusion distributions, respectively) are used to express $\dot{V}A/\dot{Q}$ inequality with larger number representing more $\dot{V}A/\dot{Q}$ inequality (54).

Information is gained about intra-pulmonary shunts, and deadspace ventilation, since these form the extremes of ventilation-perfusion inequality -i.e. $\dot{V}A/\dot{Q}$ is zero (shunt) or infinity (deadspace). In practical terms, blood flow to regions with a $\dot{V}A/\dot{Q}$ ratio less than 0.005 is characterized as shunt, whereas ventilation to regions with a $\dot{V}A/\dot{Q}$ ratio greater than 100 is characterized as deadspace ventilation.

To estimate diffusion limitation, the contribution that the measured amount of $\dot{V}A/\dot{Q}$ inequality and intrapulmonary shunt makes to the $AaDO_2$ is calculated. Since inert gases are essentially invulnerable to diffusion limitation, anything not accounted for by $\dot{V}A/\dot{Q}$ inequality can only come from diffusion limitation or extra-pulmonary non-cardiac shunts.

What is the role of ventilation-perfusion inequality in EIAH?

$\dot{V}A/\dot{Q}$ inequality increases with increasing exercise intensity (11, 13, 28) but there does not appear to be a difference $\dot{V}A/\dot{Q}$ inequality between highly fit subjects ($\dot{V}O_2$max > 60 ml/kg/min) and those of low to average aerobic fitness ($\dot{V}O_2$max < 50 ml/kg/min) (26). Although the amount of $\dot{V}A/\dot{Q}$ inequality *within* an individual generally increases with increasing exercise intensity, there does not appear to be a significant relationship between the development of $\dot{V}A/\dot{Q}$ inequality and aerobic fitness. Figure 5A shows the LogSD$\dot{Q}$. from inert gas data obtained in 55 subjects during exercise at 90-100% of $\dot{V}O_2$max with and without pulmonary gas exchange limitation as previously defined. The two groups have similar $\dot{V}A/\dot{Q}$ inequality at rest (data not shown) and the extent of the inequality is increased to a similar extent in both groups. The net effect on gas exchange is that $\dot{V}A/\dot{Q}$ inequality contributes approximate 12-15 Torr to the $AaDO_2$ (Figure 5A). In subjects without significant gas exchange limitations, this accounts for virtually all of the $AaDO_2$, however in subjects with significant gas exchange limitations it accounts for slightly less than 50% of the $AaDO_2$. That is not to say that $\dot{V}A/\dot{Q}$ inequality is not important in the development of EIAH, but since subjects in both groups develop it to the same extent, it does not distinguish those who develop EIAH from those who do not. Since $\dot{V}A/\dot{Q}$ inequality includes variations in alveolar PO_2 relative to blood flow, the potential effects of $\dot{V}A/\dot{Q}$ inequality are in part mitigated by increased alveolar ventilation relative to perfusion which acts to shift the overall $\dot{V}A/\dot{Q}$ distribution to the right. This can be though of as over-ventilation of area with limited perfusion (increased ventilation of area of high $\dot{V}A/\dot{Q}$ ratio) rather than perfusion of area with low ventilation. The next effect is to minimize the effect of heterogeneity on gas exchange.

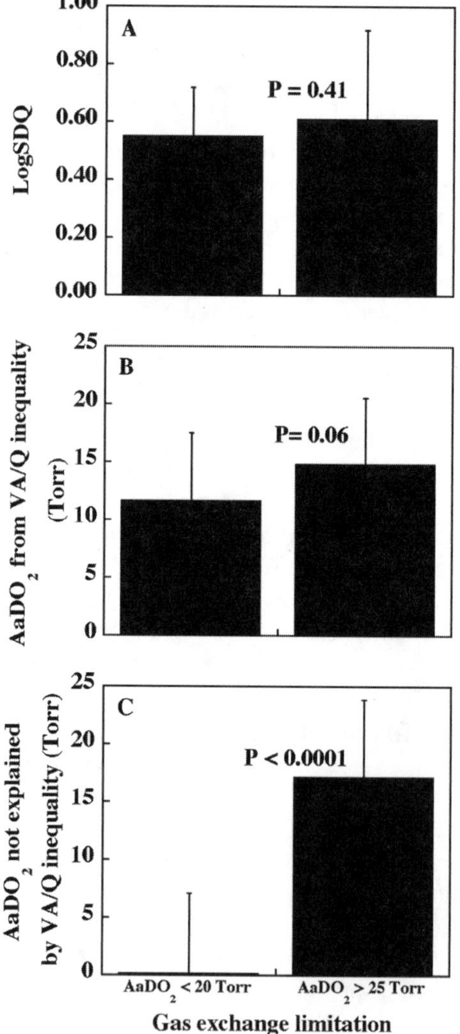

Figure 5. The contribution of $\dot{V}A/\dot{Q}$ inequality, intra-pulmonary shunting and diffusion limitation to the $AaDO_2$ in 55 subjects in whom multiple inert gas elimination data was available in subjects with and without gas exchange limitation as previously defined. The increase in $\dot{V}A/\dot{Q}$ in equality is similar between the two groups (A) and contribution of $\dot{V}A/\dot{Q}$ in equality and intrapulmonary shunting to the $AaDO_2$ is also similar in both groups (B). However the subjects who have moderate or marked gas exchange limitations have an increased $AaDO_2$ not explained by inert gases (C) mostly likely due to pulmonary diffusion limitation of oxygen transport.

What are the causes of ventilation-perfusion inequality with exercise?

The physiological basis for increased $\dot{V}_A/\dot{Q}$ inequality with exercise is not certain, but a likely cause is interstitial pulmonary edema (8). Increased pulmonary vascular pressure with exercise reduce gravitational-dependent differences in blood flow at different heights in a lung but it also increases capillary filtration. Interstitial edema fluid would be expected to distort the surrounding architecture of the alveoli and capillary network. Altered airway and blood vessel diameter resulting from the presence of cuffing would affect distribution of blood flow, and perhaps air flow, in the lung. There is less evidence for increased heterogeneity of ventilation than for perfusion during exercise. However, a reduction of gas mixing in large airways during exercise would increase apparent $\dot{V}_A\dot{Q}$ inequality measured by the inert gases (50).

Several lines of evidence implicate interstitial edema as the cause of increased $\dot{V}_A/\dot{Q}$ inequality (8). For example, $\dot{V}_A/\dot{Q}$ inequality is increased by hypoxia (11), and decreased by breathing 100% O_2, which would tend to increase and decrease, respectively, capillary pressure and filtration. Increased pulmonary artery pressure during exercise would also increase capillary filtration pressure and may have similar effects on the distribution of blood flow. Pigs, an animal that demonstrates increased $\dot{V}_A/\dot{Q}$ inequality with exercise (29) also show an increase in perivascular edema on histological examination in exercised animals, compared to resting controls (44). $\dot{V}_A/\dot{Q}$ inequality persists into recovery from heavy exercise, even after ventilation and cardiac output have returned to normal (45) and prolonged exercise results in a progressive increase in $\dot{V}_A/\dot{Q}$ inequality (25), consistent with fluid accumulation. Subjects who have a history of high altitude pulmonary edema (HAPE) also show larger increases in exercise induced $\dot{V}_A/\dot{Q}$ inequality compared to subjects without a history of HAPE (39). This has led to speculation that the underlying mechanism of increased $\dot{V}_A/\dot{Q}$ inequality with exercise and HAPE maybe the same.

Demonstrating that interstitial pulmonary edema occurs with exercise has been problematic, because many of the radiographic changes associated with edema are seen as a result of increased pulmonary blood flow, - a consequence of the increased cardiac output with exercise. Therefore to answer this question it becomes important to distinguish between intravascular and extravascular lung water. Acute clinical edema has been reported after ultra marathons, (33) and an increase in lung density is observed in subjects following a triathlon (4), and with exercise at moderate altitude (2), however this is not definite proof of the development of interstitial edema during sea level exercise. Recently, in a carefully conducted study, an increase in extravascular lung water, following sustained heavy exercise has been demonstrated using MRI (34). The MRI technique used has been validated against direct measures of water in isolated lung preparations with good results (10). These data demonstrate that interstitial edema does occur with exercise, but the corresponding effect on gas exchange remains to be demonstrated.

Is diffusion limitation of pulmonary oxygen transport important in EIAH?

As mentioned earlier, the extent of pulmonary diffusion limitation is inferred by estimating the contribution of $\dot{V}_A/\dot{Q}$ inequality and intrapulmonary shunt, measured from inert gas data to the $AaDO_2$ and attributing this to diffusion limitation. The problem with this approach is that it is an indirect estimate of the extent of diffusion limitation, and is not able to differentiate the relative contributions of pulmonary O_2 diffusion limitation and extra-pulmonary shunting (e.g. from bronchial and thebesian veins) towards the overall A-aDO_2. Pulmonary shunting at rest via the bronchial and thebesian veins is believed to comprise <2% of total cardiac output (13, 49, 51), and is unlikely to change proportionally with exercise. Studies conducted during hypoxia indicate that such shunts would have to increase to 10-20% of cardiac output to explain the contribution to the AaDO_2 (42, 49). Since such shunts are anatomic, and will not change with FIO_2 it is unlikely that extra-pulmonary shunting contributes a more than a very small amount to the overall A-aDO_2, but this cannot be definitively stated.

The cause of the pulmonary diffusion impairment of oxygen transport is unknown, but is likely because of rapid pulmonary capillary transit of red blood cells (7). Few studies have attempted to measure transit times in exercising athletes and link the results to gas exchange. A significant fall in pulmonary transit time with exercise has been shown (24, 55, 58) but unequivocal evidence to show that transit times approached the hypothetical minimum time (24, 55) for oxygen equilibration is lacking. Thus pulmonary capillary transit time has not been established as a cause of pulmonary diffusion limitation. In part this is because the techniques used to measure pulmonary transit time either measured whole lung pulmonary transit of red blood cells, (however, capillary transit time is the important variable for gas exchange), or used inspired gases that alter the physiological conditions of measurement. Subjects who develop diffusion impairment often do so at submaximal levels of exercise (43) where presumably capillary recruitment is not maximal and transit time is not minimal, which also might argue against reduced transit times as being the cause. However it is the ratio of diffusional (D) to perfusional (βQ) conductance that determines the completeness of end capillary equilibration, (37, 38) and subjects with EIAH have a lower D/Q compared to those who do not develop EIAH (43). Thus it is possible that the perfusional conductance is recruited more quickly causing diffusion impairment even at relatively low levels of exercise.

Diffusion limitation from thickening of the blood-gas barrier is unlikely, but cannot be ruled out. After prolonged, heavy exercise in humans, the diffusing capacity for carbon monoxide decreases but there is no decrease in the O_2 diffusing capacity calculated from the inert gases (8). The decrease in diffusing capacity for carbon monoxide after exercise is best explained by a decrease in pulmonary capillary volume with a redistribution of central blood flow. There may also be a change in the matching of blood flow and diffusing capacity, which impacts gas exchange similar to $\dot{V}_A/\dot{Q}$ inequality (3).

What about shunts?

A shunt is defined as blood that enters the arterial system without coming in contact with ventilated areas of the lung (21, 56). Recently, two groups working independently have demonstrated the passage of bubbles through the pulmonary circulation during exercise using agitated saline contrast echocardiography (9, 47) and have suggested that this represent intrapulmonary shunts that affect gas exchange. These potential intrapulmonary shunts are controversial, because studies using inert gas data have never demonstrated significant shunts either at rest or during exercise (11, 13, 14, 25, 28, 39, 42, 49, 51). These bubble shunts observed during exercise are discussed in the next chapter and are briefly discussed here as they relate to inert gas data. Inert gases detect intra-pulmonary and cardiac shunting because gases of low solubility such as SF_6 are ready exchanged even in regions of low $\dot{V}A/\dot{Q}$, thus significant amounts in arterial blood signify right to left shunts. In fact, right to left shunts allow passage of all inert gases without excretion irrespective of solubility, and the overall picture is an increase in the retention of gases of all solubilities without an alteration in the excretion curve (20). It has been suggested that a reason for the discrepancy in findings between the two techniques is that pre-capillary gas exchange (in the vessels that allow the passage of microbubbles) of low solubility gases such as SF_6, underestimates intrapulmonary shunt (9, 47). This essentially means that that pre-capillary gas exchange would have to occur for SF_6 but not oxygen. While it is possible that pre-capillary gas exchange could affect the excretion of SF_6, other inert gases of low solubility such as such as cyclopropane, and ethane would also be affected, but to a lesser extent. This seems an unlikely explanation for the discrepancy, since these effects should be detected in other inert gases, but are not seen. Fluorescent microsphere data in pigs, and in horses (M. Hlastala-personal communication) do not demonstrate intrapulmonary shunts in these species, consistent with the inert gas data obtained, and in dogs when shunts are introduced experimentally, they are detected by inert gases (27). Also some patients with liver disease demonstrate positive intrapulmonary shunts with echocardiography, but have normal pulmonary gas exchange (1), and in patients that do have hypoxemia, shunts are also detected using the inert gas elimination technique (19). Thus it appears that the agitated saline contrast echo technique appears to be of limited ability to distinguish shunts that affect gas exchange. Perhaps limitations of the agitated saline contrast technique, (such as small diameter bubbles passing through normal capillaries, or deformation of larger bubbles such that bubbles traverse where red cells do not) may explain why bubbles appear to be shunted but red cell do not. Certainly further work needs to be done to clarify the role, if any these shunts play in gas exchange.

SUMMARY

Understanding the role of differing components of pulmonary gas exchange on the development of exercise induced arterial hypoxemia is far from complete. While 12-15 torr on average of the $AaDO_2$ is attributable to $\dot{V}A/\dot{Q}$ inequality, it is the portion of the $AaDO_2$ that is not due to $\dot{V}A/\dot{Q}$ inequality that distinguishes those subjects with marked pulmonary gas exchange limitations from those with minimal to none. There is a large body of evidence suggesting that interstitial pulmonary edema occurs as a result of exercise, which recent MRI data confirms. How this affects gas exchange has yet to be established.

ACKNOWLEDGMENTS

Supported by NIH HL-17731. I would like to thank Mark Olfert, Peter Wagner, Jerry Dempsey, Craig Harms, Bruce Johnson, and Gerry Zavorsky for generously sharing their data.

REFERENCES

1. Abrams GA, Jaffe CC, Hoffer PB, Binder HJ, and Fallon MB. Diagnostic utility of contrast echocardiography and lung perfusion scan in patients with hepatopulmonary syndrome. *Gastroenterology* 109: 1283-1288, 1995.
2. Anholm JD, Milne EN, Stark P, Bourne JC, and Friedman P. Radiographic evidence of interstitial pulmonary edema after exercise at altitude. *J Appl Physiol* 86: 503-509, 1999.
3. Bebout DE, Storey D, Roca J, Hogan MC, Poole DC, Gonzales-Camerena R, Ueno O, Habb P, and Wagner PD. Effects of altitude acclimatization on pulmonary gas exchange during exercise. *J Appl Physiol* 67: 2286-2295, 1989.
4. Caillaud C, Serre CO, Anselme F, Capdevilla X, and Prefaut C. Computerized tomography and pulmonary diffusing capacity in highly trained athletes after performing a triathlon. *J Appl Physiol* 79: 1226-1232, 1995.
5. Dempsey JA, Hanson PG, and Henderson KS. Exercised-induced arterial hypoxaemia in healthy human subjects at sea level. *J Physiol (Lond)* 355: 161-175, 1984.
6. Dempsey JA, Sheel AW, Derchak P, and Harms C. Two types of pulmonary system limitations to exercise. *Deutsche Zeitschrift fur Sportsmedizin* 51: 318-326, 2000.
7. Dempsey JA and Wagner PD. Exercise-induced arterial hypoxemia. *J Appl Physiol* 87: 1997-2006, 1999.
8. Dempsey JA and Wagner PD. Exercise-induced arterial hypoxemia. *Journal of Applied Physiology* 87: 1997-2006, 1999.
9. Eldridge MW, Dempsey JA, Haverkamp HC, Lovering AT, and Hokanson JS. Exercise-induced intrapulmonary arteriovenous shunting in healthy humans. *J Appl Physiol* 97: 797-805, 2004.
10. Estilaei M, MacKay A, Whittall K, and Mayo J. In vitro measurements of water content and T2 relaxation times in lung using a clinical MRI scanner. *J Magn Reson Imaging* 9: 699-703, 1999.
11. Gale GE, Torre BJ, Moon RE, Saltzman HA, and Wagner PD. Ventilation-perfusion inequality in normal humans during exercise at sea level and simulated altitude. *J Appl Physiol* 58: 978-988, 1985.
12. Gavin TP and Stager JM. The effects of exercise modality on exercise-induced hypoxemia. *Respir Physiol* 155: 317-323, 1999.
13. Hammond MD, Gale GE, Kapitan KS, Ries A, and Wagner PD. Pulmonary gas exchange in humans during exercise at sea level. *J Appl Physiol* 60: 1590-1598, 1986.
14. Hammond MD, Gale GE, Kapitan KS, Ries A, and Wagner PD. Pulmonary gas exchange in humans during normobaric hypoxic exercise. *J Appl Physiol* 61: 1749-1757, 1986.
15. Hammond MD and Hempleman SC. Oxygen diffusing capacity estimates derived from measured $\dot{V}_A\dot{Q}$ distributions in man. *Respir Physiol* 69: 129-147, 1987.
16. Harms CA, McClaran SR, Nickele GA, Pegelow DF, Nelson WB, and Dempsey JA. Effect of exercise-induced arterial O2 desaturation on VO2max in women. *Med Sci Sports Exerc* 32: 1101-1108, 2000.
17. Harms CA, McClaran SR, Nickele GA, Pegelow DF, Nelson WB, and Dempsey JA. Exercise-induced arterial hypoxaemia in healthy young women. *J Physiol (Lond)*: 619-628, 1998.
18. Harms CA and Stager JM. Low chemoresponsiveness and inadequate hyperventilation contribute to exercise-induced hypoxemia. *J Appl Physiol* 79: 575-580, 1995.
19. Hedenstierna G, Soderman C, Eriksson LS, and Wahren J. Ventilation-perfusion inequality in patients with non-alcoholic liver cirrhosis. *Eur Respir J* 4: 711-717, 1991.
20. Hlastala MP, Colley PS, and Cheney FW. Pulmonary shunt: a comparison between oxygen and inert gas infusion methods. *J Appl Physiol* 39: 1048-1051., 1975.
21. Hlastala MP and Robertson HT. Inert gas elimination characteristics of the normal and

abnormal lung. *J Appl Physiol* 44: 258-266, 1978.

22. Hopkins SR, Barker RC, Brutsaert TD, Gavin TP, Entin P, Olfert IM, Veisel S, and Wagner PD. Pulmonary gas exchange during exercise in women: effects of exercise type and work increment. *J Appl Physiol* 89: 721-730, 2000.
23. Hopkins SR, Barker RC, Brutsaert TD, Gavin TP, Entin P, Olfert IM, Veisel S, and Wagner PD. Pulmonary gas exchange during exercise in women: effects of exercise type and work increment. *Journal of Applied Physiology* 89: 721-730, 2000.
24. Hopkins SR, Belzberg AS, Wiggs BR, and McKenzie DC. Pulmonary transit time and diffusion limitation during heavy exercise in athletes. *Respir Physiol* 103: 67-73, 1996.
25. Hopkins SR, Gavin TP, Siafakas NM, Haseler LJ, Olfert IM, Wagner H, and Wagner PD. Effect of prolonged, heavy exercise on pulmonary gas exchange in athletes. *J Appl Physiol* 85: 1523-1532, 1998.
26. Hopkins SR and Harms CA. Gender and pulmonary gas exchange during exercise. *Exerc Sport Sci Rev* 32: 50-56, 2004.
27. Hopkins SR, Johnson EC, Richardson RS, Wagner H, De Rosa M, and Wagner PD. Effects of inhaled nitric oxide on gas exchange in lungs with shunt or poorly ventilated areas. *Am J Respir Crit Care Med* 156: 484-491, 1997.
28. Hopkins SR, McKenzie DC, Schoene RB, Glenny RW, and Robertson HT. Pulmonary gas exchange during exercise in athletes. I. Ventilation-perfusion mismatch and diffusion limitation. *J Appl Physiol* 77: 912-917, 1994.
29. Hopkins SR, Stary CM, Falor E, Wagner H, Wagner PD, and McKirnan MD. Pulmonary gas exchange during exercise in pigs. *J Appl Physiol* 86: 93-100, 1999.
30. Johnson BD, Babcock MA, Suman OE, and Dempsey JA. Exercise-induced diaphragmatic fatigue in healthy humans. *J Physiol* 460: 385-405., 1993.
31. Johnson BD, Saupe KW, and Dempsey JA. Mechanical constraints on exercise hyperpnea in endurance athletes. *J Appl Physiol* 73: 874-886, 1992.
32. McClaran SR, Harms CA, Pegelow DF, and Dempsey JA. Smaller lungs in women affect exercise hyperpnea. *J Appl Physiol* 84: 1872-1881, 1998.
33. McKechnie JK, Leary WP, Noakes TD, Kallmeyer JC, MacSearraigh ET, and Olivier LR. Acute pulmonary oedema in two athletes during a 90-km running race. *S Afr Med J* 56: 261-265, 1979.
34. McKenzie DC, O'Hare T J, and Mayo J. The effect of sustained heavy exercise on the development of pulmonary edema in trained male cyclists. *Respir Physiol Neurobiol* 145: 209-218, 2005.
35. Mead J. Dysanapsis in normal lungs assessed by the relationship between maximal flow, static recoil, and vital capacity. *Am Rev Respir Dis* 121: 339-342., 1980.
36. Olfert IM, Balouch J, Kleinsasser A, Knapp A, Wagner H, Wagner PD, and Hopkins SR. Does gender affect human pulmonary gas exchange during exercise? *J Physiol* 557: 529-541, 2004.
37. Piiper J and Scheid P. Gas transport efficacy of gills, lungs and skin: theory and experimental data. *Respir Physiol* 23: 209-221, 1975.
38. Piiper J and Scheid P. Models for a comparative functional analysis of gas exchange organs in vertebrates. *J Appl Physiol* 53: 1321-1329, 1982.
39. Podolsky A, Eldridge MW, Richardson RS, Knight DR, Johnson EC, Hopkins SR, Johnson DH, Michimata H, Grassi B, Feiner J, Kurdak SS, Bickler PE, Severinghaus JW, and Wagner PD. Exercise-induced $\dot{V}_A\dot{Q}$ inequality in subjects with prior high-altitude pulmonary edema. *J Appl Physiol* 81: 922-932, 1996.
40. Powers SK, Lawler J, Dempsey JA, Dodd S, and Landry G. Effects of incomplete pulmonary gas exchange on VO_2 max. *J Appl Physiol* 66: 2491-2495, 1989.
41. Powers SK, Martin D, Cicale M, Collop N, Huang D, and Criswell D. Exercise-induced hypoxemia in athletes: role of inadequate hyperventilation. *Eur J Appl Physiol* 65: 37-42,

1992.
42. Rice AJ, Thornton AT, Gore CJ, Scroop GC, Greville HW, Wagner H, Wagner PD, and Hopkins SR. Pulmonary gas exchange during exercise in highly trained cyclists with arterial hypoxemia. *J Appl Physiol* 87: 1802-1812, 1999.
43. Rice AJ, Thornton AT, Gore CJ, Scroop GC, Greville HW, Wagner H, Wagner PD, and Hopkins SR. Pulmonary gas exchange during exercise in highly trained cyclists with arterial hypoxemia. *Journal of Applied Physiology* 87: 1802-1812, 1999.
44. Schaffartzik W, Arcos J, Tsukimoto K, Mathieu-Costello O, and Wagner PD. Pulmonary interstitial edema in the pig after heavy exercise. *J Appl Physiol* 75: 2535-2540, 1993.
45. Schaffartzik W, Poole DC, Derion T, Tsukimoto K, Hogan MC, Arcos JP, Bebout DE, and Wagner PD. $\dot{V}_A\dot{Q}$ distribution during heavy exercise and recovery in humans: implications for pulmonary edema. *J Appl Physiol* 72: 1657-1667, 1992.
46. Schwartz JD, Katz SA, Fegley RW, and Tockman MS. Analysis of spirometric data from a national sample of healthy 6- to 24-year-olds (NHANES II). *Am Rev Respir Dis* 138: 1405-1414, 1988.
47. Stickland MK, Welsh RC, Haykowsky MJ, Petersen SR, Anderson WD, Taylor DA, Bouffard M, and Jones RL. Intra-pulmonary shunt and pulmonary gas exchange during exercise in humans. *J Physiol* 561: 321-329, 2004.
48. Thurlbeck WM. Postnatal human lung growth. *Thorax* 37: 564-571, 1982.
49. Torre-Bueno JR, P.D. Wagner, H. A. Saltzman, G. E. Gale and R. E. Moon. Diffusion limitation in normal humans during exercise at sea level and simulated altitude. *J Appl Physiol* 58: 989-995, 1985.
50. Tsukimoto K, Arcos JP, Schaffartzik W, Wagner PD, and West JB. Effect of common dead space on $\dot{V}_A\dot{Q}$ distribution in the dog. *J Appl Physiol* 68:: 2488-2493., 1990.
51. Wagner PD, Gale GE, Moon RE, Torre BJ, Stolp BW, and Saltzman HA. Pulmonary gas exchange in humans exercising at sea level and simulated altitude. *J Appl Physiol* 61: 260-270, 1986.
52. Wagner PD, J. R. Gillespie G. L. Landgren, M. R. Fedde, B. W. Jones, R. M. de Bowes, R. L. Peischel and H. H. Erickson. Mechanism of exercise-induced hypoxemia in horses. *J Appl Physiol* 66: 1227-1233, 1989.
53. Wagner PD, Naumann PF, and Laravuso RB. Simultaneous measurement of eight foreign gases in blood by gas chromotography. *J Appl Physiol* 36: 600-605, 1974.
54. Wagner PD, Saltzman HA, and West JB. Measurement of continuous distributions of ventilation-perfusion ratios:theory. *J Appl Physiol* 36: 588-599, 1974.
55. Warren GL, Cureton KJ, Middendorf WF, Ray CA, and Warren JA. Red blood cell pulmonary capillary transit time during exercise in athletes. *Med Sci Sports Exerc* 23: 1353-1361, 1991.
56. West JB. *Respiratory Physiology: The essentials*. Baltimore, MD: Lippincott, Williams & Wilkins, 2005.
57. Yamaya Y, Bogaard HJ, Wagner PD, Niizeki K, and Hopkins SR. Validity of pulse oximetry during maximal exercise in normoxia, hypoxia, and hyperoxia. *J Appl Physiol* 92: 162-168, 2002.
58. Zavorsky GS, Walley KR, Hunte GS, McKenzie DC, Sexsmith GP, and Russell JA. Acute hypervolemia lengthens red cell pulmonary transit time during exercise in endurance athletes. *Respir Physiol Neurobiol* 131: 255-268, 2002.

Chapter 4

INTRAPULMONARY SHUNT DURING NORMOXIC AND HYPOXIC EXERCISE IN HEALTHY HUMANS

Andrew T. Lovering[1†], Michael K. Stickland[1†], Marlowe W. Eldridge[2, 3 †]

[1]Postdoctoral Fellow, The John Rankin Laboratory of Pulmonary Medicine, Department of Population Health Sciences, University of Wisconsin – Madison, Wisconsin, [2]Medical Director, The John Rankin Laboratory of Pulmonary Medicine, Department of Population Health Sciences, University of Wisconsin – Madison, [3]Assistant Professor, University of Wisconsin School of Medicine, Department of Pediatrics and Critical Care Medicine, Madison, Wisconsin, USA. [†]All authors contributed equally to this publication.

Abstract: This review presents evidence for the recruitment of intrapulmonary arteriovenous shunts (IPAVS) during exercise in normal healthy humans. Support for pre-capillary connections between the arterial and venous circulation in lungs of humans and animals have existed for over one-hundred years. Right-to-left physiological shunt has not been detected during exercise with gas exchange-dependent techniques. However, fundamental assumptions of these techniques may not allow for measurement of a small (1-3%) anatomical shunt, the magnitude of which would explain the entire A-aDO_2 typically observed during normoxic exercise. Data from contrast echocardiograph studies are presented demonstrating the development of IPAVS with exercise in 90% of subjects tested. Technetium-99m labeled macroaggregated albumin studies also found exercise IPAVS and calculated shunt to be ~2% at max exercise. These exercise IPAVS appear strongly related to the alveolar to arterial PO_2 difference, pulmonary blood flow and mean pulmonary artery pressure. Hypoxic exercise was found to induce IPAVS at lower workloads than during normoxic exercise in 50% of subjects, while all subjects continued to shunt during recovery from hypoxic exercise, but only three subjects demonstrated intrapulmonary shunt during recovery from normoxic exercise. We suggest that these previously under-appreciated intrapulmonary arteriovenous shunts develop during exercise, contributing to the impairment in gas exchange typically observed with exercise. Future work will better define the conditions for shunt recruitment as well as their physiologic consequence.

Key Words: pre-capillary gas exchange, hypoxia, intrapulmonary anastomoses, pulmonary circulation, arterial hypoxemia

Hypoxia and Exercise, edited by R.C. Roach *et al.*
Springer, New York, 2006.

INTRODUCTION

For more than one hundred years, researchers have documented pre-capillary connections between the arterial and venous circulation (54). These arteriovenous anastomoses have been found in many anatomical locations associated with dynamic changes in blood flow including the skin, muscle, penis and the lung (8, 71). The existence of intrapulmonary arteriovenous anastomoses have been reported in infant (75) and adult humans (64, 66, 67), birds (45, 60), dogs (46), cats and rabbits (45) and in the gills of amphibian larvae (38). In several of these studies synthetic beads with diameters ranging from 50-390μm were able to pass through the pulmonary circulation (45, 64, 75). Although the indentity of the vessels responsible for transpulmonary passage of these synthetic beads remains undetermined, Tobin (64) identified vessels in 47% of the lobules of human lungs which were glomus-like and suggested that these vessels may act as intrapulmonary arteriovenous shunts (IPAVS). In addition, Elliot and Reid have described small muscular arteries in human lungs that branch from the conventional pulmonary arteries at right angles and are referred to as supernumerary arteries because they do not accompany airways (16). Interestingly, these supernumerary arteries have a muscular baffle at their origin which appears to regulate blood flow (57). Accordingly, these supernumerary vessels are an attractive candidate for being able to dynamically regulate pulmonary blood flow under hyperdynamic conditions such as exercise and hypoxia.

PREVIOUS WORK IN UNDERSTANDING GAS EXCHANGE INEFFICIENCY DURING EXERCISE

Our interest in these pulmonary arteriovenous anastomoses comes from a desire to understand gas exchange as it occurs in the lung. Pulmonary gas-exchange efficiency for oxygen is defined and quantified as the difference between the alveolar partial pressure of oxygen (PAO_2) and the arterial partial pressure of oxygen (PaO_2) and is known as the alveolar-to-arterial PO_2 difference (A-aDO_2). The normal A-aDO_2 in young, healthy individuals is 5-10 mmHg at rest and increases to 15-25 mmHg at maximal exercise (Figure 1). In some elite athletes the A-aDO_2 can widen as much as 25-40 mmHg, and depending on A-aDO_2 magnitude and the ventilatory response to exercise, exercise-induced arterial hypoxemia can develop (12). Approximately one half of the A-aDO_2 during exercise is said to be due to ventilation ($\dot{V}A$) and perfusion ($\dot{Q}$) heterogeneity as measured by the multiple inert gas elimination technique (MIGET) (20, 65, 70), with the remainder due to extrapulmonary shunt, or diffusion limitation (70).

Extrapulmonary shunt results from the thebesian circulation, which empties directly into the left heart, and bronchial venus flow, which drains into the pulmonary vein. In humans, the O_2 content of the bronchial venous blood remains unknown. The contribution of these extrapulmonary shunts to arterial oxygenation would be expected to increase with exercise as mixed venous PO_2 falls (31). Although the total contribution of extrapulmonary shunt is assumed to be ~1% of the cardiac output (1, 2, 18, 19, 35, 40, 48), it should be considered an important contributor to the gas exchange inefficiency that occurs during exercise (see also anatomical shunt contribution calculations in (20)).

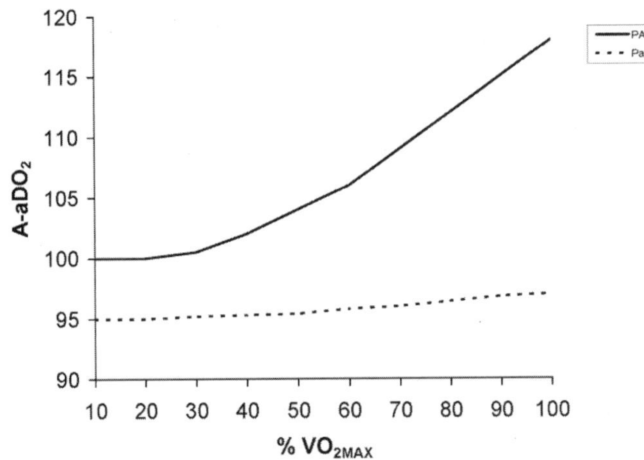

Figure 1. Alveolar PO_2 (PAO_2 - solid line) and arterial PO_2 (PaO_2 - dashed line) during progressive exercise to maximum in a healthy young adult. Despite a progressively widened $A\text{-}aDO_2$, arterial PO_2 is maintained near resting levels at all exercise intensities. Data compiled from the Rankin laboratory.

All previous studies using gas exchange-dependent methods have not documented the development of intrapulmonary shunting during exercise in healthy humans (12, 20, 23, 28, 51, 69). However, the absence of right-to-left intra-pulmonary shunt during exercise as measured by gas-dependent methods does not exclude the possibililty of exercise-induced IPAVS. Pulmonary pre-capillary gas exchange is well documented and the magnitude of pre-capillary gas exchange is critically dependent on the concentration gradient of the gas (10, 29, 30, 56, 59). Indeed Conhaim and Staub (10) have shown that pulmonary arteries can be oxygenated before reaching the alveolar capillaries, with the extent of the process dependent on time available for gas exchange and the PO_2 difference between alveolar gas and pulmonary arterial blood. For example, precapillary vessels up to 500μm are fully oxygenated when the lung is ventilated with 100% O_2. In light of evidence for pre-capillary gas exchange, Jameson suggested in 1964 that "The traditional view of the area in the pulmonary vascular bed from which diffusion occurs would appear to require revision."(30). Furthermore, in the case of the 100% oxygen technique, measurements of blood oxygen tension are not sufficiently accurate to distinguish shunts less than 10% of the cardiac output due to instrument error (50). As a result, Conhaim and Staub have stated that 100% O_2 breathing may underestimate arterial-venous shunts during normoxia. As pointed out recently, MIGET is based on early models of pulmonary gas exchange, which assumes. diffusion equilibrium between alveolar gas and end-capillary blood (26). Consequently, this technique may underestimate IPAVS because the detection of true shunt vs. low $\dot{V}_A\dot{Q}$ is dependent on the retention of any sulfur hexafluoride (SF_6), an inert gas with a very low solubility (and therefore a reduced retention) in blood (26). Accordingly, the low solubility and large concentration gradient between the blood vessels and airways may allow for pre-capillary elimination of SF_6. Recent work has reported that "...inert gases of all blood solubilities exchange in the airways..." and these authors went on to state that, "This effect complicates the interpretation of techniques that use highly soluble gases to evaluate lung function, such as MIGET"(56). As a consequence of precapillary gas exchange, the current gas exchange-dependent techniques used to determine right-to-left intrapulmonary shunt may underestimate or fail to detect IPAVS.

Intrapulmonary, or right to left, shunt can be caused by either low $\dot{V}A\dot{Q}$ regions secondary to atelectasis or alveolar flooding, or direct IPAVS. Pulmonary anastomoses as described above bypass capillaries, and therefore they should not participate in gas exchange at the capillary-alveoli interface. We hypothesized that the existence of any IPAVS during exercise would adversely affect exercise gas exchange, increasing the A-aDO_2. Indeed this right to left shunted blood is deoxygenated and would become increasingly so with exercise as oxygen extraction increases, reducing mixed venous PO_2. The magnitude of IPAVS would not need to be large during exercise, as Gledhill and associates previously calculated that an anatomical shunt of only ~2% of cardiac output would account for the entire A-aDO_2 of 17mmHg measured in their subjects during moderate intensity exercise (20). Therefore our studies examined if IPAVS developed during exercise, if these vessels are related to the widened A-aDO_2 during exercise, and whether these shunts could be modulated under different physiological conditions.

RECENT WORK IN UNDERSTANDING INTRAPULMONARY SHUNT & GAS EXCHANGE INEFFICIENCY DURING EXERCISE

We initially investigated the occurrence and prevalence of IPAVS during exercise in healthy humans using agitated saline contrast echocardiography, a non-gas exchange-dependent method (14). The validity of this standard clinical method for detecting cardiac and intrapulmonary shunting has been previously reported in detail elsewhere (7, 14, 39, 41, 42, 47, 52, 63). To detect shunt, sterile saline is agitated to create microbubbles that are injected into a peripheral vein. Contrast echocardiography distinguishes intracardiac shunting from intrapulmonary shunting, based on the number of cardiac cycles from appearance of contrast bubbles in the right heart to their appearance in the left heart. For example, if an individual has an intra-cardiac shunt due to a patent foramen ovale, contrast bubbles appear in the left heart immediately (< 3 cardiac cycles). However, if contrast bubbles appear in the left heart, after a delay (≥ 3 cardiac cycles), this is diagnostic of IPAVS (3, 21, 25, 34, 58). In these studies, agitated saline contrast echocardiograms were performed at rest and during progressive incremental cycle ergometer exercise to exhaustion. We enrolled 26 healthy active subjects. However, two subjects demonstrated atrial level shunting at rest and a third subject showed evidence of a previously unrecognized pulmonary arteriovenous malformation. These three subjects were excluded from the exercise studies. The remaining 23 healthy individuals (13♂ & 10♀, 23-48 years, mean $\dot{V}O_{2max}$ = 126% predicted) did not have evidence of shunting of contrast bubbles at rest (Figure 2). However, during exercise, ~90% of these subjects demonstrated a delayed appearance (>3 cardiac cycles) of saline contrast in the left heart which is indicative of IPAVS (Figure 2). Intrapulmonary shunting developed at submaximal exercise ($\dot{V}O_{2max}$ = 59±20 (SD)) and, once evident, persisted during all subsequent work rates. However, it appears that these shunts quickly closed following exercise, as no subject had positive contrast echocardiograms three minutes after termination of exercise (Figure 2). Fundamental limitations of this method include undetermined bubble diameter and therefore the inability to quantify shunt fraction or vessel diameter. While deformation of bubbles, and thus transpulmonary passage, is possible, Roelandt found that a perfusion pressure of 300 Torr through a firmly wedged catheter was required to force any bubble contrast through the normal pulmonary circulation (52). This suggests that with normal physiological pressures, it is highly unlikely that bubble contrast would be able to traverse the normal pulmonary circulation in the absence of large diameter intrapulmonary shunts.

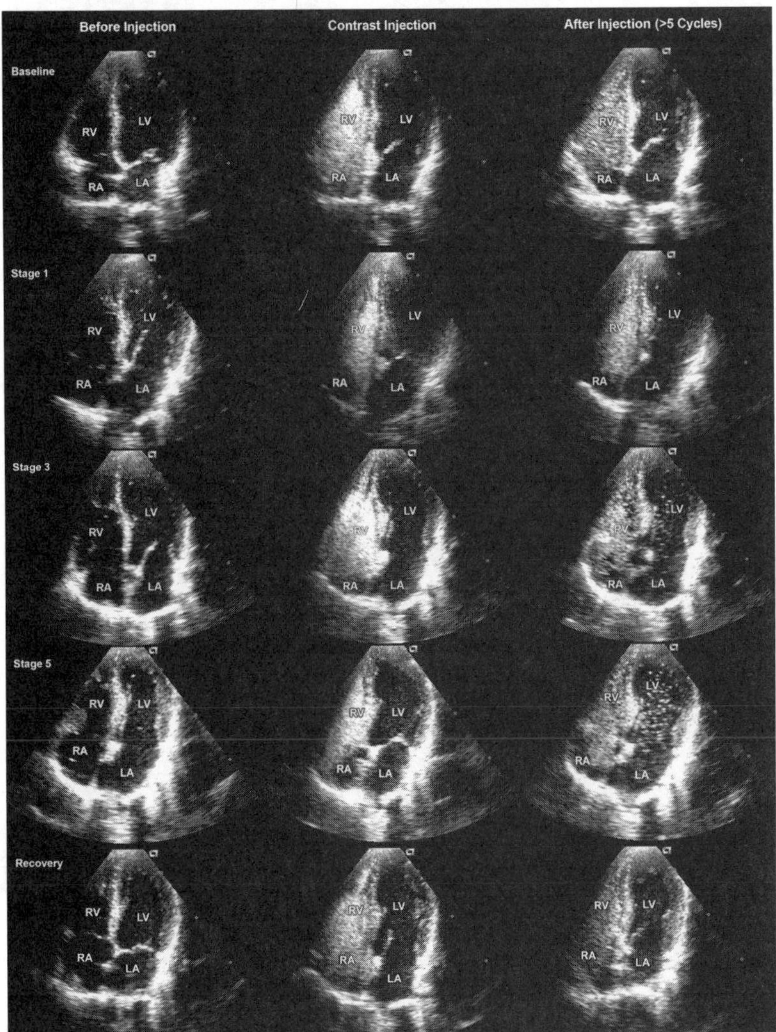

Figure 2. Exercise contrast echocardiograms at rest (Baseline) and 100, 200 and 260 watts (Stages 1, 3 & 5, respectively) in one subject. At rest (Baseline) and 100 watts (Stage 1), there is no evidence of intracardiac or intrapulmonary shunting, since the left heart is free if contrast bubbles. The first evidence of intrapulmonary shunting is seen at 200 watts (85% $\dot{V}O_{2max}$). Note the delayed appearance (>5cycles) of contrast bubbles in the left heart. The same pattern is seen at 260 watts. At three minutes post-exercise (Recovery), there is no evidence of intracardiac or intrapulmonary shunting, since the left heart is free if contrast bubbles. All images are apical 4-chamber views. RA, right atrium; RV, right ventricle; LA, left atrium; LV, left ventricle.

Subsequent to our investigations using contrast echocardiography, we utilized a standard clinical nuclear medicine technique to determine the shunt fraction (36). This technique utilizes Technetium-99m labeled macroaggregated albumin (^{99m}TcMAA) and gamma camera imaging to detect and quantify shunt. This technique is similar to contrast echocardiography in that albumin aggregates larger than the diameter of the capillaries are filtered by the pulmonary microvasculature. Thus, if a large diameter (>20μm) vascular conduit opens up, the MAA particles will escape entrapment and become lodged in sytemic capillaries. This technique is superior to contrast echocardiography because the sizes of macroaggrgates are known - ninety percent of the MAA particles are between 10 and 90μm and the average size is 20 to 40μm with no particles greater than 150μm (6). Briefly, ^{99m}TcMAA was injected intravenously at rest, while standing on the treadmill, or during the last 30 seconds of a 3-minute maximal exercise bout. Rest and exercise studies were performed on different days, separated by at least 48 hrs. Within 5 minutes of injection, subjects underwent quantitative whole body imaging in the supine position. Anterior and posterior whole body images were obtained simultaneously using a dual-head gamma camera with low energy, high-resolution collimation. Shunt fractions were determined from geometric mean counts of anterior and posterior images, using a modified approach of Whyte and associates (74). Figure 3, shows the raw images generated from a male subject at rest and immediately after maximal treadmill exercise ($\dot{V}O_2 = 3.3$ L • min^{-1}). At rest, the majority of the ^{99m}Tc MAA particles are trapped in the lung, however following maximal exercise the increased signal in the leg muscles is indicative of ^{99m}Tc MAA particles passing through the lungs and being trapped in the muscle capillaries. It was determined that in healthy males (n=4), shunt fraction increased from a resting value of 0.46 ± 0.13% (mean ± SD) to 2.17 ± 0.78% at maximal exercise ($P < 0.05$). As noted previously (see above), a 2% shunt could account for all the impairment in pulmonary gas exchange (20) . Using this technique we were able to confirm our previous contrast echocardiography data that intrapulmonary shunts develop during exercise. We cannot rule out the possibility that some smaller particles (<20μm) may be able to traverse the pulmonary circulation via dilated capillaries at maximal exercise. However, in a study by Whyte et al., microspheres with a particle range of 7-25μm were used to investigate intrapulmonary shunting at rest and during submaximal exercise in healthy humans (74). The authors reported a shunt fraction of ~3% at rest rising to ~5% with submaximal (50% $\dot{V}O_{2max}$) exercise. The larger than expected shunt fraction at rest suggests that some of these microspheres could be passing through normal pulmonary capillaries with diameters ranging between 7-10μm (72). However, if the pulmonary capillaries were dilating substantially during exercise, then the calculated shunt fraction would be expected to surpass the reported 5%, suggesting limited pulmonary capillary dilation with submaximal exercise. Thus, despite these limitations, we believe that our findings using ^{99m}Tc MAA and gamma camera imaging provides further evidence for IPAVS during exercise.

Recently a separate laboratory has found that the recruitment of anatomical intrapulmonary shunts during exercise is associated with a widening of the A-aDO_2 (63). In this study by Stickland et al. (63), presence of intrapulmonary shunting was also determined with the agitated saline technique. Arterial blood gases were obtained to calculate A-aDO_2, while a Swan-Ganz catheter was inserted to measure pulmonary vascular pressure and allow for determination of cardiac output by direct Fick. In the upright resting position, A-aDO_2 was low (< 2.0 mmHg) while no subject demonstrated intrapulmonary shunt. With incremental exercise there was a progressive widening of the A-aDO_2 in most subjects, while seven of eight subjects showed evidence of IPAVS during exercise (see Figures 4 and 5). Intrapulmonary shunting of contrast bubbles always occurred when A-aDO_2 exceeded 12 mmHg and cardiac output was greater than 24 L • min^{-1}. In the seven subjects who developed shunt, mean within-subject correlations showed that IPAVS development was related to A-aDO_2 ($r = 0.68$), cardiac output ($r = 0.76$), and mean pulmonary artery pressure ($r = 0.73$). Of note, the subject who did not develop IPAVS had the lowest $\dot{V}O_{2MAX}$, cardiac output and A-aDO_2 during exercise yet very high pulmonary vascular pressures. These results strongly suggest that the IPAVS, as assessed by contrast echocardiography, are related to the exercise-induced impairment in gas exchange.

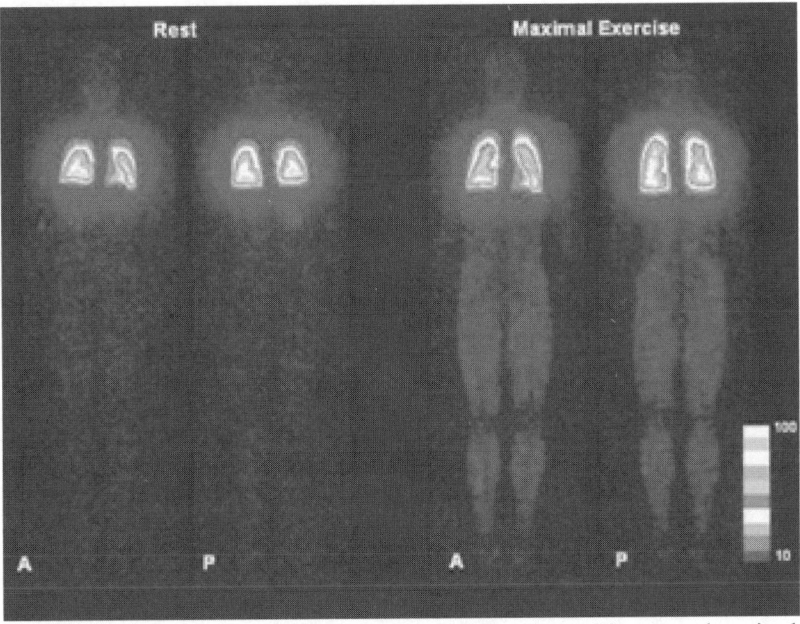

Figure 3. Anterior (A) and posterior (P) planar images obtained for rest and maximal treadmill exercise following injections with Technetium 99m-labeled macroaggregated albumin (^{99m}TcMAA). The increased number of counts in the exercising muscles (legs) indicates the transpulmonary passage of ^{99m}TcMAA. The shunt fraction in this individual at rest was 0.52% which increased to 2.83% at maximal exercise. Color bar represents increasing count intensities with lighter colors.

Next, we examined whether exercise-induced intrapulmonary shunting could be modulated with hypoxia (FiO_2=0.12). It was hypothesized that hypoxia would cause IPAVS at a lower workload than during normoxia because of the increased pulmonary vascular pressures and cardiac output that occur in response to hypoxic exercise (15). In this study, arterial lines were placed in 8 healthy males to examine the relationship between IPAVS and A-aDO_2 during hypoxic and normoxic exercise. No individuals shunted at rest during normoxia, however hypoxia caused shunting to occur at rest in 2/8 individuals. Seven of eight subjects shunted with normoxic exercise whereas all subjects shunted with hypoxic exercise (Figure 6). Unexpectedly, all subjects continued to shunt after the hypoxic exercise bout but only three of the subjects demonstrated intrapulmonary shunting of contrast bubbles after normoxic exercise. Interestingly, one subject did not demonstrate intrapulmonary shunting during normoxic exercise and this subject's A-aDO_2 did not exceed 10 Torr (Figure 6) which is similar to the findings of Stickland et al. (63). See also arrow in Figure 4.

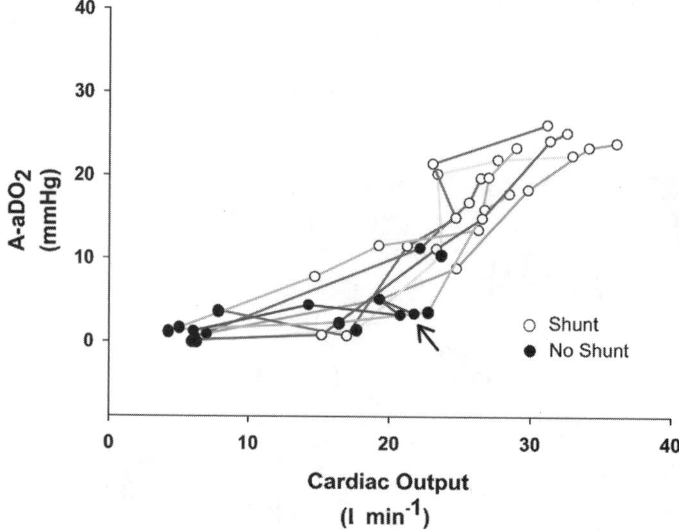

Figure 4. Individual relationships during upright rest and graded exercise between cardiac output and alveolar-arterial PO_2 difference upright at rest and during graded exercise. Note: A-aDO_2: alveolar-arterial PO_2difference.

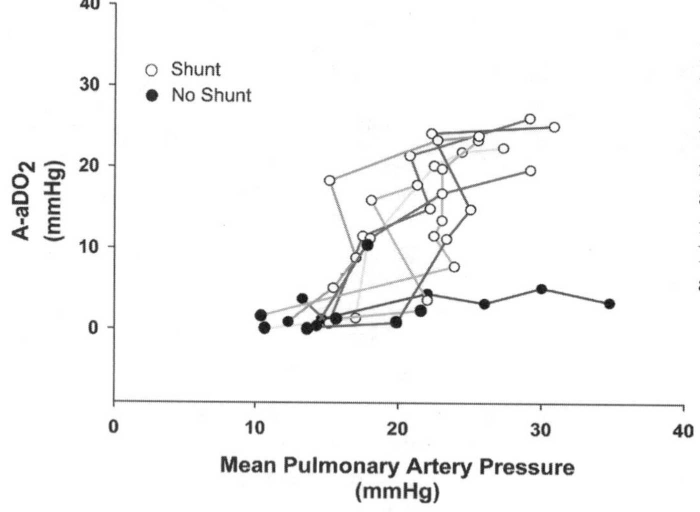

Figure 5. Individual relationships during upright rest and graded exercise between mean pulmonary artery pressure and alveolar-arterial PO_2 difference.

Note: A-aDO_2: alveolar-arterial PO_2 difference.

OTHER CONSEQUENCES OF IPAVS

In addition to the contribution to gas exchange, the recruitment of IPAVS may help to reduce pulmonary vascular pressures and right ventricular afterload during exercise. Indeed Berk *et al.* (4) first suggested that shunts may act as "pop-off valves" in response to increases in flow and pulmonary vascular resistance. The recruitment of these large diameter vessels would contribute to the reduction in pulmonary vascular pressure typically observed during exercise, limiting the driving pressure needed to maintain flow (49, 63). Based on the level of gas exchange impairment and our recent ^{99m}Tc MAA data, the total amount of blood flow shunted would have a small net effect on pulmonary artery pressure. However, MIGET has demonstrated that perfusion becomes increasingly heterogeneous with exercise (23, 44, 55, 65, 68, 70). IPAVS may be of critical importance in regulating microvascular pressures in the heterogeneously perfused lung whereby small local modulations in flow or pressure may prevent pulmonary edema or damage. The IPAVS which developed at a lower intensity during hypoxic exercise may thus serve as a protective mechanism to reduce local vascular pressures. For example, individuals prone to high altitude pulmonary edema (HAPE) appear to have a unique pulmonary vascular response to exercise with an exaggerated pulmonary vascular reactivity, higher pulmonary vascular resistances and greater exercise-induced $\dot{V}_A/\dot{Q}$ mismatch (15, 44). Approximately 10% of the subjects we have studied do not open intrapulmonary shunts during exercise. Are people who do not shunt during hyperdynamic states (e.g., exercise and exercise at altitude) more prone to pulmonary microvascular injury and thus exercise-induced alveolar hemorrhage and/or HAPE? Indeed, local recruitment of intrapulmonary shunts as regional pulmonary vascular pressures and flow increases would help divert the potentially damaging hydraulic energy away from vulnerable alveolar capillaries. It remains to be determined if these IPAVS are beneficial to the pulmonary vasculature or work capacity either under normal conditions, or extreme situations such as severe hypoxia.

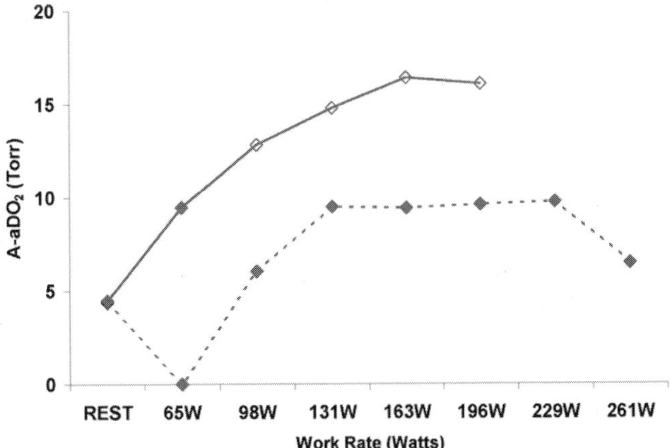

Figure 6. A-aDO$_2$ plotted against work rate in normoxia (red dashed line) and hypoxia (blue solid line). Filled symbol denotes no shunting, open symbol indicates right-to-left intrapulmonary shunting. Note than in normoxia, this subject did not shunt and the A-aDO$_2$ did not exceed 10 Torr. In hypoxia, this subject shunted at a lower workload and shunting inset occurred when the A-aDO$_2$ exceeded 10 Torr.

In addition to gas exchange, the lungs play an important protective role as blood filters. The pulmonary vasculature is generally regarded as very effective in preventing thrombi, platelet aggregates, and various other emboli from entering the systemic arterial circulation, resulting in embolic ischemic injury to the brain and heart. Indeed opening of intrapulmonary arteriovenous shunts during exertion or other hyperdynamic conditions may be important in ischemic stroke and heart disease. Indeed, even after extensive investigation 30-40% of ischemic stroke is considered cryptogenic, that is no clearly identifiable pathogenesis (24, 53). Furthermore, cryptogenic stroke is more common among young people (5, 17, 61, 62) and often associated with exertion (32). Paradoxical embolization has become an increasingly recognized cause of cryptogenic stroke (13) particularly in younger individuals without vascular risk factors (33). Paradoxical embolization occurs when emboli originating in the venous circulation bypass the normal filtering system of the pulmonary capillaries, enter the arterial circulation, and occlude arteries in various organs. Abnormal cardiovascular channels that may increase the risk of paradoxical embolization include patent foramen ovale (PFO), congenital cardiac defects, patent ductus arteriosus, and pulmonary arteriovenous malformations (PAVM). Numerous studies have found that cryptogenic stroke patients have an increased prevalence of PFO compared with patients with stroke of determined origin or normal control subjects (13, 33), and a meta-analysis found this increase to be most significant in younger patients (43). Even after surgical or percutaneous device closure, recurrent strokes occur (27). Reasons for recurrent ischemic events after either surgical or percutaneous PFO closure remain unclear. Thrombus formation at the site of surgical or device closure could serve as the potential embolic source. Furthermore, incomplete closure of a PFO may lead to subsequent paradoxical embolization. The cause for initial or subsequent stroke may not be paradoxical embolization through the PFO. Another potential channel that may increase the risk of paradoxical embolization are the inducible intrapulmonary arteriovenous conduits, we have described in this review. Indeed, these shunts maybe be invisible during standard diagnostic conditions (resting-supine). Understanding the structural and functional regulation of these inducible intrapulmonary conduits may add significantly to our understanding of a wide spectrum of diseases including cryptogenic stroke and ischemic heart disease.

INTRA-CARDIAC SHUNTING

In combination, Eldridge et al. (14) and Stickland et al. (63) observed atrial level right-to-left shunting of saline contrast in otherwise healthy, active subjects. With the original samples of both studies combined, intra-cardiac shunting was either observed at rest or developed with exercise in 9% (3/35) of the subjects. This is below the estimated frequency of intra-cardiac shunts in the general population of 27% (22). Of note, gas-dependent techniques such as MIGET have never detected intra-cardiac shunts at rest and during exercise in healthy subjects (23, 44, 65, 70). A subject with a right to left intra-cardiac shunt would be expected to develop a marked impairment in gas exchange with exercise. The data from subjects with intra-cardiac shunts were excluded from both Eldridge et al. and Stickland et al., however Stickland and colleagues did complete the exercise protocol with their one subject and observed a greater proportional increase in A-aDO_2 in the intra-cardiac shunting subject when compared to the IPAVS subjects (unpublished observation). Pulmonary physiologists and clinicians must be aware of the prevalence of intra-cardiac shunts, particularly when a large A-aDO_2 is observed in an otherwise healthy subject.

FUTURE DIRECTIONS

The recent work using contrast echocardiography and ^{99m}TcMAA, indicates strongly that IPAVS develop in healthy humans during exercise. However, these results raise several pertinent questions. For example, it is not known with certainty whether these microbubbles/albumin aggregates are traveling through distinct inducible anastomoses or dilated pulmonary capillaries. Furthermore, it is not known what effect, if any, lung volume and pulmonary pressures have on intrapulmonary shunting. To address these questions, we have opted to take a reductionist approach using an isolated heart-lung preparation from rats. In these studies, the trachea was cannulated and the lungs were inflated to 15 cm H_2O. The pulmonary artery and the left atrium were cannulated and pulmonary artery pressure was set at 20cm H_2O and left atrial pressure was set to atmospheric pressure. Lungs were perfused with phosphate-buffered saline (PBS) with 10% albumin and 250k-1.5 million fluorescent-labeled microspheres in PBS solution was continuously infused into the arterial inflow line. The entire venous outflow was collected for one minute after infusion and vacuum filtered. The filter was imaged using fluoroscopy and microspheres were counted. Preliminary results have found that a small fraction (<1%) of 10 and 15 μm microspheres, but no 30 μm microspheres, were able to traverse the pulmonary circulation of the rat under zone III conditions (37). These data suggest that some pulmonary microvessels are considerably larger than previously believed (9, 72, 73).

CHALLENGES AHEAD

Pulmonary gas exchange is not perfect at rest and this imperfection is exacerbated by exercise. The possible contributors to the gas exchange inefficiency during exercise include; $\dot{V}A/\dot{Q}$ heterogeneity, diffusion limitation as well as intra- and extrapulmonary shunt. There is long standing evidence for pulmonary anastomoses and we suggest that these vessels may contribute to the exercise-induced impairment in gas exchange. The fact that these anastomoses exist in mammals (including humans) as well as amphibians and birds suggests a common origin. It is possible that these vessels serve no "real" purpose in the adult human and are only remnant vessels from a common evolutionary pathway. Alternately, these vessels may be remnant fetal vessel that allow for blood flow through the lungs that bypass traditional gas exchange units at a time in development when gas exchange is not necessary (75). In either case, these vessels exist, but for undetermined reasons, are not detected by all techniques used to assess gas exchange at rest or during exercise. Future investigations into this area of respiratory physiology should aim to bridge the gap between the non-gas exchange and gas exchange-dependent methodology so that a more complete understanding of the complexities of gas exchange and pulmonary circulation can be determined.

ACKNOWLEDGEMENTS

We gratefully acknowledge Markus Amann for German text translations and Sarah Stickland for graphic design. Financial support from NIH HL-15469-33, A.T. Lovering is supported by T32 HL-07654-16, and M.K. Stickland is supported by the Natural Sciences and Engineering Research Council of Canada.

REFERENCES

1. Aviado DM, Daly MD, Lee CY and Schmidt CF. The contribution of the bronchial circulation to the venous admixture in pulmonary venous blood. *J Physiol* 155: 602-622, 1961.
2. Bachofen H, Hobi HJ and Scherrer M. Alveolar-arterial N_2 gradients at rest and during exercise in healthy men of different ages. *J Appl Physiol* 34: 137-142, 1973.
3. Barzilai B, Waggoner AD, Spessert C, Picus D and Goodenberger D. Two-dimensional contrast echocardiography in the detection and follow-up of congenital pulmonary arteriovenous malformations. *Am J Cardiol* 68: 1507-1510, 1991.
4. Berk JL, Hagen JF, Tong RK and Maly G. The use of dopamine to correct the reduced cardiac output resulting from positive end-expiratory pressure. A two-edged sword. *Crit Care Med* 5: 269, 1977.
5. Bogousslavsky J and Pierre P. Ischemic stroke in patients under age 45. *Neurol Clin* 10: 113-124, 1992.
6. Bracco Diagnostics Inc. Macrotec® Kit for the Preparation of Technetium Tc 99m Albumin Aggregated. 1994. New Jersey, Bracco Diagnostics Inc.
7. Butler BD and Hills BA. The lung as a filter for microbubbles. *J Appl Physiol* 47: 537-543, 1979.
8. Clara M. *Die Arterio-Venösen Anastomosen*. Vienna: Springer-Verlag, 1956.
9. Conhaim RL and Rodenkirch LA. Functional diameters of alveolar microvessels at high lung volume in zone II. *J Appl Physiol* 85: 47-52, 1998.
10. Conhaim RL and Staub NC. Reflection spectrophotometric measurement of O2 uptake in pulmonary arterioles of cats. *J Appl Physiol* 48: 848-856, 1980.
11. Conhaim RL, Watson KE, Heisey DM, Leverson GE and Harms BA. Perfusion heterogeneity in rat lungs assessed from the distribution of 4-microm-diameter latex particles. *J Appl Physiol* 94: 420-428, 2003.
12. Dempsey JA and Wagner PD. Exercise-induced arterial hypoxemia. *J Appl Physiol* 87: 1997-2006, 1999.
13. Di Tullio M, Sacco RL, Gopal A, Mohr JP and Homma S. Patent foramen ovale as a risk factor for cryptogenic stroke. *Ann Intern Med* 117: 461-465, 1992.
14. Eldridge MW, Dempsey JA, Haverkamp HC, Lovering AT and Hokanson JS. Exercise-induced intrapulmonary arteriovenous shunting in healthy humans. *J Appl Physiol* 97: 797-805, 2004.
15. Eldridge MW, Podolsky A, Richardson RS, Johnson DH, Knight DR, Johnson EC, Hopkins SR, Michimata H, Grassi B, Feiner J, Kurdak SS, Bickler PE, Wagner PD and Severinghaus JW. Pulmonary hemodynamic response to exercise in subjects with prior high-altitude pulmonary edema. *J Appl Physiol* 81: 911-921, 1996.
16. Elliott FM and Reid L. Some new facts about the pulmonary artery and its branching pattern. *Clin Radiol* 16: 193-198, 1965.
17. Foulkes MA, Wolf PA, Price TR, Mohr JP and Hier DB. The Stroke Data Bank: design, methods, and baseline characteristics. *Stroke* 19: 547-554, 1988.

18. Freeman ME, Snider GL, Brostoff P, Kimelblot S and Katz LN. Effect of training on response of cardiac output to muscular exercise in athletes. *J Appl Physiol* 8: 37-47, 1955.
19. Fritts HW, Harris P, Chidsey CAI, Clauss RH and Cournand A. Estimation of flow through bronchial-pulmonary vascular anastomoses with use of T-1824 dye. *Circulation* 23: 390-398, 1961.
20. Gledhill N, Frosese AB and Dempsey JA. Ventilation to perfusion distribution during exercise in health. In: Muscular exercise and the lung, edited by Dempsey JA and Reed CE. Madison: University of Wisconsin Press, 1977, p. 325-344.
21. Gudavalli A, Kalaria VG, Chen X and Schwarz KQ. Intrapulmonary arteriovenous shunt: diagnosis by saline contrast bubbles in the pulmonary veins. *J Am Soc Echocardiogr* 15: 1012-1014, 2002.
22. Hagen PT, Scholz DG and Edwards WD. Incidence and size of patent foramen ovale during the first 10 decades of life: an autopsy study of 965 normal hearts. *Mayo Clin Proc* 59: 17-20, 1984.
23. Hammond MD, Gale GE, Kapitan KS, Ries A and Wagner PD. Pulmonary gas exchange in humans during exercise at sea level. *J Appl Physiol* 60: 1590-1598, 1986.
24. Hart RG and Benavente O. Stroke: part I. A clinical update on prevention. *Am Fam Physician* 59: 2475-82, 2485, 1999.
25. Hernandez A, Strauss AW, McKnight R and Hartmann AF, Jr. Diagnosis of pulmonary arteriovenous fistula by contrast echocardiography. *J Pediatr* 93: 258-261, 1978.
26. Hlastala MP. Multiple inert gas elimination technique. *J Appl Physiol* 56: 1-7, 1984.
27. Homma S, Di Tullio MR, Sacco RL, Sciacca RR, Smith C and Mohr JP. Surgical closure of patent foramen ovale in cryptogenic stroke patients. *Stroke* 28: 2376-2381, 1997.
28. Hopkins SR, McKenzie DC, Schoene RB, Glenny RW and Robertson HT. Pulmonary gas exchange during exercise in athletes. I. Ventilation-perfusion mismatch and diffusion limitation. *J Appl Physiol* 77: 912-917, 1994.
29. Jameson AG. Diffusion of gases from alveolus to precapillary arteries. *Science* 139: 826-828, 1963.
30. Jameson AG. Gaseous diffusion from alveoli into pulmonary arteries. *J Appl Physiol* 19: 448-456, 1964.
31. Kitamura K, Jorgensen CR, Gobel FL, Taylor HL and Wang Y. Hemodynamic correlates of myocardial oxygen consumption during upright exercise. *J Appl Physiol* 32: 516-522, 1972.
32. Lamy C, Giannesini C, Zuber M, Arquizan C, Meder JF, Trystram D, Coste J and Mas JL. Clinical and imaging findings in cryptogenic stroke patients with and without patent foramen ovale: the PFO-ASA Study. Atrial Septal Aneurysm. *Stroke* 33: 706-711, 2002.
33. Lechat P, Mas JL, Lascault G, Loron P, Theard M, Klimczac M, Drobinski G, Thomas D and Grosgogeat Y. Prevalence of patent foramen ovale in patients with stroke. *N Engl J Med* 318: 1148-1152, 1988.
34. Lee WL, Graham AF, Pugash RA, Hutchison SJ, Grande P, Hyland RH and Faughnan ME. Contrast echocardiography remains positive after treatment of pulmonary arteriovenous malformations. *Chest* 123: 351-358, 2003.
35. Lenfant C. Measurement of factors impairing gas exchange in man with hyperbaric pressure. *J Appl Physiol* 19: 189-194, 1964.
36. Lovering AT, Haverkamp HC, Hokanson JS, Pegelow DF, Romer LM and Eldridge MW. Quantification of Exercise-Induced Intrapulmonary Shunting in Healthy Humans. In preparation: 2006.
37. Lovering, A. T., Watson, K. E., Conhaim, R. L., and Eldridge, M. W. Transpulmonary passage of 15μm and 30μm polymer microspheres in rat. Program No.368.9.2005 Abstract Viewer/Itinerary Planner. San Diego, CA: Experimental Biology, 2005.Online.

2005.

38. Malvin GM. Gill Structure and Function, Amphibian Larvae. In: Comparative Pulmonary Physiology, edited by Wood SC. New York: Marcel Dekker, INC., 1989, p. 121-151.
39. Meerbaum S. Principles of echo contrast. In: Advances in echo imaging using contrast enhancement, edited by Nanda N and Schlief R. Netherlands: Kluwer, 1993, p. 9-42.
40. Mellemgaard K, Lassen NA and Georg J. Right-to-left shunt in normal man determined by the use of tritium and krypton 85. *J Appl Physiol* 15: 778-782, 1962.
41. Meltzer RS, Klig V and Teichholz LE. Generating precision microbubbles for use as an echocardiographic contrast agent. *J Am Coll Cardiol* 5: 978-982, 1985.
42. Meltzer RS, Tickner EG and Popp RL. Why do the lungs clear ultrasonic contrast? *Ultrasound Med Biol* 6: 263-269, 1980.
43. Overell JR, Bone I and Lees KR. Interatrial septal abnormalities and stroke: a meta-analysis of case-control studies. *Neurology* 55: 1172-1179, 2000.
44. Podolsky A, Eldridge MW, Richardson RS, Knight DR, Johnson EC, Hopkins SR, Johnson DH, Michimata H, Grassi B, Feiner J, Kurdak SS, Bickler PE, Severinghaus JW and Wagner PD. Exercise-induced VA/Q inequality in subjects with prior high-altitude pulmonary edema. *J Appl Physiol* 81: 922-932, 1996.
45. Prinzmetal M, Ornitz ME, Simkin B and Bergman HC. Arterio-venous anastomoses in liver, spleen and lungs. *Am J Physiol* 152: 48-52, 1948.
46. Rahn H, Stroud RC and Tobin CE. Visualization of arterio-venous shunts in by cinefluorography in the lungs of normal dogs. *Proc Soc Exp Biol* 80: 239, 1952.
47. Raisinghani A and DeMaria AN. Physical principles of microbubble ultrasound contrast agents. *Am J Cardiol* 90(suppl): 3J-7J, 2002.
48. Ravin M, Epstein RM and Malm JR. Contribution of thebesian veins to the physiologic shunt in anesthetized man. *J Appl Physiol* 20: 1148-1152, 1965.
49. Reeves JT and Taylor AE. Pulmonary hemodynamics and fluid exchange in the lung during exercise. In: Handbook of Physiology: Section 12: Exercise: Regulation and Integration of Multiple Systems, edited by Rowell LB and Shephard JT. New York: Oxford University Press, 1996, p. 594-595.
50. Reines HD and Civetta JM. The inaccuracy of using 100% oxygen to determine intrapulmonary shunts in spite of PEEP. *Crit Care Med* 7: 301-303, 1979.
51. Rice AJ, Thornton AT, Gore CJ, Scroop GC, Greville HW, Wagner H, Wagner PD and Hopkins SR. Pulmonary gas exchange during exercise in highly trained cyclists with arterial hypoxemia. *J Appl Physiol* 87: 1802-1812, 1999.
52. Roelandt J. Contrast echocardiography. *Ultrasound Med Biol* 8: 471-492, 1982.
53. Sacco RL, Ellenberg JH, Mohr JP, Tatemichi TK, Hier DB, Price TR and Wolf PA. Infarcts of undetermined cause: the NINCDS Stroke Data Bank. *Ann Neurol* 25: 382-390, 1989.
54. Sappey PC. *Traité dánatomie descriptive* . Paris: V.A. Delahaye, 1879.
55. Schaffartzik W, Poole DC, Derion T, Tsukimoto K, Hogan MC, Arcos JP, Bebout DE and Wagner PD. VA/Q distribution during heavy exercise and recovery in humans: implications for pulmonary edema. *J Appl Physiol* 72: 1657-1667, 1992.
56. Schimmel C, Bernard SL, Anderson JC, Polissar NL, Lakshminarayan S and Hlastala MP. Soluble gas exchange in the pulmonary airways of sheep. *J Appl Physiol* 97: 1702-1708, 2004.
57. Shaw AM, Bunton DC, Fisher A, McGrath JC, Montgomery I, Daly C and MacDonald A. V-shaped cushion at the origin of bovine pulmonary supernumerary arteries: structure and putative function. *J Appl Physiol* 87: 2348-2356, 1999.
58. Shub C, Tajik AJ, Seward JB and Dines DE. Detecting intrapulmonary right-to-left shunt with contrast echocardiography. Observations in a patient with diffuse pulmonary arteriovenous fistulas. *Mayo Clin Proc* 51: 81-84, 1976.
59. Sobol BJ, Bottex G, Emirgil C and Gissen H. Gaseous diffusion from alveoli to pulmonary

vessels of considerable size. *Circ Res* 13: 71-79, 1963.

60. Spanner R. Die Drosselklappe der veno-venösen Anastomose und ihre Bedeuteng für den Abkürzungskreislauf im porto-cavalen System des Vogels; zugleich ein Beitrag zur Kenntnis der epitheloiden Zellen. *Ztschr f Anat u Entwklsg* 109: 443-492, 1939.
61. Stern BJ, Kittner S, Sloan M, Meyd C, Buchholz D, Rigamonti D, Woody R, Meyerhoff J, Bell W and Price T. Stroke in the young. (Part I). *Md Med J* 40: 453-462, 1991.
62. Stern BJ, Kittner S, Sloan M, Meyd C, Buchholz D, Rigamonti D, Woody R, Meyerhoff J, Bell W and Price T. Stroke in the young. Part II. *Md Med J* 40: 565-571, 1991.
63. Stickland MK, Welsh RC, Haykowsky MJ, Petersen SR, Anderson WD, Taylor DA, Bouffard M and Jones RL. Intra-pulmonary shunt and pulmonary gas exchange during exercise in humans. *J Physiol* 561: 321-329, 2004.
64. Tobin CE. Arteriovenous shunts in the peripheral pulmonary circulation in the human lung. *Thorax* 21: 197-204, 1966.
65. Torre-Bueno JR, Wagner PD, Saltzman HA, Gale GE and Moon RE. Diffusion limitation in normal humans during exercise at sea level and simulated altitude. *J Appl Physiol* 58: 989-995, 1985.
66. von Hayek H. Über einen Kurzschlusskreislauf (arterio-venöse Anastomosen) in der menschlichen Lunge. *Ztschr f Anat u Entwklsg* 110: 412-422, 1940.
67. von Hayek H. *The Human Lung. Translated from Die Menschliche Lunge by V.E. Krahl.* New York and London: Hafner, 1960.
68. Wagner PD, Gale GE, Moon RE, Torre-Bueno JR, Stolp BW and Saltzman HA. Pulmonary gas exchange in humans exercising at sea level and simulated altitude. *J Appl Physiol* 61: 260-270, 1986.
69. Wagner PD, Gale GE, Moon RE, Torre-Bueno JR, Stolp BW and Saltzman HA. Pulmonary gas exchange in humans exercising at sea level and simulated altitude. *J Appl Physiol* 61: 260-270, 1986.
70. Wagner PD, Laravuso RB, Uhl RR and West JB. Continuous distributions of ventilation-perfusion ratios in normal subjects breathing air and 100 per cent O2. *J Clin Invest* 54: 54-68, 1974.
71. Weibel E. (Blood vessel anastomoses in the human lungs.). *Z Zellforsch Mikrosk Anat* 50: 653-692, 1959.
72. Weibel ER. (Morphometric analysis of the number, volume and surface of the alveoli and capillaries of the human lung). *Z Zellforsch Mikrosk Anat* 57: 648-666, 1962.
73. Weibel ER. Morphometrics of the lung. In: Handbook of Physiology Section 3: Respiration, edited by Fenn WO and Rahn H. Washington, D.C.: American Physiological Society, 1964, p. 285-307.
74. Whyte MK, Peters AM, Hughes JM, Henderson BL, Bellingan GJ, Jackson JE and Chilvers ER. Quantification of right to left shunt at rest and during exercise in patients with pulmonary arteriovenous malformations. *Thorax* 47: 790-796, 1992.
75. Wilkinson MJ and Fagan DG. Postmortem demonstration of intrapulmonary arteriovenous shunting. *Arch Dis Child* 65: 435-437, 1990.

Chapter 5

EXERCISE-INDUCED ARTERIAL HYPOXEMIA: CONSEQUENCES FOR LOCOMOTOR MUSCLE FATIGUE

Lee M. Romer, Jerome A. Dempsey, Andrew Lovering and Marlowe Eldridge

John Rankin Laboratory of Pulmonary Medicine, Departments of Population Health Sciences and Pediatrics, University of Wisconsin – Madison, USA.

Abstract: Reductions in arterial O_2 saturation (-5 to -10 % SaO_2 < rest) occur over time during sustained heavy intensity exercise in a normoxic environment, due primarily to the effects of acid pH and increased temperature on the position of the HbO_2 dissociation curve. We prevented the desaturation via increased F_IO_2 (.23 to .29) and showed that exercise time to exhaustion was increased. We used supramaximal magnetic stimulation (1 – 100 Hz) of the femoral nerve to test for quadriceps fatigue. We used mildly hyperoxic inspirates (F_IO_2 .23 to .29) to prevent O_2 desaturation. We then compared the amount of quadriceps fatigue incurred following cycling exercise at SaO_2 98% vs. 91% with each trial carried out at equal exercise intensities (90% Max) and for equal durations. Preventing the normal exercise-induced O_2 desaturation prevented about one-half the amount of exercise-induced quadriceps fatigue; plasma lactate and effort perception were also reduced. We conclude that the normal exercise-induced O_2 desaturation during heavy intensity endurance exercise contributes significantly to exercise performance limitation in part because of its effect on locomotor muscle fatigue. These effects of EIAH were confirmed in mild environmental hypoxia (FIO_2 .17, SaO_2 88%) which significantly augmented the magnitude of exercise-induced quadriceps fatigue observed in normoxia.

Key Words: quadriceps fatigue, central fatigue, force:frequency

INTRODUCTION

Exercise-induced arterial hypoxemia (EIAH) is defined as a reduction in arterial O_2 saturation (SaO_2) and occurs for a variety of reasons. During short-term incremental exercise in some highly trained subjects arterial PO_2 may fall secondary to an excessively widened alveolar to arterial PO_2 difference and in the absence of significant hyperventilation (1). If this EIAH is prevented (via increased F_IO_2), $\dot{V}O_2$max is increased (5). During constant load, high intensity cycling or running exercise sustained to the point of exhaustion, SaO_2 falls progressively over time due primarily to a time- (and intensity-) dependent metabolic acidosis and rising body temperature, which shifts the O_2 dissociation curve to the right (see Figure 1). In some highly fit subjects (especially during running exercise) a reduced PaO_2 will also contribute to a reduced SaO_2 (11) (see Figure 2). Preventing this desaturation by adding small amounts of hyperoxic inspired gas mixtures (.23 - .30 F_IO_2) induces an increase in exercise time to exhaustion (See Figure 3). Furthermore, if the O_2 desaturation is exacerbated by acutely reducing F_IO2 or ascending to high altitudes, exercise time to exhaustion is further reduced (Figure 3).

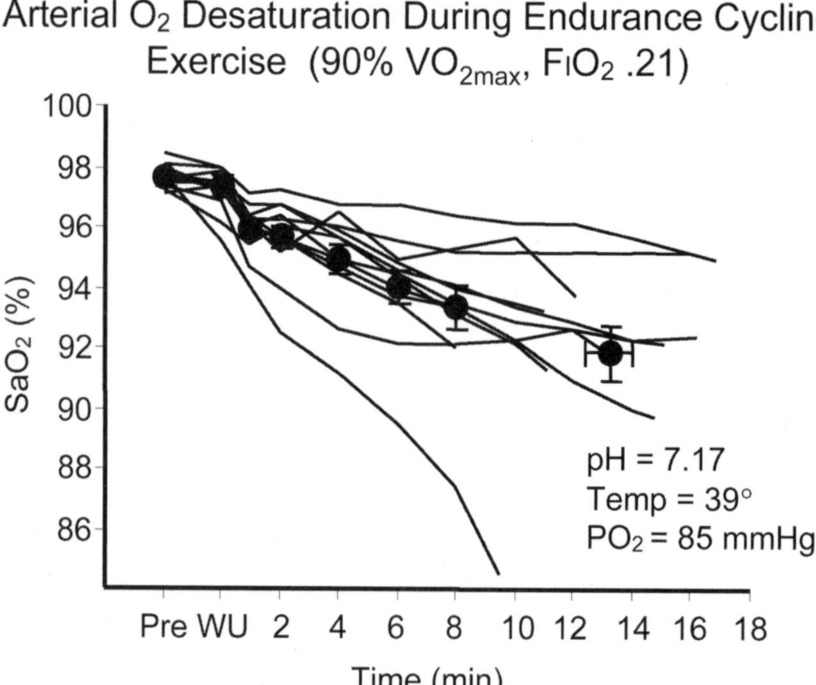

Figure 1. EIAH during heavy intensity, constant load cycling exercise in 11 fit young adult male cyclists. The O_2 desaturation was due primarily to a time-dependant metabolic acidosis (pH ~ 7.17) and rise in temperature (~ + 2°C) as PaO_2 was 80 – 90 mmHg.

HYPOTHESES

We asked the fundamental question, "Why does arterial hypoxemia—either the 6 to 10% reduction in SaO_2 induced by prolonged heavy exercise in a normoxic environment or the more severe O_2 desaturation encountered during prolonged heavy exercise at moderately high altitudes—curtail performance time?" Is this curtailment strictly a result of reduced O_2 transport to working locomotor muscle leading to "peripheral" end-organ fatigue? This peripheral fatigue effect is certainly a reasonable hypothesis given the evidence that hypoxemia will reduce Ca2+ reuptake and release in the sarcoplasmic reticulum, thereby decreasing cross-bridge activation and force output (2); and this effect may occur through a number of mechanisms, including accumulation of lactate and hydrogen ions, inorganic phosphate and/or free radical production (3). Alternatively, the long-held concept of a "central governor" limiting motor recruitment of working muscle such that the function of vital organs is protected may explain exercise limitation in the presence of hypoxemia. Hence, this latter hypothesis would require reflex inhibition of central motor output to locomotor muscles in order to protect against vital organ system failure (7, 8).

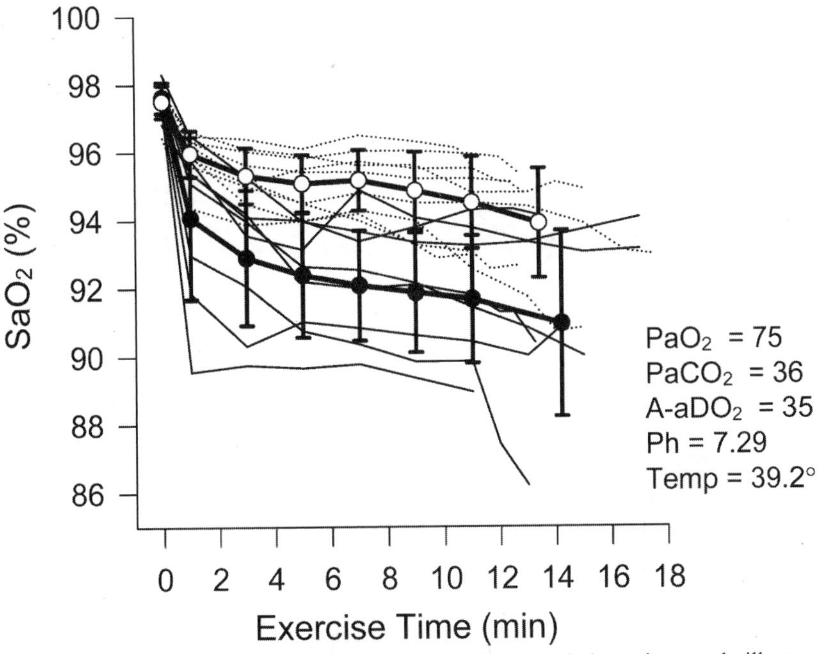

Figure 2. Arterial O_2 saturation during constant load, high intensity treadmill running to exhaustion in 17 fit young women (F_IO_2 .21). Mean values are shown for those with a low PaO_2 (~ 75 mmHg) (closed circles) and those who maintained a high PaO_2 (85 – 90 mmHg) (open circles) throughout. The $PaCO_2$ was higher and the A-aDO_2 wider in the low PaO_2 group. The time-dependant fall in SaO_2 beyond the first two minutes of running was due to the rise in temperature (+2.2°C) and fall in arterial pH (~ 7.25 pH; From Wetter et al. (11)).

Limiting the duration and/or magnitude of cerebral hypoxia may present yet another potential source of central inhibition of locomotor muscle recruitment. A recent study prevented EIAH during maximal rowing exercise and observed an increase in brain oxygenation but no change in muscle oxygenation, thereby implying that changing SaO_2 had little effect on muscle O_2 transport, per se (6). Indeed, the classic studies of John Sutton, Jack Reeves and colleagues in Operation Everest II predicted a major role for non-peripheral factors in limiting exercise performance during the simulated ascent of Everest (4, 9).

General Methods

We used supramaximal magnetic stimulation of the femoral nerve before and after cycling exercise to determine if indeed locomotor muscle fatigue, per se, was induced by changing levels of arterial oxygenation during high intensity exercise in normoxic and in hypoxic environments. This procedure consisted of paired, supra-maximal stimuli delivered over a range of frequencies (1 – 100 Hz), achieved by varying the duration of the inter-stimulus interval. The quadriceps force output in response to supramaximal nerve stimulation was shown to be highly reproducible (coefficient of variation $< \pm 6\%$) both within- and between-days. Evoked potentials in response to nerve stimulation were measured from the quadriceps muscle EMG; their magnitude remained unchanged from baseline to post exercise conditions ensuring that the motor input to the muscle was supramaximal and equal before and after the cycling exercise. Superimposition of a supramaximal twitch on a maximum voluntary quadriceps contraction produced an average 7% increase in force output, i.e., the voluntary effort produced a force that was 93% of truly maximal force output that was 7% of the potentiated twitch value at rest, indicating that subjects did not fully activate their quadriceps via voluntary effort under resting baseline conditions.

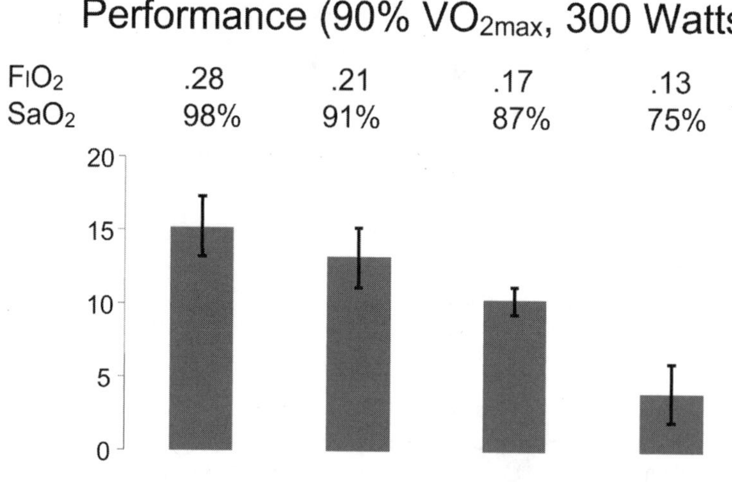

Figure 3. Effects of EIAH on time to exhaustion at a fixed, high intensity work rate. Note in a normoxic environment with an end-exercise arterial O_2 saturation which averaged 91% (see Fig. 2) time to exhaustion was about 13 minutes. Preventing this reduction in SaO_2 (via FIO_2 .23 to .29) allowed the subjects to exercise at least 16% longer, whereas reducing F_IO_2 below normoxic levels caused moderate (at F_IO_2 .17 and 87% SaO_2) and then marked (at .13 F_IO_2 and 75% SaO_2) reductions in exercise time to exhaustion.

EXPERIMENT A. PREVENTING EIAH IN A NORMOXIC ENVIRONMENT

Subjects cycled at a fixed workload at an intensity that averaged 90% of their peak maximal work rate, until they could no longer maintain a target pedaling frequency. Arterial blood was obtained periodically and magnetic stimulation was applied at baseline and at intervals from 2.5 to 70 minutes following exercise. Then the subjects returned and repeated the experiment only with supplemental inspired O_2 (.23 - .29 F_IO_2) added in amounts that were just sufficient to prevent EIAH, i.e., SaO_2 was maintained at resting levels (~98%). On this second day subjects exercised at power outputs and for durations that were identical to those under control (FIO2 .21) conditions. Thus the only difference between the two exercise conditions was the SaO2, i.e., 91% vs. 98%.

The key fatigue findings are summarized in Figure 4. Note that exercise in normoxia, which caused a progressive desaturation to 91% SaO_2 (range = 87 – 93%), resulted in a reduction of force output immediately following exercise at all stimulation frequencies (1 – 100 Hz) that averaged 33% below baseline and returned gradually to baseline levels over 70 minutes of recovery. When the EIAH was prevented and SaO_2 held at resting levels, the reduction in force output was still significant but only about one-half that which occurred under control conditions in the presence of EIAH. Thus, the prevention of EIAH, per se, significantly reduced the amount of quadriceps fatigue induced by the exercise; it also significantly lowered the absolute level and rate of rise of arterial blood lactate concentration over the final half of the exercise, and reduced the rate of rise of effort perception for both limb discomfort and dyspnea. Finally, using the twitch stimulation superimposed on the MVC, we observed that voluntary activation of the quadriceps was reduced from 93% at baseline to 85% following exercise in normoxia; and when desaturation was prevented, voluntary activation following exercise was increased to 90%.

These findings demonstrate that the arterial O_2 desaturation that normally accompanies heavy intensity sustained exercise in a normoxic environment contributes significantly to locomotor muscle fatigue. In turn, we think it reasonable to conclude that the lessening of local muscle fatigue with the prevention of O_2 desaturation contributes to an enhancement of exercise performance. While these data clearly implicate a significant effect of reduced O_2 transport on locomotor muscle fatigue and on exercise performance, they do not rule out an effect of O_2 desaturation on reducing motor output to the locomotor muscles during exercise i.e. "central fatigue." Indeed the finding that exercise significantly reduced voluntary activation of the quadriceps, and that this was largely relieved by preventing O_2 desaturation, indirectly implicates a contribution from "central fatigue" to hypoxemic effects on exercise limitation. A major outstanding problem with interpretation of these tests is whether the change in force output between the voluntary isometric effort and the sum of the voluntary effort plus superimposed twitch, as conducted in the resting subject during recovery, truly represents "central inhibition" of the volitional force produced during the preceding rhythmic exercise task. To date there is no direct evidence—pro or con—of an effect of arterial hypoxemia on reflex inhibition of central motor output to locomotor muscles during exercise. Certainly the reduced rates of rise of effort perceptions during exercise when EIAH was prevented might also have contributed to exercise performance limitation and may be classified as "central" fatigue (or "symptom limited"). However since much of the cause of enhanced effort perceptions in the presence of hypoxemia likely originated from intensified sensory feedback input from fatiguing, acidic muscles, then this type of "central" fatigue is causally linked to "peripheral" fatigue.

Nevertheless, we cannot claim a true cause: effect relationship, because we do not know how these data obtained during supramaximal nerve stimulation in recovery translate precisely into the subject's capability for sustaining a given (likely sub-maximal) power output during the preceding exercise. Indirect evidence of hypoxic effects on peripheral muscle fatigue during heavy intensity exercise is available from Taylor et al. (10) who found increases in integrated quadriceps EMG over time during exercise which were greater in severe hypoxia than in normoxia.

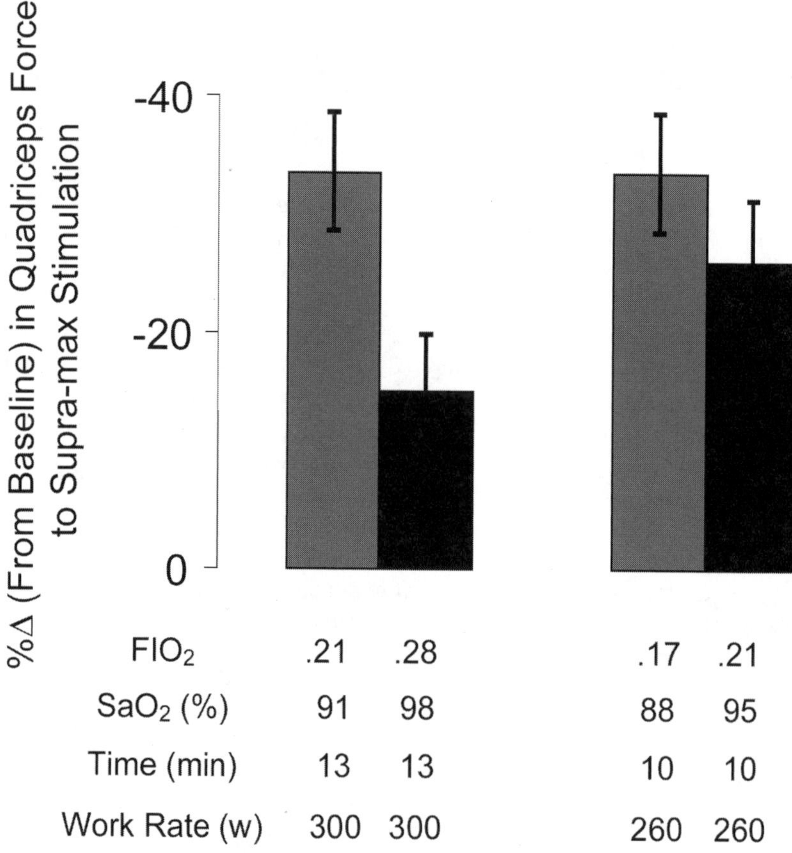

Figure 4. Cycling exercise to exhaustion in normoxia caused a reduction in force output of the quadriceps in response to supramaximal femoral nerve stimulation which averaged one-third below baseline. When the hypoxemia was prevented (.27 F_IO_2) and the exercise carried out for an identical time and work rate as at F_IO_2 .21, quadriceps fatigue was reduced by more than 50%. When EIAH was made greater by mild environmental hypoxia (F_IO_2 .17), quadriceps fatigue was enhanced.

EXPERIMENT B. EFFECT OF HYPOXIC-INDUCED MODERATE HYPOXEMIA

This experiment was conducted in those subjects who experienced minimal O_2 desaturation (~ 95%) during the exercise in normoxia. A similar design was used as in experiment A, in that the effect on quadriceps fatigue was compared following exercise of identical work rates and durations. In these subjects F_IO_2 of .17 reduced the mean exercise SaO_2 to 88% and significantly increased the amount of quadriceps fatigue by 20 – 25% over that observed at F_IO_2 .21 (SaO_2 95%) (see Figure 3). Furthermore the moderate reductions in SaO_2 below 90% increased the rate of rise of blood lactate and effort perceptions during the exercise. So again, as with the prevention of EIAH in a normoxic environment, the further reduced SaO_2 in a mildly hypoxic environment was linked to performance limitation by means of O_2 transport-induced reductions in the force output of the locomotor muscles in response to supramaximal motor nerve stimulation.

We propose that the effect of EIAH on locomotor muscle (peripheral) fatigue mechanisms were due to reductions in O_2 transport to muscle which in turn would reduce muscle capillary and mitochondrial PO_2. Since the exercise in our study required a work rate very close to $\dot{V}O_2max$, preventing the O_2 desaturation also raised mean $\dot{V}O_2$ about 5%, at end-exercise. Thus, subjects were exercising at a slightly lower relative work intensity which would account for at least some of the reduction in lactate production and fatigue.

SUMMARY

The schematic diagram in Figure 5 outlines the various types of contributions to curtailment of performance experienced in mild through moderate hypoxemia. Listed are peripheral muscle fatigue secondary to reduced O_2 transport to muscle and two types of "central" factors, namely conscious effort perception and reflex inhibition, which might limit performance by reducing motor output to the working locomotor muscles. Our results show that at all levels of hypoxemia, its effect on limiting performance time was consistently associated with significant hypoxemic-induced peripheral (i.e. locomotor muscle) fatigue. We especially emphasize that even in a normoxic (i.e. sea-level) environment, the 6 to 10% arterial O_2 desaturation normally produced during heavy intensity, sustained, exercise in healthy subjects is sufficient to significantly exacerbate locomotor muscle fatigue. An additional contribution to exercise limitation occurs from the two types of "central" influences inhibiting motor output to the limb muscles during exercise. One of these "central" factors, i.e. conscious effort perception, is strongly influenced by peripheral muscle fatigue, per se. The other, "reflex" inhibition, has not been measured directly during whole body exercise. A significant contribution from one or more of these "central" influences is likely to be present at all levels of arterial hypoxemia; and they may contribute substantially to exercise limitation in severe levels of hypoxemia.

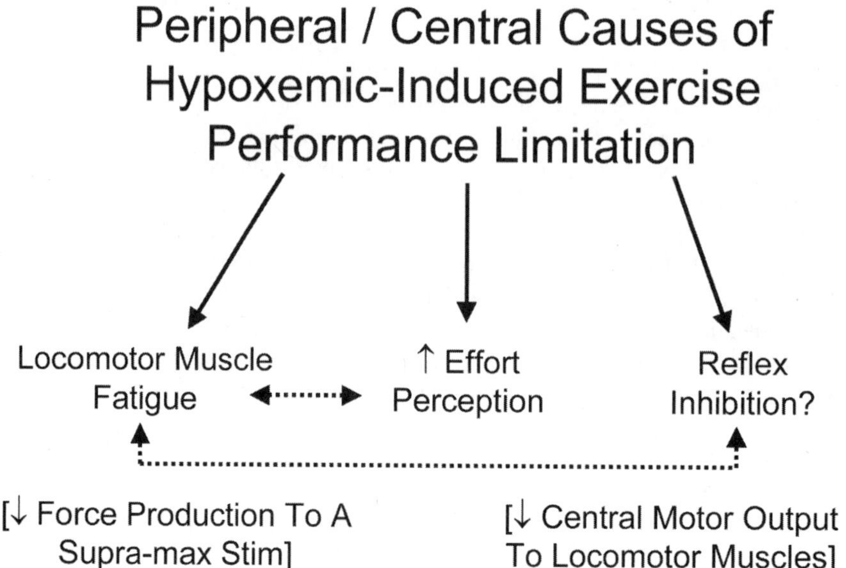

Figure 5. Schematic of the "peripheral" and "central" fatigue influences on limitations to exercise performance caused by exercise-induced arterial hypoxemia. We found peripheral locomotor muscle fatigue to be induced by all levels of arterial hypoxemia studied—including the EIAH which occurs during heavy sustained exercise in normoxia. Indirect evidence also implicates "central" fatigue contributions—especially in severe environmental hypoxia-induced arterial hypoxemia.

ACKNOWLEDGEMENTS

The original research reported in this manuscript was supported by NHLBI and the American Heart Association.

REFERENCES

1. Dempsey JA and Wagner PD. Exercise-induced arterial hypoxemia. *J Appl Physiol* 87: 1997-2006, 1999.
2. Duhamel TA, Green HJ, Sandiford SD, Perco JG, and Ouyang J. Effects of progressive exercise and hypoxia on human muscle sarcoplasmic reticulum function. *J Appl Physiol* 97: 188-196, 2004.
3. Fitts RH. Cellular mechanisms of muscle fatigue. *Physiol Rev* 74: 49-94, 1994.
4. Garner SH, Sutton JR, Burse RL, McComas AJ, Cymerman A, and Houston CS. Operation Everest II: neuromuscular performance under conditions of extreme simulated altitude. *J Appl Physiol* 68: 1167-1172, 1990.
5. Harms CA, McClaran SR, Nickele GA, Pegelow DF, Nelson WB, and Dempsey JA. Effect of exercise-induced arterial O_2 desaturation on $\dot{V}O_2$max in women. *Med Sci Sports*

Exerc 32: 1101-1108, 2000.

6. Nielsen HB, Boushel R, Madsen P, and Secher NH. Cerebral desaturation during exercise reversed by O_2 supplementation. *Am J Physiol* 277: H1045-1052, 1999.
7. Hill AV. Muscular exercise, lactic acid and the supply and utilization of oxygen. Parts VII-VIII *Proc Royal Soc Br* 97: 155-176, 1924
8. Pickar JG, Hill JM, and Kaufman MP. Stimulation of vagal afferents inhibits locomotion in mesencephalic cats. *J Appl Physiol* 74: 103-110, 1993.
9. Sutton JR, Reeves JT, Wagner PD, Groves BM, Cymerman A, Malconian MK, Rock PB, Young PM, Walter SD, and Houston CS. Operation Everest II: oxygen transport during exercise at extreme simulated altitude. *J Appl Physiol* 64: 1309-1321, 1988.
10. Taylor AD, Bronks R, Smith P, and Humphries B. Myoelectric evidence of peripheral muscle fatigue during exercise in severe hypoxia: some references to m. vastus lateralis myosin heavy chain composition. *Eur J Appl Physiol* 75: 151-159, 1997.
11. Wetter TJ, St Croix CM, Pegelow DF, Sonetti DA, and Dempsey JA. Effects of exhaustive endurance exercise on pulmonary gas exchange and airway function in women. *J Appl Physiol* 91: 847-858, 2001.

Chapter 6

MECHANISMS OF SLEEP APNEA AT ALTITUDE

William Whitelaw

Department of Medicine, University of Calgary, Calgary, Alberta, Canada.

Abstract: At altitude normal people often develop periodic breathing in sleep - regularly recurring periods of hyperpnea and apnea. This phenomenon is probably explained by instability of the negative feedback system for controlling ventilation. Such systems can be modeled by sets of differential equations that describe behavior of key components of the system and how they interact. Mathematical models of the breathing control system have increased in complexity and the accuracy with which they simulate human physiology. Recent papers by Zbigniew Topor et al. (5,6) describe a model with two separate feedback loops, one simulating peripheral and the other central chemoreceptor reflexes, as well as accurate representations of blood components, circulatory loops and brain blood flow. This model shows unstable breathing when one chemoreceptor loop has high gain while the other has low gain, but not when both have high gain. It also behaves in counter-intuitive way by becoming more stable when brain blood flow is reduced and unresponsive to blood. gas changes. Insights from such models may bring us closer to understanding high altitude periodic breathing.

Key Words: mathematical modeling, central apnea, unstable control systems, chemoreceptor feedback

INTRODUCTION

Apnea is one feature of "unstable breathing", an engineering term used to describe a pattern of breathing in which tidal volume gradually increases to maximum, then decreases to zero, where it remains during the apnea, then increases again in a recurring periodic pattern. At sea level, such recurrent apneas are typically 'obstructive'. The pharynx falls closed because of relaxation of pharyngeal dilator muscles in sleep. During the apnea, the diaphragm continues to contract but no air flows through the obstructed pharynx. CO_2 gradually rises and PO_2 falls until the chemical stimuli cause sufficient activation of pharyngeal dilator muscles to reopen the pharynx and permit breathing to resume. At altitude, or on exposure to low inspired oxygen, on the other hand, apneas are typically ?central? meaning that when tidal volume falls to zero there is no obstruction and no efforts are made by respiratory muscles during the apnea. (1)

The periodic breathing of altitude can be explained by engineering theories of negative feedback control systems. Such systems are considered unstable if they display a persistent pattern of periodic behavior in response to a disturbance in the controlled output.

A familiar example is the system that controls temperature in a shower. In the showerhead, water from a hot water source and water from a cold water source mix to produce water of a certain temperature. When the water falls on the skin of the person in the shower, temperature receptors signal the temperature to the central nervous system, which compares this temperature with the desired temperature and when necessary emits a command to correct the temperature. If the water temperature is too high, the command is sent through nerves to muscles of the hand and arm which cause the hand to reach out and turn the tap controlling the flow of hot water until the mixture of water coming from the showerhead is at the desired temperature. This is called a negative feedback system because an increase in temperature perceived at the temperature receptors leads to a decrease in the flow of hot water into the showerhead and thus to a corrective decrease in temperature.

The shower control system can be unstable if there is a long pipe between the tap that adjusts the flow of hot water and the showerhead. This causes a delay between the time the tap is adjusted and the time the resulting temperature is perceived at the temperature receptor. If somebody flushes a toilet nearby so that the flow of the cold water into the showerhead goes down and the temperature of the water striking the skin goes up, the subject reaches out and begins turning the tap down to reduce the hot water flowing into the shower. At a certain point the perfect adjustment is reached but the subject does not realize that until the water with the correct temperature has had time to go up the pipe and out the showerhead to the temperature receptors. During this delay, the subject continues to turn the flow of hot water down until the temperature of the water coming out of the showerhead is much too cold. When that cold water reaches the skin the subject reaches out again and winds the tap the other way, but once again overshoots because of the delay in the pipe and allows the temperature to get too hot. It is clear that a system like this could continue to oscillate indefinitely. It is also intuitively clear that oscillations will be more likely to happen and will be bigger when they do occur if the subject has very sensitive skin, because in that case he or she will react much more briskly to small changes in temperature and wind the tap much more quickly round, causing a much bigger overshoot.

The main factors that will make this system unstable are therefore are the *delay* in the pipe and the sensitivity or the *gain* in the feedback loop, that is the amount of change in the flow of water that results from a certain change in temperature at the temperature receptor level.

The feedback control system for arterial P_{CO2} is analogous. Arterial P_{CO2} depends on the balance between flow of $CO_{2:}$ into the lung from venous blood and out of the lung, by means of ventilation. Arterial CO_2 is sensed by chemoreceptors. There is a delay between the change in ventilation and the change in CO_2 at the chemoreceptor. This feedback system can therefore become unstable if the gain in the CO_2 feedback loop is high or if the delay is increased.

This kind of system lends itself to mathematical modeling. Numerous researchers with background in engineering have developed mathematical simulations of the respiratory feedback system. (2,4,5) Increasing sophistication of these models has meant that the various physiological mechanisms that are important to the controller have been described more and more accurately, with numerical constants based on better and better physiological data and an increasing number of adjustable components. The mathematical models become more complex as more variables are introduced, the difficulty of the mathematics increases, and major computational ability is required. An ideal model would accurately simulate all of the important components of the feedback system and would behave exactly like the physiological system it is intended to represent. All models so far have had their limitations. However, the behavior of even a moderately complex feedback system depends on interactions between the variables that are so complex that intuition proves to be a very unreliable guide to understanding how the system works. These models can therefore give us new ideas about mechanisms and how they work. In this paper, I will present some very interesting results from the most recent and most sophisticated model, developed by Zbignew Topor, John Remmers and associates. (5)

The model includes a lung, a central nervous component with brain and CSF, and a peripheral tissue component. These are linked by vascular loops, with each its own delay. The details included are a lung with variable volume, a dead space that varies with tidal volume, and blood with accurate representations of Bohr and Haldane effects, changes with the temperature and bicarbonate and interaction of all these things on oxygen carrying capacity. It has a chemosensor system with both oxygen and CO_2 sensitivity and their interaction. There are two chemoreceptors, one peripheral and one central, with different sensitivities and delays. Brain blood flow and metabolism are variable and depend on oxygen and CO_2. The mathematical model takes the form of multiple differential equations. In this model, any of the descriptive constants can be changed, for example carbon dioxide sensitivity, oxygen sensitivity, cardiac output, cerebral blood flow or inspired oxygen. (5)

One way of testing the model is to determine how it responds to a change in inspired oxygen. Figure 1 shows it behaves if, after five minutes at resting conditions, it is exposed to a sudden drop in expired oxygen, equivalent to having a subject ascend suddenly to high altitude. Arterial oxygen falls and ventilation rises. With this, arterial CO_2 drops rapidly and approaches a constant level of 25. After 50 minutes, the system begins to oscillate and the oscillations increase in amplitude. As shown in the expanded tracing of Figure 2, ventilation eventually oscillates between 20 liters a minute and zero, a pattern of recurrent central sleep apnea.

To test whether the model is stable under any circumstance, a method is to set all of the parameters, allow the system to run at stable ventilation and then perturb it, similar to flushing a toilet in the shower model. The perturbation used by Topor et al (6) was a brief drop in arterial CO_2 the equivalent of a single deep breath. When that is done ventilation immediately begins to oscillate. If the system is stable, the oscillations rapidly die away and steady breathing resumes. If it is unstable, the oscillations increase in size and a long-term pattern of periodic breathing is produced.

The introduction of two chemoreflex feedback loops with different gains and different delays has a surprising effect on behavior of the system. This is shown in Figure 3, a plot of central chemoreceptor sensitivity on the Y-axis and peripheral central chemoreceptor sensitivity on the X-axis. The sensitivity of 1.0 is normal. For this plot, all of the other parameters were set at their normal values. Inspired oxygen is normal for sea level. The model was then run many times with different combinations of central and peripheral chemosensitivity. With each setting it was tested with a disturbance equivalent to a deep breath. The plot shows circumstances when it was stable or unstable. In the central part of the graph, indicated by dark triangles, the system was stable. In the top and right side of the graph, the system was unstable. The conclusion from examining this plot is that chemoreceptor gain at sea level can be increased to more than 3 times normal without making the system unstable if both central and peripheral receptors increase their gain together. This puts the system near the upward and rightward tip of the stable area. The system will oscillate however if central chemosensitivity is high while peripheral chemosensitivity is low, or vice versa.

An explanation for this unexpected interaction of chemo-sensor feedback loops comes from recognizing that the way the signals from the central receptor and peripheral receptor interact depends on their relative delays. The central nervous system hears about a drop of oxygen in arterial blood at the peripheral chemoreceptor much earlier than it hears about the same blood arriving at the central chemoreceptor. Each of these chemoreceptors in periodic breathing is sending out an oscillating signal. Both the signals have the same period (cycle length), but there is a phase difference. At a certain point in the breathing cycle, the central nervous system controller receives a signal from the peripheral chemoreceptor when oxygen partial pressure in the carotid artery is at its peak. At that moment, oxygen partial pressure at the central chemoreceptor may be still in a trough. The two signals are then giving opposite messages and to some extent will cancel each other out. How the signals add depends on both their relative gains and their relative delays. As a special example, if the gains in the two receptors are the same but one is delayed exactly one half of the breathing cycle behind the other, the oscillations in the two signals from chemoreceptors will completely cancel each other out at the central nervous system, giving the brain the impression that blood oxygen or CO_2 tensions are constant through the cycle.

It is of interest that the oscillations predicted by the model in a subject at sea level with high central chemoreceptor gain and low peripheral chemoreceptor gain (point B in Figure 4) have characteristics similar to the Cheyne-Stokes breathing in a period of nearly one minute. On the other hand, a system with a high peripheral chemoreceptor gain and a low central chemoreceptor gain has a much shorter period, around 20 seconds, which is more like altitude periodic breathing.

To apply this model to altitude breathing, it will be necessary to construct plots like Figure 3 for different altitudes by changing the fixed value of inspired oxygen to correspond to some altitude and then testing the system for stability at various combinations of chemoreceptor gains. It can be expected that the zone of stability will shrink with increasing altitude. The original example of central apnea provoked by hypoxia shown in Figure 2 indicates that a normal system should, if the model is correct, be unstable at the (1.0,1.0) point on this graph (normal sensitivity of both central and peripheral chemoreceptors) at high altitude. However, the exact shape of the zone of stability remains to be calculated different altitudes. Matching observations of breathing in sleep at various altitudes with such predictions of the model will be an interesting test of the validity of the model.

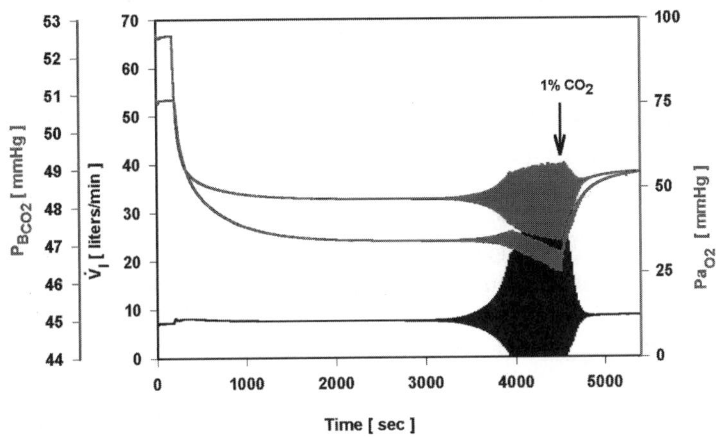

Figure 1. Response of ventilation and arterial oxygen and carbon dioxide to a sudden drop in inspired oxygen tension.

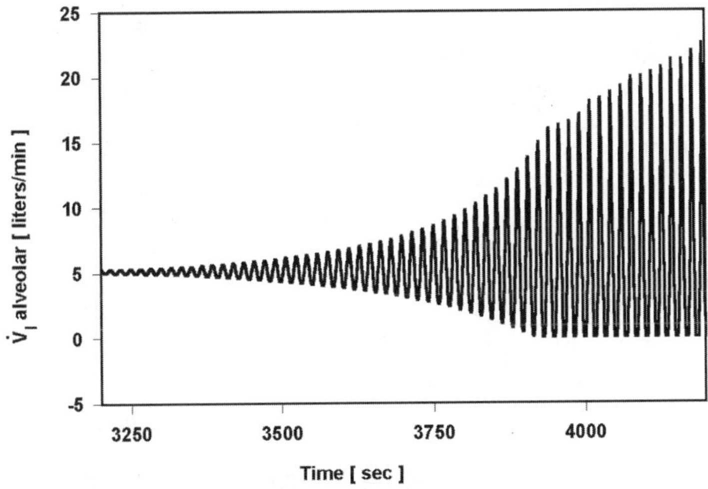

Figure 2. An expanded tracing of the ventilation tracing from Figure 1.

The model also gives hints about effect cerebral blood flow and varying cerebral blood flow on stability of breathing. An increase in cerebral blood flow does two things. It reduces the difference between PCO_2 and arterial blood and PCO_2 at the chemoreceptor itself, which is not in the blood stream but in adjacent tissue. In so doing, an increase in flow reduces the level of CO_2 stimulation at the chemoreceptor. Second, with higher flow, the wash-in and wash-out time for cerebral tissue PCO_2 is faster so that delay is effectively shorter. Cerebral blood flow is known to oscillate during periodic breathing.

When stability plots were done with cerebral blood flow twice normal, the area of stability was decreased. That is, the system was likely to oscillate at lower values of chemoreceptor gains. On the other hand, when cerebral blood flow was reduced to half normal and its ability to react to oxygen and CO_2 was eliminated, (intended to simulate cerebral vascular disease) the system became more stable, with stability independent of peripheral chemoreceptor gain, (but still unstable at very high chemoreceptor gain.)

It is very important to emphasize that mathematical models are never complete or perfectly accurate. One cannot draw conclusions with any certainty. However, they do show that even relatively straightforward additions to the system such as two chemoreceptor loops can produce surprising behavior that would be hard to predict by intuition.

The model of Topor et al. lacks a number of elements that are thought to be of possible importance in control of breathing and in generation of periodic breathing. A partial list of missing elements is: 1. After-discharge or post stimulus potentiation. This is a tendency of the mammalian respiratory control system, after a sudden change in chemical stimulus, to continue breathing the way it had been breathing. For example, a sudden drop in CO_2 is followed by a relatively slow decline in ventilation to the new value. 2. As carbon dioxide is lowered, breathing eventually stops at the apnea threshold. When the CO_2 is increased again, however, apnea does not resume at the same threshold level but at a somewhat higher one. This hysteresis in the apneic threshold would intuitively be expected to make the system les stable (3). 3. There are other feedback loops, in particular mechanical feedback, in which simple expansion and contraction of the thorax with breathing has an inhibitory effect on the respiratory control centers. 4. The mechanics of the thoracic pump are not taken into account. In particular, the upper airway constitutes a resistance to breathing. It is a variable resistance depending on tone of upper airway dilator muscles. A controller that increases upper airway dilator tone at the same time that it increases diaphragm contraction will have a higher gain than a system that always has the same upper airway resistance. Investigating these possibilities with mathematical models may soon give us a clearer idea of the interaction of all the variables and possibly some new and unexpected concepts.

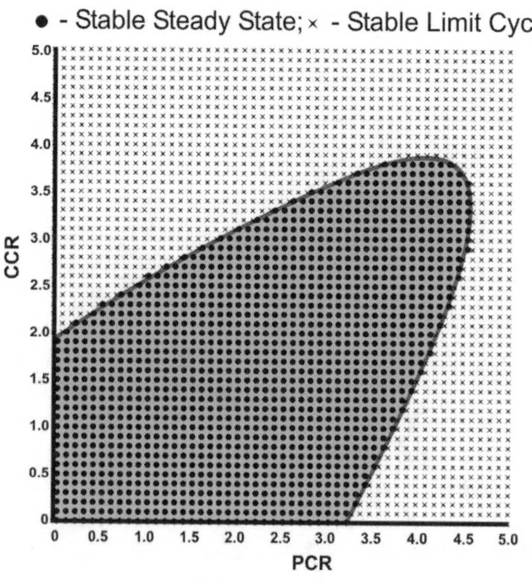

Figure 3. Conditions of central and peripheral chemoreceptor gain for which the model of the respiratory system is stable or unstable.

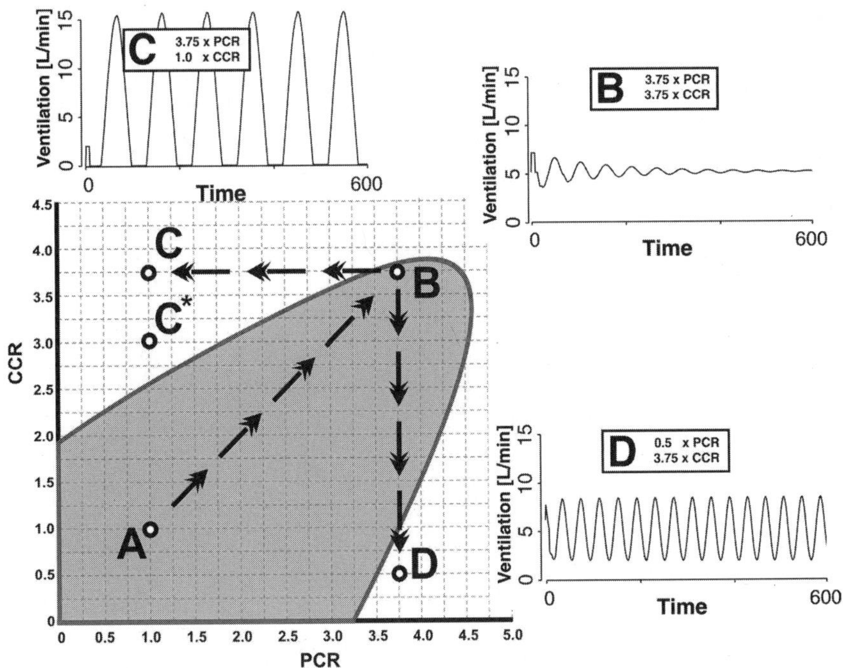

Figure 4. Same as Figure 3 showing examples of oscillations in ventilation for two points in the zone of instability.

REFERENCES

1. Berssenbrugge A, Dempsey J, Iber C, Skatrud J, and Wilson P. Mechanisms of hypoxia-induced periodic breathing during sleep in humans. *J. Physiol.* 343:507-524, 1983
2. Cherniack NS, and Longobardo GS. Cheyne-Stokes breathing ? an instability in physiological control. *N. Engl. J. Med.* 288:952-957, 1973
3. Dempsey JA. Crossing the apnoeic threshold: causes and consequences. *Exp. Physiol.* 90.1:13-24, 2004
4. Khoo MCK, Anholm JD, Ko S-W, Downey lll R, Powles PAC, Sutton JR, and Houston CS. Dynamics of periodic breathing and arousal during sleep at extreme altitude. *Respir Physiol.* 103:33-43,
5. Topor ZL, Pawlicki M, and Remmers JE. A computational model of the human respiratory control system: responses to hypoxia and hypercapnia. *Annals of Biomedical Engineering* 32(11):1530-1545, 2004
6. Topor ZL, Vasilakos K, and Remmers JE. Interaction of two chemoreflex loops in determining ventilatory stability. *Nonlinear Studies* 11(3):527-541, 2004

Chapter 7

CONTROL OF CEREBRAL BLOOD FLOW DURING SLEEP AND THE EFFECTS OF HYPOXIA

Douglas R. Corfield[1, 2] and Guy E. Meadows[2, 3]
[1]*Institute of Science and Technology in Medicine, School of Life Sciences, Keele University, Keele, UK.* [2]*Clinical and Academic Unit of Sleep and Breathing, National Heart and Lung Institute, Imperial College, London,* [3]*Sleep and Ventilation Unit, Royal Brompton Hospital, Sydney Street, London, UK.*

Abstract: During wakefulness, cerebral blood flow (CBF) is closely coupled to regional cerebral metabolism; however CBF is also strongly modulated by breathing, increasing in response to both hypercapnia and hypoxia. During stage III/IV non-rapid eye (NREM) sleep, cerebral metabolism and CBF decrease whilst the partial pressure of arterial CO_2 increases due to a reduction in alveolar ventilation. The reduction in CBF during NREM sleep therefore occurs despite a relative state of hypercapnia. We have used transcranial Doppler ultrasound to determine middle cerebral artery velocity, as an index of CBF, and have determined that NREM sleep is associated with a reduction in the cerebrovascular response to hypercapnia. This reduction in reactivity would, at least in part, allow the observed reductions in CBF in this state. Similarly, we have observed that the CBF response to hypoxia is absent during stage III/IV NREM sleep. Nocturnal hypoxia and hypercapnia are major pathogenic factor associated with cardio-respiratory diseases. These marked changes in cerebrovascular control that occur during sleep suggest that the cerebral circulation may be particularly vulnerable to cardio-respiratory insults during this period.

Key Words: transcranial Doppler ultrasound, middle cerebral artery velocity, cerebral perfusion, hypoxia, hypercapnia

INTRODUCTION

Sleep is a reversible state of reduced responsiveness to the external environment. As sleep is widely observed within the animal kingdom, it is likely that the processes occurring during this state are of functional importance and have a significant survival advantages. In spite of this, the actual function of sleep remains speculative; many theories have been proposed including energy conservation (3), thermoregulation (25), neuronal plasticity (19), and memory processing (37). It is now widely accepted that the brain, and its cellular function, is most affected by the sleep process (24).

The brain produces energy by the metabolism of oxidisable substrates; however, as the brain contains no endogenous stores of energy, it is dependent upon cerebral blood flow (CBF) for constant replenishment of oxygen and glucose and the removal of waste. Therefore, CBF is tightly regulated to meet the brain's metabolic demands. In addition, CBF must respond to alterations in the blood gas status of the blood and must safeguard the brain from fluctuations in systemic arterial pressure. When cerebral perfusion falls below a level where homeostasis can compensate, cerebral ischemia and infarction may result (6). Sleep is a state in which disturbances in cardiovascular and respiratory regulation can be particularly evident, for example in sleep-disordered breathing. Such disturbances may particularly affect cerebral perfusion and it is therefore of importance to understand the regulation of CBF during sleep. The purpose of this review is to highlight findings from some of our recent studies to investigate CBF regulation in humans, in particular its regulation during non rapid eye movement (NREM) sleep.

CBF RESPONSE TO HYPERCAPNIA DURING SLEEP

A number of studies have determined CBF during stable stage III/IV, NREM sleep in healthy humans. The predominant observation is that CBF is reduced in this state compared with wakefulness (9, 13, 20, 23, 34, 40). This reduction is believed to be linked to a decrease in the metabolic demand of brain tissue in that state (23) however this link has not been directly tested.

Carbon dioxide is a potent cerebral vasodilator and, in humans during wakefulness, CBF is very sensitive to changes in arterial PCO_2, with cerebral vascular reactivity to hypercapnia ranging from about 3.5 to 5 % increase in CBF per mmHg increase in arterial CO_2, over the normal physiological range (11, 15, 29). With sleep, ventilation is reduced and arterial PCO_2 is increased. The reported reduction in CBF during stage III/IV, NREM sleep therefore occurs despite a relative state of hypercapnia (Fig 1). This reduction would not be predicted from the wakefulness effects of CO_2 and could at least in part, be explained by a reduction in the cerebral vascular reactivity to CO_2 during sleep. Our laboratory has investigated the effects of stable stage III/IV, NREM sleep on the CBF response to CO_2 using transcranial Doppler ultrasound to determine middle cerebral artery velocity as an index of CBF (26). We determined that, in normal human subjects, hypercapnic cerebral vascular reactivity is reduced by 70% compared to wakefulness (Fig 2). This marked reduction in cerebral vascular reactivity during sleep indicates that the regulation of CBF is significantly altered compared with wakefulness. The functional advantage of such a reduction in the sleep-related cerebral vascular reactivity is not immediately apparent and, as the cerebral vascular reactivity reflects the cerebral circulation's ability to adapt to the metabolic requests of the brain, any reduction could be perceived to increase the risk of cerebral ischemia and stroke.

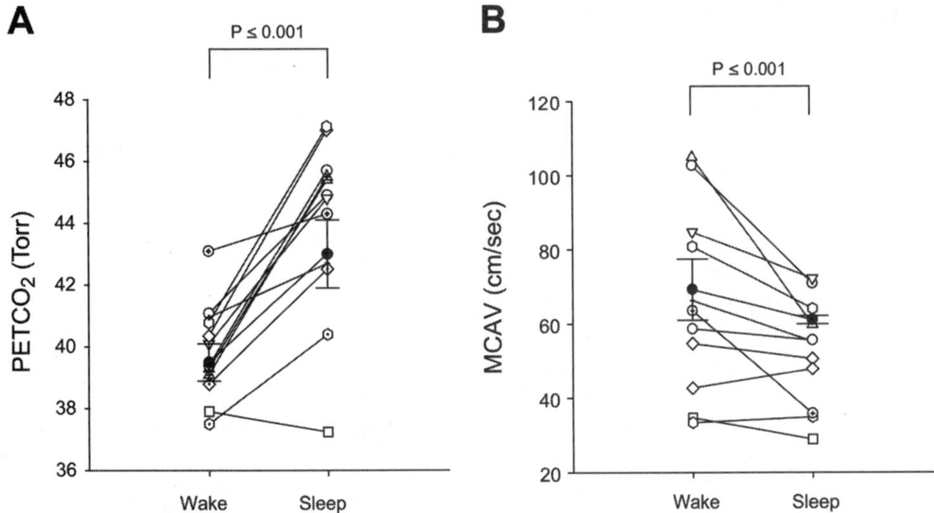

Figure 1. Sleep-related changes in PCO_2 and cerebral perfusion. (a) End tidal PCO_2 ($PETCO_2$) and (b) middle cerebral artery velocity (MCAV) during wake and stages III/IV NREM sleep. $PETCO_2$ was significantly greater, and MCAV significantly less, during sleep compared to wake. Open symbols: individual values; Solid symbols: group mean values (+/- sem). Reproduced, with permission, from (26).

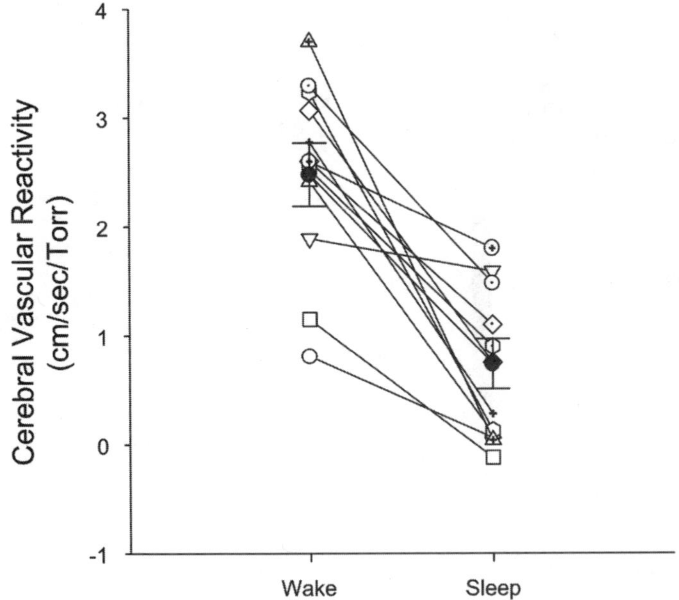

Figure 2. Changes in cerebral vascular reactivity from wake to sleep. The cerebral vascular reactivity to CO_2 from wake to NREM sleep is reduced in each individual. Open symbols: individual values; solid symbols: group mean values (+/- sem). Reproduced, with permission, from (26).

CBF RESPONSE TO HYPOXIA

Hypoxia has a well recognized vasodilator effect on the cerebral circulation (1, 7, 15). Although hypoxia is not present during wakefulness or sleep in healthy individuals, except at altitude, nocturnal hypoxia is a major pathological factor associated with cardiorespiratory diseases including obstructive sleep apnea (OSA) and congestive heart failure. Recently OSA, a condition in which cognitive function can be substantially impaired, has been associated with pathological loss of cortical grey matter (22, 28) suggesting that the nocturnal hypoxia associated with OSA may be sufficient to damage brain tissue directly.

During any hypoxic insult, protection of the brain will depend on an adequate cerebral vascular response. Normally, perfusion of the brain is dependent on a tight coupling between its oxygen supply and the metabolic demand (38). During wakefulness, a decrease in oxygen supply results in a decrease in cerebral vascular tone and a consequent increase in CBF that will mitigate the effects of the systemic hypoxia. We recently investigated the effects of isocapnic hypoxia on CBF (27). As expected CBF increased in response to hypoxia during wakefulness; in contrast, during NREM sleep, the CBF response to hypoxia was absent (Fig 3). This data is further evidence that the regulation of CBF during sleep is significantly altered compared with the waking state. As the brain is particularly sensitive to the effects of hypoxia, the inability of the cerebral vasculature to respond to hypoxic stress during sleep suggests a significant vulnerability of the brain in this state.

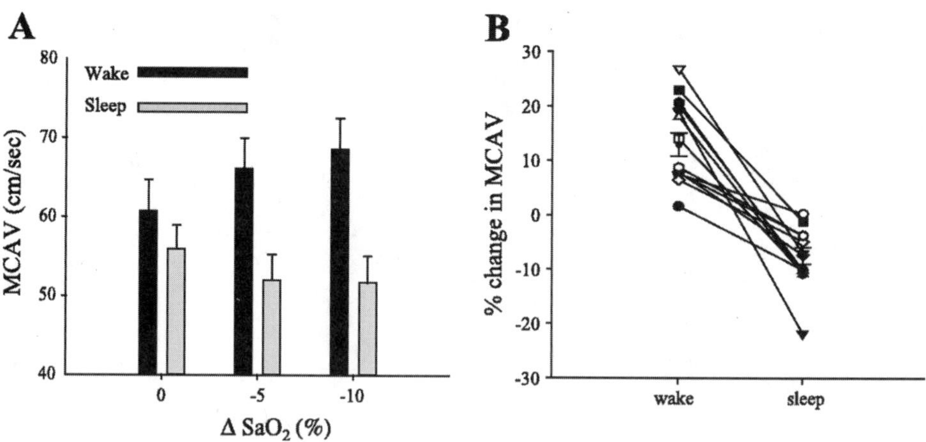

Figure 3. Reductions in cerebral vascular response to hypoxia during Stage III/IV NREM sleep. (a) Middle Cerebral Artery Velocity (MCAV) during baseline isocapnic euoxia, -5% and -10% SaO_2 (isocapnic hypoxia) during wakefulness (black bars) and sleep (grey bars; mean ± sem, n = 13). (b) Percentage changes (from baseline isocapnic euoxia to isocapnic hypoxia; -10% SaO_2) in MCAV (cm/sec) during wakefulness and sleep for each individual and for the group mean (filled circle with sem bars). Reproduced, with permission, from (27).

POTENTIAL MECHANISMS UNDERLYING CHANGES IN CEREBROVASCULAR REACTIVITY DURING SLEEP.

The mechanisms underlying the CBF response to hypercapnia and hypoxia during wakefulness remain to be elucidated; several vasoactive endothelial mediators have been proposed including prostanoids, nitric oxide, adenosine, and ATP sensitive potassium channels (4, 12, 30, 33, 35, 42, 43). Whether sleep exerts a direct effect on the production and activity of these mediators is unknown. Evidence does exist to suggest that nitric oxide is under circadian regulation, with changes during sleep that are consistent with our observed reductions in cerebrovascular reactivity (10).

During wakefulness and under physiological conditions the involvement of the central nervous system in the regulation of cerebral circulation, is controversial (14, 21). Despite this, the onset of sleep is associated with an overall reduction in neural activity that might modulate cerebral perfusion. In addition, central catecholaminergic and cholinergic systems located within the brainstem have been shown to modulate changes in cerebral vascular reactivity to CO_2. For example, cerebral vascular reactivity to CO_2 is reported to be lower following the destruction of the locus ceruleus and the ascending reticular activating system (2, 39). As these brainstem areas are intimately involved in sleep/wake functions, it is possible that changes in sleep state acting via these areas could modulate the changes in cerebral vascular reactivity.

CBF AT SLEEP ONSET

Less consistent changes in CBF have been reported during sleep onset and light sleep, than during stage III/IV sleep. One study reported that CBF was maintained at the same level during stage I sleep as wakefulness and then decreased progressively from stage II to IV NREM sleep (13). Others have reported transient increases in CBF during stage II sleep (20). A study using positron emission tomography determined regional CBF changes during stage I sleep and demonstrated relative flow increases in the occipital lobes (17). These observations suggest that the regulation of CBF during sleep onset may differ from that of established sleep; however none of these studies related the changes in CBF to the rapid changes in cortical activity that occur during this period.

Sleep onset can be considered to begin with the first occurrence of slowing of the EEG, the appearance of relatively low voltage mixed frequency EEG containing a predominance of theta activity and the absence of rapid eye movements. Sleep onset ends at the beginning of stable stage II sleep (32). During this phase the EEG contains spontaneous fluctuations in alpha and theta rhythms, including alpha-theta transitions, and theta-alpha transitions, which can be considered as transitions from wakefulness to sleep and spontaneous awakening respectively (5, 8, 41). These fluctuations in cortical state that occur during this phase are associated with marked changes in cardio-respiratory control. In particular, ventilation decreases with the alpha-theta transition and increases with the theta-alpha transition (5, 8, 41). With this context, we hypothesized that changes in blood flow would be related to changes in cortical activity, specifically, that CBF would decrease at the alpha-theta transition and increase at the theta-alpha transition (18). Contrary to our expectation, CBF increased with the alpha-theta transition (transition to sleep; Fig. 4a), coincident with a reduction in ventilation and blood pressure. Conversely with the theta-alpha transition (spontaneous awakening) CBF decreased (Fig 4b), coincident with an increase in ventilation and blood pressure, the change in CBF being more abrupt than the change with the alpha-theta transition. The increase in CBF following the alpha-theta transition might be secondary to the increase in $P_{ET}CO_2$ associated with the reduction in ventilation. However, our observations are not consistent with this interpretation. First, the CBF increase was rapid compared with the slow rise in $P_{ET}CO_2$. In addition, the relative changes in MCAV to $P_{ET}CO_2$ at the alpha-theta transition is much higher that that predicted by the hypercapnic cerebral vascular reactivity during either wakefulness or stage III-IV NREM sleep (26). Similarly the increase in MCAV following the theta-alpha transition cannot be attributed to the fall in $P_{ET}CO_2$.

The increase in CBF following the alpha-theta transition occurred despite a fall in arterial blood pressure and the decrease in CBF following the theta-alpha transition occurred despite a rise in blood pressure. Thus, it appears that the alpha-theta transition is directly associated with cerebral vasodilatation and the theta-alpha transition with cerebral vasoconstriction. As these changes in cerebral vascular tone cannot be due to the indirect effect of cardiovascular or respiratory factors, they may be directly related to changes in cortical state reflected in the changes in alpha and theta rhythms. The mechanism for such fluctuations in cerebral vascular tone during sleep onset period is not known. However, these observations suggest that the changes in CBF during sleep onset are regulated by different mechanisms from those that regulate long-term reduction in CBF associated with stable NREM sleep.

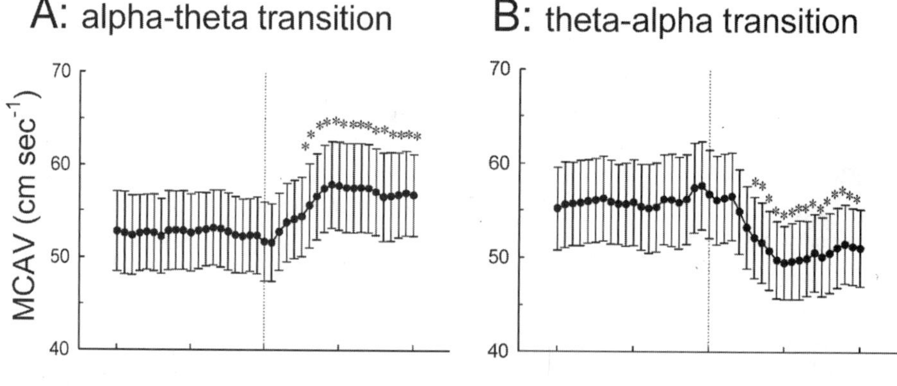

Figure 4. Middle cerebral artery velocity (MCAV) changes during sleep-wake transition; A: increase in MCAV following the alpha-theta transition, B: decrease in MCAV following the theta-alpha transition (mean ± sem; n=10; *p<0.01 compared with the pre-transition baseline. Data from (18).

CLINICAL IMPLICATIONS

Nocturnal hypoxia and hypercapnia are characteristics of cardio-respiratory diseases such as OSA and congestive heart failure. So far, our laboratory has demonstrated that cerebral vascular responses to hypercapnia and isocapnic hypoxia are drastically reduced or even abolished in healthy subjects during NREM sleep. Failure of the cerebral circulation to respond to hypoxia and hypercapnia would result in hypo-perfusion of the brain leading to impaired neural function and increased risk of cerebral ischemia and stroke (31), a condition with an increased frequency during the early hours of the morning. Such sleep related reductions in cerebral vascular reactivity may be partly responsible for the pathological loss of grey matter and cognitive dysfunction reported within OSA (22, 28) and congestive heart failure (44).

During sleep onset, the spontaneous fluctuations in alpha and theta rhythm are related to instability in breathing in normal subjects (16, 36) as well as patients with sleep disordered breathing. Whilst the increase in CBF may be interpreted as a benefit, to maintain an adequate perfusion against acute hypoxia, hypercapnia and systemic hypotension at the transition from wake to sleep, the increase in CBF may cause a reduction in extracellular carbon dioxide concentration in the brain, resulting in a decrease in central chemoreceptor stimulation, which may promote breathing instability and central apnoea. Conversely, the reduction in CBF during a spontaneous arousal during the sleep onset period, may increase chemo-stimulation, and produce an excessive increase in ventilation and breathing instability.

CONCLUSION

In conclusion, our studies indicate that the compensatory increases in CBF, in response to hypercapnia and hypoxia, are reduced or abolished in healthy humans during stable stage III/IV, NREM sleep compared to wakefulness. These findings suggest a major state-dependent vulnerability associated with the control of the cerebral circulation. The inability of the cerebral circulation to respond to the metabolic demands of the brain could therefore be linked to an increased risk of cerebral ischemia and stroke during this time.

The marked changes in CBF during the period of sleep onset could, in part, explain the relative breathing instability reported during this period. In addition, assuming that the cardio-respiratory response at the theta-alpha transition during sleep onset is similar to the arousal from stage II, slow-wave (stages III/IV) or REM sleep, these reductions in CBF with arousal would indicate a significant inability of the cerebral vascular circulation to respond to the cardio-respiratory changes induced by conditions such as sleep-disordered breathing.

REFERENCES

1. Ainslie PN and Poulin MJ. Ventilatory, cerebrovascular, and cardiovascular interactions in acute hypoxia: regulation by carbon dioxide. *J Appl Physiol* 97: 149-159, 2004.
2. Bates D, Weinshilboum RM, Campbell RJ, and Sundt TMJ. The effects of lesions in the locus ceruleus on the physiological responses of the cerebral blood vessels in cats. *Brain Res* 136: 431-443., 1977.
3. Berger RJ and Phillips NH. Energy conservation and sleep. *Behav Brain Res* 69: 65-73,

1995.

4. Brian J. Carbon dioxide and the cerebral circulation. *Anesthesiology* 88: 1365-1386, 1998.
5. Burgess HJ, Kleiman J, and Trinder J. Cardiac activity during sleep onset. *Psychophysiology* 36: 298-306, 1999.
6. Choi DW. Cerebral hypoxia: some new approaches and unanswered questions. *J Neurosci* 10: 2493-2501, 1990.
7. Cohen PJ, Alexander SC, Smith TC, Reivich M, and Wollman H. Effects of hypoxia and normocarbia on cerebral blood flow and metabolism in conscious man. *J Appl Physiol* 23: 183-189, 1967.
8. Colrain IM, Trinder J, Fraser G, and Wilson GV. Ventilation during sleep onset. *J Appl Physiol* 63: 2067-2074, 1987.
9. Droste DW, Berger W, Schuler E, and Krauss JK. Middle cerebral artery blood flow velocity in healthy persons during wakefulness and sleep: a transcranial doppler study. *Sleep* 16: 603-609, 1993.
10. Elherik K, Khan F, McLaren M, Kennedy G, and Belch JJ. Circadian variation in vascular tone and endothelial cell function in normal males. *Clin Sci (Lond)* 102: 547-552, 2002.
11. Ellingsen I, Hauge A, Nicolaysen G, Thoresen M, and Walloe L. Changes in human cerebral blood flow due to step changes in PAO2 and PACO2. *Acta Physiol Scand* 129: 157-163, 1987.
12. Faraci FM and Heistad DD. Regulation of the cerebral circulation: role of endothelium and potassium channels. *Physiol Rev* 78: 53-97, 1998.
13. Hajak G, Klingelhofer J, Schulz-Varszegi M, Matzander G, Sander D, Conrad B, and Ruther E. Relationship between cerebral blood flow velocities and cerebral electrical activity in sleep. *Sleep* 17: 11-19, 1994.
14. Jordan J, Shannon JR, Diedrich A, Black B, Costa F, Robertson D, and Biaggioni I. Interaction of carbon dioxide and sympathetic nervous system activity in the regulation of cerebral perfusion in humans. *Hypertension* 36: 383-388, 2000.
15. Kety SS and Schmidt CF. The effects of altered arterial tension of carbon dioxide and oxygen in cerebral blood flow and cerebral oxygen consumption of normal men. *J Clin Invest* 27: 484-492, 1948.
16. Khoo MC, Gottschalk A, and Pack AI. Sleep-induced periodic breathing and apnea: a theoretical study. *J Appl Physiol* 70: 2014-2024, 1991.
17. Kjaer TW, Law I, Wiltschiotz G, Paulson OB, and Madsen PL. Regional cerebral blood flow during light sleep--a $H_2^{15}O$-PET study. *J Sleep Res* 11: 201-207, 2002.
18. Kotajima F, Meadows GE, Morrell MJ, and Corfield DR. Cerebral blood flow changes associated with fluctuations in alpha and theta rhythm during sleep onset in humans. *J Physiol* 568: 305–313, 2005.
19. Krueger JM, Obal F, Jr., Kapas L, and Fang J. Brain organization and sleep function. *Behav Brain Res* 69: 177-185, 1995.
20. Kuboyama T, Hori A, Sato T, Mikami T, Yamaki T, and Ueda S. Changes in cerebral blood flow velocity in healthy young men during overnight sleep and while awake. *Electroencephalogr Clin Neurophysiol* 102: 125-131, 1997.
21. LeMarbre G, Stauber S, Khayat RN, Puleo DS, Skatrud JB, and Morgan BJ. Baroreflex-induced sympathetic activation does not alter cerebrovascular CO_2 responsiveness in humans. *J Physiol* 551: 609-616, 2003.
22. Macey PM, Henderson LA, Macey KE, Alger JR, Frysinger RC, Woo MA, Harper RK, Yan-Go FL, and Harper RM. Brain morphology associated with obstructive sleep apnea. *Am J Respir Crit Care Med* 166: 1382-1387, 2002.
23. Madsen PL, Schmidt JF, Wildschiodtz G, Friberg L, Holm S, Vorstrup S, and Lassen NA. Cerebral O_2 metabolism and cerebral blood flow in humans during deep and rapid-eye-movement sleep. *J Appl Physiol* 70: 2597-2601, 1991.

24. Maquet P, Degueldre C, Delfiore G, Aerts J, Peters J-M, Luxen A, and Franck G. Functional neuroanatomy of human slow wave sleep. *J Neurosci* 17: 2807-2812, 1997.
25. McGinty D and Szymusiak R. Keeping cool: a hypothesis about the mechanisms and functions of slow-wave sleep. *Trends Neurosci* 13: 480-487, 1990.
26. Meadows GE, Dunroy HM, Morrell MJ, and Corfield DR. Hypercapnic cerebral vascular reactivity is decreased, in humans, during sleep compared with wakefulness. *J Appl Physiol* 94: 2197-2202, 2003.
27. Meadows GE, O'Driscoll DM, Simonds AK, Morrell MJ, and Corfield DR. Cerebral blood flow response to isocapnic hypoxia during slow-wave sleep and wakefulness. *J Appl Physiol* 97: 1343-1348, 2004.
28. Morrell MJ, McRobbie, D., Cummin, A.R. and Corfield, D.R. Changes in brain morphology associated with obstructive sleep apnea. *Sleep Medicine 4: 451-454*, 2003.
29. Olesen J, Paulson OB, and Lassen NA. Regional cerebral blood flow in man determined by the initial slope of the clearance of intra-arterially injected 133Xe. *Stroke* 2: 519-540, 1971.
30. Pelligrino DA, Wang Q, Koenig HM, and Albrecht RF. Role of nitric oxide, adenosine, N-methyl--aspartate receptors, and neuronal activation in hypoxia-induced pial arteriolar dilation in rats. *Brain Research* 704: 61-70, 1995.
31. Powers WJ. Cerebral hemodynamics in ischemic cerebrovascular disiease. *Ann Neurol* 29: 231-240, 1991.
32. Rechtschaffen A and Kales A. A manual of standardised terminology, techniques, and scoring system for sleep stages of human subjects. Bethesda: National Institute of health, 1968, p. publication 204.
33. Reid JM, Davies AG, Ashcroft FM, and Paterson DJ. Effect of L-NMMA, cromakalim, and glibenclamide on cerebral blood flow in hypercapnia and hypoxia. *Am J Physiol* 269: H916-922, 1995.
34. Sakai F, Meyer JS, Karacan I, Derman S, and Yamamoto M. Normal human sleep: regional cerebral hemodynamics. *Ann Neurol* 7: 471-478, 1980.
35. Shankar V and Armstead WM. Opioids contribute to hypoxia-induced pial artery dilation through activation of ATP-sensitive K+ channels. *Am J Physiol Heart Circ Physiol* 269: H997-1002, 1995.
36. Skatrud JB and Dempsey JA. Interaction of sleep state and chemical stimuli in sustaining rhythmic ventilation. *J Appl Physiol* 55: 813-822, 1983.
37. Smith C. Sleep states and memory processes. *Behav Brain Res* 69: 137-145, 1995.
38. Sokoloff L. Local cerebral energy metabolism: its relationships to local functional activity and blood flow. *Ciba Found Symp*: 171-197, 1978.
39. Sremin OU, Rubstein EH, and Sonnenschein RR. *Cholinergic modulation of the cerebrovascular response to CO_2 in the rabbit*. Oxford: Pergamon Press, 1977.
40. Townsend RE, Prinz PN, and Obrist WD. Human cerebral blood flow during wake and sleep. *J Appl Physiol* 35: 620 - 625, 1973.
41. Trinder J, Whitworth F, Kay A, and Wilkin P. Respiratory instability during sleep onset. *J Appl Physiol* 73: 2462-2469, 1992.
42. Van Mil AH, Spilt A, Van Buchem MA, Bollen EL, Teppema L, Westendorp RG, and Blauw GJ. Nitric oxide mediates hypoxia-induced cerebral vasodilation in humans. *J Appl Physiol* 92: 962-966, 2002.
43. Winn HR, Rubio GR, and Berne RM. The role of adenosine in the regulation of cerebral blood flow. *J Cereb Blood Flow Metab* 1: 239-244, 1981.
44. Woo MA, Macey PM, Fonarow GC, Hamilton MA, and Harper RM. Regional Brain Gray Matter Loss in Heart Failure. *J Appl Physiol* 95: 677-684, 2003.

Chapter 8

NEURAL CONSEQUENCES OF SLEEP DISORDERED BREATHING: THE ROLE OF INTERMITTENT HYPOXIA

Mary J. Morrell and Gillian Twigg
Clinical and Academic Unit of Sleep and Breathing, National Heart and Lung Institute, Imperial College, Royal Brompton Campus, London, UK.

Abstract: Sleep disordered breathing is characterised by periodic breathing, episodes of hypoxia and repeated arousals from sleep; symptoms include excessive daytime sleepiness, impairment of memory, learning and attention. Recent evidence from animal studies suggests that both intermittent hypoxia and sleep fragmentation can independently lead to neuronal defects in the hippocampus and pre frontal cortex; areas known to be closely associated with neural processing of memory and executive function. We have previously shown that sleep disordered breathing is associated with loss of gray matter concentration within the left hippocampus (47). We have now confirmed and extended this finding in 22 right handed, newly diagnosed male patients (mean (sd): age 51.8 (15.4) yrs, apnea / hypopnea index 53.1 (14.0) events/hr, minimum nocturnal oxygen saturation 75 (8.4) %) and 17 controls matched for age and handedness. Voxel-based morphometry, an automated unbiased technique, was used to characterise changes in gray matter concentration. The magnetic resonance images were segmented and grey matter concentration determined voxel by voxel. Analysis of variance was then preformed, adjusted for overall image intensity, with age as a covariant. Additional to the deficit in the left hippocampus, we found more extensive loss of gray matter bilaterally in the parahippocampus. No additional focal lesions were seen in other brain regions. Based on our findings and data from other human and animal studies, we speculate that in patients with sleep disordered breathing intermittent hypoxia is associated with neural deficit, and further that such lesions may lead to cognitive dysfunction.

Key Words: sleep apnea, periodic breathing, cognitive, memory

Hypoxia and Exercise, edited by R.C. Roach *et al.*
Springer, New York, 2006.

INTRODUCTION

Sleep disordered breathing may present in several forms (I) obstructive sleep apnea / hypopnea, resulting from occlusion or partial closure of the pharyngeal airway (II) central sleep apnea, resulting from reduced efferent output to the respiratory pump muscles (III) mixed apnea, a combination of both obstructive and central events (IV) Cheyne-Stokes respiration: a periodic breathing pattern that is characterised by a crescendo-decrescendo fluctuation in tidal volume and may contain a central apnea or hypopnea. Obstructive sleep apnea / hypopnea is the most common form of sleep disordered breathing occurring in 1-4% of the middle-aged western male population (61, 67), increasing up to 24-30% in elderly males (37). Central sleep apnea and Cheyne-Stokes respiration are more often seen in patients with heart failure, or during conditions of chronic hypoxia as occurs at altitude. All forms of apnea and hypopnea produce intermittent hypoxia, to a greater or lesser extent (Figure 1).

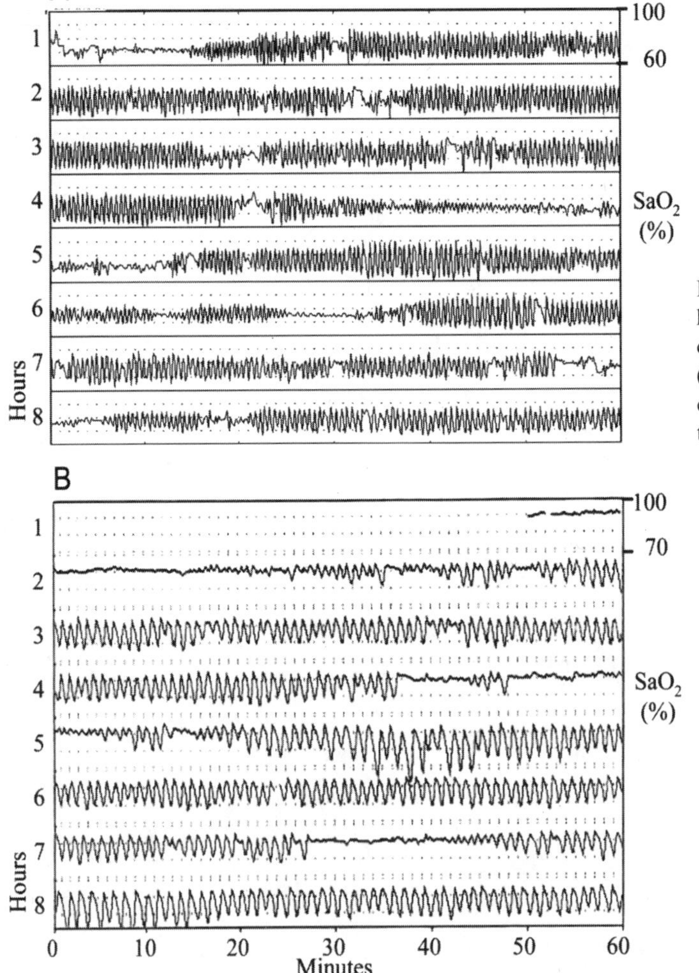

Figure 1. Intermittent hypoxia associated with obstructive sleep apnoea (Bottom Trace) and chronic hypoxia of altitude (Top Trace).

Apneic and hypopneic events are usually terminated by an arousal from sleep. As a result, sleep disordered breathing is typically associated with poor nocturnal sleep quality and excessive daytime sleepiness. The term obstructive sleep apnea / hypopnea syndrome (OSAHS) is usually taken to mean patients presenting with an apnea / hypopnea index (AHI) > 5 events / hour together with excessive daytime somnolence, not explained by other factors, or any two of the following factors: choking or gasping during sleep, recurrent awakenings during sleep, unrefreshing sleep, daytime fatigue, impaired concentration.

COGNITIVE FUNCTION AND SLEEP DISORDERED BREATHING

Cognitive dysfunction includes the impaired ability to problem solve, manipulate information, plan, inhibit responses and maintain attention (14, 15). It is a frequently reported problem in patients with sleep disordered breathing, with over 50% having some form of memory impairment (34). The mechanisms leading to the cognitive and memory deficits are unclear. Excessive daytime somnolence may result in an inability to focus and sustain attention (44), put simply patients fall asleep during boring repetitive tasks. Alternatively, sleep deprivation may lead to impaired memory by altering neural function (31). Cognitive dysfunction may be a consequence of hypoxia related neuronal deficits, in particular intermittent hypoxia (56). These mechanisms will be addressed fully in the latter sections of this paper. In the remainder of this section we will review in more detail the relationship between sleep disordered breathing and aspects of cognitive function.

Previous research has examined many aspects of cognitive functioning in patients with sleep disordered breathing, including facets of memory, attention, vigilance and executive functions. In patients with mild sleep disordered breathing (AHI 10-30 events/hour) some, but not all aspects of working memory (e.g. the ability to hold information long enough to make use of it, such as a phone number) are deficient compared to healthy controls (AHI < 5 events / hour) (54). In patients with more severe OSAHS, the recall of word lists is reduced and these patients make less efficient use of semantic cues to assist their memory. However, recognition memory and retention of previously learned information are not significantly affected (58). Taken together, these data suggest that not all aspects of memory are equally affected by sleep disordered breathing, and that the severity of the disease may influence the extent of the dysfunction.

In an important study into the effects of OSAHS on pre frontal lobe-related executive functions, Feuerstein et al found that patients were significantly impaired on a number of functions; in particular, deficits where found in tests of planning and flexibility, plus tests requiring inhibition of a learned response (21). In addition, phonemic fluency, another frontal lobe task, is impaired in OSAHS patients, compared to controls matched for age and educational status (58).

If sleep disordered breathing is associated with impairment of cognitive tasks involving the pre frontal cortex, it is reasonable to question: *to what extent treatment reverses the cognitive dysfunction?* The treatment of choice for OSAHS is continuous positive airway pressure (CPAP). This treatment has been successfully used to reduce the number of apneas / hypopneas, and the number of respiratory-related arousals, which in turn improves the quality of sleep. Patients who use CPAP frequently report a reduction in daytime somnolence, which is confirmed objectively with an increase in sleep latency (59). However, a summary review of the effectiveness of CPAP in improving cognitive function is confounded by the fact that different researchers have used different cognitive test batteries, and CPAP treatment for varying periods of time; additionally, compliance is frequently poor or not reported. Nevertheless, OSAHS patients using CPAP treatment have shown an improvement in some aspects of cognitive function. In particular, mental flexibility, such as trail making B (17, 18), psychomotor vigilance (17, 35) and measures of attention (20, 21) all improve following CPAP treatment.

The duration of CPAP treatment required to reverse cognitive dysfunction varies. Significant improvements in tests of sustained attention, spatial memory, motor agility and dexterity have been shown after fifteen days of CPAP treatment (20). When examined again at four months, these improvements had been maintained but no further significant improvements had been made. Some cognitive deficits noted prior to CPAP were not reversed by treatment; these included tests of executive function. These data are in accordance with other studies which have reported significant improvements in tests of vigilance after one night of CPAP treatment, with further significant improvements after fourteen nights (36) and six months of treatment (5); the latter study having no interim analysis at fourteen / fifteen nights.

Finally, it is important to note that not all studies of CPAP treatment have shown improvements in cognitive function. A placebo controlled study, examining the effects of CPAP on cognitive functioning after one week found no improvements in any neuropsychological tests used (2). The authors suggest that this may be due to the short duration of treatment use prior to evaluation, or poor compliance. However, this is unlikely since an earlier placebo controlled study of CPAP in OSAHS patients found that four weeks of treatment significantly improved objective and subjective measures of sleepiness, but failed to detect any improvement on the neuropsychological function (19). Similarly, sleepiness and cognitive function were compared in patients who did, and did not comply well with CPAP; in those who were compliant there was a significant improvement in sleepiness but not cognitive function (16). The results of these studies, compared to those mentioned earlier may be explained in part by the differences in cognitive test batteries. Nevertheless, the latter studies are placebo controlled and as such must be taken into account.

From this review of the literature we conclude that the use of CPAP in OSAHS leads to reversal of day time somnolence and vigilance; improvements in some, but not all aspects of cognitive dysfunction are seen in the majority of studies. We speculate that treatment of sleep disordered breathing may improve vigilance and aspects of memory by reversing daytime somnolence; whereas it has a reduced and inconsistent effect on the cognitive dysfunction, because cognitive function results from neurodegeneration associated with chronic intermittent hypoxia. This suggestion is supported by correlation studies which have shown that tests of executive functions and visuo-constructional ability correlate strongly with measures of nocturnal hypoxemia (6, 46). However, deficits in memory and attention correlated more strongly with measures of daytime somnolence (46).

STRUCTURAL CHANGES IN BRAIN MORPHOLOGY ASSOCIATED WITH SLEEP DISORDERED BREATHING

It is widely accepted that episodes of anoxia and / or hypoxia in humans can result in defuse neurodegeneration (33) and in selected cases, bilateral focal lesions of the hippocampus can occur (22). Conversely the effects of chronic intermittent hypoxia are less clear. In rats, exposure to intermittent hypoxia during sleep results in cellular damage within the CA1 region of the hippocampus and adjacent cortex (27, 55).

In humans several recent studies have investigated the suggestion that the intermittent hypoxia associated with OSAHS leads to changes in brain morphology (22, 39, 47, 48). In the first of these studies, Macey et al (39) reported widespread changes in gray matter concentration across the brain in twenty one patients with OSAHS compared to twenty one age matched controls; including the frontal and parietal cortex, the temporal lobe, anterior cingulate, hippocampus and cerebellum (Figure 2, top panel). In these patients, the decrease in gray matter concentration was related to the severity of the OSAHS disease. For each group the magnetic resonance images were analysed using voxel-based morphometry (VBM; Figure 2, top panel: A). This is an automated and unbiased technique that can be used to characterise changes in grey matter concentrations between groups (23, 26, 43, 65). It has the potential advantage of being able to detect subtle changes in relatively small structures such as the hippocampus (40). However, interpretation of the data obtained using this technique may be confounded by the statistical analysis. Macey et al (39) used a relatively low level of significance to report their findings; $p<0.001$, uncorrected for multiple comparisons, which may explain the wide spread gray matter loss in their study.

In the recent study of O'Donoghue et al (48) changes in brain morphology were examined in twenty five patients with severe OSAHS compared to twenty three healthy controls. Using VBM these authors found some reduction in gray matter concentration when the data were reported at $p<0.001$, uncorrected for multiple comparisons (Figure 2, bottom panel). However, when the data were analysed at $p<0.05$, corrected for multiple comparisons no significant reductions in gray matter in were seen. The authors corroborated their findings using a second method of MRI analysis; region of interest analysis (Figure 2, bottom panel: B)

The differences between the studies of Macey et al (39) and O'Donoghue et al (48) may in part be explained by differences in patient selection. The patients studied by O'Donoghue et al (48) had more severe OSA compared to those of Macey et al (39). However, this would have maximised the chances of O'Donoghue et al (48) finding changes in gray matter concentration. On the other hand, the study by Macey et al (39) included some patients known to have neurological and cardiovascular co-morbidity, most commonly hypertension; this could have had an independent effect on brain morphology and resulted in a reduction in gray matter concentration.

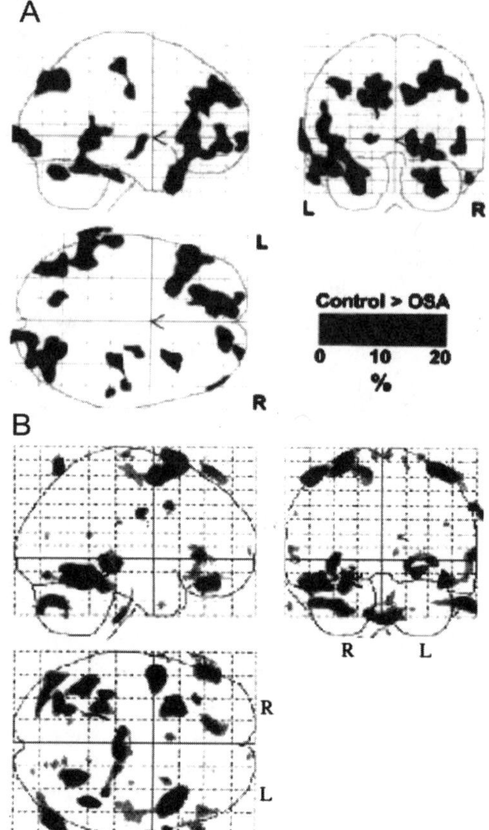

Figure 2. Glass brain display of regions of significantly reduced gray matter (p<0.001, uncorrected for multiple comparisons) in 21 subjects with OSAHS, weighted by disease severity and 21 healthy controls, matched for handedness and age (Macey et al (39) Top Panel and O'Donoghue et al (48).

Our group have also carried out a study to investigate the hypothesis that OSAHS is associated with changes in brain morphology, particularly a focal loss of grey matter within the hippocampus. Seven male right-handed, newly-diagnosed OSAHS patients were investigated using VBM. Compared to controls our study revealed a loss of grey matter concentration within the left hippocampus in patients with OSAHS (47). The level of significance used was p=0.01, corrected for multiple comparisons based on a hippocampal region of interest; this was selected on the basis of an *a priori* hypothesis of hippocampal gray matter loss in the OSA patients. We have now confirmed and extended this finding in twenty-two OSAHS patients compared to seventeen controls. See Table 1 for subject details. Additional to the deficit in the left hippocampus, this larger group of patients had more extensive loss of grey matter bilaterally in the para-hippocampus (p<0.001, a priori region of interest, uncorrected for multiple comparisons, with age as a covariant); no additional focal grey matter reductions were seen in other brain regions (p>0.05, corrected for multiple comparisons) (Figure 3). Five of our OSAHS patients and one of the control subject had a clinically diagnosed hypertension or were on antihypertensive medications. Therefore we carried out a second analysis removing these subjects. The focal lesions in the hippocampus and para hippocampus remained present on re-analysis.

Table 1. Subject characteristics.

	OSA patients (n=22)	Controls (n=17)
Age (years)	51.8 (15.4)	53.1 (14.0)
BMI (Kg/m^2)	32.4 (5.6)	24.8 (4.3)
Epworth Sleepiness Score	13.3 (4.2)	3.4 (1.2)
AHI (events/hour)	53.1 (14.0)	< 10
Minimum nocturnal oxygen saturation (%)	75 (8.4)	n/a

As we have alluded to above, sensitivity of VBM has been questioned by some. Therefore it is of significant interest that a fourth study has been published in which neuronal deficit in the hippocampus has been examined using another method of MRI analysis. In this study Gale and Hopkins (22) found bilateral hippocampal volumetric loss in 36% of the severe OSAHS patients they studied (n=14; respiratory disturbance index 84 (18) events / hour; mean percentage sleep time < 90% saturation 65 (34)%). The MRI scans were analysed using an alternative quantitative (volumetric) method (7).

So far we have discussed the impact of sleep disordered breathing on changes in gray matter concentration in humans. We conclude that some, but not all available data, supports the concept that OSAHS is associated with reduced gray matter in the hippocampus. However, before concluding this section we must mention that the relationship between OSAHS and with white matter disease has also been investigated (11, 13, 63). These studies have found no relationship between OSAHS and sub-clinical white matter disease (11, 63) or AHI and brainstem white matter disease (13).

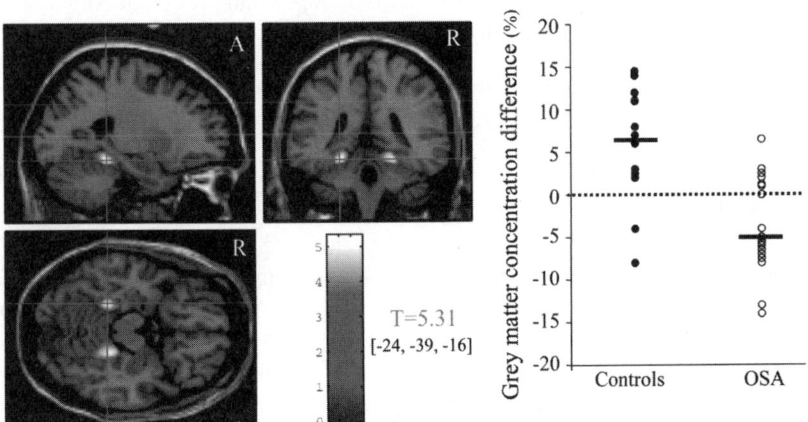

Figure 3. Shading indicates a statistically significant bilateral reduction in grey matter concentration within the para-hippocampus for the group of 22 OSAHS patients minus the 17 controls, overlaid on a standard brain template. Cross hairs indicate voxel of maximum significance ($p < 0.001$, *a priori* region of interest, uncorrected for multiple comparisons) at –24 (left), -16 (posterior), -34 (superior) mm, relative to the midline of the anterior commissure; no reductions were seen in other brain regions ($p>0.05$, corrected for multiple comparisons). Images oriented to a horizontal plane through the anterior and posterior commissures.

FUNCTIONAL IMPLICATIONS OF NEURONAL DEGENERATION IN THE HIPPOCAMPUS AND FONTAL CORTEX

To examine the functional implications of neuronal deficit in the hippocampus, studies have been carried out in patients with bilateral hippocampal degeneration, resulting from diseases other than sleep disordered breathing. In these patients aspects of memory are impaired. In one study, there was a reduction in recall of factual knowledge for several years prior to the onset of memory loss, although factual information acquired from greater than eleven years prior to onset of memory impairment remained intact (41). However, patients with bilateral hippocampal lesions do not always have complete loss of memory recall, suggesting either that other brain regions are recruited in the absence of hippocampal function, or that some cells in the hippocampus are spared (42).

Patients with damage limited to the hippocampus appear to show a reduction in source memory (41); the recognition of something as familiar and knowing the context in which it was first encountered (60). However, it must be noted that source memory is supported by other areas of the brain. Indeed studies have shown deficits in this function in patients with damage to the left prefrontal cortex, implicating this area as a vital component in the capacity for memory for source (24, 60).

Interestingly, the hippocampus has not been specifically implicated in working memory (10), whereas it does appear to be involved in spatial memory, particularly for navigation (40, 49). Bilateral dorsal hippocampal lesions have resulted in impaired spatial memory in rats, even when the lesion size encompassed as little as 30% of the total hippocampal volume (8). In addition, the medial prefrontal cortex has also been implicated in spatial memory, with lesions to either the hippocampus or the medial prefrontal cortex resulting in disruption of spatial memory capacity (62).

MECHANISMS OF NEURONAL DEGENERATION IN SLEEP DISORDERED BREATHING: THE ROLE OF INTERMITTENT HYPOXIA

As mentioned earlier at least two studies (6, 46), have examined the correlation between respiratory measures of disease severity, and performance on particular tests of cognitive function in order to address the question: *to what extent are cognitive deficits seen in patients with sleep disordered breathing attributable to hypoxemia, versus daytime somnolence?* In a large population based study, Adams et al (2001) have used factor analysis to show that respiratory disturbance index and nocturnal hypoxemia are significant predictors of declarative memory and signal discrimination (1). Furthermore, performances on tests which tap working memory, such as reverse digit span, were found to be predicted by the respiratory disturbance index (1). Performance on tasks involving attention, were significantly predicted by sleepiness (1). These data indicate that hypoxemia contributes to cognitive dysfunction in OSAHS. Consistent with this suggestion correlations between AHI and measures of visuo-spatial organisation (9, 29), visuo-motor coordination (9), reaction time (9), motor speed (29) and distractibility (9) have been shown.

From our study (47), we speculate that the changes in brain morphology which occur in patients with OSAHS resulted from the intermittent hypoxic insult. The mechanisms contributing to the hypoxic-induced hippocampal neurodegeneration are likely to have included several processes, with much of the recent research focused on the role of oxidative stress (3, 52, 53).

Brain function is critically dependent on oxygen supply. During any hypoxic insult, protection of the brain is dependent on a rapid cerebral vascular response otherwise cerebral ischemia with neuronal deficit will ensue. Recent research in healthy humans suggests that the cerebral vascular responses to both hypoxia and hypercapnia are significantly altered during stable non rapid eye movement sleep compared to wakefulness *(for a full review - see Corfield and Meadows Chapter 7 in this volume).*

Cellular responses to hypoxia include changes in the mediation ions channels, release of vasoactive substances from the endothelium and neighbouring tissues, regulation of gene expression and tissue remodelling (38). Hypoxia causes modulation of ion channels and in the hippocampal neurones immediate hyperpolerisation occurs via activation of the K_{ca} channels (32). Exposure to intermittent hypoxia during sleep results in cellular damage within the cerebella cortex (50), wake-promoting regions of the brainstem and basal forebrain (64), and CA1 region of the hippocampus and adjacent cortex (27, 30, 55). In the animals with hippocampal damage evidence of increased membrane lipid peroxidation and oxidative stress occurs, which is attenuated with administration of antioxidants (56). The susceptibility of the hippocampal neurones to neural dysfunction may be age dependent, with very young and elderly animals being more vulnerable (12, 28). The importance of this finding is that the prevalence of sleep disordered breathing increases with age (37) and in the young, sleep disordered breathing has been linked with attention deficit / hyperactivity disorder (4).

In animal experiments mentioned above the onset of intermittent hypoxia is abrupt, this is not the case in humans where the development of sleep disordered breathing is insidious. This is of interest since the neural degeneration in these experiments may be time-course dependent. In one study the neuronal deficit peaked at 3 days, returning to normoxic levels within 14 days in animals exposed to intermittent hypoxia (25). These findings lead to the suggestion that long-term potentiation, may play an important role in the impact of intermittent hypoxia on neural function (51).

MECHANISMS OF NEURONAL DEGENERATION IN SLEEP DISORDERED BREATHING: THE ROLE OF SLEEP DEPRIVATION

Although the focus of this paper is the role of intermittent hypoxia on the neural degeneration associated with sleep disordered breathing any review of sleep disordered breathing would be incomplete without considering the role of sleep *per se*.

Recent research has demonstrated the vulnerability of the hippocampus to damage in sleep deprivation (57). Selective REM sleep deprivation can also lead to a reduction in neuronal excitability in the CA1 pyramidal neurones, but not the dentate gyrus granule cells of the hippocampus (45). Sleep deprivation using a treadmill paradigm has also shown a reduction in the proliferation of cells in the dentate gyrus (31). If sleep deprivation in and of itself can result in neuronal deficits it is interesting to speculate on the combined effects of sleep deprivation and intermittent hypoxia on neuronal plasticity in humans, an area which thus far has not been investigated.

CLINICAL IMPLICATIONS OF CHANGES IN MORPHOLOGY ASSOCIATED WITH OSAHS

As outlined earlier treatment of OSAHS using CPAP produces a considerable improvement in daytime somnolence (19). However, despite the obvious benefits of CPAP treatment in patients with severe OSAHS, there remains considerable debate as to the clinical and economic benefits of treating the large number of patients with relatively-mild disease (66). In concluding this paper we suggest that if sleep disordered breathing is associated with focal changes in brain morphology, it is possible that early treatment of the disease with CPAP may prevent structural changes and subsequent cognitive dysfunction in some patients.

ACKNOWLEDGMENTS

Research supported by the Wellcome Trust and The Hammersmith Hospitals Research Council. GT was supported by an NHLI foundation studentship. The authors thank Dr DR Corfield for his partnership in all aspects of this project, including carrying out the VBM analysis.

REFERENCES

1. Adams N, Strauss M, Schluchter M, and Redline S. Relation of measures of sleep-disordered breathing to neuropsychological functioning. *Am J Respir Crit Care Med* 163: 1626-1631, 2001.
2. Bardwell WA, Ancoli-Israel S, Berry CC, and Dimsdale JE. Neuropsychological effects of one-week continuous positive airway pressure treatment in patients with obstructive sleep apnea: a placebo-controlled study. *Psychosom Med* 63: 579-584, 2001.
3. Barnham KJ, Masters CL, and Bush AI. Neurodegenerative diseases and oxidative stress. *Nat Rev Drug Discov* 3: 205-214, 2004.
4. Bass JL, Corwin M, Gozal D, Moore C, Nishida H, Parker S, Schonwald A, Wilker RE, Stehle S, and Kinane TB. The effect of chronic or intermittent hypoxia on cognition in childhood: a review of the evidence. *Pediatrics* 114: 805-816, 2004.
5. Bedard MA, Montplaisir J, Malo J, Richer F, and Rouleau I. Persistent neuropsychological deficits and vigilance impairment in sleep apnea syndrome after treatment with continuous positive airways pressure (CPAP). *J Clin Exp Neuropsychol* 15: 330-341, 1993.
6. Bedard MA, Montplaisir J, Richer F, Rouleau I, and Malo J. Obstructive sleep apnea syndrome: pathogenesis of neuropsychological deficits. *J Clin Exp Neuropsychol* 13: 950-964, 1991.

7. Blatter DD, Bigler ED, Gale SD, Johnson SC, Anderson CV, Burnett BM, Ryser D, Macnamara SE, and Bailey BJ. MR-based brain and cerebrospinal fluid measurement after traumatic brain injury: correlation with neuropsychological outcome. *AJNR Am J Neuroradiol* 18: 1-10, 1997.
8. Broadbent NJ, Squire LR, and Clark RE. Spatial memory, recognition memory, and the hippocampus. *Proc Natl Acad Sci U S A* 101: 14515-14520, 2004.
9. Cheshire K, Engleman H, Deary I, Shapiro C, and Douglas NJ. Factors impairing daytime performance in patients with sleep apnea/hypopnea syndrome. *Arch Intern Med* 152: 538-541, 1992.
10. Cowey CM and Green S. The hippocampus: a "working memory" structure? The effect of hippocampal sclerosis on working memory. *Memory* 4: 19-30, 1996.
11. Davies CW, Crosby JH, Mullins RL, Traill ZC, Anslow P, Davies RJ, and Stradling JR. Case control study of cerebrovascular damage defined by magnetic resonance imaging in patients with OSA and normal matched control subjects. *Sleep* 24: 715-720, 2001.
12. Decker MJ, Hue GE, Caudle WM, Miller GW, Keating GL, and Rye DB. Episodic neonatal hypoxia evokes executive dysfunction and regionally specific alterations in markers of dopamine signaling. *Neuroscience* 117: 417-425, 2003.
13. Ding J, Nieto FJ, Beauchamp NJ, Jr., Harris TB, Robbins JA, Hetmanski JB, Fried LP, and Redline S. Sleep-disordered breathing and white matter disease in the brainstem in older adults. *Sleep* 27: 474-479, 2004.
14. Duncan J and Owen AM. Common regions of the human frontal lobe recruited by diverse cognitive demands. *Trends Neurosci* 23: 475-483, 2000.
15. Elliott R. Executive functions and their disorders. *Br Med Bull* 65: 49-59, 2003.
16. Engleman HM, Cheshire KE, Deary IJ, and Douglas NJ. Daytime sleepiness, cognitive performance and mood after continuous positive airway pressure for the sleep apnoea/hypopnoea syndrome. *Thorax* 48: 911-914, 1993.
17. Engleman HM, Martin SE, Deary IJ, and Douglas NJ. Effect of continuous positive airway pressure treatment on daytime function in sleep apnoea/hypopnoea syndrome. *Lancet* 343: 572-575, 1994.
18. Engleman HM, Martin SE, Deary IJ, and Douglas NJ. Effect of CPAP therapy on daytime function in patients with mild sleep apnoea/hypopnoea syndrome. *Thorax* 52: 114-119, 1997.
19. Engleman HM, Martin SE, Kingshott RN, Mackay TW, Deary IJ, and Douglas NJ. Randomised placebo controlled trial of daytime function after continuous positive airway pressure (CPAP) therapy for the sleep apnoea/hypopnoea syndrome. *Thorax* 53: 341-345, 1998.
20. Ferini-Strambi L, Baietto C, Di Gioia MR, Castaldi P, Castronovo C, Zucconi M, and Cappa SF. Cognitive dysfunction in patients with obstructive sleep apnea (OSA): partial reversibility after continuous positive airway pressure (CPAP). *Brain Res Bull* 61: 87-92, 2003.
21. Feuerstein C, Naegele B, Pepin JL, and Levy P. Frontal lobe-related cognitive functions in patients with sleep apnea syndrome before and after treatment. *Acta Neurol Belg* 97: 96-107, 1997.
22. Gale SD and Hopkins RO. Effects of hypoxia on the brain: neuroimaging and neuropsychological findings following carbon monoxide poisoning and obstructive sleep apnea. *J Int Neuropsychol Soc* 10: 60-71, 2004.
23. Gitelman DR, Ashburner J, Friston KJ, Tyler LK, and Price CJ. Voxel-based morphometry of herpes simplex encephalitis. *Neuroimage* 13: 623-631, 2001.
24. Glisky EL, Rubin SR, and Davidson PS. Source memory in older adults: an encoding or retrieval problem? *J Exp Psychol Learn Mem Cogn* 27: 1131-1146, 2001.
25. Goldbart A, Row BW, Kheirandish L, Schurr A, Gozal E, Guo SZ, Payne RS, Cheng Z,

Brittian KR, and Gozal D. Intermittent hypoxic exposure during light phase induces changes in cAMP response element binding protein activity in the rat CA1 hippocampal region: water maze performance correlates. *Neuroscience* 122: 585-590, 2003.
26. Good CD, Johnsrude IS, Ashburner J, Henson RN, Friston KJ, and Frackowiak RS. A voxel-based morphometric study of ageing in 465 normal adult human brains. *Neuroimage* 14: 21-36, 2001.
27. Gozal D, Daniel JM, and Dohanich GP. Behavioral and anatomical correlates of chronic episodic hypoxia during sleep in the rat. *J Neurosci* 21: 2442-2450, 2001.
28. Gozal D, Row BW, Kheirandish L, Liu R, Guo SZ, Qiang F, and Brittian KR. Increased susceptibility to intermittent hypoxia in aging rats: changes in proteasomal activity, neuronal apoptosis and spatial function. *J Neurochem* 86: 1545-1552, 2003.
29. Greenberg GD, Watson RK, and Deptula D. Neuropsychological dysfunction in sleep apnea. *Sleep* 10: 254-262, 1987.
30. Gu XQ and Haddad GG. Decreased neuronal excitability in hippocampal neurons of mice exposed to cyclic hypoxia. *J Appl Physiol* 91: 1245-1250, 2001.
31. Guzman-Marin R, Suntsova N, Stewart DR, Gong H, Szymusiak R, and McGinty D. Sleep deprivation reduces proliferation of cells in the dentate gyrus of the hippocampus in rats. *J Physiol* 549: 563-571, 2003.
32. Haddad GG and Jiang C. Mechanisms of anoxia-induced depolarization in brainstem neurons: in vitro current and voltage clamp studies in the adult rat. *Brain Res* 625: 261-268, 1993.
33. Hopkins RO, Gale SD, Johnson SC, Anderson CV, Bigler ED, Blatter DD, and Weaver LK. Severe anoxia with and without concomitant brain atrophy and neuropsychological impairments. *J Int Neuropsychol Soc* 1: 501-509, 1995.
34. Kales A, Caldwell AB, Cadieux RJ, Vela-Bueno A, Ruch LG, and Mayes SD. Severe obstructive sleep apnea--II: Associated psychopathology and psychosocial consequences. *J Chronic Dis* 38: 427-434, 1985.
35. Kribbs NB, Pack AI, Kline LR, Getsy JE, Schuett JS, Henry JN, Maislin G, and Dinges DF. Effects of one night without nasal CPAP treatment on sleep and sleepiness in patients with obstructive sleep apnea. *Am Rev Respir Dis* 147: 1162-1168, 1993.
36. Lamphere J, Roehrs T, Wittig R, Zorick F, Conway WA, and Roth T. Recovery of alertness after CPAP in apnea. *Chest* 96: 1364-1367, 1989.
37. Levy P, Pepin JL, Malauzat D, Emeriau JP, and Leger JM. Is sleep apnea syndrome in the elderly a specific entity? *Sleep* 19: S29-38, 1996.
38. Lopez-Barneo J, Pardal R, and Ortega-Saenz P. Cellular mechanism of oxygen sensing. *Annu Rev Physiol* 63: 259-287, 2001.
39. Macey PM, Henderson LA, Macey KE, Alger JR, Frysinger RC, Woo MA, Harper RK, Yan-Go FL, and Harper RM. Brain morphology associated with obstructive sleep apnea. *Am J Respir Crit Care Med* 166: 1382-1387, 2002.
40. Maguire EA, Gadian DG, Johnsrude IS, Good CD, Ashburner J, Frackowiak RS, and Frith CD. Navigation-related structural change in the hippocampi of taxi drivers. *Proc Natl Acad Sci U S A* 97: 4398-4403, 2000.
41. Manns JR, Hopkins RO, Reed JM, Kitchener EG, and Squire LR. Recognition memory and the human hippocampus. *Neuron* 37: 171-180, 2003.
42. Manns JR, Hopkins RO, and Squire LR. Semantic memory and the human hippocampus. *Neuron* 38: 127-133, 2003.
43. May A, Ashburner J, Buchel C, McGonigle DJ, Friston KJ, Frackowiak RS, and Goadsby PJ. Correlation between structural and functional changes in brain in an idiopathic headache syndrome. *Nat Med* 5: 836-838, 1999.
44. Mazza S, Pepin JL, Naegele B, Plante J, Deschaux C, and Levy P. Most obstructive sleep apnoea patients exhibit vigilance and attention deficits on an extended battery of tests.

Eur Respir J 25: 75-80, 2005.

45. McDermott CM, LaHoste GJ, Chen C, Musto A, Bazan NG, and Magee JC. Sleep deprivation causes behavioral, synaptic, and membrane excitability alterations in hippocampal neurons. *J Neurosci* 23: 9687-9695, 2003.
46. Montplaisir J, Bedard MA, Richer F, and Rouleau I. Neurobehavioral manifestations in obstructive sleep apnea syndrome before and after treatment with continuous positive airway pressure. *Sleep* 15: S17-19, 1992.
47. Morrell MJ, McRobbie DW, Quest RA, Cummin AR, Ghiassi R, and Corfield DR. Changes in brain morphology associated with obstructive sleep apnea. *Sleep Med* 4: 451-454, 2003.
48. O'Donoghue F J, Briellmann RS, Rochford PD, Abbott DF, Pell GS, Chan CH, Tarquinio N, Jackson GD, and Pierce RJ. Cerebral Structural Changes in Severe Obstructive Sleep Apnea. *Am J Respir Crit Care Med*, 2005.
49. O'Keefe J and Conway DH. Hippocampal place units in the freely moving rat: why they fire where they fire. *Exp Brain Res* 31: 573-590, 1978.
50. Pae EK, Chien P, and Harper RM. Intermittent hypoxia damages cerebellar cortex and deep nuclei. *Neurosci Lett* 375: 123-128, 2005.
51. Payne RS, Goldbart A, Gozal D, and Schurr A. Effect of intermittent hypoxia on long-term potentiation in rat hippocampal slices. *Brain Res* 1029: 195-199, 2004.
52. Prabhakar NR, and Kumar, GK. Oxidative stress in the systemic and cellular responses to intermittent hypoxia. *Biol Chem* 385: 217-221, 2004.
53. Nanduri R, and Prabhakar NR. Sleep Apneas . An Oxidative Stress? *Am J Respir Crit Care Med* 165: 859-860, 2002.
54. Redline S, Strauss ME, Adams N, Winters M, Roebuck T, Spry K, Rosenberg C, and Adams K. Neuropsychological function in mild sleep-disordered breathing. *Sleep* 20: 160-167, 1997.
55. Row BW, Kheirandish L, Neville JJ, and Gozal D. Impaired spatial learning and hyperactivity in developing rats exposed to intermittent hypoxia. *Pediatr Res* 52: 449-453, 2002.
56. Row BW, Liu R, Xu W, Kheirandish L, and Gozal D. Intermittent hypoxia is associated with oxidative stress and spatial learning deficits in the rat. *Am J Respir Crit Care Med* 167: 1548-1553, 2003.
57. Ruskin DN, Liu C, Dunn KE, Bazan NG, and LaHoste GJ. Sleep deprivation impairs hippocampus-mediated contextual learning but not amygdala-mediated cued learning in rats. *Eur J Neurosci* 19: 3121-3124, 2004.
58. Salorio CF, White DA, Piccirillo J, Duntley SP, and Uhles ML. Learning, memory, and executive control in individuals with obstructive sleep apnea syndrome. *J Clin Exp Neuropsychol* 24: 93-100, 2002.
59. Sforza E and Krieger J. Daytime sleepiness after long-term continuous positive airway pressure (CPAP) treatment in obstructive sleep apnea syndrome. *J Neurol Sci* 110: 21-26, 1992.
60. Slotnick SD, Moo LR, Segal JB, and Hart J, Jr. Distinct prefrontal cortex activity associated with item memory and source memory for visual shapes. *Brain Res Cogn Brain Res* 17: 75-82, 2003.
61. Stradling JR and Crosby JH. Predictors and prevalence of obstructive sleep apnoea and snoring in 1001 middle aged men. *Thorax* 46: 85-90, 1991.
62. Sutherland RJ, Kolb B, and Whishaw IQ. Spatial mapping: definitive disruption by hippocampal or medial frontal cortical damage in the rat. *Neurosci Lett* 31: 271-276, 1982.
63. Thomas RJ, Rosen BR, Stern CE, Weiss JW, and Kwong KK. Functional imaging of working memory in obstructive sleep-disordered breathing. *J Appl Physiol*, 98: 2226-

2234, 2005.

64. Veasey SC, Davis CW, Fenik P, Zhan G, Hsu YJ, Pratico D, and Gow A. Long-term intermittent hypoxia in mice: protracted hypersomnolence with oxidative injury to sleep-wake brain regions. *Sleep* 27: 194-201, 2004.
65. Wright IC, McGuire PK, Poline JB, Travere JM, Murray RM, Frith CD, Frackowiak RS, and Friston KJ. A voxel-based method for the statistical analysis of gray and white matter density applied to schizophrenia. *Neuroimage* 2: 244-252, 1995.
66. Wright J and Sheldon T. The efficacy of nasal continuous positive airway pressure in the treatment of obstructive sleep apnea syndrome is not proven. *Am J Respir Crit Care Med* 161: 1776-1778, 2000.
67. Young T, Palta M, Dempsey J, Skatrud J, Weber S, and Badr S. The occurrence of sleep-disordered breathing among middle-aged adults. *N Engl J Med* 328: 1230-1235, 1993.

Chapter 9

FINDING THE GENES UNDERLYING ADAPTATION TO HYPOXIA USING GENOMIC SCANS FOR GENETIC ADAPTATION AND ADMIXTURE MAPPING

Mark D. Shriver[1], Rui Mei[2], Abigail Bigham[1], Xianyun Mao[1], Tom D. Brutsaert[3], Esteban J. Parra[4], Lorna G. Moore[5]

[1]Department of Anthropology, Penn State University, University Park, PA, [2]Affymetrix Inc., Santa Clara, CA, [3]Department of Anthropology, SUNY Albany, Albany, New York 12222 4. Department of Anthropology, University of Toronto at Mississauga, Mississauga, ON, Canada [5]Department of Anthropology and Colorado Center for Altitude Medicine and Physiology, University of Colorado at Denver and Health Sciences Center, Denver CO, USA.

Abstract: The complete sequencing the human genome and recent analytical advances have provided the opportunity to perform genome-wide studies of human variation. There is substantial potential for such population-genomic approaches to assist efforts to uncover the historical and demographic histories of human populations. Additionally, these genome-wide datasets allow for investigations of variability among genomic regions. Although all genomic regions in a population have experienced the same demographic events, they have not been affected by these events in precisely the same way. Much of the variability among genomic regions is simply the result of genetic drift (*i.e.*, gene frequency changes resulting from the effects of small breeding-population size), but some is also the result of genetic adaptation, which will only affect the gene under selection and nearby regions. We have used a new DNA typing assay that allows for the genotyping of thousands of SNPs on hundreds of samples to identify regions most likely to have been affected by genetic adaptation. Populations that have inhabited different niches (*e.g.*, high-altitude regions) can be used to identify genes underlying the physiological differences. We have used two methods (admixture mapping and genome scans for genetic adaptation) founded on the population-genomic paradigms to search for genes underlying population differences in response to chronic hypoxia. There is great promise that together these methods will facilitate the discovery of genes influencing hypoxic response.

Key Words: admixture mapping, natural selection

INTRODUCTION

There are four ways that individuals and populations can respond to physiological stress: 1) stress avoidance through cultural practices (including behaviors and technological responses), 2) acclimatization, 3) developmental acclimatization, and 4) genetic adaptation. Often these responses work together synergistically and so can confound a scientific analysis. Carefully designed studies are required to isolate the effects of each of these components of the adaptive process, and are today generally standard in research on mechanisms of physiological response to high-altitude hypoxia.

One area of research that is lagging in the search for mechanisms to explain physiological adaptation to hypoxia is the application of two particular genetic methods: 1) estimating genetic ancestry and admixture mapping and 2) screening for signatures of genetic adaptation. The application of these relatively new genetic approaches shows significant promise for understanding the processes of genetic adaptation to altitude. In this paper we will summarize the ways in which these novel genetic methods can be used to study the genetic regulation of physiological responses to hypoxia. We will also present some new data exemplifying an application of these two approaches.

Genetics, Genics, and Genomics

It is important to consider the basic evolutionary structure of the genome as these conceptions relate to the analytical methods for measuring genetic ancestry, admixture mapping and genetic adaptation. Briefly, admixture is the process by which two or more populations that had been separated join, becoming a new population. Firstly, and somewhat paradoxically, as more genetic markers are combined into an analysis, the results become less and less "genetic". Equation of genetic and genomic information is not always clear-cut and indeed, sometimes diametrically opposed. "Genetic" is the process of inheritance first described by Gregor Mendel who observed that characters were the result of the segregation of "factors" one coming from each parent. Today we call these "factors" alleles and know that they are different forms of genes. Such different forms of a gene are ultimately the result of variability in the DNA sequence comprising the gene often affecting the sequence of amino acids for the protein which the genes codes and other changes that affect the ways in which the proteins are expressed. These variations have distinct effects on the phenotype (or character), some being recessive and others showing dominant effects.

Many traits are like this; the genetic paradigm has been used with tremendous success over the past 100 years to identify more than 1460 traits that are transmitted in single gene, Mendelian fashion (12). All of these traits have distinct genetic effects, meaning they can be observed to segregate in families consistently enough to be mapped onto specific chromosomes. Most of these traits give rise to diseases. It is often the case, however, that not everyone with the risk-allele is affected with the disease; this phenomenon is known as incomplete penetrance. In addition there can be modifying loci that interact with the risk-allele, altering either the chances of showing the disease or its severity. Despite these caveats, genetic traits are those that are inherited in families and show distinct and dichotomous phenotypes.

However, variability in many traits is not the result of one gene (with or without modifying genes), but is instead the result of variation in a number of genes. These traits are called polygenic and do not segregate by Mendelian rules, but instead appear to undergo mixing.

Darwin (and others) described this as blending inheritance. Of course, there are still genes underlying this variability in polygenetic traits (*e.g.* skin pigmentation and stature); it is the combined effect of these genes that results in the continuous nature of the variation in the phenotype. Thus, polygenic traits are properly "genic" – the result of gene action, but not "genetic" in the formal sense. This may seem merely semantic, but there are important conceptual implications inherent in these terms and these distinctions are important for the population genomic paradigm on which surveys for natural selection and ancestry application are founded.

Genomic DNA is a double-stranded molecule composed of sequences of four nucleotide bases (adenine or A, cytosine or C, guanine or G, and thymine or T) organized into chromosomes 10's to 100's of millions of base pairs in length. Genetic markers such as Single Nucleotide Polymorphisms (SNPs) are discrete DNA sequences at specific locations in the genome (*e.g.,* one either has the CC, CT, or TT genotype and these are the only possibilities). SNPs are inherited by the Mendelian rules and so are analogous to simple Mendelian traits. However, as more and more SNPs are combined in an analysis, being in effect (and sometimes literally) averaged together, the result is not "genetic" in either the sense of being able to refer to a distinct phenotype or something that segregates from parents to offspring without blending. Averaging across many markers can be very informative regarding a person's or a population's history. But as more and more markers are added, there is less and less specific information about any one of those markers. (This is of course, unless some subset of the markers is correlated in their distributions across the persons or populations under consideration as is the case in ancestry analysis).

Ancestry Analyses and Admixture Mapping

Specific subsets of genetic markers can be identified which have genetic information regarding particular axes of ancestry (primary indices of genetic covariance) that exist within populations. These markers are most accurately referred to as Ancestry Informative Markers (AIMs) (19) and are basically markers where there are large differences in allele frequency among parental populations. For example, considering that Andeans today have both Indigenous American and European ancestry, a good AIM for Andeans would be one where the C allele of a C/T SNP has an 80% frequency in Europeans and a 20% frequency in Indigenous Americans. The simplest measure of how informative this marker is the delta or allele frequency differential, which in this example is 60%.

By measuring a panel of AIMs it is possible to estimate individual ancestral proportions. Provided there is variation in ancestral proportions across the population (making some persons "more" Indigenous American and others "more" European, for example), one can expect that other markers or groups of markers that are also ancestry-informative will be correlated; that is, differing in the same way across the population. In this way, individual ancestry can be used as a means to study the effects of unknown genes and to identify the locations of these genes, provided they differ between the parental populations (8,18). These associations between AIMs are formed through the process of admixture regardless of the genetic distance between markers or even whether or not they are on the same chromosome. Over time, independent assortment and recombination lead to a decay of associations among distantly-spaced markers. The result is that the level of association observed between an AIM and a phenotype is inversely proportional to the distance between the AIM and the trait gene (6,11).

Population Genetics and Population Genomics

The difference between genetics and genomics is a key point in the new paradigm of population genomics. Population genetics is different from Mendelian genetics in that it is primarily concerned with the behavior of genetic markers and trait-causing alleles in populations, not in families. Population genetics is, fundamentally, evolutionary genetics. It arose out of the "new synthesis" in which evolutionary theory was reinterpreted in the light of the rediscovery of Mendel's work in 1900. Mendelian inheritance is thus part of the foundation of population genetics, akin to an axiom in mathematics, but rarely the object of direct attention. Human population genetics research generally focuses on estimating population parameters that help us model the demographic histories of populations. Questions such as which populations are most closely related, whether particular migrations occurred over short or long periods of time, how admixture has affected contemporary populations, when and how severe were population "bottlenecks" (or reductions in the size of the breeding population) in the past, are the focus of these efforts.

Much human population genetic research has been carried out using mitochondrial DNA (mtDNA) and non-recombining Y-chromosomal (NRY) markers. Since the genes contained in mtDNA and the NRY are passed on intact, from parent to offspring, these markers do not undergo recombination. Thus, all variants are physically connected forever, regardless of the number of base pairs separating them. Since the mtDNA and NRY are very large and highly variable, they are remarkably informative regarding human demographic history. Additionally, since the mtDNA is always inherited through the maternal lineage and the NRY through the paternal lineage, these markers can be used to test hypotheses about differences between female and male migratory patterns and other aspects of mate pairing (13). But despite being very informative (26), mtDNA and NRY studies do not provide more than one measured locus and thus, there is no way to calculate confidence intervals about the point estimates of the parameters that are being studied. Since there is no recombination within the mtDNA and NRY and since these contain a number of genes, adaptation in any of the genes will affect all of the genetic variation and the assumption of selectively neutral evolution (showing no variation in fitness) will not hold.

Another branch of human population genetics has focused on averaging together as many genetic markers as possible to estimate population parameters. The same types of questions that are investigated with mtDNA and NRY markers are addressed with these many-marker averages. One procedural difference between the two methods is that for mtDNA and NRY studies, many more individuals are needed in the population samples compared to studies of large numbers of independent markers. For example, consider two population genetics papers appearing in *Science* a few years ago: the paper by Ke and colleagues focused on NRY analysis in 12,000 Asian men (14), while the paper by Rosenberg and colleagues (20) used average population samples of 20 individuals typed for 377 microsatellite markers.

Population genomics is new branch of population genetics, which is specifically focused on a consideration of both the averages across many markers as well as specific loci individually. A concise summary of this new perspective on genetic variation has been presented by Black and colleagues (3) who describe it as, "the process of simultaneously sampling numerous variable loci within a genome and the inference of locus-specific effects from the sample distributions." Translating simply, population genomics is a model of genome evolution that allows for the analysis of the unique, locus-specific patterns that result from genetic adaptation in the context of the genome-wide average and largely selectively neural demographic history. Briefly, there are four primary evolutionary forces, 1) mutation, 2) genetic drift, 3) admixture, and 4) natural selection.

Mutation (*i.e.*, a change in the sequence of nucleic acids along the strand of DNA) is the ultimate source of all genetic variation and occurs more or less at random across the genome. Mutation events are unique, occurring in just one chromosome at one particular genomic location, although some nucleotide positions are hypermutable and undergo repeated change. SNPs are an example of those most-commonly occurring types of genetic variation in the genome, and result from the point mutation of a particular base pair.

Genetic drift occurs as the result of segregation of parental alleles in the generation of the current cohort. In a population of infinite size, there is no genetic drift; that is, all alleles present in the parental generation are transmitted to the next. But in the finite population sizes in which persons live, the magnitude of the effect of drift on the genetic variation in the population is inversely proportional to the size of the mating population, increasing as population size decreases. Over time, genetic drift leads both to the loss of some alleles and fixation (*i.e.*, present in all persons) of others, and to genetic differentiation among populations (*i.e.,* populations "drift" apart after separation).

Admixture is the process of gene "flow" or "migration" of alleles from one population to another that occurs when individuals from reproductively-isolated populations interbreed and produce a new population. Admixture reduces the effects of differentiation, making populations more similar. Admixture also creates linkage disequilibrium that can be used for mapping the genes that determine variation in traits that distinguish populations. "Linkage disequilibrium" is the non-random association of alleles at different loci and an important source of statistical power for genetic association testing. Additionally, admixture creates a useful type of genetic structure within populations that might best be called admixture stratification. Admixture stratification can be an important source of information in testing the extent to which variation in a trait across populations is due to genetic differences between the parental populations.

Natural selection, or genetic adaptation, is the process of allele frequency change due to differential fitness (survival and reproduction) of individuals by genotype. Natural selection contrasts with the effects of genetic drift and admixture insofar as only the genetic region around the gene that is under natural selection undergoes change due to natural selection, whereas genetic drift and admixture affect markers across the whole genome. It is notable that, given the random nature of the effects of genetic drift, a substantial amount of variation in level of divergence is expected even though the evolutionary force of drift is applied evenly to all markers across the genome. In other words, drift alone because of the combined effects of many random events will lead to a very wide range in outcomes.

The allele frequency differential (delta), one of the simplest summary statistics, can actually be quite instructive for making comparisons across populations. Delta is calculated as the absolute value of the frequency of allele "C" in population 1 minus the frequency of the "C" allele in population 2 or simply, the difference in allele frequency. Figure 1 shows the histogram of deltas between a sample of Quechua (N=20), a Native Andean population living in Peru, and Nahua (N=20), a Meso-American population living in Mexico (23). The average delta as calculated for total of 11,555 SNPs for these populations is 0.088. This number is smaller relative to that observed when either group is compared to other populations, since these two groups are closely related by both being Indigenous Americans. For example, when an East Asian sample (N=20; 10 Japanese and 10 Chinese) is compared to the Nahua and Quechua samples, the average deltas are about twice as large, 0.167 and 0.168, respectively. Although the average is 0.088, there is a wide range of delta values for these two populations, with many markers having very low delta levels and a small number showing higher levels. Although, this overall pattern of allele frequency differential is consistent with effects due to genetic drift (akey et al, 2002,), genes that have changed in allele frequency because of the action of natural selection operating after the separation of these populations should show high levels of allele frequency differential. Since the Nahua do not live at high altitude as do the Quechua, it is reasonable to assume that, if genetic adaptation has made high-altitude populations more fit in hypoxic environments, functional alleles should show high delta levels. Thus, the high "tail" of this distribution should contain genes that have undergone genetic adaptation or, in other words, genes near clusters of high-delta markers can be considered *candidate natural-selection genes*.

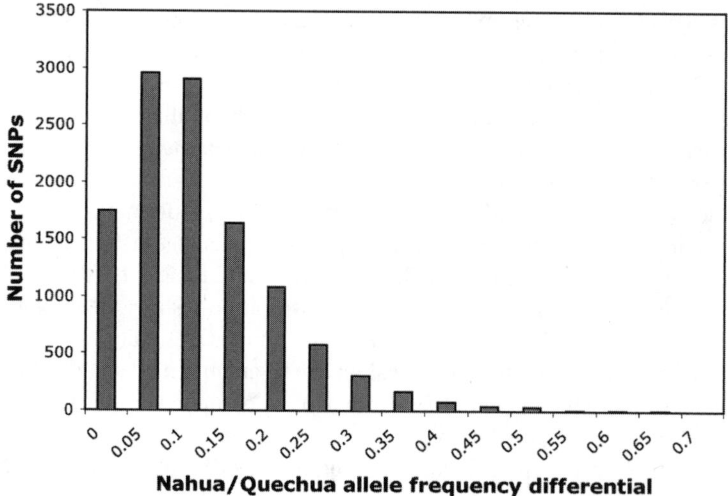

Figure 1. The histogram distribution of allele frequency differential between samples of two Indigenous American populations. The absolute value of allele frequency difference (delta) is shown for Nahua (N=20), a MesoAmerican lowland population, and Quechua (N=20), a Peruvian population from the Altiplano. A total of 11,555 SNPs were analyzed.

Although delta and related measures like F_{ST} (the measure of differentiation when more than two populations are compared), may be informative as to the likelihood that genetic adaptation has occurred near any particular marker in the dataset, more specific tests can be made with a simple modification. The problem is evident since high-delta markers between these two populations could result from either genetic adaptation to altitude (or other aspects of the environment) in the Quechua or to some change in allele frequency due to genetic adaptation in the Nahua. By including a third population, we can compute a more specific measure of differentiation called the Locus-Specific Branch Length (LSBL) as described by Shriver and collaborators (22).

To compute LSBL for three populations (A, B, and C), we use the three pairwise delta levels (d_{AB}, d_{AC}, and d_{BC}). Then using the three equations below, we can express the branch lengths of the phylogentic tree represented in Figure 2.

1) $x = (d_{AB} + d_{AC} - d_{BC}) / 2$
2) $y = (d_{AB} + d_{BC} - d_{AC}) / 2$
3) $z = (d_{AC} + d_{BC} - d_{AB}) / 2$

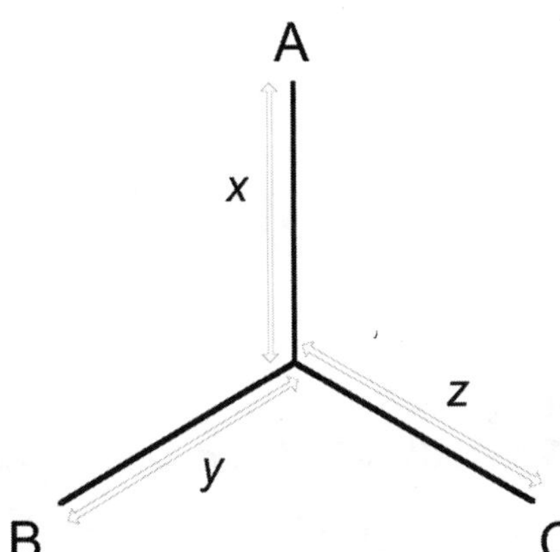

Figure 2. A diagram showing how the Locus-Specific Branch Length (LSBL) is calculated from the three pairwise delta levels. Refer to the text for formulae.

When there are three populations, there is only one topology relating populations and so the only variables are these branch lengths (*x*, *y*, and *z*). Figure 3 shows the distribution of LSBL levels for the three populations, Nahua, Quechua, and East Asian using 11,555 SNPs. As expected in this scenario, the East Asian LSBL estimates are longer, averaging 0.123, than the Nahua or Quechua, averages of 0.0438 and 0.0446, respectively.

The conceptual model of the LSBL is especially consistent with the underlying hypothesis in the case of hypoxic adaptation: we expect that the high-altitude Quechua are going to have adapted at particular loci relative to both the East Asian and Nahua populations. Evolutionary changes will have occurred in each of these populations, but those of greatest interest to hypoxia researchers are the subset of changes leading to high Quechua LSBL. Isolating the changes in one population relative to the two others is a unique facility of the LSBL measure compared to delta or F_{ST} methods. The empirical distributions of LSBL for large number of loci can be used to express the probability of observing LSBL levels of a particular magnitude (17). For example, consider that a locus of interest was measured to have an LSBL value of X. The empirical probability (P_E) is calculated as (# SNPs > X)/(total # SNPs).

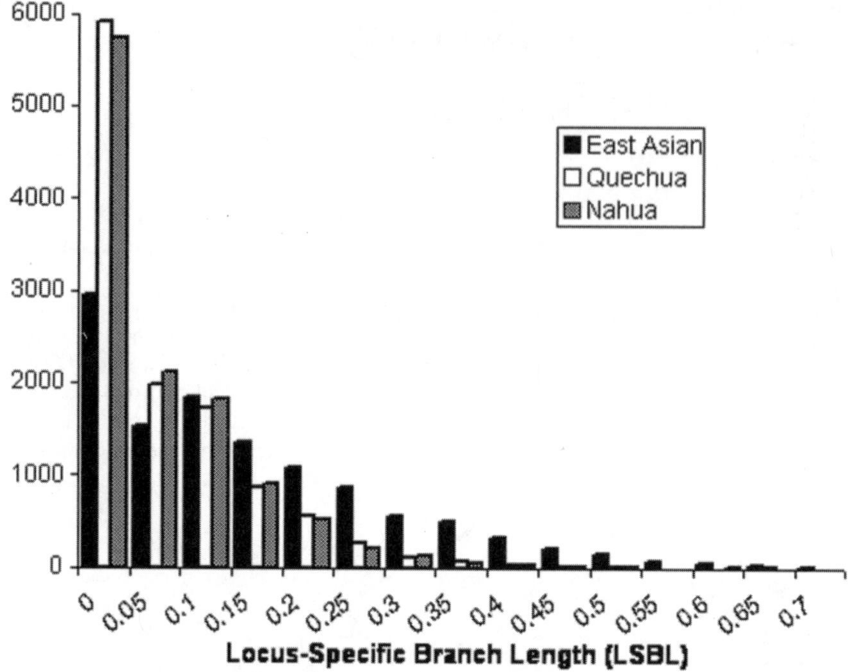

Figure 3. The histogram of the LSBL levels observed across 11,555 SNPs for three populations, Nahua (N=20), Quechua (N=20), and East Asian (N=20; 10 Japanese and 10 Chinese).

We used data generated with the Affymetrix, Inc. (Santa Clara, CA) 10K Mapping Array, a SNP genotyping platform that facilitates the simultaneous analysis of 11,555 SNPs to test a number of candidate genes for evidence of genetic adaptation. We chose four candidate genes of those approximately 40 genes known to contain a "hypoxic response element" or to be involved in the regulation of the hypoxia-inducible factors or HIFs (see Moore in this volume for a fuller explanation). These HIF pathway candidate genes were screened for proximity to any of the 11,555 SNPs. Those candidate genes showing a SNP within 40,000 bp of a SNP are shown in Table 1 along with the allele frequency in the three populations, delta, LSBL and the P_E levels. Five of these results are either suggestive P_E <0.1) or statistically significant (P_E <0.05), the most significant being a SNP near the *EDN1* gene that encodes endothelin where the delta value of 0.275 yields a P_E. = 0.036 and the LSBL value of 0.275 yields a P_E = 0.012.

These results are instructive as to how such studies can be planned and executed. For completeness, one would assay a number of SNPs (five to ten) located within a gene (that is, in either expressed or non-expressed regions embedded within the gene) and compare the deltas and LSBL levels for all of them against the empirical distributions. Genes that show several high-delta or high-LSBL SNPs should then be confirmed as such using independent replicate samples of the three populations. This is especially important when the population sample sizes for SNP markers are small (N<50) as sampling error will decrease the accuracy of allele frequency estimates. Other tests of natural selection, such as sequencing based methods and methods based on Linkage Disequilibrium (LD) can also be used to confirm these population genomic signals.

Table 1. Allele frequencies, delta levels and LSBL levels for HIF Pathway Candidate genes which have nearby SNPs on the Affymetrix 10K Mapping Array .

		Allele frequency						
Gene	**dbSNP rs#**	**Nahua**	**Quechua**	**East Asian**	**Quechua/Nahua delta**	**P_E**	**Quechua branch**	**P_E**
NOS2A	953527	0.588	0.425	0.500	0.163	0.169	0.075	0.226
NOS2A	953528	0.650	0.425	0.525	0.225	**0.074**	0.100	0.157
ADRA1B	952037	0.250	0.100	0.350	0.150	0.202	0.150	**0.093**
EDN1	1321055	0.525	0.800	0.175	0.275	**0.036**	0.275	**0.012**
FLT1	720661	1.000	1.000	1.000	0.000	0.855	0.000	0.490
FLT1	748253	0.900	0.825	0.600	0.075	0.409	0.000	0.490
TGFA	958686	0.250	0.225	0.450	0.025	0.753	0.025	0.421
CUL2	1926554	0.325	0.175	0.200	0.150	0.202	0.025	0.421
NRP2	867344	0.421	0.400	0.600	0.021	0.816	0.021	0.455
NRP2	872943	0.053	0.050	0.150	0.003	0.852	0.003	0.481
NRP1	927099	0.421	0.500	0.368	0.079	0.403	0.079	0.202
EGLN3	1769621	0.625	0.775	0.500	0.150	0.202	0.150	**0.093**
EGLN3	1809461	0.214	0.361	0.250	0.147	0.216	0.111	0.143
EGLN3	958722	0.400	0.425	0.075	0.025	0.753	0.025	0.421

Ancestry Evidence

Our preliminary studies were designed to evaluate the association of Quechua ancestry with hypoxia response traits (4,5). These studies were based on data from 151 young (age 18-35 yrs) Peruvian males and females who were born and raised in Lima, Peru (sea level), and in Cerro de Pasco, Peru (4,338 m). Originally, we used 22 ancestry-informative genetic markers (AIMs) to give estimates of Native American ancestry proportion (NAAP), European ancestry proportion (EAP), and West African ancestry proportion (AAP) for each individual in the study. Recently, as our library of markers has expanded, we have improved the precision of these estimates by using 80 AIMs (unpublished data). These studies have revealed significant associations between NAAP and the decrement in maximal oxygen consumption with altitude exposure ($\Delta\dot{V}O_2max$), the hypoxic ventilatory response to sustained hypoxia (HVR), and the level of resting and exercise ventilation ($\dot{V}_E$) at high altitude. $\Delta\dot{V}O_2max$ was evaluated by measuring the same subjects in both Lima and Cerro de Pasco. After controlling for sea-level $\dot{V}O_2max$, high NAAP was associated with a ~15% smaller $\Delta\dot{V}O_2max$ (4), consistent with earlier studies showing small $\Delta\dot{V}O_2max$ in Andeans compared to European controls (2,9,10,27). However, the ancestry association was only evident in the subset of subjects who also showed large decreases in arterial saturation at maximal exercise at 4,338 m (P=0.03). One possibility is that the ancestry-$\Delta\dot{V}O_2max$ association is easiest to detect in well-trained or highly motivated subjects who are more likely to experience pulmonary gas exchange limitation and/or exercise induced hypoxemia during exercise, particularly at altitude. Even stronger ancestry associations were detected with the HVR measured at sea-level and the altitude $\dot{V}_E$(unpublished data). NAAP was inversely related to the HVR measured after 10 minutes of isocapnic hypoxia given at sea-level (R=-0.36,P=0.04). NAAP was also inversely related to exercise $\dot{V}_E$ (R=-0.50, P=0.005) when subjects were tested at altitude in Cerro de Pasco. Thus, Quechua ancestry may be partly responsible for the well-known hypoxia tolerance of Andeans (i.e., small $\Delta\dot{V}O_2max$), their "blunted HVR" (7,17,16,21,24), and their relative exercise hypoventilation compared to European controls.

SUMMARY AND FUTURE DIRECTIONS

Given high-altitude native populations have undergone genetic adaptation making them better fit under hypoxic stress, two methods of genomic analysis can and should be used to identify the particular genes involved. The two methods, 1) Estimating genetic ancestry and admixture mapping and 2) Screening for signatures of genetic adaptation provide complementary information. Screening for genetic adaptation can be carried out on a genomic scale when sufficient numbers of genetic markers are available (25). It is unclear the number of genetic markers that will be required to properly tag the entire genome, but this number is likely to be quite high (> 100,000 evenly spaced evolutionarily informative SNPs). DNA sequence information can also be used to test for genetic adaptation on a candidate locus level now and within 5 to 10 years, on a genome-wide level as the costs of sequencing come down. The population genomic paradigm provides an appropriate context within which to identify hypoxia genes, but further theoretical and analytical developments are required to realize the full potential of these methods. Additionally, there is the need for a much more complete understanding of the demographic histories of South

American populations.

ACKNOWLEDGMENTS

We would also like to acknowledge the trust and generosity of the people and populations who contributed the DNA samples on which these studies are based. This work was supported in part by grants NIH/NHGRI (HG02154) to MDS; NIH grants HL 60131, TW 01188, and HL 079647 to LGM; NSERC grant 262080 to EJP; and NSF BCS-0129377 to TDB.

REFERENCES

1. Akey J, Zhang G, Zhang K, Jin L, and Shriver MD A high-density SNP allele frequency map reveals signatures of natural selection. *Genome Research* 12:1805-1814, 2002.
2. Baker PT. Human adaptation to high altitude. *Science* 163:1149-56, 1969.
3. Black WC, Baer CF, Antolin MF, and DuTeau NM. Population genomics: Genome-wide sampling of insect populations. *Annu Rev Entomol* 46: 441-469, 2001.
4. Brutsaert T, Parra E, Shriver M, Gamboa A, Palacios J, Rivera M, Rodriquez I, and Leaon-Velarde F. Spanish genetic admixture is associated with larger $\dot{V}O_2$max decrement from sea level to 4.338 m in Peruvan Quechua. *J Appl Physiol* 95:519-528, 2003.
5. Brutsaert T, Parra E, Shriver M, Gamboa A, Palacios J, Rivera M, Rodriquez I, and Leaon-Velarde F. Effects of birth place and individual admixture on lung volume and exercise phenotypes of Peruvian Quechua. *Am J Phys Anthro* 123:390-398, 2004.
6. Chakraborty R and Weiss KM. Admixture as a tool for finding linked genes and detecting that difference from allelic association between loci. *Proc Natl Acad Sci* 85: 9119-9123, 1988.
7. Chiodi H. Respiratory adaptations to chronic high altitude hypoxia. *J Appl Physiol* 10:81-7, 1957.
8. Halder I and Shriver MD. Measuring and using admixture to study the genetics of complex disease. *Human Genomics* 1:52-62, 2003.
9. Hochachka PW, Stanley C, Matheson GO, McKenzie DC, Allen PS, and Parkhouse WS. Metabolic and work efficiencies during exercise in Andean natives. *J Appl Physiol* 70:1720-30, 1991.
10. Hochachka PW, Stanley C, Matheson GO, McKenzie DC, Allen PS, and Parkhouse WS. Metabolic and work efficiencies during exercise in Andean natives. *J Appl Physiol* 70:1720-30, 1991.
11. Hoggart CJ, Shriver MD, Kittles RA, Clayton DG, and McKeigue PM. Design and analysis of admixture mapping studies. *Am J Hum Genet* 74: 965-978, 2004.
12. http://www.ncbi.nlm.nih.gov/Omim/mimstats.html
13. Jobling MA, Hurles ME, Tyler-Smith C. Molecular Evolutionary Genetics. London/New York: Garland Science Publishing, 2003.
14. Ke Y, Su B, Song X, Lu D, Chen L, Li H, Qi C, Marzuki S, Deka R, Underhill P, Xiao C, Shriver M, Lell J, Wallace D, Wells RS, Seielstad M, Oefner P, Zhu D, Jin J, Huang W, Chakraborty R, Chen Z, and Jin L. African origin of modern humans in east asia: a tale of 12,000 Y chromosomes. *Science* 292:1151-1153, 2001
15. Lahiri S, DeLaney RG, Brody JS, Simpser M, Velasquez T, Motoyama EK, and Polgar C. Relative role of environmental and genetic factors in respiratory adaptation to high

altitude. *Nature* 261:133-5, 1976.

16. Lahiri S, Kao FF, Velasquez T, Martinez C, and Pezzia W. Irreversible blunted respiratory sensitivity to hypoxia in high altitude natives. *Respir Physiol* 6:360-74, 1969.
17. Moore, L., Shriver, M., Bemis, L., Hickler, B., Wilson, M., Brutsaert, T., Parra, T., and Vargas, E. Maternal adaptation to high-altitude pregnancy: an experiment of nature. *Placenta* 25:S60-S71, 2004.
18. Parra EJ, Kittles RA, and Shriver, M.D. Implications of correlations between skin color and genetic ancestry for biomedical research *Nat. Genet.* 36:S54-S60, 2004.
19. Pfaff CL, Parra EJ, Bonilla C, Hiester K, McKeigue PM, Kamboh MI, Hutchinson RG, Ferrell RE, Boerwinkle E, and Shriver MD Population structure in admixed populations: Examination of African American populations from Jackson, MS and Coastal South Carolina. *Am J Hum Genet* 68:198-207, 2001.
20. Rosenberg NA, Pritchard JK, Weber JL, Cann HM, Kidd KK, Zhivotovsky LA, and Feldman MW Genetic structure of human populations. *Science* 298: 2381-2385, 2002.
21. Severinghaus JW, Bainton CR, and Carcelen A. Respiratory insensitivity to hypoxia in chronically hypoxic man. *Respir Physiol* 1:308-34, 1966.
22. Shriver MD, Kennedy GC, Parra EJ, Lawson HA, Huang J, Akey JM, and Jones KW The Genomic Distribution of Human Population Substructure in Four Populations using 8525 SNPs. *Human Genomics* 1:274-286, 2004.
23. Shriver MD, Mei R, Parra EJ, Sonpar V, Halder I, Tishkoff SA, Schurr TG, Zhadanov SI, Osipova LP, Brutsaert TD, Friedlaender J, Jorde LB, Watkins WS, Bamshad MJ, Gutierrez G, Loi H, Matsuzaki H, Kittles RA, Argyropoulos G, Fernandez JR. Akey JM, and Jones K. Large-scale SNP analysis reveals clustered and continuous human genetic variation. in press in *Human Genomics*, 2(2): 81-89, 2005
24. Sorensen SC, and Severinghaus JW. Respiratory sensitivity to acute hypoxia in man born at sea level living at high altitude. *J Appl Physiol* 25:211-6, 1968.
25. Storz JF. Using genome scans of DNA polymorphism to infer adaptive population divergence. *Molecular Ecology,* 14:671-688, 2004.
26. Torroni A, Miller JA, Moore LG, Zamudio S, Zhuang J, Droma T, Wallace DC. Mitochondrial DNA analysis in Tibet: implications for the origin of the Tibetan population and its adaptation to high altitude. *Am J Phys Anthropol* 93(2):189-199, 1994
27. Vogel JA, Hartley LH, and Cruz JC. Cardiac output during exercise in altitude natives at sea level and high altitude. *J Appl Physiol* 36:173-6, 1974.

Chapter 10

AN EVOLUTIONARY MODEL FOR IDENTIFYING GENETIC ADAPTATION TO HIGH ALTITUDE

Lorna G. Moore[1], Mark Shriver[2], Lynne Bemis[3], and EnriqueVargas[4]
[1]Colorado Center for Altitude Medicine and Physiology (Division of Emergency Medicine), PhD Program in Health and Behavioral Science, and Department of Anthropology [2]Department of Anthropology, Pennsylvania State University, State College, PA [3]Division of Medical Oncology, Department of Medicine, University of Colorado at Denver and Health Sciences Center, Denver, CO [4]Instituto Boliviano de Biología de Altura, La Paz, Bolivia.

Abstract: Coordinated maternal/fetal responses to pregnancy are required to ensure continuous O_2 delivery to the developing organism. Mammals employ distinctive reproductive strategies that afford their young an improved chance of survival through the completion or the reproductive period. Thus, mortality prior to the end of the reproductive period is concentrated in the earliest phases of the lifecycle. At high altitude, fetal growth restriction reduces birth weight and likely compromises survival during the early postnatal period. Population variation in the frequency of the altitude-associated increase in intrauterine growth restriction (IUGR) demonstrates that multigenerational Tibetan and Andean high-altitude populations are protected compared with shorter duration, European or Han (Chinese) residents. This experiment of nature permits testing the hypothesis that genetic factors (a) influence susceptibility to altitude-associated IUGR, (b) act on maternal vascular adjustments to pregnancy determining uteroplacental blood flow, and (c) involve genes which regulate and/or are regulated by hypoxia-inducible factors (HIFs). Serial, studies during pregnancy as well as postpartum in Andean and European residents of high (3600 m) and low (300 m) altitude will permit evaluation of whether uteroplacental O_2 delivery is lower in the European than Andean women and, if so, the physiological factors responsible. Comparisons of HIF-targeted vasoactive substances and SNPs in or near HIF-regulatory or targeted genes will permit determination of whether these regions are distinctive in the Andean population. Studies coupling genetic and genomic approaches with more traditional physiological measures may be productively employed for determining the genetic mechanisms influencing physiological adaptation to high altitude.

Key Words: adaptation, hypoxia, hypoxia inducible factor (HIF), IUGR, natural selection, preeclampsia, uteroplacental ischemia

Hypoxia and Exercise, edited by R.C. Roach *et al.*
Springer, New York, 2006.

INTRODUCTION

Studies of human physiological adaptation to high altitude (defined here as >2500 m or 8000 ft) have long sought to determine whether or not there are genetic factors involved. Such efforts have been hindered by the inherent difficulties in distinguishing between genetic attributes *vs.* those that are acquired as a result of prenatal, postnatal, or later-in-life influences (9). In the language of geneticists, the phenotype (P) is a function of genetic (G) and environmental (E) influences plus the interactions between them (G x E); rarely, are only genetic factors responsible for visible traits. Interaction is so ubiquitous that some have questioned whether any influence is purely genetic or environmental (47). Such interactions include the influences of age, nutrition, disease or other kinds of environmental characteristics on the expression of genetic traits. For example, at high altitude, the larger lung volumes of lifelong, Andean high-altitude residents reflect both developmental exposure and a hereditary potential for larger lung dimensions (19). In addition. Brutsaert and co-workers have shown that the extent of an individual's physical fitness -- largely a function of acquired traits such as habitual exercise levels and training -- influences the extent to which genetic factors confer protection from an altitude-associated decrement in maximal exercise capacity (8).

The purpose of this article is to describe a model for identifying the genetic and/or genomic contribution to human adaptation to high altitude. Specifically, this model lays the groundwork for applying the analytical techniques described in this volume by Shriver *et al.,* to the adaptive challenge of fetal growth restriction posed by residence at high altitude. For reasons elaborated upon below, because the risk to survival prior to the end of the reproductive period is greatest during the period of pre- and early post-natal life, we elect to focus on fetal growth restriction as our index of high-altitude adaptation. Since genetic changes occur over generations and hence require long periods of time, we also choose to compare populations with and without multigenerational exposure to high altitude, while proposing to make provision for controlling for differences between groups unrelated to high-altitude exposure.

DEFINING ADAPTATION

From a genetic perspective, evolution can be defined as change in gene (allele) frequency over time. Four factors are involved– mutation, genetic drift, gene flow and natural selection – but only one of these, natural selection, is directional. Natural selection is also the force of greatest interest to physiologists since, generally, it is the effects of genes on the organism's ability to adapt to the environment that is of paramount concern. "Adaptation" in an evolutionary context refers to the ability to live and reproduce in a given environment (17). In principle, adaptations can be grouped into those affecting fertility (the production of live offspring) and mortality (in an evolutionary context, the ability of the organism to survive until the end of its reproductive period). "Fitness" is the net result of influences on both fertility and mortality, sometimes simply referred to as reproductive success. Distinguishing between adaptations affecting fertility and mortality can be difficult, especially in mammals that, as a group, shelter their young within their mother's uterus, making early mortality difficult to detect.

Mammalian distinctions. The appearance of mammals in the paleontologic record changed natural selection from operating by an "r"- to a "k"- strategy. An "r"-based strategy is characterized by the production of a large number of young, each of which has a low probability of survival. The "k"-strategy employed by mammals relies upon the production of fewer eggs, each of which has a greater probability of being fertilized and, if fertilized, a greater probability for survival. In short, the changeover from an "r" to a "k" strategy reflects a shift from a more "quantity" to "quality" reproductive approach. Still, among mammals, probably only on the order of 20% of fertilized eggs survive until birth.

A prolonged intrauterine period greatly enhances the likelihood of survival but poses a different kind of challenge; how to house a 50% genetically dissimilar organism without the mother's immune detection and rejection? For some mammals, the answer is to protect the offspring by having a "shell" (more a leathery sort of skin) to protect the offspring from immune detection while in utero. These are "prototherian" mammals, exemplified by the duck-billed platypus. Another strategy is that employed by "metatherian" mammals, like kangaroos or wallabys, which give birth early to an extremely immature offspring that is housed in the mother's pouch where it can nurse and grow to a large enough size to be able to fend for itself. The metatherian strategy appears to have been the kind employed by the earliest mammals (105). "Eutherian" mammals' reliance on the placenta carries the "r" *vs.* "k"-approach a stage further insofar as the placenta greatly improves the conceptus' chance of survival by permiting a period of prolonged gestation for fetal growth and development. The placenta is a specialized tissue of fetal origin that not only aids in nourishing the fetus but also minimizes its detection by the mother's immune system[1].

Shape of the age vs. survival curve. The influence of the placenta on the shape of the survival curve is illustrated in Figure 1. Defining life as beginning at conception[2], mortality rates in fish are very high during hatching and then decline, as they get larger and are better able to flee from predators. The protection afforded by shelled eggs lowers mortality somewhat during early life. Protection is further enhanced in placental mammals, displacing the survival curve to the right even more. Relatively high mortality soon after conception is still present in placental mammals, likely due to implantation failure, chromosomal or other kinds of genetic abnormalities which are nearly always lethal and result in spontaneous abortion. An improved chance of survival following this early, prenatal period is carried to an extreme in humans whose smaller number of births, extended period of infancy, and social support systems reduce infantile and childhood mortality relative to other mammals. Even more remarkably in humans, survivorship extends beyond the end of the reproductive period into old age.

One point requires clarification: the difference between "lifespan" and "life expectancy." Sometime used interchangeably, "lifespan" refers to a probably, genetically-endowed maximum length of life for a given species, whereas "life expectancy" is the probability that a given organism will achieve this lifespan. For humans, the lifespan is estimated as being approximately 120 years. Life expectancy is generally calculated at birth but can, in principle, be calculated at any age. When calculated at birth, by far the greatest contributor to life expectancy is the mortality rate during infancy and childhood. If calculated at age 15, life expectancies are quite similar even when comparing societies with markedly different standards of living (21).

The point here is that humans follow a reproductive strategy in which mortality, prior to the end of the reproductive period, is concentrated in the earliest phases of the lifecycle.

In other words, once born and especially once infancy and childhood are completed, the chances of surviving through the reproductive period are very high. In relation to high altitude, the implication here is that the most important determinants of survival are likely to be those affecting intrauterine mortality or mortality soon after birth. Fertility does not seem to be adversely affected at high altitude (103); on the contrary, levels appear to be higher in some high- than low-altitude Peruvian groups (26). Therefore, the most important influences of altitude are likely to be centered on fetal growth and/or gestational age.

Importance of birth weight. For humans, the single most important predictor of neonatal mortality is small size at birth, whether due to fetal growth restriction or preterm delivery (52). This is illustrated by the continuing decline in mortality rates from the neonatal through the infant and childhood periods in Figure 1.

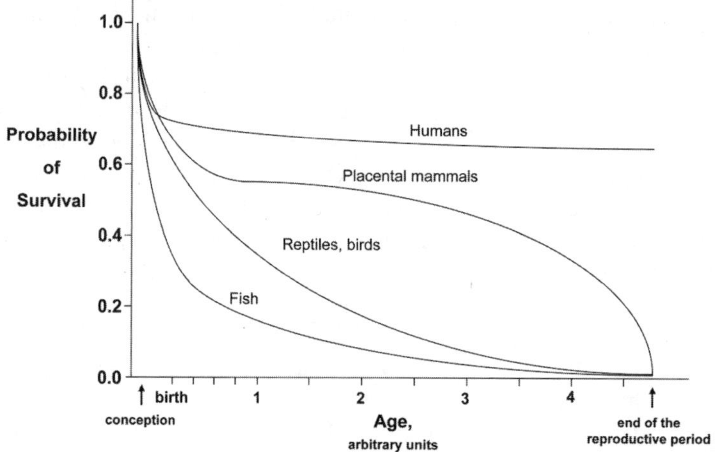

Figure 1. For fish and reptiles or birds, mortality is especially high following hatching and then gradually declines, with all individuals dying after the completion of reproduction. Placental mammals, initially, have high intrauterine mortality but an improved chance of survival relative to fish, reptiles or birds. Mortality gradually declines following birth for most placental mammals, with all deaths occurring by the end of reproduction. Humans have a distinctive pattern in which mortality is relatively low during infancy and childhood and then very low during adolesence and the adult years, with a considerable proportion surviving after the completion of the reproductive period. This graph is drawn for illustrative purposes and is not strictly to scale. Actual age-specific mortality risks vary by historical period and by society.

The contributions of gestational age and birth weight to neonatal mortality vary, depending on the particular ages and weights involved, as shown by the non-symmetric shape of the mortality boxes in the fetal growth charts first advanced by Dr. Lula Lubchenco nearly 50 years ago (Figure 2). The development of such charts, now used the world over, permits identifying whether or not a given newborn is at "risk", it ranks as one of the great public health advances of our times. Sociocultural factors also influence the effects of fetal growth and gestational age on neonatal mortality; preterm births are less likely to occur in developed countries where medical technology permits delaying labor or hastening maturation of the fetus' lungs when labor is threatened, making IUGR an especially important factor

(28). But today in the developed as well as the developing world, as well as throughout human existence, a high proportion of infant mortality is likely attributable to the influences of fetal growth restriction and preterm delivery.

While many factors contribute to IUGR[3], one of the more pervasive is uteroplacental ischemia. As elaborated below, uteroplacental blood flow increases more than 30-fold during pregnancy, fueling the exponential rise in fetal growth, and making any reductions in blood flow potentially important. While sometimes not thought of as a nutrient, oxygen can be so considered since oxygen, like other nutrients, is a source of energy (ATP supply) as well as a cofactor in numerous metabolic processes. Other nutrients required for fetal growth include glucose, amino acids, various trace minerals and vitamins.

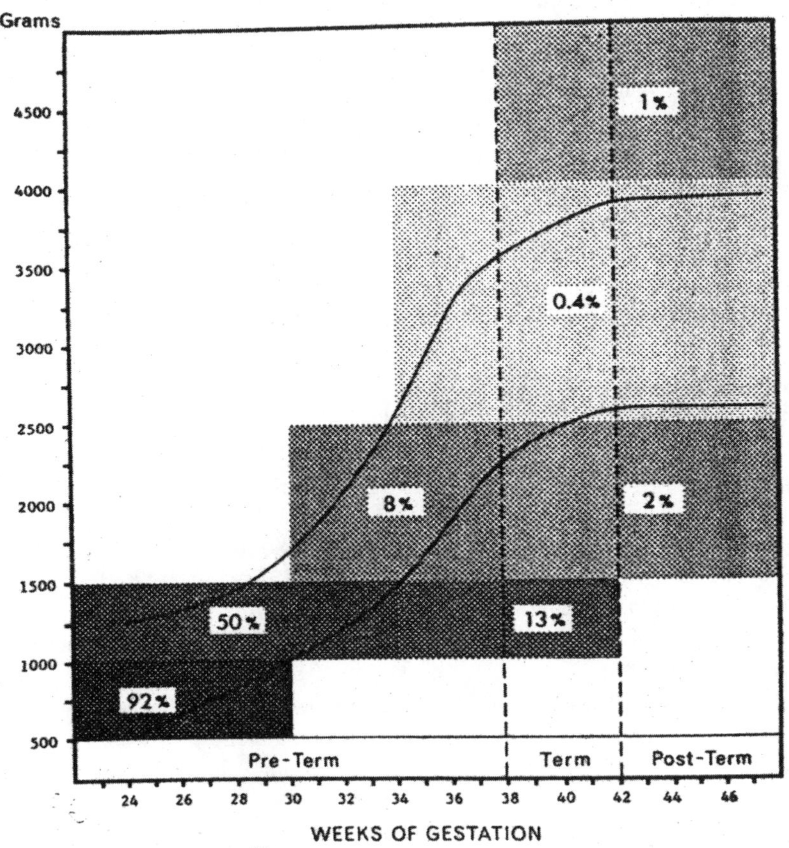

Figure 2. Birth weight (gm, y axis) and gestational age (x axis) influence neonatal mortality, shown as the percent deaths during the first 28 days of postnatal life. Mortality declines with advancing gestational age and increasing birth weight. The figure is reprinted from Lubchenco (52) who compiled data for all University of Colorado Medical Center newborn admissions from July 1, 1958 - July 1, 1968.

EFFECT OF HIGH ALTITUDE ON BIRTH WEIGHT

Epidemiological, anthropological and public health observations. High altitude occupies a special place in the history of investigating the cause(s) of low birth weight (conventionally defined as <2500 gm or 5.5 lbs). Until the 1970s, the World Health Organization and other such agencies considered any low birth weight baby to be "preterm" since gestational age information was not routinely sought. The first observations that hypoxia slows fetal growth on a population level were made at high altitude (49). In these studies, the possibility of shortened gestation was carefully considered; popular opinion held that the lack of snowplows prevented women from reaching the hospital and hence doctors delivered their patients early (65). The actual data, however, showed that gestational age did not differ from low-altitude values. Hence fetal growth restriction was identified as the primary cause in this early, as well as numerous more recent, studies (25, 37, 73). From ultrasound studies and altitude comparisons across a range of gestational ages, growth measurably begins to slow about week 30 (43, 102).

The birth weight decline averages 100 gm per 1000 m altitude gain (37). The effects of altitude are greater than those of low maternal weight gain, smoking, primiparity or preeclampsia and second only to gestational age in importance (37). Given the more than 100,000 Coloradans and 140 million persons living at high altitudes worldwide, high-altitude residents are the single largest group at risk for IUGR (41). The primary factor responsible appears to be the hypoxia associated with residence at high altitude (25, 49, 73). Additional contributors are the altitude-associated increase in preeclampsia, which accounts for about half the birth weight decline, as well as yet to be fully elucidated interactions with other factors such as smoking (37, 39, 55, 66, 78, 81).

While occurring worldwide, the magnitude of the altitude-associated birth weight reduction varies in relation to the duration (in generations) of high-altitude exposure. That is, Tibetans and Andeans who have lived at high altitudes for 10,000+ yrs show one-third the reduction present in European or Han ("Chinese") populations that have resided at high altitudes for <500 years (79). Such variation does not appear attributable to maternal body size, nutrition, health care or birth weight present at sea level (29, 64). Nor do birth weights of babies born to lifelong high-altitude residents differ from those of babies born to women moving to altitude as adults, suggesting that developmental effects are not chiefly responsible (30, 69, 106).

Given the lower birth weights present at high altitudes, the expectation would be that neonatal and, by extension, infant mortality would be increased as well. Consistent with this, Bolivia and Peru have the highest infant mortality rates in South America and, in the case of Bolivia, the highest in the western hemisphere (80). There is a proportional rise in mortality with increasing altitude within Bolivia for both urban and rural dwellers, with rural rates being higher than those seen in urban areas (7, 24). Since there is considerably greater health care access in urban than rural regions, the urban-rural differences support the importance of health care for the mortality rates observed. But since the altitude rise is present for both urban and rural residents, the data also suggest that altitude is a likely contributor. In Colorado, infant mortality was greater in the high *vs.* low-altitude regions of the state until about 1980. With the advent of specialized neonatal care services and transport systems, mortality rates fell, particularly at the higher altitudes, so that now rates are similar throughout the state or in comparison to national levels (49, 62, 102, 109). There is continuing controversy as to whether the mortality risk for a given birth weight is modified by altitude. Recent Colorado or USA data indicate a slightly lower birth weight specific mortality risk at high than low altitude (102, 109). This may, in turn, be due to the more chronic nature of the altitude-related reduction in birth weight or to evidence supporting a greater utilization of specialized health care services by the higher-altitude women (102). The lack of a vital statistics system or gestational age data in South America, Tibet, or Ladkakh prevents assessing birth weight specific mortality risk in these regions. Nonetheless, low birth weight babies have higher mortality than do their normal weight counterparts -- not only during infancy but possibly at later ages as well (4) -- suggesting that it is not good to be "small" at high (or any) altitude.

Maternal oxygen transport adjustments to pregnancy. Pregnancy alters all the components of the maternal O_2 transport system; of these, greater uteroplacental blood flow is the most important. Arterial O_2 tension rises, due to an increase in ventilation that, in turn, reflects the central as well as peripheral, stimulatory effects of progesterone and estrogen hormones and elevated metabolic rate (68). But at low altitude, this ventilation rise does not normally influence arterial O_2 saturation since values are already nearly maximal. Blood volume expands, with the rise in plasma volume exceeding that of red cell mass, such that both hemoglobin concentration and arterial O_2 content decline. Thus increased uteroplacental O_2 delivery depends entirely on greater uteroplacental blood flow. A rise in uteroplacental blood flow is accomplished by uteroplacental as well as non-uteroplacental, systemic means. There is an early fall in systemic vascular resistance (SVR) that, together with the increase in blood volume, raises resting cardiac output some 40% (11). The fall in SVR is likely due to vasodilatory effects of increased NO production, decreased sympathetic tone, and a fall in the potent vasoconstrictor endothelin-1 (ET-1) (27, 53).

In the uterine circulation, an anastomosis develops between the ovarian branch and the main uterine artery (UA), providing the uterus with dual, bilateral arterial blood supply. Because the fall in uteroplacental vascular resistance is greater than that which occurs in the rest of the systemic circulation, a large fraction of the increased cardiac output is directed to the uteroplacental vascular bed. Most (~80%) goes through the two UA, raising unilateral flow from ~10 ml/min in the non-pregnant state to ~350 ml/min near term (82). This impressive rise in UA blood flow is due both to a doubling of intraluminal diameter (which quadruples cross-sectional area) and to increased blood flow velocity. UA vasodilation, greater distensibility as well as growth in all layers of the vessel wall are responsible for the increase in UA diameter (13). Similar changes likely occur in the mesometrial and basilar arteries, but the mechanisms by which these changes interact with the trophoblast invasion occurring downstream (at the level of the spiral arterioles) are not well understood.

An important distinction arises between species with hemochorial *vs.* epithelioral placentas (*i.e.,* humans, most other primates, rodents, and guinea pigs *vs.* sheep, dogs, cows, etc) in terms of the vessels constituting the primary site of uteroplacental vasculature resistance. In hemochorial species, trophoblasts invade approximately one-third of the way through the uterine wall, whereas trophoblast invasion is only one cell layer thick in epitheliochorial species. As a result, in hemochorial species the vessels determining uteroplacental vascular resistance reside largely outside the uterus; more precisely, $2/3^{rds}$ of uteroplacental vasculature resistance is located in the mesometrial, main UA and ovarian arteries with only $1/3^{rd}$ being located in uteroplacental channels (63, 96). This is the opposite of that which occurs in species with epitheliochorial placentas where the uteroplacental vessels comprise the major site of vascular resistance. Our studies have focused on the UA since it makes a demonstrable contribution to uteroplacental vascular resistance in the hemochorial species under study and can be visualized in humans.

Mechanisms by which chronic hypoxia may alter uteroplacental oxygen delivery. While in principle, the lower birth weights at high altitudes could be due to alterations in maternal and/or placental characteristics; we suspect maternal characteristics for several reasons. First, in a limited number of women in which we were able to make measurements of both UA diameter and blood flow velocity, UA volumetric blood flows were approximately one-third lower in near term women residing at high (3100 m) *vs.* low (1600 m) altitude in Colorado (112). Second, we had previously noted that not only were birth weights lower but also the maternal complication of preeclampsia was more common at high altitude. This was an accidental outgrowth of noting a higher than expected occurrence of preeclampsia in the high-altitude residents being studied physiologically. When we compared our sample to all women delivering during the study period, we found a surprisingly high incidence of preeclampsia in the population at large (67). Later, in a more systematic study, we confirmed the increased incidence of preeclampsia at high altitudes (81). Subsequent studies have replicated this finding elsewhere (39, 54). Third, placental characteristics have not, to date, been shown to be markedly different at high *vs.* low altitude, although generalized thinning has been reported (58). TissotvanPatot *et al.,* found a smaller proportion of maternal vessels had undergone trophoblast invasion and converted to a low-resistance circuit. But a greater absolute number of vessels meant that the number of "converted" vessels was the same at low and high altitude (101). Further studies are greatly needed to indicate whether or not metabolic processes are altered in potentially significant ways in high *vs.* low altitude placentas.

At high altitude, the pregnancy-associated increase in ventilation raises arterial O_2 saturation. Near-term O_2 content still falls due to greater plasma volume than red cell mass expansion (69) (61). While the extent to which the rise in ventilation is able to defend O_2 content relates positively to infant birth weight (69), heavier birth weights in long term high-altitude natives are not due to differences in arterial oxygenation since Tibetans and Andeans do not have higher arterial O_2 content than their Han or European counterparts (71). Thus, UA blood flow is likely to be the key determinant of uteroplacental O_2 delivery at high as well as at low altitude.

Non-uteroplacental as well as uteroplacental factors may be responsible for lowering uteroplacental O_2 delivery at high altitude. Cardiac output is lower, probably as the result of lower blood volume and/or higher SVR (40). The higher SVR may be due, in turn, to increased vasoconstrictor and/or reduced vasodilator production. Acute (hours) and more chronic high-altitude exposure raise sympathetic nervous system activity and catecholamine levels in non-pregnant women (60). ET-1 levels are also elevated by chronic hypoxia (72) and in preeclampsia (20). Underscoring the potential importance of ET-1, ET-1 A receptor blockade prevents the IUGR as well as the accompanying reduction in uteroplacental blood flow that is associated with hypoxia as well as NO synthase blockade (99). A third possibility -- reduced systemic NO production -- is not strongly supported by current data (108).

Concerning the uteroplacental circulation, UA blood flow near term is one-third lower in Colorado residents of high (3100 m) *vs.* low (1600 m) altitude, due to less pregnancy-associated increase in UA diameter (111). UA diameters and volumetric flows are also lower in Han residents of high- *vs.* low altitude (12) and in our preliminary studies of European *vs.* Andean residents of high altitude (70). Our data, like those of Krampl and co-workers (42), do not indicate that the lower UA blood flows are due to higher indices of uteroplacental vascular resistance, suggesting that the factors limiting uteroplacental blood flow reside in the uterine, not primarily the placental, vessels.

Our experimental animal studies demonstrate that chronic hypoxia opposes the normal pregnancy-associated changes in the UA. During normoxic pregnancy, the UA demonsterates an increased vasodilator response to flow; this enhanced flow vasodilation is absent in UA from chronically hypoxia animals (57). Similar findings are reported in preeclampsia, where a failure of mesometrial artery flow vasodilation also occurs (44). Chronic hypoxia also inhibits UA growth such that there is only half as much rise in DNA synthesis in vessels isolated from chronically-hypoxic *vs.* normoxic animals (88). Both these flow and growth alterations may stem from a lack of pregnancy-associated increase in NO. Chronic hypoxia reduces NO-dependent vasorelaxation to acetylcholine in isolated guinea pig UA rings and inhibits the pregnancy-associated increase in endothelial NO synthase protein (NOS III) in whole vessel homogenates (107). NOS III is also known to be important for the hypertrophic outward vascular growth characteristic of pregnancy (74). Unknown is whether hypoxia also affects the pregnancy-associated alterations in other vasodilators (*e.g.,* endothelial-derived hyperpolarizing factor), growth factors (*e.g.,* VEGF, PGF) and vasoactive factors (*e.g.,* ET-1, catecholamines), although our preliminary data and limited reports in non-pregnant persons (56) suggest that it does. In contrast, in sheep which did *not* exhibit altitude-associated reductions in fetal growth or UA blood flow (40) chronic hypoxia prompts an *exaggerated* increase in vasodilator response to acetylcholine and a greater rise in NO production, NOS III protein and message than seen during pregnancy at low altitude (113). Likewise, whereas chronic hypoxia did not alter the pregnancy-associated fall in UA vasoconstrictor response to phenylephrine in the guinea pig, this was augmented in sheep UA as a result of decreased alpha1-adrenergic receptor density, binding affinity and inositol phosphate 3 production (35). Such species variation in the effects of chronic hypoxia supports an important role for genetic mechanisms in the regulation of UA vascular response to pregnancy.

THE ROLE OF THE HYPOXIA-INDUCIBLE FACTOR (HIF) SYSTEM

HIF and O_2 homeostasis. HIF plays a central role in O_2 homeostasis, regulating over 70% of hypoxia-responsive genes. Thus HIF-regulated pathways are logical targets on which selection for traits influencing susceptibility to hypoxia-related disorders could be expected to act. The molecular mechanisms by which such regulation is achieved have been the subject of intense investigation (Figure 3). HIF is a highly-conserved heterodimer consisting of class one molecules -- the constitutive HIF1beta/ARNT complex -- and one of three class two molecules -- HIF 1, 2 or 3alpha. Despite continual production, degradation is sufficiently rapid that the HIFalpha proteins are virtually undetectable in normoxia. This degradation requires trans-4-hydroxylation at proline-564 and -402, recognition and binding by the VHL protein, ubiquination by a E3 ubiquitin ligase complex (consisting elongin C/elongin B, cullin 2, and the RING-H2 finger protein Rbx-1), and transport to the proteasome (89). But under hypoxia and selected other circumstances (*e.g.,* specific oncogenes, PHD enzyme inhibition, presence of large divalent metal ions or iron chelators), HIFalpha escapes hydroxylation and recognition by VHL. This permits HIF protein levels to rise, translocate to the nucleus, heterodimerize, and transcriptionally activate genes containing the cis-acting HRE 5'ACGTG(C/G)3' (93).

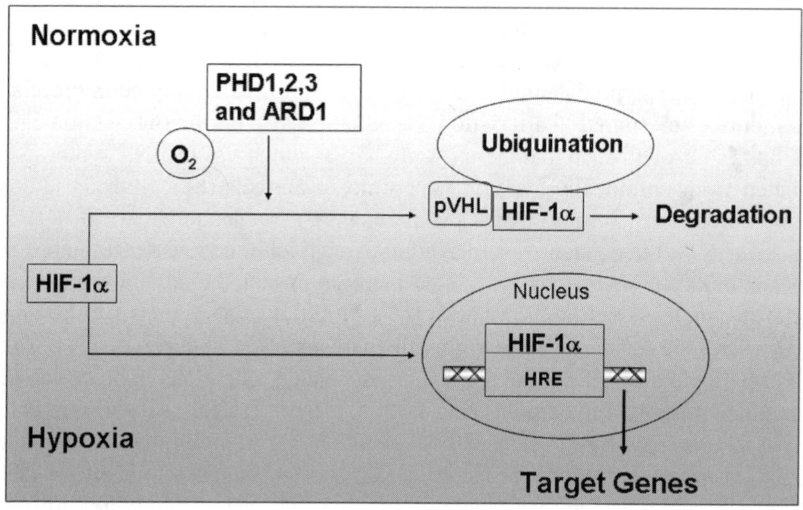

Figure 3. HIF-1 alpha regulation (schema courtesy of Kurt Stenmark).

Mechanisms and evidence of action during pregnancy. Over 40 HIF-regulated or regulatory genes have been identified whose functions influence the vascular adjustments to hypoxia and pregnancy (85; Table 1). Moreover, variation occurs in these genes and such variation alters circulating plasma levels (86). Together with previous reports demonstrating that susceptibility to preeclampsia as well as IUGR is heritable (2, 36, 50, 51, 90, 104), there is a powerful rationale for screening these genes in an effort to find those responsible for the population variation in hypoxia-associated IUGR. Additional, direct support for the involvement of HIF-regulated genes comes from recent studies showing that trophoblast cells from preeclamptic placentas over express HIF-1 and 2 alpha (10, 84). Their transcriptional targets such as ET-1 and VEGF are also likely to be altered, since both have been implicated in the characteristic vasoconstriction, endothelial damage and reduced utero-placental blood flow of preeclampsia (18, 20, 46, 59, 95, 97-100). Vascular growth and remodeling are also likely affected; hypoxia, both in vitro and in vivo, alters the production of cytokines and other growth-related factors required for trophoblasts to transition to the invasive phenotype and remodel maternal spiral arterioles (22, 23, 101).

A genetic and genomic strategy for identifying variation in HIF-targeted or regulatory genes. As noted above, long-term (multigenerational) residents are relatively protected from the altitude-associated increase in IUGR and such protection appears due to ancestry-dependent, perhaps genetic, factors that permit normal maternal vascular adaptation to pregnancy. Thus, high-altitude populations provide a natural laboratory for determining whether genetic factors influence susceptibility to IUGR and possibly other conditions characterized by uteroplacental ischemia and, if so, the pathways or mechanisms through which such genes act.

Logical next steps involve a search for variation in HIF-regulatory and -regulated genes, and linking such variation to the maternal vascular abnormalities in IUGR and preeclampsia. Our concept here is that genetic variation in these systems exists in all populations and may explain, in part, susceptibility to preeclampsia and IUGR. High-altitude residents are expected to have been acted upon by natural selection across many generations and thus to preferentially express those genetic variants conferring resistance.

The availability of single nucleotide polymorphisms (SNPs) from the Human Genome Project provides a crucial methodological tool. SNPs permit evaluating the contribution of multiple genes to disease susceptibility in conjunction with varying environmental exposures. SNPs have been described in the HIF-regulated genes listed in Table 1, including proteins of known functional significance during pregnancy such as ET-1, VEGF, tyrosine hydroxylase (the rate-limiting step in catecholamine synthesis) and glucose transporters (31, 32, 34, 76). SNPs also occur in HIF-regulatory genes. This is exemplified by VHL, a tumor suppressor gene, which contains SNPs in coding regions that influence whether the person develops phaeochromocytoma, hemanigoblastoma, or renal cell carcinoma (14). Such SNPs are functional insofar as when VHL is mutated at specific amino acids and expressed in mammalian cells, it can no longer interact with HIF1alpha and send it to the proteasome for degradation.

Genomic approaches have been infrequently applied to pregnancy complications but offer considerable power for identifying genetic involvement in complex diseases. Thus they are increasingly being used in studies of human genetic variation to provide information unavailable from other approaches (5, 91). Such genomic approaches stem from the recognition that since geographic separation of human populations is quite recent[4], most genetic variation is shared among all populations (48). Thus, we expect low levels of genetic differentiation across most genes but, given our overall hypothesis, greater divergence in the Andean population in those genes that are HIF-regulated or -regulatory. Such differences in divergence are readily detectable using statistically sophisticated methodologies as further described by Shriver et al. in chapter 9 of this volume.

SUMMARY AND CONCLUSION

The reduced O_2 availability of residence at high altitude restricts fetal growth and increases the frequency of preeclampsia, making high-altitude residents the single largest group at risk for these disorders of pregnancy/fetal life. The altitude-related increase appears due, in part, to alterations in maternal vascular reactivity, growth and remodeling that reduce uterine artery blood flow. Moreover previous studies demonstrate that multigenerational compared with shorter-term high-altitude residents are protected from the altitude-associated increase in IUGR, probably as the result of greater UA blood flow. Based on recent evidence demonstrating that hypoxia-inducible transcription factors (HIFs) play a central role in regulating O_2-sensitive genes, are implicated in pregnancy disorders, and our preliminary evidence that they are differentially regulated in long- *vs.* short-term populations, future studies will test the overall hypothesis that genetic variants in HIF-targeted or regulatory pathways protect multigenerational high-altitude residents from hypoxia-associated IUGR. Strategies that couple genetic and genomic approaches with more traditional physiological tools may permit the identification of genes influencing physiological responses to pregnancy and can be productively employed for investigating other health effects of high altitude as well. Such studies are relevant not only for the 140 million high-altitude residents worldwide, including more than 100,000 in Colorado, but also the larger number of persons whose health is compromised by hypoxia.

REFERENCES

1. Abbott BD and Buckalew AR. Placental defects in ARNT-knockout conceptus correlate with localized decreases in VEGF-R2, Ang-1, and Tie-2. *Developmental Dynamics* 219: 526-538, 2000.
2. Angrimsson R, Hayward C, Nadaud S, Baldursdottir A, Walker JJ, Liston WA, Bjarnadottir RI, Brock DJH, Geirsson RT, Connor JM, and Soubrier F. Evidence for a familial pregnancy-induced hypertension locus in the eNOS-gene region. *American Journal of Human Genetics* 61: 354-362, 1997.
3. Bae MK, Ahn MY, Jeong JW, Bae MH, Lee YM, Bae SK, Park JW, Kim KR, and Kim KW. Jab1 interacts directly with HIF-1alpha and regulates its stability. *Journal of Biological Chemistry* 277: 9-12, 2002.
4. Barker DJ. Fetal origins of cardiovascular disease. *Ann Med* 31 Suppl 1: 3-6, 1999.
5. Black WC, Baer CF, Antolin MF, and DuTeau NM. Population genomics: genome-wide sampling of insect populations. *Annu Rev Entomol* 46: 441-469, 2001.
6. Bodi I, Bishopric NH, Discher DJ, Wu X, and Webster KA. Cell-specificity and signaling pathway of endothelin-1 gene regulation by hypoxia. *Cardiovascular Research* 30: 975-984, 1995.
7. Bolivia. *Encuesta Nacional de Demografía y Salud.* Calverton, MD USA: Macro International/DHS+ Program, 1998.
8. Brutsaert T. Spanish genetic admixture is associated with larger VO2 max decrement from sea level to 4,338 m in Peruvian Quechua. *Journal of Applied Physiology* 95: 519-528, 2003.
9. Brutsaert T. Limits on inferring genetic adaptation to high altitude in Himalayan and Andean populations. *High Altitude Medicine & Biology* 2: 211-225, 2001.
10. Caniggia I and Winter JL. Hypoxia inducible factor-1: oxygen regulation of trophoblast differentiation in normal and pre-eclamptic pregnancies - a review. *Placenta* 23: S47-S57, 2002.
11. Chapman AB, Abraham WT, Osorio FV, Merouani A, Zamudio S, Young DA, Johnson A, Coffin C, Goldberg C, Moore LG, Dahms T, and Schrier RW. Temporal relationships between hormonal and hemodynamic changes in early human pregnancy. *Kidney International* 54: 2056-2063, 1998.
12. Chen D, Zhou X, Zhu Y, Zhu T, and Wang J. Comparison study on uterine and umbilical artery blood flow during pregnancy at high altitude and at low altitude. *Zhonghua Fu Chan Ke Za Zhi* 37: 69-71, 2002.
13. Cipolla M and Osol G. Hypertrophic and hyperplastic effects of pregnancy on the rat uterine arterial wall. *American Journal of Obstetrics and Gynecology* 171: 805-811, 1994.
14. Clifford SC, Cockman ME, Smallwood AC, Mole DR, Woodward ER, Maxwell PH, Ratcliffe PJ, and Maher ER. Contrasting effects on HIF-1alpha regulation by disease-causing pVHL mutations correlate with patterns of tumourigenesis in von Hippel-Lindau disease. *Hum Mol Genet* 10: 1029-1038, 2001.

15. Cope GA, Suh GS, Aravind L, Schwarz SE, Zipursky SL, Koonin EV, and Deshaies RJ. Role of predicted metalloprotease motif of Jab1/Csn5 in cleavage of Nedd8 from Cul1. *Science* 298: 608-611, 2002.
16. Coussons-Read ME, Mazzeo RS, Whitford MH, Schmitt M, Moore LG, and Zamudio S. High altitude residence during pregnancy alters cytokine and catecholamine levels. *American Journal of Reproductive Immunology* 48: 344-354, 2002.
17. Dobzhansky T. Adaptedness and fitness. In: *Population Biology and Evolution*, edited by Lewontin RC. Syracuse, NY: Syracuse University Press, 1968, p. 111-205.
18. Eremina V, Sood M, Haigh J, Nagy A, Lajoie G, Ferrara N, Gerber H-P, Kikkawa Y, Miner JH, and Quaggin SE. Glomerular-specific alterations of VEGF-A expression lead to distinct congenital and acquired renal diseases. *Journal of Clinical Investigation* 111: 707-716, 2003.
19. Frisancho AR, Frisancho HG, Albalak R, Villain M, Vargas E, and Soria R. Developmental, genetic, and environmental components of lung volumes at high altitude. *American Journal of Human Biology* 9: 191-203, 1997.
20. Furuhashi N, Kimura H, Nagae H, and Yajima A. Maternal plasma endothelin levels and fetal status in normal and preeclamptic pregnancies. *Gynecologic and Obstetric Investigation* 39: 88-92, 1995.
21. Gage T. Demography. In: *Human Biology: an evolutionary and biocultural perspective*, edited by Stinson S, Bogin B, Huss-Ashmore R and O"Rourke D. New York: John Wiley & Sons, 2000, p. 507-551.
22. Genbacev O, Krtolica A, Kaelin W, and Fisher SJ. Human cytotrophoblast expression of the von Hippel-Lindau protein is downregulated during uterine invasion in situ and upregulated by hypoxia in vitro. *Developmental Biology* 233: 526-536, 2001.
23. Genbacev O, Zhou Y, Ludlow JW, and Fisher SJ. Regulation of human placental development by oxygen tension. *Science* 277: 1669-1672, 1997.
24. Giussani D. High altitude and rural living are associated with increased infant mortality in Bolivia. *J Soc Gynecol Investig* 9: 292A, 2002.
25. Giussani DA, Seamus P, Anstee S, and Barker DJP. Effects of altitude versus economic status on birth weight and body shape at birth. *Pediatric Research* 49: 490-494, 2001.
26. Gonzales GF. Determinantes biomedicos de la fertilidad humana en la altura. In: *Reproduccion Humana en la Altura*, edited by Gonzales GF. Lima, Peru: Consejo Nacional de Ciencia y Tecnologica, 1993, p. 73-87.
27. Granger JP. Maternal and fetal adaptations during pregnancy: lessons in regulatory and integrative physiology. *American Journal of Physiology Regulatory, integrative and comparative physiology* 283: R1289-R1292, 2002.
28. Haas J, Balcazar H, and Caulfield L. Variation in early neonatal mortality for different types of fetal growth restriction. *American Journal of Physical Anthropology* 73: 467-473, 1987.
29. Haas JD. Human adaptability approach to nutritional assessment: a Bolivian example. *Federation Proceedings* 40: 2577-2582, 1981.
30. Haas JD, Frongillo EJ, Stepcik C, Beard J, and Hurtado L. Altitude, ethnic and sex differences in birth weight and length in Bolivia. *Human Biology* 52: 459-477, 1980.
31. Halushka MK, Fan J-B, Bentley K, Hsie L, Shen N, Weder A, Cooper R, Lipshutz R, and Chakravarti A. Patterns of single-nucleotide polymorphisms in candidate genes for blood-pressure homeostasis. *Nature Genetics* 22: 239-247, 1999.
32. Hanaoka M, Droma Y, Hotta J, Matsuzawa Y, Kobayashi T, Kubo K, and Ota M. Polymorphisms of the tyrosine hydroxylase gene in subjects susceptible to high-altitude pulmonary edema. *Chest* 123: 54-58, 2003.
33. Hellwig-Bürgel T, Rutkowski K, Metzen E, Fandrey J, and Jelkmann W. Interleukin-1b and tumor necrosis factor-a stimulate DNA binding of hypoxia-inducible factor-1. *Blood*

94: 1561-1567, 1999.
34. Howell WM, Bateman AC, Turner SJ, Collins A, and Theaker JM. Influence of vascular endothelial growth factor single nucleotide polymorphisms on tumour development in cutaneous malignant melanoma. *Genes and Immunity* 3: 229-232, 2002.
35. Hu XQ, Longo LD, Gilbert RD, and Zhang L. Effects of long-term high-altitude hypoxemia on alpha 1-adrenergic receptors in the ovine uterine artery. *American Journal of Physiology* 270: H1001-H1007, 1996.
36. Hubel CA, Roberts JM, and Ferrell RE. Association of pre-eclampsia with common coding sequence variations in the lipoprotein lipase gene. *Clin Genet* 56: 289-296, 1999.
37. Jensen GM and Moore LG. The effect of high altitude and other risk factors on birthweight: independent or interactive effects? *American Journal of Public Health* 87: 1003-1007, 1997.
38. Jeong JW, Bae MK, Ahn MY, Kim SH, Sohn TK, Bae MH, Yoo MA, Song EJ, Lee K, and Kim KW. Regulation and Destabilization of HIF-1alpha by ARD1-Mediated Acetylation. *Cell* 111: 709-720, 2002.
39. Keyes LE, Armaza JF, Niermeyer S, Vargas E, Young D, Villena M, and Moore LG. Intrauterine growth restriction, preeclampsia and intrauterine mortality at high altitude in Bolivia. *Pediatric Research* 54: 20-25, 2003.
40. Kitanaka T, Gilbert RD, and Longo LD. Maternal responses to long-term hypoxemia in sheep. *American Journal of Physiology* 256: R1340-R1347, 1989.
41. Krampl E. Pregnancy at high altitude. *Ultrasound Obstet Gynecol* 19: 535-539, 2002.
42. Krampl E, Espinoza-Dorado J, Lees CC, Moscoso G, and Bland JM. Maternal uterine artery Doppler studies at high altitude and sea level. *Ultrasound in Obstetrics and Gynecology* 18: 578-582, 2001.
43. Krampl E, Lees C, Bland JM, Dorado JE, Gonzalo M, and Campbell S. Fetal biometry at 4300 m compared to sea level in Peru. *Ultrasound in Obstetrics and Gynecology* 16: 9-18, 2000.
44. Kublickiene KR, Lindblom B, Kruger K, and Nisell H. Preeclampsia: evidence for impaired shear stress-mediated nitiric oxide release in uterine circulation. *American Journal of Obstetrics and Gynecology* 183: 160-166, 2000.
45. Lea RG, Riley SC, Antipatis C, Hannah L, Ashworth CJ, Clark DA, and Critchley HO. Cytokines and the regulation of apoptosis in reproductive tissues: a review. *Am J Reprod Immunol* 42: 100-109, 1999.
46. Levine RJ, Maynard SE, Qian C, Lim KH, England LJ, Yu KF, Schisterman EF, Thadhani R, Sachs BP, Epstein FH, Sibai BM, Sukhatme VP, and Karumanchi SA. Circulating angiogenic factors and the risk of preeclampsia. *N Engl J Med* 350: 672-683, 2004.
47. Lewontin R. *The triple helix: gene, organism and environment*. Cambridge: Harvard University Press, 2001.
48. Lewontin RC. Ken-Ichi Kojima September 17, 1930-November 14, 1971. *Genetics* 71: Suppl 2:s89-90, 1972.
49. Lichty JL, Ting R, Bruns PD, and Dyar E. Studies of babies born at high altitude. *American Journal of Diseases of Children* 93: 666-669, 1957.
50. Lie RT, Rasmussen S, Brunborg H, Gjessing HK, Lie-Nielsen E, and Irgens LM. Fetal and maternal contributions to risk of pre-eclampsia: population based study. *BMJ* 316: 1343-1347, 1998.
51. Lindsay RS, Kobes S, Knowler WC, and Hanson RL. Genome-wide linkage analysis assessing parent-of-origin effects in the inheritance of birth weight. *Hum Genet* 110: 503-509, 2002.
52. Lubchenco LO, Searls DT, and Brazie JV. Neonatal mortality rate: relationship to birth weight and getational age. *Journal of Pediatrics* 81: 814-822, 1972.
53. Magness RR. Maternal cardiovascular and other physiologic responses to the

endocrinology of pregnancy. In: *The Endocrinology of Pregnancy*, edited by Bazer FW. Totowas, NJ: Humana Press, 1998, p. 507-539.

54. Mahfouz AA and al-Erian RA. Hypertension in Asir region, southwestern Saudi Arabia: an epidemiologic study. *Southeast Asian Journal of Tropical Medicine and Public Health* 24: 284-286, 1993.
55. Mahfouz AA, el-Said MM, Alakija W, and al-Erian RA. Altitude and socio-biological determinants of pregnancy-associated hypertension. *International Journal of Gynaecology and Obstetrics* 44: 135-138, 1994.
56. Maloney J, Wang D, Duncan T, Voelkel N, and Ruoss S. Plasma vascular endothelial growth factor in acute mountain sickness. *Chest* 118: 47-52, 2000.
57. Mateev S, Sillau AH, Mouser R, McCullough RE, White MM, Young DA, and Moore LG. Chronic hypoxia opposes pregnancy-induced increase in uterine artery vasodilator response to flow. *American Journal of Physiology Heart and Circulatory Physiology* 284: H820-H829, 2003.
58. Mayhew TM, Jackson MR, and Haas JD. Oxygen diffusive conductances of human placentae from term pregnancies at low and high altitudes. *Placenta* 11: 493-503, 1990.
59. Maynard SE, Min J-Y, Merchan J, Lim K-H, Li J, Mondal S, Libermann TA, Morgan JP, Sellke FW, Stillman IE, Epstein FH, Sukhatme VP, and Karumanchi SA. Excess placental soluble fms-like tyrosine kinase 1 (sFlt1) may contribute to endothelial dysfunction, hypertension, and proteinuria in preeclampsia. *Journal of Clinical Investigation* 111: 649-658, 2003.
60. Mazzeo RS, Brooks GA, Butterfield GE, Podolin DA, Wolfel EE, and Reeves JT. Acclimatization to high altitude increase muscle sympathetic activity both at rest and during exercise. *American Journal of Physiology* 269: R201-R207, 1995.
61. McAuliffe F, Kametas N, Krampl E, Ernsting J, and Nicolaides K. Blood gases in pregnancy at sea level and at high altitude. *British Journal of Obstetrics and Gynaecology* 108: 980-985, 2001.
62. McCullough RE, Reeves JT, and Liljegren RL. Fetal growth retardation and increased infant mortality at high altitude. *Archives of Environmental Health* 32: 36-40, 1977.
63. Moll W and Kunzel W. The blood pressure in arteries entering the placentae of guinea pigs, rats, rabbits, and sheep. *Pflugers Archiv European Journal of Physiology* 338: 125-131, 1973.
64. Moore LG. Human genetic adaptation to high altitude. *High Altitude Medicine & Biology* 2: 257-279, 2001.
65. Moore LG. Small babies and big mountains: John Lichty solves a Colorado mystery in Leadville. In: *Attitudes on Altitude*, edited by Reeves JT and Grover FT. Boulder: Univ Colorado Press, 2001, p. 137-159.
66. Moore LG, Hershey DW, Jahnigen D, and Bowes W, Jr. The incidence of pregnancy-induced hypertension is increased among Colorado residents at high altitude. *American Journal of Obstetrics and Gynecology* 144: 423-429, 1982.
67. Moore LG, Jahnigen D, Rounds SS, Reeves JT, and Grover RF. Maternal hyperventilation helps preserve arterial oxygenation during high-altitude pregnancy. *Journal of Applied Physiology: Respiratory, Environmental and Exercise Physiology* 52: 690-694, 1982.
68. Moore LG, McCullough RE, and Weil JV. Increased HVR in pregnancy: relationship to hormonal and metabolic changes. *Journal of Applied Physiology* 62: 158-163, 1987.
69. Moore LG, Rounds SS, Jahnigen D, Grover RF, and Reeves JT. Infant birth weight is related to maternal arterial oxygenation at high altitude. *Journal of Applied Physiology: Respiratory, Environmental and Exercise Physiology* 52: 695-699, 1982.
70. Moore LG, Shriver M, Bemis L, Hickler B, Wilson M, Brutsaert T, Parra E, and Vargas E. Maternal adaptation to high-altitude pregnancy: an experiment of nature. *Placenta* 25 Suppl: S60-S71, 2004.

71. Moore LG, Zamudio S, Zhuang J, Sun S, and Droma T. Oxygen transport in Tibetan women during pregnancy at 3658 m. *American Journal of Physical Anthropology* 114: 42-53, 2001.
72. Morganti A, Giussani M, Sala C, Gazzano G, Marana I, Pierini A, Savoia MT, Ghio F, Cogo A, and Zanchetti A. Effects of exposure to high altitude on plasma endothelin-1 levels in normal subjects. *Journal of Hypertension* 13: 859-865, 1995.
73. Mortola JP, Frappell PB, Aguero L, and Armstrong K. Birth weight and altitude: a study in Peruvian communities. *Journal of Pediatrics* 136: 324-329, 2000.
74. Mulvany MJ, Baumbach GL, Aalkjaer C, Heagerty AM, Korsgaard N, Schiffrin EL, and Heistad DD. Vascular remodeling. *Hypertension* 28: 505-506, 1996.
75. NCBI. LocusLink, 2003.
76. Ng DP, Canani L, Araki S, Smiles A, Moczulski D, Warram JH, and Krolewski AS. Minor effect of GLUT1 polymorphisms on susceptibility to diabetic nephropathy in type 1 diabetes. *Diabetes* 51: 2264-2269, 2002.
77. NIEHS. Environmental Genome Project, 2003.
78. Niermeyer S, Williford D, Asmus I, Honigman B, Moore LG, and Egbert M. Low birth weight in Colorado: analysis using geographic information systems. *Adv Exp Med Biol (this volume):* page 327 (abstract), 2006.
79. Niermeyer S, Zamudio S, and Moore LG. The People. In: *Adaptations to Hypoxia*, edited by Hornbein T and Schoene RB. New York, NY: Marcel Dekker and Co., 2001, p. 43-100.
80. PAHO. *Epidemiological Bulletin* 20(3): 14-19, 1999.
81. Palmer SK, Moore LG, Young DA, Cregger B, Berman JC, and Zamudio S. Altered blood pressure course during normal pregnancy and increased preeclampsia at high altitude (3100 meters) in Colorado. *American Journal of Obstetrics and Gynecology* 180: 1161-1168, 1999.
82. Palmer SK, Zamudio S, Coffin C, Parker S, Stamm E, and Moore LG. Quantitative estimation of human uterine artery blood flow and pelvic blood flow redistribution in pregnancy. *Obstetrics and Gynecology* 80: 1000-1006, 1992.
83. Rajakumar A. The hypoxia inducible transcription factor, HIF-1a, overexpressed in preeclamptic placentas is capable of binding to the hypoxia response element. *Journal of the Society for Gynecologic Investigation* 10: 304A, 2003.
84. Rajakumar A, Doty K, Daftary A, Harger G, and Conrad KP. Impaired oxygen-dependent reduction of HIF-1alpha and -2alpha proteins in pre-eclamptic placentae. *Placenta* 24: 199-208, 2003.
85. Ratcliffe PJ, O'Rourke JF, Maxwell PH, and Pugh CW. Oxygen sensing, hypoxia-inducible factor-1 and the regulation of mammalian gene expression. *Journal of Experimental Biology* 201: 1153-1162, 1998.
86. Renner W, Kotschan S, Hoffmann C, Obermayer-Pietsch B, and Pilger E. A common 936 C/T mutation in the gene for vascular endothelial growth factor is associated with vascular endothelial growth factor plasma levels. *J Vasc Res* 37: 443-448, 2000.
87. Rinehart BK, Terrone DA, Lagoo-Deenadayalan S, Barber WH, Hale EA, Martin JN, Jr., and Bennett WA. Expression of the placental cytokines tumor necrosis factor alpha, interleukin 1beta, and interleukin 10 is increased in preeclampsia. *Am J Obstet Gynecol* 181: 915-920, 1999.
88. Rockwell LC, Keyes LE, and Moore LG. Chronic hypoxia diminishes pregnancy-associated DNA synthesis in guinea pig uteroplacental arteries. *Placenta* 21: 313-319, 2000.
89. Safran M and Kaelin WG, Jr. HIF hydroxylation and the mammalian oxygen-sensing pathway. *J Clin Invest* 111: 779-783, 2003.
90. Savvidou MD, Valance PJT, Nicolaides KH, and Hingorani AD. Endothelial nitric

oxide synthase gene polymorphism and maternal vascular adaptation to pregnancy. *Hypertension* 38: 1289-1293, 2001.

91. Schlotterer C. Hitchhiking mapping--functional genomics from the population genetics perspective. *Trends Genet* 19: 32-38, 2003.
92. SeattleSNPs. NHLBI Program for Genomic Appications, UW-FHCRC, Seattle, WA, 2004.
93. Semenza GL. Regulation of mammalian O2 homeostasis by hypoxia-inducible factor 1. *Annual Review of Cell and Developmental Biology* 15: 551-578, 1999.
94. Smiley RM and Finster M. Do receptors get pregnant too? Adrenergic receptor alterations in human pregnancy. *J Matern Fetal Med* 5: 106-114, 1996.
95. Solomon CG and Seely EW. Preeclampsia -- searching for the cause. *N Engl J Med* 350: 641-642, 2004.
96. Stock M and Metcalfe J. Maternal physiology during gestation. In: *The Physiology of Reproduction*, edited by Knobil E and Neil J. New York: Raven Press, 1994, p. 947 – 983.
97. Thaete LG, Dewey ER, and Neerhof MG. Endothelin and the regulation of uterine and placental perfusion in hypoxia-induced fetal growth restriction. *J Soc Gynecol Investig* 11: 16-21, 2004.
98. Thaete LG and Neerhof MG. Contribution of endothelin to the regulation of uterine and placental blood flow during nitric oxide synthase inhibition in the pregnant rat. *7th International Conference on Endothelin*: 222, 2001.
99. Thaete LG, Neerhof MG, and Caplan MS. Endothelin receptor A antagonism prevents hypoxia-induced intrauterine growth restriction in the rat. *American Journal of Obstetrics and Gynecology* 176: 73-76, 1997.
100. Thaete LG, Neerhof MG, and Silver RK. Differential effects of endothelin A and B receptor antagonism on fetal growth in normal and nitric oxide-deficient rats. *J Soc Gynecol Investig* 8: 18-23, 2001.
101. Tissot Van Patot M, Grilli A, Chapman P, Broad E, Tyson W, Heller DS, Zwerdlinger L, and Zamudio S. Remodeling of uteroplacental arteries is decreased in high altitude placentae. *Placenta* 24: 326-335, 2003.
102. Unger C, Weiser JK, McCullough RE, Keefer S, and Moore LG. Altitude, low birth weight, and infant mortality in Colorado. *Journal of the American Medical Association* 259: 3427-3432, 1988.
103. Vitzthum V and Wiley A. The proximate determinants of fertility in populations exposed to chronic hypoxia. *High Alt Med Biol* 4: 125-139, 2003.
104. Ward K, hata A, Jeunemaitre X, Helin C, Nelson L, Namikawa C, Farrinton PF, Ogasawara M, Suzumori K, Tomoda S, Berrebi S, Sasaki M, Corvol P, Lifton RP, and Lalouel J-M. A molecular variant of angiotensinogen associated with preeclampsia (see comments). *Nat Genet* 4: 59-61, 1993.
105. Weil A. Mammalian evolution: upwards and onwards. *Nature* 416: 798-799, 2002.
106. Weinstein RS and Haas JD. Early stress and later reproductive performance under conditions of malutrition and high altitude hypoxia. *Medical Anthropology* 1: 25-54, 1977.
107. White MM, McCullough RE, Dyckes R, Robertson AD, and Moore LG. Chronic hypoxia, pregnancy, and endothelium-mediated relaxation in guinea pig uterine and thoracic arteries. *Am J Physiol Heart Circ Physiol* 278: H2069-H2075, 2000.
108. White MM, McCullough RE, Dyckes R, Robertson AD, and Moore LG. Effects of pregnancy and chronic hypoxia on contractile responsiveness to a-1-adrenergic stimulation. *Journal of Applied Physiology* 85: 2322-2329, 1998.
109. Wilcox AJ. Birth weight and perinatal mortality: the effect of maternal smoking. *American Journal of Epidemiology* 137: 1098-1104, 1993.
110. Williams RL, Creasy RK, Cunningham GC, Hawes WE, Norris FD, and Tashiro M. Fetal

growth and perinatal viability in California. *Obstetrics and Gynecology* 59: 624-632, 1982.

111. Zamudio S, Palmer SK, Droma T, Stamm E, Coffin C, and Moore LG. Effect of altitude on uterine artery blood flow during normal pregnancy. *Journal of Applied Physiology* 79: 7-14, 1995.
112. Zamudio S, Palmer SK, Stamm E, Coffin C, and Moore LG. Uterine blood flow at high altitude. In: *Hypoxia and the Brain*, edited by Sutton JR and Houston CS. Burlington, VT, USA: Queen City Press, 1995, p. 112-124.
113. Zhang L and Ziao D. Effects of chronic hypoxia on Ca2+ mobilization and Ca2+ sensitivity of myofilaments in uterine arteries. *Am J Physiol Heart Circ Physiol* 274: H132-H138, 1998.

[1] While the placenta has been subject to intense investigation, surprisingly little attention has been devoted to the comparative physiology of the placenta or its potential influences on mammalian evolution; topics worthy of future exploration.

[2] The ongoing debate concerning abortion demonstrates that the definition of “life” is subject to cultural, as well as biological interpretations.

[3] Birth weights

Chapter 11

HYPOXIC PRECONDITIONING AND ERYTHROPOIETIN PROTECT RETINAL NEURONS FROM DEGENERATION

Christian Grimm[1], A. Wenzel[1], N. Acar[2], S. Keller[3], M. Seeliger[2], Max Gassmann[3]

[1]*Laboratory of Retinal Cell Biology, Eye Hospital Zurich and Center for Integrative Human Physiology, Zurich, Switzerland,* [2]*Retinal Electrodiagnostics Research Group, Universitäts-Augenklinik Tübingen, Tübingen, Germany,* [3]*Institute of Veterinary Physiology, Vetsuisse Faculty and Center for Integrative Human Physiology, University of Zurich, Zurich, Switzerland,* [4]*Ophthalmology, University Eye Hospital Zurich, Zurich, Switzerland.*

Abstract: Reduced tissue oxygenation stabilizes the alpha-subunit of the transcription factor hypoxia-inducible factor-1 (HIF-1). This leads to the induction of a number of hypoxia responsive genes. One of the best known HIF-1 targets is erythropoietin that exerts neuroprotective effects on ischemia-related injury in the brain. Thus, pre-exposure to low environmental oxygen concentrations might be exploited as a preconditioning procedure to protect tissues against a variety of harmful conditions. We present recent work on neuroprotection of retinal photoreceptors induced by hypoxic preconditioning or by systemically elevated levels of Epo in mouse plasma.

Key Words: hypoxia-inducible factor-1, apoptosis, photoreceptor, blinding disease, overexpression of EPO

INTRODUCTION

Reduced oxygenation triggers several adaptive responses in mammals including man. At the cellular level, low oxygen supply induces expression of a variety of oxygen-regulated genes such as erythropoietin (Epo), vascular endothelial growth factor (VEGF) and several glycolytic enzymes. Once 'loaded' with the products of hypoxically activated genes, the organism is able to cope with hypoxia. Expression of oxygen-dependent genes is transient and the return to normoxic conditions will gradually reduce the intra- and extracellular concentrations of induced proteins to pre-hypoxic levels. Upon re-oxygenation, however, there is a given period of time in which the tissue is still 'loaded' with gene products that were upregulated during the antecedent hypoxic period. If re-exposed to hypoxia, these tissues are better protected against hypoxic injury compared to non-preexposed ones. We call this concept *hypoxic preconditioning* (Grimm et al; submitted).

It is conceivable that hypoxic preconditioning of cells, tissues, animals or even patients has a clinical potential (reviewed in (16)). We propose that the full set of oxygen-dependent genes will include some that can provide tissue- or cell-protective effects. This protection may not be limited to hypoxic/ischemic insults but may also protect against other stimuli that otherwise might harm an organism. It is therefore desirable to identify such protective genes or gene products that have a potential as therapeutical drugs. We show that hypoxic preconditioning increases the resistance of neuronal tissue against harmful insults and that Epo is one of several putative factors involved in this protection.

THE MOLECULAR RESPONSE TO HYPOXIA IS VERY FAST

Many reviews on the oxygen-sensing mechanism and the involved hypoxia-inducible factors and prolyl hydroxylases have been published recently (24, 25, 53, 54). In brief, hypoxic exposure of cells leads to the accumulation of the α-subunit of the hypoxia-inducible factor-1 (HIF-1). Heterodimerization of HIF-1α with its partner HIF-1β (also termed ARNT for arylhydrocarbon receptor nuclear translocator) leads to the formation of the HIF-1 complex that binds to the hypoxic response element that is present in all HIF-target genes described so far (3) and enhances their transcription. While hypoxia quickly stabilizes HIF-1α protein, normoxia leads to immediate degradation of HIF-1α (28). Stabilization of HIF-1α is highly efficient also *in vivo*: upon exposure of mice to 6% oxygen, we observed accumulation of HIF-1α protein in several organs within 60 minutes (58). This observation implies that hypoxic preconditioning for less than one hour might be sufficient to provide tissue protective effects.

EPO PROVIDES NEUROPROTECTION IN THE BRAIN

Until recently, the function of Epo was thought to be restricted to erythropoiesis. Binding of Epo to its receptor (EpoR) present on erythroid progenitor cells was shown to repress apoptosis, thereby allowing red blood cells to mature (27). However, we and others discovered expression of Epo and EpoR in the brain (13, 39, 59). The presence of the blood-brain-barrier made a systemic erythropoietic function of brain-derived Epo unlikely and suggested a local role of Epo in the brain by binding to local EpoR's. In analogy to the kidney, Epo gene expression in brain is regulated in an oxygen-dependent manner. Considering that Epo is a HIF-1-target gene, we were not surprised to find elevated Epo protein levels in the hypoxic brain (58).

Why do we need Epo in the brain? Sasaki and co-workers reported for the first time that Epo protects neurons from ischemic damage *in vivo* (51) and many subsequent animal stroke models confirmed that Epo protects against this ischemic brain injury (reviewed in (40)). By now, several reports have enlarged the possible use of Epo in ischemic-related injuries (including spinal cord) and the involved protective mechanisms have been summarized recently (17, 18, 38). At the same time, Ehrenreich and co-workers (14) pioneered the first clinical trial applying rhEpo on patients suffering from acute stroke. They reported that Epo-treated patients showed markedly enhanced neurological recovery and an improved clinical outcome. The fact that no side effects of Epo therapy were identified makes the therapeutic use of Epo in ischemia-related neuronal injuries very promising.

TRANSGENIC MICE OVEREXPRESSING HUMAN EPO

Encouraged by the beneficial effects of Epo in the brain of stroke patients and animal models we started to study the potential neuroprotective capacity of Epo in the retina by three different approaches: i) by upregulation of Epo (among other factors) through hypoxic preconditioning, ii) by application of rhEpo and iii) by transgenic overexpression of hEpo. For the latter approach, a transgenic mouse line was generated that expresses human Epo cDNA driven by the human platelet-derived growth factor (PDGF) B-chain promoter. This promoter directs expression of the transgene preferentially, but not exclusively, to neuronal cells. The resulting transgenic mouse line termed tg6 showed a dramatic increase of cerebral and plasma Epo levels, the latter leading to excessive erythrocytosis with hematocrit values of up to 90% (50, 55, 62). Unexpectedly, blood pressure was not elevated nor was the cardiac output altered in tg6 mice. Despite concomitant activation of the endothelin system (46), elevated NO-levels observed in tg6 mice led to a generalized vasodilation (50). In concert with regulated blood viscosity (61), the observed vasodilation protected tg6 animals from cardiovascular complications.

EPO IS OVEREXPRESSED IN THE TRANSGENIC RETINA

The transgene caused more than 20-fold elevated levels of Epo in the retina (21). The high levels of Epo did not influence retinal development, and the adult retina showed normal morphology and thickness without obvious alterations, and also a normal content and regeneration of visual pigments (21). However, the retinal vessels were massively dilated, in particular the veins (Fig. 1A). The functional analysis was performed to answer the question whether enhanced hematocrit would lead to a reduction (e.g. via a reduced capillar flow) or an enhancement of the electrophysiological activity. It turned out that retinal function was enhanced in tg6 mutant mice. Both rod and cone system function as measured by the scotopic (Fig. 1B) and photopic (not shown) electroretinogram (ERG) were increased in comparison to normal, especially at higher stimulus intensities (Fig. 1B). The exact reason for the enlarged ERGs is not clear but presumably involves alterations in the blood and oxygen supply to the retina and/or the retinal pigment epithelium (RPE), caused by the high hematocrit values, vasodilation and altered blood viscosity in tg6 mice. Alternatively, subtle changes in retinal architecture, especially in the inner nuclear layer (INL) and Muller cells may contribute to the increased b-wave amplitudes. Such potential structural changes in the tg6 retina may not be detectable in histological sections examined by conventional light microscopy. A more detailed analysis of the tg6 retina with respect to the observed functional alterations is currently in progress. Although these experiments are not yet completed, we used the tg6 mouse to test the potential benefit of increased Epo levels on the survival of retinal cells in mouse models of induced and inherited retinal degeneration.

Light is considered a risk- or cofactor for many human retinal degenerations (10-12, 57, 60). Furthermore, degeneration in many animal models is accelerated by light and light-induced retinal degeneration in wildtype mice has been used to study pathophysiological mechanisms in the retina (8, 9, 33, 44, 52, 63, 66). Short exposure of mice to high levels of white light induces a synchronized burst of apoptosis in a large number of photoreceptors. This process leads to cell death, loss of retinal function and blindness (47, 48, 66). Since apoptosis is the final common death pathway in most human retinal diseases, this system can be used to study signaling pathways and apoptotic cascades in the retina with respect to human pathology.

Many transgenic and spontaneously arised mouse lines exist that represent models for inherited retinal degenerations (22). Results obtained in the induced system can be tested in some of these models especially to analyze effectivity of therapeutical approaches like gene therapy, implantation of prosthetic devices and neuroprotective treatments (see below).

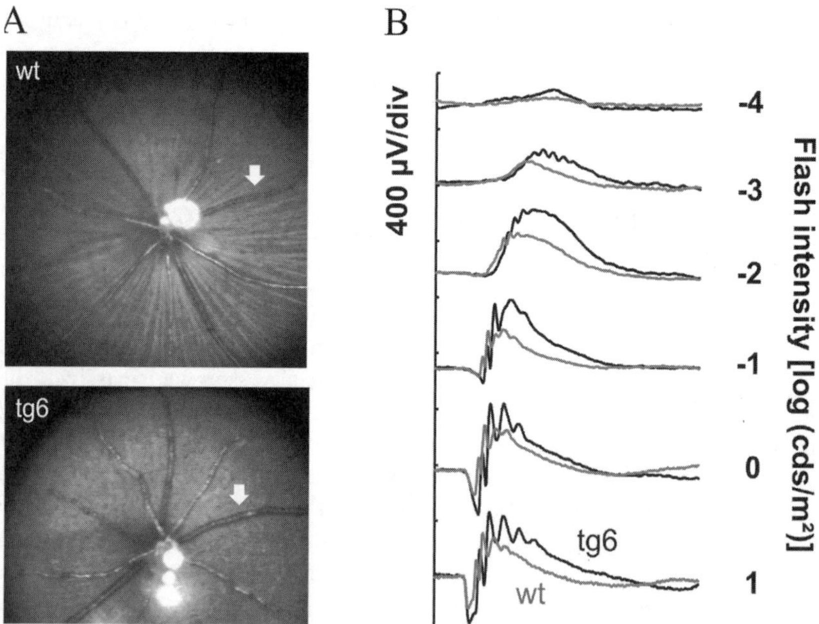

Figure 1. Functional and morphological *in vivo* analysis of tg6 mutant mice (see Ref (26) for methodological details on the scanning laser ophthalmoscope (SLO) and ERG analysis). A) Analysis of retinal vessels *in vivo* by SLO reveals dilatated retinal vessels in the tg6 mouse. The comparison between wt and tg6 mice shows that particularly the veins have a massive increase in diameter (arrows). B) Enlargement of ERG amplitudes in tg6 mice. Both the negative (a-wave) and positive (b-wave) portion of the signals is increased.

WHY THE RETINA?

The retina is a highly specialized and easily accessible 'outpost' of the brain designed to convert light into an electrical signal that can be interpreted by the brain. This demanding task is carried out by the different cells of the retina with photoreceptors being the light-absorbing cells. The extreme specialization of these cells renders them highly vulnerable and their physical and physiological integrity is easily disturbed by environmental factors as well as by gene mutations.

Many human blinding diseases exist in which cells of the retina, in particular photoreceptors, are lost through an apoptotic cell death. As a consequence, the retina degenerates leading to partial or complete loss of vision. In the gene for the visual pigment rhodopsin, over a hundred mutations are known that lead to Retinitis Pigmentosa (RP). To date, no effective treatment exists for most degenerative diseases of the retina. Strategies to develop therapies include retinal prosthesis, stem cell transplantation, gene therapy, surgery and anti-apoptotic or neuroprotective measures to interfere with the cell death program. To inhibit cell death in various models of retinal degeneration, several anti-apoptotic factors have been used with different success. Tested factors included members of the Bcl-2 family of proteins, growth factors and cytokines (66). Similarly, several protocols of preconditioning, including hyperthermia, food deprivation, light exposure or injury of the retina were shown to protect the retina against degeneration (1, 5, 30, 35-37, 41-43, 67). Likewise, ischemic preconditioning conferred protection against apoptotic stimuli like ischemia-induced death of ganglion cells and light-induced photoreceptor degeneration (6, 37, 69).

HIF-1α IS UPREGULATED DURING POSTNATAL DEVELOPMENT OF THE RETINA

The mouse retina fully develops during the first three weeks after birth. This postnatal development is characterized by the final differentiation of the various retinal cell types, the expression of the visual pigment and the development of the retinal vasculature. Until retinal vessels have fully developed, the retina may experience reduced oxygen concentrations. Using RT-PCR, we show that during this critical period of retinal development as well as in the adult mouse retina, both HIF-1α and HIF-1β/ARNT are expressed at constantly high levels (Fig. 2A). HIF-1α protein, however, can be detected at high levels only during early postnatal development (Fig. 2B). Concomitant with the development of the retinal vessels of the inner retina, HIF-1α protein levels decrease, presumably because the retina becomes more and more oxygenized. High levels of HIF-1 transcription factor during postnatal retinal development most likely secures proper retinal vasculogenesis by regulating expression of proteins involved in angiogenesis like VEGF. In the adult retina, HIF-1α is barely detectable. Nevertheless, the genes for both HIF-1 subunits are still highly expressed suggesting that the retina may be able to quickly react to any reduction in oxygen tension. Stabilization of HIF-1α with subsequent differential regulation of HIF-1 target genes in reduced oxygen conditions may be an important neuroprotective mechanism in the adult retina. This may particularly be necessary during nighttime, when the retina has the highest energy demand and oxygen conditions are borderline hypoxic in the retina.

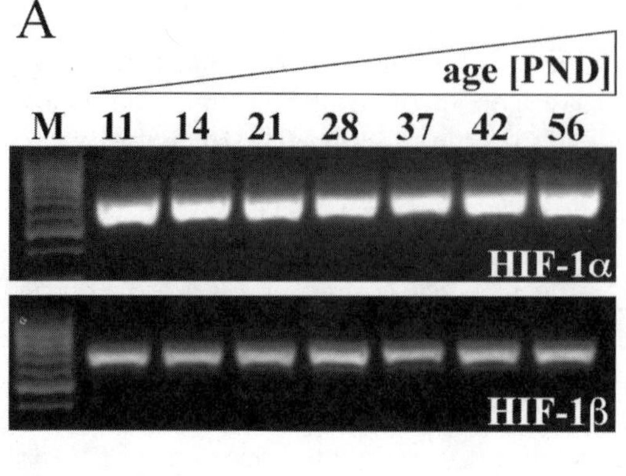

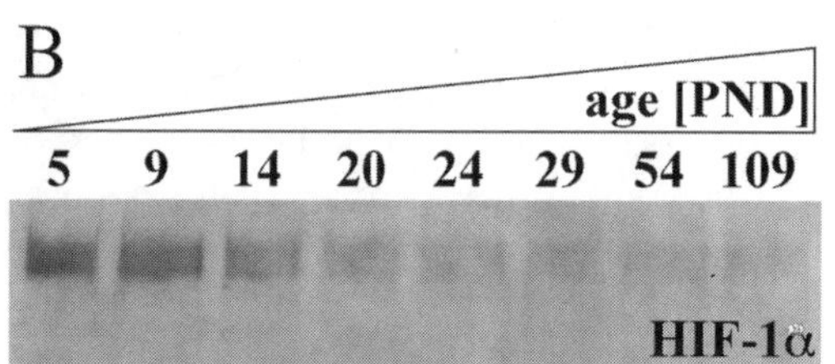

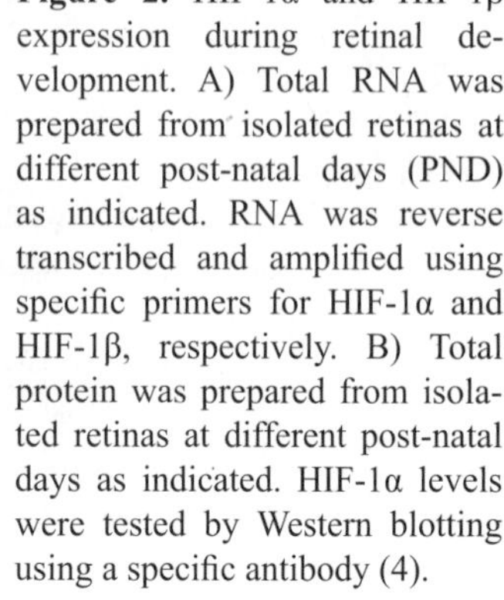
Figure 2. HIF-1α and HIF-1β expression during retinal development. A) Total RNA was prepared from isolated retinas at different post-natal days (PND) as indicated. RNA was reverse transcribed and amplified using specific primers for HIF-1α and HIF-1β, respectively. B) Total protein was prepared from isolated retinas at different post-natal days as indicated. HIF-1α levels were tested by Western blotting using a specific antibody (4).

NEUROPROTECTION IN THE RETINA THROUGH HYPOXIC PRECONDITIONING AND HIF-1 ACTIVATION.

We intended to prepare the adult mouse retina to cope with a strong apoptotic stimulus by a short exposure to low environmental oxygen concentrations. We then analyzed the molecular response of the retina to this hypoxic preconditioning and tested the neuroprotective capacity of this treatment (20). Hypoxic preconditioning stabilized HIF-1α in the retina and levels of retinal HIF-1α protein followed a dose-response function: exposure to 6% and 10% oxygen for 6 hours strongly stabilized HIF-1α, while exposure to 14% oxygen had an intermediate effect on HIF-1α levels, and 18% and 21% (normoxia) conditions did not cause any notable stabilization of the transcription factor. As noticed in other tissues, HIF-1α was quickly destabilized upon reoxygenation and protein levels reached basal values already after 1 hour in normal room air (20). The functionality of the stabilized HIF-1α protein was shown by the increased expression of HIF-1 target genes in the retina. Of particular interest was the strong induction of erythropoietin (up to 10-fold) (20).

Hypoxic preconditioning induced a neuroprotective response in the retina rendering photoreceptors resistant against exposure to high levels of white light, a strong apoptotic insult (48, 66). Without preconditioning, exposure to 5'800 lux of white fluorescent light for one hour was sufficient to induce apoptosis in a large number of photoreceptors leading to cell loss and retinal degeneration. Photoreceptors of mice preconditioned by hypoxic exposure, however, were completely protected against the light insult when exposed after a 4-hour period of reoxygenation (Fig. 3A). Importantly, not only retinal morphology was protected but also retinal function as determined by ERG recordings (20). After 16 hours of reoxygenation, photoreceptors were again susceptible to light damage and light exposure resulted in photoreceptor loss and thinning of the outer nuclear layer (ONL) as well as of the layer of rod inner (RIS) and rod outer segments (ROS). All other layers including the RPE remained remarkably intact (Fig. 3B). The transient nature of the neuroprotective effect indicates that that the protective factors induced by hypoxic preconditioning are short-lived and implies that these factors might be deactivated immediately upon reoxygenation to restore a physiological retinal environment. Neuroprotection induced by hypoxic preconditioning most likely was dependent on the transcription factor HIF-1 since protection correlated directly with retinal levels of HIF-1α and inversely with oxygen concentrations during the preconditioning period (20).

Other potential protective mechanisms involve stress-mediated protection (67) or severely affected rhodopsin regeneration in the visual cycle (31, 56, 68). Light damage as applied here utilizes signaling cascades involving the activation of the transcription factor AP-1 (23, 64, 67). Stress was shown to inhibit AP-1 DNA binding via the activation of the glucocorticoid receptor (GR) in the retina (67). Although hypoxic preconditioning indeed imposed a stress on the animals leading to an activation and nuclear translocation of the glucocorticoid receptor (GR) immediately at the end of the hypoxic period, nucleo-cytoplasmic distribution of GR was normal and indistinguishable form normoxic controls after the 4-hour period of reoxygenation that preceded light exposure (20). Furthermore, light exposure of hypoxic preconditioned mice strongly activated AP-1 activity without leading to photoreceptor apoptosis. This suggests that protection was not mediated through the inhibition of AP-1 and that hypoxic preconditioning interrupts the apoptotic signaling cascade downstream of AP-1. Another important parameter for light induced retinal degeneration is the speed of the visual cycle. Upon photon absorption 11-cis retinal is photoisomerized to all-trans retinal in the visual pigment rhodopsin. Before rhodopsin can absorb another photon, 11-cis retinal has to be regenerated from all-trans retinal in the visual cycle, a complex reaction cascade involving a multitude of enzymes in both the RPE and the photoreceptors. Slowing or blocking the visual cycle renders the retina resistant against light damage due to the reduced number of photon absorptions by rhodopsin (31, 56, 65, 68). It has been shown that hypoxic exposure alters rhodopsin regeneration in mice (45) as well as dark adaptation in humans (2, 32, 34). However, after 4 hours of reoxygenation – at the timepoint of light exposure – rhodopsin regeneration was comparable in preconditioned and control mice (20). Neuroprotection against light toxicity might therefore not be mediated by alterations in the visual cycle but rather by factors differentially regulated by the hypoxic period. Such factors may not be stably expressed under normoxic conditions and their production might depend on oxygen-sensing molecules like HIF-1.

EPO AS NEUROPROTECTIVE AGENT IN THE RETINA

One of the most prominent genes induced by hypoxia via HIF-1 is Epo. Using real-time PCR, we showed that Epo was strongly upregulated in the retina upon hypoxic exposure (20). In addition, Epo receptor was found to be expressed on photoreceptor cells (20) and retinal ganglion cells (29). Epo protects neuronal cells from apoptotic cell death in a variety of models for neuronal damage (15) including the retina (29). We therefore tested whether Epo is responsible for the retinal protection observed after hypoxic preconditioning. Recombinant human Epo (rhEpo) was injected intraperitoneally into normal mice before or after light exposure. This treatment reduced light damage susceptibility of the mice, suggesting that Epo-mediated activation of the Epo receptor directly induces protection of the visual cells. However, protection by rhEpo was less complete than the protection observed after hypoxic preconditioning. It is possible that the limited protective capacity of rhEpo was due to a poor translocation of the protein across the blood-retina barrier leading to an insufficient availability of Epo in the retina. However, even the 20-fold increased retinal Epo levels in tg6 mice did not induce the same complete protection as observed after hypoxic preconditioning (21). This result suggests that pretreatment with low oxygen induces several factor(s) (Epo being one of them) that may need to act in concert to fully protect photoreceptors against a light-induced injury.

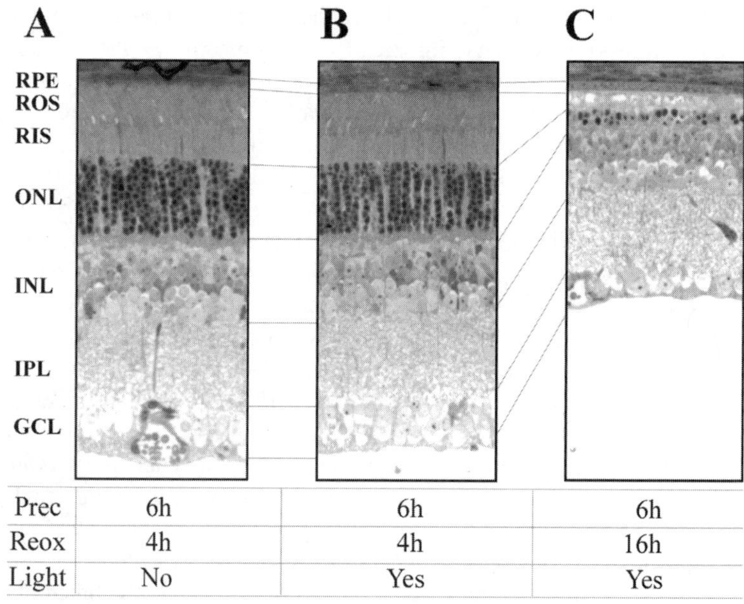

Prec	6h	6h	6h
Reox	4h	4h	16h
Light	No	Yes	Yes

Figure 3. Hypoxic preconditioning induces a transient neuroprotection of the retina against light-induced photoreceptor apoptosis. All BALB/c mice were preconditioned (Prec) for 6h with 6% oxygen, reoxygenized (Reox) for 4 hours (A, B) or 16 hours (C) prior to exposure to 1 hour of 5'800 lux of white light (Light; B, C). Retinal morphology was assayed on plastic embedded sections by light microscopy 10 days after light exposure. A) Retinal morphology of a control mouse without light exposure. B) Retinal morphology of a light exposed mouse preconditioned with hypoxia followed by a 4-hour reoxygenation period. The retina was completely protected against light induced apoptosis. C) Retinal morphology of a light exposed mouse preconditioned with hypoxia followed by a 16-hour reoxygenation period. The retina was susceptible to light induced apoptosis. Retinal degeneration and loss of photoreceptor cells is indicated by the thinning of the outer nuclear layer (ONL), rod inner segments (RIS) and rod outer segments (ROS). The other layers of the retina were not affected by the exposure to light. Shown are representative sections of at least 4 different animals. RPE: retinal pigment epithelium, INL: inner nuclear layer, IPL; inner plexiform layer, GCL: ganglion cell layer.

EPO IN MODELS OF INHERITED DEGENERATION OF PHOTORECEPTORS

Many mouse models of inherited retinal degeneration exist (22). To test the therapeutic potential of Epo, we used two models: the retinal degeneration mouse 1 (rd1) as a model for autosomal recessive Retinitis Pigmentosa (RP) and the VPP transgenic mouse resembling an autosomal dominant form of RP. The rd1 mouse carries a spontaneous insertion of a retrovirus in the gene encoding the β-subunit of phosphodiesterase leading to aberrant splicing and a null phenotype (7, 66). The lack of phosphodiesterase activity increases levels of cGMP in photoreceptors resulting in constantly open ion channels and, as a consequence, elevated intracellular Ca^{2+} levels. Either the elevated cGMP and/or the high levels of Ca^{2+} might be the cause of the observed early onset (around post natal day 10) and rapid degeneration of the photoreceptor cell layer. Already ten days after onset of degeneration, retinas of rd1 mice are mostly devoid of rods.

The VPP mouse expresses a transgene encoding a mutant form of rod opsin with three amino acid substitutions at the N-terminal end of the protein (19). One of these mutations causes the substitution of prolin at residue 23 by histidine (P23H). This mutation is the most frequent mutation found in opsin of human RP patients and accounts for about 10% of autosomal dominant RP in the USA.

Two approaches were used to investigate the potential neuroprotective capacity of Epo in inherited retinal degeneration: i) recombinant human Epo (rhEpo) was systemically applied by intraperitoneal (ip) injections into rd1 and VPP mice every other day before onset and during the first phase of degeneration. ii) using classical breeding schemes, both mouse models for inherited retinal degeneration were combined with the transgene in tg6 that expresses Epo at high levels especially in neuronal tissue including the retina (see above). However, neither the transgene nor the systemic application of rhEpo protected the rd1 or the VPP mouse against retinal degeneration (21). Protection of photoreceptors in the rd1 and the VPP mouse may therefore require other or additional factors. We are currently attempting to identify the postulated (see above) additional neuroprotective molecules induced by hypoxic preconditioning. Once identified, it will be important to test these factors in the inherited models. Recently, it has been suggested that only systemically but not locally produced Epo is neuroprotective in the retina (49). Since the tg6 mice seem to produce most of their Epo locally in neuronal tissue, this observation might additionally explain the weaker neuroprotective capacity – as compared to hypoxic preconditioning – of the transgene against light toxicity. Additional experiments have to be conducted in order to establish the physiological and neuroprotective role of Epo produced locally in the retina.

ACKNOWLEDGEMENTS

Our work was supported by the Swiss National Science Foundation, the Theodore Ott Foundation, the Hartmann Muller Foundation, and the Roche Research Foundation, the German Research Council (DFG), the Messerli Foundation, a fortune grant Univ. of Tübingen, and a BMBF grant (IZKF University of Tübingen). The Epo-overexpressing mouse line tg6 was generated by Max Gassmann.

REFERENCES

1. Barbe MF, Tytell M, Gower DJ, and Welch WJ. Hyperthermia protects against light damage in the rat retina. *Science* 241: 1817-1820, 1988.
2. Brinchmann-Hansen O and Myhre K. The effect of hypoxia upon macular recovery time in normal humans. *Aviat Space Environ Med* 60: 1183-1186, 1989.
3. Camenisch G, Stroka DM, Gassmann M, and Wenger RH. Attenuation of HIF-1 DNA-binding activity limits hypoxia-inducible endothelin-1 expression. *Pflugers Arch* 443: 240-249, 2001.
4. Camenisch G, Tini M, Chilov D, Kvietikova I, Srinivas V, Caro J, Spielmann P, Wenger RH, and Gassmann M. General applicability of chicken egg yolk antibodies: the performance of IgY immunoglobulins raised against the hypoxia-inducible factor 1alpha. *Faseb J* 13: 81-88, 1999.
5. Casson RJ, Chidlow G, Wood JP, Vidal-Sanz M, and Osborne NN. The effect of retinal ganglion cell injury on light-induced photoreceptor degeneration. *Invest Ophthalmol Vis Sci* 45: 685-693, 2004.
6. Casson RJ, Wood JP, Melena J, Chidlow G, and Osborne NN. The effect of ischemic preconditioning on light-induced photoreceptor injury. *Invest Ophthalmol Vis Sci* 44: 1348-1354, 2003.
7. Chang B, Hawes NL, Hurd RE, Davisson MT, Nusinowitz S, and Heckenlively JR. Retinal degeneration mutants in the mouse. *Vision Res* 42: 517-525, 2002.
8. Chen CK, Burns ME, Spencer M, Niemi GA, Chen J, Hurley JB, Baylor DA, and Simon MI. Abnormal photoresponses and light-induced apoptosis in rods lacking rhodopsin kinase. *Proc Natl Acad Sci USA* 96: 3718-3722, 1999.
9. Chen J, Simon MI, Matthes MT, Yasumura D, and LaVail MM. Increased susceptibility to light damage in an arrestin knockout mouse model of Oguchi disease (stationary night blindness). *Invest Ophthalmol Vis Sci* 40: 2978-2982, 1999.
10. Cideciyan AV, Hood DC, Huang Y, Banin E, Li ZY, Stone EM, Milam AH, and Jacobson SG. Disease sequence from mutant rhodopsin allele to rod and cone photoreceptor degeneration in man. *Proc Natl Acad Sci U S A* 95: 7103-7108, 1998.
11. Cruickshanks KJ, Klein R, and Klein BE. Sunlight and age-related macular degeneration. The Beaver Dam Eye Study. *Arch Ophthalmol* 111: 514-518, 1993.
12. Cruickshanks KJ, Klein R, Klein BE, and Nondahl DM. Sunlight and the 5-year incidence of early age-related maculopathy: the beaver dam eye study. *Arch Ophthalmol* 119: 246-250, 2001.
13. Digicaylioglu M, Bichet S, Marti HH, Wenger RH, Rivas LA, Bauer C, and Gassmann M. Localization of specific erythropoietin binding sites in defined areas of the mouse brain. *Proc Natl Acad Sci U S A* 92: 3717-3720., 1995.
14. Ehrenreich H, Hasselblatt M, Dembowski C, Cepek L, Lewczuk P, Stiefel M, Rustenbeck HH, Breiter N, Jacob S, Knerlich F, Bohn M, Poser W, Ruther E, Kochen M, Gefeller O, Gleiter C, Wessel TC, De Ryck M, Itri L, Prange H, Cerami A, Brines M, and Siren AL. Erythropoietin therapy for acute stroke is both safe and beneficial. *Mol Med* 8: 495-505, 2002.
15. Eid T and Brines M. Recombinant human erythropoietin for neuroprotection: what is the evidence? *Clin Breast Cancer* 3 Suppl 3: S109-115, 2002.
16. Eisen A, Fisman EZ, Rubenfire M, Freimark D, McKechnie R, Tenenbaum A, Motro M, and Adler Y. Ischemic preconditioning: nearly two decades of research. A comprehensive review. *Atherosclerosis* 172: 201-210, 2004.
17. Gassmann M, Heinicke K, Soliz J, and Ogunshola OO. Non-erythroid functions of erythropoietin. *Adv Exp Med Biol* 543: 323-330, 2003.
18. Ghezzi P and Brines M. Erythropoietin as an antiapoptotic, tissue-protective cytokine. *Cell*

Death Differ 11 Suppl 1: S37-44, 2004.

19. Goto Y, Peachey NS, Ziroli NE, Seiple WH, Gryczan C, Pepperberg DR, and Naash MI. Rod phototransduction in transgenic mice expressing a mutant opsin gene. *J Opt Soc Am A* 13: 577-585., 1996.
20. Grimm C, Wenzel A, Groszer M, Mayser H, Seeliger M, Samardzija M, Bauer C, Gassmann M, and Reme CE. HIF-1-induced erythropoietin in the hypoxic retina protects against light-induced retinal degeneration. *Nat Med* 8: 718-724, 2002.
21. Grimm C, Wenzel A, Stanescu D, Samardzija M, Hotop S, Groszer M, Naash M, Gassmann M, and Reme C. Constitutive overexpression of human erythropoietin protects the mouse retina against induced but not inherited retinal degeneration. *J Neurosci* 24: 5651-5658, 2004.
22. Hafezi F, Grimm C, Simmen BC, Wenzel A, and Reme CE. Molecular ophthalmology: an update on animal models for retinal degenerations and dystrophies. *Br J Ophthalmol* 84: 922-927, 2000.
23. Hafezi F, Steinbach JP, Marti A, Munz K, Wang ZQ, Wagner EF, Aguzzi A, and Reme CE. The absence of c-fos prevents light-induced apoptotic cell death of photoreceptors in retinal degeneration in vivo. *Nat Med* 3: 346-349, 1997.
24. Hopfl G, Ogunshola O, and Gassmann M. HIFs and tumors--causes and consequences. *Am J Physiol Regul Integr Comp Physiol* 286: R608-623, 2004.
25. Hopfl G, Ogunshola O, and Gassmann M. Hypoxia and high altitude. The molecular response. *Adv Exp Med Biol* 543: 89-115, 2003.
26. Huttl S, Michalakis S, Seeliger M, Luo DG, Acar N, Geiger H, Hudl K, Mader R, Haverkamp S, Moser M, Pfeifer A, Gerstner A, Yau KW, and Biel M. Impaired channel targeting and retinal degeneration in mice lacking the cyclic nucleotide-gated channel subunit CNGB1. *J Neurosci* 25: 130-138, 2005.
27. Jelkmann W. Erythropoietin: structure, control of production, and function. *Physiol Rev* 72: 449-489., 1992.
28. Jewell UR, Kvietikova I, Scheid A, Bauer C, Wenger RH, and Gassmann M. Induction of HIF-1alpha in response to hypoxia is instantaneous. *Faseb J* 15: 1312-1314., 2001.
29. Junk AK, Mammis A, Savitz SI, Singh M, Roth S, Malhotra S, Rosenbaum PS, Cerami A, Brines M, and Rosenbaum DM. Erythropoietin administration protects retinal neurons from acute ischemia-reperfusion injury. *Proc Natl Acad Sci U S A* 99: 10659-10664, 2002.
30. Kaldi I, Martin RE, Huang H, Brush RS, Morrison KA, and Anderson RE. Bright cyclic rearing protects albino mouse retina against acute light-induced apoptosis. *Mol Vis* 9: 337-344, 2003.
31. Keller C, Grimm C, Wenzel A, Hafezi F, and Reme C. Protective effect of halothane anesthesia on retinal light damage: inhibition of metabolic rhodopsin regeneration. *Invest Ophthalmol Vis Sci* 42: 476-480, 2001.
32. Kobrick JL, Zwick H, Witt CE, and Devine JA. Effects of extended hypoxia on night vision. *Aviat Space Environ Med* 55: 191-195, 1984.
33. LaVail MM, Gorrin GM, Yasumura D, and Matthes MT. Increased susceptibility to constant light in nr and pcd mice with inherited retinal degeneration. *Invest Ophthalmol Vis Sci* 40: 1020-1024, 1999.
34. Leber LL, Roscoe SN, and Southward GM. Mild hypoxia and visual performance with night vision goggles. *Aviat Space Environ Med* 57: 318-324, 1986.
35. Li F, Cao W, and Anderson RE. Protection of photoreceptor cells in adult rats from light-induced degeneration by adaptation to bright cyclic light. *Exp Eye Res* 73: 569-577, 2001.
36. Li Y, Roth S, Laser M, Ma JX, and Crosson CE. Retinal preconditioning and the induction of heat-shock protein 27. *Invest Ophthalmol Vis Sci* 44: 1299-1304, 2003.

37. Liu C, Peng M, Laties AM, and Wen R. Preconditioning with bright light evokes a protective response against light damage in the rat retina. *J Neurosci* 18: 1337-1344, 1998.
38. Marti HH. Erythropoietin and the hypoxic brain. *J Exp Biol* 207: 3233-3242, 2004.
39. Marti HH, Wenger RH, Rivas LA, Straumann U, Digicaylioglu M, Henn V, Yonekawa Y, Bauer C, and Gassmann M. Erythropoietin gene expression in human, monkey and murine brain. *Eur J Neurosci* 8: 666-676., 1996.
40. Marti HJ, Bernaudin M, Bellail A, Schoch H, Euler M, Petit E, and Risau W. Hypoxia-induced vascular endothelial growth factor expression precedes neovascularization after cerebral ischemia. *Am J Pathol* 156: 965-976., 2000.
41. Nir I, Harrison JM, Liu C, and Wen R. Extended photoreceptor viability by light stress in the RCS rats but not in the opsin P23H mutant rats. *Invest Ophthalmol Vis Sci* 42: 842-849, 2001.
42. Nir I, Liu C, and Wen R. Light treatment enhances photoreceptor survival in dystrophic retinas of Royal College of Surgeons rats. *Invest Ophthalmol Vis Sci* 40: 2383-2390, 1999.
43. O'Steen WK, Bare DJ, Tytell M, Morris M, and Gower DJ. Water deprivation protects photoreceptors against light damage. *Brain Res* 534: 99-105, 1990.
44. Organisciak DT, Li M, Darrow RM, and Farber DB. Photoreceptor cell damage by light in young Royal College of Surgeons rats. *Curr Eye Res* 19: 188-196, 1999.
45. Ostroy SE, Gaitatzes CG, and Friedmann AL. Hypoxia inhibits rhodopsin regeneration in the excised mouse eye. *Invest Ophthalmol Vis Sci* 34: 447-452, 1993.
46. Quaschning T, Ruschitzka F, Stallmach T, Shaw S, Morawietz H, Goettsch W, Hermann M, Slowinski T, Theuring F, Hocher B, Luscher TF, and Gassmann M. Erythropoietin-induced excessive erythrocytosis activates the tissue endothelin system in mice. *Faseb J* 17: 259-261, 2003.
47. Reme CE, Grimm C, Hafezi F, Iseli HP, and Wenzel A. Why study rod cell death in retinal degenerations and how? *Doc Ophthalmol* 106: 25-29, 2003.
48. Reme CE, Grimm C, Hafezi F, Marti A, and Wenzel A. Apoptotic cell death in retinal degenerations. *Prog Retin Eye Res* 17: 443-464, 1998.
49. Rex TS, Allocca M, Domenici L, Surace EM, Maguire AM, Lyubarsky A, Cellerino A, Bennett J, and Auricchio A. Systemic but not intraocular Epo gene transfer protects the retina from light-and genetic-induced degeneration. *Mol Ther* 10: 855-861, 2004.
50. Ruschitzka FT, Wenger RH, Stallmach T, Quaschning T, de Wit C, Wagner K, Labugger R, Kelm M, Noll G, Rulicke T, Shaw S, Lindberg RL, Rodenwaldt B, Lutz H, Bauer C, Luscher TF, and Gassmann M. Nitric oxide prevents cardiovascular disease and determines survival in polyglobulic mice overexpressing erythropoietin. *Proc Natl Acad Sci U S A* 97: 11609-11613, 2000.
51. Sakanaka M, Wen TC, Matsuda S, Masuda S, Morishita E, Nagao M, and Sasaki R. In vivo evidence that erythropoietin protects neurons from ischemic damage. *Proc Natl Acad Sci U S A* 95: 4635-4640., 1998.
52. Sanyal S and Hawkins RK. Development and degeneration of retina in rds mutant mice: effects of light on the rate of degeneration in albino and pigmented homozygous and heterozygous mutant and normal mice. *Vision Res* 26: 1177-1185, 1986.
53. Schofield CJ and Ratcliffe PJ. Oxygen sensing by HIF hydroxylases. *Nat Rev Mol Cell Biol* 5: 343-354, 2004.
54. Semenza GL. Hydroxylation of HIF-1: oxygen sensing at the molecular level. *Physiology* 19: 176-182, 2004.
55. Shibata J, Hasegawa J, Siemens HJ, Wolber E, Dibbelt L, Li D, Katschinski DM, Fandrey J, Jelkmann W, Gassmann M, Wenger RH, and Wagner KF. Hemostasis and coagulation at a hematocrit level of 0.85: functional consequences of erythrocytosis. *Blood* 101:

4416-4422, 2003.
56. Sieving PA, Chaudhry P, Kondo M, Provenzano M, Wu D, Carlson TJ, Bush RA, and Thompson DA. Inhibition of the visual cycle in vivo by 13-cis retinoic acid protects from light damage and provides a mechanism for night blindness in isotretinoin therapy. *Proc Natl Acad Sci U S A* 98: 1835-1840, 2001.
57. Simons K. Artificial light and early-life exposure in age-related macular degeneration and in cataractogenic phototoxicity. *Arch Ophthalmol* 111: 297-298, 1993.
58. Stroka DM, Burkhardt T, Desbaillets I, Wenger RH, Neil DA, Bauer C, Gassmann M, and Candinas D. HIF-1 is expressed in normoxic tissue and displays an organ-specific regulation under systemic hypoxia. *Faseb J* 15: 2445-2453., 2001.
59. Tan CC, Eckardt KU, Firth JD, and Ratcliffe PJ. Feedback modulation of renal and hepatic erythropoietin mRNA in response to graded anemia and hypoxia. *Am J Physiol* 263: F474-481, 1992.
60. Taylor HR, Munoz B, West S, Bressler NM, Bressler SB, and Rosenthal FS. Visible light and risk of age-related macular degeneration. *Trans Am Ophthalmol Soc* 88: 163-173, 1990.
61. Vogel J, Kiessling I, Heinicke K, Stallmach T, Ossent P, Vogel O, Aulmann M, Frietsch T, Schmid-Schonbein H, Kuschinsky W, and Gassmann M. Transgenic mice overexpressing erythropoietin adapt to excessive erythrocytosis by regulating blood viscosity. *Blood* 102: 2278-2284, 2003.
62. Wagner KF, Katschinski DM, Hasegawa J, Schumacher D, Meller B, Gembruch U, Schramm U, Jelkmann W, Gassmann M, and Fandrey J. Chronic inborn erythrocytosis leads to cardiac dysfunction and premature death in mice overexpressing erythropoietin. *Blood* 97: 536-542, 2001.
63. Wang M, Lam TT, Tso MO, and Naash MI. Expression of a mutant opsin gene increases the susceptibility of the retina to light damage. *Vis Neurosci* 14: 55-62, 1997.
64. Wenzel A, Grimm C, Marti A, Kueng-Hitz N, Hafezi F, Niemeyer G, and Reme CE. c-fos controls the "private pathway" of light-induced apoptosis of retinal photoreceptors. *J Neurosci* 20: 81-88, 2000.
65. Wenzel A, Grimm C, Samardzija M, and Reme CE. The genetic modifier Rpe65Leu(450): effect on light damage susceptibility in c-Fos-deficient mice. *Invest Ophthalmol Vis Sci* 44: 2798-2802, 2003.
66. Wenzel A, Grimm C, Samardzija M, and Reme CE. Molecular mechanisms of light-induced photoreceptor apoptosis and neuroprotection for retinal degeneration. *Prog Retin Eye Res* 24: 275-306, 2005.
67. Wenzel A, Grimm C, Seeliger MW, Jaissle G, Hafezi F, Kretschmer R, Zrenner E, and Reme CE. Prevention of photoreceptor apoptosis by activation of the glucocorticoid receptor. *Invest Ophthalmol Vis Sci* 42: 1653-1659, 2001.
68. Wenzel A, Reme CE, Williams TP, Hafezi F, and Grimm C. The Rpe65 Leu450Met variation increases retinal resistance against light-induced degeneration by slowing rhodopsin regeneration. *J Neurosci* 21: 53-58, 2001.
69. Zhang C, Rosenbaum DM, Shaikh AR, Li Q, Rosenbaum PS, Pelham DJ, and Roth S. Ischemic preconditioning attenuates apoptotic cell death in the rat retina. *Invest Ophthalmol Vis Sci* 43: 3059-3066, 2002.

Chapter 12

BLOCKING STRESS SIGNALING PATHWAYS WITH CELL PERMEABLE PEPTIDES

Christophe Bonny
Unit of Molecular Genetics, CHUV, Lausanne, Switzerland.

Abstract: Cells are continuously adapting to changes in their environment by activating extra-cellular stimuli-dependent signal transduction cascades. These cascades, or signaling pathways, culminate both in changes in genes expression and in the functional regulation of pre-existing proteins. The Mitogen-Activated Protein Kinases (MAPKs) constitute a structurally related class of signaling proteins whose distinctive feature is their ability to directly phosphorylate, and thereby modulate, the activity of the transcription factors that are targets of the initial stimuli. The specificity of activation of MAPK signaling modules is determined, at least for an important part, by the specificity of the protein-protein contacts that are required for the propagation of the signal. We will discuss how we may interfere with MAPK signaling by using short cell-permeable peptides able to block, through a competitive mechanisms, relevant protein-protein contacts, and their effects on signaling and cell function.

Key Words: signaling, apoptosis, cell-permeable peptides, MAPK

INTRODUCTION

Extracellular stimuli activate different signal transduction pathways that culminate in modification of pre-existing proteins, changes in mitochondrial permeability, ER responses and changes in gene expression, ultimately, robust and durable stimuli may lead to apoptosis. Amongst other signaling components, MAPK (Mitogen-Activated Protein Kinases) constitute the final elements of a series of signaling events that transduce external stressful events to the nucleus, the mitochondria, the ER, and other cell components. The distinctive feature of MAPKs is their ability to directly phosphorylate, and thereby modulate the activity of the transcription factors that are targets of the initial stimuli.

Regulation and activation of MAPKs appears to require sophisticated signaling events,

Hypoxia and Exercise, edited by R.C. Roach *et al.*
Springer, New York, 2006.

thus providing different therapeutic opportunities. MAPK core module pathways are com posed of three conserved kinases that proceed through a phosphorylation cascade creating a sequential activation pathway. The first kinase in the module is a MAPK kinase kinase (MKKK), a serine/threonine kinase that when activated phosphorylates and activates the next kinase in the module, a MAPK kinase (MKK). The MKKs are dual specific kinases that phosphorylate a Thr-X-Tyr motif in the activation loop of MAPKs. MAPKs are the final kinases in the module and phosphorylate different substrates on serine and threonine residues. Three major conserved groups of MAPKs have been described: the Extra-cellular signal Regulated Kinases (ERK1/2/3) (10), the p38 kinases (p38 α/ß/γ/and θ) (27), and the c-Jun NH_2-terminal kinases (JNK1/2/3) (13).

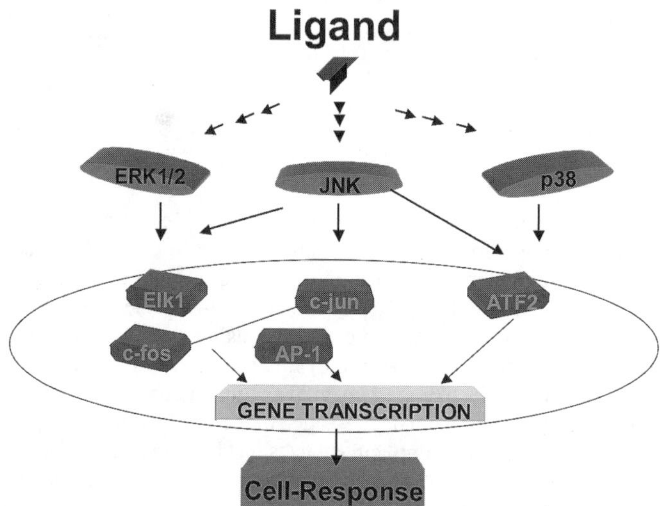

Figure 1. MAPK signaling unit is made up of three sequential kinases. The signal is transmitted to the nucleus through three MAPKs, ERK, p38 and JNK.

In mammals, these MAPKs can be activated by six MKKs: MKK1 and MKK2 are upstream activators of ERK1/2, MKK3 and MKK6 are activators of p38, and MKK4 and MKK7 regulate JNK. It has also been shown that MKK4 can activate p38 in addition to JNK. Both JNK and p38 activate downstream nuclear transcription factors that participate to the cellular response. Amongst these, activation of the activator protein-1 (AP-1) ?formed of heteromers of c-Fos, c-Jun and ATF2- is required for some forms of apoptosis, notably in neuronal cells. A major transcriptional target of JNK and p38 is the c-fos gene. The p38 kinases and JNKs primarily respond to a variety of stimuli collectively designated as «stress-signals». These include for example cytokine treatments (IL-1ß, TNFα), but also environmental stresses including osmotic shocks, heat and cold shocks, lack of survival factors, uncoupling from the cell-matrix, shearing stresses, reactive oxygen species (12, 37) and many others.

JNK

10 different isoforms of JNK arising from the expression of three genes have been described. Amongst these, the JNK3 isoforms appear particularly interesting as they show expression restricted to neurons and heart, and they have been clearly associated with apoptotic events in the brain, potentially through the induction of Bim and Fas and the mitochondrial release of cytochrome c (30, 48), JNK3 KO mice are substantially resistant against and survive kainic acid-induced seizures (11). Furthermore, the JNK1, 2 and 3 isoforms show clear substrate specificities (21), explaining at least in part why only the JNK3 protein has been associated with cell-death in some neuronal populations. Excluding transcription factors, JNK also phosphorylates a whole battery of cytoplasmic, membrane-bound and mitochondrial targets. These include: bcl-2, bcl-xL, MADD or IRS-1.

P38

The family of the p38 proteins regroups 4 major isoforms: α/ß/γ/θ. The p38α and ß isoforms, which are 75% homologous, are ubiquitously expressed and have been intensively studied, as numerous inhibitors are readily available, the most widely used being the SB203580 and SB202190 agents (38). It is important to note here that these inhibitors do not affect the γ and θ isoforms, although they strongly inhibit a whole battery of other kinases, rendering the interpretation of data generated using these chemicals extremely difficult (the same situation being true as well for the commercially available JNK inhibitors) (4). No chemical inhibitor is available to block neither the p38γ nor the θ isoforms. The expression of the p38γ form is limited to muscles, whereas p38θ shows preferential expression in the pancreas. All p38 isoforms are activated by the same upstream kinases ? MAP kinase kinase (MKK)3 or MKK6 ? in response to inflammatory and stressful stimuli. A major substrate of p38α and ß is MAPK-activated protein kinase (MAPKAPK)-2. The p38γ and θ forms are less effective at activating the downstream kinases and better at phosphorylating transcription factors such as activating-transcription-factor (ATF)2, Elk-1 and SAP-1 (38). As we will show, there is clear overlapping between the substrate specificities of p38θ and JNK, both being for example able to phosphorylate the N-terminal transcriptional activation domain of c-Jun. Finally, the activity of p38θ is regulated by the scaffold protein IB2 (35, 40), the second member of the Islet-Brain (IB) family of proteins, a genetic defect in IB1, which regulates JNK signaling, has been linked to diabetes (47).

Ample evidence suggests a correlation between the activation of the p38 pathway and apoptosis. Such a correlation is based on the concomitant activation of p38, caspase activation and apoptosis induced by a variety of agents including NGF withdrawal and Fas ligation (this being true for JNK as well). Overexpression of dominant active MKK6ß can induce caspase activity and cell death (16), the mechanism by which this pathway might influence caspase activity being currently not fully characterized. Also, SB203580 can block sodium salicylate-induced FS-4 fibroblast apoptosis, glutamate-induced cerebellar granule cell apoptosis, serum depletion induced Rat-1 cell death, NGF withdrawal-induced PC12 cell apoptosis, and TL1-induced bovine pulmonary artery endothelial cell apoptosis (see (36) for a review on the p38 signal transduction pathway). Activation of p38θ has been shown to be required for anoikis of enterocytes induced by inhibition of focal adhesion kinase or beta1 integrins, or by maintaining cells in suspension (46). The respective roles of the p38ß and p38θ isoforms might be clearly antagonist, as for example the former isoform increases LPS-dependent induction of Heme Oxygenase (HO)-1 gene expression, whereas activation of the latter prevents its expression (54). In keratinocytes, activation of p38θ is associated with apoptosis (16). In these cells, okadaic acid, which is a strong activator of p38θ but not the other p38 isoforms, as well as overexpression of p38θ inhibits ERK1/2 activity without reducing ERK1/2 levels. In keratinocytes again, p38θ activity is associated with increased levels of AP1 binding protein factors. This response is maintained in the presence of SB203580, whereas dominant-negative p38θ inhibits AP-1 activity (15). Thus, p38θ may directly suppress ERK1/2 activity at the same time as activating AP-1.

EVIDENCE THAT JNK AND P38 SIGNALING IS ORDERED BY SPECIALIZED SCAFFOLD PROTEINS

Many intracellular components that participate to signaling events are presumably physically ordered through distinct protein-protein interactions. The specificity of activation and function of MAP-kinase signaling modules appears determined, in part, by scaffold proteins that create multienzyme complexes. These scaffold proteins facilitate MAP-kinase activation in response to specific physiological stimuli, and insulate the bound MAP-kinase module against activation by irrelevant stimuli. Scaffold proteins are therefore critical components of MAP-kinase modules to ensure signalling specificity (14, 52).

In *Saccharomyces cerevisiae*, two MAP- kinase-scaffold proteins have been identified. In mammals, different scaffolds with no intrinsic enzymatic activity have been described that aggregate sequential components of MAP-kinases signaling. One such protein, MP1, tether the ERK kinase MEK1 to ERK (39). Two other scaffolds aggregate the JNK signaling unit: MLK-MKK7-JNK. These are JIP-1 (IB1) and JIP-3/JSAP-1, whereas JIP-2 (IB2) is a scaffold for p38θ (7, 24, 29, 35, 51, 60).

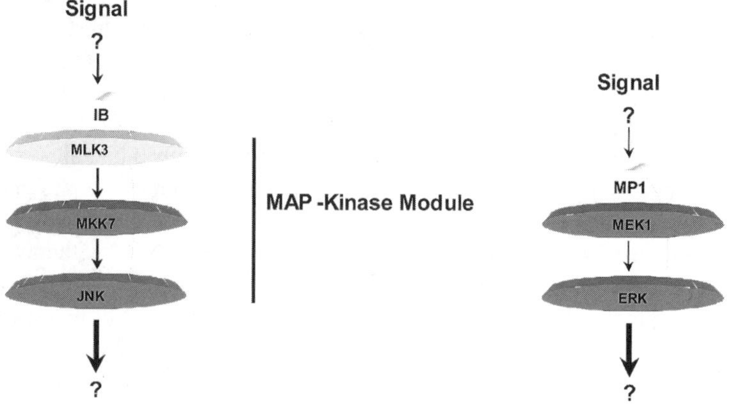

Figure 2. The IB and MP1 scaffolds aggregate sequential components of a signalling module (55, 71).

JIP-3 belongs to a structurally distinct family of proteins than the highly related JIP-1/IB1 and JIP-2/IB2. Despite their differences in structure, it is noteworthy that all these scaffolds are expressed almost exclusively in brain and also in heart (7, 29, 34, 35, 51, 60). Except for the JIP/IB proteins that are able to interact with the ApoER2 receptors and presumably with other components of LDL-receptor signaling, the known scaffolds are currently «orphan», *i.e.* no convincing association with either upstream or downstream components of the signaling cascade have been described. Results in yeast where scaffolds were known for many years and in human (47, 52), indicate that malfunction of these molecules may result in major physiopathological states (53).

USE OF CELL-PENETRATING PEPTIDES TO BLOCK SIGNALING EVENTS

Inhibiting kinase activities along intracellular pathways is usually used to block signaling. An alternative is to prevent essential protein-protein interaction between necessary factors within signaling cascades. This might be efficiently performed in cell lines, tissue or animals by cell-penetrating peptides (41) that take advantage of the often small size of the amino acids sequences mediating interaction between two protein partners. The blockade is achieved by introducing a molar excess of one of the two protein interaction domains inside cells. Importantly, this process does not require any intrinsic enzymatic activity from any of the protein partners. Intracellular delivery is achieved by linking these sequences to special peptidic transporters such as "TAT_{48-57}", "Antennapedia" and others. Probably because of its short length (10 amino acids) and its good efficacy in crossing cell-membranes from different cell-types, the TAT_{48-57} sequence from HIV seems now the most generally used for intracellular delivery of peptides. To date, different cell-penetrating peptides acting on different signaling pathways have been shown to confer biological activity in either animal or cell culture models. They include BH4 domain peptides from Bcl-xL, NEMO-Binding-Domain peptides (NBD, blocks NF-κB signaling), TRAF peptides, peptides derived from the signaling protein PSD95 (TAT-NR2B9c), cyclinD:Cdk4/6 derived peptides, hypoxia-inducible factor-1 (HIF) peptides and many others (1, 20, 33, 44, 55, 61). We have engineered similar peptides to block the interaction between JNK and its target c-Jun (6, 8), and shown their biological activity in animals (9, 49).

MAPK INHIBITORY PEPTIDES

The substrate specificity of MAPKs is determined by two components: 1? the sequence and local context of the phospho-acceptor motifs (MAPKs phosphorylate serine and threonine residues followed by proline residues) and 2° the sequence of the docking site on the substrate. The MAPK-docking sites locate usually outside the catalytic domain of the MAPK-interacting molecules. The first MAPK docking site or binding motif identified was the θ domain of c-Jun (42), which acts as a binding site for JNK. The θ domain is important for efficient phosphorylation of c-Jun and the regulation of its transcriptional activation.

v-Jun, the oncogenic counterpart of c-Jun, does not posses the θ domain and therefore looses the ability to bind JNK (32). While JunB, which contains a functional JNK docking site, cannot be phosphorylated by JNKs owing to the absence of sequence specificity conferred by residues surrounding its phospho-acceptors (19), insertion of specific residues can bring JunB under JNK control. JunD, by contrast, possesses a phospho-acceptor region essentially identical to that of c-Jun but lacks an effective JNK docking site, resulting in a weak phosphorylation by JNK. Nevertheless it can be phosphorylated by JNK through heterodimerization with docking competent partners (25). By using a peptide encoding the θ domain and purified JNK, it has been demonstrated that this peptide inhibits phosphorylation of the amino terminus of both c-Jun and JunD, by competing with the substrate for binding to the kinase (2).

Similar docking motifs related to the θ domain and called the docking domain or D domain, are found in MAPK-interacting proteins (18, 45, 58, 59). This docking site is typically less than 20 amino acid long and shows limited sequence similarity, but is characterized by a «slashcircle»A-X-øB motif, where øA and øB are hydrophobic residues (Leu, Val or Ile), separated by 2-6 residues from a cluster of a least two basic residues (Lys, Arg) (5, 43, 50, 56). The basic and hydrophobic residues of the D domain have been shown to be important for recognition, binding, specificity and phosphorylation. For example, the N-terminal portion of MKK4 contains a MAPK-docking site and serves as a binding site for its upstream activator, MEKK1, and its downstream target JNK. Furthermore, the N-terminal portion of MEK1 and the C-terminal portion of RSK2, both of which include the MAPK-docking site, are sufficient for binding to ERK2 (57). Further studies showed that ERK and JNK target Elk-1 via the D domain, and that this targeting is essential for efficient Elk-1 phosphorylation. However, different residues in the D domain are important for ERK and JNK binding. In contrast, p38 is not targeted to Elk-1 via the D domain. ATF2 also contains a docking domain for JNK. Deletion of the binding domain of c-Jun or ATF2 blocks their phosphorylation by JNK.

A peptide derived from the N-terminal sequence of MEK1 and containing the ERK docking domain completely inhibits the interactions between ERK and its substrates and regulators, but is much less efficient in affecting the interaction between p38 and its substrate and regulators. Experiments performed using a p38-derived peptide gave reciprocal results. Similarly, we have produced a peptide from the docking domain of IB1 that specifically prevents the interaction between JNK and its substrate, but not between p38 or ERK and their respective targets (8). By linking this domain to the HIV TAT_{48-57} transporter, we were able to produce cell-permeable molecules capable of blocking JNK signaling in vivo. Others have taken a similar approach to block either ERK (28) or p38 signaling (17).

CELL-PENETRATING PEPTIDE INHIBITORS OF JNK

As indicated above, we designed the first cell-penetrating inhibitors of JNK (JNKi peptides) by linking the minimal 20 amino acids JBD's (*J*NK *B*inding *D*omains) of IB1 or IB2 to the 10 amino acid TAT transporter (8). We showed that these inhibitors efficiently concentrated into a variety of cell types and organs in animals, prevented phosphorylation of c-Jun and ATF2 by JNK (Figures 3 & 4), and blocked the apoptotic response under different stress conditions. These molecules now represent established tools to manipulate the

JNK signaling pathway in animals (6, 8, 31). Furthermore, these JNK-inhibitory peptides have shown real therapeutic perspectives, as they were able to restore normoglycaemia in two models of type 2 diabetes, C57BL/KsJ-db/db mice and C57BL6 mice treated with a high-fat, high sucrose diet, the effect occurred mainly by improvement of insulin-resistance through blockage of JNK-mediated IRS-1 inactivation (3, 26), the same peptides also decreased brain lesions in mice and rats models of stroke (9, 23), and they conferred protection against noise- and antibiotic induced hearing loss (49).

To more precisely define the inhibitory properties of the JNKi peptides, we further analyzed 18 substrates of JNK in *in vitro* protein kinase assays, as well as the effect of the peptide on the activity of 40 different kinases. Our results indicate that the peptide does not inhibit binding of JNK to all its substrates, *i.e* some substrates, including p53 and PPARγ, are efficiently phosphorylated by JNK even in the presence of JNKi. It is not yet clear whether this partial inhibition of JNK-mediated signaling plays any role in the anti-apoptotic activity of the peptide (*i.e.*, would the protective effect be less efficient if the access of JNK to *all* its substrates had been prevented?-it is possible that some of the substrates modified by JNK in presence of the peptide might have anti-apoptotic activities (22)). Apart from its action on the three JNK isoforms and the two upstream JNK-kinases MKK4 and MKK7, JNKi did not appear to significantly impair the activity of any of the other kinases tested (see also (9)).

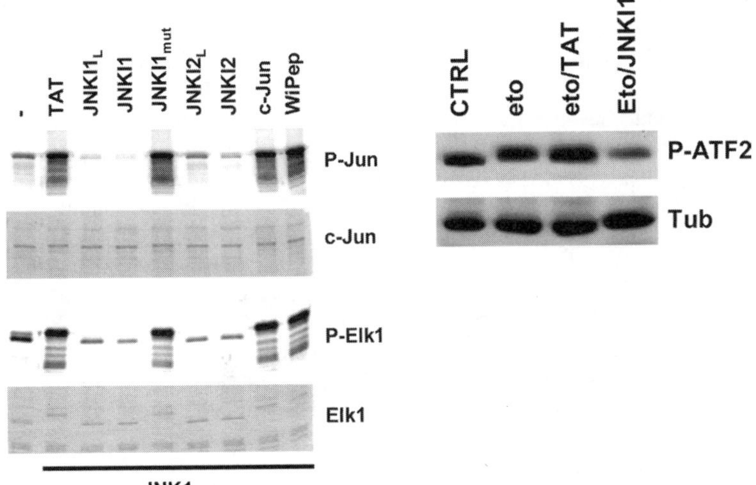

Figure 3. Left, inhibition of c-Jun and Elk1 phosphorylation by recombinant JNK *in vitro*. Right, inhibition of ATF2 phosphorylation in intact HeLa cells (eto: etoposide).

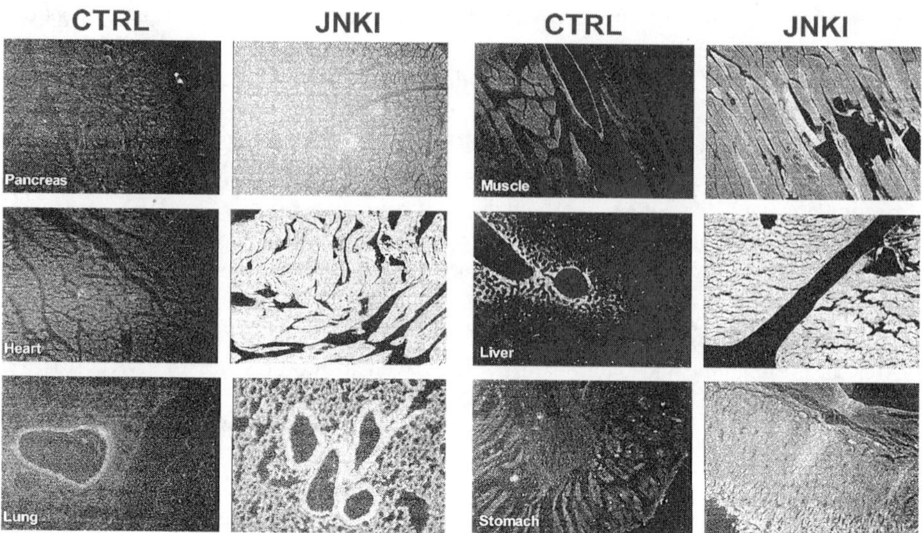

Figure 4. Penetration of JNKi in mouse tissues. 30 μl of a 1 mM solution of FITC-labelled JNKI were injected *ip* in a mouse. Tissues were mounted 1 hour later.

REFERENCES

1. Aarts M, Liu Y, Liu L, Besshoh S, Arundine M, Gurd JW, Wang YT, Salter MW and Tymianski M. Treatment of ischemic brain damage by perturbing NMDA receptor- PSD-95 protein interactions. *Science* 298: 846-850, 2002.
2. Adler V, Unlap T and Kraft AS. A peptide encoding the c-Jun delta domain inhibits the activity of a c-jun amino-terminal protein kinase. *J Biol Chem* 269: 11186-11191, 1994.
3. Aguirre V, Uchida T, Yenush L, Davis R and White MF. The c-Jun NH(2)-terminal kinase promotes insulin resistance during association with insulin receptor substrate-1 and phosphorylation of Ser(307). *J Biol Chem* 275: 9047-9054, 2000.
4. Bain J, McLauchlan H, Elliott M and Cohen P. The specificities of protein kinase inhibitors: an update. *Biochem J* 371: 199-204, 2003.
5. Bardwell L and Thorner J. A conserved motif at the amino termini of MEKs might mediate high-affinity interaction with the cognate MAPKs. *Trends Biochem Sci* 21: 373-374, 1996.
6. Barr RK, Kendrick TS and Bogoyevitch MA. Identification of the critical features of a small peptide inhibitor of c-Jun N-terminal kinase (JNK) activity. *J Biol Chem* 2002.
7. Bonny C, Nicod P and Waeber G. IB1, a JIP-1-related nuclear protein present in insulin-secreting cells. *J Biol Chem* 273: 1843-1846, 1998.
8. Bonny C, Oberson A, Negri S, Sauser C and Schorderet DF. Cell-permeable peptide inhibitors of JNK: Novel blockers of «beta»-cell death. *Diabetes* 50: 77-82, 2001.
9. Borsello T, Clarke PGH, Hirt L, Vercelli A, Repici M, Schorderet DF, Bogousslavsky J and Bonny C. A peptide inhibitor of c-Jun N-terminal kinase protects against excitotoxicity and cerebral ischemia. *Nature Medicine* 9: 1180-1186, 2003.
10. Boulton TG, Nye SH, Robbins DJ, Ip NY, Radziejewska E, Morgenbesser SD, DePinho RA, Panayotatos N, Cobb MH and Yancopoulos GD. ERKs: a family of protein-serine/threonine kinases that are activated and tyrosine phosphorylated in response to insulin

and NGF. *Cell* 65: 663-675, 1991.
11. Brecht S, Kirchhof R, Chromik A, Willesen M, Nicolaus T, Raivich G, Wessig J, Waetzig V, Goetz M, Claussen M, Pearse D, Kuan CY, Vaudano E, Behrens A, Wagner E, Flavell RA, Davis RJ and Herdegen T. Specific pathophysiological functions of JNK isoforms in the brain. *Eur J Neurosci* 21: 363-377, 2005.
12. Clerk A, Fuller SJ, Michael A and Sugden PH. Stimulation of «stress-regulated» mitogen-activated protein kinases (stress-activated protein kinases/c-Jun N-terminal kinases and p38-mitogen-activated protein kinases) in perfused rat hearts by oxidative and other stresses. *J Biol Chem* 273: 7228-7234, 1998.
13. Davis RJ. Signal transduction by the c-Jun N-terminal kinase. *Biochem Soc Symp* 64: 1-12, 1999.
14. Davis RJ. Signal transduction by the JNK group of MAP kinases. *Cell* 103: 239-252, 2000.
15. Efimova T, Broome AM and Eckert RL. A regulatory role for p38 delta MAPK in keratinocyte differentiation. Evidence for p38 delta-ERK1/2 complex formation. *J Biol Chem* 278: 34277-34285, 2003.
16. Efimova T, Broome AM and Eckert RL. Protein kinase Cdelta regulates keratinocyte death and survival by regulating activity and subcellular localization of a p38delta-extracellular signal-regulated kinase 1/2 complex. *Mol Cell Biol* 24: 8167-8183, 2004.
17. Enslen H, Brancho DM and Davis RJ. Molecular determinants that mediate selective activation of p38 MAP kinase isoforms. *EMBO J* 19: 1301-1311, 2000.
18. Enslen H and Davis RJ. Regulation of MAP kinases by docking domains. *Biol Cell* 93: 5-14, 2001.
19. Franklin CC, Sanchez V, Wagner F, Woodgett JR and Kraft AS. Phorbol ester-induced amino-terminal phosphorylation of human JUN but not JUNB regulates transcriptional activation. *Proc Natl Acad Sci U S A* 89: 7247-7251, 1992.
20. Gius DR, Ezhevsky SA, Becker-Hapak M, Nagahara H, Wei MC and Dowdy SF. Transduced p16INK4a peptides inhibit hypophosphorylation of the retinoblastoma protein and cell cycle progression prior to activation of Cdk2 complexes in late G1. *Cancer Res* 59: 2577-2580, 1999.
21. Gupta S, Barrett T, Whitmarsh AJ, Cavanagh J, Sluss HK, Derijard B and Davis RJ. Selective interaction of JNK protein kinase isoforms with transcription factors. *EMBO J* 15: 2760-2770, 1996.
22. Hess P, Pihan G, Sawyers CL, Flavell RA and Davis RJ. Survival signaling mediated by c-Jun NH(2)-terminal kinase in transformed B lymphoblasts. *Nat Genet* 32: 201-205, 2002.
23. Hirt L, Badaut J, Thevenet J, Granziera C, Regli L, Maurer F, Bonny C and Bogousslavsky J. D-JNKI1, a Cell-Penetrating c-Jun-N-Terminal Kinase Inhibitor, Protects Against Cell Death in Severe Cerebral Ischemia. *Stroke* 2004.
24. Ito M, Yoshioka K, Akechi M, Yamashita S, Takamatsu N, Sugiyama K, Hibi M, Nakabeppu Y, Shiba T and Yamamoto KI. JSAP1, a novel jun N-terminal protein kinase (JNK)-binding protein that functions as a Scaffold factor in the JNK signaling pathway. *Mol Cell Biol* 19: 7539-7548, 1999.
25. Kallunki T, Deng T, Hibi M and Karin M. c-Jun can recruit JNK to phosphorylate dimerization partners via specific docking interactions. *Cell* 87: 929-939, 1996.
26. Kaneto H, Nakatani Y, Miyatsuka T, Kawamori D, Matsuoka TA, Matsuhisa M, Kajimoto Y, Ichijo H, Yamasaki Y and Hori M. Possible novel therapy for diabetes with cell-permeable JNK-inhibitory peptide. *Nat Med* 2004.
27. Keesler GA, Bray J, Hunt J, Johnson DA, Gleason T, Yao Z, Wang SW, Parker C, Yamane H, Cole C and Lichenstein HS. Purification and activation of recombinant p38 isoforms alpha, beta, gamma, and delta. *Protein Expr Purif* 14: 221-228, 1998.
28. Kelemen BR, Hsiao K and Goueli SA. Selective in Vivo Inhibition of Mitogen-activated

Protein Kinase Activation Using Cell-permeable Peptides. *J Biol Chem* 277: 8741-8748, 2002.
29. Kelkar N, Gupta S, Dickens M and Davis RJ. Interaction of a mitogen-activated protein kinase signaling module with the neuronal protein JIP3. *Mol Cell Biol* 20: 1030-1043, 2000.
30. Kuan CY, Whitmarsh AJ, Yang DD, Liao G, Schloemer AJ, Dong C, Bao J, Banasiak KJ, Haddad GG, Flavell RA, Davis RJ and Rakic P. A critical role of neural-specific JNK3 for ischemic apoptosis. *Proc Natl Acad Sci U S A* 100: 15184-15189, 2003.
31. Lee YH, Giraud J, Davis RJ and White MF. c-Jun N-terminal kinase (JNK) mediates feedback inhibition of the insulin signaling cascade. *J Biol Chem* 278: 2896-2902, 2003.
32. May GH, Funk M, Black EJ, Clark W, Hussain S, Woodgett JR and Gillespie DA. An oncogenic mutation uncouples the v-Jun oncoprotein from positive regulation by the SAPK/JNK pathway in vivo. *Curr Biol* 8: 117-120, 1998.
33. May MJ, D'Acquisto F, Madge LA, Glockner J, Pober JS and Ghosh S. Selective Inhibition of NF-kappaB Activation by a Peptide That Blocks the Interaction of NEMO with the IkappaB Kinase Complex. *Science* 289: 1550-1554, 2000.
34. Mooser V, Maillard A, Bonny C, Steinmann M, Shaw P, Yarnall DP, Burns DK, Schorderet DF, Nicod P and Waeber G. Genomic organization, fine-mapping, and expression of the human islet- brain 1 (IB1)/c-Jun-amino-terminal kinase interacting protein-1 (JIP-1) gene. *Genomics* 55: 202-208, 1999.
35. Negri S, Oberson A, Steinmann M, Nicod P, Waeber G, Schorderet DF and Bonny C. cDNA Cloning and Mapping of a Novel Islet-Brain/JNK Interacting Protein . *Genomics* 64: 324-330, 2000.
36. Ono K and Han J. The p38 signal transduction pathway: activation and function. *Cell Signal* 12: 1-13, 2000.
37. Raingeaud J, Gupta S, Rogers JS, Dickens M, Han J, Ulevitch RJ and Davis RJ. Pro-inflammatory cytokines and environmental stress cause p38 mitogen- activated protein kinase activation by dual phosphorylation on tyrosine and threonine. *J Biol Chem* 270: 7420-7426, 1995.
38. Saklatvala J. The p38 MAP kinase pathway as a therapeutic target in inflammatory disease. *Curr Opin Pharmacol* 4: 372-377, 2004.
39. Schaeffer HJ, Catling AD, Eblen ST, Collier LS, Krauss A and Weber MJ. MP1: a MEK binding partner that enhances enzymatic activation of the MAP kinase cascade. *Science* 281: 1668-1671, 1998.
40. Schoorlemmer J and Goldfarb M. FGF homologous factors and the islet brain-2 scaffold protein regulate activation of a stress-activated protein kinase. *J Biol Chem* 277: 49111-49119, 2002.
41. Schwarze SR, Ho A, Vocero-Akbani A and Dowdy SF. In Vivo Protein Transduction: Delivery of a Biologically Active Protein into the Mouse. *Science* 285: 1573-1576, 1999.
42. Sharrocks AD, Yang SH and Galanis A. Docking domains and substrate-specificity determination for MAP kinases. *Trends Biochem Sci* 25: 448-453, 2000.
43. Sharrocks AD, Yang SH and Galanis A. Docking domains and substrate-specificity determination for MAP kinases. *Trends Biochem Sci* 25: 448-453, 2000.
44. Sugioka R, Shimizu S, Funatsu T, Tamagawa H, Sawa Y, Kawakami T and Tsujimoto Y. BH4-domain peptide from Bcl-xL exerts anti-apoptotic activity in vivo. *Oncogene* 22: 8432-8440, 2003.
45. Tanoue T, Adachi M, Moriguchi T and Nishida E. A conserved docking motif in MAP kinases common to substrates, activators and regulators. *Nat Cell Biol* 2: 110-116, 2000.
46. Vachon PH, Harnois C, Grenier A, Dufour G, Bouchard V, Han J, Landry J, Beaulieu JF, Vezina A, Dydensborg AB, Gauthier R, Cote A, Drolet JF and Lareau F. Differentiation state-selective roles of p38 isoforms in human intestinal epithelial cell anoikis.

Gastroenterology 123: 1980-1991, 2002.
47. Waeber G, Delplanque J, Bonny C, Mooser V, Steinmann M, Widmann C, Maillard A, Miklossy J, Dina C, Hani EH, Vionnet N, Nicod P, Boutin P and Froguel P. The gene MAPK8IP1, encoding islet-brain-1, is a candidate for type 2 diabetes. *Nat Genet* 24: 291-295, 2000.
48. Waetzig V and Herdegen T. A single c-Jun N-terminal kinase isoform (JNK3-p54) is an effector in both neuronal differentiation and cell death. *J Biol Chem* 278: 567-572, 2003.
49. Wang J, Van de Water TR, Bonny C, de Ribaupierre F, Puel JL and Zine A. A peptide inhibitor of c-Jun N-terminal kinase protects against both aminoglycoside and acoustic trauma-induced auditory hair cell death and hearing loss. *Journal of Neuroscience* 23: 8596-8607, 2003.
50. Weston CR and Davis RJ. The JNK signal transduction pathway. *Curr Opin Genet Dev* 12: 14-21, 2002.
51. Whitmarsh AJ, Cavanagh J, Tournier C, Yasuda J and Davis RJ. A mammalian scaffold complex that selectively mediates MAP kinase activation. *Science* 281: 1671-1674, 1998.
52. Whitmarsh AJ and Davis RJ. Structural organization of MAP-kinase signaling modules by scaffold proteins in yeast and mammals. *Trends Biochem Sci* 23: 481-485, 1998.
53. Widmann C, Gibson S, Jarpe MB and Johnson GL. Mitogen-activated protein kinase: conservation of a three-kinase module from yeast to human. *Physiol Rev* 79: 143-180, 1999.
54. Wijayanti N, Huber S, Samoylenko A, Kietzmann T and Immenschuh S. Role of NF-kappaB and p38 MAP kinase signaling pathways in the lipopolysaccharide-dependent activation of heme oxygenase-1 gene expression. *Antioxid Redox Signal* 6: 802-810, 2004.
55. Willam C, Masson N, Tian YM, Mahmood SA, Wilson MI, Bicknell R, Eckardt KU, Maxwell PH, Ratcliffe PJ and Pugh CW. Peptide blockade of HIFalpha degradation modulates cellular metabolism and angiogenesis. *Proc Natl Acad Sci U S A* 99: 10423-10428, 2002.
56. Xia Y, Wu Z, Su B, Murray B and Karin M. JNKK1 organizes a MAP kinase module through specific and sequential interactions with upstream and downstream components mediated by its amino-terminal extension. *Genes Dev* 12: 3369-3381, 1998.
57. Xu B, Stippec S, Robinson FL and Cobb MH. Hydrophobic as well as charged residues in both MEK1 and ERK2 are important for their proper docking. *J Biol Chem* 276: 26509-26515, 2001.
58. Yang SH, Whitmarsh AJ, Davis RJ and Sharrocks AD. Differential targeting of MAP kinases to the ETS-domain transcription factor Elk-1. *EMBO J* 17: 1740-1749, 1998.
59. Yang SH, Yates PR, Whitmarsh AJ, Davis RJ and Sharrocks AD. The Elk-1 ETS-domain transcription factor contains a mitogen-activated protein kinase targeting motif. *Mol Cell Biol* 18: 710-720, 1998.
60. Yasuda J, Whitmarsh AJ, Cavanagh J, Sharma M and Davis RJ. The JIP group of mitogen-activated protein kinase scaffold proteins. *Mol Cell Biol* 19: 7245-7254, 1999.
61. Ye H, Arron JR, Lamothe B, Cirilli M, Kobayashi T, Shevde NK, Segal D, Dzivenu OK, Vologodskaia M, Yim M, Du K, Singh S, Pike JW, Darnay BG, Choi Y and Wu H. Distinct molecular mechanism for initiating TRAF6 signalling. *Nature* 418: 443-447, 2002.

Chapter 13

JNK PATHWAY AS THERAPEUTIC TARGET TO PREVENT DEGENERATION IN THE CENTRAL NERVOUS SYSTEM

Mariaelena Repici[1] and Tiziana Borsello[1,2]

[1]*University of Lausanne, Lausanne, Switzerland,* [2]*Biol. Neurodeg. Disorders Lab, Istituto di ricerche Farmacologiche "Mario Negri", Milano, Italy.*

Abstract: JNKs (c-Jun N- terminal kinases) are important transducing enzymes involved in many faces of cellular regulation such as gene expression, cell proliferation and programmed cell death. The activation of JNK pathway is critical for naturally occurring neuronal death during development as well as for pathological death of adult brain following different insults. In particular, JNKs play an important role in excitotoxicity and all related phenomena. Initial research concentrated on defining the components and organization of JNK signalling cascades, but more recent studies have begun to see JNK as the appropriate target for prevent cell loss. We used a specific JNK inhibitor, the cell permeable peptide D-JNKI1, to block JNK action in neuronal death following excitotoxicity in vitro and cerebral ischemia in vivo. Here we review our recent findings and we discuss the possibility of using D-JNKI1 as a therapeutic agent to prevent cell loss in the central nervous system.

Key Words: JNK inhibitors, excitotoxicity, neurodegeneration, ischemic damage

INTRODUCTION

Excitotoxicity is defined as the excessive activation of glutamate receptors, in which *N*-methyl-D-aspartate (NMDA) receptors play a key role, owing to their high Ca^{2+} permeability. The overactivation of the NMDA receptors induces downstream cascade of events resulting in neuronal death. Excitotoxicity is responsible for many brain injuries such as ischemia (43), epilepsy (30) and it plays an important role also in several neurodegenerative diseases (42), (22).

Excitotoxicity has been studied extensively, but the downstream mechanisms coupling increased intracellular Ca^{2+} to cell death are still poorly understood. Several studies have

Hypoxia and Exercise, edited by R.C. Roach *et al.*
Springer, New York, 2006.

tried to obtain neuroprotection by blocking NMDA receptors, the major agent representing this category is the NMDA-r antagonist MK-801: notwithstanding the promising results in animal models (reduction of the excitotoxic damage), they had to be abandoned for the emergence of unacceptable psychotomimetic side effects. These side effects are strongly correlated with the physiological NMDA receptor activity, which is essential for normal neuronal cell functions. A second possible approach in the prevention of excitotoxicity is to target specific intracellular pathways, which normally act downstream from the glutamate receptor, without blocking synaptic activity. A peptide that disrupts the interaction of NMDArs with the postsynaptic density protein PSD-95 has been used against excitotoxicity in cultured neurons and ischemic damage in vivo (1).

The first evidence of the JNK involvement in excitotoxicity derived from the analysis of JNK3 deficient mice: after a systemic injection of kainate these mice showed a reduction in seizures activity and a prevention of apoptosis (39). Moreover, mice with an inactive form of c-jun (Jun AA, in which serines 63 and 73 are mutated to alanines) also showed resistance to excitotoxic neuronal death, thus suggesting that preventing JNK from accessing c-jun might confer neuroprotection (3). It has been shown that in cortical neurons NMDA mediated neurotoxicity activates JNK in dependence on entry of extracellular calcium (23). Moreover in an immortalized rat hippocampal neuronal cell line, the post-synaptic density protein 95 (PSD95) links GluR6-mediated excitotoxicity with JNK via MLK2/3 (29). A recent paper by Brecht (11), has proved distinct roles for the different JNK isoforms in four models of neurodegeneration in vivo, including permanent ischemia and excitotoxicity by application of kainic acid.

JNK INHIBITORS

Several research laboratories have proposed JNK inhibitors in order to find effective drugs for the treatment of a variety of pathologies. These inhibitors could be divided in two classes: chemical compounds and cell permeable peptide inhibitors.

Chemical compounds

This approach consists in producing small organic compounds that are competitive inhibitors of the ATP-binding site of the kinase. This technique has given a couple of efficient JNK inhibitors. Two of them, CEP-1347 and SP600125 have been the subjects of peer-reviewed studies as described in Bozyczko-Coyne and Bogoyevitch reviews (10), (5) but the published information on their efficacy in clinical trials remains limited.

CEP-1347 is a semi-synthetic inhibitor of the MLK group of MAPKKK (see Figure 1). It blocks the upstream component in the JNK pathway, and derives from the naturally occurring small molecule K252a. It competes with ATP to bind MLKs, with IC_{50} values of 38nM (MLK1), 51nM (MLK2), and 23nM (MLK3) (26). CEP-1347 is able to prevent neuronal cell death in vivo models of Alzheimer's disease (AD), Parkinson's disease (PD) and cochlear hair cell death (37, 38).

SP600125, developed by Celgene, is an ATP competitive inhibitor of JNK (see Figure 1). It inhibits all three JNK isoforms, with IC_{50} values of 40, 40, and 90nM for JNK1, JNK2 and JNK3 respectively. It also has an inhibitory activity against other MAPKs, such as ERK and p38 (4). In vivo this compound inhibited leukocyte recruitment in a rat inflamed lung model (16) and was active in the rat rheumatoid arthritis model (18).

It also protected dopaminergic neurons in the MPTP model of Parkinson's disease (38) and it was used to attenuate apoptosis in a model of Alzheimer's disease neurotoxicity (25).

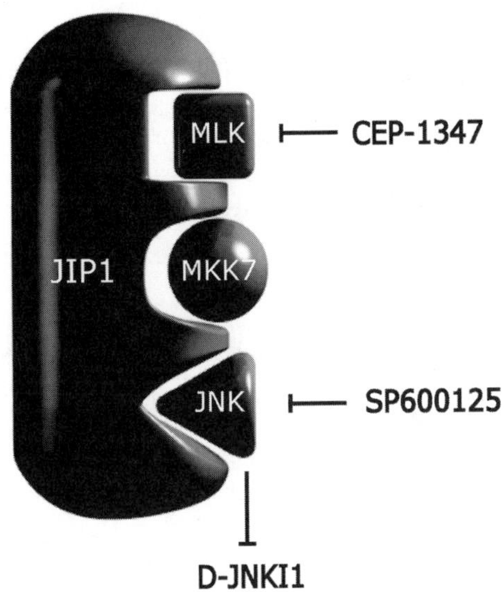

Figure 1. Modular organization of the JNK signaling pathway. JIP-1 scaffold protein binds to JNK, MKK7, one of the two JNK activators, and to members of the mixed-lineage protein kinases (MLK) group. The assembly of the JNK module by a scaffold may lead to a more efficient activation of JNK. The two small chemical inhibitors of the JNK pathway are acting at different levels of the cascade: whilst CEP-1347 inhibits MLK, SP600125 inhibits JNK activation. The cell permeable peptide D-JNKI-1 prevents JNK action without interfere with JNK activation/ phosphorylation.

Cell permeable peptide inhibitor

D-JNKI-1 inhibitor produces an allosteric modulation of JNK by blocking the access of the kinase to some of its targets, preventing protein-protein interactions, without interfering with its activation (Figure 1).

In 2001 Bonny showed that a new efficient and specific inhibitor of JNK action was able to protect pancreatic ß-cells from IL1 ß induced apoptosis. D-JNKI-1 peptide (which is the D-retro-inverso form, made of aminoacids in reversed sequence order) has been engineered by linking the 20 amino acid JNK-inhibitory sequence of IB1/JIP-1 scaffold protein (JBD_{20}) to the 10 amino acid HIV- transporter sequence (6). The $TAT_{48\text{-}57}$ peptide penetrates in a variety of cells and could be useful for delivering macromolecules, also to animal tissues (32). Between the TAT sequence and the JBD_{20} sequence two proline-residues were inserted as spacer to allow for maximal flexibility. JIP-1 scaffold protein and c-Jun, JNK main target, share a similar binding motif for interact with JNK. However JNK binding affinity to JIP-1 is about 100-fold higher than to c-Jun, for this reason the inhibitor peptide is able to block the access of JNK to its substrates. Barr and collaborators (2) found that a shorter peptide sequence (RPKRPTTLNLF=TI-JIP) based on amino acids 143-153 on the $JBD_{20}$of JIP-1, partly overlapped with the sequence described by Bonny (6) and was also able to prevent c-Jun phosphorylation. Thus the inhibitory action of D-JNKI-1 peptide is fundamentally different from that of classical small chemical inhibitors (7), (8). D-JNKI-1 does not inhibit JNK's enzymatic activity, but selectively blocks access to many of its substrates by a competitive mechanism

(6), (7), (8). To determine the specificity of the peptide in blocking JNK action, we characterized the effects of the peptide on the activity of 40 different kinases (10 μM peptide, 10 μM ATP) towards their respective substrates in cell free system. It did not interfere with the activities of the other kinases (7), (8), proving its exceptional superiority.

In a recent study we showed that the D-JNKI-1 peptide completely inhibited excitotoxicity in primary culture and strongly prevented neuronal loss against two different models, transient and permanent, of middle cerebral artery occlusion (MCAo) (8). However other authors have demonstrated powerful protection in different models of CNS injury: D-JNKI-1 protects against toxic drug and acoustic trauma induced auditory hair cell death (36) and against retinal ganglion cells death following optic nerve crush (34). This cell permeable peptide inhibitor offers interesting possibilities for therapeutic application in preventing neuronal loss.

OUR OWN RESULTS BY USING D-JNKI-1

We investigated the protective D-JNKI-1 action at three different levels: i) in vitro in cortical neurons cultures, ii) in organotypic hippocampal cultures, and iii) in vivo in focal cerebral ischemia.

Cortical neurons

D-JNKI-1 completely inhibited cell death induced by excitotoxicity (100μM NMDA) in primary cortical neurons (Figure 2)(8). JNK activation in NMDA-treated neurons appeared maximal after 30 min of NMDA, and resulted into an elevated c-Jun phosphorylation. Addition of D-JNKI-1 completely prevented the increase in phosphorylated c-Jun after 5h exposure to 100 μM NMDA (despite a normal level of JNK activation), bringing the level of P-c-Jun below even that in the control. NMDA-induced activation of the c-fos gene, transcription of which is under the positive control of the JNK target Elk-1, was also completely prevented by the peptide. In fact, c-fos expression in D-JNKI-1/NMDA treated neurons, evaluated by real-time RT-PCR, was comparable to control levels whereas in neurons treated with only NMDA it increased and strongly correlated with the NMDA time course.

Organotypic cultures

NMDA treatment (100 μM) in organotypic hippocampal cultures (9) resulted in death of pyramidal neurons in the CA1 and CA3 already detectable within two hours of NMDA administration. In the same regions, following two hours of NMDA, c-Jun was selectively phosphorylated and c-fos was up-regulated. Pretreatment of 2 μM D-JNKI-1 prevented pyramidal neurons cell death and completely inhibited c-Jun phosphorylation and c-fos expression (Figure 3).

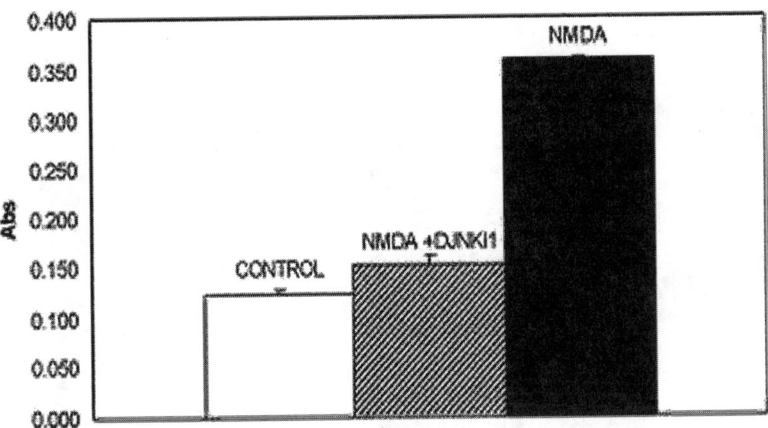

Figure 2. Neuronal death at 5 h after exposure to 100 μM NMDA evaluated by LDH activity in the culture medium in presence (black and white) or absence (black) of D-JNKI1 2 μM.

In vivo

D-JNKI-1 effect has been tested on two different models of cerebral ischemia (8), transient ischemia in adult mice and permanent focal ischemia in P14 rats. The peptide was able to confer strong protection against ischemic damage in both models. The infarcted volumes were traced on serial sections by using the Neurolucida software program after 24h from insult (17), allowing the quantification of brain damage (Figure 4). In the transient ischemia model we obtained a reduction of the infarct of 88% following an intracerebroventricular injection 1 hour before the lesion, and the strongest reduction (93%) following D-JNKI-1 administration 6 hours after ischemia. In the permanent middle cerebral artery occlusion (MCAo) model we injected the peptide intraperitoneally 30 min before, 6 hours after or 12 hours after ischemia and we obtained an infarcted volume decrease of respectively 68%, 78% and 49%. Actually, the only approved therapy for ischemic stroke is the administration of tissue plasminogen activator (tPA) within 3 hours of the onset of the ischemia, since after 3 hours the risk of a hemorrhage caused by tPA becomes too high. The most prominent feature of the protection observed with D-JNKI-1 is that the peptide is still effective when administered 6-12 hours after the onset of stroke. This is particularly relevant, as most patients will access medical centres only 6-10 hours following the onset of stroke.

To assess whether the peptide really prevented neuronal death or only delayed it, we analyzed lesion volumes one week (permanent ischemia) or two weeks (transient ischemia) after lesion in animals treated with D-JNKI-1 6 hours following ischemia, compared to control animals. In permanent ischemia D-JNKI-1-treated rats and control rats presented a shrunken infarct, but there was still a significant protection by the peptide (54%). In transient ischemia of adult mice we obtained 93% reduction of lesion volume, exactly the same protection shown at the shorter survival time (24h after ischemia).

Furthermore, the powerful neuroprotection obtained is accompanied by behavioral benefits; we have not so far detected negative side effects at the dose-levels required for protection.

Therefore, JNK inhibition using D-JNKI-1 might prove useful in the treatment of stroke damage.

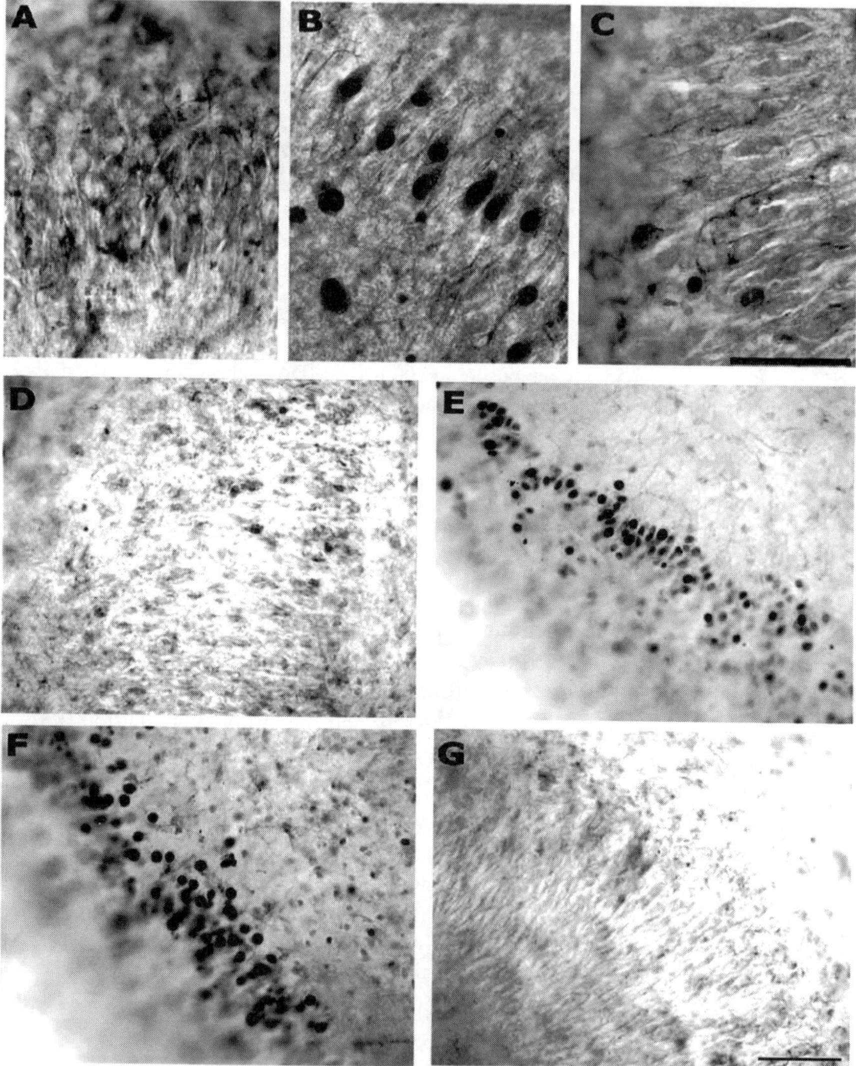

Figure 3. Immunohistochemistry in organotypic hippocampal cultures. (A-C):phosphorylated c-jun immunolabelling. (A): control condition, (B): 2h of 100μM NMDA, (C): 2h of 100μM NMDA in presence of 2μM D-JNKI1. (D-G): c-fos immunolabelling. (D): control condition, (E):1h of 100μM NMDA, (F): 2h of 100μM NMDA, (G): 2h of 100μM NMDA in presence of 2μM D-JNKI1. Reprinted, with permission from the Eur. J. Neurosci. 2003, 18(3): 473-85.

JNK TARGETS RELATED TO NEURODEGENERATION

JNK substrates related to cell death can be nuclear or cytoplasmic, and this means that JNK could act at transcriptional or at post-transductional level.

Concerning nuclear substrates, JNKs activate several members of the AP-1 group of transcription factors, the most important of which is c-Jun, activated by phosphorylation on Ser 63 and 73 (27). ATF-2 and Elk-1 are also activated by JNKs (21), (12). Transcriptional activity enhanced by these proteins is responsible for cells biologic response. JNK2 and JNK3 seem to be responsible for the activation of transcription factors whereas the basal constitutive presence of activated JNK1 is not effective in phosphorylation of transcription factors including c-Jun (13), (14). c-Jun phosphorylation was also linked to the protection or regeneration (19) and it has not been clarified if JNK can also contribute to pro-survival action.

Regarding cytoplasmic substrates, it has been shown that there is interdependency between JNK signaling and mitochondrial apoptosis (31). Oxygen-glucose deprivation in hippocampal neurons from Jnk3-null mice compared to WT mice suggests a critical JNK3 role in both the apoptotic process and the release of cytochrome c from mitochondria (24). The release of cytochrome c from mitochondria is controlled by specific members of the Bcl-2 family protein, whose phosphorylation could be regulated by JNKs (28), (35).

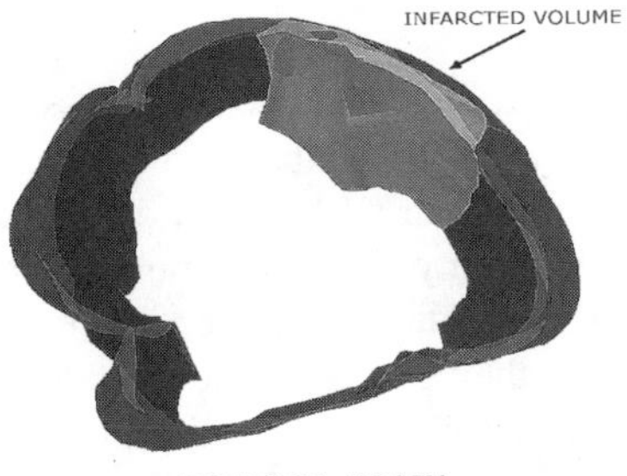

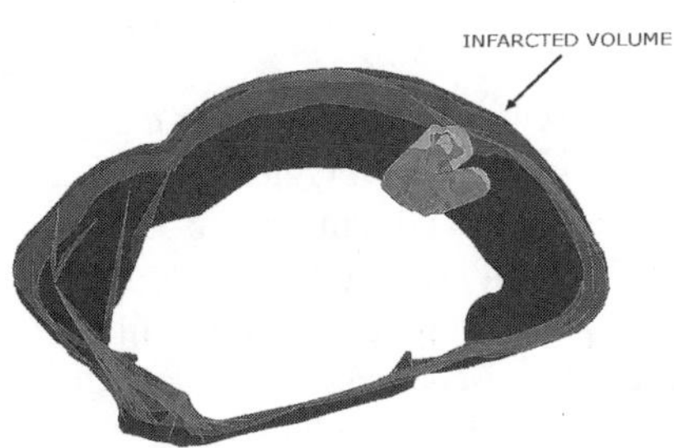

Figure 4. Three-dimensional reconstruction showing examples of lesion in control rat and D-JNKI-1 treated rat 6 hours after permanent ischemia (middle cerebral artery occlusion). This ischemic lesion results in a unilateral degeneration of the parietal cortex 24 hours following ischemia. The areas of the ischemic lesion and of the whole brain were traced using the Neurolucida software program for computer-aided microscopy.

DENN/MADD is also a JNK cytoplasmic substrate implicated in cell death. It has a death domain and was identified as a substrate for JNK3, which is the isoform mostly present in the CNS (41). The meaning of this phosphorylation is still unclear, but increasing evidences support a correlation between low MADD expression and neuronal loss: it has recently been shown that MADD down-regulation correlates with neuronal cell death in

Alzheimer's disease brain and hippocampal neurons (15).

Finally, JNK is involved in the phosphorylation of Tau and APP, two proteins strongly related to neurodegenerative diseases. In fact, hyperphosphorylation and accumulation of Tau in neurons (and glial cells) is one of the main pathologic hallmarks in Alzheimer's disease and other tauopathies. Many of the hyperphosphorylated sites are serine/threonine-proline sequences. Recently it has been shown that all three JNK isoforms phosphorylate Tau at many serine/threonine-prolines, as assessed by the generation of the epitopes of phosphorylation-dependent anti-Tau antibodies (40). Phosphorylation by JNK isoforms resulted in a greatly reduced ability of Tau to promote microtubule assembly, which would compromise neuronal transport and would result in neuronal dysfunction.

APP is efficiently phosphorylated in its cytoplasmic region by JNK3 in vitro (33) and APP phosphorylation by JNK is enhanced by the association of APP with scaffold protein JIP-1b (20). Moreover, an enhanced activation of JNK pathway and an attenuation of apoptosis by SP600125, the ATP competitive JNK inhibitor, through protection of mitochondrial dysfunction and reduction of caspase 9 activity have been demonstrated (25). These results put in evidence that JNK could play an important role in the pathogenesis of Alzheimer's disease.

CONCLUSIONS

JNK could provide a suitable target for the protection against neuronal loss and considerable effort is being directed to the development of JNK inhibitors. This resulted in a couple of chemical inhibitors: CEP-1347, an inhibitor of the MLK family of JNK pathway activators, and SP600125, a direct inhibitor of JNK activity. These commonly used inhibitors have demonstrated efficacy for use in vivo, with the successful intervention in animal models. An alternative approach is represented by the cell permeable peptide D-JNKI-1, which is a new powerful neuroprotective agent. D-JNKI-1 is an efficient and specific inhibitor of JNK action. It does not inhibit JNK's enzymatic activity, like the classical small chemical inhibitors, but it selectively blocks access to many of its substrates by a competitive mechanism and results as the most selective inhibitor proving its exceptional superiority.

D-JNKI-1 protects against several forms of excitotoxicity in vitro (8), (9), and it confers the strongest protection even reported before against ischemic cell loss in vivo with extended therapeutic window, since it still protects when administered 6-12 hours after the ischemic insult (8). Moreover it has been shown that it is really able to completely prevent the death program and not just to delay it, as a significant protection was still seen after one or two weeks following ischemic lesion in transient ischemia: this confirms that it could be a promising agent to obtain neuroprotection in stroke. D-JNKI-1 protective action has also been tested with positive results in two other models of CNS injury, hair cell death and hearing loss following ototoxic drug or acoustic trauma exposure (36) and retinal ganglion cells death following optic nerve crush (34): these results provide strong evidence that JNK inhibition with D-JNKI-1 could be a very interesting therapeuthic approach to prevent cell loss in the CNS.

Despite these promising results further studies will be necessary in order to detect D-JNKI-1 side effects, and caution is required in view of JNK's involvement in metabolic regulation and neuronal plasticity and regeneration. In fact, it has to be admitted that the underlying cell biology of this powerful neuroprotection is still largely unknown.

A deep understanding of the organization and function of the JNK signaling cascade will be crucial to improve the specificity of the JNK inhibitors. In fact, due to the complex cross-talk within different signaling cascades, as well as peculiar neuronal response, it is difficult to predict potential adverse events that might arise from JNK inhibition. However, it appears clear that further studies are needed to offer greater specificity in order to prevent only the pathological responses of this signaling, that extent its physiological functions in such a large range.

Detailed studies about D-JNKI-1 toxicity and its potential side effects are now essential. Until these aspects are clarified the question will remain if D-JNKI-1 could represent an important molecule in human therapy and whether it can be extended to clinical trails.

ACKNOWLEDGEMENTS

Supported by the Botnar Foundation grant. Special thanks to Architettura Laboratorio Communication for the graphic figures and representations (*www.archilab.it*).

We thank the authors and publishers for the permission to use the material from Eur J Neurosci 2003, 18 (3):473-85, published by Blackwell.

REFERENCES

1. Aarts M, Liu Y, Liu L, Besshoh S, Arundine M, Gurd JW, Wang YT, Salter MW, and Tymianski M. Treatment of ischemic brain damage by perturbing NMDA receptor- PSD-95 protein interactions. *Science* 298: 846-850, 2002.
2. Barr RK, Kendrick TS, and Bogoyevitch MA. Identification of the critical features of a small peptide inhibitor of JNK activity. *J Biol Chem* 277: 10987-10997, 2002.
3. Behrens A, Sibilia M, and Wagner EF. Amino-terminal phosphorylation of c-Jun regulates stress-induced apoptosis and cellular proliferation. *Nat Genet* 21: 326-329, 1999.
4. Bennett BL, Sasaki DT, Murray BW, O'Leary EC, Sakata ST, Xu W, Leisten JC, Motiwala A, Pierce S, Satoh Y, Bhagwat SS, Manning AM, and Anderson DW. SP600125, an anthrapyrazolone inhibitor of Jun N-terminal kinase. *Proc Natl Acad Sci U S A* 98: 13681-13686, 2001.
5. Bogoyevitch MA, Boehm I, Oakley A, Ketterman AJ, and Barr RK. Targeting the JNK MAPK cascade for inhibition: basic science and therapeutic potential. *Biochim Biophys Acta* 1697: 89-101, 2004.
6. Bonny C, Oberson A, Negri S, Sauser C, and Schorderet DF. Cell-permeable peptide inhibitors of JNK: novel blockers of ß-cell death. *Diabetes* 50: 77-82, 2001.
7. Borsello T and Bonny C. Use of cell-permeable peptides to prevent neuronal degeneration. *Trends Mol Med* 10: 239-244, 2004.
8. Borsello T, Clarke PG, Hirt L, Vercelli A, Repici M, Schorderet DF, Bogousslavsky J, and Bonny C. A peptide inhibitor of c-Jun N-terminal kinase protects against excitotoxicity and cerebral ischemia. *Nat Med* 9: 1180-1186, 2003.
9. Borsello T, Croquelois K, Hornung JP, and Clarke PG. N-methyl-d-aspartate-triggered neuronal death in organotypic hippocampal cultures is endocytic, autophagic and mediated by the c-Jun N-terminal kinase pathway. *Eur J Neurosci* 18: 473-485, 2003.

10. Bozyczko-Coyne D, Saporito MS, and Hudkins RL. Targeting the JNK pathway for therapeutic benefit in CNS disease. *Curr Drug Target CNS Neurol Disord* 1: 31-49, 2002.
11. Brecht S, Kirchhof R, Chromik A, Willesen M, Nicolaus T, Raivich G, Wessig J, Waetzig V, Goetz M, Claussen M, Pearse D, Kuan CY, Vaudano E, Behrens A, Wagner E, Flavell RA, Davis RJ, and Herdegen T. Specific pathophysiological functions of JNK isoforms in the brain. *Eur J Neurosci* 21: 363-377, 2005.
12. Cavigelli M, Dolfi F, Claret FX, and Karin M. Induction of c-fos expression through JNK-mediated TCF/Elk-1 phosphorylation. *Embo J* 14: 5957-5964, 1995.
13. Coffey ET, Hongisto V, Dickens M, Davis RJ, and Courtney MJ. Dual Roles for c-Jun N-Terminal Kinase in Developmental and Stress Responses in Cerebellar Granule Neurons. *J Neurosci* 20: 7602-7613, 2000.
14. Coffey ET, Smiciene G, Hongisto V, Cao J, Brecht S, Herdegen T, and Courtney MJ. c-Jun N-terminal protein kinase (JNK) 2/3 is specifically activated by stress, mediating c-Jun activation, in the presence of constitutive JNK1 activity in cerebellar neurons. *J Neurosci* 22: 4335-4345, 2002.
15. Del Villar K and Miller CA. Down-regulation of DENN/MADD, a TNF receptor binding protein, correlates with neuronal cell death in Alzheimer's disease brain and hippocampal neurons. *Proc Natl Acad Sci U S A* 101: 4210-4215, 2004.
16. Eynott PR, Nath P, Leung SY, Adcock IM, Bennett BL, and Chung KF. Allergen-induced inflammation and airway epithelial and smooth muscle cell proliferation: role of Jun N-terminal kinase. *Br J Pharmacol* 140: 1373-1380, 2003.
17. Glaser JR and Glaser EM. Neuron imaging with Neurolucida--a PC-based system for image combining microscopy. *Comput Med Imaging Graph* 14: 307-317, 1990.
18. Han Z, Boyle DL, Chang L, Bennett B, Karin M, Yang L, Manning AM, and Firestein GS. c-Jun N-terminal kinase is required for metalloproteinase expression and joint destruction in inflammatory arthritis. *J Clin Invest* 108: 73-81, 2001.
19. Herdegen T, Skene P, and Bahr M. The c-Jun transcription factor--bipotential mediator of neuronal death, survival and regeneration. *Trends Neurosci* 20: 227-231, 1997.
20. Inomata H, Nakamura Y, Hayakawa A, Takata H, Suzuki T, Miyazawa K, and Kitamura N. A scaffold protein JIP-1b enhances amyloid precursor protein phosphorylation by JNK and its association with kinesin light chain 1. *J Biol Chem* 278: 22946-22955, 2003.
21. Ip YT and Davis RJ. Signal transduction by the c-Jun N-terminal kinase (JNK)--from inflammation to development. *Curr Opin Cell Biol* 10: 205-219, 1998.
22. Kim HS, Park CH, Cha SH, Lee JH, Lee S, Kim Y, Rah JC, Jeong SJ, and Suh YH. Carboxyl-terminal fragment of Alzheimer's APP destabilizes calcium homeostasis and renders neuronal cells vulnerable to excitotoxicity. *Faseb J* 14: 1508-1517, 2000.
23. Ko HW, Park KY, Kim H, Han PL, Kim YU, Gwag BJ, and Choi EJ. Ca2+-mediated activation of c-Jun N-terminal kinase and nuclear factor kappa B by NMDA in cortical cell cultures. *J Neurochem* 71: 1390-1395, 1998.
24. Kuan CY, Whitmarsh AJ, Yang DD, Liao G, Schloemer AJ, Dong C, Bao J, Banasiak KJ, Haddad GG, Flavell RA, Davis RJ, and Rakic P. A critical role of neural-specific JNK3 for ischemic apoptosis. *Proc Natl Acad Sci U S A* 100: 15184-15189, 2003.
25. Marques CA, Keil U, Bonert A, Steiner B, Haass C, Muller WE, and Eckert A. Neurotoxic mechanisms caused by the Alzheimer's disease-linked Swedish amyloid precursor protein mutation: oxidative stress, caspases, and the JNK pathway. *J Biol Chem* 278: 28294-28302, 2003.
26. Murakata C, Kaneko M, Gessner G, Angeles TS, Ator MA, O'Kane TM, McKenna BA, Thomas BA, Mathiasen JR, Saporito MS, Bozyczko-Coyne D, and Hudkins RL. Mixed lineage kinase activity of indolocarbazole analogues. *Bioorg Med Chem Lett* 12: 147-150, 2002.
27. Pulverer BJ, Kyriakis JM, Avruch J, Nikolakaki E, and Woodgett JR. Phosphorylation of

c-jun mediated by MAP kinases. *Nature* 353: 670-674, 1991.

28. Putcha GV, Le S, Frank S, Besirli CG, Clark K, Chu B, Alix S, Youle RJ, LaMarche A, Maroney AC, and Johnson EM, Jr. JNK-mediated BIM phosphorylation potentiates BAX-dependent apoptosis. *Neuron* 38: 899-914, 2003.
29. Savinainen A, Garcia EP, Dorow D, Marshall J, and Liu YF. Kainate receptor activation induces mixed lineage kinase-mediated cellular signaling cascades via post-synaptic density protein 95. *J Biol Chem* 276: 11382-11386, 2001.
30. Schauwecker PE. Seizure-induced neuronal death is associated with induction of c-Jun N-terminal kinase and is dependent on genetic background. *Brain Res* 884: 116-128, 2000.
31. Schroeter H, Boyd CS, Ahmed R, Spencer JP, Duncan RF, Rice-Evans C, and Cadenas E. c-Jun N-terminal kinase (JNK)-mediated modulation of brain mitochondria function: new target proteins for JNK signalling in mitochondrion-dependent apoptosis. *Biochem J* 372: 359-369, 2003.
32. Schwarze SR, Ho A, Vocero-Akbani A, and Dowdy SF. In vivo protein transduction: delivery of a biologically active protein into the mouse. *Science* 285: 1569-1572, 1999.
33. Standen CL, Brownlees J, Grierson AJ, Kesavapany S, Lau KF, McLoughlin DM, and Miller CC. Phosphorylation of thr(668) in the cytoplasmic domain of the Alzheimer's disease amyloid precursor protein by stress-activated protein kinase 1b (Jun N-terminal kinase-3). *J Neurochem* 76: 316-320, 2001.
34. Tezel G, Chauhan BC, LeBlanc RP, and Wax MB. Immunohistochemical assessment of the glial mitogen-activated protein kinase activation in glaucoma. *Invest Ophthalmol Vis Sci* 44: 3025-3033, 2003.
35. Tournier C, Hess P, Yang DD, Xu J, Turner TK, Nimnual A, Bar-Sagi D, Jones SN, Flavell RA, and Davis RJ. Requirement of JNK for stress-induced activation of the cytochrome c-mediated death pathway. *Science* 288: 870-874, 2000.
36. Wang J, Van De Water TR, Bonny C, de Ribaupierre F, Puel JL, and Zine A. A peptide inhibitor of c-Jun N-terminal kinase protects against both aminoglycoside and acoustic trauma-induced auditory hair cell death and hearing loss. *J Neurosci* 23: 8596-8607, 2003.
37. Wang LH, Besirli CG, and Johnson EM, Jr. Mixed-lineage kinases: a target for the prevention of neurodegeneration. *Annu Rev Pharmacol Toxicol* 44: 451-474, 2004.
38. Wang W, Shi L, Xie Y, Ma C, Li W, Su X, Huang S, Chen R, Zhu Z, Mao Z, Han Y, and Li M. SP600125, a new JNK inhibitor, protects dopaminergic neurons in the MPTP model of Parkinson's disease. *Neurosci Res* 48: 195-202, 2004.
39. Yang DD, Kuan CY, Whitmarsh AJ, Rincon M, Zheng TS, Davis RJ, Rakic P, and Flavell RA. Absence of excitotoxicity-induced apoptosis in the hippocampus of mice lacking the Jnk3 gene. *Nature* 389: 865-870, 1997.
40. Yoshida H, Hastie CJ, McLauchlan H, Cohen P, and Goedert M. Phosphorylation of microtubule-associated protein tau by isoforms of c-Jun N-terminal kinase (JNK). *J Neurochem* 90: 352-358, 2004.
41. Zhang Y, Zhou L, and Miller CA. A splicing variant of a death domain protein that is regulated by a mitogen-activated kinase is a substrate for c-Jun N-terminal kinase in the human central nervous system. *Proc Natl Acad Sci U S A* 95: 2586-2591, 1998.
42. Zhu X, Raina AK, Rottkamp CA, Aliev G, Perry G, Boux H, and Smith MA. Activation and redistribution of c-jun N-terminal kinase/stress activated protein kinase in degenerating neurons in Alzheimer's disease. *J Neurochem* 76: 435-441, 2001.
43. Zipfel GJ, Babcock DJ, Lee JM, and Choi DW. Neuronal apoptosis after CNS injury: the roles of glutamate and calcium. *J Neurotrauma* 17: 857-869, 2000.

Chapter 14

SALVAGE OF ISCHEMIC MYOCARDIUM: A FOCUS ON JNK

Hervé Duplain
Department of Internal Medicine and Botnar Center for Clinical Research, Centre Hospitalier Universitaire Vaudois, Lausanne, Switzerland.

Abstract: Myocardial infarction is a problem of utmost clinical significance, associated with an important morbidity and mortality. Actual treatment of this affection is focusing on the reperfusion of the occluded coronary-artery. A complementary approach would be to prevent the death of the ischemic myocardium by interacting with detrimental intracellular pathways. Several strategies have been successfully used to reduce the size of myocardial infarction in animal models. In this article, we will focus on the c-Jun N-terminal kinase (JNK), a member of the mitogen-activated (MAPK) protein kinase family and an important determinant of cell survival/death. We will review the role of JNK in cardiac ischemia/reperfusion and summarize recent advances in the use of JNK inhibitors to protect the myocardium.

Key Words: myocardial infarction, ischemia/reperfusion, treatment, JNK, MAPK

INTRODUCTION

Myocardial infarction is a problem of utmost clinical significance, associated with an important mortality and morbidity. In 2002, over 850000 persons suffered from a myocardial infarction in the United States, with an associated mortality of roughly 25%. The resulting annual economical burden was estimated at 142 billion dollars (2). Since the prevalence of cardiovascular diseases is rapidly increasing in developing countries, ischemic heart disease is becoming one of the leading causes of mortality worldwide (1).

Initially, treatment of myocardial infarction was limited to bed rest and fighting potential complications. In a pioneering editorial in 1974, E. Braunwald wrote:"… it is now fair to accept the position that just because myocardial tissue lies within the distribution of a recently occluded coronary artery does not mean that it is necessarily condemned to death."

(8) Most of the ensuing work, aimed at rescuing the ischemic myocardium, focused on coronary artery reperfusion, leading to a dramatic improvement of the clinical outcome after myocardial infarction. More recently, a novel focus of intense research is the prevention myocardial cell death during ischemia. This approach could be complementary to reperfusion.

CARDIAC PROTECTION STRATEGIES

One of the earliest attempts to protect the ischemic myocardium was the treatment with glucose-insulin-potassium infusions. The rationale was to provide metabolic support to the cardiomyocytes by shifting the source of myocardial energy from free fatty acid oxidation (FFA) to glucose oxidation, rendering the heart more "oxygen effective". Furthermore, during acute myocardial infarction, FFAs levels rapidly increase because of lipolytic effects of catecholamines, in turn leading to membrane damage. Treatment with glucose-insulin-potassium was able to decrease circulating levels of FFA and in turn protecting the myocardial cells. However, so far, clinical studies with glucose-insulin-potassium infusions after myocardial infarction provided highly controversial results regarding the benefits of this adjunctive therapy (4). Recently, a double-blind prospective study including more than 20000 patients with acute myocardial infarction showed no benefit of glucose-insulin-potassium infusion on mortality, cardiac arrest or cardiogenic schock (26).

Interestingly, the beneficial effects of the beta-blocker carvedilol could also be related to a direct effect on the cardiomyocytes. Indeed, in animal models of ischemia/reperfusion, carvedilol was able to directly prevent cell death of cardiomyocytes (40).

Due to the clinical significance of ischemic heart disease, several cardioprotective strategies are currently under investigation in animal models of myocardial ischemia/reperfusion. The common goal of these therapies is to interfere with intracellular pathways in order to promote cell survival and/or reduce cell death. Successfully reducing infarct size in animal models was achieved with a number of treatment such as erythropoietin (10), rosiglitazone (36) and even carbon monoxide (19), for example.

NECROSIS AND APOPTOSIS

Two distinct types of cell death occur in the myocardium, namely necrosis and apoptosis. The mechanisms underlying the development of cell necrosis are still poorly understood. Originally considered as a passive cellular event, data obtained in C. elegans suggests that necrosis involves activation of specific, energy-dependant cellular pathways (38).

On the other hand, the cellular and molecular mechanisms leading to apoptosis have been studied extensively in the last decades. Apoptosis is a highly regulated, energy-dependent form of cell death. Central to apoptosis are the disabling of mitochondrial function and the activation of caspases, a subclass of cysteine proteases, ultimately leading to proteolytic destruction of the cell (35). In vivo, apoptosis of cardiac myocytes is present after ischemia (32) especially when followed by reperfusion (18), heart failure (28) and viral myocarditis (23).

Originally only necrosis was thought to mediate ischemic cell death. To date, the relative contributions of apoptosis and necrosis during ischemia/reperfusion are not clearly established. However, the importance of apoptosis have been highlighted by demonstrating that genetic manipulations aimed at inhibiting apoptosis in mice resulted in a 60 to 70% reduction of the size of the myocardial infarction following ischemia/reperfusion (9) (25).

THE JNK PATHWAY

During the course of life, the heart has to adapt to a series of physiological and pathological stresses, such as exercise, hypoxia, pressure overload, ischemia or infections. Several regulatory pathways are critical signal transducers involved in the dynamical adaptation of the myocardium to stresses. Amongst them are the mitogen-activated protein kinases (MAPKs). MAPKs are serine-threonine protein kinases that are activated by diverse stimuli ranging from cytokines, growth factors, neurotransmitters, hormones, cellular stress, and cell adherence; acting as central regulators of cell survival, growth and transformation (37). The MAPK activation module includes three levels of kinases, comprising a MAPK kinase kinase (MKKK), MAPK kinase (MKK), and MAPK, leading to sequential activation of the downstream target. In mammals three families of MAPK have been identified: the c-Jun N-terminal kinase (JNK), the extracellular signal-regulated protein kinase (ERK 1/2, ERK 3/4, ERK 5 or big MAPK-1) and p38.

The JNK proteins are encoded by three different genes. JNK1 and JNK2 are ubiquitously expressed, whereas JNK3 is mostly restricted to brain but seems to be also found in testis, and very weakly in the heart. Two different transcripts results in the formation of a 46 kDa and 55 kDa isoform for each JNK gene, but the functional significance of these splice variants is still unclear. Mice with genetically disruption of the genes encoding for JNK1 or 2 appear morphologically normal but are immunodeficient due to T cell function defects (12).

Activation of JNK starts at the cell membrane where small GTP-binding proteins activate MAPK kinase kinase 1, 2, 3 (MEKK 1, 2, 3) and apoptosis signal-regulating kinase 1 (ASK1) in turn phosphorylating MAPK kinase 4 and 7 (MKK4 and 7), resulting in direct JNK activation. Since protein-protein interactions are important for JNK activation, the assembly of the JNK module by scaffold proteins enables efficient JNK phosphorylation. The protein islet-brain 1 and 2 (IB-1 and -2), also called JNK interacting protein (JIP 1 and 2) are molecular scaffolds bringing the different component of the module in close proximity and therefore facilitating JNK activation (12). These proteins are highly expressed in the brain and insulin-secreting cells of the pancreas. Lowers levels are also found in the heart, ovary and small intestine.

Although the activation of JNK during myocardial ischemia has not been clearly proven, it is now well established that JNK is dramatically activated during reperfusion (5; 22). In rodent models of ischemia-reperfusion, cardiac JNK activation starts as early as 1 minute post reperfusion and lasts up to 3 hours (27). In a rat model of myocardial infarction, increased JNK activity was present after 15 min and returned to normal after 24 hours (34). Finally in humans, JNK activation has been demonstrated in patients with heart failure secondary to ischemic heart disease (11). Regarding the mechanisms of JNK activation during ischemia/reperfusion, it appears that increased oxidative stress plays a major role. In cultured rat neonatal myocytes, exposure to hypoxia/reoxygenation results in a dramatic increase in the generation of reactive oxygen species that is associated with JNK activation. Pretreatment with antioxidant could prevent this activation (14). In a perfused rat heart model, treatment with superoxide dismutase or catalase was able to prevent, at least in part, ischemia/reperfusion-induced JNK activation (22).

Regarding the significance of JNK activation on cell survival, studies in cultured cardiomyocytes have given equivocal results. While some authors found that activation of JNK promoted to apoptosis (3; 20), another report showed that activated JNK protected the cardiomyocytes after oxidative stress (15). In contrast, cardiac JNK activation in vivo is clearly detrimental. In mice, targeted cardiac activation of JNK due to transgenic, cardiac-restricted expression of a constitutively active mutant of MMK7 induced the induction of the fetal gene program and the development of congestive heart failure, associated with conduction defects (30). In line with this concept, preventing the activation of JNK due to oxidative-stress resulted in reduction of apoptosis (24). Similarly, treatment with carvedilol prevented the ischemia/reperfusion-induced activation of JNK and decreased apoptosis (40).

Over the past several years, various epidemiological studies have strongly suggested that mild-to-moderate alcohol consumption, in particular red wine, is associated with a reduced incidence of mortality and morbidity from coronary heart disease (The French Paradox) (31). Interestingly, the grape seed proanthocyanidin has been shown to prevent, at least in part, ischemia/reperfusion-induced JNK activation and to decrease cardiomyocytes apoptosis and prevent left-ventricular dysfunction in a perfused heart model of ischemia/reperfusion (33).

Several downstream mechanisms may explain the pro-apoptotic effects of activated JNK. It has been demonstrated that during ischemia/reperfusion activated JNK was associated with mitochondria (20), where it induced cytochrome C release, consequently promoting apoptosis (3). Furthermore anti-apoptotic proteins from the Bcl-2 family were found to be phosphorylated by JNK, leading to their inactivation (39). JNK also directly phosphorylates and activates the pro-apoptotic factor Bad (13).

Taken together these data show that ischemia/reperfusion-induced activation of cardiac JNK leads to cardiomyocytes apoptosis and provide the rational for JNK inhibition as a mean to protect the myocardium from ischemia/reperfusion injury.

INHIBITION OF JNK

In cultured rat neonatal cardiomyocytes, inhibition of JNK1, but not JNK2 translation with gene specific antisense oligonucleotides, resulted in a 50% decrease of the number of apoptotic cells (21). In vivo, in a rat model or ischemia/reperfusion, the non-peptidic JNK inhibitor AS601245 has been shown to decrease infarct size by 40% when given during the whole reperfusion period (Figure 1). The effect was associated with 85% reduction in JNK activation, whereas the other member of the MAPKs appeared to be unaffected by the treatment (17).

However, one of the issues that may occur with chemical inhibitors is their lack of specificity and potential side effects. To circumvent this problem a novel approach to JNK inhibition was developed. JNK interacts with its substrate via a 15-20 amino acids sequence called JNK-binding domain (JBD). For example, JIP-1/IB1 and c-Jun share a similar binding motif, but JNK's affinity of binding to JIP-1/IB1 is about 100-fold higher. It has been demonstrated that expression of the IB1-derived binding domain could selectively block the access of JNK to c-Jun and other substrates by a competitive mechanism, and in turn prevent its detrimental effects (29). To make this novel peptide cell permeable, the 10-amino-acid HIV Tat transporter peptide was fused to the 20-amino-acid JNK-binding motif of JIP-1/IB1. In addition, it was synthesized as a protease-resistant *all-D-retroinverso* form (D-JNKi) to expand its half-life *in vivo*. In vitro, this peptide protects insulin-secreting TC-3 cell lines against IL-1-induced apoptosis (6). In a murine stroke model, intraventricular administration of the peptide reduced the size of the lesion by 90% and prevented long-term behavioral consequences (7).

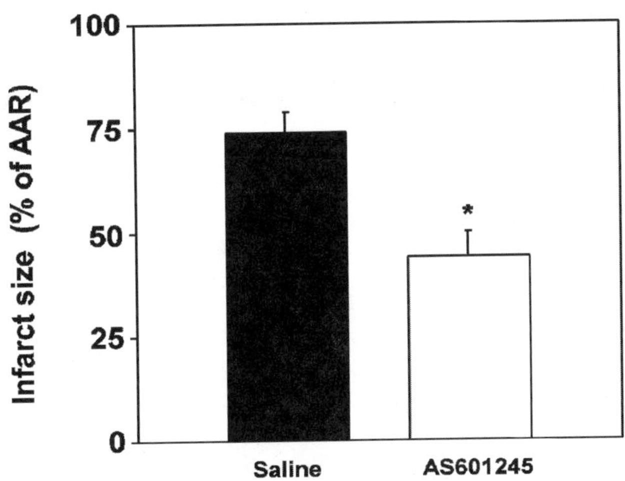

Figure 1. Reduction of myocardial infact size by AS601245.

With these data at hand, we tested the effects of D-JNKi in a mouse model of cardiac ischemia/reperfusion. Our preliminary results show that intraperitoneal treatment with D-JNKi, when administered prior to ischemia significantly reduced the size of the infarct by roughly 70%. Most interestingly, even when administered after ischemia and reperfusion, this peptide significantly reduced, albeit to a lesser extend, the size of the infarct (16). Therefore, these very promising data give us the rationale for the use of specific peptide inhibitors of JNK as potential treatment of myocardial infarction (Figure 2).

FUTURE PERSPECTIVES

Advances in molecular medicine have enabled us to identify critical pathways involved in cell survival or death in the myocardium. Furthermore, critical regulators of these pathways have been identified, leading to the development of novel therapeutic approaches of ischemic heart disease. Preliminary results in murine models in vivo are promising, however further studies are granted before a clinical application, where coronary-artery reperfusion and prevention of cardiomyocytes death will be the gold standard of the treatment of myocardial infarction.

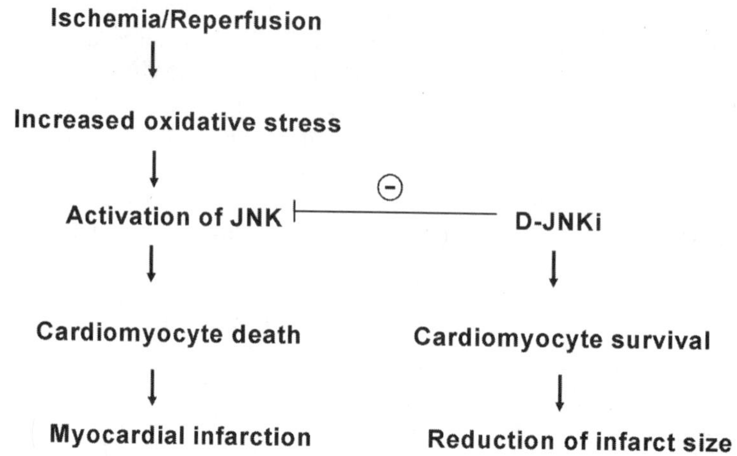

Figure 2. JNK-mediated cell death during myocardial ischemia/reperfusion and effects of D-JNKi, a novel peptide inhibitor of JNK.

ACKNOWLEDGMENTS

I am indebted to Professors Pascal Nicod and Urs Scherrer for continued support, to Christophe Bonny for kindly providing us with D-JNKi, to Stéphane Cook and Caroline Mathieu for expert technical assistance.

REFERENCES

1. Anonymous, Neglected Global Epidemics: three growing threats. In: World Health Report 2003, World Health Organization, 2003, p. 83-102.
2. Anonymous, Coronary Heart Disease,Acute Coronary Syndrome and Angina Pectoris. In: Heart Disease and Stroke Statistics-2005 Update, American Heart Association, 2005, p. 10-16.
3. Aoki H, Kang PM, Hampe J, Yoshimura K, Noma T, Matsuzaki M and Izumo S. Direct activation of mitochondrial apoptosis machinery by c-Jun N-terminal kinase in adult cardiac myocytes. *J Biol Chem* 277: 10244-10250, 2002.
4. Apstein CS. The benefits of glucose-insulin-potassium for acute myocardial infarction (and some concerns). *J Am Coll Cardiol* 42: 792-795, 2003.
5. Bogoyevitch MA, Gillespie-Brown J, Ketterman AJ, Fuller SJ, Ben Levy R, Ashworth A, Marshall CJ and Sugden PH. Stimulation of the stress-activated mitogen-activated protein kinase subfamilies in perfused heart. p38/RK mitogen-activated protein kinases and c-Jun N-terminal kinases are activated by ischemia/reperfusion. *Circ Res* 79: 162-173, 1996.
6. Bonny C, Oberson A, Negri S, Sauser C and Schorderet DF. Cell-permeable peptide inhibitors of JNK: novel blockers of beta-cell death. *Diabetes* 50: 77-82, 2001.
7. Borsello T, Clarke PG, Hirt L, Vercelli A, Repici M, Schorderet DF, Bogousslavsky J and Bonny C. A peptide inhibitor of c-Jun N-terminal kinase protects against excitotoxicity

and cerebral ischemia. *Nat Med* 9: 1180-1186, 2003.
8. Braunwald E. Editorial: Reduction of myocardial-infarct size. *N Engl J Med* 291: 525-526, 1974.
9. Brocheriou V, Hagege AA, Oubenaissa A, Lambert M, Mallet VO, Duriez M, Wassef M, Kahn A, Menasche P and Gilgenkrantz H. Cardiac functional improvement by a human Bcl-2 transgene in a mouse model of ischemia/reperfusion injury. *J Gene Med* 2: 326-333, 2000.
10. Calvillo L, Latini R, Kajstura J, Leri A, Anversa P, Ghezzi P, Salio M, Cerami A and Brines M. Recombinant human erythropoietin protects the myocardium from ischemia-reperfusion injury and promotes beneficial remodeling. *Proc Natl Acad Sci U S A* 100: 4802-4806, 2003.
11. Cook SA, Sugden PH and Clerk A. Activation of c-Jun N-terminal kinases and p38-mitogen-activated protein kinases in human heart failure secondary to ischaemic heart disease. *J Mol Cell Cardiol* 31: 1429-1434, 1999.
12. Davis RJ. Signal transduction by the JNK group of MAP kinases. *Cell* 103: 239-252, 2000.
13. Donovan N, Becker EB, Konishi Y and Bonni A. JNK phosphorylation and activation of BAD couples the stress-activated signaling pathway to the cell death machinery. *J Biol Chem* 277: 40944-40949, 2002.
14. Dougherty CJ, Kubasiak LA, Frazier DP, Li H, Xiong WC, Bishopric NH and Webster KA. Mitochondrial signals initiate the activation of c-Jun N-terminal kinase (JNK) by hypoxia-reoxygenation. *FASEB J* 18: 1060-1070, 2004.
15. Dougherty CJ, Kubasiak LA, Prentice H, Andreka P, Bishopric NH and Webster KA. Activation of c-Jun N-terminal kinase promotes survival of cardiac myocytes after oxidative stress. *Biochem J* 362: 561-571, 2002.
16. Duplain, H, Cook, S., Mathieu, C., Bonny, C., Scherrer, U., and Nicod, P. Myocardial Salvage through a Novel Peptidic c-Jun NH2-terminal kinase inhibitor (Abstract) Circulation 110(suppl). 2004.
17. Ferrandi C, Ballerio R, Gaillard P, Giachetti C, Carboni S, Vitte PA, Gotteland JP and Cirillo R. Inhibition of c-Jun N-terminal kinase decreases cardiomyocyte apoptosis and infarct size after myocardial ischemia and reperfusion in anaesthetized rats. *Br J Pharmacol* 142: 953-960, 2004.
18. Fliss H and Gattinger D. Apoptosis in ischemic and reperfused rat myocardium. *Circ Res* 79: 949-956, 1996.
19. Fujimoto H, Ohno M, Ayabe S, Kobayashi H, Ishizaka N, Kimura H, Yoshida K and Nagai R. Carbon monoxide protects against cardiac ischemia--reperfusion injury in vivo via MAPK and Akt--eNOS pathways. *Arterioscler Thromb Vasc Biol* 24: 1848-1853, 2004.
20. He H, Li HL, Lin A and Gottlieb RA. Activation of the JNK pathway is important for cardiomyocyte death in response to simulated ischemia. *Cell Death Differ* 6: 987-991, 1999.
21. Hreniuk D, Garay M, Gaarde W, Monia BP, McKay RA and Cioffi CL. Inhibition of c-Jun N-terminal kinase 1, but not c-Jun N-terminal kinase 2, suppresses apoptosis induced by ischemia/reoxygenation in rat cardiac myocytes. *Mol Pharmacol* 59: 867-874, 2001.
22. Knight RJ and Buxton DB. Stimulation of c-Jun kinase and mitogen-activated protein kinase by ischemia and reperfusion in the perfused rat heart. *Biochem Biophys Res Commun* 218: 83-88, 1996.
23. Knowlton KU and Duplain H. Viral infections of the heart. In: Molecular Basis of Cardiovascular Disease, edited by Chien KR. Philadelphia: Saunders, 2004, p. 667-683.
24. Li WG, Coppey L, Weiss RM and Oskarsson HJ. Antioxidant therapy attenuates JNK activation and apoptosis in the remote noninfarcted myocardium after large myocardial infarction. *Biochem Biophys Res Commun* 280: 353-357, 2001.

25. Matsui T, Tao J, del Monte F, Lee KH, Li L, Picard M, Force TL, Franke TF, Hajjar RJ and Rosenzweig A. Akt activation preserves cardiac function and prevents injury after transient cardiac ischemia in vivo. *Circulation* 104: 330-335, 2001.
26. Mehta SR, Yusuf S, Diaz R, Zhu J, Pais P, Xavier D, Paolasso E, Ahmed R, Xie C, Kazmi K, Tai J, Orlandini A, Pogue J and Liu L. Effect of glucose-insulin-potassium infusion on mortality in patients with acute ST-segment elevation myocardial infarction: the CREATE-ECLA randomized controlled trial. *JAMA* 293: 437-446, 2005.
27. Naito Z, Kudo M, Xu G, Nishigaki R, Yokoyama M, Yamada N and Asano G. Immunohistochemical localization of mitogen-activated protein kinase (MAPK) family and morphological changes in rat heart after ischemia-reperfusion injury. *Med Electron Microsc* 33: 74-81, 2000.
28. Narula J, Haider N, Virmani R, DiSalvo TG, Kolodgie FD, Hajjar RJ, Schmidt U, Semigran MJ, Dec GW and Khaw BA. Apoptosis in myocytes in end-stage heart failure. *N Engl J Med* 335: 1182-1189, 1996.
29. Negri S, Oberson A, Steinmann M, Sauser C, Nicod P, Waeber G, Schorderet DF and Bonny C. cDNA cloning and mapping of a novel islet-brain/JNK-interacting protein. *Genomics* 64: 324-330, 2000.
30. Petrich BG, Eloff BC, Lerner DL, Kovacs A, Saffitz JE, Rosenbaum DS and Wang Y. Targeted activation of c-Jun N-terminal kinase in vivo induces restrictive cardiomyopathy and conduction defects. *J Biol Chem* 279: 15330-15338, 2004.
31. Renaud S and de Lorgeril M. Wine, alcohol, platelets, and the French paradox for coronary heart disease. *Lancet* 339: 1523-1526, 1992.
32. Saraste A, Pulkki K, Kallajoki M, Henriksen K, Parvinen M and Voipio-Pulkki LM. Apoptosis in human acute myocardial infarction. *Circulation* 95: 320-323, 1997.
33. Sato M, Bagchi D, Tosaki A and Das DK. Grape seed proanthocyanidin reduces cardiomyocyte apoptosis by inhibiting ischemia/reperfusion-induced activation of JNK-1 and C-JUN. *Free Radic Biol Med* 31: 729-737, 2001.
34. Shimizu N, Yoshiyama M, Omura T, Hanatani A, Kim S, Takeuchi K, Iwao H and Yoshikawa J. Activation of mitogen-activated protein kinases and activator protein-1 in myocardial infarction in rats. *Cardiovasc Res* 38: 116-124, 1998.
35. Thornberry NA and Lazebnik Y. Caspases: enemies within. *Science* 281: 1312-1316, 1998.
36. Wayman NS, Hattori Y, McDonald MC, Mota-Filipe H, Cuzzocrea S, Pisano B, Chatterjee PK and Thiemermann C. Ligands of the peroxisome proliferator-activated receptors (PPAR-gamma and PPAR-alpha) reduce myocardial infarct size. *FASEB J* 16: 1027-1040, 2002.
37. Widmann C, Gibson S, Jarpe MB and Johnson GL. Mitogen-activated protein kinase: conservation of a three-kinase module from yeast to human. *Physiol Rev* 79: 143-180, 1999.
38. Xu K, Tavernarakis N and Driscoll M. Necrotic cell death in C. elegans requires the function of calreticulin and regulators of Ca(2+) release from the endoplasmic reticulum. *Neuron* 31: 957-971, 2001.
39. Yamamoto K, Ichijo H and Korsmeyer SJ. BCL-2 is phosphorylated and inactivated by an ASK1/Jun N-terminal protein kinase pathway normally activated at G(2)/M. *Mol Cell Biol* 19: 8469-8478, 1999.
40. Yue TL, Ma XL, Wang X, Romanic AM, Liu GL, Louden C, Gu JL, Kumar S, Poste G, Ruffolo RR, Jr. and Feuerstein GZ. Possible involvement of stress-activated protein kinase signaling pathway and Fas receptor expression in prevention of ischemia/reperfusion-induced cardiomyocyte apoptosis by carvedilol. *Circ Res* 82: 166-174, 1998.

Chapter 15

MITOCHONDRIAL REACTIVE OXYGEN SPECIES ARE REQUIRED FOR HYPOXIC HIFα STABILIZATION

M. Celeste Simon
Investigator, Howard Hughes Medical Institute, Professor, Dept. of Cell and Dev. Biology and Abramson Family Cancer Research Institute, University of Pennsylvania School of Medicine, Philadelphia, PA , USA.

Abstract: Multicellular organisms initiate adaptive responses when oxygen (O_2) availability decreases. The underlying mechanisms of O_2 sensing remain unclear. Mitochondria have been implicated in many hypoxia-inducible factor (HIF) –dependent and –independent hypoxic responses. However, the role of mitochondria in mammalian cellular O_2 sensing has remained controversial, particularly regarding the use pharmacologic agents to effect hypoxic HIFα stabilization, which has produced conflicting data in the literature. Using murine embryonic cells lacking cytochrome c, we show that mitochondrial reactive O_2 species (ROS) are essential for O_2 sensing and subsequent HIFα stabilization at 1.5% O_2. In the absence of this signal, HIFα subunits continue to be hydroxylated and degraded via the proteasome. Importantly, exogenous treatment with H_2O_2 and severe O_2 deprivation is sufficient to stabilize HIFα even in the absence of functional mitochondrial. These results demonstrate that mitochondria function as O_2 sensors and signal hypoxic HIFα stabilization by releasing ROS to the cytoplasm. The cytochrome c mutant embryonic cells provide a unique reagent to further dissect the role of mitochondria in O_2 mediated-intracellular events.

Key Words: transcription, signal transduction, HIF prolyl hydroxylases

INTRODUCTION

Molecular oxygen is essential for aerobic energy metabolism, whereby the oxidoreduction energy of mitochondrial electron transport is converted into the high-energy phosphate bond of ATP. Oxygen (O_2) serves as the final electron acceptor for electron transport at complex IV (cytochrome c oxidase). However, where excess O_2 can be toxic, a significant decrease in O_2 impairs ATP generation and cell viability. Therefore, most prokaryotic and eukaryotic life is restricted to a narrow range of pO_2. Most mammalian cells exist at an *in vivo* pO_2 of 30 mm Hg to 50 mm Hg (4-7% O_2). As O_2 levels drop below this range, a number of cellular responses are engaged, including inhibition of ion channel activity, cell division, ribosome biogenesis, and mRNA translation. Cells have also developed transcriptional responses to hypoxia mostly regulated by hypoxia-inducible factors (HIFs) (12). HIFs activate transcription of genes encoding proteins that enhance glycolytic ATP production or increase O_2 delivery to affected tissues. This review will focus on models of O_2 sensing and their impact on the HIF signaling pathway (Figure 1).

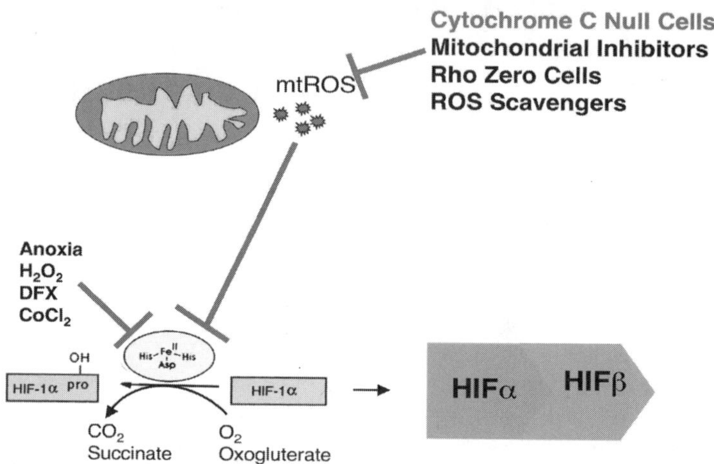

Figure 1. Proposed role of mitochondria in cellular oxygen sensing. This figure documents the experimental evidence supporting a role for mitochondrial reactive oxygen species (ROS) in the modulation of HIF stability, including cytochrome c null cells, mitochondrial inhibitors, Rho 0 cells, and ROS scavengers. We believe that mitochondrial ROS inhibit prolyl hydroxylase enzymatic activity in a similar fashion to anoxia, H_2O_2, DFX, and cobalt chloride. Inhibition of hydroxylase activity leads to HIFα accumulation, dimerization with HIFα (ARNT), and HIF-mediated gene expression.

OXYGEN SENSORS AND HYPOXIC SIGNAL TRANSDUCTION

The mechanisms by which eukaryotic cells sense decreased O_2 and transduce this signal to the HIF pathway have been debated for at least a decade. HIFs are heterodimeric transcription factors consisting of alpha (HIF-1α, HIF-2α, and HIF-3α), and beta (ARNT, ARNT2) subunits. The beta subunits are constitutively transcribed and translated and reside in the nucleus. In contrast, while the alpha subunits are transcribed and translated at a high rate in normoxic conditions (21% O_2), they are rapidly degraded via the proteasome. HIF-1α, HIF-2α, and HIF-3α contain 200 amino acid "oxygen dependent degradation domains" (ODDs) (5). These ODDs include a highly conserved binding domain for the tumor suppressor Von Hippel-Lindau protein (pVHL). pVHL coordinates the assembly of an E3 ubiquitin ligase complex containing Elongin B, Elongin C, Cullin 2, and RBX 1, and this complex ubiquitylates HIFα's, targeting their degradation via the proteasome (6) (7).

Recent data have shown that the interaction between HIFα's and pVHL is regulated via hydroxylation of proline residues in the ODD (6) (7). There are at least three HIF prolyl hydroxylases in mammalian cells (4). In the absence of O_2, prolyl hydroxylases are inactive; the unmodified HIFα no longer interacts with pVHL and accumulates. The absolute requirement for O_2 by HIF prolyl hydroxylases indicates that these enzymes may function as direct oxygen sensors. However, the precise sensor for the HIF pathway remains contentious. Previous models have included heme-binding proteins, membrane associated NADPH oxidases, and mitochondrial reactive oxygen species (10).

The model based on NADPH oxidase was first proposed in 1996 (8) (15). NADPH oxidases convert O_2 into reactive oxygen species (ROS); decreased pO_2 would therefore result in *reduced* formation of ROS to stabilize HIFα subunits. However, oxygen sensing and HIFα stabilization during hypoxia are preserved in gp91-*phox*-deficient cells isolated from knockout mice or patients with chronic granulomatous disease (1). These and other observations have shed doubt on a role for NADPH oxidase in oxygen sensing and HIF activation. A third model proposed in 1998 by Chandel et al. (2) suggests that hypoxia results in *increased* production of ROS by the mitochondria. Here, linear decreases in pO_2 result in a progressive increase in ROS. Pharmacological inhibitors of different complexes of the mitochondrial respiratory chain support the hypothesis of mitochondria as a key intracellular source of ROS. Inhibition of complex I (via rotenone) suppresses ROS production while inhibition of complex III or IV (antimycin A) increases ROS. Moreover, HIF activation directly correlates with ROS accumulation. Antioxidants such as ebselen and PDTC attenuate the ROS signal and abolish HIF stabilization. Importantly, Rho 0 cells (where mitochondria are deficient in electron transport and oxidative phosphorylation) fail to induce HIF activity. These results were not reproduced using other cell types: Srinivas et al. (13) and Vaux et al. (14) observed that Rho 0 cells display a normal response to hypoxia based on HIF stabilization. Vaux et al. used mutant cell lines with specific genetic defects in the electron transport chain and demonstrated that HIF activation by hypoxia was preserved. Taken together, these results failed to support the model implicating mitochondrial ROS during hypoxia as effectors in HIFα stabilization. However, Schroedl et al. accounted for this discrepancy by comparing HIFα stabilization under hypoxic conditions (1.5% O_2) versus anoxic conditions (less than 0.1% O_2) (11). Both the Srinivas and Vaux studies observed hypoxic HIFα stabilization using extremely low levels of O_2. The Schroedl et al. paper showed that mitochondrial ROS are essential for HIF stabilization at 1% O_2, while extremely low levels of O_2 (less than 0.01% O_2) are independent of mitochondrial electron transport. These results provide a plausible explanation, as the HIF prolyl hydroxylase enzymes are dependent on O_2 as a cofactor and at anoxic conditions could become substrate limited.

Both of these models suggest ROS are key players in O_2 sensing by the HIF pathway. However, the effector(s) regulated by ROS that transduces the signal to HIF remain unknown. Further investigation is also required to identify these intermediates and determine if they modulate prolyl hydroxylase enzymatic activity.

CYTOCHROME C IS REQUIRE FOR CELLULAR OXYGEN SENSING AND HYPOXIC HIFA ACTIVATION

While cellular responses to hypoxia have been studied extensively, the precise identity of mammalian cellular O_2 sensors remains controversial. Because of their O_2 dependence and relatively high kM for O_2 *in vitro*, it has been proposed that the HIF prolyl hydroxylases directly sense O_2 deprivation to stabilize HIF. However, mitochondrial ROS have been implicated in many cellular processes including HIFα stability and transcriptional activity, myocyte contraction, IL-6 production, glutathione depletion, NA,K-ATPase activity, and adipocyte differentiation (15). Despite this evidence, the role of mitochondria in mammalian cellular oxygen sensing has remained controversial. The use of pharmacological agents to affect HIFα stabilization has produced conflicting data in the literature. Therefore, we investigated this controversy by repeating and extending previous observations.

Mitochondria-deficient Hep3B Rho 0 cells have been shown to be defective in HIFα stabilization (3). Nevertheless, later work suggests this may be an artifact due to their selection with the mitochondrial inhibitor rotenone (14). We initially chose to address this discrepancy by generating Hep3B Rho 0 cell using ethidium bromide and avoiding selection with mitochondrial inhibitors (9). Of note, Hep3B cells exposed to steady doses of ethidium bromide for 3 weeks exhibit no mitochondrial DNA or oxygen consumption. Upon exposure to 1.5% O_2, Rho 0 cells failed to stabilized either HIF-1α or HIF-2α. We also generated HEK293 Rho 0 cells and used human osteosarcoma-derived 143B Rho 0 cells and obtained similar results. Hep3B, HEK293, and 143B cells retained responsiveness to desferrioxamine (DFX) with regard to HIF stabilization. These findings indicate that mitochondrial electron transport is required for hypoxic HIFα stabilization at 1.5% O_2, indicating that all cells retained active prolyl hydroxylation.

Due to concerns about long-term metabolic adaptation or genetic alteration of Rho 0 cells, we also employed acute mitochondrial inhibition of complex I (rotenone) or complex III (myxothiazol), minimizing non-specific effects by utilizing extremely low nanomolar doses. Treatment of Hep3B cells with rotenone or myxothiazol inhibited respiration and prevented hypoxic HIF-1α and HIF-2α stabilization after 2 hours of treatment. Importantly, myxothiazol treatment also affected HIFα stabilization in response to cobalt chloride, especially at higher doses. These results highlight difficulties inherent to direct pharmacological treatment and have prevented widespread acceptance of mitochondrial ROS during mammalian O_2 sensation.

We, therefore, employed a novel genetic model to further investigate the role of mitochondrial ROS in cellular oxygen sensing avoiding the non-specific effects of ethidium bromide or pharmacological inhibition all together. The murine somatic cytochrome c gene has been targeted previously. Loss of cytochrome c prevents oxidation of cytochrome c1, keeping the Reiske's iron sulfur protein reduced. This prevents oxidation of ubiquinol and the formation of the ubisemiquinone radical, eliminating one important source of superoxide anion (O_2^-) (and therefore H_2O_2) that has been implicated in hypoxic HIFα stabilization. We generated wild type, heterozygous, and null cell lines for cytochrome c using day 8.5 mouse embryos. While wild type and heterozygous cells exhibit similar respiratory rates while null cells are devoid of any measurable mitochondrial O_2 assumption or cytochrome c protein.

We next investigated *in vivo* ROS production in the cells using oxidant sensitive dichlorofluorescein (DCFH) and a ROS-sensitive FRET probe. Where wild type and heterozygous cells rapidly and dramatically increase oxidation and FRET activation, cytochrome c null cells exhibit an attenuated response. Importantly, unlike their wild type or heterozygous counterparts, cytochrome c null cells are unable to stabilize HIF-1α or HIF-2α in response to treatment with 1.5% O_2. The null cells, however, retain an appropriate response to DFX. These results argue strongly that the increased ROS production in hypoxic heterozygous cells are mitochondrial, and supports the hypothesis that mitochondrial ROS generated by complex III are responsible for hypoxic HIF-1α and HIF-2α stabilization.

Stable reintroduction of cytochrome c into an independent null cell line restores mitochondrial function and hypoxic mitochondrial ROS accumulation. This correlated with restoration of properly stabilized HIF-1α and HIF-2α levels similar to wild type cells. We concluded that the inhibility of null cells to properly sense O_2 is due to the lack of a functional mitochondrial electron transport chain resulting from cytochrome c loss. All cell lines respond similarly to DFX, suggesting that cytochrome c null cells maintain normal HIFα transcription, translation, and degradation even in the absence of functional mitochondrial. However, to test that they continue to hydroxylate and degrade HIF-1α and HIF-2α under hypoxic conditions, cytochrome c wild type and null cells were treated with 1.5% O_2 in the presence of the proteasome inhibitor MG132. While the null cells failed to stabilize HIFα in response to hypoxia, inhibition of proteasome degradation by MG132 leads to HIFα accumulation similar to data obtained with wild type cells. This demonstrates that hydroxylation and degradation of HIFα continue to occur in the cytochrome c null cells even at this reduced O_2 concentration.

We next determined if HIFα stabilization can be bypassed by severe O_2 deprivation (anoxia or approximately 0% O_2) where prolyl hydroxylases appear to be substrate limited. Importantly, the null cells fail to stabilize HIF-1α or HIF-2α in response to 1.5% O_2. However, exposure to 0% O_2 induces both HIF-1α or HIF-2α in a mitochondria-independent manner. These results suggest functional mitochondria are not necessary for cellular responses to severe O_2 deprivation. To test whether ROS production is also sufficient to stabilize HIF-1α or HIF-2α, Hep3B cells were treated with exogenous hydrogen peroxide (H_2O_2) as previously described (3). This resulted in normoxic stabilization of HIF-1α or HIF-2α similar to that induced by hypoxia in the same period of time. Furthermore, incubation of Hep3B cells with an H_2O_2 generating enzyme, glucose oxidase, is sufficient to stabilize both HIFα subunits. This is shown to be H_2O_2-dependent as inclusion of catalase abolishes HIFα stabilization. Finally, treatment of cytochrome c null cells with T-butyl hydroperoxide (TBP) a stable H_2O_2 analog, also induces HIFα stabilization similar to the hypoxia mimetic cobalt chloride. These results indicate that ROS production is sufficient for HIFα stabilization and likely functions downstream of mitochondria.

In summary, cytochrome c null cells provide novel genetic evidence supporting a role for mitochondrial ROS in the mammalian O_2 sensing pathway that leads to HIFα stabilization. How mitochondrial ROS effect HIF prolyl hydroxylase activity is important to understanding cellular O_2 sensing. These experiments are ongoing in the laboratory and suggest that ROS may directly inhibit the prolyl hydroxylases perhaps by oxidizing Fe^{2+} at the active site. It is likely that a number of mammalian cellular O_2 sensor exist, controlling various hypoxic responses depending on the cell type, O_2 tension, and other cellular conditions. The cytochrome c null cells provide valuable tools for investigating the role of the mitochondria and other hypoxic responses such as the inhibition of protein synthesis and cell cycle progression.

REFERENCES

1. Archer SL, Reeve HL, Michelakis E, Puttagunta L, Waite R, Nelson DP, Dinauer MC, and Weir EK. O2 sensing is preserved in mice lacking the gp91 phox subunit of NADPH oxidase. *Proc Natl Acad Sci U S A* 96: 7944-7949, 1999.
2. Chandel NS, Maltepe E, Goldwasser E, Mathieu CE, Simon MC, and Schumacker PT. Mitochondrial reactive oxygen species trigger hypoxia-induced transcription. *Proc Natl Acad Sci USA* 95: 11715-11720, 1998.
3. Chandel NS, McClintock DS, Feliciano CE, Wood TM, Melendez JA, Rodriguez AM, and Schumacker PT. Reactive oxygen species generated at mitochondrial complex III stabilize hypoxia-inducible factor-1alpha during hypoxia: a mechanism of O2 sensing. *J Biol Chem* 275: 25130-25138., 2000.
4. Epstein AC, Gleadle JM, McNeill LA, Hewitson KS, O'Rourke J, Mole DR, Mukherji M, Metzen E, Wilson MI, Dhanda A, Tian YM, Masson N, Hamilton DL, Jaakkola P, Barstead R, Hodgkin J, Maxwell PH, Pugh CW, Schofield CJ, and Ratcliffe PJ. C. elegans EGL-9 and mammalian homologs define a family of dioxygenases that regulate HIF by prolyl hydroxylation. *Cell* 107: 43-54, 2001.
5. Huang LE, Gu J, Schau M, and Bunn HF. Regulation of hypoxia-inducible factor 1alpha is mediated by an O2- dependent degradation domain via the ubiquitin-proteasome pathway. *Proc Natl Acad Sci U S A* 95: 7987-7992, 1998.
6. Ivan M, Kondo K, Yang H, Kim W, Valiando J, Ohh M, Salic A, Asara JM, Lane WS, and Kaelin WG, Jr. HIFalpha targeted for VHL-mediated destruction by proline hydroxylation: implications for O2 sensing. *Science* 292: 464-468., 2001.
7. Jaakkola P, Mole DR, Tian YM, Wilson MI, Gielbert J, Gaskell SJ, Kriegsheim A, Hebestreit HF, Mukherji M, Schofield CJ, Maxwell PH, Pugh CW, and Ratcliffe PJ. Targeting of HIF-alpha to the von Hippel-Lindau ubiquitylation complex by O2-regulated prolyl hydroxylation. *Science* 292: 468-472., 2001.
8. Jones RD, Hancock JT, and Morice AH. NADPH oxidase: a universal oxygen sensor? *Free Radic Biol Med* 29: 416-424, 2000.
9. Mansfield KD, Guzy RD, Pan Y, Young RD, Schumacker PT, and Simon MC. Cytochrome C is required for cellular oxygen sensing and hypoxic HIF activation. *Cell Metabolism, manuscript submitted*, 2005.
10. Michiels C, Minet E, Mottet D, and Raes M. Regulation of gene expression by oxygen: NF-kappaB and HIF-1, two extremes. *Free Radic Biol Med* 33: 1231-1242, 2002.
11. Schroedl C, McClintock DS, Budinger GR, and Chandel NS. Hypoxic but not anoxic stabilization of HIF-1alpha requires mitochondrial reactive oxygen species. *Am J Physiol Lung Cell Mol Physiol* 283: L922-931., 2002.
12. Semenza GL. Regulation of mammalian O2 homeostasis by hypoxia-inducible factor 1. *Annu Rev Cell Dev Biol* 15: 551-578, 1999.
13. Srinivas V, Leshchinsky I, Sang N, King MP, Minchenko A, and Caro J. Oxygen sensing and HIF-1 activation does not require an active mitochondrial respiratory chain electron-transfer pathway. *J Biol Chem* 276: 21995-21998, 2001.
14. Vaux E, Metzen E, Yeates K, and Ratcliffe P. Regulation of hypoxia-inducible factor is preserved in the absence of a functioning mitochondrial respiratory chain. *Blood* 98: 296-302, 2001.
15. Zhu H and Bunn H. Oxygen Sensing and signaling: impact on the regulation of physiologically important genes. *Respiration Physiology* 115: 239-247, 1999.

Chapter 16

HYPOXIA-INDUCED GENE ACTIVITY IN DISUSED OXIDATIVE MUSCLE

Christoph Däpp[1], Max Gassmann[2], Hans Hoppeler[1], Martin Flück[1]
[1]Department of Anatomy, University of Berne, Switzerland. [2]Vetsuisse Faculty and Zurich Center for Integrative Human Physiology, University if Zurich, Switzerland.

Abstract: Hypoxia is an important modulator of the skeletal muscle's oxidative phenotype. However, little is known regarding the molecular circuitry underlying the muscular hypoxia response and the interaction of hypoxia with other stimuli of muscle oxidative capacity. We hypothesized that exposure of mice to severe hypoxia would promote the expression of genes involved in capillary morphogenesis and glucose over fatty acid metabolism in active or disused soleus muscle of mice. Specifically, we tested whether the hypoxic response depends on oxygen sensing via the alpha-subunit of hypoxia-inducible factor-1 (HIF-1α). Spontaneously active wildtype and HIF-1α heterozygous deficient adult female C57Bl/6 mice were subjected to hypoxia (PiO_2 70 mmHg). In addition, animals were subjected to hypoxia after 7 days of muscle disuse provoked by hindlimb suspension. Soleus muscles were rapidly isolated and analyzed for transcript level alterations with custom-designed AtlasTM cDNA expression arrays (BD Biosciences) and cluster analysis of differentially expressed mRNAs. Multiple mRNA elevations of factors involved in dissolution and stabilization of blood vessels, glycolysis, and mitochondrial respiration were evident after 24 hours of hypoxia in soleus muscle. In parallel transcripts of fat metabolism were reduced. A comparable hypoxia-induced expression pattern involving complex alterations of the IGF-I axis was observed in reloaded muscle after disuse. This hypoxia response in spontaneously active animals was blunted in the HIF-1α heterozygous deficient mice demonstrating 35% lower HIF-1α mRNA levels. Our molecular observations support the concept that severe hypoxia provides HIF-1-dependent signals for remodeling of existing blood vessels, a shift towards glycolytic metabolism and altered myogenic regulation in oxidative mouse muscle and which is amplified by enhanced muscle use. These findings further imply differential mitochondrial turnover and a negative role of HIF-1α for control of fatty acid oxidation in skeletal muscle exposed to one day of severe hypoxia.

Key Words: HIF-1α, microarray, angiogenesis, altitude, ischemia

INTRODUCTION

Ever since the early observations on ischemia and altitude exposure, hypoxia has been seen as an important modulator of the muscular phenotype (reviewed by 1). Subsequent studies laid out a picture whereby hypoxia alone may affect glycolytic flux, protein synthesis and mitochondrial oxidative capacity (18,29).

In fact, skeletal muscle is a particular hypoxia-sensitive tissue as muscular oxygen tension is subject to large variations during daily use. Rapidly after the onset of exercise, a significant 2-fold drop in muscular oxygen tension is apparent (reviewed by 20, 36). Similarly, muscle pO_2 drops to low levels in consequence of reduced oxygen pressure of the inspired air (32, 41). Concomitant exercise additionally lowers the oxymyoglobin concentration in muscle (36).

While this hypoxia-based drop in oxygen tension certainly represents an important stimulus, it has been argued that many of the muscular adjustments to hypoxia such as alterations in fiber size and aerobic enzymes depend on a number of additional factors. These co-variables include the level of exercise and hypoxia (4). These studies also pointed out that hypoxia alone does not alter capillary number (26). Endurance exercise in fact, exerts pronounced control over similar aspects of muscular processes as the hypoxic stimulus. For instance, endurance training is known to ameliorate energy metabolic processes mainly via enhancing mitochondrial oxidative capacity and increasing capillarity (17).

The understanding of the molecular mechanisms underlying hypoxia-dependent muscular adaptations and the interaction with exercise stimuli is still incomplete. Altered expression of gene messenger, i.e. mRNAs, has been recognized as a possible strategy involved in the integration of the hypoxia stimuli into a phenotypic response. Several hypoxia sensitive mRNAs have been identified in muscle tissue. The recent systematic analysis of the expressional response of cultured endothelial cells and skeletal muscle to hypoxia or ischemia indicates that the mRNA response is more complex than previously assumed. These changes involve specific alterations of the total pool of RNAs, i.e. the transcriptome (30, 31). With respect to trans-activation of hypoxia-dependent genes, the HIF-1 system has been recognized to be crucial for hypoxia sensing in various systems (14, 38). This master switch is a dimeric complex, termed hypoxia-inducible factor-1 (HIF-1), the α subunit of which is tagged for degradation in normoxia. Conversely, HIF-1α is rapidly stabilized in severe hypoxia thereby causing its association with the HIF-1β subunit to form the DNA-binding HIF-1 complex which initiates transcription of various oxygen responsive genes (40). HIF-1α therefore promotes angiogenesis and a shift towards glycolysis in conditions of ischemia (14, 38). The importance of HIF-1α in the hypoxia response is underlined by the observation that HIF-1α null mice die at midgestation and that ablation of one HIF-1α allele produces defective tissue response in situations where muscular oxygen tension is suspected to drop (25, 38). For instance, multiple systemic defects to chronic hypoxia (10% O_2) involving polycythemia, right ventricular hypertrophy, pulmonary hypertension, and defect pulmonary vascular remodeling are apparent in HIF-1α heterozygous mice (45). Analogously, the partial ablation of the HIF-1α gene in conditional knock-out mice produces measurable muscular aberrations. These involve a metabolic shift away from glycolysis towards enhanced capacity for the mitochondrial Krebs cycle and beta oxidative enzymes thereby improving exercise endurance (25).

We have developed a muscle-specific cDNA microarray to map the transcriptome alterations which underlie the structural adjustments with disuse of mouse soleus muscle in the hindlimb suspension-reloading model (6). The current exploration applied this technology in combination with transgenic technology to identify gene expressional alterations in the soleus muscle of mice induced by short term severe hypoxia. Additionally, we intended to reveal the interaction of the hypoxia response in this anti-gravitational muscle with mechanical stimuli and to identify the underlying hypoxia-sensing mechanism. It was hypothesized that exposure of mice to severe hypoxia (PiO_2 70 mmHg) for 24 hours would promote a distinct enhancement of expression for genes involved in capillary morphogenesis and glucose metabolism over the combustion of fatty acids in the oxidative soleus muscle. We tested whether this expressional response depends on sensing via HIF-1α by subjecting wildtype and HIF-1α heterozygous deficient adult female C57Bl/6 mice to hypoxia. Alternatively, animals were subjected to hypoxia after 7 days of muscle disuse provoked by hindlimb suspension to reveal whether the hypoxia signature of gene expression would be preserved when the hypoxia stimuli was combined with mechanical stress.

METHODS

Spontaneously active mice: 3-4 months old wildtype (wt) or HIF-1α heterozygous deficient (HIF-1α+/-) female mice (C57BL/6) were acclimatized for 7 days to housing in single cages (Makrolon type III, Indulab, Italy). Wt and HIF-1α+/- mice were then randomly assigned to a normoxia or hypoxia group. For details see paragraph on "hypoxia exposure" (see Fig. 1). 24 hours after hypoxia exposure the animals were anesthetized while still under the respective hypoxic/normoxic condition. The body weight of animals was determined and soleus muscles were rapidly dissected (<5 minutes), weighed and frozen in liquid nitrogen-cooled isopentane. Muscle weighing was avoided in the hypoxia group to reduce the exposure to "normoxic air".

Muscle disuse and reloading: Muscle disuse was provoked by 7 days of hindlimb suspension before the hindlimbs were reloaded for 24 hours in normoxia or hypoxia (see Fig. 1). Appearance, behavior and activity levels of animals were regularly observed and recorded during the interventions on an analogue scale. Animals were kept at a 12:12 light: dark cycle with water and standard chow *ad libitum*. Start time of the experiments was held constant to permit constant interval between nocturnal activity cycle and muscle harvesting.

Hypoxia exposure: The cages of singly housed mice were rapidly flushed with a mixture of nitrogen and oxygen under application of a continuous pump system (AltiTrainer200, SMTEC, Switzerland). Oxygen and carbon dioxide content was monitored online (Servomex Oxygen Analyzer 570 A; Zurich, Switzerland) and set to a PiO_2 of 70 mmHg for the hypoxia group, i.e. 10.5% O_2 ad 23°C @ 560 meters above sea level (21). This corresponds to an O_2 concentration at 5360 meters above sea level. Control animals were exposed to a PiO_2 of 138 mmHg, i.e. 20.9% O_2 ad 23°C @ 560 meters above sea level. Animals were observed twice to monitor the level of spontaneous activity and health status during the hypoxia exposure. Differences in body and soleus weight were statistically verified with a one-way ANOVA and an ANOVA with repeated measurements, respectively, with a post-hoc test for highest significance difference (HSD; STATISTICA 6.1, StatSoft Inc, www.statsoft.com).

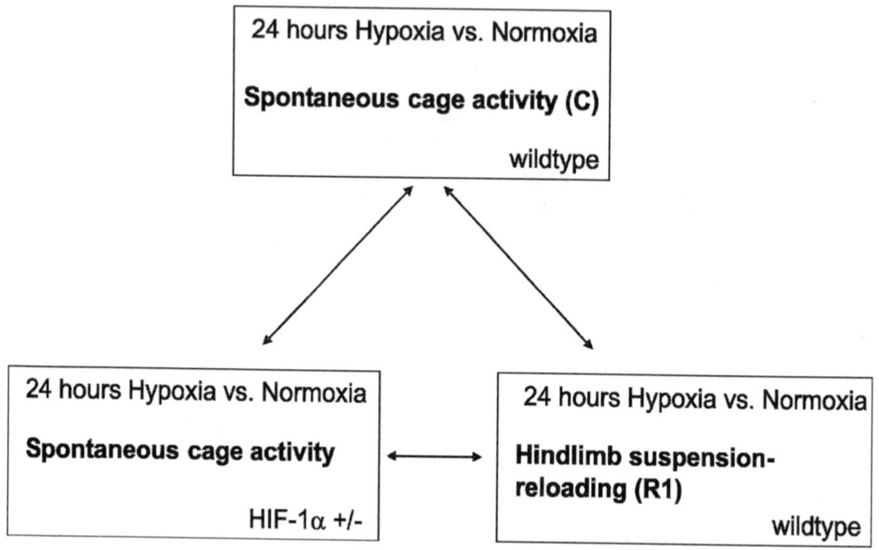

Figure 1. Experimental setup. Arrows separate between the different experimental groups.

Microarray analysis: Microarray analysis with custom-designed low-density AtlasTM cDNA expression arrays (BD Biosciences AG, Allschwil, Switzerland) for 222 mouse cDNAs associated with skeletal muscle form and function was carried out as described (6). In brief, total RNA was isolated and reverse-transcribed in parallel into labelled cDNA with 222 mRNA-specific primers and ribosomal 18S/28S rRNA using Superscript II (Life Technologies AG, Basel, Switzerland). mRNA-specific and 1:900 diluted 18S/28S cDNAs were mixed, hybridized to nylon arrays and signals of the washed filters were detected after 5 days of exposure with a phosphoImager (Molecular Dynamics, Sunnyvale, CA, USA). Batches of 4 samples were always processed simultaneously with 6 biological replica for each treatment. Data sets have been deposited at Gene Expression Omnibus (GEO, http://www.ncbi.nlm.nih.gov/geo) under series GSE2384 according to the minimal information on gene expression (Brazma MIAME).

Statistical analyses for differential mRNA expression: Testing for transcript level differences between two experimental groups was carried out as described (43). In brief, 141 mRNAs which detection level was 30% above background (on ≥4 filters) were analyzed. The significance of an mRNA level alteration was tested with permutation analyses on L1 regression models of logarithmized raw values in scatter plots for the comparison of 2 treatments under application of the sign-test (STATISTICA 6.1). To correct for multiple tests, the False Discovery Rate method introduced by Benjamini and Hochberg was applied at a two-tailed p=0.05 (12). The expression ratio for each transcript was estimated from the mean of potentiated residues (to the base of 10) from the individual scatterplots.

The effect of reloading after muscle disuse vs. spontaneous activity on hypoxia-induced gene expression was verified using 28S-related signal ratios of the two hypoxia group after normalization to the mean of the respective normoxia group. A one-way ANOVA at $p<0.05$ was used to test the combined effect of treatment on the hypoxia-response (STATISTICA 6.1).

Hierarchical cluster analysis: For the identification of major hypoxia-dependent expression patterns, background-corrected signals of the 141 detected transcripts were normalized to the signal of stably expressed mRNAs (pixel intensity between 10,000-100,000 counts). Normalized values from the hypoxia treatments were then related to the mean normalized signal of the respective normoxia group. Following, the values of 63 mRNAs which were significantly altered with 24 hours of hypoxia vs. normoxia (and/or with reloading after muscle disuse) were extracted, log-transformed, mean-centered for genes and arrays and subjected to hierarchical cluster analysis for genes and arrays using centered correlations with public Cluster and Treeview software (8).

RESULTS

The hypoxia signature of the anti-gravitational soleus muscle-Exposure of wt mice to 24-hours of severe hypoxia had a significant effect on expression of multiple genes in soleus muscle of spontaneously active mice (table 1). These adaptations were in most cases less than 2-fold. Detailed inspection revealed that these changes involved distinct upregulation of mRNA levels of glycolytic factors (ALDOA, ALDOC, GAPDH, LDH3, PFKFB1) as well as small increases of abundant mitochondrial respiration chain constituents (CYTC, COX4A, COX5B, COX6A2) and the main oxygen transporter myoglobin (MB) (see table 1). Strikingly, a down-regulation of a main factor involved in the uptake of endothelial derived lipids (LPL) and 2 members of beta-oxidation (ACADL, HADH) was observed. Conversely, the main factor of myocellular fatty acid transport (FABP3) was increased while mRNA levels of facilitative glucose transporters were not affected in spontaneously active mice after 24 hours of hypoxia exposure. With regard to the detected factors of capillary morphogenesis, transcript expression levels of factors involved in vessel dissolution (Ang-1, Ang-2, Tenascin-C), stabilization (CD31, CDH5, Ephrin B2, VEGF-R1, VEGF-R3, TSP-1) and proliferation (PAI-1, PDGFRb) were increased (44). Finally, myogenic regulatory factors including the IGF-system and myogenic transcription factors were complex affected. The body weight of mice exposed to 10.5% hypoxia, unlike normoxia, was significantly reduced (see table 2).

The HIF-1 system and the muscular hypoxia response-We analyzed the involvement of the HIF-1 system in the transduction of the hypoxia signal. Qualitative structural analysis did not indicate significant differences in RNA content, soleus or body weight between matched HIF-1α+/- and wt mice (table 2). In normoxia, soleus muscles of spontaneously active HIF-1α+/- mice demonstrated a 35%-reduced HIF-1α mRNA level in soleus muscle vs. matched wildtype animals (table 3). Several other gene transcript involving known HIF-1 targets were moderately different expressed in soleus muscles of HIF-1α+/- vs. wt mice. These mRNA level differences concerning factors involved in fatty acid metabolism, myogenic regulation replication, capillary dissolution and hypoxia signaling

Table 1. Summary of hypoxia-induced mRNA level alterations. Hypoxia (Hyp) to normoxia (Nor) ratio of transcript levels in mouse soleus muscle ordered per gene ontology for wildtype (wt) and HIF-1α+/- cage controls, and wt mice after reloading from previous disuse. Known HIF-1 regulated genes are printed in white on black background. Transcripts which are subject to opposite regulation in wt versus HIF-1α+/- mice are highlighted in grey. Significant differences are underlined and printed in bold.

Category		Gene	GenBank ID	Cage control Hyp/Nor				Reloaded Hyp/Nor	
				wt		HIF-1α+/-		wt	
				p value	fold change	p value	fold change	p value	fold change
Metabolism	CHO metabolism	GLUT1	M23384		0.96	1.4E-03	**1.01**		1.04
		GLUT2	X16986		1.09	1.0E-07	**1.51**	5.5E-06	**1.37**
		GLUT3	M75135		0.96		n.d.	1.4E-03	**1.05**
		GLUT4	M23383	9.2E-09	**0.80**		1.00		1.04
	Glycolysis	ALDOA	Y00516	1.2E-04	**1.20**		0.96	8.7E-03	**1.23**
		ALDOC	S72537	4.4E-04	**1.29**		1.19	1.5E-11	**2.80**
		ENO2	X52380	8.6E-07	**0.82**		0.94		0.88
		GAPDH	M32599	2.8E-05	**1.21**		0.97	1.4E-03	**1.16**
		HK1	J05277		n.d.		n.d.	1.4E-03	**0.90**
		LDH1	U13687		0.90	2.8E-05	**0.87**	3.7E-03	**0.83**
		LDH3	M17587	8.7E-03	**1.14**		0.88	1.2E-04	**1.18**
		PFKFB1	X98848	1.8E-02	**1.19**		0.96	4.4E-04	**1.35**
	FA mobilization	LDLR	Z19521		0.97		n.d.	2.8E-05	**0.84**
		VLDLR	L33417		0.95	9.2E-09	**1.25**	3.7E-03	**0.84**
		FAT/CD36	L23108		1.23	1.0E-07	**1.66**	1.0E-07	**1.45**
		Scarb2	AB008553		0.97		0.93	1.0E-07	**0.75**
		LPL	M60847	9.2E-09	**0.84**	1.8E-02	**1.09**	1.4E-03	**0.78**
	FA transport	FABP4	K02109		0.95	9.2E-09	**1.49**		1.12
		FABP3	X14961	2.8E-05	**1.36**	3.7E-03	**1.28**	1.2E-04	**1.32**
	krebs cycle	PDHA1	M76727	4.4E-04	**0.85**	9.2E-09	**1.34**		0.86
	beta oxidation	ACADL	U21489	4.4E-04	**0.80**	9.2E-09	**1.23**		0.90
		HADH	D29639	5.5E-06	**0.76**		1.06		0.88
	O_2 storage	MB	X04405	2.8E-05	**1.18**		0.96	1.0E-07	**1.28**
		HO-1	M33203	2.8E-05	**1.17**	1.4E-03	**1.17**	1.2E-04	**0.66**
	respiration	CYCT	X55771	3.7E-03	**1.13**		n.d.		0.95
		COX4A	X54691	1.8E-02	**1.05**		1.05		1.07
		COX5B	X53157	4.4E-04	**1.16**		1.03	8.6E-07	**1.35**
		COX6A2	U08439	9.2E-09	**1.21**		0.90	1.0E-07	**1.33**
myogenic regulation	cell cycle	MEF2A	U30823	3.7E-03	**0.78**		0.98	1.2E-04	**0.86**
		MEF2C	L13171	1.0E-07	**0.68**	3.7E-03	**1.10**	1.0E-07	**0.72**
		MYOD	M84918		1.12		0.76	3.7E-03	**0.66**
		SRF	NM020493		0.90		0.99	8.7E-03	**1.03**
		CCND1	S78355	9.2E-09	**0.81**		n.d.	0.0E+00	**0.61**
		CDK4	L01640	1.4E-03	**1.18**		n.d.		0.84
	hormonal	GHR	M33324	4.4E-04	**0.86**		0.89		**1.02**
		IGF-I	X04480		1.34		0.63	1.4E-03	**1.82**
		MGF	NM010512		1.22		0.65	1.4E-03	**1.61**
		IGF2R	U04710		0.99		0.97	9.2E-09	**0.74**
		IGFBP4	X81582	1.0E-07	**0.85**		1.00	2.8E-05	**0.88**
		IGFBP5	L12447	0.0E+00	**0.54**	1.0E-07	**0.85**	0.0E+00	**0.66**
		IGFBP6	X81584	4.4E-04	**1.44**		1.01	8.6E-07	**1.76**
	dissolution	ADAM 2	U16242	3.7E-03	**0.80**		0.99		0.89
		Ang-1	U22516	4.4E-04	**1.64**		1.08		1.14
capillary remodeling		Angpt-2	AF004326		1.33		1.16	8.6E-07	**2.00**
		Ang-2	U22519	1.4E-03	**1.42**		1.00	1.4E-03	**1.59**
		MMP-10	Y13185		n.d.		n.d.	4.4E-04	**0.69**
		Tenascin-C	D90343	8.7E-03	**1.31**		0.88		1.25
	proliferation	ACE	J04946		1.11	8.6E-07	**1.23**	3.7E-03	**0.88**
		CD44	M27129		n.d.		n.d.	2.8E-05	**0.69**
		EGF-R	X78987	5.5E-06	**0.88**		1.04		1.02
		iNOS 2	M87039		1.31		n.d.	1.4E-03	**1.37**
		PAI-1	M33960	8.7E-03	**1.41**	1.4E-03	**0.84**		1.31
		PDGFRb	X04367	2.8E-05	**1.11**		0.97	5.5E-06	**0.88**
		MMP-14	X83536		0.95		1.03	1.4E-03	**0.89**
		Tie-2	S67051		1.00		n.d.	8.7E-03	**1.08**
		u-PA	X02389		n.d.	1.4E-03	**1.15**	1.4E-03	**1.34**
		VEGF	M95200		0.97	5.5E-06	**0.84**		1.00
		VEGF-B	U43836		0.99	1.8E-02	**1.06**		1.03
		VEGF-R2	X70842		0.95	4.4E-04	**0.92**		1.02
	stabilisation /anti-angiogenic	CD31/PECAM	L06039	8.7E-03	**1.68**		0.86	5.5E-06	**1.83**
		CDH5	X83930	1.8E-02	**1.21**		1.14	4.4E-04	**1.22**
		Ephrin B2	L25890	3.7E-03	**1.12**		0.97		0.98
		lama 4	Y09827		1.05	1.2E-04	**0.86**	5.5E-06	**1.11**
		TIMP-1	X04684	4.4E-04	**0.88**		0.94	8.6E-07	**0.76**
		TIMP-2	X62622	3.7E-03	**0.90**	1.2E-04	**1.17**		0.89
		TIMP-3	L19622		0.98	2.8E-05	**1.33**	1.4E-03	**0.78**
		TSP1	M62470	1.4E-03	**1.21**		0.88	1.4E-03	**1.22**
		VEGF-R1	X78568	3.7E-03	**1.16**		n.d.		0.99
		VEGF-R3	L07296	1.8E-02	**1.42**		n.d.	5.5E-06	**1.66**

were small but systematically affected.

Hierarchical cluster analysis of the differentially expressed mRNAs revealed that these HIF-1α heterozygous mice demonstrate systematic shifts of the hypoxia-induced gene expression patterns during spontaneous cage activity (Fig. 2). For instance the hypoxia-induced transcript levels in wt mice of gene ontologies involved in glycolysis and mitochondrial respiration were blunted (see table 1 and Fig. 3). Conversely, the down-regulated muscular mRNA levels for factors involved in fatty acid mobilization, except FABP3, were now enhanced with 24 hours of severe hypoxia in the HIF-1α+/- mice. In hypoxia, the mRNA response of several angiogenic factors and most myogenic regulators was reduced and some were oppositely affected in HIF-1α+/- vs. wt littermates.

Interaction of hypoxia with mechanical stimuli-We next evaluated the interaction of the hypoxia stress with mechanical stimuli in mice by reloading after muscle disuse. The hypoxia-induced transcript level alterations were significantly different between reloading and spontaneous cage activity ($p<0.05$; one way ANOVA). This divergence was substantiated by cluster analysis demonstrated that the hypoxia transcript signature differentiated between the two experimental groups (Fig. 2). This cluster analysis also revealed that components of the hypoxia-induced transcript signature were preserved and expanded in disused soleus muscles after 24 hours of reloading in hypoxia (Fig. 2). Interestingly, from the 50 transcripts which were significantly altered upon hypoxia, 24 follow the same expression pattern upon reloading in hypoxia. Detailed inspection revealed that the amplitude rather than the involvement of most transcripts, hypoxia-modulated level adjustments of gene ontologies involved in glycolysis, mitochondrial respiration, and capillary remodeling were reduced with reloading of disused soleus muscle compared to spontaneous cage activity (Table 1). Conversely, hypoxia-induced transcript level alterations of myogenic regulators IGF-I, MGF and IGF-BP-6 were more pronounced during reloading.

Table 2. Alterations in RNA content, soleus and body weight with 24 hours of normoxia and hypoxia.

		Normoxia		*Hypoxia*	
		total	***Δ24h***	***total***	***Δ24h***
Cage control	*RNA*	3.3 ± 0.5 μg		3.3 ± 0.3 μg	
	soleus	7.3 ± 0.2 mg *		na	
	body	22.6 ± 0.5 gr *	+0.1	20.9 ± 0.9 gr	-1.8 †
Hindlimb suspension-reloading	*RNA*	2.0 ± 0.3 μg		1.8 ± 0.3 μg	
	soleus	5.5 ± 0.4 mg		na	
	body	20.45± 0.4 gr	+0.2	20.0 ± 0.6 gr	-1.2 †
HIF-1α+/-	*RNA*	4.0 ± 0.6 μg		3.5 ± 0.5 μg	
	soleus	7.8 ± 0.4 mg *		na	
	body	22.4 ± 0.9 gr	0.0	20.2 ± 0.7 gr	-2.5 †

Values represent the mean ± SE after the 24 hour interventions (n=6). Δ denotes the mean difference values after the 24 hours of intervention. na, not assessed *, p< 0.05 vs. disuse-reloading in normoxia. †, p< 0.01 vs. values before exposure to hypoxia (ANOVA, HSD post hoc test).

DISCUSSION

Systemic hypoxia is a main stimulus of muscle phenotypical adaptations. The addition of hypoxia is known to pronounce the effects of enhanced contractile activity and muscle loading on vessel growth, protein synthesis and metabolic pathways (1, 18, 29). This hypoxia-promoted activation of biological processes in skeletal muscle may be the direct consequence of the enhanced induction of signaling cascades by local reduction of oxygen supply in muscle or mediated by central effects of hypoxia (i.e. on blood flow) (1). Thus, we reasoned that exposure of mice to a hypoxic environment for 24 hours results in a specific muscular transcript "signature" that relates to the known effects of hypoxia and which would prevail with reloading after muscle disuse. 24 hours of hypoxia was selected to reveal the sustained rather than early, and possibly muscle tissue-specific expressional adaptations to this stimulus (30, 31). The assessment of alterations of selected muscular mRNAs was carried out with validated microarray filters and accepted statistical tests (6, 43). In order to study the interaction of hypoxia with contractile activity/muscle loading, we focused on the soleus muscle in mice. This muscle's homeostasis is particularly mechano-dependent and undergoes severe atrophy and a pronounced metabolic shift with hindlimb suspension (6). This model of muscle disuse and a transgenic model for HIF-1α deficiency were thus used to pinpoint at the role of muscle activity and the HIF-1 hypoxia sensor in the muscular response to severe systemic hypoxia.

Our microarray study identifies that the hypoxia response involves distinct gene expressional adaptations that discriminates between experimental treatments but shows that basic features were preserved during reloading after muscle disuse (Fig. 2). The recorded molecular adjustments (see below) must seen in context of previous observations on muscle structural adjustments to hypoxia and resemble recent molecular observations on the response of cultured endothelial cells to hypoxia (31) and HIF-1α conditional knock-out mice to running exercise (25). In combination with the blunted RNA response to hypoxia in HIF-1α+/- mice, our molecular observations imply a key role of the hypoxia sensor HIF-1α and muscle use in the response of muscle tissue to the assumed local hypoxia.

Limitations–This is the first systematic study analyzing the broad expressional response of muscle-relevant factors to a non-lethal hypoxia stimulus. Due to the exploratory nature of this mRNA study, several considerations apply with regard to potential limitations of our conclusions. These concerns relate to the cellular origin and the translation of the observed hypoxia-induced transcript level adaptations at the protein level. Missing biochemical data on HIF-1α protein accumulation cast some uncertainty with regard to the suspected direct role of the HIF-1α subunit in the sensing mechanism that governs hypoxia-induced 0transcript expression in soleus muscle. Thus we can not rule out that the altered hypoxia response of transcript levels in HIF-1α+/- vs. wt animals is a consequence of alternative hypoxia-sensing pathways in muscle or nerve-dependent hypoxia reflexes of blood supply lines (see 1, 13).

The significant drop in body weight after 24 hours of severe hypoxia indicates that our results must be seen with regard to systemic events related to wasting (see table 2). Despite this, only a few transcript level alterations point in the similar direction as seen previously with food deprivation in the gastrocnemius muscle of mice (22), i.e. IGFBP-5, ENO1 and CD36. In fact, the majority of mRNA level alterations in mouse soleus such as those

Table 3. mRNA level differences in normoxia between HIF-1α+/- and wt mice. Significant alterations at $p<0.05$ as determined from microarray experiments (n=6) are indicated with an asterisk. Δ% refers to the mean percentage change (HIF-1α+/-vs.wt) of the corresponding transcript group *, determined with RT-PCR (HIF-1α+/-, n=4 vs. wt n=3).

ontology	*general trend*	*genes*	*genbank*
CHO uptake	↑Δ*+20%*	GLUT2 GLUT3	X16986 M75135
glycolysis	↑Δ*+60%*	ALDOA ALDOC PFKFB1	Y00516 S72537 X98848
	↓Δ*-28%*	ENO2 LDH1 LDH3	X52380 U13687 M17587
fatty acid metabolism	↑Δ*+39%*	FAT/CD36 VLDLR FABP4 HADH PDHA1	L23108 L33417 K02109 D29639 M76727
	↓	Scarb2	AB008553
mitochondrial respiration	↓Δ*-10%* ↑	COX4A COX6A2 COX VIIIa	X54691 U08439 U37721
myogenic regulation	↑Δ*+69%*	GHR IGF-I IGF-II IGFBP6	M33324 X04480 M14951 X81584
	↓Δ*-13%*	IGF2R CCND1	U04710 S78355
replication	↓Δ*-20%*	Pola Pole2 Top1	D17384 AF036898 D10061
capillary remodeling dissolution	↑Δ*+62%*	ADAM 2 (↓) Ang-1 Angpt-2 Ang-2 Tenascin-C	U16242 U22516 AF004326 U22519 D90343
proliferation	↑Δ*+46%*	EGF-R FGF R2 PAI-1 VEGF-R2	X78987 M86441 M33960 X70842
	↓Δ*-22%*	Itgav iNOS 2 MMP-14 PDGFRb PDGFb PDGFRa Tie-2	U14135 M87039 X83536 X04367 M84453 M57683 S67051
stabilisation	↑Δ*+22%*	CDH5 Ephrin B1 Ephrin B2	X83930 U12983 L25890
	↓Δ*-20%*	Lama 5 Tsp2 VEGF-C	U37501 L07803 U73620
hypoxia signaling	↓Δ*-20%*	HIF-1α * HIF-1β	U59496 U14333

related to glycolytic and oxidative metabolism were different to the ones observed in starved gastrocnemius. This implies that our molecular observations in hypoxia do not correlate with starvation. Finally, the uncertainty of the level of muscle use during spontaneous cage activity in hypoxia vs. normoxia in our experiments and the particular tonic, oxidative phenotype of the muscle under study argue for caution in the extrapolation of identified relationships to the muscular hypoxia response in other models and species. Nevertheless, the "molecular features" of the hypoxia response of soleus muscle as exposed by our microarray exploration allow to hypothesize on the interaction of muscle use with the HIF-1α-mediated muscular hypoxia response.

The pattern of hypoxia-induced transcript level alterations-The contention of a specific molecular hypoxia "signature" is indicated by our findings showing a preservation of this signature for transcript levels in the soleus muscle in mice after disuse atrophy (see Fig. 2). This is suggestive for hypoxia to represent an important stimulus setting the direction of the muscular gene responses. The molecular hypoxia signature involved enhanced gene expression of capillary remodeling factors, opposite mRNA adaptations of oxidative, glycolytic and lipidic metabolic pathways and modified expression of myogenic regulators (see Fig. 4). These observations thus extend the historical assumptions on enhanced mitochondrial biogenesis and the increased glycolytic energy production in hypoxia to the mechanistic level. At the same time, this adds novel evidence for alterations of fatty acid transport and enhanced remodeling of the capillary network (Fig. 3).

Particularly, the co-incident upregulation of factors involved in distinct metabolic pathways indicates expressional reprogramming of distinct energy metabolic processes in hypoxia-exposed soleus muscle. The increased mRNA levels in glycolytic factors thereby reflect those enzymatic adaptations as previously noted in gastrocnemius muscle (33). This contention on a comprehensive shift from fatty acid to carbohydrate consumption is supported by the down-regulation of the verified factors involved in uptake of lipids from the vasculature into muscular tissues, i.e. VLDLR, LDLR and LPL, and mitochondrial beta oxidation, i.e. ACADL and HADH, in the soleus muscle with reloading in hypoxia. In this regard, the increased mRNA level of respiration factors is puzzling as this suggests enhanced turnover or accumulation of constituents of the mitochondrial oxidative pathway in hypoxia.

HIF-1α and the hypoxic response in soleus muscle-The setting of ambient air to 10.5% O_2 represents a severe insult for the exposed mice. A rapid drop in muscular oxygen tension due to this lowering of FiO_2 to a simulated altitude of 5360 meter above sea level is indicated from recent studies (28, 32, 41, 39). Evidence for global tissue hypoxia in our study was provided by the visual de-oxygenation of animals as seen due to the shift form a red to a bluish body color within minutes of exposure to 10.5% O_2. Consequently, important hypoxia-dependent processes may be initiated in muscle tissues.

In various organs HIF-1α protein is known to be stabilized with a specific time-course in response to a lowering of FiO_2 to 6% (40). Our western blot analysis with several antibodies failed to detect a suspected accumulation of stabilized HIF-1α protein in whole cell lysates of the soleus muscle during the time course of the 24 hour response in 10.5% (and 6%) O_2 (data not shown). Subsequent experiments with more specific antisera and nuclear fractions are now necessary to provide the ultimate biochemical proof for a direct muscular involvement of HIF-1α protein in the observed muscular transcript response in hypoxia. The blunted hypoxia response of multiple transcripts in the HIF-1α+/- animals with a 35%-

reduced basal level of HIF-1α mRNA therefore were the confounding observation of our study. This indeed points towards an active role of HIF-1α in the mRNA response of hypoxic muscle (see Fig. 4). The notion of a master role of HIF-1α in hypoxia-induced gene expression in muscle is corroborated with the similitude of biological processes which response to endurance exercise is blunted in conditional-knock-out HIF-1α animals demonstrating a 40% reduction of the HIF-1α allele (25).

In this regard, the up-regulation of transcripts for factors involved in vascular lipid uptake and mitochondrial beta oxidation in HIF-1α+/- animals was a surprising observation because these concentrations were reduced upon hypoxia exposure in wild type mice. This invokes the existence of HIF-1α dependent negative feedback mechanism which controls transcript synthesis or degradation of the former mRNAs. Decreased oxygenation initiates a variety of signals that lead to the growth of blood vessels (1). The blunted response of remodeling factors therefore provides evidence that the suspected remodeling response of the endothelium is mediated by HIF-1-dependent hypoxia sensing.

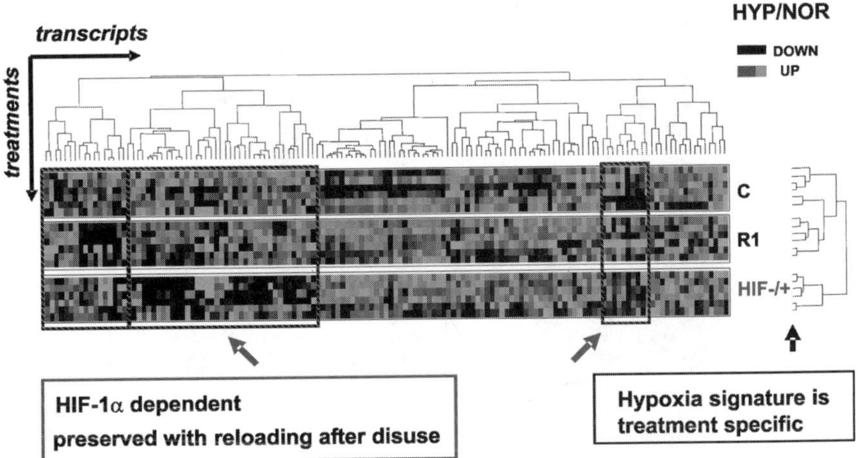

Figure 2. Muscular hypoxia expression "signature". Graph depicts that the muscular hypoxia-induced gene expression patterns distinguish between experimental groups. Hypoxia vs. normoxia expression ratios of hypoxia-modified transcripts in soleus muscle from wildtype mice during spontaneous cage activity (C) or one day of reloading of after disuse (R1) or HIF-1α+/- mice was analyzed by hierarchical cluster analysis. Clusters of mRNA levels with a particular level of co-regulation are demarcated.

Interaction with muscle use-Our findings showing a moderately reduced but expanded, muscular hypoxia signature of transcript levels in reloaded animals after disuse atrophy extend the evidence for a possible interference of muscle use and hypoxia with regard to muscular adjustments to the molecular level (reviewed by 11, 29). Meanwhile meta analysis demonstrated a certain overlap in the gene ontologies for HIF-1α-dependent muscular transcript adaptations to hypoxia in our study and in the previous report on endurance exercise in HIF-1α-dependent mice (25). This possibly relates to the lowering of the muscular HIF-1α mRNA level increase with reloading in hypoxia (minus 20%) or a lower uptake of contractile activity in disused than normal skeletal muscle.

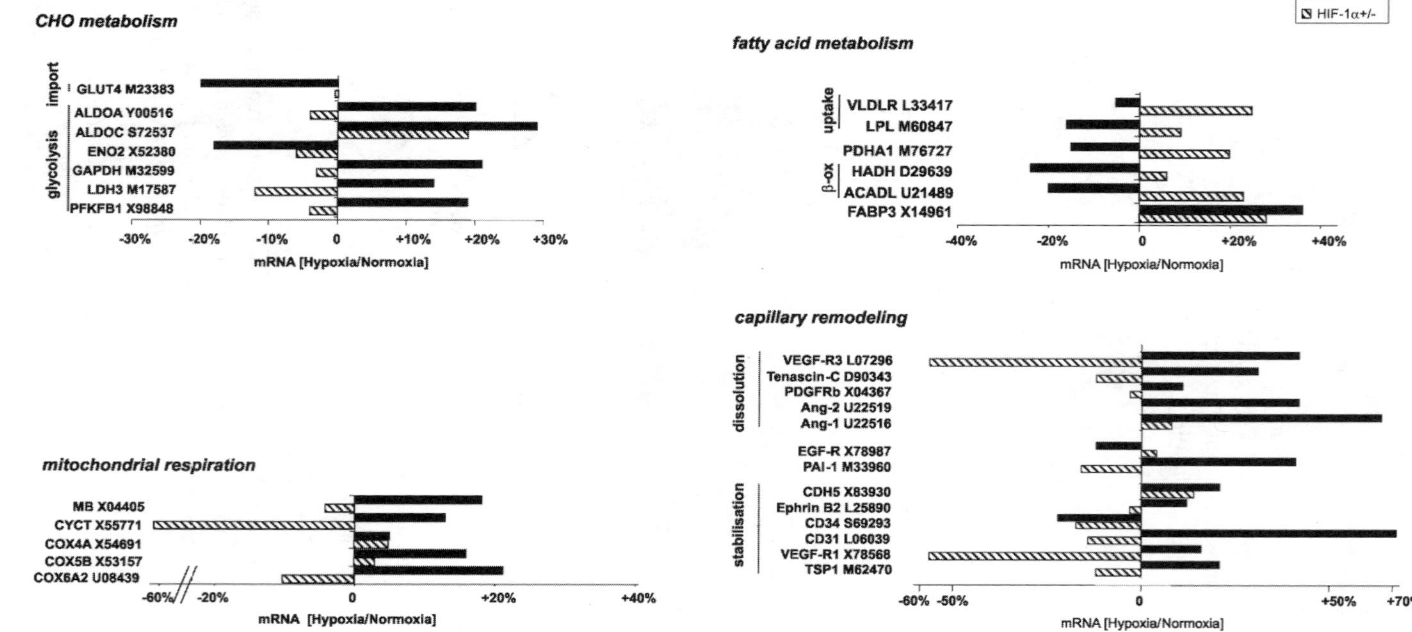

Figure 3. Hypoxia-induced alterations and HIF-1α-dependence of transcripts within individual gene ontologies

In this regard, the lower amplitude of hypoxia-induced mRNA alterations in disused soleus muscle may reflect reduced HIF-1-mediated oxygen sensing due to reduced potential for stabilization of HIF-1α signaling molecules during reloading in hypoxia (see Fig. 4). On the other hand, animal monitoring indicated an initial drop in the spontaneous physical activity of mice upon exposure to 10.5% hypoxia.

In parallel, reloading of disused muscle provides a relative high increase in muscle loading vs. the load changes seen with spontaneous activity in the cage controls. This "predominance" of mechano-dependent events is also manifested by the additional upregulation of expression levels for the mechano-sensitive insulin-like growth factor I (IGF-I) transcripts and the related MGF splice form and IGFBP6 after reloading of disused muscle in hypoxia (see Fig. 2 and table 1; 10). The novel observation of hypoxia-induced expressional regulation of the IGF-I system therefore is seen to be related to the reported effect of hypoxia on protein synthesis (reviewed in 10, 18, 29). Our data therefore indicate that the muscle hypoxia response is part of a potential part of an auto-/paracrine loop involved in the anabolic effects of hypoxia exposure (10, 18). Overall our observations provide a molecular counterpart for the structural observations that muscle activity is an important co-variable of hypoxia-induced alterations in muscle fiber phenotoype (4, 26).

The (sub)cellular mechanism of the hypoxia response-The measure of mRNA level alterations in a homogenate begs the question as on the cellular origin and functional implications of the gene expressional response. In this regard, the expression of several of the quantified transcripts is confined to one particular cell type. Consequently, these level changes are indicative for activation of distinct cellular populations in muscle by 24 hours of severe hypoxia. For instance, several of the altered mRNA levels of factors involved in capillary remodeling are preferentially/uniquely expressed in the endothelial cell type (CD31, CDH5, Ephrin B2). Similarly, the match in several mRNA level adaptations of soleus muscle with the ones seen in hypoxic endothelial cultures (see table 3) suggests a major contribution of endothelial cells to the muscular transcript alterations after 24 hours of hypoxia in our study (30, 31). Likewise, muscle fibers represent the major source of glycolytic and mitochondrial respiratory factors (5, 34).

Concerning the transcript level alterations for endothelial-specific factors, evidence for a distinct kind of capillary remodeling becomes manifest. For instance, the increase in mRNAs involved in vessel dissolution (Ang-1, Ang-2, Tenascin-C, VEGF-R3, PDGFRb) and stabilization (CD31, Ephrin B2, CDH5, VEGF-R1, TSP-1), concomitant with the absence of consistent alterations for promoters of vascular proliferation (VEGF, EGF-R, PDGFRb) supports that hypoxia *per se* is not a sufficient stimulus for capillary neo-formation in muscle (19, 26). Similar complex expressional induction of dissolution (proliferation) and stabilization factors of capillaries has been noted recently during capillary formation (23) and the hypoxic response of different vascular beds (30). Moreover, inconsistent changes in factors related to cell proliferation, i.e. CCND1, PCNA, EGF-R, mimics the anti-proliferative response seen in endothelial cells under hypoxic stress (31). The observed mRNA alterations in our study therefore may indicate proliferation-independent shape alterations of the capillary bed such as those related to intussuseptive vessel growth (1, 7, 21, 44). This is in line with the initiation of morphological alterations in capillaries (reviewed by 11) and long held speculations on the changes of vascular tortuosity in hypoxia exposed muscle (42) .

With regard to the alterations of mitochondrial transcripts two potentially important relationships become apparent. First, the upregulation of myoglobin (MB), CYTC, COX4A, COX5B, COX6A2 mRNAs (Table 1, Fig. 3) represent the first evidence for an expressional regulation of respiratory chain constituents in muscle upon severe hypoxia alone. This observation is compatible with the initially supported but later refused contention of Reynafarie that hypoxia alone may increase mitochondrial performance (see 4, 19). Secondly, the opposite transcript level alterations of factors involved in beta-oxidation provides evidence for a differential regulation of the expressional makeup of mitochondria. We do not know whether these transcript responses necessarily translate into corresponding change of mitochondrial protein composition. Future studies now need to test whether the hypoxia stimulus alone is sufficient to promote selective turnover or compositional alterations of mitochondrial content.

Outlook-Muscle disuse and hypoxia take important part in the onset of clinical syndromes such as chronic obstructive pulmonary disease, chronic heart failure and peripheral arterial occlusive disease (9). For instance, deconditioned muscles of chronic obstructive pulmonary disease (COPD) patients experience frequent episodes of tissue hypoxia during rehabilitation (3, 24). The peripheral muscle abnormalities observed with these syndromes include a shift from oxidative to glycolytic energy metabolism and a limitation of blood flow via a reduction of vasculature supply (reviewed in 9, 27, 35). These adaptations are of striking similarity to the adjustments seen with muscle disuse and hypoxia in the hindlimb suspension model. The molecular observations on the transcriptome response to hypoxia in disused muscle therefore are of potential relevance for the understanding of the role of ischemia in deconditioned human muscle tissues. This notion is supported by the fact that in accordance with our study, cytochrome oxidase activity is paradoxically increased in skeletal muscle of COPD patients when the mitochondrial machinery involved in the generation of reduction equivalents from organic C2 substrates was reduced (2, 37).

CONCLUSION

The present microarray study demonstrates that 24 hours of severe hypoxia provokes a specific gene expressional response in anti-gravitational mouse soleus muscle via the hypoxia sensor HIF-1α and interacts with mechanical signals as modified by the level of muscle use. The mapped transcript "signature" implicates a scenario for distinct expressional mechanisms to be involved in the early muscular adaptations to severe hypoxia. For most, these mRNA level adjustments resemble the response of endothelial cells to severe hypoxia and link to the reported metabolic consequences of chronic hypoxia and muscle use on skeletal muscle makeup. This molecular picture suggests that short term severe hypoxia promotes capillary remodeling via an activation of the endothelial cell population and supports a shift toward an enhanced potential for glycolysis and mitochondrial respiration with a concomitant down-regulation of vascular import and beta oxidation of fatty acids.

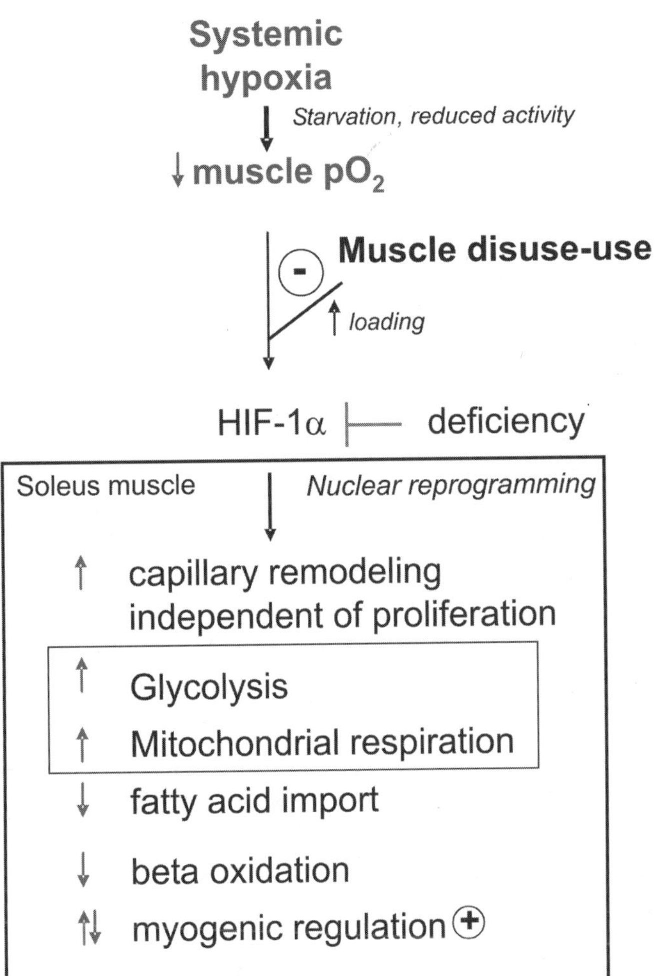

Figure 4. Synopsis and proposed model of hypoxia signal integration. Systemic hypoxia provokes nuclear programming of different gene ontologies (boxed) in soleus muscle via a drop in muscle oxygen tension (piO_2) and the activation of the hypoxia sensor HIF-1α. Consequently, this hypoxia response is blunted in HIF-1α heterozygous deficient mice. Other potential co-stimuli involved in the muscular response during systemic hypoxia are indicated in italics. Enhanced muscle activity such as with reloading after muscle disuse reduces the amplitude of hypoxia-induced transcript level alterations via enhanced muscle loading (except for myogenic factors whose transcript response is enhanced).

ACKNOWLEGEMENTS

The study was supported by Swiss National Science Foundation grant 3100-065276.

ABBREVIATIONS

ACADL, Acyl-CoA dehydrogenase; ALDOA, Aldolase A; ALDOC, Aldolase C; Ang-1, Angiogenin; Ang-2, Angiogenin-2; CCND1, cyclin D1; CD31, Platelet endothelial cell adhesion molecule precursor; CDH5, Vascular endothelial-cadherin precursor; CYTC, Cytochrome C; COX4A, Cytochrome C oxidase subunit 4A; COX5B, Cytochrome C oxidase subunit 5B; COX6A2, Cytochrome C oxidase subunit 6A2; EGF-R, Epidermal growth factor receptor; Ephrin B2, Ephrin type-B receptor 2, GAPDH, Glyceraldehyde-3-phosphate dehydrogenase; HADH, Short chain 3-hydroxyacyl-CoA dehydrogenase; HIF-1α, hypoxia-inducible factor-1 alpha;HIF-1α, hypoxia-inducible factor-1 beta LDH3,lactate dehydrogenase 3; LDLR, low-density lipoprotein receptor; LPL, Lipoprotein lipase; FABP3, (heart) fatty acid binding protein 3; IGF-I, Insulin-like growth factor I; IGFBP6, Insulin-like growth factor binding protein 6; MB, Myoglobin; MGF, mechano-growth factor (IGF-I splice form); PAI-1, Plasminogen activator inhibitor-1; PCNA, Proliferating cell nuclear antigen; PDGFRb, Beta platelet-derived growth factor receptor; PFKFB1, 6-phosphofructo-2-kinase/fructose-2,6-biphosphatase 1; TSP-1, Thrombospondin 1; VEGF, Vascular endothelial growth factor; VEGF-R1, Vascular endothelial growth factor receptor 1; VEGF-R3, Vascular endothelial growth factor receptor 3; VLDLR, Very low-density lipoprotein receptor

REFERENCES

1. Adair TH, Gay WJ and Montani JP. Growth regulation of the vascular system: evidence for a metabolic hypothesis. *Am J Physiol* 259: R393-R404, 1990.
2. Allaire J, Maltais F, Doyon JF, Noel M, LeBlanc P, Carrier G, Simard C and Jobin J. Peripheral muscle endurance and the oxidative profile of the quadriceps in patients with COPD. *Thorax* 59: 673-678, 2004.
3. Antonucci R, Berton E, Huertas A, Laveneziana P and Palange P. Exercise physiology in COPD. *Monaldi Arch Chest Dis* 59: 134-139, 2003.
4. Banchero N. Cardiovascular responses to chronic hypoxia. *Annu Rev Physiol* 49: 465-476, 1987.
5. Bass A, Brdiczka D, Eyer P, Hofer S and Pette D. Metabolic differentiation of distinct muscle types at the level of enzymatic organization. *Eur J Biochem* 10: 198-206, 1969.
6. Dapp C, Schmutz S, Hoppeler H and Fluck M. Transcriptional reprogramming and ultrastructure during atrophy and recovery of mouse soleus muscle. *Physiol Genomics* 20: 97-107, 2004.
7. Djonov V, Baum O and Burri PH. Vascular remodeling by intussusceptive angiogenesis. *Cell Tissue Res* 314: 107-117, 2003.
8. Eisen MB, Spellman PT, Brown PO and Botstein D. Cluster analysis and display of genome-wide expression patterns. *Proc Natl Acad Sci USA* 95: 14863-14868, 1998.
9. Gosker HR, Wouters EF, van der Vusse GJ and Schols AM. Skeletal muscle dysfunction in chronic obstructive pulmonary disease and chronic heart failure: underlying mechanisms and therapy perspectives. *Am J Clin Nutr* 71: 1033-1047, 2000.
10. Haddad F and Adams GR. Selected contribution: acute cellular and molecular responses to resistance exercise. *J Appl Physiol* 93: 394-403, 2002.
11. Hepple RT. Skeletal muscle: microcirculatory adaptation to metabolic demand. *Med Sci Sports Exerc* 32: 117-123, 2000.

12. Hochberg Y and Benjamini Y. More powerful procedures for multiple signifi cance testing. *Stat Med* 9: 811-818, 1990.
13. Hofer T, Wenger RH, Kramer MF, Ferreira GC and Gassmann M. Hypoxic up-regulation of erythroid 5-aminolevulinate synthase. *Blood* 101: 348-350, 2003.
14. Hopfl G, Ogunshola O and Gassmann M. HIFs and tumors--causes and consequences. *Am J Physiol Regul Integr Comp Physiol* 286: R608-R623, 2004.
15. Hopfl G, Ogunshola O and Gassmann M. Hypoxia and high altitude. The molecular response. *Adv Exp Med Biol* 543: 89-115, 2003.
16. Hoppeler H and Vogt M. Muscle tissue adaptations to hypoxia. *J Exp Biol* 204: 3133-3139, 2001.
17. Hoppeler H, Luthi P, Claassen H, Weibel ER and Howald H. The ultrastructure of the normal human skeletal muscle. A morphometric analysis on untrained men, women and well-trained orienteers. *Pfl ugers Arch* 344: 217-232, 1973.
18. Hoppeler H and Desplanches D. Muscle structural modifi cations in hypoxia. *Int J Sports Med* 13 Suppl 1: S166-S168, 1992.
19. Hoppeler H. Vascular growth in hypoxic skeletal muscle. *Adv Exp Med Biol* 474: 277-286, 1999.
20. Hoppeler H, Vogt M, Weibel ER and Fluck M. Response of skeletal muscle mitochondria to hypoxia. *Exp Physiol* 88: 109-119, 2003.
21. Hudlicka O. Is physiological angiogenesis in skeletal muscle regulated by changes in microcirculation? *Microcirculation* 5: 5-23, 1998.
22. Jagoe RT, Lecker SH, Gomes M and Goldberg AL. Patterns of gene expression in atrophying skeletal muscles: response to food deprivation. *FASEB J* 16: 1697-1712, 2002.
23. Kilic N, Oliveira-Ferrer L, Wurmbach JH, Loges S, Chalajour F, Vahid SN, Weil J, Fernando M and Ergun S. Pro-angiogenic signaling by the endothelial presence of CEACAM1. *J Biol Chem* 280: 2361-2369, 2005.
24. Mador MJ and Bozkanat E. Skeletal muscle dysfunction in chronic obstructive pulmonary disease. *Respir Res* 2: 216-224, 2001.
25. Mason SD, Howlett RA, Kim MJ, Olfert IM, Hogan MC, McNulty W, Hickey RP, Wagner PD, Kahn CR, Giordano FJ and Johnson RS. Loss of skeletal muscle HIF-1alpha results in altered exercise endurance. *PLoS Biol* 2: e288, 2004.
26. Mathieu-Costello O. Muscle adaptation to altitude: tissue capillarity and capacity for aerobic metabolism. *High Alt Med Biol* 2: 413-425, 2001.
27. McGuigan MR, Bronks R, Newton RU, Sharman MJ, Graham JC, Cody DV and Kraemer WJ. Resistance training in patients with peripheral arterial disease: effects on myosin isoforms, fi ber type distribution, and capillary supply to skeletal muscle. *J Gerontol A Biol Sci Med Sci* 56: B302-B310, 2001.
28. Millis RM, Stephens TA, Harris G, Anonye C and Reynolds M. Relationship between intracellular oxygenation and neuromuscular conduction during hypoxic hypoxia. *Life Sci* 35: 2443-2451, 1984.
29. Narici MV and Kayser B. Hypertrophic response of human skeletal muscle to strength training in hypoxia and normoxia. *Eur J Appl Physiol Occup Physiol* 70: 213-219, 1995.
30. Nilsson I, Shibuya M and Wennstrom S. Differential activation of vascular genes by hypoxia in primary endothelial cells. *Exp Cell Res* 299: 476-485, 2004.
31. Ning W, Chu TJ, Li CJ, Choi AM and Peters DG. Genome-wide analysis of the endothelial transcriptome under short-term chronic hypoxia. *Physiol Genomics* 18: 70-78, 2004.
32. Nioka S, McCully K, McClellan G, Park J and Chance B. Oxygen transport and intracellular bioenergetics on stimulated cat skeletal muscle. *Adv Exp Med Biol* 510: 267-272, 2003.
33. Pastoris O, Foppa P, Catapano M and Dossena M. Effects of hypoxia on enzyme activities

in skeletal muscle of rats of different ages. An attempt at pharmacological treatment. *Pharmacol Res* 32: 375-381, 1995.
34. Pette D and Spamer C. Metabolic properties of muscle fi bers. *Fed Proc* 45: 2910-2914, 1986.
35. Raguso CA, Guinot SL, Janssens JP, Kayser B and Pichard C. Chronic hypoxia: common traits between chronic obstructive pulmonary disease and altitude. *Curr Opin Clin Nutr Metab Care* 7: 411-417, 2004.
36. Richardson RS, Noyszewski EA, Kendrick KF, Leigh JS and Wagner PD. Myoglobin O2 desaturation during exercise. Evidence of limited O2 transport. *J Clin Invest* 96: 1916-1926, 1995.
37. Sauleda J, Garcia-Palmer F, Wiesner RJ, Tarraga S, Harting I, Tomas P, Gomez C, Saus C, Palou A and Agusti AG. Cytochrome oxidase activity and mitochondrial gene expression in skeletal muscle of patients with chronic obstructive pulmonary disease. *Am J Respir Crit Care Med* 157: 1413-1417, 1998.
38. Semenza GL. HIF-1: mediator of physiological and pathophysiological responses to hypoxia. *J Appl Physiol* 88: 1474-1480, 2000.
39. Slate RK, Ryan M and Bongard FS. Dependence of tissue oxygen on oxygen delivery. *J Surg Res* 61: 201-205, 1996.
40. Stroka DM, Burkhardt T, Desbaillets I, Wenger RH, Neil DA, Bauer C, Gassmann M and Candinas D. HIF-1 is expressed in normoxic tissue and displays an organ-specifi c regulation under systemic hypoxia. *FASEB J* 15: 2445-2453, 2001.
41. Tsai AG, Johnson PC and Intaglietta M. Oxygen gradients in the microcirculation. *Physiol Rev* 83: 933-963, 2003.
42. Weineck J. *Optimales Training*. Erlangen: Perimed Fachbuch-Verlagsgesellschaft, 1983.
43. Wittwer M, Billeter R, Hoppeler H and Fluck M. Regulatory gene expression in skeletal muscle of highly endurance-trained humans. *Acta Physiol Scand* 180: 217-227, 2004.
44. Yancopoulos GD, Davis S, Gale NW, Rudge JS, Wiegand SJ and Holash J. Vascularspecifi c growth factors and blood vessel formation. *Nature* 407: 242-248, 2000.
45. Yu AY, Shimoda LA, Iyer NV, Huso DL, Sun X, McWilliams R, Beaty T, Sham JS, Wiener CM, Sylvester JT and Semenza GL. Impaired physiological responses to chronic hypoxia in mice partially defi cient for hypoxia-inducible factor 1alpha. *J Clin Invest* 103: 691-696, 1999.

Chapter 17

ROLE OF THE RED BLOOD CELL IN NITRIC OXIDE HOMEOSTASIS AND HYPOXIC VASODILATION

Mark T. Gladwin

Vascular Medicine Branch, National Heart, Lung and Blood Institute; Critical Care Medicine Department, Clinical Center; National Institutes of Health, Bethesda, Maryland, USA.

Abstract: Nitric oxide (NO) regulates normal vasomotor tone and modulates important homeostatic functions such as thrombosis, cellular proliferation, and adhesion molecule expression. Recent data implicate a critical function for hemoglobin and the erythrocyte in regulating the bioavailability of NO in the vascular compartment. Under normoxic conditions the erythrocytic hemoglobin scavenges NO and produces a vasopressor effect that is limited by diffusional barriers along the endothelium and in the unstirred layer around the erythrocyte. In hemolytic diseases, intravascular hemolysis releases hemoglobin from the red blood cell into plasma (decompartmentalizes the hemoglobin), which is then able to scavenge endothelial derived NO 600-fold faster than erythrocytic hemoglobin, thereby dysregulating NO homoestasis. In addition to releasing plasma hemoglobin, the red cell contains arginase which when released into plasma further dysregulates arginine metabolism. These data support the existence of a novel mechanism of human disease, hemolysis associated endothelial dysfunction, that potentially participates in the vasculopathy of iatrogenic and hereditary hemolytic conditions. In addition to providing an NO scavenging role in the physiological regulation of NO-dependent vasodilation, hemoglobin and the erythrocyte may deliver NO as the hemoglobin deoxygenates. Two mechanisms have been proposed to explain this principle: 1) Oxygen linked allosteric delivery of S-nitrosothiols from S-nitrosated hemoglobin (SNO-Hb), and 2) a nitrite reductase activity of deoxygenated hemoglobin that reduces nitrite to NO and vasodilates the human circulation along the physiological oxygen gradient. The later newly described role of hemoglobin as a nitrite reductase is discussed in the context of hypoxic vasodilation, blood flow regulation and oxygen sensing.

Key Words: SNO-Hb, hemoglobin, vasodilation, nitrite, nitric oxide, hemolysis, arginase

INTRODUCTION

Hypoxic vasodilation is a highly conserved physiological response required to match blood flow and oxygen delivery to tissue metabolic demand. This systemic response has been appreciated for more than 100 years since the initial description by Roy and Brown in 1879 (76). Feedback hypoxic vasodilation requires oxygen or pH sensing to detect an "error signal" in the normal relationship between delivered blood oxygen content and tissue oxygen consumption (90). This error signal leads to the feedback generation of vasodilatory effectors that increase blood flow to maintain the balance of oxygen delivery and oxygen consumption. In mammals such vasodilation occurs as the hemoglobin desaturates from 60 to 40%, around a partial pressure of oxygen ranging from 40-20 mm Hg (75). Recent measurements of microcirculatory oxygen tension and hemoglobin oxygen saturation suggest that this degree of deoxygenation occurs within the resistance arterioles, especially in the case of skeletal muscle (87). In other tissues, such as heart and brain, more oxygen is extracted within the capillary network. Work by Segal and Duling suggests that NO or ATP delivery to the capillary circulation produces retrograde intracellular propagation of a vasodilating signal to the precapillary resistance vessels (80-82). These data in aggregate suggest that the oxygen or pH sensor is responsive to tissue oxygen partial pressures of 20-40 mm Hg and hemoglobin saturations of 40-60% (around the hemoglobin P_{50}).

Despite the physiological appreciation of this conserved blood flow response to hypoxia, the identity of the oxygen sensor mechanism and the specific feedback vasodilators remains uncertain and controversial. Even the site of sensing remains unknown with oxygen sensing and vasodilation either occurring within the A3-A4 arterioles or in the capillary network with retrograde propagation of a vasodilating signal through endothelium to the precapillary resistance arterioles. A number of mediators have been considered, including adenosine, nitric oxide (NO), K_{ATP} channels, endothelium derived hyperpolarizing factor (candidates include CO, H_2O_2 or $ONOO^-$), and prostacyclin, however, blockade of many of these pathways fails to completely inhibit hypoxic vasodilation (90, 91). These studies suggest that the system is either intricate and overbuilt with multiple effectors or that other undiscovered pathways exist.

An alternative paradigm has been advanced since 1995: That hemoglobin per se is the oxygen sensor with the oxygen linked allosteric structural transition of the hemoglobin tetramer from the oxygenated conformation (relaxed or R state) to the deoxygenated conformation (tense or T state) signaling the release or generation of a vasodilating signal from the erythrocyte (12). The first such hypothesis suggested that this R-to-T transition produced a release of ATP from the erythrocyte, which by binding to purinergic receptors in endothelium resulted in vasodilation (8, 12, 24, 37). This mechanism is supported by the observation of increasing concentrations of ATP in venous blood following hypoxia, and the in vitro generation of ATP from hypoxic or acidic erythrocytes. Evidence for retrograde propogation of the ATP/purinergic receptor/eNOS signal from the capillaries to precapillary arterioles further supports this hypothesis (12). The details and experimental evidence supporting this hypothesis will be covered in detail by Dr. Sprague's contribution to this series.

The second two hypotheses suggest that hemoglobin deoxygenation results in NO (equivalent) release from the red blood cell and subsequent NO-dependent vasodilation, however, the proposed mechanisms are fundamentally different. The first prosposed mechanism is that S-nitrosated hemoglobin (SNO-Hb) releases S-nitrosothiols during hemoglobin deoxygenation with subsequent generation of NO and vasodilation (25, 26, 38, 86). The second proposed mechanism suggests that hemoglobin is an allosterically regulated nitrite reductase which reduces nitrite to NO by deoxyheme as hemoglobin deoxygenates (5, 56). The present review will briefly review the overall role of the erythrocyte in vascular NO homeostasis, the specific mechanistic challenges facing the SNO-Hb hypothesis and then summarize the mechanism and emerging data supporting the nitrite reductase hypothesis.

NITRIC OXIDE AS A PARACRINE AND ENDOCRINE VASODILATOR (Figure 1)

Nitric oxide is produced from endothelial NO synthase and participates in the regulation of basal blood vessel tone and vascular homeostasis (antiplatelet activity, modulation of oxidant stress, endothelial and smooth muscle proliferation and adhesion molecule expression) (15, 33, 34, 64, 65). NO is a paracrine signaling molecule as it is produced in endothelium and then diffuses to vicinal smooth muscle, binds avidly to the heme of soluble guanylyl cyclase which produces cGMP, activates cGMP dependent protein kinases ultimately leading to smooth muscle relaxation. NO that diffuses into the lumen of the blood vessel is expected to react at a nearly diffusion limited rate (10^7 $M^{-1}sec^{-1}$) with both oxy- and deoxyhemoglobin to form methemoglobin/nitrate and iron-nitrosyl-hemoglobin ($HbFe^{II}$-NO), respectively (62). These reactions limit the half life and diffusional distance of NO in blood (<2 millisecond half time) and maintain NO as a paracrine vasoregulator . The rapid irreversible nature of these NO-hemoglobin reactions and the massive concentration of hemoglobin in blood (10,000 μM heme) also suggest a great paradox in vascular biology: while we know that NO is a paracrine vasodilator, kinetic calculations suggest that all of the NO produced by endothelium should be inactivated by hemoglobin and the sphere of diffusion of NO should be extremely limited, i.e. diffusion to adjacent smooth muscle should be impossible (44).

However, we know that such diffusion is indeed possible, and the proposed solution to the paradox is illustrated in the central panel of Figure 1: during normal physiology the reaction of NO with hemoglobin is limited by compartmentalization of hemoglobin within the erythrocyte membrane (79). This compartmentalization of hemoglobin from endothelium creates two diffusional barriers: a cell free diffusion barrier along the endothelium in laminar flowing blood (3, 46) and an unstirred bulk diffusional barrier around the erythrocyte membrane (49). Additional studies suggest an intrinsic barrier within the membrane and submembrane protein matrix that further limits NO entry (29). Similar diffusional barriers modulate oxygen diffusion across the erythrocyte (4). Such barriers suggest a potential role for plasma enrichment in the microcirculation in NO homeostasis (the "Fahreus-Lindqvist" effect) and explain the morbidity and mortality of stroma-based blood substitutes and hemolytic disease (62, 73).

Hemolysis associated endothelial dysfunction and vasculopathy

Indeed, hemolytic diseases such as sickle cell disease and paroxysmal nocturnal hemoglobinuria are associated with relative hypertension (compared to the hypotension of non-hemolytic anemias) (74), pulmonary hypertension (19, 39), esophageal and smooth muscle dystonias during paroxysms of hemolysis (28), and recently, in the case of sickle cell disease, the characterization of a state of NO resistance (73). Vasodilation during infusions of NO donors (nitroprusside, nitroglycerin, NONOates) is blunted in patients with sickle cell disease (10, 73) and in transgenic mouse models of sickle cell disease (41, 42, 60), and this resistance to NO correlates with plasma hemoglobin levels (42, 73). Not only does cell free plasma hemoglobin released during hemolysis disrupt the normal diffusional barriers but may also extravate into the extracellular space and directly intercept NO diffusing between endothelium to smooth muscle (58, 62). In addition to the release of hemoglobin during hemolysis, the red blood cell also contains large quantities of arginase, such that hemolysis increases plasma levels of this enzyme and metabolizes arginine to ornithine, reducing the substrate for endothelial NO synthase (19, 55, 83). Impairment of endothelium-dependent vasodilation leads to a state of hemolysis associated endothelial dysfunction, and with chronic hemolysis, a progressive proliferative vasculopathy. It is increasingly clear that multiple systems have evolved to limit the toxicity of cell free plasma hemoglobin, including the high molecular weight haptoglobin system (prevents extravasation of hemoglobin and limits NO scavenging) (11, 57, 92), hemopexin, CD163 hemoglobin scavenger protein (which not only mediates haptoglobin-hemoglobin clearance but also upregulates IL-10 and hemeoxygenase 1) (69), and the hemeoxygenase 1/biliverdin reductase/p21 pathways which exert anti-inflammatory, anti-oxidant and anti-proliferative effects (1, 13, 59, 63, 77).

Endocrine properties of NO

In addition to a paracrine vasodilator function, there is increasing appreciation that NO may be stabilized by the formation of NO modified proteins, peptides and lipids, as well as by oxidation to the anion nitrite. The principle that NO may be thus stabilized in blood, and the inactivation reactions with hemoglobin thus limited, was first proposed by Loscalzo and Stamler. They hypothesized that NO (abstraction of an electron required) could form a covalent bond with cysteine residues on albumin to form S-nitrosated albumin (SNO-albumin) (78, 85). This paradigm was later extended by the Stamler group to S-nitrosated hemoglobin (SNO-Hb) (38). While this field is extremely controversial, largely secondary to major questions about the concentrations and importance of SNO-albumin and SNO-hemoglobin in the human circulation (reported values range from a few μM to undetectable, with more modern methodologies documenting levels of less than 10 nM) (18, 20, 50, 70, 71, 84, 92), it is likely that there are a number of intravascular species capable of endocrine vasodilation, including S-nitrosothiols (61, 85), nitrite (5), N-nitrosamines (27, 48, 70), iron-nitrosyls (18), and recently identified nitrated lipids (47). This review will briefly review the SNO-Hb hypothesis, the major challenges to this theory, and then focus on the role of nitrite in vasoregulation and hypoxic vasodilation.

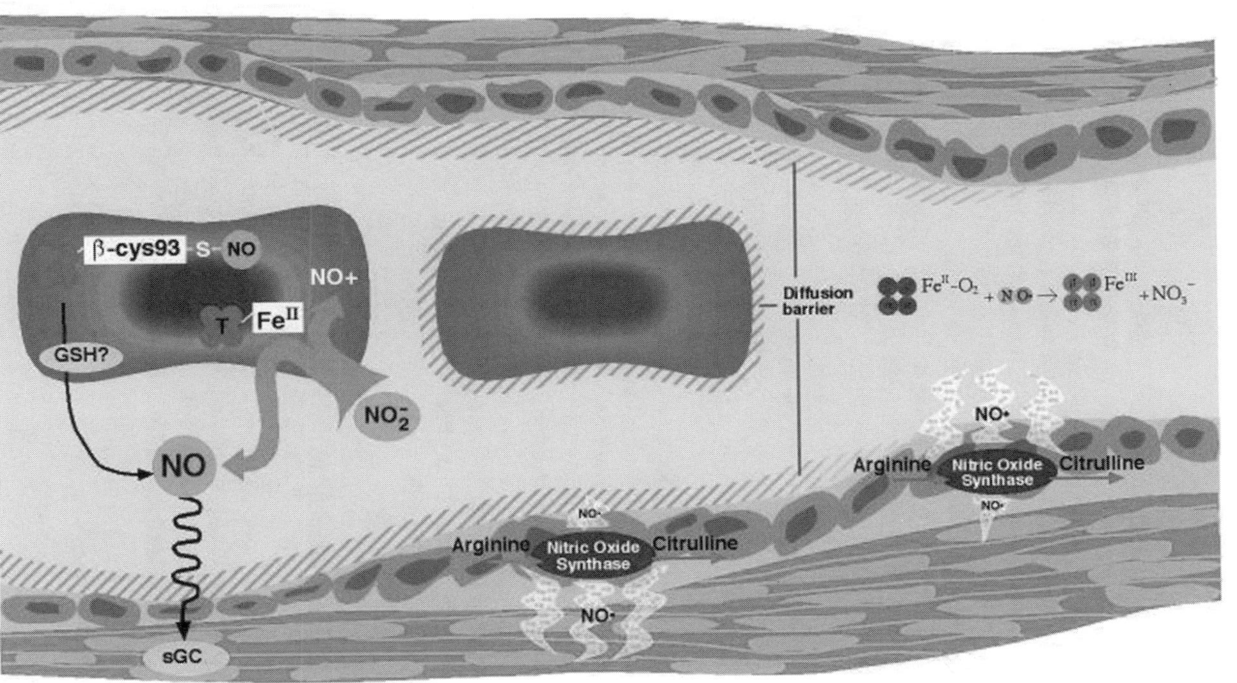

Figure 1. Endocrine, paracrine and autocrine properties of NO. Nitric oxide as a paracrine vasodilator (middle of figure), whose scavenging by hemoglobin is limited by the compartmentalization of hemoglobin within the intact erythrocyte. Nitric oxide as an endocrine vasodilator (left side of figure) being transported in blood as nitrite or an S-nitrosothiol. Nitric oxide as an autocrine vasodilator (right side of figure), whose diffusion is limited by scavenging by cell free plasma hemoglobin released during pathological hemolysis. Adapted with permission from: Schechter AN and Gladwin MT. Hemoglobin and the paracrine and endocrine functions of nitric oxide. *N Engl J Med* 348: 1483-1485, 2003.

The SNO-hemoglobin hypothesis

Based on observed artery-to-vein gradients in SNO-Hb in the rat and the ability of S-nitrosated hemoglobin to vasodilate aortic ring preparations and the rat circulation it was proposed that NO represented a third gas molecule in the human respiratory cycle (26, 38, 86). A complicated mechanism was proposed suggesting that NO produced by the endothelium would react with a vacant heme on oxygenated hemoglobin (three $HbFe^{II}$-O_2 per tetramer and one $HbFe^{II}$-NO per tetramer) and thus trap and "preserve" the NO on hemoglobin (25, 52). The NO would lose an electron (mechanism not demonstrated) and then migrate to the ß-globin chain cysteine 93 residue to form an S-nitrothiol bond. This SNO-Hb would then transfer the NO+ group by transnitrosation to the erythrocyte membrane anion exchange protein (AE1 or band 3) thiols followed by export of a yet to be identified intermediate species (called X-NO) (68). This would presumably be an S-nitrosothiol which would need to be reduced to NO to activate soluble guanylate cyclase.

While the principle was elegant, the mechanism has been severely challenged (Figure 2) (17). Multiple laboratories have now shown that NO does not bind preferentially to vacant hemes on oxygenated hemoglobin (cooperative NO binding is not observed) (18, 30, 31, 40, 96). The required transfer of NO from the heme to the cysteine has not been observed using electron paramagnetic resonance spectroscopy (unless large concentrations of nitrite contaminate the experiment) (95). Importantly, this transfer requires the abstraction of an electron from the NO and a mechanism for this reduction has not been determined over the last 9 years. Finally, multiple groups have been unable to reproduce the levels of both SNO-albumin or SNO-hemoglobin reported by the Stamler group, and the artery-to-vein gradients have not been detected in the human circulation by other groups (18, 22, 50, 61, 70-72, 95). Finally, SNO-Hb is not stable in the reductive intra-erythrocytic environment at 37°C and is rapidly reduced by intracellular glutathione and ferrous heme (6, 7, 22). Thus the mechanism for formation, levels in the circulation, and oxygen dependent delivery of the S-NO group have all been challenged.

While our work suggests that SNO-Hb does not participate in the process of hypoxic vasodilation in the basal human circulation, we do find support for the principle that the red blood cell and hemoglobin participates in oxygen dependent NO homeostasis. Rather than hemoglobin being a reservoir of S-nitrosated hemoglobin, we find that hemoglobin is an enzymatic nitrite reductase with a deoxyheme-nitrite reaction generating NO as hemoglobin deoxygenates within the circulation (5, 16).

Vasoactivity of nitrite in the human circulation

While large doses of nitrite given as an antidote for cyanide poisoning clearly produces hypotension in humans (94), the large concentrations of nitrite required to vasodilate aortic ring bioassay systems led to a dismissal of nitrite as a vasoactive reservoir of NO in the circulation. Indeed, nitrite at concentrations exceeding 100 μM was shown to vasodilate aortic ring bioassays by Furchgott as far back as 1952, and shown by Murad and Ignarro to activate guanylate cyclase in the mid 1970's and early 1980's (14, 35, 36, 54). However, studies published by Laur and colleagues suggested that nitrite had no intrinsic vasodilator activity and led to a premature dismissal of nitrite as a physiological vasodilator (45, 51, 67).

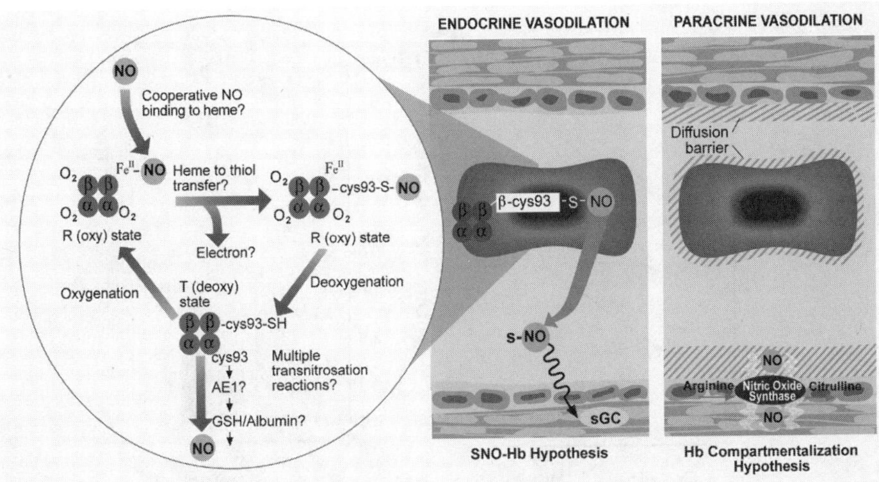

Figure 2. Mechanism proposed for SNO-hemoglobin mediated hypoxic vasodilation (left panel). A complicated mechanism was proposed suggesting that NO produced by the endothelium would react with a vacant heme on oxygenated hemoglobin (three $HbFe^{II}$-O_2 per tetramer and one $HbFe^{II}$-NO per tetramer) and thus trap and "preserve" the NO on hemoglobin (25, 52). The NO would lose an electron (mechanism not demonstrated) and then migrate to the ß-globin chain cysteine 93 residue to form an S-nitrothiol bond. This SNO-Hb would then transfer the NO+ group by transnitrosation to the erythrocyte membrane anion exchange protein (AE1 or band 3) thiols followed by export of a yet to be identified intermediate species (called X-NO) (68). This would presumably be an S-nitrosothiol which would need to be reduced to NO to activate soluble guanylate cyclase. The question marks reflect specific challenges to the mechanism discussed in the text. Figure reproduced with permission from: Gladwin MT, Lancaster JR, Freeman BA, and Schechter AN. Nitric oxide's reactions with hemoglobin: a view through the SNO-storm. *Nat Med* 9: 496-500, 2003.

Despite the apparent lack of bioactivity of nitrite in these more recent studies, we observed arterial-to-vein gradients in nitrite across the human forearm, with increased consumption of nitrite during exercise stress, suggesting that nitrite was metabolized across the peripheral circulation (21). We therefore hypothesized that nitrite might be reduced to NO during hypoxic and acidic stress by the actions of xanthine oxidoreductase (23, 53) or by acidic reduction (disproportionation) (97). To test this we infused nitrite into the forearm brachial artery of 18 healthy volunteers and to our surprise, observed substantial vasodilation, even without exercise stress. Nitrite was remarkable potent, increasing blood flow by 170% at 200 μM and by 22% at 2.5 μM. Even levels of 900 nM vasodilated during exercise stress with concurrent NO synthase inhibition with L-NMMA (Figure 3) (5). A vasodilation at these concentrations under normal physiological non-stress conditions was inconsistent with a mechanism of reduction by xanthine oxidoreductase or disproportionation, as both of these pathways require very low pH and extreme hypoxia, thus suggesting an alternative mechanism of nitrite bioactivation. Additional studies have been published in the last year confirming the vasodilating effects of nitrite (32, 43, 88, 89, 93).

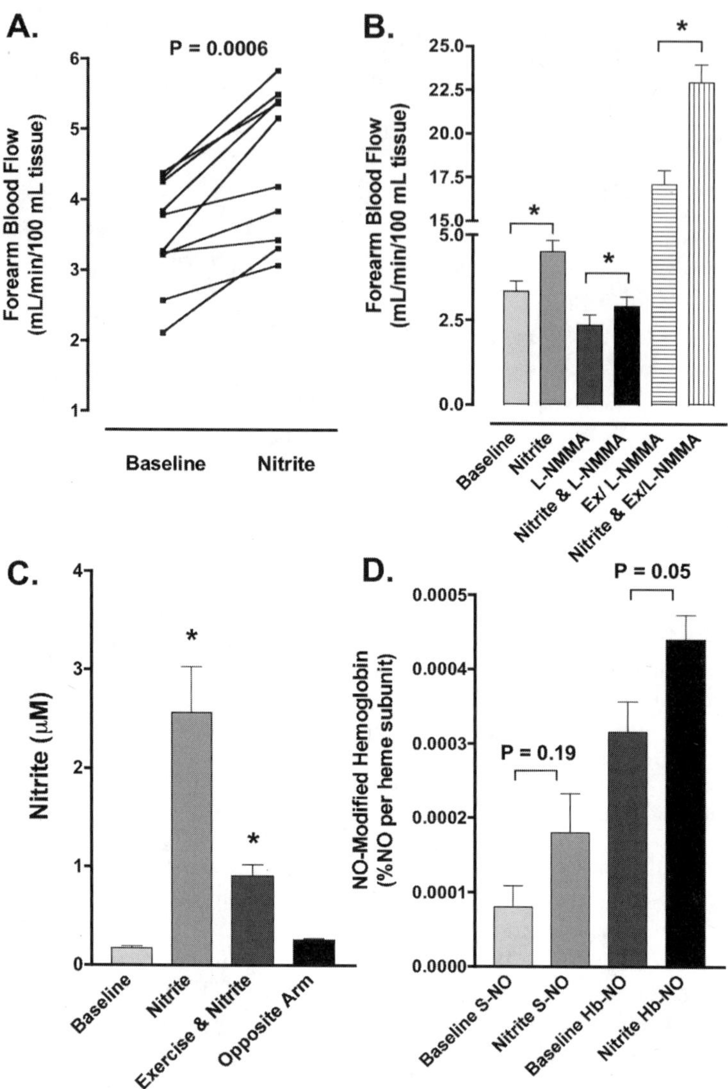

Figure 3. Nitrite vasodilates the human circulation at near physiological concentrations. Panel A: Nitrite infusion increases blood flow 22% in ten normal volunteers. Panel B: Increase in blood flow occurs at rest, during exercise and during exercise with NO synthase inhibition and L-NMMA infusion. Panel C: Blood flow increases with regional nitrite concentrations of 2.5 μM at rest and 900 nM during exercise. Panel D: Blood flow increases during nitrite infusions are associated with the formation of iron-nitrosyl-hemoglobin from artery-to-vein. Figure reproduced with permission from Cosby K, Partovi KS, Crawford JH, Patel RP, Reiter CD, Martyr S, Yang BK, Waclawiw MA, Zalos G, Xu X, Huang KT, Shields H, Kim-Shapiro DB, Schechter AN, Cannon RO, and Gladwin MT. Nitrite reduction to nitric oxide by deoxyhemoglobin vasodilates the human circulation. *Nat Med* 9: 1498-1505, 2003.

Hemoglobin as an allosterically and electronically regulated nitrite reductase

During nitrite infusions into the brachial artery we observed the artery-to-venous formation of iron-nitrosyl-hemoglobin ($HbFe^{II}$-NO) suggesting that nitrite was being reduced to NO rapidly within one half-circulatory time (5). An analysis of the iron-nitrosyl-hemoglobin levels during all experimental conditions revealed a striking inverse correlation with oxyhemoglobin saturation, i.e. as hemoglobin deoxygenated more NO formed. These physiological observations were consistent with a reaction between nitrite and deoxyhemoglobin to form NO as described by Doyle and colleagues in 1981 (9):

$$NO_2^- + HbFe^{II} \text{ (deoxyhemoglobin) } + H^+ \rightarrow NO \text{ (nitric oxide) } + HbFe^{III} + OH^-$$

Much of the formed NO is then captured as iron nitrosyl-hemoglobin ($HbFe^{II}$-NO) on viscinal hemes and measured as a "dosimeter" of NO production in venous blood:

$$NO + HbFe^{II} \text{ (deoxyhemoglobin) } \rightarrow HbFe^{II}\text{-NO (iron-nitrosyl-hemoglobin)}$$

Consider the potential physiological implications of this simple equation. The reaction requires deoxyhemoglobin and a proton, providing oxygen and pH sensor chemistry, and generates NO, a potent vasodilator. Methemoglobin formed during the reaction will not autocapture and inactivate the NO formed. In additional experiments we found that nitrite, red cells (or hemoglobin), and hypoxia were required for in vitro hypoxic vasodilation of rat aortic rings. Indeed, in the presence of hypoxia and erythrocytes (conditions never tested in historical aortic ring bioassay studies) nitrite now vasodilated aortic rings at physiological concentrations of 200-500 nM (Figure 4) (5).

Using an in vitro aortic ring bioassay systems designed by the Patel lab to simultaneously measure vessel force tension and oxygen tension, we find that vasodilation is measureably potentiated by as low as 200 nM nitrite under hypoxic conditions (5). Importantly, these studies reveal that nitrite-red blood cell dependent vasodilation is initiated at an oxygen tension around the intrinsic hemoglobin P_{50} (PaO_2 of 40 mm Hg for rat erythrocytes and 30 mm Hg for human erythrocytes). In ongoing unpublished work from four laboratories (the Gladwin, Patel, Kim-Shapiro, and Hogg groups) we have now found that this vasodilation occurs as hemoglobin unloads oxygen to 50% saturation, and that this vasodilation is mediated by a maximal nitrite reductase activity of hemoglobin allosterically linked to its intrinsic P_{50}. This maximal reductase activity is allosterically regulated as oxygen binding to one heme decreases the redox potential of the other hemes in the tetramer, thus increasing the ability of the hemes to donate an electron and reduce nitrite. An ideal balance of available deoxyhemes for nitrite binding and oxyhemes - required to lower redox potential of the vacant hemes - is met at the 50% hemoglobin saturation (the P_{50}). Indeed the measured rate of nitrite reduction by hemoglobin is maximal at a hemoglobin-oxygen saturation between 40-60%. Such a maximal reductase activty at P_{50} is biochemically consistent with a role in hypoxic vasodilation because physiological studies demontrate an onset of hypoxic vasodilation at 40-60% hemoglobin oxygen saturation (75).

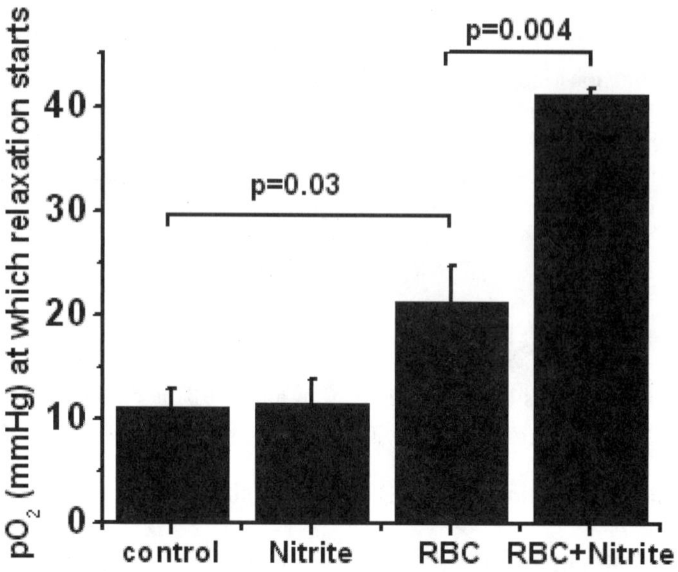

Figure 4. In the presence of hypoxia and erythrocytes nitrite vasodilates aortic rings at a PaO_2 of 30-40 mm Hg. Using an in vitro aortic ring bioassay system designed by the Patel laboratory to simultaneously measure vessel force tension and oxygen tension, we find that vasodilation is measureably potentiated by nitrite under hypoxic conditions. While control rat aortic rings and nitrite alone vasodilate at an oxygen tension of approximately 10 mm Hg, nitrite and red blood cells vasodilate at an oxygen tension around the intrinsic hemoglobin P_{50} (PaO_2 of 40 mm Hg for rat erythrocytes as shown in this figure and 30 mm Hg for human erythrocytes - data not shown). This experiment utilizes 2 μM nitrite and 0.3% red cell hematocrit. Figure based on data from Cosby K, Partovi KS, Crawford JH, Patel RP, Reiter CD, Martyr S, Yang BK, Waclawiw MA, Zalos G, Xu X, Huang KT, Shields H, Kim-Shapiro DB, Schechter AN, Cannon RO, and Gladwin MT. Nitrite reduction to nitric oxide by deoxyhemoglobin vasodilates the human circulation. *Nat Med* 9: 1498-1505, 2003.

INTEGRATED BIOCHEMICAL PHYSIOLOGY

Nitrite appears to fit requirements for a physiological mediator of hypoxic vasodilation as it maximally reacts with hemoglobin at 40-60% hemoglobin saturation, an oxygen tension (20-40 mm Hg) significantly higher than that required for SNO-hemoglobin deoxygenation, i.e. cysteine 93 liganded hemoglobins have very high oxygen affinities (2, 66). In the normal skeletal muscle circulation oxygen tension decreases from the A1 caliber arterioles (100 μmeter diameter) to the A4 caliber arterioles (20 μmeter diameter) to values as low as 20 mm Hg prior to the capillary circulation (87). These data suggest that much of the oxygen delivery occurs within the arterioles allowing for spacially linked oxygen delivery and vasomotor control. Additional mechanisms suggest that NO or ATP delivery to the capillary circulation produces retrograde intracellular propagation of vasodilating

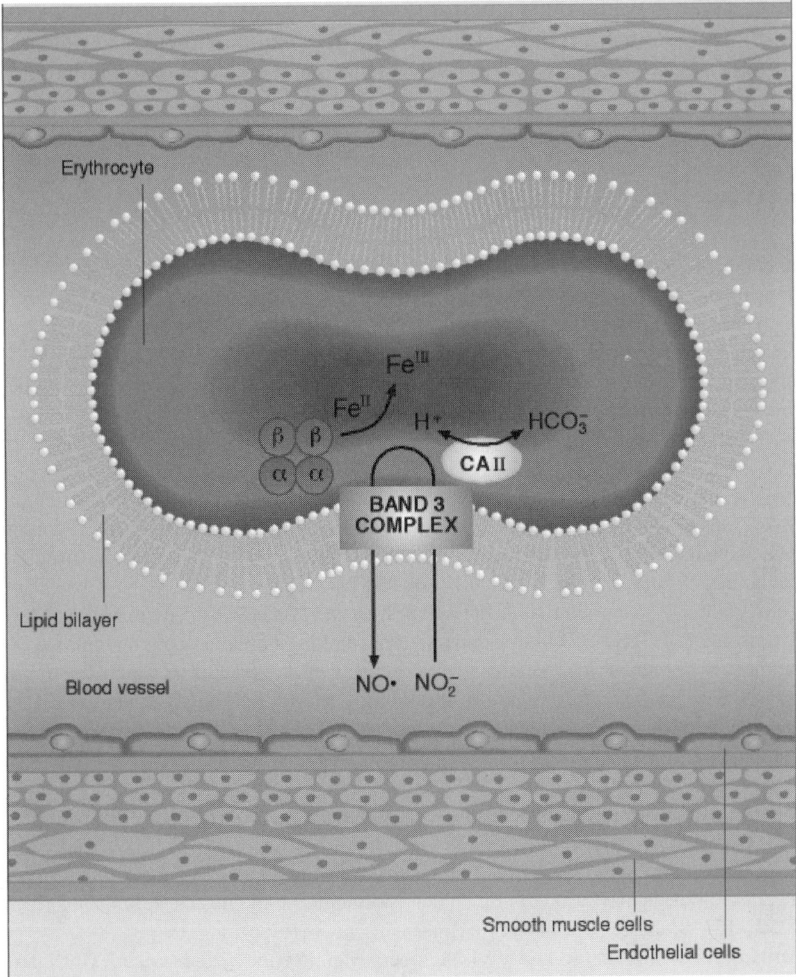

Figure 5. Putative nitrite reductase metabolon. We speculate that the erythrocyte membrane proteins provide a potential nitrite reductase metabolon function composed of deoxyhemoglobin and methemoglobin, anion exchange protein, carbonic anhydrase, aquaporin and Rh channels. Such as system would concentrate nitrite, proton, deoxyheme and highly hydrophobic channels at the membrane complex. Reproduced with permission from: Gladwin MT, Crawford JH, and Patel RP. The biochemistry of nitric oxide, nitrite, and hemoglobin: role in blood flow regulation. *Free Radic Biol Med* 36: 707-717, 2004.

signal to the precapillary resistance vessels (80-82). Thus a maximal nitrite reductase activity at the hemoglobin P_{50} appears ideal for oxygen sensing and hypoxic vasodilation as this allosteric point iş thermally, chemically and electronically responsive to physiologically relevant tissue metabolic stress. We speculate that the erythrocyte membrane proteins provide a potential nitrite reductase metabolon function composed of deoxyhemoglobin and methemoglobin, anion exchange protein, carbonic anhydrase, aquaporin and Rh channels

(16). Such as system would concentrate nitrite, proton, deoxyheme and highly hydrophobic channels at the membrane complex (Figure 5) (16). The lipophilicity and potency of NO (EC_{50} of only 1-5 nM) requires very little NO escape to regulate vasodilation, especially considering that flow is proportional to the radius to the fourth power.

REFERENCES

1. Baranano DE, Rao M, Ferris CD, and Snyder SH. Biliverdin reductase: a major physiologic cytoprotectant. *Proc Natl Acad Sci U S A* 99: 16093-16098, 2002.
2. Bonaventura C, Ferruzzi G, Tesh S, and Stevens RD. Effects of S-nitrosation on oxygen binding by normal and sickle cell hemoglobin. *J Biol Chem* 274: 24742-24748, 1999.
3. Butler AR, Megson IL, and Wright PG. Diffusion of nitric oxide and scavenging by blood in the vasculature. *Biochim Biophys Acta* 1425: 168-176., 1998.
4. Coin JT and Olson JS. The rate of oxygen uptake by human red blood cells. *J Biol Chem* 254: 1178-1190., 1979.
5. Cosby K, Partovi KS, Crawford JH, Patel RP, Reiter CD, Martyr S, Yang BK, Waclawiw MA, Zalos G, Xu X, Huang KT, Shields H, Kim-Shapiro DB, Schechter AN, Cannon RO, and Gladwin MT. Nitrite reduction to nitric oxide by deoxyhemoglobin vasodilates the human circulation. *Nat Med* 9: 1498-1505, 2003.
6. Deem S, Kim JU, Manjula BN, Acharya AS, Kerr ME, Patel RP, Gladwin MT, and Swenson ER. Effects of S-nitrosation and cross-linking of hemoglobin on hypoxic pulmonary vasoconstriction in isolated rat lungs. *Circ Res* 91: 626-632., 2002.
7. Deem S, Kim SS, Min JH, Eveland R, Moulding J, Martyr S, Wang X, Swenson ER, and Gladwin MT. Pulmonary vascular effects of red blood cells containing S-nitrosated hemoglobin. *Am J Physiol Heart Circ Physiol*, 2004.
8. Dietrich HH, Ellsworth ML, Sprague RS, and Dacey RG, Jr. Red blood cell regulation of microvascular tone through adenosine triphosphate. *Am J Physiol Heart Circ Physiol* 278: H1294-1298, 2000.
9. Doyle MP, Pickering RA, DeWeert TM, Hoekstra JW, and Pater D. Kinetics and mechanism of the oxidation of human deoxyhemoglobin by nitrites. *J Biol Chem* 256: 12393-12398, 1981.
10. Eberhardt RT, McMahon L, Duffy SJ, Steinberg MH, Perrine SP, Loscalzo J, Coffman JD, and Vita JA. Sickle cell anemia is associated with reduced nitric oxide bioactivity in peripheral conduit and resistance vessels. *Am J Hematol* 74: 104-111, 2003.
11. Edwards DH, Griffith TM, Ryley HC, and Henderson AH. Haptoglobin-haemoglobin complex in human plasma inhibits endothelium dependent relaxation: evidence that endothelium derived relaxing factor acts as a local autocoid. *Cardiovasc Res* 20: 549-556, 1986.
12. Ellsworth ML, Forrester T, Ellis CG, and Dietrich HH. The erythrocyte as a regulator of vascular tone. *Am J Physiol* 269: H2155-2161, 1995.
13. Ferris CD, Jaffrey SR, Sawa A, Takahashi M, Brady SD, Barrow RK, Tysoe SA, Wolosker H, Baranano DE, Dore S, Poss KD, and Snyder SH. Haem oxygenase-1 prevents cell death by regulating cellular iron. *Nat Cell Biol* 1: 152-157, 1999.
14. Furchgott RF and Bhadrakom S. Reactions of strips of rabbit aorta to epinephrine, isopropylarterenol, sodium nitrite and other drugs. *J Pharmacol Exp Ther* 108: 129-143, 1953.
15. Furchgott RF and Zawadzki JV. The obligatory role of endothelial cells in the relaxation of arterial smooth muscle by acetylcholine. *Nature* 288: 373-376, 1980.
16. Gladwin MT, Crawford JH, and Patel RP. The biochemistry of nitric oxide, nitrite, and

hemoglobin: role in blood flow regulation. *Free Radic Biol Med* 36: 707-717, 2004.
17. Gladwin MT, Lancaster JR, Freeman BA, and Schechter AN. Nitric oxide's reactions with hemoglobin: a view through the SNO-storm. *Nat Med* 9: 496-500, 2003.
18. Gladwin MT, Ognibene FP, Pannell LK, Nichols JS, Pease-Fye ME, Shelhamer JH, and Schechter AN. Relative role of heme nitrosylation and beta -cysteine 93 nitrosation in the transport and metabolism of nitric oxide by hemoglobin in the human circulation. *Proc Natl Acad Sci U S A* 97: 9943-9948, 2000.
19. Gladwin MT, Sachdev V, Jison ML, Shizukuda Y, Plehn JF, Minter K, Brown B, Coles WA, Nichols JS, Ernst I, Hunter LA, Blackwelder WC, Schechter AN, Rodgers GP, Castro O, and Ognibene FP. Pulmonary hypertension as a risk factor for death in patients with sickle cell disease. *N Engl J Med* 350: 886-895, 2004.
20. Gladwin MT and Schechter AN. NO contest: nitrite versus S-nitroso-hemoglobin. *Circ Res* 94: 851-855, 2004.
21. Gladwin MT, Shelhamer JH, Schechter AN, Pease-Fye ME, Waclawiw MA, Panza JA, Ognibene FP, and Cannon RO, 3rd. Role of circulating nitrite and S-nitrosohemoglobin in the regulation of regional blood flow in humans. *Proc Natl Acad Sci U S A* 97: 11482-11487, 2000.
22. Gladwin MT, Wang X, Reiter CD, Yang BK, Vivas EX, Bonaventura C, and Schechter AN. S-nitrosohemoglobin is unstable in the reductive red cell environment and lacks O2/NO-linked allosteric function. *J Biol Chem* 21: 21, 2002.
23. Godber BL, Doel JJ, Sapkota GP, Blake DR, Stevens CR, Eisenthal R, and Harrison R. Reduction of nitrite to nitric oxide catalyzed by xanthine oxidoreductase. *J Biol Chem* 275: 7757-7763, 2000.
24. Gonzalez-Alonso J, Olsen DB, and Saltin B. Erythrocyte and the regulation of human skeletal muscle blood flow and oxygen delivery: role of circulating ATP. *Circ Res* 91: 1046-1055, 2002.
25. Gow AJ, Luchsinger BP, Pawloski JR, Singel DJ, and Stamler JS. The oxyhemoglobin reaction of nitric oxide. *Proc Natl Acad Sci U S A* 96: 9027-9032, 1999.
26. Gow AJ and Stamler JS. Reactions between nitric oxide and haemoglobin under physiological conditions. *Nature* 391: 169-173, 1998.
27. Gruetter CA, Barry BK, McNamara DB, Kadowitz PJ, and Ignarro LJ. Coronary arterial relaxation and guanylate cyclase activation by cigarette smoke, N'-nitrosonornicotine and nitric oxide. *J Pharmacol Exp Ther* 214: 9-15, 1980.
28. Hillmen P, Hall C, Marsh JC, Elebute M, Bombara MP, Petro BE, Cullen MJ, Richards SJ, Rollins SA, Mojcik CF, and Rother RP. Effect of eculizumab on hemolysis and transfusion requirements in patients with paroxysmal nocturnal hemoglobinuria. *N Engl J Med* 350: 552-559, 2004.
29. Huang KT, Han TH, Hyduke DR, Vaughn MW, Van Herle H, Hein TW, Zhang C, Kuo L, and Liao JC. Modulation of nitric oxide bioavailability by erythrocytes. *Proc Natl Acad Sci U S A* 98: 11771-11776., 2001.
30. Huang Z, Louderback JG, Goyal M, Azizi F, King SB, and Kim-Shapiro DB. Nitric oxide binding to oxygenated hemoglobin under physiological conditions. *Biochim Biophys Acta* 1568: 252-260., 2001.
31. Huang Z, Ucer KB, Murphy T, Williams RT, King SB, and Kim-Shapiro DB. Kinetics of nitric oxide binding to R-state hemoglobin. *Biochem Biophys Res Commun* 292: 812-818., 2002.
32. Hunter CJ, Dejam A, Blood AB, Shields H, Kim-Shapiro DB, Machado RF, Tarekegn S, Mulla N, Hopper AO, Schechter AN, Power GG, and Gladwin MT. Inhaled nebulized nitrite is a hypoxia-sensitive NO-dependent selective pulmonary vasodilator. *Nat Med* 10: 1122-1127, 2004.
33. Ignarro LJ, Buga GM, Wood KS, Byrns RE, and Chaudhuri G. Endothelium-derived

relaxing factor produced and released from artery and vein is nitric oxide. *Proc Natl Acad Sci U S A* 84: 9265-9269., 1987.
34. Ignarro LJ, Byrns RE, Buga GM, and Wood KS. Endothelium-derived relaxing factor from pulmonary artery and vein possesses pharmacologic and chemical properties identical to those of nitric oxide radical. *Circ Res* 61: 866-879, 1987.
35. Ignarro LJ and Gruetter CA. Requirement of thiols for activation of coronary arterial guanylate cyclase by glyceryl trinitrate and sodium nitrite: possible involvement of S-nitrosothiols. *Biochim Biophys Acta* 631: 221-231., 1980.
36. Ignarro LJ, Lippton H, Edwards JC, Baricos WH, Hyman AL, Kadowitz PJ, and Gruetter CA. Mechanism of vascular smooth muscle relaxation by organic nitrates, nitrites, nitroprusside and nitric oxide: evidence for the involvement of S-nitrosothiols as active intermediates. *J Pharmacol Exp Ther* 218: 739-749, 1981.
37. Jagger JE, Bateman RM, Ellsworth ML, and Ellis CG. Role of erythrocyte in regulating local O2 delivery mediated by hemoglobin oxygenation. *Am J Physiol Heart Circ Physiol* 280: H2833-2839, 2001.
38. Jia L, Bonaventura C, Bonaventura J, and Stamler JS. S-nitrosohaemoglobin: a dynamic activity of blood involved in vascular control (see comments). *Nature* 380: 221-226, 1996.
39. Jison ML and Gladwin MT. Hemolytic anemia-associated pulmonary hypertension of sickle cell disease and the nitric oxide/arginine pathway. *Am J Respir Crit Care Med* 168: 3-4, 2003.
40. Joshi MS, Ferguson TB, Jr., Han TH, Hyduke DR, Liao JC, Rassaf T, Bryan N, Feelisch M, and Lancaster JR, Jr. Nitric oxide is consumed, rather than conserved, by reaction with oxyhemoglobin under physiological conditions. *Proc Natl Acad Sci U S A* 17: 17, 2002.
41. Kaul DK, Liu XD, Chang HY, Nagel RL, and Fabry ME. Effect of fetal hemoglobin on microvascular regulation in sickle transgenic-knockout mice. *J Clin Invest* 114: 1136-1145, 2004.
42. Kaul DK, Liu XD, Fabry ME, and Nagel RL. Impaired nitric oxide-mediated vasodilation in transgenic sickle mouse. *Am J Physiol Heart Circ Physiol* 278: H1799-1806., 2000.
43. Kozlov AV, Costantino G, Sobhian B, Szalay L, Umar F, Nohl H, Bahrami S, and RedlH. Mechanisms of vasodilatation induced by nitrite instillation in intestinal lumen: possible role of hemoglobin. *Antioxid Redox Signal* 7: 515-521, 2005.
44. Lancaster JR, Jr. A tutorial on the diffusibility and reactivity of free nitric oxide. *Nitric Oxide* 1: 18-30., 1997.
45. Lauer T, Preik M, Rassaf T, Strauer BE, Deussen A, Feelisch M, and Kelm M. Plasma nitrite rather than nitrate reflects regional endothelial nitric oxide synthase activity but lacks intrinsic vasodilator action. *Proc Natl Acad Sci U S A* 98: 12814-12819., 2001.
46. Liao JC, Hein TW, Vaughn MW, Huang KT, and Kuo L. Intravascular flow decreases erythrocyte consumption of nitric oxide. *Proc Natl Acad Sci U S A* 96: 8757-8761., 1999.
47. Lim DG, Sweeney S, Bloodsworth A, White CR, Chumley PH, Krishna NR, Schopfer F, O'Donnell VB, Eiserich JP, and Freeman BA. Nitrolinoleate, a nitric oxide-derived mediator of cell function: synthesis, characterization, and vasomotor activity. *Proc Natl Acad Sci U S A* 99: 15941-15946, 2002.
48. Lippton HL, Gruetter CA, Ignarro LJ, Meyer RL, and Kadowitz PJ. Vasodilator actions of several N-nitroso compounds. *Can J Physiol Pharmacol* 60: 68-75, 1982.
49. Liu X, Miller MJ, Joshi MS, Sadowska-Krowicka H, Clark DA, and Lancaster JR, Jr. Diffusion-limited reaction of free nitric oxide with erythrocytes. *J Biol Chem* 273: 18709-18713, 1998.
50. Marley R, Feelisch M, Holt S, and Moore K. A chemiluminescense-based assay for S-nitrosoalbumin and other plasma S- nitrosothiols. *Free Radic Res* 32: 1-9, 2000.

51. McMahon TJ. Hemoglobin and nitric oxide. *N Engl J Med* 349: 402-405; author reply 402-405, 2003.
52. McMahon TJ, Moon RE, Luschinger BP, Carraway MS, Stone AE, Stolp BW, Gow AJ, Pawloski JR, Watke P, Singel DJ, Piantadosi CA, and Stamler JS. Nitric oxide in the human respiratory cycle. *Nat Med* 3: 3, 2002.
53. Millar TM, Stevens CR, Benjamin N, Eisenthal R, Harrison R, and Blake DR. Xanthine oxidoreductase catalyses the reduction of nitrates and nitrite to nitric oxide under hypoxic conditions. *FEBS Lett* 427: 225-228, 1998.
54. Mittal CK, Arnold WP, and Murad F. Characterization of protein inhibitors of guanylate cyclase activation from rat heart and bovine lung. *J Biol Chem* 253: 1266-1271, 1978.
55. Morris CR, Morris SM, Hagar W, Van Warmerdam J, Claster S, Kepka-Lenhart D, Machado L, Kuypers FA, and Vichinsky EP. Arginine Therapy: A New Treatment for Pulmonary Hypertension in Sickle Cell Disease? *Am J Respir Crit Care Med*, 2003.
56. Nagababu E, Ramasamy S, Abernethy DR, and Rifkind JM. Active nitric oxide produced in the red cell under hypoxic conditions by deoxyhemoglobin mediated nitrite reduction. *J Biol Chem*, 2003.
57. Nakai K, Ohta T, Sakuma I, Akama K, Kobayashi Y, Tokuyama S, Kitabatake A, Nakazato Y, Takahashi TA, and Sadayoshi S. Inhibition of endothelium-dependent relaxation by hemoglobin in rabbit aortic strips: comparison between acellular hemoglobin derivatives and cellular hemoglobins. *J Cardiovasc Pharmacol* 28: 115-123, 1996.
58. Nakai K, Sakuma I, Ohta T, Ando J, Kitabatake A, Nakazato Y, and Takahashi TA. Permeability characteristics of hemoglobin derivatives across cultured endothelial cell monolayers. *J Lab Clin Med* 132: 313-319, 1998.
59. Nath KA, Katusic ZS, and Gladwin MT. The perfusion paradox and vascular instability in sickle cell disease. *Microcirculation* 11: 179-193, 2004.
60. Nath KA, Shah V, Haggard JJ, Croatt AJ, Smith LA, Hebbel RP, and Katusic ZS. Mechanisms of vascular instability in a transgenic mouse model of sickle cell disease. *Am J Physiol Regul Integr Comp Physiol* 279: R1949-1955., 2000.
61. Ng ES, Jourd'heuil D, McCord JM, Hernandez D, Yasui M, Knight D, and Kubes P. Enhanced S-nitroso-albumin formation from inhaled NO during ischemia/reperfusion. *Circ Res* 94: 559-565, 2004.
62. Olson JS, Foley EW, Rogge C, Tsai AL, Doyle MP, and Lemon DD. No scavenging and the hypertensive effect of hemoglobin-based blood substitutes. *Free Radic Biol Med* 36: 685-697, 2004.
63. Otterbein LE, Bach FH, Alam J, Soares M, Tao Lu H, Wysk M, Davis RJ, Flavell RA, and Choi AM. Carbon monoxide has anti-inflammatory effects involving the mitogen-activated protein kinase pathway. *Nat Med* 6: 422-428, 2000.
64. Palmer RM, Ashton DS, and Moncada S. Vascular endothelial cells synthesize nitric oxide from L-arginine. *Nature* 333: 664-666, 1988.
65. Palmer RM, Ferrige AG, and Moncada S. Nitric oxide release accounts for the biological activity of endothelium-derived relaxing factor. *Nature* 327: 524-526, 1987.
66. Patel RP, Hogg N, Spencer NY, Kalyanaraman B, Matalon S, and Darley-Usmar VM. Biochemical Characterization of Human S-Nitrosohemoglobin. Effects on oxygen binding and transnitrosation. *J Biol Chem* 274: 15487-15492, 1999.
67. Pawloski JR. Hemoglobin and nitric oxide. *N Engl J Med* 349: 402-405; author reply 402-405, 2003.
68. Pawloski JR, Hess DT, and Stamler JS. Export by red blood cells of nitric oxide bioactivity. *Nature* 409: 622-626., 2001.
69. Philippidis P, Mason JC, Evans BJ, Nadra I, Taylor KM, Haskard DO, and Landis RC. Hemoglobin Scavenger Receptor CD163 Mediates Interleukin-10 Release and Heme Oxygenase-1 Synthesis. Antiinflammatory Monocyte-Macrophage Responses In Vitro, in

Resolving Skin Blisters In Vivo, and After Cardiopulmonary Bypass Surgery. *Circ Res*, 2003.

70. Rassaf T, Bryan NS, Kelm M, and Feelisch M. Concomitant presence of N-nitroso and S-nitroso proteins in human plasma. *Free Radic Biol Med* 33: 1590-1596., 2002.
71. Rassaf T, Bryan NS, Maloney RE, Specian V, Kelm M, Kalyanaraman B, Rodriguez J, and Feelisch M. NO adducts in mammalian red blood cells: too much or too little? *Nat Med* 9: 481-483, 2003.
72. Rassaf T, Feelisch M, and Kelm M. Circulating no pool: assessment of nitrite and nitroso species in blood and tissues. *Free Radic Biol Med* 36: 413-422, 2004.
73. Reiter CD, Wang X, Tanus-Santos JE, Hogg N, Cannon RO, Schechter AN, and Gladwin MT. Cell-free hemoglobin limits nitric oxide bioavailability in sickle-cell disease. *Nat Med* 8: 1383-1389., 2002.
74. Rodgers GP, Walker EC, and Podgor MJ. Is "relative" hypertension a risk factor for vaso-occlusive complications in sickle cell disease? *Am J Med Sci* 305: 150-156, 1993.
75. Ross JM, Fairchild HM, Weldy J, and Guyton AC. Autoregulation of blood flow by oxygen lack. *Am J Physiol* 202: 21-24, 1962.
76. Roy CS, and Brown, J.G. *Journal of Physiology, London* 2: 323, 1879.
77. Ryter SW, Otterbein LE, Morse D, and Choi AM. Heme oxygenase/carbon monoxide signaling pathways: regulation and functional significance. *Mol Cell Biochem* 234-235: 249-263, 2002.
78. Scharfstein JS, Keaney JF, Jr., Slivka A, Welch GN, Vita JA, Stamler JS, and Loscalzo J. In vivo transfer of nitric oxide between a plasma protein-bound reservoir and low molecular weight thiols. *J Clin Invest* 94: 1432-1439, 1994.
79. Schechter AN and Gladwin MT. Hemoglobin and the paracrine and endocrine functions of nitric oxide. *N Engl J Med* 348: 1483-1485, 2003.
80. Segal SS and Duling BR. Communication between feed arteries and microvessels in hamster striated muscle: segmental vascular responses are functionally coordinated. *Circ Res* 59: 283-290, 1986.
81. Segal SS and Duling BR. Conduction of vasomotor responses in arterioles: a role for cell-to-cell coupling? *Am J Physiol* 256: H838-845, 1989.
82. Segal SS and Duling BR. Flow control among microvessels coordinated by intercellular conduction. *Science* 234: 868-870, 1986.
83. Spector EB, Rice SC, Kern RM, Hendrickson R, and Cederbaum SD. Comparison of arginase activity in red blood cells of lower mammals, primates, and man: evolution to high activity in primates. *Am J Hum Genet* 37: 1138-1145, 1985.
84. Stamler JS. S-nitrosothiols in the blood: roles, amounts, and methods of analysis. *Circ Res* 94: 414-417, 2004.
85. Stamler JS, Jaraki O, Osborne J, Simon DI, Keaney J, Vita J, Singel D, Valeri CR, and Loscalzo J. Nitric oxide circulates in mammalian plasma primarily as an S-nitroso adduct of serum albumin. *Proc Natl Acad Sci U S A* 89: 7674-7677, 1992.
86. Stamler JS, Jia L, Eu JP, McMahon TJ, Demchenko IT, Bonaventura J, Gernert K, and Piantadosi CA. Blood flow regulation by S-nitrosohemoglobin in the physiological oxygen gradient. *Science* 276: 2034-2037, 1997.
87. Tsai AG, Johnson PC, and Intaglietta M. Oxygen gradients in the microcirculation. *Physiol Rev* 83: 933-963, 2003.
88. Tsuchiya K, Kanematsu Y, Yoshizumi M, Ohnishi H, Kirima K, Izawa Y, Shikishima M, Ishida T, Kondo S, Kagami S, Takiguchi Y, and Tamaki T. Nitrite is an alternative source of NO in vivo. *Am J Physiol Heart Circ Physiol*, 2004.
89. Tsuchiya K, Takiguchi Y, Okamoto M, Izawa Y, Kanematsu Y, Yoshizumi M, and Tamaki T. Malfunction of vascular control in lifestyle-related diseases: formation of systemic hemoglobin-nitric oxide complex (HbNO) from dietary nitrite. *J Pharmacol Sci* 96: 395-

400, 2004.
90. Tune JD, Gorman MW, and Feigl EO. Matching coronary blood flow to myocardial oxygen consumption. *J Appl Physiol* 97: 404-415, 2004.
91. Tune JD, Richmond KN, Gorman MW, and Feigl EO. K(ATP)(+) channels, nitric oxide, and adenosine are not required for local metabolic coronary vasodilation. *Am J Physiol Heart Circ Physiol* 280: H868-875, 2001.
92. Wang X, Tanus-Santos JE, Reiter CD, Dejam A, Shiva S, Smith RD, Hogg N, and Gladwin MT. Biological activity of nitric oxide in the plasmatic compartment. *Proc Natl Acad Sci U S A* 101: 11477-11482, 2004.
93. Webb A, Bond R, McLean P, Uppal R, Benjamin N, and Ahluwalia A. Reduction of nitrite to nitric oxide during ischemia protects against myocardial ischemia-reperfusion damage. *Proc Natl Acad Sci U S A* 101: 13683-13688, 2004.
94. Weiss S, Wilkins, R.W., and Haynes F.W. The nature of circulatory collapse induced by sodium nitrite. *Journal of Clinical Investigation* 16: 73-84, 1937.
95. Xu X, Cho M, Spencer NY, Patel N, Huang Z, Shields H, King SB, Gladwin MT, Hogg N, and Kim-Shapiro DB. Measurements of nitric oxide on the heme iron and beta-93 thiol of human hemoglobin during cycles of oxygenation and deoxygenation. *Proc Natl Acad Sci U S A* 100: 11303-11308, 2003.
96. Zhang Y and Hogg N. Mixing artifacts from the bolus addition of nitric oxide to oxymyoglobin: implications for S-nitrosothiol formation. *Free Radic Biol Med* 32: 1212-1219., 2002.
97. Zweier JL, Wang P, Samouilov A, and Kuppusamy P. Enzyme-independent formation of nitric oxide in biological tissues (see comments). *Nat Med* 1: 804-809, 1995.

Chapter 18

EXPRESSION OF THE HETEROTRIMERIC G PROTEIN Gi AND ATP RELEASE ARE IMPAIRED IN ERYTHROCYTES OF HUMANS WITH DIABETES MELLITUS

Randy Sprague, Alan Stephenson, Elizabeth Bowles, Madelyn Stumpf, Gregory Ricketts and Andrew Lonigro
Saint Louis University, School of Medicine, Department of Pharmacological and Physiological Science, St. Louis, MO, USA.

Abstract: Erythrocytes of humans have been reported to stimulate nitric oxide (NO) synthesis in the circulation as a consequence of their ability to release ATP in response to both mechanical deformation and exposure to reduced oxygen tension. It has been proposed that the ability of the erythrocyte to affect local vascular resistance permits it to participate in the regulation of blood flow such that oxygen delivery is matched with metabolic need. A signal transduction pathway that relates deformation and exposure to reduced oxygen tension to ATP release from human erythrocytes has been described. The heterotrimeric G protein, Gi, is a critical component of this pathway. Importantly, stimulation of Gi results in activation of adenylyl cyclase and ATP release from these cells. Recently, in a model of diabetes mellitus in rats, expression of Gi was reported to be decreased in the aorta. We report that expression of $G\alpha_{i2}$ is selectively decreased in erythrocytes of humans with type 2 diabetes (DM2) and that these erythrocytes fail to release ATP in response to incubation with mastoparan 7 (10 μM), an agent that activates Gi. These results provide support for the hypothesis that ATP release from erythrocytes of humans with DM2 is impaired and this defect in erythrocyte physiology could contribute to the vascular disease associated with this clinical condition.

Key Words: mastoparan 7, heterotrimeric G proteins, western analysis

INTRODUCTION

Previously, we reported that human erythrocytes release ATP in response to both mechanical deformation (28,29,30) and exposure to reduced oxygen tension (3,8,9). In the vasculature, P_{2y} purinergic receptors are found on endothelial cells (5,7,16). Binding of ATP to these receptors results in the synthesis of NO (5,16). We have proposed that ATP released from the erythrocyte acts locally on endothelial cells to evoke NO release which, in turn, affects vascular caliber permitting the erythrocyte to participate in local regulation of the circulation. Indeed, the erythrocyte has been suggested to be an important determinant of the matching of oxygen supply with tissue metabolic demand (8,9,11).

The fact that ATP does not readily cross cell membranes suggests that its release from erythrocytes requires a specific mechanism. We reported that, in human erythrocytes, Gs (22) and Gi (21,23), adenylyl cyclase (30), cyclic AMP-dependent protein kinase (PKA) (30) and the cystic fibrosis transmembrane conductance regulator (CFTR) (27) are components of a signal-transduction pathway that relates physiological stimuli such as mechanical deformation or exposure to reduced oxygen tension to ATP release (Figure 1).

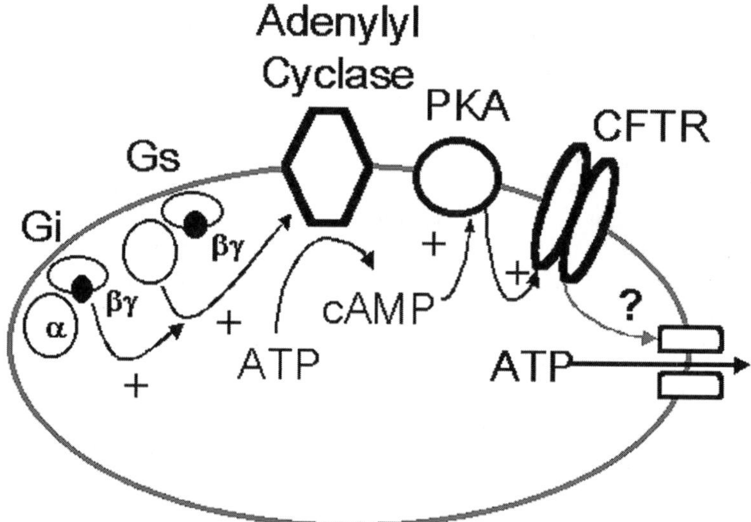

Figure 1. Proposed pathway for regulated ATP release from human erythrocytes. Abbreviations: Gs and Gi - heterotrimeric G proteins; ATP - adenosine triphosphate; cAMP - 3'5'-cyclic-adenosine monophosphate; PKA - protein kinase A; CFTR - cystic fibrosis transmembrane conductance regulator; **?** - a yet unidentified conduit for ATP release; + - stimulates.

Recently, altered expression of one of the components of this pathway, Gi, has been reported to occur in an animal model of diabetes mellitus (12). In rats made diabetic with streptozotocin, significant reductions in the expression of the heterotrimeric G-proteins, $G\alpha i_2$ and $G\alpha i_3$ were detected in the aorta (12). This finding is of particular interest as we have demonstrated that Gi is a necessary component of a signal-transduction pathway for ATP release from erythrocytes of humans (21,23) in response to mechanical deformation and exposure to reduced oxygen tension. Importantly, Gi activation results in stimulation of adenylyl cyclase and ATP release from these erythrocytes (21,23).

The finding that activation of Gi is a critical component of a signal transduction pathway for ATP release from erythrocytes in response to physiological stimuli, coupled with reports that expression of this G protein is reduced in experimental diabetes, suggested to us that erythrocytes of humans with diabetes might have a defect in ATP release from erythrocytes that could, ultimately, lead to a decreased stimulus for endogenous NO synthesis. Here, we investigated the hypothesis that expression of the heterotrimeric G protein, Gi, is reduced in erythrocytes of humans with type 2 diabetes (DM2) and that this defect is associated with decreased ATP release in response to an agent that activates that G protein, mastoparan 7 (MAS 7) (15,21,23).

METHODS

Generation of washed erythrocytes: Blood was obtained from healthy humans as well as humans with type 2 diabetes mellitus (DM2) by venipuncture (antecubital fossa). Blood was collected into a heparinized syringe and centrifuged at 500 x g at 4°C for 10 min. The plasma and buffy coat were discarded. Erythrocytes were resuspended and washed x 3 in buffer (in mM, 4.7 KCl, 2.0 $CaCl_2$, 140.5 NaCl 1.2 $MgSO_4$, 21.0 tris(hydroxymethyl)amino methane, 5.5 glucose with 0.5% bovine serum albumin (final pH 7.4)). Cells were prepared on the day of use.

ATP assay: ATP was measured by the luciferin-luciferase technique (3,21-23,27-30) in which the amount of light generated by the reaction of ATP with firefly tail extract is dependent on ATP concentration. Sensitivity was augmented by addition of synthetic D-luciferin. A 200 µl sample of erythrocyte-containing solution (or ATP standard) was injected into a cuvette containing 100 µl firefly tail extract (10 mg/ ml distilled water, FLE 50, Sigma, St. Louis, MO) and 100 µl of a solution of synthetic D-luciferin (5 mg/10 ml distilled water, Sigma, St. Louis, MO). The peak light efflux was determined using a luminometer (Turner Designs, Sunnyvale, CA, model 20/20). A standard curve was obtained on the day of each experiment. Values for ATP were normalized to an erythrocyte count of 4 x 10^5 cells/mm^3.

Measurement of hemoglobin: To exclude the possibility that concentrations of extracellular ATP represent that released by the lysis of erythrocytes, after ATP determinations, erythrocyte suspensions were centrifuged at 500 x g at 4°C for 10 min and the presence of hemoglobin in the supernatant was determined by light absorption at a wavelength of 405 nm (33). The assays for ATP and hemoglobin have similar sensitivities such that an increase in ATP, if unaccompanied by an increase in hemoglobin, represents active ATP release from erythrocytes and is not the result of cell lysis. If increases in hemoglobin were detected, the study was excluded.

Preparation of erythrocyte membranes: Erythrocyte membranes were prepared as follows. All lytic steps were conducted at 4°C. Washed RBCs (2 ml) were added to 200 ml of hypotonic buffer (in mM; 5 Tris-HCl, 2 EDTA with pH adjusted to 7.4) and stirred vigorously for 20 min. The mixture was centrifuged at 23,300 x g for 15 min. The supernatant was discarded and the membranes were re-suspended in buffer. The mixture was centrifuged at 23,300 x g for 15 min and the supernatant discarded. The membranes were pooled, re-suspended in buffer, and centrifuged again at 23,300 x g for 15 min. The protein concentration was determined with the BCA Protein Assay (Pierce).

Identification of the α subunit of heterotrimeric G proteins in erythrocyte membranes: Erythrocyte membranes were solubilized in SDS sample buffer (0.277 M sodium dodecyl sulfate (SDS), 60% glycerol, 0.4 M dithiothreitol, 0.25 M Tris HCl, and 0.004% bromophenol blue) and heated (5 min, 100°C) before loading onto a precast 4-20% gradient Tris-HCl Ready Gel (Bio-Rad). Gels were subjected to electrophoresis at 150 V for 1.5 h with buffer containing 25 mM Tris, 192 mM glycine and 0.1% w/v SDS, pH 8.3. After electrophoresis, proteins were transferred for 1 h on ice onto a polyvinylidene difluoride (PVDF) membrane with transfer buffer (25 mM Tris and 192 mM glycine with 20% v/v methanol at pH 8.3) at 100 V. PVDF membranes were blocked (overnight, 4 °C) with 5% non-fat dry milk in phosphate-buffered saline (10 mM sodium phosphate, pH 7.4, 150 mM NaCl), then incubated with antibodies directed against the alpha subunit of Gs, (rabbit polyclonal), Gi_2 (mouse monoclonal), and Gi_3 (rabbit polyclonal) (Biomol). In addition, membranes were incubated with antibody directed against ß-actin, a structural protein in erythrocytes. PVDF membranes were then incubated (4 h, 25 °C) with donkey anti-rabbit or sheep anti-mouse IgG linked to horseradish peroxidase (Amersham Biosciences) as the secondary antibody in 1% non-fat dry milk in phosphate-buffered saline containing 0.1% Tween 20. After labeling with the secondary antibody, PVDF membranes were exposed to enhanced chemiluminescence using ECL (Amersham Biosciences).

Determination of relative amounts of G protein α subunits present in erythrocyte membranes: Amounts of membrane protein loaded on the gels were standardized by determination of the protein content of each preparation prior to loading and by determination of the amount of ß-actin present in each sample on separate gels with protein diluted 5 fold. Amounts of G protein in individual membrane preparations were calculated as the ratio of G protein to β-actin . Values measured in humans with DM2 are expressed as the percentage of that detected in the membranes of healthy humans run on the same gel. All studies were performed in duplicate.

Study of Patients with Diabetes Mellitus Type 2 (DM2): Patients with diabetes mellitus type 2 (DM2) were identified by physicians in the Endocrine Clinic at Saint Louis University. A history form was completed for each individual studied (both healthy volunteers and humans with DM2). The information obtained included a medication history, a detailed listing of all medications and age, as well as the most recent HbA1c level (values within four weeks of blood removal). The mean age of healthy humans and humans with DM2 was 40±5 and 51±5 respectively. Patients with DM2 (n=9) were treated with insulin (n=8), lipid lowering agents (n=8) oral hypoglycemic agents(n=6), anti-platelet agents (n=6), diuretics (n=5), β blockers (n=5), angiotensin converting enzyme inhibitors (n=5) and calcium channel blockers (n=3). All record keeping was in strict compliance with HIPPA regulations.

Incubation of erythrocytes with MAS7: After washing, erythrocytes were diluted with wash buffer (see above) to achieve a hematocrit of 20%. Erythrocytes of healthy humans or humans with DM2 (HbA1c values of 8 or greater, range 8.1 to 11.8) were incubated with either mastoparan 7 (MAS 7, activator of Gi, 10 μM) or its vehicle (saline). ATP release was measured at 5, 10 and 15 minutes after addition of MAS 7 or buffer. ATP was measured by adding 200 μl of erythrocyte suspension diluted 250 fold to the luciferin/luciferase mixture. The amount of free hemoglobin in each sample was measured.

Statistical methods: Statistical significance between experimental periods was determined with an analysis of variance. In the event that the F ratio indicated that changes had occurred, a least significant difference test was used to identify individual differences. P values of 0.05 or less were considered statistically significant. Results are reported as means ± SE.

RESULTS

Quantification of heterotrimeric G protein α subunits in erythrocyte membranes: Erythrocyte membranes of humans with DM2 were found to contain amounts of Gsα (n=4, HbA1c=12.3±1.8) and $G\alpha i_3$ (n=5, HbA1c=12.2±1.4) that were not different from those found in heathy humans (n=6 and 5, respectively) (Figure 2). In contrast, expression of $G\alpha i_2$ (n=5, HbA1c=12.2±1.4) was reduced to 56±2 % of that found in healthy humans (n=8) (Figures 2 and 3).

ATP release from erythrocytes in response to MAS 7: Incubation of erythrocytes of healthy humans with 10 μM MAS 7 resulted in 7 ± 1 fold increase in ATP release (n=8, $P<0.01$) (figure 4). In contrast, incubation of erythrocytes of humans with DM2 (HbA1c= 10.1± 0.7, n=5) with MAS 7 did not result in increased ATP release (Figure 4).

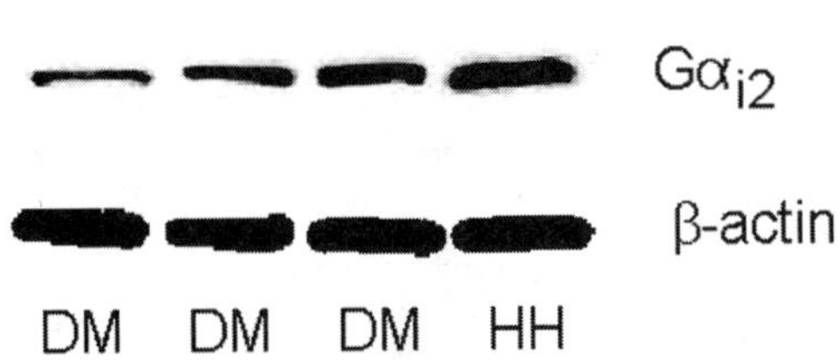

Figure 2: Measurement of the heterotrimeric G protein $G\alpha i_2$ and β-actin in erythrocyte membranes in a healthy human (HH) and humans with diabetes mellitus type 2 (DM). Membranes were prepared and the proteins were resolved using a 4-20% gradient TRIS-HCl pre-cast gel. Protein was transferred to a PVDF membrane and incubated with a mouse monoclonal anti-$G\alpha i_2$ antibody.

DISCUSSION

In humans with diabetes mellitus (DM), cardiovascular disease accounts for 66% of deaths (14,20). The most prevalent form of human DM (90-95% of individuals) is classified as type 2 (DM2) (20). DM2 is characterized by peripheral insulin resistance with an insulin secretory defect that varies in severity. It occurs typically in individuals over

40 years of age who have a family history of diabetes. Over 90% of these individuals are obese. Patients with DM2 retain the ability to secrete some endogenous insulin, therefore, they do not develop diabetic ketoacidosis. Thus, these individuals may require insulin and/or oral hypoglycemic agents to control blood sugar levels, but do not depend on them to prevent ketoacidosis.

The observation that vascular reactivity is altered in humans with DM2 is widely accepted (14,20). Indeed, both endothelium-dependent and -independent vasodilation is impaired in humans with DM2 (1,19,34,35). Impaired vasodilation in DM2 has been attributed to decreased NO synthesis (34), increased NO degradation (1) and/or to abnormalities in the vascular smooth muscle (35). Mechanism(s) notwithstanding, NO-mediated vasodilation is reduced in humans with DM2. It is possible that, in addition to the endothelium, other sources of endogenous NO may be compromised in these individuals. In addition, changes in erythrocyte physiology have also been reported to be present in humans with DM.

Erythrocytes of patients with DM have been reported to have reduced glutathione concentration (6) although this observation has not been confirmed by others (17). However, it is agreed that the oxidant stress to which erythrocytes are exposed is increased in a high glucose environment (6,17). It has been hypothesized that this oxidant stress leads to increased glycation of erythrocyte proteins (4). Glycated hemoglobin (HbA1c) has been accepted as a measure of the degree of glycemic control in patients with diabetes such that the lower the HbA1c level, the better the glycemic control (26,32). Indeed, HbA1c levels correlate with diabetic complications (17,32), i.e., better glycemic control is associated with reduced complications.

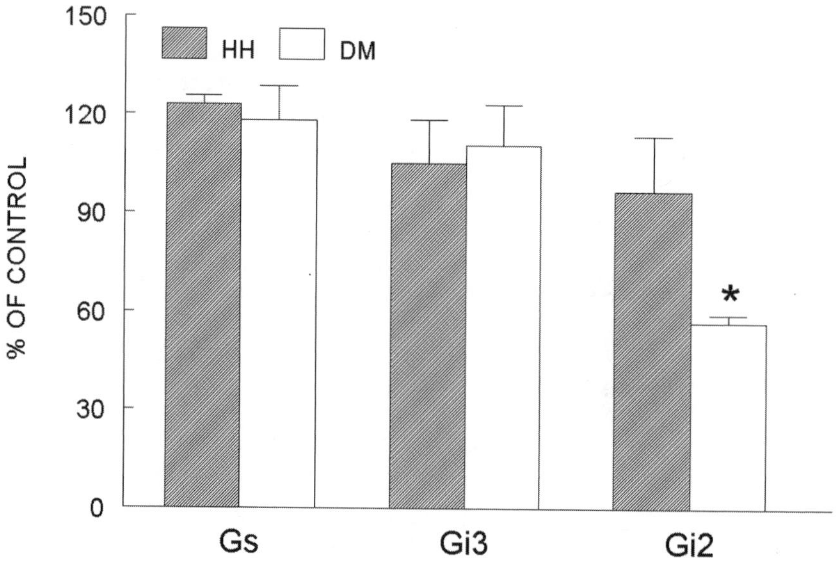

Figure 3. Expression of heterotrimeric G protein α subunits in erythrocyte membranes of healthy humans (HH, cross hatched bars) and humans with diabetes mellitus type 2 (DM, open bars). Numbers of humans studied are: Gs, 5 HH and 4 DM; Gi3, 4 HH and 5 DM and Gi2, 7 HH and 5 DM. Values are calculated as the % of the amount of G protein α subunit found in a control human erythrocyte preparation. Values are the mean ± SEM. *, $p<0.05$ compared to all other groups.

In addition to glycated hemoglobin, several properties of the membranes of RBCs of patients with diabetes differ from those of healthy humans (13,24,25). For example, exposure of erythrocytes to increased concentrations of D-glucose results in altered conductivity of the cell membrane (13). Erythrocytes of diabetics have also been reported to be less deformable that those of healthy humans (18). More important to this study, erythrocytes of patients with diabetes demonstrate a defect in ATP release in response to osmotic stress (24) and contain increased amounts of ATP (24), the latter finding possibly reflecting a failure of those mechanisms that result in ATP release. Here we investigated the hypothesis that such a defect in ATP release from erythrocytes of humans with DM2 is the result of the failure of a component or components of a signal transduction pathway for ATP release.

As stated above, we have defined a signal transduction pathway that relates physiological stimuli to ATP release from erythrocytes of rabbits and humans (figure 1). Recently, altered expression of one of the components of this pathway, Gi, has been reported in an animal model of diabetes (12). Thus, in rats made diabetic with streptozotocin, significant reductions in the expression of the heterotrimeric G-proteins, Gαi2 and Gαi3 were detected in the aorta (12). This finding is of particular interest in that we have demonstrated previously that Gi is a necessary component of a signal-transduction pathway for deformation- and reduced oxygen tension-induced ATP release from erythrocytes of healthy humans (21,23).

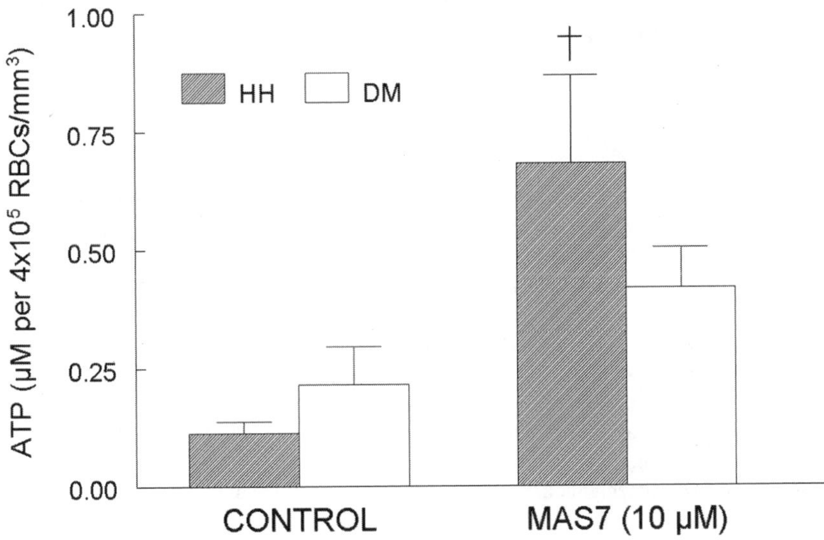

Figure 4. Effect of mastoparan 7 (MAS7) on ATP release from erythrocytes of healthy humans (HH, n=8) and humans with diabetes mellitus type 2 (DM, n=5). Washed erythrocytes were incubated with MAS7 or its vehicle (saline, control). ATP release was measured at 5, 10 and 15 min after MAS7 and the maximal response is reported. Values are the mean ± SEM. †, $p<0.05$ compared to respective control.

It is now recognized that, in addition to the α subunits of heterotrimeric G proteins, the βγ subunit is capable of activating at least three of eight membrane associated isoforms of adenylyl cyclase, specifically, subtypes II, IV and VII (table 1) (10,31). The heterotrimeric G proteins most clearly associated with this property are of the Gi/o subclass (31). The ability of the βγ subunit to activate adenylyl cyclase subtypes II, IV and VII has been shown to reside with the β component of that dimer, of which five types have been defined (31). Of five β subunit types that have been identified, the ability to stimulate adenylyl cyclase has been associated with types 1, 2, 3 and 4, but not type 5 (2). We have reported that β subunits 1,2,3,and 4 are components of the erythrocyte membranes of humans (28). Thus, G proteins of both the Gs and Gi subclasses, as well as β subunits capable of stimulating adenylyl cyclase, are present in human erythrocytes.

The finding that activation of Gi is a critical component of a signal transduction pathway for ATP release from erythrocytes in response to physiological stimuli, coupled with the finding that expression of this G protein is reduced in the erythrocyte membranes of humans with DM2, suggests that erythrocytes of humans with DM2 could have a defect in ATP release from erythrocytes that leads to a decreased stimulus for endogenous NO synthesis. Thus, we conclude that defects in the ability of erythrocytes to release ATP in response to physiological stimuli could contribute to vascular disease in humans with DM2.

ACKNOWLEDGMENTS

This work is supported by National Heart Lung and Blood Institute Grants HL-51298, HL- 64180 and an Innovation Award from the American Diabetes Association. The authors thank J. L. Sprague for inspiration.

REFERENCES

1. Bagi, Z., Koller, A. and Kaley, G.: Superoxide-NO interaction decreases flow- and agonist-induced dilations of coronary arterioles in Type 2 diabetes mellitus. *Am. J. Physiol* 285: H1404-H1410, 2003.
2. Bayewitch, M.L., Avidor-Reiss, T., Levy, R., Pfeuffer, T. et al.: Differential modulation of adenylyl cyclase I and II by various Gβ subunits. *J. Biol. Chem.* 273:2273-2276, 1998.
3. Bergfeld, G.R. and T. Forrester. Release of ATP from human erythrocytes in response to a brief period of hypoxia and hypercapnea. *Cardiovasc. Res.* 26:40-47, 1992.
4. Brownlee, M., Cerami, A. and Vlassara, H.: Advanced glycosylation end producs in tissues and the biochemical basis of diabetic complications. *N.E.J.M.* 318, 1315-1321, 1988.
5. Communi, D., Raspe, E., Pirotton, S. and Boeynaems, J.M.: Coexpression of P_{2y} and P_{2u} receptors on aortic endothelial cells: Comparison of cell localization and signaling pathways. *Circ. Res.* 76:191-198, 1991.
6. Costagliola, C.: Oxidative state of glutathione in red blood cells and plasma of diabetic patients: In vivo and in vitro study. *Clin. Physiol. Biochem.* 8:204-210, 1990.
7. Dazel, H.H. and Westfall, D.P.: Receptors for adenine nucleotides and nucleosides: Subclassification, distribution and molecular characterization. *Pharmacological Reviews* 46:449-466, 1994.
8. Ellsworth, M.L.: Red blood cell derived atp as a regulator of skeletal muscle perfusion: *Med. Sci. Sports Exerc.*, Vol. 36, No. 1, pp. 3541, 2004.
9. Ellsworth, M.L.: The red blood cell as an oxygen sensor: what is the evidence? *Acta. Physiol. Scand.* 168:551-559, 2000.
10. Federman, A.D., Conklin, B.R., Schrader, K.A., Reed, R.R. and Bourne, H.R.: Hormonal

stimulation of adenylyl cyclase therough Gi-protein beta gamma subunits. *Nature* 356:159-161, 1992.

11. Gonzalez-Alonzo, J., Olsen, D.B., Saltin, B.: Erythrocyte and the regulation of human skeletal muscle blood flow and oxygen delivery. *Circ. Res*. 91:1046-1055, 2002.
12. Hashim, S., Liu, Y.Y., Wand, R. and Anand-Srivastava, M.B.: Streptozotocin-induced diabetes impairs G-protein linked signal transduction in vascular smooth muscle. *Molecular and Cellular Biochemistry* 240:57-63, 2000
13. Hayashi, Y., Leishits, L., Caduff, A. and Feldman, Y.: Dielectric spectroscopy study of specific glucose influence on humans erythrocyte membranes. *J Physics D: Applied Physics* 36:369-374, 2003.
14. Hsueh, W.A. and Quinones, M.J.: Role of endothelial dysfunction in insulin resistance. *Am. J. Cardiol*. 92(suppl):10j-17j, 2003.
15. Katsu, T., Kuroko, M., Morikawa, K., Sanchika, K., Yamanaka, H., Shinoda, S. and Fujita, Y.: Interaction of wasp venom mastoparan with biomembranes. *Biochemica et Biophysica Acta* 1027:185-190, 1990.
16. Kennedy, C., Delbro, D. and Burnstock, G.: P_2-purinoceptors mediate both vasodilation (via the endothelium) and vasoconstriction of the isolated rat femoral artery. *Eur. J. Pharmacol.* 1072:161-168, 1985.
17. McLellan, A.C., Thornalley, P.J., Benn, J. and Sonksen, P.H.: Glyoxalase system in clinical diabetes mellitus and correlation with diabetic complications. *Clin. Sci*. 87:21-29, 1994.
18. McMillan, D.E., Utterback, N.G. and La Puma, J.: Reduce erythrocyte deformability in diabetes. *Diabetes* 27:895-901, 1978.
19. Hayes, J.R.: Impared endothelium-dependent and independent vasodilation in patients with type 2 (non-insulin-dependent) diabetes mellitus. Diabetologia 35:771-776, 1992.
20. Mokdad, A.H., et al.: Diabetes trends in the U.S.:1990-1998, *Diabetes Care*, 23:1278-1283, 2000.
21. Olearczyk, JJ, Ellsworth, ML, Stephenson, AH, Lonigro, AJ and Sprague, RS: Nitric oxide inhibits ATP release from rrythrocytes. *J Pharmacol. Exp. Ther*. 309: 1079-1084, 2004.
22. Olearczyk, JJ, Stephenson, AH, Lonigro, AJ and Sprague, RS: Receptor-mediated Activation of the Heterotrimeric G-protein Gs results in ATP Release from Erythrocytes. *Med. Sci. Monit*. 7:669-674, 2001.
23. Olearczyk, JJ, Stephenson, AH, Lonigro, AJ and Sprague, RS: Heterotrimeric G protein Gi is involved in a signal transduction pathway for ATP release from erythrocytes *Am. J. Physiol* 286:H940-H945, 2004.
24. Petruzzi, E., Orlando, C., Pinzani, P., et al.: ATP release by osmotic shock and HbA1c in diabetic subject's erythrocytes. *Metabolism* 43:435-440, 1994.
25. Rabini, R.A., Petruzzi, E., Staffolani, R., Tesei, M., Fumelli, P., Pazzagli, M. and Mazzanti, L.: Diabetes mellitus and subjects's ageing: a study on the ATP content and ATP-related enzyme activities in humans erythrocytes. *Eur. J. Clin. Invest*. 27:327-332, 1997.
26. Sowers, J.R. and Haffner, S.: Treatment of cardiovascular and renal rick factors in the diabetic hypertensive. *Hypertension* 40:781-788, 2002.
27. Sprague, R.S., Ellsworth, M.L., Stephenson, A.H., Kleinhenz, M.E. and A.J. Lonigro. Deformation-induced ATP release from red blood cells requires cystic fibrosis transmembrane conductance regulator activity. *Am. J. Physiol*. 275:H1726-H1732, 1998.
28. Sprague, RS, Bowles, EA, Olearczyk, JJ, Stephenson, AH and Lonigro, AJ: The role of G protein β subunits in the release of ATP from human erythrocytes. *J. Physiol & Pharmacol* 53:667-674, 2002.
29. Sprague, R.S., M.L. Ellsworth, A.H. Stephenson, and A.J. Lonigro. ATP: the red blood cell link to NO and local control of the pulmonary circulation. *Am. J. Physiol*. 271:H2717-H2722, 1996.

30. Sprague, RS, Ellsworth, ML, Stephenson AH and Lonigro, AJ: Participation of cAMP in a signal-transduction pathway relating erythrocyte deformation of ATP release *Am. J. Physiol.* 281:C1158-C1164, 2001.

31. Tang, W. and Gilman, A.G.: Type-specific regulation of adenylyl cyclase by G protein βγ subunits. *Science* 254:1500-1503, 1991.

32. The Diabetes Control and Complications Trial Research Group: The effect of intensive treatment of diabetes on the development and progression of long-term complicationof inulin-dependent diabetes mellitus. *N.E.J.M.* 329:977-986, 1993.

33. van Kampen, E.J. and W.G. Zijlstra. Spectrophotometry of hemoglobin and hemoglobin derivatives. *Adv. Clin. Chem.* 23:199-257, 1983.

34. van Etten, R.W., de Koning, E.J.P., Verhaar, M.C., Gaillard, C.A.J.M. and Rabelink, T.J.: Impaired NO-dependent vasodilation in patients with Type II (non-insulin-dependent) diabetes mellitus is restored by acute administration of folate. *Diabetologia* 45:1004-1010, 2002.

35. Yugar-Toledo, J.C. et al.: Uncontrolled hypertension, uncompensated type II diabetes, and smoking have different patterns of vascular dysfunction. *Chest* 125:823-830, 2004.

Chapter 19

RED BLOOD CELLS AND HEMOGLOBIN IN HYPOXIC PULMONARY VASOCONSTRICTION

Steven Deem

Departments of Anesthesiology and Medicine, University of Washington, Harborview Medical Center, Seattle, WA, USA.

Abstract: Nitric oxide (NO) plays an important role in the modulation of hypoxic pulmonary vasoconstriction; in turn, red blood cells (RBCs) augment HPV by hemoglobin-mediated oxidation and inactivation of NO. In addition, scavenging of reactive oxygen species by RBCs may play a role in augmentation of HPV. NO delivery and/or production by RBCs does not appear to be important in the control of pulmonary vasomotor tone. This review will discuss regulation of HPV by RBCs with an emphasis on hemoglobin-NO interactions. In addition, the review will discuss how biologic (S-nitrosation) or pharmacologic (cross-linking) modification of hemoglobin may affect pulmonary circulatory-hemoglobin interactions.

Key Words: pulmonary blood flow, gas exchange, oxygen delivery

INTRODUCTION

Vasoconstriction of small pulmonary arteries and arterioles occurs in response to alveolar hypoxia. (43, 75, 78) In the presence of regional shunt or low ventilation-to-perfusion, this hypoxic pulmonary vasoconstriction (HPV) acts to divert blood flow away from hypoxic lung regions, thus minimizing the effects of lung pathology on the arterial PO_2.(13, 62). In the presence of global lung hypoxia, HPV results in pulmonary hypertension.

HPV kinetics are rapid, and HPV is undoubtedly an intrinsic property of pulmonary vascular smooth muscle. (55, 61, 81, 83) It is generally agreed that HPV is initiated by opening of L-type calcium channels and an increase in intracellular calcium (2, 4, 34, 68, 80, 87, 88). The location of the "hypoxia sensor" may be the mitochondria, but the role of reactive oxygen species (ROS) in transducing this signal is a subject of intense debate.(59, 82) Despite the localization of sensor and effector mechanisms for hypoxic pulmonary

Hypoxia and Exercise, edited by R.C. Roach *et al.*
Springer, New York, 2006.

vasoconstriction to pulmonary vascular smooth muscle cells, extrinsic factors certainly modify the response. In particular, the pulmonary vascular endothelium modulates hypoxic pulmonary vasoconstriction through production of arachidonic acid derivatives, nitric oxide (NO), and endothelin, and perhaps other yet undefined mediators.(1) In addition, it is clear that the red blood cell is necessary for the full expression of hypoxic pulmonary vasoconstriction via a variety of potential mechanisms, including interactions with nitric oxide (NO), other reactive oxygen species, purines, and endothelial interactions. The remainder of this review will discuss the roles that red blood cells play in the modulation of hypoxic pulmonary vasoconstriction, with particular emphasis on the importance of NO and hemoglobin (Hb) in this interaction.

MODULATION OF HPV BY NO

Multiple levels of evidence suggest an important role for NO in the modulation of HPV, including marked augmentation of HPV in isolated lungs, intact animals, and human subjects after inhibition of NO synthesis, (3, 8, 12, 24, 41, 53, 66, 72, 74, 76), and in mice with targeted disruption of the endothelial nitric oxide synthase (eNOS) gene. (31) Administration of inhaled NO results in inhibition of hypoxic pulmonary vasoconstriction. (33, 67, 75) There appear to be species differences in the role that NO plays in regulation of pulmonary vascular resistance during normoxia and hypoxia, with NO playing an important role in mice, rats, rabbits, pigs, sheep, and humans, but less so in dogs.(18)

Given that NO is continually produced by pulmonary vascular endothelium and airway epithelium, it is remarkable that HPV is not tonically inhibited. The inhibitory effect of NO on HPV appears to be blunted by the capacity for red blood cells to take up and inactivate NO, as discussed below. In addition, an immediate fall in NO production during acute hypoxia due to reduced NOS activity may act to enhance hypoxic pulmonary vasoconstriction (29, 46, 70).

MODULATION OF HPV BY RED BLOOD CELLS AND HEMOGLOBIN: INITIAL STUDIES

Augmentation of HPV by blood was demonstrated by Duke et al in isolated, perfused cat lungs more than 50 years ago.(28) McMurtry et al later identified the role of the red blood cell in this response when they showed that isolated rat lungs perfused with colloid solution, plasma, or plasma plus platelets had rapidly decaying hypoxic pulmonary vasoconstriction when compared to lungs perfused with blood or plasma plus red blood cells. (58) Although they showed that cyclooxygenase played no role in augmentation of HPV by red blood cells, they were unable to identify a mechanism to explain their observations.

Later, potentiation of hypoxic pulmonary vasoconstriction by red blood cells was described in both rat and cat lungs, but not in lungs from swine and hamsters (39, 40). Later investigations by Hakim suggested that species differences in augmentation of HPV by red blood cells were due to differences in muscular pulmonary vessel size, and/or red blood cell deformability changes in response to hypoxia. (38, 39) Weissmann et al found that red blood cells augmented HPV at very low concentrations (hematocrit of 1-5%), but with no further augmentation beyond that level. (84) However, the mechanism by which red blood cells augmented hypoxic pulmonary vasoconstriction remained unproven.

HEMOGLOBIN-NO INTERACTIONS

The biochemical interactions between NO and hemoglobin are discussed in detail elsewhere in this symposium. Briefly, there are four reactions that are of potential import to the regulation of vascular tone: 1) Oxidation of nitric oxide (NO) by oxyhemoglobin (oxyHb) to form methemoglobin (metHb) and nitrate irreversibly inactivates NO.(65) 2) Addition of NO to deoxyheme to form nitrosyl(heme)Hb in a reaction that is reversible under certain conditions.(14, 16, 35, 79) 3) S-nitrosation of Hb at the ß-cysteine 93 (ß-cys93) residue to form S-nitrosoHb (SNO-Hb).(45) This reaction is also reversible, particularly in the presence of low-molecular weight thiols such as GSH.(45, 85) It has also been proposed that the Hb S-nitrosation reaction is under the allosteric influence of deoxygenation, although this is controversial as will be discussed in a following section.(9, 46, 57, 77) 4) Reduction of nitrite by deoxyHb to form NO.(17, 27, 50) Of these reactions, the oxidation and addition reactions have the potential to limit the magnitude and duration of NO's vasorelaxant effects during hypoxia, whereas the S-nitrosation and reduction reactions have the potential to generate NO during hypoxia.

HEMOGLOBIN, NO, AND HPV

Given the large capacity for oxidation of NO by ferrous Hb, largely through irreversible oxidation to form metHb and nitrate, we postulated that red blood cells augment hypoxic pulmonary vasoconstriction by reducing local NO availability. Indeed, several studies have demonstrated augmentation of HPV by free Hb. (41, 42, 56) Furthermore, Heller et al showed that NOS inhibition by L-NAME did not further augment hypoxic pulmonary vasoconstriction in lungs perfused with buffer containing free Hb. (42)

Isolated, perfused rabbit lungs are particularly suited to the study of the interactions between red blood cells, NO, and HPV, in that they have a moderately strong pressor response to hypoxia, and also demonstrate a high concentration of NO in the exhaled breath, with the latter being highly and rapidly sensitive to changes in perfusate and alveolar conditions. (7, 15, 37) Accordingly, using this model we found that both HPV and exhaled NO varied with changes in perfusate hematocrit; HPV was augmented and exhaled NO depressed as hematocrit was increased within the physiologic range (10-30%) (Figure 1).(24) Nitric oxide synthase (NOS) inhibition with the L-arginine analog N^{Ω}-nitro-L-arginine (L-NA) resulted in a reduction in exhaled NO in buffer-perfused lungs to the level of that in lungs perfused with a hematocrit of 30%, and markedly enhanced HPV in buffer-perfused lungs, but not in lungs perfused with red blood cells (Figure 2). Other investigators corroborated our findings, and showed that red blood cells but not leukocytes or platelets augment hypoxic pulmonary vasoconstriction and reduce intravascular NO in isolated rat lungs. (47)

In later studies, we provided more direct evidence that red cells augment HPV by inactivating NO. When isolated, perfused rabbit lungs were exposed to a very low concentration of free Hb (~4 μM), exhaled NO was reduced and HPV was augmented to a similar degree as when perfusate contained an approximately 400 fold greater concentration of intraerythrocytic Hb (perfusate hematocrit 30%) (Figure 2). (19)

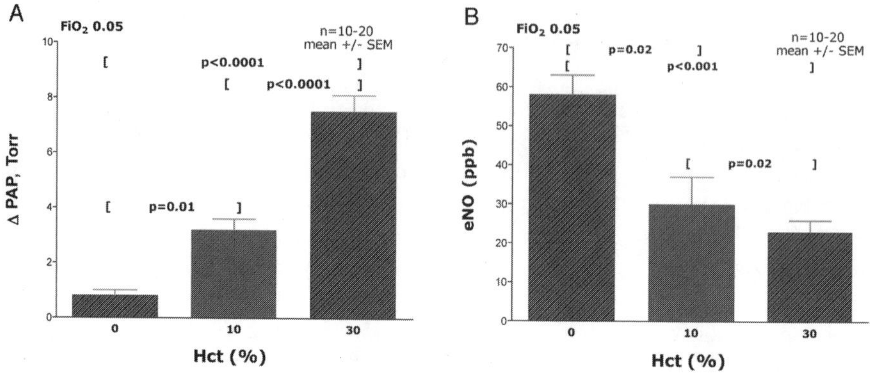

Figure 1. A. Hypoxic pulmonary vasoconstriction (HPV) represented as the change in pulmonary artery pressure (ΔPAP) from baseline 5 minutes after initiation of hypoxic ventilation. HPV increases with the addition of red blood cells to the perfusate in a "dose-dependent" fashion. B. Exhaled NO (eNO) in lungs perfused with buffer, or with buffer containing red blood cells at hematocrits of 10 and 30%.

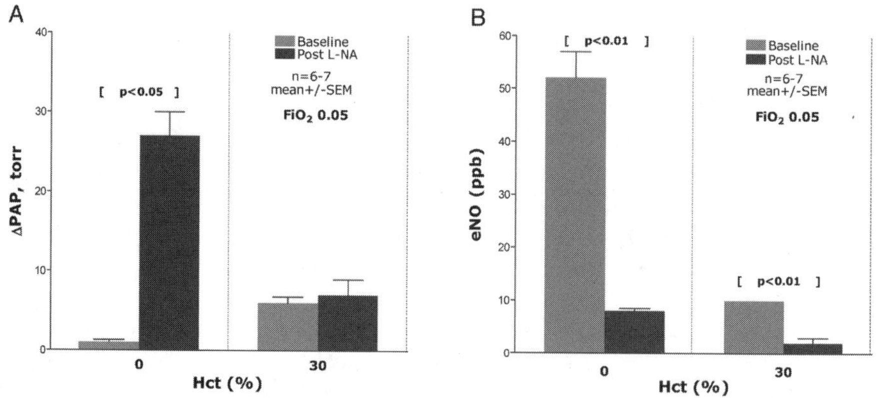

Figure 2. A. HPV before and after nitric oxide synthase (NOS) inhibition in lungs perfused with buffer, or buffer plus red blood cells (Hct 30%). NOS inhibition augments HPV in buffer but not red cell-perfused lungs. B. Exhaled NO (eNO) before and after NOS inhibition in lungs perfused with buffer, or buffer plus red blood cells (Hct 30%). NOS inhibition reduces exhaled NO in both conditions, but the change is more dramatic in buffer-perfused lungs.

Treatment of free Hb with potassium ferricyanate to form cyanometHb to prevent all interactions of heme with NO (oxidation and nitrosylation), prevented augmentation of HPV and reduction of exhaled NO in this model (Figure 3). (21) These data provide convincing evidence that the red cell augments HPV by Hb-mediated NO inactivation. The data also illustrate the remarkable ability of the red blood cell membrane to protect NO from degradation by heme.

There may be a Hct threshold effect for inactivation of NO and augmentation of HPV by red blood cells. Loer and Peters demonstrated that HPV was augmented in isolated rabbit lungs when perfusate hematocrit was increased from 0-1% to 16-18% and then to 34-36%, but an increase in hematocrit to 49-51% did not further increase HPV. (54) Alternately, a high hematocrit may have other effects on the pulmonary circulation (see discussion below) that negate the scavenging capacity of Hb for NO.

Limited *in vivo* work supports the notion that red cells are important in the modulation of HPV. In anesthetized rabbits with lobar atelectasis, hemodilution caused a relative increase in intrapulmonary shunt and blood flow to the collapsed lung.(20) This increase in shunt could not be explained by the purely physical effects of reduced blood viscosity, and thus likely represented a reduction of hypoxic pulmonary vasoconstriction in the atelectatic lung. Anesthetized dogs ventilated with a hypoxic gas mixture exhibited an approximately 50% reduction in HPV when they were hemodiluted from a Hct of 40% to 20%.(48)

No studies have directly tested the hypothesis that red blood cells modulate HPV in humans. However, indirect evidence is demonstrated by the observation that polycythemic patients with chronic hypoxemic lung disease have attenuated vasodilation in response to acetylcholine infusion (25). Vasodilation by acetylcholine can be restored by a reduction in hematocrit. In summary, these data suggest that augmentation of hypoxic pulmonary vasoconstriction by red blood cells/Hb is a measurable and likely important physiologic effect.

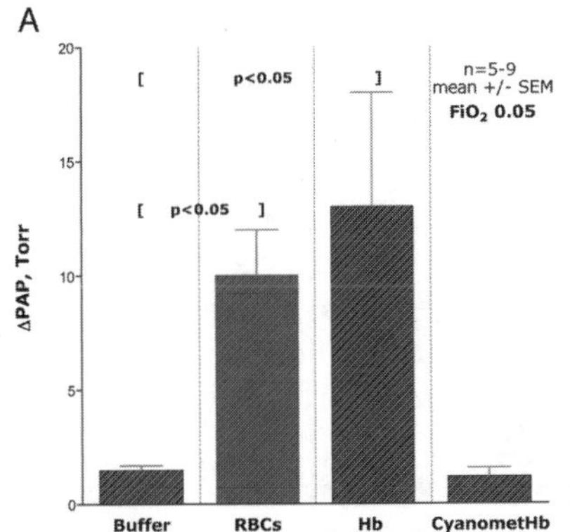

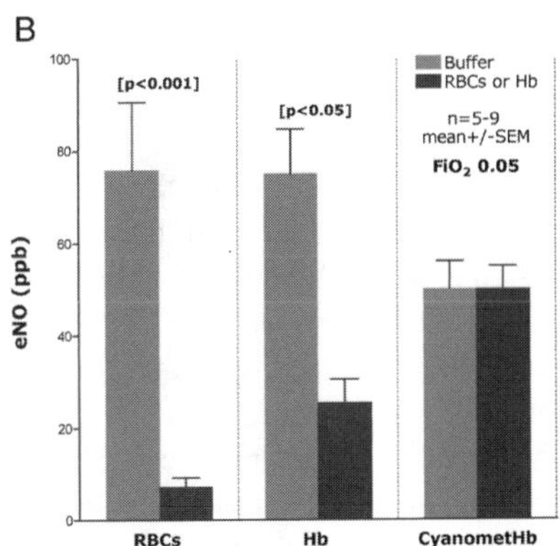

Figure 3. A. HPV in lungs perfused with buffer, or buffer plus RBCs (Hct 30%), buffer plus free Hb (3.6 μM), or buffer plus Hb treated with potassium ferricyanate (cyanometHb) to block oxidation and addition reactions of Hb with NO. Free Hb augments HPV at a concentration 400-fold less than that found in RBCs at Hct 30%, whereas cyanometHb has no effect on HPV. B. Exhaled NO in lungs before and after adding the RBCs, Hb, or cyanometHb to the perfusate. RBCs and Hb reduce eNO, whereas cyanometHb does not.

As noted above, we found that concentrations of free Hb as low as 4 μM resulted in evidence of NO inactivation and augmentation of HPV. Free Hb concentrations of this magnitude and higher have been described in patients undergoing massive blood transfusion (64) and with sickle cell disease (69). This suggests the potential for augmented pulmonary (and systemic) vasoconstriction in these and other conditions associated with hemolysis.

As mentioned previously, the role of the red cell in modulation of HPV appears to predominantly one of augmentation, largely due to inactivation (oxidation) of NO by oxyHb. However, recent work suggests that red blood cells may have the capacity to release NO under certain conditions. The S-nitrosylhemoglobin hypothesis suggests that SNO-Hb is formed in the pulmonary circulation in conjunction with uptake of O_2 by Hb, and that Hb then releases SNO in hypoxic systemic tissues, where it either directly or through NO causes local vasodilation. This Hb-NO-O_2 linkage would act to maximize O_2 delivery to hypoxic tissues. How SNO-Hb might effect HPV is unclear; since SNO-Hb is putatively formed as Hb takes on oxygen in the lung, it would appear that little SNO-Hb would be formed in hypoxic lung units and that there would be little or no effect of SNO-Hb biochemistry in regions where HPV is operant. However, the isolated, perfused lung model provides the unique environment to test the effects of SNO-Hb on vascular smooth muscle and NO production. Hypoxic ventilation reverses the normal flux of O_2 from alveolus to blood, and thus mimics the movement of O_2 to tissues in the systemic circulation; this will result in deoxygenation of Hb and provide conditions for the release of NO from SNO-Hb. The pulmonary circulation also constricts in direct response to hypoxia, unlike the systemic circulation, and thus provided a strong signal for the measurement of vasodilator activity. Given these considerations, we utilized the isolated, perfused lung to study the allosteric and vasodilatory properties of SNO-Hb.

In isolated, perfused rabbit lungs SNO-Hb augmented HPV and reduced exhaled NO to the same magnitude as non-S-nitrosated oxyHb. (21) The rate of release of SNO from Hb was unaffected by hypoxia, and metHb levels increased as SNO-Hb levels fell. One limitation of this study was that the perfusate PO_2 was well above the p50 for SNO-Hb, and may have not provided a strong stimulus for Hb deoxygenation and SNO release; therefore, we repeated the study using an isolated, perfused rat lung model in which the perfusate PO_2 was reduced to an average of 11 Torr (22). Once again, SNO-Hb augmented hypoxic pulmonary vasoconstriction to the same magnitude as free oxyHb (Figure 4), and deoxygenation had no influence of the rate of loss of SNO from Hb. In both studies, glutathione (GSH) accelerated the rate of SNO loss from Hb and commensurate metHb formation. In aggregate, these data suggest that the oxidation reaction of NO with heme predominates over any effect of release of SNO/NO from Hb, and that there is not an allosteric influence of deoxygenation on the release of SNO from Hb.

It is likely that SNO-Hb encapsulated by the red cell membrane behaves entirely differently than when in the free form. Thus, we tested whether red blood cells loaded with supraphysiologic concentrations of SNO-Hb (SNO-RBCs) would vasodilate the pulmonary circulation when hypertension was induced by hypoxic ventilation or infusion of a thromboxane analog during normoxic ventilation. Using an isolated, perfused rat lung model, we found that "SNO-RBCs" did indeed reduce the pressor response to hypoxia, but they equally reduced the pressor response to thromboxane infusion during normoxia (Figure 5).(23) Moreover, the inhibitory concentration of SNO-Hb within red cells was several-fold higher than that measured the mammalian circulation, and the loss of SNO from red cells was not affected by the perfusate PO_2. These data provide further evidence against the allosteric regulation of SNO-Hb formation and degradation, and suggest that SNO-Hb is unlikely to be an important regulator of pulmonary vascular tone.

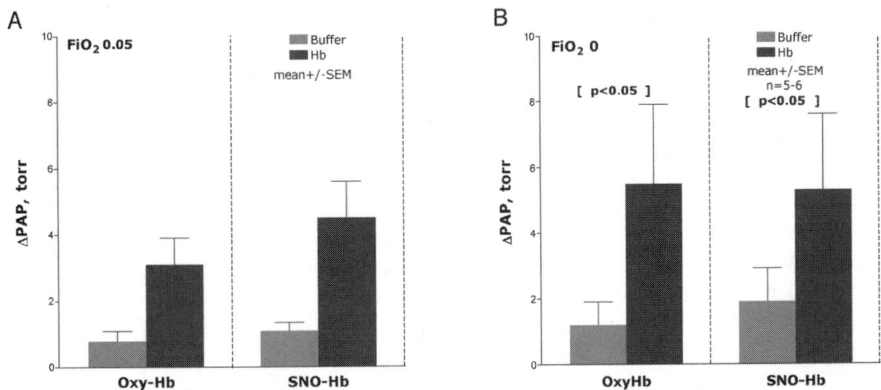

Figure 4. A. HPV before and after addition of oxyHb or SNO-Hb to buffer perfused rabbit lungs. Perfusate PO_2 in these experiments was approximately 60 Torr. OxyHb and SNO-Hb have similar effects on HPV. B. As for panel A, rat lungs. PO_2 in these experiments was approximately 11 Torr, near the p50 for free SNO-Hb.

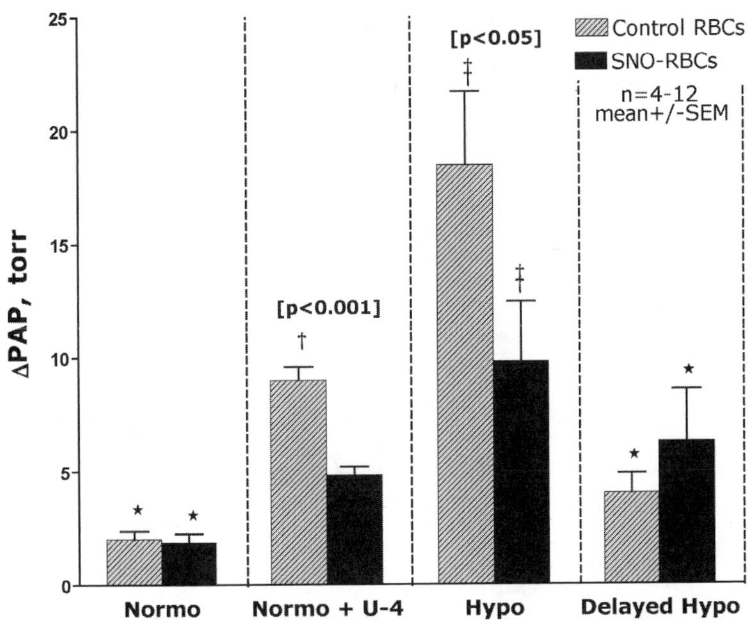

Figure 5. Effect of RBCs containing SNO-Hb (SNO-RBCs) on pulmonary artery pressure during normoxic (infusion of U-46619) or hypoxic pulmonary hypertension in isolated rat lungs, compared to the effect of control RBCs (no SNO-Hb). SNO-RBCs reduce PAP under both normoxic and hypoxic conditions, but the effect is lost at lower SNO concentrations (late hypoxia).

Nitrite has also been postulated to be an important modulator of vascular tone, serving as a storage pool for NO. NO is converted to nitrite in hypoxic conditions, and deoxyhemoglobin has been postulated to play an important role in NO generation from nitrite by serving as a nitrite "reductase".(27, 50, 63) Nitrite at low concentrations has been shown to relax systemic vascular smooth muscle in vitro, and to increase forearm blood flow in vivo.(17, 36) Furthermore, Hunter et al have shown that inhaled, nebulized nitrite reduces hypoxia-induced pulmonary artery pressure in fetal sheep.(44) However, in the latter study local lung concentrations of nitrite where likely high, and systemic blood nitrite concentrations were several times that measured in the normal circulation.

In preliminary studies, we have found that relatively low perfusate concentrations of nitrite (5 μM) reduce HPV in isolated, perfused rat lungs (Figure 6). However, addition of red cells to the perfusate attenuated the effect of nitrite on HPV, in contrast to the effect seen when nitrite is applied to aortic rings. The reasons for the discrepancy in our findings from those of others are not evident, and the role of circulating nitrite in the modulation of HPV is unclear. Nonetheless, inhaled, nebulized nitrite may have therapeutic application in the treatment of pulmonary hypertension and refractory hypoxia.

Although much of the previous discussion focuses on how the red blood cell affects NO, it is also important to recognize that NO may affect the red blood cell. NO increases red cell deformability, which in turn may have important effects on microvascular blood flow(5, 11, 51) . Given that hypoxia reduces red cell deformability (38), a combination of NO deficiency and hypoxia may have additive detrimental effects on the ability of red cells to traverse the microcirculation, and contribute to pulmonary hypertension in these conditions (26).

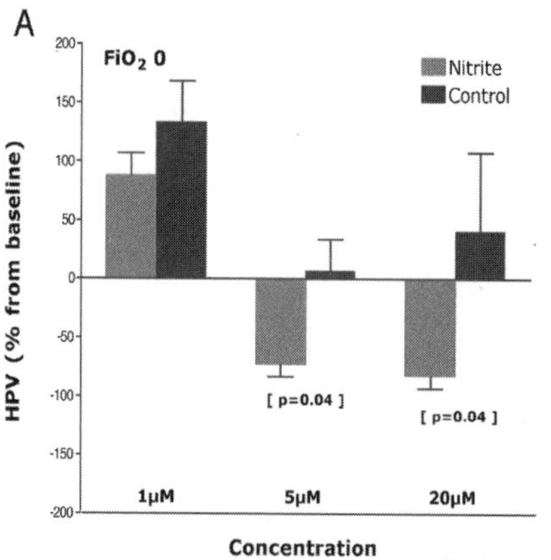

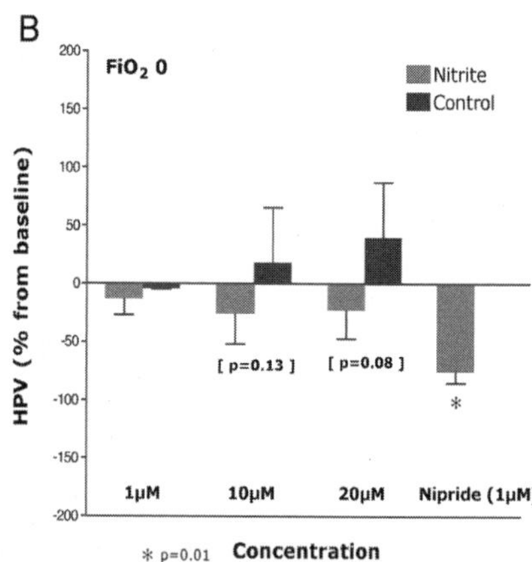

Figure 6. A. Effect of nitrite on HPV in buffer-perfused rat lungs. HPV is reported as the a percentage change from baseline response. Nitrite inhibits HPV at a concentration of 5 μM. B. Effect of nitrite on HPV in lungs perfused with buffer containing RBCs (Hct 15%). Inhibition of HPV by nitrite is lost in the presence of RBCs.

RED BLOOD CELLS AND MODULATION OF HYPOXIC PULMONARY VASOCONSTRICTION: OTHER MECHANISMS

The role of reactive oxygen species in the initiation and modulation of HPV is controversial, and the interested reader is directed elsewhere for reviews of this issue.(59, 82) Suffice it to say there is evidence that HPV may be provoked or inhibited by reactive oxygen species, and that the anti-oxidant capacity of red cells may play a role in the modulation of HPV. Red blood cells are rich in antioxidant enzymes, including superoxide dismutase (SOD), catalase, and glutathione peroxidase. Yamaguchi et al found that lungs subjected to oxidant stress by addition of xanthine and xanthine oxidase exhibited diminished HPV, which could be restored by addition of red blood cells to the perfusate. Inhibition of SOD, but not catalase, in red blood cells prevented restoration of hypoxic vasoconstriction; addition of exogenous SOD once again restored vasoconstriction (86). Thus, inactivation of superoxide radical (but not H_20_2) by red blood cells during high oxidant stress appears to be important in maintaining hypoxic pulmonary vasoconstriction.

Kerbaul et al found that the antioxidant n-acetylcysteine restored HPV to baseline values in dogs that had undergone hemodilution to a Hct of 20%.(48) They postulated that the reduced antioxidant capacity induced by anemia was responsible for a reduction in HPV. However, no measurements of NO or oxidant stress were reported, thus limiting the implications of this study. N-acetylcysteine may reduce NO production by inhibiting arginase, which would also explain their observations.(30)

In addition to augmentation of HPV, the red cell may also have an inhibitory effect, with the former predominating under most conditions. This inhibitory effect is suggested by the observation that NOS inhibition dramatically augments HPV in buffer-perfused lungs, but not in red cell-perfused lungs (Figure 2).(24) This relative inhibition of HPV by red cells may be due to effects of viscosity. Although modeling of pulmonary arterial pressure changes with variations in blood viscosity predict a diminution of HPV as Hct falls, (48) the experimental evidence suggests the opposite. In 1975, Benumof demonstrated that increased blood viscosity inhibited HPV in intact dogs.(6) We confirmed this finding in isolated, perfused rabbit lungs, and also demonstrated that the isolated red blood cell membrane (red blood cell ghosts) inhibits HPV (Figure 7).(19) Inhibition of HPV by increased perfusate viscosity was not prevented by either cyclooxygenase or NOS inhibition, but it appears likely that increased viscosity produces shear-stress effects that have an inhibitory effect on HPV.

HEMOGLOBIN-BASED OXYGEN CARRIERS (HBOCS)

Structural modification of Hb in order to create a safe and effective HBOC is an area of intense research. One limitation of HBOCs lies in the increased capacity for any free Hb solution to inactivate NO (65). Accordingly, HBOCs cause pulmonary vasoconstriction both *in vitro* and *in vivo* (10, 52, 60, 73), an effect which appears to be due to NO scavenging (32, 49). Furthermore, genetic modification of a recombinant HBOC to reduce NO scavenging by heme prevents pulmonary vasoconstriction and augmentation of hypoxic pulmonary vasoconstriction (71).

Theoretically, inter- or intra-molecular cross-linking of free Hb may reduce the NO scavenging and vasoconstrictive effects of HBOCs by preventing Hb tetramer dissociation and extra-luminal movement of dimers. However, we found no difference in either baseline pulmonary artery pressure or hypoxic pulmonary vasoconstriction when free Hb that was intramolecularly cross-linked at the ß-cysteine 93 residue was compared to native Hb in isolated rat lungs (22). It is likely that more specific modifications of Hb to reduce or prevent NO scavenging, as described above, will be necessary to significantly limit the vasoconstrictive effects of HBOCs (71).

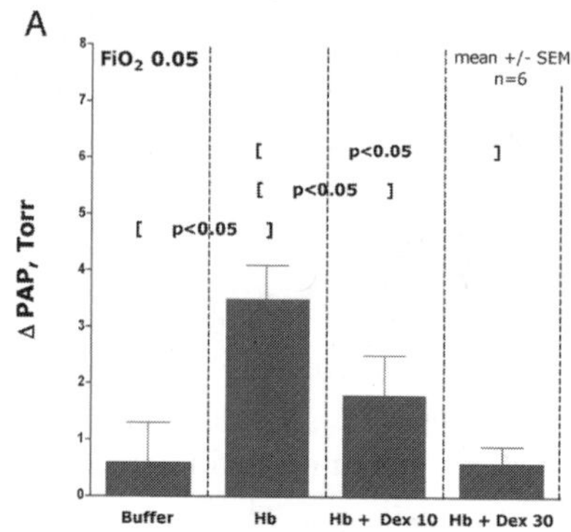

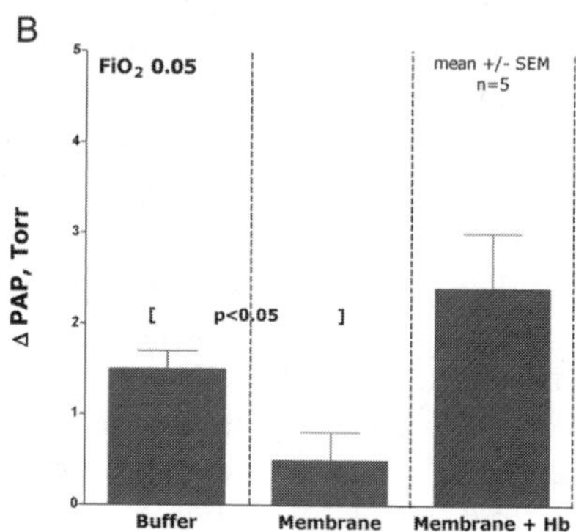

Figure 7. A. HPV in lungs perfused with buffer, or buffer containing Hb, or Hb plus dextran to raise perfusate viscosity to that comparable to a Hct of 10 and 30%. Increasing perfusate viscosity inhibits HPV. B. HPV in lungs perfused with buffer, or buffer plus RBC membrane, or membrane plus Hb. RBC membrane inhibits HPV.

CONCLUSIONS

Continuous production of NO in the lung acts to attenuate, or "brake", HPV. Red blood cells counteract this effect, predominantly by hemoglobin-mediated oxidation and inactivation of NO, and also possibly through scavenging of reactive oxygen species. Despite evidence that RBC transport and production of NO may play a role in the control of systemic vasomotor tone via hypoxic vasodilation, production of NO by RBCs does not appear to be important in the modulation of HPV. RBC-NO-HPV interactions are likely important factors in the optimization of gas exchange in health and disease, and are limiting factors in the therapeutic use of HBOCs. Further research is necessary to complete our understanding of lung-red cell interactions and their important interplay in health and disease.

ACKNOWLEGDMENTS

Dr. Deem is the 2003 recipient of the Frontiers in Anesthesia Research Award from the International Anesthesia Research Society. Supported by NIH HL 03796-01 and the International Anesthesia Research Society.

REFERENCES

1. Aaronson PI, Robertson TP, and Ward JP. Endothelium-derived mediators and hypoxic pulmonary vasoconstriction. *Respir Physiol Neurobiol* 132: 107-120, 2002.
2. Archer SL, Huang J, Henry T, Peterson D, and Weir EK. A redox-based O2 sensor in rat pulmonary vasculature. *Circ Res* 73: 1100-1112, 1993.
3. Archer SL, Tolins JP, Raij L, and Weir EK. Hypoxic pulmonary vasoconstriction is enhanced by inhibition of the synthesis of an endothelium derived relaxing factor. *Biochemical and Biophysical Research Communications* 164: 1198-1205, 1989.
4. Barman SA. Potassium channels modulate hypoxic pulmonary vasoconstriction. *Am J Physiol* 275: L64-70., 1998.
5. Bateman RM, Jagger JE, Sharpe MD, Ellsworth ML, Mehta S, and Ellis CG. Erythrocyte deformability is a nitric oxide-mediated factor in decreased capillary density during sepsis. *Am J Physiol Heart Circ Physiol* 280: H2848-2856, 2001.
6. Benumof JL and Wahrenbrock EA. Blunted hypoxic pulmonary vasoconstriction by increased lung vascular pressures. *J Appl Physiol* 38: 846-850, 1975.
7. Berg JT, Deem S, Kerr ME, and Swenson ER. Hemoglobin and red blood cells alter the response of expired nitric oxide to mechanical forces. *Am J Physiol Heart Circ Physiol* 279: H2947-2953., 2000.
8. Blitzer ML, Loh E, Roddy M-A, Stamler JS, and Creager MA. Endothelium-derived nitric oxide regulates systemic and pulmonary vascular resistance during acute hypoxia in humans. *J Am Coll Cardiol* 28: 591-596, 1996.
9. Bonaventura C, Ferruzzi G, Tesh S, and Stevens RD. Effects of S-nitrosation on oxygen binding by normal and sickle cell hemoglobin. *J Biol Chem* 274: 24742-24748., 1999.
10. Bone HG, Waurick R, Van Aken H, Jahn UR, Booke M, and Meyer J. The hemodynamic effects of cell-free hemoglobin during general and epidural anesthesia. *Anesth Analg* 89: 1131-1136, 1999.
11. Bor-Kucukatay M, Wenby RB, Meiselman HJ, and Baskurt OK. Effects of nitric oxide on red blood cell deformability. *Am J Physiol Heart Circ Physiol* 284: H1577-1584, 2003.
12. Brashers VL, Peach MJ, and Edward CR, Jr. Augmentation of hypoxic pulmonary vasoconstriction in the isolated perfused rat lung by in vitro antagonists of endothelium-dependent relaxation. *J Clin Invest* 82: 1495-1502, 1988.
13. Brimioulle S, LeJeune P, and Naeije R. Effects of hypoxic pulmonary vasoconstriction on pulmonary gas exchange. *J Appl Physiol* 81: 1535-1543, 1996.
14. Cannon RO, 3rd, Schechter AN, Panza JA, Ognibene FP, Pease-Fye ME, Waclawiw MA, Shelhamer JH, and Gladwin MT. Effects of inhaled nitric oxide on regional blood flow are consistent with intravascular nitric oxide delivery. *J Clin Invest* 108: 279-287., 2001.
15. Carlin RE, Ferrario L, Boyd JT, Camporesi EM, McGraw DJ, and Hakim TS. Determinants of nitric oxide in exhaled gas in the isolated rabbit lung. *Am J Respir Crit Care Med* 155: 922-927., 1997.
16. Cooper CE. Nitric oxide and iron proteins. *Biochim Biophys Acta* 1411: 290-309., 1999.
17. Cosby K, Partovi KS, Crawford JH, Patel RP, Reiter CD, Martyr S, Yang BK, Waclawiw MA, Zalos G, Xu X, Huang KT, Shields H, Kim-Shapiro DB, Schechter AN, Cannon RO, 3rd, and Gladwin MT. Nitrite reduction to nitric oxide by deoxyhemoglobin vasodilates the human circulation. *Nat Med* 9: 1498-1505, 2003.
18. Cremona G, Wood AM, Hall LW, Bower EA, and Higenbottam T. Effect of inhibitors of nitric oxide release and action on vascular tone in isolated lungs of pig, sheep, dog and man. *J Physiol* 481 (Pt 1): 185-195, 1994.
19. Deem S, Berg JT, Kerr ME, and Swenson ER. Effects of the RBC membrane and increased perfusate viscosity on hypoxic pulmonary vasoconstriction. *J Appl Physiol* 88: 1520-1528., 2000.

20. Deem S, Bishop MJ, and Alberts MK. Effect of anemia on intrapulmonary shunt during atelectasis in rabbits. *J Appl Physiol* 79: 1951-1957., 1995.
21. Deem S, Gladwin MT, Berg JT, Kerr ME, and Swenson ER. Effects of S-Nitrosation of Hemoglobin on Hypoxic Pulmonary Vasoconstriction and Nitric Oxide Flux. *Am J Respir Crit Care Med* 163: 1164-1170., 2001.
22. Deem S, Kim JU, Manjula BN, Acharya AS, Kerr ME, Patel RP, Gladwin MT, and Swenson ER. Effects of S-nitrosation and cross-linking of hemoglobin on hypoxic pulmonary vasoconstriction in isolated rat lungs. *Circ Res* 91: 626-632, 2002.
23. Deem S, Kim SS, Min JH, Eveland R, Moulding J, Martyr S, Wang X, Swenson ER, and Gladwin MT. Pulmonary vascular effects of red blood cells containing S-nitrosated hemoglobin. *Am J Physiol Heart Circ Physiol*, 2004.
24. Deem S, Swenson ER, Alberts MK, Hedges RG, and Bishop MJ. Red-blood-cell augmentation of hypoxic pulmonary vasoconstriction: hematocrit dependence and the importance of nitric oxide. *Am J Respir Crit Care Med* 157: 1181-1186., 1998.
25. Defouilloy C, Teiger E, Sediame S, Andrivet P, Roudot-Thoraval F, Chouaid C, Housset B, and Adnot S. Polycythemia impairs vasodilator response to acetylcholine in patients with chronic hypoxemic lung disease. *Am J Respir Crit Care Med* 157: 1452-1460, 1998.
26. Doyle MP, Galey WR, and Walker BR. Reduced erythrocyte deformability alters pulmonary hemodynamics. *J Appl Physiol* 67: 2593-2599, 1989.
27. Doyle MP, Pickering RA, DeWeert TM, Hoekstra JW, and Pater D. Kinetics and mechanism of the oxidation of human deoxyhemoglobin by nitrites. *J Biol Chem* 256: 12393-12398, 1981.
28. Duke H and Killick E. Pulmonary vasomotor responses of isolated perfused cat lungs to anoxia. *J Physiol* 117: 303-316, 1952.
29. Dweik RA, Laskowski D, Abu-Soud HM, Kaneko F, Hutte R, Stuehr DJ, and Erzurum SC. Nitric oxide synthesis in the lung. Regulation by oxygen through a kinetic mechanism. *J Clin Invest* 101: 660-666, 1998.
30. Erbas H, Aydogdu N, and Kaymak K. Effects of N-acetylcysteine on arginase, ornithine and nitric oxide in renal ischemia-reperfusion injury. *Pharmacol Res* 50: 523-527, 2004.
31. Fagan KA, Fouty BW, Tyler RC, Morris KG, Jr., Hepler LK, Sato K, LeCras TD, Abman SH, Weinberger HD, Huang PL, McMurtry IF, and Rodman DM. The pulmonary circulation of homozygous or heterozygous eNOS-null mice is hyperresponsive to mild hypoxia. *J Clin Invest* 103: 291-299., 1999.
32. Freas W, Llave R, Jing M, Hart J, McQuillan P, and Muldoon S. Contractile effects of diaspirin cross-linked hemoglobin (DCLHb) on isolated porcine blood vessels. *J Lab Clin Med* 125: 762-767, 1995.
33. Frostell CG, Blomqvist H, Hedenstierna G, Lundberg J, and Zapol WM. Inhaled nitric oxide selectively reverses human hypoxic pulmonary vasoconstriction without causing systemic vasodilation. *Anesthesiology* 78: 427-435., 1993.
34. Gelband CH and Gelband H. Ca2+ release from intracellular stores is an initial step in hypoxic pulmonary vasoconstriction of rat pulmonary artery resistance vessels. *Circulation* 96: 3647-3654, 1997.
35. Gladwin MT, Ognibene FP, Pannell LK, Nichols JS, Pease-Fye ME, Shelhamer JH, and Schechter AN. Relative role of heme nitrosylation and beta-cysteine 93 nitrosation in the transport and metabolism of nitric oxide by hemoglobin in the human circulation. *Proc Natl Acad Sci U S A* 97: 9943-9948., 2000.
36. Gladwin MT, Shelhamer JH, Schechter AN, Pease-Fye ME, Waclawiw MA, Panza JA, Ognibene FP, and Cannon RO, 3rd. Role of circulating nitrite and S-nitrosohemoglobin in the regulation of regional blood flow in humans. *Proc Natl Acad Sci U S A* 97: 11482-11487., 2000.
37. Grimminger F, Spriestersbach R, Weissmann N, Walmrath D, and Seeger W. Nitric oxide

generation and hypoxic vasoconstriction in buffer-perfused rabbit lungs. *J Appl Physiol* 78: 1509-1515., 1995.

38. Hakim TS and Macek AS. Effect of hypoxia on erythrocyte deformability in different species. *Biorheology* 25: 857-868, 1988.
39. Hakim TS and Macek AS. Role of erythrocyte deformability in the acute hypoxic pressor response in the pulmonary vasculature. *Respir Physiol* 72: 95-107., 1988.
40. Hakim TS and Malik AB. Hypoxic vasoconstriction in blood and plasma perfused lungs. *Respir Physiol* 72: 109-121., 1988.
41. Hasunuma K, Yamaguchi T, Rodman DM, O'Brien RF, and McMurtry IF. Effects of inhibitors of EDRF and EDHF on vasoreactivity of perfused rat lungs. *Am J Physiol* 260: L97-104., 1991.
42. Heller A, Ragaller M, Schmeck J, Fluth H, Muller M, Albrecht DM, and Koch T. Role of NO and endothelin in hemoglobin-induced pulmonary vasoconstriction. *Shock* 10: 401-406, 1998.
43. Hillier SC, Graham JA, Hanger CC, Godbey PS, Glenny RW, and Wagner WW, Jr. Hypoxic vasoconstriction in pulmonary arterioles and venules. *J Appl Physiol* 82: 1084-1090, 1997.
44. Hunter CJ, Dejam A, Blood AB, Shields H, Kim-Shapiro DB, Machado RF, Tarekegn S, Mulla N, Hopper AO, Schechter AN, Power GG, and Gladwin MT. Inhaled nebulized nitrite is a hypoxia-sensitive NO-dependent selective pulmonary vasodilator. *Nat Med* 10: 1122-1127, 2004.
45. Jia L, Bonaventura C, Bonaventura J, and Stamler JS. S-nitrosohaemoglobin: a dynamic activity of blood involved in vascular control. *Nature* 380: 221-226., 1996.
46. Kantrow SP, Huang YC, Whorton AR, Grayck EN, Knight JM, Millington DS, and Piantadosi CA. Hypoxia inhibits nitric oxide synthesis in isolated rabbit lung. *Am J Physiol* 272: L1167-1173, 1997.
47. Kao SJ, Wei J, Hwang CP, Lieu MW, Jiang JS, Wang D, and Chen HI. Modulatory effect of blood cells on hypoxic vasoconstriction response and nitric oxide release in rat lungs. *J Formos Med Assoc* 98: 39-44, 1999.
48. Kerbaul F, Van der Linden P, Pierre S, Rondelet B, Melot C, Brimioulle S, and Naeije R. Prevention of hemodilution-induced inhibition of hypoxic pulmonary vasoconstriction by N-acetylcysteine in dogs. *Anesth Analg* 99: 547-551, table of contents, 2004.
49. Kim HW and Greenburg AG. Hemoglobin mediated vasoactivity in isolated vascular rings. *Artif Cells Blood Substit Immobil Biotechnol* 23: 303-309, 1995.
50. Kim-Shapiro DB, Gladwin MT, Patel RP, and Hogg N. The reaction between nitrite and hemoglobin: the role of nitrite in hemoglobin-mediated hypoxic vasodilation. *J Inorg Biochem* 99: 237-246, 2005.
51. Korbut R and Gryglewski RJ. Nitric oxide from polymorphonuclear leukocytes modulates red blood cell deformability in vitro. *Eur J Pharmacol* 234: 17-22, 1993.
52. Lee R, Neya K, Svizzero TA, and Vlahakes GJ. Limitations of the efficacy of hemoglobin-based oxygen-carrying solutions. *J Appl Physiol* 79: 236-242, 1995.
53. Liu S, Crawley DE, Barnes PJ, and Evans TW. Endothelium-derived relaxing factor inhibits hypoxic pulmonary vasoconstriction in rats. *Am Rev Respir Dis* 143: 32-37, 1991.
54. Loer SA and Peters J. Effects of haemoconcentration and haemodilution on acute hypoxia-induced pulmonary hypertension and changes in vascular compliance of isolated rabbit lungs. *Intensive Care Med* 26: 1124-1130., 2000.
55. Madden JA, Vadula MS, and Kurup VP. Effects of hypoxia and other vasoactive agents on pulmonary and cerebral artery smooth muscle cells. *Am J Physiol* 263: L384-393, 1992.
56. Mazmanian G-M, Baudet B, Brink C, Cerrina J, Kirkiacharian S, and Weiss M. Methylene blue potentiates vascular reactivity in isolated rat lungs. *J Appl Physiol* 66: 1040-1045,

1989.
57. McMahon TJ, Moon RE, Luschinger BP, Carraway MS, Stone AE, Stolp BW, Gow AJ, Pawloski JR, Watke P, Singel DJ, Piantadosi CA, and Stamler JS. Nitric oxide in the human respiratory cycle. *Nat Med* 3: 3, 2002.
58. McMurtry IF, Hookway BW, and Roos SD. Red blood cells but not platelets prolong vascular reactivity of isolated rat lungs. *Am J Physiol* 234: H186-191., 1978.
59. Michelakis ED, Thebaud B, Weir EK, and Archer SL. Hypoxic pulmonary vasoconstriction: redox regulation of O2-sensitive K+ channels by a mitochondrial O2-sensor in resistance artery smooth muscle cells. *J Mol Cell Cardiol* 37: 1119-1136, 2004.
60. Muldoon SM, Ledvina MA, Hart JL, and Macdonald VW. Hemoglobin-induced contraction of pig pulmonary veins. *J Lab Clin Med* 128: 579-584, 1996.
61. Murray TR, Chen L, Marshall BE, and Macarak EJ. Hypoxic contraction of cultured pulmonary vascular smooth muscle cells. *Am J Respir Cell Mol Biol* 3: 457-465, 1990.
62. Naeije R and Brimioulle S. Physiology in medicine: importance of hypoxic pulmonary vasoconstriction in maintaining arterial oxygenation during acute respiratory failure. *Crit Care* 5: 67-71, 2001.
63. Nagababu E, Ramasamy S, Abernethy DR, and Rifkind JM. Active nitric oxide produced in the red cell under hypoxic conditions by deoxyhemoglobin-mediated nitrite reduction. *J Biol Chem* 278: 46349-46356, 2003.
64. Nishiyama T and Hanaoka K. Free hemoglobin concentrations in patients receiving massive blood transfusion during emergency surgery for trauma. *Can J Anaesth* 47: 881-885, 2000.
65. Patel RP. Biochemical aspects of the reaction of hemoglobin and NO: implications for Hb-based blood substitutes. *Free Radic Biol Med* 28: 1518-1525., 2000.
66. Persson MG, Gustafsson LE, Wiklund NP, Moncada S, and Hedquist P. Endogenous nitric oxide as a probably modulator of pulmonary circulation and hypoxic pressor response in vivo. *Acta Physiol Scand* 140: 449-457, 1990.
67. Pison U, Lopez FA, Heidelmeyer CF, Rossaint R, and Falke KJ. Inhaled nitric oxide reverses hypoxic pulmonary vasoconstriction without impairing gas exchange. *J Appl Physiol* 74: 1287-1292., 1993.
68. Post JM, Hume JR, Archer SL, and Weir EK. Direct role for potassium channel inhibition in hypoxic pulmonary vasoconstriction. *Am J Physiol* 262: C882-890., 1992.
69. Reiter CD, Wang X, Tanus-Santos JE, Hogg N, Cannon RO, 3rd, Schechter AN, and Gladwin MT. Cell-free hemoglobin limits nitric oxide bioavailability in sickle-cell disease. *Nat Med* 8: 1383-1389, 2002.
70. Rengasamy A and Johns RA. Determination of Km for oxygen of nitric oxide synthase isoforms. *J Pharmacol Exp Ther* 276: 30-33, 1996.
71. Resta TC, Walker BR, Eichinger MR, and Doyle MP. Rate of NO scavenging alters effects of recombinant hemoglobin solutions on pulmonary vasoreactivity. *J Appl Physiol* 93: 1327-1336, 2002.
72. Sander M, Welling K-LK, Ravn JB, Boberg B, and Amtorp O. Endogenous NO does not regulate baseline pulmonary pressure, but reduces acute pulmonary hypertension in dogs. *Acta Physiol Scand* 178: 269-277, 2003.
73. Sefton W, Pudimat P, Bina S, Lojeski E, Mongan P, and Muldoon S. Inhaled nitric oxide attenuates increased pulmonary artery pressure following diaspirin crosslinked hemoglobin (DCLHB) administration. *Artif Cells Blood Substit Immobil Biotechnol* 27: 203-213, 1999.
74. Shirai M, Shimouchi A, Kawaguchi AT, Ikeda S, Sunagawa K, and Ninomiya I. Endogenous nitric oxide attenuates hypoxic vasoconstriction of small pulmonary arteries and veins in anaesthetized cats. *Acta Physiol Scand* 159: 263-264, 1997.
75. Shirai M, Shimouchi A, Kawaguchi AT, Sunagawa K, and Ninomiya I. Inhaled nitric

oxide: diameter response patterns in feline small pulmonary arteries and veins. *Am J Physiol* 270: H974-980, 1996.

76. Sprague RS, Thiemermann C, and Vane JR. Endogenous endothelium-derived relaxing factor opposes hypoxic pulmonary vasoconstriction and supports blood flow to hypoxic alveoli in anesthetized rabbits. *Proc Natl Acad Sci U S A* 89: 8711-8715, 1992.
77. Stamler JS, Jia L, Eu JP, McMahon TJ, Demchenko IT, Bonaventura J, Gernert K, and Piantadosi CA. Blood flow regulation by S-nitrosohemoglobin in the physiological oxygen gradient. *Science* 276: 2034-2037., 1997.
78. Staub NC. Site of hypoxic pulmonary vasoconstriction. *Chest* 88: 240S-245S, 1985.
79. Toothill C. The chemistry of the in vivo reaction between haemoglobin and various oxides of nitrogen. *Br J Anaesth* 39: 405-412., 1967.
80. Vadula MS, Kleinman JG, and Madden JA. Effect of hypoxia and norepinephrine on cytoplasmic free Ca2+ in pulmonary and cerebral arterial myocytes. *Am J Physiol* 265: L591-597, 1993.
81. Voelkel NF. Mechanisms of hypoxic pulmonary vasoconstriction. *Am Rev Respir Dis* 133: 1186-1195, 1986.
82. Waypa GB and Schumacker PT. Hypoxic pulmonary vasoconstriction: redox events in oxygen sensing. *J Appl Physiol* 98: 404-414, 2005.
83. Weissmann N, Grimminger F, Olschewski A, and Seeger W. Hypoxic pulmonary vasoconstriction: a multifactorial response? *Am J Physiol Lung Cell Mol Physiol* 281: L314-317, 2001.
84. Weissmann N, Grimminger F, Walmrath D, and Seeger W. Hypoxic vasoconstriction in buffer-perfused rabbit lungs. *Respir Physiol* 100: 159-169., 1995.
85. Wolzt M, MacAllister RJ, Davis D, Feelisch M, Moncada S, Vallance P, and Hobbs AJ. Biochemical characterization of S-nitrosohemoglobin. Mechanisms underlying synthesis, no release, and biological activity. *J Biol Chem* 274: 28983-28990., 1999.
86. Yamaguchi K, Asano K, Takasugi T, Mori M, Fujita H, Oyamada Y, Suzuki K, Miyata A, Aoki T, and Suzuki Y. Modulation of hypoxic pulmonary vasoconstriction by antioxidant enzymes in red blood cells. *Am J Respir Crit Care Med* 153: 211-217, 1996.
87. Yuan XJ, Tod ML, Rubin LJ, and Blaustein MP. Contrasting effects of hypoxia on tension in rat pulmonary and mesenteric arteries. *Am J Physiol* 259: H281-289, 1990.
88. Zhang F, Carson RC, Zhang H, Gibson G, and Thomas HM, 3rd. Pulmonary artery smooth muscle cell (Ca2+)i and contraction: responses to diphenyleneiodonium and hypoxia. *Am J Physiol* 273: L603-611, 1997.

Chapter 20

DOSE-RESPONSE OF ALTITUDE TRAINING: HOW MUCH ALTITUDE IS ENOUGH?

Benjamin D. Levine[1], James Stray-Gundersen[2]

[1]Institute for Exercise and Environmental Medicine, Presbyterian Hospital of Dallas, Professor of Medicine, University of Texas Southwestern Medical Center at Dallas, [2]Department of Health, University of Utah, Dallas, TX , USA.

Abstract: Altitude training continues to be a key adjunctive aid for the training of competitive athletes throughout the world. Over the past decade, evidence has accumulated from many groups of investigators that the "living high -- training low" approach to altitude training provides the most robust and reliable performance enhancements. The success of this strategy depends on two key features: 1) living high enough, for enough hours per day, for a long enough period of time, to initiate and sustain an erythropoietic effect of high altitude; and 2) training low enough to allow maximal quality of high intensity workouts, requiring high rates of sustained oxidative flux. Because of the relatively limited access to environments where such a strategy can be practically applied, numerous devices have been developed to "bring the mountain to the athlete," which has raised the key issue of the appropriate "dose" of altitude required to stimulate an acclimatization response and performance enhancement. These include devices using molecular sieve technology to provide a normobaric hypoxic living or sleeping environment, approaches using very high altitudes (5,500m) for shorter periods of time during the day, and "intermittent hypoxic training" involving breathing very hypoxic gas mixtures for alternating 5 minutes periods over the course of 60-90 minutes. Unfortunately, objective testing of the strategies employing short term (less than 4 hours) normobaric or hypobaric hypoxia has failed to demonstrate an advantage of these techniques. Moreover individual variability of the response to even the best of living high -- training low strategies has been great, and the mechanisms behind this variability remain obscure. Future research efforts will need to focus on defining the optimal dosing strategy for these devices, and determining the underlying mechanisms of the individual variability so as to enable the individualized "prescription" of altitude exposure to optimize the performance of each athlete.

Key Words: hypoxic training, athletics, hemoglobin, erythropoietin

INTRODUCTION

Altitude training is frequently included as a cornerstone of the training plans for elite endurance athletes(65). Since the publication of the "living high-training low" model in 1997(34), this approach to altitude training has become increasingly adopted by many teams in the United States and around the world. For example, the US speed skating team used it to great advantage in the 2002 Salt Lake City Olympic Games, living in Park City, Utah at an altitude of 2,000-2,500m and training at the Olympic Oval at 1,400m, sometimes even using supplemental oxygen to allow increased training loads(38). This approach, incorporated into a highly focused training plan, contributed to the largest number of medals awarded to the most number of skaters in US Skating history. More recently, both US medalists in the Olympic marathon at the Athens Games in 2004 incorporated LHTL into their training plans by living at Mammoth, California (2,500m), and performing intermittent high intensity interval training at low altitude in Bishop (1,250m). This effort resulted in the first ever medals awarded to US men and women athletes in the marathon in the same Olympics.

The essential features of the LHTL model appear to be living high enough, long enough to acquire the essential features of altitude acclimatization that may improve sea level performance, combined with performing enough high intensity training sessions at a low enough altitude to maintain work out quality by ensuring high rates of oxidative flux(33, 34). The key question for this presentation is how much altitude is required to stimulate a robust and sustainable adaptive response? In order to frame this discussion, it is useful to consider both exercise training and the interactive effect of altitude as a "dose" of a medication that leads to a specific physiological response. Such a "dose-response" curve is shown in figure 1.

Conceptually, at very low levels of exercise training, there is very limited adaptive response (i.e., sitting quietly, or slow walking won't lead to much of a training effect?); after some threshold level of training is achieved, with increasing doses of exercise (frequency, duration, intensity) there is a corresponding increase in the adaptive response, which can be quantified physiologically (increased maximal aerobic power, improved endurance, augmented anaerobic capacity) or by enhanced performance. In pharmacology terms, the "ED 50" would then be the "effective dose" at which 50% of the physiological effect is achieved. At some point, more training does not necessarily lead to a greater response and a plateau is achieved. Along with this dose-response relationship, there is also a toxicity curve that can be drawn. Thus for exercise, the toxic effects are relatively low at most doses of training. However there is a point at which increasing training (particularly increasing the intensity of "recovery" sessions) may lead to side effects such as staleness, over reaching or over training. Again in an analogy with a pharmacological therapy, the "LD 50" would then be the dose at which 50% of the toxic (or "lethal" -- used figuratively here...) effect is suffered. Ultimately the "therapeutic range" is the range of exercise training which is at the ED 50 or above, but also is below the rapid rise in toxic side effects.

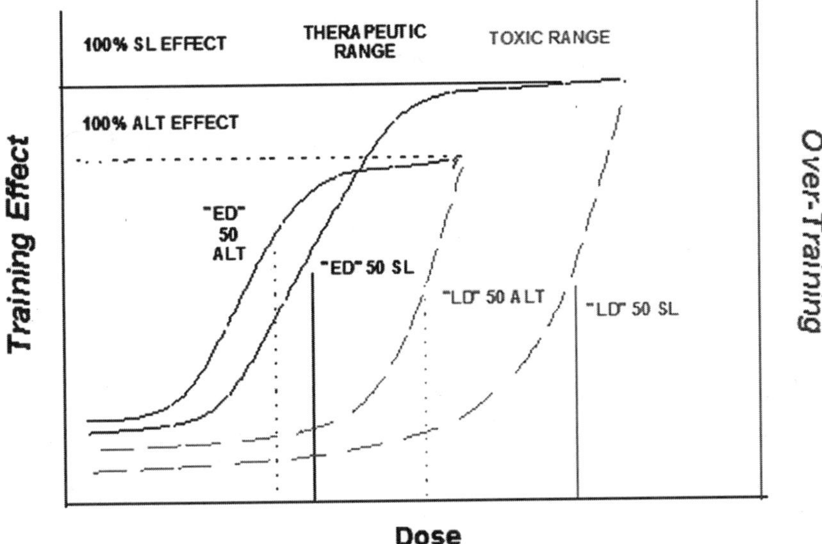

Figure 1. "Dose-Response" relationship between exercise training and the adaptive response at sea level (in black) and at altitude (in grey). See text for details.

Altitude has specific effects on this relationship. First of all, because exercise under hypoxic conditions is associated with prominent reductions in maximal power output, oxygen flux through mitochondrial systems, and work capacity, the peak response to endurance training under high altitude conditions is depressed(9, 20, 34, 35, 59). Because at submaximal levels, the same absolute power output at altitude is a greater fraction of the maximal capacity compared with sea level, the dose-response curve may also be shifted to the left. However the toxic effects of exercise are also more prominent and athletes may be more prone to over training while at altitude. The therapeutic range is therefore smaller with exercise training at altitude. Like exercise training, the effect of altitude by itself has its own "dose-response" curve (not shown), though each of the manifestations of the altitude acclimatization response likely has its own specific curve with different threshold, therapeutic range, and toxic profiles.

Although many possible mechanisms have been proposed as mediating a beneficial effect on performance from altitude training (including LHTL)(24), our own studies have drawn us inexorably towards the hematopoietic system(33). In addition, it is abundantly clear that increasing blood volume from direct transfusion or exogenous erythropoietin increases performance at sea level in virtually all athletes(11, 14, 15). To the best of our knowledge, this is the only effect of altitude acclimatization that has directly, and unequivocally been shown to improve sea level performance in athletes. In other words, there is no other effect of altitude acclimatization that can be (or has been) manipulated *independently* and demonstrated to improve athletic performance over a sustained period of time (weeks).

The erythropoietic effect of altitude acclimatization is clear and compelling, particularly when the exposure is high enough, and sustained for a long enough period of time. This evidence has been reviewed recently(33) and will not be repeated here. For the purposes of the discussion regarding "dose" of altitude however, one study does bear brief discussion. For example, half a century ago, Reynafarje exposed 10 sea level natives to full time residence (i.e., 24 hr/d) at an altitude of 4,500m, and measured both plasma and red cell compartment volumes over a year at this altitude(39). After the first month, there was a small, but measurable increase in the red cell compartment (slightly less than 10%), along with a small decrease in the plasma compartment, such that total blood volume did not change. Over the subsequent half a year, the red cell mass and blood volume steadily increased, reaching its peak after 8 months of full time altitude residence (about 35% increase in red cell volume), and then increasing no further out to a year.

There are a number of key important points that deserve emphasis from this study: a) the high altitude, and long duration of continuous exposure likely make this study an example of the most vigorous erythropoietic effect that could be expected from sea level natives ascending to altitude; b) even at this "dose", the observed effect was at the limits of detection after the first 4 weeks, making it less likely that shorter duration exposures would be associated with a large effect; c) the red cell mass continued to increase for a full 8 months, despite the fact that erythropoietin levels were almost certainly near "normal" after the first few weeks. This observation emphasizes that erythropoiesis may be accelerated even in the face of apparently normal EPO levels, which are therefore elevated for the level of the red cell mass; d) plasma volume re-expanded rapidly on return to sea level, and both total blood volume and red cell volume remained above baseline for at least 2-4 weeks after descent. However after 2 months at sea level, all compartment volumes had returned to baseline.

THE LIVE HIGH -- TRAIN LOW MODEL OF ALTITUDE TRAINING

If this kind of exposure represents the maximal possible effect of altitude acclimatization, what happens with "submaximal" exposures? For the "classic' LHTL studies(13, 34, 35, 55), every effort was made for the athletes to spend as much time as possible at moderate altitude. There are a number of important design features of these studies that deserve emphasis: 1) all studies began with a 2 week "lead-in" phase where athletes were brought from their home cities to Dallas, TX (150m above sea level) for familiarization with laboratory equipment and testing procedures, and a focused period of controlled training; 2) this lead-in phase was followed by 4 weeks of training at sea level where all athletes trained together prior to randomization to bring all athletes up to an equivalent degree of training readiness. The key point to be made here is that virtually all athletes improved performance with experience and training. Therefore studies involving measures of performance which only include pre-post measurements may falsely conclude that an intervention is successful, simply because of the "training camp effect"; 3) athletes were then randomized into one of three training groups where they were exposed for 4 weeks to: a) the primary experimental group where the athletes lived at 2,500m and traveled down to a lower altitude of 1,250m once or twice per day to train. These athletes thus spent 20-22 hr/d at moderate altitude; b) an altitude control, where the athletes lived at 2,500m together with the LHTL athletes, but did all their training at the same altitude or higher (2,500-3,000m). These athletes spent 24 hr/d at altitude; c) a sea level control where the athletes traveled to a new, training camp environment with mountainous terrain, but at sea level altitude. The volume and relative intensity of training was closely matched among groups, and followed the same pattern as the previous 4 weeks of training at sea level. All subjects then returned to sea level for post-intervention testing acutely, and then 3 weeks later.

The details of these studies have recently been summarized in some detail and will only be reviewed briefly here. (33) The essential results of these studies were as follows: 1) the athletes living for more than 20hr/d at moderate altitude (8,000 ft.) had a significant increase in erythropoietin concentration which led to a significant increase in the erythrocyte volume (blood volume -- plasma volume); neither changed significantly in a sea level control group; 2) Coincident with the increase in erythrocyte volume, there was an increase in maximal oxygen uptake in both groups living at 8,000 ft., that was proportional to the increase in erythrocyte volume, and that was not observed in the control group performing similar training in an outstanding training camp environment, but at sea level; 3) Despite an increase in $\dot{V}O_{2max}$ in both groups of subjects living at moderate altitude, only the group performing all their training at low altitude improved 5,000m racing time by 1.3%. For the LHTL athletes, this quality of training maintained muscle fiber size, myoglobin concentration, and muscle buffer capacity, all of which decreased in the athletes attempting to do all their training at moderate altitude.(57) Functionally, this preservation of muscle structure allowed an increase in both the $\dot{V}O_2$ at the ventilatory threshold, and the velocity at $\dot{V}O_{2max}$ which were present only in the high-low group.(34); 4) There was no relationship between the skill of the athlete, and the magnitude of improvement observed after 4 weeks of LHTL(55). Even elite US runners, including US Olympians achieved on average, the same 1-2% improvement in performance associated with clear evidence of accelerated erythropoiesis and increased maximal aerobic power(55).

Despite the clear superiority of living high-training low over traditional altitude or sea level training, there remains substantial individual variability in the magnitude of improvement achieved with such a regimen.(13) To address the mechanisms of this variability, we performed a retrospective review of all 39 athletes in our previous studies (34, 58) who lived at 2,500m and trained between 1,250m and 3,000m, and divided them into two groups: those athletes who improved their 5,000m race by more than the group mean ("responders"); and those that got worse ("non-responders") (13). There were no differences between these groups with respect to baseline demographic variables (age, $\dot{V}O_{2max}$, running performance, hemoglobin concentration) or many physiological variables that might determine the magnitude of the acclimatization response to altitude including pulmonary diffusing capacity, oxygen saturation either at rest, during sleep, or during exercise at 2,500m.

The key distinguishing feature between "responders" and "non-responders" was that the responders had a significantly greater increase in erythropoietin concentration which remained elevated after 2 weeks at altitude. Moreover, the responders had an increase in erythrocyte volume and increased aerobic power while the non-responders did not. This model was confirmed prospectively in a group of elite US runners(13, 55). Recently, our group has sought to determine the mechanisms of this variability in erythropoietic response to altitude (44). For example, the increase in EPO in response to acute hypobaric hypoxia equivalent to altitude of 2,800m varies dramatically among individuals, ranging from a 40% decrease to a 400% increase in EPO after 24 hours. Although preliminary work suggested that there might be specific genetic markers on the erythropoietin gene that regulate this response (66), more detailed evaluation has been unable to identify a unique single nucleotide polymorphism (SNP) in candidate genes of the hypoxia response pathway that can explain this variability(29).

In summary, these studies demonstrated quite convincingly that: 1) the "living high-training low" model of intermittent hypoxic training works to improve sea level performance; 2) the mechanism is highly likely to be a stimulation of erythropoiesis leading to an increase in hemoglobin concentration, red cell mass, and aerobic power; 3) the effect of this increase in oxygen transport capacity is maximized by maintaining normal, sea level oxygen flux during intense exercise avoiding the down regulation of skeletal muscle structure and function that may occur in athletes who attempt to perform all their training under hypoxic conditions.

It is important to emphasize that although our results have led us to focus on the erythropoietic pathway, this was not an exclusive hypothesis at the beginning of our experiments. For example, we made detailed measurements of anaerobic capacity using the accumulated oxygen deficit method of Medbo et al(37), which in 10 years of study and more than 100 athletes, never changed over the course of any intervention(33-35). Moreover, muscle biopsy measures of buffer capacity in these same athletes failed to demonstrate an increase in buffer capacity, or increase in oxidative enzymes(34). Although we did not specifically measure the sodium-potassium pump function, which has been suggested recently to possibly contribute to altitude acclimatization(22), carefully controlled studies without harsh field conditions have failed to confirm a prominent effect of this mechanism in healthy controls (Lundby et al, personal communication) or athletes(7). Similarly, careful measures of running economy using very precise techniques have failed to identify any changes in economy in large numbers of runners(34, 35) or other athletes or healthy individuals(36). Thus the weight of evidence argues strongly for the primary effect of altitude acclimatization on sea level performance in competitive athletes being on the erythropoietic pathways.

WHAT IS THE OPTIMAL ALTITUDE?

All the published studies by our group have used an altitude of 2,500m as the primary living altitude. However one key question is what is the best living altitude for competitive athletes? To address this question, we studied 48 competitive runners at sea level, and then again after 4 weeks of living at one of 4 different altitudes: 1780m, 2,085m, 2,454m, and 2805m (n=12 each). The response to acute hypobaric hypoxia in an altitude chamber for these subjects has been published(44), though the outcome data have only been presented in abstract form(67). The key results can be summarized as follows: a) there was a progressive increase in both the mean and dispersion around the mean of the rise in EPO with increasing altitude, with the two lowest altitudes (1800m and 2100m) having significantly smaller responses than the two highest altitudes(45); b) this pattern was generally matched by the response in the field, with the major difference being that the higher altitudes resulted in a more sustained increase in EPO than the lower altitudes; c) after 4 weeks, there was a “dose-dependent” increase in VO2 max of 8 ml, 206 ml, 308 ml, and 301 ml at 1780m, 2085m, 2454m and 2805m respectively(67); d) surprisingly, the change in performance followed a somewhat different pattern -- there was only a minimal improvement in performance (3K time) at the lowest (1.1%) and highest (1.4%) altitudes, but a much more robust improvement at the two middle altitudes (2.8% and 2.7%)(67); e) the highest altitude was associated with a significant increase in ventilation during submaximal exercise. These data suggested that there may be a relatively narrow window of “optimal dose” of altitude for competitive athletes using the LHTL model, and spending at least 20 hr/d at altitude. This altitude appears to be between 2,000 and 2,500m -- altitudes that are too low are associated with inadequate erythropoietic response, while altitudes that are too high may be complicated by other aspects of acclimatization that may be detrimental to competitive athletes, such as excessive ventilatory acclimatization, or possibly even muscle atrophy (not measured in these studies).

HOW LONG TO SPEND AT ALTITUDE?

All the studies by our group have used a minimum of 4 weeks at altitude. However many athletes use shorter training camps of 2-3 weeks for altitude training. Although we have not addressed this question specifically in our published studies, some insight can be gained from the literature. First of all, even when EPO is injected directly, there is no change in haemoglobin or hematocrit for the first week to 10 days, and then only a barely detectable increase after 2 weeks(6, 8). Thereafter, erythropoiesis accelerates, particularly between weeks 3-4 during which time hemoglobin and hematocrit increase prominently(8). Therefore altitude camps that last < 2 weeks are not likely to generate much of an improvement in aerobic power due to accelerated erythropoiesis. A compilation of published and unpublished studies carried out by the authors is shown in figure 2.

Note that there is no appreciable effect from exposures of < 2 weeks, whether to real or simulated altitude. With increasing duration of exposure, and particularly with extension of the duration at altitude to 4 weeks, there is a substantial increase in the magnitude of the erythropoietic effect. Ultimately, 4 weeks of altitude exposure above 2,000-2,500m appears equivalent in magnitude to a similar duration of low dose erythropoietin injection (50 IU/kg x 3 wk followed by 20 IU/kg x 3 wk). A recent meta analysis of studies involving varying degrees of altitude exposure by Rusko and colleagues (49)has confirmed that altitude exposures of at least 3-4 weeks are necessary to see an increase in red cell mass in the majority of athletes. The fact that the effect of 4 weeks of exposure to moderate altitude is equivalent in magnitude (erythrocyte volume, $\dot{V}O_{2max}$, and performance) to low dose erythropoietin injection provides further evidence in support of the erythropoietic pathway being a major component of the altitude effect for competitive athletes.

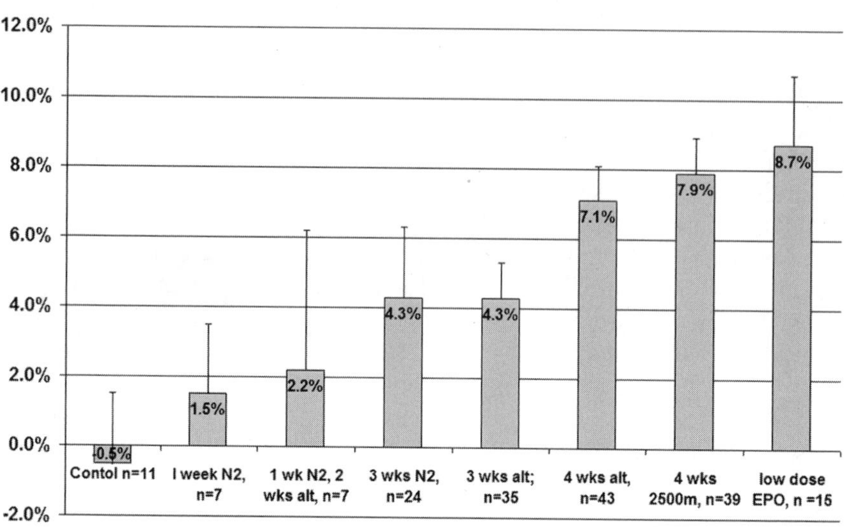

Figure 2. The columns indicate percent change in the volume of red cell mass from before to after the particular perturbation. The error bars represent the standard deviation of the percent change. Volume of red cell mass was estimated by Evans blue dye technique. A p value is associated with the column if < 0.10. All subjects were male and female currently endurance training athletes (age 18-30). Starting on the far left, Control (n=11) represents 11 athletes who were measured twice with 4-6 weeks time in between. The second column represents before and after 1 week of 12 hours per day in a nitrogen room (n=7). The third column represents the change associated with 1 week in a nitrogen room and a 2 week stay at 2100m altitude (n=7). The fourth column (n=24) represents before and after a 3 week stay (~12 hours/day) in a nitrogen room. The fifth column represents the change after a 3 week stay at natural altitude (n=35). Living altitudes ranged from 2000 to 2500m. The sixth column represents the change after a 4 week stay at natural altitude (n=43). Living altitudes ranged from 1800-2800m. The seventh column represents the change after a 4 week stay at 2500m (n=26). The far right column represents the change after a 4 week course of low dose rhEPO (50 IU/kg 3x/wk for 3 weeks, followed by 20 IU/kg 3x/wk for 3 weeks, staying below the regulatory limits for hematocrit (50) or hemoglobin (18.5) set by international organizations for the purposes of doping control).

HOW MANY HOURS PER DAY?

The compelling results from the LHTL model have led to the development of strategies designed to "bring the mountain to the athlete", particularly for athletes who do not have access to environments of sufficiently diverse altitudes to engage in a true LHTL training camp(32). A variety of approaches have been developed which involve breathing normobaric or hypobaric hypoxic gas mixtures for varying periods of time. To date, no systematic effort to examine the minimal duration of altitude exposure that is necessary to lead to sufficient sustained acclimatization responses to improve sea level performance has been accomplished.

One recent strategy that has generated a lot of interest among the athletic community has been the use of small portable hypoxia generating devices that allow individuals to breathe a hypoxic gas mixture without having to otherwise alter their living environment or behaviour patterns. Originally developed in the former Soviet Union(54) these devices are designed to provide brief periods (5 minutes) of intense hypoxia (FIO2=0.10) alternating with periods of normoxia and repeating for 70-90 minutes/d. The authors recently investigated these devices in collaboration with Randy Wilber from the USOC, Chris Gore from the Australian Institute for Sport, and Jack Daniels from Stanford University, which has been published.(31) In a randomized, double blind, placebo controlled trial, this type of intermittent hypoxia had no effect on indices of accelerated erythropoiesis, $\dot{V}O_{2max}$ or performance in highly trained runners (n=14). This study provides convincing evidence that very short periods of hypoxia, interspersed with periods of normoxia do not produce a sufficiently robust acclimatization response to increase red cell production, improve oxygen transport, or improve exercise performance (at sea level).

Most recently, the authors assembled an international group of collaborators including Ferran Rodriquez from Spain, Martin Truijens from Amsterdam, and Chris Gore from Australia to examine critically the protocol popularized by Rodriguez and colleagues(12, 46) involving a longer duration of exposure -- 3 hr/day of hypobaric hypoxia equivalent to 5,500m for 4 weeks, using 23 highly trained runners and swimmers, in a randomized, double blind, placebo controlled design (21, 47, 56, 60, 62). In order to maintain the blinding, even the subjects exposed to normobaric hypoxia experienced rapid changes in chamber pressure so that they would feel the pressure changes in their ears and other air containing spaces. With this exposure, we were able to confirm an acute increase in erythropoietin concentration, measured 2 hours after hypobaric hypoxia in the 2nd and 4th week of the experiment.(56)

However despite this transient increase in erythropoietin, there was no increase in reticulocytes, reticulocyte hemoglobin, hemoglobin concentration, soluble transferrin receptor, or total hemoglobin mass/red cell volume, measured either with carbon monoxide rebreathing or Evans blue dye(21, 56). Not only was there no evidence of erythropoietic acclimatization with this protocol (despite uncontrolled studies using relatively non-specific methods suggesting otherwise), there also was no evidence for ventilatory acclimatization, with no change in ventilation at rest or during exercise, no change in end-tidal CO_2 concentrations, and no change in the hypercapnic or hypoxic ventilatory response (HVR) which was measured weekly in runners and pre-post in swimmers(60).

This result was surprising, because the literature is more consistent with the ability of relatively short periods of hypoxia to induce ventilatory acclimatization. For example, Poulin et al have shown significant increases in the hypoxic ventilatory response (HVR), also called "short term facilitation" after only 5 days of normobaric hypoxia (1). Townsend et al, (61) using 8-10 hr/night of normobaric hypoxia have also shown an increase in HVR and a decrease in end-tidal CO_2 concentrations measured at rest. Ricart et al (40), have observed an increase in ventilation and decrease in $ETCO_2$ after only 2 hr/d of simulated hypobaric hypoxia up to 5,000m, though this increase was only manifest during submaximal exercise. It is important to note however, that all these measurements were made within the first 24 hours after the last hypoxia exposure. In contrast, our post exposure measurements were made 72 hours after completion of the last hypobaric hypoxic exposure and were unable to demonstrate lasting effects on resting or exercise ventilation. It thus may be that the ventilatory response to such short periods of hypoxia is not very robust, and may extinguish within a relatively short period of time -- certainly not a very practical acclimatization response in terms improving sea level performance of athletes.

Lastly, in keeping with the lack of any measurable evidence of altitude acclimatization with this regimen of 3 hours/day of severe hypobaric hypoxia, we observed no improvement in sea level endurance performance in this group of athletes, either in terms of running or swimming economy(62), $\dot{V}O_{2max}$, or race times(47).

NITROGEN HOUSES OR TENTS -- "SLEEP HIGH" -- TRAIN LOW

A number of authors have attempted to administer normobaric hypoxia during sleep, both to minimize the confinement necessary with simulated altitude devices, and to allow more extended durations of exposure. An example of three such studies is shown in figure 3 suggesting a "dose-limiting" effect.

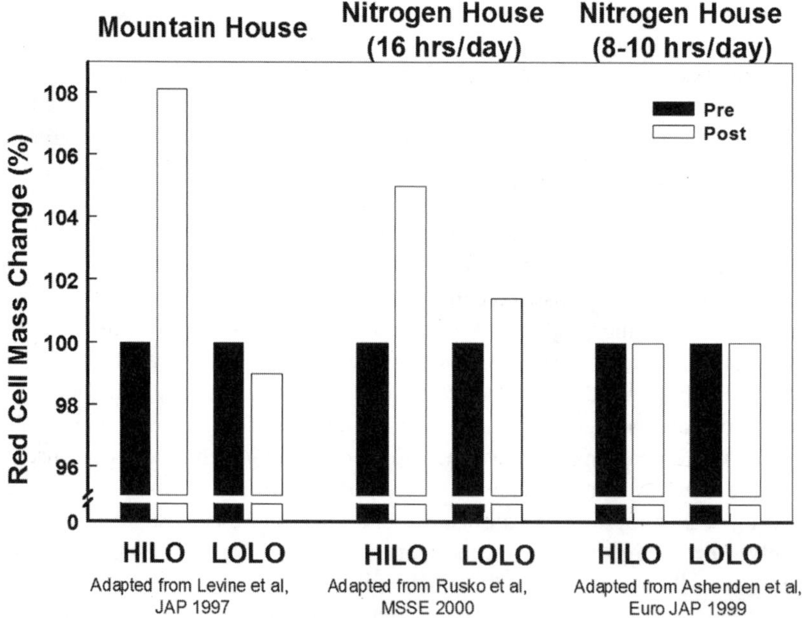

Figure 3. (HiLo=living at altitude, training at sea level; lolo=sea level control; Mountain house = field altitude 20-22hr/d). Data from (5, 32, 34).

For example, studies by the authors using 22 hours/day of altitude (2,500m) in the field ("Mountain House") for 4 weeks clearly demonstrate an erythropoietic effect of altitude exposure and an improvement in sea level performance in competitive distance runners (34). These observations have been confirmed recently by Swiss investigators in national level orienteers, (64), in Swiss national biathletes(25), in German national junior swimmers(18), and cross-sectionally in Bolivian professional cyclists(50). Thus despite rare reports to the contrary(19) more recent publication and presentation of data from multiple different research groups around the world using the most sensitive and precise tools for assessing the hemoglobin mass (i.e., CO rebreathing) have confirmed that moderate altitude exposure for nearly 24 hr/day increases the red cell mass even in elite, highly trained athletes.

But do lesser durations of exposure also increase the red cell mass? As noted above, 3 hr/d is not sufficient to do so despite transient increases in erythropoietin(21, 56). However Finnish investigators have employed 12-16 hours/day for 4 weeks of simulated altitude in a nitrogen house (2,500m equivalent altitude), which closely replicates the results observed in the field studies (32, 48) (Fig 3). These results have been confirmed recently by Richalet and colleagues who demonstrated a similar increase in hemoglobin mass in elite French skiers and runners spending 14 hr/night in a N2 house equivalent to 3,000m for 3 weeks(10). In contrast, Australian investigators using only 8-10 hours/day of simulated altitude exposure (2,500-3,000m) for 10 days -- 21 days failed to demonstrate an increase in the red blood cell mass, though other changes in ventilation, anaerobic performance and peak power output were identified (5) (Fig 3).

Recent advances in the understanding of the biological pathways involved in the adaptive response to hypoxia have the potential to contribute substantially to this debate. For example, the principal transcriptional activator of gene expression in hypoxic cells is hypoxia-inducible factor 1 alpha (HIF-1) (51-53, 63). Under normal, well oxygenated conditions, HIF-1 is hydroxylated via a highly conserved prolyl hydroxylase (the putative cellular "oxygen sensor" in peripheral tissues), which then binds to the Von Hipple-Lindau factor, targeting the entire complex for rapid degradation via the ubiquitin- proteosome pathway (16, 27, 28). In fact, this process is so rapid, that in the presence of oxygen and iron, HIF-1 alpha has one of the shortest half-lives of any known protein (28). In contrast, under hypoxic conditions, the HIF-1 complex is stable, allowing for transcriptional activation and ultimate stimulation of proteins such as erythropoietin and vascular endothelial growth factor (63).

Moreover, when altitude natives, or even altitude sojourners return to sea level, there is a suppression of erythropoietin (13, 17, 23, 30, 34, 43), a prominent reduction in iron turnover and bone marrow production of erythroid cell lines (26, 39), and a marked decrease in red cell survival time (39). This increase in red cell destruction with suppression of EPO levels has been termed "neocytolysis" and has been observed under other conditions of a relative increase in oxygen content (2-4, 41, 42). Both the rapid ubiquitination and destruction of HIF-1 alpha, and neocytolysis (which may be its clinical manifestation), may compromise the ability of short duration, intermittent hypoxic exposures to induce a sustained increase in the red cell mass.

In conclusion, it appears from the available evidence that real or simulated altitude exposures have the potential to increase the red cell mass, maximal aerobic power, and endurance performance in competitive athletes. However the "dose" of altitude must be at least that equivalent to 2,000-2,500m, for the majority of the day (i.e., more than 12 hrs), lasting at least 3-4 weeks to stimulate a sustained adaptive response in the majority of athletes. It is likely that some athletes, based on genetic predisposition may well have a beneficial response to lower "doses", and that some athletes may never respond positively, even to higher doses which then may be limited by toxicity. Future research should be directed to understanding the biological underpinnings of this diversity and defining more explicitly the optimal combinations of duration, frequency, and intensity for both individual and groups of athletes. Finally, it should be emphasized that the majority of this discussion is primarily relevant to well trained athletes who are using altitude exposure for discrete periods of time to boost sea level performance. There is much less information regarding longer durations of exposures (months to years) on athletic performance at sea level, or of the effects of these types of altitude exposures on performance at altitude. Both of these areas would be fruitful for further investigation.

REFERENCES

1. Ainslie PN, Kolb JC, Ide K, and Poulin MJ. Effects of five nights of normobaric hypoxia on the ventilatory responses to acute hypoxia and hypercapnia. *Respir Physiol Neurobiol* 138: 193-204, 2003.
2. Alfrey CP, Rice L, Udden MM, and Driscoll TB. Neocytolysis: physiological down-regulator of red-cell mass. *Lancet* 349: 1389-1390., 1997.
3. Alfrey CP, Udden MM, Huntoon CL, and Driscoll T. Destruction of newly released red blood cells in space flight. *Med Sci Sports Exerc* 28: S42-44., 1996.
4. Alfrey CP, Udden MM, Leach-Huntoon C, Driscoll T, and Pickett MH. Control of red blood cell mass in spaceflight. *J Appl Physiol* 81: 98-104., 1996.
5. Ashenden MJ, Gore CJ, Dobson GP, and Hahn AG. "Live high, train low" does not change the total haemoglobin mass of male endurance athletes sleeping at a simulated altitude of 3000 m for 23 nights. *Eur J Appl Physiol Occup Physiol* 80: 479-484., 1999.
6. Ashenden MJ, Hahn AG, Martin DT, Logan P, Parisotto R, and Gore CJ. A comparison of the physiological response to simulated altitude exposure and r-HuEpo administration. *J Sports Sci* 19: 831-837, 2001.
7. Aughey RJ, Gore CJ, Hahn AG, Garnham AP, Clark SA, Petersen AC, Roberts AD, and McKenna MJ. Chronic intermittent hypoxia and incremental cycling exercise independently depress muscle in vitro maximal Na+-K+-ATPase activity in well-trained athletes. *J Appl Physiol* 98: 186-192, 2005.
8. Birkeland KI, Stray-Gundersen J, Hemmersbach P, Hallen J, Haug E, and Bahr R. Effect of rhEPO administration on serum levels of sTfR and cycling performance. *Med Sci Sports Exerc* 32: 1238-1243, 2000.
9. Brosnan MJ, Martin DT, Hahn AG, Gore CJ, and Hawley JA. Impaired interval exercise responses in elite female cyclists at moderate simulated altitude. *J Appl Physiol* 89: 1819-1824., 2000.
10. Brugniaux JV, Schmitt L, Robach P, Fouillot J-P, Nicolet G, Lasne F, Moutereau S, Olsen NV, and Richalet JP. Living high-training low: effects on acclimatization, erythropoiesis and aerobic performance in elite middle distance runners. *High Alt Med Biol* 5: 477-478 (abstr), 2004.
11. Buick FJ, Gledhill N, Froese AB, Spriet L, and Meyers EC. Effect of induced erythrocythemia on aerobic work capacity. *J Appl Physiol* 48: 636-642., 1980.
12. Casas M, Casas H, Pages T, Rama R, Ricart A, Ventura JL, Ibanez J, Rodriguez FA, and Viscor G. Intermittent hypobaric hypoxia induces altitude acclimation and improves the lactate threshold. *Aviat Space Environ Med* 71: 125-130, 2000.
13. Chapman RF, Stray-Gundersen J, and Levine BD. Individual variation in response to altitude training. *J Appl Physiol* 85: 1448-1456, 1998.

14. Ekblom B and Berglund B. Effect of erythropoietin administration on maximal aerobic power. *Scand J Med Sci Sports* 1: 88-93, 1991.
15. Ekblom B, Goldbarg AN, and Gullbring B. Response to exercise after blood loss and reinfusion. *J Appl Physiol* 33: 175-180, 1972.
16. Epstein AC, Gleadle JM, McNeill LA, Hewitson KS, O'Rourke J, Mole DR, Mukherji M, Metzen E, Wilson MI, Dhanda A, Tian YM, Masson N, Hamilton DL, Jaakkola P, Barstead R, Hodgkin J, Maxwell PH, Pugh CW, Schofield CJ, and Ratcliffe PJ. C. elegans EGL-9 and mammalian homologs define a family of dioxygenases that regulate HIF by prolyl hydroxylation. *Cell* 107: 43-54, 2001.
17. Faura J, Ramos J, Reynafarje C, English E, Finne P, and Finch CA. Effect of altitude on erythropoiesis. *Blood* 33: 668-676, 1969.
18. Friedmann B, Frese F, Menold E, Kauper F, Jost J, and Bartsch P. Individual variation in the erythropoietic response to altitude training in elite junior swimmers. *Br J Sports Med* 39: 148-153, 2005.
19. Gore CJ, Hahn A, Rice A, Bourdon P, Lawrence S, Walsh C, Stanef T, Barnes P, Parisotto R, Martin D, Pyne D, and Gore C. Altitude training at 2690m does not increase total haemoglobin mass or sea level $\dot{V}O_{2max}$ in world champion track cyclists. *J Sci Med Sport* 1: 156-170., 1998.
20. Gore CJ, Hahn AG, Scroop GC, Watson DB, Norton KI, Wood RJ, Campbell DP, and Emonson DL. Increased arterial desaturation in trained cyclists during maximal exercise at 580 m altitude. *J Applied Physiol* 80: 2204-2210, 1996.
21. Gore CJ, Stray Gundersen J, Rodriguez FA, Truijens MJ, Townsend NE, and Levine BD. Comparison of Blood Volume via Co Re-Breathing and Evans Blue Dye. *Medicine and Science in Sports and Exercise* 36: S336 (abstr), 2004.
22. Green H, Roy B, Grant S, Burnett M, Tupling R, Otto C, Pipe A, and McKenzie D. Downregulation in muscle Na(+)-K(+)-ATPase following a 21-day expedition to 6,194 m. *J Appl Physiol* 88: 634-640, 2000.
23. Gunga HC, Rocker L, Behn C, Hildebrandt W, Koralewski E, Rich I, Schobersberger W, and Kirsch K. Shift working in the Chilean Andes (>3600 m) and its influence on erythropoietin and the low-pressure system. *J Appl Physiol* 81: 846-852, 1996.
24. Hahn AG, Gore CJ, Martin DT, Ashenden MJ, Roberts AD, and Logan PA. An evaluation of the concept of living at moderate altitude and training at sea level. *Comp Biochem Physiol A Mol Integr Physiol* 128: 777-789., 2001.
25. Heinicke K, Heinicke I, Schmidt W, and Wolfarth B. A three-week traditional altitude training increases hemoglobin mass and red cell volume in elite biathlon athletes. *Internal Journal of Sports Medicine* 26(5): 350-355, 2005.
26. Huff RL, Lawrence JH, Siri WE, Wasserman LR, and Hennessy TG. Effects of changes in altitude on hematopoietic activity. *Medicine* 30: 197-217, 1951.
27. Ivan M, Kondo K, Yang H, Kim W, Valiando J, Ohh M, Salic A, Asara JM, Lane WS, and Kaelin WG, Jr. HIFalpha targeted for VHL-mediated destruction by proline hydroxylation: implications for O2 sensing. *Science* 292: 464-468, 2001.
28. Jaakkola P, Mole DR, Tian YM, Wilson MI, Gielbert J, Gaskell SJ, Kriegsheim A, Hebestreit HF, Mukherji M, Schofield CJ, Maxwell PH, Pugh CW, and Ratcliffe PJ. Targeting of HIF-alpha to the von Hippel-Lindau ubiquitylation complex by O2-regulated prolyl hydroxylation. *Science* 292: 468-472, 2001.
29. Jedlickova K, Stockton DW, Chen H, Stray-Gundersen J, Witkowski S, Ri-Li G, Jelinek J, Levine BD, and Prchal JT. Search for genetic determinants of individual variability of the erythropoietin response to high altitude. *Blood Cells Mol Dis* 31: 175-182, 2003.
30. Jelkman W. Erythropoietin: structure, control of production, and function. *Physiological Reviews* 72: 449-489, 1992.
31. Julian CG, Gore CJ, Wilber RL, Daniels JT, Fredericson M, Stray-Gundersen J, Hahn AG,

Parisotto R, and Levine BD. Intermittent normobaric hypoxia does not alter performance or erythropoietic markers in highly trained distance runners. *J Appl Physiol* 96: 1800-1807, 2004.

32. Laitinen H, Alopaeus K, Heikkinen R, Hietanen H, Mikkelsson L, Tikkanen H, and Rusko HK. Acclimatization to living in normobaric hypoxia and training in normoxia at sea level in runners (Abstract). *Med Sci Sport Exerc* 27: S617, 1995.
33. Levine BD. Intermittent hypoxic training: fact and fancy. *High Alt Med Biol* 3: 177-193, 2002.
34. Levine BD and Stray-Gundersen J. "Living high-training low": effect of moderate-altitude acclimatization with low-altitude training on performance. *J Appl Physiol* 83: 102-112, 1997.
35. Levine BD and Stray-Gundersen J. A practical approach to altitude training: where to live and train for optimal performance enhancement. *Intl J Sport Med* 13: S209-S212, 1992.
36. Lundby C, Calbet J, Sander M, van Hall G, Mazzeo RS, Stray-Gundersen J, Saltin B, and Levine BD. Exercise economy does not change during or after acclimatization to moderate to very high altitude. *Journal of Applied Physiology* in press, 2006.
37. Medbo JI, Mohn AC, Tabata I, Bahr R, Vaage O, and Sejersted OM. Anaerobic capacity determined by maximal accumulated O2 deficit. *J Appl Physiol* 64: 50-60., 1988.
38. Morris DM, Kearney JT, and Burke ER. The effects of breathing supplemental oxygen during altitude training on cycling performance. *J Sci Med Sport* 3: 165-175, 2000.
39. Reynafarje C, Lozano R, and Valdivieso J. The polycythemia of high altitudes: iron metabolism and related aspects. *Blood* 14: 433-455, 1959.
40. Ricart A, Casas H, Casas M, Pages T, Palacios L, Rama R, Rodriguez FA, Viscor G, and Ventura JL. Acclimatization near home? Early respiratory changes after short-term intermittent exposure to simulated altitude. *Wilderness Environ Med* 11: 84-88, 2000.
41. Rice L and Alfrey CP. Modulation of red cell mass by neocytolysis in space and on Earth. *Pflugers Arch* 441: R91-94., 2000.
42. Rice L, Ruiz W, Driscoll T, Whitley CE, Tapia R, Hachey DL, Gonzales GF, and Alfrey CP. Neocytolysis on descent from altitude: a newly recognized mechanism for the control of red cell mass. *Ann Intern Med* 134: 652-656., 2001.
43. Richalet JP, Souberbielle JC, and Antezana AM. Control of erythropoiesis in humans during prolonged exposure to the altitude of 6542 m. *Am J Physiol* 266: R756-R764, 1993.
44. Ri-Li G, Witkowski S, Zhang Y, Alfrey C, Sivieri M, Karlsen T, Resaland GK, Harber M, Stray-Gundersen J, and Levine BD. Determinants of erythropoietin release in response to short term, hypobaric hypoxia. *J Appl Physiol* 92: 2361-2367, 2002.
45. Ri-Li G, Witkowski S, Zhang Y, Alfrey C, Sivieri M, Karlsen T, Resaland GK, Harber M, Stray-Gundersen J, and Levine BD. Determinants of erythropoietin release in response to short-term hypobaric hypoxia. *J Appl Physiol* 92: 2361-2367, 2002.
46. Rodriguez FA, Casas H, Casas M, Pages T, Rama R, Ricart A, Ventura JL, Ibanez J, and Viscor G. Intermittent hypobaric hypoxia stimulates erythropoiesis and improves aerobic capacity. *Med Sci Sports Exerc* 31: 264-268, 1999.
47. Rodriguez FA, Truijens MJ, Townsend NE, Martini ER, Stray-Gundersen J, Gore SM, and Levine BD. Effects of four weeks of intermittent hypobaric hypoxia on sea level running and swimming performance. *Medicine and Science in Sports and Exercise* 36: S 338 (abstr), 2004.
48. Rusko HK, Tikkanen H, Paavolainen L, Hamalainen I, Kalliokoski K, and Puranen A. Effect of living in hypoxia and training in normoxia on sea level $\dot{V}O_2$max and red cell mass. *Medicine and Science in Sports and Exercise* 31: S86, 1999.
49. Rusko HK, Tikkanen HO, and Peltonen JE. Altitude and endurance training. *J Sports Sci* 22: 928-944; discussion 945, 2004.

50. Schmidt W, Heinicke K, Rojas J, Manuel Gomez J, Serrato M, Mora M, Wolfarth B, Schmid A, and Keul J. Blood volume and hemoglobin mass in endurance athletes from moderate altitude. *Med Sci Sports Exerc* 34: 1934-1940, 2002.
51. Semenza GL. Regulation of erythropoietin production. New insights into molecular mechanisms of oxygen homeostasis. *Hemat/Onc Clin NA* 8: 863, 1994.
52. Semenza GL, Agani F, Booth G, Forsythe J, Iyer N, Jiang BH, Leung S, Roe R, Wiener C, and Yu A. Structural and functional analysis of hypoxia-inducible factor 1. *Kidney Int* 51: 553-555, 1997.
53. Semenza GL, Roth PH, Fang HM, and Wang GL. Transcriptional regulation of genes encoding glycolytic enzymes by hypoxia-inducible factor 1. *J Biol Chem* 269: 23757-23763, 1994.
54. Serebrovskaya TV. Intermittent hypoxia research in the former soviet union and the commonwealth of independent States: history and review of the concept and selected applications. *High Alt Med Biol* 3: 205-221, 2002.
55. Stray-Gundersen J, Chapman RF, and Levine BD. "Living high - training low" altitude training improves sea level performance in male and female elite runners. *J Appl Physiol* 91: 1113-1120, 2001.
56. Stray-Gundersen J, Gore CJ, and Rodriguez FA TM, Townsend NE, Levine BD. Effect of Intermittent Hypobaric Hypoxia on Erythropoiesis. *Medicine and Science in Sports and Exercise* 36: S335 (abstr), 2004.
57. Stray-Gundersen J and Levine BD. Effect of altitude training on runners' skeletal muscle. *Medicine and Science in Sports and Exercise* 31: S182, 1999.
58. Stray-Gundersen J and Levine BD. "Living high-training high and low" is equivalent to "living high-training low for sea level performance. *Medicine and Science in Sports and Exercise* 29: S136, 1997.
59. Terrados N, Mizuno M, and Andersen H. Reduction in maximal oxygen uptake at low altitudes. Role of training status and lung function. *Clin Physiol* 5: 75-79, 1985.
60. Tonwnsend NE, Gore SM, Truijens MJ, Rodriguez FA, Stray Gundersen J, and Levine BD. Ventilatory acclimatization to intermittent hypoxia in well trained runners and swimmers. *Medicine and Science in Sports and Exercise* 36: S337 (abstr), 2004.
61. Townsend NE, Gore CJ, Hahn AG, McKenna MJ, Aughey RJ, Clark SA, Kinsman T, Hawley JA, and Chow CM. Living high-training low increases hypoxic ventilatory response of well-trained endurance athletes. *J Appl Physiol* 93: 1498-1505, 2002.
62. Truijens MJ, F.A. R, Palmer D, Townsend NE, Gore SM, Stray-Gundersen J, and Levine BD. The effect of intermittent hypobaric hypoxic exposure on economy in runners and swimmers. *Medicine and Science in Sports and Exercise* 36: S 338 (abstr), 2004.
63. Wang GL and Semenza GL. Molecular basis of hypoxia-induced erythropoietin expression. *Curr Opin Hematol* 3: 156-162., 1996.
64. Wehrlin J, Zuest G, Clenin J, Hallen J, and Marti B. Live high train low increases red cell volume, running performance and $\dot{V}O_2$max in endurance trained athletes. *J Appl Physiol* in press, 2006
65. Wilber RL. Current trends in altitude training. *Sports Med* 31: 249-265, 2001.
66. Witkowski S, Chen H, Stray-Gundersen J, Ri-Li G, Alfrey C, Prchal JT, and Levine BD. Genetic marker for the erythropoietic response to altitude. *Medicine and Science in Sports and Exercise* 34(5): Supplement 1, S246, 2002.
67. Witkowski S, Karlsen T, Resaland G, Sivieri M, R.Yates, Ri-Li G, Stray-Gundersen J, and Levine BD. Optimal altitude for "living high-training low". *Medicine and Science in Sports and Exercise* 33: S292 (abstr), 2001.

Chapter 21

THE EYE AT ALTITUDE

Daniel S Morris[1], John Somner[2], Michael J Donald[3], Ian JC McCormick[2], Rupert RA Bourne[4], Suber S Huang[5], Peter Aspinall[6], Baljean Dhillon[7]

[1]Royal Victoria Infirmary, Newcastle-upon-Tyne, UK, [2]Royal Infirmary of Edinburgh, Edinburgh, UK, [3]Royal North Shore Hospital, Sydney, Australia, [4]Moorfields Eye Hospital, London, UK, [5]Retinal Diseases Image Analysis Reading Center, Cleveland, Ohio, USA [6]Heriot-Watt University, Edinburgh, UK, [7]Princess Alexandra Eye Pavilion, Edinburgh, UK.

Abstract High altitude retinopathy (HAR) was first described in 1969 as engorgement of retinal veins with occasional papilloedema and vitreous hemorrhage. Since then various studies have attempted to define the incidence, etiology and significance of this phenomenon, usually with small numbers of subjects. Recently studies on relatively large groups of subjects in Nepal, Bolivia and Tibet have confirmed that the retinal vasculature becomes engorged and tortuous in all lowlanders ascending above 2500m. Sometimes this leads to hemorrhages, cotton wool spots and papilloedema, which is the pathological state better known as high altitude retinopathy. These studies have also shown a significant change in both corneal thickness and intraocular pressure at altitude. The retinal blood vessels are the only directly observable vascular system in the human body and also supply some of the most oxygen-demanding tissue, the photoreceptors of the retina. New techniques are being applied in both hypobaric chamber and field expeditions to observe changes in retinal function during conditions of hypobaric hypoxia. This work allows better advice to be given to lowlanders traveling to altitude either if they have pre-existing ocular conditions or if they suffer from visual problems whilst at altitude. This especially applies to the effect of altitude on refractive eye surgery and results of recent studies will be discussed so that physicians can advise their patients using the latest evidence. Retinal hypoxia at sea level accounts for the developed world's largest cause of blindness, diabetic retinopathy. The investigation of retinal response to hypobaric hypoxia in healthy subjects may open new avenues for treatment of this debilitating disease.

Key Words: altitude, high altitude retinopathy, corneal pachymetry, intraocular pressure, refractive surgery

INTRODUCTION

The eye, like every other organ, is affected by the hypobaric hypoxia of high altitude. This can cause decreased vision which can be life-threatening in a mountain environment, and is of interest to the clinician treating hypoxic eye disease at sea level.

There have been no previous measurements of corneal thickness at altitude in man; studies of intraocular pressure (IOP) have been hampered by small numbers of subjects and hostile conditions. High altitude retinopathy (HAR) was first recognized in 1969(71) but since then many studies have tried to assess its incidence and clinical significance with little success.

The preliminary results of ocular studies carried out on three large medical expeditions are discussed in this paper, the Medex expedition to Chamlang base camp in Nepal, the Apex 2 expedition to Chacaltaya in Bolivia and the Irvine Lovett Everest Expedition to the north side of Mount Everest in Tibet. These research expeditions had large numbers of subjects and different ascent profiles; as such they provided an excellent model for studying the effect of altitude on the eye.

An excellent review is available of the risks associated with ascent to altitude with pre-existing ocular conditions, so this will not be covered.(46) However the popularity of refractive surgery amongst high altitude mountaineers warrants discussion, as this has opened up new potential visual problems.

INTRAOCULAR PRESSURE

Intraocular pressure (IOP) at high altitude has been the subject of controversy for many years. In 1918 Wilmer and Berens measured IOP in 14 aviators in a hypobaric chamber but came to no significant conclusion.(83) More recently some groups have found decreased IOP,(10) whereas others have found increased IOP,(15) and normal IOP.(5, 17) Butler et al reported a significant relationship between IOP and flame hemorrhages associated with high altitude retinopathy(14) and one previous study showed a reduction in IOP that occurred within hours of ascent and recovered during acclimatization.(18)

IOP is determined by the rate of aqueous secretion, the resistance encountered in outflow channels and the level of episcleral venous pressure. The distribution of IOP within the normal population has a range of 11mmHg to 21mmHg (mean 16±2.5mmHg).(37) However IOP varies with the time of day, heart beat, blood pressure and respiration. The mean range of diurnal IOP fluctuations in normal eyes is 5mmHg with a tendency to be higher in the morning and lower in the afternoon and evening. It is therefore important to standardize the time of day when IOP readings are taken.

Approximately 80% of aqueous is produced by the non-pigmented ciliary epithelium as a result of an active metabolic process.(37) Therefore aqueous secretion should be diminished by factors that inhibit active metabolism such as hypoxia and hypothermia. Aqueous drainage is also partially an active process. There is no data on IOP changes in other chronic hypoxic conditions at sea level, such as chronic obstructive pulmonary disease and congenital cyanotic heart disease, and subsequently it is not known at what arterial oxygen saturation the autoregulatory control of IOP fails.

During the Apex 2 expedition, the opportunity arose to measure the IOP of 104 healthy young lowlanders all ascending to 5200m with minimal exertion using the same ascent profile.

Materials and Methods

104 healthy subjects (56 male and 48 female) with a median age of 21 years (range 18-60) were selected to join the Apex 2 research expedition. At a pre-expedition meeting, subjects were consented, screened and sea-level measurements were recorded. There was no history of prior ocular disease and 18 subjects wore contact lenses. Subjects were then flown to La Paz (3700m) in Bolivia where they acclimatized for 4 days before being driven over 2 hours to the Cosmic Physics Laboratory at Chacaltaya (5200m). Testing took place on the first, third and seventh day in the laboratory. After the seventh day, the subjects were driven back down to La Paz. A post-expedition measurement was taken when at least one month after all subjects had returned to sea level. The ascent profile is shown in Figure 1.

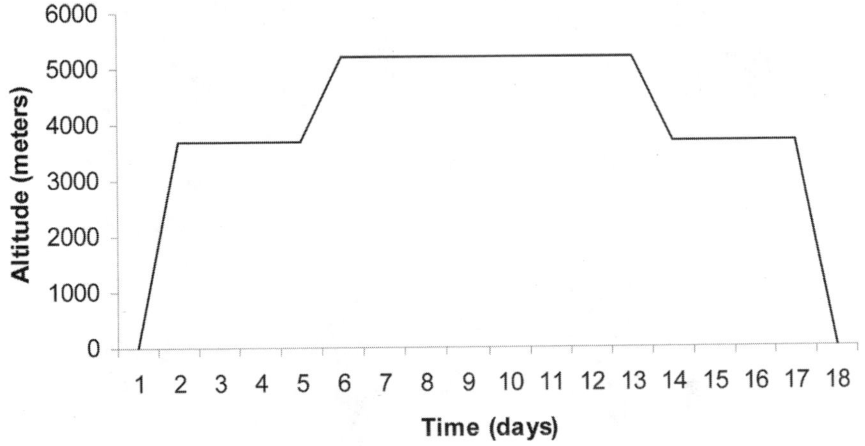

Figure 1. Apex 2 ascent profile.

In La Paz (3700m), subjects were advised to avoid any strenuous activity and were not allowed to descend below 2000m. In the laboratory (5200m), subjects were not formally restricted in their activity but were advised to rest for the first 2 days. After this they were allowed to exercise moderately if they wished but were not allowed to descend below 5000m. Cigarette smoking and alcohol consumption were prohibited for the duration of the experiment. AMS scores were recorded using the Lake Louise scale(66)

The subjects were also part of a double blind randomized controlled trial to compare the effect of sildenafil, anti-oxidants and placebo (see separate report) so use of medication was restricted to their experimental drug only, unless one of the expedition doctors had given permission. The effect of these trial drugs is discussed in the results section.

Choice of instrument for measuring IOP at altitude is difficult. Goldmann tonometry would be ideal but unfortunately requires a bulky slit lamp and is often poorly tolerated by young people. The Perkins tonometer is less accurate and difficult to calibrate. The air-puff tonometer has not been evaluated at altitude and is heavy and it is likely that the decrease in barometric air pressure would affect results.

In contrast the Tono-Pen is light, easy to calibrate and uses a pressure transducer. It is also well tolerated and has been proven in several trials to be comparable to the Goldmann applanation tonometer, especially in the normal range of intraocular pressure.(3, 24, 53) The Tono-Pen has a tendency to underestimate IOP above 30mmHg and overestimate IOP under 9mmHg.(38) However most readings at altitude are likely to be within the normal range of 11-21mmHg. The Tono-Pen is certainly the instrument of choice for field trials.(4)

IOP was measured for each eye with the Tono-Pen XL instrument (Figure 2). Each day the Tono-pen was calibrated to ensure accuracy and measurements were always taken in the early afternoon to avoid any diurnal variation. The intraocular pressure was measured 3 times for each eye after topical anesthesia with amethocaine. Visual acuity was measured at 6 meters under standard lighting conditions with a LogMAR chart.

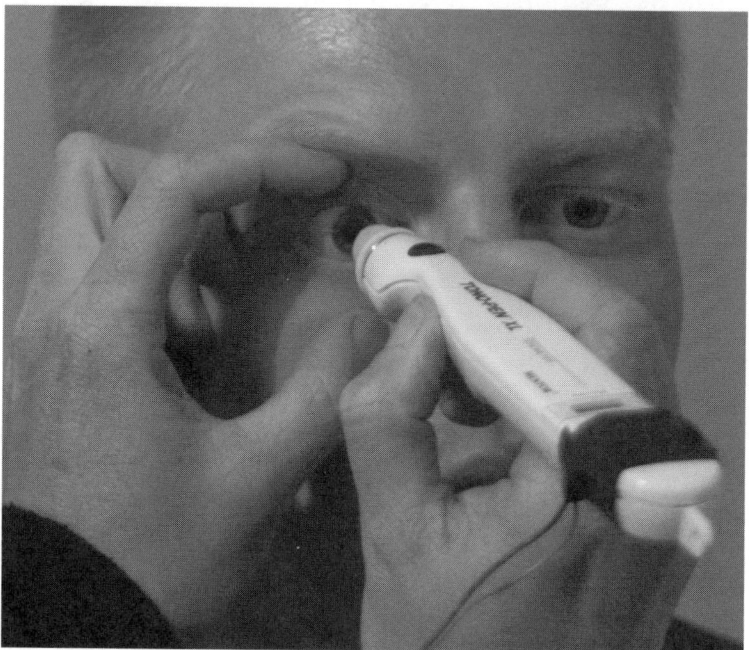

Figure 2. Measuring IOP with the Tono-Pen XL (A Simpson)

Results

96 subjects (92 %) consented to take part in the eye study, 82 (78 %) consenting to the invasive testing of IOP measurement. Of these 89 (93 %) completed the first altitude testing session, 80 (83 %) the second and 73 (76 %) all three. The 23 (24 %) drop outs from the study were due to acute mountain sickness (AMS) in 17 cases and gastroenteritis and other conditions in the remaining 6 cases.

Analysis of the 3 sub-groups in the drug trial showed that neither sildenafil or the antioxidant preparation had any effect on the change in IOP. None of the subjects were allowed to take acetazolamide which is used as an IOP-lowering agent. There was also no statistical change in visual acuity from sea level.

The average IOP measurements are shown in Figure 3. A repeated ANOVA test was carried out on these results. Mauchly's test of sphericity was non significant (Chi-Square=10.1, df=5, p=0.07) but the multivariate F ratio was significant (F=3.07, df = 3, p=.037). Follow up paired comparison tests showed a significant difference between sea level and the first day at 5200m (p=0.006), borderline significance between sea level and the third day at 5200m (p=0.067) and no significant difference between the seventh day at 5200m and sea level (p=0.680).

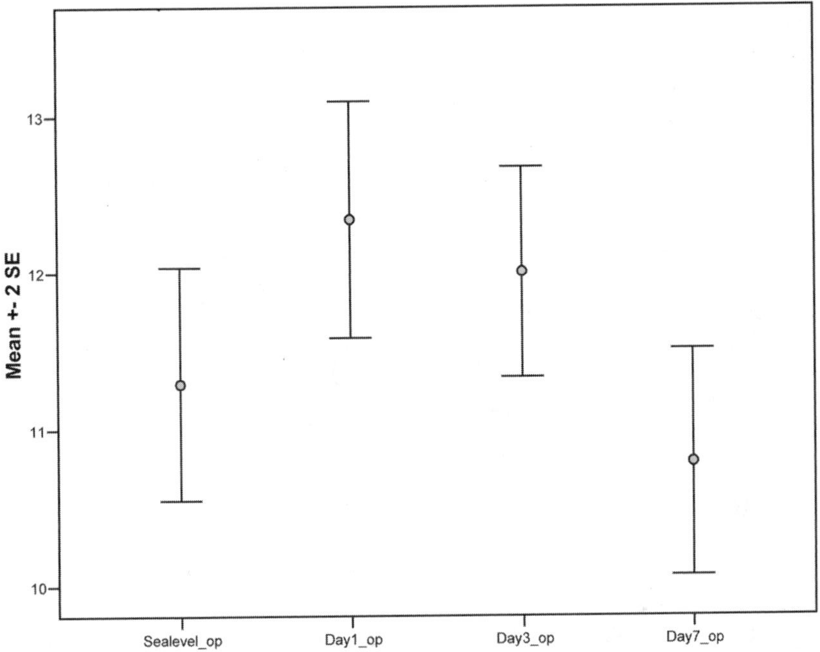

Figure 3. Change in intraocular pressure at altitude. There is an increase on the first day at 5200m which is significant, but IOP returns to sea level values by the seventh day at 5200m.

Discussion

Previous confusion over IOP at altitude may stem from poorly designed studies, small numbers of subjects, change in corneal thickness or because of a genuine change in IOP during acclimatization. Exercise has also been shown to reduce IOP as part of a hypotensive and sympathetic response.(44) Exercise conditioning can also significantly reduce baseline intraocular pressure.(61) This may be another confounding factor as subjects at altitude are often exercising more than normal and become increasingly fit during a sojourn to high altitude.

In contrast this study had a relatively large number of subjects and was rigorously designed as part of the Apex 2 expedition. Exertion was avoided as subjects were driven to 5200m. The results showed a significant increase in IOP on the first day at 5200m, which was less but still significant at the third day at altitude but had returned to near sea level values by the seventh day.

These results do not fit with any previous investigation but may explain some of the past confusion. It appears that IOP rises on arrival at altitude but soon returns to normal. Therefore the timing of previous studies would have been crucial, as those testing IOP immediately on arrival at altitude would find an increase in IOP whereas those testing after the third day would find normal IOP or even decreased IOP because of the exertional factor.

This study used a fast ascent profile, designed to provoke altitude pathology. Normal ascent profiles may not identify this change in IOP as the IOP regulating mechanisms appear to acclimatize at the same time as the rest of the body.

Why is there an increase in IOP on arrival at altitude? As explained above IOP is determined by the rate of aqueous secretion, the resistance encountered in outflow channels and the level of episcleral venous pressure. It is unlikely the rate of aqueous secretion would increase at altitude as it is governed by active transport mechanisms that would be affected by hypoxia making a decrease in secretion more likely. The resistance in the outflow channels is also unlikely to change at altitude. However the episcleral venous pressure may increase as vessels dilate to cope with the decrease in oxygen saturation; this is the most likely cause of a transient rise in IOP during acclimatization.

This rise in IOP is unlikely to have an effect on the retinal circulation as the IOP still remains within normal limits, but further analysis is being carried out on optic disc photographs and frequency doubled perimetry that was carried out at 5200m to assess the impact of this IOP change on retinal function.

THE CORNEA

Corneal swelling due to hypoxia is a well known phenomenon, especially in relation to contact lens wear, but changes in corneal thickness due to the hypobaric hypoxia of altitude are less well described. Early studies showed that the normal human cornea will swell by 7% every hour in an oxygen-free environment.(63) Diurnal variation of central corneal thickness has also been described, with swelling up to 3.9% overnight, probably due to the hypoxia of lid closure; this swelling resolved by early afternoon.(74)

Corneal swelling is not just related to oxygen tension. Endothelial function and corneal metabolic activity are also important and various studies have attempted to determine the importance of each of these factors.(9, 59) For example it has been shown that contact lens wearers, whose corneas are in a constant state of mild hypoxia, do not adapt by modifying oxygen consumption but by using glucose more efficiently.(9) This raises the possibility that the cornea may be able to acclimatize to low atmospheric oxygen at altitude and that contact lens wearers may be less affected by altitude.

Diabetic subjects are more vulnerable to corneal hypoxia and have a reduced ability to recover after transient hypoxic edema, possibly due to enzymatic dysfunction of the endothelial pumps and a shift towards anaerobic metabolism.(84) However there are no reports of this affecting visual function outside the laboratory setting.

Previous studies have indicated that the physiological response of the cornea to soft contact lens wear at altitude are subject to higher levels of manifested stresses, but these occurred without measurable degradation in vision and do not preclude normal wear of soft contact lenses.(21) Rigid contact lenses tend to cause more corneal swelling than soft contact lenses.(6) The aging cornea has a slower hypoxia-induced edema response compared with the younger group; whether this is caused by a decreased corneal lactate production or an increased resistance to physical expansion is unknown.(16, 62) One case study described a 77-year-old patient with low corneal endothelial cell counts who sustained acute unilateral endothelial decompensation when he traveled to an elevation of 12,500 feet. The corneal edema gradually increased after his return to sea level, and penetrating keratoplasty was required to restore vision.(40)

Once again, the Apex 2 expedition provided an excellent setting for measuring central corneal thickness in a large group of healthy lowlanders exposed to acute altitude.

Materials and methods

The subjects and experimental setting are as described previously, the only difference being that contact lens wearers were excluded from this study.

There are several methods available for measuring corneal thickness, such as specular microscopy, optical pachymetry, Orbscan Slitscan pachymetry and ultrasound pachymetry. Studies have shown that each technique delivers slightly different results, but the reliability of each individual technique is good.(49, 54) The ultrasound pachymeter is portable, reliable and depends on direct contact perpendicular to the cornea. It appears that central corneal thickness by ultrasound pachymetry can be adequately assessed in the majority of eyes by taking three measurements per eye.(64)

Corneal thickness was therefore measured with the Tomey SP-2000 ultrasound pachymeter (kindly loaned by the Princess Alexandra Eye Pavilion in Edinburgh). Measurements were taken 9 times for each eye after topical anesthesia with amethocaine (Figure 4). Corneal pachymetry was performed pre and post expedition and on the first, third and seventh day at 5200m, always early afternoon to avoid diurnal variation.

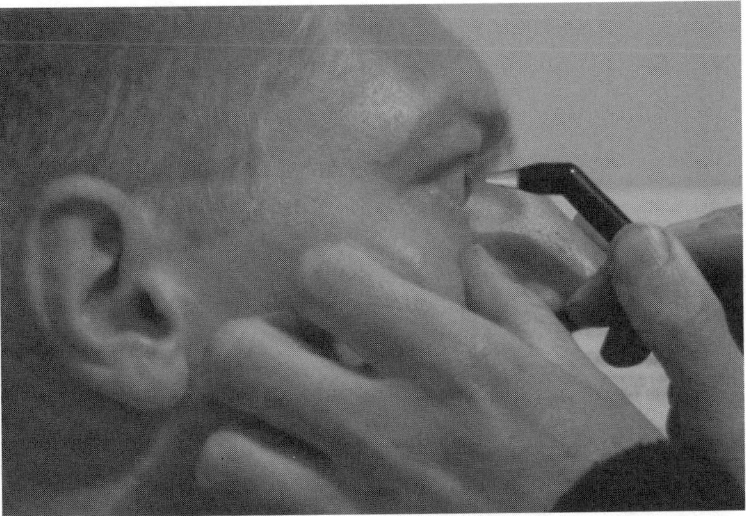

Figure 4. Measuring corneal thickness with ultrasound pachymetry (A Simpson)

Results

Analysis of the 3 sub-groups in the drug trial showed that neither sildenafil or the antioxidant preparation had any effect on the change in corneal thickness. As before there was no change in visual acuity.

The average corneal thickness measurements are shown in Figure 5 and a repeated ANOVA test was undertaken on the results. As Mauchly's test of sphericity was significant (Chi-Square=1, df=4, $p<0.001$) a multivariate analysis was used. This showed that the comparison between the two sea level values was not significant ($p=0.45$) but that all other altitude measures are highly significantly different from sea level ($p<0.001$). The pattern of the change in corneal thickness at altitude is shown in Figure 1. In addition to a significant increase in corneal thickness at altitude compared to sea level, there is also an apparent increase in corneal thickness with time spent at altitude. This was also found to be significant ($p=0.01$).

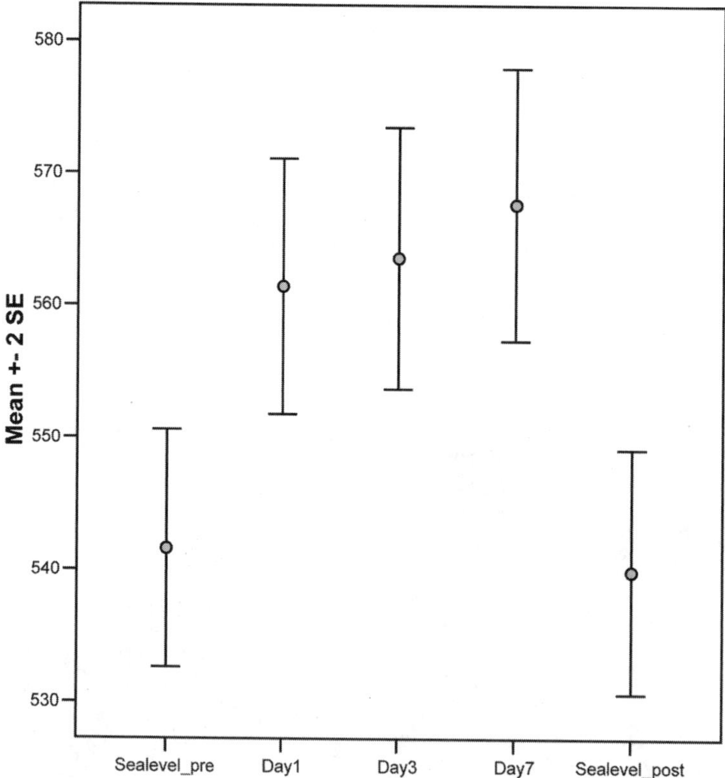

Figure 5. Change in corneal thickness at altitude. There is a clear difference between the sea level and altitude values and also an increase with time spent at altitude, both of which are significant.

DISCUSSION

For the first time there is evidence that hypobaric hypoxia causes a significant increase in corneal thickness in healthy lowlanders. This is significant from the point of view of IOP measurement and refractive surgery, as explained below.

There was marked variation between individuals dispute the majority being young and all contact lens wearers being excluded. There is evidence of individual susceptibility to corneal hypoxia; one study using a closed contact lens system to simulate a hypoxic environment over 3 hours.(68) The results showed a large variation in the amount of increased corneal thickness. This could be an indicator of the individual's capability to deal with hypoxia and acclimatize.

Which part of the cornea expands? Ultrastructural analysis of the rat cornea after exposure to a simulated altitude of 5,500 m for 30 days showed no change in the corneal epithelium.(50) This has been corroborated by evidence using optical coherence topography to measure corneal thickness after 3 hours of closed-eye contact lens wear which also showed no increase in epithelial thickness.(76) However the corneal stroma showed vascularization with advanced vessel differentiation and signs of active proliferation. The endothelium of hypoxic cornea showed swollen mitochondria and large empty cytoplasmic areas, and the endothelial intercellular junctions could hardly be identified in the hypoxic condition. Descemet's membrane was considerably thickened to approximately twice that of the control specimen. It therefore appears that the active transport mechanisms in the endothelium of the cornea, which normally maintain the cornea in its dehydrated state, are affected by hypoxia. This allows water to collect in the stroma causing the thickening seen in this experiment. Increased expression of both corneal epithelial vascular endothelial growth factor (VEGF) and cytochrome p450 4B1 was found in a rabbit model of closed eye contact lens wear, suggesting further evidence for the basic mechanism of hypoxic corneal swelling.(51)

It is interesting to compare these results with a group of similar subjects at sea level. A recent study of 1000 young, healthy, emmetropic eyes showed a range of 518-589um for central corneal thickness.(67) At altitude, the average corneal thickness did not exceed this normal range, explaining why there was no change in visual acuity. However within this range the average changed considerably from sea level to 5200m.

The cornea is dependent on aqueous humor for nourishment and the Fick equation shows that IOP measurement is dependent on corneal thickness.(37) If corneal thickness changes at altitude, then measured IOP changes may be artefactual. Previous studies have shown that a thickened cornea will give artificially high IOP readings and a thin cornea (for example following from excimer laser surgery(25)) will cause artificially low IOP readings.(13,36,77) However a recent study has cast doubt on these results by measuring central corneal thickness, IOP using applanation tonometry and IOP directly with an intracameral probe.(20) This showed no systematic error of applanation tonometry with corneal thickness. Regardless of these new findings, the corneal thickness and IOP are closely related and both need to be measured to accurately assess change at high altitude; in this case as the cornea thickened at altitude, the IOP decreased, suggesting that this was a real effect.

REFRACTIVE SURGERY AT ALTITUDE

The cornea is the main refractive structure in the eye. It is has been possible for some time to weaken or strengthen the power of the cornea surgically to avoid the use of spectacles and contact lenses. This type of refractive surgery has therefore become popular with active people who enjoy sports and outdoor recreation. However there are risks associated with the procedures, as with any surgery, and altitude can transiently affect the visual outcome. This could be life-threatening, as was demonstrated by the case of Dr Beck Weathers on Mount Everest in 1996. He had radial keratotomy and his vision became so blurred that he was unable to navigate back to his tent, losing his hands and nearly his life.

Radial Keratotomy (RK) was pioneered by the Russians in the 1980's. Deep radial incisions are made in the cornea to weaken and therefore flatten the surface. This makes the eye more hyperopic (long-sighted). Results were generally very encouraging, although it was difficult to predict exactly the final outcome, results were not always stable and occasionally the incisions were made too deep causing corneal perforation. Some climbers who had received RK noticed their vision became blurred at altitude and this was first reported in 1993 when a climber who had been under-corrected during RK noticed an improvement in his vision at 10,000 feet. (78) Refraction showed that he had become less myopic and therefore closer to his target refraction. The same authors investigated this phenomenon further trying to quantify and explain this change in refraction at altitude, using a variety of techniques including hypobaric chambers and sealed goggles to create a controlled environment and to separate the hypoxic and hypobaric elements of altitude which could potentially be causing this problem.(45,47,48,58,82)

They found a general trend towards hyperopia in subjects at altitude who had RK. This appears to be related to the decreased atmospheric pressure causing the weakened cornea to expand circumferentially. However there was a delay in the onset of refractive change at altitude so they hypothesized that this was not just a mechanical pressure effect, but there was also hypoxic expansion of the cornea around the radial incisions where there was sometimes endothelial cell loss.(7)

RK has now been superceded by excimer laser keratectomy, where a laser beam has replaced the traditional blade to shave layers off the cornea in a controlled, highly accurate fashion. There are two main techniques in use at present, laser in-situ keratomileusis (LASIK) and photo-refractive keratectomy (PRK). During the LASIK procedure a flap is made on the front of the cornea with a microkeratome and the excimer laser is then applied to remove a pre-determined amount of the corneal stroma. Once the flap is replaced, there is immediate, almost pain-free, visual recovery. However, there are occasionally flap-related complications, such as infection. During PRK, the corneal epithelium is removed and the laser applied directly to the cornea. However, there is a slight delay in visual recovery as the epithelium heals and it is more painful.

As both the lasers and the software controlling them becomes more sophisticated, there is now the possibility of super-vision, where the procedure can essentially remove all the tiny imperfections in the cornea as well as correcting the refractive error. This is obviously extremely attractive to pilots and those involved in outdoor pursuits.

Despite being superior to RK, LASIK and PRK do change the inherent structure and strength of the cornea, so the hypobaria and hypoxia of altitude can affect the refractive error. This was first reported in 2000 when a climber who had received LASIK experienced blurred vision at 19,500 feet which cleared on descent.(79) Refraction showed this to be a myopic (short-sighted) shift, the opposite of the hyperopic shift from RK and this was confirmed by other case reports.(8) Mechanically, the anterior fibers of the cornea are cut when creating the LASIK flap, thus allowing the cornea to steepen at altitude, as opposed to the circumferential fibers that are severed during RK, causing corneal flattening. Sealed goggle experiments showed that hypoxia caused a slight steepening of the cornea in LASIK-treated eyes that was not statistically significant.(56)

The most impressive experiment to date involved six climbers on Mount Everest who all had LASIK.(19) Four reached the summit and all spent at least 24 hours above 26,400 feet. Although less people ascend to these extreme altitudes, it is here that altered vision could be potentially fatal. Three of the subjects had visual problems, one at 16,000 feet which cleared with acclimatization, one at 26,400 feet which made his vision hazy but did not stop him reaching the summit and finally one who turned around at 27,000 feet because of blurred vision.

The LASIK altitude myopic shift appears to be less common and less pronounced than the RK altitude hyperopic shift, which is logical as the procedure is less invasive. There is also an element of individual susceptibility as many people who have had refractive surgery experience no problems whatsoever, and this is corroborated by results in this paper on corneal thickness at altitude.

Physicians should be aware of these potential changes in patients who have had refractive surgery and intend to go to high altitude. As the results of refractive surgery can take some months to stabilize, patients should be advised not to receive treatment within 3 months of leaving on an expedition. Eyes treated with any refractive surgery are more susceptible to both dryness and infection, so patients and expedition doctors should be equipped to deal with these potential sight-threatening hazards.

HIGH ALTITUDE RETINOPATHY

In 1969, Singh et al published their observations of 1,925 Indian soldiers at high altitude. (71) 17 subjects complained of blurred vision (0.009%); on examination they noted engorgement of retinal veins in all 17 cases with papilloedema in 4 cases and vitreous hemorrhage in 3 cases.

Although Singh et al(71) are credited with the first description of HAR, Wilmer and Berens published a paper in 1918 on the effect of altitude on ocular functions.(83) They mention that Dr Guilbert of the French Air Service noted that "...at 2000m, in general, the visual acuity decreases by a third by reason of the congestion of all the organs of the head, and in particular of the choroid and retina." This is the first mention of retinal vascular engorgement at altitude in the literature.

It also appears that two other groups in North America discovered HAR at the same time as Singh et al but were slower to publish their findings. Frayser, Houston et al observed HAR on Mount Logan in 1969(22) as did Schumacher and Petajan on Mount McKinley in 1968 but did not publish their results until 1975.(69)

High altitude retinopathy (HAR) is a pathological response by the retina to the hypoxia of altitude (Figure 6). Flame hemorrhages are most commonly seen but cotton wool spots, dot and blot and pre-retinal hemorrhages have also been reported.(27) This should be distinguished from the normal physiological retinal response to the hypoxia of high altitude which includes retinal vascular tortuosity and engorgement and optic disc hyperemia.

Although HAR is usually asymptomatic, when a hemorrhage occurs over the macula, vision can be affected. This is occasionally reported in ocular studies at altitude as above but more often as individual case reports in the literature.(33, 73, 80) Macular involvement may be rare because there the area is avascular or because local factors ensure that nutrient supply to the macula is preserved in the hypoxic environment. Hemorrhages usually resolve without sequelae, but persistent field defects have been reported.(34, 70)

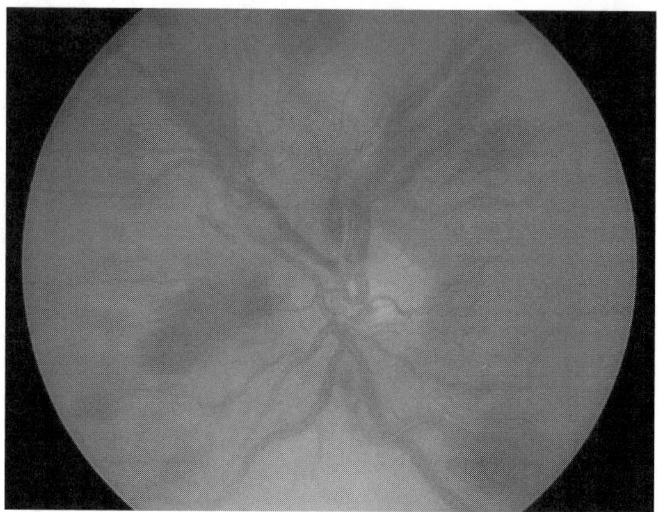

Figure 6. HAR - several flame hemorrhages and optic disk hyperemia.

Incidence of HAR

Table 1 shows the varying incidence of HAR described in the literature. The large range of incidence, from 3.8% to 90.5 %, reflects many different studies but may also provide a clue as to the pathophysiology of HAR. The maximum altitude attained appears to be a risk factor, and the low incidence of HAR in hypobaric chambers suggests that exertion may also be important.(11, 39, 72)

Digital fundal photography was performed before, during and after the 3 different expeditions mentioned earlier (Figure 7). HAR was defined as one or more hemorrhages in either eye and the incidences in table 2 below were recorded.

All subjects had their visual acuity assessed using a LogMAR chart but this was unaffected by altitude. AMS scores were recorded using the Lake Louise scale(66) and this data is still undergoing analysis. Incidence of HAR ranged from 10% to 64.2% but the maximum altitude attained did not appear to be significant as the Everest summiteers had the lowest incidence of HAR. This contradicts previous work,(81) but these mountaineers used supplemental oxygen above 7400m and when their overall ascent rate is examined, it was far lower than those who went to the north col of Everest, and who subsequently had the highest incidence of HAR (Figure 8). This raises the possibility that acclimatization is important in preventing HAR. However, one would then expect the Apex 2 subjects to have a high rate of HAR with their extremely fast rate of ascent. But this was not the case, and the only difference was that these subjects were driven up to 5200m with no exertion. So these results point to a combination of poor acclimatization and exertion being the key risk factors in the development of HAR.

Table 1. The incidence of HAR in the literature.

Year	1st Author	Subjects	Max altitude	HAR (%)
1970	Frayser(22)	25	2959	36
1975	Schumacher(69)	39	6194	36
1989	Brinchmann-Hansen(10)	23	4000-5850	13
1975	Rennie(65)	15	5227-8167	33
1975	Shults(70)	6	5366-6890	67
1976	Clarke(17)	20	6500-8848	30
1979	Hackett(26)	340	5545	3.8
1981	McFadden(52)	39	5360	56.4
1983	Kramar(41)	7	6798	28.8
1992	Butler(14)	14	5300-8182	29
1999	Wiedman(81)	40	<7620	73.6
			>7620	90.5
2000	Müllner-Eidenböck(55)	7	7500-8201	25

Table 2. Incidence of HAR on 3 different expeditions.

Expedition	Subjects	Max altitude (m)	Ascent rate (m/day)	HAR (%)
Everest summit	20	8848	140	10
Everest north col	14	7100	338	64.2
Medex 2003	52	6500	210	28.3

Pathophysiology of HAR

There have been many proposed theories for the development of HAR, but none of them have been thoroughly tested (table 3).

One hypothesis that has been recently tested is that of changed blood viscosity. Erythropoietin is released in response to the lowered arterial oxygen saturation at altitude which causes a rise in hematocrit.(35) This response varies considerably between individuals and the increased blood viscosity has been suggested as another mechanism for the development of HAR.(42) The Medex expedition in 2003 provided the opportunity to test this hypothesis.

Volunteers were recruited and consented at a pre-expedition weekend. They then trekked from Tumlingtar (300m) to Chamlang base camp (5100m) in Nepal over 19 days following a safe acclimatization regime. All measurements were taken at sea level and at 5100m. Capillary hematocrit was assessed using a Clinispin Hct Benchtop Centrifuge; samples were spun at 3,000 rpm for 15 minutes and the proportion of packed red blood cells to plasma was measured immediately against a visual scale. Digital fundal photography of the posterior pole was carried out using a Nidek NM-100 camera. Subjects with co-existing ocular pathology and those who took acetazolamide were excluded.

Forty six subjects fit the criteria for the study. There were 25 males and 21 females with a mean age of 33.3 years, the oldest being 53 and the youngest being 21. Mean hematocrit at sea level was 40.4 % (SD 3.7). This increased to 48.1 % at 5100m (SD 4.7). A paired t-test showed this change to be highly significant ($p<0.05$). HAR, defined as one or more hemorrhages at 5100m in either eye, was found in 13 out of 46 subjects (28.3 %). None of these subjects reported any visual symptoms and the hemorrhages cleared within 2 weeks without sequelae. These subjects did not have any significantly greater or smaller change in hematocrit, as measured by the two-tailed Wilcoxon rank sum test ($p=0.66$).

The incidence of 28.3 % in this study would fit with a cohort ascending sensibly to moderately high altitude. However these results do not support the hypothesis that increased blood viscosity secondary to raised hematocrit at altitude is a causative factor in the development of HAR. In this study, hematocrit rose as expected but the extent of this increase was not predictive of HAR.

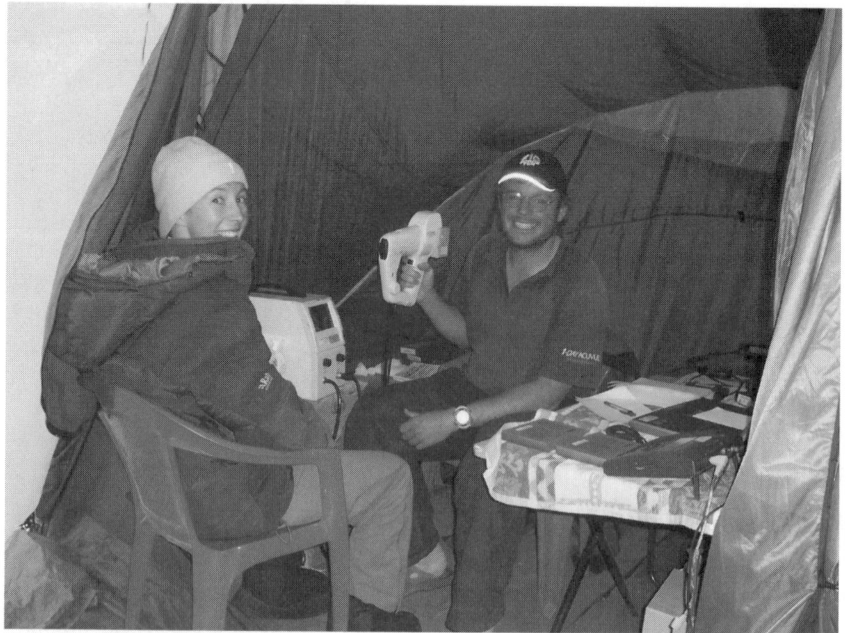

Figure 7. Digital retinal photography at Everest basecamp (5200 m).

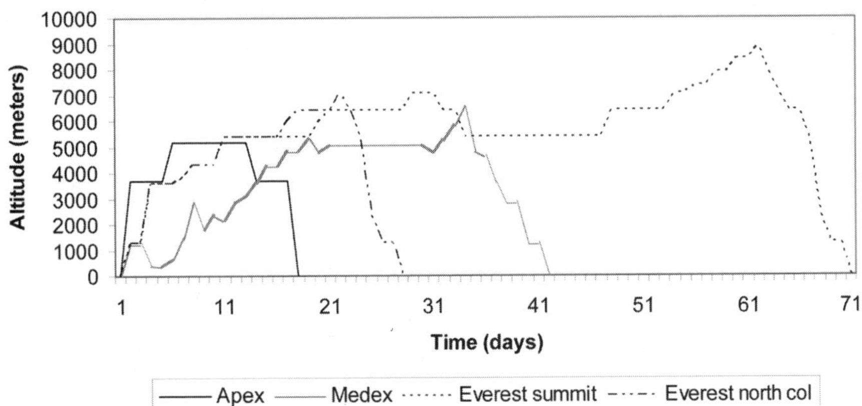

Figure 8. Different ascent profiles of each expedition; Apex 2 had the fastest rate of ascent and the Everest summiteers the slowest rate of ascent.

Retinal blood flow regulation

Regulation of blood flow to the retina and optic nerve remains constant over a range of elevated intraocular pressure or mean arterial pressure, independent of sympathetic activation (pressure autoregulation). In addition, increased metabolic activity in these tissues proportionally increases blood flow (metabolic autoregulation). At constant metabolic rate, altered arterial oxygen content reciprocally alters blood flow, leaving total oxygen delivery constant, while blood flow rises and falls with the arterial carbon dioxide tension. These responses are similar to those of the cerebral circulation.(30) In retinal circulation, systemic controls have only a minor influence, while local factors (e.g. nitric oxide, prostaglandins, endothelin, and the renin-angiotensin system(28)) dominate regulation.(60)

At sea level, the main factor for retinal vascular smooth muscle is the arterial carbon dioxide tension; blood flow varies directly with the PCO_2.(29) However at altitude there is evidence that hypoxia, rather than hypocapnia, becomes the controlling factor in retinal circulation.(23)

There is also an apparent change in retinal arterial response to exercise at simulated altitude after 7 weeks acclimatization; relative constriction to exercise was replaced with dilation. This provides a clue to a change in the autoregulatory pattern, possibly illustrating an increased state of readiness for exercise in the hypoxic state.(12)

With currently available evidence, it would appear that the pathophysiology of HAR is a two-stage process; firstly the hypoxic stress of altitude causes retinal vascular engorgement to maintain adequate oxygen supply for the metabolically-demanding photoreceptors; this is a normal physiological response. Secondly there is some overload of the vascular system, such as exertion, which pushes the regulatory system beyond its physiological limits, causing the pathological breakdown of the capillary endothelium and hemorrhage.

Table 3. Theories for the pathophysiology of HAR

- Increased ocular blood flow (80)
- Retinal venous outflow obstruction (22)
- Increased IOP (22)
- Valsalva retinopathy (65)(70)
- Increased blood pressure (22)
- Raised intracranial pressure (17,22,81)
- Vascular headache mechanism (69)
- Vascular dysregulation (55)
- Increased blood viscosity (42,65,70)
- Hypoxic vascular weakness (65)
- Decreased atmospheric ozone (70)
- Hypoxic endothelial decompensation (41,80)
- Platelet microemboli (34)

FUTURE DIRECTIONS

The clear optical media of the eye allow direct observation of a vascular bed at altitude and recent technological advances have allowed investigators to take advantage of this window. Müllner-Eidenböck et al recently used the Heidelberg retinal flowmeter in an altitude study.(55) This device uses laser Doppler flowmetry and laser scanning tomography to produce a reading for retinal blood volume, flow and velocity. Instruments such as this and the Paradigm ocular blood flowmeter, will provide a more dynamic picture of changes to the vasculature in the eye at altitude and may explain exactly what precipitates retinal hemorrhages. Magnetic resonance imaging has also been performed on 2 subjects who had HAR after ascending Aconcagua (6986m) which showed no significant changes.(43)

Vascular endothelial growth factor (VEGF) is an angiogenic protein and vasopermeability factor which is released at high altitude.(75) Intraocular VEGF concentrations are closely correlated with active neovascularization in patients with diabetes mellitus, central retinal vein occlusion, retinopathy of prematurity and rubeosis iridis.(1) In-vitro experiments have shown that hypoxia increases VEGF expression in retinal cells.(2) VEGF has also been found in hypoxic corneal epithelial cells as described above.(51) The role of VEGF in ocular altitude problems is not yet understood, but clearly warrants further research.

The optic nerve sheath is continuous with the dura mater and its diameter can be measured using ocular ultrasound. This has been shown to be a reliable non-invasive measure of intra-cranial pressure.(31, 32, 57) A recent pilot study in Colorado showed a small increase in optic nerve sheath diameter after brief decompression to 14,000 feet. This will be further investigated and may prove important in the early diagnosis of HACE.

Visual acuity is a coarse measure of retinal function and therefore rarely changes during studies at altitude. More sensitive measurements include contrast sensitivity, luminance thresholds, dark adaptation, macular recovery time, visual fields and color vision. As more sophisticated tests emerge, they will be used in altitude experiments to asses the effect of altitude on retinal function, rather than just examining the retinal vasculature (Figure 10).

Most altitude research is carried out on lowlanders ascending for a short time to high altitude. There are a large number of people throughout the world who live above 2500m and studying the retinal circulation in these people may provide an insight into the effect of chronic hypoxia on the retina.

There is a need for hypothesis-driven research with larger numbers of subjects on research-orientated expeditions. This should be combined with controlled experiments in hypobaric chambers and perhaps the development of an animal model for HAR.

Figure 9. Measuring color vision with a prototype instrument at Everest north col (7100m).

CONCLUSION

These studies have begun to shed light on corneal and IOP changes at altitude. However it is now over 35 years since the original observation that retinal hemorrhages occur at high altitude and despite a considerable amount of work on the subject, the cause and possible clinical implications of HAR remain obscure. A better understanding of the pathophysiology of HAR may shed light on the basic mechanisms of hypoxic illness at sea level; diabetic retinopathy and retinopathy of prematurity are caused by retinal hypoxia.

There has been an attempt to classify HAR(81) but as most people observing this phenomenon are not ophthalmologists, it would be better to simplify the definition of HAR to "one or more hemorrhages in either eye of a person ascending above 2500m" with secondary signs of decreased visual acuity, papilloedema and cotton wool spots. Retinal vascular engorgement and tortuosity should be viewed as the normal physiological response to hypoxia.

HAR is not confined to the realms of extreme altitude and every year more people venture above 2500m for recreation, for example Honigman et al recently described a case of HAR in a Colorado skier.(33) Any change in vision at altitude warrants descent, as the cause is not always obvious as it could be a benign change in the cornea after refractive surgery or a potentially fatal episode of cerebral hypoxia.

ACKNOWLEDGEMENTS

DM is a member of Medical Expeditions (Medex) and Altitude Physiology Expeditions (Apex) which are both charities that promote research and education into high altitude physiology and medicine. Thanks to all members of Apex especially Roger Thompson, Alistair Simpson, Anna Thompson, Kirsten Scott, Shaima Elnor and David Cavanagh. Thanks to all members of Medex, especially Annabel Nickol, Simon Currin, David Collier and Denzil Broadhurst. Thanks to Chris Hogg and Geoff Arden at Moorfields Eye Hospital, Jill Inglis, everyone at the Colorado Centre for Altitude Medicine and Physiology (CCAMP) and the staff at the Retinal Diseases Image Analysis Reading Center (REDIARC) in Ohio. Thanks to the following companies for the loan of equipment : Nidek, AccuScene, Paradigm and Zeiss. This work was partly funded by the Royal College of Ophthalmologists, the Royal College of Physicians and Surgeons of Glasgow, the Carnegie Trust for the Universities of Scotland and the Royal Society of Medicine.

ABBREVIATIONS

AMS - Acute mountain sickness
BP - Blood pressure
CCAMP - Colorado Centre for Altitude Medicine and Physiology
CSF - Cerebrospinal fluid
HAR – High altitude retinopathy
HAPE – High altitude pulmonary edema
HACE – High altitude cerebral edema
ICP - Intracranial pressure
IOP - Intraocular pressure
LASIK - Laser in-situ keratomileusis
NSAID - Non-steroidal anti-inflammatory drugs
PRK - Photo-refractive keratectomy
RK – Radial Keratotomy
REDIARC - Retinal Diseases Image Analysis Reading Center
VEGF – Vascular endothelial growth factor.

REFERENCES

1. Aiello LP, Avery RL, and Arrigg PG. Vascular endothelial growth factor in ocular fluid of patients with diabetic retinopathy and other retinal disorders. *N Engl J Med* 331 : 1480-1487, 1994.
2. Aiello LP, Northrup JM, Keyt BA, Takagi H, and Iwamoto MA. Hypoxic regulation of vascular endothelial growth factor in retinal cells. *Arch Ophthalmol* 113(12) : 1538-1544, 1995.
3. Bafa M, Lambrinakis I, Dayan M, and Birch M. Clinical comparison of the measurement of the IOP with the ocular blood flow tonometer, the Tono-Pen XL and the Goldmann applanation tonometer. *Acta Ophthalmol Scand* 79(1) : 15-18, 2001.
4. Bandyopadhyay M, Raychaudhuri A, Lahiri SK, Schwartz EC, Myatt M, and Johnson GJ. Comparison of Goldmann applanation tonometry with the Tono-Pen for measuring IOP in a population-based glaucoma survey in rural West Bengal. *Ophthalmic Epidemiol* 9(3) : 215-224, 2002.
5. Bayer A, Yumusak E, and Sahin OF. Intraocular pressure measured at ground level and 10,000 feet. *Aviat Space Environ Med* 75 : 543-545, 2004.
6. Bergmanson JP, and Chu LW. Corneal response to rigid contact lens wear. *Br J Ophthalmol* 66 : 667-675, 1982.
7. Binder PS, Stainer GA, Zavala EY, Deg JK, and Akers PH. Acute morphologic features of Radial Keratotomy. *Arch Ophthalmol* 101 : 1113-1116, 1983.
8. Boes DA, Omura AK, and Hennessy MJ. Effect of high altitude exposure on myopic LASIK. *J Cataract Refract Surg*; 27 : 1937-1941, 2001.
9. Bonanno JA, Nyguen T, Biehl T, Soni S. Can variability in corneal metabolism explain the variability in corneal swelling? *Eye and Contact Lens : Science and Clinical Practice* 29 (1 Supp) : S7-9, 2003.
10. Brinchmann-Hansen O, and Myhre K. Blood pressure, intraocular pressure and retinal vessels after high altitude mountain exposure. *Aviat Space Environ Med* 60 : 970-976, 1989.
11. Brinchmann-Hansen O, Myhre K. Vascular response of retinal arteries and veins to acute hypoxia of 8,000, 10,000, 12,500, and 15,000 feet of simulated altitude. *Aviat Space Environ Med* 61(2) :112-116, 1990.
12. Brinchmann-Hansen O, Myhre K, and Sandvik L. Retinal vessel responses to exercise and hypoxia before and after high altitude acclimatization. *Eye* 3 : 768-776, 1989.
13. Brubaker RF. Tonometry and corneal thickness. *Arch Ophthalmol* 117(1) : 104-105, 1999.
14. Butler FK, Harris DJ Jr, and Reynolds RD. Altitude retinopathy on Mount Everest, 1989. *Ophthalmol* 99 : 739-746, 1992.
15. Carapancea M. Experimental and clinical hyperophthalmotony of high altitudes. *Arch Ophthalmol Rev Gen Ophthalmol* 37 : 775-784, 1977.
16. Cheung AK, Siu AW, Cheung DW, and Mo EC. Production of hypoxia-induced corneal edema in aged eyes. *Yen Ko Hsueh Pao (Eye Science)*. 20(1) :1-5, 2004.
17. Clarke C, and Duff J. Mountain sickness, retinal haemorrhages and acclimatisation on Mount Everest in 1975.*Br Med J* ii : 495-497, 1976.
18. Cymerman A, Rock PB, Muza SR, Lyons TP, Fulco CS, Mazzeo RS, Butterfield G, and Moore LG. Intraocular pressure and acclimatization to 4300 M altitude *Aviat Space Environ Med* 71(10) : 1045-1050, 2000.
19. Dimming JW, and Tabin G. The ascent of Mount Everest following LASIK. *J Refract Surg*, 19 : 48-52, 2003.
20. Feltgen N, Leifert D, and Funk J. Correlation between central corneal thickness, applanation tonometry and direct intracameral IOP readings. *Br J Ophthalmol* 85 : 85-87, 2001.

21. Flynn WJ, Miller RE 2nd, Tredici TJ, and Block MG. Soft contact lens wear at altitude : effects of hypoxia. *Aviat Space Environ Med* 59(1) : 44-8, 1988.
22. Frayser R, Houston CS, Bryan AC, Rennie ID, and Gray G. Retinal hemorrhage at high altitude. *New Eng J Med* 282(21) : 1183-1184, 1970.
23. Frayser R, Gray GW, and Houston CS. Control of the retinal circulation at altitude. *J Appl Physiol* 37(3) : 302-304, 1974.
24. Frenkel REP, Hong YJ, and Shin DS. Comparison of the Tono-pen to the Goldmann Applanation Tonometer. *Arch Ophthalmol* 106 : 750-753, 1988.
25. Garzozi HJ, Chung HS, and Lang Y. Intraocular pressure and PRK : a comparison of 3 different tonometers. *Cornea* 20 : 33-36, 2001.
26. Hackett PH and Rennie D. Rales, peripheral oedema, retinal hemorrhage and acute mountain sickness. *Am J Med* 67 : 214-218, 1979.
27. Hackett PH and Rennie ID. *Cotton wool spots : A new addition to high altitude retinopathy*. In : *High altitude physiology and medicine.* Editors : Brendel W, Zink RA. New York : Springer-Verlag, 1982, 215-218.
28. Haefliger I, Meyer P, Flammer J, and Luscher T. The vascular endothelium as a regulator of the ocular circulation : a new concept in ophthalmology? *Surv Ophthalmol* 39 : 123-129, 1994.
29. Harris A, Arend O, Wolf S, Cantor L, and Martin B. CO<cpSubscript>2 dependence of retinal arterial and capillary blood velocity. *Acta Ophthalmologica* 73 : 421-424, 1995.
30. Harris A, Ciulla TA, Chung HS, and Martin B. Regulation of retinal and optic nerve blood flow. *Arch Ophthalmol* 116(11) : 1491-1495, 1998.
31. Helmke H, and Hansen HC. Fundamentals of transorbital sonographic evaluation of the optic nerve sheath expansion under intracranial hypertension. I Experimental study *Paediatr Radiol* 26 : 701-705, 1996.
32. Helmke H, and Hansen HC. Fundamentals of transorbital sonographic evaluation of the optic nerve sheath expansion under intracranial hypertension. II Patient study. Paediatr Radiol 26 : 706-710, 1996.
33. Honigman B, Noordewier E, Kleinman D, and Yaron M. High altitude retinal hemorrhages in a Colorado skier. *High Alt Med Biol* 2(4) : 539-544, 2001.
34. Houston CS, and McFadden DM. Long term effects of altitude on the eye. *Lancet* 338 : 49, 1979.
35. Jedlickova K, Stockton DW and Chen H. Search for genetic determinants of individual variability of the erythropoietin response to high altitude. *Blood Cells Molecules & Diseases* 31(2) : 175-82, 2003.
36. Johnson M, Kass MA, Moses RA, and Grodzki WJ. Increased corneal thickness simulating elevated IOP. *Arch Ophthalmol* 96 : 664-665, 1978.
37. Kanski JJ. In : *Clinical Ophthalmology- a systematic approach (4th edition)*. Oxford : Butterworth-Heinemann, 1999, 168.
38. Kao SF, Lichter PR, Bergstrom TJ, Rowe S, and Musch DC. Clinical comparison of the Oculab Tono-Pen to the Goldmann applanation tonometer. *Ophthalmol* 94 : 1541-1544, 1987.
39. Kobrick JL, and Appleton B. Effects of extended hypoxia on visual performance and retinal vascular state. *J Appl Physiol* 31(3) : 357-362, 1971.
40. Koch DD. Knauer WJ 3rd, and Emery JM. High altitude corneal endothelial decompensation. *Cornea* 3(3) :189-91, 1984.
41. Kramar PO, Drinkwater BL, Folinsbee J, and Bedi JF. Ocular functions and incidence of acute mountain sickness. *Aviat Space Environ Med* 54(2) : 116-120, 1983.
42. Lang GE, and Kuba GB. High altitude retinopathy. *Am J Ophthalmol* 123(3) : 418-420, 1997.
43. Lee AG, Aldana AE, Harper RL. High altitude retinopathy. *J Neuro-ophthalmol* 19(3) :

205-206, 1999.

44. Lempert P, Cooper KH, Culver JF, and Tredici, TJ. The effect of exercise on intraocular pressure. *Am J Ophthalmol* 63(6) : 1673-1676, 1967.
45. Mader TH, Blanton CL, Gilbert BN, Kubis KC, Schallhorn SC, White LJ, Parmley VC, and Ng JD. Refractive changes during 72 hour exposure to high altitude after refractive surgery. *Ophthalmol* 103 : 1188-1195, 1996.
46. Mader TH, and Tabin G. Going to high altitude with pre-existing ocular conditions. *High Alt Med Biol* 4(4) : 419-430, 2003.
47. Mader TH, and White LJ. Refractive changes at extreme altitude after RK. *Am J Ophthalmol* 119 : 733-737, 1995.
48. Mader TH, White LJ, Johnson DS, and Barth FC. The ascent of Mount Everest following radial keratotomy. *Wildern Environ Med* 13 : 53-54, 2002.
49. Marsich MM, and Bullimore MA, The repeatability of corneal thickness measures. *Cornea* 19(6) : 792-795, 2000.
50. Mastropasqua L, Ciancaglini M, Di Tano G, Carpineto P, Lobefalo L, Loffredo B, Bosco D, Columbaro M, and Falcieri E. Ultrastructural changes in rat cornea after prolonged hypobaric hypoxia. *J Submicroscopic Cytol & Pathol* 30(2) : 285-93, 1998.
51. Mastyugin V, Mosaed S, Bonazzi A, Dunn MW and Schwartzman ML. Corneal epithelial VEGF and cytochrome p450 4B1 expression in a rabbit model of closed eye contact lens wear. *Curr Eye Res* 23(1) : 1-10, 2001.
52. McFadden DM, Houston CS, Sutton JR, Powles ACP, Gray GW, and Roberts RS. High Altitude Retinopathy. *JAMA* 245 : 581-586, 1981.
53. Minkler DS, Baerveldt G, Heuer DK, Quillen-Thomas B, Walonker AF, and Weiner J. Clinical evaluation of the Oculab Tono-pen. *Am J Ophthalmol* 104 : 168-173, 1987.
54. Modis L, Langenbucher A, and Seitz B. Scanning-slit and specular microscopic pachymetry in comparison with ultrasonic determination of corneal thickness. *Cornea* 20(7) : 711-714, 2001.
55. Müllner-Eidenböck A, Rainer G, Strenn K, and Zidek T. High altitude retinopathy and retinal vascular dysregulation. *Eye* 14 : 724-729, 2000.
56. Nelson ML, Brady S, Mader TH, White LJ, Parmley VC and Winkle RK. Refractive changes caused by hypoxia after LASIK. *Ophthalmol* 108 : 542-544, 2001.
57. Newman WD, Hollman AS, Dutton GN and Carachi R. Measurement of optic nerve sheath diameter by ultrasound : a means of detecting acute raised intracranial pressure in hydrocephalus. *Br J Ophthalmol* 86 : 1109-1113, 2002.
58. Ng JD, White LJ, Parmley VC, Hubickey W, Carter J, and Mader TH. Effects of simulated high altitude on patients who have had RK. *Ophthalmol* 103 : 453-457, 1996.
59. Nguyen T, Soni PS, Brizendine E, and Bonanno JA. Variability in hypoxia-induced corneal swelling is associated with variability in corneal metabolism and endothelial function. *Eye and Contact Lens : Science and Clinical Practice* 29 (2) : 117-125, 2003.
60. Palmer RM, Ferrige AG, and Moncada S. Nitric oxide release accounts for the biological activity of endothelium-derived relaxing factor. *Nature* 327 : 524-526, 1987.
61. Passo MS, Goldberg L, Elliot DL, and Van Buskirk EM. Exercise conditioning and Intraocular Pressure. *Am J Ophthalmol* 103 : 754-757, 1987.
62. Polse KA, Brand R, Mandell R, Vastine D, DeMartini D, and Flom R. Age differences in corneal hydration control. *Invest Ophthalmol Vis Sci* 30(3) : 392-399, 1989.
63. Polse KA, and Mandell RB. Critical oxygen tension at the corneal surface. *Arch Ophthalmol* 84 : 505-508, 1970.
64. Realini T, and Lovelace K. Measuring central corneal thickness with ultrasound pachymetry. *Optom Vis Sci* 80(6) : 437-439, 2003.
65. Rennie D, and Morrisey J. Retinal changes in Himalayan climbers. *Arch Ophthalmol* 93 : 395-400, 1975.

66. Roach RC, Bartcsh P, Oelz O, Hackett PH, and Lake Louise AMS Scoring Consensus Committee. The Lake Louise Acute Mountain Sickness Scoring System. In : Sutton JR, Houston CS, Coates G, eds. *Hypoxia and molecular medicine.* Burlington, VT. : Charles S Houston, 1993 : 272-274.
67. Sanchis-Gimeno JA, Lleo-Perez A, Alonso L, Rahhal MS, and Martinez-Soriano F. Anatomic study of the corneal thickness of young emmetropic subjects. *Cornea* 23 : 669-673, 2004.
68. Sarver MD, Polse KA, and Baggett DA. Intersubject difference in corneal response to hypoxia. *Am J of Optom and Physiological Optics* 60(2) : 128-131, 1983.
69. Schumacher GA, and Petajan JH. High altitude stress and retinal hemorrhage- relation to vascular headache mechanisms. *Arch Environ Health* 30 : 217-221, 1975.
70. Shults WT, and Swan KC. High altitude retinopathy in mountain climbers. *Arch Ophthalmol* 93 : 404-408, 1975.
71. Singh I, Khanna PK, Srivastava MC, Lal M, Roy SB, and Subramanyam CSV. Acute Mountain Sickness. *New Eng J Med* 280(4) : 175-184, 1969.
72. Sutton JR, Coates G, Gray GW, Mansell AL, Powles P, and Zahoruk R. Retinal studies at 466 torr in a hypobaric chamber. *Aviat Space Environ Med* 51(4) : 407-408, 1980.
73. Tingay DG, Tsimnadis P, and Basnyat B. A blurred view from Everest. *Lancet* 362 : 1978, 2003.
74. du Toit R, Vega JA, Fonn D, and Simpson T. Diurnal variation of corneal sensitivity and thickness. *Cornea* 22(3) : 205-209, 2003.
75. Walter R. Maggiorini M. Scherrer U. Contesse J. and Reinhart WH. Effects of high-altitude exposure on vascular endothelial growth factor levels in man. *Eur J Appl Physiol* 85(1-2) :113-7, 2001.
76. Wang J, Fonn D, Simpson TL, and Jones L. The measurement of corneal epithelial thickness in response to hypoxia using optical coherence topography. *Am J Ophthalmol* 133(3) : 315-319, 2002.
77. Whitacre MM, Stein RA, and Hassanein K. The effect of corneal thickness on applanation tonometry. *Am J Ophthalmol* 115 : 592-596, 1993.
78. White LJ, and Mader TH. Refractive changes with increasing altitude after RK. *Am J Ophthalmol* 115(6) : 821-823, 1993.
79. White LJ, and Mader TH. Refractive changes at high altitude after LASIK. *Ophthalmol* 107(12) : 2118, 2000.
80. Wiedman M. High altitude retinal hemorrhage. *Arch Ophthalmology* 93 : 401-403, 1975.
81. Wiedman M, and Tabin GC. High Altitude Retinopathy and Altitude Illness. *Ophthalmol* 106 : 1924-1927, 1999.
82. Winkle RK, Mader TH, Parmley VC, White LJ, and Polse KA. The etiology of refractive changes at high altitude after RK. *Ophthalmol* 105 :282-286, 1998.
83. Wilmer WH and Berens C. The effect of altitude on ocular functions. *JAMA* 71 : 1382-1400, 1918.
84. Ziadi M, Moiroux P, d'Athis P, Bron A, Brun J-M, and Creuzot-Garcher C. Assessment of induced corneal hypoxia in diabetic patients. *Cornea* 21(5) : 453-457, 2002.

Chapter 22

LAKE LOUISE CONSENSUS METHODS FOR MEASURING THE HYPOXIC VENTILATORY RESPONSE

Frank L. Powell
Department of Medicine and White Mountain Research Station, University of California San Diego, La Jolla, CA, USA.

BACKGROUND

The hypoxic ventilatory response (HVR) is the body's first line of defense against environmental hypoxia, for example, at high altitude. In acute hypoxia, the HVR is a reflex increase in ventilation in response to decreased arterial PO_2, which is rapidly sensed by arterial chemoreceptors primarily in the carotid bodies.With sustained exposure to hypoxia, the HVR changes (8). For example, after 5 to 20 minutes of hypoxia, ventilation "rolls off" relative to the acute hypoxic response and this is called hypoxic ventilatory decline (HVD). With continuous hypoxia, for example during acclimatization to high altitude, ventilation increases above the level of the acute HVR with ventilatory acclimatization to hypoxia (VAH). The different time domains of the HVR raise many questions about the physiological mechanisms of oxygen sensing and the control of breathing. They also raise many issues about experimental methods to measure the HVR and comparing results between laboratories. At the 13th International Hypoxia Symposium, John Severinghaus proposed consensus methods for measuring the HVR in humans, and the discussion continued at the 14th International Hypoxia Symposium in Lake Louise. The goal of this report is to stimulate further discussion and experiments so we can adopt a "Lake Louise Consensus for Measuring the HVR" at the 15th International Hypoxia Symposium in 2007.

METHODS AND RESULTS

An example of a study using methods that are similar to early drafts of a consensus for measuring the HVR in humans is found in an abstract in these proceedings (12). It uses steady-state measurements of the HVR so ventilation is measured as a function of constant

Hypoxia and Exercise, edited by R.C. Roach *et al.*
Springer, New York, 2006.

level of hypoxic stimulation, in contrast to methods relying on continuously changing PaO_2 (13) or cyclic changes in PaO_2 (6). Breathing circuits for this kind of measurement are described in the literature (11).

Ventilation was measured from subjects wearing a face mask. PIO_2 and $PICO_2$ were adjusted to obtain desired levels of arterial O_2 saturation estimated with a pulse oximeter (SpO_2), and end-tidal PCO_2 ($PETCO_2$). Figure 1 illustrates the key points of the protocol to measure HVR and shows average results from Steinbeck and co-workers (12).

After acclimating to the apparatus while breathing room air (ca. 15 min), PIO_2 is rapidly decreased to produce a target SpO_2 of 80%, while $PICO_2$ is kept at 0 Torr, to measure the poikilocapnic HVR. This level of PIO_2 is maintained for 20 min. Because the change in V. E is so small with hypocapnia from the hypoxic hyperventilation, the poikilocapnic HVR is quantified as: $pHVR = \Delta PETCO_2 / \Delta SpO_2$. The pHVR5 measured after 5 min of poikilocapnic hypoxia is a measure of the acute poikilocapnic HVR before significant HVD occurs. The $pHVR_{20}$ measured after 20 min of hypoxia quantifies the poikilocapnic HVR in the presence of HVD.

Subjects then rested 1 hr before measuring the isocapnic HVR using a similar protocol. $PETCO_2$ was increased 1 Torr above the level measured during the first 5 min of mild hyperoxia and held at that level for another 10 min of hyperoxia. PIO_2 was decreased to give a target SpO_2 of 80% and $PICO_2$ was adjusted as necessary to maintain $PETCO_2$ throughout 20 min of sustained isocapnic hypoxia. The isocapnic HVR was quantified as: $iHVR = \Delta \dot{V}E / \Delta SpO_2$. The $iHVR_5$ measured the acute isocapnic HVR before significant HVD and $iHVR_{20}$ measured the HVR after HVD had stabilized under isocapnic conditions.

In Steinbeck et al's. subjects, $iHVR_5 = 2.37 \pm 0.61$ (L/min%) and this decreased with HVD so $iHVR_{20} = 0.75 \pm 0.27$ (L/min%). These values are similar to other publications using similar methods and protocols (3, 10, 11). The effects of HVD on the measure of poikilocapnic HVR were much smaller: $pHVR_5 = 0.33 \pm 0.05$ (Torr/%) and $pHVR_{20} = 0.28 \pm 0.08$ (Torr/%).

DISCUSSION

The results presented above demonstrate a relatively simple and short protocol can generate reproducible measures of the HVR that are comparable between different laboratories. However, there are many questions that need further discussion and study before endorsing consensus methods. These are presented briefly below.

Steady state method

This approach is chosen because it is relatively simple and requires only the most basic respiratory physiology equipment. Additional information about the physiology of the various time domains of the HVR may be obtained by more sophisticated methods relying on rapid, cyclic changes in O_2 level. HVD may start decreasing ventilation within 2 min of sustained hypoxia (1) so $iHVR_5$ may not be a perfect measure of the acute HVR but it is robust. Rebreathing methods may offer an advantage when gases are not available to control steady PIO_2 and $PICO_2$ levels (e.g. at altitude) but the results are more difficult to interpret given with simultaneous time-dependent changes in the HVR and stimulus levels.

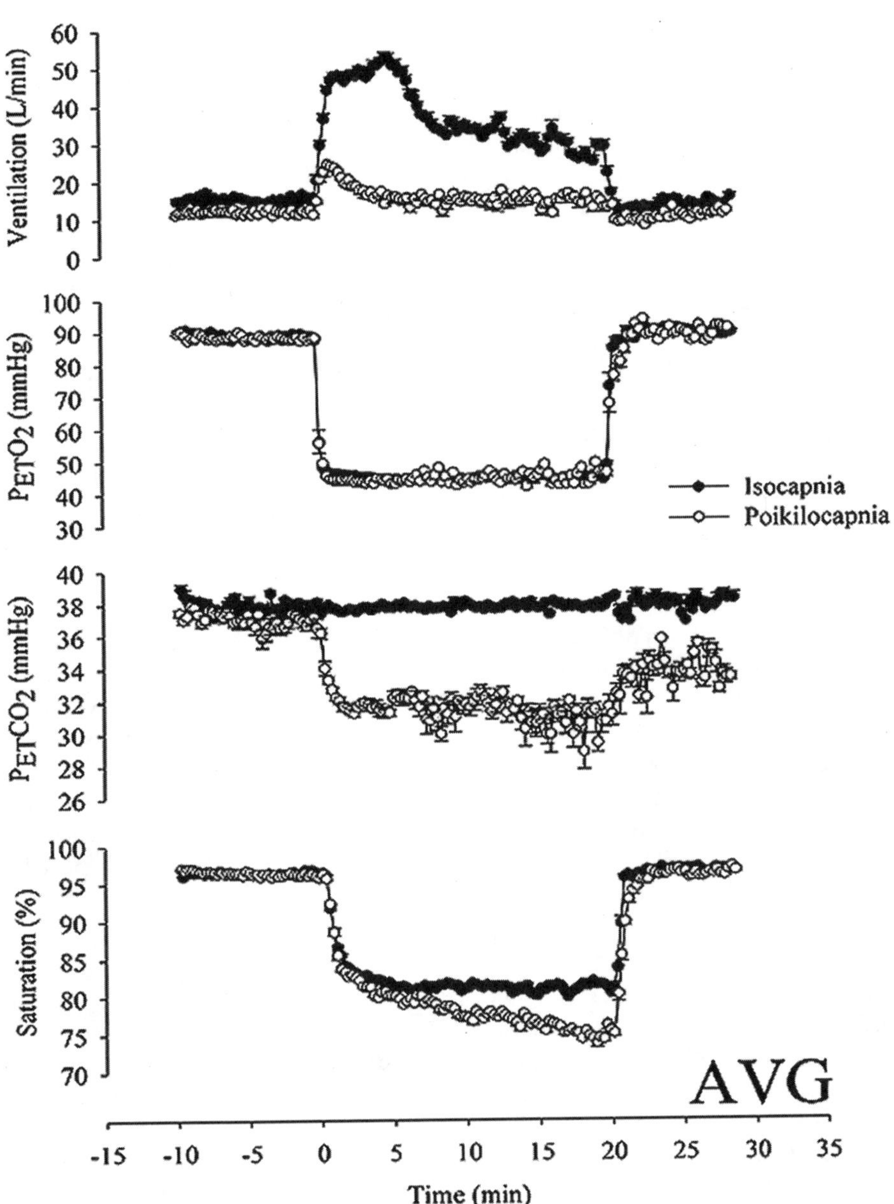

Figure 1. Average respiratory variables for normal humans (n=7) during normoxia, 20 min of hypoxia and normoxic recovery (12).

Ventilatory baseline

Most subjects show small decreases in $\dot{V}E$ and increases in $PETCO_2$ breathing 30% O_2 versus room air (21%) at sea level. Hence, mild hyperoxia (PIO_2 = 200 Torr) has been used to minimize O_2-sensitive ventilatory drive from arterial chemoreceptors (11). However, animal studies indicate that even such mild hyperoxia may be a ventilatory stimulant and there is also some evidence for this in some human studies that should be evaluated further (cf. (2)). The ideal duration for increasing O_2 level to establish the ventilatory baseline needs to be determined. For subjects acclimatized to 3,800 m, additional time at high O_2 levels was necessary to remove underlying HVD with chronic hypoxia at altitude (11).

Hypoxic stimulus

The hypoxic stimulus to carotid body chemoreceptors is arterial PO_2 and not arterial O_2 content or saturation. However, $\dot{V}E$ is a linear function of SaO_2 between 100% and 70% (9, 11) allowing the HVR to be expressed independent of the exact level of hypoxia within this range as $\Delta\dot{V}E/\Delta SpO_2$. This is not meant to imply that the stimulus is SaO_2, however. This protocol held PIO_2 constant after achieving the initial target for hypoxic stimulation but other approaches include adjusting PIO_2 to maintain constant $PETO_2$ or SpO_2 during sustained hypoxia.

CO_2 level for isocapnia

Results appear similar in different studies that have maintained isocapnia either (1) 1-2 Torr above the level measured during normoxia (this study), (2) 1-2 Torr above the level measured during mild hyperoxia (3), or (3) at the level necessary to increase $\dot{V}E$ with PIO_2 = 200 Torr to a target level(4, 11). However, choosing the $PETCO_2$ level for the isocapnic HVR during acclimatization to altitude is more difficult because the arterial CO_2 set point decreases as ventilatory drive increases with VAH. Efforts to maintain ventilatory drive constant at different time points during acclimatization are difficult to interpret because interactions between the HVR and other ventilatory drives being manipulated experimentally (e.g. central CO_2 drive, cf. (11)) could be changing during VAH.

Time points and measurements

The 5 min time point for measuring the HVR is a compromise between using simple methods to establish a constant stimulus level (SpO_2 = 80% and constant $PETCO_2$) and the desire to measure the HVR as soon as possible before significant HVD can occur. Sophisticated methods show some HVD occurs as soon as 2 min after the start of hypoxia but the changes are minimal compared to those measured between 5 and 20 min of hypoxia (1). Of course it is ideal if continuous measurements are possible but agreeing on specific time points is necessary for a consensus to compare between different experiments and investigators.

The order of measuring the isocapnic and poikilocapnic HVR should also be considered if they are studied in an individual on the same day. Steinbeck and co-workers found a tendency for $\dot{V}E$ to remain elevated for more than 20 min following isocapnic hypoxia in some individuals, presumably because of lactic acidosis. Hence, it may be preferable to measure the poikilocapnic HVR before the isocapnic HVR if they must be measured sequentially on the same day.

Finally, the individual components of $\dot{V}_E$, i.e. respiratory frequency and tidal volume, should be measured and reported.

Other factors

Other factors that may influence the HVR and should be at least reported, if not standardized, include: posture (e.g. semi-recumbent 30° head up (11)), open versus closed eyes (affects resting $PETCO_2$, JW Severinghaus, personal communication), auditory stimuli (listening to music or watching a movie should not drive breathing), coaching by the investigators on how to breathe (should alleviate stress response and unmask reflex responses), a facemask or a mouthpiece (different effects on pattern of breathing in some subjects), the phase of the menstrual cycle or birth control pills in women (hormones affects the HVR), medications (e.g. aspirin enhances the HVR), fasting versus post-prandial state and wakefulness.

Physiological significance and interpretation

The goal of measuring the HVR is frequently to investigate a physiological mechanism of hypoxic sensitivity. For example, people reading this volume and attending the International Hypoxia Symposia may be interested in the physiological mechanisms of change in the HVR during ventilatory acclimatization to high altitude. However, the HVR is a reflex measurement, so it is a challenge to distinguish differences between O_2 sensing, integration within the central nervous system, and changes in respiratory motor output (7). Still, the effort to develop a consensus method for measuring the HVR should prove valuable even if it does not include standard physiological interpretation of the results. For example, the Lake Louise scoring system for AMS has been extremely useful for increasing our understanding of the physiology and pathology of acute mountain sickness (5).

FUTURE DIRECTIONS

The draft consensus methods for measuring HVR are available on the hypoxia web site: http://www.hypoxia.net. Interested parties are encouraged to access the web site and use the contact information found there to expand the discussion of this topic. An updated draft will be posted before the 15th International Hypoxia Symposium in 2007 with the goal of adopting a "Lake Louise consensus for measuring the HVR" at that meeting.

ACKNOWLEDGEMENTS

John Severinghaus is responsible for initiating the effort to develop a consensus method for measuring the hypoxic ventilatory response. Jerry Dempsey and Tom Hornbein stimulated many provocative discussions on this problem and continue to provide valuable guidance in efforts to understand the hypoxic ventilatory response.

REFERENCES

1. Bascom DA, Clement ID, Cunningham DA, Painter R and Robbins PA. Changes in peripheral chemoreflex sensitivity during sustained, isocapnic hypoxia. *Respir Physiol* 82: 161-176, 1990.
2. Dean JB, Mulkey DK, Henderson RA, III, Potter SJ and Putnam RW. Hyperoxia, reactive oxygen species, and hyperventilation: oxygen sensitivity of brain stem neurons. *J Appl Physiol* 96: 784-791, 2004.
3. Garcia N, Hopkins SR, Elliott AR, Aaron EA, Weinger MB and Powell FL. Ventilatory response to 2-h sustained hypoxia in humans. *Respir Physiol* 124: 11-22, 2000.
4. Garcia N, Hopkins SR and Powell FL. Intermittent versus continuous hypoxia: effects on ventilation and erythropoiesis in man. *Wilderness and Environmental Medicine* 2000.
5. Hackett PH and Oelz O. The Lake Louise consensus on the definition and quantitation of acute mountain illness. In: *Hypoxia and Mountain Medicine*, edited by Sutton JR, Coates G and Houston CS. Burlington: Queen City Printers, 1992, p. 327-330.
6. Howard LSGE and Robbins PA. Alterations in respiratory control during 8 h of isocapnic and poikilocapnic hypoxia in humans. *J Appl Physiol* 78: 1098-1107, 1995.
7. Powell FL, Dwinell MR and Aaron EA. Measuring ventilatory acclimatization to hypoxia: comparative aspects. *Respir Physiol* 122: 271-284, 2000.
8. Powell FL, Milsom WK and Mitchell GS. Time domains of the hypoxic ventilatory response. *Respir Physiol* 112: 123-134, 1998.
9. Rebuck AS and Campbell EJM. A clinical method for assessing the ventilatory respnse to hypoxia. *Am Rev Respir Dis* 109: 345-350, 1974.
10. Sato M, Severinghaus JW and Bickler PE. Time course of augmentation and depression of hypoxic ventilatory responses at altitude. *J Appl Physiol* 77: 313-316, 1994.
11. Sato M, Severinghaus JW, Powell FL, Xu FD and Spellman MJ, Jr. Augmented hypoxic ventilatory response in men at altitude. *J Appl Physiol* 73: 101-107, 1992.
12. Steinbeck CD, Severinghaus JW, Ainslie PN and Poulin MJ. Isocapnic and pikilocapnic hypoxia ventilatory response consensus methods in humans. This volume, page 332, 2006.
13. Weil JV and Zwillich CW. Assessment of ventilatory response to hypoxia. Chest 70: 124-128, 1976.

Chapter 23

PULMONARY HYPERTENSION IN HIGH-ALTITUDE DWELLERS: NOVEL MECHANISMS, UNSUSPECTED PREDISPOSING FACTORS

Urs Scherrer[1], Pierre Turini[1], Sébastien Thalmann[1], Damian Hutter[2], Carlos Salinas Salmon[4], Thomas Stuber[2], Sidney Shaw[3], Pierre-Yves Jayet[1], Céline Sartori-Cucchia[1], Mercedes Villena[4], Yves Allemann[2] and Claudio Sartori[1]

[1]Department of Internal Medicine and the Botnar Center for Clinical Research, Centre Hospitalier Universitaire Vaudois, Lausanne; [2]Swiss Cardiovascular Center, [3]Department of Clinical Research (S.S.), University Hospital, Berne; all in Switzerland, and [4]Instituto Boliviano de Biologia de Altura, La Paz, Bolivia.

Abstract: Studies of high-altitude populations, and in particular of maladapted subgroups, may provide important insight into underlying mechanisms involved in the pathogenesis of hypoxemia-related disease states in general. Over the past decade, studies involving short-term hypoxic exposure have greatly advanced our knowledge regarding underlying mechanisms and predisposing events of hypoxic pulmonary hypertension. Studies in high altitude pulmonary edema (HAPE)-prone subjects, a condition characterized by exaggerated hypoxic pulmonary hypertension, have provided evidence for the central role of pulmonary vascular endothelial and respiratory epithelial nitric oxide (NO) for pulmonary artery pressure homeostasis. More recently, it has been shown that pathological events during the perinatal period (possibly by impairing pulmonary NO synthesis), predispose to exaggerated hypoxic pulmonary hypertension later in life. In an attempt to translate some of this new knowledge to the understanding of underlying mechanisms and predisposing events of chronic hypoxic pulmonary hypertension, we have recently initiated a series of studies among high-risk subpopulations (experiments of nature) of high-altitude dwellers. These studies have allowed to identify novel risk factors and underlying mechanisms that may predispose to sustained hypoxic pulmonary hypertension. The aim of this article is to briefly review this new data, and demonstrate that insufficient NO synthesis/bioavailability, possibly related in part to augmented oxidative stress, may represent an important underlying mechanism predisposing to pulmonary hypertension in high-altitude dwellers.

Hypoxia and Exercise, edited by R.C. Roach *et al.*
Springer, New York, 2006.

Key Words: re-entry pulmonary edema, preeclampsia, oxidative stress, trisomy 21

INTRODUCTION

High altitude constitutes an exciting natural laboratory for medical research. Over the past decade, the scope of high altitude research has broadened considerably, since it has become clear that besides of being of importance for the prevention and/or treatment of altitude related diseases in climbers, the results of this research also may have important implications for the treatment of patients at low altitude, and for the understanding of diseases in the millions of people living permanently at high altitude.

Our group, after having devoted a decade or so, to the study of short-term adaptation to high altitude in mountaineers, has recently started to translate some of this new knowledge gained during these studies, to the study of long-term adaptation in high-altitude dwellers. In this article, we will first briefly summarize some of the salient results gathered during the short-term high altitude studies (with particular focus on pulmonary artery pressure and mechanisms of pulmonary edema), and then demonstrate the potential importance of this new knowledge for the long-term adaptation of high-altitude dwellers.

SHORT-TERM ADAPTATION TO HYPOXIA

Mechanisms underlying exaggerated pulmonary vasoconstrictor responsiveness during short-term high altitude exposure

Over the past two decades, studies in subjects susceptible to high-altitude pulmonary edema (HAPE), a condition characterized by exaggerated hypoxia-induced pulmonary vasoconstriction, have provided important new insight into the regulation of pulmonary-artery pressure at high altitude.(41)

Nitric oxide

These studies have provided evidence for the importance of pulmonary vascular endothelial and alveolar epithelial nitric oxide (NO) synthesis in the regulation of pulmonary vascular responsiveness to high-altitude exposure. The evidence is as follows: NO plays an important role in the regulation of pulmonary vascular tone in humans, because inhibition of NO synthesis by L-NMMA infusion potentiates the pulmonary vasoconstrictor response evoked by short-term hypoxic breathing. (6) In certain populations, HAPE susceptibility has been found to be associated with eNOS polymorphisms and impaired vascular NO synthesis. (1, 15) NO, when administered by inhalation, lowers pulmonary-artery pressure to a much larger extent in HAPE-susceptible subjects than in control subjects who never experienced HAPE.(42) These observations suggest that defective pulmonary endothelial NO synthesis is one of the mechanisms contributing to exaggerated hypoxic pulmonary hypertension in humans. Parenthetically, it is interesting to note here that at physiological concentrations, NO attenuates oxidative stress, a mechanism that has been implicated in the pathogenesis of hypoxic pulmonary hypertension. (7, 22, 25) In eNOS deficient states, loss of NO inhibition of oxidative stress may therefore represent an additional mechanism facilitating pulmonary hypertension.

In the respiratory system, NO is not only produced by the pulmonary vascular endothelium, but also by the respiratory epithelium, and there is evidence that the latter also regulates pulmonary artery pressure.(43) Respiratory epithelial, but not pulmonary endothelial, NO synthesis can be assessed by measuring NO in the exhaled air.(11, 37) In HAPE prone subjects, exhaled NO at high altitude is lower than in control subjects (Figure 1A), and there exists an inverse relationship between pulmonary-artery pressure and exhaled NO at high altitude (Figure 1B).(16) Taken together, these findings indicate that defective pulmonary endothelial and respiratory epithelial NO synthesis contributes to exaggerated pulmonary hypertension during short term high altitude exposure.

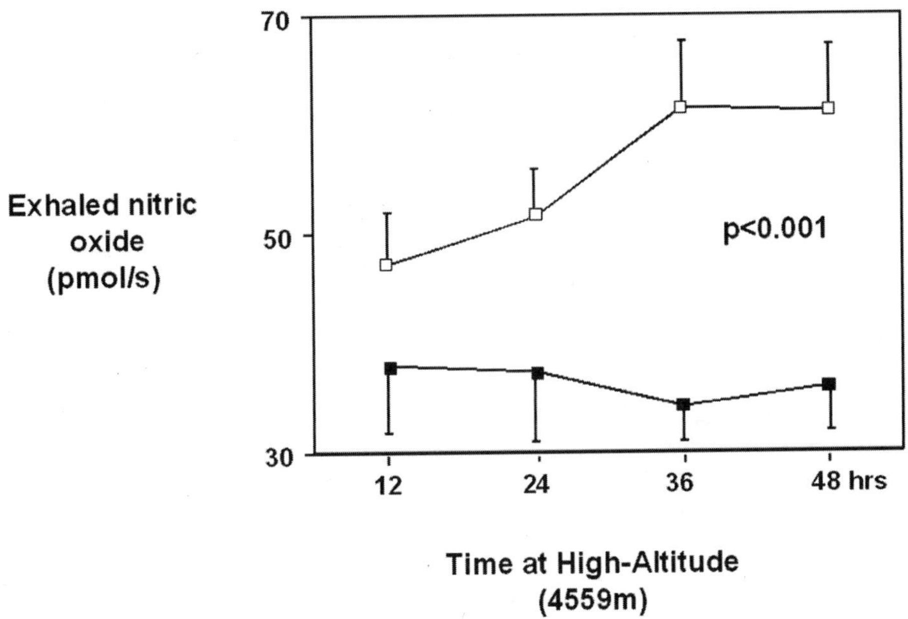

Figure 1A. Line graphs showing the effects of high-altitude exposure on exhaled pulmonary NO in HAPE-prone and resistant subjects. In the HAPE-prone subject, exhaled NO was significantly lower ($p<0.001$) than in HAPE-resistant subjects. (Adapted from Duplain et al. (16))

Endothelin-1

Recent evidence suggest that not only impaired pulmonary synthesis of the vasodilator NO, but also augmented production of the potent pulmonary vasoconstrictor ET-1, may contribute to exaggerated pulmonary vasoconstriction at high altitude. Indeed, it is well established that high-altitude exposure stimulates ET-1 synthesis in humans, and we found that there exists a direct relationship between the altitude-induced stimulation of ET-1 synthesis and the increase in pulmonary-artery pressure in humans.(40) Interestingly, defective pulmonary NO synthesis and augmented ET-1 synthesis could be causally related, because NO inhibits hypoxia-induced stimulation of ET-1 synthesis in human endothelial cells in vitro. (28)

Sympathetic nervous system

There is abundant evidence that cardiovascular adjustments to hypoxia are mediated, at least in part, by the sympathetic nervous system. (29) Studies in HAPE-susceptible humans indicate that hypoxia-induced sympathetic over-activity may represent an underlying mechanism for exaggerated pulmonary hypertension at high altitude. (17) Most interestingly, studies in experimental animals and humans indicate that central neural NO plays an important role in buffering sympathetic outflow.(32, 38) This observation could be consistent with the hypothesis that defective NO synthesis could lead to exaggerated pulmonary hypertension by the combination of loss of NO-induced vasodilatation, and facilitation of ET-1- and sympathetically-mediated vasoconstriction.

In conclusion, while these studies provided important insight into mechanisms involved into exaggerated pulmonary vasoconstriction during short-term high-altitude exposure in humans, the equally important issue of factors or events predisposing and/or protecting humans from exaggerated hypoxic pulmonary hypertension remained largely "terra incognita". Recent studies have started to shed some light on this issue.

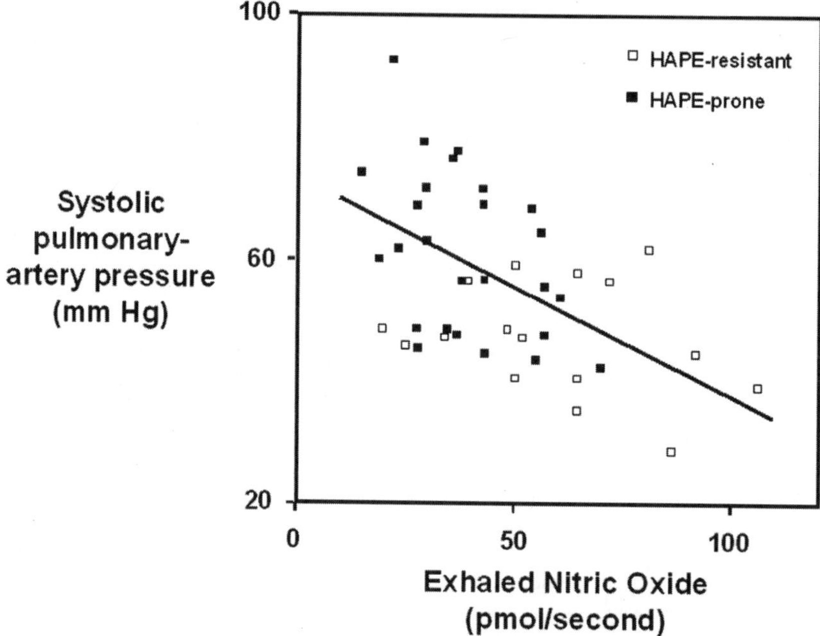

Figure 1B. Plot of the relationship between exhaled pulmonary NO and systolic pulmonary artery pressure at high altitude (4,559 m). r=-0.51, P<0.001. (Adapted from Duplain et al. (16))

Factors predisposing to exaggerated pulmonary hypertension during short-term hypoxic exposure

Perinatal hypoxia

Epidemiological studies suggest that adverse events in utero may predispose to cardiovascular and metabolic disease in adulthood. (2) In mammals and humans, at birth, the transition from gas exchange by the placenta to gas exchange by the lungs, requires dramatic changes in the pulmonary blood vessels which during this period are particularly vulnerable to noxious stimuli such as hypoxia. (30) In rats, exposure to hypoxia during the first days of life induces a transient increase of pulmonary artery pressure, and predisposes to exaggerated pulmonary vasoconstrictor responses to hypoxia and monocrotaline in the adult life.(20) During studies at the high-altitude research laboratory Capanna Regina Margherita in the Alps (4559 m), we have demonstrated a similar phenomenon in young healthy adults who had suffered from transient lack of oxygen during the first few days after birth.(35; Figure 2) The mechanism underlying this exaggerated vasoconstrictor response is not known yet, but there is evidence that this pathologic response is related to a functional rather than a structural defect. Data in rats show that transient hypoxia during the first few days leads to decreased eNOS expression in the lungs. (45) Thus, impaired NO synthesis may represent a potential mechanism. In line with this hypothesis, NO inhalation caused a substantially larger decrease in pulmonary artery pressure in the subjects with a perinatal insult than in control subjects.(35)(Figure 2) These findings demonstrate that in humans, a transient insult to the pulmonary circulation during the perinatal period, leaves a persistent and potentially fatal imprint (possibly defective NO synthesis) which, when activated later in the life, predisposes to a pathological response. This observation suggests that survivors of perinatal pulmonary hypertension may be at risk of developing this disorder later in life.

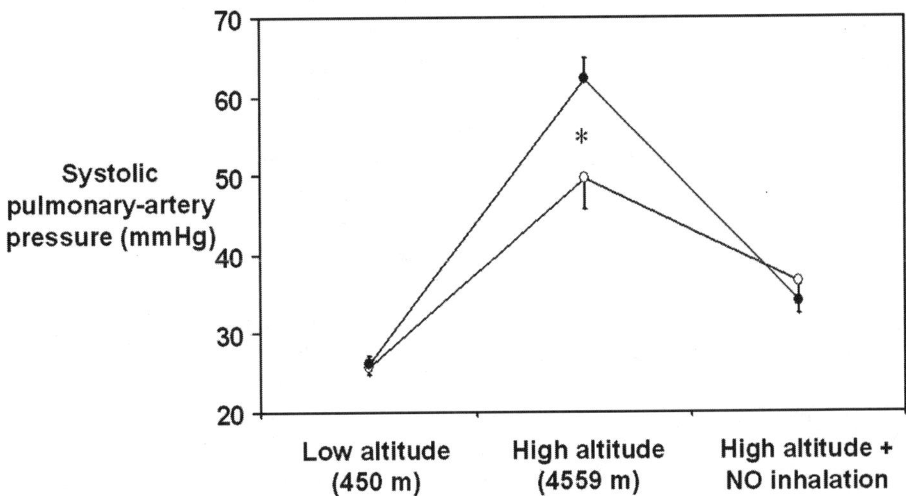

Figure 2. Effects of high-altitude exposure (4559 m) and nitric oxide inhalation at high altitude on mean[±SE] systolic pulmonary-artery pressure in 10 healthy young adults with a history of transient perinatal pulmonary hypertension (filled symbols) and in 10 control subjects (open symbols). The high-altitude induced increase in pulmonary artery pressure was significantly (p=0.01) larger in patients than in control subjects. During NO inhalation pulmonary artery pressure was comparable in the two groups because the NO-induced decrease in pulmonary artery pressure was much larger (p< 0.001) in the patients than in the control subjects (Adapted from Sartori et al. (35))

Parenthetically, exaggerated pulmonary hypertension in these young adults, while of similar magnitude as the one found in HAPE-prone mountaineers, did not cause pulmonary edema in any of these subjects.(36) This important observation suggests that exaggerated pulmonary hypertension per se may not always be sufficient to trigger HAPE, and that additional mechanisms play a role. In subsequent studies, we provided direct evidence that impaired alveolar fluid clearance (related to a defect of the transepithelial respiratory sodium transport) represents such an additional mechanism.(19, 34)

Trisomy 21

In a recent study, Durmowicz reported 6 cases of HAPE in children with trisomy 21 occurring during travel at moderate altitudes.(18) These observational studies did not establish the underlying mechanism leading to HAPE in these children. While two of these children had been treated for congenital heart defects, and thus may have suffered from a perinatal insult to the pulmonary vasculature predisposing them to exaggerated pulmonary vasoconstriction (see above), this was not the case in the other four, and alternative explanations need to be considered.

Conclusion

Based on these observations, we suggest that defective NO synthesis may represent a central event in the pathogenesis of exaggerated pulmonary hypertension during short-time hypoxic exposure. The evidence is as follows:

In HAPE-prone subjects, a condition characterized by exaggerated hypoxic pulmonary hypertension, defective pulmonary vascular endothelial and respiratory epithelial NO production impairs pulmonary vasodilation. On the other hand, loss of NO inhibition of three major pulmonary vasoconstrictor mechanisms, namely ET-1 synthesis, sympathetic central neural outflow, and oxidative stress, promotes pulmonary vasoconstriction (Figure 3).

While these important studies in HAPE-prone subjects shed light on underlying mechanisms involved in exaggerated pulmonary hypertension during short-term hypoxia, the factors or events predisposing to/protecting from exaggerated hypoxia-induced pulmonary hypertension remained largely unknown. Recent studies suggest that pathological events during the perinatal period (possibly by impairing pulmonary NO synthesis), and trisomy 21, may represent conditions predisposing to exaggerated hypoxic pulmonary hypertension.

In an attempt to translate some of this new knowledge gained during studies involving short-term hypoxic exposure to the understanding of underlying mechanisms and predisposing events of chronic hypoxic pulmonary hypertension, we have recently initiated a series of studies in high-altitude dwellers.

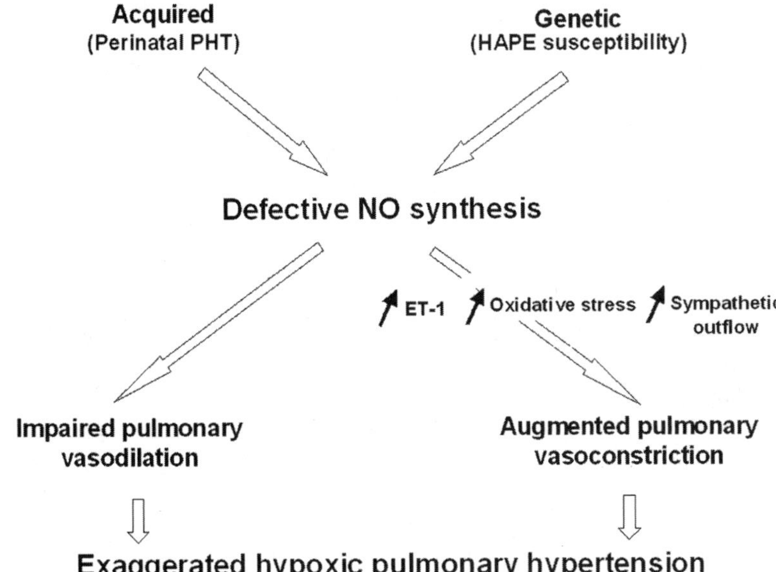

Figure 3. Mechanisms involved in the pathogenesis of exaggerated pulmonary hypertension in HAPE-prone subjects.

LONG-TERM ADAPTATION TO HYPOXIA IN HIGH-ALTITUDE DWELLERS

Due to its critical role in energy production, oxygen is essential for the survival of the cells. A reduction in tissue oxygen availability stimulates a complex series of adjustments, both at the cellular and at the systemic level. As the adaptation to hypoxia proceeds, these responses are generally limited by inhibitory feedback mechanisms. There exist, however, situations in which, for unknown reasons, these feedback mechanisms are impaired, leading to exaggerated compensatory responses to hypoxia with detrimental consequences for the organism. The underlying mechanisms regulating the delicate balance between positive (self-limited) and negative (exaggerated) adjustments to hypoxia are incompletely understood. Studies of populations permanently living at high altitude, and in particular of maladapted subgroups, may provide important insight into adaptation/maladaptation to hypoxia and, even more importantly, into underlying mechanisms involved in the pathogenesis of hypoxemia-related disease states in general.

Adaptive mechanisms differ between Tibetans, Ethiopians and Andeans

While the abovementioned studies have provided important insight regarding the cardiopulmonary adjustments to short-term hypoxia, for the clinician, the long-term adjustments to chronic hypoxia may be even more important. To this end, in collaboration with Bolivian researchers at the Instituto Boliviano de Biologia de Altura, we have recently started to study cardiopulmonary adaptation in high-altitude dwellers living in La Paz,

Bolivia (3600-4000 m). In contrast to Tibetans (normal venous hemoglobin concentration, arterial hypoxemia) and Ethiopians (normal hemoglobin concentration and normal arterial oxygenation), Andeans present the "classic" pattern of human adaptation to high altitude (erythrocytosis and arterial hypoxemia) (3, 4) making them a potentially more relevant model for hypoxemia-related disease states in lowland residents of the Western hemisphere.

Is sustained high-altitude exposure invariably associated with pulmonary hypertension?

Pulmonary artery vasoconstriction is a hallmark of the adaptation to hypoxia. It occurs very rapidly after exposure to hypoxia, and is intended to reduce blood flow through poorly ventilated alveoli. When self-limited, this vasoconstriction helps to match alveolar perfusion to ventilation. It thereby decreases the shunt effect and attenuates systemic hypoxemia. When sustained, however, hypoxic pulmonary vasoconstriction may have detrimental consequences, such as exaggerated pulmonary hypertension, right ventricular hypertrophy, and right heart failure, diseases which are associated with a high morbidity and mortality. (48)

Surprisingly little information is available on pulmonary-artery pressure in young healthy high-altitude dwellers, but the general thinking is that pulmonary hypertension is present in high-altitude native children, since invasive studies showed elevated pulmonary-artery pressure in a few children studied at high altitude in the Andes. (33, 44) However, the data to support this assumption is extremely sparse. To address this issue, we have recently measured systolic pulmonary-artery pressure in a large group of Bolivian high-altitude native children of Aymara origin in the surroundings of La Paz. Our preliminary findings indicate that pulmonary artery pressure in Aymara children is considerably lower than the one measured in Caucasian children who were born at high altitude or long-term residents of La Paz, and, indeed, appears to be quite similar to the one measured in children at low altitude. The lower pulmonary-artery pressure in the Aymara children was not related to better arterial oxygenation. Finally, there is some preliminary evidence that Aymara girls may be even better protected against hypoxic pulmonary hypertension than Aymara boys. (39) These data challenge the paradigm that sustained high-altitude exposure invariably leads to pulmonary hypertension in young healthy subjects. Protection from hypoxia-induced pulmonary hypertension may represent a specific high-altitude adaptation of the Aymaran ethnicity, but the underlying mechanism is not clear.

Does respiratory nitric oxide offset hypoxic pulmonary vasoconstriction?

In a recent study, exhaled NO at high altitude was found to be elevated in healthy Bolivian Aymara and Tibetans, when compared with a low-altitude reference sample from the United States. (5) The authors suggested that the augmented amount of NO produced in the lungs may reduce pulmonary-artery pressure in high-altitude dwellers, and improve oxygen delivery to the tissues. While this is an interesting speculation, this study does not provide any direct evidence for this concept, because measurements of pulmonary artery pressure were not performed during these observational studies. Moreover, a large part of the high-altitude dwellers (in particular among the Bolivian Aymaras) had exhaled NO concentrations that were comparable to those measured in the low altitude sample, and the authors did not measure exhaled NO in high-altitude dwellers of Caucasian origin. Further study is needed, to determine whether augmented respiratory NO production represents a protective mechanism offsetting pulmonary hypertension in Bolivian Aymaras and/or Tibetans.

Re-entry HAPE, a marker of sustained pulmonary hypertension in high altitude dwellers?

In the surroundings of La Paz, millions of people have to deal permanently with lack of oxygen in the inspired air due to high altitude. Some high-altitude dwellers suffer from a very particular form of high-altitude pulmonary edema when they return from a sojourn at low altitude, the so called "edema pulmonar de reentrada" or re-entry HAPE. The underlying mechanism is not known. As discussed above, in mountaineers, classical HAPE is caused by the conjunction of defective alveolar fluid clearance and augmented alveolar fluid flooding related to exaggerated pulmonary hypertension. We speculated that if in high-altitude dwellers susceptible to re-entry pulmonary edema, a similar dysfunction of the pulmonary blood vessels exists, they should display a persistent elevation of the pulmonary-artery pressure at high altitude. This is exactly what we found. These subjects had markedly more elevated pulmonary-artery pressure than control subjects who never experienced re-entry pulmonary edema.(47) These important findings indicate that a history of re-entry HAPE allows to identify a subgroup of otherwise healthy high-altitude dwellers, suffering from chronic pulmonary hypertension.

The underlying mechanism causing sustained pulmonary hypertension in re-entry HAPE prone high-altitude dwellers is not known yet. Exaggerated hypoxic pulmonary vasoconstriction was not related to more severe hypoxemia, because arterial oxygen saturation in these subjects was comparable to the one observed in control subjects. Therefore, alternative explanations need to be considered. There is increasing evidence that oxidative stress may play an important role in the pathogenesis of pulmonary vasoconstriction. In fetal lambs, ductus arteriosus ligation-induced pulmonary hypertension has been found to be associated with oxidative stress, and superoxide scavengers augmented vascular relaxation to exogenous NO in this model. (9) In rats, the anti-oxidant N-acetylcysteine attenuated the hypoxia-induced pulmonary hypertension and right ventricular hypertrophy. This favourable effect appears be related to attenuation of oxidative stress, because N-acetylcysteine attenuated the hypoxia-induced stimulation of lung phosphatidylcholine hydroperoxide. (22) Finally, in humans hypoxia also appears to stimulate oxidative stress. (26) In line with this concept, preliminary data suggest that re-entry HAPE prone subjects appear to display exaggerated oxidative stress. In line with this speculation, treatment with an anti-oxidant pharmacological agent led to a dramatic decrease of pulmonary-artery pressure in a few of these subjects. Thus, these exciting preliminary findings provide the very first evidence for a pathogenic role of oxidative stress in a human form of pulmonary hypertension.(47)

The unexpected finding of a normalization of pulmonary-artery pressure in a few of these subjects suffering from chronic hypoxic pulmonary hypertension deserves an additional comment. It is generally thought that structural changes in the pulmonary vascular bed underlie chronic hypoxic pulmonary hypertension. If this were the case, pharmacological interventions would not be expected to normalize pulmonary artery pressure in these subjects. Recent studies in experimental animal models have called into question this long-held paradigm. Studies in chronically hypoxic rats, using novel techniques to examine pulmonary vascular structure, demonstrated that hypoxia did not reduce the luminal diameter. (23) In line with this concept, Rho kinase inhibitors, a vasodilating agent, rapidly normalized pulmonary artery pressure. (31) We speculate that pulmonary vasoconstriction in re-entry-HAPE-prone high altitude dwellers is functional rather than structural.

We made two additional potentially very important observations during these studies. We noticed that an unexpected large proportion of the subjects having experienced re-entry pulmonary edema in the past, were offspring of mothers suffering from preeclampsia on the one hand, and subjects suffering from trisomy 21 on the other hand.

Offspring of preeclampsia are predisposed to exaggerated hypoxic pulmonary vasoconstriction?

This intriguing observation suggested that preeclampsia may predispose the offspring to pulmonary hypertension at high altitude. In a recent field study in the surroundings of La Paz, we confirmed this finding in a larger group of children of mothers suffering from preeclampsia. The exact mechanism by which preeclampsia of the mother predisposes the offspring to hypoxic pulmonary hypertension is not clear. Our studies demonstrating exaggerated hypoxic pulmonary hypertension in young adults having suffered from transient perinatal hypoxia (see above) suggest that pathologic events during the fetal/perinatal period may leave a persistent damage to the pulmonary circulation of the newborn. It is well established that during preeclampsia, the diseased placenta produces a number of circulating molecules that are known to interfere with the vascular function of the mother. (21, 46) Most importantly, some of these molecules also have the potential to cross the placental barrier. It appears thus possible that vasculotoxic molecules produced by the diseased placenta, may cause a persistent damage to the vascular system of the fetus that under certain pathological conditions, predisposes the offspring to a pathological response later in life. Life in the oxygen poor environment of high altitude appears to represent an example of a condition that triggers such a pathological response in the pulmonary circulation.

Trisomy 21 predisposes to pulmonary hypertension in high-altitude dwellers?

Circumstantial evidence suggests that children with Down syndrome may be at risk for HAPE (see above). Exaggerated pulmonary hypertension is a prerequisite for HAPE. We, therefore, hypothesized that Down syndrome predisposes to pulmonary hypertension at high altitude. To address this issue, we recently performed echocardiographic measurements of pulmonary-artery pressure in Bolivian high-altitude natives with Down syndrome. Subjects with associated cardiac malformations were excluded from these studies. Our preliminary findings suggest that pulmonary artery pressure is considerably higher in the children with Down syndrome than in control subjects. Pulmonary hypertension in Down syndrome did not appear to be related to more severe hypoxia or increased blood viscosity, because values for arterial oxygen saturation and hemoglobin were comparable to those observed in control subjects. These findings suggest that Down syndrome predisposes to pulmonary hypertension at high altitude. The underlying mechanism is not clear yet. We speculate that smaller than normal lungs and cross-sectional area of the pulmonary vascular bed and/or endothelial dysfunction related to augmented oxidative stress, which are both associated with trisomy 21, could be factors predisposing to exaggerated hypoxia-induced pulmonary hypertension in Down syndrome.

With regard to the latter, there is evidence that augmented oxidative stress, is involved in the pathogenesis of the central neural and ocular manifestations of trisomy 21. (8, 12, 24) Augmented oxidative stress in trisomy 21(27) has been attributed to augmented generation of hydrogen peroxide and hydroxy radicals related to the extra gene for superoxide dismutases located on the chromosome 21. (10) We speculate that in subjects with trisomy 21, augmented oxidative stress may also predispose to pulmonary hypertension in high -altitude dwellers. In line with this speculation, the antioxidant vitamin C decreased pulmonary artery pressure in children with trisomy 21 living at high altitude, whereas it had no detectable effect on pulmonary artery pressure in control subjects.

Pulmonary hypertension associated with erythrocytosis (Monge disease)

Erythrocytosis is another well known adaptive mechanism to chronic hypoxia. As for hypoxia-induced pulmonary vasoconstriction, the beneficial effects of this compensatory adjustment are lost, if this adjustment is non-limited, as evidenced by the Monge disease. The large majority of these subjects also suffer from severe pulmonary hypertension and right ventricular failure. The underlying mechanisms are unclear. It appears possible that reduced NO bioavailability, related to erythrocytosis, may contribute to pulmonary hypertension in Monge disease, since the rapid oxidation of nitric oxide by oxyhemoglobin to form methemoglobin and nitrate, could limit the magnitude and duration of NO-induced vasorelaxation. (13, 14) Moreover, the higher viscosity per se may contribute to augmented vascular resistance in these patients.

CONCLUSION

Based on our results, we suggest the following new concepts regarding the regulation of pulmonary-artery pressure in high-altitude dwellers (Figure 4).

In contrast to the long-held belief, pulmonary-artery pressure does not appear to be elevated in young healthy children of Aymara origin living between 3’600 and 4’000 meters. The situation appears to be different for subjects of Caucasian origin living at high altitude who display pulmonary hypertension. The mechanism protecting Aymaras from hypoxic pulmonary hypertension is not clear, but possibly could include augmented pulmonary NO synthesis.

Preliminary studies have identified, for the first time, 3 subgroups of high altitude dwellers suffering from sustained pulmonary hypertension, namely, re-entry-HAPE-prone subjects, offspring of preeclampsia, and subjects with trisomy 21. The underlying predisposing mechanisms are not known yet, but augmented oxidative stress (facilitated by impaired pulmonary NO synthesis?) may represent a candidate mechanism.

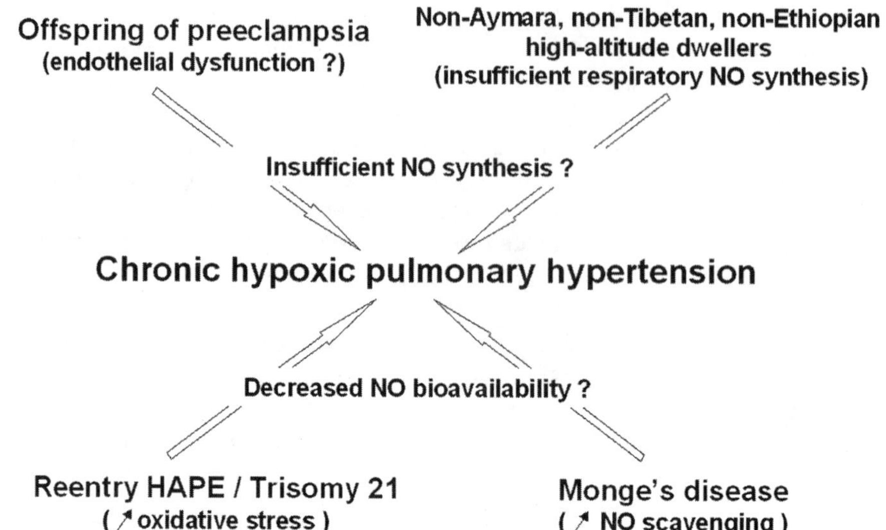

Figure 4. Mechanisms/factors predisposing to sustained pulmonary hypertension in high-altitude dwellers.

ACKNOWLEDGMENTS

The author's research was supported by grants from the Swiss National Science Foundation, the Cloëtta Foundation, the Emma Muschamp Foundation, the Novartis Foundation, and the Placide Nicod Foundation. We would like to thank Drs. Hilde Spielvogel and Armando Rodriguez, and Mrs. Loyola Riveros and Cristina Gonzales for invaluable help with these studies, and Professor Pascal Nicod for his continued support and many stimulating discussions.

REFERENCES

1. Ahsan A, Charu R, Pasha MA, Norboo T, Afrin F, and Baig MA. eNOS allelic variants at the same locus associate with HAPE and adaptation. *Thorax* 59: 1000-1002, 2004.
2. Barker DJP. *Mothers, babies, and disease in later life.* London: BMJ Books, 1994.
3. Beall CM. Tibetan and Andean patterns of adaptation to high-altitude hypoxia. *Hum Biol* 72: 201-228, 2000.
4. Beall CM, Decker MJ, Brittenham GM, Kushner I, Gebremedhin A, and Strohl KP. An Ethiopian pattern of human adaptation to high-altitude hypoxia. *Proc Natl Acad Sci U S A* 99: 17215-17218, 2002.
5. Beall CM, Laskowski D, Strohl KP, Soria R, Villena M, Vargas E, Alarcon AM, Gonzales C, and Erzurum SC. Pulmonary nitric oxide in mountain dwellers. *Nature* 414: 411-412, 2001.

6. Blitzer ML, Loh E, Roddy MA, Stamler JS, and Creager MA. Endothelium-derived nitric oxide regulates systemic and pulmonary vascular resistance during acute hypoxia in humans. *J Am Coll Cardiol* 28: 591-596, 1996.
7. Bowers R, Cool C, Murphy RC, Tuder RM, Hopken MW, Flores SC, and Voelkel NF. Oxidative stress in severe pulmonary hypertension. *Am J Respir Crit Care Med* 169: 764-769, 2004.
8. Bras A, Monteiro C, and Rueff J. Oxidative stress in trisomy 21. A possible role in cataractogenesis. *Ophthalmic Paediatr Genet* 10: 271-277, 1989.
9. Brennan LA, Steinhorn RH, Wedgwood S, Mata-Greenwood E, Roark EA, Russell JA, and Black SM. Increased superoxide generation is associated with pulmonary hypertension in fetal lambs: a role for NADPH oxidase. *Circ Res* 92: 683-691, 2003.
10. Carratelli M, Porcaro L, Ruscica M, De Simone E, Bertelli AA, and Corsi MM. Reactive oxygen metabolites and prooxidant status in children with Down's syndrome. *Int J Clin Pharmacol Res* 21: 79-84, 2001.
11. Cook S, Vollenweider P, Menard B, Egli M, Nicod P, and Scherrer U. Increased NOS and pulmonary iNOS expression in eNOS null mice. *Eur Respir J* 21: 770-773, 2003.
12. de Haan JB, Susil B, Pritchard M, and Kola I. An altered antioxidant balance occurs in Down syndrome fetal organs: implications for the "gene dosage effect" hypothesis. *J Neural Transm Suppl*: 67-83, 2003.
13. Deem S, Gladwin MT, Berg JT, Kerr ME, and Swenson ER. Effects of S-nitrosation of hemoglobin on hypoxic pulmonary vasoconstriction and nitric oxide flux. *Am J Respir Crit Care Med* 163: 1164-1170, 2001.
14. Deem S, Swenson ER, Alberts MK, Hedges RG, and Bishop MJ. Red-blood-cell augmentation of hypoxic pulmonary vasoconstriction: hematocrit dependence and the importance of nitric oxide. *Am J Respir Crit Care Med* 157: 1181-1186, 1998.
15. Droma Y, Hanaoka M, Ota M, Katsuyama Y, Koizumi T, Fujimoto K, Kobayashi T, and Kubo K. Positive association of the endothelial nitric oxide synthase gene polymorphisms with high-altitude pulmonary edema. *Circulation* 106: 826-830, 2002.
16. Duplain H, Sartori C, Lepori M, Egli M, Allemann Y, Nicod P, and Scherrer U. Exhaled nitric oxide in high-altitude pulmonary edema. Role In the regulation of pulmonary vascular tone and evidence for a role against inflammation. *Am J Respir Crit Care Med* 162: 221-224, 2000.
17. Duplain H, Vollenweider L, Delabays A, Nicod P, Bärtsch P, and Scherrer U. Augmented sympathetic activation during short-term hypoxia and high-altitude exposure in subjects susceptible to high altitude pulmonary edema. *Circulation* 99: 1713-1718, 1999.
18. Durmowicz AG. Pulmonary edema in 6 children with Down syndrome during travel to moderate altitudes. *Pediatrics* 108: 443-447, 2001.
19. Egli M, Duplain H, Lepori M, Cook S, Nicod P, Hummler E, Sartori C, and Scherrer U. Defective respiratory amiloride-sensitive sodium transport predisposes to pulmonary oedema and delays its resolution in mice. *J Physiol* 560: 857-865, 2004.
20. Hakim TS and Mortola JP. Pulmonary vascular resistance in adult rats exposed to hypoxia in the neonatal period. *Can J Physiol Pharmacol* 68: 419-424, 1990.
21. Hayman R, Brockelsby J, Kenny L, and Baker P. Preeclampsia: the endothelium, circulating factor(s) and vascular endothelial growth factor. *J Soc Gynecol Investig* 6: 3-10, 1999.
22. Hoshikawa Y, Ono S, Suzuki S, Tanita T, Chida M, Song C, Noda M, Tabata T, Voelkel NF, and Fujimura S. Generation of oxidative stress contributes to the development of pulmonary hypertension induced by hypoxia. *J Appl Physiol* 90: 1299-1306, 2001.
23. Howell K, Preston RJ, and McLoughlin P. Chronic hypoxia causes angiogenesis in addition to remodelling in the adult rat pulmonary circulation. *J Physiol* 547: 133-145, 2003.

24. Iannello RC, Crack PJ, de Haan JB, and Kola I. Oxidative stress and neural dysfunction in Down syndrome. *J Neural Transm Suppl* 57: 257-267, 1999.
25. Irodova NL, Lankin VZ, Konovalova GK, Kochetov AG, and Chazova IE. Oxidative stress in patients with primary pulmonary hypertension. *Bull Exp Biol Med* 133: 580-582, 2002.
26. Joanny P, Steinberg J, Robach P, Richalet JP, Gortan C, Gardette B, and Jammes Y. Operation Everest III (Comex'97): the effect of simulated sever hypobaric hypoxia on lipid peroxidation and antioxidant defence systems in human blood at rest and after maximal exercise. *Resuscitation* 49: 307-314, 2001.
27. Jovanovic SV, Clements D, and MacLeod K. Biomarkers of oxidative stress are significantly elevated in Down syndrome. *Free Radic Biol Med* 25: 1044-1048, 1998.
28. Kourembanas S, McQuillan LP, Leung GK, and Faller DV. Nitric oxide regulates the expression of vasoconstrictors and growth factors by vascular endothelium under both normoxia and hypoxia. *J Clin Invest* 92: 99-104, 1993.
29. Krasney JA. A neurogenic basis for acute altitude illness. *Med Sci Sports Exerc* 26: 195-208, 1994.
30. Morin FC and Stenmark KR. Persistent pulmonary hypertension of the newborn. *Am J Respir Crit Care Med* 151: 2010-2032, 1995.
31. Nagaoka T, Morio Y, Casanova N, Bauer N, Gebb S, McMurtry I, and Oka M. Rho/Rho kinase signaling mediates increased basal pulmonary vascular tone in chronically hypoxic rats. *Am J Physiol Lung Cell Mol Physiol* 287: L665-672, 2004.
32. Owlya R, Vollenweider L, Trueb L, Sartori C, Lepori M, Nicod P, and Scherrer U. Cardiovascular and sympathetic effects of nitric oxide inhibition at rest and during exercise in humans. *Circulation* 96: 3897-3903, 1997.
33. Penaloza D, Arias-Stella J, Sime F, Recavarren S, and Marticorena E. The Heart and Pulmonary Circulation in Children at High Altitudes: Physiological, Anatomical, and Clinical Observations. *Pediatrics* 34: 568-582, 1964.
34. Sartori C, Allemann Y, Duplain H, Lepori M, Egli M, Lipp E, Hutter D, Turini P, Hugli O, Cook S, Nicod P, and Scherrer U. Salmeterol for the prevention of high-altitude pulmonary edema. *N Engl J Med* 346: 1631-1636, 2002.
35. Sartori C, Allemann Y, Trueb L, Delabays A, Nicod P, and Scherrer U. Augmented vasoreactivity in adult life associated with perinatal vascular insult. *Lancet* 353: 2205-2207, 1999.
36. Sartori C, Allemann Y, Trueb L, Lepori M, Maggiorini M, Nicod P, and Scherrer U. Exaggerated pulmonary hypertension is not sufficient to trigger high- altitude pulmonary oedema in humans. *Schweiz Med Wochenschr* 130: 385-389, 2000.
37. Sartori C, Lepori M, Busch T, Duplain H, Hildebrandt W, Bartsch P, Nicod P, Falke KJ, and Scherrer U. Exhaled nitric oxide does not provide a marker of vascular endothelial function in healthy humans. *Am J Respir Crit Care Med* 160: 879-882, 1999.
38. Sartori C, Lepori M, and Scherrer U. Interaction between nitric oxide and the cholinergic and sympathetic system in cardiovascular control in humans. *Pharmacology & Therapeutics* 106: 209-220, 2005.
39. Sartori C, Turini P, Allemann Y, Salinas C, Rodriguez A, Hutter D, Thalmann S, Villena M, and Scherrer U. Protective effect of female sex hormones against pulmonary hypertension in bolivian high altitude natives. *High Altitude Medicine and Biology* 3: A430, 2003.
40. Sartori C, Vollenweider L, Loffler BM, Delabays A, Nicod P, Bartsch P, and Scherrer U. Exaggerated endothelin release in high-altitude pulmonary edema. *Circulation* 99: 2665-2668, 1999.
41. Scherrer U, Sartori C, Lepori M, Allemann Y, Duplain H, Trueb L, and Nicod P. High-altitude pulmonary edema: from exaggerated pulmonary hypertension to a defect in

transepithelial sodium transport. *Adv Exp Med Biol* 474: 93-107, 1999.

42. Scherrer U, Vollenweider L, Delabays A, Savcic M, Eichenberger U, Kleger G-R, Fikrle A, Ballmer PE, Nicod P, and Bärtsch P. Inhaled nitric oxide for high-altitude pulmonary edema. *N Engl J Med* 334: 624-629, 1996.
43. Settergren G, Angdin M, Astudillo R, Gelinder S, Liska J, Lundberg JO, and Weitzberg E. Decreased pulmonary vascular resistance during nasal breathing: modulation by endogenous nitric oxide from the paranasal sinuses. *Acta Physiol Scand* 163: 235-239, 1998.
44. Sime F, Banchero N, Penaloza D, Gamboa R, Cruz J, and Marticorena E. Pulmonary hypertension in children born and living at high altitudes. *Am J Cardiol* 11: 143-149, 1963.
45. Smith APL, Emery CJ, and Higenbottam TW. Perinatal chronic hypoxia decreases endothelial nitric oxide synthase (NOS III) and increases preproendothelin-1 (ppET-1) mRNA levels in rat. *Eur Respir J* 10: 433s (Abstract), 1997.
46. Taylor RN, de Groot CJ, Cho YK, and Lim KH. Circulating factors as markers and mediators of endothelial cell dysfunction in preeclampsia. *Semin Reprod Endocrinol* 16: 17-31, 1998.
47. Thalmann S, Allemann Y, Jayet PY, Hutter D, Salinas C, Stuber T, Shaw S, Villena M, Sartori C, and Scherrer U. Oxidative stress mediated chronic pulmonary hypertension in re-entry pulmonary edema-prone high altitude dwellers. *FASEB J* 19(5): A1333, 2005.
48. Ward MP, Milledge JS, and West JB. *High Altitude Medicine and Physiology*. Philadelphia: University of Pennsylvania Press, 1989.

Chapter 24

GENE HUNTING IN HYPOXIA AND EXERCISE

Kenneth B. Storey
Institute of Biochemistry, Carleton University, 1125 Colonel By Drive, Ottawa, Ontario, Canada.

Abstract: New technologies in genomics and proteomics are revolutionizing the study of adaptation to environmental stress. These approaches provide a comprehensive overview of the responses of thousands of genes/proteins to stress and enormously expand our view of the molecular and metabolic changes that underlie physiological responses. Several new technologies can help physiological labs to become gene hunters. DNA array screening is particularly effective for two purposes: (1) identifying coordinated responses by functional groups of gene/proteins such as multiple members of a signal transduction cascade or enzymes of a metabolic pathway, and (2) highlighting cell functions that have never before been linked with the stress under consideration. We have shown that heterologous screening of DNA arrays can be a highly effective method of gene hunting for the comparative biochemist provided that it is followed up by species-specific analyses including PCR to quantify transcript levels and Western blotting to analyze protein responses. Recent work in my lab has used cDNA array screening to evaluate responses to low oxygen by multiple hypoxia/anoxia tolerant systems, revealing common gene responses across phylogeny. Analysis of vertebrate facultative anaerobiosis in freshwater turtles reveals an interesting mixture of gene responses, including up-regulation of antioxidant enzymes, protease inhibitors, and proteins of iron metabolism; a few of these are coordinated by the hypoxia inducible factor in other systems but most are not. Array screening is also providing new insights into how exercise stimulates the growth of differentiated muscle cells and studies in our lab are identifying the gene responses associated with "anti-exercise" – gene up-regulation that aids hibernating mammals to maintain their muscle mass despite months of inactivity.

Key Words. anoxia tolerance, hibernation, cDNA array screening, metabolic rate depression

INTRODUCTION

Major advances in molecular biology technology over the last decade have fundamentally changed the approach that my lab uses to identify biochemical adaptations that support animal survival in extreme environments. We have become gene hunters. The traditional approach to studying stress responses by cells and organisms has been a "top-down" one – begin with a highly "visible" phenotypic response (e.g. 2 M glycerol accumulated by a cold-hardy insect, a massive synthesis of heat shock proteins, etc.) and work backwards to trace the protein/enzyme and gene modifications that underlie it. This approach continues to be excellent in many cases but has one key limitation in that to begin it requires the identification of a major metabolic response (phenotype change) in either qualitative or quantitative terms. Sometimes this leads to a perhaps inordinate focus on a selected phenotypic response (e.g. thousands of papers on cryoprotectant levels in cold-hardy animals) that can obscure or delay discovery of other adaptive responses that are just as important to stress survival but have no readily detectable "signature". Gene hunters take a different approach. Using multiple new technologies, particularly DNA microarray screening, organismal response to a stress can be examined in a "bottom-up" direction that provides an unbiased assessment of the responses to stress of thousands of different genes, representing hundreds of different cell functions, and reveals the totality of gene expression changes that underlie the physiological response to stress.

The two most important gene discovery techniques available to the gene hunter are cDNA library screening and DNA microarray screening and we have used both in our analysis of diverse animal models of anoxia tolerance, freeze tolerance, cold hardiness and hibernation (7,44-47,49). Construction and screening of a cDNA library is an arduous job and screening favours the discovery of high abundance mRNA transcripts but the technique has one key advantage for researchers working with unusual animal models. That is the opportunity to find novel genes that are unique to the species/stress under study. For example, our screening of a cDNA library made from tissues of the anoxia tolerant marine snail, *Littorina littorea*, identified two anoxia-responsive genes that have, to date, no equivalents in other species (28,30,45). We have not yet defined their functions but structural features of the gene *kvn* suggest that it may encode an iron-sulfur protein related to the ferredoxin family (28) whereas *sarp* contains two putative EF-hand calcium binding domains that suggest a role for SARP-19 protein in calcium-activated signalling or calcium sequestering during anaerobiosis (30). Similarly, our cDNA library screening studies of freeze tolerant wood frogs discovered three novel freeze-responsive genes of as yet unknown functions but that encode proteins with distinctly different physical characteristics, organ distribution, and responses to intracellular second messengers (47).

DNA microarray screening provides even greater opportunities for the gene hunter. The number of species for which homologous arrays are available is growing rapidly and provides the opportunity to screen the responses to an imposed stress by thousands of genes. Major effort is being put into perfecting array screening in both qualitative and quantitative terms in order to be able to rely on the technology as a predictive and diagnostic tool, particularly in medicine. We have taken a different approach and shown that excellent information can also be derived from heterologous screening using arrays made from cDNA of one species (e.g. human, rat, *Drosophila*) but probed with cDNA of another (7,47,49). Clearly, because of DNA sequence differences, cross-hybridization during heterologous probing is never 100%. A substantial number of genes on the array will go unevaluated (including some that may be stress-responsive) and a potential for false positives also exists (experimental cDNA binding to a sequence that is not its gene homologue). However, we have found that good levels of cross-hybridization can be achieved during heterologous probing, particularly after initial manipulations of hybridization and washing conditions to optimize binding. For example, we used human 19,000 gene chips from the Microarray Centre (Ontario Cancer Institute, Toronto; *http://www.microarrays.ca/*) to screen for anoxia-, freeze-, or hibernation-responsive gene expression in multiple systems, with cross-hybridization percentages of 85-90% using cDNA from hibernating mammals (ground squirrels or bats), 60-80% for frog tissues, and 18.35% for hepatopancreas of the marine snail *Littorina littorea*) (7,45-47). Although this last number for snails seems low, we were still able to evaluate the expression of nearly 3500 genes on the 19K array and found over 300 that were putatively up-regulated by anoxia exposure, providing many new leads for follow-up in the hunt for genes that support anoxia survival in molluscs.

Heterologous screening is not appropriate for gathering quantitative data – that is derived from various follow-up techniques (see below) – but this form of screening is excellent in qualitative terms. Gene hunting by this method is particularly exciting for two reasons: (a) the hunt often reveals previously unsuspected genes and proteins (and their corresponding cell functions) that participate in the adaptive response, and (b) the responses of related groups of genes (proteins) can be assessed – e.g. families of proteins, components of signal transduction cascades, enzymes of a metabolic pathway – to gain a broad overview of the areas of cell function that respond in creating the coordinated adaptive response to stress. These features are key to allowing us to build a "big picture" of gene responses to an imposed stress and they point the way into targeted studies of specific areas of metabolism.

For example, our recent analyses of hibernating ground squirrels and anoxia tolerant turtles (44,46) showed the completely unexpected up-regulation in both systems of selected *ser*ine *p*rotease *in*hibitor*s* (serpins) in the experimental state (torpid or anoxic), suggesting that these have a role to play in animals entering hypometabolism (a key survival strategy of both hibernation and anaerobiosis is metabolic rate suppression (51)). Most serpins are plasma proteins (typically secreted by liver) that act as irreversible covalent inhibitors of proteases that cleave specific proteins. Many inhibit the proteases that act at critical checkpoints in self-perpetuating proteolytic cascades such as the proteases involved in blood coagulation, fibrinolysis, inflammation, and complement activation (16). Enhanced levels of selected serpins during entry into a hypometabolic state could be key for inhibiting specific proteolytic reactions and cascades that could otherwise cause damage to tissues during long term hypometabolism. Suppression of proteolytic cascades as part of metabolic rate depression would also contribute to lowering net protein turnover during hypometabolism, thereby contributing to ATP savings (44,51).

Because of the nature of heterologous array screening, the information that derived from arrays must be confirmed, validated and quantified by other means. Typically genes showing at least 2-fold higher signal in experimental versus control states are good candidates for follow-up studies. The basic plan that we have used for follow-up in recent studies (9,10,34) includes the following: (1) design of DNA primers for the gene of interest based on a consensus sequence put together from available sequences in Genbank, (2) use of the primers to retrieve the species-specific cDNA via PCR, (3) nucleotide sequencing of the retrieved cDNA to confirm its identity followed by design and synthesis of a species-specific probe, (4) use of the species-specific probe to evaluate organ-, time-, and stress-specific gene expression via Q-PCR or RT-PCR, (5) as appropriate, 3' or 5'RACE to retrieve the full nucleotide sequence for analysis of possible adaptive changes in amino acid sequence compared with other species, and (5) use of the putative amino acid sequence to design and synthesize peptide antibodies (or use of commercial antibodies if appropriate) to quantify patterns of protein expression. This latter is especially important because, while it is generally true that enhanced gene expression leads to elevated protein levels, exceptions occur and so quantification of relative mRNA levels in control versus stress situations does not always correlate with changes in protein levels. Indeed, some proteins are subject to primary regulation at other levels, through regulation of translation (e.g. ferritin) or proteoloysis (e.g. hypoxia-inducible factor 1α [HIF-1α]) (17,18). Our studies with hypometabolic systems have also noted instances of time-frame differences between transcription and translation. For example, in kidney of hibernating ground squirrels, mRNA transcripts of the organic cation transporter type 2 (*Oct2*) were 2-3 fold higher than in euthermic animals as assessed by both Northern blots and cDNA arrays but the transcripts remained sequestered with translationally silent monosomes during torpor (23). As a result, Western blots showed that OCT2 protein levels in kidney dropped by 66% during hibernation but after arousal, newly assembled polysomes can quickly produce OCT2 protein from existing *Oct2* transcripts.

A few final points about array screening can be made. The technology for array screening is now widespread and highly automated and screening is offered as a service by many companies. My lab now finds it cost-effective to out-source our screening needs rather than invest in expensive equipment and expensive mistakes while training personnel. We use array screening as the initial identification tool to highlight interesting genes but then turn to other techniques to validate array results and to further investigate the regulation and the function of the interesting genes/proteins. Hence, the modern lab in molecular physiology need only invest in validation technologies such as PCR for quantifying stress-induced changes in mRNA transcript levels and Western blotting for analyzing the corresponding changes in protein levels. These technologies, together with activity assays and other investigative techniques, are the ones that are needed to analyze the functional role of gene/protein expression

Other new technologies are also available to gene hunters to gain information about the regulation of the gene/protein of interest. A cDNA sequence can be used as the starting point to screen a genomic library to retrieve the full genomic sequence (introns plus exons) as well as promotor (5'untranslated) regions. Genomic sequence is often crucial to understanding the evolution of novel genes (13) and identification of transcription factor binding sites in the promoter region unlock regulatory aspects of gene function. Bioinformatics programs can be applied to analyze amino acid sequences to detect regulatory motifs (e.g. phosphorylation sites) and to analyze species-specific differences in amino acid sequence that may be adaptive (21,30). Rapidly advancing proteomics technologies are also making it increasingly easy to directly analyze stress-responsive changes in the proteome (Figure 1)(10,32). Proteins are separated by two dimensional gel electrophoresis and protein spots that differ in intensity between control and experimental states are excised, digested, and analyzed by mass spectrometry based methods such as MALDI-TOF for peptide mass fingerprinting and tandem MS/MS for de novo peptide sequencing (32). Peptide fingerprints are now known for hundreds of cellular proteins so that identification can often be achieved by evaluating the pattern alone or with the additional selective sequencing of one or more of the peptide peaks. Proteins that are subject to reversible phosphorylation can also be studied using phospho-specific antibodies (raised against the peptide segment containing the phosphorylated amino acid) to quantify stress-responsive changes in the relative level of phosphorylated versus dephosphorylated protein which typically mirrors the activity state of the protein (Figure 1). Use of phospho-specific antibodies is especially key for tracing multi-component signal transduction cascades leading from cell surface to nuclear gene activation. Hence, we now have the molecular tools to evaluate almost any metabolic system and to search for the breadth and depth of biochemical adaptations that define the differences between stress-tolerant and stress-intolerant organisms.

GENE HUNTING IN HYPOXIA AND ANOXIA

The strategies and approaches for gene hunting outlined above are being used to explore animal responses to low oxygen and illuminate differences between hypoxia/anoxia tolerant and intolerant species. Most organisms are adversely affected by low oxygen availability because the supply of ATP from mitochondrial oxidative catabolism is reduced and falls below the pace of cellular ATP consumption; if not corrected, this imbalance can become lethal rapidly. The response to low oxygen by most vertebrates, including man, is a suite of compensatory strategies at behavioural, physiological and biochemical levels that address two main goals: (1) increase oxygen delivery to tissues, and (2) elevate glycolytic ATP output. These strategies are accomplished in part by increased transcription and translation of genes under the control of the HIF-1 transcription factor (5,17,54). The HIF-1α subunit is oxygen sensitive. At high oxygen tensions, O_2-dependent hydroxylation of two proline residues sets up the alpha subunit for rapid proteolysis so that net HIF-1α levels in cells remain low whereas under low oxygen conditions HIF-1α is stabilized, dimerizes with HIF-1ß, and activates gene transcription. The list of HIF-1 regulated genes is large and includes most glycolytic enzymes as well as glucose transporter isoforms 1 and 3. Various proteins associated erythropoiesis and capillary growth are also up-regulated under direct control by HIF-1α or secondary control by erythropoietin or vascular endothelial growth factor (VEGF), themselves both regulated by HIF-1 (5,17,54).

Compensatory strategies allow many species to adjust to short or long term reductions in oxygen availability (hypoxia) and even brief periods of anoxia but some animals are challenged by environments or lifestyles where oxygen deprivation is continuous for days, weeks or months. Survival of long term oxygen lack requires a different strategy – a conservation strategy that dramatically lowers tissue energy needs to a level that can be sustained over the long term by anaerobic pathways of ATP production. Research over the last 20-30 years by my lab and others has illuminated many of the biochemical adaptations and regulatory mechanisms that support facultative anaerobiosis (for review 2,25,31) and emphasized the importance of metabolic rate depression (often by >90%) as the key element for energy savings in anoxic state (51).

The premier facultative anaerobes among vertebrate species are various freshwater turtles of the *Trachemys* and *Chrysemys* genera (25,26). Adults can typically survive in cold deoxygenated water (<10°C) for ~3 months. They do so by lowering their metabolic rate to ~10% of the corresponding value that they exhibit in air at the same temperature.

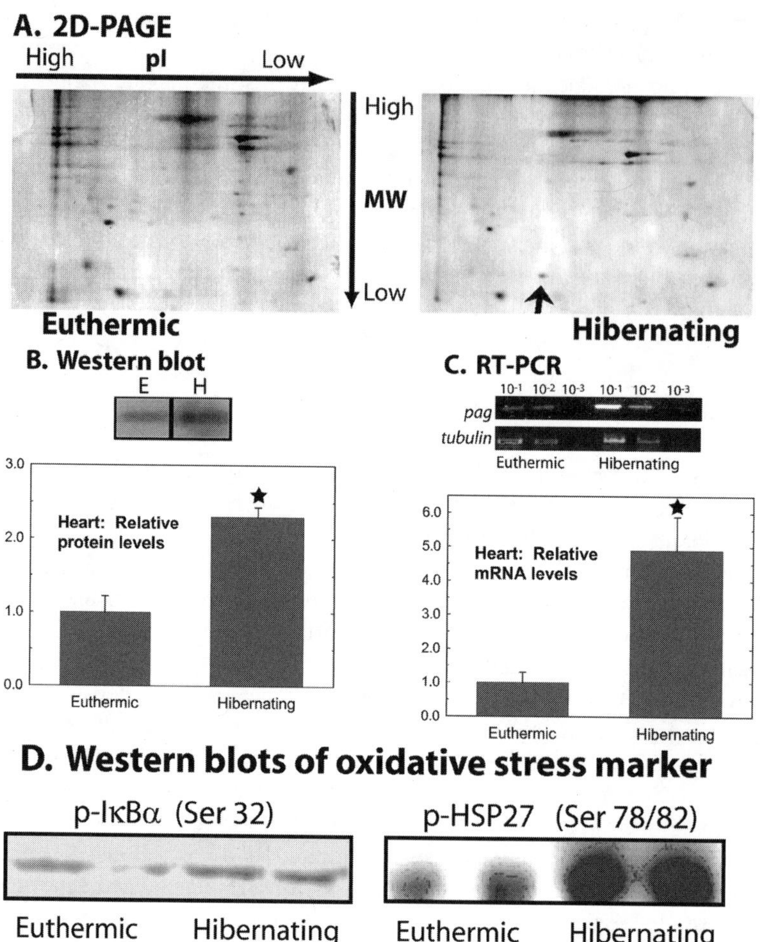

Figure 1. Strategies for stress-responsive protein hunting: identification and analysis of a protein called proliferation-associated gene (PAG) (also known as thioredoxin peroxidase 1 or peroxiredoxin 1) in heart of hibernating bats, *Myotis lucifugus*. (A) Two dimensional polyacrylamide gel electrophoresis separated 150 µg aliquots of heart soluble protein. Coomassie blue staining revealed stronger expression in hibernator heart of a protein with an isoelectric point of ~7 and a molecular weight of ~22 kD (indicated by arrow). The protein spot was excised, subjected to tryptic digestion, analyzed by mass spectrometry and two tryptic peptides were obtained (GLFIIDGK and QITVNDLPVGR) and used for identification. (B) Western blotting with antibody to human PAG showed 2.30 ± 0.13 fold (n=3, P<0.05) higher protein in heart of hibernating versus euthermic bats. (C) Consensus primers for the *pag* gene were designed from the sequences of human, rat and mouse *pag* and used to clone bat *pag*. The full nucleotide sequence was obtained (Genbank accession number AY680839), showing 92% nucleotide and 99% amino acid sequence identity with the human protein. RT-PCR was performed on three dilutions of bat *pag*; amplification of α-tubulin message in the same samples was used to normalize *pag* expression levels. Using data from the 10^{-2} dilution, bat *pag* transcripts were 4.9 ± 1.6 fold (n=3, P<0.05) higher in heart of hibernating animals. (D) Protein markers of oxidative stress in bat heart were assessed by Western blotting. Antibodies assessed relative amounts of phosphorylated IκB-α(Ser32) and phosphorylated HSP27(Ser78/82) in euthermic and hibernating heart. Complied from (10).

Huge organ reserves of glycogen are mobilized to fuel glycolytic ATP production and metabolic poisoning from lactate build-up is avoided by two measures: (a) buffering by calcium and magnesium carbonates released by the shell, and (b) storing a high percentage of the lactate produced in the shell (26). Metabolic rate depression is achieved by targeting and coordinating the rates of energy-producing pathways and energy-utilizing cell functions to "turn down the fires of life" and reorganize the priorities for ATP expenditure (2,51). Studies with isolated turtle hepatocytes provide an excellent example of this. Incubation of these cells under anoxic conditions decreased ATP turnover by 94% and dramatically changed the portion of ATP turnover that was devoted to five main ATP-consuming processes: ion motive ATPases, protein synthesis, protein degradation, gluconeogenesis, and urea synthesis (24). As a result, the $Na^{+}K^{+}$ATPase pump became the dominant energy sink in anoxic hepatocytes, consuming 62% of total ATP turnover compared with 28% in normoxia. Protein synthesis and degradation were largely shut down (by >90%) and urea synthesis was halted. A primary mechanism used for metabolic suppression is reversible protein phosphorylation, using the addition (by protein kinases) or removal (by protein phosphatases) of covalently-bound phosphate to partially or fully inactivate proteins/enzymes. This mechanism reappears across phylogeny as the means of making major changes in metabolic rate in numerous animal models of metabolic suppression including hibernation, estivation, diapause, dormancy, torpor, anhydrobiosis and anaerobiosis (51). Reversible phosphorylation controls have been linked with the suppression of multiple cell functions during anoxia in turtles including glycolytic enzymes, voltage-gated ion channels (Na^{+}, Ca^{2+}, K^{+}), membrane receptors (e.g. *N*-methyl-D-aspartate-type glutamate receptor), and protein synthesis (e.g. ribosomal initiation and elongation factors) (2,25,51). Another consumer of cellular energy is gene transcription and, not surprisingly, the global rate of gene transcription is suppressed in hypometabolic states. This is done with little net change in total mRNA which is sequestered intact in association with translationally-silent monosomes or ribonuclear proteins and preserved until polysomes can be reassembled again (51). However, selected genes are also specifically repressed or activated to resculpt organs for long term anaerobic survival. For example, in anoxic turtle brain, mRNA transcripts of voltage-dependent potassium channels were reduced to just 18.5% of normoxic levels after 4 h of anoxia but rebounded after reoxygenation (37).

Of greater interest to us are the genes that are up-regulated under anoxia. Clearly, these must important to the anaerobic phenotype because gene transcription and protein translation are ATP-expensive processes that are minimized under anoxia (24). Hence, ATP would not be wasted on the synthesis of nonessential proteins. Furthermore, we would not expect anoxia-responsive genes in facultative anaerobes to be those that are up-regulated under HIF-1 control in hypoxia-sensitive species. Anoxia tolerant species do not increase their net glycolytic ATP production; indeed, they reduce it during anaerobiosis (51). Furthermore, both erythropoiesis and capillary growth during natural hypoxia/anoxia excursions is counter-intuitive as it is energy-expensive at a time when energy savings are crucial and unproductive since low tissue oxygen levels cannot be improved by enhanced oxygen delivery under apnoic, anoxic conditions.

So, what genes do turtles, the champion vertebrate facultative anaerobes, up-regulate when challenged with low oxygen stress? Quite a variety as it turns out. Our studies using cDNA library and DNA array screening tell an interesting story about which cell functions need adjustment for anoxia survival. Our first work on anoxia-induced gene expression focused on submergence anoxia (20 h in N_2-bubbled water at 7°C) in adult red-eared sliders, *Trachemys scripta elegans*. Differential screening of a cDNA library made from heart produced a surprising result – up-regulation of two genes encoded on the mitochondrial genome: *Cox1* that encodes cytochrome C oxidase subunit 1 (COX1) and *Nad5* that encodes subunit 5 of NADH-ubiquinone oxidoreductase (ND5) (4). Transcripts rose within 1 h of anoxia exposure to 3-4.5 fold higher than aerobic control values, remained high after 20 h, and then declined during aerobic recovery. Expression of both genes also rose during anoxia in muscle, brain and kidney. A second study found that other mitochondrially encoded genes were anoxia responsive in liver: transcripts of *Cytb*, encoding cytochrome b, and *Nad4*, encoding subunit 4 of ND, rose by 5- and 13-fold, respectively, within 1 h under anoxia (55). The reason for mitochondrial gene up-regulation in anoxia is not yet known but the phenomenon also occurs during freezing (which causes ischemia) in freeze tolerant turtles and wood frogs (4,47) and in mammalian hibernation (43,51).

In recent work we have applied cDNA array screening to an evaluation of anoxia-responsive gene expression in both adult *T. s. elegans* and hatchling painted turtles, *Chyrsemys picta marginata*. The young of this species are remarkable because, after hatching in September, they remain in their shallow nests (<10 cm deep, typically on exposed river or lake banks) over their first winter and employ strategies of cold hardiness to survive at temperatures below 0°C. Near the northern limits of their range, such as in Algonquin Park, Ontario where we study them, the hatchlings survive freezing, enduring the conversion of ~50% of total body water into extracellular ice (50). A significant element in natural freeze tolerance is ischemia/anoxia resistance necessitated because plasma freezing halts oxygen delivery to organs. We used heterologous screening with human 19K gene chips to search for differential gene expression in adult *T. s. elegans* given 4 hours of anoxic submergence in nitrogen-bubbled water and hatchling *C. p. marginata* given 4 hours exposure under a nitrogen gas atmosphere, each compared with aerobic controls and all animals held at 7°C.

ANOXIA RESPONSIVE GENE UP-REGULATION IN TURTLE HEART AND LIVER

Array screening of heart and liver of hatchling *C. p. marginata* revealed a variety of genes that showed enhanced expression in anoxic turtles, binding intensities of labeled probe being 1.5-3.5 fold higher than in aerobic controls. Of these, I will comment here on three outstanding groups of genes that were consistently up-regulated: (1) iron storage proteins, (2) enzymes of antioxidant defense, and (3) selected serpins.

Iron storage proteins: Hatchling turtle heart and liver both showed enhanced expression of ferritin heavy (H) and light (L) chains and transferrin receptor 2 (TfR2) during anoxia exposure. Iron is a vital component of many proteins, including cytochromes and haemoglobin, but free iron in the ferrous state (Fe^{2+}) participates in the Fenton reaction with hydrogen peroxide and lipid peroxides to generate highly reactive hydroxyl radicals and lipid radicals (18,20). Hence, intracellular free iron levels are kept low by storing the metal in ferritin, a huge protein consisting of 24 H and L subunits that surrounds a core of up to 4500 iron atoms locked in a low reactivity ferrihydrite state (18). In plasma, iron is bound tightly to another protein, transferrin (Tf), and iron uptake into cells involves endocytosis of Tf after docking with the cell surface transferrin receptor (TfR). Acidification of the endosomes releases the iron and Tf and TfR are recycled. The TfR1 isoform is ubiquitous but in mammals TfR2 is restricted to tissues such as liver and erythroid cells. Both ferritin and TfR proteins are induced by hypoxia in mammals and the Tf and TfR genes are under HIF-1 control (41,52,54). What is the reason for ferritin and TfR2 up-regulation under anoxia in turtles? Clearly, an increase in cellular iron uptake and storage is indicated. Interestingly, in comparable studies of anoxia tolerance in marine snails, we also found anoxia-responsive up-regulation of ferritin H chain mRNA and protein and ferritin mRNA remained in the polysome fraction during anoxia, indicating that it is one of just a few actively translated proteins in anoxia (29). It is doubtful that the purpose of ferritin up-regulation in anoxia tolerant species is related to haemoglobin production; one would expect biosynthesis to strongly suppressed in anoxic turtles and snails do not have haemoglobin. Alternative reasons for iron sequestering in anoxia tolerant animals could include: (a) to minimize free Fe^{2+} so as to limit the potential for generating reactive oxygen species (ROS), particularly when oxygen is rapidly reintroduced into tissues, or (b) storage of excess iron during hypometabolism when the net rate of biosynthesis of iron-containing proteins is low. The first reason seems quite likely especially when put together with the simultaneous up-regulation of antioxidant genes in turtle organs.

Antioxidant defenses: Anoxia exposure stimulated up-regulation of several antioxidant enzymes (AOEs) in heart and liver of hatchling *C. p. marginata*: superoxide dismutase 1 (SOD-1), glutathione peroxidase (GPX) isozymes 1 and 4, glutathione-S-transferase (GST) isozymes M5 and A2, and peroxiredoxin 1. Many of the damaging effects of hypoxia or ischemia in mammals can be traced to ROS attack on cellular macromolecules occurring particularly during the transition from hypoxia/ischemia back to normal oxygen levels. This is because cellular antioxidant defenses can be overwhelmed by a burst of ROS generation when oxygen levels rise rapidly (20). Hence, hypoxia/anoxia survival requires not just adaptations that deal with problems of the anoxic state (low ATP availability, toxicity of accumulated end products, etc.) but also adaptations that deal with the reintroduction of oxygen (19,20). Studies by our lab and others have shown that anoxia tolerant species have two strategies for dealing with oxidative stress during natural transitions from low to high oxygen availability: (a) high constitutive antioxidant defenses, both AOEs and metabolites, and (b) inducible increases in AOE activities typically occurring in the low oxygen state in anticipation of their need when oxygen levels rise again (19,20). Indeed, the best facultative anaerobes that experience routine anoxic excursions, such as adult *T. s. elegans*, have constitutive AOE activities that are comparable to values seen in mammals and many-fold higher than in other cold-blooded vertebrates (20). Species that face anoxia less often show anoxia-induced enhancement of defenses. The responses of the hatchling *C. p. marginata* indicate readily inducible antioxidant defenses, a response that would be important for enduring ischemia/reperfusion insults during winter freeze/thaw exposures. The very high constitutive antioxidant enzyme activities characteristic of adult turtles would probably appear only in subsequent years when the animals are challenged by routine low oxygen excursions during diving or wintering underwater.

The up-regulation of peroxiredoxin 1 deserves a special mention because it may indicate a new principle of metabolic adjustment for anoxia tolerance. The traditional view of ROS is that they are bad and the purpose of antioxidant defenses, therefore, is to prevent or repair the damage done by ROS to cellular macromolecules. This view began to change when it was recognized that nitric oxide (˙NO) and peroxynitrite ($OONO^-$) have second messenger functions and is now undergoing radical revision with the recent demonstration that both superoxide and hydrogen peroxide are effective intracellular second messengers (39). Therefore, it would be expected that one or more enzymes would be present in cells to modulate the levels of these ROS with respect to their signalling functions. Peroxiredoxins (Prx) may have this role (in addition to a general role in antioxidant defense). They are relatively recent additions to the known antioxidant defenses of cells (15,57). Six isoforms of Prx occur in mammals, all containing a reactive Cys in a conserved region near the N-terminus that can reduce H_2O_2 or various alkyl hydroperoxides. Prx1, which is anoxia-responsive in both heart and liver of turtles, is a cytosolic dimer that uses either thioredoxin or reduced glutathione (GSH) as the electron donor. Prx1 is induced by oxidative and other stresses on cells and cells transfected with Prx1 exhibit resistance to apoptosis caused by hydrogen peroxide (15). Substantial support for H_2O_2 as an intracellular second messenger has accumulated recently including: (a) transient elevations of intracellular H_2O_2 occur in response to various cytokines and peptide growth factors, (b) elevated H_2O_2 affects the function of various protein kinases and phosphatases, transcription factors, and G proteins, and (c) inhibition of H_2O_2 generation results in a complete blockage of signalling by growth factors including PDGF, EGF and angiotensin II (39). The overriding critical mechanism of anoxia tolerance is metabolic rate depression – the coordinated suppression of the rates of ATP-producing and ATP-utilizing to stabilize a new much lower rate of ATP turnover (51). As noted earlier, biosynthetic processes (e.g. protein synthesis) are major targets of suppression when ATP is limiting (24,51). Predictably, then, another element of metabolic suppression should be a blockage of cell responsiveness to growth signals. One way to do this could be to strongly suppress the levels of intracellular second messengers, such as H_2O_2, that mediate growth factor and cytokine effects. Up-regulation of Prx1 could facilitate this as Prx1 is known to catabolize H_2O_2 produced from cell surface signalling (39). Prx1 is also regulated by cyclin dependent kinases; Cdc2 kinase-mediated phosphorylation reduced Prx1 activity by 80% and Prx1 was phosphorylated in cells in mitotic phase but not during interphase.

Serpins: As mentioned earlier, serpins are specific inhibitors of selected proteolytic enzymes, often of proteases circulating in the plasma. Most are synthesized and secreted by liver. Anoxia exposure of adult *T. s. elegans* turtles triggered enhanced expression of selected serpins in liver and heart: SERPINC1 (antithrombin), D1 (heparin cofactor II; liver only), and F1 (pigment epithelium derived factor (PEDF)) as well as another inhibitor, called tissue factor pathway inhibitor (46). Our analysis of hatchling *C. p. marginata* also found enhanced expression of SERPINC1 and D1 expression in liver and SERPINF1 and G1 (complement inhibitor) in heart of anoxia exposed turtles, compared with aerobic controls. SERPINC1 and SERPIND1 both inhibit thrombin and, thereby, suppress the clotting cascade. Predictably, clotting capacity should be reduced during anaerobiosis to minimize the risk of thrombosis in the microvasculature under the low blood flow conditions caused by bradycardia during hypometabolism.

SERPINF1 or PEDF is also interesting. It does not inhibit a protease but instead antagonizes VEGF with potent anti-angiogenic effects that have been shown to inhibit vascular growth in several tissues (6,35). HIF-1 triggers a wide range of gene responses, not all of which may be needed in any given situation of low oxygen availability. Anoxia tolerant organisms must clearly retain and use HIF-1 in many circumstances (e.g. to regulate vascular growth during development or erythropoiesis after blood loss) but under environmental anoxia, up-regulation of some of the genes under HIF-1 appears appropriate (e.g. TfR) but others seem counter-intuitive (e.g. VEGF to trigger vascular growth). The putative up-regulation of PEDF in both adult and hatchling anoxia-tolerant turtles is highly intriguing for it suggests a way of blocking an unnecessary angiogenic response during natural anaerobic excursions.

GENE HUNTING IN EXERCISE AND "ANTI-EXERCISE"

The principles and methods for gene hunting are applicable to analyzing the effects of all forms of physiological and environmental stress on organisms. Muscle metabolism is no exception. Many recent studies have applied microarray screening to analyzing multiple aspects of human muscle performance (38) such as the patterns of gene changes seen during endurance exercise (14,56). For example, in a comparison of endurance trained versus untrained cyclists, trained athletes showed significantly higher levels of mRNA for eight genes including DNA repair enzymes, transcription factors, signal transducers, and a glycolytic enzyme (56). Endurance exercise increases the volume density of type I (red) fibers and their mitochondrial volume density and capillarity. Capacity for the oxidation of both fatty acids (lipoprotein lipase, acyl-CoA dehydrogenase, carnitine palmitoyl transferase, fatty acid translocase) and glucose (GLUT4 transporters, hexokinase) increases and Krebs cycle (pyruvate and succinate dehydrogenases) and electron transport enzymes (e.g. COX1, COX4, ND6) are elevated (14).

Studies in my lab have been examining the gene responses of what could be the ultimate "couch potato" or anti-exerciser – the hibernating mammal. Species such as ground squirrels and bats can spend 6-9 months of the year hibernating; long bouts of cold torpor (days-weeks) are interspersed with brief periods of arousal (a day or less) back to euthermic conditions. During torpor, metabolic rate drops to 1-5% of normal, physiological functions (e.g. heart beat, breathing, kidney filtration, and others) are strongly suppressed, body temperature (Tb) can drop to near 0°C, and skeletal muscles go largely unused (53). Hibernators experience some muscle atrophy, but it is much less than would expected from equivalent periods of inactivity in humans (11,42). Gene hunting techniques can provide the answers to multiple questions about skeletal muscle responses during hibernation including: (a) how is torpor induced and coordinated among all cell functions, (b) how are the normally injurious effects of hypothermia on mammalian tissues avoided, (c) how are fuel metabolism and cellular energetics managed, and (d) how is atrophy minimized.

Gene expression supporting hibernation can occur on two time scales: (a) seasonal, and (b) induced during entry into each torpor bout. Recent studies by my lab and others have used diverse techniques of gene screening to analyze the latter in ground squirrels. To date, known hibernation responsive genes have been found in many organs including α_2-macroglobulin in liver, moesin in intestine, isozyme 4 of pyruvate dehydrogenase kinase (PDK4) and pancreatic lipase in heart, isoforms of uncoupling proteins (UCPs) and fatty acid binding proteins (FABPs) in multiple tissues, the ventricular isoform of myosin light chain 1 ($MLC1_v$) in heart and skeletal muscle, six kinds of membrane transporters in kidney, the melatonin receptor, eight types of serpins in multiple organs (A1, A3, A7, B9, C1, E2, F2, G1), several antioxidant enzymes, and four genes on the mitochondrial genome (reviewed in 1,43,44,48). Although the genes identified to date are a disparate group, some principles of adaptation are emerging. Themes include:

(a) Myosin restructuring – studies with heart of ground squirrels and hamsters suggest that changes in the proportions of myosin heavy and light chain isoforms resculpt the contractile apparatus for the new work load and thermal conditions of the torpid state.

(b) Minimizing thrombosis risk – up-regulation of α_2-macroglobulin and multiple plasma serpins, reduced platelet numbers, and reduced levels of several clotting factors all contribute to reduced clotting capacity during torpor to minimize the risk of thrombosis in the microvasculature under the very low blood flow (ischemic) conditions of the hibernating state (reviewed in 44,43). Note that this is mechanism was also seen in anoxic turtles.

(c) Mitochondrial metabolism – some genes encoded on the mitochondrial genome are up-regulated during entry into torpor including subunits of electron transport proteins (ND2, COX1) and the F_1F_0-ATPase (ATPase 6 & 8) but, significantly, nuclear-encoded subunits of these proteins (e.g. COX4, ATPα) are not altered during hibernation (22). Recall that the same phenomenon was seen under anoxia and freezing stress and this suggests that it may be a general principle of hypometabolism. Mitochondrial UCPs that function in thermogenesis are also up-regulated during hibernation.

(d) Reorganization of fuel metabolism – carbohydrate catabolism is suppressed (PDK4 phosphorylates and inhibits pyruvate dehydrogenase) and lipid and ketone body transport and catabolism are enhanced (up-regulation of FABPs, monocarboxylate transporter, lipase).

(e) Antioxidant defenses – use of nylon macroarrays revealed significant up-regulation (>2-fold) of GST, GPX and SOD in kidney and these plus Prx and metallothionein in liver (43). It has long been known that hibernators elevate AOE activities in brown adipose to deal with high rates of ROS generation during thermogenesis (3) but it now appears that this may be a general phenomenon in all organs.

In new studies, we have focused on gene/protein expression during hibernation in little brown bats, *Myotis lucifugus,* with some interesting findings. FABPs are prominently up-regulated in bat organs during hibernation (9), as they are in ground squirrels (21). The control of *fabp* gene expression is linked to the transcription factor PPARγ (peroxisome proliferator-activated receptor) and its coactivator PGC-1 which promote lipid oxidation, both of which are also up-regulated in bat organs during hibernation (8,43). Application of proteomics technology identified a new hibernation-responsive gene in bat heart, a member of the thioredoxin peroxidase family called proliferation associated gene (PAG) (10), also known as Prx 1. Two dimensional electrophoresis revealed a prominent increase in a protein with an isoelectric point of ~7 and a molecular weight of ~22 kD that was subsequently identified after tryptic digestion and mass spectrometry as PAG (Figure 1). Subsequent analysis via RT-PCR and Western blotting showed 2.3- and 4.9-fold increases in *pag* mRNA and PAG protein in bat heart during hibernation. The thioredoxin peroxidases (peroxiredoxins) are a family of enzymes that reduce ROS in cells using thiol groups on conserved cysteine residues (positions 52 and 173) and thioredoxin as the source of reducing equivalents. As noted earlier, members of this family appear to be involved in mediating H_2O_2 levels in signalling pathways and they are up-regulated in response to stresses that elevate peroxide levels (39). Prx is also directly involved with the activation of nuclear factor kappa B (NF-κB) (27), an transcription factor that regulates gene expression, often in response to oxidative stress. With the demonstrated up-regulation of PAG (Prx1) in hibernator heart, we also wondered how markers of oxidative stress responded in hibernation. Two of these are NF-κB and the heat shock protein, HSP27. Activation of NF-κB occurs when its inhibitor protein, IκB-α, is phosphorylated at serine 32 leading to its dissociation from NF-κB, followed by ubiquitination and degradation of IκB-α. Hence, NF-κB activation status is proportional to the relative levels of phospho-IκB-α (Ser32) which increased during hibernation by 2- and 6-fold, in heart and skeletal muscle, respectively (Figure 1) (10). Similarly, levels of phospho-HSP27 rose during hibernation by 2.2-fold in heart and 3.2-fold in muscle (10).

The elevated levels of PAG (Prx1) in bat heart (10) indicate that enhanced antioxidant defenses are important in hibernation (as was also shown in ground squirrels) and this idea is further supported by our new results from microarray screening of bat skeletal muscle. Using the 19K human DNA arrays we found enhanced expression of a variety of genes in skeletal muscle of hibernating bats (Tb = 6°C) compared with aroused animals (Tb = 37°C). Binding intensities of labeled probe were 1.9-7.2 fold higher than in euthermic controls. Significantly, many of these were genes/proteins that we encountered before in hibernation or other systems of metabolic arrest. They included: (1) iron storage proteins – ferritin H and L chains, TfR2, (2) AOEs: GST A2, GPX 1 and 2, Prx 1, (3) protease inhibitors: SERPINF1 (PEDF), (4) H-FABP, the isoform in muscle and heart, and (5) several muscle motor proteins – myosin alkali light chain isoforms 4 and 6, myosin heavy chain isoforms Vc, VIIa and IXb, and actin alpha 2. The results for Prx1 and H-FABP agree with our identification of these proteins as hibernation-responsive by other means (9,10) and also validate array screening as a reliable way of finding hibernation-responsive genes. For example, four loci on the array assessed *h-fabp* and all agreed in showing 2.8-4.3 fold higher probe binding in muscle samples from hibernating versus euthermic bats; this concurs with the 1.8 ± 0.3 fold higher *h-fabp* transcript levels in hibernator muscle found by Northern blotting (9). Enhanced expression of SERPINF1 or PEDF again suggests, as discussed for anoxia tolerant turtles, that measures are taken to counteract angiogenic responses under natural states of ischemia/hypoxia that would not be improved by enhanced vascular growth. During torpor, some level of self-imposed hypoxia may occur due to the apnoic breathing patterns used by hibernators and this could trigger increased HIF-1 mediated gene transcription. Indeed, compared with euthermic ground squirrels, HIF-1α protein levels were 60-70% higher during hibernation in brown adipose and skeletal muscle, the two organs responsible for thermogenesis, and HIF-1 binding to DNA was 6-fold higher in nuclear extracts of hibernator brown adipose (34).

It is also significant that iron storage proteins and antioxidant enzymes are both up-regulated during hibernation. This emphasizes the importance of minimizing damage by ROS during hibernation and probably serves multiple purposes. One is the maintenance of long term cell viability and health during many days or weeks of continuous torpor during which strong inhibition of protein synthesis and other biosynthetic pathways (51) severely limit the possibility of replacing macromolecules that are damaged by ROS. Another reason for good antioxidant defenses in skeletal muscle during torpor could be to minimize atrophy. Much recent evidence has implicated oxidative stress as a potential regulator of proteolytic pathways leading to muscle atrophy during periods of prolonged disuse (36). As much as possible, hibernators need to maintain their muscle mass and, without the option of exercise as a positive stimulus to counteract atrophy, the next best option may be to minimize ROS levels and the signals that stimulate atrophy. Finally, well-developed antioxidant defenses in muscle are also key to preparing for, and preventing damage from, the huge increase in ROS production that occurs within minutes when animals initiate thermogenesis and begin arousal; organ O_2 consumption can rise by 10-20 fold within minutes as the animal rewarms.

Array screening also highlighted increased levels of transcripts of selected myosin subunits and actin α2. These results suggest that remodeling of the skeletal muscle myosin motor of bats occurs during hibernation, similar to previous reports of myosin restructuring in heart of hibernating ground squirrels and hamsters (12,33). Unlike most hibernators that lie curled up in their burrows while in torpor, bats hang by their legs in their roosts and may, therefore, require a continuous level of muscle contractility. Myosin remodelling may optimize the contractile properties of skeletal muscle for two purposes: (1) to function at temperatures near 0°C during torpor, and (2) to provide effective shivering thermogenesis during arousal from torpor (initial heating is done by brown adipose but muscle shivering begins to contribute when Tb reaches ~15°C). Interestingly, two of the muscle proteins highlighted from the screening suggest that other aspects of contractile protein restructuring may also be important in hibernation. Actin α2 is a smooth muscle isoform found in the vasculature and its appearance on the list of up-regulated genes suggests that muscle restructuring for successful hibernation extends also to the smooth muscles of the blood vessels that infiltrate the skeletal muscles. Class V myosins do not participate in the contractile work of skeletal muscle but function as motors for organelle trafficking. Interestingly, overexpression studies have shown that the myosin Vc colocalizes with TfR and perturbs Tf trafficking (43). Hence, modification of iron storage or of endosome processing during hibernation may extend to a need for altered function of cytoskeletal motors.

The power of modern genomics and proteomics is impressive and is allowing us to make major advances in our understanding of how organisms adapt their metabolism to endure stresses imposed by lifestyle and environment. More importantly, the "global view" that is offered by gene screening is critical in showing us both the breadth of cellular responses and the commonalities of mechanisms that underlie organismal adaptation to environmental stress.

ACKNOWLEDGEMENTS

Thanks to recent members of my lab, especially S. Eddy, K. Larade, D. McMullen, P. Morin and D. Hittel for their exploration of array screening, and to J.M. Storey for critical commentary on the manuscript. Research in my lab is supported by a discovery grant from the Natural Sciences and Engineering Research Council of Canada and the Canada Research Chairs program. Visit *www.carleton.ca/~kbstorey* for more information on gene hunting.

REFERENCES

1. Andrews MT. Genes controlling the metabolic switch in hibernating mammals. Biochem Soc Trans 32: 1021-1024, 2004.
2. Bickler PE, Donohoe PH, and Buck LT. The hypoxic brain: suppressing energy-expensive membrane functions by regulation of receptors and ion channels. In: *Molecular Mechanisms of Metabolic Arrest*, edited by Storey KB. Oxford: BIOS Scientific, 2001, p. 77-102.
3. Buzadzic B, Spasic M, Saicic ZS, Radojicic R, Petrovic VM, Halliwell B. Antioxidant defenses in the ground squirrel *Citellus citellus*. 2. The effect of hibernation. *Free Radic Biol Med* 9: 407-413, 1990.
4. Cai Q, and Storey KB. Anoxia-induced gene expression in turtle heart: up-regulation of mitochondrial genes for NADH-ubiquinone oxidoreductase subunit 5 and cytochrome C oxidase subunit 1. *Eur J Biochem* 241: 83-92, 1996.
5. Douglas RM, and Haddad GG. Genetic models in applied physiology: invited review: effect of oxygen deprivation on cell cycle activity: a profile of delay and arrest. *J Appl Physiol* 94: 2068-2083, 2003.
6. Duh EJ, Yang HS, Suzuma I, Miyagi M, Youngman E, Mori K, Katai M, Yan L, Suzuma K, West K, Davarya S, Tong P, Gehlbach P, Pearlman J, Crabb JW, Aiello LP, Campochiaro PA, and Zack DJ. Pigment epithelium-derived factor suppresses ischemia-induced retinal neovascularization and VEGF-induced migration and growth. *Invest Ophthalmol Vis Sci* 43: 821-829, 2002.
7. Eddy SF, and Storey KB. Dynamic use of cDNA arrays: heterologous probing for gene discovery and exploration of animal adaptations in stressful environments. In: *Cell and Molecular Responses to Stress,* edited by Storey KB and Storey JM. Amsterdam: Elsevier 2002, vol. 3, p. 315-325.
8. Eddy SF, and Storey KB. Differential expression of Akt, PPAR-γ and PGC-1 during hibernation in bats. *Biochem Cell Biol* 81: 269-274, 2003.
9. Eddy SF, and Storey KB. Up-regulation of fatty acid-binding proteins during hibernation in the little brown bat, *Myotis lucifugus*. *Biochim Biophys Acta* 1676: 63-70, 2004.
10. Eddy SF, McNally JD, and Storey KB. Up-regulation of a thioredoxin peroxidase-like protein, proliferation associated gene, in hibernating bats. *Arch Biochem Biophys* 435: 101-111, 2005.
11. Egginton S, Fairney J, and Bratcher J. Differential effects of cold exposure on muscle fibre composition and capillary supply in hibernator and non-hibernator rodents. *Exp Physiol* 86: 629-639, 2001.
12. Fahlman A, Storey JM, and Storey KB. Gene up-regulation in heart during mammalian hibernation. *Cryobiology* 40: 332-342, 2000.
13. Fletcher GL, Hew CL, and Davies PL. Antifreeze proteins of teleost fish. *Ann Rev Physiol* 63: 359-390, 2001.
14. Fluck M, and Hoppeler H. Molecular basis of skeletal muscle plasticity – from gene to form and function. *Rev Physiol Biochem Pharmacol* 146: 159-216, 2003.
15. Fujii J, and Ikeda Y. Advances in our understanding of peroxiredoxin, a multifunctional, mammalian redox protein. *Redox Rep* 7: 123-130, 2002.
16. Gettins PGW. Serpin structure, mechanism and function. *Chem Rev* 102: 4751-4803, 2002.
17. Haddad JJ. Oxygen-sensing mechanisms and the regulation of redox-responsive transcription factors in development and pathophysiology. Respir Res. 3: 26, 2002. *http://respiratory-research.com/content/3/1/26*
18. Hentze MW, Muckenthaler MU, and Andrews NC. Balancing acts: molecular control of mammalian iron metabolism. *Cell* 117: 285-297, 2004.
19. Hermes-Lima M, Zenteno-Savin T. Animal response to drastic changes in oxygen

availability and physiological oxidative stress. *Comp Biochem Physiol C* 133: 537-556, 2002.

20. Hermes-Lima M, Storey JM, Storey KB. Antioxidant defenses and animal adaptation to oxygen availability during environmental stress. In: *Cell and Molecular Responses to Stress* edited by Storey KB and Storey JM. Amsterdam: Elsevier Press, 2001, vol. 2, p. 263-287.
21. Hittel D, and Storey KB. Differential expression of adipose and heart type fatty acid binding proteins in hibernating ground squirrels. *Biochim Biophys Acta* 1522: 238-243, 2001.
22. Hittel D, and Storey KB. Differential expression of mitochondria-encoded genes in a hibernating mammal. *J Exp Biol* 205: 1625-1631, 2002.
23. Hittel D, and Storey KB. The translation state of differentially expressed mRNAs in the hibernating thirteen-lined ground squirrel (*Spermophilus tridecemlineatus*). *Arch Biochem Biophys* 401: 244-254, 2002.
24. Hochachka PW, Buck LT, Doll CJ, and Land SC. Unifying theory of hypoxia tolerance: molecular/metabolic defense and rescue mechanisms for surviving oxygen lack. *Proc Natl Acad Sci USA* 93: 9493-9498, 1996.
25. Hochachka PW, and Lutz PL. Mechanism, origin and evolution of anoxia tolerance in animals. *Comp Biochem Physiol B* 130: 435-459, 2001.
26. Jackson DC. How a turtle's shell helps it survive prolonged anoxic acidosis. News Physiol Sci 15: 181-185, 2000.
27. Jin DY, Chae HZ, Rhee SG, Jeang KT. Regulatory role for a novel human thioredoxin peroxidase in NF-κB activation. *J Biol Chem* 272: 30952-30961, 1997.
28. Larade K, and Storey KB. Characterization of a novel gene up-regulated during anoxia exposure in the marine snail *Littorina littorea. Gene* 283: 145-154, 2002.
29. Larade K, and Storey KB. Accumulation and translation of ferritin heavy chain transcripts following anoxia exposure in a marine invertebrate. *J Exp Biol* 207: 1353-1360, 2004.
30. Larade K, and Storey KB. Anoxia-induced transcriptional up-regulation of *sarp-19*: cloning and characterization of a novel EF-hand containing gene expressed in hepatopancreas of *Littorina littorea. Biochem Cell Biol* 82: 285-293, 2004.
31. Lutz PL, and Storey KB. Adaptations to variations in oxygen tension by vertebrates and invertebrates. In: *Handbook of Physiology, Section 13: Comparative Physiology*, edited by Dantzler WH. Oxford: Oxford University Press, 1997, Vol. 2, pp. 1479-1522.
32. MacDonald JA, and Borman MA. Analyzing biological function with emerging proteomic technologies. *Int Cong Ser* 1275: 14–21, 2004.
33. Morano I, Adler K, Agostini B, and Hasselbach W. Expression of myosin heavy and light chains and phosphorylation of myosin light chain in the heart ventricle of the European hamster during hibernation and in summer. *J Muscle Res Cell Motil* 13: 64-70, 1992.
34. Morin P, and Storey KB. Cloning and expression of hypoxia-inducible factor 1α from the hibernating ground squirrel, *Spermophilus tridecemlineatus. Biochim Biophys Acta*, 1729(1): 32-40, 2005.
35. Petersen SV, Valnickova Z, and Enghild JJ. Pigment-epithelium-derived factor (PEDF) occurs at a physiologically relevant concentration in human blood: purification and characterization. *Biochem J* 374: 199-206, 2003.
36. Powers SK, Kavazis AN, and DeRuisseau KC. Mechanisms of disuse muscle atrophy: role of oxidative stress. *Am J Physiol* 288: R337-R344, 2005.
37. Prentice HM, Milton SL, Scheurle D, and Lutz PL. Gene transcription of brain voltage-gated potassium channels is reversibly regulated by oxygen supply. *Am J Physiol* 285: R1317-1321, 2003.
38. Rankinen T, Perusse L, Rauramaa R, Rivera MA, Wolfarth B, and Bouchard C. The human gene map for performance and health-related fitness phenotypes: the 2003 update.

Med Sci Sports Exerc 36: 1451-1469, 2004.
39. Rhee SG, Chang T-S, Bae YS, Lee S-R, and Kang SW. Cellular regulation by hydrogen peroxide. *J Am Soc Nephrol* 14: S211-S215, 2003.
40. Rodriguez OC, and Cheney RE. Human myosin-Vc is a novel class V myosin expressed in epithelial cells. *J Cell Sci* 115: 991-1004, 2002.
41. Smith JJ, O'Brien-Ladner AR, Kaiser CR, and Wesselius LJ. Effects of hypoxia and nitric oxide on ferritin content of alveolar cells. *J Lab Clin Med* 141: 309-317, 2003.
42. Steffen JM, Koebel DA, Musacchia XJ, and Milsom WK. Morphometric and metabolic indices of disuse in muscles of hibernating ground squirrels. *Comp Biochem Physiol B* 99: 815-819, 1991.
43. Storey KB. Mammalian hibernation: transcriptional and translational controls. *Adv Exp Med Biol* 543: 21-38, 2003.
44. Storey KB. Cold, ischemic organ preservation: lessons from natural systems. *J Invest Med* 52: 315-322, 2004.
45. Storey KB. Gene regulation in physiological stress. *Int Cong Ser* 1275: 1-13, 2004.
46. Storey KB. Molecular mechanisms of anoxia tolerance. *Int Cong Ser* 1275: 47-54, 2004.
47. Storey KB. Strategies for exploration of freeze responsive gene expression: advances in vertebrate freeze tolerance. *Cryobiology* 48: 134-145, 2004.
48. Storey KB. Hibernating mammals: can natural cryoprotective mechanisms help prolong lifetimes of transplantable organs? In: *Extending the Life Span*, edited by Sames K, Sethe S. and Stolzing A. Transaction Publishers, NY, 2005.
49. Storey KB, and McMullen DC. Insect cold-hardiness: new advances using gene screening technology. In: *Life in the Cold: Evolution, Mechanisms, Adaptation, and Application.* Edited by Barnes BM, and Carey HV. Fairbanks: Biological Papers of the University of Alaska, 2004, #27, p. 275-281.
50. Storey KB, and Storey JM. Natural freeze tolerance in ectothermic vertebrates. *Ann Rev Physiol* 54: 619-637, 1992.
51. Storey KB, and Storey JM. Metabolic rate depression in animals: transcriptional and translational controls. *Biol Rev Camb Philos Soc* 79: 207-233, 2004.
52. Tacchini L., Fusar Poli D, Bernelli-Zazzera A, and Cairo G. Transferrin receptor gene expression and transferrin-bound iron uptake are increased during postischemic rat liver perfusion. Hepatology 36: 103-111, 2002.
53. Wang LCH, and Lee TF. Torpor and hibernation in mammals: metabolic, physiological, and biochemical adaptations. In: *Handbook of Physiology: Environmental Physiology*, edited by Fregley MJ, and Blatteis CM. New York: Oxford University Press, 1996, sect. 4, vol. 1, p. 507-532.
54. Wenger RH. Cellular adaptation to hypoxia: O_2-sensing protein hydroxylases, hypoxia-inducible transcription factors, and O_2-regulated gene expression. *FASEB J* 16: 1151-1162, 2002.
55. Willmore WG, English TE, and Storey KB. Mitochondrial gene responses to low oxygen stress in turtle organs. *Copeia* 2001, 628–637, 2001.
56. Wittwer M, Billeter R, Hoppeler H, and Fluck M. Regulatory gene expression in skeletal muscle of highly endurance-trained humans. *Acta Physiol Scand* 180: 217-227, 2004.
57. Wood ZA, Schroder E, Harris JR, and Poole LB. Structure, mechanism and regulation of peroxiredoxins. *Trends Biochem Sci* 28: 32-40, 2003.

LATE ABSTRACTS

103. LIVING WITH HYPOXEMIA: AN ANALYSIS OF MUSCLE SARCOPLASMIC RETICULUM PROPERTIES IN CHRONIC OBSTRUCTIVE PULMONARY DISEASE

H.J. Green[1], T.A. Duhamel[1], C. D'Arsigny[2], D. O'Donnell[2], I. McBride[2], and J. Ouyang[1].

1Department of Kinesiology, University of Waterloo, Waterloo, Ontario, Canada. 2Respiratory Investigation Unit, Kingston General Hospital, Kingston, Ontario, Canada. Email: green@healthy.uwaterloo.ca

The objective of this study was to investigate the hypothesis that alterations in sarcoplasmic reticulum (SR) Ca^{2+}-cycling properties would occur in skeletal muscle of patients with moderate to severe chronic obstructive lung disease (COPD). To investigate this hypothesis, tissue samples were obtained from the vastus lateralis of 8 patients with COPD (age 67.4±2.4 yrs; FEV_1/FVC=44±2%; ±SE) and 10 healthy-matched controls (CON, age 67.5±2.4 yrs; FEV_1/FVC=77±2%) and analyzed for a wide range of SR properties. Resting PaO_2 was 83.8±2.2 mm Hg and 61.4±2.3 mm Hg in CON and COPD, respectively. As compared to CON, COPD displayed a 16% lower ($P<0.05$) maximal Ca^{2+}-ATPase activity (V_{max}, 158±vs 133±7 μmol.g protein.min^{-1}), and a 17% lower ($P<0.05$) Ca^{2+}-uptake (4.65±0.039 vs 3.85±0.26 μmol.g protein.min^{-1}) which occurred in the absence of differences in Ca^{2+}-release. The lower V_{max} in COPD was also accompanied by an 11% lower ($P<0.05$) Ca^{2+}-sensitivity, as defined by the Hill coefficient. For the Ca^{2+}-ATPase isoforms, SERCA 1a was 16% higher ($P<0.05$) and SERCA 2a was 14% lower ($P<0.05$) in COPD. It is concluded that moderate to severe COPD results in abnormalities in SR Ca^{2+}-ATPase properties, as evidenced by the dissociation between the functional and isoform phenotypes. The reduced Ca^{2+}-ATPase, which appears to be mediated by a reduction in V_{max}, suggests impairment in the ability of the muscle to relax after contraction.

Supported by Department of Medicine Research (Queen's University)

104. MONITORING HYPOXIA INDUCED ANGIOGENESIS IN BRAIN USING STEADY STATE MRI

Jeff Dunn[1], Marcie Roche[2], Michelle Abajian[2].
[1]University of Calgary, [2]Dartmouth Medical School. Email: dunnj@ucalgary.ca

Angiogenesis is known to occur in brain in response to hypoxia. This study introduces an MRI method for monitoring angiogenesis in brain during hypoxic exposure using steady state R2 (STAR2) MRI, and shows the results over a time-course of 17 days exposure to ½ atm hypobaric hypoxia. Multiple measurements of CBV were made in the same animals over a time course of hypoxic exposure. Multi-echo spin echo MRI imaging was performed before and after infusion of the intravascular contrast agent, monocrystaline iron-oxide nanoparticals (MION). CBV was calculated as deltaR2t/deltaR2b, where delta=the difference in R2 before and after MION injection, t=cortical tissue and b=blood. Blood samples were obtained before and after infusion for MRI quantification of serum R2. deltaR2b was corrected for hematocrit (Hct) by deltaR2s • (1-Hct), where s=serum. CBV at day 0 measured 3.52±1.05 v/v (n=5; mean±SD). After 3 days of hypoxia, CBV significantly increased to 5.81±1.60 v/v and after 17 days CBV was 6.85±1.35 v/v. In an earlier study, we measured a CBV of 6.42±0.54 v/v (n=4; mean±SD) after 3 weeks of the same hypoxia. There was no significant difference between day 3, 17 or 21 days. Thus, after 72 hours, CBV reached a level commensurate with that obtained after 3 weeks of chronic hypoxia.This study indicates that steady-state imaging with MION is useful for quantification of CBV as a marker of angiogenesis in the same animal over a time-course study and that, within 3 days of onset of acclimation, the effective CBV has approached the final adapted volume.

Acknowledgements: Supported by NIH NS045466 and EB002085

105. CLIMBING THE EDUCATION MOUNTAIN: EDUCATIONAL APPRAISAL OF THE FIRST TWO YEARS EXPERIENCE OF THE UK DIPLOMA IN MOUNTAIN MEDICINE

Peter Barry[1], Kyle Pattinson[2], David Hillebrandt[3], On behalf of the UK Diploma in Mountain Medicine Faculty[4].
[1]University of Leicester, [2]University of Oxford, [3]Holsworthy Health Centre, [4]Medical Expeditions. Email: pwb1@le.ac.uk

30 students have now completed the diploma; we describe the candidates and course methods. Appraisal of candidates application forms, evaluation forms, and formal assessments. Description of teaching and assessment methods. Students have been from anaesthetics (34%); internal medicine (32%); or general practice (26%). They plan to use the course to help in work as an expedition doctor (47%); or in pre-hospital care (24%). A variety of teaching methods are used, including traditional lectures and seminars, but making extensive use of field work, simulations and scenario-based problem solving. A practical wilderness emergency care course has been developed and evaluated as a popular learning tool. Assessment methods include multiple choice question papers (MCQ); short answer papers (SAQ); and practical skills assessments. MCQs were difficult to write and contentious to mark, but did generate discussion and were popular for formative assessment. They were not sufficiently rigorous for summative assessment. SAQ papers were marked by two

faculty separately and the results pooled, There was good correlation between markers. Borderline papers were remarked by senior faculty. Practical skills assessment in navigation, mountain craft and wilderness medical care was by British mountain guides based upon adaptation of formal mountain qualifications, and experienced wilderness medicine practitioners in the faculty. Satisfactory assessment in both written and practical tests was required. Two candidates have been required to repeat SAQ and two subjects asked to get more experience & to present themselves for skills reassessment. Students may progress from the UIAA Diploma to a University Accredited Diploma and Masters qualification by the completion of reflective papers and a dissertation. As well as demonstrating academic rigour, these will contribute to the research base of mountain medicine.Adult learning has been successfully adapted to combine theoretical medicine & practical mountaineering skills essential for safe mountain medicine practice.

Acknowledgements: The UK Diploma in Mountain Medicine is supported by Medical Expeditions and Accredited by the University of Leicester

106. INTERMITTENT HYPOXIC TRAINING TO ENHANCE ATHLETES PERFORMANCE

Alexander Brovko[1], Nikolai Volkov[2]

[1]PRAXSEP Inc., Guelph, Ontario, Canada, [2]Russian State University of Physical Education, Sport and Tourism, Moscow, Russia. Email: alexbrovko@praxsep.com.

The improvement of sports achievements occuring in the process of athletes training reflects the process of adaptation under the influence of means and methods used in training. Intermittent Hypoxic Training (IHT) – discontinuous normobaric hypoxia - has been used as an additional method to enhance results of endurance athletes. Twelve swimmers of high qualification were divided into two groups: control and experimental. The control group was training with usual capacity using traditional techniques. Experimental group of swimmers together with the same traditional methods of training used different variants of IHT during the recovery periods followed the main training loads. Hypoxicator 'Everest' (joint project of Climbi Ltd., Russia and Praxsep Inc., Canada) was used for creating hypoxic atmosphere. Each single hypoxic exposure was 1-5 min followed by 1-5 min 'rest' period when athletes were breathing regular air. Combined exposure did not exceed 1.5 hours within one day. The period of experimental training continued for three months. Before and immediately after the end of experiment the athletes of both groups were tested in standard ergonomic procedures for the maximum of aerobic and anaerobic work capacity. Under the conditions of the given experiment IHT resulted in significant increase in parameters of maximum aerobic capacity for the experimental group: VO_2 max increased on average 11%; Ve – 6.4%; Wer – 10.8%; pH – 44.6%; Exc CO_2 -23%, and Wmax – 9.8%. Results for the control group were significantly lower. According with these findings the greater improvement in swimming performance was to be expected for athletes in the experimental group in middle distances such as 200, 400, and 800 m. The use of IHT as additional training method for qualified swimmers made it possible to considerably improve sports results in short period of training.

107. CRF RECEPTOR TYPE 1 AND SOMATOSTATIN MODULATE PITUITARY GROWTH HORMONE AND HEPATIC INSULIN-LIKE GROWTH FACTOR-I OF RATS DURING HYPOXIA

Xue-Qun Chen[1], Ji-Zeng Du[1], Ning-Yi Xu[1], Yi Wang[1], Cunming Duan[2].
[1]Zhejiang University, Yuquan Campus, China, [2]Michigan University, USA. Email: chewyg@cls.zju.edu.cn

This study presents the responses of pituitary growth hormone (GH) and hepatic insulin-like growth factor-I (IGF-I) in rats to hypoxia and combination with cold or restraint, as well as the involvements of corticotropin-releasing factor receptor type 1 (CRFR1) and somatostatin (SS) in hypoxia-induced GH and IGF-I. Continual hypobaric hypoxia of altitude 5km (CH5km) was performed for 1 through 25d; did the combination of intermittent hypoxia of altitude 5km (IH5km) with cold (4°C) or restraint for 2d(4h/d); CRFR1 antagonist (CP154526, 30mg/kg/d, s.c.) or SS antagonist (cysteamine, CSH, 200mg/kg/d, s.c.) were applied following exposure to 5d CH5km. Pituitary GHmRNA and hepatic IGF-I mRNA were analyzed using RT-PCR. Pituitary GH or hepatic IGF-I was measured using immunohistochemistry. During CH5km immunostaining pituitary GH (ipGH) and hepatic IGF-I (ihIGF-I) were increased for 1 and 2d, and recovered afterward; the pituitary GH mRNA was decrease on day 5, while the hepatic IGF-I mRNA reduced on day 1 and increased on day 5. IH5km, cold, restraint, and combination increased ipGH and ihIGF-I, but the restraint powerfully acted on ipGH than the IH5km or cold, and the IH5km + restraint was much potential than IH5km or IH5km + cold. Besides restraint induced a higher ihIGF-I than cold, did IH5km + restraint than IH5km, and did IH5km + cold than IH5km or cold. CP154526 and CSH significantly blocked CH5km (for 5d)-decreased pituitary GH mRNA and increased hepatic IGF-I mRNA, but remarkably induced ipGH and ihIGF-I decreases vs. CH5km + vehicle. These data suggest that CH5km could modulate the expressions of pituitary GH and hepatic IGF-I in a time-course dependent manner; restraint acts much powerfully on pituitary GH and hepatic IGF-I than hypoxia or cold, combinative stress may enlarge responses than individual one; SS and CRFR1 are involved in mediating the pituitary GH and hepatic IGF-I during CH5km.

Acknowledgements: This work is supported by the grant from NSFC (Major Project No. 30393134 and Project No. 30270232; 30470648; 30070289).

108. HYPOXIC ENDOTHELIN-1 EXPRESSION IN THE HEART OF MICE, OCHOTONA CURZONIAE, AND MICROTUS OECONOMUS BY COCL2-INDUCED AND HYPOBARIC HYPOXIA

Xue-Qun Chen[1], Ji-Zeng Du[1], Jun-Jun He[1], Xiao-Cheng Chen[2].
[1]Zhejiang University, Yuquan Campus, China, [2]Northwest Plateau Institute of Biology, Chinese Academy of Sciences, China. Email: chewyg@cls.zju.edu.cn

Ochotona curzoniae and Microtus oeconomus are native mammals at Qinghai-Tibetan plateau. The responses of ET-1 in the heart of these mammals to hypoxia have been unclear.In this study, both CoCl2-induced hypoxia and hypobaric altitude hypoxia (HAH) were applied. CoCl2-induced hypoxia was performed with intraperitoneal injection of CoCl2 (20, 40, and 60 mg/kg). HAH was performed in a hypobaric chamber setting at equal to altitude of 5km (10.8%O_2) and 7km (8.2%O_2). ET-1 and HIF-1α were measured after hypoxia exposure for 6h using radioimmunoassay and Western blot, respectively. We also tested the involvement of the transcriptional factor of NF-kB in hypoxia-induced ET-1 increase through an injection (s.c.) of NF-κB antagonist.The results showed: 1. ET-1 and HIF-1a in mice heart were markedly increased intensity-dependently following an injection of three doses of CoCl2. In M. oeconomus, the increased HIF-1 α resulted from CoCl2 40 or 60mg/kg but only 60mg/kg caused ET-1 increase. However there were no changes of HIF-1α and ET-1 presented in O. curzoniae at all dosages. 2. ET-1 was markedly increased in mice heart subjecting to 5km and 7km for 6h, and 5km or 7km hypoxia-induced increased ET-1 was blocked by treatment (s.c.) with NF-κB antagonist. In M. oeconomus 5km or 7km-hypoxia caused an increased ET-1, and 5km hypoxia-induced increase was blocked by NF-κB. In O. curzoniae only 7km-hypoxia stimulated ET-1, which could not be blocked by NF-κB.These data indicate that the dramatic enhancement of ET-1 and HIF-1α in mice heart is highly sensitive to CoCl2-hypoxia or hypobaric altitude hypoxia, whereas those in O. curzoniae are entirely not sensitive compared with the mice, suggesting that O. curzoniae is well-acclimatized to environment hypoxia. Although M. oeconomus is also an inhabitant at plateau, his abilities against hypoxia are not competition with O. curzoniae. Both NF-κB and HIF-1α may be the joint transcriptional factor for ET-1 gene in mice heart, but NF-κB probably correlates with ET-1 gene in plateau mammals.

Acknowledgements: This work is supported by the grant from NSFC (Major Project No. 30393134 and Project No. 30270232; 30470648; 30070289).

109. CORTICOTROPIN-RELEASING FACTOR RECEPTOR 1 MEDIATES THE CONTINUAL HYPOXIA-ACTIVATED ENDOTHELIN-1 MRNA EXPRESSION IN PARAVENTRICULAR NUCLEUS OF RAT HYPOTHALAMUS

Ji-Zeng Du[1], Xue-Qun Chen[1], Jun-Jun He[1], Jian-Fen Xu[1].

[1]*Zhejiang University, Yuquan Campus, China. Email: dujz@cls.zju.edu.cn.*

This work aims at investigating the patterns of endothelin-1 (ET-1) changes in rat hypothalamic PVN induced by the continual hypobaric altitude hypoxia 5km (CHAH5km) and the correlation with corticotropin-releasing factor (CRF) and its receptor subtype 1 (CRFR1) in PVN activated by CHAH5km. CHAH5km (10.8 % O_2) was performed in a hypobaric chamber. ET-1 mRNA, ET-1, and CRF protein were measured using in situ hybridization and immunohistochemistry, respectively. We found that CHAH5km caused a programmed ET-1 drop and return over 1 to 25d, and the lowest point occurred on day5 of the exposure but CRF reached its peak at the same time through an early-declined phase on day 1 and 2. CHAH5km triggered ET-1 mRNA up-expression following a sharp reduction of ET-1 protein on day 5, which were completely reversed by treatment with five daily injection (s.c.) of CRFR1 antagonist (30 mg/kg/d of CP 154,526), meanwhile this treatment led to that CHAH5km-triggered increased CRF and CRF mRNA expression in PVN were also partly/completely reversed. These suggest that hypoxia-activated ET-1 release and ET-1 mRNA expression as well as CRF and CRF mRNA in PVN are mediated through CRFR1. Hypoxia activating CRFR1 in PVN positively stimulates CRF which triggers further the ET-1 release and ET-1 mRNA expression.

Acknowledgements: This work is supported by the grant from NSFC (Major Project No. 30393134 and Project No. 30270232; 30470648; 30070289).

110. WHOLE BODY PROTEIN TURNOVER AT HIGH ALTITUDE

Carsten Lundby[1], Paul Robach[2], Kirsten Møller[3], Gerrit van Hall[1].

[1]Copenhagen Muscle Research Centre, [2]Ecole National de Ski et D'Alpinisme, [3]Rigshospitalet, Copenhagen, Denmark. Email: carsten@cmrc.dk.

Skeletal muscle loss has often been reported as a common feature of long term exposure to high altitude. Although the muscle loss has been reported for decades the underlying regulating mechanisms are relatively unknown. We studied protein turnover in nine male subjects at sea level and after seven days exposure to 4559 m. Three days prior to experiments subjects were confined to live in our laboratory or inside the Margeritha hut at 4559 m. For this period diet and activity levels were matched. Protein turnover was studied during 4 hours of supine rest by a primed constant infusion of [1-13C]leucine and sodium bicarbonate. Blood and pulmonary CO_2 samples were obtained, before and every hour after the start of the isotope infusion. Muscle biopsies were obtained pre-infusion, and then after one and four hours. Whole body protein synthesis for the last 2 hours of the study was similar at sea level and altitude with 0.22±0.02 and 0.24±0.01 g.(kg.h)-1, respectively. Also the net whole body protein balance was similar at sea level and altitude with a net protein degradation of 0.025±0.002 and 0.030±0.002 g.(kg.h)-1, respectively. In conclusion, whole body protein synthesis and the net protein balance are unchanged after 7-9 days of acclimatization to 4559 m if activity level and diet are maintained. In addition, the previous reported altitude depended muscle loss might be related to decreased energy intake and/or activity level.

111. NEONATAL EXPOSURE TO INTERMITTENT HYPOXIA ENHANCES MICE PERFORMANCE IN WATER MAZE AND 8-ARM RADIAL MAZE TASKS

Ji-Zeng Du[1], Xue-Qun Chen[1], Jia-Xing Zhang[1], Qing-Mei Chen[1], Chao-Yang Zhu[2].

[1]Zhejiang University, Yuquan Campus, China, [2]Zhejiang University, Hubing Campus, China. Email: dujz@cls.zju.edu.cn.

Hypoxia has generally been reported to impair learning and memory behavior. The aim of this study was to investigate whether intermittent hypoxia (IH) might improve mice learning and memory. IH was simulated at 2 km (16.0% O_2) or 5 km (8.2% O_2) in a hypobaric chamber for 4h/d from birth to 1, 2, 3 or 4 week(s), respectively. Spatial learning and memory ability was tested in the Morris water maze (MWM) task at ages of postnatal day 36 (P36)-P40 and P85-89, respectively, and in 8-arm maze task at P60-68. The long-term potentiation (LTP), synaptic density, and phosphorylated cAMP-responsive element-binding protein (p-CREB) level in hippocampus were tested in mice at P36 under the IH for 4w (IH-4w). The results showed that IH-3w and IH-4w at 2 km significantly reduced the escape latencies of mice at P36-40 in MWM task with the significantly enhanced retention, and IH-4w-improved abilities in MWM was maintained in mice up to P85-89. At 2 km, IH-4w markedly decreased the number of error choices of mice at P60-68 in 8-arm maze task. IH-4w at 2 km or 5 km significantly increased amplitude of LTP, the number of synapse, and the p-CREB level in the hippocampus in P36 mice. We concluded that neonatal mice subjected to IH (4h/d) at 2 km for 3w or 4w improved spatial learning and memory, which was associated with the increased p-CREB, LTP, and synapses of hippocampus in this model.

This work is supported by the grant from NSFC (Major Project No. 30393134 and Project No. 30070289; 30270232, 30470648).

112. THE VARIATIONS OF RESPONSIVE MANNERS BETWEEN MICE AND QINGHAI-TIBETAN PLATEAU MAMMALS TO COCL2-INDUCED HYPOXIA

JiZeng Du[1], ShiJun Wang[1], XueQun Chen[1], Cunming Duan[2,3].
1Zhejiang University, 2University of Michigan, 3Northwest Plateau Institute of Biology, China.
Email: dujz@cls.zju.edu.cn.

Ochotona curzoniae and Microtus oeconomus are native mammals at Qinghai-Tibetan plateau, and well acclimatized to environmental hypoxia, but the adaptive principle has not been entirely explored. This study reports the acute response of HIF-1, IGF-I, IGFBP-1, and key metabolic enzyme genes of LDH-A, ICD and SDH in liver to CoCl2-induced hypoxia. The parameters were tested 6h after CoCl2 injection i.p. (20, 40 and 60 mg/kg) to mice and plateau native mammals.The results firstly demonstrated that HIF-1a expression (transcriptional factor, steady and inducible under hypoxia) in mice was markedly increased with i.p. CoCl2 (20 or 40mg/kg), and no response in either O. curzoniae or M. oeconomus at any dose; CoCl2 significantly increased hepatic IGF-I expression in a dose-dependent manner in M. oeconomus, but not in O. curzoniae and mice; CoCl2 induced an increased hepatic IGFBP-1 in dose dependent reducing in mice, and not in M. oeconomus. In the contrast, a dramatic increasd IGFBP-1 was caused by all doses of CoCl2 in O. curzoniae, and 40 mg/kg CoCl2-induced IGFBP-1 increase maintained up to 12h (last point of observation), CoCl2 (20 mg/kg) stimulated LDH-A mRNA but reduced ICD mRNA in mice and no change in plateau native mammals.These data suggest that in contrast with lowland lab animal, plateau-acclimated native mammals are de-sensitive or high endurance to CoCl2-induced hypoxia, and maintaining the aerobic TCA may be of the characteristic manner of energy metabolism for the hypoxia-well-acclimatized plateau mammals, but the increased anaerobic LDH and reduced TCA may be the signal for triggered glycolysis pathway and/or hepatic damage for lowland mice. The IGF/IGFBP-1 systems are distinguishing for those classes, and may differentially contribute to hypoxic protection at cellular or molecular levels in the liver.

Acknowledgements: This work is supported by the grant from NSFC (Major Project No. 30393134 and Project No. 30070289; 30270232).

113. EFFECTS OF SILDENAFIL ON EXERCISE CAPACITY AT THE ALTITUDE OF 5000 M ON MOUNT CHIMBORAZO

Vitalie Faoro[1], Michel Lamotte[2], Gael Deboeck[1], Adriana Pavelescu[2], Hervé Guenard[3], Jean-Benoit Martinot[4], Robert Naeije[1].

[1]Department of Physiology, Erasme Campus, Free University of Brussels, Belgium, [2]Department of Cardiology, Erasme University Hospital, Brussels, Belgium, [3]Department of Physiology, Université de Bordeaux 2, France, [4]Department of Pneumology, St Elisabeth Hospital, Namur, Belgium. Email: rnaeije@ulb.ac.be.

Phosphodiesterase-5 inhibition with sildenafil has been reported to improve exercise capacity in patients with pulmonary arterial hypertension (Sastry et al, J Am Coll Cardiol 2004;43:1149-53) or with congestive heart failure (Guazzi et al, J Am Coll Cardiol 2004;44:2339-48) and in normal subjects at high altitude (Ghofrani et al, Ann Intern Med 2004;141:169-77 and Richalet et al Am J Respir Crit Care Med 2005;171:275-81). Sildenafil has been the only pharmacologic treatment until now reported to limit altitude-associated decrease in aerobic exercise capacity. We investigated the effects of the intake of 50 mg of sildenafil versus placebo in 14 healthy young adults, 6 women and 8 men, on exercise capacity as evaluated by an incremental 25 W/min cycle ergometer cardiopulmonary exercise test (CPET) at the altitude of 5000 m, in the Whymper hut, on the slopes of Mount Chimborazo, in Ecuador. Sildenafil and placebo were given on 2 consecutive days following a randomized, double blind, placebo controlled cross-over design. The subjects had been acclimatized by seven days residence at the altitude of 3800 m, with hiking at altitudes between 2800 and 4800 m. None of the subjects presented with a significant increase of the acute mountain sickness Lake Louise score at the time of the CPET. Sildenafil compared to placebo had no effect on resting O_2 saturation (81.6 ± 1.3 vs 82.7 ± 1.2 %), maximum exercise O_2 saturation (75.1 ± 1.2 vs 74.8 ± 1.0 %) resting heart rate (92 ± 4 vs 90 ± 4 bpm) or maximum workload (180 ± 15 vs 182 ± 15 W). Sildenafil had no effect on maximum O_2 uptake, maximum CO_2 ouput, maximum ventilation, ventilatory threshold, ventilatory equivalent for CO_2 at the ventilatory threshold, O_2 pulse, and maximum effort dyspnea score. The only significant changes observed after sildenafil intake were an increase in maximum heart rate (161 ± 3 vs 155 ± 4, $P < 0.05$) and a decrease in diastolic blood pressure after 2 min recovery (75 ± 4 vs 85 ± 3 mmHg, $P < 0.05$). We conclude that in the conditions of the present experiment, sildenafil did not increase aerobic exercise capacity at high altitude.

Acknowledgements: Cardiopulmonary exercise equipment was loaned by Medisoft Inc, Dinant, Belgium Sildenafil (Viagra®) was a gift from Pfizer Inc, Sandwich, UK

114. OXYGEN-INDUCED PULMONARY VASODILATION IN PULMONARY ARTERIAL HYPERTENSION

Sebastiaan Holverda[1], Tji-Joong Gan[1], Anco Boonstra[1], Pieter Postmus[1], Anton Vonk-Noordegraaf[1].

1VU University medical centre, Amsterdam, The Netherlands. Email: bholverda@vumc.nl.

Pulmonary vascular resistance (PVR) is elevated in pulmonary arterial hypertension (PAH). Because of relatively normal alveolar oxygen tension in PAH, hypoxic pulmonary vasoconstriction should not be present and affect PVR. However, decreased mixed venous oxygen tension ($PmvO_2$) might be of disadvantageous for the PVR. Aim: Show that increased PVR in PAH is partly due to decreased mixed venous oxygen tension, and that supplementation of oxygen can improve PVR. Methods: 16 PAH patients (10 female) underwent right heart catheterization. Mean pulmonary artery pressure and mixed venous oxygen pressure were measured. Cardiac output was calculated by the Fick method and the PVR was calculated from the cardiac output and pressure measurements. PVR was assessed during 5 minutes of breathing (1) ambient air (2) 100 % O_2 (3) 20 ppm NO and (4) 100%O_2 and 20 ppm NO. In between steps was a 5 minutes normalization period. Results: The mean PVR at baseline was 753±369 dynes.s-1.cm-5 (range: 299-1615). The overall changes in PVR from baseline to the three conditions were, (1) during NO: -24±16%, (2) during O2: -38±13%, (3) during NO and O2: -46±22%. There was no correlation between the change in PVR during NO and the change in PVR during O_2. $PmvO_2$ did not correlate with either the response of PVR to NO or the response of PVR to O_2. Even next to a vasodilator as NO, oxygen has an additive effect on the decrease in PVR in PAH, suggesting a different pathway of vasodilation by oxygen and NO. $PmvO_2$ is not predictive for the response of PVR to NO or O_2.

115. HYPOXIA AND COMBINED EXERCISE CHANGE METABOLIC ENZYME ACTIVITIES OF RAT HEART

Yuqi Gao[1], Mingchun Cai*[2], Qingyuan Huang[1], Wenxiang Gao[1].
[1]Institute of High Altitude Medicine, Third Military Medical University, Chongqing,China,
[2]Institute of High Altitude Medicine, Third Military Medical Universit, Chongqing,Chinay.
Email: gaoy66@yahoo.com.

This study was designed to determine the effects of chronic hypobaric hypoxia solo and combined with exercise on the activity of oxidative and glycolytic enzymes. Wistar rats were divided into 4 groups: Control (C), hypoxic group (H), exercising group (E) and hypoxia-combined exercise group (HE). Rats of H and HE groups were subjected to simulated 5 000 m hypobaric hypoxia for 5 weeks (24 h/d, 7d/week), except that animals of both groups were descended to 4 000 m for 1 h/day (6 d/week) from the second week to the end, during which the HE group was forced to swim ceaselessly. Twenty four hours after the last bout of exercise training, animals were sacrificed at 4 000 m (H and HE groups) or at sea level (C and R groups), ventricles were collected and the activities of oxidative enzymes succinate dehydrogenase (SDH) and citrate synthase(CS) as well as glycolytic enzymes hexokinase (HK) and lactate dehydrogenase (LDH) were determined. SDH and CS in left ventricle (LV) were significantly lower in H than in C ($p<0.05$), but no significant difference was found between HE and C. HK, CS and LDH were significantly lower in H than in C in right ventricle (RV) ($p<0.05$), but CS and LDH exhibited no significant difference between HE and C. SDH of RV was significantly higher in HE than in C ($p<0.05$). Chronic hypoxia can diminish the activity of oxidative and glycolytic enzymes, while moderate exercise under hypoxic environment benefit to maintain these enzymes. It may be an important mechanism by which moderate exercise under hypoxic environment promote the acclimatization to hypoxia.

(*Correspondence, gaoy66@yahoo.com. Supported by NSFC 30393131, 30200130.)

116. CEREBRAL HYPOXIA INDUCES PULMONARY EDEMA: A PILOT STUDY

David Irwin[1], Eric Monnet[2], Lisa Klopp[2], E.J. Ehrhart[2], Dave Peterson[3], Damian Bailey[4], Andy Subudhi[4], Martha Tissot-van-Patot[4], Robert Roach[4].

[1]Colorado State University and University Colorado Health Science Center, [2]Colorado State University, [3]Poudre Valley Hospital, [4]Colorado Center for Altitude Medicine and Physiology, Depts Surgery and Anesthesiology, University of Colorado at Denver Health Sciences Center, Email: Davidcirwin@earthlink.net.

High altitude pulmonary edema (HAPE), acute respiratory distress syndrome and neurogenic pulmonary edema are permeability-induced pulmonary edemas. Pathophysiological studies of these illnesses in animals have concentrated on inducing whole body hypoxia, sepsis or increasing intracranial pressure, and have neglected the influence of cerebral hypoxia alone. A series of published studies from one laboratory (Moss, 1968-1972) suggests a link between pulmonary edema (PE) in an animal model where the brain is hypoxic in the presence of systemic normoxia. These studies have not been replicated. Thus, we hypothesized that cerebral hypoxia (CH) coupled with whole body normoxia would induce pulmonary edema in mongrel dogs. Methods: Indices of pulmonary edema, hemodynamic parameters and norepinephrine (NE) values were measured in anesthetized adult Walker hounds in which one carotid artery was ligated and the other delivered a venous (n=3) or arterial (n=1; CTRL) perfusate. In CH PO_2, PCO_2 and SaO_2 were maintained for 2 h at 38±1, 44±1,and 63±7 vs. 83±4, 40±1, and 94±1 in CTRL, while the systemic PO_2, PCO_2 and SaO_2 were maintained as in normoxia. After 2 h of CH, normoxic cerebral blood perfusion was reinstated and dogs breathed room air spontaneously for an additional 2 h before euthanasia. Results: Lung wet weight-to-dry weight ratios were increased in the CH group compared to CTRL (6±1 vs. 2). Histology revealed areas of marked increases of neutrophils and macrophages, acute hemorrhage, congestion and alveolar edema in the CH animals, but not CTRL. In CH arterial PO_2, SaO_2 and pH decreased to 42±3, 63±4 and 7.22±0.02 respectively during the 2 hr of "recovery" while PCO_2 increased to 51±2 mm Hg. There were no significant differences in mean arterial, pulmonary wedge and pulmonary artery pressures or cardiac output between the CH and CTRL. However, NE increased 5-fold more in the CH vs. CTRL animal. Discussion: CH increases NE and induces PE. We speculate that the increase in permeability may be directly modulated by NE, however other hypoxia-initiated factors may be involved. For example, neuropeptide-Y is often elevated in conjunction with elevated NE, and NPY can cause increases in vascular permeability. Further research is necessary to answer these questions, and to establish if this model can serve as an animal model for HAPE. It may be that the cerebral hypoxia induced in our model activates a series of pathophysiological responses similar to those encountered by the apneic, hypoxemic climber sleeping at very high altitudes. In that case, the brain is certainly hypoxic and its contribution to HAPE may be explored using the cerebral hypoxia model.

Acknowledgements. We thank Eric Monnet for providing the surgical expertise and the laboratory space to carry out this research project at Colorado State University's Veterinary Teaching Hospital. This grant was funded by the College Research Council (CRC) # 1168 (Lisa Klopp and Eric Monnet)

117. LAKE LOUISE SCORING SYSTEM UNDERESTIMATES SYMPTOMS OF ACUTE MOUNTAIN SICKNESS IN 4-11 YEAR OLD CHILDREN

Andrew Southard[1], Jason Roosa[1], Morgan Skurky-Thomas[1], Heather Prouty[1], Logan McDaneld[1], Susan Niermeyer[2,5], Michael Yaron[3,4,5].
University of Colorado Health Sciences Center, [1]School of Medicine, [2]Department of Pediatrics, [3]Division of Emergency Medicine, [4]Colorado Emergency Medicine Research Center, [5]Colorado Center for Altitude Medicine and Physiology, Denver, Colorado. Email: Michael.Yaron@UCHSC.edu.

The Lake Louise Scoring System (LLSS) is a self-reporting tool designed to evaluate adults for symptoms of acute mountain sickness (AMS). Our objective was to evaluate if age appropriate language alters the results of the AMS diagnostic score in 4-11 yr old children. In this prospective study, subjects completed both the LLSS and an equivalent modified language symptom score (MLS) once daily for 3 days. The MLS included an additional "faces pain scale" to quantify headache symptoms. Parents were allowed to assist children with questions on both surveys. Measurements were made at 1605m, in the subject's homes, without any altitude change. Equivalent symptom questions between the two surveys were assessed for agreement on the day when the most symptoms were recorded for each question. Thirty-seven children (19 girls), ages 4 to 11 (mean age 7.38 ± 2.28 years) completed the study. Six children enrolled were lost to follow-up. Kappa values: headache (K=0.22), gastrointestinal (K=0.34), fatigue (K=0.88), dizziness (K=0.65) and sleep (K=0.88) ranged from fair to very good. The MLS resulted in higher mean symptom scores (1.14 ± .98) compared to LLSS questions (.61 ± .82) ($p<.01$). The AMS diagnostic threshold, including both a headache and a total score of 3 or greater, was reached in 9% (95%CI, 4-16) of measurements using the MLS and 4.5% (95%CI, 1.5-10) with the LLSS. The LLSS underestimates symptoms associated with AMS in 4-11 year old children. Age appropriate language must be used in the development of any AMS diagnostic tools; particularly for headache (the key symptom of AMS) and gastrointestinal symptoms. After normal values are established, the numerical threshold for AMS diagnosis may require modification in this age population.

118. FOOD CHOICES FOCUSING ON CARBOHYDRATE AND FAT CONSUMPTION AT FIVE ALTITUDES ON A CLIMBING EXPEDITION TO MOUNT EVEREST

Julie Ann Lickteig[1], Robert D. Reynolds[2], Patricia A. Deuster[3].
[1]Cardinal Stritch University, Milwaukee Wisconsin 53217, [2]University of Illinois, Chicago, Illinois, [3]Uniformed Services University of the Health Sciences, Bethesda, Maryland. Email: gnewuch@wirural.net.

The initial field study was designed to determine the overall consumption of energy, the distribution of the macronutrients which provided the energy, and the effects of increasing altitude on total energy consumption and on changes in energy-providing macronutrients. The 9-week dietary study included three meals and daily snacks on a 10-day rotation. A detailed record of energy intake was kept by five subjects who remained in base camp (5300m) and by 10 subjects who climbed to altitudes up to and including the summit of

Mt. Everest (8848m). Free choice of individual items and amounts within the diet was permitted. Intake of food and fluid was determined by means of monitored entries in 843 daily food records. It is commonly assumed that there is a natural increase in preference for consumption of higher carbohydrate foods at the highest altitudes. Contrary to these beliefs, the climbers did successfully self-select an average of 28.5% fat, 55.5% carbohydrate and 14.5% protein. A practical outgrowth of the study was the derivation of food frequency lists itemizing the top 25 choices in descending order for the five camps. Energy intake percentages for fat and carbohydrate were also determined for each of these 25 food selections. Upon reviewing the reported food items, it appears that higher fat foods should not be excluded from the packs of climbers going to higher altitudes. Energy-dense foods may be encouraged to provide extra energy and alleviate loss of weight.

119. THE EFFECT OF CARBON DIOXIDE ON CEREBRAL AND SKELETAL MUSCLE TISSUE OXYGENATION RESPONSES DURING ACUTE HYPOXIA

Sarah-Jane Lusina[1], Michael S. Koehle[2], A. William Sheel[1].
[1]Health and Integrative Physiology Laboratory, School of Human Kinetics, University of British Columbia, [2]Department of Family Medicine, Allan McGavin Sport Medicine Centre, University of British Columbia. Email: slusina@interchange.ubc.ca.

This study was conducted to test the hypothesis that during hypoxia, hypercapnia would increase mean arterial blood pressure (MAP), minute ventilation (VE), and maintain cerebral tissue oxygenation (cTOI) to a greater degree than normocapnia. A secondary purpose was to explore the effect of our intervention on skeletal muscle tissue oxygenation (mTOI). Eight healthy males completed two hypoxic protocols (SaO_2=80.3 ± 0.7%, mean ± SEM), defined by either increased (+5 Torr) or eupnic end-tidal PCO_2 ($PETCO_2$). Each protocol was delivered in random order on two separate days and consisted of five segments: three 10 min resting periods separated by a hypoxic ventilatory response test (HVR) and then a 20 min hypoxic exposure. Near infrared spectroscopy was applied to the left cerebral cortex and vastus lateralis muscle. During the 20 min hypoxic exposure, a trend towards a greater reduction in cTOI was observed for normocapnia compared with hypercapnia (8.2 ± 0.8 vs. 6.2 ± 0.8 %, $p=0.08$). A main effect for time was observed during the hypoxic exposure, showing a progressive reduction in cTOI ($p<0.01$) which was greater during the hypercapnic protocol ($p=0.05$). The reduction in mTOI was not significantly different between each protocol, however, a main effect for time showed that mTOI progressively decreased ($p<0.01$). The HVR values were not different between protocols (0.74 ± 0.1 L min-1 % SaO_2^{-1}, range: 0.21-1.23). Throughout the hypoxic exposure, hypercapnia compared to normocapnia resulted in greater increases in MAP (8.3 ± 1.4 vs 3.8 ± 1.4 mmHg, $p=0.04$) and VE (18.1 ± 2.9 vs 4.3 ± 2.9 L min-1, $p<0.01$).When hypoxia is combined with hypercapnia, cTOI is maintained to a greater degree than during normocapnia, a likely result of CO_2-mediated cerebral vasodilatation. The mTOI demonstrated no differential effect between protocols, and therefore the skeletal vascular responses do not appear to be modulated by CO_2 in the same way as the cerebral vasculature.

Acknowledgements: NSERC, MSFHR, CFI

120. ESTIMATING VA FROM FRESH GAS FLOW AND END-TIDAL FCO2 USING A SEQUENTIAL REBREATHING CIRCUIT

Alexandra Mardimae[1], David Preiss[2], Marat Slessarev[1], Joseph A. Fisher[3].
[1]Department of Physiology, University of Toronto, Toronto, Canada, [2]Department of Biomedical Engineering, University of Toronto, Toronto, Canada, [3]Department of Anaesthesia, Toronto General Hospital, Toronto, Canada. Email: a.mardimae@utoronto.ca.

To maintain isocapnia using a sequential rebreathing circuit, fresh gas flow (FGF) must be set equal to alveolar ventilation (VA). Simple observation can identify when FGF is equal to minute ventilation (VE), but not when it is equal to VA. We devised and validated a method of setting FGF to VA.Seven healthy subjects breathed via a commercial sequential rebreathing circuit supplying fresh gas and previously exhaled gas in sequence. Initially, FGF was set at approximately equal to VE. Minute CO_2 production ($VCO_{2)}$ was calculated as the product of the FGF and the fractional concentration of CO_2 in the exhaled gas reservoir. The VA was calculated as VCO_2 divided by the end-tidal fractional CO_2 concentration ($FETCO_2$). FGF was decreased to the calculated VA for a control period, following which subjects were asked to increase their ventilation. FGF was confirmed to be equal to VA if $FETCO_2$ did not change with marked hyperpnea.$FETCO_2$ did not change significantly from control breathing (41.22 ± 0.39 mmHg) to hyperventilation (40.89 ± 0.27 mmHg) ($p = 0.820$), despite increases in VE from 11.16 ± 2.70 L/min to 40.30 ± 2.68 L/min ($p < 0.001$). When breathing via a sequential rebreathing circuit, VA can be approximated from FGF, $FETCO_2$ and CO_2 concentrations in mixed exhaled gas, all of which are readily measurable parameters. The result is sufficiently accurate to maintain isocapnia at increased minute ventilation.

121. POSSIBLE ROLE OF LUNG VOLUMES, ALVEOLAR PO2 AND PCO2 ON BREATH HOLDING TIME

Shigeru Masuyama[1], Atsuko Masuda[2], Chikako Yoshino[3].
[1]Ryotokuji College, [2]Tokyo Medical and Dental University, [3]Chiba College of Allied Medical Sciences. Email: s_masu@za2.so-net.ne.jp.

To evaluate the effect of lung volume, alveolar hypoxia and hypercapnia on breath holding time (BHT), 10 healthy subjects participated in this study. They conducted breath holding (BH) starting from three different lung volume, i.e., TLC, FRC and RV (air trials: TLC-air, FRC-air and RV-air). In addition, to cancel alveolar hypoxia due to progress of BH, subjects started BH following 100% oxygen inhalation (oxygen trials: TLC-O_2, FRC-O_2 and RV-O_2). Furthermore they also performed BH from TLC right after inhalation air or 100% oxygen containing 5% CO_2 (CO_2 trials: TLC-airCO_2, TLC-O_2CO_2). Therefore, each subject challenged eight BH trials. $PETO_2$ and $PETCO_2$ at breaking point (BP) were also monitored. Mean BHT in TLC-air, FRC-air and RV-air were 86.5, 40.0 and 30.4 sec, respectively. And mean BHT in TLC-O_2, FRC-O_2 and RV-O_2 were 123.3, 84.4 and 45.3 sec, respectively. In all O_2 trials, $PETO_2$ at BP were higher than 400mmHg with higher $PETCO_2$ at BP than air trials. From these results, we confirmed that BHT was prolonged in accordance with starting lung volume and determined by combined effect of alveolar hypoxia and hypercapnia. However, when BHT was plotted against actual lung volumes, we found dogleg-like relationship between these two variables, which was not linear. On the other hand, when we cancelled alveolar hypocapnia by breathing mixed gases containing 5% CO_2 in TLC trials (CO_2 trials), BHT became shorter and the dogleg shape disappeared. Correlation of BHT with lung volume became linear significantly.These results suggest that a part of prolongation of BHT from TLC is explained by initial low alveolar hypocapnia, which is cancelled by 5% CO_2 inhalation, induced by CO_2 dilution by deep breath at TLC.

122. GASTRIC TONOMETRY AT REST AND DURING EXERCISE AT 5100M

Stuart McCorkell[1], Michael Grocott[1], Daniel Martin[1], Mark Cox[2], John Dick[1], Paul Gunning[3], André Vercueil[1], Michael Mythen[1].

[1]Centre for Aviation, Space and Extreme Environment Medicine, University College London, [2]Chelsea and Westminster NHS Trust, [3]Hammersmith Hospitals NHS Trust. Email: hypoxia@bellew.demon.co.uk

To determine the effect of exercise on intragastric CO_2 levels, measured using a gastric tonometer, at 5100m. Background: Reduced gastric perfusion (indicated by abnormal gastric CO_2 tonometry) is associated with an adverse outcome in critically ill patients(1). Location: Chamlang basecamp (5100m), Hongu Valley, Solu Khumbu, Nepal. Subjects: 5 well acclimatised healthy male volunteers. Preparation: Ranitidine 150mg 12 and 2 hours prior to study, nil by mouth 12 hours prior to study. Intervention: Stepping on and off 0.2m step, 6 Kg backpack, 30 minutes rest, 15 minutes at heart rate 110 (HR110), 15 minutes at heart rate 140 (HR140), 15 minutes rest. Measurements: Heart rate and oxygen saturation (Novametrix model 513 pulse oximeter), end-tidal(et)PCO_2 and gastric(g)PCO_2 (TONOCAP, Datex-Ohmeda, Finland). Gastric/end-tidal PCO_2 gap ($P(g\text{-}et)CO_2$) was calculated by subtracting gastric PCO_2 from end-tidal PCO_2 at each time point. Statistical analysis: Mean values were compared using 2 tailed paired t-tests. All subjects (Age range: 30-38) completed the protocol. Mean oxygen saturations: When compared with rest (SpO_2 91.2) HR110 (SpO_2 79.3, $p<0.05$) and HR140 (SpO_2 80.7, $p<0.05$) were reduced. Mean gastric/end-tidal CO_2 gap: When compared with rest (P(g-et)CO2 0.22) there was no increase at HR110 ($P(g\text{-}et)CO_2$ -0.18, NS) but a significant increase at HR140 ($P(g\text{-}et)CO_2$ 0.77, $p<0.05$).These are the first data demonstrating that intragastric PCO_2 during exercise in a hypoxic environment falls relative to end tidal PCO_2 suggesting that gastric perfusion may be reduced.

Reference

1. Mythen MG, Webb AR: Perioperative plasma volume expansion reduces the incidence of gut mucosal hypoperfusion during cardiac surgery. *Arch Surg* 1995, 130: 423-429

123. MODIFIED OXYGEN MASK TO INDUCE TARGET LEVELS OF HYPEROXIA AND HYPERCARBIA: A MORE EFFECTIVE ALTERNATIVE TO CARBOGEN

Eitan Prisman[1], Marat Slessarev[1], Takafumi Azami[2], Dan Nayot[1], David Preiss[1], Michael Milosevic[3], Joseph Fisher[1].

[1]Department of Anesthesiology, University Health Network and the University of Toronto, Toronto, Canada., [2]Department of Anesthesiology and Resuscitology, Nagoya City University Medical School, Nagoya, Japan, [3]Department of Radiation Oncology, Ontario Cancer Institute/ Princess Margaret Hospital, Toronto, Canada. Email: eitan.prisman@utoronto.ca

Carbogen (95-98% O_2, 5-2% CO_2) inhalation during radiotherapy is designed to enhance tumor radiosensitivity by increasing cellular PO_2. CO_2 is administered to increase tumor perfusion. In practice, however, carbogen is inconsistent in raising PCO_2. We investigated a partial rebreathing method to raise PCO_2, and compared its efficacy to that of carbogen. Ten healthy volunteers breathed 1.5, 3 and 5% carbogen in 5 minute stages via a non-rebreathing circuit. At the end of the 5% carbogen stage, four volunteers voluntarily hyperventilated. All the volunteers then breathed 100% oxygen through a commercial sequential gas delivery oxygen mask modified by attaching a reservoir to its exhalation port. Oxygen flow to the circuit was reduced to induce hypercapnia. At the end of the study, the same four subjects voluntarily hyperventilated. In all experiments minute ventilation and end-tidal PCO_2 ($PETCO_2$) were measured at steady-state. $PETCO_2$ did not increase from baseline (40±1.5 mmHg) when 1.5 ($p=0.26$) and 3% carbogen ($p=0.38$) were inhaled. Breathing 5% carbogen increased $PETCO_2$ to 45±1.6 mmHg ($p<0.001$); however, voluntary hyperventilation reduced $PETCO_2$ back to control levels ($p=0.987$). With the sequential gas delivery method, reducing O2 flow to 4.3±0.7 L/min increased $PETCO_2$ from 41±2.0mmHg (baseline) to 46±2.1 mmHg ($p<0.001$). In contrast to carbogen, however, voluntary hyperventilation at the same O_2 flow did not reduce $PETCO_2$ ($p=0.379$). Precise $PETCO_2$ can be reliably induced and maintained by controlling O_2 flow into a modified sequential gas delivery system. We suggest that this is a simpler and more reliable means than carbogen, of raising arterial PCO_2 during radiotherapy.

124. LOW BIRTH WEIGHT IN COLORADO: ANALYSIS USING GEOGRAPHIC INFORMATION SYSTEMS

Susan Niermeyer[1], Devon Williford[2], Ingrid Asmus[2], Benjamin Honigman[1], Lorna G. Moore[1], Mark Egbert[2].

1University of Colorado Denver and Health Sciences Center; Denver, Colorado USA, 2Colorado Department of Public Health and Environment, Denver, Colorado, USA. Email: susan.niermeyer@uchsc.edu

The rate of low birth weight (< 2500 grams) in Colorado consistently exceeds the national average. Analyzing risk factors for low birth weight at altitude has been difficult due to the inability to precisely define the elevation of the mother during pregnancy. The use of geographic information systems (GIS) in the analysis of low birth weight in Colorado results in greater accuracy in altitude assignment for births, new methods for examining the interaction of altitude with social and medical factors, and enhanced graphic representation of results as compared with previous analyses. To advance understanding of the interaction between the environment (altitude) and potentially modifiable health and behavioral factors, 560,840 birth records from 1993-2002 were assigned latitude, longitude, and accurate elevation based on the mother's residence. Statistical tools were used to detect significant clusters of events (SatScan and spatial statistics tools found in ArcGIS 9.0). Clusters of low weight births and maternal smoking were identified both within prescribed ranges of altitude and across all altitudes. ArcGIS software was then used to create maps that linked altitude, demographic, and health services data.GIS analysis offers unique advantages for the study of altitude-related health conditions.

Acknowledgements: Funded by the Colorado Tobacco Research Program. Dedicated to John T. Reeves, who nurtured the idea and served as consultant.

125. EFFECTS OF SPRINT INTERVAL TRAINING UNDER NORMOBARIC NORMOXIA AND HYPOXIA ON MYOSIN HEAVY CHAIN COMPOSITION AND BIOENERGETIC PROPERTIES IN RAT DIAPHRAGM

Yuji Ogura[1], Hisashi Naito[1], Jin Uchimaru[1], Takao Sugiura[2], Shizuo Katamoto[1].

[1]Juntendo University, Chiba, Japan, [2]Yamaguchi University, Yamaguchi, Japan. Email: yuji_ogura@nifty.com

The purposes of the present study were to examine 1) whether sprint interval training (SIT) could alter the myosin heavy chain (MyHC) composition and bioenergetic properties of rat diaphragm, 2) whether hypoxia could enhance the effects of SIT on rat diaphragm. The present study was approved by the Juntendo University Animal Care and Use Committee. Male Wistar rats (7 weeks old) were divided into 3 groups with matched weight, control: CON (n=7), normoxic training: NT (n=7), hypoxic training: HT (n=7). SIT (1 min/sprint, 6-10 repetitions/day and 5-6 days/week for 9 weeks) was conducted on an animal treadmill under oxygen concentration of 20.9% for NT and 14.5% for HT. The treadmill speed was 75-80 m/min at the final week. Costal diaphragm portions were removed 48 hours after the last training session to analyze MyHC composition (sodium dodecyl sulfate polyacrylamide gel electrophoresis), and citrate synthase (CS) and lactate dehydrogenase (LDH) activities (spectrophotometry). In MyHC composition, type IIa isoforms were increased (CON: 20.5 < NT: 24.6 < HT: 30.1%, $P < 0.05$) and type IId isoform were decreased (CON: 51.7 > NT: 47.2 > HT: 42.1%, $P < 0.05$) by SIT. Thus, hypoxia resulted in greater changes of MyHC composition. CS activities were increased (CON: 293 ± 31 < NT: 342 ± 38 < HT: 391 ± 15 nM/min/mg protein, $P < 0.05$) by SIT, and the activity of HT was significantly higher than NT ($P < 0.05$). But, LDH activities were decreased by SIT. SIT could induce the increasing of oxidative capacity and the fast-to-slow shift of MyHC composition in diaphragm, which would contribute to improve the diaphragmatic endurance ability. In addition hypoxia could enhance such improvements.

126. NON-INVASIVE MEASUREMENT OF CARDIAC OUTPUT DURING SPONTANEOUS BREATHING

David Preiss[1], Takafumi Azami[2], George Volgyesi[3], Arthur Slutsky[1], Ludwik Fedorko[3], George Djaiani[3], Joseph Fisher[1].

[1]University of Toronto, Toronto Canada, [2]Nagoya City University Hospital, Nagoya City, Japan, [3]Toronto General Hospital, Toronto Canada. Email: david.preiss@utoronto.ca

All respiratory-based methods of measuring cardiac output depend on imposing a step-change in alveolar ventilation (VA) for a particular gas. For CO_2, this can be accomplished by interposing respiratory deadspace in the breathing circuit, but therefore requires a uniform breathing pattern. We developed a method of reducing VA that is independent of breathing pattern using a new breathing circuit. We evaluated this method's accuracy by comparing its measurements (QNI) with those of thermodilution (QTD) on cardiac patients in the ICU, as well as its precision by performing repeated tests on subjects in a laboratory. Our subjects consisted of 31 extubated post cardiac surgery patients in the cardiovascular intensive care unit. The reduction in VA was induced by a step reduction in gas flow to the circuit. The balance of ventilation was composed of previously exhaled gas and no respiratory manoeuvre was required by the patient. QTD was measured simultaneously. We also conducted measurements to evaluate precision by performing 8 repeated tests on 24 subjects in a laboratory setting. In our validation study, QNI was highly correlated with QTD (R2 = 0.89) despite a wide range of breathing patterns. The bias and precision of the non-invasive method were -0.08 and 0.80 L/min, respectively. The repeatability of QNI, measured as the SD of repeated tests, was 0.73 L/min, which is slightly less that the repeatability of QTD, which is usually reported as 0.60 L/min.We have developed and tested a new method for measuring cardiac output non-invasively in spontaneously breathing subjects. Although measures to improve accuracy are still needed, our method correlated well with thermodilution and may eventually provide researchers with a new, clinically useful, non-invasive test.

127. HIGH ALTITUDE PULMONARY EDEMA FOLLOWING MARIJUANA SMOKE INHALATION

Piotr Szawarski[1], Tommy O'Neill[2], Annabel Nickol[3], Paul Richards[4]

[1]Department of Anaesthesia, Whittington Hospital, Highgate Hill, London, UK, [2]Department of Anaesthesia, Trafford Hospital, Manchester, UK, [3]Chest Unit, Churchill Hospital Oxford OX3 7LJ, UK, [4]The Surgery, London Rd, Wickford, Essex, UK Email: zmierzchowiec@aol.com (P Szawarski)

Association between cannabis smoke and high altitude pulmonary edema (HAPE) has not been described. This is a case report of HAPE in a non-smoker following inhalation of marijuana smoke. We believe marijuana may modulate hypoxic pulmonary vasoconstriction. A healthy, non-smoking 26 year-old male participated in a high altitude expedition. The ascent profile allowed for acclimatization. At 2550m and having asymptomatically been to 3100m he smoked a large quantity of marijuana. He developed dry cough, exertional dyspnoea and was disproportionately tired. He continued with the trek that day crossing a pass at 3050m, descending to camp at 2800m. There he subjectively worsened. On examination he was apyrexial, alert, with pulse 102min^{-1}, blood pressure 130/88mmHg, respiratory rate 18min-1, bilateral basal crepitations and finger plethysmography oxygen saturation 89% falling to 79% on minimal exertion. HAPE was diagnosed. The treatment was descent by 600m, nifedipine (SR 20mg tds), azithromycin and acetazolamide (250mg bd). Following rest, taking nifedipine and acetazolamide, he uneventfully continued the ascent to 5100m. Pulmonary Doppler showed significant increase in pulmonary arterial pressure in spite of nifedipine. It is known that marijuana does not cause severe changes in pulmonary capillary permeability [1] though chronic use may cause airway inflammation [2]. It is possible that marijuana smoke has an effect on hypoxic pulmonary vasoconstriction (HPV). Animal studies suggest smoking can augment HPV [3]. Effect of smoking and cannabis use on HPV in humans deserves further studies.

References:

1. Gil E et al Acute and chronic effects of marijuana smoking on pulmonary alveolar permeability Life Sci 1995;56:2193-9;
2. Roth MD et al Airway inflammation in young marijuana and tobacco smokers Am J Resp Crit Care Med 1998;157(3pt1):928-37;
3. Yang GT, Wang DX Influence of cigarette smoking on the hypoxic pulmonary vasoconstriction in isolated rat lung-the role of prostaglandins and leukotrienes. J Tongji Med Univ 1992;12:6-10

Acknowledgement: This work was carried out in association with Medical Expeditions.

128. EXPRESSION OF PROTEINS OF IRON METABOLISM IN HUMAN SKELETAL MUSCLE AT HIGH ALTITUDE

Paul Robach[1], Gaetano Cairo[2], José AL Calbet[3], Francesca Bernuzzi[2], Paolo Santambrogio[4], Stéphane Moutereau[5], Carsten Lundby[6].

[1]Ecole Nationale de Ski et d'Alpinisme, 74401 Chamonix, France, [2]Institute of General Pathology, University of Milan, 20133 Milan, Italy, [3]Department of Physical Education, University of Las Palmas de Gran Canaria, Spain, [4]Protein Engineering Unit, Dibit, IRCCS H.S. Raffaele, Milan, Italy, [5]Laboratoire de Biochimie, Hôpital Henri-Mondor, 94000 Créteil, France, [6]The Copenhagen Muscle Research Centre, Rigshospitalet, 2200 Copenhagen N, Denmark. Email: paul.robach@ensa.jeunesse-sports.fr.

Hypoxia enhances the synthesis of several hemoproteins. In cell lines exposed to hypoxia, transferrin receptor (TfR) – a membrane protein that controls cellular iron uptake and contributes to heme synthesis - was previously found upregulated. Other iron-related proteins were also found modulated by hypoxia. However, the regulation of these proteins during hypoxia at the muscle level is unknown. The present study therefore evaluated the effect of hypobaric hypoxia on the expression of proteins involved in iron metabolism in human skeletal muscle. Nine male lowlanders were evaluated at sea-level (SL) and after 7-9 days spent at high altitude (HA, 4,559 m). Soluble TfR (sTfR), ferritin and erythropoietin (EPO) were determined in venous serum by standard methods. Muscle biopsy specimens were obtained from the vastus lateralis to assess the expression of TfR by immunoblot analysis, H and L ferritin subunits by ELISA, Iron Regulatory Protein (IRP) binding activity by bandshift analysis and Hypoxia Inducible Factor (HIF)-1α; and -2α; mRNAs by real-time RT-PCR. Serum analysis showed that HA induced a two-fold increase in sTfR levels, a significant increase in EPO and a strong decrease in ferritin concentrations. Analysis of muscle samples revealed that both HIF-1α and HIF-2α mRNAs levels were 2-3 fold higher in HA. Surprisingly, TfR content was diminished by 50 % (average decrease) in HA, along with a decreased IRP binding activity. HA did not alter the content of H ferritin subunits, but decreased the content of L ferritin subunits. Expression of iron-related proteins was decreased in skeletal muscle during prolonged hypoxia, at a time when erythropoiesis was enhanced. This unexpected response into the muscle tissue suggests that the strong iron demand associated with high erythropoiesis would trigger a mobilization of muscle iron stores.

Acknowledgements: This work was supported by grants from Novo Nordisk and Sundhedsvidenskabligt Forskningsråd

129. RELIABILITY OF INDUCTION OF HYPOXIA FOR HYPOXIC TRAINING WITH A NEW CIRCUIT COMPARED TO THAT WITH ALTIPOWER

Lisa Rodrigues[1], David Preiss[2], Marat Slessarev[3], Joseph A. Fisher[4].
[1]Department of Anesthesia, Toronto General Hospital, Toronto, Canada, [2]Department of Biomedical Engineering, University of Toronto, Toronto, Canada, [3]Department of Physiology, University of Toronto, Toronto, Canada, [4]Department of Anesthesia, Toronto General Hospital, Toronto, Canada. Email: lisa_j_rodrigues@hotmail.com

Intermittent hypoxic training has been shown to enhance athletic performance and high altitude acclimatization. However, efficacy of a training device may be limited by the reliability of induction of hypoxia. We devised a semi-closed breathing circuit designed to reliably attain and maintain target levels of $FETO_2$ independent of increases in minute ventilation. The purpose of the study was to compare the performance of our circuit to a popular commercial hypoxic training device (Altipower) that also does not require any electronics or compressed gases. Five subjects participated in the study. Each subject breathed through Altipower at each of the 4 settings set by the manufacturer, for 5 min and then hyperventilated for 1 min. Subjects breathed room air at rest between each test. The same protocol was followed while breathing via the new circuit. $FETO_2$ and SpO_2% was measured continuously. In our circuit, the precise flow of ambient air was set at 60% of the participant's alveolar ventilation (as estimated by the Radford nomogram) for the first level, followed by 3 further reductions of approximately 5% of VA. With the Altipower there was no consistent reduction in $FETO_2$ at any of the settings. In some subjects there was no reduction and in others the reductions were to $FETO_2$ less than 6% (at levels 3 and 4), which the subjects found intolerable. Hyperventilation returned the $FETO_2$ to control in the majority of the subjects. With our circuit the reductions in O_2 were consistent from subject to subject (FETO2 were within a small range) and were further reduced at each incremental setting. Hyperventilation had little effect on $FETO_2$ (changes were less than 1% at all settings). Our hypoxic circuit allows reliable setting of $FETO_2$, which is well maintained even with hyperventilation.

130. THE PROFILE OF HYPOXIA EXPOSURE INFLUENCES THE RELATIONSHIP BETWEEN BLOOD PRESSURE & INOS RESPONSE

George Rodway[1], Jigme Sethi[2], Leslie Hoffman[2], Yvette Conley[2], Stefan Ryter[2], Augustine Choi[2], Thomas Zullo[2], Mark Sanders[2].

[1]The Ohio State University, The University of Pittsburgh, [2]The University of Pittsburgh. Email: rodway.1@osu.edu.

Determinants of the nature and magnitude of the hemodynamic responses to hypoxia may include the specific profile of exposure and variation in the expression of relevant genes such as those responsible for inducible nitric oxide synthase (iNOS). The purpose of this investigation was to examine the relationship between blood pressure (BP) and iNOS mRNA to daily comparable total exposure time of intermittent hypoxia (IH) vs. continuous hypoxia (CH). Ten normal males had six 10-min. hypoxic exposures (oxyhemoglobin saturation [SpO_2] = 80-90%) separated by 10 min. of normoxia on 3 consecutive days. Subjects also had 3 consecutive days of CH (60 min/day; SpO_2: 80-90%). A washout period of >7 days separated IH and CH exposure blocks. Heart rate, BP, SpO_2, and $ETCO_2$ were recorded during the 5 min. prior to the start of each day's IH and CH session, as well as during the last 5 min. of hypoxia exposure on each day. Venous blood for iNOS mRNA was obtained (using PAXgene Blood RNA System) before IH and CH exposure on day 1, and 2 hours after the last exposure on day 3. The relationship between the hemodynamic and molecular parameters was determined via nonparametric correlation. Usable data for analysis were available on 9 subjects. At the end of the day 3 IH session, there was a significant negative correlation ($p<0.01$) between both diastolic and mean BP with iNOS mRNA. The negative correlation between BP and iNOS mRNA in conjunction with IH, but not CH, exposure suggests that the hemodynamic response to IH, but not CH, may be modulated by iNOS. The inter-individual differences in the iNOS/BP relationship during IH may provide further insight into hypertension development in humans undergoing regular episodic hypoxia exposure.

This work was supported by the American Lung Association Lung Health Dissertation Award LH-12-N, NRSA Predoctoral Fellowship F31 NR 08458-01, Sigma Theta Tau International (Eta Chapter), and Division of Pulmonary, Allergy & Critical Care Medicine, Univers

131. SENSITIVITY ANALYSIS OF THE FACTORS INFLUENCING VO2,MAX IN BIRDS DURING NORMOXIA AND HYPOXIA

Graham Scott, William Milsom.

Department of Zoology, University of British Columbia. Email: scott@zoology.ubc.ca.

The objective of this study was to examine how various factors may influence maximal oxygen consumption in birds during normoxia, moderate hypoxia, and severe hypoxia. In doing so, we hope to reveal the traits that may be adaptive in high altitude species. We used a theoretical approach involving a numerical model of three equations to calculate oxygen consumption, namely mass conservation across the lungs and a version of the Fick equation at both the lungs and tissues. Physiological traits were then varied to determine the relative influence each has on VO_2max. Of those traits that were analyzed, increasing the diffusional conductance of the tissue for O_2 (DT) had the greatest influence on VO_2,max for all environmental oxygen concentrations, while conductance at the lungs (DL) had a much more modest effect. In normoxia, low haemoglobin (Hb) oxygen affinity (high P50), high Hb-O_2 cooperativity (Hill coefficients above 2.8), and high Bohr shift all had beneficial effects on oxygen consumption. In contrast, severe hypoxia favoured a lower P50 and less cooperativity, while a pronounced Bohr shift had less influence. Ventilation rate, cardiac output, and Hb concentration all had a greater influence on VO_2,max during severe hypoxia, but only ventilation had appreciable effects. Perhaps most interesting was the interaction between P50 and DT: at lower P50, DT had a much greater influence on oxygen consumption at all environmental oxygen concentrations. Indeed, the greatest relative increases in VO_2,max were always observed when P50 decreased and DT increased concurrently. These results suggest that high Hb-O_2 affinity increases the selective advantage of high tissue O_2 conductance, and that concurrent changes in both P50 and DT may be required for performance at high altitude in birds.

132. GENDER-SPECIFIC EFFECT OF NMDA GLUTAMATE RECEPTORS ON RESPIRATORY AND METABOLIC ADAPTATION TO CHRONIC HYPOXIA IN NEWBORN RATS

Mirza Shafiulla Baig, Vincent Joseph

University Laval, Dpt Pediatrics, Quebec, Canada. Email: joseph.vincent@crsfa.ulaval.ca

Newborn mammals exposed to chronic hypoxia develop several mechanisms including metabolic and ventilatory adjustments, but the neural mechanisms involved in these modifications are not known. Since previous studies have reported that the expression of glutamatergic NMDA receptor is drastically upregulated during chronic hypoxia in rat pups, we tested the hypothesis that the function of NMDA receptors on respiratory and metabolic homeostasis is altered in newborn rats raised under chronic hypoxia. Respiratory and metabolic recordings were performed in 10 days-old rat pups (P10) raised from one day before birth in chronic hypoxia (CHx: 12-13% O_2) or normoxia (Nx: 21% O_2). Using whole body plethysmography, we recorded minute ventilation (Ve-mL/min/100g), Rectal Temperature (Tb-°C) and oxygen consumption (VO_2 -mL/min/100g), 30 minutes after intraperitonial injection of vehicle or NMDA receptor antagonist MK-801 (1mg/kg). Recording chamber was maintained at 32°C. Recordings were performed in males and females under conditions used during growth (CHx or Nx).CHx pups had lower body weight (males -29%; females -27% - both $p<0.0001$) and Tb (males -0.5 °C ; females -0.9°C - both $p<0.0001$) than Nx. Hypoxic male and female pups had similar VO_2 than normoxic, while Ve was increased in CHx males (+40% - p=0.001) but not in CHx females (+2% - p=ns). In normoxic rats MK-801 had no effect. In hypoxic males, after MK-801 injection Tb, VO_2 and Ve dropped (Tb: -0,9°C - $p<0.01$; VO2: -21% - $p<0.02$; Ve: -20% - $p<0.05$ vs. saline) while in females only Tb dropped significantly (-0.9 °C - $p<0.01$; VO_2: -13% - p=ns; Ve: +18% p=ns).Male rat pups raised in hypoxia relied on NMDA glutamate receptors function to maintain VO_2, Ve and Tb at an optimal level.

Acknowledgements: Funded by Natural Sciences and Engineering Research Council of Canada (NSERC), MSB holds a fellowship from Fondation de la Recherche des Maladies Infantiles.

133. CEREBRAL BLOOD FLOW AND METABOLISM IN SEVERELY HEAD-INJURED PATIENTS WITH HYPOTHERMIA

Naoko Shiga[1], Yasutaka Naoe[1], Norihumi Ninomiya[1], Osamu Tone[2], Hiroki Tomita[2].

[1]Department of Emergency and Critical Care Medicine, Nippon Medical School Tama Nagayama Hospital, [2]Department of Neurosurgery, Musashino Red Cross Hospital. Email: shigan@nms.ac.jp.

The effect of therapeutic hypothermia for head injury is controversial. Clifton mentioned the impact of hypothermia on admission in severely head-injured patients (N Engl J Med 2001 Feb). We compared severely head-injured patients of accidental hypothermia (AH group) and those who were not hypothermia on admission and treated by therapeutic hypothermia (TH group) by measuring cerebral blood flow (CBF) and cerebral metabolic rates for oxygen (CMRO2). In five cases of acute subdural hematoma (Glasgow Coma Scale scores of 6 or less on admission), CBF and $CMRO_2$ were measured within 5 days after injury by Kety-Schmidt technique using N_2O as the indicator. Three cases of AH group and 2 cases of TH group were all treated with mild hypothermia (33-34degrees Celsius) after evacuation of hematoma. Three cases except for moderate hypothermia cases were sedated with Midazolam during cooling. Outcomes were determined at discharge using Glasgow Outcome Scale.In AH group, two cases of moderate hypothermia on admission (29.5-31degrees Celsius) showed extremely low CBF (15.4 and 6.9ml/100g/min) and $CMRO_2$ (0.17 and 0.21ml/100g/min), and both of them died. In the rest of AH group, the case of mild hypothermia (34.5degrees Celsius), CBF was 32.9 and $CMRO_2$ was 2.87ml/100g/min, and outcome was SD. In TH group, CBF were 29.4 and 49.3 ml/100g/min, CMRO2 were 1.48 and 2.52ml/100g/min, and outcomes were SD and MD.

134. NEW CHEMICAL OXYGEN GENERATOR TESTED IN MT. FUJI

Tadashi Shinozuka[1], Akio Konishi[2].

[1]Japanese Society of Travel Medicine, TOKYO, JAPAN, [2]Shin-TOKYO Hospital, Matsudo, JAPAN. Email: shinozuka@obm-med.co.jp

In Japan, 5.6 million people enjoy mountaineering. So, we (the members of Japaense Society of Travel Medicine) give them practical safety advice of mountaineering, including of AMS (Acute Mountain Sickness) prevention and self-treatment. We tested the effectiveness of New Chemical Oxygen Generator (O_2 Forest, ACS Co.Ltd.,Tokyo,Japan) in Mt. Fuji (3,776m).We measured oxygen saturation of 33 healthy volunteers at the hight of 2,500m, 2,700m, 3,000m, 3,300m, 3,600m, 3,776m, using portable pulse-oxymeter (FO-0001-3A, Casio Co.Ltd.,Tokyo, Japan). After each measurement, low flow oxygen (0.4 L/Min.), generated by New Chemical Oxygen Generator, was inhaled for 3 minutes, and oxygen saturation was again measured and recorded. Oxygen saturation average values without oxygen inhalation are as follows: 93.2%(2,500m), 92.9%(2,700m), 92.3%(3,000m), 83.6%(3,600m), 81.4%(3.776m). Oxygen saturation after 3 minutes oxygen inhalation are as follows: 93.7%(2,500m), 93.5%(2,700m), 93.6%(3,000m), 92.2%(3,300m), 91.6%(3,600m), 90.7%(3,776m). New Chemical Oxygen Generator enhances oxygen saturation at the height from 2,500m up to 3,776m in Mt. Fuji. So, this new portable oxygen generator could be an excellent modality for the treatment of mild and moderate case of AMS.

Acknowledgements: 33 sets of portable oxygen generators were donated from ACS Co.Ltd. Japanese Society of Travel Medicine Resarch Fund was given to this project.

135. CEREBROVASCULAR RESPONSE TO ULTRA-SHORT CYCLIC ALTERATIONS IN END-TIDAL PCO2

Marat Slessarev[1], Eitan Prisman[1], David Preiss[1], James Duffin[1], Joseph Fisher[1].

[1]University Health Network, University of Toronto, Toronto, Canada. Email: marat.slessarev@ utoronto.ca.

Assessment of cerebrovascular reactivity with functional MRI requires rapid cycling of end-tidal PCO_2 ($PETCO_2$) between two steady-states. To optimize signal to noise ratio we devised a method of iso-oxic cycling between $PETCO_2$ of 30 and 40 mmHg with 15 s transitions and steady state (<2 mmHg variation in $PETCO_2$) of 30 s at each level (rapid cycling). We used trans-cranial Doppler to confirm that the protocol provides sufficient time for full cerebrovascular response. In addition, we tested whether there is hysteresis or fatigue of response with repeated cycles. We alternated 'rapid cycles' with periods of 'slow cycles' in which the steady state components were prolonged to 2 min but transition rates remained unchanged. The protocol was carried out for 15 min in 4 subjects. Time constants for the rising MCAV were the same in fast and slow cycles, as were those of the falling MCAV. MCAV reached the same levels at each respective 'steady state' phase of the rapid and slow cycles. MCAV response to each level of $PETCO_2$ did not change over the course of the experiment. Rapid square-wave cycles with steady-state phases as short as 30 seconds exhibit full MCAV response to changes in $PETCO_2$ without fatigue or hysteresis. We speculate that similar results could be expected with the regional blood flow as measured by MRI.

136. HOW HIGH CAN YOU GET: RAISING THE ANTE ON OXYGEN DELIVERY

Marat Slessarev[1], Ron Somogyi[1], David Preiss[1], Alex Vesely[1], Hiroshi Sasano[2], Joseph Fisher[1].

[1]University Health Network, University of Toronto, Toronto, Canada, [2]Department of Anesthesiology and Resuscitology, Nagoya City University Medical School, Nagoya, Japan. Email: marat.slessarev@utoronto.ca

Non-rebreathing (NRM) and Venturi O_2 masks cannot consistently provide high inspired fractional concentrations of oxygen (FIO_2) to breathless or severely hypoxic patients. We compared the performance of these masks to a new O_2 mask (HiOx80) that exploits efficiencies afforded by sequential gas delivery. Eight volunteers breathed through each of the masks at rest and at 10, 14, 18, 24 and 30 L/min. O_2 flow to the HiOx80 mask was 2, 4 and 8 L/min, but 8 L/min to the other masks. We used end tidal partial pressures of O_2 and CO_2 and the alveolar gas equation to calculate FIO_2.The HiOx80 was the only mask to provide $FIO_2 > 0.8$ and it consistently provided the highest FIO_2 among the three masks (from 0.95 ± 0.03 at resting ventilation to 0.47 ± 0.03 at 30 L/min) when oxygen flow was set to 8 L/min ($p<0.001$). HiOx80 provided an $FIO_2 > 0.4$ at minute ventilations of ≤ 18 L/min with oxygen flow of only 4 L/min ($p<0.001$). When oxygen flow was further reduced to 2 L/min an $FIO_2 > 0.4$ was achieved at minute ventilations of <10 L/min ($p<0.05$). FIO_2 delivered by Hudson and HiOx80 masks decreased significantly ($p<0.05$) with increasing minute ventilations, whereas FIO_2 with the Venturi mask did not change significantly from 0.4 ($P>0.05$).We conclude that HiOx80 should be used preferentially to provide high $FIO_{2,}$ as well as for efficient delivery of O_2 when supplies are limited.

137. THE TIEN SHAN MOUNTAINS (KAZAKHSTAN): THE NEW FRONTIER OF ALTITUDE RESEARCH

Marat Slessarev[1], Ron Somogyi[1], David Preiss[1], Joseph Fisher[1].
[1]*University Health Network, University of Toronto, Toronto, Canada. Email: ron.somogyi@utoronto.ca.*

Suitable facilities must be readily accessible, inexpensive, and have adequate infrastructure to support instruments used for high altitude research. Researchers tend to frequent the same, but limited facilities in the Alps, Himalayas and Andes. We engaged in a pilot project to explore the feasibility of adding the Tien Shen Mountains in Kazakhstan to the list of suitable venues. A group of 4 Canadian altitude researchers joined The Kazakhstan Centre for Disaster Medicine and Republican Search & Rescue Team to carry out three studies. The local teams arranged for local transportation, shelter, electrical access, communications, backup medical and rescue support, and necessary provisions for the destination altitudes. They stayed on to provide continuous logistic support including volunteering as study subjects. Among the resources we used were all-terrain vehicles, horses, electrical generators, large tents, heaters, portable blood gas and biochemical laboratory. Helicopters are available but we did not require them. Accessible altitudes include 2200 m (Chimbulak) and 4000 m (Amangeldi). Access to altitudes up to 7000 m requires advanced climbing skills. Local search and rescue personnel are prepared to pre-install safety lines along the rout to camp and provide climbing support. Heavy equipment can be delivered by helicopter. The entire region is found within close vicinity of major cities with access to modern medical, communication and transportation facilities. The high altitude region is most accessible from mid-July to mid-September. Cost is on the basis of cost recovery (fuel, personnel). Cost is further defrayed in collaborative studies by each party bearing expenses.Contact information will be provided.

Acknowledgements: The Kazakhstan Centre for Disaster Medicine and Republican Search & Rescue Team

138. ALTERATIONS IN COGNITIVE FUNCTION WITH O2 SUPPLEMENTATION AT MODERATE ALTITUDE

Ron Somogyi[1], Marat Slessarev[1], David Preiss[1], Joseph Bleiberg[2], Joseph Fisher[1].
[1]*University of Toronto, University Health Network, Department of Anesthesia, Toronto, Canada,* [2]*Center for Cognitive Neuroscience, National Rehabilitation Hospital, Washington, D.C. Email: ron.somogyi@utoronto.ca.*

It is not clear to what extent cognitive function is altered by hypoxia or oxygen supplementation at moderate altitude. We performed a randomized double blind study of physiological and cognitive response at 800 m and 3200 m before and after administration of supplemental O_2 via HiOx80 at 1 L/min in 8 healthy male volunteers. The ANAM battery of tests was used to assess reaction time, mathematical processing, procedural memory and code substitution. In comparison to 800 m, at 3200 m, oxygen saturation decreased (to 90±1% from 97±0 %) and heart rate increased (to 107±4 bpm from 80±4 bpm). Supplemental O_2 at 3200 m significantly increased arterial oxygen saturation (90±1 vs. 97±0 %) and decreased heart rate (94±5 vs. 107±4 bpm), but had no effect on these variables at 800 m. No changes in cognitive function were identified under any condition. The ANAM tests did not detect cognitive deterioration with acute exposure to low-moderate altitude, possibly because of inadequate hypoxic stimulus. Low flow O_2 supplementation at 3200 m ameliorates select physiological effects of altitude.

139. DOES CEREBRAL VASCULAR REACTIVITY ACCLIMATIZE

Alex Vesely[1], Ron Somogyi[1], Takafumi Azami[2], Eitan Prisman[1], David Preiss[1], James Duffin[1], Joseph Fisher[1].

[1]University of Toronto, Toronto, Canada, [2]Nagoya City University Medical School, Nagoya, Japan. Email: alex.vesely@utoronto.ca.

At altitude, hypoxia and hypocapnia result in changes in cerebral blood flow (CBF), as defined by the subject's underlying cerebral vascular reactivity (CVR) curve. It is important to characterize the exact nature of this response in order to understand its role in maintaining cerebral oxygen delivery, and its possible role in the pathogenesis of HACE. We hypothesized that, similar to ventilatory chemoreflexes, CVR may show acclimatization. One female and five male healthy volunteers were studied at sea level and after 5 days at 3480 m. Cerebral blood flow velocity (CBFv) was measured using transcranial doppler ultrasound. CVR was assessed as the response of CBFv over a continuous range of $PetCO_2$ at two iso-oxic values of $PetO_2$, using modified Read rebreathing tests with iso-oxia maintained at $PetO_2$ of 50 mmHg or 150 mmHg. Each subject performed one hypoxic and one hyperoxic rebreathing test at sea level prior to ascent (SL), and after 5 days at altitude (Alt). T-test was used to compare slopes of linear fits to CBFv versus $PetCO_2$ data. In three subjects, CBFv increased continuously with rising PCO_2, however surprisingly, in the other three subjects, CBFv plateaued before maximally tolerated PCO_2 was reached – this was not an artifact from signal cutoff. A trend towards increased CVR at altitude was seen but did not reach statistical significance due to intersubject variability. Resting PCO_2 (mmHg) - SL: 39.9 +/- 1.5, Alt: 31.6 +/- 1.7 ($p<0.05$); Resting CBF (cm/s) - SL: 47 +/- 2, Alt: 50 +/- 3; CVR (cm/s/mmHg) - SL: 1.33 +/- 0.12, Alt: 1.43 +/- 0.24.1. Further study is needed, however these data imply that cerebral vascular reactivity may acclimatize by increasing in sensitivity. This may help to preserve CBFv and cerebral oxygen delivery in the face of falling $PetCO_2$ due to ventilatory acclimatization. It appears that in some subjects CBFv can reach a maximum at relatively low PCO_2.

140. ISOCAPNIC AND POIKILOCAPNIC HYPOXIA VENTILATORY RESPONSE CONSENSUS METHODS IN HUMANS

Craig Steinback[1], John Severinghaus[2], Philip Ainslie[1], Marc Poulin[1].
[1]University of Calgary, Calgary, Canada, [2]University of California - San Francisco, San Francisco, USA. Email: poulin@ucalgary.ca.

At the 13th Hypoxia Symposia (2003), consensus methods were proposed for measuring hypoxic ventilatory responses (HVR) during 20 min of both isocapnic (IH) and poikilocapnic (PH) hypoxia, and for better predicting success in altitude acclimatization. During IH, HVR at 5 min quantifies peripheral chemoreceptor stimulation to hypoxia per se while HVR at 20 min measures hypoxic ventilatory decline (HVD). During PH, HVR at 5 min tests the interaction of peripheral chemosensitivity with the concomitant hypocapnic alkalosis while the value at 20 min includes HVD, as occurs at altitude. We examined IH and PH HVR in 7 normal adults, age 26±3yrs, during two randomly assigned 20 min protocols. During IH, $PETCO_2$ was held at 38±1.0 Torr (1 Torr above resting values) while $PETO_2$, was reduced stepwise using dynamic end-tidal gas forcing to 45 Torr. During PH, $PETO_2$ was reduced stepwise to 45 Torr with zero inspired CO_2. Tests were separated by 1 hour. During IH, iHVR calculated as $\Delta VE/\Delta SpO_2$ (L/min/%) was 2.37±0.61 and 0.78±0.27 at 5 and 20 min, respectively ($P<0.05$). HVD was thus 43.7±5.4 %. During PH, $PETCO_2$ fell 5 and 6 Torr at 5 and 20 min, respectively, although VE was not measurably increased. pHVR reported as $\Delta PETCO_2/\Delta SpO_2$ (mmHg/%) was 0.33±0.05 and 0.28±0.08 at 5 and 20 min, respectively during PH. During IH, SpO_2 was 81% while during PH it fell from 80.2±1.6% (5 min) to 74.8±1.8% (20 min). During IH, iHVR was correlated to both pHVR ($r = 0.63$, $P<0.05$) and change in $PETCO_2$ ($r = -0.41$, $P<0.05$) during PH. Further research is required to assess whether these combined indices of HVR are useful for predicting acclimatization success to altitude.

Acknowledgements: This study was approved by the local Ethics Board and supported by AHFMR, HSFA, CIHR.

141. DO THE CAROTID CHEMORECEPTORS MODULATE REGIONAL BLOOD FLOW DISTRIBUTION AND VASCULAR CONDUCTANCE DURING EXERCISE

Michael Stickland, Jordan Miller, Curtis Smith, Jerome Dempsey.
University of Wisconsin School of Medicine, Madison, USA. Email: stickland@wisc.edu

Stimulation of the carotid chemoreceptors (CC) causes increased sympathetic vasoconstrictor outflow to skeletal muscle. We examined the effect of inhibiting/stimulating CC on cardiac output (QT), hind-limb flow (QL), total (GT) and hindlimb (GL) conductance and blood pressure (BP) during exercise (2.5 mph, 5% grade) in the dog.Bolus injections (<0.5 ml) of Dopamine (10 ug/kg) or NaCN (2 ug/kg) were administered via a chronically implanted carotid arterial catheter. Dopamine has been previously shown to have a bi-phasic response on carotid sinus nerve activity, with a 1-2 sec excitatory period followed by a prolonged (5-10 sec) inhibitory period, while NaCN injections cause only excitation (Bisgard et al., 1979). During exercise, injections of Dopamine elicited a bi-phasic response; first, a short (2 sec) reduction in GT (7%) and GL (15%) was observed. This was followed by a pronounced vasodilation (5-10 sec) as indicated by increases in GT (24%), GL (31%), QT (7%), and QL (14%), and a 10% reduction in BP. NaCN caused a similar initial transient decrease in both GT (-7%) and GL (-11%), however there was no evidence of a reflex vasodilation as little change in GT (5%), GL (5%), and BP (-2%) was observed during the ensuing period. Isovolumetric control injections of saline elicited no cardiovascular response. These preliminary results indicate that modulation of the carotid chemoreceptors can affect the distribution of blood flow during exercise, likely by influencing sympathetic nervous activity.

Acknowledgements: Funded by: NHLBI

142. ERYTHROPOIETIN AND ACCLIMATISATION: MORE THAN JUST ERYTHROPOIESIS

AI Sutherland[1], EC Davies[2], CJA Lockie[3], JK Ballie[4], AAR Thompson[4], RA Sherwood[2].

[1]Nuffield Depatment of Surgery, Oxford University, UK, [2]Department of Clinical Biochemistry, Kings College Hospital, London, UK, [3]Guys,Kings and Thomas; Medical School, London, UK, [4]APEX (Altitude Physiology Expeditions), c/o College of Medicine, University of Edinburgh, UK. Email: andrew.sutherland@surgery.ox.ac.uk.

Erythropoietion has a long appreciated role in adaption to high altitude in relation to haemopoiesis. More recently erythropoietin has been shown to have cytoprotective properties, protecting the brain, heart and kidneys from ischaemic injury. We hypothesised that erythropoietin may play a role in the early phase of acclimatisation independent of its erythropoietic activity. On a recent expedition to Bolivia (APEX2) we examined the relationship between serum erythropoietin and Acute Mountain Sickness (AMS). 41 healthy lowlanders (25 male, median age 21 range 18 to 31) flew to La Paz, Bolivia (3650m) spending 4 or 5 days before ascending in 90 minutes to Chacaltaya (5,200m). We measured serum erythropoietin in venous blood at sea level (SL1), within 6 hours of arrival at 5,200m (CH1), day 3 (CH3) day 6 (CH6), and again at sea level 2 months later (SL2). AMS was scored using the Lake Louise Scoring system (LLS).There was a 78% incidence of AMS in the first 3 days at 5200m (LLS>3). Maximum AMS scores in the first 3 days following ascent to 5200m were used to compare serum erythropoietin responses of subjects with little or no AMS ('AMS-ve', LLS<3, n=9) to those with moderate to severe AMS ('AMS+ve', LLS>4, n=32). Mean erythropoietin levels (IU/L±SEM) were as follows: AMS-ve 10.3±1.6 (SL1), 24.1±2.4 (CH1), 124.8±29.0 (CH3), 79.3±22.4 (CH6), 11.2±1.5 (SL2); AMS+ve 10.3±0.6 (SL1), 21.0±1.6 (CH1), 57.0±4.9 (CH3), 54.1±9.4 (CH6), 10.2±0.7 (SL2). Mean serum erythropoietin 48 hours after arrival at 5200m (CH3) was markedly higher in the AMS-ve group (124.8±29.0 vs. 57.0±4.9, p<0.007, two-tailed Mann-Whitney test).These results suggest that a blunted erythropoietin response to acute altitude exposure may be associated with AMS. The potential for erythropoietin to protect the brain and other organs from hypoxic injury in altitude acclimatisation deserves further investigation.

Acknowledgements: Volunteers and researchers, Apex 2 expedition; Marken, our international couriers; the IIF, Universidad Mayor de San Andres, Bolivia and IBBA, La Paz, Bolivia.

143. ORTHOSTATIC HYPOTENSION IS COMMON AT ALTITUDE AND ASSOCIATED WITH PRE-SYNCOPE

AI Sutherland[1], OT Mytton[2], A Simpson[3], R Oram[2], AAR Thompson[3], A Darowski[4], AJ Pollard[5].

[1]Nuffield Deaprtment of Surgery, University of Oxford,UK, [2]Oxford University Medical School, John Radcliffe Hospital, Oxford, UK, [3]APEX (Altitude Physiology Expeditions),c/o College of Medicine, University of Edinburgh, UK, [4]Nuffield Department of Medicine, John Radcliffe Hospital, Oxford, UK, [5]Department of Paediatrics, Oxford University, John Radcliffe Hospital, Oxford,UK. Email: Andrew.Sutherland@surgery.oxford.ac.uk.

Orthostatic hypotension, assessed by tilt table, is greater at altitude. The blood pressure (BP) response on standing upright is of interest because of the increased incidence of syncope at altitude and the increased prevalence of dizziness, a symptom of acute mountain sickness.We investigated orthostatic hypotension at altitude and its association with symptoms of pre-syncope on standing up from a supine position, in healthy volunteers. 36 lowlanders (22 males, 14 females) flew into La Paz, Bolivia (3650m) and after 4-5 days acclimatization ascended over 90 minutes to the Chacaltaya laboratory (5200m) by off-road vehicle. BP was measured on five occasions, three times at 5200m, and twice at sea-level, before and after the expedition. BP was measured with a mercury sphygmomanometer; a supine measurement and an erect measurement, within 15 seconds of standing, were recorded. The mean fall in BP for males at the first sea-level sample day was 11.9 mmHg, compared to 20.7 mmHg (paired t-test, $p = 0.0224$, $n = 19$), 27.8 mmHg ($p < 0.0001$, $n = 17$) and 25.0 mmHg ($p = 0.002$, $n = 17$) on the first, third and seventh days at altitude respectively. For females the fall in systolic BP was greater at altitude, but the difference was not significant. Symptoms (feeling faint on standing) were more prevalent on all altitude sample days, although only significant ($p < 0.01$) on the first day (81%), in comparison with sea-level sample days (45% and 50%). Symptoms were associated with a greater fall in systolic BP at altitude, although the differences were not significant. Orthostatic hypotension is more severe at altitude, particularly amongst men, and is likely to be associated with symptoms of pre-syncope. Dehydration or changes in the regulation of venomotor tone are the likely aetiology.

Acknowledgements: APEX2 Volunteers

144. EFFECT OF INTERMITTENT NORMOBARIC HYPOXIA ON PLASMA GLUTAMINE CONCENTRATION IN TRAINED MEN

Kohei Takahashi[1], Jin Uchimaru[1], Yuji Ogura[1], Shizuo Katamoto[1], Hisashi Naito[1], Junichiro Aoki[1].

[1]Juntendo University, Chiba, Japan. Email: kohey_t@ybb.ne.jp

The purpose of the present study was to investigate the effect of intermittent normobaric hypoxia on plasma glutamine, which is one of the energy substrates for immune cells, and on immune parameter in trained men.Eight male triathletes and five male cyclists volunteered for this study. They were randomly divided into a hypoxic (H) group (n=7) or control (C) group (n=6). H group stayed in a normobaric hypoxic room (15.4% O_2) for 10 hours a day (22:00-8:00) over 10 days whereas C group stayed in normobaric normoxic condition. Both groups maintained their usual training routine at sea level during the experimental period. To measure plasma glutamine concentration and parameters of CBC/differential and reticulocyte, blood samples were drown from antecubital vein at baseline before the experiment, and in the morning of day 1, 3, 6 and 10. Maximal oxygen uptake was also evaluated before and after the experimental period. The plasma glutamine concentration in H group significantly ($P<0.001$) decreased by 23% within one day and then gradually recovered to basal level by day 6, but it once again significantly dropped on day 10. Lymphocyte count in H group was significantly ($P<0.01$) lower on day 1 and 6 compared to baseline. There was no change in maximal oxygen uptake over the period. The results suggest that a significant decrease in plasma glutamine associated with an intermittent normobaric hypoxia may have a negative influence on immune function in trained men.

145. THE EFFECT OF SILDENAFIL ON CEREBRAL OXYGENATION AT ALTITUDE

Colin Chan[1], Helen Hoar[1], Kyle Pattinson[2], Jo Bradwell[1], Alex Wright[1], Chris Imray[3].

[1]Birmingham Medical Research Expeditionary Society, Birmingham, United Kingdom, [2]John Radcliffe Hospital, Oxford, United Kingdom, [3]University Hospitals Coventry & Warwickshire NHS Trust, Coventry, United Kingdom. Email: colin@cpwchan.demon.co.uk.

Sildenafil has been shown to reduced pulmonary hypertension and improve arterial oxygenation at altitude. We studied the effect of sildenafil on cerebral perfusion and oxygenation at altitude. Previously, we have shown middle cerebral artery velocity (MCAV) tends to fall and cerebral oxygenation (rSO_2) rises one hour after sildenafil when given three days after arrival at altitude. We have extended these observations to 1 and 2 hours after sildenafil and on one and three days after arrival at altitude (3480m) in a larger group of subjects (n=10). Results are given as mean (standard error). Results Day 1: Heart rate increased, blood pressure decreased and arterial oxygen saturation increased at both 1 and 2 hours after sildenafil. MCAV was unchanged but rSO_2 increased from 59.35% (1.3) to 62.7 (0.8) ($p<0.05$) at 1hour and to 65.3 (0.9) at 2 hours. End tidal CO_2 was unchanged. Results Day 3: Heart rate and blood pressure changes were similar as on day 1 but arterial oxygen saturation was unchanged at 1 and 2 hours. MCAV was reduced from 65.3 cm.sec-1 (1.8) to 61.3 (1.5) ($p<0.01$) and to 60.9 (1.7) ($p<0.0001$) at 1 and 2 hours respectively. rSO_2 increased from 61.7 % (0.9) to 65.0 (1.0) ($p<0.0001$) at 1hour and to 64.0 (0.9) ($p<0.0001$) at 2 hours. End tidal CO_2 decreased from 4.088 kPa before sildenafil to 4.010 kPa at 2 hours ($p<0.01$). Sildenalfil increases cerebral oxygenation at altitude. On day 1 rSO_2 increased still further at 2 hours without any change in MCAV. On day 3 no further rise in rSO_2 was found after 1hr and the rise in rSO_2 was accompanied by a fall in MCAV. The mechanisms whereby sildenafil increases rSO_2 may be different on acute exposure to altitude and after acclimatisation.

146. HYPOXIA INDUCIBLE FACTOR-1A REGULATES IN VIVO T CELL RESPONSES

Shuhei Tomita.
University of Tokushima, Tokushima, Japan. Email: tomita@genome.tokushima-u.ac.jp.

A basic HLH-PAS transcription factor, hypoxia inducible factor-1a (HIF-1α) facilitates the adaptation of cells to oxygen deprivation, by regulating the genes that are involved in glucose uptake, angiogenesis, erythropoiesis, and cell survival. The roles of HIF-1α in immune system have been identified in myeloid cells and in developing B cells. To investigate the role of HIF-1α in T cells, HIF-1α -floxed mice were crossed with proximal lck promoter-driven Cre-transgenic mice. We found that HIF-1α -deficient T cells were normally generated in the thymus and their distribution in the spleen and lymph nodes was unimpaired. In the in vitro culture conditions, HIF-1α -deficient T cells exhibited undiminished IL-2/IL-2R production and proliferation upon stimulation with either anti-CD3 antibody or Con A. However, any T cell-mediated responses measured in vivo by Con A-induced IL-2R expression, SEB-induced increase and decrease of Vb8+ cells, and SRBC-induced antibody production were severely diminished in T cell-specific HIF-1α -deficient mice. Con A treatment in T cell-specific HIF-1α -deficient mice caused less severe hepatitis.These results indicate that HIF-1α in T cells plays a crucial role in the in vivo immune responses, suggesting a pivotal role of hypoxic responses in intravital T cell-mediated immunity.

147. WEIGHT LOSS AT HIGH ALTITUDE: A BENEFICIAL EFFECT FOR OBESE SUBJECTS

Ge Ri-Li[1], Wang Xiujuan[1], Yamg Huihuang[2], Liu Yineng[2].
[1]Research Center for High Altitude Medicine, Qinghai University, Xining, Qinghai, P.R. China, [2]The hospital of the 5th Railway Engineering group at Golmud-Lhasa Railway, Golmud, Qinghai, P.R. China. Email: gerili@public.xn.qh.cn.

Loss of weight is frequently observed at high altitude and is believed a harmful effect for people who live at high altitude. However, the beneficial effect of weight reduction at high altitude has currently not been determined. The present study was performed to evaluate high-altitude weight loss as a nonpharmcotherapic effect for obese subjects when they are exposed to high altitude. A 120 subjects (age 34.5± 4.6 yr) who worked in the construction of Golmud-Lhasa Railway (4600m), which is the highest railway in the world, participated in the study. 85 subjects came from sea level (sea-level group) and 35 came from moderate altitude (2200m; moderate-altitude group). Body weight and body mass index (BMI) were measured at Golmud (baseline; 2800m) and after one month after they ascended to an altitude of 4600m. Among the sea-level group, the body weight of 20 subjects at 4600m was measured each morning for 33days continuous before they went to work. The average weight loss for the see-level group (n=85) was 10.2±3.8%, with the highest one of 29%, and 2.3%± 0.6% for the moderate-altitude group. The degree of weight loss (Δ weight loss) in the sea level group was significantly correlated with their baseline BMI ($r=0.678$; $p<0.001$) but this was not true in the moderate-altitude group ($r=0.009$). In the 20 subjects who had continuous measurements of body weight significant weight loss was observed within 20days of ascent but was a stable thereafter. The main findings of the present study are that 1) high altitude exposure markedly reduces body weight in sea level subjects but not in moderate -altitude subjects; 2) the degree of weight loss is closely related to initial

BM in the sea-level group; 3) a sufficient weight loss occurs within three weeks when people from near sea-level ascend to high altitude. Conclusion: These results suggest that weight loss at high altitude may be a safe, but previously unrecognized nonpharmcologic strategy for the treatment of obesity.

Acknowledgements: The work was funded by Natural Science Foundation of China (302600354, 30393130)

148. INDEPENDENT AND COMBINED EFFECTS OF HYPOXIA AND ELEVATED ESOPHAGEAL TEMPERATURE ON THE PATTERN OF HUMAN EXERCISE VENTILATION

Matthew D. White[1], Aaron L. Chu[1], Ollie Jay[1].

[1]*Simon Fraser University, Burnaby, BC CANADA. Email: matt@sfu.ca.*

The independent and combined effects of hypoxia and elevated esophageal temperature (Tes) were investigated for their effects on the pattern of exercise ventilation (VE). Eleven college-aged, healthy males volunteered for the study. In either a 'hyperthermic' Tes or a 'normothermic' Tes exercise session, participants were immersed to their shoulders and pedalled on a head-out, underwater cycle ergometer at a steady-state oxygen consumption (O2) of 0.87 (SD 0.07) L•min-1. A bath temperature of 31.5°C (SD 1.4) gave a steady state Tes of ~37.1°C for the normothermic exercise and a bath temperature of 38.2°C (SD 0.1) gave a steady state Tes of ~38.6°C for hyperthermic exercise. After a 30-min rest in air, participants were immersed and performed a 20-min warm-up followed by a 30-min steady-state cycling period when they inhaled air for 10 min, then hypoxic gas (12% O2 and 88% N2) for the next 10 min and then air again for 10 min. End-tidal CO2 (PETCO2) was maintained at an isocapnic level of 5.19 kPa (SD 0.71) during exercise. Results showed a main effect of core temperature (P = 0.007) was evident for breathing frequency (f), with an increased f in hyperthermic relative to the normothermic exercise. Significant decreases in inspiratory time (TI; P = 0.035) and expiratory time (TE; P = 0.014) were evident and these decreases were independent of any changes in tidal volume (VT). Inspiratory flow (VT•TI-1) was significantly increased in hyperthermic relative to normothermic (P = 0.003) exercise, an increase that was pronounced (P = 0.013) during hyperthermic hypoxia. In conclusion, during low intensity, steady-state exercise, a hyperthermic relative to a normothermic Tes caused a significant increase in VE due to an increase in f on account of decreases of TI and TE. This gave evidence of a thermally-induced tachypnea with increases of inspiratory flow that were accentuated in hyperthermic, hypoxic exercise.

Acknowledgements: This study was supported by NSERC and CFI.

149. GINKGO BILOBA PROPHYLAXIS DOES NOT PREVENT ACUTE MOUNTAIN SICKNESS

Vaughn Browne[1], Tony Chow[2], Heather Heileson[3], Desiree Wallace[4], James Anholm[5], Steven Green[6]

[1]Division of Emergency Medicine University of Colorado Health Sciences Center, [2]Dept. of Emergency Medicine Loma Linda University Medical Center, [3]Department of Emergency Medicine, Rose Medical Center, [4]Department of Pharmacy, Loma Linda University Medical Center, [5]Department of Medicine, Loma Linda University and the Jerry L. Pettis Veterans Medical Center, [6]Department of Emergency Medicine, Loma Linda University Medical Center. Email: Vaughn.Browne@UCHSC.edu.

Acetazolamide and ginkgo biloba have both been recommended for AMS prophylaxis; however, there is conflicting evidence of efficacy for ginkgo. We performed a prospective randomized, placebo-controlled trial of acetazolamide versus ginkgo biloba for AMS prophylaxis.We randomized unacclimatized adults to receive acetazolamide, ginkgo biloba, or placebo in a double-blinded fashion and took them to elevation (3800m) for 24 hours. For 5 days prior to ascent, subjects took identically appearing capsules twice daily containing either placebo, or Ginkgo biloba 120 mg. Subjects randomized to the acetazolamide group received placebo for 5 days, then were switched to acetazolamide 250 mg twice daily one day prior to ascent . We graded AMS symptoms using the Lake Louise Score (LLS) and compared the incidence of AMS (defined as LLS >3 and headache). Fifty seven subjects completed the trial (20 acetazolamide, 17 ginkgo biloba, 20 placebo). LLS scores were significantly different between groups; the median acetazolamide score was significantly lower than placebo (p=0.0124, effect size 2, 95%CI 0, 3) unlike ginkgo biloba (p=0.889, effect size 0, 95%CI -2, 2). AMS occurred less frequently in acetazolamide subjects compared to placebo (effect size 30%, 95%CI 61%, -15%), and was similar between ginkgo biloba subjects compared to placebo (effect size -5%, 95%CI -37%, 28%). In this small study, prophylactic acetazolamide decreased the severity and incidence of AMS. We found no evidence of similar efficacy for ginkgo biloba.

150. A ROLE FOR ACTIGRAPHY AS AN ADJUNCT TO SLEEP MONITORING AT HIGH ALTITUDE

Michael Schupp[1], Chris Hanning[2], Annabel Nickol[3].

[1]Glenfield Hospital , Leicester, UK, [2]General Hospital, Leicester, UK, [3]Chest Unit, Churchill Hospital, Oxford, UK. Email: mbschupp@aol.com.

Sleep-disruption is almost universal at high altitude, however many sleep systems are cumbersome to use in a remote environment. Actigraphs, or movement sensors, may be used as an indicator of sleep or wakefulness. Their simplicity is attractive for altitude use, but they have not to our knowledge previously been evaluated in this environment. Objectives: (1) Evaluation of nocturnal-movement with ascent (2) Determination of the relationship with subjective sleep quality. 15 volunteers underwent a graduated 17-day ascent from Tumlingtar (350m) to Chamlang base-camp (5000m). They wore an Actigraph (Cambridge Neurotechnology, UK) on the non-dominant wrist. At basecamp data was downloaded and the Fragmentation Index (FI) for each night determined. VAS was recorded each morning, using a 100 mm rule (0= 'best night's sleep ever': 100= 'worst night's sleep ever'). Examining data for new ascents only: FI increased significantly from 22.2 +/- 10.0/hour at 410m, through sequential altitudes to 37.1 +/- 17.9/hour at 5000m ($p=0.001$, ANOVA). There was no significant change in subjective sleep quality (VAS score 64.6 +/- 22.0 at 410m and 57.5 +/- 22.3mm at 5000m, $p=0.25$). There was a significant relationship between FI vs altitude ($r2=0.40$; $p=0.006$, Pearson's correlation coefficient) and FI vs VAS ($r2=0.33$; $p=0.019$), and a trend towards a relationship between VAS and altitude ($r2=0.22$; $p=0.058$). We have demonstrated that nocturnal movement increases sequentially with ascent. Using VAS as the primary outcome, subjective sleep quality did not significantly deteriorate with altitude, and this may be attributable to our slow ascent profile. Despite this, we demonstrated a significant relationship between nocturnal movement and subjective sleep. We have also demonstrated this simple device to be robust and reliable in the remote high altitude environment, despite the restriction of a sleeping bag. It may make a useful adjunct to sleep monitoring at altitude.

151. ELEVATED CEREBRAL BLOOD VOLUME DURING HYPOBARIC HYPOXIA PROTECTS AGAINST THE DEVELOPMENT OF AMS

C. Matthew Kinsey[1,2] and Robert Roach[2].

[1]Beth Israel Deaconess Medical Center, Boston MA and [2]The Colorado Center for Altitude Medicine and Physiology, UCHSC Depts Surgery and Anesthesiology, Denver CO. Email: mkinsey@caregroup.harvard.edu.

Acute mountain sickness (AMS) is a common ailment among individuals who travel too high too fast. The etiology of AMS remains poorly understood, in part due to the difficulty in obtaining non-invasive measurements of many cerebral parameters. Elevated cerebral blood volume (CBV) has been implicated by several authors as a contributor to the development of AMS. Traditionally, measurement of CBV has required creating a change in blood arterial oxygen saturation levels and comparing the change in concentration of oxygenated hemoglobin monitored by near infrared spectroscopy (NIRS), to that occurring in a peripheral pulse oximeter. In most reports this technique, known as the oxygen method, has been limited by poor reproducibility. Alternatively, NIRS can be used to monitor changes in total hemoglobin, as a surrogate for changes in CBV, but is limited by an inability to absolutely quantitate CBV. To apply this technique to longer duration studies we developed a unique NIRS optode holder and placement technique that allowed us to reproducibly replace the optodes (coefficient of variation = 1.3%) and sample the same "walnut" of cerebral tissue over time. We used the two different techniques to measure changes in CBV in altitude naive individuals exposed to hypobaric hypoxia (Pb =426 mmHg) for nine hours. Using the total hemoglobin method, we found that CBV increased in all subjects. Interestingly, these changes were largest in the AMS negative individuals ($p<.01$ at 9hrs). The magnitude of this difference correlates to a change in total CBV of 0.45 ml/100g. A similar although non-significant, trend was seen using the quantitative CBV technique. We hypothesize that individuals who will develop AMS may not be able to further increase their CBV, and subsequently increase oxygen delivery, secondary to poor craniospinal capacitance.

152. INHIBITION OF EXTRACELLULAR CARBONIC ANHYDRASE DOES NOT PREVENT HYPOXIC PULMONARY VASOCONSTRICTION

Philipp Pickerodt[1], Willehad Boemke[1], Roland Francis[1], Erik Swenson[2], Claudia Hoehne[1].

Univ Medicine, Berlin, Germany[1], Univ Washington, Seattle, USA[2]. Email: claudia.hoehne@charite.de.

Objective: Combined inhibition of both intra- and extracellular carbonic anhydrase (CA) by acetazolamide has been shown to prevent hypoxic pulmonary vasoconstriction (HPV). This study investigates, whether this effect is primarily due to extracellular CA inhibition, using benzolamide (BZ) - a powerful, hydrophilic, nonpermeant CA inhibitor - to inhibit extracellular luminal membrane bound CA isoenzyme IV. Methods: Six Beagle dogs were studied twice in randomized order. Protocol 1: Controls; Protocol 2: benzolamide IV (BZ) (2mg/kg bolus, followed by 2mg/kg/h continuously). During all experiments the conscious dogs were breathing spontaneously through a face mask: first hour normoxia (FiO_2=0.21), followed by 2 hours of hypoxia (FiO_2=0.1 in Controls and 0.09-0.08 in the BZ protocol, to match the PaO_2 observed during hypoxia in Controls). Mean pulmonary artery pressure (MPAP) and pulmonary vascular resistance (PVR) were recorded. Arterial blood gases were measured during normoxia and after 2 hours of hypoxia. Data are means±SEM; $p<0.05$ (GLM-ANOVA). Results: PaO_2 and $PaCO_2$ during hypoxia were 35.8±2.4mmHg and 29.1±0.9 mmHg in Controls and 38.3±1.2mmHg and 27.8±0.7mmHg with BZ. MPAP increased from 13.3±1 (normoxia) to 20.7±1.3mmHg (hypoxia), and PVR increased from 324±33 to 528±37dyn.s-1 .cm-5 in Controls. These values were comparable in the BZ protocol (MPAP 11.6±0.7 vs 18.6+1.1mmHg; PVR 251±14 vs 508±46dyn.s-1.cm-5). Arterial pH increased from 7.39±0.01 (normoxia) to 7.46±0.01 (hypoxia) in Controls while base excess (-2±0.6mmol/l) did not change. With BZ, arterial pH was 7.36±0.01 (normoxia) and 7.41±0.01 (hypoxia), while base excess decreased from -4.25±0.2 to -6.2±0.4mmol/l. Conclusions: BZ could not prevent HPV in conscious, spontaneously breathing dogs, suggesting that prevention of HPV by CA inhibition is not primarily related to extracellular vascular endothelial CA (IV) inhibition and changes of systemic pH.

CORRECTIONS

The following abstracts are presented here with corrections from the original as printed in the Hypoxia Abstract issue of High Altitude Medicine and Biology. The corrections will appear in the summer 2005 edition of High Altuitude Medicine and Biology.

The author line was mis-printed on the following abstracts.

6. EFFECTS OF SHORT-TERM NORMOBARIC HYPOXIA ON ANAEROBIC AND AEROBIC PERFORMANCE IN HIGHLY TRAINED ATHLETES

Fabien A. Basset[1], Denis R. Joanisse[2], François Billaut[3], Frédéric Boivin[2], Jean Doré[2], Josée St-Onge[2], Richard Chouinard[2], Guy Falgairette[3], Denis Richard[2], and Marcel R. Boulay[2].

School of Human Kinetics and Recreation, Memorial Univ Newfoundland, St. John, Canada[1]. Faculté de Médecine, Univ Laval, Québec, Canada[2]. STAPS, Univ du Sud Toulon-Var, France[3]. Email: fbasset@mun.ca.

82. INFLUENCE OF HYPOXIA ON EXHALED NITRIC OXIDE, PULMONARY FUNCTION, AND PULMONARY VASCULAR PRESSURES IN HEALTHY HUMANS

Eric Snyder, Ken Beck, Robert Frantz, Bruce Johnson.

Mayo Clinic. Email: johnson.bruce@mayo.edu.

92. REGULAR SILDENAFIL DOES NOT INHIBIT ALTITUDE-INDUCED PULMONARY HYPERTENSION; A RANDOMISED DOUBLE BLIND PLACEBO-CONTROLLED TRIAL

Roger Thompson[1], Matthew Bates[1], Kenneth Baillie[1], Nikhil Hirani[2], David Webb[3].

Apex (altitude physiological expeditions), c/o College of Medicine, Univ Edinburgh, UK[1], Respiratory Medicine, Univ Edinburgh, Royal Infirmary of Edinburgh, UK[2], Clinical Pharmacology Unit, Univ Edinburgh, Western General Hospital, Edinburgh, UK[3]. Email: rogerthompson@doctors.org.uk

The body of the following abstract was not properly reproduced in HAMB:

14. PULMONARY FUNCTION AND NOCTURNAL VENTILATION IN MOUNTAINEERS DEVELOPING HAPE

Andreas L Christ[1], Christian F Clarenbach[1], Oliver Senn[1], Manuel Fischler[2], Heimo Mairbauerl[3], Marco Maggiorini[2], Konrad E Bloch[1].

Pulmonary Divison, Univ Hospital Zurich, Switzerland[1], Medical Intensive Care Unit, Univ Hospital Zurich, Switzerland[2], Sports Medicine, Univ Heidelberg, Germany[3]. Email: christian.clarenbach@usz.ch.

Introduction: To investigate changes in lung function, breathing patterns, and oxygenation in montaineers developing HAPE. Methods: We studied 18 mountaineers in Zurich (490m) and after ascent to Capanna Margherita (4559m), within <24 hours. Eight mountaineers developed HAPE, 10 remained well (controls). Lung function, nocturnal breathing pattern by calibrated inductive plethysmography, and oxygen saturation were measured in Zurich (490m) and at 4559m over 3 consecutive days or until HAPE was clinically and radiographically diagnosed. Results: HAPE developed in 8 subjects within the 3 days at 4559m. Their FVC progressively decreased from a mean ±SD of 108±17 %pred at 490m to 87±15 %pred at 4559m (P<0.05, last measurement before overt HAPE). FEV1 fell in proportion to FVC. Closing volume increased from 0.33±0.06 to 0.51±0.05 L (P<0.05). Maximal inspiratory pressure remained unchanged. Diffusing capacity decreased from 102±11 to 91±8 %pred (P<0.05). Mean oxygen saturation in the night before HAPE occurred was 60±8%, the number of periodic breathing cycles was 97±45 h-1, minute ventilation was 8.6±3.1 L/min, breath rate was 27±5 min-1, mean inspiratory flow was 0.33±0.01 Lmin-1. In controls, FVC and FEV1 decreased to a similar degree as in subjects developing HAPE, but changes in closing volume (from 0.40±0.10 L at 490m to 0.41±0.07 L at 4559m, P=NS) and diffusing capacity (from 103±14 %pred at 490m to 102±16 %pred at 4559m, P=NS) were less pronounced. Nocturnal oxygen saturation in controls was higher (73±3 %), periodic breathing cycles (48±44 h-1), minute ventilation (5.1±1.8 Lmin-1), breath rate (20±3 min-1), and mean inspiratory flow (0.19±0.06 Lsec-1) were lower than in subjects developing HAPE (P< 0.05, all comparisons). Conclusion: Overt HAPE is preceeded by changes in pulmonary function, gas exchange and breathing pattern suggesting insterstitial fluid accumulation but not a reduced respiratory center drive. Measurement of pulmonary function and nocturnal breathing pattern might assist in early detection of HAPE.

Acknowledgements: Polygraphic equipment was provided by VivoMetrics, Ventura, CA, USA. Lung function equipment was provided by Pilger AG, Zofingen, Switzerland

AUTHOR INDEX

A

B

C

D

E

F

G

H

I

J

K

L

M

N

O

P

R

S

T

U

V

W

X

Y

Z

SUBJECT INDEX

A

B

C

D

E

F

G